BRITISH HISTORICAL STATI

BRITISH HISTORICAL STATISTICS

BY

B. R. MITCHELL

CAMBRIDGE UNIVERSITY PRESS

CAMBRIDGE UNIVERSITY PRESS
Cambridge, New York, Melbourne, Madrid, Cape Town,
Singapore, São Paulo, Delhi, Tokyo, Mexico City

Cambridge University Press
The Edinburgh Building, Cambridge CB2 8RU, UK

Published in the United States of America by Cambridge University Press, New York

www.cambridge.org
Information on this title: www.cambridge.org/9781107402447

First published 1988
Reprinted 1990, 1994
First paperback edition 2011

A catalogue record for this publication is available from the British Library

Library of Congress Cataloguing in Publication data
Mitchell, B. R. (Brian R.)
British historical statistics.
Includes index.
1. Great Britain – Statistics – History I. Title.
HA1134.M58 1988 314.1 86-24513

ISBN 978-0-521-33008-4 Hardback
ISBN 978-1-107-40244-7 Paperback

CONTENTS

PREFACE

This volume is the successor to the *Abstract of British Historical Statistics*, which I compiled in collaboration with Phyllis Deane about a quarter-of-a-century ago, and its supplementary volume, the *Second Abstract of British Historical Statistics*, for which I had the collaboration of Hywel Jones. The origin of these books lay in the development of interest in the historical record of economic growth which began after the Second World War, with Simon Kuznets as its main inspiration. The first volume was also, in a sense, a by-product of the analytical work on the British case undertaken by Phyllis Deane and W. A. Cole, the original idea being to present a collection of the 'raw' statistics which lay behind their quantitative manipulations and analyses. In the event, it went some way beyond that, and the extension from economic to other kinds of statistics and the inclusion of more processed statistics have been carried still further in the present volume.

The objective remains the same as that of the original *Abstract of British Historical Statistics*, namely to provide the user of historical statistics with informed access to a wide range of economic data, without the labour of identifying sources or of transforming many different annual sources into comparable time series. A somewhat wider selection of social statistics is now included, but unquestionably the emphasis remains on economic history.

The statistics selected for presentation have been arranged in sixteen chapters. The classification, which differs slightly from the original version, and conforms more closely with that adopted in national statistical yearbooks, has necessarily been arbitrary in some respects, and some series could easily have been included in different chapters. The index should, however, make it possible to locate a particular series fairly easily. The introductions to each chapter provide the non-specialist with information on the sources, coverage, and major problems of the series presented, whilst the notes and footnotes to the tables point to detailed difficulties and qualifications. The most important additional statistical sources are also referred to there, though the bibliographies included in the original version have now been dropped because of a combination of shortage of space and the vast increase in relevant publications in the last twenty years.

In general, the majority of the statistical series included are 'raw', that is, unprocessed. However, there are some topics for which it is impossible to avoid manipulated statistics, and others for which it would be undesirable. Some of these, indeed, are the only statistics available on their subject. This applies to wage, price, and aggregate industrial production indices, to the recent demographic estimates for periods up to the early nineteenth century, and to all the national accounts figures. Even on other subjects, there has been no policy of avoiding processed statistics.

Most of the series shown cover substantial numbers of years, but isolated figures which are of particular interest have not been excluded as a matter of principle. However, the inclusion of a great many poorly connected statistics would lead to very disjointed tables, and would often make clarity of presentation impossible to achieve. Their use has therefore been sparing.

This is not the place to deal with the many problems which beset the user of statistics, but attention may be drawn to some of the major ones peculiar to historical time series. Three general ones may be singled out. First, there are often changes in definitions or in breadth of coverage which are unadvertised in the sources, and are even, in a sense, concealed by an unchanged description. It is hoped that where the effects of this have not been overcome, at least they have all been signposted in the tables. Second, there is no way of knowing what variations took place in the efficiency of those who collected, compiled, and printed statistics in the past. This is one of those problems which, having looked it squarely in the eye, we must pass on. All we can do is to keep a vigilant rein on our credulity. Third, some statistics collected in the past – in the present, too, for that matter – were not collected for their own sakes, but as a by-product of some administrative purpose, often taxation. In that case especially, there was good reason to keep out of the record if possible; but there is not usually any way of knowing how successful people were in this. Once again, there is little that can be done about this except remain wary, cross-check everything possible, and try to assess the mutual compatibility of different but related statistics.

The Irish statistics raised certain problems, especially around the time of the Act of Union, both because they were generally less complete and because changes in administrative relationships brought unavoidable breaks in continuity. The order of magnitude of these breaks is indicated wherever possible, but that is usually all that can be done. There were similar breaks in 1923 at the time of the secession of southern Ireland; but, except for the external trade statistics, it is usually easy to assess their magnitude; and on this occasion many of the series are continued separately for the twenty-six counties which became the Republic of Ireland. This nomenclature, incidentally, has been used throughout, even though it is an anachronism prior to 1949.

Since this book, though roughly double the size of the original, reproduces a good deal of the data compiled then, it may be said to have been twenty-eight years in the making. During that time, I have incurred a great many obligations which must be recorded. First amongst these is my debt to Phyllis Deane, who inspired and planned the original project, and was always at hand to give advice during the compilation. There were many others who helped with advice at that time, and the list given in Phyllis Deane's preface to the first book should, in effect, be carried over into this. Others contributed similarly to the *Second Abstract*, above all Hywel Jones, who shared in its compilation; and yet others have helped in this way with the present volume, and I am most happy to acknowledge their assistance, even if I have not always followed their advice. Those concerned are:

M. D. Bailey
N. F. R. Crafts
C. H. Feinstein
Roderick Floud
Peter Mathias
Robin Matthews
Barry Supple
Donald McCloskey
Cormac Ó Gráda
Jeffrey Williamson
E. A. Wrigley

Various people have kindly allowed me to include copyright or previously unpublished material, and I must record a particular debt of gratitude in that respect to Professor Charles Feinstein. My debt to him in chapter 16 will be very obvious. Other individuals who have helped in this way are:

the late Professor T. S. Ashton
the late Lord Beveridge
Dr Forrest Capie and Dr Alan Webber
Professor W. A. Cole
Professor N. F. R. Crafts
Mr F. W. S. Craig
the late Mrs Selma Goldsmith
Professor J. Parry Lewis
Professor John J. McCusker
the late Professor P. Rousseaux
Mr J. R. Wells
Professor E. A. Wrigley and Dr R. S. Schofield

Others to whom acknowledgement must be made are the editors and officials of the following journals and organisations which publish (or have published) regular statistical series:

the British Iron and Steel Federation
the British Road Federation
the Commonwealth Economic Committee
the Cotton Board
the Department of Employment
Economica
The Economic History Review
the Economic History Society
Explorations in Economic History
the Governor and Company of the Bank of England
Her Majesty's Stationery Office
the International Tin Council
The Journal of Economic History
the National Bureau of Economic Research (New York)
the Registrar General for Scotland

Research in Economic History
the Royal Statistical Society
The Scottish Journal of Political Economy
the Trustee Savings Banks Association

and the following publishing firms:

Basil Blackwell
Cambridge University Press
the Clarendon Press
Harvard University Press
Leicester University Press
Longmans, Green & Co.
Manchester University Press

Finally, I must record certain other obligations incurred whilst working on this book. First, there is the long-standing debt to the Cambridge University Department of Applied Economics, which sponsored the original project thirty years ago and has provided many facilities, both then and since. Then there are the various librarians, of whom I have been a demanding client, especially Mrs Olga Peppercorn of the Department of Applied Economics, Mr Finkell of the Marshall Library, and Mr Vickery and Mr Noblett of the Official Publications Department of the Cambridge University Library. Proofreading a work of this nature is particularly demanding, and it gives me pleasure to be able to record my thanks to those members of the staff of the Department of Applied Economics who have undertaken the task. Chief amongst them have been Ms Margaret Clarke and Mr John Turner, whilst Mrs Ann Newton gave much helpful advice at this stage. And lastly, Francis Brooke of the Cambridge University Press, who has been encouraging and sympathetic at the right moments, and has seen this volume almost through to publication.

LIST OF ABBREVIATIONS

The following abbreviations are used:

–	=	nil
––	=	less than half of the smallest digit used in the table
...	=	not available
Abstract	=	*Statistical Abstract of the United Kingdom* or *Annual Abstract of Statistics*
C.S.O.	=	Central Statistical Office
E.H.R.	=	*Economic History Review*
E.J.	=	*Economic Journal*
H.M.S.O.	=	Her Majesty's Stationery Office
H.C.J.	=	*House of Commons Journal*
J.[R]S.S.	=	*Journal of the [Royal] Statistical Society*
L.C.E.S.	=	London and Cambridge Economic Service
P.P.	=	*Parliamentary Papers*, 1st series
Porter's Tables	=	*Tables of Revenues, Population, Commerce, etc.*, published in *Sessional Papers* in 1833 and from 1835 to 1854
R.E.S.	=	*Review of Economic Statistics*
S.J.P.E.	=	*Scottish Journal of Political Economy*
S.P.	=	*Sessional Papers of Parliament* (followed by date and volume)
T.M.S.S.	=	*Transactions of the Manchester Statistical Society*

CHAPTER 1

POPULATION AND VITAL STATISTICS

TABLES

Statistics of the population of scattered small units of the polities of the British Isles have long been available for periods prior to the first British census: but those for large aggregates were little more than informed guesswork until the publication of the first major volume of Wrigley and Schofield's work in 1981. Some of these earlier figures are reproduced in table 1a, mainly for their historiographical interest. The quite wide variations between the different estimators, especially before 1750, are testimony to the lack of a firm basis on which they could work. The best of these figures – those of Farr, Griffith, and Brownlee – could perhaps be regarded as reasonably reliable so far as the overall population of England and Wales was concerned; but they were unhelpful for gauging short-period variations, and of no use in estimating movements in vital statistics since they were actually based on assumptions about such ratios.

The estimates of English population since the first half of the sixteenth century which result from Wrigley and Schofield's work are a long way removed from enumeration records, and there was surely some justification for Flinn's statement that 'however well founded and skilfully devised the techniques employed may be, the multiplicity of assumptions and sheer number of cumulative modifications to the raw data must diminish the accuracy of the end-products'.[1] The key question, though, is by how much? Wrigley and Schofield themselves describe their series as 'tolerably reliable';[2] by which they presumably meant that they would not mislead anyone as to the direction and order of magnitude of demographic movements. Flinn, and Hollingsworth too,[3] warned, in effect, that this might not be so if their assumptions about the age-structure of mortality and about migration are seriously wrong. Doubtless this is correct, as is also Flinn's belief that 'the sheer density and complexity of the book will discourage careful reading and will lead to the uncritical quarrying of a handful of basic tables'. It must be admitted that this is what is done here in tables 1, 10, 13, 17, and 19. But as Flinn wisely realised, it is unavoidable. In defence it may be said that Wrigley and Schofield were seldom, if ever, uncritical of their own assumptions and adjustments – indeed the 'density' of the work is itself a reflection of that – and it is clear that in many cases alternatives were run through their computer in order to let the figures jostle each other, as it were, until they settled into a mutually compatible pattern. Nevertheless, it is clear that Wrigley and Schofield's figures are, as Hollingworth puts it, 'by no means beyond controversy', and the user would do well to remember this. Hollingsworth himself appears to be somewhat sceptical of Wrigley and Schofield's implied assumption that their sample parishes' registers 'are only regarded as poor for the period during which their inaccuracy is indisputable'. This suggests that the vital events and rates estimated may be too low. But he also suggests that the particular life-table used in the back projection technique exaggerates infant and child mortality before the nineteenth century and understates adult mortality, and so possibly results in overestimates of population in earlier periods. Obviously, those who wish to use Wrigley and Schofield's work as the basis of further detailed demographic calculations must go back to the source and test the effects of alternative assumptions for themselves. But for most of the purposes for which economic and

[1] M. W. Flinn, 'The Population History of England, 1541–1871', *Economic History Review*, second series XXXV, 3 (1982)

[2] E. A. Wrigley and R. S. Schofield, *The Population History of England 1541–1871* (London, 1981)

[3] T. H. Hollingsworth, review in *Population Studies*, XXXVI (1981).

social historians are likely to want statistics of population and vital events, it would seem that Wrigley and Schofield's own 'tolerably reliable' verdict may be accepted. As Hollingsworth concludes: 'Even if the population history of England was not exactly as sketched here, it was certainly something like this'.

Controversy over the course of Irish population change before the 1821 census, or even later, has been as fierce as that over English pre-censal population used to be. Connell's estimates, published in 1950, and shown in table 1 here, escaped much criticism for a long time, though Drake disputed the mechanisms by which Connell suggested that the population changed.[4] This has not been the case recently, and Ó Gráda and others have suggested rather different figures, which are also reproduced here. In all cases, though, it is well to bear in mind Connell's own statement that 'we can do little more than guess at the dimensions of the problem'.[5] The early censuses of Ireland were probably more defective than in the case of Great Britain, and the first two were even said by McDowall to be of 'dubious value',[6] whilst that for 1841 is a 'statistical trap' according to Joseph Lee[7] – admittedly with reference to its figures on age-structure and on marriages rather than its overall totals. These criticisms are probably overstated, and Ó Gráda's contention that 'as indicators of the rates of growth at least down to the county level, the 1821 and 1841 census data are surely sufficient'[8] seems more acceptable.

From the first censuses of Great Britain in 1801 and of Ireland in 1821 an increasing flow of information is available, and by 1851 all the population series included here had been started. But it is necessary to be aware of deficiencies and doubts about the censuses. The level of overall omissions cannot be accurately estimated, at least until very recent times. Taylor reckoned that they came to less than 5 per cent in 1801, and, by implication, could be ignored subsequently.[9] Krause, on the other hand, regarded the 5 per cent figure (and 3 per cent for 1811 and 1 per cent for 1821) as 'moderate'.[10] However, Wrigley and Schofield, having made what they admit to be rather 'cursory checks', conclude that their investigation 'lends greater weight to the view that the 1801 census tended to exaggerate population totals than to the opposite view'.[11] But this was more a matter of failure to record properly in the figures actually published than of anything else, and the suspicion of some failure to enumerate altogether must remain.

[4] M. Drake, 'Marriage and Population Growth in Ireland, 1750–1845', *Economic History Review*, second series XVI, 2 (1963).

[5] K. H. Connell in R. B. McDowell (ed.), *Social Life in Ireland 1800–45* (Dublin, 1957), p. 80.

[6] R. B. McDowall in R. D. Edwards and T. D. Williams (eds.), *The Great Famine* (Dublin, 1956).

[7] Joseph Lee, 'Marriage and Population in Pre-Famine Ireland', *Economic History Review*, second series XXI, 2 (1968).

[8] Cormac Ó Gráda, 'The Population of Ireland 1700–1900: A Survey', *Annales de Demographie Historique* (1979).

[9] Arthur J. Taylor, 'The Taking of the Census, 1801–1951', *British Medical Journal* (7 April 1951).

[10] J. T. Krause, 'Changes in English Fertility and Mortality, 1781–1850', *Economic History Review*, second series XI, 1 (1958).

[11] *op. cit.*, p. 125.

Later British censuses have received less criticism, though there appears to be little reason to expect those of 1821 and 1831 to have been better than 1811, since collection of data was undertaken by the same method in all of them – essentially, on tally-sheets by largely unsupervised local overseers. John Rickman, director of the early censuses, however, said that with the end of the wars 'there remains no reason to suspect the least deficiency in the Returns of 1821',[12] and, as Wrigley and Schofield have pointed out, this census has not 'been suspected of general under-enumeration by those who have used it in the past'. However, apart from the omission of men in the armed forces and merchant marine, alluded to in the footnotes to table 2, they do point to the under-enumeration of young children. However, this seems to have been largely offset by over-enumeration of older people, and they are prepared to regard the 1821 census, as well as that of 1841 when methods of data collection were much improved, as 'tolerably accurate'.[13] They attempted to calculate the extent of under-enumeration of children for the years up to 1871, and their conclusions are that omissions in the age-groups under ten years old amounted to 1.127 per cent of the total population in 1821 – the only year prior to 1841 in which any information about age-structure is available. They assume that this ratio would apply to other years prior to 1841, but the improved methods of that year brought their calculated figure of overall omission on account of under-enumeration of young children down to about 0.8 per cent, with a further reduction to about 0.5 per cent by 1851.[14] These estimates should be born in mind in using tables 4 and 5, since it must be presumed that similar under-enumeration affected other parts of the British Isles as well as England; but they do encourage belief that overall population totals after 1811 can be regarded as reliable for all practical purposes. Wrigley and Schofield make certain adjustments to them for their own purposes,[15] but in the tables shown here, from 2 to 9, the only alterations to the original census figures are those which have been made retrospectively, in later censuses.

The table of town populations presented more difficulties than most, mainly because of the problem of dealing with boundary changes. Since these were few, and largely untraceable in their effects before 1851, the population figures for the first half of the nineteenth century are related so far as possible to the 1851 area. For later years, the results of each intercensal expansion of area on population are shown, and for some of the larger towns, the effects of such expansions are traced back beyond a single decade.

The beginning of civil registration in each of the various parts of the United Kingdom has almost as great an effect on the information available on vital statistics as the coming of the census has for overall population. But the first year of registration in each country produced seriously defective figures, and in none was registration virtually complete until the 1860s at the earliest. However, it is generally reckoned that both marriages and deaths were better

[12] Census, 1821, *Preliminary Observations*, p. xxix.
[13] *op. cit.*, p. 118.
[14] *op. cit.*, appendix 6.
[15] See their chapter 5 and appendix 6.

covered than births – indeed, the marriage series may well be hardly affected at all by the advent of civil registration. In order to allow for the deficiencies of registration up to 1871, Wrigley and Schofield made estimates of its extent for both births and deaths, and the resulting figures are reproduced here in tables 10 and 11, as well as the raw data from the Registrar General, to which they are preferable for ordinary purposes. In Ireland, where civil registration did not begin until 1864, Ó Gráda has said that due to recalcitrant Catholic priests and careless medical officers, the returns are seriously incomplete for the first three or four decades at least'.[16] No one has yet made any systematic attempt to supply the deficiency, however.

In addition to the tables of birth, deaths, and marriages, and the appropriate rates derived from them by using the estimated mid-year populations shown in table 3 (or, in the case of the Wrigley and Schofield rates, by using their own population estimates), three tables of death rates by age-groups are shown here for the different parts of the British Isles. They have been included in preference to standardised death rates for two reasons. First, no death rate standardised to a single year has been published for the whole period of civil registration; and second, the age-group death rates give additional information, though a single series of rates genuinely comparable over a long period is admittedly lacking.

Tables 18 to 26 give a selection of the available statistics relating to migration. Wrigley and Schofield's estimates for the sixteenth to nineteenth centuries, though amongst the most speculative of their statistics, seem to be adequate as a guide, and for the nineteenth century they may well be preferable to any which can be derived simply from the shipping passenger figures. The general conclusion to be drawn from Ferenczi and Willcox's work, which is the immediate source of the early data, and of Brinley Thomas's discussion in his *Migration and Economic Growth*,[17] is that these figures are not very useful before the 1850s, and that even a century later they were by no means complete. The two principal deficiencies were the omission of all movements between Britain and the continent of Europe (including the Mediterranean coastlands), and the lack of statistics of migration, as opposed to passenger movement, down to 1912. A further deficiency, until the 1950s, is the lack of any record of movements by air. Apart from these major omissions, the statistics which do exist are far from perfect. The passenger movements from United Kingdom ports were underestimated quite seriously in the early years, since it was easy for small sailing ships to evade inspection. Thomas regards this as significant until the large steamship became dominant on the Atlantic run in the 1850s. Moreover, until 1853, there was no distinction between citizens and aliens in the passenger lists, and for ten years after that, the large number recorded as of unknown nationality render the figures of little use. According to Leak and Priday, distinction of nationality was imperfect as late as the early 1900s.[18]

[16] Cormac Ó Gráda, 'The Population of Ireland 1700–1900: A Survey', *Annales de Demographie Historique* (1979).

[17] (Cambridge, 1954).

[18] H. Leak and T. Priday, 'Migration from and to the United Kingdom', *Journal of the Royal Statistical Society*, XCVI (1933).

Inward movements, while recorded from 1855, did not distinguish nationality until 1876, and so it is only from that date that we can strike a balance, however imperfectly, of net movements of British passengers. This balance is a rough indicator of net migration, for though the increasing volume of business and pleasure trips was by that time having a noticeable effect on the aggregate of movements, this type of movement was virtually self-offsetting. Thomas believes that 'in the first half of the century ending in 1912 the number of British passengers recorded as leaving the United Kingdom is too low and in the second half is too high', but 'as a measure of aggregate net emigration the total outward balance of passengers is a good approximation for the entire period'.[19]

Irish passenger statistics in the nineteenth century were similar to the British ones, and, according to Ó Gráda, are not so good as the figures from United States sources given in table 27.[20] From 1851 an attempt was also made to collect statistics on emigration properly so called, though the resulting figures are clearly incomplete. The statistics resulted from information supplied voluntarily at the main Irish ports, and, from 1876, a question about destination was asked. So far as the answers of those who said that they were going to the United States are concerned, comparison with the figures from American sources suggests that deficiences were not too serious. However, as Ó Gráda has shown, the official figures 'are quite misleading in their implications for emigration to Britain'.[21] When tested against the data from the British censuses of those born in Ireland they are much too low. The overall total of emigrants in the period 1852 to 1910 was recorded as about 4.0 million, but 'this must be discarded. The real figure [was] probably nearer 5 million', with most of the omissions being emigrants to Britain. These strictures should be born in mind when table 26 is used.

[19] *op. cit.*, p. 41.

[20] Cormac Ó Gráda, 'A Note on Nineteenth-Century Irish Emigration on Statistics', *Population Studies*, XXIX (1975).

[21] *ibid.*, p. 147.

Population and Vital Statistics 1. Pre-censal Estimates of Population – British Isles, 1541–1801

NOTE

SOURCES: Part A – E. A. Wrigley and R. S. Schofield, *The Population History of England* (London, 1981), table A3.3.
Part B – Alexander Webster's census of Scotland, published in J. G. Kyd (ed.), *Scottish Population Statistics* (Edinburgh, 1952).
Part C – K. H. Connell, The Population of Ireland, 1750–1845 (Oxford, 1950), p. 25; and Stuart Daultrey, David Dickson, and Cormac Ó Gráda, "Eighteenth Century Irish Population: New Perspectives from Old Sources," *J.E.H.* XLI, 3 (1981), p. 624.

A. England (excluding Monmouthshire), 1541–1801

(in thousands)

1541	2,774	1586	3,806	1631	4,893	1676	5,003	1721	5,350
1542	2,812	1587	3,824	1632	4,906	1677	5,021	1722	5,353
1543	2,829	1588	3,812	1633	4,957	1678	5,056	1723	5,371
1544	2,861	1589	3,849	1634	4,997	1679	5,024	1724	5,388
1545	2,857	1590	3,896	1635	5,035	1680	4,989	1725	5,406
1546	2,854	1591	3,899	1636	5,058	1681	4,930	1726	5,450
1547	2,856	1592	3,906	1637	5,075	1682	4,900	1727	5,480
1548	2,898	1593	3,904	1638	5,083	1683	4,886	1728	5,425
1549	2,928	1594	3,938	1639	5,051	1684	4,888	1729	5,336
1550	2,969	1595	3,985	1640	5,055	1685	4,871	1730	5,269
1551	3,011	1596	4,012	1641	5,092	1686	4,865	1731	5,263
1552	3,035	1597	4,010	1642	5,112	1687	4,879	1732	5,284
1553	3,060	1598	3,985	1643	5,137	1688	4,897	1733	5,310
1554	3,090	1599	4,020	1644	5,121	1689	4,917	1734	5,363
1555	3,115	1600	4,066	1645	5,130	1690	4,916	1735	5,409
1556	3,159	1601	4,110	1646	5,177	1691	4,931	1736	5,450
1557	3,153	1602	4,135	1647	5,214	1692	4,935	1737	5,481
1558	3,085	1603	4,156	1648	5,226	1693	4,963	1738	5,504
1559	2,986	1604	4,166	1649	5,229	1694	4,950	1739	5,537
1560	2,963	1605	4,215	1650	5,221	1695	4,951	1740	5,565
1561	2,985	1606	4,253	1651	5,228	1696	4,962	1741	5,576
1562	3,016	1607	4,303	1652	5,240	1697	4,978	1742	5,516
1563	3,048	1608	4,340	1653	5,234	1698	4,998	1743	5,512
1564	3,060	1609	4,376	1654	5,219	1699	5,015	1744	5,548
1565	3,102	1610	4,390	1655	5,246	1700	5,027	1745	5,603
1566	3,128	1611	4,416	1656	5,281	1701	5,058	1746	5,635
1567	3,155	1612	4,439	1657	5,284	1702	5,092	1747	5,658
1568	3,204	1613	4,459	1658	5,206	1703	5,134	1748	5,669
1569	3,230	1614	4,459	1659	5,136	1704	5,157	1749	5,703
1570	3,255	1615	4,494	1660	5,130	1705	5,167	1750	5,739
1571	3,271	1616	4,510	1661	5,141	1706	5,182	1751	5,772
1572	3,303	1617	4,515	1662	5,116	1707	5,199	1752	5,811
1573	3,323	1618	4,546	1663	5,105	1708	5,215	1753	5,856
1574	3,344	1619	4,590	1664	5,129	1709	5,225	1754	5,900
1575	3,377	1620	4,635	1665	5,110	1710	5,238	1755	5,943
1576	3,413	1621	4,693	1666	5,067	1711	5,230	1756	5,993
1577	3,455	1622	4,756	1667	5,059	1712	5,218	1757	6,021
1578	3,493	1623	4,772	1668	5,047	1713	5,225	1758	6,039
1579	3,526	1624	4,756	1669	5,037	1714	5,242	1759	6,063
1580	3,568	1625	4,752	1670	5,022	1715	5,246	1760	6,102
1581	3,598	1626	4,720	1671	4,983	1716	5,276	1761	6,147
1582	3,637	1627	4,738	1672	4,973	1717	5,310	1762	6,173
1583	3,687	1628	4,791	1673	4,993	1718	5,344	1763	6,162
1584	3,734	1629	4,832	1674	5,008	1719	5,378	1764	6,195
1585	3,763	1630	4,884	1675	5,009	1720	5,358	1765	6,246

A. England (excluding Monmouthshire), 1541–1801 *continued*

(in thousands)

1766	6,277	1774	6,602	1781	7,069	1788	7,543	1795	8,198
1767	6,295	1775	6,674	1782	7,127	1789	7,648	1796	8,285
1768	6,314	1776	6,740	1783	7,145	1790	7,740	1797	8,399
1769	6,358	1777	6,808	1784	7,217	1791	7,842	1798	8,501
1770	6,405	1778	6,882	1785	7,289	1792	7,937	1799	8,606
1771	6,448	1779	6,949	1786	7,371	1793	8,025	1800	8,664
1772	6,499	1780	6,989	1787	7,462	1794	8,101	1801	8,728
1773	6,552								

B. Scotland, 1755

1755	1,265

C. Ireland, 1687–1791

	Connell	Daultrey *et al.*		Connell	Daultrey *et al.*		Connell	Daultrey *et al.*		Connell	Daultrey *et al.*
1687	2,167	...	1726	3,031	...	1754	3,191	...	1785	4,019	...
1706	...	1,750–2,060	1732	3,018	2,160–2,530	1767	3,480	...	1788	4,389	...
1712	2,791	1,980–2,320	1744	...	1,910–2,230	1772	3,584	...	1790	4,591	...
1718	2,894	...	1749	...	1,950–2,280	1777	3,740	...	1791	4,753	4,420
1725	3,042	2,180–2,560	1753	...	2,200–2,570	1781	4,048	...			

Population and Vital Statistics 1A. Early Estimates of Eighteenth-Century Population

NOTES

[1] Sources: Rickman (1)—*Observations on the Results of the Population Act*, 41 *Geo III*, p. 9 (in *S.P.* 1802, VII); Rickman (2)—1841 Census, *Enumeration Abstract*, preface pp. 36–7; Malthus—T. Malthus, *Essay on Population* (5th edition, London, 1817), vol. II, p. 95; Finlaison—1831 census, *Enumeration Abstract*, p. xiv; Farr—1861 Census, *General Report*, p. 22; Brownlee—J. Brownlee, 'History of the Birth and Death Rates in England and Wales ...', in *Public Health* (June and July 1916); Griffith—G. Talbot Griffith, *Population Problems in the Age of Malthus* (Cambridge University Press, 1926), p. 18.

[2] Rickman's, Finlaison's and Griffith's estimates are for 1700, 1710, etc., with Rickman and Griffith ending in 1801 and Finlaison in mid-1800. The remaining estimates are for 1701, 1711, etc.

(in thousands)

	Rickman (1)	Rickman (2)	Malthus	Finlaison	Farr	Brownlee	Griffith
1700/1	5,475	6,045	...	5,135	6,122	5,826	5,835
1710/1	5,240	...	...	5,066	6,252	5,981	6,013
1720/1	5,565	...	...	5,345	6,253	6,001	6,048
1730/1	5,796	...	...	5,688	6,183	5,947	6,008
1740/1	6,064	...	...	5,830	6,153	5,926	6,013
1750/1	6,467	6,517	...	6,040	6,336	6,140	6,253
1760/1	6,736	...	...	6,480	6,721	6,569	6,665
1770/1	7,428	...	...	7,228	7,153	7,052	7,124
1780/1	7,953	...	7,721	7,815	7,574	7,531	7,581
1785/6	8,016	...	7,998	...	...	...	7,826
1790/1	8,675	...	8,415	8,541	8,256	8,247	8,216
1795/6	9,055	...	8,831	...	...	...	8,656
1800/1	9,168	...	9,287	9,187	9,193	9,156	9,168

Population and Vital Statistics 2. Population (by Sex) and Intercensal Increases – British Isles, 1801–1981

NOTES

[1] SOURCES: *Reports* of the Censuses of 1981 for England & Wales, Scotland, and Northern Ireland, of 1911 for Ireland, and of 1981 for the Irish Republic.

[2] The population of Islands in the British Seas has not been included.

[3] The figures of intercensal increase are given here as a percentage per year (i.e. compounded), whereas in the first *Abstract of British Historical Statistics* the percentage increase between censuses was shown.

A. England & Wales

	Total Population (thousands)			Increase since Previous Census (thousands)			Intercensal Increase (per cent per year)			Females per 1,000 Males
	Persons	Males	Females	Persons	Males	Females	Persons	Males	Females	
1801 Mar. 9/10	8,893	4,255	4,638	...	...	...	...	...	...	1,057 (*a*)
1811 May 26/27	10,164	4,874	5,291	1,272	619	653	1·32	1·34	1·30	1,054 (*a*)
1821 May 27/28	12,000	5,850	6,150	1,836	977	859	1·67	1·84	1·52	1,036 (*a*)
1831 May 29/30	13,897	6,771	7,126	1,897	921	976	1·48	1·47	1·48	1,040 (*a*)
1841 June 6/7	15,914	7,778	8,137	2,017	1,006	1,011	1·36	1·39	1·33	1,046
1851 Mar. 30/31	17,928	8,781	9,146	2,013	1,004	1,010	1·22	1·24	1·20	1,042
1861 Apr. 7/8	20,066	9,776	10,290	2,139	995	1,144	1·13	1·08	1·18	1,053
1871 Apr. 2/3	22,712	11,059	11,653	2,646	1,283	1,363	1·25	1·24	1·25	1,054
1881 Apr. 3/4	25,974	12,640	13,335	3,262	1,581	1,681	1·35	1·34	1·36	1,055
1891 Apr. 5/6 (*b*)	29,003	14,060	14,942	3,028	1,420	1,608	1·11	1·07	1·14	1,063
1901 Mar. 31/ Apr. 1	32,528	15,729	16,799	3,525	1,668	1,857	1·16	1·13	1·18	1,068
1911 Apr. 2/3	36,070	17,446	18,625	3,543	1,717	1,826	1·04	1·04	1·04	1,068
1921 June 19/20	37,887	18,075	19,811	1,816	630	1,187	0·48	0·35	0·61	1,096
1931 Apr. 26/27	39,952	19,133	20,819	2,066	1,058	1,008	0·54	0·58	0·50	1,088
(*1939 mid-year estimate*	*41,460*	*19,920*	*21,540*	*1,508*	*787*	*721*	*0·37*	*0·41*	*0·34*	*1,081*)
1951 Apr. 8/9	43,758	21,016	22,742	2,298 (*c*)	1,096 (*c*)	1,202 (*c*)	0·54 (*c*)	0·53 (*c*)	0·54 (*c*)	1,082
1961 Apr. 23/24	46,105	22,304	23,801	2,347	1,288	1,058	0·52	0·59	0·45	1,067
1971 Apr. 25/26	48,750	23,683	25,067	2,645	1,379	1,266	0·56	0·60	0·52	1,058
1981 Apr. 5/6	49,155	23,873	25,281	405	190	215	0·08	0·08	0·08	1,059

B. Scotland

	Total Population (thousands)			Increase since Previous Census (thousands)			Intercensal Increase (per cent per year)			Females per 1,000 Males
	Persons	Males	Females	Persons	Males	Females	Persons	Males	Females	
1801	1,608	739	869	...	...	...	...	...	...	1,176
1811	1,806	826	980	197	87	110	1·14	1·10	1·18	1,185
1821	2,092	983	1,109	286	156	129	1·48	1·75	1·25	1,129
1831	2,364	1,114	1,250	273	132	141	1·23	1·27	1·20	1,122
1841	2,620	1,242	1,378	256	127	128	1·03	1·09	0·98	1,110
1851	2,889	1,375	1,513	269	134	135	1·00	1·05	0·96	1,100
1861	3,062	1,450	1,612	174	74	99	0·58	0·53	0·64	1,112
1871	3,360	1,603	1,757	298	153	144	0·93	1·01	0·86	1,096
1881	3,736	1,799	1,936	376	196	179	1·06	1·16	0·98	1,076
1891 (*b*)	4,026	1,943	2,083	290	143	147	0·75	0·77	0·73	1,072
1901	4,472	2,174	2,298	446	231	215	1·06	1·13	0·99	1,057
1911	4,761	2,309	2,452	289	135	154	0·63	0·60	0·65	1,062
1921	4,882	2,348	2,535	122	39	83	0·25	0·16	0·33	1,080
1931	4,843	2,326	2,517	−40	−22	−17	−0·08	−0·10	−0·07	1,083
(*1939 mid-year*	*5,007*	*2,412*	*2,594*	*164*	*87*	*77*	*0·41*	*0·45*	*0·37*	*1,076*)
1951	5,096	2,434	2,662	90 (*c*)	22 (*c*)	68 (*c*)	0·15 (*c*)	0·08 (*c*)	0·22 (*c*)	1,094
1961	5,179	2,483	2,697	83	48	35	0·16	0·20	0·13	1,087
1971	5,229	2,515	2,714	50	32	18	0·10	0·13	0·07	1,079
1981	5,131	2,466	2,664	−98	−49	−49	−0·19	0·20	−0·19	1,080

See p. 10 for footnotes

Population and Vital Statistics 2. *continued*

C. Ireland

	Total Population (thousands)			Increase since Previous Census (thousands)			Intercensal Increase (per cent per year)			Females per 1,000 Males
	Persons	Males	Females	Persons	Males	Females	Persons	Males	Females	
1821 (*d*)	6,802	3,342	3,460	...	...	...	...	...	...	1,035
1831 (*d*)	7,767	3,795	3,973	966	453	513	1.34	1·28	1·39	1,047
1841	8,178	4,022	4,156	411	227	183	0·52	0·58	0·45	1,033
1851	6,554	3,192	3,362	−1,624	−830	−794	−2·19	−2·28	−2·10	1,053
1861	5,799	2,837	2,962	−753	−353	−400	−1·22	−1·17	−1·26	1,044
1871	5,412	2,640	2,773	−387	−198	−189	−0·69	−0·72	−0·66	1,050
1881	5,175	2,533	2,642	−238	−106	−131	−0·45	−0·41	−0·48	1,042
1891 (*b*)	4,705	2,319	2,386	−470	−214	−256	−0·95	−0.88	−1·01	1,029
1901	4,459	2,200	2,259	−246	−119	−127	−0·54	−0·53	−0·55	1,027
1911	4,390	2,192	2,198	−69	−8	−61	−0·16	−0·04	−0·27	1,003

D. Northern Ireland

	Persons	Males	Females	Persons	Males	Females	Persons	Males	Females	Females per 1,000 Males
1926 Apr. 18/19	1,257	608	648	6	6	--	0·03	0·06	0·00	1,066
1937 Feb. 28/ Mar. 1	1,280	623	657	23	15	8	0·16	0·22	0·13	1,054
1951	1,371	668	703	91	45	47	0·49	0·50	0·49	1,053
1961	1,425	694	731	54	26	28	0·38	0·38	0·39	1,053
1966 Oct 9/10	1,485	724	761	60	30	30	0·75	0·76	0·74	1,051
1971	1,536	755	781	51	31	20	0·34	0·42	0·26	1,034
1981	1,510	740	770	−26	−15	−11	−0·17	−0·20	−0·14	1,041

E. Republic of Ireland

	Persons	Males	Females	Persons	Males	Females	Persons	Males	Females	Females per 1,000 Males
1926	2,972	1,507	1,465	−168	−83	−85	−0·37	−0·36	−0·38	972
1936	2,968	1,520	1,448	−4	14	−17	−0·01	0·09	−0·12	952
1946	2,955	1,495	1,460	−13	−26	12	−0·04	−0·17	0·08	977
1951	2,961	1,507	1,454	6	12	−6	0·04	0·16	−0·08	965
1956	2,898	1,463	1,435	−62	−44	−19	−0·43	−0·59	−0·26	981
1961	2,818	1,417	1,402	−70	−46	−34	−0·56	−0·64	−0·46	990
1966	2,884	1,449	1,435	66	32	33	0·46	0·45	0·47	990
1971	2,978	1,496	1,482	94	47	48	0·64	0·64	0·65	991
1979	3,368	1,693	1,675	390	198	192	1·55	1·56	1·54	989
1981	3,443	1,729	1,714	75	36	39	1·11	1·06	1·16	991

(*a*) In computing the proportion of females to males the following estimates of the numbers of men in the Army, Navy, and Merchant Service at home have been adopted:

1801	1811	1821	1831
131,818	145,137	87,740	78,968

(*b*) The figures for this year have been adjusted to counteract a tendency by certain enumerators to confuse males and females in completion of a new type of enumeration book introduced at this census.

(*c*) The increases are reckoned from mid-1939.

(*d*) Excluding members of the Armed Forces stationed at home.

Population and Vital Statistics 3. Estimated Mid-Year Home Population (by Sex) – British Isles, 1801–1980

NOTES

[1] SOURCES: England & Wales—*Registrar General's Statistical Review of England & Wales* and subsequent publications of the Office of Population Censuses and Surveys; Scotland—*Annual Report of the Registrar General for Scotland*; Ireland—*Annual Report of the Registrar General for Ireland*, subsequently *Annual Report of the Registrar General for Northern Ireland*.

[2] The sex breakdown for Scotland for 1855–1910 has not been published in the *Annual Report*, but has been supplied to us by courtesy of the Registrar General for Scotland, as have certain corrections to published figures.

[3] From 1952 figures for the Irish Republic relate to early April.

(in thousands)

	England & Wales Area: 37,342,463 acres			Scotland Area: 20,075,023 acres			Ireland Area: 20,862,864 acres		
	Persons	Males	Females	Persons	Males	Females	Persons	Males	Females
1801	9,061	4,404	4,657	1,625	752	873	5,216	2,592	2,625
1802	9,130	4,441	4,689	1,644	761	883	5,286	2,625	2,661
1803	9,235	4,494	4,741	1,663	769	894	5,357	2,658	2,698
1804	9,367	4,559	4,808	1,682	778	904	5,428	2,692	2,736
1805	9,513	4,631	4,882	1,702	787	915	5,501	2,727	2,774
1806	9,656	4,700	4,956	1,722	796	926	5,574	2,762	2,812
1807	9,794	4,768	5,026	1,742	805	936	5,649	2,797	2,851
1808	9,924	4,832	5,092	1,762	815	947	5,724	2,833	2,891
1809	10,056	4,895	5,161	1,783	824	959	5,800	2,869	2,931
1810	10,186	4,958	5,228	1,803	834	970	5,878	2,906	2,972
1811	10,322	5,025	5,297	1,824	843	981	5,956	2,943	3,013
1812	10,480	5,103	5,377	1,851	858	993	6,036	2,981	3,055
1813	10,650	5,191	5,459	1,878	872	1,006	6,117	3,019	3,098
1814	10,820	5,280	5,540	1,905	887	1,018	6,198	3,057	3,141
1815	11,004	5,376	5,628	1,933	902	1,031	6,281	3,097	3,185
1816	11,196	5,475	5,721	1,959	916	1,044	6,365	3,136	3,229
1817	11,378	5,568	5,810	1,986	929	1,057	6,450	3,176	3,274
1818	11,555	5,659	5,896	2,014	944	1,070	6,536	3,217	3,319
1819	11,723	5,748	5,975	2,042	959	1,083	6,624	3,258	3,366
1820	11,903	5,843	6,060	2,071	974	1,097	6,712	3,300	3,412
1821	12,106	5,947	6,159	2,100	990	1,110	6,802	3,342	3,460
1822	12,320	6,051	6,269	2,126	1,002	1,123	6,893	3,385	3,508
1823	12,529	6,153	6,376	2,152	1,015	1,137	6,985	3,428	3,557
1824	12,721	6,246	6,475	2,179	1,028	1,151	7,078	3,472	3,606
1825	12,903	6,334	6,569	2,205	1,041	1,164	7,173	3,516	3,656
1826	13,074	6,417	6,657	2,233	1,054	1,179	7,269	3,561	3,707
1827	13,247	6,500	6,747	2,259	1,066	1,193	7,366	3,607	3,759
1828	13,438	6,592	6,846	2,288	1,081	1,207	7,464	3,653	3,811
1829	13,625	6,681	6,944	2,316	1,095	1,221	7,564	3,700	3,864
1830	13,805	6,767	7,038	2,345	1,108	1,236	7,665	3,747	3,918
1831	13,994	6,859	7,135	2,374	1,123	1,251	7,767	3,795	3,973
1832	14,165	6,944	7,221	2,398	1,134	1,263	7,810	3,819	3,991
1833	14,328	7,023	7,305	2,422	1,147	1,276	7,852	3,842	4,010
1834	14,520	7,116	7,404	2,447	1,159	1,288	7,895	3,866	4,028
1835	14,724	7,214	7,510	2,472	1,171	1,301	7,938	3,890	4,047
1836	14,928	7,310	7,618	2,497	1,184	1,314	7,981	3,915	4,066
1837	15,104	7,392	7,712	2,523	1,196	1,326	8,024	3,939	4,085
1838	15,288	7,479	7,809	2,548	1,209	1,339	8,068	3,963	4,104
1839	15,514	7,586	7,928	2,574	1,222	1,353	8,111	3,988	4,123
1840	15,731	7,689	8,042	2,601	1,235	1,366	8,156	4,013	4,143
1841	15,929	7,785	8,144	2,622	1,243	1,379	8,200	4,038	4,162
1842	16,130	7,887	8,243	2,653	1,259	1,394	8,221	4,048	4,173
1843	16,332	7,990	8,342	2,684	1,274	1,409	8,240	4,057	4,183
1844	16,535	8,093	8,442	2,713	1,289	1,424	8,277	4,074	4,202
1845	16,739	8,196	8,543	2,742	1,304	1,438	8,295	4,083	4,212

Population and Vital Statistics 3. *continued*

(in thousands)

	England & Wales Area: 37,342,463 acres			Scotland Area: 20,075,023 acres			Ireland Area: 20,862,864 acres		
	Persons	Males	Females	Persons	Males	Females	Persons	Males	Females
1846	16,944	8,298	8,646	2,770	1,318	1,452	8,288	4,079	4,209
1847	17,150	8,401	8,749	2,797	1,331	1,466	8,025	3,944	4,081
1848	17,357	8,503	8,854	2,823	1,344	1,479	7,640	3,746	3,893
1849	17,564	8,605	8,959	2,849	1,356	1,492	7,256	3,551	3,705
1850	17,773	8,707	9,066	2,873	1,368	1,505	6,878	3,361	3,517
1851	17,983	8,809	9,174	2,896	1,379	1,517	6,514	3,181	3,333
1852	18,193	8,910	9,283	2,918	1,389	1,529	6,337	3,095	3,242
1853	18,404	9,011	9,393	2,939	1,399	1,540	6,199	3,031	3,168
1854	18,616	9,111	9,505	2,959	1,408	1,551	6,083	2,977	3,106
1855	18,829	9,212	9,617	2,978	1,417	1,561	6,015	2,946	3,069
1856	19,042	9,311	9,731	2,996	1,424	1,572	5,973	2,926	3,047
1857	19,256	9,410	9,846	3,012	1,431	1,581	5,919	2,898	3,022
1858	19,471	9,509	9,962	3,028	1,437	1,590	5,891	2,882	3,009
1859	19,687	9,607	10,080	3,042	1,443	1,599	5,862	2,866	2,996
1860	19,902	9,704	10,198	3,055	1,448	1,607	5,821	2,845	2,976
1861	20,119	9,801	10,318	3,069	1,454	1,616	5,788	2,832	2,957
1862	20,371	9,923	10,448	3,098	1,468	1,630	5,776	2,827	2,948
1863	20,626	10,047	10,579	3,127	1,483	1,644	5,718	2,800	2,919
1864	20,884	10,172	10,712	3,156	1,498	1,658	5,641	2,762	2,879
1865	21,145	10,299	10,846	3,185	1,513	1,672	5,595	2,741	2,854
1866	21,410	10,427	10,983	3,215	1,528	1,687	5,523	2,701	2,822
1867	21,677	10,557	11,120	3,245	1,544	1,701	5,487	2,681	2,805
1868	21,949	10,689	11,260	3,275	1,559	1,716	5,466	2,669	2,797
1869	22,223	10,822	11,401	3,306	1,575	1,731	5,449	2,660	2,789
1870	22,501	10,956	11,545	3,337	1,591	1,746	5,419	2,642	2,777
1871	22,789	11,093	11,696	3,369	1,608	1,761	5,398	2,631	2,767
1872	23,096	11,242	11,854	3,405	1,626	1,778	5,373	2,616	2,757
1873	23,408	11,394	12,014	3,441	1,645	1,796	5,328	2,590	2,738
1874	23,724	11,548	12,176	3,478	1,664	1,813	5,299	2,576	2,723
1875	24,045	11,704	12,341	3,515	1,684	1,831	5,279	2,569	2,709
1876	24,370	11,862	12,508	3,552	1,703	1,849	5,278	2,572	2,705
1877	24,700	12,023	12,677	3,590	1,723	1,867	5,286	2,579	2,707
1878	25,033	12,185	12,848	3,628	1,743	1,885	5,282	2,580	2,691
1879	25,371	12,350	13,021	3,667	1,763	1,903	5,266	2,575	2,691
1880	25,714	12,517	13,197	3,706	1,784	1,922	5,203	2,543	2,659
1881	26,046	12,673	13,373	3,743	1,803	1,940	5,146	2,519	2,627
1882	26,334	12,808	13,526	3,771	1,817	1,954	5,101	2,497	2,604
1883	26,627	12,945	13,682	3,799	1,831	1,968	5,024	2,462	2,562
1884	26,922	13,083	13,839	3,827	1,845	1,983	4,975	2,440	2,535
1885	27,220	13,222	13,998	3,856	1,859	1,997	4,939	2,424	2,514
1886	27,522	13,363	14,159	3,885	1,873	2,012	4,906	2,410	2,496
1887	27,827	13,505	14,322	3,914	1,888	2,027	4,857	2,387	2,470
1888	28,136	13,649	14,487	3,944	1,902	2,041	4,801	2,361	2,441
1889	28,448	13,795	14,653	3,973	1,917	2,056	4,757	2,341	2,417
1890	28,764	13,942	14,822	4,003	1,932	2,072	4,718	2,323	2,395
1891	29,086	14,093	14,993	4,036	1,948	2,088	4,680	2,306	2,374
1892	29,421	14,252	15,169	4,079	1,970	2,109	4,634	2,282	2,351
1893	29,761	14,414	15,347	4,122	1,992	2,130	4,607	2,268	2,339
1894	30,104	14,577	15,527	4,166	2,015	2,151	4,589	2,260	2,329
1895	30,451	14,742	15,709	4,210	2,038	2,172	4,560	2,247	2,313

Population and Vital Statistics 3. *continued*

(in thousands)

	England & Wales Area: 37,342,463 acres			Scotland Area: 20,075,023 acres			Ireland Area: 20,862,864 acres		
	Persons	Males	Females	Persons	Males	Females	Persons	Males	Females
1896	30,803	14,909	15,894	4,254	2,061	2,193	4,542	2,239	2,303
1897	31,158	15,078	16,080	4,299	2,084	2,215	4,530	2,234	2,296
1898	31,518	15,249	16,269	4,345	2,108	2,237	4,518	2,230	2,289
1899	31,881	15,421	16,460	4,391	2,131	2,259	4,502	2,222	2,280
1900	32,249	15,596	16,653	4,437	2,156	2,281	4,469	2,205	2,264
1901	32,612	15,769	16,843	4,479	2,177	2,302	4,447	2,196	2,251
1902	32,951	15,934	17,017	4,507	2,190	2,317	4,435	2,194	2,241
1903	33,293	16,099	17,194	4,536	2,203	2,332	4,418	2,189	2,228
1904	33,639	16,267	17,372	4,564	2,217	2,347	4,408	2,188	2,220
1905	33,989	16,437	17,552	4,593	2,230	2,362	4,399	2,187	2,213
1906	34,342	16,608	17,734	4,621	2,244	2,378	4,398	2,187	2,211
1907	34,699	16,781	17,918	4,650	2,257	2,393	4,388	2,183	2,205
1908	35,059	16,955	18,104	4,680	2,271	2,409	4,385	2,184	2,201
1909	35,424	17,132	18,292	4,709	2,285	2,424	4,387	2,188	2,199
1910	35,792	17,311	18,481	4,739	2,298	2,440	4,385	2,188	2,197
1911	36,136	17,471	18,665	4,751	2,304	2,447	4,381	2,187	2,194
1912	36,327	17,571	18,756	4,741	2,299	2,442	4,368	2,182	2,186
1913	36,574	17,687	18,887	4,728	2,293	2,435	4,346	2,170	2,176
1914	36,967	17,885	19,082	4,747	2,302	2,445	4,334	2,166	2,168
1915	35,284 (*a*)	16,003 (*a*)	19,281	4,771	2,308	2,463	4,278	2,111	2,167
1916	34,642 (*a*)	15,222 (*a*)	19,420	4,795	2,314	2,481	4,273	2,108	2,165
1917	34,197 (*a*)	14,661 (*a*)	19,536	4,810	2,316	2,494	4,273	2,113	2,160
1918	34,024 (*a*)	14,433 (*a*)	19,591	4,812	2,309	2,503	4,280	2,119	2,161
1919	35,427 (*a*)	15,868 (*a*)	19,559	4,820	2,305	2,515	4,352	2,203	2,149
1920	37,247 (*a*)	17,582 (*a*)	19,665	4,864	2,338	2,527	4,361	2,210	2,151
1921	37,932	18,098	19,834	4,882	2,348	2,535	4,354	2,209	2,145

	England and Wales			Scotland			Northern Ireland Area: 3,495,617 acres			Republic of Ireland Area: 17,367,247 acres		
	Persons	Males	Females	Persons	Males	Females	Persons	Males	Females	Persons	Males	Females
1922	38,205	18,249	19,956	4,898	2,358	2,540	1,269	619	650	3,022	1,529	1,493
1923	38,449	18,366	20,083	4,888	2,353	2,536	1,259	609	650	3,014	1,526	1,488
1924	38,795	18,571	20,224	4,862	2,329	2,533	1,258	608	650	3,005	1,521	1,484
1925	38,935	18,625	20,310	4,867	2,334	2,533	1,257	608	649	2,985	1,512	1,473
1926	39,114	18,722	20,392	4,864	2,333	2,531	1,254	607	647	2,971	1,507	1,464
1927	39,286	18,802	20,484	4,853	2,327	2,526	1,250	604	646	2,957	1,502	1,455
1928	39,483	18,897	20,586	4,848	2,324	2,523	1,247	602	645	2,944	1,498	1,446
1929	39,600	18,961	20,639	4,832	2,317	2,516	1,240	599	641	2,937	1,496	1,441
1930	39,801	19,072	20,729	4,828	2,316	2,512	1,237	598	639	2,927	1,493	1,434
1931	39,988	19,160	20,828	4,843	2,326	2,517	1,243	601	642	2,933	1,497	1,436
1932	40,201	19,280	20,921	4,883	2,348	2,535	1,251	607	644	2,949	1,505	1,444
1933	40,350	19,357	20,993	4,912	2,364	2,549	1,258	611	647	2,962	1,512	1,450
1934	40,467	19,412	21,055	4,934	2,375	2,559	1,265	616	649	2,971	1,518	1,453
1935	40,645	19,500	21,145	4,953	2,385	2,567	1,271	619	652	2,971	1,520	1,451
1936	40,839	19,591	21,248	4,966	2,392	2,574	1,276	622	654	2,967	1,520	1,447
1937	41,031	19,705	21,326	4,977	2,397	2,580	1,281	624	657	2,948	1,510	1,438
1938	41,215	19,792	21,423	4,993	2,405	2,588	1,286	625	661	2,937	1,505	1,432
1939	41,460	19,920	21,540	5,007	2,412	2,594	1,295	630	665	2,934	1,503	1,431
	...	...	...	...	...	...	...	...	...			
1940 (*b*)	41,862	20,216	21,646	5,065	2,454	2,611	1,299	634	665	2,958	1,515	1,443
1941 (*b*)	41,748	20,141	21,607	5,160	2,492	2,668	1,308	633	675	2,993	1,533	1,460

See p. 14 for footnotes.

Population and Vital Statistics 3. *continued*

(in thousands)

	England and Wales			Scotland			Northern Ireland Area: 3,495,617 acres			Republic of Ireland Area: 17,367,247 acres		
	Persons	Males	Females	Persons	Males	Females	Persons	Males	Females	Persons	Males	Females
1942 (*b*)	41,897	20,180	21,717	5,174	2,508	2,666	1,329	648	681	2,963	1,499	1,464
1943 (*b*)	42,259	20,397	21,862	5,189	2,521	2,668	1,341	656	685	2,946	1,490	1,456
1944 (*b*)	42,449	20,473	21,976	5,210	2,534	2,676	1,357	665	692	2,944	1,487	1,457
1945 (*b*)	42,636	20,549	22,087	5,187	2,508	2,679	1,359	666	693	2,952	1,490	1,462
1946 (*b*)	42,700	20,611	22,089	5,167	2,509	2,658	1,350	662	688	2,957	1,496	1,461
1947 (*b*)	43,050	20,822	22,228	5,120	2,476	2,643	1,350	661	689	2,974	1,505	1,469
1948 (*b*)	43,502	21,091	22,411	5,150	2,496	2,654	1,362	667	695	2,985	1,512	1,473
1949 (*b*)	43,785	21,239	22,546	5,156	2,501	2,655	1,371	672	699	2,981	1,513	1,468
1950 (*b*)	44,020	21,357	22,663	5,168	2,506	2,662	1,377	674	703	2,969	1,510	1,459
	...	...	...	...	...	...	...	...	...			
1951	43,815	21,044	22,771	5,102	2,439	2,664	1,373	669	704	2,961	1,507	1,454
1952	43,955	21,110	22,845	5,101	2,437	2,664	1,375	670	705	2,953	1,501	1,452
1953	44,109	21,206	22,903	5,099	2,436	2,664	1,384	675	709	2,949	1,498	1,451
1954	44,274	21,288	22,986	5,104	2,437	2,667	1,387	676	711	2,941	1,493	1,448
1955	44,441	21,389	23,052	5,112	2,442	2,669	1,394	679	715	2,921	1,479	1,442
1956	44,667	21,517	23,150	5,120	2,447	2,673	1,397	681	716	2,898	1,463	1,435
1957	44,907	21,648	23,259	5,125	2,450	2,675	1,399	681	717	2,885	1,456	1,429
1958	45,109	21,744	23,365	5,141	2,461	2,680	1,402	684	719	2,853	1,439	1,414
1959	45,386	21,885	23,501	5,162	2,473	2,689	1,408	686	722	2,846	1,435	1,411
1960	45,775	22,097	23,678	5,177	2,483	2,694	1,420	692	728	2,832	1,427	1,405
1961	46,196	22,347	23,849	5,184	2,485	2,699	1,427	696	732	2,818	1,417	1,402
1962	46.657	22,631	24,026	5,198	2,495	2,703	1,437	700	737	2,824	1,419	1,405
1963	46,973	22,787	24,186	5,205	2,500	2,705	1,447	705	741	2,841	1,427	1,414
1964	47,324	22,978	24,346	5,209	2,501	2,707	1,458	711	747	2,849	1,431	1,418
1965	47,671	23,151	24,521	5,210	2,501	2,709	1,468	716	752	2,855	1,433	1,422
1966	47,966	23,296	24,671	5,201	2,496	2,704	1,476	719	757	2,884	1,449	1,435
1967	48,272	23,451	24,821	5,198	2,496	2,702	1,489	726	763	2,899	1,456	1,443
1968	48,511	23,554	24,957	5,200	2,498	2,702	1,503	733	770	2,910	1,461	1,449
1969	48,738	23,666	25,072	5,209	2,503	2,706	1,514	739	776	2,921	1,466	1,455
1970	48,891	23,738	25,153	5,214	2,507	2,707	1,527	747	781	2,944	1,479	1,466
1971	49,152	23,897	25,255	5,217	2,507	2,710	1,538	756	782	2,978	1,496	1,483
1972	49,327	23,989	25,338	5,210	2,503	2,707	1,545	762	782	3,024	1,519	1,505
1973	49,459	24,060	25,398	5,212	2,504	2,708	1,547	766	781	3,073	1,554	1,529
1974	49,468	24,074	25,393	5,217	2,508	2,709	1,547	766	781	3,124	1,570	1,544
1975	49,470	24,091	25,378	5,206	2,504	2,702	1,537	761	777	3,177	1,597	1,580
1976	49,459	24,089	25,370	5,205	2,504	2,702	1,538	762	777	3,228	1,623	1,605
1977	49,440	24,076	25,364	5,196	2,501	2,695	1,537	761	776	3,272	1,645	1,627
1978	49,442	24,067	25,375	5,179	2,494	2,685	1,539	762	777	3,314	1,666	1,648
1979	49,508	24,113	25,395	5,167	2,490	2,678	1,543	763	780	3,368	1,693	1,675
1980	49,603	24,156	25,448	5,153	2,480	2,673	1,547	764	783	3,428	1,724	1,704

(a) These figures are for civilians only.

(b) These figures relate, so far as England & Wales, Scotland and Northern Ireland are concerned, to total population, i.e. to home population plus members of H.M. Forces overseas, less members of the Armed Forces of other countries temporarily in the United Kingdom. In 1951 figures of total population were as follows: England & Wales 44,008; Scotland 5,169. No figure of total population in 1951 was published for Northern Ireland in the source. The difference between home and total population is almost entirely represented by differences in the male population.

Population and Vital Statistics 4. Population by Sex and Age-Groups (Quinary) – 1841–1981

NOTES

[1] SOURCES: *Reports* of the censuses of 1951, 1961, 1971 and 1981 for the separate parts of the United Kingdom, of the census of 1911 for Ireland, and of 1981 for the Republic of Ireland.

[2] Partial returns to a question on ages were secured in Great Britain at the census of 1821. The results were as follows (in thousands):

(in thousands)

	England & Wales		Scotland	
	Males	Females	Males	Females
Total Population	5,850	6,150	983	1,109
Number Answering	5,151	5,380	924	1,033
Ages of Those Answering				
0–4	791·6	774·7	138·0	133·7
5–9	693·9	682·5	125·3	121·6
10–14	603·6	569·4	115·2	109·2
15–19	509·6	535·6	95·3	108·3
20–29	755·8	901·5	137·6	182·7
30–39	593·7	649·5	101·1	124·4
40–49	482·3	501·0	82·7	97·0
50–59	342·2	352·2	60·0	73·5
60–69	231·5	249·2	42·3	51·9
70–79	115·0	124·6	20·0	23·3
80–89	29·6	36·3	5·4	6·7
90–99	2·3	3·3	0·6	0·8
100 and over	0·06	0·12	0·04	0·06

A. England & Wales

(in thousands)

PERSONS	1841 (*a*)	1851	1861	1871	1881	1891	1901	1911	1921	1931	1951	1961	1971	1981
All Ages	15,914·1	17,927·6	20,066·3	22,712·2	25,974·4	29,002·5	32,527·8	36,070·5	37,886·7	39,952·4	43,757·8	46,104·5	48,749·6	48,521·6
0–4	2,106·3	2,348·1	2,700·7	3,071·2	3,520·7	3,553·4	3,716·7	3,854·3	3,321·8	2,990·3	3,717·8	3,597·0	3,904·7	2,910·2
5–9	1,904·9	2,092·3	2,344·1	2,706·4	3,147·3	3,395·2	3,487·2	3,696·8	3,518·9	3,322·6	3,161·9	3,262·3	4,044·1	3,206·6
10–14	1,732·1	1,913·4	2,105·2	2,424·3	2,800·2	3,223·6	3,341·8	3,499·7	3,659·8	3,207·2	2,811·9	3,725·2	3,627·0	3,846·3
15–19	1,586·8	1,757·2	1,932·6	2,180·4	2,547·3	2,950·9	3,246·1	3,336·6	3,503·0	3,434·6	2,704·5	3,200·7	3,313·6	4,020·0
20–24	1,550·5	1,666·7	1,829·5	2,004·7	2,328·3	2,646·4	3,120·9	3,175·8	3,151·5	3,494·5	2,927·4	2,878·3	3,731·2	3,564·2
25–29	1,282·9	1,470·4	1,569·2	1,780·6	2,048·0	2,350·2	2,824·5	3,079·1	2,960·3	3,357·1	3,279·9	2,846·2	3,191·3	3,274·8
30–34	1,167·0	1,276·1	1,386·8	1,560·0	1,745·5	2,027·5	2,431·4	2,877·2	2,800·9	3,055·3	3,078·5	2,984·3	2,871·3	3,656·1
35–39	884·5	1,088·6	1,224·6	1,341·3	1,541·4	1,781·8	2,145·4	2,613·2	2,745·2	2,803·0	3,323·2	3,241·9	2,786·2	3,092·4
40–44	888·0	968·6	1,134·2	1,229·8	1,399·4	1,547·0	1,850·6	2,232·6	2,601·2	2,663·5	3,365·2	3,036·6	2,935·1	2,792·4
45–49	638·6	799·0	930·8	1,053·0	1,151·4	1,336·8	1,573·2	1,925·6	2,406·2	2,554·0	3,172·2	3,228·8	3,135·5	2,689·1
50–54	634·4	708·8	806·6	944·7	1,022·1	1,160·1	1,329·0	1,602·6	2,014·1	2,381·6	2,824·8	3,221·1	2,897·4	2,785·0
55–59	391·8	526·3	614·0	718·2	806·5	884·2	1,052·6	1,278·4	1,630·7	2,068·4	2,423·0	2,927·8	2,975·6	2,877·5
60–64	439·8	481·3	556·2	622·7	727·7	772·9	890·6	1,020·0	1,282·0	1,657·0	2,142·8	2,458·1	2,840·9	2,532·8
65–69	259·6	327·5	376·5	441·3	502·4	572·0	629·7	806·8	986·1	1,270·7	1,829·4	1,978·8	2,399·8	2,426·2
70–74	224·3	250·1	281·3	324·0	349·9	417·9	446·4	553·6	656·8	870·8	1,427·8	1,541·7	1,778·1	2,061·7
75–79	119·9	146·1	160·7	182·0	202·3	233·3	264·5	310·0	392·5	499·9	923·7	1,068·9	1,185·5	1,458·4
80–84	70·5	73·9	79·7	89·9	95·8	105·6	128·7	144·2	179·9	225·8	446·0	605·1	707·2	821·2
85 and over	32·2	33·2	33·6	37·7	38·2	43·7	48·5	64·0	75·8	96·1	197·8	302·0	425·1	506·8
MALES	1841 (*a*)	1851	1861	1871	1881	1891	1901	1911	1921	1931	1951	1961	1971	1981
All Ages	7,777·6	8,781·2	9,776·3	11,058·9	12,639·9	14,060·4	15,728·6	17,445·6	18,075·2	19,133·0	21,015·6	22,303·8	23,682·0	23,624·7
0–4	1,048·4	1,176·9	1,354·9	1,536·4	1,757·6	1,775·1	1,855·3	1,936·0	1,681·5	1,510·2	1,903·7	1,846·1	2,002·8	1,492·4
5–9	953·2	1,050·2	1,173·0	1,350·8	1,568·6	1,693·4	1,738·9	1,847·3	1,766·5	1,677·8	1,616·4	1,670·6	2,074·3	1,647·0
10–14	880·4	964·0	1,059·9	1,220·8	1,402·1	1,610·9	1,671·0	1,747·6	1,837·1	1,620·4	1,428·6	1,907·3	1,865·3	1,971·8
15–19	781·6	873·2	957·9	1,084·7	1,268·3	1,465·2	1,607·5	1,654·9	1,727·8	1,709·6	1,335·3	1,622·0	1,696·1	2,053·6
20–24	723·4	795·5	860·2	951·9	1,112·4	1,247·3	1,472·6	1,502·7	1,448·4	1,699·1	1,427·2	1,434·4	1,876·1	1,804·7
25–29	610·9	699·3	734·3	843·3	981·3	1,111·1	1,328·3	1,455·8	1,340·0	1,629·0	1,625·8	1,446·0	1,612·1	1,647·7
30–34	564·7	617·9	661·7	746·3	840·3	977·9	1,157·7	1,375·9	1,281·3	1,433·3	1,513·9	1,501·6	1,460·3	1,834·6
35–39	435·0	532·7	590·3	640·8	744·9	865·5	1,034·5	1,261·4	1,273·3	1,283·0	1,632·5	1,616·2	1,409·8	1,554·4
40–44	435·6	474·2	551·1	590·1	673·0	745·5	897·5	1,075·1	1,223·1	1,229·3	1,657·9	1,493·8	1,466·8	1,405·3
45–49	313·5	393·9	453·3	506·9	547·5	642·2	760·0	926·1	1,162·2	1,186·6	1,556·4	1,583·8	1,551·8	1,351·1
50–54	307·3	346·1	392·2	455·8	485·8	549·6	636·3	768·2	971·0	1,116·3	1,317·9	1,575·4	1,412·0	1,380·6
55–59	189·7	254·9	299·0	345·9	382·0	413·3	497·5	608·0	781·6	987·4	1,089·3	1,407·8	1,433·7	1,403·4
60–64	209·1	227·2	265·5	294·7	340·6	356·9	410·4	477·2	601·2	778·1	938·8	1,096·3	1,330·2	1,195·8
65–69	120·8	151·6	175·5	205·4	231·5	259·7	282·4	365·9	449·4	578·0	780·6	818·9	1,063·3	1,099·9

Population and Vital Statistics 4. *continued*

A. England & Wales *continued*

(in thousands)

MALES	1841 (a)	1851	1861	1871	1881	1891	1901	1911	1921	1931	1951	1961	1971	1981
70–74	104·1	114·7	128·4	149·9	158·3	185·2	195·5	236·9	280·5	376·5	591·2	599·6	692·0	870·9
75–80	55·6	65·0	71·8	82·1	89·8	101·7	113·1	127·5	158·5	204·2	374·5	389·1	409·7	544·0
80–84	31·1	31·7	34·3	38·6	41·2	43·7	52·1	56·4	67·0	83·6	164·8	204·6	217·0	248·4
85 and over	13·2	13·2	13·0	14·5	14·7	16·2	18·0	22·7	24·8	30·6	60·8	90·2	109·8	119·2
FEMALES	1841 (a)	1851	1861	1871	1881	1891	1901	1911	1921	1931	1951	1961	1971	1981
All Ages	8,136·5	9,146·4	10,290·0	11,653·3	13,334·5	14,942·1	16,799·2	18,624·9	19,811·5	20,819·4	22,742·2	23,800·7	25,066·6	24,896·9
0–4	1,057·9	1,171·2	1,345·8	1,534·8	1,763·1	1,778·3	1,861·4	1,918·3	1,640·3	1,480·1	1,814·1	1,750·9	1,901·9	1,417·7
5–9	951·7	1,042·1	1,171·1	1,355·6	1,578·7	1,701·8	1,748·3	1,849·5	1,752·4	1,644·8	1,545·5	1,591·7	1,969·8	1,559·5
10–14	851·7	949·4	1,045·3	1,203·5	1,398·1	1,612·7	1,670·8	1,752·1	1,822·7	1,586·8	1,383·3	1,817·9	1,761·7	1,874·5
15–19	805·2	884·0	974·7	1,095·7	1,279·0	1,485·7	1,638·6	1,681·7	1,775·2	1,725·0	1,369·2	1,578·7	1,617·5	1,966·4
20–24	827·1	871·2	969·3	1,052·8	1,215·9	1,399·1	1,648·3	1,673·1	1,703·1	1,795·4	1,500·2	1,443·9	1,855·1	1,759·5
25–29	672·0	771·1	834·9	937·3	1,066·7	1,239·1	1,496·2	1,623·3	1,620·3	1,728·1	1,654·1	1,400·2	1,579·2	1,627·1
30–34	602·3	658·2	725·1	813·7	905·2	1,049·6	1,273·7	1,501·3	1,519·6	1,622·0	1,564·6	1,482·7	1,411·0	1,821·5
35–39	449·5	555·9	634·3	700·5	796·5	916·3	1,110·9	1,351·8	1,471·9	1,520·0	1,690·7	1,625·7	1,376·4	1,538·0
40–44	452·4	494·4	583·1	639·7	726·4	801·5	953·1	1,157·5	1,378·1	1,434·2	1,707·3	1,542·8	1,468·3	1,387·1
45–49	325·1	406·1	477·5	546·1	603·9	694·6	813·2	999·5	1,224·0	1,367·4	1,615·8	1,645·0	1,583·7	1,338·1
50–54	327·1	362·7	414·4	488·9	536·3	610·5	692·7	834·4	1,043·1	1,265·3	1,506·9	1,645·7	1,485·4	1,404·4
55–59	202·1	271·4	315·0	372·3	424·5	470·9	555·1	670·4	849·1	1,081·0	1,333·7	1,519·9	1,542·0	1,474·0
60–64	230·7	254·1	290·7	328·0	387·1	416·0	480·2	542·8	680·8	878·9	1,204·0	1,361·8	1,510·7	1,337·0
65–69	138·8	175·9	201·0	235·9	270·9	312·3	347·3	440·9	536·7	692·7	1,048·8	1,159·9	1,336·4	1,326·3
70–74	120·2	135·4	152·9	174·1	191·6	232·7	250·9	316·7	376·3	494·3	836·6	942·1	1,086·1	1,190·9
75–79	64·3	81·1	88·9	99·9	112·5	131·6	151·4	182·5	234·0	295·7	549·2	679·8	775·8	914·3
80–84	39·4	42·2	45·4	51·3	54·6	61·9	76·6	87·8	112·9	142·2	281·2	400·5	490·1	572·9
85 and over	19·0	20·0	20·6	23·2	23·5	27·5	30·5	41·3	51·0	65·5	137·0	211·8	315·4	387·5

B. Scotland

(in thousands)

PERSONS	1841 (a)	1851	1861	1871	1881	1891	1901	1911	1921	1931	1951	1961	1971	1981
All Ages	2,620·2	2,888·7	3,062·3	3,360·0	3,735·6	4,025·6	4,472·1	4,760·9	4,882·5	4,843·0	5,096·4	5,179·3	5,229·0	5,035·3
0–4	342·8	371·5	417·3	455·6	510·6	502·4	533·0	532·7	472·4	423·3	470·8	469·2	444·3	308·4
5–9	313·5	339·9	363·2	404·8	450·0	477·6	492·7	513·8	477·3	455·7	397·8	420·7	468·4	344·4
10–14	296·9	317·5	322·7	372·1	405·0	452·2	469·3	490·1	490·0	425·8	386·5	449·1	442·1	425·2
15–19	270·2	299·8	307·4	335·6	378·3	418·4	456·0	462·7	478·1	439·3	361·8	374·1	392·3	446·6
20–24	254·5	280·4	280·3	292·4	343·7	363·6	433·3	419·5	428·8	421·6	364·1	333·0	390·4	394·3
25–29	205·9	230·3	232·8	254·8	288·5	312·6	379·0	385·7	376·3	389·0	381·2	327·0	316·4	342·2
30–34	187·9	193·5	202·2	220·3	237·2	270·4	315·2	355·5	337·9	349·5	344·9	332·5	300·6	358·7
35–39	141·8	164·9	174·0	189·3	211·8	237·4	277·9	324·6	324·2	316·2	368·5	347·3	300·8	300·3
40–44	145·9	153·6	162·5	175·7	196·4	205·2	245·4	275·8	308·4	292·2	370·1	320·5	311·3	288·1
45–49	98·4	122·1	135·4	147·4	162·2	182·6	208·8	241·0	290·0	280·6	349·5	342·6	322·8	285·7
50–54	101·3	118·6	124·3	134·7	147·4	162·6	176·5	205·7	244·5	266·5	308·0	342·2	295·8	289·6
55–59	63·0	80·8	94·2	105·0	113·2	124·0	142·8	166·3	200·6	238·0	260·2	312·5	306·3	289·8
60–64	76·5	78·1	94·0	98·4	105·4	113·6	125·6	129·6	161·4	191·8	224·7	259·5	293·0	251·3
65–69	39·2	51·3	57·4	67·5	72·8	79·2	86·8	104·5	123·4	148·8	192·2	204·6	247·3	240·8
70–74	37·4	41·6	43·5	54·4	55·4	60·7	64·1	80·5	83·5	106·2	151·3	153·9	179·3	203·5
75–79	19·9	23·6	26·0	28·8	32·5	35·7	37·3	42·6	49·8	60·2	97·7	105·4	115·2	142·5
80–84	13·8	14·5	15·3	15·9	18·1	18·9	19·9	20·5	24·6	26·5	45·8	57·9	65·6	78·3
85 and over	6·5	6·9	6·9	7·3	7·2	8·6	8·4	9·3	10·6	11·5	19·8	27·2	37·2	45·6
not stated	4·9	—	2·7	—	—	—	—	0·4	0·8	0·2	1·1	—	—	—
MALES	1841 (a)	1851	1861	1871	1881	1891	1901	1911	1921	1931	1951	1961	1971	1981
All Ages	1,241·9	1,375·5	1,449·8	1,603·1	1,799·5	1,942·7	2,173·8	2,308·8	2,347·6	2,325·5	2,434·4	2,482·7	2,514·6	2,428·5
0–4	173·8	189·1	212·0	230·8	258·4	254·8	268·4	268·2	238·6	213·6	241·0	240·1	228·5	158·3
5–9	158·7	172·1	184·3	204·6	227·8	241·7	249·3	257·9	240·2	229·4	202·5	215·1	240·1	176·3
10–14	150·8	162·6	165·1	189·9	205·7	229·2	238·3	246·8	246·6	214·5	195·7	230·1	226·5	218·2
15–19	128·2	145·9	150·4	167·3	189·7	211·0	230·4	233·4	238·8	219·2	173·2	187·4	194·9	227·8
20–24	113·4	128·6	127·5	138·4	166·6	174·1	210·4	201·8	202·9	205·8	172·4	159·4	196·6	199·8
25–29	92·8	104·3	101·2	116·0	137·0	145·1	181·3	182·0	172·5	186·5	187·2	161·0	158·3	172·2
30–34	85·8	88·5	90·7	100·1	112·1	129·0	150·9	170·2	155·0	162·2	166·1	162·8	148·1	180·5
35–39	64·9	75·9	78·5	84·7	98·0	113·7	132·6	157·6	150·1	143·9	177·6	170·5	147·4	149·5
40–44	66·7	70·9	73·8	80·0	90·7	97·3	118·7	133·1	145·8	134·5	180·0	153·2	151·4	141·3

B. Scotland *continued*

(in thousands)

Males	1841 (a)	1851	1861	1871	1881	1891	1901	1911	1921	1931	1951	1961	1971	1981
45–49	45·9	56·6	62·4	67·3	73·6	84·7	100·5	115·2	141·9	129·9	168·7	163·9	157·0	139·5
50–54	45·0	53·6	56·4	60·9	66·5	74·0	83·7	98·2	119·3	126·7	141·3	164·3	139·6	139·6
55–59	28·7	56·5	43·0	47·5	50·9	55·6	65·6	79·1	96·5	115·5	115·8	147·3	143·2	138·4
60–64	33·5	33·3	40·6	43·0	45·5	49·6	55·6	59·9	75·9	91·7	97·9	113·2	133·7	114·4
65–69	17·4	22·0	24·5	29·2	31·2	33·7	37·0	46·1	56·8	68·1	83·2	83·4	106·6	105·7
70–74	16·2	17·5	17·8	22·8	22·9	24·8	26·3	32·2	34·8	46·0	65·7	60·2	67·9	83·2
75–79	8·7	9·9	10·7	11·8	13·4	14·2	14·8	16·5	19·4	24·5	41·6	40·2	39·4	50·9
80–84	5·6	5·7	5·9	6·2	7·1	7·1	7·3	7·4	8·7	9·8	17·8	21·7	20·5	22·5
85 and over	2·6	2·6	2·5	2·6	2·5	3·0	2·8	3·0	3·3	3·5	6·4	9·0	10·4	10·5
not stated	3.2	—	2·5	—	—	—	—	0·2	0·4	0·1	0·5	—	—	—

Females	1841 (a)	1851	1861	1871	1881	1891	1901	1911	1921	1931	1951	1961	1971	1981
All Ages	1,378·3	1,513·3	1,612·4	1,756·9	1,936·1	2,082·9	2,298·3	2,452·1	2,534·9	2,517·5	2,662·1	2,696·6	2,714·3	2,606·8
0–4	169·0	182·5	205·3	224·8	252·2	247·6	264·7	264·6	233·8	209·7	229·8	229·1	215·8	150·1
5–9	154·8	167·7	178·9	200·2	222·2	235·9	243·4	255·9	237·2	226·3	195·3	205·7	228·3	168·1
10–14	146·1	154·9	157·6	182·2	199·2	223·0	231·0	243·4	243·4	211·3	190·8	219·1	215·5	207·0
15–19	142·0	154·0	157·0	168·3	188·6	207·4	225·7	229·3	239·3	220·1	188·7	186·7	192·9	218·8
20–24	141·1	151·8	152·8	154·0	177·1	189·5	222·9	217·7	225·9	215·8	191·7	173·7	193·8	194·6
25–29	113·2	126·0	131·6	138·8	151·5	167·5	197·6	203·7	203·9	202·5	194·0	166·0	158·1	170·0
30–34	102·1	105·0	111·5	120·2	125·1	141·4	164·3	185·3	182·9	187·2	178·8	169·7	152·4	178·3
35–39	76·9	89·1	95·5	104·6	113·8	123·7	145·3	167·1	174·0	172·3	190·8	176·9	153·4	150·8
40–44	79·2	82·7	88·6	95·7	105·8	107·9	126·7	142·6	162·5	157·8	190·1	167·2	159·9	146·9
45–59	52·5	65·5	73·0	80·1	88·6	98·0	108·3	125·8	148·0	150·7	180·9	178·8	165·8	146·2
50–54	56·3	65·0	67·9	73·8	80·9	88·6	92·8	107·5	125·2	139·8	166·6	177·9	156·2	150·1
55–59	34·2	44·4	51·3	57·5	62·3	68·4	77·2	87·1	104·1	122·5	144·9	165·2	163·1	151·3
60–64	43·1	44·7	53·4	55·3	59·9	64·0	70·0	69·7	85·4	100·1	126·8	146·4	159·3	136·8
65–69	21·8	29·2	32·9	38·4	41·5	45·5	49·8	58·4	66·5	80·7	108·9	121·1	140·6	135·1
70–74	21·2	24·0	25·7	31·6	32·5	35·9	37·8	48·3	48·7	60·2	85·6	93·7	111·4	120·3
75–79	11·2	13·7	15·3	17·1	19·1	21·5	22·5	26·2	30·4	35·7	56·2	65·2	75·9	91·6
80–84	8·1	8·8	9·4	9·7	11·1	11·8	12·6	13·1	15·9	16·7	28·0	36·2	45·1	55·8
85 and over	3·8	4·3	4·0	4·7	4·7	5·5	5·6	6·3	7·3	8·0	13·4	18·2	26·8	35·1
not stated	1·7	—	0·2	—	—	—	—	0·2	0·4	0·1	0·6	—	—	—

C. Ireland

(in thousands)

Persons	1861	1871	1881	1891	1901	1911
All Ages	5,799·0	5,412·4	5,174·8	4,704·8	4,458·8	4,390·2
0–4	693·7	653·3	576·0	470·4	442·7	435·7
5–9	611·2	632·2	621·6	508·8	450·9	437·9
10–14	597·0	629·8	616·4	549·9	459·6	427·1
15–19	672·8	531·6	559·0	549·9	472·8	423·0
20–24	615·1	457·7	477·3	444·5	444·2	376·2
25–34	758·1	732·7	633·8	598·1	656·6	636·0
35–44	595·8	544·0	558·8	488·1	482·8	536·8
45–54	547·5	476·8	443·1	458·6	413·5	394·2
55–64	429·0	424·9	364·1	334·1	351·2	282·5
65–74	184·1	224·8	213·6	191·2	190·9	314·2
75–84	76·5	83·5	93·7	90·2	77·8	110·8
85 and over	14·3	17·3	14·6	19·1	15·8	15·9
not stated	3·8	3·8	3·0	1·8	—	—

Northern Ireland

Persons	1926	1937	1951	1961	1971	1981
All Ages	1,256·6	1,279·7	1,370·9	1,425·0	1,536·1	1,556·0
0–4	127·8	111·9	137·8	146·5	156·2	130·6
5–9	116·9	114·2	129·2	132·4	157·1	134·3
10–14	119·7	120·7	111·7	133·2	143·7	148·6
15–19	119·9	113·7	108·5	120·2	126·4	148·3
20–24	109·2	105·2	100·9	93·8	114·9	124·8
25–29	99·0	101·4	99·5	85·2	101·9	102·1
30–35	82·3	90·8	91·2	86·5	86·7	100·8
35–39	76·4	88·2	94·1	90·9	82·4	94·6
40–44	70·0	75·9	89·1	85·1	84·3	82·9
45–49	70·0	67·6	80·8	87·0	86·0	77·8
50–54	65·6	62·0	76·3	82·0	80·0	78·9
55–59	54·4	58·1	62·2	72·5	78·5	78·0
60–64	43·5	54·2	54·5	65·7	72·0	70·5
65–69	39·1	47·1	47·4	52·2	60·3	65·5
70–74	31·6	35·3	40·5	40·1	47·9	52·2
75–79	17·6	19·9	27·2	27·0	29·9	33·9
80–84	8·8	9·2	13·7	16·2	17·5	20·0
85 and over	4·7	4·2	6·1	8·4	10·4	12·2

See p. 19 for footnotes.

Population and Vital Statistics 4. *continued*

C. Ireland *continued*

(in thousands)

MALES	1861	1871	1881	1891	1901	1911
All Ages	2,837·4	2.639·8	2,533·3	2,319·0	2,200·0	2,192·0
0–4	352·2	331·0	292·2	238·9	224·8	220·8
5–9	309·7	319·8	314·5	258·4	228·4	222·1
10–14	306·0	322·4	315·0	280·4	234·2	217·3
15–19	329·4	258·7	274·0	276·3	235·0	214·9
20–24	297·7	214·2	231·8	223·9	217·3	191·3
25–34	367·0	342·8	296·3	286·2	320·9	312·1
35–44	277·3	260·4	262·7	227·0	233·8	273·2
45–54	261·9	224·5	213·6	217·9	194·5	198·1
55–64	204·8	204·7	171·8	163·1	169·2	137·7
65–74	87·2	111·8	106·0	92·5	96·3	144·0
75–84	35·4	39·1	46·8	44·1	38·1	53·0
85 and over	6·4	8·1	6·8	9·4	7·5	8·4
not stated	2·5	2·2	1·8	0·9	—	—

FEMALES	1861	1871	1881	1891	1901	1911
All Ages	2,961·6	2,772·6	2,641·6	2,385·8	2,258·7	2,198·2
0–4	341·5	322·3	283·7	231·5	217·9	214·9
5–9	301·5	312·4	307·2	250·4	222·5	215·7
10–14	291·1	307·4	301·4	269·6	225·4	209·8
15–19	343·5	273·0	284·9	273·6	237·8	208·1
20–24	317·4	243·5	245·5	220·6	226·9	184·9
25–34	391·2	389·9	337·5	311·8	335·7	323·9
35–44	318·5	283·6	296·1	261·1	249·0	263·6
45–54	285·6	252·3	229·4	240·7	219·0	196·0
55–64	224·2	220·2	192·3	171·1	182·0	144·8
65–74	96·9	113·0	107·6	98·7	94·6	170·2
75–84	41·0	44·3	46·8	46·1	39·7	57·8
85 and over	7·9	9·2	7·8	9·7	8·2	8·4
not stated	1·4	1·6	1·2	0·9	—	—

NORTHERN IRELAND

MALES	1926	1937	1951	1961	1971	1981
All Ages	608·1	623·3	667·8	694·2	754·7	761·9
0–4	65·0	57·1	70·6	75·4	80·3	66·7
5–9	59·3	58·1	66·1	68·1	81·1	69·2
10–14	60·3	61·5	56·9	68·1	73·7	76·1
15–19	59·4	56·7	55·4	60·3	65·1	76·4
20–24	52·5	51·0	48·7	46·9	59·3	64·1
25–29	45·9	48·4	47·9	41·6	51·6	52·2
30–34	38·0	43·6	44·7	41·6	43·5	50·8
35–39	35·3	41·6	45·5	43·9	40·7	47·1
40–44	32·7	35·8	43·0	41·6	40·7	40·9
45–49	33·5	31·9	38·8	42·1	41·7	37·9
50–54	32·3	29·4	36·1	39·6	39·1	37·7
55–59	26·8	27·9	28·9	34·4	37·4	36·9
60–64	21·3	26·6	24·4	29·4	33·1	32·6
65–69	18·8	22·8	21·6	23·0	26·4	29·1
70–74	13·8	16·1	18·3	17·0	19·5	21·7
75–79	7·5	8·8	12·4	11·3	11·6	12·6
80–84	3·7	3·9	6·0	6·7	6·4	6·5
85 and over	1·9	1·6	2·4	3·2	3·5	3·4

FEMALES	1926	1937	1951	1961	1971	1981
All Ages	648·5	656·6	703·1	730·8	781·4	794·2
0–4	62·8	54·8	67·2	71·2	75·9	63·9
5–9	57·6	56·1	63·1	64·3	76·0	65·1
10–14	59·4	59·2	54·8	65·0	69·9	72·5
15–19	60·5	57·1	53·1	60·0	61·2	71·8
20–24	56·7	54·2	52·2	46·9	55·6	60·8
25–29	53·9	52·8	51·6	43·6	50·3	49·9
30–34	44·3	47·1	46·6	44·9	43·2	50·1
35–39	41·1	46·6	48·6	47·0	41·7	47·4
40–44	37·3	40·0	46·0	43·4	43·6	42·1
45–49	36·6	35·7	42·0	44·9	44·4	39·9
50–54	33·3	32·6	40·3	42·5	41·0	41·2
55–59	27·6	30·2	33·3	38·2	41·1	41·1
60–64	22·2	27·6	30·1	36·3	39·0	37·9
65–69	20·3	24·3	25·8	29·2	33·8	36·4
70–74	17·8	19·2	22·2	23·1	28·4	30·5
75–79	10·0	11·1	14·8	15·7	18·3	21·3
80–84	5·1	5·3	7·3	9·4	11·1	13·4
85 and over	2·8	2·6	3·7	5·2	6·9	8·8

Population and Vital Statistics 4. *continued*

(in thousands)

D. Republic of Ireland

PERSONS	1926	1936	1951	1961	1971	1981
All Ages	2,972·0	2,958·4	2,960·6	2,818·3	2,978·3	3,443·4
0–4	287·7	268·3	312·8	300·8	315·6	353·0
5–9	284·6	269·3	281·0	287·7	316·9	349·5
10–14	295·5	282·8	260·9	288·8	298·5	341·2
15–19	286·2	268·3	241·2	233·8	267·8	326·4
20–24	240·2	254·5	202·2	158·0	215·3	276·1
25–29	215·4	216·8	198·4	145·4	173·0	246·1
30–34	183·3	183·3	191·6	152·8	151·3	232·0
35–39	165·8	192·4	200·9	166·8	149·1	193·8
40–44	169·1	162·9	180·3	170·3	152·7	165·9
45–49	168·9	156·6	160·9	174·6	160·1	151·9
50–54	162·7	152·7	163·0	157·1	159·0	148·7
55–59	125·7	143·4	128·8	136·1	154·8	149·9
60–64	105·1	130·4	122·0	131·1	134·0	139·3
65–69	101·2	113·0	107·5	103·5	111·8	133·9
70–74	82·2	84·2	100·1	92·8	99·0	103·2
75–79	46·0	53·0	64·5	63·2	61·8	68·5
80–84	27·4	23·2	30·9	37·0	36·4	40·5
85 and over	14·9	11·5	13·3	18·5	20·9	23·0
MALES	1926	1936	1951	1961	1971	1981
All Ages	1,506·9	1,520·5	1,506·6	1,416·5	1,495·8	1,729·4
0–4	146·2	136·4	160·2	153·4	161·8	181·0
5–9	144·8	136·3	143·5	147·0	161·8	179·1
10–14	150·8	143·7	132·7	148·3	152·1	175·3
15–19	146·0	138·1	125·7	120·3	136·8	166·7
20–24	124·5	134·7	105·4	80·4	110·0	140·4
25–29	106·6	113·3	100·0	72·3	87·7	124·4
30–34	92·5	94·1	96·4	75·2	76·8	118·3
35–39	87·3	96·8	102·3	81·6	75·5	99·3
40–44	86·1	83·7	94·0	84·8	76·4	85·3
45–49	87·0	80·5	82·4	89·0	79·5	77·8
50–54	85·6	78·7	82·9	81·7	80·0	75·3
55–59	67·1	75·1	65·0	68·6	78·4	73·3
60–64	53·7	68·1	61·3	64·4	68·1	68·0
65–69	51·5	60·1	54·1	51·1	54·5	64·3
70–74	37·5	40·8	49·1	44·1	44·6	48·4
75–79	20·9	24·6	31·6	29·7	27·8	29·2
80–84	12·1	10·5	14·6	16·7	15·7	15·4
85 and over	6·6	4·9	5·5	7·7	8·1	7·9
FEMALES	1926	1936	1951	1961	1971	1981
All Ages	1,465·1	1,448·0	1,454·0	1,401·8	1,482·5	1,714·1
0–4	141·5	131·9	152·6	147·4	153·8	172·0
5–9	139·9	133·0	137·6	140·7	155·1	170·4
10–14	144·7	139·1	128·2	140·5	146·4	166·0
15–19	140·1	130·2	115·4	113·5	131·0	159·8
20–24	115·7	119·8	96·8	77·6	105·3	135·7
25–29	108·8	103·5	98·8	73·1	85·3	121·7
30–34	90·8	89·2	95·1	77·5	74·5	113·7
35–39	88·4	95·6	98·6	85·2	73·6	94·5
40–44	83·0	79·2	86·3	85·5	76·3	80·6
45–49	81·9	76·1	78·5	85·6	80·6	74·1
50–54	77·1	74·1	80·1	75·4	79·0	74·4
55–59	58·6	68·3	63·8	67·5	76·4	76·3
60–64	51·5	62·3	60·7	66·6	65·9	71·3
65–69	49·7	52·9	53·4	52·3	57·3	69·6
70–74	44·8	45·1	51·0	48·7	54·4	54·8
75–79	25·0	28·3	32·9	33·5	34·0	39·3
80–84	15·3	12·8	16·2	20·4	20·7	25·0
85 and over	8·3	6·6	7·8	10·8	12·8	15·1

(*a*) Figures for 1841 are only approximate ones.

Population and Vital Statistics 5. Proportions of Each Age-Group (by Sex) according to Marital Condition – England & Wales, and Scotland 1851–1981

NOTES

[1] SOURCE: *Reports* of the Census of 1961 for England & Wales, and for Scotland.

[2] The divorced were not separately enumerated before 1921.

[3] In Scotland, persons who failed to state their marital condition were excluded from the statistics from 1911 onwards.

A. England & Wales, Males

(per thousand of the appropriate sex in each age-group)

		1851	1861	1871	1881 (*a*)	1891 (*a*)	1901 (*b*)	1911	1921	1931	1951	1961	1971	1981
All Ages	S	625	612	613	619	620	608	592	550	518	438	437	439	438
	M	337	351	351	346	345	357	372	414	444	523	530	525	504
	W	38	37	36	34	35	35	35	36	38	35	30	28	28
	D								0	1	4	4	8	24
15 and over	S	411	388	384	392	406	411	403	365	356	265	256	251	284
	M	529	554	559	553	540	536	545	584	593	684	700	701	650
	W	60	58	57	55	54	53	52	50	50	46	39	38	36
	D								1	1	5	6	10	30
15–19	S	996	995	994	995	996	997	998	996	997	995	989	979	989
	M	4	5	5	5	4	3	2	4	3	5	11	20	11
	W	..	..	..	..	..	..	..	..	..	..	..	..	..
	D								..	..	..	..	..	..
20–24	S	797	775	767	777	806	826	857	822	861	762	690	632	748
	M	200	223	230	221	193	173	142	177	138	237	309	366	246
	W	3	2	3	2	2	1	1	1	1	..	..	..	..
	D								..	..	..	..	2	6
25–29	S	441	402	392	392	429	450	492	446	471	349	294	257	341
	M	547	587	596	598	563	544	503	548	525	646	702	732	625
	W	12	11	11	10	8	6	5	6	4	2	1	1	1
	D								1	..	3	3	10	33
30–34	S	259	226	230	229	244	254	272	231	218	190	175	138	166
	M	718	755	750	751	739	732	716	756	771	799	818	844	784
	W	23	20	21	20	17	14	12	12	9	4	2	2	2
	D								1	1	7	6	15	48
35–39	S	180	153	151	152	163	174	186	163	137	133	132	111	112
	M	785	817	818	818	809	802	794	818	847	851	856	869	833
	W	35	30	31	30	28	24	20	18	14	7	4	3	3
	D								1	2	9	8	17	53
40–44	S	142	130	122	123	128	140	148	137	113	109	107	108	93
	M	806	826	834	834	830	822	820	837	863	872	876	869	848
	W	52	44	44	43	42	38	32	25	22	11	7	6	5
	D								1	2	9	9	16	54
45–49	S	121	108	99	99	104	116	127	124	110	98	95	99	89
	M	810	831	842	842	835	826	824	837	855	878	882	872	852
	W	69	62	59	59	61	58	49	38	33	17	12	12	9
	D								1	2	7	10	16	50
50–54	S	107	102	96	94	96	104	114	115	107	86	89	87	94
	M	794	809	821	821	817	810	809	824	839	876	880	877	846
	W	98	88	83	85	87	86	77	60	53	31	22	20	18
	D								1	1	6	10	15	41
55–59	S	101	90	88	81	83	87	98	106	104	77	86	82	91
	M	771	789	799	806	798	790	789	802	814	867	870	870	843
	W	128	121	113	113	119	123	113	91	81	51	37	34	32
	D								1	1	5	8	14	33
60–64	S	95	91	91	84	86	90	100	100	100	79	79	79	82
	M	721	729	739	748	740	732	729	758	771	830	849	852	839
	W	184	179	170	168	174	178	171	141	128	87	65	57	52
	D								1	1	4	6	12	27

Population and Vital Statistics 5. *continued*

A. England & Wales, Males (*cont.*)

(per thousand of the appropriate sex in each age-group)

		1851	1861	1871	1881 (*a*)	1891 (*a*)	1901 (*b*)	1911	1921	1931	1951	1961	1971	1981
65–69	S	86	86	83	81	76	80	88	94	96	84	73	77	80
	M	666	668	679	685	688	668	665	688	708	771	812	816	811
	W	248	246	238	234	236	252	247	217	195	143	111	97	88
	D								1	1	3	4	9	22
70–74	S	84	81	80	76	73	75	80	86	85	85	76	70	77
	M	574	572	582	586	588	577	577	599	621	682	734	755	753
	W	342	347	338	338	339	348	343	314	293	231	187	169	142
	D								1	1	2	3	6	17
75–79	S	78	75	74	72	71	67	71	75	76	82	79	63	78
	M	489	474	477	484	487	476	475	501	507	568	624	666	683
	W	433	451	449	444	442	457	454	424	416	348	295	267	227
	D									1	1	2	4	12
80–84	S	66	71	67	66	66	63	64	67	63	74	77	63	72
	M	395	363	373	378	380	373	370	391	392	443	487	534	561
	W	538	566	560	556	554	564	565	542	544	482	435	400	358
	D									1	1	1	3	8
85 and over	S	76	74	62	63	63	62	61	70	56	65	73	65	68
	M	290	272	270	271	274	263	258	272	268	311	337	360	391
	W	634	654	668	666	663	675	681	657	676	623	589	573	536
	D								1	1	1	1	2	6

B. England & Wales, Females

		1851	1861	1871	1881 (*a*)	1891 (*a*)	1901 (*b*)	1911	1921	1931	1951	1961	1971	1981
All Ages	S	598	587	586	592	596	585	571	535	500	405	388	380	369
	M	330	339	339	333	329	340	356	383	413	488	498	498	485
	W	72	74	75	75	75	74	73	82	86	102	106	111	113
	D									1	6	7	12	32
15 and over	S	385	369	361	367	387	395	390	368	354	248	219	200	216
	M	504	519	522	516	499	496	506	520	534	616	636	643	602
	W	111	112	116	116	114	108	104	111	111	129	136	143	140
	D								1	1	7	9	15	40
15–19	S	975	969	968	974	980	984	988	982	982	956	934	913	989
	M	25	30	32	25	19	15	12	18	18	44	66	87	11
	W	--	--	--	--	--	--	--	--	--	--	--	--	--
	D								--	--	--	--	--	--
20–24	S	687	664	652	665	701	726	757	726	742	518	420	397	748
	M	308	331	343	331	296	272	242	270	257	480	577	597	246
	W	5	5	5	4	3	2	1	3	1	1	1	1	--
	D								--	--	1	1	5	6
25–29	S	398	368	356	353	394	410	434	410	406	217	157	133	341
	M	584	613	624	630	593	579	558	568	587	770	835	847	625
	W	19	19	20	17	13	11	8	21	6	5	3	2	1
	D								1	1	8	6	18	33
30–34	S	249	232	224	221	245	257	270	260	249	146	109	78	166
	M	711	729	735	741	724	718	711	697	733	827	875	892	784
	W	40	39	41	38	31	25	19	42	16	14	6	5	2
	D								1	2	13	9	24	48
35–39	S	179	173	168	165	177	200	210	204	206	133	98	70	112
	M	758	765	766	770	765	752	752	740	755	831	875	894	833
	W	63	62	66	65	58	48	38	55	37	23	13	11	3
	D								1	2	13	14	24	53
40–44	S	145	142	141	140	149	168	180	179	181	142	97	74	93
	M	756	760	758	760	756	750	755	751	749	810	859	881	848
	W	100	97	100	100	95	82	66	69	67	35	27	22	5
	D								1	2	13	17	23	54

Population and Vital Statistics 5. *continued*

B. England & Wales, Females (*cont.*)

(per thousand of the appropriate sex in each age-group)

		1851	1861	1871	1881 (*a*)	1891 (*a*)	1901 (*b*)	1911	1921	1931	1951	1961	1971	1981
45–49	S	126	122	124	123	129	143	165	168	168	152	105	78	89
	M	739	744	740	734	728	726	729	739	733	780	828	855	852
	W	135	134	136	143	143	131	107	93	97	58	50	43	9
	D								1	2	11	17	23	50
50–54	S	119	116	117	115	118	129	150	159	159	150	122	83	94
	M	688	692	690	684	680	680	685	700	707	737	778	815	846
	W	193	192	193	201	202	191	165	140	132	104	84	80	18
	D								1	1	9	15	22	41
55–59	S	114	107	109	110	113	122	135	155	157	155	138	96	91
	M	639	643	637	627	616	612	624	638	656	668	706	746	843
	W	248	251	255	263	271	266	241	206	186	170	143	138	32
	D								1	1	6	13	20	33
60–64	S	116	111	109	107	107	111	128	151	155	156	144	115	78
	M	536	532	535	530	523	520	534	551	574	574	610	649	682
	W	347	357	356	363	370	369	338	297	270	265	237	218	205
	D								..	1	5	10	17	35
65–69	S	110	104	104	106	109	112	120	139	158	154	152	132	92
	M	448	449	441	433	425	417	424	441	461	477	493	526	566
	W	442	447	454	461	466	471	456	419	380	366	349	329	314
	D								..	1	3	6	12	28
70–74	S	112	106	104	105	107	112	123	139	156	157	155	139	112
	M	337	336	327	319	314	300	307	325	342	368	367	385	433
	W	551	558	570	576	579	588	570	535	501	472	475	467	435
	D								..	..	2	4	8	21
75–79	S	109	103	97	100	104	110	120	133	149	162	155	150	131
	M	243	232	234	225	215	204	206	214	223	257	250	258	289
	W	648	665	670	675	681	686	674	653	627	579	592	586	566
	D								..	..	1	2	5	14
80–84	S	110	100	97	99	107	111	121	132	144	167	161	155	137
	M	150	142	147	141	130	121	118	131	128	154	152	153	167
	W	740	757	756	760	763	768	760	738	728	679	686	689	686
	D								..	..	1	1	3	9
85 and over	S	107	91	91	95	105	119	126	130	142	172	172	160	152
	M	81	77	74	69	64	59	55	67	61	77	71	71	75
	W	812	832	835	836	831	823	818	802	796	751	756	767	768
	D								..	..	..	1	2	6
C. Scotland, Males														
All Ages	S	668	658	661	663	663	655	642	607	583	500	486	476	458
	M	298	309	306	304	304	312	322	355	376	458	478	488	495
	W	34	33	33	33	33	33	36	38	40	40	33	31	31
	D								..	1	2	3	5	16
15 and over	S	463	441	444	452	463	471	462	431	419	322	290	276	299
	M	482	505	502	495	485	478	485	514	524	621	661	674	641
	W	55	54	54	53	53	51	54	55	56	54	46	43	40
	D								1	1	3	4	7	21
15–19	S	996	996	997	997	998	997	998	995	996	996	988	977	984
	M	4	3	3	3	2	3	2	5	4	4	12	23	16
	W	..	..	..	..	..	..	..	..	..	..	..	..	..
	D								..	..	..	..	..	..
20–24	S	834	833	842	848	866	874	884	854	882	800	704	616	702
	M	163	165	156	150	132	125	115	145	117	199	295	381	292
	W	2	2	2	2	2	1	1	1	1	..	..	..	..
	D								..	..	..	..	2	6

Population and Vital Statistics 5. *continued*

C. Scotland, Males (*cont.*)

(per thousand of the appropriate sex in each age-group)

		1851	1861	1871	1881 (*a*)	1891 (*a*)	1901 (*b*)	1911	1921	1931	1951	1961	1971	1981
25–29	S	513	477	487	493	536	550	582	538	564	418	308	251	306
	M	477	513	502	496	455	443	412	456	431	577	689	741	669
	W	10	10	11	11	9	7	6	6	5	3	1	1	1
	D								1	..	2	2	7	24
30–34	S	322	283	286	287	318	334	360	316	307	240	189	142	155
	M	656	698	693	692	663	649	625	668	681	749	806	845	809
	W	23	19	21	21	19	17	15	14	11	6	2	2	2
	D								1	1	5	4	11	34
35–39	S	226	199	195	197	214	232	252	233	201	172	153	116	113
	M	739	772	774	771	755	741	723	744	779	812	836	869	846
	W	34	30	31	32	32	27	25	22	19	10	5	4	4
	D								1	2	6	5	11	37
40–44	S	183	164	163	158	172	187	202	194	170	145	132	117	98
	M	765	793	791	797	783	771	759	772	800	835	852	864	856
	W	52	43	45	45	45	41	40	33	29	15	9	7	7
	D								1	2	5	6	11	38
45–49	S	152	138	134	130	137	152	169	176	165	135	124	117	96
	M	776	801	804	808	800	787	772	776	791	837	852	857	856
	W	71	61	62	62	63	61	59	47	43	24	17	15	13
	D								1	2	5	7	11	35
50–54	S	141	132	129	125	129	139	150	160	159	125	121	110	103
	M	766	781	786	791	785	771	766	766	776	829	844	854	845
	W	94	86	84	85	86	90	84	73	64	42	29	26	24
	D								1	1	4	6	10	28
55–59	S	121	126	120	112	113	120	130	147	154	116	121	109	107
	M	756	761	767	771	770	757	750	743	750	813	824	837	828
	W	123	113	113	116	117	123	120	109	96	68	49	44	42
	D								1	1	3	5	9	23
60–64	S	118	126	122	111	116	122	126	136	145	120	119	110	103
	M	713	716	720	727	720	705	700	706	709	768	791	809	812
	W	168	158	158	162	164	173	174	157	145	109	85	73	67
	D								1	1	3	4	8	18
65–69	S	101	113	119	109	106	107	117	122	136	131	112	114	108
	M	675	668	673	670	671	655	639	651	650	690	742	760	769
	W	224	219	208	221	223	238	244	226	213	177	143	121	110
	D								1	1	2	3	6	14
70–74	S	100	110	121	108	106	107	111	114	123	130	117	109	111
	M	603	600	594	588	588	573	560	561	574	594	654	686	709
	W	297	289	285	304	306	320	329	325	303	274	227	200	170
	D								1	1	1	2	5	10
75–79	S	87	98	110	108	106	103	102	97	109	119	124	101	116
	M	540	516	515	499	509	481	475	466	472	490	531	585	620
	W	373	386	375	393	385	417	423	436	418	389	343	311	257
	D								..	1	1	1	3	7
80–84	S	78	84	105	108	96	98	98	93	102	108	122	106	113
	M	445	445	437	407	423	395	373	364	355	379	406	453	491
	W	477	471	458	485	481	507	529	543	542	512	471	440	391
	D								..	..	1	1	2	6
85 and over	S	83	81	97	81	89	95	95	82	92	94	113	108	109
	M	358	338	311	317	304	280	266	263	252	251	272	289	337
	W	559	581	591	603	606	625	639	655	655	655	615	602	551
	D								..	1	..	..	1	4

Population and Vital Statistics 5. *continued*

D. Scotland, Females

(per thousand of the appropriate sex in each age-group)

		1851	1861	1871	1881 (*a*)	1891 (*a*)	1901 (*b*)	1911	1921	1931	1951	1961	1971	1981
All Ages	S	637	630	629	629	631	623	615	586	565	475	447	425	397
	M	279	286	287	290	290	300	311	333	353	427	448	457	465
	W	84	84	84	82	79	76	74	80	81	94	99	109	116
	D								1	1	4	5	9	23
15 and over	S	455	443	432	430	442	445	440	424	415	316	270	240	245
	M	419	431	439	444	438	443	452	464	475	556	592	604	582
	W	126	127	129	126	119	112	108	111	109	122	131	144	145
	D								1	1	5	7	11	29
15–19	S	979	979	978	982	988	983	986	979	977	965	942	921	950
	M	21	21	22	18	12	16	14	21	23	35	58	79	50
	W	..	..	..	..	..	..	..	..	..	..	..	..	..
	D								..	..	..	..	..	..
20–24	S	748	741	738	735	764	764	782	754	771	602	482	420	523
	M	247	255	258	261	233	234	216	242	228	396	516	574	461
	W	5	4	4	3	2	2	2	4	1	1	1	1	2
	D								..	..	1	1	5	14
25–29	S	466	460	443	431	478	475	502	480	495	290	190	146	185
	M	512	520	537	553	511	515	491	501	498	698	803	837	769
	W	23	20	20	17	12	10	7	19	6	6	3	3	3
	D								1	1	6	4	14	42
30–34	S	316	311	301	288	312	318	333	322	324	190	144	92	89
	M	634	645	653	673	657	657	648	637	657	784	842	882	853
	W	49	44	45	39	31	25	20	40	17	17	8	7	6
	D								1	2	9	7	19	52
35–39	S	249	253	250	233	240	256	259	259	261	171	136	88	69
	M	673	672	677	699	703	695	701	685	697	793	835	880	863
	W	78	75	73	68	57	49	40	54	39	28	17	14	13
	D								1	2	9	12	18	55
40–44	S	223	220	219	206	206	219	223	226	232	186	131	101	65
	M	650	662	667	683	697	696	707	703	699	765	820	852	857
	W	127	117	114	111	97	84	70	70	68	41	36	29	24
	D								1	2	7	13	17	53
45–49	S	209	199	202	194	188	197	213	211	219	203	142	114	74
	M	624	642	640	650	668	671	675	691	683	720	783	813	835
	W	167	159	158	156	144	132	112	97	96	70	63	54	48
	D								1	2	7	12	19	43
50–54	S	207	204	199	193	185	186	203	203	211	203	167	118	92
	M	560	574	580	589	605	615	627	649	656	672	720	766	784
	W	234	222	221	217	210	199	170	147	131	119	103	100	90
	D								1	2	6	10	17	35
55–59	S	205	198	192	192	181	179	190	206	206	207	192	135	108
	M	499	516	528	526	548	550	567	581	606	601	632	686	714
	W	296	287	280	281	271	272	244	213	187	187	167	166	148
	D								1	1	5	8	13	30
60–64	S	211	212	203	196	192	183	188	203	207	211	203	163	114
	M	404	409	423	428	443	446	476	494	516	509	529	575	619
	W	386	379	374	376	366	371	336	302	275	276	261	251	242
	D								1	1	4	6	11	24
65–69	S	205	207	201	195	190	184	187	198	216	215	213	191	136
	M	336	335	349	349	361	356	369	388	410	420	418	444	493
	W	459	457	451	455	449	459	444	413	373	363	364	357	353
	D								1	1	2	5	8	18

D. Scotland, Females (*cont.*)

(per thousand of the appropriate sex in each age-group)

		1851	1861	1871	1881 (*a*)	1891 (*a*)	1901 (*b*)	1911	1921	1931	1951	1961	1971	1981
70–74	S	211	214	209	205	200	197	196	200	218	219	220	205	165
	M	250	244	251	252	260	250	259	278	297	320	305	313	360
	W	539	542	540	543	540	554	544	522	484	459	472	476	463
	D									1	2	3	5	13
75–79	S	208	209	208	200	191	201	200	193	211	220	227	220	195
	M	176	175	174	178	187	167	167	173	186	212	205	205	227
	W	616	616	618	622	622	632	633	633	602	566	566	572	570
	D										1	2	3	8
80–84	S	217	210	214	208	212	204	210	195	212	223	233	227	207
	M	104	105	105	104	111	91	101	97	102	123	117	116	122
	W	679	685	681	688	677	706	689	708	686	653	648	655	666
	D										1	2	3	6
85 and over	S	191	186	194	194	203	207	212	188	202	225	235	239	229
	M	56	53	61	55	64	40	41	47	52	58	52	53	51
	W	753	761	745	751	733	753	747	765	745	716	712	706	716
	D										1	1	1	4

(*a*) The proportions for 1881 and 1891 have been estimated from data for 10-year age-groups between the ages of 25 and 64 and the age-group 65 and over, in the case of England & Wales.

(*b*) The proportions for 1901 have been estimated from data for 10-year age-groups between the ages of 25 and 84.

Population and Vital Statistics 6. Population of Conurbations – Great Britain, 1801–1981

NOTES

[1] SOURCE: Census of England & Wales and of Scotland for 1951, 1971, and 1981.

[2] All figures, except as indicated in footnotes b and c, are adjusted to the present area of the conurbation, but for 1911 and preceding years it is not possible to give truly comparable figures; but the errors were small.

(in thousands)

	Greater London	South-East Lancashire	West Midlands	West Yorkshire	Merseyside	Tyneside	Clydeside (*a*)
1801	1,117	...	...	...	...	...	...
1811	1,327	...	...	...	...	...	...
1821	1,600	...	...	...	...	...	...
1831	1,907	...	...	...	...	...	...
1841	2,239	...	...	...	...	...	...
1851	2,685	...	...	...	...	...	...
1861	3,227	...	...	...	...	...	...
1871	3,890	1,386	969	1,064	690	346	...
1881	4,770	1,685	1,134	1,269	824	426	...
1891	5,638	1,894	1,269	1,410	908	551	...
1901	6,586	2,117	1,483	1,524	1,030	678	...
1911	7,256	2,328	1,634	1,590	1,157	761	...
1921	7,488	2,361	1,773	1,614	1,263	816	1,638
1931	8,216	2,427	1,933	1,655	1,347	827	1.690
1951	8,348	2,423	2,237	1,693	1,382	836	1,758
1961	8,183 ...(*b*)	2,428	2,347	1,704	1,338	832	1,802
1971	7,452	2,393 ...(*c*)	2,372	1,728	1,267	805	1,728
1981	7,678	2,219	2,244	1,682	1,127	738	...

(*a*) The census for 1951 does not give figures for censuses prior to 1921. Approximate figures can be extracted from the two censuses before that, as follows (in thousands):–

1901 1,343 1911 1,461

(*b*) Subsequent figures are for the area administered by the Greater London Council, the population of which was 7,992 thousand in 1961 and 8,197 thousand in 1951.

(*c*) The 1981 figure excludes the former Disley Rural District, which had a population of 4 thousand in 1971.

Population and Vital Statistics 7. Population of Principal Towns – British Isles, 1801–1981

NOTES

[1] SOURCES: *Reports* of the censuses of 1851–1951.

[2] Figures for the period 1801–51 (first column) are for the area of the towns in 1851, as nearly as is possible. For the census from 1851 onwards two figures are given – the first as shown in the census for the year concerned (first column), and the second as shown in that census for the area of the town as given at the subsequent census.

(in thousands)

	1801	1811	1821	1831	1841	1851	1851	1861	1861	1871	1871	1881	1881	1891	1891
Aberdeen	27	35	44	57	63	72	72	74	74	88	88	105	106	125	125
Bath	33	38	47	51	53	54	54	53	53	53	53	52	52	52	52
Belfast	...	...	37	53	70	87	103	122	122	174	174	208	208	256	273
Birkenhead				3	8	24	25	38	38	45	66	84	84	100	100
Birmingham	71	83	102	144	183	233	233	296	296	344	344	401	437	478	478
environs of Birmingham later incorporated (*c*)	...	...	...	...	19	32	32	55	55	91	91	145	...	156	156
Blackburn	12	15	22	27	37	47	47	63	63	76	85(*a*)	101	104	120	120
Blackpool		1	1	1	2	3	3	4	4	6	...	14	14	24	24
Bolton	18	25	32	42	51	61	61	70	70	83	...	105	105	115	156
Bournemouth	...	...	...	...	...	...	...	...	...	6	...	...	19	38	38
Bradford	13	16	26	44	67	104	104	106	106	146	147	183	194	216	266
Brighton	7	12	24	41	47	66	66	78	78	90	93(*a*)	108	108	116	116
Bristol	61	71	85	104	124	137	137	154	154	183	183	207	207	222	289
Cambridge	10	11	14	21	24	28	28	26	26	30	30	35	35	37	37
Cardiff	2	2	4	6	10	18	18	33	33	40	57	83	83	129	129
Carlisle	9	11	14	19	22	26	26	29	29	31	31	36	37	39	39
Chester	15	16	20	21	24	28	28	31	31	35	35	37	37	37	37
Colchester	12	13	14	16	18	19	19	24	24	26	26	28	28	35	35
Cork	...	...	...	...	83	88	88	80	80	79	79	75	75	76	76
Coventry	16	18	21	27	31	36	36	41	41	38	38	42	45	53	59
Derby	11	13	17	24	33	41	41	43	43	50	61	81	81	94	94
Dublin	...	...	...	...	246	272	272	271	271	263	263	268	268	269	269
Dudley	10	14	18	23	31	38	38	45	45	44	44	46	46	46	46
Dundee	26	30	31	45	63	79	79	90	91	119	119	140	140	154	154
Edinburgh (including Leith)	83	103	138	162	166	194	202	203	203	242	244	295	295	332	342
Exeter	17	19	23	28	31	33	33	34	34	35	35	38	37	37	46
Gateshead	9	9	12	15	20	26	26	34	34	49	49	66	66	86	86
Glasgow	77	101	147	202	275	345	357	420	420	522	522	587	587	658	658
environs of Glasgow later incorporated (*d*)				10	12	18	18	23	23	46	46	86	86	108	108
Greenock	17	19	22	27	36	37	37	43	43	58	58	67	67	63	63
Halifax	12	13	17	22	28	34	34	37	47(*a*)	66	66	74	81	90	98
Huddersfield	7	10	13	19	25	31	31	35	61	70	70	82	87	95	95
Hull	30	37	45	52	67	85	85	98	98	122	122	154	166	200	200
Ipswich	11	14	17	20	25	33	33	38	38	43	43	51	51	57	57
King's Lynn	10	10	12	13	16	19	19	16	16	17	17	19	19	18	18
Leeds	53	63	84	123	152	172	172	207	207	259	259	309	309	368	368
Leicester	17	19	26	41	53	61	61	68	68	95	95	122	137	175	175
Limerick	...	...	...	...	49	54	54	44	44	39	39	39	39	37	37
Liverpool	82	104	138	202	286	376	376	444	444	493	493	553	553	518	630
environs of Liverpool later incorporated (*e*)				8	13	19	19	28	28	47	47	74	74	113	
Luton	...	...	3	4	6	11	11	15	15	17	...	24	24	30	30
Macclesfield	11	15	21	30	33	39	39	36	36	35	35	38	38	36	36
Manchester	75	89	126	182	235	303	303	339	339	351	351	341	462	505	505
environs of Manchester later incorporated (*f*)		7	9	12	17	26	26	43	43	57	57	95			
environs of Manchester later incorporated (*g*)						9	9	17	17	36	36	66	...	70	70
Middlesbrough					6	8	8	19	19	40	40(*a*)	55	55	76	76
Newcastle-upon-Tyne	33	33	42	54	70	88	88	109	109	128	128	145	145	186	186

See p. 29 for footnotes.

Population and Vital Statistics 7. *continued*

(in thousands)

	1801	1811	1821	1831	1841	1851	1851	1861	1861	1871	1871	1881	1881	1891	1891
Newport (Mon.)	...	...	...	...	10	19	19	23	23	27	27	35	38	55	55
Northampton	7	8	11	15	21	27	27	33	33	41	41	52	52	61	75
Norwich	36	37	50	61	62	68	68	75	75	80	80	88	88	101	101
Nottingham	29	34	40	50	52	57	57	75	75	87	139(*a*)	187	187	214	214
Oldham	12	17	22	32	43	53	53	72	72	83	83	111	111	131	131
Oxford	12	13	16	21	24	28	28	28	28	31	31	35	41	46	46
Paisley	25	29	38	46	48	48	48	47	47	48	48	56	56	66	66
Plymouth (including Devonport)	40	51	55	66	70	90	90	113	113	118	118	123	123	139	145
Poole	6	6	8	8	9	9	9	10	10	10	10	12	12	15	15
Portsmouth	33	42	47	50	53	72	72	95	95	114	114	128	128	159	159
Preston	12	17	25	34	51	70	70	83	83	85	88(*a*)	97	97	108	108
Reading	10	11	13	16	19	21	21	25	25	32	32	42	49	60	60
St. Helens	...	...	...	...	...	15	15	18	32	45	45	57	57	71	72
Salford	14	19	26	41	53	64	85	102	102	125	125	176	176	198	198
Sheffield	46	53	65	92	111	135	135	185	185	240	240	285	285	324	324
Shrewsbury	15	17	20	21	18	20	20	22	22	23	23	26	26	27	27
Southampton	8	10	13	19	28	35	35	47	47	54	54	60	60	65	82
Southend-on-Sea	...	...	...	...	...	...	...	3	3	5	5	8	8	12	13
South Shields	11	15	17	19	23	29	29	35	35	45	45	57	57	78	78
Stockport	17	21	27	36	50	54	54	55	55	53	53	60	60	70	70
Stoke-upon-Trent (*h*)	...	28	35	35	54	66	66	78	78	101	101	113	125	145	193
Sunderland	24	25	31	39	43	65	64	78	80	98	98	117	117	131	132
Swansea	10	12	15	20	25	31	31	42	41	52	52	66	76	91	91
Tynemouth	13	18	23	23	25	29	29	34	34	39	39	44	44	47	47
Wakefield	11	11	14	16	19	22	23	23	23	28	28	31	31	33	39
Wallasey	1	1	1	3	6	8	8	11	11	15	15	21	21	33	33
Walsall	10	11	12	15	20	26	26	38	38	46	51	59	59	72	72
Warrington	11	13	15	18	21	23	23	26	26	32	32	41	43	53	55
Wigan	11	14	18	21	26	32	32	38	38	39	39	48	48	55	55
Wolverhampton	13	15	18	25	36	50	50	61	61	68	68	76	76	83	83
Worcester	11	14	17	19	27	28	28	31	31	33	33	34	40	43	43
Yarmouth	17	20	21	25	28	31	31	35	35	42	42	46	47	49	49
York	17	19	22	26	29	36	36	40	40	44	44	50	62	67	68

(in thousands)

	1901	1901	1911	1911	1921	1921	1931	1931	1951	1951	1961	1961	1971	1971	1981
Aberdeen	154	154	164	164	159	159	167	170	183	183	185	185	182	212	204
Bath	50	50	51	69	69	69	69	69(*b*)	79	79	81	84	85	84	81
Belfast (figures for 1926 and 1937 instead of 1921 and 1931)	349	349	387	387	415	415	438	438	444	444	416	416	362	417	306
Birkenhead	111	111	131	131	146	148	148	152	143	143	142	142	138	138	124
Birmingham	522	523	526	840	919	922	1,003	1,003	1,113	1,113	1,107	1,111	1,015	1,098	1,007
environs of Birmingham later incorporated (*c*)	238	238	314												
Blackburn	128	129	133	133	127	127	123	123	111	111	106	106	102	141	142(*i*)
Blackpool	47	47	58	61	100	100	102	106	147	147	153	153	152	152	148
Bolton	168	168	181	181	179	179	177	177	167	167	161	161	154	260	261(*i*)
Bournemouth	47	47	79	79	92	96	117	117	145	145	154	154	154	154	146
Bradford	280	280	288	288	286	291	298	299	292	292	296	296	294	462	457(*i*)
Brighton	123	123	131	131	142	147	147	147	156	158	163	163	161	161	147
Bristol	329	339	357	357	377	377	397	404(*b*)	443	443	437	438	427	438	391

See p. 29 for footnotes.

Population and Vital Statistics 7. *continued*

(in thousands)

	1901	1901	1911	1911	1921	1921	1931	1931	1951	1951	1961	1961	1971	1971	1981
Cambridge	38	38	40	56	59	59	67	70	82	82	96	96	99	99	91
Cardiff	164	164	182	182	200	220	224	227(*b*)	244	244	257	284	279	288	275
Carlisle	45	45	46	52	53	53	57	57	68	68	71	71	72	72	73
Chester	38	38	39	39	41	41	41	46	48	57	59	59	63	63	58
Colchester	38	38	43	43	43	43	49	49	57	57	65	65	77	77	82
Cork (figures for 1926 and 1936 instead of 1921 and 1931)	76	76	77	77	78	78	81	81	75	75	112	112	129	129	136
Coventry	70	70	106	106	128	148	167	178	258	258	306	317	335	337	314
Derby	106	115	123	123	130	131	142	143	141	141	132	213	220	220	217
Dublin (figures for 1926 and 1936 instead of 1921 and 1931)	291	291	305	305	317	404	473	473	522	522	537	537	566	568	526
Dudley	49	49	51	51	56	56	60	60	63	64	63	162	186	294	300(*i*)
Dundee	161	161	165	176	168	168	176	177	177	177	183	183	182	197	180
Edinburgh (including Leith)	394	395	401	424	420	420	439	439	467	467	468	468	454	477	437
Exeter	47	47	49	59	60	60	66	68	76	76	80	89	96	96	97
Gateshead	110	112	117	117	125	125	125	125	115	115	103	103	94	225	211(*i*)
Glasgow	762	776	784	1,000	1,034	1,052	1,088	1,093	1,090	1,090	1,055	1,055	898	982	766
environs of Glasgow later incorporated (*d*)	142	142	169												
Greenock	68	68	75	75	81	81	79	79	76	77	75	75	70	70	68
Halifax	105	105	102	102	99	99	98	98	98	98	96	96	91	91	87
Huddersfield	95	95	108	108	110	110	113	123	129	129	131	131	131	131	124
Hull	240	240	278	278	287	291	314	314	299	299	303	304	286	286	270
Ipswich	67	67	74	74	79	79	88	88	105	107	117	117	123	123	121
King's Lynn	20	20	20	20	20	20	21	24	26	26	28	28	30	30	33
Leeds	429	429	446	453	458	463	483	483	505	506	511	511	496	739	705(*i*)
Leicester	212	212	227	227	234	234	239	258	285	285	273	288	284	284	280
Limerick (figures for 1926 and 1936 instead of 1921 and 1931)	38	38	39	39	39	39	41	41	51	51	51	51	83	83	101
Liverpool	685	704	746	753	803	805	856	856	789	791	746	746	610	610	510
environs of Liverpool later incorporated (*e*)															
Luton	36	36	50	50	57	60	69	70	110	110	132	140	161	161	165
Macclesfield	35	35	35	35	34	34	35	36	36	36	38	38	44	44	47
Manchester	544	645	714	714	730	736	766	766	703	703	662	662	544	544	449
environs of Manchester later incorporated (*f*)															
environs of Manchester later incorporated (*g*)	101														
Middlesbrough	91	91	105	120	131	131	138	139	147	147	157	164	159	159	149
Newcastle-upon-Tyne	215	247	267	267	275	275	283	286	292	292	270	270	222	308	278(*i*)
Newport (Mon./Gwent)	67	67	84	84	92	92	89	98	106	106	108	109	112	137	134
Northampton	87	87	90	90	91	91	92	97	104	104	105	118	127	127	145
Norwich	112	114	121	121	121	121	126	...	121	121	120	121	122	122	123
Nottingham	240	240	260	260	263	263	269	276	306	308	312	312	301	301	272
Oldham	137	137	147	147	145	145	140	...	121	123	115	115	106	224	220(*i*)
Oxford	49	49	53	53	57	67	81	81	99	99	106	106	109	109	99
Paisley	79	79	84	84	85	85	86	88	94	94	96	96	95	95	85
Plymouth (including Devonport)	178	178	194	207	210	210	208	202(*b*)	208	208	204	230	239	239	246
Poole	19	28	39	39	44	46	60	60	83	83	92	92	107	107	119
Portsmouth	188	189	231	234	247	247	249	252	234	234	215	215	197	197	180
Preston	113	113	117	117	117	117	119	120	119	121	113	113	98	135	126(*i*)
Reading	72	81	88	88	92	92	97	97	114	114	120	120	133	140	134

Population and Vital Statistics 7. *continued*

(in thousands)

	1901	1901	1911	1911	1921	1921	1931	1931	1951	1951	1961	1961	1971	1971	1981
St. Helens	84	84	97	97	103	103	107	107	110	113	109	109	104	189	190(*i*)
Salford	221	221	231	231	234	234	223	223	178	178	155	155	131	280	244(*i*)
Sheffield	381	409	455	465	491	512	512	518	513	513	494	540	520	573	538(*i*)
Shrewsbury	28	28	29	29	31	31	32	37	45	45	50	50	56	56	60
Southampton	105	105	119	145	161	161	176	176	178	190	205	205	215	215	205
Southend-on-Sea	29	29	63	72	106	106	120	130	152	152	165	165	163	163	157
South Shields	97	101	109	109	117	119	113	113(*b*)	107	107	110	110	101	177	160(*i*)
Stockport	79	93	109	120	123	123	125	126	142	142	143	143	140	292	290(*i*)
Stoke-upon-Trent (*h*)	215	215	235	235	240	268	277	277	275	275	265	277	265	265	253
Sunderland	146	146	151	151	159	182	186	186(*b*)	182	182	190	219	217	293	295(*i*)
Swansea	95	95	115	144	158	158	165	165	161	161	167	167	173	190	187(*i*)
Tynemouth	51	51	59	59	64	64	65	66	67	67	70	70	69	69	60
Wakefield	41	48	52	52	53	53	59	59 (*b*)	60	60	61	61	60	60	61
Wallasey	54	54	79	79	91	95	98	98	101	101	103	103	97	97	90
Walsall	86	86	92	92	97	98	103	103	115	115	118	176	184	273	267(*i*)
Warrington	64	64	72	72	77	77	79	82	81	81	76	76	68	163	169(*i*)
Wigan	61	82	89	89	89	89	85	85	85	85	79	79	81	81	80
Wolverhampton	94	94	95	95	102	121	133	139	163	163	151	262	269	269	255
Worcester	47	47	48	49	49	49	51	52	60	62	66	66	73	74	75
Yarmouth	51	51	56	56	61	61	57	57	51	51	53	53	50	76	81(*i*)
York	78	78	82	82	84	84	85	94	105	105	104	108	105	105	100

(*a*) These figures are approximate, but are generally accurate to within 0.5 per cent.

(*b*) In the second column for 1931 it was not always possible to take account of boundary changes between 1931 and 1951 because of the destruction of records during the war. Incomplete figures are indicated by this footnote, and seriously defective ones have been omitted.

(*c*) The parishes or townships of Aston, Handsworth, King's Norton, Northfield, and Yardley (except such parts as were already incorporated in Birmingham)—i.e. such an area which at the end of the nineteenth century comprised Aston Manor county borough, Erdington, Handsworth, King's Norton, and Northfield urban districts, and Yardley, rural district. A part of the area was incorporated in Birmingham between 1881 and 1891, and the remainder between 1911 and 1921.

(*d*) The town of Pollokshaws and the parish of Govan—i.e. the area which at the end of the nineteenth century comprised the burghs of Govan, Partick, and Pollokshaws, and was incorporated in Glasgow between 1911 and 1921. Other areas, namely Crosshill, Govanhill, Maryhill, Hillhead, and Pollokshields, which were incorporated in Glasgow between 1881 and 1891, were previously classed as suburbs, and are here included with the city throughout.

(*e*) The parishes of West Derby, Toxteth Park, Walton-on-the-Hill and Wavertree (except such parts as were already incorporated in Liverpool). The whole of this area was incorporated in the city between 1891 and 1901.

(*f*) The parishes of Blackley, Harpurhey, Crumpsall, Bradford, Moston, Newton, Openshaw, and Rusholme, all of which were incorporated in Manchester between 1881 and 1891.

(*g*) The parishes of Moss Side, Gorton, Levenshulme, and Withington (except such parts as were already incorporated in Manchester). A part of this area was incorporated in the city between 1881 and 1891 and the remainder between 1901 and 1911.

(*h*) The townships of Hanley, Longton, Stoke, and Burslem for the period 1811–91. Thereafter the urban districts of Fenton and Tunstall are included.

(*i*) The 1981 populations of the 1971 boundaries of the following towns which underwent major boundary changes in the early 1970s were:–

Blackburn	88				
Bolton	147	Oldham	95	Stockport	136
Bradford	281	Preston	87	Sunderland	196
Dudley	187	St. Helens	99	Swansea	168
Gateshead	75	Salford	98	Walsall	179
Leeds	449	Sheffield	477	Warrington	57
Newcastle-upon-Tyne	192	South Shields	87	Yarmouth	48

Population and Vital Statistics 8. Population of the Old Counties – British Isles, 1801–1981

NOTES

[1] SOURCES: *Reports* of the census of 1951, 1961, and 1971 for the separate parts of the United Kingdom, of 1911 for Ireland, and of 1981 for the Republic of Ireland.

[2] The population of Belfast county borough is not shown in any of the counties of Northern Ireland after 1821.

[3] Members of the armed forces serving in Ireland were not included in the population at any census before 1861.

A. England

(in thousands)

	1801	1811	1821	1831	1841	1851	1861	1871
Bedfordshire	63	70	84	95	108	124	135	146
Berkshire	111	120	133	147	162	170	176	196
Buckinghamshire	108	118	135	147	156	164	168	176
Cambridgeshire (whole)	89	101	122	144	164	185	176	187
(Isle of Ely								
Cheshire	192	227	270	334	396	456	505	561
Cornwall	192	221	261	301	342	356	369	362
Cumberland	117	134	156	169	178	195	205	220
Derbyshire	162	186	214	237	272	296	339	379
Devonshire	340	383	438	494	533	567	584	601
Dorsetshire	114	125	145	159	175	184	189	196
Durham	149	165	194	239	308	391	509	685
Essex (*c*)	228	252	289	318	345	369	405	466
Gloucestershire	251	286	336	387	431	459	486	535
Hampshire (whole)	219	246	283	314	355	405	482	544
(Isle of Wight								
Herefordshire	88	94	103	111	113	115	124	125
Hertfordshire	97	111	130	143	157	167	173	192
Huntingdonshire	38	42	49	53	59	64	64	64
Kent (*c*)	259	306	355	399	448	486	546	631
Lancashire	673	828	1,053	1,337	1,667	2,031	2,429	2,819
Leicestershire	130	150	174	197	216	230	237	269
Lincolnshire (whole)	209	238	283	317	363	407	412	437
(Holland								
(Kesteven								
(Lindsey								
London (*c*)	959	1,139	1,380	1,656	1,949	2,363	2,808	3,261
Middlesex (*c*)	71	84	99	113	132	141	176	253
Monmouthshire	46	62	76	98	134	157	175	195
Norfolk	273	292	344	390	413	443	435	439
Northamptonshire (whole)	132	141	163	179	199	212	228	244
(Soke of Peterborough								
Northumberland	168	183	213	237	266	304	343	387
Nottinghamshire	140	163	187	225	250	270	294	320
Oxfordshire	112	120	138	154	163	170	171	178
Rutland	16	16	18	19	21	23	22	22
Shropshire	170	185	198	214	226	229	241	248
Somerset	274	303	356	404	436	444	445	463
Staffordshire	243	295	346	409	509	609	747	858
Suffolk (whole)	214	234	272	296	315	337	337	349
(Suffolk East								
(Suffolk West								
Surrey (*c*)	106	121	139	157	182	197	246	342
Sussex (whole)	159	190	233	273	300	337	364	417
(Sussex East								
(Sussex West								
Warwickshire	207	229	274	337	402	475	562	634
Westmorland	41	46	51	55	56	58	61	65
Wiltshire	184	192	219	237	256	254	249	257
Worcestershire	146	169	194	223	248	277	307	339
Yorkshire (East Riding)	111	133	154	168	194	219	238	265

Population and Vital Statistics 8. *continued*

A. England (*cont.*)

(in thousands)

	1801	1811	1821	1831	1841	1851	1861	1871
Yorkshire (North Riding)	158	169	187	191	203	213	242	290
Yorkshire (West Riding)	591	684	833	1,013	1,195	1,366	1,553	1,882
B. Wales								
Anglesey	34	37	45	48	51	57	55	51
Brecknockshire	32	38	44	48	56	61	62	60
Caernarvonshire	42	50	58	67	81	88	96	106
Cardiganshire	43	50	58	65	69	71	72	73
Carmarthenshire	67	77	90	101	106	111	112	116
Denbighshire	60	64	76	83	88	93	101	105
Flintshire	39	46	54	60	67	68	70	76
Glamorganshire	71	85	102	127	171	232	318	398
Merionethshire	30	31	34	35	39	39	47	52
Montgomeryshire	48	52	60	67	70	67	67	68
Pembrokeshire	56	61	74	81	88	94	96	92
Radnorshire	19	20	23	25	25	25	25	25
C. Scotland								
Aberdeenshire	121	134	155	178	192	212	222	245
Angusshire	99	107	113	140	170	191	204	238
Argyllshire	81	87	97	101	97	89	80	76
Ayrshire	84	104	127	145	164	190	199	210
Banffshire	37	38	44	48	50	54	59	62
Berwickshire	30	31	33	34	34	36	37	36
Buteshire	12	12	14	14	16	17	16	17
Caithness-shire	23	23	29	35	36	39	41	40
Clackmannanshire	11	12	13	15	19	23	21	24
Dumfriesshire	55	63	71	74	73	78	76	75
Dunbartonshire	21	24	27	33	44	45	52	59
East Lothianshire	30	31	35	36	36	36	38	38
Fifeshire	94	101	115	129	140	154	155	161
Inverness-shire	73	78	90	95	98	97	89	88
Kincardineshire	26	27	29	31	33	35	34	35
Kinross-shire	7	7	8	9	9	9	8	7
Kirkcudbrightshire	29	34	39	41	41	43	42	42
Lanarkshire	148	191	244	317	427	530	632	765
Midlothianshire	123	149	192	219	225	259	274	328
Morayshire	28	28	31	34	35	39	43	44
Nairnshire	8	8	9	9	9	10	10	10
Orkney	24	23	27	29	31	31	32	31
Peeblesshire	9	10	10	11	10	11	11	12
Perthshire	126	134	138	142	137	139	134	128
Renfrewshire	79	93	112	133	155	161	178	217
Ross & Cromarty	56	61	69	75	79	83	81	81
Roxburghshire	34	37	41	44	46	52	54	54
Selkirkshire	5	6	7	7	8	10	10	14
Shetland	22	23	26	29	31	31	32	32
Stirlingshire	51	58	65	73	82	86	92	98
Sutherlandshire	23	24	24	26	25	26	25	24
West Lothianshire	18	19	23	23	27	30	39	41
Wigtownshire	23	27	33	36	39	43	42	39

Population and Vital Statistics 8. *continued*

D. Northern Ireland

(in thousands)

	1801	1811	1821	1831	1841	1851	1861	1871
Antrim			234	272	291	274	257(*b*)	246
Armagh			197	220	233	196	190	179
Down			325	352	361	321	299	277
Fermanagh			131	150	157	116	106	93
Londonderry			194	222	222	192	184	174
Tyrone			262	304	313	256	239	216
E. Irish Republic								
Carlow			79	82	86	68	57	52
Cavan			195	228	243	174	154	141
Clare			208	258	286	212	166	148
Cork			730	811	854	649	545	517
Donegal			248	289	296	255	237	218
Dublin			336	380	373	405	410	405
Galway			337	415	440	322	271	248
Kerry			216	263	294	238	201	197
Kildare			99	108	114	96	91	84
Kilkenny			182	194	202	159	125	109
Laoighis (Queen's)			134	146	154	112	91	80
Leitrim			125	142	155	112	105	96
Limerick			277	315	330	262	217	192
Longford			108	113	115	82	72	65
Louth			119	125	128	108	91	84
Mayo			293	366	389	274	255	246
Meath			159	177	184	141	110	96
Monaghan			175	196	200	142	126	115
Offaly (King's)			131	144	147	112	90	76
Roscommon			209	250	254	173	157	141
Sligo			146	172	181	129	125	115
Tipperary			347	403	436	332	249	217
Waterford			157	177	196	164	134	123
Westmeath			129	137	141	111	91	78
Wexford			171	183	202	180	144	133
Wicklow			111	122	126	99	86	79

Population and Vital Statistics 8. *continued*

A. England

(in thousands)

	1881	1891 (*a*)	1891 (*a*)	1901	1911	1921	1931	1951
Bedfordshire	149	161	161	172	195	206	221	312
Berkshire	218	239	241	259	281	295	311	403
Buckinghamshire	176	185	187	197	219	236	271	386
Cambridgeshire (whole)	186	189	185	186	199	207	221	256
(Isle of Ely			64	65	71	77	81	89
Cheshire	644	730	755	842	962	1,020	1,088	1,259
Cornwall	331	323	323	322	328	321	318	345
Cumberland	251	267	267	267	266	273	263	285
Derbyshire	462	528	511	596	679	709	750	826
Devonshire	604	632	633	662	700	710	733	798
Dorsetshire	191	195	192	200	221	225	239	291
Durham	867	1,016	1,017	1,187	1,370	1,479	1,486	1,464
Essex (*c*)	576	785	783	1,084	1,351	1,470	1,755	2,045
Gloucestershire	572	600	656	710	738	760	791	939*
Hampshire (whole)	593	690	694	801	953	1,008	1,103	1,293
(Isle of Wight			79	82	88	95	88	96
Herefordshire	121	116	116	114	114	113	112	127
Hertfordshire	203	220	227	258	311	333	401	610
Huntingdonshire	59	58	55	54	56	55	56	69
Kent (*c*)	710	807	830	961	1,046	1,142	1,219	1,564
Lancashire	3,454	3,927	3,897	4,373	4,762	4,934	5,040	5,118
Leicestershire	321	373	376	438	477	494	542	631
Lincolnshire (whole)	470	473	474	500	564	602	624	706
(Holland			76	77	83	86	92	102
(Kesteven			103	101	107	108	110	131
(Lindsey			295	321	374	409	422	474
London (*c*)	3,830	4,228	4,228	4,536	4,522	4,485	4,397	3,348
Middlesex (*c*)	370	564	543	792	1,126	1,253	1,639	2,269
Monmouthshire	211	252	258	297	395	450	432	425
Norfolk	445	455	468	476	498	501	502	548
Northamptonshire (whole)	273	302	300	336	349	349	361	423
(Soke of Peterborough			35	41	45	47	52	64
Northumberland	434	506	506	603	697	746	757	798
Nottinghamshire	392	446	446	514	604	641	713	841
Oxfordshire	180	185	185	180	190	190	210	276
Rutland	21	21	21	20	20	18	17	21
Shropshire	248	236	237	240	246	243	244	290
Somerset	469	484	428	433	455	462	470	551
Staffordshire	981	1,083	1,053	1,184	1,286	1,356	1,434	1,621
Suffolk (whole)	357	371	362	373	394	400	401	443
(Suffolk East			241	256	277	291	295	322
(Suffolk West			121	118	117	109	106	121
Surrey (*c*)	439	542	522	654	846	930	1,181	1,602
Sussex (whole)	491	550	548	602	663	728	770	937
(Sussex East			407	451	487	532	547	619
(Sussex West			141	151	176	196	223	319
Warwickshire	737	805	921	1,087	1,250	1,393	1,533	1,862
Westmorland	64	66	66	64	64	66	65	67
Wiltshire	259	265	262	271	286	292	303	387
Worcestershire	380	414	337	360	380	398	420	523
Yorkshire (East Riding)	309	342	342	385	433	461	483	511
Yorkshire (North Riding)	341	360	359	377	419	456	467	525
Yorkshire (West Riding)	2,237	2,507	2,521	2,843	3,131	3,270	3,446	3,586

* *See footnote (a).*

See p. 37 for footnotes.

Population and Vital Statistics 8. *continued*

B. Wales

(in thousands)

	1881	1891 (*a*)	1891 (*a*)	1901	1911	1921	1931	1951
Anglesey	51	50	50	51	51	52	49	51
Brecknockshire	58	57	51	54	59	61	58	57
Caernarvonshire	119	118	116	123	123	128	121	124
Cardiganshire	70	63	63	61	60	61	55	53
Carmarthenshire	125	131	131	135	160	175	179	172
Denbighshire	112	118	121	134	147	158	158	171
Flintshire	81	77	77	81	93	107	113	145
Glamorganshire	511	687	688	861	1,122	1,254	1,229	1,203
Merionethshire	52	49	49	49	46	45	43	41
Montgomeryshire	66	58	58	55	53	51	48	46
Pembrokeshire	92	89	88	88	90	92	87	91
Radnorshire	24	22	22	23	23	24	21	20

C. Scotland

	1881	1891 (*a*)	1891 (*a*)	1901	1911	1921	1931	1951
Aberdeenshire	268	281	283	304	312	301	300	308
Angusshire	266	278	278	284	281	271	270	275
Argyllshire	76	75	74	74	71	77	63	63
Ayrshire	218	226	226	254	268	299	285	321
Banffshire	63	64	61	60	61	57	55	50
Berwickshire	35	32	32	31	30	28	27	25
Buteshire	18	18	18	19	18	34	19	19
Caithness-shire	39	37	37	34	32	28	26	23
Clackmannanshire	26	28	32	32	31	33	32	38
Dumfriesshire	76	74	74	73	73	75	75	86 (*b*)
Dunbartonshire	75	94	98	114	140	151 (*b*)	148	164
East Lothianshire	39	37	37	39	43	47	47	52
Fifeshire	172	187	190	219	268	293	276	307
Inverness-shire	90	89	90	90	87	82	82	85
Kincardineshire	34	36	36	41	41	42	41	47
Kinross-shire	7	6	7	7	8	8	7	7
Kirkcudbrightshire	42	40	40	39	38	37	37	31 (*b*)
Lanarkshire	904	1,046	1,136	1,339	1,447	1,539 (*b*)	1,586 (*b*)	1,614
Midlothianshire	389	434	434	489	508	506	526	566
Morayshire	44	43	43	45	43	42	41	48
Nairnshire	10	10	9	9	9	9	8	9
Orkney	32	30	30	29	26	24	22	21
Peeblesshire	14	15	15	15	15	15	15	15
Perthshire	129	126	122	123	124	126	121	128
Renfrewshire	263	291	225	269	315	299 (*b*)	289 (*b*)	325
Ross & Cromarty	78	78	79	76	77	71	63	61
Roxburghshire	53 (*b*)	54	53	49	47	45	46	46
Selkirkshire	26 (*b*)	27	28	23	25	23	23	22
Shetland	30	29	29	28	28	26	21	19
Stirlingshire	112	126	119	142	161	162	166	188
Sutherlandshire	23	22	22	21	20	18	16	14
West Lothianshire	44	53	53	66	80	84	81	89
Wigtownshire	39	36	36	33	32	31	29	32

D. Northern Ireland

	1881	1891 (*a*)	1891 (*a*)	1901	1911	1926	1937	1951
Antrim	238	215	208	196	194	192	197	231
Armagh	163	143	138	125	120	110	109	114
Down	248	224	219	206	204	209	211	241
Fermanagh	85	74	74	65	62	58	55	53
Londonderry	165	152	152	144	141	140	143	156
Tyrone	198	171	171	151	143	133	128	132

See p. 37 for footnotes.

Population and Vital Statistics 8. *continued*

E. Irish Republic

(in thousands)

	1881	1891 (*a*)	1891 (*a*)	1901	1911	1926	1936	1951
Carlow	47	41	42	38	36	34	34	34
Cavan	129	112	112	98	91	82	77	66
Clare	141	124	126	112	104	95	90	81
Cork	496	438	438	405	392	366	356	341
Donegal	206	186	186	174	169	153	142	132
Dublin	419	419	417	448	477	506	587	693
Galway	242 (*b*)	215	211	193	182	169	168	160
Kerry	201	179	179	166	160	149	140	127
Kildare	76	70	70	64	67	58	58	66
Kilkenny	100	87	89	79	75	71	69	65
Laoighis (Queen's)	73	65	64	57	55	52	50	48
Leitrim	90	79	79	69	64	56	51	41
Limerick	181	159	159	146	143	140	141	141
Longford	61	53	53	47	44	40	38	35
Louth	78	71	71	66	64	63	64	69
Mayo	245 (*b*)	219	219	199	192	173	161	142
Meath	87	77	77	67	65	63	61	66
Monaghan	103	86	86	75	71	65	61	55
Offaly (King's)	73	66	66	60	57	53	51	53
Roscommon	132	114	119	102	94	84	78	68
Sligo	112	98	94	84	79	71	67	61
Tipperary	200	173	173	160	152	141	138	133
Waterford	113	98	96	87	84	79	78	75
Westmeath	72	65	65	62	60	57	55	54
Wexford	124	112	112	104	102	96	94	90
Wicklow	70	62	64	61	61	58	59	63

A. England

(in thousands)

	1961	1961 (*d*)	1971
Bedfordshire	381	383	464
Berkshire	504	504	637
Buckinghamshire	488	484	588
Cambridgeshire (whole)	279	277	303
(Isle of Ely	89	87	90
Cheshire	1,369	1,369	1,546
Cornwall	342	343	382
Cumberland	294	294	292
Derbyshire	878	845	885
Devonshire	824	822	898
Dorsetshire	313	314	362
Durham	1,516	1,402	1,410
Essex (*c*)	2,288	1,104	1,358
Gloucestershire	1,002	1,002	1,077
Hampshire (whole)	1,433	1,337	1,565
(Isle of Wight	96	96	110
Herefordshire	131	131	139
Hertfordshire	833	788	925
Huntingdonshire (*e*)	80	159	203
Kent (*c*)	1,702	1,199	1,399
Lancashire	5,129	5,129	5,118
Leicestershire	683	683	772
Lincolnshire (whole)	743	744	809
(Holland	103	103	106
(Kesteven	135	135	158
(Lindsey	505	505	545
London (*c*)	3,200	7,992	7,452
Middlesex (*c*)	2,235	...	...
Monmouthshire	445	445	462

See p. 37 for footnotes.

Population and Vital Statistics 8. *continued*

A. England (*cont*)

(in thousands)

	1961	1961 (*d*)	1971
Norfolk	561	561	618
Northamptonshire (whole)	473	398	469
(Soke of Peterborough	75	...	...
Northumberland	821	821	796
Nottinghamshire	903	903	976
Oxfordshire	309	309	382
Rutland	24	24	27
Shropshire	297	298	337
Somerset	599	599	683
Staffordshire	1,734	1,689	1,858
Suffolk (whole)	472	472	547
(Suffolk East	343	343	381
(Suffolk West	129	129	165
Surrey (*c*)	1,731	906	1,003
Sussex (whole)	1,078	1,078	1,239
(Sussex East	666	666	748
(Sussex West	412	412	492
Warwickshire	2,025	2,017	2,082
Westmorland	67	67	73
Wiltshire	423	423	487
Worcestershire	570	623	693
Yorkshire (East Riding)	527	527	543
Yorkshire (North Riding)	554	665	726
Yorkshire (West Riding)	3,645	3,681	3,785

B. Wales

	1961	1961 (*d*)	1971
Anglesey	52	52	60
Brecknockshire	55	55	53
Caernarvonshire	122	122	123
Cardiganshire	54	54	55
Carmarthenshire	168	168	163
Denbighshire	174	174	185
Flintshire	150	150	176
Glamorganshire	1,230	1,230	1,259
Merionethshire	38	38	35
Montgomeryshire	44	44	43
Pembrokeshire	94	94	99
Radnorshire	18	18	18

C. Scotland

	1961	1971
Aberdeenshire	322	320
Angusshire	278	280
Argyllshire	59	60
Ayrshire	343	361
Banffshire	46	44
Berwickshire	22	21
Buteshire	15	13
Caithness-shire	27	28
Clackmannanshire	41	46
Dumfriesshire	88	88
Dumbartonshire	185	238
East Lothianshire	53	56
Fifeshire	321	327
Inverness-shire	83	90
Kincardineshire	26	26
Kinross-shire	7	6
Kirkcudbrightshire	29	28
Lanarkshire	1,626	1,524
Midlothianshire	580	596
Morayshire	49	52
Nairnshire	8	11

Population and Vital Statistics 8. *continued*

(in thousands)

C. Scotland (*cont.*)

	1961	1971
Orkney	19	17
Peeblesshire	14	14
Perthshire	127	127
Renfrewshire	339	362
Ross & Cromarty	58	58
Roxburghshire	43	42
Selkirkshire	21	21
Shetland	18	17
Stirlingshire	195	209
Sutherland	14	13
West Lothianshire	93	108
Wigtownshire	29	27

D. Northern Ireland

	1961	1971
Antrim	274	356
Armagh	118	134
Down	267	312
Fermanagh	52	50
Londonderry	165	183
Tyrone	134	139

E. Irish Republic

	1961	1971	1981
Carlow	33	34	40
Cavan	57	53	54
Clare	74	75	88
Cork	330	353	402
Donegal	114	108	125
Dublin	718	852	1,003
Galway	150	149	172
Kerry	116	113	123
Kildare	64	72	104
Kilkenny	62	61	71
Laoighis (Queen's)	45	45	51
Leitrim	33	28	28
Limerick	133	140	162
Longford	31	28	31
Louth	67	75	89
Mayo	123	110	115
Meath	65	72	95
Monaghan	47	46	51
Offaly (King's)	52	52	58
Roscommon	59	54	55
Sligo	54	50	55
Tipperary	124	124	135
Waterford	71	77	89
Westmeath	53	54	62
Wexford	83	86	99
Wicklow	58	66	87

(*a*) The first column headed 1891 relates (for England & Wales) to the Ancient County as altered by the operation of the Counties (Detached Parts) Act of 1844; whilst the second column relates to the Administrative County. For all counties (except London) the figures prior to 1891 relate to the area of the Ancient County in 1891. Figures subsequent to 1891, except the last two columns, relate to the area of the Administrative County in 1961. The exceptions are marked * They are Gloucestershire in which case the figures before 1951 have not been adjusted for a boundary change effective on 1st April 1951, and Aberdeenshire and Kincardineshire, where the part of Aberdeen City in Kincardineshire has been transferred to Aberdeenshire in 1961. Its population was 19 thousand in 1951. The first column headed 1891 relates (for Scotland and for Ireland) to the area in 1891, and the second column to the area in 1901.

(*b*) Except as indicated in (*a*), all figures for Scotland and Ireland relate to the counties as constituted at the time of the census concerned. The principal transfers of population resulting from boundary changes were as follows: Between 1871 and 1881—an area transferred from Roxburgh to Selkirk, with a population in 1871 of 5,245; areas transferred from Renfrew to Lanark between 1911 and 1921, with a population in 1911 of about 31,500, and between 1921 and 1931, with a population in 1921 of about 15,000; between 1911 and 1921—an area transferred from Dunbarton to Lanarak, with a population in 1921 of 3,825; between 1931 and 1951—an area transferred from Kirkcudbright to Dumfries, with a population in 1931 of 6,175; between 1851 and 1861—an area transferred from Antrim to the city of Belfast, with a population in 1851 of 20,670; between 1871 and 1881—an area transferred from Mayo to Galway, with a population in 1881 of 1,166.

(*c*) The population of the County of London is for the 1961 area, except in the last two columns, which relate to the area administered by the Greater London County Council. It has been deducted from the counties previously forming part.

(*d*) This column relates to the area of the county in 1971.

(*e*) Huntingdonshire & Peterborough in the last two columns.

Population and Vital Statistics 9. Population of the New Counties and Regions – Great Britain, 1891–1981

A. England

(in thousands)

	1891	1901	1911	1921	1931	*1939 (a)*	1951	1961	1971	1981
Avon	511	569	603	634	664	*702*	775•	829	906	915
Bedfordshire	163	174	197	209	223	*268*	313	383	464	507
Berkshire	211	237	261	277	304	*337*	405•	517	631	681
Buckinghamshire	167	173	191	203	226	*247*	304•	378	476	568
Cambridgeshire	277	283	302	309	329	*347*•	391	437	506	579
Cheshire	462	485	527	545	578	*609*	687•	730	867	930
Cleveland	290	338	379	418	439	*440*•	473	526	568	568
Cornwall	323	322	328	321	318	*310*•	346	343	382	432
Cumbria	432	436	436	461	437	*429*	464	470	476	487
Derbyshire	509	593	675	706	746	*764*	810•	847	887	910
Devon	633	662	700	710	733	*747*•	959	797	823	898
Dorset	245	269	311	330	369	*394*	459•	500	554	595
Durham	407	452	557	603	597	*578*	597•	605	607	607
East Sussex	370	410	443	486	498	*515*•	554	586	647	657
Essex	367	405	488	554	643	*719*•	839	1,104	1,358	1,474
Gloucestershire	301	305	314	313	316	*322*•	391	426	467	502
Greater London	5,572	6,507	7,160	7,387	8,110	*8,615*•	8,197	7,992	7,452	7,678
Greater Manchester	2,155	2,404	2,638	2,674	2,727	*2,714*	2,716•	2,720	2,729	2,596
Hampshire	562	651	775	808	885	*959*	1,030•	1,151	1,373	1,466
Herefordshire & Worcestershire	341	350	360	365	372	*383*•	453	492	560	632
Hertfordshire	214	242	290	311	373	*456*•	561	788	925	957
Humberside	453	522	610	660	702	*734*•	756	797	839	852
Isle of Wight	79	82	88	95	88	*86*	96	96	110	119
Kent	710	806	869	938	959	*1,015*•	1,091	1,199	1,399	1,468
Lancashire	890	1,025	1,115	1,161	1,171	*1,171*	1,239•	1,261	1,345	1,377
Leicestershire	397	457	497	513	559	*587*•	652	706	800	845
Lincolnshire	359	361	388	399	405	*413*•	457	469	503	551
Merseyside	1,078	1,233	1,378	1,497	1,587	*1,607*	1,663•	1,718	1,657	1,512
Norfolk	468	476	498	504	505	*506*	552•	566	626	695
Northamptonshire	264	295	304	302	309	*319*•	360	398	469	528
Northumberland	194	219	252	274	264	*263*	273•	274	280	299
North Yorkshire	424	448	471	495	506	*520*	573•	575	627	667
Nottinghamshire	445	514	604	641	712	*757*	840•	901	975	985
Oxfordshire	232	224	236	238	260	*291*	353•	403	498	519
Shropshire	237	240	246	243	244	*245*•	290	298	337	376
Somerset	272	268	277	274	281	*282*	325•	345	386	427
South Yorkshire	663	805	963	1,068	1,173	*1,192*	1,253•	1,303	1,323	1,304
Staffordshire	544	603	654	680	707	*728*	794•	849	964	1,016
Suffolk	360	371	391	397	398	*402*	439•	467	538	598
Surrey	271	325	393	423	507	*628*	750•	906	1,002	1,004
Tyne & Wear	800	969	1,105	1,181	1,201	*1,188*	1,201•	1,244	1,212	1,143
Warwickshire	186	206	236	260	277	*296*	339•	387	455	476
West Midlands	1,356	1,587	1,780	1,955	2,143	*2,335*	2,547•	2,732	2,793	2,649
West Sussex	177	192	221	242	272	*327*•	383	492	594	662
West Yorkshire	1,598	1,747	1,852	1,876	1,939	*1,940*•	1,986	2,005	2,067	2,037
Wiltshire	262	271	286	292	303	*311*•	387	423	487	519

B. Wales

	1891	1901	1911	1921	1931	*1939 (a)*	1951	1961	1971	1981
Clwyd	196	214	239	263	269	*277*•	314	322	359	391
Dyfed	282	284	310	328	321	*307*	316	316	316	330
Gwent	248	286	376	427	409	*380*	405•	424	441	440
Gwynedd	216	224	220	226	215	*207*	218	214	221	230

B. Wales (*cont.*)

(in thousands)

	1891	1901	1911	1921	1931	*1939* (*a*)	1951	1961	1971	1981
Mid Glamorgan	330	426	585	645	591	*526*	530*	519	532	538
Powys	117	118	118	118	112	*103*	108	102	99	111
South Glamorgan	178	232	268	304	316	*315**	351	380	390	384
West Glamorgan	203	228	304	345	360	*351**	357	366	373	368
C. Scotland										
Borders	130	120	118	113	112	*108*	109	102	98	100
Central	165	185	205	208	212	*220*	233	245	263	273
Dumfries & Galloway	150	145	143	143	141	*141*	148	146	143	145
Fife	187	219	268	293	276	*285*	307	321	327	325
Grampian	422	448	455	439	433	*443*	451	440	439	472
Highland	201	194	188	172	164	*161*	162	164	175	200
Lothian	513	580	615	623	639	*678*	691	710	746	723
Orkney	30	29	26	24	22	*22*	21	19	17	19
Shetland	29	28	28	26	21	*20*	19	18	17	27
Strathclyde	1,758	2,079	2,270	2,410	2,400	*2,505*	2,524	2,584	2,576	2,405
Tayside	395	399	398	388	384	*385*	396	398	398	392
Western Isles	45	46	47	44	39	*39*	36	33	30	32

*Comparability with the 1981 area is as close as possible up to this point, but not exact.

(*a*) Mid-year estimates.

Population and Vital Statistics 10. Births and Birth Rates – British Isles 1539–1980

NOTE TO PART A

SOURCE: E. A. Wrigley and R. S. Schofield, *The Population History of England, 1541–1871* (London, 1981), tables A2.3 and A3.3

A. England (excluding Monmouthshire), 1539–1871

	Births in thousands	Rate per 1,000 of population		Births in thousands	Rate per 1,000 of population		Births in thousands	Rate per 1,000 of population		Births in thousands	Rate per 1,000 of population
1539	114	...	1584	130	34·7	1629	159	32·9	1674	146	29·2
1540	112	...	1585	130	34·6	1630	160	32·8	1675	138	27·6
1541	94	34·0	1586	125	32·9	1631	135	27·7	1676	155	31·1
1542	114	40·5	1587	112	29·3	1632	158	32·1	1677	155	31·0
1543	108	38·3	1588	127	33·2	1633	166	33·4	1678	150	29·6
1544	101	35·4	1589	141	36·6	1634	161	32·3	1679	139	27·6
1545	105	36·8	1590	122	31·3	1635	159	31·7	1680	146	29·2
1546	108	37·7	1591	115	29·6	1636	165	32·6	1681	148	30·1
1547	98	34·3	1592	128	32·8	1637	161	31·7	1682	150	30·7
1548	117	40·3	1593	129	33·1	1638	154	30·3	1683	160	32·7
1549	112	38·4	1594	140	35·6	1639	147	29·0	1684	158	32·3
1550	123	41·5	1595	131	32·9	1640	175	34·7	1685	153	31·3
1551	119	39·6	1596	122	30·4	1641	164	32·2	1686	163	33·5
1552	114	37·7	1597	117	29·1	1642	167	32·7	1687	162	33·2
1553	114	37·2	1598	116	29·1	1643	172	33·5	1688	164	33·6
1554	103	33·3	1599	146	36·3	1644	157	30·7	1689	161	32·7
1555	112	36·0	1600	139	34·1	1645	169	32·9	1690	155	31·6
1556	111	35·2	1601	129	31·3	1646	166	32·2	1691	158	32·1
1557	86	27·3	1602	129	31·1	1647	157	30·1	1692	154	31·2
1558	96	31·2	1603	149	35·8	1648	145	27·7	1693	152	30·6
1559	81	27·2	1604	144	34·5	1649	137	26·2	1694	139	28·2
1560	102	34·6	1605	149	35·3	1650	134	25·7	1695	159	32·2
1561	111	37·1	1606	144	33·9	1651	151	28·8	1696	166	33·5
1562	115	38·0	1607	150	34·8	1652	141	26·8	1697	160	32·0
1563	109	35·7	1608	141	32·5	1653	139	26·5	1698	158	31·7
1564	116	38·0	1609	141	32·3	1654	159	30·5	1699	156	31·1
1565	121	39·1	1610	144	32·9	1655	168	32·1	1700	162	32·3
1566	111	35·6	1611	151	34·2	1656	164	31·1	1701	173	34·2
1567	112	35·6	1612	143	32·3	1657	144	27·2	1702	173	34·0
1568	120	37·5	1613	133	29·9	1658	128	24·7	1703	172	33·5
1569	101	31·3	1614	141	31·6	1659	118	22·9	1704	165	32·1
1570	111	34·2	1615	149	33·2	1660	144	28·2	1705	167	32·2
1571	109	33·3	1616	140	31·0	1661	146	28·4	1706	164	31·6
1572	110	33·4	1617	142	31·5	1662	132	25·8	1707	155	29·8
1573	106	31·8	1618	145	31·9	1663	148	29·1	1708	159	30·5
1574	106	31·7	1619	155	33·7	1664	154	30·1	1709	149	28·5
1575	111	33·0	1620	163	35·2	1665	154	30·2	1710	146	27·9
1576	118	34·6	1621	162	34·5	1666	154	30·4	1711	151	28·9
1577	119	34·6	1622	154	32·3	1667	149	29·4	1712	150	28·7
1578	122	34·9	1623	133	27·9	1668	150	29·7	1713	158	30·2
1579	123	34·8	1624	141	29·8	1669	151	29·9	1714	162	30·9
1580	121	34·0	1625	152	32·0	1670	146	29·2	1715	164	31·3
1581	122	33·8	1626	141	29·9	1671	137	27·6	1716	176	33·3
1582	126	34·6	1627	150	31·6	1672	153	30·8	1717	169	31·9
1583	126	34·2	1628	161	33·7	1673	151	30·2	1718	176	32·9

Population and Vital Statistics 10. *continued*

A. England (excluding Monmouthshire), 1539–1871

	Births in thousands	Rate per 1,000 of population		Births in thousands	Rate per 1,000 of population		Births in thousands	Rate per 1,000 of population		Births in thousands	Rate per 1,000 of population
1719	181	33·7	1758	190	31·4	1796	310	37·9	1834	496	36·0
1720	164	30·6	1759	204	33·7	1797	330	39·8	1835	495	35·6
1721	169	31·6	1760	205	33·6	1798	330	39·3	1836	505	35·8
1722	180	33·7	1761	214	34·8	1799	320	37·6	1837	504	35·3
1723	189	35·3	1762	212	34·4	1800	315	36·6	1838	509	35·2
1724	184	34·1	1763	206	33·4	1801	294	33·9	1839	531	36·3
1725	179	33·2	1764	217	35·1	1802	340	39·0	1840	534	36·1
1726	187	34·4	1765	221	35·4	1803	365	41·3	1841	538	36·0
1727	188	34·3	1766	211	33·6	1804	373	41·6	1842	539	35·6
1728	157	29·0	1767	213	33·9	1805	373	40·9	1843	544	35·5
1729	156	29·3	1768	213	33·8	1806	375	40·4	1844	553	35·6
1730	166	31·5	1769	226	35·5	1807	377	40·1	1845	551	35·0
1731	192	36·4	1770	235	36·7	1808	380	39·8	1846	575	36·1
1732	187	35·4	1771	227	35·2	1809	372	38·6	1847	541	33·7
1733	195	36·6	1772	232	35·7	1810	385	39·5	1848	562	34·7
1734	195	36·3	1773	236	36·1	1811	395	40·0	1849	576	35·2
1735	197	36·4	1774	230	34·9	1812	391	39·1	1850	589	35·7
1736	192	35·3	1775	244	36·5	1813	407	40·1	1851	609	36·4
1737	190	34·7	1776	243	36·1	1814	416	40·5	1852	616	36·4
1738	194	35·2	1777	252	37·0	1815	464	44·3	1853	604	35·2
1739	198	35·8	1778	254	36·9	1816	450	42·2	1854	625	36·0
1740	187	33·7	1779	256	36·9	1817	454	41·9	1855	625	35·7
1741	174	31·2	1780	252	36·1	1818	448	40·8	1856	646	36·4
1742	170	30·8	1781	250	35·5	1819	447	40·1	1857	651	36·1
1743	187	33·9	1782	247	34·9	1820	450	39·8	1858	643	35·3
1744	188	34·0	1783	248	34·8	1821	469	40·9	1859	675	36·6
1745	191	34·1	1784	252	35·3	1822	490	41·9	1860	669	35·8
1746	187	33·2	1785	271	37·5	1823	485	40·8	1861	680	35·9
1747	186	32·8	1786	280	38·5	1824	481	39·9	1862	695	36·2
1748	191	33·7	1787	275	37·3	1825	485	39·6	1863	708	36·4
1749	187	32·8	1788	292	39·1	1826	490	39·5	1864	719	36·5
1750	200	34·8	1789	286	37·9	1827	468	37·3	1865	725	36·4
1751	197	34·2	1790	301	39·4	1828	491	38·5	1866	730	36·2
1752	192	33·0	1791	297	38·4	1829	462	35·7	1867	742	36·4
1753	199	33·9	1792	317	40·4	1830	466	35·6	1868	759	36·6
1754	199	33·7	1793	311	39·2	1831	468	35·2	1869	745	35·5
1755	203	34·2	1794	307	38·2	1832	472	35·2	1870	762	35·9
1756	201	33·6	1795	311	38·4	1833	500	36·8	1871	767	35·7
1757	191	31·7									

NOTES TO PARTS B, C, and D

[1] SOURCES: *Annual Report of the Registrar General for England & Wales, for Scotland, for Ireland,* and *for Northern Ireland* and the *Republic of Ireland*. (In later years the volume for England & Wales was called *The Registrar General's Statistical Review of England and Wales*, and since 1973 has been replaced by various publications of the Office of Population Censuses and Surveys.)

[2] In each of the countries, the first year shown is a serious understatement, owing to deficiencies in registration. In no case was registration virtually complete until well into the 1860s.

B. England & Wales, 1838–1980

	Numbers of Births (thousands)				Births	
	Males	Females	Total	Legitimate	per 1,000 Population	per 1,000 Women Aged 15–44
1838	...	...	464	...	30·3	...
1839	252	240	493	...	31·8	...
1840	257	245	502	...	32·0	...
1841	263	249	512	...	32·2	134
1842	265	253	518	483	32·1	134
1843	271	257	527	...	32·3	135
1844	277	263	541	...	32·7	137
1845	278	265	544	505	32·5	137
1846	293	279	573	534	33·8	142
1847	276	264	540	504	31·5	133
1848	288	275	563	526	32·5	137
1849	295	283	578	539	32·9	139
1850	303	291	593	553	33·4	141
1851	315	301	616	574	34·3	145
1852	319	305	624	582	34·3	145
1853	314	299	612	573	33·3	141
1854	324	310	634	594	34·1	145
1855	324	311	635	594	33·8	143
1856	336	322	657	615	34·5	147
1857	340	323	663	620	34·4	146
1858	335	320	655	612	33·7	143
1859	353	337	690	645	35·0	149
1860	350	334	684	640	34·3	146·5
1861	356	340	696	652	34·6	147·4
1862	364	349	713	667	35·0	149·4
1863	372	355	727	680	35·3	150·7
1864	378	363	740	693	35·4	151·7
1865	381	367	748	701	35·4	151·7
1866	385	369	754	708	35·2	151·4
1867	392	376	768	723	35·4	152·6
1868	400	386	787	741	35·8	154·8
1869	395	379	773	729	34·8	150·5
1870	404	388	793	748	35·2	152·9
1871	406	392	797	753	35·0	152·1
1872	421	405	826	781	35·6	155·4
1873	423	407	830	787	35·4	153·9
1874	435	419	855	812	36·0	156·5
1875	434	416	851	810	35·4	153·6
1876	452	436	888	846	36·3	156·7
1877	452	436	888	846	36·0	156·1
1878	455	437	892	850	35·6	154·8
1879	448	432	880	838	34·7	150·7
1880	449	433	882	839	34·2	149·1
1881	450	433	884	841	33·9	147·6
1882	453	436	889	846	33·8	146·2

Population and Vital Statistics 10. *continued*

B. England & Wales, 1838–1980 (*cont.*)

	Numbers of Births (thousands)				Births	
	Males	Females	Total	Legitimate	per 1,000 Population	per 1,000 Women Aged 15–44
1883	453	438	891	848	33·5	144·4
1884	463	444	907	864	33·6	144·9
1885	456	438	894	851	32·9	140·8
1886	460	443	904	861	32·8	140·4
1887	452	435	886	844	31·9	135·7
1888	447	433	880	839	31·2	132·9
1889	451	435	886	845	31·1	132·0
1890	442	428	870	832	30·2	127·9
1891	466	448	914	875	31·4	132·6
1892	457	441	898	860	30·4	128·2
1893	466	449	915	876	30·7	128·2
1894	453	437	890	852	29·6	121·2
1895	469	453	922	883	30·3	124·9
1896	466	450	915	877	29·6	121·9
1897	469	452	922	883	29·6	120·9
1898	469	454	923	885	29·3	119·1
1899	473	455	929	892	29·1	118·0
1900	471	455	927	890	28·7	115·9
1901	474	456	930	894	28·5	114·5
1902	479	461	941	904	28·5	114·6
1903	482	466	948	911	28·5	114·3
1904	481	464	945	908	28·0	112·7
1905	472	456	929	892	27·3	109·7
1906	477	458	935	898	27·2	109·2
1907	468	450	918	882	26·5	106·2
1908	478	462	940	903	26·7	107·6
1909	466	448	914	877	25·8	103·6
1910	457	440	897	860	25·1	100·7
1911	449	432	881	844	24·3	98·0
1912	445	428	873	835	23·9	96·6
1913	449	433	882	844	24·1	97·1
1914	447	432	879	842	23·8	96·2
1915	415	399	815	778	21·9	88·8
1916	402	383	786	748	20·9	85·2
1917	341	327	668	631	17·8	72·1
1918	339	324	663	621	17·7	71·1
1919	356	336	692	651	18·5	73·9
1920	471	467	958	943	25·5	101·7
1921	435	414	849	810	22·4	89·7
1922	399	381	780	746	20·4	82·1
1923	387	371	758	727	19·7	79·4
1924	373	357	730	700	18·8	75·8
1925	363	347	711	682	18·3	73·5
1926	354	340	695	665	17·8	71·9
1927	334	320	654	625	16·6	67·5
1928	337	323	660	631	16·7	67·9
1929	329	315	644	614	16·3	65·8
1930	331	317	649	619	16·3	66·2
1931	324	309	632	604	15·8	64·4
1932	314	300	614	587	15·3	62·6

B. England & Wales, 1838–1980 (*cont.*)

	Numbers of Births (thousands)				Births	
	Males	Females	Total	Legitimate	per 1,000 Population	per 1,000 Women Aged 15–44
1933	297	284	580	555	14·4	59·4
1934	307	291	598	572	14·8	61·5
1935	308	291	599	574	14·7	61·0
1936	311	295	605	580	14·8	61·2
1937	314	297	611	585	14·9	61·4
1938	318	303	621	595	15·1	62·4
1939	316	299	614	588	14·8	61·3
1940	303	288	590	564	14·1	58·7
1941	297	282	579	548	13·9	57·9
1942	336	316	652	616	15·6	65·2
1943	353	332	684	640	16·2	68·6
1944	388	364	751	696	17·7	75·7
1945	350	330	680	617	15·9	68·8
1946	422	398	821	767	19·2	83·7
1947	454	427	881	834	20·5	90·6
1948	399	376	775	733	17·8	80·2
1949	376	354	731	694	16·7	76·0
1950	359	338	697	662	15·8	73·0
1951	349	329	678	645	15·5	71·6
1952	346	328	674	641	15·3	71·8
1953	352	332	684	651	15·5	73·5
1954	346	327	674	642	15·2	72·9
1955	344	324	668	637	15·0	72·8
1956	360	340	700	666	15·7	77·0
1957	372	351	723	688	16·1	70·0
1958	381	360	741	705	16·4	82·1
1959	386	363	749	711	16·5	83·0
1960	404	381	785	742	17·1	86·7
1961	418	394	811	763	17·6	89·1
1962	432	407	839	784	18·0	90·5
1963	438	416	854	795	18·2	90·9
1964	451	425	876	813	18·5	92·6
1965	443	420	863	796	18·1	91·2
1966	437	413	850	783	17·7	90·2
1967	428	404	832	762	17·2	88·5
1968	421	398	819	750	16·9	87·0
1969	410	387	798	730	16·4	84·7
1970	403	381	784	720	16·0	83·3
1971	403	380	783	717	15·9	83·6
1972	374	351	725	663	14·7	77·0
1973	349	327	676	618	13·7	71·7
1974	329	310	640	583	12·9	67·6
1975	311	293	603	549	12·2	63·3
1976	300	284	584	531	11·8	60·8
1977	293	276	569	514	11·5	58·7
1978	307	289	596	536	12·1	60·7
1979	328	310	638	569	12·9	64·1
1980	336	320	656	579	13·2	65·0

Population and Vital Statistics 10. *continued*

C. Scotland, 1855–1980

	Numbers of Births (thousands)				Births	
	Males	Females	Total	Legitimate	per 1,000 Population	per 1,000 Women Aged 15–44
1855	47·8	49·6	93·3	86·0	31·3	129·6
1856	52·2	45·5	101·8	93·1	34·0	140·8
1857	53·2	50·3	103·4	94·2	34·3	142·5
1858	53·7	50·3	104·0	94·7	34·4	142·8
1859	54·6	51·9	106·5	96·8	35·0	145·6
1860	54·4	51·2	105·6	95·9	35·6	143·8
1861	54·6	52·4	107·0	97·1	34·9	145·2
1862	55·3	51·8	107·1	96·7	34·6	144·4
1863	56·2	53·1	109·3	98·4	35·0	146·5
1864	57·4	55·0	112·3	101·1	35·6	149·6
1865	58·2	54·9	113·1	101·8	35·5	149·8
1866	58·4	55·3	113·7	102·0	35·4	149·7
1867	58·5	55·5	114·0	102·9	35·1	149·3
1868	59·2	56·3	115·5	104·2	35·3	150·3
1869	58·3	55·0	113·4	102·3	34·3	146·8
1870	59·0	56·4	115·4	104·4	34·6	149·8
1871	60·0	56·1	116·1	105·1	34·5	148·6
1872	61·3	57·5	118·8	107·8	34·9	150·5
1873	61·5	58·2	119·7	108·8	34·8	150·1
1874	63·6	60·1	123·7	113·7	35·6	153·5
1875	63·4	60·1	123·6	112·8	35·2	151·9
1876	64·8	61·7	126·5	115·5	35·6	153·9
1877	65·1	61·7	126·8	116·3	35·3	152·8
1878	65·2	61·6	126·8	116·1	34·9	151·3
1879	64·3	61·4	125·7	115·0	34·3	148·5
1880	63·8	60·8	124·6	114·0	33·6	145·9
1881	64·7	61·5	126·2	115·7	33·7	146·4
1882	64·5	61·7	126·2	115·6	33·5	145·2
1883	63·9	60·6	124·5	114·3	32·8	141·9
1884	66·4	62·8	129·2	118·7	33·7	146·1
1885	64·5	61·6	126·1	115·4	32·7	141·3
1886	65·9	62·0	127·9	117·4	32·9	142·2
1887	63·8	60·6	124·4	114·0	31·8	137·1
1888	63·1	60·1	123·3	113·3	31·3	134·8
1889	63·3	59·5	122·8	113·0	30·9	133·1
1890	62·2	59·3	121·5	112·3	30·4	130·7
1891	64·8	61·2	126·0	116·3	31·2	134·4
1892	64·4	60·7	125·0	115·8	30·7	131·3
1893	65·0	62·1	127·1	117·6	30·8	131·5
1894	63·9	60·5	124·4	115·3	29·9	126·6
1895	64·8	61·7	126·5	117·3	30·0	127·1
1896	66·2	63·0	129·2	119·8	30·4	127·9
1897	65·8	63·1	128·9	119·8	30·0	125·8
1898	66·8	64·0	130·9	122·0	30·1	126·0
1899	66·8	64·0	130·7	122·2	29·8	124·1
1900	67·1	64·3	131·4	122·9	29·6	123·0
1901	67·8	64·4	132·2	123·7	29·5	122·1
1902	67·4	64·8	132·3	124·0	29·3	120·6
1903	68·1	65·4	133·5	125·2	29·4	120·6
1904	67·8	64·8	132·6	123·6	29·1	118·6

Population and Vital Statistics 10. *continued*

C. Scotland, 1855–1980 (*cont.*)

	Numbers of Births (thousands)				Births	
	Males	Females	Total	Legitimate	per 1,000 Population	per 1,000 Women Aged 15–44
1905	66·8	64·7	131·4	122·3	28·6	116·4
1906	67·5	64·5	132·0	122·7	28·6	115·8
1907	65·9	62·9	128·8	120·0	27·7	111·9
1908	66·8	64·5	131·4	122·3	28·1	113·0
1909	65·7	62·9	128·7	119·3	27·3	112·7
1910	63·1	60·9	124·1	115·0	26·2	108·0
1911	62·3	59·6	121·9	112·7	25·6	106·6
1912	62·9	59·9	122·8	113·8	25·9	107·6
1913	61·5	59·1	120·5	112·0	25·5	105·9
1914	63·0	61·0	123·9	115·1	26·1	108·5
1915	58·4	55·8	114·2	106·3	23·9	99·1
1916	56·5	53·5	109·9	102·1	22·8	94·7
1917	50·0	47·4	97·4	90·1	20·1	83·4
1918	50·4	48·2	98·6	90·7	20·2	83·8
1919	54·8	51·5	106·3	98·8	21·7	90·2
1920	69·7	66·8	136·5	126·3	28·1	115·3
1921	63·1	60·1	123·2	114·4	25·2	103·7
1922	58·8	56·3	115·1	107·2	23·5	96·7
1923	57·3	54·6	111·9	104·4	22·9	94·4
1924	54·9	52·0	106·9	99·8	22·0	90·8
1925	53·4	50·7	104·1	97·3	21·4	88·5
1926	52·4	50·1	102·4	95·4	21·1	87·6
1927	49·3	47·4	96·7	89·7	19·9	83·1
1928	49·6	47·2	96·8	89·7	20·0	83·4
1929	47·8	45·1	92·9	85·7	19·2	80·0
1930	48·1	46·5	94·5	87·6	19·6	81·6
1931	47·0	45·2	92·2	85·6	19·0	79·8
1932	46·6	44·4	91·0	84·5	18·6	78·4
1933	44·8	41·8	86·5	80·6	17·6	74·5
1934	45·4	43·4	88·8	82·7	18·0	76·5
1935	45·0	43·0	87·9	82·2	17·8	74·9
1936	45·3	43·6	88·9	83·2	17·9	75·1
1937	45·0	42·8	87·8	82·4	17·6	73·7
1938	45·4	43·2	88·6	83·2	17·7	74·0
1939	44·7	42·2	86·9	81·7	17·4	72·1
1940	44·2	42·2	86·4	81·3	17·1	71·4
1941	46·1	43·6	89·7	83·8	17·5	73·5
1942	46·4	44·3	90·7	84·2	17·6	74·2
1943	48·5	46·2	94·7	87·5	18·4	78·7
1944	49·5	46·4	95·9	88·3	18·5	79·9
1945	44·8	42·2	86·9	89·4	16·9	73·1
1946	53·9	50·6	104·4	97·5	20·3	89·5
1947	58·0	55·1	113·1	106·8	22·3	97·1
1948	51·9	48·5	100·3	94·5	19·7	86·6
1949	49·2	46·5	95·7	90·5	18·8	83·4
1950	47·8	44·7	92·5	87·7	18·1	81·0
1951	46·7	43·9	90·6	86·0	17·8	79·5
1952	46·3	44·2	90·4	86·1	17·7	80·0
1953	46·9	44·1	90·9	86·7	17·8	81·3
1954	47·4	44·9	92·3	88·1	18·1	83·5

C. Scotland, 1855–1980 (*cont.*)

	Numbers of Births (thousands)				Births	
	Males	Females	Total	Legitimate	per 1,000 Population	per 1,000 Women Aged 15–44
1955	47·5	45·0	92·5	88·5	18·1	84·4
1956	49·0	46·4	95·3	91·2	18·6	87·9
1957	50·4	47·6	98·0	94·0	19·1	91·3
1958	51·0	48·5	99·5	95·4	19·4	93·4
1959	51·1	48·1	99·3	95·2	19·2	93·6
1960	51·9	49·4	101·3	96·9	19·6	96·4
1961	52·0	49·2	101·2	96·6	19·5	96·9
1962	53·9	50·4	104·3	99·3	20·1	99·0
1963	52·7	50·0	102·7	97·4	19·7	97·1
1964	53·7	50·7	104·4	98·8	20·0	98·6
1965	52·0	48·6	100·7	94·8	19·3	96·6
1966	49·8	46·8	96·5	90·4	18·6	93·8
1967	49·6	46·6	96·2	89·6	18·6	94·7
1968	48·9	45·9	94·8	87·8	18·3	93·8
1969	46·7	43·6	90·3	83·6	17·4	89·5
1970	45·0	42·3	87·3	80·6	16·8	86·5
1971	44·5	42·3	86·7	79·7	16·6	85·6
1972	40·3	38·3	78·6	71·9	15·1	77·7
1973	38·6	35·8	74·4	67·9	14·3	73·4
1974	35·8	34·3	70·1	64·6	13·4	68·3
1975	35·0	32·9	67·9	61·6	13·1	66·1
1976	33·5	31·4	64·9	58·7	12·5	62·5
1977	32·0	30·3	62·3	56·4	12·0	59·4
1978	33·1	31·2	64·3	58·0	12·4	60·8
1979	35·4	33·0	68·4	61·4	13·2	63·9
1980	35·4	33·5	68·9	61·2	13·4	63·8

D. (i) Ireland, 1864–1921

	Males	Females	Total	Legitimate	per 1,000 Population	per 1,000 Women Aged 15–44
1864	70·1	66·3	136·4	131·2	24·2	103·6
1865	74·4	70·6	145·0	139·6	25·9	111·7
1866	75·1	71·0	146·1	141·2	26·5	114·1
1867	74·3	70·1	144·4	139·7	26·3	114·4
1868	75·2	70·9	146·1	141·5	26·7	117·4
1869	74·9	70·7	145·7	141·5	26·7	118·8
1870	76·9	73·1	149·8	145·8	27·7	124·0
1871	77·3	74·0	151·4	147·2	28·1	127·2
1872	76·9	72·4	149·3	145·5	27·8	125·8
1873	74·2	70·1	144·4	140·9	27·1	121·9
1874	72·5	68·8	141·3	138·0	26·6	119·5
1875	71·1	67·2	138·3	135·2	26·1	117·2
1876	72·2	68·3	140·5	137·2	26·4	119·4
1877	71·7	68·0	139·7	136·3	26·2	118·9
1878	68·5	65·6	134·1	131·0	25·1	114·4
1879	69·9	65·5	135·3	132·0	25·2	115·7
1880	66·0	62·1	128·1	124·9	24·7	109·8
1881	64·8	61·1	125·8	122·6	24·5	108·1
1882	63·0	59·6	122·6	119·4	24·0	106·2
1883	60·7	57·5	118·2	115·1	23·5	103·3

D. (i) Ireland, 1864–1921 (*cont.*)

	Numbers of Births (thousands)				Births	
	Males	Females	Total	Legitimate	per 1,000 Population	per 1,000 Women Aged 15–44
1884	61·2	57·7	118·9	115·7	23·9	104·8
1885	59·4	56·5	116·0	112·7	23·5	103·1
1886	58·9	55·0	113·9	110·9	23·2	102·1
1887	57·8	54·6	112·4	109·2	23·1	101·6
1888	56·2	53·4	109·6	106·4	22·8	100·0
1889	55·2	52·7	107·8	104·8	22·7	99·2
1890	54·3	51·0	105·3	102·4	22·3	97·8
1891	55·5	52·6	108·1	105·2	23·1	101·3
1892	53·6	50·7	104·2	101·6	22·5	97·8
1893	54·3	51·8	106·1	103·3	23·0	99·8
1894	53·9	51·4	105·4	102·5	22·9	99·2
1895	54·7	51·5	106·1	103·2	23·3	100·1
1896	55·3	52·3	107·6	104·8	23·7	101·7
1897	54·7	52·0	106·7	103·9	23·5	101·0
1898	54·3	51·2	105·5	102·6	23·3	100·3
1899	53·4	50·5	103·9	101·2	23·1	98·7
1900	52·2	49·2	101·5	98·8	22·7	96·6
1901	52·0	49·0	101·0	98·4	22·7	96·2
1902	52·6	49·3	101·9	99·2	23·0	97·7
1903	52·2	49·7	101·8	99·2	23·1	98·3
1904	53·2	50·7	103·8	101·2	23·6	100·9
1905	52·5	50·3	102·8	100·1	23·4	100·6
1906	53·4	50·2	103·5	100·8	23·5	102·0
1907	52·2	49·6	101·7	99·2	23·2	100·9
1908	52·4	49·6	102·0	99·4	23·3	101·9
1909	52·7	50·0	102·8	100·0	23·4	103·4
1910	52·1	49·9	102·0	99·1	23·3	103·3
1911	52·4	49·3	101·8	99·0	23·2	103·8
1912	51·7	49·3	101·0	98·2	23·0	103·5
1913	51·2	48·9	100·1	97·3	22·8	102·9
1914	50·7	48·1	98·8	95·9	22·6	102·0
1915	49·3	46·3	95·6	92·6	22·0	99·1
1916	47·2	44·3	91·4	88·7	20·9	95·2
1917	44·3	42·1	86·4	83·7	19·7	90·3
1918	44·7	42·7	87·3	84·6	19·8	91·6
1919	51·2	48·9	89·3	97·3	20·0	94·1
1920	51·3	48·3	99·5	96·2	22·8	105·3
1921	46·5	44·2	90·7	87·7	20·8	96·4

D. (ii) Republic of Ireland, 1922–1980

	Males	Females	Total	Legitimate	per 1,000 Population	per 1,000 Women Aged 15–44
1922	30·3	28·5	58·8	57·3	19·5	
1923	31·8	29·9	61·7	60·1	20·5	
1924	32·7	30·7	63·4	61·7	21·1	
1925	31·8	30·3	62·1	60·4	20·8	
1926	31·4	29·8	61·2	59·5	20·6	
1927	30·6	29·4	60·1	58·3	20·3	
1928	30·3	28·8	59·2	57·4	20·1	
1929	29·6	28·7	58·3	56·4	19·8	
1930	29·9	28·4	58·4	56·5	19·9	
1931	29·4	27·7	57·1	55·2	19·5	

D. (ii) Republic of Ireland, 1922–1980 (*cont.*)

	Numbers of Births (thousands)				Births	
	Males	Females	Total	Legitimate	per 1,000 Population	per 1,000 Women Aged 15–44
1932	28·8	27·4	56·2	54·4	19·1	
1933	29·4	28·0	57·4	55·4	19·4	
1934	29·8	28·1	57·9	55·9	19·5	
1935	29·9	28·4	58·3	56·3	19·6	
1936	29·6	28·5	58·1	56·2	19·6	
1937	28·9	27·6	56·5	54·7	19·2	
1938	29·1	27·8	56·9	55·0	19·4	
1939	28·8	27·3	56·1	54·3	19·1	
1940	29·0	27·3	56·3	54·8	19·1	
1941	29·2	27·6	56·8	54·8	19·0	
1942	34·0	32·1	66·1	63·7	22·3	
1943	33·2	31·1	64·4	61·9	21·9	
1944	33·6	31·8	65·4	62·9	22·2	
1945	34·3	32·5	66·9	64·2	22·7	
1946	35·1	32·8	67·9	65·3	22·9	
1947	35·7	33·3	69·0	66·6	23·2	
1948	34·0	31·9	65·9	63·8	22·0	
1949	32·9	31·3	64·2	62·1	21·5	
1950	32·9	30·7	63·6	61·9	21·4	
1951	32·3	30·6	62·9	61·3	21·2	
1952	33·0	31·6	64·6	63·0	21·9	
1953	32·2	30·3	62·6	61·2	21·2	
1954	32·1	30·4	62·5	61·2	21·3	
1955	31·5	30·1	61·6	60·4	21·1	
1956	31·3	29·5	60·7	59·6	21·0	
1957	31·3	29·9	61·2	60·2	21·2	
1958	30·5	29·0	59·5	58·5	20·9	
1959	30·7	29·5	60·2	59·2	21·2	
1960	31·1	29·6	60·7	59·8	21·5	
1961	30·7	29·1	59·8	58·9	21·2	
1962	31·7	30·1	61·8	60·7	21·8	
1963	32·5	30·8	63·2	62·1	22·1	
1964	32·8	31·3	64·1	62·8	22·4	
1965	32·4	31·1	63·5	62·1	22·1	
1966	32·2	30·0	62·2	60·7	21·6	
1967	31·6	29·7	61·3	59·8	21·2	
1968	31·5	29·5	61·0	59·4	21·0	
1969	32·1	30·8	62·9	61·3	21·5	
	. . .(*a*)	. . .(*a*)	. . .(*a*)	. . .(*a*)	. . .(*a*)	
1970	33·1	31·3	64·4	62·6	21·9	
1971	34·8	32·8	67·6	65·7	22·7	
1972	35·4	33·2	68·5	67·5	22·7	
1973	35·3	33·4	68·7	65·9	22·4	
1974	35·4	33·5	68·9	66·6	22·1	
1975	34·5	32·6	67·2	64·7	21·2	
1976	34·8	32·9	67·7	65·2	21·0	
1977	35·5	33·4	68·9	66·0	21·1	
1978	35·8	34·5	70·3	67·3	21·2	
1979	37·2	35·1	72·4	69·0	21·5	
1980	38·5	35·9	74·4	70·7	21·9	

See p. 51 for footnote.

Population and Vital Statistics 10. *continued*

D. (iii) Northern Ireland, 1922–80

	Numbers of Births (thousands)				Births	
	Males	Females	Total	Legitimate	per 1,000 Population	per 1,000 Women Aged 15–44
1922	15·1	14·4	29·5	28·3	23·3	100·1
1923	15·3	14·8	30·1	28·8	23·9	102·2
1924	14·8	13·7	28·5	27·3	22·7	96·9
1925	14·2	13·5	27·7	26·5	22·0	94·2
1926	14·6	13·6	28·2	26·9	22·5	96·1
1927	13·7	13·0	26·7	25·4	21·3	90·7
1928	13·4	12·5	26·0	24·8	20·8	88·2
1929	13·0	12·4	25·4	24·2	20·4	85·9
1930	13·2	12·7	25·9	24·6	20·8	87·5
1931	13·2	12·5	25·7	24·4	20·5	86·7
1932	12·9	12·2	25·1	23·8	19·9	84·5
1933	12·6	12·0	24·6	23·4	19·6	84·0
1934	13·2	12·2	25·4	24·1	20·1	86·1
1935	12·8	12·0	24·7	23·5	19·5	83·2
1936	13·3	12·6	25·9	24·7	20·3	86·3
1937	13·0	12·4	25·4	24·2	19·8	85·2
1938	13·2	12·5	25·7	24·6	20·0	85·2
1939	12·9	12·3	25·2	24·1	19·5	82·5
1940	13·2	12·2	25·4	24·2	19·5	83·2
1941	14·1	12·8	26·9	25·6	20·5	85·4
1942	15·3	14·4	29·6	28·2	22·3	93·5
1943	16·3	15·2	31·5	29·8	23·5	99·5
1944	15·8	15·1	30·9	29·2	22·8	96·7
1945	14·9	14·1	29·0	27·4	21·3	91·0
1946	15·5	14·7	30·1	28·8	22·3	95·8
1947	16·0	15·2	31·3	30·1	23·2	100·5
1948	15·3	14·3	29·5	28·5	21·7	94·5
1949	15·0	14·1	29·1	28·0	21·2	92·8
1950	14·9	13·9	28·8	27·8	21·0	91·8
1951	14·6	13·8	28·5	27·6	20·7	91·1
1952	14·8	13·9	28·8	27·8	20·9	98·3
1953	15·0	13·9	29·0	28·2	20·9	98·3
1954	14·8	14·0	28·8	28·0	20·8	98·2
1955	15·1	13·9	29·0	28·3	20·8	98·7
1956	15·1	14·4	29·5	28·7	21·1	101·7
1957	15·5	14·6	30·1	29·4	21·5	104·8
1958	15·7	14·6	30·3	29·6	21·6	105·9
1959	15·9	14·9	30·8	30·1	21·9	107·3
1960	16·6	15·4	32·0	31·2	22·5	110·8
1961	16·4	15·5	31·9	31·1	22·4	111·5
1962	16·8	15·8	32·6	31·8	22·7	112·7
1963	17·3	16·1	33·4	32·5	23·1	114·4
1964	17·6	16·7	34·3	33·3	23·6	116·5
1965	17·7	16·2	33·9	32·9	23·1	114·5
1966	17·3	15·9	33·2	32·2	22·5	111·9
1967	17·2	16·2	33·4	32·2	22·4	114·3
1968	17·2	16·1	33·2	31·9	22·1	113·4
1969	16·6	15·8	32·4	31·2	21·4	110·3
1970	16·5	15·5	32·1	30·9	21·1	108·8
1971	16·5	15·3	31·8	30·6	20·7	108·6

D. (iii) Northern Ireland, 1922–80 (*cont.*)

	Numbers of Births (thousands)				Births	
	Males	Females	Total	Legitimate	per 1,000 Population	per 1,000 Women Aged 15–44
1972	15·6	14·4	30·0	28·7	19·4	101·3
1973	15·2	14·0	29·2	28·0	18·9	98·4
1974	14·0	13·2	27·2	25·9	17·6	91·3
1975	13·5	12·7	26·1	24·8	17·0	87·7
1976	13·5	12·8	26·4	25·0	17·1	87·8
1977	13·2	12·3	25·4	24·1	16·5	83·7
1978	13·2	13·1	26·2	24·7	17·1	85·3
1979	14·5	13·7	28·2	26·5	18·3	90·1
1980	14·7	13·9	28·6	26·8	18·5	90·2

(*a*) Subsequent figures relate to births occurring in the year shown rather than to births registered.

Population and Vital Statistics 11. Deaths and Death Rates – England (excluding Monmouthshire) 1539–1871

NOTE
SOURCE: E. A. Wrigley and R. S. Schofield, *The Population History of England, 1541–1871* (London, 1981), tables A2.3 and A3.3.

	Deaths in thousands	Rate per 1,000 of population		Deaths in thousands	Rate per 1,000 of population		Deaths in thousands	Rate per 1,000 of population		Deaths in thousands	Rate per 1,000 of population
1539	67	...	1584	84	22·5	1629	115	23·8	1674	131	26·1
1540	100	...	1585	90	23·9	1630	117	23·9	1675	145	29·0
1541	72	26·1	1586	83	21·9	1631	131	26·8	1676	137	27·5
1542	71	25·3	1587	108	28·2	1632	115	23·4	1677	125	24·9
1543	97	34·3	1588	109	28·6	1633	112	22·6	1678	135	26·7
1544	85	29·6	1589	90	23·3	1634	112	22·5	1679	187	37·2
1545	103	36.0	1590	91	23·4	1635	123	24·4	1680	168	33·8
1546	95	33·3	1591	111	28·4	1636	146	28·8	1681	192	38·9
1547	83	29·2	1592	111	28·3	1637	130	25·6	1682	171	35·0
1548	80	27·6	1593	121	31·1	1638	160	31·5	1683	156	31·8
1549	64	21·9	1594	82	20·8	1639	158	31·2	1684	164	33·6
1550	80	27·1	1595	84	21·1	1640	143	28·2	1685	162	33·3
1551	84	27·9	1596	97	24·1	1641	132	26·0	1686	153	31·5
1552	82	27·1	1597	133	33·2	1642	133	25·9	1687	141	28·9
1553	81	26·6	1598	105	26·4	1643	163	31·8	1688	143	29·3
1554	68	22·1	1599	92	22·8	1644	155	30·3	1689	151	30·6
1555	80	25·8	1600	87	21·3	1645	123	24·1	1690	150	30·5
1556	77	24·4	1601	84	20·5	1646	107	20·8	1691	135	27·3
1557	134	42·5	1602	101	24·4	1647	125	24·0	1692	136	27·5
1558	166	53·9	1603	142	34·2	1648	121	23·2	1693	136	27·4
1559	141	47·3	1604	97	23·3	1649	130	24·9	1694	150	30·2
1560	94	31·6	1605	91	21·6	1650	131	25·2	1695	152	30·7
1561	77	25·9	1606	98	23·0	1651	116	22·2	1696	143	28·9
1562	73	24·2	1607	95	22·0	1652	131	25·0	1697	140	28·1
1563	106	34·6	1608	105	24·1	1653	136	26·0	1698	134	26·8
1564	81	26·3	1609	102	23·2	1654	143	27·5	1699	139	27·7
1565	74	23·7	1610	127	28·9	1655	123	23·5	1700	140	27·9
1566	81	25·9	1611	108	24·6	1656	124	23·5	1701	135	26·7
1567	80	25·2	1612	123	27·8	1657	170	32·1	1702	128	25·2
1568	73	22·8	1613	116	26·0	1658	198	38·0	1703	127	24·8
1569	76	23·6	1614	120	26·8	1659	142	27·7	1704	139	27·0
1570	85	26·2	1615	112	25·0	1660	125	24·4	1705	163	31·5
1571	82	25·0	1616	131	29·1	1661	143	27·8	1706	138	26·6
1572	77	23·2	1617	117	25·8	1662	137	26·8	1707	131	25·2
1573	79	23·9	1618	108	23·7	1663	129	25·2	1708	141	27·0
1574	78	23·5	1619	101	22·0	1664	129	25·1	1709	134	25·7
1575	76	22·5	1620	104	22·5	1665	220	43·0	1710	138	26·4
1576	71	20·9	1621	100	21·3	1666	142	28·1	1711	149	28·5
1577	74	21·4	1622	101	21·3	1667	151	29·8	1712	157	30·1
1578	84	24·0	1623	144	30·3	1668	145	28·7	1713	135	25·8
1579	81	22·9	1624	131	27·6	1669	165	32·8	1714	149	28·4
1580	89	24·9	1625	197	41·6	1670	163	32·4	1715	137	26·2
1581	72	20·0	1626	119	25·2	1671	151	30·2	1716	140	26·5
1582	80	22·1	1627	109	23·0	1672	133	26·8	1717	132	24·9
1583	71	19·2	1628	107	22·3	1673	128	25·7	1718	137	25·6

Population and Vital Statistics 11. *continued*

	Deaths in thousands	Rate per 1,000 of population		Deaths in thousands	Rate per 1,000 of population		Deaths in thousands	Rate per 1,000 of population		Deaths in thousands	Rate per 1,000 of population
1719	171	31·8	1758	165	27·4	1796	206	25·1	1834	307	22·3
1720	174	32·4	1759	166	27·3	1797	226	27·2	1835	307	22·0
1721	168	31·4	1760	161	26·4	1798	209	24·9	1836	306	21·7
1722	159	29·7	1761	163	26·5	1799	213	25·1	1837	325	22·8
1723	168	31·3	1762	193	31·3	1800	230	26·7	1838	328	22·7
1724	162	30·1	1763	200	32·4	1801	243	28·1	1839	325	22·3
1725	137	25·4	1764	168	27·2	1802	236	27·0	1840	345	23·3
1726	151	27·7	1765	163	26·1	1803	251	28·4	1841	329	22·0
1727	194	35·5	1766	188	30·0	1804	220	24·6	1842	335	22·1
1728	216	39·8	1767	186	29·5	1805	218	23·9	1843	332	21·6
1729	239	44·7	1768	176	27·8	1806	215	23·2	1844	342	22·0
1730	191	36·2	1769	173	27·2	1807	245	26·1	1845	334	21·3
1731	179	34·1	1770	183	28·6	1808	247	25·9	1846	372	23·4
1732	158	29·8	1771	175	27·2	1809	239	24·7	1847	402	25·0
1733	154	29·0	1772	178	27·3	1810	273	27·9	1848	378	23·4
1734	139	26·0	1773	181	27·6	1811	262	26·5	1849	415	25·4
1735	145	26·9	1774	164	24·8	1812	248	24·8	1850	346	21·0
1736	153	28·1	1775	173	25·9	1813	242	23·8	1851	370	22·1
1737	167	30·6	1776	166	24·6	1814	269	26·1	1852	381	22·5
1738	151	27·4	1777	178	26·2	1815	263	25·1	1853	394	23·0
1739	152	27·5	1778	178	25·9	1816	277	26·0	1854	410	23·6
1740	173	31·1	1779	194	28·0	1817	269	24·8	1855	399	22·8
1741	194	34·7	1780	202	29·0	1818	282	25·7	1856	366	20·6
1742	202	36·7	1781	209	29·7	1819	278	24·9	1857	393	21·8
1743	160	29·0	1782	200	28·4	1820	271	24·0	1858	421	23·1
1744	139	25·0	1783	209	29·3	1821	269	23·4	1859	413	22·4
1745	141	25·2	1784	203	28·5	1822	276	23·6	1860	396	21·2
1746	157	27·9	1785	197	27·3	1823	292	24·6	1861	408	21·6
1747	162	28·6	1786	195	26·7	1824	291	24·2	1862	410	21·3
1748	162	28·6	1787	190	25·8	1825	297	24·3	1863	445	22·9
1749	153	26·8	1788	200	26·8	1826	300	24·2	1864	465	23·6
1750	158	27·5	1789	193	25·6	1827	286	22·8	1865	461	23·1
1751	152	26·3	1790	197	25·8	1828	278	21·8	1866	470	23·3
1752	148	25·4	1791	196	25·4	1829	286	22·1	1867	442	21·7
1753	145	24·8	1792	203	25·9	1830	271	20·7	1868	451	21·8
1754	150	25·4	1793	225	28·4	1831	299	22·5	1869	464	22·1
1755	150	25·2	1794	216	26·9	1832	309	23·0	1870	484	22·8
1756	154	25·7	1795	236	29·1	1833	297	21·8	1871	483	22·5
1757	158	26·2									

Population and Vital Statistics 12. Deaths – England and Wales 1838–1980, Scotland 1855–1980, Ireland 1864–1980

NOTES

[1] SOURCE: *Annual Report of the Registrar General* (and its successors) for each country.

[2] In each country the first year shown is a serious understatement, owing to deficiencies in registration. In no case was registration virtually complete until well into the 1860s.

(in thousands)

	England & Wales		Scotland		Ireland	
	Males	Females	Males	Females	Males	Females
1838	175	168	...	...	...	...
1839	173	166	...	...	...	...
1840	182	177	...	...	...	...
1841	174	170	...	...	...	...
1842	177	173	...	...	...	...
1843	176	171	...	...	...	...
1844	181	176	...	...	...	...
1845	178	172	...	...	...	...
1846	198	192	...	...	...	...
1847	212	207	...	...	...	...
1848	202	196	...	...	...	...
1849	222	219	...	...	...	...
1850	186	183	...	...	...	...
1851	201	195	...	...	...	...
1852	207	200	...	...	...	...
1853	215	206	...	...	...	...
1854	222	215	...	...	...	...
1855	217	209	30·6	31·4	...	...
1856	199	192	29·4	29·1	...	...
1857	212	207	30·9	31·0	...	...
1858	227	222	31·7	31·9	...	...
1859	224	217	30·6	31·1	...	...
1860	215	207	33·6	34·6	...	...
1861	222	213	30·9	31·5	...	...
1862	223	214	33·2	34·0	...	...
1863	242	232	35·6	35·9	...	...
1864	254	242	37·0	37·4	46·3	46·8
1865	252	239	35·2	35·7	46·2	46·9
1866	256	244	35·4	36·0	46·1	46·9
1867	243	228	34·4	34·7	46·9	46·6
1868	247	234	34·7	34·8	43·4	42·8
1869	255	240	37·9	38·0	45·0	44·6
1870	266	250	36·9	37·3	45·5	45·0
1871	266	249	36·8	37·9	44·2	44·1
1872	255	237	37·9	37·4	49·0	48·3
1873	255	238	39·0	37·9	49·0	48·6
1874	272	254	40·7	40·0	46·5	45·5
1875	282	264	40·3	41·4	48·9	49·2
1876	265	245	37·4	36·7	46·1	46·2
1877	261	240	37·2	36·8	47·2	46·4
1878	279	261	38·4	38·4	50·1	49·5
1879	271	255	36·3	37·1	52·3	52·8
1880	273	255	38·1	37·1	51·6	51·3
1881	254	238	36·1	36·2	45·1	45·0
1882	266	251	36·3	36·7	43·6	44·9

Population and Vital Statistics 12. *continued*

(in thousands)

	England & Wales		Scotland		Ireland			
	Males	Females	Males	Females	Males	Females		
1883	269	254	38·3	38·6	47·6	48·7		
1884	274	257	37·6	37·6	43·4	43·8		
1885	268	254	36·9	37·7	45·1	45·6		
1886	276	261	36·4	37·2	43·5	43·8		
1887	272	259	36·8	37·7	43·9	44·7		
1888	263	248	35·0	36·2	42·5	43·4		
1889	266	252	36·3	36·9	41·1	41·8		
1890	290	272	39·1	39·9	42·1	43·7		
1891	302	285	41·1	42·5	42·1	43·9		
1892	286	274	37·5	38·1	44·0	46·0		
1893	292	278	39·6	40·1	40·8	42·0		
1894	256	243	35·2	36·0	41·4	42·2		
1895	291	278	40·7	41·2	41·8	42·6		
1896	271	256	35·3	35·4	37·4	38·3		
1897	280	261	39·5	39·6	41·6	42·3		
1898	284	268	39·3	39·1	40·7	41·7		
1899	299	282	39·9	39·7	39·7	40·0		
1900	304	284	41·3	41·0	43·0	44·7		
1901	286	266	40·2	39·9	39·3	39·8		
1902	277	258	39·2	38·8	38·6	39·1		
1903	266	248	38·1	37·9	38·3	39·1		
1904	283	267	38·9	39·1	39·3	40·2		
1905	268	252	37·2	37·3	37·3	37·8		
1906	274	257	37·7	37·9	37·1	37·3		
1907	269	255	38·2	39·1	38·6	38·7		
1908	269	252	38·9	39·0	38·2	38·7		
1909	265	253	37·1	37·5	37·1	37·9		
1910	249	234	36·0	36·2	37·1	37·8		
1911	273	255	35·8	35·9	36·2	36·3		
1912	250	237	36·1	36·3	36·0	36·2		
1913	262	243	36·5	36·6	37·5	37·2		
1914	267	249	36·8	36·8	35·8	35·5		
1915	292	270	41·1	40·5	38·1	38·0		
1916	265	243	35·6	35·0	36·0	35·4		
1917	262	237	35·4	34·1	36·3	36·4		
1918	315	297	39·1	39·2	39·2	39·5		
1919	258	246	37·5	37·6	39·0	39·6		
1920	240	226	34·6	33·5	33·1	33·4		
1921	234	224	33·1	33·1	63·8			
					Northern Ireland		Republic of Ireland	
					Males	Females	Males	Females
1922	247	240	36·2	36·7	9·5	10·3	22·7	21·8
1923	227	218	31·7	31·6	9·0	9·7	21·6	20·7
1924	241	233	35·2	35·2	9·8	10·5	22·8	22·4
1925	241	232	33·0	32·5	9·6	10·2	22·1	21·5
1926	232	222	32·0	31·8	9·2	9·7	20·8	20·9
1927	247	238	33·1	32·7	8·7	9·5	21·8	21·9
1928	236	225	32·6	32·7	8·7	9·3	20·9	20·9
1929	270	263	35·4	35·5	9·5	10·4	21·5	21·4
1930	234	221	32·4	31·8	8·4	8·8	21·1	20·6
1931	250	242	32·2	32·0	8·8	9·2	21·8	21·2

Population and Vital Statistics 12. *continued*

(in thousands)

	England & Wales		Scotland		Northern Ireland		Republic of Ireland	
	Males	Females	Males	Females	Males	Females	Males	Females
1932	246	238	32·7	33·3	8·7	9·1	21·8	21·2
1933	251	246	32·6	32·3	9·0	9·2	20·6	19·9
1934	243	234	32·1	31·6	8·7	8·8	19·9	19·2
1935	243	234	32·8	32·5	9·2	9·4	21·5	20·0
1936	253	242	33·9	32·9	9·0	9·4	21·9	20·7
1937	260	250	35·0	34·0	9·4	9·9	23·3	21·8
1938	247	232	31·8	31·1	8·7	8·9	20·6	19·4
1939	256	244	33·0	31·4	8·7	8·8	21·6	20·2
1940	303	278	37·6	35·1	9·6	9·4	21·6	20·3
1941	281	254	37·7	34·9	10·2	9·9	22·6	21·2
1942	251	229	33·8	31·1	9·1	8·4	21·9	19·8
1943	259	242	34·3	32·4	9·1	8·6	22·7	20·8
1944	258	234	33·3	31·3	8·6	8·4	23·5	21·7
1945	252	236	32·0	30·7	8·2	8·2	22·3	20·5
1946	252	240	32·7	31·9	8·4	8·3	21·9	19·6
1947	268	250	33·8	32·4	8·6	8·3	23·5	20·6
1948	243	227	30·8	30·1	7·7	7·4	19·1	17·2
1949	261	250	31·9	31·6	7·9	7·7	19·9	18·2
1950	261	249	32·2	31·8	8·0	7·8	20·0	17·7
1951	282	268	33·1	32·7	8·9	8·7	22·5	19·9
1952	258	240	31·4	30·1	7·7	7·1	18·9	16·2
1953	259	244	30·3	28·6	7·7	7·1	18·4	16·2
1954	260	242	31·5	29·9	7·7	7·4	19·2	16·3
1955	267	252	31·3	30·3	7·9	7·5	19·8	17·0
1956	268	253	31·7	30·1	7·6	7·2	18·3	15·6
1957	266	248	31·6	29·5	7·9	7·3	18·4	16·0
1958	271	256	31·8	30·3	7·9	7·2	18·5	15·8
1959	270	258	32·5	30·6	8·0	7·4	18·6	15·6
1960	269	257	31·7	30·1	7·9	7·4	17·5	15·2
1961	281	271	32·8	31·1	8·4	7·7	18·8	16·0
1962	285	272	32·7	30·5	7·9	7·3	18·4	15·5
1963	292	280	34·1	31·4	8·3	7·6	18·2	15·6
1964	275	260	31·8	29·3	8·0	7·3	17·6	15·0
1965	282	267	32·6	30·3	8·2	7·4	18·0	15·1
1966	289	275	32·5	31·2	8·7	7·8	19·1	16·0
1967	277	265	30·6	29·0	7·7	6·9	17·0	14·4
1968	293	284	32·1	31·2	8·2	7·7	18·0	15·1
1969	297	283	32·6	31·2	8·6	7·7	18·3	15·4
							- - -(*a*)	- - -(*a*)
1970	293	282	32·5	31·1	8·8	7·8	18·4	15·2
1971	288	279	31·6	30·0	8·6	7·6	17·4	14·5
1972	300	292	33·2	31·8	9·0	8·0	18·7	15·7
1973	297	291	33·0	31·6	9·3	8·4	18·7	15·5
1974	295	290	32·7	32·0	9·2	8·1	18·9	16·0
1975	294	289	32·2	31·0	8·7	7·8	18·1	15·1
1976	300	298	33·0	32·3	8·9	8·2	18·5	15·6
1977	290	286	31·3	31·0	8·9	8·1	18·3	15·3
1978	296	290	32·4	32·7	8·5	7·7	18·4	15·4
1979	298	295	32·9	32·9	8·8	8·0	18·1	14·7
1980	292	290	31·7	31·6	8·8	8·0	18·0	14·9

(*a*) Subsequent figures are of deaths occurring in the year shown rather than of deaths registered.

Population and Vital Statistics 13. Crude Death Rates and Infant Mortality – England & Wales 1838–1980, Scotland 1855–1980, Ireland 1864–1980

NOTES

[1] SOURCES: *Annual Report of the Registrar General* (and its successors) for each country.

[2] In each country the first year shown is a serious understatement owing to deficiencies in registration. In no case was registration virtually complete until well into the 1860s, and infant mortality for Ireland as a whole may be understated right up to 1920.

[3] From 3 September 1939 to 31 December 1949 for males, and from 1 June 1941 to 31 December 1949 for females, the mortality rates are based upon civilian deaths and estimated civilian population in the United Kingdom.

	Deaths per 1,000 Persons			Deaths per 1,000 Males			Deaths per 1,000 Females			Deaths of Infants under one year per 1,000 Live Births		
	England & Wales	Scotland	Ireland	England & Wales	Scotland	Ireland	England & Wales	Scotland	Ireland	England & Wales	Scotland	Ireland
1838	22·4	...	...	23·4	...	...	21·5	...	...	...	...	...
1839	21·8	...	...	22·8	...	...	21·0	...	...	151	...	...
1840	22·9	...	...	23·7	...	...	22·0	...	...	154	...	...
1841	21·6	...	...	22·4	...	...	20·8	...	...	145	...	...
1842	21·7	...	...	22·4	...	...	21·0	...	...	152	...	...
1843	21·2	...	...	22·0	...	...	20·5	...	...	150	...	...
1844	21·6	...	...	22·4	...	...	20·8	...	...	148	...	...
1845	20·9	...	...	21·7	...	...	20·1	...	...	142	...	...
1846	23·0	...	...	23·9	...	...	22·2	...	...	164	...	...
1847	24·7	...	...	25·4	...	...	23·8	...	...	164	...	...
1848	23·0	...	...	23·9	...	...	22·2	...	...	153	...	...
1849	25·1	...	...	25·8	...	...	24·5	...	...	160	...	...
1850	20·8	...	...	21·4	...	...	20·1	...	...	162	...	...
1851	22·0	...	...	22·8	...	...	21·2	...	...	153	...	...
1852	22·4	...	...	23·2	...	...	21·6	...	...	158	...	...
1853	22·9	...	...	23·8	...	...	22·0	...	...	159	...	...
1854	23·5	...	...	24·4	...	...	22·7	...	...	157	...	...
1855	22·6	20·8	...	23·5	21·6	...	21·7	20·0	...	153	125	...
1856	20·5	19·5	...	21·4	20·7	...	19·7	18·5	...	143	118	...
1857	21·8	20·6	...	22·6	21·6	...	21·1	19·6	...	156	118	...
1858	23·1	21·0	...	23·9	22·0	...	22·3	20·1	...	151	121	...
1859	22·4	20·3	...	23·3	21·2	...	21·5	19·4	...	153	108	...
1860	21·2	22·3	...	22·1	23·2	...	20·3	21·5	...	148	127	...
1861	21·6	20·3	...	22·7	21·3	...	20·6	19·5	...	153	111	...
1862	21·4	21·7	...	22·4	22·6	...	20·5	20·9	...	142	117	...
1863	23·0	22·9	...	24·1	24·0	...	21·9	21·8	...	149	120	...
1864	23·7	23·6	16·5	24·9	24·7	16·8	22·5	22·6	16·3	153	126	98
1865	23·2	22·3	16·7	24·5	23·3	16·9	22·0	21·4	16·4	160	125	98
1866	23·4	22·2	16·8	24·6	23·1	17·1	22·2	21·3	16·6	160	122	94
1867	21·7	21·3	17·0	23·0	22·3	17·6	20·5	20·4	16·6	153	119	97
1868	21·8	21·2	15·8	23·1	22·2	16·3	20·7	20·3	15·3	155	118	95
1869	22·3	23·0	16·4	23·6	24·0	16·9	21·0	22·0	16·0	156	129	93
1870	22·9	22·2	16·7	24·2	23·2	17·2	21·6	21·4	16·2	160	123	95
1871	22·6	22·2	16·4	23·9	22·9	16·8	21·3	21·5	15·9	158	130	91
1872	21·3	22·3	18·1	22·6	23·3	18·8	19·9	21·0	17·5	150	124	97
1873	21·0	22·4	18·3	22·4	23·7	18·9	19·8	21·1	17·7	149	125	96
1874	22·2	23·2	17·3	23·6	24·4	18·1	20·9	22·1	16·6	151	125	94
1875	22·7	23·3	18·5	24·1	23·9	19·0	21·4	22·6	18·0	158	132	95
1876	20·9	20·9	17·3	22·3	22·0	17·9	19·6	19·9	16·9	146	121	94
1877	20·3	20·6	17·5	21·7	21·6	18·2	18·9	19·7	16·9	136	115	92
1878	21·6	21·2	18·6	22·9	22·0	19·3	20·3	20·4	18·0	152	123	97
1879	20·7	20·0	19·6	22·0	20·6	20·1	19·6	19·5	19·1	135	108	101
1880	20·5	20·5	19·8	21·8	21·3	20·4	19·3	19·6	19·0	153	125	112
1881	18·9	19·3	17·5	20·0	20·0	17·9	17·8	18·7	17·1	130	113	91
1882	19·6	19·4	17·3	20·7	20·0	17·4	18·5	18·8	17·2	141	118	95

Population and Vital Statistics 13. *continued*

	Deaths per 1,000 Persons			Deaths per 1,000 Males			Deaths per 1,000 Females			Deaths of Infants under one year per 1,000 Live Births		
	England & Wales	Scotland	Ireland	England & Wales	Scotland	Ireland	England & Wales	Scotland	Ireland	England & Wales	Scotland	Ireland
1883	19·6	20·2	19·2	20·8	20·9	19·4	18·5	19·6	19·0	137	119	98
1884	19·7	19·6	17·5	20·8	20·3	17·9	18·5	19·0	17·3	147	118	92
1885	19·2	19·3	18·4	20·3	19·8	18·7	18·2	18·9	18·2	138	121	95
1886	19·5	19·0	17·8	20·6	19·4	18·0	18·5	18·5	17·5	149	116	94
1887	19·1	19·0	18·2	20·2	19·4	18·4	18·1	18·6	18·0	145	122	95
1888	18·1	18·0	17·9	19·2	18·3	18·0	17·0	17·8	17·7	136	113	97
1889	18·2	18·4	17·4	19·3	18·9	17·6	17·2	18·0	17·2	144	121	94
1890	19·5	19·7	18·2	20·8	20·3	18·2	18·3	19·3	18·2	151	131	95
1891	20·2	20·7	18·4	21·5	21·1	18·2	19·0	20·3	18·5	149	128	95
1892	19·0	18·5	19·4	20·0	19·0	19·2	18·0	18·1	19·6	148	117	105
1893	19·2	19·3	18·0	20·3	19·9	17·9	18·1	18·8	18·0	159	136	102
1894	16·6	17·1	18·2	17·6	17·5	18·2	15·6	16·7	18·1	137	117	102
1895	18·7	19·4	18·5	19·7	20·0	18·4	17·7	19·0	18·5	161	133	104
1896	17·1	16·6	16·7	18·1	17·1	16·5	16·1	16·1	16·7	148	115	95
1897	17·4	18·4	18·5	18·6	19·0	18·4	16·2	17·9	18·5	156	138	109
1898	17·5	18·0	18·2	18·6	18·7	18·0	16·5	17·5	18·3	160	134	110
1899	18·2	18·1	17·7	19·4	18·7	17·6	17·2	17·6	17·6	163	131	108
1900	18·2	18·5	19·6	19·5	19·2	19·5	17·1	18·0	19·7	154	128	109
1901	16·9	17·9	17·8	18·1	18·5	17·9	15·8	17·3	17·7	151	129	101
1902	16·3	17·3	17·5	17·4	17·9	17·6	15·2	16·7	17·5	133	113	100
1903	15·5	16·8	17·5	16·5	17·3	17·5	14·4	16·2	17·5	132	118	96
1904	16·3	17·1	18·0	17·4	17·5	18·0	15·3	16·7	18·1	145	123	100
1905	15·3	16·2	17·1	16·3	16·7	17·1	14·4	15·8	17·1	128	116	95
1906	15·5	16·4	16·9	16·5	16·8	17·1	14·5	15·9	16·9	132	115	93
1907	15·1	16·6	17·6	16·0	16·9	17·8	14·2	16·3	17·6	118	110	92
1908	14·8	16·6	17·5	15·8	17·1	17·6	13·9	16·2	17·6	120	121	97
1909	14·6	15·8	17·1	15·5	16·2	17·1	13·8	15·5	17·2	109	108	92
1910	13·5	15·3	17·1	14·4	15·7	17·1	12·7	14·8	17·2	105	108	95
1911	14·6	15·1	16·5	15·6	15·6	16·6	13·7	14·7	16·5	130	112	94
1912	13·3	15·3	16·5	14·2	15·7	16·4	12·6	14·9	16·5	95	105	86
1913	13·8	15·5	17·1	14·8	15·9	17·2	12·9	15·0	17·0	108	110	97
1914	14·0	15·5	16.3	15·0	16·0	16·4	13·1	15·1	16·2	105	111	87
1915	15·7(*a*)	17·1	17·6	17·7(*a*)	17·8	17·8	13·9	16·5	17·3	110	126	92
1916	14·3(*a*)	14·7	16·3	16·7(*a*)	15·4	16·8	12·4	14·1	16·1	91	97	83
1917	14.2(*a*)	14·4	16·6	17·1(*a*)	15·2	17·0	12·1	13·7	16·6	96	107	88
1918	17·3(*a*)	16·3	17·9	20·1(*a*)	17·0	18·0	15·1	15·7	17·9	97	100	86
1919	14·0(*a*)	15·6	17·6	15·7(*a*)	16·2	17·3	12·5	15·0	17·9	89	102	88
1920	12·4(*a*)	14·0	14·8	13·5(*a*)	14·8	14·6	12·0	13·3	15·1	80	92	83
1921	12·1	13·6	14·2	12·4	14·1	...	10·9	13·1	...	83	90	...

Population and Vital Statistics 13. *continued*

	Deaths per 1,000 Persons				Deaths per 1,000 Males				Deaths per 1,000 Females				Deaths of Infants under one year per 1,000 Live Births			
	England & Wales	Scotland	Northern Ireland	Republic of Ireland	England & Wales	Scotland	Northern Ireland	Republic of Ireland	England & Wales	Scotland	Northern Ireland	Republic of Ireland	England & Wales	Scotland	Northern Ireland	Republic of Ireland
1922	12·7	14·9	15·4	14·7	13·5	15·4	15·1	14·9	12·0	14·4	15·7	14·6	77	101	77	69
1923	11·6	12·9	14·7	14·0	12·4	13·5	14·6	14·1	10·9	12·5	14·8	13·9	69	80	77	66
1924	12·2	14·5	15·9	15·0	13·0	15·1	15·8	15·0	11·5	13·9	16·0	15·1	75	98	85	72
1925	12·1	13·5	15·7	14·6	12·9	14·2	15·7	14·6	11·4	12·8	15·7	14·6	75	91	86	68
1926	11·6	13·1	15·0	14·1	12·4	13·7	15·1	13·9	10·9	12·6	14·9	14·3	70	83	85	74
1927	12·3	13·6	14·6	14·8	13·1	14·2	14·4	14·6	11·6	13·0	14·7	15·0	70	89	78	71
1928	11·7	13·5	14·4	14·2	12·5	14·0	14·4	14·0	10·9	13·0	14·4	14·4	65	86	78	68
1929	13·4	14·7	15·9	14·6	14·2	15·3	15·7	14·4	12·7	14·1	16·1	14·8	74	87	86	70
1930	11·4	13·3	13·8	14·2	12·3	14·0	14·0	14·1	10·7	12·7	13·6	14·2	60	83	68	68
1931	12·3	13·3	14·4	14·5	13·0	13·9	14·6	14·5	11·6	12·7	14·3	14·6	66	82	73	69
1932	12·0	13·5	14·1	14·6	12·7	13·9	14·2	14·5	11·4	13·1	14·1	14·7	64	86	83	72
1933	12·3	13·2	14·3	13·7	12·9	13·8	14·5	13·6	11·7	12·7	14·1	13·7	63	81	80	65
1934	11·8	12·9	13·9	13·2	12·5	13·5	14·2	13·1	11·1	12·4	13·5	13·2	59	78	70	63
1935	11·7	13·2	14·6	14·0	12·5	13·8	14·8	14·2	11·1	12·7	14·4	13·8	57	77	86	68
1936	12·1	13·4	14·4	14·4	12·9	14·2	14·5	14·4	11·4	12·8	14·4	14·3	59	82	77	74
1937	12·4	13·9	15·1	15·3	13·2	14·6	15·1	15·5	11·7	13·2	15·0	15·1	58	80	78	73
1938	11·6	12·6	13·7	13·6	12·5	13·2	14·0	13·7	10·8	12·0	13·5	13·6	53	70	75	67
1939	12·1	12·9	13·5	14·2	13·0	13·7	13·9	14·2	11·3	12·1	13·2	14·1	51	69	71	66
1940	14·4	14·9	14·6	14·2	16·1	16·6	15·2	14·3	12·9	13·4	14·1	14·1	57	78	86	66
1941	13·5	14·7	15·2	14·6	15·7	16·7	15·6	14·8	11·8	13·1	14·9	14·5	60	83	77	73
1942	12·3	13·3	13·3	14·1	14·4	15·2	14·0	14·6	10·7	11·8	12·7	13·5	51	69	76	69
1943	13·0	14·0	13·4	14·8	15·3	15·9	13·9	15·2	11·3	12·4	12·9	14·3	49	65	78	83
1944	12·7	13·6	12·8	15·3	15·3	15·7	13·2	15·8	10·8	12·0	12·4	14·9	45	65	67	79
1945	12·6	13·2	12·3	14·5	15·0	15·1	12·6	14·9	10·8	11·7	12·1	14·0	46	56	68	71
1946	12·0	13·1	12·5	14·0	13·4	14·1	13·0	14·6	10·9	12·1	12·1	13·4	43	54	54	65
1947	12·3	13·1	12·6	14·8	13·6	13·9	13·2	15·6	11·3	12·3	12·1	14·0	41	56	53	68
1948	11·0	12·0	11·2	12·1	11·9	12·7	11·7	12·6	10·1	11·4	10·7	11·6	34	45	46	50
1949	11·8	12·5	11·5	12·7	12·6	13·0	12·0	13·2	11·1	11·9	11·1	12·3	32	41	45	53
1950	11·6	12·5	11·6	12·7	12·3	13·1	12·1	13·3	11·0	12·0	11·1	12·1	30	39	41	46
1951	12·5	12·9	12·8	14·3	13·4	13·6	13·3	14·9	11·8	12·3	12·4	13·7	30	37	41	46
1952	11·3	12·1	10·8	11·9	12·2	12·9	11·4	12·6	10·5	11·3	10·1	11·2	28	35	39	41
1953	11·4	11·5	10·7	11·7	12·2	12·5	11·4	12·3	10·7	10·7	10·1	11·2	27	31	38	39
1954	11·3	12·0	10·9	12·1	12·2	12·9	11·5	12·9	10·5	11·2	10·4	11·3	25	31	33	38
1955	11·7	12·1	11·1	12·6	12·5	12·8	11·6	13·4	10·9	11·4	10·6	11·8	25	30	32	37
1956	11·7	12·1	10·6	11·7	12·5	12·9	11·2	12·5	10·9	11·3	10·1	10·9	24	29	29	36
1957	11·5	11·9	10·9	11·9	12·3	12·9	11·6	12·6	10·7	11·0	10·1	11·2	23	29	29	33
1958	11·7	12·1	10·8	12·0	12·4	12·9	11·6	12·9	11·0	11·3	10·0	11·1	23	28	28	35
1959	11·6	12·2	10·9	12·0	12·3	13·1	11·6	13·0	11·0	11·4	10·3	11·1	22	28	28	32
1960	11·5	11·9	10·8	11·5	12·2	12·8	11·4	12·2	10·9	11·2	10·2	10·8	22	26	27	29
1961	11·9	12·3	11·3	12·3	12·6	13·2	12·1	13·2	11·4	11·5	10·5	11·4	21	26	27	30
1962	12·0	12·2	10·6	12·0	12·6	13·1	11·3	12·9	11·3	11·3	9·9	11·0	22	26	27	29
1963	12·2	12·6	11·0	11·9	12·8	13·6	11·8	12·8	11·6	11·6	10·2	11·0	21	26	27	27
1964	11·3	11·7	10·5	11·4	12·0	12·7	11·3	12·3	10·7	10·8	9·8	10·6	20	24	26	27
1965	11·5	12·1	10·6	11·5	12·2	13·0	11·4	12·5	10·9	11·2	9·8	10·6	19	23	25	25
1966	11·8	12·3	11·1	12·2	12·4	13·0	12·0	13·2	11·1	11·5	10·3	11·1	19	23	25	25
1967	11·2	11·5	9·8	10·8	11·8	12·2	10·6	11·7	10·7	10·7	9·1	10·0	18	21	24	24
1968	11·9	12·2	10·6	11·4	12·4	12·9	11·2	12·3	11·4	11·5	10·0	10·4	18	21	24	21
1969	11·9	12·3	10·8	11·6	12·5	13·0	11·7	12·5	11·3	11·5	10·0	10·6	18	21	24	21
				...(a)				...(a)				...(a)				..(a)
1970	11·8	12·2	10·9	11·4	12·3	13·0	11·8	12·5	11·2	11·5	10·0	10·4	18	20	23	20
1971	11·5	11·8	10·5	10·7	12·1	12·6	11·4	11·6	11·0	11·1	9·8	9·8	18	20	23	18
1972	12·0	12·5	11·0	11·4	12·5	13·3	11·8	12·4	11·5	11·8	10·2	10·4	17	19	21	18
1973	11·9	12·4	11·4	11·1	12·3	13·2	12·1	12·1	11·5	11·7	10·7	10·1	17	19	21	18
1974	11·8	12·4	11·2	11·2	12·3	13·0	12·0	12·1	11·4	11·8	10·4	10·3	16	19	21	18
1975	11·7	12·1	10·7	10·4	12·2	12·9	11·4	11·3	11·4	11·5	10·1	9·6	16	17	20	18
1976	12·1	12·5	11·1	10·6	12·5	13·2	11·6	11·4	11·8	12·0	10·5	9·7	14	15	18	16
1977	11·6	12·0	11·1	10·3	12·0	12·5	11·7	11·1	11·3	11·5	10·4	9·4	14	16	17	16
1978	11·9	12·6	10·5	10·2	12·3	13·0	11·1	11·1	11·4	12·2	9·9	9·3	13	13	16	15
1979	12·0	12·7	10·9	9·7	12·4	13·2	11·6	11·0	11·6	12·3	10·2	9·0	13	12	15	13
1980	11·7	12·3	10·9	9·7	12·1	12·8	11·6	10·7	11·4	11·8	10·2	9·0	12	11	13	11

(*a*) Subsequent figures are of deaths occurring in the year shown rather than of deaths registered.

Population and Vital Statistics 14. Death Rates per 1,000 in Different Age-Groups – England & Wales 1838–1980

NOTE
SOURCE: *The Registrar General's Statistical Review of England & Wales* (and its successors).

A. Males

	0–4	5–9	10–14	15–19	20–24	25–34	35–44	45–54	55–64	65–74	75–84	85 and over
1838	70·7	9·1	5·3	7·4	9·9	10·7	13·4	19·1	33·6	68·0	148·4	316·0
1839	71·8	9·1	5·1	7·2	9·4	9·9	12·6	17·7	31·6	63·4	139·1	291·2
1840	75·4	10·8	5·4	7·5	9·3	9·9	12·7	17·7	31·2	66·2	144·9	312·2
1841	68·4	9·6	5·1	7·2	9·2	9·8	12·2	17·7	31·3	64·5	142·6	303·0
1842	70·4	9·0	5·0	6·9	8·9	9·3	12·0	17·2	30·3	65·7	145·6	300·6
1843	68·8	8·4	4·8	6·7	8·9	9·2	12·2	17·0	30·0	65·5	140·7	293·5
1844	69·7	9·0	4·7	6·5	8·9	9·4	12·3	17·3	30·4	67·1	146·6	320·7
1845	66·5	8·2	4·6	6·6	9·1	9·2	12·1	17·0	29·6	64·7	143·7	308·4
1846	77·4	8·2	5·1	7·3	10·0	10·2	12·8	17·8	31·1	67·4	150·4	328·9
1847	76·0	9·7	5·5	8·0	10·8	11·0	14·5	20·5	36·5	77·1	173·6	364·6
1848	73·8	10·4	5·3	7·3	10·0	10·3	13·1	18·4	32·5	67·8	149·6	310·3
1849	75·0	11·2	6·5	8·0	11·1	12·4	15·9	22·4	36·4	72·4	151·7	304·7
1850	66·8	8·1	4·7	6·2	8·2	8·8	11·7	17·0	29·7	63·1	140·1	289·7
1851	72·9	8·7	4·9	6·8	8·8	9·5	12·4	17·7	30·2	64·1	140·6	288·6
1852	74·8	9·1	5·2	6·9	9·2	9·8	12·4	18·0	30·5	62·9	142·1	293·4
1853	73·0	8·5	5·1	7·2	9·6	10·3	13·2	19·3	32·4	69·1	159·8	328·3
1854	77·3	9·4	5·5	7·3	9·7	10·5	13·6	19·3	31·8	66·5	149·2	296·0
1855	71·5	8·2	5·0	6·7	8·9	9·8	12·8	18·6	32·8	70·7	162·9	349·2
1856	67·2	7·2	4·5	6·4	8·5	9·1	11·8	16·6	29·1	60·8	131·1	284·2
1857	72·2	7·8	4·7	6·4	8·4	9·2	12·0	17·3	29·9	63·3	143·9	306·1
1858	76·5	10·5	5·0	6·8	8·7	9·3	12·3	17·7	30·9	66·2	147·0	323·5
1859	74·7	9·2	4·8	6·4	8·4	9·2	12·3	17·8	30·8	64·2	140·2	298·9
1860	67·3	6·8	4·1	6·1	8·2	9·0	12·4	17·8	31·5	67·3	151·2	314·9
1861	71·8	6·7	4·3	6·4	8·3	9·2	12·3	17·6	30·9	65·4	146·5	315·7
1862	69·8	7·7	4·4	6·2	8·2	9·2	12·4	18·1	31·3	63·3	139·9	296·7
1863	77·8	10·3	5·0	6·4	8·5	9·4	12·8	18·2	31·7	63·9	139·4	309·7
1864	75·8	9·8	4·9	6·5	9·1	10·3	14·3	20·1	35·2	70·3	151·4	334·4
1865	75·0	8·1	4·7	6·4	9·2	10·6	14·2	20·5	34·7	68·6	151·8	325·6
1866	74·9	7·8	4·6	6·5	9·2	10·9	14·7	20·9	34·7	68·9	150·6	323·5
1867	69·3	6·5	4·0	6·0	8·4	10·0	13·6	19·1	33·5	68·3	152·5	332·4
1868	72·8	7·8	4·2	5·9	8·0	9·7	13·2	18·9	31·9	63·8	139·1	282·4
1869	72·5	8·3	4·3	5·7	7·9	9·9	13·5	19·3	33·3	68·4	149·1	308·9
1870	75·0	8·9	4·5	5·9	8·0	10·1	13·8	19·6	33·9	69·6	152·1	320·7
1871	71·7	8·3	4·4	6·4	9·2	11·1	14·4	20·0	33·9	67·5	145·2	312·8
1872	67·6	7·0	4·1	6·0	8·7	10·3	14·0	19·4	32·5	65·5	140·3	292·0
1873	66·4	6·0	3·7	5·3	7·5	9·5	13·6	19·8	34·1	70·9	150·6	324·9
1874	71·8	7·4	3·9	5·3	7·5	9·6	14·3	20·9	35·8	71·4	146·4	322·8
1875	71·9	6·9	3·8	5·6	7·6	9·7	15·0	21·5	37·7	74·7	165·0	363·8
1876	67·6	6·3	3·5	5·3	7·3	9·3	13·8	19·9	34·3	67·2	145·8	302·6
1877	63·9	6·1	3·5	4·9	7·0	9·1	13·7	19·7	34·7	68·2	145·8	324·9
1878	71·2	6·6	3·6	4·9	6·8	8·8	13·6	20·0	35·1	69·5	154·8	353·9
1879	63·3	6·3	3·3	4·7	6·4	8·6	13·3	20·4	36·8	74·0	168·7	365·5
1880	69·2	6·4	3·3	4·5	6·1	7·9	12·5	19·1	33·7	68·1	145·8	310·9
1881	56·6	5·8	3·2	4·5	6·1	8·3	13·0	19·3	34·0	67·7	144·8	293·5
1882	63·5	6·3	3·2	4·6	5·9	8·2	12·6	19·0	33·8	66·2	139·3	287·1
1883	61·0	6·2	3·3	4·7	6·2	8·3	13·0	19·7	35·1	70·1	149·1	303·2
1884	64·9	5·8	3·2	4·5	6·0	8·0	12·7	19·4	33·5	68·3	142·2	290·1
1885	60·6	5·1	2·9	4·3	5·8	8·0	12·6	19·3	34·4	71·3	151·5	316·2
1886	64·5	4·8	2·8	4·3	5·7	7·6	12·1	19·2	34·7	72·8	153·4	339·1
1887	62·5	5·1	2·9	4·2	5·4	7·3	11·9	18·7	35·0	72·1	149·4	310·1

Population and Vital Statistics 14. *continued*

A. Males (*cont.*)

	0–4	5–9	10–14	15–19	20–24	25–34	35–44	45–54	55–64	65–74	75–84	85 and over
1888	57·7	4·7	2·7	4·0	5·4	7·1	11·7	19·0	34·4	71·6	144·5	304·7
1889	61·8	4·7	2·6	3·9	5·1	7·0	11·3	18·3	33·4	68·5	138·9	298·6
1890	62·9	5·0	2·8	4·3	5·7	8·0	13·2	21·7	38·6	75·3	153·3	316·5
1891	64·6	4·7	2·6	4·2	5·6	7·9	13·4	22·4	41·0	81·3	167·9	327·1
1892	62·4	4·7	2·6	4·0	5·2	7·1	12·1	19·8	36·6	75·7	154·6	305·4
1893	65·6	5·0	2·8	4·3	5·4	7·3	12·5	19·9	35·6	71·4	142·5	272·8
1894	56·1	4·2	2·3	3·8	5·0	6·5	10·8	17·3	31·4	62·8	127·6	243·6
1895	66·0	4·1	2·5	3·8	5·0	6·6	11·0	18·5	34·9	71·3	154·1	306·1
1896	61·2	4·5	2·3	3·5	4·8	6·2	10·6	17·3	31·6	63·0	128·6	251·9
1897	62·5	3·9	2·4	3·6	4·8	6·4	10·8	17·7	32·9	65·8	141·7	272·1
1898	63·4	3·8	2·2	3·5	4·8	6·3	10·7	17·6	33·2	66·4	140·3	282·6
1899	63·4	4·1	2·3	3·6	5·0	6·7	11·6	19·2	35·5	72·0	150·3	302·1
1900	61·6	4·2	2·3	3·7	5·1	6·7	11·7	19·9	37·1	74·2	153·7	304·3
1901	59·0	4·0	2·3	3·5	4·7	6·2	10·6	18·0	33·5	67·8	139·8	276·5
1902	54·1	3·9	2·2	3·3	4·6	6·2	10·4	17·8	33·3	66·7	138·5	270·0
1903	52·5	3·5	2·0	3·0	4·2	5·8	9·4	16·6	31·6	63·3	132·8	160·3
1904	57·4	3·6	2·1	3·1	4·3	5·7	9·4	16·5	32·3	65·5	139·7	287·6
1905	50·3	3·4	2·1	3·1	4·2	5·6	9·0	16·1	31·5	63·3	137·2	278·2
1906	51·2	3·5	2·0	3·2	4·1	5·5	9·1	16·1	32·4	64·3	137·3	298·5
1907	46·8	3·4	2·0	3·0	4·0	5·5	9·0	16·1	32·3	65·2	138·8	291·7
1908	46·9	3·3	2·0	2·9	4·0	5·3	8·6	15·4	31·4	64·3	138·4	277·2
1909	42·8	3·4	2·0	3·0	3·9	5·2	8·5	15·6	31·1	66·4	142·5	289·9
1910	39·7	3·0	1·9	2·7	3·7	4·7	7·9	14·5	29·4	61·8	131·6	259·7
1911	46·7	3·5	2·1	3·1	3·8	5·0	8·1	14·9	29·6	63·2	140·5	268·0
1912	35·8	3·1	1·8	2·9	3·6	4·8	7·9	14·6	29·4	63·9	137·1	266·7
1913	40·3	3·2	1·9	2·8	3·6	4·8	7·9	14·7	29·9	64·2	138·0	258·1
1914	39·4	3·4	2·1	3·1	3·9	5·1	8·3	14·9	30·0	64·7	135·3	269·5
1915 (*a*)	42·0	3·9	2·3	3·3	5·8	6·5	8·9	15·4	31·9	70·7	155·2	309·3
1916 (*a*)	32·4	3·3	2·2	3·4	6·8	7·2	8·6	14·4	29·5	67·9	150·3	296·3
1917 (*a*)	31·8	3·3	2·2	3·6	7·9	8·5	9·1	14·1	29·2	67·5	149·4	286·5
1918(*a*)	38·9	5·5	3·5	6·2	13·8	19·6	12·6	16·4	29·3	65·7	132·1	234·4
1919 (*a*)	32·8	3·5	2·3	3·6	5·5	8·1	8·6	13·3	27·2	63·5	145·5	277·6
1920 (*a*)	36·2	3·3	1·9	2·9	3·9	4·7	7·0	12·0	24·5	56·0	124·6	235·2
1921	32·3	2·8	1·8	2·8	3·6	4·2	6·5	11·4	24·4	55·8	128·7	262·8
1922	30·2	2·6	1·7	2·7	3·7	4·4	6·9	12·0	26·0	61·2	143·9	271·3
1923	24·3	2·3	1·6	2·6	3·4	4·0	6·3	11·2	24·1	56·0	130·2	262·0
1924	25·1	2·5	1·7	2·6	3·3	3·9	6·3	11·6	24·5	59·6	140·2	290·0
1925	25·3	2·5	1·5	2·5	3·1	3·7	6·1	11·1	23·3	56·8	132·7	282·0
1926	23·3	2·5	1·5	2·5	3·2	3·6	6·1	11·0	23·6	55·9	131·1	284·3
1927	23·7	2·5	1·6	2·5	3·4	3·8	6·5	11·9	24·9	59·9	139·8	312·2
1928	21·9	2·4	1·7	2·6	3·2	3·6	6·0	11·2	23·6	56·5	128·0	290·9
1929	26·2	2·6	1·7	2·7	3·5	3·9	6·7	12·9	26·3	64·1	151·5	343·6
1930	20·4	2·4	1·6	2·6	3·2	3·5	5·7	11·2	23·4	55·2	126·6	263·5
1931	22·4	2·3	1·5	2·6	3·3	3·5	5·8	11·6	23·9	58·7	138·4	295·9
1932	21·0	2·2	1·5	2·5	3·2	3·3	5·3	10·8	23·4	57·9	138·0	289·7
1933	19·9	2·3	1·5	2·6	3·3	3·5	5·7	11·7	23·8	56·6	139·4	286·3
1934	19·3	2·5	1·5	2·4	3·1	3·2	5·1	10·9	23·4	55·4	129·3	256·4
1935	17·9	2·1	1·4	2·1	2·9	3·1	5·0	10·8	23·3	55·2	131·8	268·9
1936	19·1	2·1	1·3	2·1	2·9	2·9	4·9	10·8	24·2	56·3	137·3	291·8
1937	18·6	2·0	1·2	2·1	2·8	3·0	5·0	11·1	24·9	57·1	138·5	292·3

See p. 65 for footnote.

A. Males (*cont.*)

	0–4	5–9	10–14	15–19	20–24	25–34	35–44	45–54	55–64	65–74	75–84	85 and over
1938	17·1	1·9	1·3	2·0	2·7	2·8	4·6	10·2	23·1	53·7	130·1	263·6
1939 (*a*)	15·2	1·7	1·1	1·9	2·6	2·7	4·4	10·3	24·3	55·4	139·1	280·8
1940 (*a*)	17·5	2·1	1·5	2·8	4·8	4·1	5·8	12·5	28·3	61·3	151·8	303·2
1941 (*a*)	18·2	2·3	1·5	2·9	5·6	4·6	5·6	11·0	25·1	55·2	134·6	258·8
1942 (*a*)	15·6	1·7	1·2	2·1	4·8	3·9	4·7	9·6	22·4	51·2	120·7	232·9
1943 (*a*)	15·6	1·6	1·1	2·1	5·0	4·0	4·8	10·0	22·8	51·4	122·6	234·1
1944 (*a*)	14·8	1·6	1·2	2·0	4·8	4·3	9·6	4·8	22·7	50·6	116·5	212·0
1945 (*a*)	13·7	1·4	1·0	1·8	4·8	3·8	4·2	9·1	22·3	50·3	115·7	204·7
1946 (*a*)	13·4	1·0	0·9	1·5	2·7	2·2	3·6	8·9	22·3	49·7	117·4	232·3
1947 (*a*)	13·5	1·0	0·8	1·6	2·1	2·1	3·4	9·0	22·9	52·5	125·9	266·5
1948 (*a*)	9·7	0·9	0·6	1·3	1·5	1·9	3·2	8·2	21·6	49·0	108·6	210·2
1949 (*a*)	8·7	0·8	0·6	1·3	1·6	1·8	3·1	8·4	22·6	53·2	120·7	249·0
1950	7·5	0·8	0·6	1·0	1·4	1·7	2·9	8·3	22·5	53·3	122·5	250·4
1951	7·4	0·7	0·6	0·9	1·4	1·6	3·0	8·6	24·3	58·8	136·9	307·8
1952	7·0	0·6	0·5	0·9	1·3	1·4	2·8	7·9	22·2	53·1	122·1	265·1
1953	7·1	0·6	0·5	0·8	1·2	1·4	2·6	7·8	22·2	53·7	123·4	258·1
1954	6·7	0·5	0·4	0·8	1·1	1·3	2·7	7·7	21·9	53·3	123·0	249·6
1955	6·6	0·5	0·5	0·9	1·2	1·3	2·5	7·7	22·0	54·2	128·5	256·2
1956	6·5	0·5	0·4	0·8	1·1	1·2	2·5	7·5	22·1	54·2	127·5	256·2
1957	6·4	0·5	0·4	0·9	1·2	1·2	2·5	7·5	22·3	54·0	119·9	226·8
1958	6·3	0·5	0·4	0·8	1·1	1·2	2·4	7·4	21·9	54·3	124·6	242·6
1959	6·1	0·5	0·4	0·9	1·1	1·1	2·4	7·2	21·8	53·6	122·2	240·0
1960	6·2	0·5	0·4	0·9	1·2	1·1	2·4	7·2	21·4	52·5	119·6	232·1
1961	6·1	0·5	0·4	0·9	1·1	1·2	2·4	7·3	21·9	54·7	124·5	256·9
1962	6·2	0·4	0·4	0·9	1·1	1·1	2·4	7·3	22·1	55·3	125·2	261·1
1963	6·0	0·5	0·4	0·9	1·1	1·1	2·5	7·5	22·3	55·8	128·0	272·8
1964	5·6	0·5	0·4	1·0	1·1	1·1	2·5	7·4	21·2	51·7	113·8	234·2
1965	5·2	0·5	0·4	1·0	1·1	1·1	2·5	7·4	21·4	53·0	118·4	242·4
1966	5·1	0·4	0·4	1·1	1·0	1·1	2·4	7·3	21·4	53·6	120·8	258·2
1967	4·7	0·4	0·4	1·0	1·0	1·0	2·3	6·9	20·6	51·1	112·4	238·6
1968	4·8	0·4	0·4	0·9	0·9	1·0	2·3	7·0	21·1	53·7	123·2	267·4
1969	4·7	0·4	0·4	0·9	0·9	1·0	2·3	7·3	21·6	55·2	119·4	249·9
1970	4·7	0·4	0·4	0·9	1·0	1·0	2·3	7·0	21·0	53·4	118·6	253·3
1971	4·6	0·4	0·4	0·9	0·9	1·0	2·3	7·1	20·3	51·8	118·7	243·1
1972	4·3	0·4	0·4	0·9	1·0	1·0	2·3	7·3	20·8	54·2	123·9	255·7
1973	4·1	0·4	0·3	0·9	1·1	1·0	2·3	7·2	20·4	51·5	117·7	242·1
1974	3·9	0·4	0·3	0·9	1·0	1·0	2·2	7·3	20·2	51·3	115·1	241·1
1975	3·6	0·3	0·3	0·9	1·0	1·0	2·1	7·1	19·5	50·3	115·3	240·3
1976	3·4	0·3	0·3	0·9	1·0	0·9	2·1	7·0	19·7	50·7	117·8	249·9
1977	3·3	0·3	0·3	0·8	0·9	0·9	2·0	6·8	18·8	48·9	111·1	232·2
1978	3·5	0·3	0·3	0·9	1·0	0·9	2·0	6·8	18·9	49·1	112·2	233·8
1979	3·6	0·3	0·3	0·9	0·9	0·9	2·0	6·6	18·8	48·5	112·4	240·2
1980	3·4	0·3	0·3	0·8	0·9	0·9	1·9	6·4	18·3	46·9	109·2	230·6

B. Females

	0–4	5–9	10–14	15–19	20–24	25–34	35–44	45–54	55–64	65–74	75–84	85 and over
1838	61·1	8·6	5·8	8·2	9·3	10·6	13·0	16·4	29·3	58·4	131·4	278·4
1839	61·7	9·0	5·7	8·2	9·0	10·1	12·4	15·4	27·0	55·0	124·2	263·4
1840	64·5	10·6	6·0	8·6	8·9	10·4	12·6	15·6	28·1	58·7	134·7	294·3
1841	58·6	9·2	5·4	8·0	8·8	10·1	12·3	15·4	27·3	58·3	133·5	291·3
1842	60·2	8·9	5·3	7·9	8·7	10·0	12·2	15·3	27·4	60·0	130·6	291·4

See p. 65 for footnote.

Population and Vital Statistics 14. *continued*

B. Females (*cont.*)

	0–4	5–9	10–14	15–19	20–24	25–34	35–44	45–54	55–64	65–74	75–84	85 and over
1843	59·0	8·2	5·0	7·3	8·4	9·7	12·3	14·9	26·9	58·6	130·2	286·0
1844	58·8	8·8	5·2	7·5	8·6	10·0	12·1	15·3	27·7	60·3	134·8	292·3
1845	56·5	7·8	4·9	7·6	8·6	9·8	12·0	14·7	26·6	58·4	130·2	282·9
1846	66·7	8·0	5·5	8·0	9·3	10·4	12·5	15·7	27·8	61·3	137·8	314·6
1847	65·7	9·4	5·9	8·4	9·9	11·7	14·4	18·1	32·3	69·6	159·9	333·0
1848	63·9	9·8	5·7	8·0	9·4	10·8	13·2	16·0	28·6	60·5	136·0	286·1
1849	64·8	10·9	6·6	9·0	10·9	13·4	16·4	20·2	33·6	65·7	140·3	285·3
1850	57·4	8·1	4·9	7·2	8·3	9·8	11·9	14·9	26·3	56·9	126·9	268·2
1851	63·0	8·6	5·3	7·5	8·8	9·9	12·1	15·4	26·8	58·3	128·3	273·6
1852	64·3	8·8	5·4	7·8	8·8	10·2	12·3	15·3	26·6	56·8	132·3	283·8
1853	63·2	8·1	5·4	8·1	9·0	10·6	12·6	16·0	28·3	60·8	141·8	303·2
1854	67·5	9·2	5·6	7·9	9·2	11·0	13·4	16·7	28·3	59·2	134·3	277·8
1855	61·3	8·0	4·9	7·5	8·7	10·0	12·6	15·6	29·1	63·3	149·3	322·4
1856	58·6	7·3	4·5	6·9	8·0	9·3	11·6	14·2	24·9	53·1	121·1	249·4
1857	63·5	7·7	4·6	7·1	8·4	9·5	11·8	14·8	26·7	58·5	132·6	290·5
1858	67·2	10·4	5·3	7·4	8·7	9·8	12·1	14·9	27·0	60·6	139·1	305·4
1859	65·0	9·4	5·2	7·2	8·3	9·8	12·0	15·2	26·3	57·6	130·1	282·9
1860	57·2	6·9	4·4	6·7	7·8	9·5	11·8	15·0	27·5	60·6	136·7	301·3
1861	62·0	6·8	4·4	7·0	8·1	9·5	11·4	14·7	26·9	57·3	131·2	274·6
1862	60·3	7·4	4·6	6·8	7·8	9·4	11·7	14·8	26·9	57·7	128·7	274·9
1863	67·5	9·9	5·2	6·8	8·1	9·7	12·0	14·9	27·1	56·7	129·1	290·2
1864	65·8	9·4	5·1	7·0	8·4	10·3	12·6	16·5	29·8	63·4	141·1	302·3
1865	65·1	7·8	4·6	6·8	8·5	10·2	12·6	16·6	28·8	60·4	138·4	296·7
1866	65·6	7·2	4·5	6·9	8·6	10·5	13·2	16·9	29·3	61·3	139·8	295·7
1867	59·6	6·1	3·9	6·4	7·8	9·5	12·0	15·6	27·5	59·5	139·4	287·3
1868	63·9	7·4	4·1	6·3	7·7	9·4	11·5	14·9	26·4	55·0	125·8	261·5
1869	63·0	7·8	4·3	6·1	7·3	9·3	11·7	15·7	27·6	59·2	135·4	277·1
1870	64·2	8·3	4·5	6·4	7·6	9·5	11·9	15·8	28·8	60·6	140·2	290·3
1871	62·4	7·5	4·5	6·6	8·2	9·7	12·2	15·9	28·5	60·4	133·6	276·4
1872	58·5	6·5	4·0	6·2	7·6	9·3	11·8	15·1	26·6	56·6	124·7	269·0
1873	56·4	5·6	3·6	5·5	6·8	8·6	11·4	15·6	28·3	61·9	135·2	303·5
1874	61·4	7·1	3·9	5·7	7·3	9·2	12·2	15·9	29·2	61·6	134·0	290·0
1875	61·2	6·4	3·8	5·7	7·3	9·3	12·4	17·0	31·1	65·7	148·8	330·3
1876	57·3	5·9	3·6	5·2	6·7	8·3	11·7	15·4	27·9	58·4	128·7	287·0
1877	53·6	5·6	3·6	5·1	6·3	8·2	11·3	15·3	27·7	58·9	129·1	291·6
1878	61·1	6·1	3·6	5·2	6·3	8·0	11·3	15·4	29·2	61·7	140·5	312·7
1879	52·9	5·8	3·4	4·9	6·0	8·0	11·3	16·0	30·7	66·6	150·2	328·7
1880	59·2	6·0	3·3	4·8	5·9	7·6	10·6	14·7	27·5	58·2	129·1	274·9
1881	48·0	5·7	3·2	4·7	6·0	7·9	11·0	14·9	28·0	58·4	126·4	263·8
1882	54·4	6·0	3·3	4·7	5·9	7·9	11·0	15·0	27·6	56·9	124·1	256·0
1883	51·1	5·8	3·4	4·9	6·1	8·1	11·1	15·6	28·8	60·2	134·2	277·0
1884	54·9	5·8	3·4	4·7	5·9	7·8	10·9	15·3	27·5	57·7	126·8	247·4
1885	51·0	5·1	3·1	4·5	5·7	7·7	10·8	15·2	28·7	62·0	133·2	282·8
1886	54·2	4·8	3·1	4·4	5·3	7·2	10·4	15·0	29·1	63·2	136·5	302·1
1887	52·7	5·1	3·0	4·2	5·4	7·0	10·3	15·2	28·8	62·2	131·6	272·1
1888	48·0	4·7	2·9	4·0	5·1	6·9	9·9	14·5	27·9	60·1	130·0	270·1
1889	51·9	4·7	2·8	3·9	4·9	6·5	9·8	14·3	27·4	58·7	126·5	260·3
1890	53·3	5·0	2·9	4·2	5·1	7·1	10·9	15·9	30·7	64·2	136·9	276·6
1891	53·7	4·7	2·9	4·3	5·2	7·1	11·1	17·1	33·4	70·6	148·1	300·7
1892	52·5	4·6	2·7	4·0	4·7	6·7	10·3	15·5	30·4	66·0	140·9	274·4

Population and Vital Statistics 14. *continued*

B. Females (*cont.*)

	0–4	5–9	10–14	15–19	20–24	25–34	35–44	45–54	55–64	65–74	75–84	85 and over
1893	55·2	5·1	3·0	4·3	5·1	7·0	10·7	15·2	29·2	62·4	128·7	250·0
1894	47·4	4·3	2·6	3·7	4·5	6·0	9·2	13·5	25·1	53·7	113·6	219·6
1895	55·2	4·2	2·6	3·7	4·5	6·1	9·5	14·8	29·6	62·6	140·9	276·2
1896	52·3	4·5	2·4	3·4	4·2	5·7	8·9	13·6	25·8	53·4	113·9	233·4
1897	52·4	4·0	2·4	3·4	4·1	5·6	8·9	13·7	26·2	55·7	121·2	252·6
1898	53·5	3·9	2·3	3·3	4·1	5·5	8·9	13·9	26·7	57·5	126·0	259·6
1899	53·6	4·2	2·4	3·3	4·1	5·7	9·4	15·0	28·7	62·3	136·3	273·2
1900	51·8	4·2	2·5	3·3	4·2	5·7	9·3	15·3	29·6	63·2	136·8	273·9
1901	49·5	4·1	2·4	3·2	3·8	5·3	8·7	13·8	26·5	56·5	122·6	247·1
1902	45·0	4·2	2·3	3·1	3·9	5·3	8·4	13·4	25·9	55·7	122·1	252·3
1903	43·7	3·6	2·1	2·9	3·5	4·9	7·9	12·8	24·4	52·9	114·7	233·9
1904	48·5	3·6	2·2	3·0	3·5	4·9	7·7	12·8	25·6	55·1	123·2	256·1
1905	42·1	3·5	2·2	2·9	3·6	4·8	7·5	12·5	24·8	53·8	117·2	256·7
1906	43·1	3·7	2·3	2·9	3·5	4·7	7·5	12·4	24·8	52·5	119·6	258·7
1907	39·1	3·5	2·1	2·9	3·4	4·6	7·4	12·4	25·3	55·1	122·6	259·4
1908	39·0	3·4	2·0	2·7	3·4	4·4	6·9	12·1	24·2	52·7	119·4	248·8
1909	35·7	3·5	2·1	2·8	3·3	4·4	6·9	12·1	24·8	55·5	124·2	256·2
1910	33·1	3·1	2·0	2·6	3·1	4·1	6·5	11·1	22·4	49·8	112·3	232·8
1911	39·5	3·4	2·1	2·7	3·3	4·2	6·6	11·4	22·8	50·9	115·1	229·4
1912	29·8	3·1	2·0	2·7	3·2	4·0	6·3	11·1	22·3	51·6	115·1	239·3
1913	33·3	3·2	2·0	2·6	3·2	4·0	6·4	11·3	22·3	50·7	111·4	230·9
1914	32·9	3·4	2·2	2·7	3·2	4·1	6·5	11·5	22·4	51·4	113·8	238·7
1915	34·4	3·8	2·3	3·0	3·4	4·2	6·5	11·7	23·6	56·2	129·8	269·9
1916	26·4	3·2	2·2	3·0	3·4	4·0	6·1	10·6	21·5	52·2	122·6	262·5
1917	26·3	3·2	2·2	3·2	3·4	3·9	5·8	10·1	20·7	49·2	118·9	246·8
1918	34·1	5·9	4·0	6·0	7·9	9·8	8·5	12·3	21·4	48·3	107·5	216·7
1919	26·4	3·6	2·3	3·4	4·3	5·4	6·1	10·1	20·5	48·8	120·4	251·7
1920	28·8	3·2	2·0	2·7	3·3	4·2	5·4	8·9	18·1	42·6	104·9	213·6
1921	25·8	2·7	1·8	2·7	3·2	3·7	5·2	8·8	18·2	43·6	108·9	232·3
1922	24·5	2·5	1·8	2·6	3·2	3·9	5·3	9·3	19·7	48·6	120·9	251·0
1923	19·6	2·2	1·6	2·5	3·0	3·4	4·8	8·5	18·2	44·1	108·5	231·9
1924	20·2	2·4	1·7	2·5	3·1	3·4	4·8	8·6	18·1	46·2	115·8	269·1
1925	20·7	2·3	1·5	2·4	2·9	3·3	4·6	8·2	17·4	43·9	108·0	254·2
1926	18·8	2·3	1·5	2·4	2·9	3·3	4·7	8·3	17·6	42·7	105·4	240·2
1927	18·9	2·2	1·5	2·4	3·0	3·4	4·9	8·8	18·5	45·9	115·2	262·3
1928	17·3	2·2	1·5	2·4	3·0	3·3	4·6	8·2	17·3	42·7	102·6	242·9
1929	21·6	2·3	1·7	2·5	3·1	3·5	4·9	9·1	19·6	49·9	126·7	298·2
1930	16·0	2·2	1·5	2·3	2·8	3·2	4·4	7·9	16·9	40·7	102·2	226·5
1931	17·4	2·0	1·5	2·4	2·9	3·3	4·5	8·3	17·6	44·4	114·4	255·3
1932	16·8	1·9	1·3	2·2	2·8	3·1	4·3	8·0	17·1	43·2	111·4	253·0
1933	15·8	2·1	1·4	2·3	2·9	3·2	4·7	8·4	17·4	43·8	113·5	256·9
1934	15·6	2·4	1·4	2·2	2·6	3·0	4·1	7·7	16·5	41·7	102·8	227·1
1935	14·2	1·9	1·3	2·0	2·6	2·9	4·0	7·5	16·4	41·2	103·4	234·4
1936	14·9	1·9	1·1	1·8	2·5	2·7	3·9	7·6	16·5	42·2	106·2	253·2
1937	14·7	1·8	1·1	1·8	2·5	2·8	4·0	7·7	16·9	42·5	108·2	261·9
1938	13·4	1·8	1·1	1·7	2·3	2·5	3·6	7·0	15·5	38·8	98·1	228·9
1939	12·1	1·3	1·0	1·6	2·3	2·5	3·5	7·1	15·7	40·5	106·2	251·1
1940	13·6	1·8	1·3	2·3	2·9	2·9	4·1	8·0	17·7	45·0	116·4	267·5
1941 (*a*)	14·5	1·9	1·2	2·3	2·8	2·9	3·8	7·3	15·4	39·5	101·5	241·7
1942 (*a*)	12·3	1·3	0·9	1·7	2·4	2·4	3·2	6·4	13·9	35·4	91·0	209·2

Population and Vital Statistics 14. *continued*

B. Females (*cont.*)

	0–4	5–9	10–14	15–19	20–24	25–34	35–44	45–54	55–64	65–74	75–84	85 and over
1943 (*a*)	12·4	1·2	1·0	1·7	2·4	2·5	3·3	6·4	13·9	36·4	95·9	213·5
1944 (*a*)	11·7	1·2	0·9	1·6	2·4	2·4	3·1	6·2	13·4	34·6	89·7	188·8
1945 (*a*)	10·8	1·0	0·8	1·4	2·1	2·1	2·9	5·9	13·3	34·6	90·2	189·5
1946 (*a*)	10·3	0·8	0·7	1·2	1·8	2·0	2·8	5·8	13·3	34·6	92·4	206·2
1947 (*a*)	10·6	0·8	0·6	1·2	1·8	1·9	2·7	5·7	13·1	35·2	96·6	219·8
1948 (*a*)	7·6	0·6	0·6	1·1	1·6	1·8	2·5	5·3	12·2	32·1	84·5	183·5
1949 (*a*)	6·7	0·6	0·5	1·0	1·4	1·7	2·5	5·4	12·8	35·5	95·8	217·5
1950	5·9	0·5	0·4	0·8	1·1	1·5	2·3	5·3	12·6	34·7	96·6	216·9
1951	5·7	0·5	0·4	0·6	0·9	1·3	2·3	5·3	13·0	36·9	104·4	249·1
1952	5·4	0·4	0·3	0·5	0·8	1·1	2·1	4·9	11·9	32·3	89·6	212·3
1953	5·6	0·4	0·4	0·5	0·7	1·1	2·1	4·8	11·6	32·1	90·7	218·8
1954	5·1	0·3	0·3	0·5	0·6	1·0	2·1	4·8	11·4	31·6	87·4	209·7
1955	5·1	0·4	0·3	0·4	0·6	0·9	1·9	4·7	11·3	32·3	90·9	222·9
1956	5·0	0·3	0·3	0·4	0·5	0·9	1·9	4·5	11·2	31·8	90·1	222·7
1955	5·1	0·3	0·3	0·5	0·5	0·9	1·9	4·6	11·2	30·9	84·2	199·2
1958	4·9	0·3	0·2	0·4	0·5	0·8	1·8	4·5	10·9	30·9	87·5	215·6
1959	4·9	0·3	0·3	0·4	0·5	0·8	1·8	4·4	10·8	30·5	86·3	215·4
1960	4·8	0·3	0·3	0·4	0·4	0·7	1·7	4·4	10·6	29·5	84·4	210·4
1961	4·8	0·3	0·3	0·4	0·5	0·7	1·8	4·5	10·8	30·9	87·8	214·1
1962	4·7	0·3	0·3	0·4	0·5	0·8	1·8	4·4	10·8	30·2	86·9	213·8
1963	4·7	0·3	0·3	0·4	0·4	0·7	1·8	4·5	10·8	30·8	88·0	220·2
1964	4·4	0·3	0·3	0·4	0·5	0·7	1·8	4·4	10·2	28·4	77·9	190·4
1965	4·0	0·3	0·3	0·4	0·5	0·7	1·8	4·4	10·3	28·3	79·2	197·1
1966	3·9	0·3	0·3	0·4	0·5	0·7	1·7	4·4	10·3	28·6	81·1	204·0
1967	3·8	0·3	0·3	0·4	0·4	0·6	1·7	4·2	10·0	27·1	75·3	192·1
1968	3·7	0·3	0·3	0·4	0·4	0·6	1·7	4·3	10·4	28·2	80·2	214·1
1969	3·6	0·3	0·2	0·4	0·4	0·6	1·7	4·4	10·6	28·6	77·4	201·4
1970	3·6	0·3	0·2	0·4	0·5	0·6	1·6	4·3	10·2	27·8	76·1	203·3
1971	3·5	0·3	0·2	0·4	0·4	0·6	1·6	4·3	10·1	26·5	77·8	193·0
1972	2·9	0·3	0·2	0·4	0·4	0·6	1·6	4·5	10·5	27·5	80·4	200·6
1973	2·8	0·3	0·2	0·4	0·4	0·6	1·6	4·4	10·2	26·8	76·6	196·0
1974	3·0	0·3	0·2	0·4	0·4	0·5	1·5	4·4	10·4	26·5	74·7	193·6
1975	2·9	0·2	0·2	0·4	0·4	0·6	1·5	4·3	10·1	25·8	73·5	192·9
1976	2·6	0·2	0·2	0·3	0·4	0·6	1·5	4·3	10·2	26·1	75·3	201·4
1977	2·6	0·2	0·2	0·3	0·4	0·5	1·4	4·1	9·9	25·2	70·8	188·6
1978	2·8	0·2	0·2	0·4	0·4	0·6	1·4	4·2	9·8	25·3	70·2	190·7
1979	2·8	0·2	0·2	0·3	0·4	0·6	1·4	4·1	9·9	25·3	70·4	194·7
1980	2·7	0·2	0·2	0·3	0·4	0·5	1·3	3·9	9·7	24·6	67·5	188·2

(*a*) Based upon civilian deaths and estimated civilian population (from 3 September in 1939 for males and from 1 June 1941 for females).

Population and Vital Statistics 15. Death Rates per 1,000 in Different Age-Groups – Scotland 1860–2 to 1980

NOTES

[1] SOURCE: *Annual Report of the Registrar General for Scotland.*

[2] The figures for 1860–2 to 1900–2 are obtained by dividing the appropriate census figure of population in each age-group into the average yearly number of deaths in that age-group in the census year itself and in the year on either side of that.

A. Males

	0–1	1–4	5–9	10–14	15–24	25–34	35–44	45–54	55–64	65–74	75–84	85 & over
1860–2	152·0	37·4	9·1	5·2	8·7	10·3	12·4	17·3	29·6	64·8	166·9	
1870–2	159·5	35·2	9·8	5·4	9·3	11·2	14·0	20·0	32·5	64·1	159·7	
1880–2	149·6	29·5	7·8	4·3	7·1	8·9	12·5	19·4	33·4	63·6	148·1	
1890–2	159·0	27·5	5·7	3·5	6·5	8·3	12·2	20·8	37·2	72·1	165·2	
1900–2	158·4	22·8	4·3	2·8	5·0	7·5	11·7	19·5	38·0	71·6	158·5	
1911	140·9	17·8	3·7	2·3	4·1	5·5	8·4	15·5	30·6	65·2	148·6	
1912	133·6	17·8	3·5	2·3	4·0	5·6	8·7	15·8	32·8	67·0	156·0	
1913	122·8	16·9	3·6	2·4	3·8	5·4	8·5	14·7	29·8	60·5	151·5	
1914	140·9	17·4	3·7	2·5	3·9	5·7	8·6	15·8	33·3	66·5	165·8	
1915	147·0	22·2	4·1	2·7	4·7	5·9	9·3	17·4	37·3	74·0	182·2	
1916	107·8	16·1	3·5	2·3	4·1	5·3	8·0	15·8	34·2	70·3	174·6	
1917	105·7	17·4	3·4	2·2	3·7	4·7	8·0	15·7	34·0	69·7	171·4	
1918	100·3	18·6	4·4	3·3	6·2	9·1	10·1	17·2	33·7	66·7	158·7	
1919	112·8	15·5	3·7	2·3	4·8	7·2	8·9	16·7	36·0	72·5	185·6	
1920	130·0	10·5	2·9	2·1	3·8	4·7	7·8	16·1	34·4	68·0	165·2	
1921	115·0	10·7	2·7	1·9	3·3	4·3	6·8	14·5	32·7	68·6	163·4	311·8
1922	116·8	21·7	2·8	1·8	3·3	4·9	7·0	12·6	28·2	65·3	148·2	279·5
1923	88·6	14·3	2·5	1·7	3·1	4·2	6·2	11·9	26·8	63·5	137·5	274·8
1924	105·8	19·4	2·5	2·0	3·3	4·3	6·7	12·2	28·1	68·1	156·7	311·2
1925	96·9	13·9	2·7	1·7	3·2	4·1	6·7	11·6	28·0	67·3	144·9	310·7
1926	86·3	12·6	2·5	1·8	2·9	4·1	6·1	12·0	27·8	67·3	146·1	322·1
1927	85·8	12·2	2·7	1·8	2·9	4·3	6·6	12·2	28·8	71·9	154·6	333·7
1928	104·3	12·3	2·6	1·8	3·1	4·0	6·7	11·2	24·3	62·1	144·4	300·5
1929	103·0	13·0	2·5	2·0	3·3	4·1	7·7	12·8	26·7	67·9	163·6	330·8
1930	102·1	10·6	2·8	1·9	3·0	3·7	7·0	11·7	24·5	61·7	151·1	314·1
1931	100·5	10·1	2·6	1·7	3·0	3·9	6·3	11·6	24·5	60·4	140·8	293·8
1932	100·4	10·6	2·7	1·6	3·0	3·8	6·6	11·6	24·1	60·1	142·1	273·7
1933	94·1	8·5	2·4	1·7	3·0	4·0	6·4	12·2	24·9	59·8	139·4	290·5
1934	93·5	9·8	2·9	1·6	2·8	3·8	6·1	11·6	24·0	57·3	135·7	275·7
1935	92·3	7·2	2·4	1·7	2·7	3·5	6·1	11·8	24·2	61·0	145·5	314·5
1936	98·6	7·9	2·4	1·5	2·8	3·5	6·1	12·6	24·6	61·2	145·4	318·6
1937	96·2	7·2	2·2	1·5	2·8	3·8	6·3	12·8	25·8	63·0	150·3	351·2
1938	81·6	7·0	1·9	1·4	2·5	3·2	5·6	11·6	23·8	57·0	137·7	319·9
1939	82·1	4·8	1·9	1·4	2·5	3·2	5·6	12·0	25·2	59·5	146·1	356·2
1940 (*a*)	95·0	7·0	2·4	1·5	3·3	4·1	6·6	13·2	27·8	63·6	156·1	408·7
1941 (*a*)	100·5	6·5	2·5	1·7	3·7	4·9	6·8	13·3	26·6	58·4	146·3	299·0
1942 (*a*)	85·4	4·6	1·7	1·4	3·3	4·0	5·8	11·9	23·9	54·0	132·4	278·3
1943 (*a*)	79·1	4·4	1·9	1·4	3·5	4·4	6·3	11·6	23·9	53·8	131·0	300·7
1944 (*a*)	80·5	4·0	1·8	1·4	3·2	3·8	5·8	11·0	24·1	52·5	121·3	289·3
1945 (*a*)	65·0	3·5	1·5	1·2	2·9	4·1	5·6	10·8	23·7	51·6	118·2	284·9
1946 (*a*)	73·2	3·5	1·4	1·1	2·3	2·6	4·8	11·4	24·4	54·4	121·2	279·3
1947	66·7	3·2	1·4	0·9	2·1	2·6	4·4	11·1	25·0	55·1	135·0	295·0
1948	53·7	2·6	1·1	1·0	1·9	2·5	4·2	10·1	24·1	51·3	120·1	257·4
1949	47·9	2·2	1·1	0·8	1·8	2·3	4·1	10·2	25·1	55·2	128·0	272·5
1950	45·1	2·1	0·8	0·6	1·5	2·0	3·7	10·3	26·0	56·3	132·4	280·1
1951	43·5	1·8	0·9	0·5	1·3	2·1	3·6	10·4	26·4	59·0	140·0	298·4
1952	41·7	1·6	0·8	0·5	1·2	1·8	3·3	9·7	25·3	56·6	131·4	270·8
1953	36·6	1·5	0·8	0·6	1·2	1·8	3·5	9·1	24·9	55·6	122·6	242·4
1954	36·7	1·5	0·6	0·4	1·1	1·7	3·2	9·5	26·1	56·4	129·1	274·2
1955	34·9	1·4	0·6	0·5	1·0	1·6	3·3	9·5	25·2	57·2	127·5	280·5

A. Males (*cont.*)

	0–1	1–4	5–9	10–14	15–24	25–34	35–44	45–54	55–64	65–74	75–84	85 & over
1956	34·3	1·2	0·5	0·5	1·0	1·6	3·1	9·2	25·2	59·1	129·9	277·6
1957	34·8	1·3	0·7	0·5	1·0	1·5	3·1	9·5	25·6	57·8	123·6	269·8
1958	32·5	1·0	0·5	0·5	1·0	1·4	3·2	9·0	24·9	59·6	127·1	272·8
1959	33·4	1·3	0·5	0·5	0·9	1·4	3·1	9·2	25·5	60·1	131·7	274·8
1960	31·5	1·2	0·6	0·5	0·9	1·5	2·9	9·1	25·1	58·0	126·2	250·5
1961	30·6	1·2	0·6	0·4	1·0	1·4	3·2	9·1	26·1	59·4	131·5	275·8
1962	32·7	1·1	0·5	0·5	0·9	1·4	3·3	9·2	25·4	59·6	129·6	266·2
1963	29·6	1·2	0·6	0·5	0·9	1·4	3·3	9·6	26·8	62·6	137·1	279·2
1964	28·5	0·9	0·5	0·4	0·9	1·2	3·2	9·3	25·7	58·2	121·1	250·4
1965	26·2	1·0	0·6	0·5	1·0	1·3	3·1	9·2	25·6	59·7	125·0	265·7
1966	26·7	1·0	0·5	0·4	1·1	1·4	3·1	9·1	24·9	58·0	128·2	271·1
1967	23·9	1·0	0·5	0·5	1·0	1·4	3·0	8·5	23·7	54·8	115·7	238·1
1968	24·9	1·1	0·5	0·5	1·1	1·3	3·0	8·8	24·0	58·2	123·0	254·7
1969	23·8	0·9	0·5	0·5	1·1	1·3	3·1	8·6	24·7	59·0	123·5	258·9
1970	22·8	1·0	0·5	0·4	1·0	1·3	3·0	8·8	24·7	58·4	121·2	259·0
1971	22·6	0·8	0·4	0·5	1·1	1·2	2·8	8·7	23·3	56·7	118·6	236·2
1972	20·1	0·9	0·6	0·3	1·0	1·3	3·1	8·9	24·3	59·3	128·5	259·4
1973	21·8	1·0	0·5	0·3	1·0	1·2	2·9	9·3	24·5	58·5	125·9	248·8
1974	20·7	0·9	0·4	0·4	1·0	1·2	3·3	9·0	24·4	57·5	123·0	257·1
1975	19·3	0·7	0·5	0·4	1·0	1·2	2·9	8·8	23·3	56·8	122·0	242·3
1976	16·5	0·7	0·4	0·4	1·0	1·3	2·8	8·9	23·8	57·4	127·6	254·2
1977	18·5	0·7	0·4	0·3	1·0	1·2	2·8	8·6	22·7	53·2	118·7	239·7
1978	15·1	0·6	0·3	0·3	1·0	1·3	2·9	8·7	23·0	56·0	122·3	246·6
1979	14·4	0·6	0·4	0·3	0·9	1·2	2·7	9·1	23·0	56·4	122·3	267·3
1980	13·9	0·7	0·3	0·3	1·0	1·2	2·6	8·2	22·2	53·5	119·5	254·7

B. Females

	0–1	1–4	5–9	10–14	15–24	25–34	35–44	45–54	55–64	65–74	75–84	85 & over
1860–2	126·4	37·4	8·8	5·2	7·6	9·6	11·5	14·4	24·9	56·6	155·1	
1870–2	130·8	35·3	9·3	5·8	8·5	10·4	12·4	16·1	27·8	54·6	150·3	
1880–2	121·3	28·8	7·3	4·7	7·0	9·2	11·2	14·9	26·9	53·4	136·6	
1890–2	129·6	27·1	6·0	4·0	6·2	8·8	11·6	15·8	30·4	61·8	149·8	
1900–2	126·0	21·5	4·8	3·2	5·1	7·1	10·0	15·6	32·7	60·2	142·8	
1911	112·2	16·8	3·8	2·6	3·9	5·7	8·1	12·4	24·6	52·4	132·0	
1912	106·1	17·1	3·6	2·4	3·9	5·3	8·2	12·6	25·9	53·6	143·2	
1913	107·6	16·5	3·6	2·6	3·8	5·3	8·2	13·1	26·5	54·9	145·9	
1914	112·5	16·4	3·7	2·6	3·6	5·4	8·4	13·2	26·2	53·5	145·7	
1915	117·8	20·6	3·9	2·8	3·9	5·7	8·4	13·4	28·9	57·1	168·2	
1916	86·4	14·8	3·6	2·5	3·8	4·8	7·5	12·1	25·8	50·5	154·6	
1917	83·6	16·1	3·1	2·5	3·7	4·7	7·4	12·0	24·5	48·0	146·1	
1918	76·3	18·2	4·7	3·7	6·4	8·9	9·3	13·9	26·5	48·9	139·6	
1919	84·1	14·8	3·7	2·8	4·4	6·6	7·7	13·4	27·5	54·2	163·4	
1920	96·9	9·7	2·9	2·0	3·5	5·1	7·1	11·5	25·5	47·5	144·5	
1921	85·3	9·8	2·5	1·9	3·4	4·6	6·8	14·5	32·7	68·6	163·4	311·5
1922	89·2	19·9	2·6	2·0	3·4	5·0	7·0	10·8	22·6	52·6	124·5	267·1
1923	67·4	12·9	2·4	1·7	3·0	4·3	5·8	9·6	21·4	49·9	113·1	240·1
1924	79·5	17·1	2·5	1·8	3·1	4·5	6·1	10·8	22·5	54·2	128·8	278·2
1925	70·0	12·8	2·3	1·8	3·0	4·1	5·5	10·0	22·4	51·3	118·6	274·2
1926	64·3	10·9	2·3	1·6	3·0	4·2	5·7	10·1	21·7	51·2	119·0	272·7
1927	66·0	10·5	2·4	1·5	2·7	4·0	5·9	10·6	22·5	54·1	127·3	286·2
1928	79·5	10·9	2·6	1·6	2·9	4·0	5·6	9·7	19·4	49·6	121·1	284·0
1929	78·7	10·8	2·2	1·7	3·1	4·2	6·2	10·8	21·1	55·0	141·3	327·7
1930	78·2	9·6	2·4	1·7	2·8	3·7	5·5	9·4	19·2	48·5	124·9	278·8

Population and Vital Statistics 15. *continued*

B. Females (*cont.*)

	0–1	1–4	5–9	10–14	15–24	25–34	35–44	45–54	55–64	65–74	75–84	85 & over
1931	74·4	9·5	2·3	1·4	2·9	3·7	5·3	9·2	19·5	47·0	118·6	266·2
1932	80·0	9·7	2·3	1·7	2·9	4·0	5·5	9·4	19·8	47·7	119·7	268·5
1933	73·6	7·4	2·1	1·5	2·8	3·7	5·3	9·1	19·4	47·8	117·9	257·1
1934	73·0	8·3	2·5	1·5	2·8	3·6	5·0	8·9	19·2	45·0	110·9	246·6
1935	69·6	6·4	2·0	1·4	2·7	3·4	5·1	9·0	19·3	47·4	119·9	265·0
1936	75·6	7·3	1·9	1·2	2·6	3·2	4·9	9·2	18·9	47·8	117·4	263·5
1937	73·5	6·6	1·9	1·2	2·7	3·4	4·9	9·1	19·5	50·0	121·2	288·6
1938	65·7	6·2	1·9	1·3	2·5	3·0	4·4	8·3	18·2	45·2	108·6	261·0
1939	61·5	4·1	1·7	1·1	2·3	3·0	4·3	8·5	17·8	45·6	114·9	281·2
1940 (*a*)	68·3	6·4	2·1	1·3	2·7	3·3	4·6	8·5	19·7	48·6	122·3	317·3
1941 (*a*)	75·8	6·6	2·0	1·6	3·2	3·5	4·6	8·5	18·0	45·3	113·4	274·5
1942 (*a*)	65·2	4·1	1·4	1·2	3·0	3·3	4·0	7·2	16·5	40·3	100·7	246·7
1943 (*a*)	60·9	3·9	1·6	1·2	3·2	3·3	4·1	7·5	17·0	40·9	100·0	272·9
1944 (*a*)	60·8	3·2	1·4	1·1	2·9	3·1	3·7	7·1	15·7	38·9	97·3	256·3
1945 (*a*)	47·2	3·0	1·1	1·0	2·6	3·1	3·5	7·0	15·4	39·8	95·8	257·3
1946 (*a*)	56·5	2·8	1·1	0·9	2·4	3·3	3·4	6·8	15·8	40·7	98·1	271·0
1947	50·8	2·9	1·1	1·0	2·5	2·9	3·4	6·7	15·8	40·5	104·3	253·3
1948	38·7	2·0	0·9	0·9	2·4	2·7	3·3	6·6	15·0	38·5	98·2	218·4
1949	37·5	1·9	0·7	0·6	2·2	2·6	3·2	6·6	15·4	41·5	107·1	233·0
1950	34·9	1·6	0·6	0·4	1·6	2·3	3·1	6·4	15·8	41·4	109·6	244·6
1951	33·2	1·6	0·6	0·5	1·2	1·9	3·0	6·3	15·6	43·5	115·6	267·9
1952	32·5	1·4	0·5	0·4	1·0	1·6	2·7	6·1	14·6	40·3	102·6	234·1
1953	27·6	1·3	0·5	0·4	0·8	1·4	2·6	6·0	13·5	36·9	98·4	221·8
1954	28·0	1·1	0·4	0·4	0·7	1·3	2·6	6·2	14·4	37·5	103·0	233·9
1955	28·5	1·0	0·5	0·4	0·6	1·3	2·4	5·6	14·1	39·1	103·8	248·1
1956	25·4	1·0	0·4	0·3	0·5	1·1	2·2	5·5	13·8	38·1	103·2	249·7
1957	26·1	0·8	0·4	0·4	0·5	1·0	2·5	5·4	13·6	36·8	95·8	239·0
1958	25·4	0·9	0·3	0·3	0·5	1·1	2·4	5·5	13·6	37·0	100·1	238·5
1959	25·1	1·1	0·3	0·3	0·5	0·9	2·3	5·2	13·7	37·0	100·5	245·2
1960	24·4	0·9	0·5	0·3	0·5	0·9	2·2	5·2	12·9	36·2	97·3	228·1
1961	22·8	0·9	0·3	0·3	0·4	0·8	2·2	5·5	13·4	36·7	100·3	232·9
1962	22·8	1·0	0·4	0·3	0·4	0·9	2·2	5·3	13·2	35·0	97·0	223·3
1963	23·0	0·9	0·3	0·2	0·4	1·0	2·3	5·5	13·7	35·9	98·5	225·3
1964	22·0	0·9	0·3	0·3	0·4	0·8	2·0	5·5	12·7	33·9	86·0	204·4
1965	20·9	0·8	0·3	0·3	0·5	0·8	2·1	5·3	12·6	34·2	88·6	211·0
1966	21·0	0·8	0·3	0·3	0·5	0·8	2·1	5·4	12·5	34·3	90·8	221·5
1967	19·0	0·7	0·3	0·3	0·5	0·6	2·0	5·1	11·9	31·3	81·5	199·5
1968	18·4	0·8	0·3	0·2	0·4	0·7	2·1	5·4	12·5	32·6	87·1	224·3
1969	18·5	0·9	0·2	0·3	0·4	0·7	2·0	5·6	12·8	32·7	84·8	211·4
1970	16·8	0·7	0·4	0·2	0·4	0·8	2·0	5·6	12·6	31·4	84·8	206·1
1971	17·6	0·6	0·3	0·3	0·3	0·7	1·9	5·4	12·4	30·1	79·5	188·9
1972	16·3	0·7	0·3	0·1	0·4	0·7	2·0	5·5	12·6	31·5	84·2	202·4
1973	15·7	0·6	0·3	0·2	0·4	0·7	2·0	5·5	12·6	30·5	81·7	203·7
1974	17·0	0·7	0·3	0·2	0·4	0·7	2·0	5·3	13·3	30·5	80·7	203·8
1975	15·0	0·7	0·3	0·1	0·4	0·7	1·9	5·1	12·5	29·2	77·1	194·3
1976	12·1	0·6	0·2	0·2	0·4	0·7	1·9	5·4	12·9	29·9	79·0	206·9
1977	14·1	0·5	0·2	0·2	0·5	0·6	1·9	5·1	12·1	29·1	75·8	185·8
1978	11·5	0·6	0·2	0·3	0·4	0·7	2·0	5·4	12·9	30·8	76·7	198·8
1979	12·2	0·6	0·2	0·3	0·4	0·7	1·8	5·4	12·7	30·2	76·8	201·1
1980	10·6	0·4	0·2	0·2	0·3	0·6	1·8	5·0	12·2	28·9	73·0	189·7

(*a*) Based upon civilian deaths and estimated civilian population.

Population and Vital Statistics 16. Death Rates per 1,000 in Different Age-Groups – Ireland 1870–2 to 1978–80

NOTES

[1] SOURCES: *Annual Report of the Registrar General for Ireland*, up to 1910–2, and *for Northern Ireland* thereafter, and *Statistical Abstract of Ireland*.

[2] All figures are obtained by dividing the census population of each age-group into the average yearly number of deaths in the census years and the years on each side of that.

	0–4	5–9	10–14	15–19	20–24	25–34	35–44	45–54	55–64	65–74	75–84	85 & over
A. Males												
1870–2	38·0	5·4	3·2	5·4	8·1	9·0	9·9	14·4	25·4	59·0	126·9	258·9
1880–2	40·0	5·3	3·4	5·5	8·0	8·8	10·5	15·7	29·9	63·5	135·8	300·4
1890–2	38·3	4·1	2·9	4·9	7·6	9·3	10·8	15·8	29·9	66·3	143·8	291·2
1900–2	39·4	3·9	2·9	4·8	7·1	9·0	10·6	15·6	29·5	63·1	140·0	317·1
1910–2	34·7	3·2	2·3	4·0	5·8	7·1	8·8	14·1	27·7	48·9	102·5	248·9
Northern Ireland												
1925–7	29·4	2·6	1·9	3·1	4·4	4·8	6·6	12·8	25·9	56·5	116·9	236·0
1936–8	25·0	2·0	1·5	2·3	3·4	3·8	6·1	12·3	24·1	58·7	125·4	234·8
1950–2	10·8	0·8	0·6	0·9	1·6	1·9	3·6	9·0	21·9	53·1	118·3	243·8
1960–2	6·6	0·6	0·4	0·8	1·0	1·2	2·5	7·6	22·2	50·9	118·4	255·0
1965–7	5·5	0·5	0·4	0·8	1·1	1·1	2·8	7·5	21·7	51·2	113·7	241·0
1970–2	5·6	0·5	0·4	1·2	1·4	1·2	2·7	8·0	22·6	54·3	119·8	270·8
Republic of Ireland												
1925–7	24·2	2·5	1·7	3·2	4·4	5·3	7·0	11·2	23·7	48·5	109·3	218·5
1935–7	23·8	2·2	1·6	2·6	3·8	4·4	6·1	11·7	24·3	55·4	105·8	206·1
1940–2	21·3	2·0	1·3	2·7	3·8	4·0	5·6	10·5	23·2	51·8	117·1	184·4
1945–7	20·9	1·4	1·1	1·4	3·2	3·5	5·0	9·8	22·3	53·9	125·8	229·3
1950–2	12·1	0·9	0·6	1·2	2·0	2·5	3·9	8·9	20·8	51·4	127·3	258·6
1955–7	9·5	0·6	0·5	0·7	1·2	1·6	2·9	7·7	19·4	47·3	121·5	249·9
1960–2	7·8	0·5	0·4	0·7	1·0	1·4	2·7	7·2	19·6	47·8	117·8	282·5
1965–7	6·3	0·5	0·4	0·7	1·1	1·2	2·6	7·2	19·9	50·0	114·6	275·0
1970–2	5·0	0·5	0·4	0·8	1·3	1·2	2·6	7·6	20·3	50·7	114·9	262·9
1978–80	3·6	0·4	0·4	0·8	1·2	1·2	2·3	7·2	20·0	48·9	119·0	254·9
B. Females												
1870–2	34·2	5·4	3·7	5·5	6·4	8·1	9·5	12·2	24·1	59·4	126·0	249·1
1880–2	36·1	5·8	4·1	6·1	7·4	8·9	10·3	14·2	28·8	63·8	134·4	281·9
1890–2	34·5	4·7	4·0	6·2	7·4	9·5	10·4	15·2	31·1	70·3	144·0	283·7
1900–2	35·0	4·8	3·9	6·0	6·6	8·6	10·8	14·9	29·6	67·2	142·2	292·6
1910–2	30·2	3·7	3·2	4·7	5·7	7·3	9·2	13·7	27·5	45·7	96·0	236·3
Northern Ireland												
1925–7	24·3	2·6	2·3	3·8	5·1	6·0	6·8	13·1	25·3	52·7	101·6	193·2
1936–8	21·8	2·1	1·7	2·4	3·5	4·3	5·2	10·7	19·6	52·3	111·1	218·2
1950–2	8·6	0·5	0·6	0·7	1·1	1·8	2·9	6·4	15·7	41·2	107·8	225·4
1960–2	5·2	0·3	0·2	0·5	0·6	0·8	1·9	5·0	11·8	34·9	96·3	221·3
1965–7	4·8	0·2	0·2	0·4	0·4	0·8	1·9	4·6	11·1	31·3	85·1	197·6
1970–2	4·5	0·3	0·2	0·4	0·4	0·7	1·8	4·8	11·5	31·5	84·2	203·9
Republic of Ireland												
1925–7	21·0	2·7	2·1	3·7	4·9	5·9	7·4	11·3	23·4	46·2	97·7	190·8
1935–7	19·2	2·3	1·8	2·8	4·2	5·1	6·3	10·6	22·4	50·7	98·0	188·3
1940–2	17·1	1·6	1·5	2·8	4·2	4·4	5·7	9·7	21·2	46·6	105·0	167·3
1945–7	14·8	1·3	1·1	2·5	3·7	4·0	5·3	8·8	18·5	45·8	109·5	198·8
1950–2	9·6	0·7	0·7	1·3	2·0	2·5	3·7	7·1	16·4	42·8	109·6	222·1
1955–7	7·3	0·5	0·4	0·5	0·9	1·4	2·7	6·0	13·8	37·7	105·5	235·4
1960–2	6·1	0·4	0·3	0·3	0·7	1·1	2·2	7·3	12·6	35·0	97·5	235·9
1965–7	4·9	0·4	0·2	0·3	0·5	0·8	1·9	5·2	12·3	33·1	91·9	227·3
1970–2	4·1	0·3	0·2	0·5	0·5	0·7	1·8	5·0	12·2	31·9	90·2	222·2
1978–80	2·9	0·2	0·2	0·3	0·4	0·6	1·4	4·3	11·2	28·6	84·8	215·6

Population and Vital Statistics 17. Marriages and Marriage Rates – British Isles, 1539–1980

NOTE TO PART A

SOURCE: E. A. Wrigley and R. S. Schofield, *The Population History of England, 1541–1871* (London, 1981), tables A2.3 and A3.3.

A. England (excluding Monmouthshire), 1539–1838

	Marriages in thousands	Rate per 1,000 of population		Marriages in thousands	Rate per 1,000 of population		Marriages in thousands	Rate per 1,000 of population		Marriages in thousands	Rate per 1,000 of population
1539	57	...	1584	37	10·0	1629	42	8·6	1674	33	6.5
1540	37	...	1585	38	10·1	1630	38	7·8	1675	32	6.4
1541	39	14·0	1586	33	8·8	1631	37	7·5	1676	34	6·9
1542	42	15·0	1587	35	9·1	1632	41	8·4	1677	38	7·5
1543	35	12·4	1588	41	10·7	1633	40	8·1	1678	35	6·9
1544	32	11·2	1589	40	10·4	1634	42	8·3	1679	35	7·0
1545	30	10·6	1590	35	9·0	1635	42	8·4	1680	42	8·3
1546	36	12·7	1591	36	9·3	1636	38	7·6	1681	40	8·1
1547	40	14·0	1592	37	9·6	1637	41	8·2	1682	39	7·9
1548	44	15·1	1593	39	9·9	1638	38	7·4	1683	44	8·9
1549	33	11·1	1594	39	10·0	1639	47	9·3	1684	37	7·6
1550	35	11·8	1595	35	8·8	1640	48	9·6	1685	38	7·9
1551	34	11·2	1596	34	8·4	1641	51	10·0	1686	39	8·1
1552	38	12·5	1597	29	7·3	1642	45	8·9	1687	41	8·5
1553	40	13·2	1598	35	8·9	1643	32	6·3	1688	39	7·9
1554	21	6·7	1599	38	9·6	1644	31	6·1	1689	34	6·8
1555	30	9·6	1600	38	9·4	1645	43	8·3	1690	34	7·0
1556	24	7·6	1601	35	8·5	1646	43	8·3	1691	32	6·6
1557	23	7·3	1602	36	8·8	1647	39	7·4	1692	30	6·1
1558	34	11·0	1603	40	9·5	1648	29	5·5	1693	30	6·0
1559	34	11·4	1604	40	9·6	1649	31	5·9	1694	30	6·2
1560	42	14·1	1605	41	9·7	1650	37	7·2	1695	41	8·2
1561	40	13·4	1606	38	8·9	1651	38	7·3	1696	40	8·0
1562	35	11·6	1607	36	8·4	1652	35	6·7	1697	38	7·6
1563	31	10·3	1608	38	8·8	1653	35	6·7	1698	40	8·1
1564	32	10·5	1609	39	8·8	1654	51	9·7	1699	41	8·1
1565	29	9·3	1610	40	9·1	1655	64	12·1	1700	42	8·3
1566	26	8·5	1611	44	9·9	1656	56	10·7	1701	42	8·3
1567	33	10·4	1612	40	9·0	1657	47	8·8	1702	42	8·2
1568	31	9·7	1613	38	8·5	1658	43	8·3	1703	41	8·0
1569	32	9·8	1614	37	8·4	1659	46	9·0	1704	38	7·4
1570	32	9·8	1615	39	8·7	1660	36	7·0	1705	41	7·9
1571	31	9·4	1616	37	8·3	1661	31	6·0	1706	41	7·8
1572	33	10·0	1617	36	7·9	1662	38	7·4	1707	39	7·5
1573	31	9·4	1618	42	9·2	1663	43	8·4	1708	37	7·0
1574	35	10·6	1619	41	9·0	1664	44	8·5	1709	36	6·8
1575	35	10·3	1620	41	8·8	1665	39	7·6	1710	39	7·5
1576	35	10·1	1621	39	8·3	1666	36	7·2	1711	38	7·3
1577	32	9·2	1622	32	6·7	1667	38	7·4	1712	40	7·7
1578	38	10·7	1623	30	6·2	1668	34	6·6	1713	44	8·5
1579	33	9·2	1624	37	7·7	1669	35	6·9	1714	46	8·8
1580	39	10·8	1625	34	7·2	1670	35	7·0	1715	46	8·7
1581	34	9·4	1626	37	7·9	1671	40	8·0	1716	42	8·0
1582	33	9·0	1627	40	8·5	1672	37	7·5	1717	43	8·0
1583	34	9·3	1628	41	8·6	1673	35	7·0	1718	49	9·1

Population and Vital Statistics 17. *continued*

	Marriages in thousands	Rate per 1,000 of population		Marriages in thousands	Rate per 1,000 of population		Marriages in thousands	Rate per 1,000 of population		Marriages in thousands	Rate per 1,000 of population
1719	44	8·2	1749	47	8·3	1779	59	8·5	1809	74	7·7
1720	44	8·2	1750	48	8·4	1780	63	9·0	1810	76	7·7
1721	46	8·6	1751	47	8·1	1781	60	8·5	1811	83	8·4
1722	50	9·4	1752	47	8·1	1782	59	8·3	1812	80	8·0
1723	54	10·1	1753	49	8·3	1783	62	8·7	1813	78	7·7
1724	51	9·5	1754	47	7·9	1784	62	8·7	1814	90	8·7
1725	48	8·9	1755	50	8·4	1785	71	9·8	1815	95	9·0
1726	51	9·4	1756	51	8·6	1786	65	9·0	1816	89	8·4
1727	46	8·3	1757	45	7·4	1787	64	8·8	1817	83	7·7
1728	45	8·2	1758	49	8·1	1788	65	8·8	1818	89	8·1
1729	46	8·6	1759	56	9·2	1789	63	8·4	1819	86	7·7
1730	58	10·9	1760	60	9·8	1790	68	8·8	1820	93	8·3
1731	59	11·2	1761	60	9·8	1791	67	8·6	1821	93	8·1
1732	54	10·3	1762	55	8·8	1792	71	9·1	1822	98	8·4
1733	49	9·3	1763	58	9·4	1793	71	8·9	1823	98	8·3
1734	48	8·9	1764	59	9·5	1794	66	8·3	1824	98	8·1
1735	48	8·9	1765	56	9·0	1795	61	7·5	1825	106	8·7
1736	44	8·0	1766	55	8·8	1796	70	8·5	1826	98	7·9
1737	46	8·4	1767	52	8·3	1797	72	8·7	1827	93	7·4
1738	46	8·4	1768	57	9·0	1798	77	9·1	1828	109	8·5
1739	48	8·6	1769	61	9·5	1799	70	8·2	1829	94	7·3
1740	45	8·2	1770	60	9·4	1800	64	7·4	1830	96	7·3
1741	41	7·3	1771	58	9·0	1801	60	6·9	1831	105	7·9
1742	45	8·2	1772	58	9·0	1802	85	9·7	1832	109	8·1
1743	50	9·0	1773	57	8·7	1803	89	10·0	1833	114	8·4
1744	50	8·9	1774	58	8·8	1804	82	9·1	1834	112	8·1
1745	46	8·2	1775	58	8·6	1805	76	8·3	1835	109	7·9
1746	45	8·0	1776	59	8·8	1806	74	8·0	1836	115	8·1
1747	49	8·7	1777	62	9·0	1807	80	8·6	1837	106	7·5
1748	48	8·5	1778	61	8·9	1808	77	8·0	1838	111	7·7

NOTES TO PART B

[1] SOURCES: *Annual Report of the Registrar General for England & Wales, for Scotland, for Ireland* and *for Northern Ireland* (and their successors).

[2] Figures for the earlier years in each country may be somewhat lower than they should be owing to deficiencies in registration.

B. British Isles, 1838–1980

	Thousands of Marriages			Rate per 1,000 of Population		
	England & Wales	Scotland	Ireland	England & Wales	Scotland	Ireland
1838	118	...	...	15·4	...	...
1839	123	...	...	15·9	...	...
1840	123	...	...	15·6	...	...
1841	122	...	...	15·4	...	...
1842	119	...	...	14·7	...	...
1843	124	...	...	15·2	...	...
1844	132	...	...	16·0	...	...
1845	144	...	...	17·2	...	...
1846	146	...	...	17·2	...	...
1847	136	...	...	15·9	...	...
1848	138	...	...	15·9	...	...
1849	142	...	...	16·2	...	...
1850	153	...	...	17·2	...	...
1851	154	...	...	17·2	...	...
1852	159	...	...	17·4	...	...
1853	165	...	...	17·9	...	...
1854	160	...	...	17·2	...	...
1855	152	19·7	...	16·2	13·2	...
1856	159	20·7	...	16·7	13·8	...
1857	159	21·4	...	16·5	14·2	...
1858	156	19·7	...	16·0	13·0	...
1859	168	21·2	...	17·0	13·9	...
1860	170	21·2	...	17·1	13·9	...
1861	164	20·9	...	16·3	13·6	...
1862	164	20·6	...	16·1	13·3	...
1863	174	22·2	...	16·8	14·3	...
1864	180	22·7	27·4	17·6	14·4	9·7
1865	185	23·6	30·8	17·5	14·8	11·0
1866	188	23·7	30·1	17·5	14·7	10·9
1867	179	22·6	29·7	16·5	13·9	10·8
1868	177	21·9	27·7	16·1	13·3	10·1
1869	177	22·1	27·3	15·9	13·4	10·0
1870	182	23·9	28·7	16·1	14·3	10·6
1871	190	24·0	29·0	16·7	14·3	10·7
1872	201	25·6	26·9	17·4	15·1	10·0
1873	206	26·7	25·7	17·6	15·5	9·6
1874	202	26·4	24·5	17·0	15·2	9·2
1875	201	26·0	24·0	16·7	14·8	9·1
1876	202	26·6	26·4	16·5	15·0	9·9
1877	194	25·8	24·7	15·7	14·4	9·3
1878	190	24·4	25·3	15·2	13·4	9·5
1879	182	23·5	23·3	14·4	12·8	8·7
1880	192	24·5	20·4	14·9	13·2	7·8
1881	197	26·0	21·8	15·1	13·9	8·5
1882	204	26·6	22·0	15·5	14·1	8·6

Population and Vital Statistics 17. *continued*

B. British Isles, 1838–1980 (*cont.*)

	Thousands of Marriages				Rate per 1,000 of Population			
	England & Wales	Scotland	Ireland		England & Wales	Scotland	Ireland	
1883	206	26·9	21·4		15·5	14·1	8·5	
1884	204	26·1	22·6		15·1	13·6	9·1	
1885	198	25·3	21·2		14·5	13·1	8·6	
1886	196	24·5	20·6		14·2	12·6	8·4	
1887	201	24·9	20·9		14·4	12·7	8·6	
1888	204	25·3	20·1		14·4	12·8	8·4	
1889	214	26·3	21·5		15·0	13·3	9·0	
1890	223	27·5	21·0		15·5	13·7	8·9	
1891	227	28·0	21·5		15·6	13·9	9·2	
1892	227	28·7	21·5		15·4	14·1	9·3	
1893	219	27·1	21·7		14·7	13·2	9·4	
1894	226	27·6	21·6		15·0	13·3	9·4	
1895	228	28·4	23·1		15·0	13·5	10·1	
1896	243	30·3	23·1		15·7	14·2	10·2	
1897	249	31·1	22·9		16·0	14·4	10·1	
1898	255	32·1	22·6		16·2	14·8	10·0	
1899	262	33·0	22·3		16·5	15·0	9·9	
1900	257	32·4	21·3		16·0	14·6	9·5	
1901	259	31·4	22·6		15·9	14·0	10·1	
1902	262	31·9	22·9		15·9	14·2	10·4	
1903	261	32·4	23·0		15·7	14·3	10·4	
1904	258	32·3	23·0		15·3	14·1	10·4	
1905	261	31·3	23·1		15·3	13·6	10·5	
1906	271	33·1	22·7		15·7	14·3	10·3	
1907	276	33·3	22·5		15·9	14·3	10·3	
1908	265	31·6	22·7		15·1	13·5	10·4	
1909	261	30·1	22·7		14·7	12·8	10·3	
1910	268	30·9	22·1		15·0	13·0	10·1	
1911	275	31·8	23·5		15·2	13·4	10·7	
1912	284	32·5	23·3		15·6	13·7	10·6	
1913	287	33·8	22·3		15·7	14·2	10·2	
1914	294	35·0	23·7		15·9	14·8	10·8	
1915	361	36·2	24·2		19·4	15·2	11·1	
1916	280	31·4	22·2		14·9	13·1	10·2	
1917	259	30·4	21·1		13·8	12·6	9·6	
1918	287	34·5	22·6		15·3	14·3	10·3	
1919	369	44·1	27·2		19·7	18·3	12·2	
1920	380	46·8	26·8		20·2	19·2	12·0	
1921	321	39·2	23·2		16·9	16·1	10·4	
			Northern Ireland	Republic of Ireland			Northern Ireland	Republic of Ireland
1922	300	34·4	8·1	15·1	15·7	14·0	12·6	10·0
1923	292	35·2	8·0	15·6	15·2	14·4	12·5	10·4
1924	296	32·3	7·5	14·8	15·3	13·3	11·9	9·9
1925	296	32·5	7·7	13·8	15·2	13·3	12·2	9·3
1926	280	31·2	7·2	13·6	14·3	12·8	11·5	9·1
1927	308	32·6	7·2	13·4	15·7	13·4	11·5	9·1
1928	303	32·9	7·3	13·7	15·4	13·6	11·7	9·3
1929	313	33·0	7·4	13·6	15·8	13·6	12·0	9·2
1930	315	33·3	7·5	13·6	15·8	13·8	12·2	9·3
1931	312	32·7	7·4	13·1	15·6	13·5	11·9	8·9
1932	307	33·2	7·0	13·0	15·3	13·6	11·1	8·8

Population and Vital Statistics 17. *continued*

B. British Isles, 1838–1980 (*cont.*)

	Thousands of Marriages				Rate per 1,000 of Population			
	England & Wales	Scotland	Northern Ireland	Republic of Ireland	England & Wales	Scotland	Northern Ireland	Republic of Ireland
1933	318	34·2	7·6	14·0	15·8	13·9	12·1	9·4
1934	342	36·9	8·2	14·3	16·9	15·0	13·0	9·6
1935	350	38·0	8·8	14·3	17·2	15·3	13·9	9·7
1936	355	37·9	9·1	14·8	17·4	15·3	14·3	10·0
1937	359	38·4	8·6	14·8	17·5	15·4	13·5	10·0
1938	362	38·7	8·6	14·9	17·6	15·5	13·4	10·1
1939	440	46·2	9·2	15·2	21·2	18·5	14·2	10·4
1940	471	53·5	9·8	15·2	22·5	21·2	15·1	10·3
1941	389	47·6	12·0	15·0	18·6	18·6	18·3	10·0
1942	370	47·4	11·7	17·5	17·7	18·4	17·6	11·8
1943	296	38·2	10·2	17·3	14·0	14·8	15·1	11·8
1944	303	37·0	9·5	16·8	14·3	14·3	14·0	11·4
1945	398	48·6	10·5	17·3	18·7	18·9	15·4	11·7
1946	386	45·8	9·8	17·5	18·1	17·8	14·5	11·8
1947	401	44·4	9·5	16·3	18·6	17·5	14·1	11·0
1948	397	43·7	9·4	16·1	18·2	17·2	13·8	10·8
1949	375	41·7	9·2	16·0	17·1	16·4	13·4	10·8
1950	358	40·5	9·1	16·0	16·3	15·8	13·3	10·8
1951	361	41·4	9·4	16·0	16·5	16·2	13·7	10·8
1952	349	41·2	9·3	15·9	15·9	16·1	13·5	10·8
1953	345	40·9	9·4	15·9	15·6	16·0	13·6	10·8
1954	342	42·0	9·2	15·8	15·4	16·4	13·2	10·8
1955	358	43·2	9·5	16·4	16·1	16·9	13·7	11·3
1956	353	44·0	9·4	16·8	15·8	17·2	13·4	11·6
1957	347	42·7	9·4	14·7	15·4	16·7	13·4	10·2
1958	340	41·2	9·3	15·1	15·1	16·0	13·2	10·6
1959	340	40·4	9·6	15·4	15·0	15·7	13·7	10·8
1960	344	40·1	9·9	15·5	15·0	15·5	13·9	10·9
1961	347	40·6	9·9	15·3	15·0	15·7	13·8	10·9
1962	348	40·2	9·8	15·6	15·0	15·5	13·7	11·0
1963	351	39·7	10·2	15·6	14·9	15·2	14·1	10·9
1964	359	40·2	10·6	16·1	15·2	15·4	14·6	11·3
1965	371	40·5	10·5	16·9	15·6	15·5	14·2	11·8
1966	384	41·9	10·7	16·8	16·0	16·1	14·6	11·7
1967	386	42·1	10·9	17·9	16·0	16·2	14·6	12·3
1968	408	43·7	11·2	19·0	16·8	16·8	15·0	13·1
1969	397	43·3	11·6	20·3	16·3	16·6	15·4	14·0
1970	415	43·2	12·3	20·8	17·0	16·6	16·2	14·1
1971	405	42·5	12·2	22·0	16·5	16·3	15·8	14·8
1972	426	42·1	11·9	22·3	17·3	16·2	15·4	14·8
1973	400	42·0	11·2	22·8	16·2	16·1	14·4	14·9
1974	384	41·2	10·8	22·8	15·5	15·8	13·9	14·6
1975	381	39·2	10·9	21·3	15·4	15·1	14·2	13·4
1976	359	37·5	9·9	20·6	14·5	14·4	12·8	12·8
1937	357	37·3	9·7	20·0	14·4	14·4	12·6	12·2
1978	368	37·8	10·3	21·2	14·9	14·6	13·4	12·8
1979	369	37·9	10·2	20·9	14·9	14·7	13·2	12·4
1980	370	38·5	9·9	21·7	14·9	14·9	12·8	12·8

Population and Vital Statistics 18. Divorces – England & Wales 1858–1980, Scotland 1855–1980

NOTES

[1] SOURCES: England & Wales Decrees for Dissolution, 1858–1909 – Appendix III to *Report* of the Royal Commission on Divorce (*S.P.* 1912/13 xx); other figures for England & Wales – *Registrar General's Statistical Review of England & Wales* and its successors; Scottish figures – *Annual Reports of the Registrar General for Scotland* (especially that for 1920).

[2] The Registrar General does not give annual figures for England & Wales before 1906, but he does give the following quinquennial averages of divorces and nullity decrees:

1876–80	277·0	1896–1900	490·0
1881–5	335·6	1901–5	563·2
1886–90	353·4		
1891–5	371·8		

	England & Wales Decrees for Dissolution	Scotland Divorce and Nullity Decrees		England & Wales Decrees for Dissolution	England & Wales Divorce and Nullity Decrees	Scotland Divorce and Nullity Decrees
1855	...	11	1895	478	...	117
1856	...	16	1896	486	...	133
1857	...	18	1897	583	...	142
1858	179	12	1898	436	...	135
1859	141	24	1899	525	...	176
1860	127	23	1900	494	...	144
1861	118	27	1901	601	...	158
1862	153	26	1902	608	...	204
1863	160	9	1903	614	...	194
1864	166	2	1904	634	...	182
1865	147	4	1905	623	...	167
1866	146	4	1906	650	546	173
1867	144	5	1907	598	644	200
1868	181	13	1908	672	638	189
1869	186	7	1909	685	694	192
1870	194	17	1910	...	581	223
1871	190	11	1911	...	580	234
1872	203	12	1912	...	587	249
1873	238	25	1913	...	577	250
1874	281	38	1914	...	856	347
1875	304	33	1915	...	680	242
1876	283	40	1916	...	990	267
1877	322	29	1917	...	703	297
1878	380	66	1918	...	1,111	485
1879	300	55	1919	...	1,657	829
1880	340	80	1920	...	3,090	776
1881	302	71	1921	...	3,522	500
1882	345	69	1922	...	2,588	382
1883	361	65	1923	...	2,667	363
1884	337	87	1924	...	2,286	438
1885	316	76	1925	...	2,605	451
1886	387	97	1926	...	2,622	425
1887	390	80	1927	...	3,190	474
1888	392	107	1928	...	4,018	504
1889	370	100	1929	...	3,396	519
1890	400	87	1930	...	3,563	469
1891	342	107	1931	...	3,764	569
1892	354	118	1932	...	3,894	488
1893	362	112	1933	...	4,042	510
1894	381	120	1934	...	4,287	468

Population and Vital Statistics 18. *continued*

	England & Wales Divorce and Nullity Decrees	Scotland Divorce and Nullity Decrees		England & Wales Divorce and Nullity Decrees	Scotland Divorce and Nullity Decrees
1935	4,069	498	1960	23,868	1,823
1936	4,057	642	1961	25,394	1,825
1937	4,886	649	1962	28,935	2,035
1938	6,250	788	1963	32,052	2,235
1939	7,955	884	1964	34,868	2,446
1940	7,755	780	1965	37,785	2,688
1941	6,368	762	1966	39,067	3,570
1942	7,618	1,017	1967	43,093	3,033
1943	10,012	1,312	1968	45,794	4,797
1944	12,312	1,731	1969	51,310	4,242
1945	15,634	2,223	1970	58,239	4,613
1946	29,829	2,924	1971	74,437	4,808
1947	60,254	2,513	1972	119,025	5,530
1948	43,698	2,047	1973	106,003	7,127
1949	34,856	2,438	1974	113,500	7,215
1950	30,870	2,196	1975	120,522	8,317
1951	28,767	1,944	1976	126,694	8,685
1952	33,922	2,718	1977	129,053	8,820
1953	30,326	2,365	1978	143,667	8,458
1954	28,027	2,216	1979	138,706	8,837
1955	26,816	2,073	1980	148,301	10,529
1956	26,265	1,883			
1957	23,785	1,739			
1958	22,654	1,781			
1959	24,286	1,699			

Population and Vital Statistics 19. Net Emigration by Quinquennium – England (excluding Monmouthshire) 1541–1871

NOTE
SOURCE: E. A. Wrigley and R. S. Schofield, *The Population History of England, 1541–1871* (London, 1981), table 7.11.

(in thousands)

1541–5	18·1	1626–30	24·1	1711–5	27·5	1796–1800	22·6
1546–50	20·4	1631–5	31·3	1716–20	27·6	1801–5	28·3
1551–5	21·8	1636–40	39·9	1721–5	28·1	1806–10	33·5
1556–60	19·2	1641–5	49·2	1726–30	26·0	1811–5	40·7
1561–5	17·0	1646–50	57·6	1731–5	24·2	1816–20	50·4
1566–70	18·5	1651–5	63·1	1736–40	24·8	1821–5	62·6
1571–5	21·0	1656–60	62·2	1741–5	25·9	1826–30	77·8
1576–80	23·3	1661–5	55·2	1746–50	27·8	1831–5	90·3
1581–5	26·4	1666–70	45·2	1751–5	31·4	1836–40	101·5
1586–90	30·8	1671–5	34·8	1756–60	35·0	1841–5	115·1
1591–5	34·7	1676–80	25·8	1761–5	35·3	1846–50	123·7
1596–1600	36·2	1681–5	19·4	1766–70	31·3	1851–5	121·5
1601–5	36·0	1686–90	18·1	1771–5	26·3	1856–60	109·5
1606–10	34·1	1691–5	19·6	1776–80	22·0	1861–5	101·6
1611–5	29·7	1696–1700	22·1	1781–5	17·2	1866–70	117·3
1616–20	24·9	1701–5	25·0	1786–90	15·4		
1621–5	22·1	1706–10	27·0	1791–5	18·2		

Population and Vital Statistics 20. Passengers from United Kingdom Ports to Extra-European Countries – 1815–1964

NOTES

[1] SOURCES: 1815–1924 – Ferenczi and Willcox, *International Migrations* (2 vols., National Bureau of Economic Research, New York, 1929–31), vol. 1; 1924–64 – *Board of Trade Journal*.

[2] The distinction between Commonwealth citizens and aliens cannot be made in this table after 1962 owing to changes in the merchant shipping regulations.

(in thousands)

	U.K. Citizens	Aliens	Nationality Unknown	Total		U.K. Citizens	Aliens	Nationality Unknown	Total
1815	...	...	...	2	1861	65	4	23	92
1816	...	...	...	13	1862	98	3	20	121
1817	...	...	...	21	1863	193	8	23	224
1818	...	...	...	28	1864	187	17	5	209
1819	...	...	...	35	1865	175	29	6	210
1820	...	...	...	26	1866	170	27	8	205
1821	...	...	...	18	1867	157	31	8	196
1822	...	...	...	20	1868	138	52	6	196
1823	...	...	...	17	1869	186	66	6	258
1824	...	...	...	14	1870	203	48	6	257
1825	...	...	...	15	1871	193	53	6	252
1826	...	...	...	21	1872	210	79	6	295
1827	...	...	...	28	1873	228	72	10	311
1828	...	...	...	26	1874	197	38	5	241
1829	...	...	...	31	1875	141	31	2	174
1830	...	...	...	57	1876	109	26	3	138
1831	...	...	...	83	1877	95	21	3	120
1832	...	...	...	103	1878	113	32	3	148
1833	...	...	...	63	1879	164	49	3	217
1834	...	...	...	76	1880	228	100	4	332
1835	...	...	...	44	1881	243	144	5	393
1836	...	...	...	75	1882	279	130	4	413
1837	...	...	...	72	1883	320	73	4	397
1838	...	...	...	33	1884	242	58	4	304
1839	...	...	...	62	1885	208	54	3	264
1840	...	...	...	91	1886	233	94	4	331
1841	...	...	...	119	1887	281	109	6	396
1842	...	...	...	128	1888	280	113	5	398
1843	...	...	...	57	1889	254	83	5	343
1844	...	...	...	71	1890	218	95	3	316
1845	...	...	...	94	1891	219	112	4	335
1846	...	...	...	130	1892	210	107	4	321
1847	...	...	...	258	1893	209	95	4	308
1848	...	...	...	248	1894	156	67	4	227
1849	...	...	...	299	1895	185	83	4	272
1850	...	...	...	281	1896	162	76	4	242
1851	...	...	...	336	1897	146	63	4	213
1852	...	...	...	369	1898	141	61	4	205
1853	278	31	20	330	1899	146	90	4	241
1854	267	38	19	323	1900	169	125	5	299
1855	150	11	16	177	1901	172	124	7	303
1856	148	9	19	177	1902	206	174	7	387
1857	181	13	19	213	1903	260	182	8	449
1858	95	5	14	114	1904	271	174	8	454
1859	97	4	19	120	1905	262	188	9	460
1860	96	5	28	128	1906	325	229	3	557

Population and Vital Statistics 20. *continued*

(in thousands)

	U.K. Citizens	Aliens	Nationality Unknown	Total
1907	396	239	..	635
1908	263	123	—	386
1909	289	186		474
1910	398	221		619
1911	455	169		623
1912	468	189		657
1913	470	232		702
1914	293	158		451
1915	105	22		127
1916	76	17		94
1917	21	7		28
1918	17	6		23
1919	180	21		202
1920	353	85		438
1921	268	109		378
1922	248	95		344
	...	...		...
1923(*a*)	338	126		463
	...	...		...
1924	263	108		371
1925	250	105		355
1926	284	116		402
1927	277	137		414
1928	271	127		397
1929	281	119		399
1930	221	107		328
1931	150	63		213
	...	...		...
1932(*b*)	166	56		222
1933	177	49		226
1934	187	54		240
1935	183	61		245
1936	198	80		278
1937	194	93		287
1938	185	79		264
1939–45	...	...		...
1946	...	...		214
1947	...	...		245

	Commonwealth Citizens	Aliens	Total
1947(*c*)	190	54	244
1948	245	63	307
1949	256	61	316
1950	258	68	325
1951	283	80	363
1952	301	82	383
1953	277	82	359
1954	277	82	359
1955	276	85	361
1956	293	87	380
1957	302	77	379
1958	251	75	326
1959	241	70	311
1960	225	65	290
	...	...	...
1961	220(*d*)	60(*d*)	280(*d*)
	...	...	...
1962	216(*e*)	71(*e*)	287(*e*)
1963	...	...	296
1964	...	...	284

(*a*) From 1st April 1923 the figures are exclusive of passengers who departed from ports in southern Ireland.
(*b*) From 1932 onwards the figures are inclusive of passengers on pleasure cruises.
(*c*) Subsequently including passengers travelling indirectly via continental ports or ports in the Republic of Ireland.
(*d*) With effect from 1961 countries in Africa and the Middle East which bordered on the Mediterranean Sea were classified as European.
(*e*) From 1 June 1962 South Africans were classified as aliens instead of Commonwealth citizens.

Population and Vital Statistics 21. Passengers to United Kingdom Ports from Extra-European Countries – 1855–1964

NOTES

[1] SOURCE: 1855–1924 – Ferenczi and Willcox, *International Migrations* (2 vols., National Bureau of Economic Research, New York, 1929–31), vol. 1; 1925–64 – *Board of Trade Journal*.

[2] The figures up to 1870 are only approximations.

(in thousands)

	U.K. Citizens	Aliens	Total		U.K. Citizens	Aliens	Total
1855	...	...	23	1898	91	48	139
1858	...	...	24	1899	100	62	162
1859	...	...	20	1900	98	78	176
1860	...	...	24	1901	100	65	165
1861	...	...	32	1902	104	67	171
1862	...	...	...	1903	113	87	200
1863	...	...	18	1904	145	97	242
1864	...	...	26	1905	123	82	205
1865	...	...	34	1906	130	100	230
1866	...	...	31	1907	161	133	294
1867	...	...	37	1908	172	171	343
1868	...	...	...	1909	149	112	261
1869	...	...	36	1910	164	135	299
1870	...	...	42	1911	193	158	350
1871	...	...	45	1912	199	142	341
1872	...	...	42	1913	228	145	373
1873	...	...	75	1914	230	130	360
1874	...	...	118	1915	130	18	147
1875	...	...	94	1916	85	14	99
1876	71	22	94	1917	21	13	34
1877	64	18	82	1918	15	11	26
1878	55	23	78	1919	153	40	194
1879	38	16	54	1920	180	104	284
1880	47	21	68	1921	149	78	228
1881	53	24	77	1922	148	76	224
1882	55	28	83	1923	147	63	211
1883	74	27	101	1924	175	78	253
1884	91	32	123	1925	163	78	241
1885	85	28	114	1926	161	77	237
1886	80	29	109	1927	174	86	260
1887	85	34	119	1928	188	89	277
1888	94	35	129	1929	188	90	278
1889	103	44	147	1930	197	93	290
1890	109	46	156	1931	185	71	256
1891	103	48	151	1932	215	62	277
1892	98	46	144	1933	206	47	253
1893	102	39	141	1934	199	50	249
1894	118	67	186	1935	194	58	252
1895	109	66	176	1936	208	74	282
1896	102	58	160	1937	198	80	278
1897	95	60	155	1938	182	62	244
				1939–45	...	...	116
				1946	...	...	182

Population and Vital Statistics 21. *continued*

(in thousands)

	Commonwealth Citizens	Aliens	Total
1938	160	62	222
1939–46	...	...	...
1947	134	46	181
1948	172	58	230
1949	196	56	252
1950	200	62	262
1951	202	63	265
1952	209	81	290
1953	212	80	292
1954	233	83	316
1955	238	89	327
1956	229	89	318
1957	207	81	288
1958	210	80	290
1959	215	74	289
1960	227	76	303
	---(*a*)	---(*a*)	---(*a*)
1961	223	66	289
	---(*b*)	---(*b*)	
1962	200	76	276
1963	...	...	251
1964	...	...	245

(*a*) With effect from 1961 countries in Africa and the Middle East which bordered on the Mediterranean Sea were classified as European.

(*b*) From 1 June 1962 South Africans were classified as aliens instead of Commonwealth citizens.

Population and Vital Statistics 22. Inward and Outward Movements of United Kingdom Citizens between United Kingdom Ports and Extra-European Countries – 1853–1914

NOTE

SOURCE: Ferenczi and Willcox, *International Migrations* (2 vols., National Bureau of Economic Research, New York, 1929–31), vol. 1.

A. Outward Movements, 1853–1914

(in thousands)

	Total	To: U.S.A.	British North America	Australasia	British South Africa		Total	To: U.S.A.	British North America	Australasia	British South Africa
1853	278	191	32	55	...	1884	242	155	31	44	4
1854	267	154	36	78	...	1885	208	138	20	39	3
1855	150	86	16	47	...	1886	233	153	25	43	4
1856	148	95	11	41	...	1887	281	202	32	34	5
1857	181	106	17	58	...	1888	280	196	35	31	6
1858	95	49	7	36	...	1889	254	169	28	28	14
1859	97	57	2	29	...	1890	218	152	23	21	10
1860	96	68	3	21	...	1891	219	156	22	20	9
1861	65	38	4	21	...	1892	210	150	23	16	10
1862	98	49	8	39	...	1893	209	149	25	11	13
1863	193	131	10	50	...	1894	156	104	17	11	13
1864	187	130	11	40	...	1895	185	127	17	11	20
1865	175	118	14	37	...	1896	162	99	15	10	25
1866	170	132	10	24	...	1897	146	85	16	12	21
1867	157	126	12	14	...	1898	141	80	18	11	20
1868	138	108	12	12	...	1899	146	92	16	11	14
1869	186	147	21	14	...	1900	169	103	18	15	21
1870	203	153	27	17	...	1901	172	104	16	15	23
1871	193	151	25	12	...	1902	206	108	26	14	43
1872	210	162	24	15	...	1903	260	124	60	12	50
1873	228	167	29	25	...	1904	271	146	70	14	27
1874	197	114	21	53	...	1905	262	122	82	15	26
1875	141	81	12	35	...	1906	325	145	115	19	23
1876	109	55	9	32	...	1907	396	170	151	25	21
1877	95	45	8	30	5	1908	263	97	81	34	20
1878	113	55	11	36	4	1909	289	110	86	38	22
1879	164	92	18	41	7	1910	398	132	157	46	27
1880	228	167	21	24	9	1911	455	122	185	81	31
1881	243	176	24	23	13	1912	468	117	186	97	28
1882	279	182	40	37	12	1913	470	129	196	78	26
1883	320	192	44	71	6	1914	293	93	94	48	21

Population and Vital Statistics 22. *continued*

B. Difference between Outward and Inward Movements, 1876–1914 (Excess Inward +, Outward −)

(in thousands)

	Total	To or from: U.S.A.	British North America	Australasia	British South Africa
1876	− 38	+ . .	− 3	−30	. . .
1877	− 31	− 1	− 2	−26	. . .
1878	− 58	− 21	− 4	−32	. . .
1879	−126	− 72	−14	−36	. . .
1880	−181	−140	−16	−18	. . .
1881	−190	−146	−18	−17	. . .
1882	−225	−153	−34	−30	− 6
1883	−246	−145	−37	−64	+ . .
1884	−151	− 94	−22	−36	+ 2
1885	−122	− 80	−11	−31	+ 1
1886	−153	−100	−18	−34	− . .
1887	−196	−143	−25	−24	− 2
1888	−186	−132	−26	−21	− 3
1889	−151	− 97	−20	−18	− 9
1890	−109	− 78	−13	−11	− 4
1891	−115	− 88	−13	−10	− 3
1892	−112	− 87	−14	− 5	− 4
1893	−107	− 82	−16	− 1	− 7
1894	− 38	− 20	− 7	− 2	− 6
1895	− 76	− 55	− 6	− 1	−12
1896	− 60	− 40	− 6	− 1	−10
1897	− 51	− 32	− 6	− 5	− 6
1898	− 49	− 30	− 8	− 4	− 6
1899	− 46	− 39	− 8	− 4	+ 6
1900	− 71	− 48	− 8	− 6	− 7
1901	− 72	− 46	− 7	− 7	− 9
1902	−102	− 52	− 15	− 4	−28
1903	−147	− 65	− 46	− 4	−28
1904	−127	− 67	− 51	− 5	+ 1
1905	−139	− 61	− 63	− 7	− 3
1906	−195	− 86	− 91	−10	+ 3
1907	−235	−100	−118	−14	+ 5
1908	− 91	− 31	− 41	−20	+ 5
1909	−140	− 56	− 52	−25	− 2
1910	−234	− 74	−116	−33	− 8
1911	−262	− 50	−135	−66	− 8
1912	−268	− 46	−134	−80	− 4
1913	−242	− 52	−128	−57	− . .
1914	− 63	− 16	− 30	−26	+ 4

Population and Vital Statistics 23. Balance of Extra-European Migration of United Kingdom/Commonwealth Citizens by Main Countries of Last or Future Permanent Residence – 1912–63

NOTES

[1] SOURCES: 1912–24 – Ferenczi and Willcox, *International Migrations* (2 vols, National Bureau of Economic Research, New York, 1929–31), vol. 1; 1925–63 – *Board of Trade Journal*.

[2] This table relates only to travel by sea.

(in thousands)
(Excess Inward +, Outward −)

	Total	To or from: British North America	Australasia	British South Africa (*a*)	Other British Empire (*b*)	U.S.A.
1912 (*c*)	−267	−132	−62	− 3	− 3	−65
1913	−304	−165	−56	−..	− 2	−78
1914	−110	− 45	−24	+ 4	+ 1	−49
1915	+ 15	+ 22	− 2	+ 1	+ 1	−13
1916	+ 5	+ 10	+ 1	+ 3	+ 1	−12
1917	+ 2	− 1	+ 1	+ 1	+ 1	−..
1918	− 2	+..	− 2	− 1	−..	−..
1919	− 54	− 45	− 9	+ 1	+ 3	− 3
1920	−199	− 94	−28	− 8	− 4	−60
1921	−128	− 47	−29	− 7	− 2	−42
1922	−106	− 30	−41	− 1	+ 3	−37
	....	....	...	...	...	...
1923 (*d*)	−199	− 76	−39	− 1	+ 3	−86
	....	....	...	...	...	...
1924	− 91	− 47	−39	− 1	+ 2	− 6
1925	− 84	− 25	−37	− 2	+..	−22
1926	−116	− 39	−51	− 3	−..	−22
1927	− 98	− 40	−38	− 2	+..	−19
1928	− 78	− 39	−22	− 2	+..	−16
1929	− 87	− 53	−11	− 1	+ 2	−25
1930	− 26	− 15	+ 3	−..	+ 4	−19
1931	+ 37	+ 10	+ 9	+ 1	+ 6	+ 9
1932	+ 49	+ 18	+ 5	+ 4	+ 6	+14
1933	+ 33	+ 14	+ 3	+ 2	+ 4	+ 8
1934	+ 21	+ 10	+ 2	+ 1	+ 3	+ 4
1935	+ 16	+ 8	+ 1	− 1	+ 4	+ 3
1936	+ 17	+ 8	+ 2	− 1	+ 5	+ 3
1937	+ 11	+ 6	+..	− 2	+ 3	+ 1
1938	+ 6	+ 4	− 2	− 2	+ 4	+ 1
1946 (*e*)	−104	− 43	− 8	− 2	− 2	−46
1947	− 65	− 15	−12	−22	+ 1	−17
1948	− 96	− 27	−35	−28	+10	−17
1949	− 85	− 13	−54	− 9	+..	−13
1950	− 64	− 6	−54	− 2	+ 6	− 9
1951	− 83	− 23	−54	− 5	+ 5	−10
1952	− 97	− 30	−53	− 8	+ 4	−13
1953	− 75	− 34	−30	− 3	+ 5	−13
1954	− 53	− 29	−27	− 2	+14	−11
1955	− 44	− 16	−32	− 3	+15	− 9
1956	− 66	− 34	−30	− 5	+13	−11
1957	− 98	− 51	−35	− 6	+ 6	−12
1958	− 44	− 4	−37	− 5	+ 7	− 6
1959	− 28	+..	−33	− 1	+ 9	− 4
1960	− 9	+..	−28	+ 4	+19	− 4
1961	− 7	+ 1	−34	+ 6	+23	− 2
				... (*f*)		
1962	− 23	− 3	−30	+..	+13	− 3
1963	− 60	− 9	−40	− 4	+..	− 4

(*a*) Includes the High Commission territories and Rhodesia (later the whole Central African Federation).

(*b*) As constituted at the date concerned.

(*c*) Nine months only.

(*d*) The figures for the fourth quarter of 1923 and for all later years are exclusive of migrants travelling via ports in southern Ireland.

(*e*) Figures are not available for 1939–45, and those for 1946 are stated by the Board of Trade to be about 5 per cent deficient.

(*f*) South Africa left the Commonwealth as from 1 June 1962. South African citizens were subsequently treated as aliens, but migration to or from South Africa continues to be included in this column.

Population and Vital Statistics 24. U.K. International Migration, 1964–80

NOTE
SOURCE: Office of Population Censuses & Surveys, *International Migration*.

A. By Citizenship

(in thousands)

	Immigrants					Emigrants					
			Commonwealth Citizens (*a*)					Commonwealth Citizens (*a*)			Overall Net
	Total	U.K. Citizens	Old	New	Aliens	Total	U.K. Citizens	Old	New	Aliens	Balance
1964	211.0	71.3	12.7	60.0	67.0	271.4	202.4	12.6	17.3	39.3	−60.4
1965	206.3	71.4	16.6	52.0	66.3	284.3	219.2	12.3	19.1	33.7	−78.0
1966	219.2	77.7	14.9	49.7	76.9	301.6	229.9	11.8	21.2	38.7	−82.4
1967	225.0	82.8	16.6	57.5	68.0	309.0	238.2	12.7	17.7	40.5	−84.0
1968	221.6	93.4	14.2	57.6	56.5	277.7	208.3	12.9	19.0	37.5	−56.0
1969	205.6	82.0	15.0	48.9	59.7	292.7	220.7	12.4	19.7	39.8	−87.1
1970	225.6	95.1	19.2	40.8	70.4	290.7	214.5	12.8	20.6	42.8	−65.1
1971	199.7	92.0	17.3	36.0	54.4	240.0	170.6	13.0	16.3	40.1	−40.4
1972	221.9	111.2	18.7	34.6	57.4	233.2	159.9	15.1	20.3	37.9	− 11.4
1973	195.7	82.6	21.1	23.8	68.3	245.8	175.7	15.0	13.5	41.6	− 50.1
1974	183.8	78.9	16.1	27.2	61.6	269.0	198.8	15.9	13.6	40.7	− 85.3
1975	197.2	85.3	18.2	34.9	58.8	238.3	169.4	14.0	13.5	41.5	− 41.2
1976	191.3	86.6	16.2	33.5	55.0	210.4	137.3	14.7	13.5	44.9	− 19.1
1977	162.6	73.1	14.0	25.4	50.1	208.7	143.7	15.4	13.3	36.3	− 46.1
1978	187.0	73.5	15.9	33.7	63.9	192.4	126.5	12.0	13.4	40.6	− 5.5
1979	194.8	78.2	15.3	41.4	59.8	188.6	126.0	12.6	15.0	35.0	+ 6.2
1980	173.7	66.7	13.0	29.6	64.4	229.1	150.4	15.4	14.9	48.4	− 55.4

B. By Country of Last or Next Residence

	Immigrants						Emigrants					
	Australia & New Zealand	Canada	Indian Sub-continent	Other Common-wealth	U.S.A.	E.E.C.	Australia & New Zealand	Canada	Indian Sub-continent	Other Common-wealth	U.S.A.	E.E.C.
1964	21.6	9.7	27.8	58.7	19.0	32.3	97.0	31.7	8.8	32.3	30.2	29.6
1965	25.6	9.3	23.8	54.6	20.1	37.8	106.1	42.2	9.1	32.5	27.8	26.6
1966	27.0	9.2	26.7	49.7	22.7	36.7	101.9	63.8	9.2	32.5	27.1	25.8
1967	35.7	10.1	39.6	46.5	22.0	30.3	99.1	64.0	7.6	32.0	34.2	27.3
1968	37.1	12.5	40.1	48.1	18.9	27.4	92.1	40.1	6.8	33.1	31.0	28.6
1969	32.7	13.2	32.0	41.1	20.5	28.9	105.7	34.0	10.1	34.2	23.2	31.4
1970	39.1	15.3	27.5	42.9	22.8	32.5	98.7	28.7	9.7	35.3	21.5	33.7
1971	38.9	13.4	24.3	41.5	22.2	20.6	83.4	15.3	7.9	30.8	16.6	31.1
1972	38.9	11.2	22.8	61.1	20.0	24.3	72.6	18.1	12.8	32.4	17.9	28.2
1973	38.5	11.4	17.0	41.7	20.5	23.5	81.5	28.8	8.4	26.1	20.3	32.2
1974	32.6	7.2	16.4	40.5	18.9	29.3	92.2	36.9	6.4	26.0	19.0	29.6
1975	35.9	7.3	20.2	45.6	16.6	22.9	43.7	37.3	5.9	25.4	22.1	28.1
1976	32.7	7.4	27.1	39.3	16.4	25.0	40.7	22.7	5.8	24.4	20.9	31.1
1977	28.0	6.8	22.8	31.0	12.3	18.2	40.1	18.7	6.1	30.0	20.7	29.0
1978	27.2	6.7	37.9	30.6	15.2	23.7	34.8	14.6	5.2	22.2	25.0	31.7
1979	24.7	6.0	33.3	42.4	13.4	22.6	31.2	19.0	5.7	22.0	26.3	28.8
1980	17.9	5.2	25.3	34.3	16.8	23.1	46.0	19.4	6.1	29.4	28.6	33.7

(*a*) including Pakistanis throughout.

Population and Vital Statistics 25. Emigration of Natives of Ireland, 1825–1925

NOTES

[1] SOURCE: *Commission on Emigration and Other Population Problems, 1948–1954: Reports* (Dublin, 1956).

[2] Part A relates to Irish passengers for overseas countries at all United Kingdom ports. Part B relates, in principle, to emigrants from the main Irish ports. It is clear, however, that, as mentioned in the introduction to this section, many emigrants, to Great Britain especially, were omitted.

A. Total Irish Passengers to extra-European Countries, 1825–1925

(in thousands)

1825	11	1851	255	1876	26	1901	39
1826	16	1852	225	1877	23	1902	42
1827	20	1853	193	1878	29	1903	46
1828	14	1854	150	1879	41	1904	58
1829	18	1855	79	1880	94	1905	50
1830	32	1856	72	1881	76	1906	52
1831	56	1857	86	1882	84	1907	64
1832	55	1858	43	1883	106	1908	38
1833	28	1859	53	1884	73	1909	44
1834	44	1860	61	1885	60	1910	51
1835	23	1861	36	1886	61	1911	49
1836	43	1862	50	1887	79	1912	43
1837	46	1863	116	1888	73	1913	44
1838	13	1864	115	1889	65	1914	31
1839	33	1865	101	1890	57	1915	15
1840	55	1866	99	1891	58	1916	10
1841	32	1867	89	1892	53	1917	0·8
1842	41	1868	65	1893	52	1918	0·4
1843	38	1869	73	1894	42	1919	4·3
1844	54	1870	74	1895	54	1920	30
1845	75	1871	71	1896	42	1921	26
1846	106	1872	73	1897	36	1922	21
1847	220	1873	84	1898	34	1923	34
1848	181	1874	60	1899	43	1924	27
1849	219	1875	41	1900	46	1925	39
1850	214						

B. Emigrants from Ireland by Main Destination, 1851–1921

(in thousands)

	Total	U.S.A.	Canada	Australasia	Great Britain		Total	U.S.A.	Canada	Australasia	Great Britain
1851	[152] (*a*)	...	...	...	...	1887	83	70	4	4	5
1852	190	...	...	...	...	1888	79	67	3	3	6
1853	173	...	...	...	...	1889	70	60	2	3	4
1854	141	...	...	...	...	1890	61	53	2	2	4
1855	92	...	...	...	...	1891	60	52	1	2	4
1856	91	...	...	...	...	1892	51	47	1	1	2
1857	95	...	...	...	...	1893	48	45	1	1	1
1858	64	...	...	...	...	1894	36	33	1	1	2
1859	81	...	...	...	...	1895	49	45	1	1	2
1860	85	...	...	...	...	1896	39	35	1	1	2
1861	64	...	...	...	...	1897	33	29	--	1	2
1862	70	...	...	...	...	1898	32	28	--	1	3
1863	117	...	...	...	...	1899	41	35	--	1	4
1864	114	...	...	...	...	1900	45	38	--	1	6
1865	101	...	...	...	...	1901	40	32	1	1	6
1866	99	...	...	...	...	1902	40	34	1	1	5
1867	81	...	...	...	...	1903	40	34	1	--	4
1868	61	...	...	...	...	1904	37	31	2	--	3
1869	67	...	...	...	...	1905	31	24	2	--	3
1870	75	...	...	...	...	1906	35	27	3	--	4
1871	71	...	...	...	...	1907	39	30	4	1	4
1872	78	...	...	...	...	1908	23	17	3	1	3
1873	90	...	...	...	...	1909	29	22	3	1	3
1874	73	...	...	...	...	1910	32	25	4	1	2
1875	51	...	...	...	...	1911	31	22	5	1	2
1876	38	15	1	5	17	1912	29	20	6	1	2
1877	39	12	--	6	20	1913	31	22	7	1	1
1878	41	15	1	7	19	1914	20	15	3	1	1
1879	47	23	2	6	15	1915	11	7	1	--	3
1880	96	75	3	4	14	1916	7	4	--	--	2
1881	78	61	3	3	11	1917	2	--	--	--	2
1882	89	66	7	5	11	1918	1	--	--	--	1
1883	109	80	11	8	10	1919	3	1	1	--	1
1884	76	57	4	6	9	1920	16	12	2	--	1
1885	62	50	2	4	6	1921	14	11	1	--	--
1886	63	51	3	4	5						

(*a*) Eight months only.

Population and Vital Statistics 26. Passenger Movement – Republic of Ireland 1924–80

NOTES

[1] SOURCE: *Statistical Abstract of Ireland*.

[2] Data to 1938 are of passengers by sea only. Subsequently they include people moving by rail, bus, and air (other than transit passengers).

(in thousands)

	Total		to or from Britain and Northern Ireland		to or from extra-European Countries	
	Inward	Outward	Inward	Outward	Inward	Outward
1924	...	...	...	...	2·5	19
1925	...	...	...	...	2·2	30
1926	...	...	318	322	1·8	30
1927	...	...	340	350	1·9	27
	...	...			2.2	25
1928	----(a)	----(a)	350	362	----(a)	----(a)
	366	392			15	29
1929	381	403	364	375	15	26
1930	380	393	364	370	15	22
1931	387	387	372	377	14	8
1932	406	399	370	377	33	19
1933	374	377	356	364	14	11
1934	401	412	382	395	12	10
1935	434	448	416	434	12	10
1936	481	503	462	489	13	10
1937	523	549	506	534	14	12
1938	534	552	520	539	13	11
	----	----	to or from Britain		to or from Northern Ireland	
			Inward	Outward	Inward	Outward
1939	1,337	1,324	448	433	879	881
1940	931	914	106	95	825	816
1941	1,237	1,260	109	127	1,127	1,132
1942	1,379	1,432	143	168	1,231	1,261
1943	1,568	1,605	183	209	1,379	1,392
1944	1,556	1,550	138	137	1,415	1,410
1945						
1946	2,150	2,159	483	483	1,594	1,600
1947	1,985	1,973	471	480	1,580	1,486
1948	2,428	2,440	728	729	1,596	1,578
1949	2,472	2,480	762	752	1,599	1,589
1950	2,437	2,437	787	783	1,511	1,492
1951	2,419	2,429	786	815	1,607	1,585
1952	2,226	2,245	828	861	1,372	1,355
1953	2,048	2,068	798	827	1,220	1,206
1954	1,943	1,970	822	857	1,082	1,067
1955	1,992	2,019	887	928	1,068	1,049
1956	2,011	2,040	975	1,009	994	981
1957	1,952	2,005	959	1,004	940	932
1958	1,956	1,989	994	1,022	888	880
1959	1,986	2,019	1,041	1,071	881	876
1960	2,041	2,071	1,101	1,139	863	851
1961	2,114	2,140	1,188	1,208	839	838
1962	2,104	2,125	1,169	1,184	832	833
1963	2,147	2,170	1,210	1,223	820	821
1964	2,290	2,321	1,335	1,349	811	820
1965	2,364	2,394	1,429	1,448	767	770
1966	2,420	2,441	1,442	1,467	787	782
1967	2,541	2,582	1,491	1,533	827	819
1968	2,734	2,730	1,626	1,629	855	847

Population and Vital Statistics 26. *continued*

(in thousands)

	Total		to or from Britain		to or from Northern Ireland	
	Inward	Outward	Inward	Outward	Inward	Outward
1969	2,816	2,819	1,706	1,724	793	787
1970	2,815	2,817	1,709	1,716	758	755
1971	2,802	2,801	1,708	1,710	690	690
1972	2,531	2,527	1,521	1,512	602	602
1973	2,774	2,761	1,725	1,707	600	597
1974	2,796	2,792	1,703	1,684	624	629
1975	2,910	2,907	1,707	1,693	672	674
1976	2,822	2,829	1,677	1,673	614	613
1977	3,047	3,062	1,862	1,863	597	599
1978	3,460	3,445	2,162	2,159	622	615
1979	3,578	3,607	2,200	2,215	602	604
1980	3,515	3,520	2,209	2,204	545	546

(*a*) Data previously relate to Irish and U.K. citizens describing themselves as migrants.

Population and Vital Statistics 27. Immigrants to the U.S.A. from Great Britain and Ireland, 1820–1979

NOTES

[1] SOURCES: *Historical Statistics of the United States* (U.S. Bureau of the Census, Washington, 1975), vol. I, pp. 105–6.

[2] Arrivals at Pacific ports were not included until 1850, those at Alaska ports until 1871 and irregularly only from then until 1904, those in Hawaii until 1901, in Puerto Rico until 1902, and in the American Virgin Islands until 1942. Arrivals at land borders were counted very irregularly until 1905 and not fully until 1908, but those who arrived at Canadian ports with the declared intention of proceeding to the United States were included from 1894. Arrivals at ports under Confederate Control in 1861–5 were not recorded.

[3] Temporary visitors are included for 1856–57, when they constituted about 1½ per cent of all arrivals.

[4] Changes in definitions or procedures which affected the exact comparability of the series are noted in footnotes.

[5] Statistics are for years ending 30 June except as follows: 1820–31 and 1844–49 are for years ending 30 September; 1833–42 and 1851–67 are for calendar years, with the 1832 and 1850 figures being for 15 months ending 31 December, the 1843 figures 9 months ending 30 September, and the 1868 figures for 6 months ending 30 June.

(in thousands)

	Great Britain	Ireland		Great Britain	Ireland		Great Britain	Ireland
1820	2·4	3·6	1845	19	45	1870	104	57
1821	3·2	1·5	1846	22	52	1871	85	57
1822	1·2	2·3	1847	23	106	1872	85	69
1823	1·1	1·9	1848	35	113	1873	90	77
1824	1·3	2·3	1849	55	159	1874	62	54
1825	2·1	4·9	1850	[51](*a*)	[164](*a*)	1875	48	38
1826	2·3	5·4	1851	51	221	1876	29	20
1827	4·2	9·8	1852	41	160	1877	24	15
1828	5·4	12	1853	38	163	1878	22	16
1829	3·2	7·4	1854	59	102	1879	30	20
1830	1·2	2·7	1855	48	50	1880	73	72
				- -(*b*)	- - -(*b*)			
1831	2·5	5·8	1856	45	54	1881	81	72
1832	[5·3](*a*)	[12](*a*)	1857	58	54	1882	103	76
1833	4·9	8·6	1858	29	27	1883	77	81
1834	10	24	1859	26	35	1884	66	63
1835	9·0	21	1860	30	49	1885	58	52
1836	13	31	1861	20	24	1886	63	50
1837	12	29	1862	25	23	1887	93	68
1838	5·4	13	1863	67	56	1888	109	74
1839	10	24	1864	53	64	1889	88	66
1840	2·6	39	1865	82	30	1890	70	53
1841	16	38	1866	95	37	1891	67	56
							- - -(*b*)	- -(*b*)
1842	22	51	1867	53	73	1892	42	51
				- -(*b*)	- - -(*b*)			
1843	[8·4](*a*)	[20](*a*)	1868	[24](*a*)	[32](*a*)	1893	35	44
1844	14	33	1869	84	41	1894	23	30
1895	29	46	1924	59	17	1953	17	4·3
1896	25	40	1925	27	27	1954	17	4·7
1897	13	28	1926	26	25	1955	16	5·2
	- - -(*c*)	- - -(*c*)						
1898	13	25	1927	24	29	1956	19	5·6
1899	13	32	1928	20	25	1957	24	8·2
1900	13	36	1929	21	20	1958	24	9·1
1901	15	31	1930	31	23	1959	18	6·6
1902	17	29	1931	9·1	7·3	1960	20	6·9
1903	34	35	1932	2·1	0·5	1961	19	5·7
1904	51	36	1933	1·0	0·3	1962	18	5·1
	- - -(*c*)	- - -(*c*)						
1905	84	53	1934	1·3	0·4	1963	23	5·7
	- - -(*d*)	- - -(*d*)	1935	1·4	0·5	1964	26	6·1
1906	67	35	1936	1·3	0·4	1965	24	5·2
1907	79	35	1937	1·7	0·5	1966	19	3·3
1908	63	31	1938	2·3	1·1	1967	23	2·8
1909	47	25						

See p. 90 for footnotes.

Population and Vital Statistics 27. *continued*

(in thousands)

	Great Britain	Ireland		Great Britain	Ireland		Great Britain	Ireland
1910	69	30	1939	3·1	1·2	1968	26	3·0
1911	73	29	1940	6·2	0·8	1969	15	2·0
1912	57	26	1941	7·7	0·3	1970	14	1·2
1913	60	28	1942	0·9	0·1	1971	12	1·2
1914	49	25	1943	1·0	0·2	1972	12	1·4
1915	27	14	1944	1·3	0·1	1973	12	1·6
1916	16	8·6	1945	3·0	0·4	1974	12	1·3
1917	11	5·4	1946	34	1·8	1975	12	1·1
1918	2·5	0·3	1947	24	2·6	1976	13	1·0
1919	6·8	0·5	1948	26	7·5	1977	14	1·0
1920	38	9·6	1949	21	8·7	1978	16	0·9
1921	51	28	1950	13	5·8	1979	16	0·8
1922	25	11	1951	15	3·1			
1923	46	16	1952	22	3·5			

(*a*) See note 5 above.
(*b*) See note 3 above.
(*c*) From 1892 to 1904 figures relate only to steerage passengers. There were other changes in 1892, the main one being the adoption of admissions rather than arrivals (a practice discontinued from 1898) and in 1905 (see note 2 above).
(*d*) Subsequently excluding resident aliens returning from a visit abroad.

CHAPTER II

LABOUR FORCE

TABLES

Official collection and publication of statistics pertaining to labour in Britain sprang from a House of Commons resolution passed in 1886, which was implemented in a sustained fashion from the establishment of the Board of Trade Labour Department – ancestor of today's Department of Employment – in 1893, and the inauguration of its monthly journal, the *Labour Gazette*. However, statistics for earlier dates than this are available for some aspects of labour – notably for numbers in different occupations and industries, for wages, and for some sorts of information about trade unions. Representatives of all these aspects are included in this chapter.

It is only comparatively recently that the distinction between a person's occupation and the category of economic activity in which he is engaged has been properly appreciated. Statistics of the numbers of the labour force in different occupations or industries tended, therefore, to be defined with less than perfect clarity until into the twentieth century, though almost from the first, the directors of the census were interested in eliciting information about occupations. Prior to that, some of the practitioners of 'political arithmetic', most notably Gregory King, made estimates which, though themselves concerned with the sources of incomes, throw some light on occupational distribution. The first table in this chapter springs from a modern reworking of some of these estimates to make them accord better with the categories used today. The original figures may be deemed unreliable, perhaps, and certainly they were presented with different aims from ours today. Moreover, though Lindert and Williamson corrected some of the errors and adjusted the categories, it may still be felt that the results cannot be trusted fully. Nevertheless, they are the only quantitative evidence available before the nineteenth century, and provided one tests the sensitivity of one's conclusions to error in the estimates, it seems preferable to make use of what is there.

The attempt to elicit information about occupations at the 1801 census is generally regarded to have been a failure; but the even rougher classification of families by agricultural and non-agricultural branches of activity made in the next three censuses may well have been more successful, so far as it went, and these are shown here as part of table 2. The 1831 census also provided a more detailed analysis of the occupations of males of twenty years old and over. The first full-scale analysis of occupations of the whole population was attempted in 1841; but no provision had been made in advance for a classification or standardised designations of activities, and the officials were completely surprised by the enormous variety that were returned when individuals were left to describe themselves. A very general classification was devised *ex post*, but it is not comparable with later censuses. Apart from that, the detailed lists were printed with little explanation of the terms used, and with some aggregation under headings which in later censuses were separated or assigned to different categories. An attempt has been made here to fit the information gathered in 1841 into the pattern of the 1911 classification; but it is clear that the degree of comparability between 1841 and later censuses is relatively poor for many occupations. Charles Booth, in the 1880s, noted that 'owing to the different methods of tabulation as to ages and the imperfections of the returns, the figures for 1841 do not ... offer a very safe basis of comparison',[1] and that remains true to quite a large extent, as may be deduced from the notes to table 2. However, it is worth noting that the uncertainties are much greater for tertiary sector occupations than for others.

By 1851 the officials were prepared, and the principle of classification then adopted survives, in essentials, to this day, though there have been many trivial and some important changes; and the occupational classification has been supplemented by an industrial one since 1921. The changes between censuses have been such as to render exact comparisons impossible over the period as a whole, though broad ones can be made except across the two major breaks in 1871–1881 and 1911–1921. In the latter case, however, comparisons are possible for quite a considerable number of occupations, as the *General Report* of the 1921 census pointed out – most professions, some activities dealt with on occupational rather than industrial lines in 1911, and some which are necessarily confined to certain industries.[2] In cases where comparison in a particular occupation is likely to be especially inaccurate, this is indicated in tables 2 and 3.

Throughout the period from 1881 onwards, comparison of the totals occupied and unoccupied is broadly valid, provided account is taken of changes in the lower age-limit of people covered by the returns. Comparisons between 1871 (and earlier) and 1881 is vitiated by the inclusion, prior to 1881, of retired people in their former occupations. The effect of this, however, appears to have been relatively quite small – much less, in fact, than the effects of the Education and Factory Acts. If attention is concentrated on people aged fifteen and over, there was actually a slight rise in the total occupied proportion between 1861 and 1881, despite the exclusion of the retired at the later date – from 40.80 to 40.99 per cent. Presumably, when state pensions did not exist, and occupational schemes were quite rare, there was little voluntary retirement; and many who became unfit to carry on their occupation took other, less demanding jobs.

The accuracy of all occupation statistics can be called in question on the ground of likely errors in the returns by householders. This has long been recognised, but the criticism has been discounted generally. Stevenson, for example, discussed the matter in the introduction

[1] Charles Booth, 'Occupations of the People of the United Kingdom, 1801–1881', *Journal of the Statistical Society*, XLIX (1886).

[2] *loc. cit.*, p. 87.

to the mortality tables of 1910–12,[3] and concluded that, for groups at any rate, the errors were unlikely to be significant. A similar conclusion was reached in the *General Report* of the 1951 census on the basis of a sample enquiry: 'In summary, it may be said that, while the occupational classification sometimes falls victim to the combined forces of its own specificity and the human capacity for variation in description, the general impression emerges that the level of reliability of occupational assignment at the census justifies the statistical analyses which are based thereon.'[4]

Statistics of the numbers engaged in agriculture, coal-mining, iron and steel, and the textile industries, derived from other sources than the census, can be found in chapters 3 to 6; and the numbers in the armed forces are shown here in table 6. However, census data have been adjusted by Feinstein to give broadly comparable series for a wider selection of industries for the period 1861 to 1911, and these are shown in table 4. Then, with the coming of widespread compulsory insurance for manual workers late in 1920, annual figures relating to a substantial proportion of the numbers occupied in different industries became available, though the Ministry of Labour's industrial classification was not brought into line with the census of population system until 1923. Changes in the scope of the insurance scheme seriously affect the comparability of the figures for some industries over the period 1923 to 1948, and there are later problems caused both by administrative changes and by alterations in the Standard Industrial Classification. But with the obvious exceptions, which are clearly indicated, these statistics are particularly useful for year-to-year comparisons; and they do also give a good idea of long-term trends if used with care.

Table 5 is the basis of the percentage figures of unemployment by industry, given in tables 11 and 12, and of the percentages of total insured employees out of work given in part B of table 8. The total numbers unemployed shown in table 10 are, however, more complete, at least until 1948, since they are derived from Labour Exchange (Job Centre) records, and include both insured and uninsured workers registered for employment. It must be noted, though, that they exclude salaried workers and some wage-earners (mainly married women) who would normally be regarded as unemployed, but who did not register. Whether any of these figures are 'true' indicators of the level of unemployment, even in the post-1948 period, has been a matter of considerable dispute. There is a large literature, much of which, for the period covered here, is cited and discussed in W. R. Garside's *The Measurement of Unemployment*,[5] a thorough treatment of the problems of the statistics of unemployment from 1850 onwards. In the light of this work, it is clearly no longer possible to regard the unemployment figures derived from the insurance schemes or the Labour Exchange registers as having a completely clear and unambiguous meaning.

Prior to 1922 there are no general statistics of unemployment in Britain, but certain trade unions which paid out-of-work benefit to their members kept records, and made these

[3] Supplement to the 75th *Annual Report of the Registrar General for England and Wales*, part IV, pp. iv–vii.
[4] *loc cit.*, p. 51.
[5] (Oxford, 1980).

available (together with later returns) to the Labour Department. These records cover quite a wide variety of industries from the late 1880s, and for a few unions in the engineering, shipbuilding and metal group they go back to 1851. Prior to that there is no usable statistical series of a general nature, though K.D.M. Snell has much useful discussion of long-run changes in seasonal unemployment from the late seventeenth century to the mid nineteenth in his *Annals of the Labouring Poor*.[6]

The percentages computed from the trade union records were commonly used as a general indicator of unemployment at one time, though in view of the small numbers of workers covered by them this is obviously a hazardous procedure. They consist almost exclusively of skilled male workers, and, naturally, only of those – usually a minority – who were union members. They tend to over-represent industries which were vulnerable to cyclical employment fluctuations, although they under-represent textiles and, at least until 1889, mining, both of which normally reacted to slack demand by using short-time working rather than laying off workers completely. Moreover, they have no coverage of some of the more stable economic activities – agriculture, domestic service, and the railways, for example. The industries covered by the records changed in relative importance over the period: before 1867 the engineering, metal and shipbuilding trades were preponderant; and in the 1880s still accounted for three-fifths of the totals covered. The gradual reduction in the overriding influence of this group, and the emergence of a better balance amongst groups generally, doubtless improved the representative nature of the overall averages, but nevertheless, it did mean that comparisons made between different years are not necessarily of like with like.

For all these doubts and criticisms, the official view of the Ministry of Labour in 1926 (by which time it was possible to compare the trade union returns with insurance data) was that for the period after 1881, 'the general percentages provide a valuable guide to the direction of the changes in unemployment and a rough indication of the comparative state of employment at different periods, although they cannot be relied upon as an absolute measure of the total amount of unemployment in all industries at any particular date'.[7]

Various attempts have been made to adjust and improve the trade union returns. Feinstein summarises the best of these and links them to his own adjustments of the insurance data. The resulting statistics are shown here in table 8. It is likely that these adjusted trade union figures are indeed an improvement on the representative nature of the series, but as Feinstein notes: 'It does not appear to be possible to make any statistical assessment of the possible under- and over-statement involved in the use of the trade union series as a measure of the *general* unemployment rate.'[8] Feinstein's adjustment to the insurance data has been

[6] (Cambridge, 1985).

[7] In a memorandum submitted to the Balfour Committee on Trade and Industry and published in its *Survey of Industrial Relations* (H.M.S.O., 1926), pp. 218–19. Further discussion of the reliability of this material can be found on pp. 244–5.

[8] C. H. Feinstein, *National Income, Expenditure and Output of the United Kingdom, 1856–1965* (Cambridge, 1972, p. 225. Feinstein incorporates the Board of Trade 'corrections' to 1881, leaves them uncorrected for 1882–1911, and uses Hilton's adjustments from 1912 (as given in his 'Statistics of Unemployment Derived from the Working of the Unemployment Insurance Acts', *Journal of the Royal Statistical Society*, LXXXVI (1923).

characterised as, if anything, an overestimate – by Booth and Glyn[9] – and probably an underestimate – by Garside. However, there is no way of proving either proposition, and, as Garside eventually concludes, 'it will remain a matter of conjecture how far the available unemployment data are a reasonably accurate guide to conditions over the entire period from the 1860s to 1939'.[10]

It is rather surprising that the trade union Royal Commission and the legislation of the 1860s and 1870s did not lead to the establishment of more annual returns on labour matters in the way that the wages enquiry of 1886 eventually did. But, in fact, it was not until then that, with the establishment of the Labour Department, official series of trade union membership and finances and of industrial disputes began to be collected and published. These series, shown in tables 13 to 18, are believed to be both complete, to all intents and purposes, and reliable. The break caused by the partition of Ireland is much less important in these (as in practically all labour series) than might have been expected, because of the smallness of its industrial workforce. Its size may be gauged from the separate southern Irish figures in tables 14 and 18.

By far the most detailed study of hours of work in Britain is Bienefeld's book,[11] which summarises (and discusses and offers an explanation for) the scattered material which exists prior to the second half of the nineteenth century. But it nevertheless remains just that – scattered. Essentially, no firm and consistent *series* exists until after the First World War, other than that created by Matthews, Feinstein, and Odling-Smee, which is shown here as table 19. From 1920, however, the Ministry of Labour published statistics of 'normal' hours (shown here as table 20), and from 1940 they also collected data on actual hours worked, which have not been included here because of limitations of space.

In travelling backwards from the twentieth century to the nineteenth, the student of wages passes from a highway, not without its twists and turns, to a thorny path; but in passing to earlier periods he crosses into a morass with but few firm places.[12] In the present century, a great deal of information on wages is available, and this has been used to produce statistics relating to rates of pay which have been generally accepted as definitive. It is true that these are, generally speaking, to be regarded as minimum (or standard) rates, rather than average ones, and that they are still further removed from average earnings. But prior to the First World War, these distinctions were of less importance than they became later, for normal hours of work were much longer, and overtime working was less frequent. And after 1919 separate data on earnings become available, such as those shown here in tables 34 to 36. A more serious difficulty with the wage rate statistics before 1914 is that national agreements or awards were few. Indices, which were compiled officially from 1874, were therefore based on a selection of representative grades, industries, and places – or so it was hoped.

[9] A. E. Booth and Sean Glyn, 'Unemployment in the Interwar Period: a Multiple Problem', *Journal of Contemporary History* (1975), pp. 613–14.

[10] W. R. Garside, *op. cit.*, pp. 59–60.

[11] M. A. Bienefeld, *Working Hours in British Industry: An Economic History* (London, 1972).

[12] J. E. T. Rogers, *A History of Agriculture and Prices in England* (7 vols., Oxford, 1866–1902).

For earlier in the nineteenth century a fair amount of rather scattered material is available, much of which has been organised into a reasonably comprehensive statistical picture. But before 1800 or so, with one major group of exceptions, even scattered references are quite scarce – scarcer, indeed, as Thorold Rogers found, for the eighteenth century than for some earlier periods. Such eighteenth-century references as there are in Rogers's work, moreover, are subject to the major criticism that they are not in the main critically examined and qualitatively assessed, and that they are not differentiated by regions.

The major group of exceptions referred to is the building trades, for which Phelps-Brown and Hopkins produced indices going back to 1264 (together with a crude index of prices to enable approximations to real wages to be calculated). The most important of their series are reproduced here as tables 30 and 31. The bases of their work were Rogers' wage data to 1700, and material collected by Elizabeth Gilboy for the eighteenth century and by Bowley for the nineteenth, together with price data from Rogers and from Beveridge,[13] which were mainly wholesale or institutional rather than retail. Their wage data, on the whole, have escaped serious criticism, save perhaps that they are stronger for craftsmen than for labourers; but their price series have not. Indeed, they themselves were the first to point to many of the drawbacks – lack of continuity in some components, difficulties in dealing with new commodities, the high volatility of wholesale prices (and the stability of institutional prices), and so on. For all that, it is not yet possible to propose any fundamental alteration to their indices, though a continuous and smoother series, involving no spurious sharp jumps, was offered by Wrigley and Schofield, albeit rather tentatively.[14]

The importance of regional variations, both in the level and the direction of wage movements, is brought out fully in the only major published work on eighteenth-century wages since Rogers, that of Elizabeth Gilboy. However, this is itself limited in scope by the scarcity of information, and in particular by the fact that it relates mainly to the building trades and to agriculture, and therefore tells us little about the wages of those in industrial occupations, which were probably more flexible. This limitation should be born in mind when using both the Phelps Brown and Hopkins and the Gilboy indices. For full details about the construction of these – as, indeed, of all indices in this chapter – the original sources must be consulted. Here it is sufficient to say that, though Gilboy's cost-of-living index is mainly based on institutional prices, we may accept as still valid today her view that 'crude as our index is, it is based on the most complete, consistent, and homogeneous series now available'.[15]

A major synthesis of existing data on eighteenth- and early nineteenth-century wages was undertaken by Flinn in 1974,[16] which is still of great value despite minor critical comments

[13] See the notes on sources to tables 21, 24 and 25, and W. H. Beveridge *et al.*, *Prices and Wages in England*, vol. 1 (London, 1939).
[14] *op cit.*, appendix 9.
[15] E. W. Gilboy, 'The Cost of Living and Real Wages in Eighteenth-Century England', *The Review of Economic Statistics* (1936), p. 141.
[16] M. W. Flinn, 'Trends in Real Wages, 1750–1850', *Economic History Review*, second series XXVII, 3 (1974).

from Gourvish and Von Tunzelmann.[17] But the most important effort made actually to improve the data on wages for the eighteenth and early nineteenth centuries since Gilboy's has been that of Lindert and Williamson, who have added several new series, mainly for service occupations. These were converted into annual full-time earnings estimates, and by means of a new cost-of-living index, into real earnings – without allowance for unemployment or short-time working, of course, though these are discussed in the source. These are shown in tables 22 and 23. The main criticisms of these statistics have related to the cost-of-living index, though most people would probably agree with Crafts that it is, in fact, 'better suited to the measurement of changes in workers' purchasing power than earlier price indices'.[18] It is more appropriately weighted, it is more comprehensive, and it makes at least a gesture in including a rent component, though the basis for this is confined to a few dozen cottages in Trentham, Staffordshire. Nevertheless, criticisms have been levelled both at this rent limitation and its treatment of clothing prices, and Lindert and Williamson partially accepted the latter.[19] The resulting revisions are incorporated in the tables here.

As has been said, most of the criticism of Lindert and Williamson's work has concentrated on their cost-of-living indices. However, their wage series, though certainly more comprehensive than previous ones, cannot go entirely without comment. Their use of Bowley and Wood's indices of colliers' wages will certainly tend to understate the rise in wages, especially for the period up to 1820, for which their figures derive from the still relatively well-paid Scottish miners. But there is likely to be an opposite tendency springing from the absence from their component groups of any of those workers whose position was most drastically affected at some time or other by changing technology. The handloom weavers, the nailers, the woolcombers, the coachmen, for instance, are not represented. It may well be, therefore, that Lindert and Williamson's conclusions about average annual earnings are, for this reason, too 'optimistic', especially for the period from about 1820 onwards – and, maybe, insufficiently 'optimistic' twenty or thirty years earlier. These same omissions surely also undermine their conclusion that changes in the occupational structure had little influence on average earnings.

That the regional variation of wage rates did not abate much until quite late in the nineteenth century is apparent from E. H. Hunt's *Regional Wage Variations in Britain, 1850–1914*.[20] However, there is a much greater variety of material available from about 1790 onwards, both regionally and occupationally, and it has been used to compile indices which have some genuine claim to be called national – though it should be borne in mind that

[17] T. R. Gourvish, 'Flinn and Real Wage Trends in Britain, 1750–1850: A Comment', *Economic History Review*, second series XXIX, 1 (1976) with a reply by Flinn; and G. N. Von Tunzelmann, 'Trends in Real Wages, 1750–1850, Revisited', *Economic History Review*, second series XXXII, 1 (1979).

[18] N. F. R. Crafts, *British Economic Growth during the Industrial Revolution* (Oxford, 1985), p. 99.

[19] In their reply to N. F. R. Crafts, 'English Workers' Real Wages During the Industrial Revolution: Some Remaining Problems', *Journal of Economic History*, XLV, 1 (1985).

[20] (Oxford, 1973).

national averages *do* conceal wide differences in local experience; and, as Hunt pertinently asks: 'Is not a great deal obscured by averages purporting to show increases in wages throughout Britain as a whole?'[21] Clearly, local studies, such as those by Neale, Gourvish, and Barnsby have shown that the answer is 'yes'.[22] However, it is worth pointing out in this connection that local studies showing little change in real wages in an area may be revealing the effects of the immigration of people from areas where wages were lower.

The main work in the field of wages during the nineteenth century was done in the 1890s and 1900s by G. H. Wood, who was in the Labour Department at the time, and by A. L. Bowley, and was published in a series of articles between 1898 and 1910.[23] The work done then has remained largely untouched, apart from some refining and continuation in Bowley's *Wages and Income since 1860*,[24] which reflects both the respect in which their work has been held, and the absence of large discoveries of new data. This work is the basis of parts A to C of table 21, and the main individual industry indices in table 25. One improvement which could undoubtedly be made to the latter would be by using the indices for coal hewers in table 32; but the changes in the overall national indices would not be large.

Although links between before and after the First World War are rather poor, as is pointed out in the notes to tables 21 and 26, by the beginning of the 1920s interest in wages was such that there was plentiful material available for the statisticians. From early in the decade two or three indices were published – notably one in the London and Cambridge Economic Service *Bulletin*,[25] a similar one in Bowley's *Wages and Income since 1860*, and one by E. C. Ramsbottom of the Ministry of Labour in the *Journal of the Royal Statistical Society*.[26] There is little difference between these indices, though the last is probably based on the most complete information, and it is the one used here in table 26 for occupational wage rates. It is also, in effect, the one incorporated into the overall average official indices shown in the last part of table 21.

With the exception of the tables based on Lindert and Williamson's work, the wage series

[21] *Ibid.*, pp. 2–3.

[22] R. S. Neale, 'The Standard of Living, 1780–1844; a Regional and Class Study', *Economic History Review*, second series, XIX, 3 (1966); T. R. Gourvish, 'The Cost of Living in Glasgow in the Early Nineteenth Century', *Economic History Review*, second series XXV, 1 (1972); G. J. Barnsby, 'The Standard of Living in the Black Country during the Nineteenth Century', *Economic History Review*, second series XXIV, 2 (1971).

[23] A. L. Bowley, 'Comparison of the Changes in Wages in France, the U.S. and the U.K. from 1840–1891', *Economic Journal* (1898); A. L. Bowley, 'Statistics of Wages in the United Kingdom during the Nineteenth Century: Agricultural Wages', *Journal of the Royal Statistical Society* (1890–1900); 'Building Trades', *ibid.* (1900); 'Printers', *ibid.* (1900); Worsted and Woollen Manufacture of the West Riding of Yorkshire', *ibid.* (1902); 'Engineering and Shipbuilding', *ibid.* (1905–6 – with G. H. Wood). G. H. Wood, 'The Course of Average Wages between 1790 and 1860', *Economic Journal* (1899). G. H. Wood, 'Real Wages and the Standard of Comfort since 1850', *Journal of the Royal Statistical Society* (1909). G. H. Wood, 'The Statistics of Wages in the United Kingdom during the Nineteenth Century: The Cotton Industry', *ibid.* (1910).

[24] (Cambridge, 1937).

[25] Summarised in A. L. Bowley, 'Index Numbers of Wage Rates and Cost of Living', *Journal of the Royal Statistical Society* CXV (1952).

[26] Issues of 1935, 1938, and 1939. Indices not published for certain years were kindly supplied to me in the 1950s by the Ministry of Labour.

referred to hitherto have been concerned with wage rates rather than earnings,[27] and this applies also to the other tables relating to individual occupational groups and to the Irish tables. Some statistics of annual earnings in the period 1736–1845 are now available for southern and eastern counties in Snell's book,[28] though they are too detailed for inclusion here. But apart from that, and a few more isolated figures, it is not until 1920 that data on earnings become readily available. Some of these are shown in the last three tables. Tables 34 and 35 cover both the averages of all wage-earners and each of the main industrial groups, based respectively on the work of Chapman and Knight and of the statisticians of the Ministry of Labour and its successors. Table 36 relates only to coal mines, but is of particular interest as a reasonably long and continuous series for a major industry.

It is perhaps necessary to make a few general comments on the wages and earnings indices shown here, for all are subject to certain disadvantages when used, as they often have been, as indicators of the standard of living. Even the earnings statistics relate to employed persons only, and whilst Wood's series in part B of table 21 attempts to allow for unemployment, it is obviously done in a very rough-and-ready fashion; and none of the other statistics even go thus far. Perhaps R. S. Tucker was right to suggest that allowance for unemployment would not alter the trend of real wages,[29] and certainly this has been argued convincingly for the first half of the nineteenth century by Lindert and Williamson, who conclude their detailed discussion by saying that 'the trend in unemployment could not have detracted greatly from the improvement in workers' real wages, and it may even have contributed to their improvement.'[30] Such conclusions, however, do not apply to individual years, such as 1858, 1879, or 1886 (and earlier, perhaps, 1841–2),[31] or to longer periods in the interwar years, and it is necessary to remember this when putting wage data into the context of discussion of living standards.

Aside from unemployment and short-time working, there are other points to bear in mind in this context. One is possible differences between individual (almost wholly male) wages and earnings about which information is relatively ample, and family earnings, about which it is difficult to say anything precise. However, there is no doubt as to the direction of the changes in the century between 1750 and 1850 at any rate, for, as McKendrick has argued, 'long hours of work for women were not new, but the machinery to make these hours of work as productive as the work of men *was* new – and so, therefore, was the motive to offer greater rewards than ever before to women workers and to employ a greater number of them than ever before . . . as separate, independent wage-earners'.[32]

27 The indices of coal hewers' shift earnings are an apparent exception, but these are much closer to a daily wage rate than to weekly, let alone annual, earnings.

28 Referred to p. 95 above.

29 R. S. Tucker, 'The Wages of London Artisans', *Journal of the American Statistical Association* (1936), p. 77.

30 Peter H. Lindert and Jeffrey G. Williamson, 'English Workers' Living Standards during the Industrial Revolution: A New Look', *Economic History Review*, second series XXXVI, 1 (1983), p. 16.

31 For which see E. J. Hobsbawm, *Labouring Men* (London, 1964), pp. 72–82 and Lindert and Williamson's comments in *loc. cit.*, p. 13.

32 Neil McKendrick in *Historical Perspectives: Studies in English Thought and Society* (London, 1974), p. 164.

Another factor is that the indices take no account of the effect on standards of living of changes in normal hours of work, which, as was indicated above, are rather inadequately documented in the first half of the nineteenth century and earlier. Yet another factor which does not show up in wages indices is the increase in services provided by the state (especially since 1907), and (since the Second World War) in employers' contributions to state or private insurance funds. Finally, there have clearly been undocumented changes, not completely reflected in prices, in the quality of the goods included in the various cost-of-living indices. An important example of this is housing; but it also applies to many manufactured goods.

Labour Force 1. Lindert & Williamson's Social Tables – England & Wales 1688, 1759, 1801/3

NOTE

SOURCE: Peter H. Lindert & Jeffrey G. Williamson, "Revising England's Social Tables 1688–1812", *Explorations in Economic History*, 19 (1982)

	1688				1759				1801/3			
	Families		Incomes		Families		Incomes		Families		Incomes	
	Numbers	% of Total	£ million	% of Total	Numbers	% of Total	£ million	% of Total	Numbers	% of Total	£ million	% of Total
High Titles and Gentlemen	19,626	1·4	8·81	16·2	18,070	1·2	11·74	17·6	27,203	1·2	27·54	13·9
Professions	42,960	3·1	4·46	8·2	57,000	3·7	5·09	7·6	74,840	3·4	17·31	8·7
Military and Maritime	94,000	6·8	2·13	3·9	86,000	5·6	2·13	3·2	244,348	11·1	10·38	5·2
Commerce (*a*)	128,025	9·2	10·90	20·0	200,500	13·0	14·01	21·0	205,800	9·4	39·21	19·7
Industry and Building	256,866	18·5	9·58	17·6	366,252	23·8	11·72	17·5	541,026	24·7	51·07	25·7
Agriculture (*b*)	227,440	16·4	12·21	22·4	379,008	24·6	16·66	24·9	320,000	14·6	38·00	19·1
Labourers (*c*)	284,997	20·5	4·27	7·8	240,000	15·6	4·20	6·3	340,000	15·5	10·54	5·3
Cottagers and Paupers (*d*)	313,183	22·5	2·04	3·7	178,892	11·6	1·25	1·9	260,179	11·9	2·60	1·3
Vagrants	23,489	1·7	0·04	0·1	13,418	0·9	0·04	0·1	179,718	8·2	1·92	1·0
TOTAL	1,390,586		54·44		1,539,140		66·84		2,193,114		198·58	

(*a*) Including tradesmen, some of whom should be in 'Industry and Building'.
(*b*) Excluding labourers.
(*c*) Including both agricultural and non-agricultural labourers in 1688 and 1759. Only "labourers in husbandry" in 1801/3, with other labourers included in 'Industry and Building'.
(*d*) 'Paupers' only in 1801/3.

Labour Force 2. Occupations at Censuses – Great Britain 1811–1981

NOTES TO PARTS A and B

[1] SOURCES: *Census Reports*, 1811–1921.

[2] For part B slight modifications have been made to the census categories of 1911 in order to achieve comparability over a greater period than would otherwise have been possible. The main occupations under each heading (where these are not obvious) and the modifications of the 1911 census categories are detailed below. The major general difference between this part and part C is that in 1911 and earlier censuses, owners, general labourers, and dealers were so far as possible counted according to the raw material with which they worked. In addition to this major break, there is another of almost as great significance between 1871 and 1881. In the former and earlier censuses, retired persons were included in the occupation which they had formerly followed, if this was stated by them.

Modified 1911 Categories – Principal Features

(i) *Public Administration* – includes government messengers and clerks and Post Office Workers, but not telephonists and telegraphists (except for Scotland in 1911 only).
(ii) *Armed Forces* – includes retired officers, but not other-rank pensioners.
(iii) *Professional Occupations, etc.* – includes professional entertainers and sportsmen. Veterinary surgeons have been excluded throughout, as have chemists and druggists.
(iv) *Domestic Offices, etc.* – catering trades and hairdressers are included, but domestic coachmen, grooms and gardeners have been excluded (except as indicated in note 3).
(v) *Transport, etc.* – government telephonists and telegraphists, and domestic coachmen and grooms are included (except as indicated in note 3).
(vi) *Commercial Occupations* – includes clerks and typists (though not railway clerks except in 1841).
(vii) *Agriculture, etc.* – veterinary surgeons and domestic gardeners are included.
(viii) *Metal Manufacture, etc.* – includes those engaged in making musical and surgical instruments, games tackle, toys, etc. All builders of vehicles and ships are included, whether using wood or metal. Gasfitters, plumbers, locksmiths, and their assistants have been excluded.
(ix) *Wood, etc.* – includes French polishers, undertakers, cane and cork workers, carvers and gilders.
(x) *Building, etc.* – includes carpenters, gasfitters, plumbers, locksmiths, and their assistants.
(xi) *Chemicals, etc.* – includes chemists and druggists, and workers in rubber and waterproof goods.
(xii) *Clothing* – hairdressers and wigmakers are excluded. Boot and shoe makers and repairers are in this category.
(xiii) *Food, Drink, and Tobacco* – the catering trades are excluded.

This modified classification has been followed so far as possible in all years from 1841–1921, though changes in each census render exact comparisons usually impossible. A vertical line has been inserted wherever an approximate comparison is inappropriate.

[3] The 1841 census is particularly difficult to splice on to later figures, since there was scarcely any classification of occupations by the compilers. The following are the principal causes of lack of comparability between 1841 and later years:

Public Administration – some who would later have been included under this heading were simply described as messengers and are included under *Transport and Communications*; others, who were also engaged in trade, are included with *All Others Occupied*.

Professional Occupations, etc. – nurses were returned as domestic servants in Scotland in 1841 (and may have been in England also to a fair extent).

Domestic Offices, etc. – many who in later censuses were returned as domestic coachmen, grooms, and gardeners, were simply described as servants in 1841, thus greatly swelling this category so far as males are concerned.

Commercial Occupations – includes railway clerks in 1841, and also, it seems clear, many who were described as clerks in 1841 who would later have been more precisely defined, and attributed to other categories.

Transport, etc. – many domestic coachmen and grooms were not included in 1841, nor were railway clerks. From the very small number of dockers returned in 1841, it must be presumed that many described themselves as general labourers, and so are included in *All Others Occupied*.

[4] The 1841 census describes as unoccupied many who would later have been assigned to an occupation. This is clear from a comparison of the Totals Occupied and Unoccupied in 1841 and 1851. At the later date there appears to have been a decline of over half-a-million men unoccupied and an increase in the women occupied of over a million. Changes of this magnitude are clearly due to differences in the methods and efficiency of enumeration.

[5] The 1841 figures include Islands in the British Seas. The totals occupied in these islands were 29,663 males and 11,898 females, and the totals unoccupied aged 20 and over were 4,753 males and 29,424 females.

[6] The 1911 census reference numbers of occupations used for each heading here are: *Public Administration* 2–9, *Armed Forces* 10–18, *Professional Occupations, etc.* 19–29 and 31–49, *Domestic Offices, etc.* 50–51, 55–65, 396, and 425–432, *Commercial Occupations* 66–77, *Transport, etc.* 78–116, *Agriculture, etc.* 30, 54, and 117–129, *Fishing* 130, *Mining, etc.* 131–154, *Metal Manufacture, etc.* 155–200 and 203–241, *Building, etc.* 84–85, 201–202, and 242–265, *Wood, etc.* 266–282, *Bricks, etc.* 283–290, *Chemicals, etc.* 291–307, 363, and 447, *Skins, etc.* 308–315, *Paper, etc.* 316–334 and 439–441, *Textiles* 335–375, *Clothing* 376–395, 397–399, and 467 (females only), *Food, etc.* 400–424, and 433, *Gas, etc. Supply* 434–436.

[7] The following numbers of children under ten years old were recorded as occupied:

	1851	1861	1871
Males	26,492	22,755	11,592
Females	15,434	13,760	10,244

With these exceptions, and unrecorded numbers in 1841 and 1881 (the latter very small), the figures for the years before 1921 apply to persons over ten years old. Those for 1921 apply to people of at least twelve years old.

[8] So far as possible, those not gainfully employed are included in the heading *Total Unoccupied*. For 1871 and earlier censuses, therefore, persons returned as land proprietors, house proprietors, capitalists, students, wives (of all kinds), farmers' female relatives, Chelsea pensioners, etc. have been counted as unoccupied. In order to maintain comparability over as long a period as possible, farmers' wives and female relatives have continued to be counted as unoccupied throughout part B.

A. 1811–41

(in thousands)

	Number of Families			Males 20 or over	
	1811	1821	1831	1831	1841
Agricultural Occupations	896	979	961	1,243	1,208
Trade, Manufactures, and Handicraft	1,129	1,350	1,435	1,564	2,028
Others	519	612	1,018	1,137	1,422

Labour Force 2. *continued*

B. 1841–1921 – based on the 1911 Census Categories

(in thousands)

Males	1841	1851	1861	1871	1881	1891	1901	1911	1921
Public Administration	40	64	72	106	109	146	191	271	383
Armed Forces	51	63	118	124	114	134	176	221	250
Professional Occupations and their Subordinate Services (*a*)	113	162	179	204	254	287	348	413	415
Domestic Offices and Personal Services	255	193	195	230	238	293	341	456	371
Commercial Occupations	94	91	130	212	352	449	597	739	904
Transport and Communications	196	433	579	654	870	1,104	1,409	1,571	1,530
of which: railways	2	29	60	96	157	212	318	370	354
roads	70	139	193	229	315	407	565	600	595
sea, canals and docks	76	153	202	191	205	235	263	292	311
Agriculture, Horticulture and Forestry	1,434	1,788	1,779	1,634	1,517	1,422	1,339	1,436	1,344
Fishing	24	36	39	47	58	53	51	53	51
Mining and Quarrying, and Workers in the Products of Mines and Quarries	218	383	457	517	604	751	931	1,202	1,240
Metal Manufacture, Machines, Implements, Vehicles, Precious Metals, etc.	396	536	747	869	977	1,151	1,485	1,795	2,125
Building and Construction	376	496	593	712	875	899	1,216	1,140	894
Wood, Furniture, Fittings, and Decorations	107	152	171	186	185	206	267	287	511
Bricks, Cement, Pottery, and Glass	48	75	93	97	111	119	152	145	100
Chemicals, Oil, Soap, Resin, etc.	23	42	47	61	72	89	116	155	93
Skins, Leather, Hair, and Feathers	47	55	61	68	73	80	87	90	72
Paper, Printing, Books, and Stationery	44	62	79	94	134	178	212	253	193
Textiles	525	661	612	584	554	593	557	639	409
Clothing	358	418	413	399	379	409	423	432	315
Food, Drink, and Tobacco	268	348	386	448	494	597	701	806	228
Gas, Water, and Electricity Supply	2	7	12	18	24	38	62	86	...
All Others Occupied	474	490	510	917	851	1,009	887	741	2,130
TOTAL OCCUPIED (*b*)	5,093	6,554	7,271	8,182	8,844	10,010	11,548	12,930	13,670
Total Unoccupied (*b*)	1,604	1,041	1,054	1,169	1,778	2,028	2,242	2,515	2,002
Females	1841	1851	1861	1871	1881	1891	1901	1911	1921
Public Administration	3	3	4	7	9	17	29	50	81
Armed Forces	—	—	—	—	—	—	—	—	..
Professional Occupations and their Subordinate Services (*a*)	49	103	126	152	203	264	326	383	441
Domestic Offices and Personal Services	989	1,135	1,407	1,678	1,756	2,036	2,003	2,127	1,845
Commercial Occupations	1	..	2	5	11	26	76	157	587
Transport and Communications	4	13	11	16	15	20	27	38	72
of which: railways	..	..	..	..	1	1	2	3	3
roads	1	3	3	3	2	2	1	3	7
sea, canals and docks	..	3	1	1	1	1	1	1	3
Agriculture, Horticulture, and Forestry	81	229	163	135	116	80	67	60	90
Fishing	..	1	1	1	3	1	..	..	..
Mining and Quarrying, and Workers in the Products of Mines and Quarries	7	11	6	11	8	7	6	8	9
Metal Manufacture, Machines, Implements, Vehicles, Precious Metals, etc.	14	36	45	46	49	59	84	128	175
Building and Construction	1	1	1	4	2	3	3	5	5
Wood, Furniture, Fittings, and Decorations	5	8	15	26	21	25	30	35	31
Bricks, Cement, Pottery and Glass	10	15	19	25	27	32	37	42	45
Chemicals, Oil, Soap, Resin, etc.	1	4	3	5	9	17	31	46	35
Skins, Leather, Hair, and Feathers	3	5	8	10	16	20	27	32	33
Paper, Printing, Books, and Stationery	6	16	23	31	53	78	111	144	12
Textiles	358	635	676	726	745	795	795	870	70
Clothing	200	491	596	594	667	759	792	825	60
Food, Drink, and Tobacco	42	53	71	78	98	163	216	308	12
Gas, Water, and Electricity Supply	—	—	..	..	..	..	..	..	...
All Others Occupied (*b*)	41	61	76	21	81	89	75	98	68
TOTAL OCCUPIED (*b*)	1,815	2,819	3,252	3,570	3,887(*c*)	4,489(*c*)	4,732	5,356	5,684
Total Unoccupied (*b*)	5,369	5,192	5,762	6,535	7,567(*c*)	8,572(*c*)	10,247	11,432	11,983

(*a*) Includes persons engaged in entertainment and sport.

(*b*) The Total Occupied, like the items above it, includes children under 10 years of age, whereas the Total Unoccupied does not.

(*c*) These figures were calculated by assuming where necessary (i.e. Scotland in 1881 and 1891, England and Wales in 1881) that all children in the 5–14 age-group who were occupied were aged 10 or over.

NOTES TO PART C

[1] SOURCES: *Census Reports*, 1921–51.

[2] The Standard Industrial Classification as used in the 1951 census has been adopted here with one exception, namely the formation of the heading *Public Administration*. The principal features to be noted are:

(i) *Public Administration* – composed of Civil Service and Local Authority Officials and staff (other than clerks and typists in 1931 and 1951, but including them in 1921), and the police force.

(ii) *Armed Forces* – only effectives are counted.

(iii) *Professional and Technical Occupations* – includes veterinary surgeons.

(iv) *Commercial, etc. Occupations* – wholesale and retail dealers are included.

(v) *Metal Manufacture, etc.* – includes plumbers and gasfitters and some categories which in 1911 came under the heading of gas, water and electricity supply.

(vi) *Wood, etc.* – includes carpenters, but not upholsterers or bedding and mattress workers.

(vii) *Building, etc.* – does not include plumbers, gasfitters or carpenters.

(viii) *Treatment of Non-Metalliferous Mining Products other than Coal* – corresponds closely to the 1911 heading bricks, cement, pottery and glass.

(ix) *Coal-gas and Coke, Chemicals, etc.* – includes many who came under the heading gas, water and electricity supply in 1911, and no longer includes workers in rubber or waterproof goods.

(x) *Textile Goods and Clothing* – includes upholsterers and bedding mattress workers.

(xi) *Administrators, etc.* – higher Civil Service and Local Authority officials are here excluded.

[3] The figures for 1921 relate to persons of twelve years old and over, those for 1931 to 14-year-olds and over, and those for 1951 to all aged fifteen and over.

C. 1921–51 – based on the 1951 Census categories

(in thousands)

	Males			Females		
	1921	1931	1951	1921	1931	1951
Public Administration	261	141	214	78	3	21
Armed Forces	221	189	560	..	—	18
Professional and Technical Occupations	378	490	788	408	443	588
Professional Entertainers and Sportsmen	74	100	90	30	24	23
Personal Service	372	516	512	1,845	2,129	1,610
Commercial Finance and Insurance Occupations (excluding clerical staff)	1,180	1,621	1,357	579	701	856
Clerks, Typists, etc.	581	778	932	492	648	1,409
Transport and Communications	1,591	1,748	1,569	75	82	149
of which: railways	354	303	310	3	2	8
roads	595	761	811	7	8	37
sea, canals and docks	311	303	217	3	2	1
Agriculture, Horticulture and Forestry	1,341	1,282	1,105	107	71	114
Fishing	51	40	26	..	..	..
Mining and Quarrying	1,204	1,083	675	7	4	2
Metal Manufacture, Engineering and Allied Trades	1,888	1,765	2,517	123	147	208
Building and Contracting (including Painting and Decorating)	738	970	1,268	10	17	14
Wood, Cane and Cork (including Furniture)	453	497	492	10	8	15
Treatment of Non-Metalliferous Mining Products other than Coal	69	82	86	36	46	48
Coal, Gas and Coke, Chemicals and Allied Trades	41	52	102	4	5	14
Leather, Leather Goods (including boots and shoes) and Fur	178	178	125	59	66	67
Paper, Books and Printing	155	178	178	97	108	93
Textiles	314	324	220	634	663	413
Textile Goods and Clothing (other than boots and shoes)	155	164	135	544	544	474
Food, Drink and Tobacco	147	161	175	77	73	97
Administrators and Managers in Extractive or Manufacturing Industries	287	350	347	25	26	30
Warehousemen, Storekeepers, Packers, Bottlers, etc.	243	268	379	141	162	199
All Others Occupied	1,749	1,851	1,794	319	317	497
TOTAL OCCUPIED	13,656	14,790	15,649	5,701	6,265	6,961
Total Unoccupied	2,016	1,552	2,213	11,966	12,055	13,084

NOTES TO PART D

[1] SOURCE: Census *Report*, 1961 (General Volume).

[2] The new classification of occupations used in 1961 'introduced a number of changes in principle which make it impossible to make direct comparisons even between fairly large aggregates of occupation codes' between 1961 and earlier censuses. The figures shown here result from an attempt to make a comparison between 1951 and 1961 by recording a sub-sample of 100,000 out of the 10 per cent sample part of the 1961 data to the occupation code they would have had in 1951. The 1961 figures were not adjusted for sample bias.

D. 1951–1961, England & Wales – based on 1951 Census

(in thousands)

	Males		Females	
	1951	1961	1951	1961
Agriculture, Horticulture, and Forestry	961·3	741·4	97·5	70·8
Fishing	15·2	10·8	—	—
Mining and Quarrying	589·7	469·6	1·3	0·2
Treatment of Non-Metalliferous Mining Products (other than coal)	81·2	76·6	46·4	40·2
Gas and Coke Manufacture, and Chemicals and Allied Trades	93·0	108·8	11·1	10·0
Metal Manufacture, Engineering, and Allied Trades	2,260·2	2,460·6	197·9	199·6
Textiles	197·6	144·6	359·1	245·4
Leather, Leather Goods, and Fur	116·9	83·6	64·9	65·2
Clothing, etc. (other than shoes)	124·2	96·8	437·2	364·4
Food, Drink, and Tobacco	148·9	134·8	83·9	65·6
Wood, Cane, and Cork	433·3	428·4	13·3	12·0
Paper and Printing	161·7	200·8	81·1	84·4
Other Manufactures	84·5	94·2	40·7	43·4
Building and Contracting	840·5	838·2	1·4	1·0
Painting and Decorating	298·6	283·0	10·4	9·2
Administrators, Managers (n.e.s.), and Directors	406·2	525·6	45·9	67·6
Transport and Communications	1,403·7	1,400·4	130·1	147·6
Commerce, Finance, and Insurance (excl. clerical staff)	1,227·5	1,462·4	757·8	910·6
Professional and Technical Occupations (excl. clerical staff)	714·2	1,108·0	523·1	674·6
Armed Forces	527·7	295·4	16·7	11·2
Civilian Defence Services	158·2	190·8	2·9	2·4
Entertainment and Sport	82·1	77·0	21·7	21·8
Personal Service	465·6	492·4	1,464·1	1,555·8
Clerks, Typists, etc.	861·7	956·2	1,270·5	1,725·4
Warehousemen, Storekeepers, Packers, and Bottlers	348·3	398·8	181·2	213·6
Stationary Engine Drivers, Crane Drivers, Tractor Drivers, etc.	225·9	226·0	2·0	1·8
Workers in Unskilled Occupations (not elsewhere specified)	1,118·9	1,193·6	378·4	437·0
Others	116·7	150·2	32·4	64·6

NOTES TO PART E

[1] SOURCES: *Census Reports*, 1961–81.

[2] The 1961 figures for England & Wales and the 1981 figures are based on a 10% sample.

E. 1961–1981 – based on 1961/1971 Census Categories

(in thousands)

	Males					Females				
	England & Wales 1961	Scotland 1961	England & Wales 1971	Scotland 1971	Great Britain 1981	England & Wales 1961	Scotland 1961	England & Wales 1971	Scotland 1971	Great Britain 1981
Agriculture, Horticulure, and Forestry	739·84	119·37	542·20	84·72	518·42	78·46	10·33	81·38	9·75	80·06
Fishing	14·31	9·42	10·17	6·07	14·58	—	0·02	0·05	0·11	0·08
Mining and Quarrying	457·55	69·16	228·81	27·76	163·25	0·35	0·09	0·44	0·04	0·65
Gas, Coke, and Chemical Manufacture	117·95	11·41	114·30	11·88	108·13	13·33	2·36	11·28	1·89	11·14
Glass and Ceramics	65·85	5·12	59·34	3·99	47·89	35·76	1·07	28·11	0·81	18·89
Furnaces, Forges, Foundries, and Rolling Mills	205·16	25·16	144·73	14·81	113·94	10·24	0·80	8·31	0·62	7·94
Electrical and Electronic Goods	433·31	45·12	478·17	51·15	535·35	54·57	1·38	81·02	7·85	76·84
Engineering and Allied Trades	2,157·06	224·03	2,279·68	219·71	2,286·11	252·66	19·56	273·07	21·50	189·17
Woodworking	392·69	52·90	366·15	49·00	383·06	10·53	0·77	11·65	0·63	9·52
Leatherworking	86·51	5·55	54·58	2·54	35·39	62·97	2·05	55·42	1·54	33·48
Textiles	146·70	21·38	126·10	16·78	81·49	252·37	45·32	139·94	26·55	94·30
Clothing	86·04	7·04	72·50	5·75	65·02	361·43	29·22	297·60	31·48	230·86
Food, Drink, and Tobacco	253·28	41·09	228·79	33·10	232·42	88·03	13·88	96·84	17·06	96·35
Paper and Printing	202·87	19·70	202·75	16·92	195·95	100·12	13·23	84·77	10·87	81·44
Other Manufactures	173·76	11·02	192·75	13·93	177·95	118·13	5·23	103·05	5·95	107·08
Construction	513·75	56·31	500·30	52·42	616·70	0·50	0·05	1·56	0·11	4·65
Painting and Decorating	294·38	28·04	253·46	25·57	258·60	11·92	1·51	7·84	0·76	6·97
Drivers of Stationary Engines, Cranes, etc.	280·12	30·44	274·64	33·24	247·90	2·79	0·17	3·52	0·29	4·20
Labourers (not elsewhere specified)	1,100·32	142·58	965·75	135·44	802·76	91·91	5·81	121·56	13·14	57·27
Transport and Communications	1,236·22	147·25	1,141·24	125·60	1,141·01	131·35	16·83	140·20	15·46	157·89
Warehousemen, Storekeepers, Packers, and Bottlers	478·25	45·58	459·77	42·64	473·51	274·93	26·60	270·22	25·39	285·44
Clerical Workers	1,045·38	91·74	995·68	79·73	894·79	1,795·97	176·97	2,280·14	206·37	2,856·18
Sales Workers	1,165·12	114·23	1,085·37	95·90	1,164·52	898·05	112·60	947·40	116·15	1,081·27
Services, Sport and Recreation	740·28	80·95	824·83	86·09	1,056·00	1,512·72	161·57	1,837·15	204·06	2,236·75
Administrators and Managers	562·63	40·06	787·96	57·16	1,139·16	38·53	1·89	72·96	5·04	203·43
Professional and Technical Services, and Artists	1,172·77	106·39	1,545·03	137·61	1,982·28	707·32	82·37	956·43	110·11	1,517·16
Armed Forces	296·56	20·85	220·30	20·99	242·96	11·52	0·89	11·31	0·64	18·08
Inadequately described	231·42	11·50	251·71	23·43	547·57	128·93	3·89	339·91	35·01	410·59
TOTAL POPULATION AGED 15 AND OVER (*a*)	16,992·30	1,818·49	19,496·10	1,813·40		18,705·94	2,052·37	21,438·90	2,050·23	
Total Economically Inactive	2,343·22	235·10	3,612·20	339·53		11,660·55	1,315·91	12,301·40	1,181·10	

(*a*) These figures are sums of the economically active and inactive, and because of sample bias are slightly larger than the recorded totals aged 15 and over.

Labour Force 3. Occupations at Censuses – Ireland 1871–1971

NOTES TO PART A

[1] SOURCES: Census Reports, 1881–1911

[2] Since the same detail is not available in the Irish censuses up to 1911 as in those for Great Britain, it has not been possible to achieve so high a degree of comparability between years as in table 2. The remarks in note 2 to Parts A and B of table 2 apply to this table, however, with the exception that the following categories have been left as they were defined in each census: Public Administration (except the army); Professional Occupations; Transport and Communications; Agriculture etc. (including people "working about animals"); Metal Manufacture etc.; Building and Construction.

A. Ireland 1871–1911

(in thousands)

	Males					Females				
	1871	1811	1891	1901	1911	1871	1881	1891	1901	1911
Public Administration (*a*)	25	27	27	30	32	1	1	3	4	3
Armed Forces	37	40	38	32	34	—	—	—	—	—
Professional Occupations and their Subordinate Services (*b*)	30	31	31	31	38	17	20	23	25	34
Domestic Offices and Personal Services (*c*)	60	40	41	33	32	363	241	226	199	150
Commercial Occupations	21	22	28	35	39	1	1	2	5	9
Transport and Communications	53	48	53	58	62	1	1	1	1	1
Agriculture, Horticulture, and Forestry	879	891	834	780	713	98	96	91	86	59
Fishing	9	11	11	10	9	..	..	..	..	..
Mining and Quarrying	4	3	2	3	2	—	—	—	—	..
Metal Manufacture, Machines, Implements, Vehicles, Precious Metals, etc.	42	39	42	47	52	1	..	1	..	..
Building and Construction	50	49	47	54	52	..	..	..	..	..
Wood, Furniture, Fittings, and Decorations	15	13	12	11	10	1	1	1	1	1
Bricks, Cement, Pottery, and Glass	1	1	1	1	1	..	..	..	..	..
Chemicals, Oils, Soap, Resin, etc.	..	1	2	2	3	..	..	..	..	..
Skins, Leather, Hair, and Feathers	1	2	2	1	1	1	3	1	..	..
Paper, Printing, Books, and Stationery	6	7	7	7	8	2	3	4	4	4
Textiles	60	48	46	38	37	134	82	84	72	68
Clothing	48	43	38	32	30	128	118	116	106	66
Food, Drink, and Tobacco	42	46	46	46	43	14	13	13	12	10
Gas and Water Supply	1	1	1	2	2	—	..	..	—	—
All Others Occupied	265	169	150	155	180	77	39	28	31	24
TOTAL OCCUPIED	1,635	1,572	1,504	1,414	1,387	1,242(*d*)	815	641	550	430
Total Unoccupied	78(*e*)	961	815	786	805	213(*d*)	1,827(*e*)	1,744	1,709	1,768

(*a*) including naval personnel.

(*b*) including persons engaged in recreational activities but excluding unspecified students.

(*c*) including the catering trades.

(*d*) including wives as occupied.

(*e*) over 16 years old only.

Labour Force 3. *continued*

NOTES TO PARTS B and C.

[1] SOURCES: *Census Reports* for Northern Ireland, 1926–71.

[2] Part B is based on the 1951 census categories and Part C on those of 1961.

B. Northern Ireland, 1926–51

(in thousands)

	Males		Females	
	1926	1951	1926	1951
Armed Forces	4·3	8·3	1·4	0·6
Professional and Technical Occupations	8·6	16·0	9·6	14·1
Professional Entertainers and Sportsmen	1·4	2·3	0·3	0·2
Personal Service	8·3	10·7	41·0	32·9
Commercial, Finance and Insurance Occupations (excluding clerical staff)	34·3	36·6	13·4	16·9
Clerks, Typists, etc.	10·2	16·6	9·4	25·5
Transport and Communications	30·7	37·4	0·8	1·6
Agriculture, Horticulture, and Forestry	134·0	99·1	15·9	5·9
Fishing	1·1	..	0·8	..
Mining and Quarrying	2·2	2·8	..	—
Metal Manufacture, Engineering, and Allied Trades	38·2	47·0	..	0·7
Building and Contracting (including Painting and Decorating)	22·8	35·2	..	..
Wood, Cane, and Cork (including furniture)	14·4	14·0	..	..
Treatment of Non-metalliferous Mining Products other than Coal	1·6	0·9	..	0·4
Coal, Gas, Coke, Chemicals and Allied Trades	0·6	0·7	..	..
Leather, Leather Goods (including Boots and Shoes), and Fur	3·5	2·2	0·1	0·5
Paper, Books and Printing	3·0	2·1	2·0	1·4
Textiles	24·2	11·5	47·6	32·7
Textile Goods and Clothing (other than Boots and Shoes)	5·9	3·6	34·2	31·3
Food, Drink, and Tobacco	6·9	2·0	5·2	4·4
Administrators and Managers in Industry	4·3	8·3	1·4	0·6
Warehousemen, Storekeepers, Packers, Bottlers, etc.	4·8	6·5	1·4	3·0
All Others Occupied	23·9	53·6	0·9	9·8
TOTAL OCCUPIED	390	421	180	183
Total Unoccupied	70	65	325	346

C. Northern Ireland, 1961–1971

	Males		Females	
	1961	1971	1961	1971
Agriculture, Horticulture, and Forestry	75·4	47·2	3·2	2·1
Fishing	0·7	0·8	—	—
Mining and Quarrying	1·3	0·9	..	..
Gas, Coke, and Chemical Manufacture	1·5	4·9	0·1	0·2
Glass and Ceramics	0·8	1·0	0·4	0·5
Furnaces, Forges, Foundries and Rolling Mills	2·1	1·1	..	..
Electrical and Electronic Goods	9·4	12·7	0·9	3·3
Engineering and Allied Trades	43·4	47·5	1·1	1·9
Woodworking	13·1	13·7	0·1	0·1
Leatherworking	1·5	1·3	0·7	1·5
Textiles	9·0	8·6	20·4	9·3
Clothing	3·0	2·7	29·7	23·9
Food, Drink, and Tobacco	9·4	10·6	6·2	5·4
Paper and Printing	2·6	2·8	2·0	1·4
Other Manufactures	2·0	6·2	1·5	1·9
Construction	13·3	18·5	..	..
Painting and Decorating	6·2	6·1	0·1	0·1
Drivers of Stationary Engines, Cranes, etc.	5·2	7·3	..	..
Labourers (not elsewhere specified)	51·9	42·0	0·7	1·0
Transport and Communications	35·0	30·9	1·3	1·9
Warehousemen, Storekeepers, Packers, and Bottlers	9·9	10·9	6·2	5·3
Clerical Workers	18·9	20·5	33·1	44·2
Sales Workers	36·1	32·0	21·2	23·3
Services, Sport, and Recreation	22·0	23·1	37·2	43·6
Administrators and Managers	7·6	11·1	0·5	0·8
Professional and Technical Services, and Artists	22·9	32·8	18·6	27·2
Armed Forces	6·6	11·6	0·3	0·1
Inadequately described	4·4	3·0	1·5	1·4
TOTAL POPULATION AGED 15 AND OVER	483	515	530	557
Total Economically Inactive	67	103	343	356

Labour Force 3. *continued*

NOTES TO PART D.

[1] SOURCES: *Census Reports* for the Republic of Ireland, 1926–1971.

[2] The main difference between the classification up to 1951 and that used subsequently is the earlier inclusion of proprietors, managers and foremen in the industrial categories. The second column for 1951 is an attempt to derive figures comparable with later censuses.

D. Republic of Ireland, 1926–71

(in thousands)

	Males							Females						
	1926	1936	1946	1951	1951	1961	1971	1926	1936	1946	1951	1951	1961	1971
Agriculture, Horticulture, and Forestry	550	537	512	445	445	348	261	122	107	82	68	68	42	25
Fishing	6	4	4	3	3	2	3	..	..	..	..	..	—	..
Mining and Quarrying	3	3	3	4	4	6	5	..	..	..	..	..	..	—
Treatment of Non-Metalliferous Mining Products other than Coal	1	1	1	2	1(*b*)	1(*b*)	2(*b*)	..	..	..	..	..(*b*)	..(*b*)	..(*b*)
Gas, Coke, and Chemical Manufacture	2	1	1	1	..	1	2	..	..	..	..	..	..	..
Metal Manufacture, Engineering, and Allied Trades	28	27	28	34	40	35	49	..	..	1	1	1	1	1
Electrical Goods	3	4	5	8	7	9	18	..	..	..	..	..	1	3
Textiles	3	3	4	5	4	5	3	5	5	5	8	8	9	25
Leatherworking	8	9	8	9	8	6	4	1	2	2	3	3	3	3
Clothing other than Boots and Shoes	8	8	7	8	7	5	9	18	21	19	22	22	16	23
Food, Drink, and Tobacco	18	11	13	13	10	11	15	5	4	4	6	6	5	5
Woodworking	24	24	21	25	25	17	22	1	1	1	..	..	..	..
Paper and Printing	4	4	4	5	4	5	6	2	2	2	3	3	3	3
Other manufactures	2	2	2	2	2	3	6	..	1	1	1	1	2	2
Building	48	62	54	75	71	49	16	..	..	..	..	..	..	..
Painting and Decorating	5	5	5	7	6	7	8	..	..	..	..	..	..	..
Transport and Communications	64	67	58	68	65	55	58	1	1	1	5	4	2	4
Commercial, Finance and Insurance Occupations (excluding Clerical Staff)	57	63	56	73	74	66	73	28	31	32	40	40	39	36
Public Administration	18	19	21	28	...	...	...	4	4	8	5	...	...	...
Armed Forces	15	7	14	8	8	9	9	—	—	..	..	..	..	..
Drivers of Stationary Engines, Cranes, etc.	2	2	3	4	4	5	8	—	—	—	..	..	—	—
Warehousemen, Storekeepers, Packers, Bottlers, etc.	5	11	6	9	9	12	15	2	4	5	7	7	9	8
Professional and Technical Occupations	20	29	34	36	37	38	53	30	33	37	39	39	41	51
Services, Sport, Recreation, etc.	22	24	26	19	27	25	31	110	110	103	80	79	62	50
Clerical Workers	17	18	20	22	30	32	36	13	19	24	31	35	46	67
Administrative, Executive, Management, etc.	...	...	...	...	12	12	17	...	...	...	...	2	1	1
Foremen and Supervisors of Manual Workers	...	...	...	...	6	7	13	...	...	...	...	1	1	1
Others Occupied	26	47	55	46	46	49	92	1	4	8	4	4	3	2
TOTAL POPULATION AGED 14 AND OVER (*a*)	1,157(*a*)	1,133	1,102	1,097	1,097	997	1,050	1,127	1,072	1,081	1,062	1,062	1,001	1,056
Total Unoccupied aged 14 and over(*a*)	193(*a*)	146	138	150	150	176	218	783	721	746	737	737	715	768

(*a*) Aged 12 and over in 1926.
(*b*) Glass and ceramics only.

Labour Force 4. Industrial Classification of the Working Population – United Kingdom, 1861–1911

NOTES

[1] SOURCE: C. H. Feinstein, *National Income, Expenditure, and Output of the United Kingdom, 1855–1965* (Cambridge, 1972), table 60, based on census material (the exact sources being given on pp. 223–4 and 226).

[2] The following notes indicate the classification used; the numbers given are the *reference numbers* adopted for the 1911 Census of England and Wales, vol. x, *Occupations and Industries* Table 25, p. 524. In addition to the numbers listed below (or the corresponding occupations – estimated where necessary – for 1861 to 1901) the following *general occupations* were allocated (as explained on p. 226) to two or more individual industries, but are *not* listed separately in industries 1–12 below:

Caretakers, office keepers (58–9)
Others engaged in service (64–5)
Commercial or business clerks (73)
Carmen, carriers, carters, van guards etc. (93, 95–6)
Messengers, porters, watchmen (115)
Carpenters, painters and other building workers (mainly 244–9, 254, 258–9 and 265)
General labourers (463) (except in Ireland, where all were allocated to agriculture)
Engine-drivers, stokers etc. (464)

1. Agriculture: 117–29
2. Fishing: 130
3. Mining and quarrying: (*a*) 131–52
4. Manufacturing: * 155–200, 203–27, 230–9, 266–9, 271–2, 275–81, 283–9, 291–7, 299–305, 308–14, 316–22, 325–31, 333, 335–73, 376–81, 383, 385–9, 391–3, 395, 397–8, 402, 404, 406, 408, 410, 412–14, 417–18, 420, 422–4, 447–51, 465–7.
5. Building and contracting: 201–2 (plus majority of workers in 242–65)
6. Gas, electricity and water: 434–6
7. Transport and communications: 1–4, 78–92, 94, 97–114, 116 plus merchant seamen abroad less foreign seamen in U.K.
8. Distributive trades: 66–9, 71–2, 53–4, 228–9, 240–1, 273–4, 282, 290, 298, 306–7, 315, 323–4, 332, 334, 374–5, 382, 384, 390, 394, 399–401, 403, 405, 407, 409, 411, 415–16, 419, 421, 433, 443–6, 453–62
9. Insurance, banking, finance: 71, 74–7, 439–42.
10. Public administration and defence
    (*a*) Central Government: † 5–6
    (*b*) Local authorities: † 7–9, 437–8
    (*c*) Defence: 10–18 plus Armed Forces abroad
11. Professional services
    (*a*) Teachers, lecturers, etc: 34–5
    (*b*) Doctors, dentists, nurses etc.: 28–33
    (*c*) Other (including domestic service in hospitals, schools etc.): 19–27, 36–44, 57, 70
12. Miscellaneous services
    (*a*) Private domestic service: 51–5, 61–2
    (*b*) Catering, hotels etc.: 50, 56, 60, 425–32
    (*c*) Other (entertainment and sport, laundries, hairdressing, photography etc.): 45–9, 63, 270, 396, 452

(in thousands)

Industry	1861	1871	1881	1891	1901	1911
1. Agriculture	3,470	3,060	2,790	2,560	2,360	2,340
2. Fishing	50	60	70	70	60	60
3. Mining and quarrying	490	570	680	840	1,020	1,290
4. Manufacturing	4,300	4,700	4,920	5,520	5,990	6,550
5. Building and contracting	550	660	830	840	1,090	1,030
6. Gas, electricity and water	25	30	40	60	100	120
7. Transport and communication	590	760	860	1,110	1,450	1,580
8. Distributive trades	850	1,050	1,300	1,640	1,990	2,460
9. Insurance, banking, finance	20	40	70	110	150	230
10. Public administration and defence						
(*a*) Central Government	40	40	50	70	80	120
(*b*) Local authorities	100	130	170	200	270	320
(*c*) Defence	310	250	240	280	530	400
11. Professional services						
(*a*) Education	140	160	210	240	280	310
(*b*) Medical and dental	65	70	80	100	120	150
(*c*) Other	130	160	240	260	320	370
12. Miscellaneous services						
(*a*) Private domestic service	1,510	1,790	1,850	1,940	1,980	2,000
(*b*) Catering, hotels etc.	200	240	350	430	460	610
(*c*) Other	250	280	320	390	430	450
TOTAL	13,090	14,050	15,060	16,660	18,680	20,390

* A number of blacksmiths, fitters, turners and other general engineering workers (mainly 170–2) were allocated to mining and quarrying but the majority are in manufacturing.

† The following categories are *not* included: teachers, doctors, nurses and ancillary workers in local authority schools and hospitals, workers in government dockyards, manufacturing establishments etc. and in local authority trading services.

Labour Force 5. Estimated Numbers of Employees (by Industry) in June/July in Each Year – United Kingdom 1923–80

NOTES TO PART A

[1] SOURCE: *Ministry of Labour Gazette*, though for the years 1923–36 the figures are to be found more conveniently in the 18th–22nd *Abstract of Labour Statistics*.

[2] All figures include unemployed workers attached to particular industries, but the grand total also includes some unemployed not attached to any industry.

[3] Certain classes of employee were excluded from the scope of the insurance scheme in this period. Briefly these consisted of agricultural workers until the establishment of a special scheme in 1936, most non-manual workers, and certain workers under public authorities, railways and public utilities.

[4] The three major changes in the scope of the insurance scheme during this period were in 1928, when people aged 65 or over were excluded, in 1934, when those aged 14 and 15 were included, and in 1940, when women aged 60 and over were excluded and non-manual workers earning from £250 to £420 per year were included. The first two of these breaks are indicated by giving two figures for 1927 and 1935, one on the old basis and the second on the new.

[5] We are grateful to the Department of Employment and Productivity for pointing out the omission in our original source for 1931–3 of people in Northern Ireland insured under the special scheme for commerce etc.

A. 1923–47 – Insured Employees in July (in thousands)

Males	1923	1924	1925	1926	1927	1927	1928	1929	1930	1931	1932
Agriculture											
Fishing	24	26	27	27	28	27	27	27	27	30	30
Mining	1,337	1,353	1,329	1,323	1,299	1,260	1,211	1,173	1,169	1,146	1,142
Non-Metalliferous Mining Products	40	40	42	44	46	44	44	46	46	47	48
Brick, Tile, Pipe, etc. Making	54	63	70	75	80	75	74	75	77	80	81
Pottery, Earthenware, etc.	36	38	34	35	35	32	33	35	36	35	36
Glass Trades	37	38	37	37	36	35	35	37	37	38	37
Chemicals, etc.	160	161	159	157	159	152	161	164	162	155	160
Metal Manufacture	342	340	327	326	326	314	304	308	309	293	289
Engineering, Shipbuilding and Repairing, and Metal Trades	1,613	1,583	1,576	1,566	1,557	1,506	1,509	1,537	1,563	1,550	1,521
Textile Trades	521	519	519	523	522	499	506	508	507	470	495
Leather and Leather Goods	49	49	48	46	46	45	44	44	43	42	44
Clothing	203	204	205	202	200	193	192	196	193	195	197
Food, Drink, and Tobacco	297	300	300	308	306	296	295	296	300	303	312
Woodworking, etc	162	166	169	174	180	172	177	182	185	192	195
Paper, Printing, etc.	213	221	220	229	233	224	230	236	243	251	260
Building and Contracting	835	851	900	962	1,008	961	967	980	1,008	1,118	1,136
Other Manufactures	81	85	88	92	95	91	96	101	102	98	98
Gas, Water, and Electricity Supply	166	165	171	177	165	157	157	156	160	166	167
Transport and Communications	762	760	769	774	768	743	755	775	787	837	840
Distributive Trades	750	811	885	917	964	939	974	1,015	1,064	1,137	1,202
Commerce, Banking, Finance and Insurance	147	150	148	149	151	150	149	155	158	162	167
Miscellaneous Trades and Services	663	665	692	700	695	663	680	709	756	820	848
TOTAL INSURED	8,493	8,586	8,717	8,844	8,899	8,576	8,622	8,755	8,932	9,188	9,304

	1933	1934	1935	1935	1936	1937	1938	1939	1945	1946	1947
Agriculture						544	540	533	512	562	574
Fishing	31	31	32	32	34	34	33	32	11	20	25
Mining	1,119	1,078	1,034	1,069	1,025	999	990	968	776	792	807
Non-Metalliferous Mining Products	48	49	52	53	54	59	61	61	40	57	65
Brick, Tile, Pipe, etc. Making	83	90	95	101	103	106	107	99	30	55	63
Pottery, Earthenware, etc.	35	35	33	36	36	36	36	34	15	23	28
Glass Trades	39	40	40	42	42	43	43	42	28	37	43
Chemicals, etc.	162	158	157	162	166	174	185	194	233	218	228
Metal Manufacture	284	288	284	291	304	326	325	336	283	296	320
Engineering, Shipbuilding and Repairing, and Metal Trades	1,499	1,507	1,549	1,650	1,722	1,906	1,977	2,064	2,373	2,253	2,441
Textile Trades	485	478	471	499	488	480	459	493	231	292	340
Leather and Leather Goods	46	47	47	50	51	51	48	48	28	36	44
Clothing	199	195	194	211	207	202	204	203	110	135	164
Food, Drink, and Tobacco	321	328	330	347	348	356	356	359	256	304	341
Woodworking, etc.	194	200	200	219	227	230	230	224	128	179	206
Paper, Printing, etc.	262	264	264	283	286	292	292	294	148	211	248
Building and Contracting	1,150	1,188	1,242	1,273	1,329	1,347	1,393	1,417	637	1,036	1,172
Other Manufactures	102	101	102	110	109	107	105	109	86	138	168
Gas, Water, and Electricity Supply	175	186	192	195	204	212	215	214	142	191	218

Labour Force 5. *continued*

A. 1923–47 – Insured Employees in July (in thousands)

Males

	1933	1934	1935	1935	1936	1937	1938	1939	1945	1946	1947
Transport and Communications	825	833	842	860	877	885	875	863	764	910	978
Distributive Trades	1,236	1,262	1,267	1,427	1,441	1,418	1,422	1,394	635	827	951
Commerce, Banking, Finance and Insurance	169	176	179	184	183	187	186	181	88	136	146
Miscellaneous Trades and Services	883	900	927	960	978	997	1,115	1,152	1,036	1,262	1,387
TOTAL INSURED	9,346	9,435	9,531	10,055	10,243	11,130	11,358	11,428	8,602	10,647	11,100

Females

	1923	1924	1925	1926	1927	1927	1928	1929	1930	1931	1932
Agriculture											
Fishing	1	1	1	1	1	1	1	1	1	1	1
Mining	10	10	11	10	9	9	8	8	8	8	7
Non-Metalliferous Mining Products	1	2	2	2	2	2	2	3	2	3	3
Brick, Tile, Pipe, etc. Making	7	8	8	8	8	8	7	7	7	7	6
Pottery, Earthenware, etc.	36	36	39	38	38	38	38	39	43	43	39
Glass Trades	7	7	8	7	8	7	7	8	8	9	8
Chemicals, etc.	54	53	52	52	54	54	54	54	56	59	56
Metal Manufacture	18	18	19	18	17	17	17	16	17	17	16
Engineering, Shipbuilding and Repairing, and Metal Trades	224	231	248	254	251	250	259	272	289	290	281
Textile Trades	791	808	812	813	806	797	806	807	832	823	776
Leather and Leather Goods	21	21	21	22	23	23	23	24	24	24	24
Clothing	377	375	379	380	384	383	385	386	394	412	408
Food, Drink, and Tobacco	203	211	220	215	217	216	212	217	226	232	223
Woodworking, etc.	30	29	30	30	31	31	31	32	33	34	34
Paper, Printing, etc.	135	140	142	145	146	145	144	151	157	160	158
Building and Contracting	9	9	9	9	9	9	10	10	11	11	11
Other Manufactures	46	48	49	51	50	50	53	56	56	59	56
Gas, Water, and Electricity Supply	7	6	7	7	6	6	7	6	6	8	7
Transport and Communications	30	27	29	28	29	29	30	32	34	35	34
Distributive Trades	504	544	580	597	617	614	640	664	701	738	749
Commerce, Banking, Finance and Insurance	80	76	73	71	72	72	72	74	75	75	78
Miscellaneous Trades and Services	402	418	437	442	453	447	454	474	494	535	530
TOTAL INSURED	2,993	3,078	3,175	3,197	3,232	3,208	3,260	3,339	3,474	3,583	3,506

Agriculture

	1933	1934	1935	1935	1936	1937	1938	1939	(a) 1945	1946	1947
						41	47	50	143	109	96
Fishing	1	1	1	1	1	1	1	1	—	—	—
Mining	7	6	6	7	6	6	6	6	14	13	13
Non-Metalliferous Mining Products	2	2	2	2	2	3	3	3	8	7	7
Brick, Tile, Pipe, etc. Making	6	6	6	7	6	7	7	7	5	6	6
Pottery, Earthenware, etc.	41	40	40	45	45	46	46	45	24	32	36
Glass Trades	9	9	9	10	10	11	11	11	17	17	15
Chemicals, etc.	59	59	58	67	67	71	73	77	196	129	113
Metal Manufacture	16	16	15	17	18	20	20	21	71	56	47
Engineering, Shipbuilding and Repairing, and Metal Trades	279	289	302	346	367	400	402	419	1,109	712	649
Textile Trades	761	740	715	783	779	778	746	732	430	458	480
Leather and Leather Goods	24	25	25	29	30	31	30	31	22	25	27
Clothing	415	418	413	477	486	488	492	500	309	364	387
Food, Drink, and Tobacco	235	226	223	260	266	271	278	283	226	231	231

See p. 120 for footnotes.

Labour Force 5. *continued*

A. 1923–47 – Insured Employees in July (in thousands)

Females

	1933	1934	1935	1935	1936	1937	1938	1939	(a) 1945	1946	1947
Woodworking, etc.	33	33	33	39	40	42	44	43	58	50	44
Paper, Printing, etc.	160	157	156	186	189	194	199	201	124	144	155
Building and Contracting	12	12	12	13	14	15	15	16	25	26	24
Other Manufactures	59	59	58	67	65	67	66	69	72	105	113
Gas, Water, and Electricity Supply	8	9	8	8	10	10	12	12	27	22	19
Transport and Communications	34	35	37	39	41	44	42	43	190	142	112
Distributive Trades	756	743	740	831	854	874	908	924	850	873	862
Commerce, Banking, Finance and Insurance	78	81	81	84	87	91	96	99	144	124	127
Miscellaneous Trades and Services	542	557	584	631	657	690	841	877	1,319	1,245	1,248
TOTAL INSURED	3,539	3,525	3,527	3,947	4,042	4,205	4,385	4,424	5,398	4,925	4,820

See p. 120 for footnotes.

NOTES TO PARTS B and C.

[1] SOURCES: *Ministry of Labour Gazette* (and its successors) and *British Labour Statistics: Historical Abstract, 1886–1968*.

[2] All figures include unemployed workers attached to particular industries, and the grand total also includes some unemployed workers not attached to particular industries.

B. 1948–58 – Insured Employees in June (in thousands)

Males

	1948	1949	1950	1951	1952	1953	1954	1955	1956	1957	1958
Agriculture and Forestry	689	682	676	645	600	590	585	576	548	537	523
Fishing	37	36	33	32	32	30	29	27	27	26	26
Mining and Quarrying	872	871	847	847	862	865	855	849	845	854	841
Bricks and Fireclay Goods	71	74	76	75	78	79	79	77	76	75	70
Pottery and Earthenware	34	35	37	36	36	34	34	34	34	31	31
Glass	50	52	53	55	53	50	52	55	56	58	58
Other Non-Metalliferous Mining Products	85	84	87	90	92	94	96	98	98	98	96
Chemicals, etc.	314	322	336	345	354	351	357	370	377	384	393
Metal Manufacture	475	480	485	488	495	490	489	503	514	517	511
Engineering, Shipbuilding, and Electrical Goods	1,465	1,473	1,475	1,490	1,547	1,558	1,583	1,639	1,682	1,706	1,731
Vehicles	828	844	864	884	931	952	995	1,035	1,058	1,038	1,055
Metal Goods not elsewhere specified	330	327	321	323	323	316	314	326	331	335	337
Precision Instruments, Jewellery, etc.	83	85	88	88	85	85	86	90	92	93	93
Textiles	412	429	456	461	420	433	443	432	423	428	414
Leather, Leather Goods, and Fur	51	49	49	48	43	44	43	43	40	40	39
Clothing	191	198	198	201	190	192	192	187	184	188	180
Food, Drink, and Tobacco	448	468	481	487	491	499	503	506	511	514	530
Manufactures of Wood and Cork	237	245	251	251	240	241	242	244	235	234	231
Paper and Printing	296	310	325	328	332	328	341	354	362	373	378
Other Manufacturing Industries	146	142	147	156	150	150	158	167	169	173	176
Building and Contracting	1,335	1,321	1,325	1,314	1,313	1,330	1,341	1,357	1,397	1,389	1,363
Gas, Water, and Electricity	302	311	329	333	343	343	343	346	345	347	345
Transport and Communications	1,563	1,553	1,559	1,517	1,527	1,502	1,486	1,473	1,478	1,480	1,474
Distributive Trades	1,096	1,124	1,135	1,132	1,135	1,143	1,165	1,183	1,203	1,235	1,247
Insurance, Banking, and Finance	268	281	277	273	274	273	278	282	282	290	294
Public Administration (*b*)	1,013	1,029	1,025	1,008	1,009	1,013	1,014	985	988	988	987
Professional Services	474	477	512	529	548	552	567	573	594	614	632
Miscellaneous Services	503	486	469	459	449	451	442	431	427	429	435
GRAND TOTAL (*d*)	13,778	13,828	13,937	13,906	13,966	14,001	14,123	14,224	14,389	14,487	14,512

See p. 120 for footnotes.

Labour Force 5. *continued*

B. 1948–58 – Insured Employees in June (in thousands)

Females

	1948	1949	1950	1951	1952	1953	1954	1955	1956	1957	1958
Agriculture and Forestry	128	114	112	105	103	103	100	100	97	98	94
Fishing	1	1	1	1	1	1	1	1	1	..	..
Mining and Quarrying	16	17	18	18	19	20	20	21	21	28	24
Bricks and Fireclay Goods	7	7	8	8	9	9	9	9	9	8	8
Pottery and Earthenware	42	43	45	45	46	45	44	45	44	40	39
Glass	18	17	18	19	19	17	18	20	19	19	19
Other Non-Metalliferous Mining Products	12	12	12	13	13	13	13	14	14	14	13
Chemicals, etc.	133	136	139	141	142	142	147	151	154	154	151
Metal Manufacture	62	61	63	66	68	66	67	71	70	68	66
Engineering, Shipbuilding, and Electrical Goods	385	365	376	405	434	411	430	480	477	477	475
Vehicles	131	130	138	148	159	162	170	183	184	178	180
Metal Goods not elsewhere specified	181	172	180	190	189	176	181	193	191	185	180
Precision Instruments, Jewellery, etc.	47	49	52	51	50	51	54	58	57	57	58
Textiles	589	612	633	650	587	612	625	600	584	581	538
Leather, Leather Goods, and Fur	29	28	29	31	28	30	30	31	29	29	27
Clothing	447	476	504	505	475	496	496	486	492	488	468
Food, Drink, and Tobacco	308	327	338	356	367	376	387	400	407	405	409
Manufactures of Wood and Cork	57	58	60	62	59	60	62	65	64	63	62
Paper and Printing	176	182	194	200	194	187	198	205	210	211	209
Other Manufacturing Industries	102	104	108	118	106	108	118	122	119	118	116
Building and Contracting	40	38	38	40	46	48	50	52	60	63	65
Gas, Water, and Electricity	27	30	34	37	38	38	39	40	41	42	42
Transport and Communications	235	230	233	241	252	248	249	252	259	256	252
Distributive Trades	972	1,014	1,021	1,049	1,083	1,126	1,176	1,216	1,259	1,306	1,301
Insurance, Banking and Finance	164	162	161	169	174	179	188	194	203	211	215
Public Administration (*b*)	424	420	398	394	387	369	369	357	365	371	376
Professional Services	852	868	945	963	993	1,014	1,052	1,088	1,127	1,161	1,192
Miscellaneous Services	1,366	1,281	1,259	1,230	1,228	1,223	1,227	1,223	1,220	1,199	1,192
GRAND TOTAL (*d*)	6,954	6,954	7,118	7,271	7,286	7,351	7,535	7,689	7,791	7,848	7,778

See p. 120 for footnotes.

Labour Force 5. *continued*

C. 1959–71 – Insured Employees in June
Males

(in thousands)

	1959	1960	1961	1962	1963 (*c*)	1964	1965	1966 (*d*)		1967	1968	1969 (*e*)		1970	1971
Agriculture and Forestry	526	504	480	461	463	439	401	380	381	355	337	317	316	299	280
Fishing	27	26	25	26	25	24	23	23	23	24	22	21	21	21	21
Mining and Quarrying	817	752	718	698	673	645	611	563	561	541	489	450	451	425	408
Bricks, Fireclay, and Refractory Goods	69	71	72	71	68	69	68	64	64	63	61	59	59	56	52
Pottery	30	30	29	31	30	30	30	31	31	29	29	29	30	30	30
Glass	58	58	59	60	59	60	60	61	63	61	62	64	63	62	62
Other Non-Metalliferous Mining Products	98	105	109	112	112	120	124	119	129	127	134	132	129	126	123
Chemicals, etc.	379	387	388	381	379	374	379	383	383	383	372	386	392	398	395
Metal Manufacture	511	547	561	531	529	552	560	548	551	530	519	522	524	531	507
Engineering and Electrical Goods	1,441	1,508	1,583	1,617	1,596	1,617	1,675	1,704	1,740	1,752	1,717	1,736	1,671	1,688	1,664
Shipbuilding and Marine Engineering	292	278	263	251	230	216	212	207	207	206	195	189	194	194	196
Vehicles	759	800	780	771	765	765	758	749	743	721	711	730	733	743	733
Metal Goods not elsewhere specified	332	353	366	368	371	378	391	395	397	388	390	396	443	453	450
Textiles	403	405	402	396	393	395	391	392	392	378	376	394	391	386	369
Leather, Leather Goods, and Fur	38	37	37	37	37	37	36	34	35	34	33	34	34	32	32
Clothing	154	156	159	155	151	148	146	144	145	138	133	136	138	130	130
Food, Drink, and Tobacco	467	468	475	488	488	485	490	489	502	504	493	500	521	531	529
Timber, Furniture, etc.	230	236	234	235	234	238	244	239	259	252	270	260	260	250	249
Paper, Printing, and Publishing	374	393	402	409	414	415	421	427	429	427	430	434	434	439	426
Other Manufacturing Industries	171	182	184	188	192	199	206	209	212	208	221	230	221	226	229
Construction	1,414	1,436	1,480	1,533	1,576	1,628	1,657	1,674	1,633	1,597	1,567	1,497	1,499	1,380	1,331
Gas, Water, and Electricity	342	337	344	351	359	363	367	378	378	379	368	350	350	336	322
Transport and Communications	1,451	1,433	1,445	1,460	1,449	1,431	1,414	1,383	1,390	1,388	1,370	1,331	1,336	1,341	1,340
Distributive Trades	1,373	1,390	1,384	1,421	1,447	1,441	1,429	1,409	1,374	1,325	1,310	1,269	1,261	1,220	1,205
Insurance, Banking, and Finance	311	313	321	329	342	352	357	355	355	356	367	378	449	469	477
Public Administration	954	947	952	974	1,016	960	966	982	982	1,013	1,019	997	991	991	1,003
Professional and Scientific Services	668	680	711	745	771	799	833	860	856	890	908	921	928	952	981
Miscellaneous Services	834	840	857	904	932	962	976	996	988	961	965	969	890	859	859
GRAND TOTAL (*d*)	14,565	14,719	14,869	15,064	15,144	15,163	15,243	15,220	15,220	15,056	14,901	14,764	14,764	14,604	14,453

See p. 120 for footnotes.

Labour Force 5. *continued*

C. 1959–71 – Insured Employees in June
Females

(in thousands)

	1959	1960	1961	1962	1963 (*c*)	1964	1965	1966 (*d*)		1967	1968	1969 (*e*)		1970	1971
Agriculture and Forestry	94	93	90	90	93	89	84	83	82	79	79	76	77	73	68
Fishing	--	1	1	1	1	--	--	--	--	--	--	--	--	--	--
Mining and Quarrying	25	23	24	23	22	23	23	23	23	22	21	19	19	18	18
Bricks, Fireclay, and Refractory Goods	7	7	8	7	7	7	7	7	7	7	7	7	7	6	6
Pottery	38	38	39	38	36	37	35	36	36	35	32	32	32	31	30
Glass	18	19	19	20	19	20	20	21	21	20	20	20	20	20	20
Other Non-Metalliferous Mining Products	15	16	16	17	16	17	18	18	19	18	18	18	18	17	17
Chemicals, etc.	145	148	147	143	142	143	145	149	149	143	137	142	148	150	144
Metal Manufacture	72	76	77	74	74	76	77	76	77	73	73	72	72	73	70
Engineering and Electrical Goods	508	555	573	582	582	614	628	647	651	630	628	655	624	629	603
Shipbuilding and Marine Engineering	14	14	13	13	12	12	12	12	12	13	13	12	13	14	15
Vehicles	118	124	122	119	118	119	117	116	115	112	110	110	113	112	107
Metal Goods not elsewhere specified	183	198	199	193	189	200	205	206	207	194	191	192	205	200	191
Textiles	515	512	501	469	454	450	438	426	426	390	375	370	364	345	312
Leather, Leather Goods, and Fur	27	27	27	27	27	27	26	25	26	24	25	24	25	23	22
Clothing	426	441	441	440	427	423	417	411	413	395	391	394	396	378	380
Food, Drink, and Tobacco	358	360	366	369	362	361	359	361	369	365	360	363	374	379	374
Timber, Furniture, etc.	59	61	61	59	57	59	61	60	63	60	62	60	59	58	58
Paper, Printing, and Publishing	205	214	219	223	218	219	222	225	226	220	218	221	221	224	211
Other Manufacturing Industries	113	123	126	123	124	128	133	136	140	139	140	144	140	140	135
Construction	66	70	76	81	82	83	89	95	92	87	91	91	91	89	88
Gas, Water, and Electricity	43	44	45	47	49	51	54	55	55	58	58	61	61	62	64
Transport and Communications	249	252	263	264	259	258	264	268	267	274	274	274	275	284	289
Distributive Trades	1,430	1,480	1,508	1,554	1,576	1,597	1,627	1,657	1,644	1,589	1,580	1,555	1,549	1,540	1,498
Insurance, Banking, and Finance	228	237	247	260	275	286	295	300	300	310	318	333	465	508	521
Public Administration	350	356	371	382	394	381	389	416	415	439	448	451	452	466	486
Professional and Scientific Services	1,302	1,345	1,393	1,458	1,505	1,575	1,638	1,722	1,722	1,805	1,859	1,921	1,927	1,942	2,018
Miscellaneous Services	1,208	1,196	1,189	1,226	1,224	1,275	1,283	1,281	1,278	1,242	1,224	1,221	1,081	1,035	1,030
GRAND TOTAL	7,864	8,098	8,242	8,368	8,414	8,543	8,677	8,845	8,845	8,751	8,766	8,839	8,839	8,842	8,781

See p. 120 for footnotes.

NOTES TO PART D
[1] SOURCES: *Department of Employment (and Productivity) Gazette.*
[2] Unemployed workers are not included in this Part.

D. 1971–8 – Persons in Employment in June (in thousands)

Males

	1971	1972	1973	1974	1975	1976	1977	1978
Agriculture and Forestry	317	315	307	298	290	286	287	283
Fishing	11	11	11	10	9	9	8	7
Mining and Quarrying	381	364	349	335	338	333	335	337
Bricks, Fireclay, and Refractory Goods	45	45	45	43	37	36	36	36
Pottery	27	27	28	29	29	30	30	29
Glass	58	56	56	56	53	50	53	55
Other Non-Metalliferous Mining Products	112	110	111	105	93	88	82	85
Chemicals, etc	354	343	340	342	342	338	345	348
Metal Manufacture	492	457	460	448	444	416	428	405
Engineering and Electrical Goods	1,494	1,416	1,403	1,418	1,392	1,349	1,350	1,359
Shipbuilding and Marine Engineering	181	175	175	173	171	172	170	168
Vehicles	710	688	699	692	663	654	659	663
Metal Goods not elsewhere specified	406	396	400	408	391	376	386	394
Textiles	333	322	321	318	291	284	280	269
Leather, Leather Goods, and Fur	27	26	25	24	23	23	23	21
Clothing	112	111	106	102	96	91	89	88
Food, Drink, and Tobacco	465	458	450	452	435	430	425	420
Timber, Furniture, etc.	219	224	236	229	213	213	208	206
Paper, Printing and Publishing	402	392	387	394	381	370	365	367
Other Manufacturing Industries	215	217	224	223	210	212	213	210
Construction	1,178	1,212	1,284	1,232	1,214	1,204	1,165	1,155
Gas, Water, and Electricity	316	295	284	283	285	285	281	273
Transport and Communications	1,307	1,286	1,265	1,243	1,249	1,217	1,207	1,212
Distributive Trades	1,180	1,200	1,231	1,221	1,224	1,210	1,227	1,246
Insurance, Banking, and Finance	480	485	511	536	538	542	553	571
Public Administration	996	1,014	1,022	997	1,026	1,018	1,005	986
Professional and Scientific Services	1,002	1,035	1,081	1,111	1,149	1,172	1,158	1,174
Miscellaneous Services	893	924	960	936	947	976	994	1,018
GRAND TOTAL	13,713	13,606	13,771	13,659	13,532	13,388	13,363	13,385

See p. 120 for footnotes.

Labour Force 5. *continued*

D. 1971–8 – Persons in Employment in June (in thousands)

Females

	1971	1972	1973	1974	1975	1976	1977	1978
Agriculture and Forestry	104	102	115	107	102	100	92	92
Fishing	..	..	..	..	..	..	..	..
Mining and Quarrying	15	15	14	14	14	15	15	16
Bricks, Fireclay, and Refractory Goods	5	5	4	5	4	4	4	4
Pottery	28	28	29	31	30	29	29	27
Glass	18	17	17	17	16	15	16	16
Other Non-Metalliferous Mining Products	15	15	15	15	13	12	12	12
Chemicals, etc	128	125	128	132	128	122	127	132
Metal Manufacture	64	59	58	59	57	53	55	53
Engineering and Electrical Goods	534	507	533	562	504	469	478	481
Shipbuilding and Marine Engineering	12	12	12	12	13	13	12	13
Vehicles	106	96	98	99	93	89	91	91
Metal Goods not elsewhere specified	169	160	167	174	155	146	149	148
Textiles	289	275	272	267	238	229	232	221
Leather, Leather Goods, and Fur	20	19	19	19	18	17	18	21
Clothing	343	339	334	325	307	291	299	290
Food, Drink, and Tobacco	305	297	303	314	290	284	286	284
Timber, Furniture, etc.	50	51	56	54	51	51	50	51
Paper, Printing and Publishing	194	187	188	195	184	172	172	174
Other Manufacturing Industries	124	122	129	135	120	118	118	118
Construction	83	87	95	96	98	104	105	109
Gas, Water, and Electricity	61	60	61	64	68	68	66	67
Transport and Communications	261	257	260	263	269	258	261	270
Distributive Trades	1,430	1,440	1,512	1,540	1,539	1,512	1,525	1,534
Insurance, Banking, and Finance	496	510	547	580	565	561	592	629
Public Administration	514	537	562	599	629	609	609	619
Professional and Scientific Services	1,987	2,072	2,168	2,263	2,407	2,482	2,489	2,506
Miscellaneous Services	1,053	1,116	1,193	1,189	1,255	1,323	1,349	1,396
GRAND TOTAL	8,408	8,512	8,891	9,131	9,174	9,151	9,255	9,372

(*a*) As from 1940 women aged 60–64 ceased to be included in the statistics, whilst non-manual workers earning from £250 to £420 per year were included.

(*b*) The estimates for 1948 and 1949 do not include civil servants stationed overseas.

(*c*) The estimates for 1964 and 1965 were calculated by a revised method which was described in the *Ministry of Labour Gazette* (March and May 1966). The totals for 1950–1964 were recalculated by this method, and the revised totals are shown here. This was not done, however, for the individual industries for the period before 1964. The break between 1963 and 1964 is negligible except in the case of some of the larger industrial groups for females. Figures for these on the unrevised basis for the year 1964 are as follows:

Engineering and Electrical Goods	611
Textiles	447
Distributive Trades	1,587
Professional and Scientific Services	1,564
Miscellaneous Services	1,268

(*d*) Between 1966 and 1967 the industrial classifications of many establishments were corrected. The estimates for 1966 are shown on both corrected and uncorrected bases.

(*e*) Estimates for 1969 are shown on both the old and the new industrial classifications.

Labour Force 6. Numbers in the Armed Forces – United Kingdom, 1855–1980

NOTE
SOURCE: C. H. Feinstein, *National Income, Expenditure, and Output of the United Kingdom, 1855–1965* (Cambridge, 1972), table 57; and *Abstract*.

(in thousands)

1855	250	1887	270	1919	2,130	1950	721(*a*)
1856	280	1888	270	1920	760	1951	838(*a*)
1857	230	1889	270	1921	491	1952	878(*a*)
1858	250	1890	270	1922	392	1953	868(*a*)
1859	270	1891	280	1923	348	1954	844(*a*)
1860	300	1892	280	1924	346	1955	805(*a*)
1861	300	1893	290	1925	350	1956	775(*a*)
1862	290	1894	290	1926	349	1957	693(*a*)
1863	280	1895	300	1927	347	1958	613(*a*)
1864	270	1896	310	1928	336	1959	562(*a*)
1865	270	1897	310	1929	333	1960	515
1866	250	1898	320	1930	327	1961	469
1867	250	1899	340	1931	325	1962	439
1868	250	1900	490	1932	323	1963	426
1869	240	1901	530	1933	323	1964	424
1870	240	1902	500	1934	325	1965	422
1871	250	1903	420	1935	333	1966	418
1872	250	1904	410	1936	349	1967	417
1873	240	1905	400	1937	377	1968	405
1874	240	1906	390	1938	432	1969	383
1875	240	1907	380	1939	480	1970	373
1876	240	1908	380	1940	2,270	1971	368
1877	250	1909	390	1941	3,380	1972	371
1878	260	1910	390	1942	4,090	1973	367
1879	250	1911	400	1943	4,780(*a*)	1974	349
1880	240	1912	400	1944	4,990(*a*)	1975	338
1881	240	1913	400	1945	5,130(*a*)	1976	337
1882	240	1914	810	1946	2,730(*a*)	1977	331
1883	240	1915	2,490	1947	1,460(*a*)	1978	321
1884	240	1916	3,500	1948	940(*a*)	1979	315
1885	250	1917	4,250	1949	790(*a*)	1980	321
1886	260	1918	4,430				

(*a*) For 1943–59 includes ex-members of H.M. Forces on release but not yet in employment. The numbers were below 10 thousand except as follows:-

1943	20	1945	40	1947	155
1944	20	1946	700	1948	92

Labour Force 7. Percentages Unemployed in Certain Trade Unions – 1851–1926

NOTES

[1] SOURCES: *S.P.* 1905, LXXXIV for 1851–1903, and the *Abstract of Labour Statistics* thereafter.

[2] The figures in columns headed A are partly computed from expenditure on unemployment benefit; those in columns headed B are from returns of unemployment at the end of each month.

[3] From 1867 onwards the total of unions making returns included others besides those separately shown here.

	All Unions Making Returns		Engineering, Metal and Shipbuilding Unions		Amalgamated Society of Carpenters and Joiners	Woodworking and Furnishing Unions		Printing and Bookbinding Unions		All Others Making Returns	
	A	B	A	B	B	A	B	A	B	A	B
1851	3·9		3·9								
1852	6·0		6·0								
1853	1·7		1·7								
1854	2·9		2·9								
1855	5·4		5·4								
1856	4·7		4·9					1·6			
1857	6·0		6·1					2·3			
1858	11·9		12·2					2·5			
1859	3·8		3·9					1·4			
1860	1·9		1·9		0·2			2·1			
1861	5·2		5·5		1·8			3·1			
1862	8·4		9·0		1·8			3·5			
1863	6·0		6·7		1·2			3·2			
1864	2·7		3·0		0·4			1·3			
1865	2·1		2·4		0·3			2·0			
1866	3·3		3·9		1·1			1·8			
1867	7·4		9·1		3·0	4·8		2·7		5·9	
1868	7·9		10·0		2·9	5·0		2·5		6·2	
1869	6·7		8·9		3·6	4·5		2·8		0·4	
1870	3·9		4·4		3·7	4·8		3·5		0·2	
1871	1·6		1·3		2·5	3·5		2·0		0·3	
1872	0·9		0·9		1·2	2·4		1·5		0·0	
1873	1·2		1·4		0·9	1·8		1·3		0·3	
1874	1·7		2·3		0·8	2·1		1·6		0·1	
1875	2·4		3·5		0·6	2·0		1·6		0·3	
1876	3·7		5·2		0·7	2·4		2·4		1·3	
1877	4·7		6·3		1·2	3·5		2·6		2·8	
1878	6·8		9·0		3·5	4·4		3·2		3·0	
1879	11·4		15·3		8·2	8·3		4·0		3·3	
1880	5·5		6·7		6·1	3·2		3·2		2·2	
1881	3·5		3·8		5·2	2·7		2·8		1·5	
1882	2·3		2·3		3·5	2·5		2·4		0·9	
1883	2·6		2·7		3·6	2·5		2·2		1·2	
1884	8·1		10·8		4·7	3·0		2·1		1·4	
1885	9·3		12·9		7·1	4·1		2·5		1·8	
1886	10·2		13·5		8·2	4·7		2·6		5·2	
1887	7·6		10.4		6·5	3·6		2·2		1·9	
1888	4·6	4·9	5·5	6·0	5·7	3·6	3·1	2·5	2·4	1·2	3·2
1889	2·1	2·1	2·0	2·3	3·0	2·6	2·4	2·1	2·5	0·9	0·0
1890	2·1	2·1	2·4	2·2	2·2	1·5	2·5	1·9	2·2	0·6	1·6
1891	3·2	3·5	4·4	4·1	1·9	1·7	2·1	2·9	4·0	0·7	1·7
1892	5·8	6·3	8·2	7·7	3·1	2·4	3·8	3·6	4·3	1·3	5·6
1893		7·5		11·4	3·1		4·1		4·1		2·6
1894		6·9		11·2	4·3		4·4		5·7		1·9
1895		5·8		8·2	4·4		3·6		4·9		3·3

Labour Force 7. *continued*

	All Unions Making Returns		Engineering, Metal and Shipbuilding Unions		Amalgamated Society of Carpenters and Joiners	Woodworking and Furnishing Unions		Printing and Bookbinding Unions		All Others Making Returns	
	A	B	A	B	B	A	B	A	B	A	B
1896		3·3		4·2	1·3		2·0		4·3		2·3
1897		3·3		4·8	1·2		2·2		3·9		1·8
1898		2·8		4·0	0·9		2·3		3·7		1·5
1899		2.0		2·4	1·2		2·1		3·9		1·2
1900		2·5		2·6	2·6		2·8		4·2		1·6
1901		3·3		3·8	3·9		3·7		4·5		2·1
1902		4·0		5·5	4·0		4·1		4·6		1·9
1903		4·7		6·6	4·4		4·7		4·4		2·5
1904		6·0		8·4	7·3		6·8		4·7		3·0
1905		5·0		6·6	8·0		5·8		5·1		2·3
1906		3·6		4·1	6·9		4·8		4·5		1·9
1907		3·7		4·9	7·3		4·6		4·4		1·6
1908		7·8		12·5	11·6		8·3		5·5		2·9
1909		7·7		13·0	11·7		7·6		5·6		2·6
1910		4·7		6·8	8·3		5·4		4·9		2·2
1911		3·0		3·4	4·2		3·3		5·1		2·1
1912		3·2		3·6	3·7		3·1		5·2		2·1
1913		2·1		2·2	3·3		2·4		4·0		1·4
1914		3·3		3·3	3·3		4·1		4·5		2·9
1915		1·1		0·6	2·2		2·1		3·1		
1916		0·4		0·3	0·9		1·0		1·3		
1917		0·7		0·2	0·5		0·6		0·6		
1918		0·8		0·2	0·2		0·5		0·3		
1919		2·4		3·2	1·2		1·3		1·6		
1920		2·4		3·2	0·3		1·4		1·6		
1921		14.8		22·1	3·9		9·4		7·3		
1922		15·2		27·0	7·5		7·6		6·6		
1923		11·3		20·6	5·0		5·8		4·7		
1924		8·1		13·8	1·9		4·5		3·3		
1925		10·5		13·5	2·2		4·4		2·8		
1926		12·2		18·2	5·2		8·2		4·3		

Labour Force 8. Adjusted Estimates of Overall Percentages Unemployed, 1855–1965, and Percentages of Insured Unemployed, 1913–1980

NOTE

SOURCES: C. H. Feinstein, *National Income, Expenditure, and Output of the United Kingdom, 1855–1965* (Cambridge, 1972) table 57; Department of Employment and Productivity, *British Labour Statistics: Historical Abstract, 1886–1968* (London, 1971); and *Abstract*.

	Feinstein		Feinstein	National Insurance		Feinstein	National Insurance		Feinstein	National Insurance
1855	(3·7)	1890	2·1	...	1920	2·0	3·9	1950	1·3	1·6
1856	3·2	1891	3·5	...	1921	11·3	16·9	1951	1·1	1·3
1857	4·2	1892	6·3	...	1922	9·8	14·3	1952	1·6	2·2
1858	7·3	1893	7·5	...	1923	8·1	11·7	1953	1·5	1·8
1859	2·6	1894	6·9	...	1924	7·2	10·3	1954	1·2	1·5
1860	1·8	1895	5·8	...	1925	7·9	11·3	1955	1·0	1·2
1861	3·7	1896	3·3	...	1926	8·8	12·5	1956	1·1	1·3
1862	6·0	1897	3·3	...	1927	6·8	9·7	1957	1·3	1·6
1863	4·7	1898	2·8	...	1928	7·5	10·8	1958	1·9	2·2
1864	1·9	1899	2·0	...	1929	7·3	10·4	1959	1·9	2·3
1865	1·8	1900	2·5	...	1930	11·2	16·1	1960	1·5	1·7
1866	2·6	1901	3·3	...	1931	15·1	21·3	1961	1·4	1·6
1867	6·3	1902	4·0	...	1932	15·6	22·1	1962	1·9	2·1
1868	6·7	1903	4·7	...	1933	14·1	19·9	1963	2·1	2·6
1869	5·9	1904	6·0	...	1934	11·9	16·7	1964	1·5	1·7
1870	3·7	1905	5·0	...	1935	11·0	15·5	1965	1·3	1·5
1871	1·6	1906	3·6	...	1936	9·4	13·1	1966	...	1·5
1872	0·9	1907	3·7	...	1937	7·8	10·8	1967	...	2·3
1873	1·1	1908	7·8	...	1938	9·3	12·9	1968	...	2·5
1874	1·6	1909	7·7	...	1939	5·8	10·5 / 9·3 (a)	1969	...	2·5
1875	2·2	1910	4·7	...	1940	3·3	6·0	1970	...	2·6
1876	3·4	1911	3·0	...	1941	1·2	2·2	1971	...	3·4
1877	4·4	1012	3·3	...	1942	0·5	0·8	1972	...	3·8
1878	6·2	1913	2·1	3·6	1943	0·4	0·6	1973	...	2·7
1879	10·7	1914	3·3	4·2	1944	0·4	0·5	1974	...	2·6(c)
1880	5·2	1915	1·1	1·2	1945	0·5	1·3	1975	...	4·0
1881	3·5	1916	0·4	0·6	1946	1·9	2·5	1976	...	5·5(d)
1882	2·3	1917	0·6	0·7	1947	1·4	3·1	1977	...	5·8
1883	2·6	1918	0·8	0·8	1948	1·3	(2·0) / (1·6) (b)	1978	...	5·7
1884	8·1	1919	3·4	...	1949	1·2	1·6	1979	...	5·3
1885	9·3							1980	...	6·8
1886	10·2									
1887	7·6									
1888	4·9									
1889	2·1									

(*a*) Allowances for those still unemployed who had ceased to register were discontinued after 1939. The two figures shown here are comparable on a before-and-after basis.

(*b*) The first figure shown is for the first half and the second figure is for the second half. The comprehensive National Insurance scheme came into effect in July 1948.

(*c*) Based on the first eleven months, but excluding the West Midlands in October and November.

(*d*) Average of eleven months.

Labour Force 9. Percentages of Registered Unemployed by Regions – 1923–1980

NOTES

[1] SOURCES: Department of Employment and Productivity, *British Labour Statistics: Historical Abstract, 1886–1968*, and *Abstract*.

[2] The figures to 1939 are based on the total numbers of registered unemployed and the numbers of insured employees. This has the effect of inflating the percentages to a small degree.

[3] Workers temporarily stopped are included in the figures.

[4] All figures are averages of 12 monthly observations, except in 1943 to September, 1945, when they are averages of quarterly figures, and in 1939.

	London	South-East	South-West	Midlands	North-East	North-West	North (*d*)	Wales	Scotland	Great Britain	Northern Ireland
1923	9·9	9·2	10·4	9·9	11·5	14·2	...	6·3	13·8	11·2	16·4
1924 (*a*)	8·6	7·1	8·7	8·3	10·4	12·3	...	9·0	13·3	9·9	15·5
1925 (*a*)	7·1	5·5	8·0	8·5	14·6	10·9	...	16·9	14·7	10·7	22·8
1926 (*b*)	6·3	5·0	7·8	10·4	16·8	14·0	...	18·2	15·8	11·9	21·1
1927	5·3	4·7	7·1	8·1	13·5	10·3	...	20·0	10·1	9·4	12·0
	5·5	4·8	7·3	8·3	13·9	10·6	...	20·7	10·4	9·7	12·3
1928 (*a*)	5·2	5·2	8·1	9·8	15·5	12·5	...	23·2	11·6	10·8	16·3
1929 (*a*)	5·3	5·6	8·3	9·2	14·1	12·3	...	19·9	12·3	10·6	14·0
1930 (*a*)	7·9	8·0	10·5	14·9	20·8	23·9	...	26·7	18·7	16·3	22·6
1931 (*a*)	11·6	11·8	14·4	20·7	27·4	28·2	...	32·4	26·5	21·4	26·4
1932 (*a*)	12·9	14·3	17·2	19·6	28·8	25·6	...	36·8	28·2	22·1	25·7
1933	11·4	11·8	16·0	17·0	26·7	23·6	...	35·3	27·1	20·2	25·7
1934	8·9	9·0	13·8	12·7	23·0	21·3	...	33·5	24·5	17·2	21·2
1935 (*a*) (*c*)	8·2	8·5	12·3	11·1	21·8	20·4	...	33·3	23·2	16·1	25·3
1936 (*c*)	7·7(*e*)	7·5(*e*)	9·8	8·9	17·7		...	31·8	20·2	13·6	23·2
1937 (*a*) (*c*)	6·0	7·2(*e*)	8·3(*e*)	7·1(*e*)	11·4(*e*)	14·4	19·4	24·2	17·4	11·2	24·6
1938	7·8	8·9	8·8	10·1	14·1	18·4	19·8	26·6	17·9	13·3	30·5
1939 (to Aug.) (*a*)	7·4	8·6	7·2	8·1	11·8	15·4	18·7	22·0	16·1	11·1	26·2

	London & South-East	East	South	South-West	Midlands	North Midlands	East & West Ridings	North	North-West	Wales	Scotland	Great Britain	Northern Ireland
1945	0·5	0·5	0·5	0·6	0·7	0·4	0·7	2·1	1·0	4·0	2·0	1·0	5·6
1946	1·0	1·1	1·1	1·3	1·2	0·8(*e*)	1·4	5·0(*e*)	2·9(*e*)	8·6	4·6	2·4	8·4
1947	2·0	2·3	1·5	1·5	3·2	2·1	2·2	4·2	4·3	6·9	4·0	3·0	7·9

See p. 126 for footnotes.

Labour Force 9. *continued*

	South-East	East Anglia	South-West	West Midlands	East Midlands	Yorkshire & Humberside	North-West	North	Wales	Scotland	Great Britain	Northern Ireland
1949	1·1		1·4	0·6	0·7		1·7	2·6	4·0	3·0	1·5	6·5
1950	1·1		1·5	0·5	0·8		1·6	2·8	3·7	3·1	1·5	5·8
1951	0·9		1·2	0·4	0·7		1·2	2·2	2·7	2·5	1·2	6·1
1952	1·3		1·5	0·9	1·5		3·7	2·6	2·8	3·3	2·0	10·3
1953	1·2		1·6	1·1	1·0		2·1	2·4	2·9	3·0	1·6	8·1
1954	1·0		1·4	0·6	0·8		1·5	2·3	2·4	2·8	1·3	7·0
1955	0·7		1·1	0·5	0·6		1·4	1·8	1·8	2·4	1·1	6·8
1956	0·8		1·3	1·1	0·7		1·3	1·5	2·0	2·4	1·2	6·4
1957	1·1		1·8	1·3	0·9		1·6	1·7	2·6	2·6	1·4	7·3
1958	1·4		2·2	1·6	1·8		2·7	2·4	3·8	3·8	2·1	9·3
1959	1·3		2·1	1·5	1·7		2·8	3·3	3·8	4·4	2·2	7·8
1960	1·0		1·7	1·0	1·1		1·9	2·9	2·7	3·6	1·6	6·7
1961	1·0		1·4	1·4	1·0		1·6	2·5	2·6	3·1	1·5	7·5
1962	1·3		1·7	1·8	1·5		2·5	3·7	3·1	3·8	2·0	7·5
1963	1·6		2·1	2·0	1·9		3·1	5·0	3·6	4·8	2·5	7·9
1964	1·0		1·5	0·9	1·1		2·1	3·3	2·6	3·6	1·6	6·6
1965	0·9	1·3	1·6	0·9	0·9	1·1	1·6	2·6	2·6	3·0	1·4	6·1
1966	1·0	1·4	1·8	1·3	1·1	1·2	1·5	2·6	2·9	2·9	1·5	6·1
1967	1·7	2·1	2·5	2·5	1·8	2·1	2·5	4·0	4·1	3·9	2·4	7·7
1968	1·6	2·0	2·5	2·2	1·9	2·6	2·5	4·7	4·0	3·8	2·4	7·2
1969	1·6	1·9	2·7	2·0	2·0	2·6	2·5	4·8	4·1	3·7	2·4	7·3
1970	1·7	2·1	2·8	2·3	2·3	2·9	2·8	4·8	4·0	4·3	2·6	7·0
1970 (g)	1·6	2·1	2·8	1·9	2·2	2·8	2·7	4·6	3·8	4·2	2·5	6·8
1971	2·0	3·2	3·3	2·9	2·9	3·8	3·9	5·7	4·4	5·8	3·4	7·9
1972	2·2	2·9	3·4	3·6	3·0	4·2	4·8	6·3	4·8	6·4	3·7	8·0
1973	1·5	1·9	2·4	2·2	2·0	2·8	3·5	4·7	3·4	4·5	2·6	6·1
1974	1·5	1·9	2·6	...	2·2	2·6	3·5	4·6	3·7	4·0	2·6	5·7
1975	2·8	3·4	4·7	4·1	3·6	4·0	5·3	5·9	5·6	5·2	4·1	7·9
1976	4·2	4·8	6·4	5·8	4·7	5·5	7·0	7·5	7·3	7·0	5·6	10·0
1977	4·5	5·3	6·8	5·8	5·0	5·8	7·4	8·3	8·0	8·1	6·0	11·0
1978	4·2	5·0	6·4	5·6	5·0	6·0	7·5	8·9	8·3	8·2	6·0	11·5
1979	3·7	4·5	5·7	5·5	4·6	5·7	7·1	8·7	7·9	8·0	5·6	11·3
1980	4·8	5·7	6·7	7·8	6·4	7·8	9·3	10·9	10·3	10·0	7·3	13·7

(*a*) Changes in regulations resulted in increases or decreases in the numbers registered as unemployed in these years. The approximate effects on the percentages for Great Britain (where they can be estimated) are as follows: 1924 +1·1, 1928 +0·3, 1930 +0·5, 1931–32 −1·5, 1935 +0·2, 1937 −0·2, 1939 +0·4.
(*b*) Excluding coalminers absent from work due to the dispute.
(*c*) The extension of unemployment insurance to agriculture etc, in May 1936, to gardeners in February 1937, and to some domestic workers in April 1938 resulted in the inclusion of an indeterminate number of people who might not otherwise have registered as unemployed.
(*d*) Created out of parts of the North-East and the North-West.
(*e*) Transfers between regions have been allowed for in calculating these figures.
(*f*) No regional breakdown of the numbers of uninsured workers registered as unemployed is available from October 1945 to June 1948. The difference to the U.K. percentage if they are included is 0·1 or less.
(*g*) Subsequently excluding temporarily stopped workers.

Labour Force 10. Total Numbers Registered as Unemployed – United Kingdom, 1923–80

NOTES

[1] SOURCE: *Ministry of Labour Gazette* (and its successors); Department of Employment and Productivity, *British Labour Statistics. Historical Abstract, 1886–1968* (London, 1971) for Totals to 1947.

[2] The figures are averages of twelve monthly figures in each year, except in 1943 to September 1945, when they are averages of quarterly figures.

(in thousands)

	Great Britain					Northern Ireland				
	Wholly Unemployed		Temporarily Stopped			Wholly Unemployed		Temporarily Stopped		
	Males	Females	Males	Females	Total	Males	Females	Males	Females	Total
1923	...	...	...	...	1,250·6	...	...	...	...	41·5
1924 (*a*)	...	...	...	...	1,112·8	...	...	...	...	40·1
1925 (*a*)	...	...	...	...	1,228·1	...	...	...	...	60·6
1926 (*b*)	737·6	131·6	288·3	152·3	1,385·2	32·7	13·9	2·0	4·9	56·0
1927	640·6	111·7	215·9	76·6	1,109·3	21·3	4·5	1·0	1·8	30·6
1928 (*a*)	719·9	129·8	232·7	89·9	1,246·0	21·8	10·6	1·8	4·5	40·8
1929 (*a*)	728·1	154·2	191·6	87·3	1,239·9	20·9	8·4	1·6	2·6	36·1
1930 (*a*)	1,010·0	307·7	352·2	187·8	1,954·0	29·7	18·2	2·7	5·3	60·1
1931 (*a*)	1,499.6	439·7	417·9	167·5	2,647·1	42·0	18·7	2·4	5·0	71·3
1932 (*a*)	1,759·9	318·1	352·2	187·8	2,744·8	44·0	15·2	2·4	6·5	68·2
1933	1,695·2	283·3	338·6	112·0	2,520·6	44·8	14·1	2·3	3·8	65·0
1934	1,460·7	248·9	258·7	105·1	2,159·2	40·9	13·5	1·7	2·5	61·8
1935 (*a*)	1,385·5	260·5	215·4	83·8	2,036·4	43·6	17·1	1·7	11·8	69·7
1936 (*a*)	1,188·4	243·8	176·2	70·8	1,755·0	42·1	16·8	1·4	3·2	66·7
1937 (*a*)	1,000.8	216·9	132·3	68·6	1,484·4	48·1	17·5	1·5	3·1	72·6
1938 (*a*)	1,067.8	286·1	235·5	136·4	1,790·7	54·1	25·2	2·5	6·0	90·7
	----(*c*)	----(*c*)	----(*c*)	----(*c*)		----(*c*)	----(*c*)	----(*c*)	----(*c*)	
1939 (*a*)	982·9	315·0	137·2	78·5	1,513·6	52·3	18·7	1·5	3·7	76·3
1940 (*a*)	507·7	295·2	100·6	59·2	962·7	42·9	22·9	1·6	4·1	72·0
1941	153·2	139·2	29·3	28·1	349·8	16·4	20·6	1·2	3·6	41·7
1942 (*a*)	740·0	43·2	3·2	2·8	123·2	8·5	8·6	1·5	2·5	20·9
1943	53·1	26·9	0·8	0·8	81·6	11·0	4·0	1·6	1·0	17·5
1944	50·7	22·9	0·4	0·5	74·5	9·1	3·5	1·3	0·8	15·1
1945	83·7	52·1	0·6	0·7	137·1	14·0	4·4	1·3	0·6	20·3
1946	257·5	113·5	2·1	1·2	374·3	26·1	4·3	0·2	0·5	31·1
1947	239·0	86·5	102·7	52·0	480·2	[24·7](*d*)	[3·1](*d*)	[0·5](*d*)	[0·7](*d*)	29·9
1948 (*a*)	227·5	75·0	4·3	3·2	310·0	22·2	4·4	0·4	0·8	27·8
1949	223·2	76·9	4·8	3·1	308·0	21·4	6·9	0·4	1·2	30·0
1950	215·0	90·6	5·1	3·5	314·2	20·7	5·7	0·3	0·2	26·9
1951	153·4	83·6	8·1	7·8	252·9	20·5	6·6	0·3	1·1	28·5
1952	196·1	132·6	31·8	53·8	414·3	25·0	14·7	1·8	6·7	48·3
1953	204·3	115·6	13·9	8·2	342·0	26·8	9·6	0·5	1·3	38·0
1954	176·5	95·1	7·9	5·3	284·8	23·4	7·9	0·4	1·3	33·0
1955	137·4	75·7	9·3	9·8	232·2	22·3	8·1	0·5	1·3	32·3
1956	151·0	78·6	17·8	9·6	257·0	21·7	7·0	0·5	0·9	30·1
1957	204·3	90·2	12·3	5·7	312·5	24·8	7·8	0·5	0·6	34·7
1958	293·8	116·3	27·6	19·7	457·4	29·1	11·2	1·0	2·1	43·5
1959	322·6	121·9	21·2	9·5	475·2	25·4	10·3	0·4	0·8	36·9
1960	248·3	97·6	11·5	3·0	360·4	23·6	7·8	0·5	0·5	32·4
1961	226·3	85·8	23·3	5·3	340·7	25·2	9·2	0·6	1·1	36·1
1962	321·9	110·0	22·9	8·3	463·3	25·0	10·5	0·4	0·8	36·7
1963	393·8	126·7	46·2	6·4	573·2	27·4	10·2	0·8	0·7	39·0
1964	279·6	92·6	6·6	1·8	380·6	23·3	8·9	0·3	0·4	32·8
1965	240·6	76·4	9·7	2·1	328·8	21·8	8·4	0·6	0·3	30·9
1966	259·6	71·3	25·5	3·4	359·7	22·2	8·0	0·5	0·5	31·2
1967	420·7	100·2	30·5	8·0	559·5	27·0	10·9	0·5	1·3	39·6

See p. 128 for footnotes.

Labour Force 10. *continued*

(in thousands)

	Great Britain					Northern Ireland				
	Wholly Unemployed		Temporarily Stopped			Wholly Unemployed		Temporarily Stopped		
	Males	Females	Males	Females	Total	Males	Females	Males	Females	Total
1968	460·7	88·8	13·1	1·6	564·1	27·4	9·2	0·3	0·3	37·2
1969	461·9	81·9	14·0	1·5	559·3	28·7	8·4	0·5	0·2	37·8
1970	495·3	86·9	18·7	2·4	603·4	27·6	8·2	0·5	0·3	36·5
1971	639·8	118·6	41·9	6·5	800·1	31·3	9·5	0·6	0·5	41·5
1972	705·1 ----(*e*) 698·6	139·0 ----(*e*) 136·4	63·2	14·7	924·0 ----(*e*) 912·9	30·5 ----(*e*) 30·0	10·9 ----(*e*) 10·6	0·9	0·4	41·9 ----(*e*) 41·1
1973	492·4	95·3	10·0	1·1	598·8	22·8	8·3	0·3	0·2	31·6
1974	491·6	93·6	...	...	536·5	22·2	7·8	1·0	0·9	31·8
1975	747·4	188·4	48·9(*f*)	11·9(*f*)	...	29·7	12·1	0·9	1·0	43·9
1976	986·0	318·6	18·7(*g*)	5·1(*g*)	...	37·5	17·4	0·5	0·5	55·9
1977	1,027·5	395·2	15·3	2·2	1,440·2	41·7	19·1	2·0	0·4	63·3
1978	995·2	414·4	9·0	1·3	1,420·0	45·0	20·4	0·7	0·2	66·3
1979	919·6	405·9	10·7	1·6	1,337·8	44·3	20·6	0·7	0·1	65·7
1980	1,180·0	535·8	14·5	2·9	1,733·3	53·6	25·3	0·6	0·2	79·6

(*a*) Changes in regulations resulted in increases or decreases in the numbers registered in these years. The approximate effects on the numbers in the United Kingdom (where they can be estimated) were as follows in the month of change: Feb. 1924 +13·5; Aug. 1924 +70·0; Oct. 1924 +3·7; Aug. 1925 −10·0; Jan. 1928 −25·0; Apr. 1928 +40·0; July 1928 +25·0; June 1929 +5·0; March 1930 +60·0; between Oct. 1931 and May 1932 −180·0 to 190·0; Jan. 1932 −14·0; Jan. 1935 +20·0; Apr. 1937 +20·0; Aug. 1937 −50·5; Sept. 1939 +50·0; July 1940 −7·8; Feb. 1942 −18·6.

(*b*) Excluding coalminers absent from work due to the dispute.

(*c*) Casual workers are only included in the totals to 1938.

(*d*) Excluding February.

(*e*) Subsequently excluding adult students temporarily seeking vacation jobs.

(*f*) Excluding January.

(*g*) Excluding November and December.

Labour Force 11. Percentages of Insured Workers Unemployed by Industry – United Kingdom 1923–39

NOTE
SOURCE: *Ministry of Labour Gazette*.

(Averages of the Percentages in January and July each year, excluding workers under 16)

	1923 (a)	1924	1925	1926	1927	1928 (b)	1929	1930	1931	1932	1933	1934	1935	1936	1937 (c)	1938	1939
Fishing	12·0	14·1	12·5	16·7	13·8	11·6	11·8	13·3	18·0	22·0	22·8	23·2	21·1	22·0	24·2	26·4	24·6
Coalmining	3·0	5·8	11·5	9·5	19·0	23·6	19·0	20·6	28·4	34·5	33·5	29·7	27·2	22·8	16·1	16·7	12·5
Brick, Tile, Pipe, etc. Manufacture	7·6	7·9	6·8	15·2	6·9	12·4	11·5	13·0	18·0	21·5	20·2	13·3	11·9	11·7	8·2	9·1	10·9
Pottery, Earthenware, etc.	13·2	13·3	18·1	38·6	16·6	18·6	17·0	23·7	36·3	36·2	30·9	23·8	22·3	21·8	17·5	20·7	22·0
Chemicals	11·8	9·9	9·1	10·9	7·2	6·1	6·5	10·0	17·6	17·3	15·2	11·3	11·0	9·2	6·8	7·4	6·4
Pig Iron	10·1	14·1	21·5	43·4	16·4	18·7	14·4	20·3	37·7	43·8	41·5	27·7	22·3	16·0	10·7	12·9	17·6
Steel Melting and Iron Puddling, and Iron and Steel Rolling and Forging	21·2	22·0	25·0	40·4	19·4	22·4	20·1	28·2	45·5	47·9	41·5	27·3	23·5	17·4	11·4	19·5	15·1
General Engineering: Engineers' Iron and Steel Founding	20·5	16·9	13·3	15·1	11·8	9·8	9·9	14·2	27·0	29·1	27·4	18·4	13·6	9·6	5·8	7·0	6·6
Electrical Engineering	7·3	5·5	5·6	7·5	5·9	4·8	4·6	6·6	14·1	16·8	16·5	9·6	7·0	4·8	3·1	4·7	4·4
Construction and Repair of Motors, Cycles and Aircraft	9·7	8·9	7·1	8·2	8·1	8·1	7·1	12·1	19·3	22·4	17·6	10·8	9·0	6·9	5·0	7·2	4·4
Shipbuilding and Repairing	43·6	30·3	33·5	39·5	29·7	24·5	25·3	27·6	51·9	62·0	61·7	51·2	44·4	33·3	24·4	21·4	20·9
Stove, Grate, Pipe, etc. and General Ironfounding	17·7	13·2	11·4	14·7	10·0	12·0	10·9	14·7	24·8	28·6	25·0	15·3	14·4	9·8	7·0	12·7	11·9
Electric Cable, Apparatus, Lamps, etc. Manufacture	16·2	7·7	7·2	7·4	7·7	5·6	5·3	7·5	13·9	13·3	14·5	10·0	8·8	7·9	5·0	8·1	6·2
Cotton Textiles	21·6	15·9	8·8	18·3	15·4	12·5	12·9	32·4	43·2	30·6	25·1	23·7	22·3	16·7	10·9	23·9	16·9
Wool Textiles	9·5	8·4	16·9	17·4	11·0	12·0	15·5	23·3	33·8	22·4	17·0	17·8	15·5	10·3	8·8	21·3	11.0
Linen Textiles	19·8	11·8	25·0	28·2	12·2	19·8	15·7	25·2	35·3	29·7	23·1	17·7	24·0	21·4	16·2	40·3	21·5
Hosiery Manufacture	7·9	7·4	9·8	10·3	7·6	5·8	7·1	12·5	20·8	13·5	12·8	10·9	13·7	9·4	8·1	12·6	7·9
Tailoring	6·7	10·4	11·9	11·2	9·2	9·2	10·0	12·3	17·7	17·6	18·2	16·3	15·4	13·8	12·3	15·5	12·6
Dressmaking and Millinery	6·3	8·6	9·0	7·7	6·2	5·9	6·1	6·6	9·7	11·5	11·7	8·9	8·3	8·8	7·5	9·2	9·4
Boots, Shoes, etc. Manufacture	10·6	8·6	11·3	11·5	11·3	13·4	15·5	15·2	22·2	18·0	19·5	21·4	17·1	14·6	12·1	14·3	10·4
Bread, Biscuits, Cakes, etc. Manufacture	9·9	9·8	9·3	8·4	7·2	6·6	7·2	9·1	12·4	12·2	11·8	10·7	10·6	10·3	8·7	8·8	8·3
Drink Industries	6·4	6·8	6·9	6·3	6·3	6·2	6·8	8·7	12·9	14·4	13·1	10·9	10·6	9·6	7·7	8·0	7·4
Sawmilling and Machined Woodwork	11·5	10·6	9·8	11·1	8·4	9·2	10·0	11·9	18·4	22·0	20·0	16·8	15·8	13·6	10·7	11·9	11·2
Furniture Manufacture and Upholstery	7·8	8·2	6·9	7·8	6·5	5·9	6·5	10·0	19·0	21·7	20·6	15·4	13·9	11·6	9·8	13·4	12·8
Printing, Publishing, and Bookbinding	5·6	5·6	5·2	5·4	5·2	4·6	4·6	6·0	9·8	11·0	10·3	9·2	8·7	8·1	6·7	6·9	7·1
Building	12·2	12·5	10·5	12·1	11·1	13·9	14·3	16·2	22·7	30·2	29·0	21·3	19·7	19·8	14·6	16·7	17·6
Gas, Water, and Electricity Supply	7·2	6·3	6·2	6·0	5·4	5·8	6·1	7·0	8·9	10·9	11·0	10·1	10·4	9·7	8·3	8·3	7·7
Railway Service	6·0	6·4	6·5	12·3	6·1	6·5	6·5	6·9	12·1	15·7	16·7	12·3	10·0	8·5	6·5	7·3	8·4
Tramway and Omnibus Service	3·1	3·1	3·6	4·3	3·7	3·1	3·1	3·8	5·0	5·9	6·1	5·6	4·8	4·0	3·3	3·2	3·1
Other Road Transport	17·3	15·6	13·9	14·0	11·8	11·7	12·0	14·8	19·3	22·2	22·6	20·1	18·7	16·1	12·3	12·5	11·9
Docks, Harbours Canals, etc. Service	27·5	25·8	29·0	29·7	24·5	29·1	30·7	33·4	39·8	33·3	33·3	31·1	31·0	29·3	27·5	25·0	24·1
Distributive Trades	5·9	6·4	6·7	6·7	5·5	5·5	6·2	8·1	11·6	12·6	12·4	11·3	11·3	9·8	8·9	9·2	9·0
National Goverment Service	11·1	9·8	8·2	7·3	6·2	6·2	6·9	8·2	10·3	12·4	13·3	14·5	13·8	12·9	11·7	12·1	10·0
Local Government Service	6·0	6·9	8·6	9·0	8·2	8·6	9·6	10·7	13·7	18·2	19·6	20·3	20·2	19·7	17·6	17·2	14·6
Hotel, Public House, Club, etc. Service	9·8	11·3	11·4	9·0	7·9	7·6	8·7	11·8	17·6	17·5	16·7	15·2	15·5	15·0	13·9	15·5 (d)	15·3
Laundry and Dry-cleaning Service	5·0	5·8	5·8	4·5	4·1	3·8	4·3	6·1	9·8	9·4	9·0	7·7	7·6	6·9	6·0	6·8	7·0
TOTAL INSURED WORKERS OVER 16 (except those in the Agricultural Scheme)	11·6	10·9	11·2	12·7	10·6	11·2	11·0	14·6	21·5	22·5	21·3	17·7	16·4	14·3	11·3	13·3	11·7

(*a*) The figures for 1923 are for July only.
(*b*) In the figures for 1928 and later, people over 65 years old are not counted.
(*c*) The method of counting the unemployed was changed in September 1937, resulting in a reduction in the total recorded of about 50,000. The effect on the percentage is scarcely significant.
(*d*) Domestic servants in clubs, hospitals, etc. were included for the first time in 1938.

Labour Force 12. Unemployment among Insured Persons by Industry – United Kingdom 1938–80

NOTES

[1] SOURCE: *Ministry of Labour Gazette* (and its successors).

[2] The figures include both wholly unemployed and temporarily stopped up to 1972 (1st line), but are subsequently of the wholly unemployed only.

[3] The figures are for mid-July up to 1948, and for mid-June to 1976 and for mid-May subsequently, i.e. they are at the closest possible date to the employment figures given in table 5.

A. 1938–47

	Males					Females				
	1938	1939	1945	1946	1947	1938	1939	1945	1946	1947
Agriculture and Forestry	28,091	27,171	1,739	4,092	4,446	2,775	3,189	410	747	641
Fishing	5,813	5,755	176	643	755	106	120	3	1	2
Mining and Quarrying	203,018	122,351	7,175	13,995	1,820	707	570	47	295	151
Non-Metalliferous Mining Products	6,549	5,260	252	1,020	905	232	167	34	162	134
Brick, Tile, Pipe, etc., Making	8,194	8,368	200	877	813	733	867	28	115	138
Pottery and Earthenware	5,866	4,743	97	335	302	8,580	8,049	43	108	100
Glass	6,059	5,136	135	621	588	904	684	86	387	498
Chemicals, etc.	13,087	10,541	4,014	14,099	6,052	2,878	2,660	6,902	11,508	4,644
Metal Manufacture	71,792	28,978	1,804	5,683	6,493	2,239	1,030	982	3,562	2,611
Engineering, Shipbuilding and Repairing, and Metal Trades	223,101	130,691	24,328	67,353	42,905	35,094	21,021	13,083	20,231	11,093
Textiles	97,892	50,539	1,801	6,603	5,031	182,439	83,580	1,838	3,619	2,919
Leather and Leather Goods	6,416	3,806	129	683	516	2,930	2,150	56	248	240
Clothing	28,803	19,546	492	1,973	3,076	54,752	28,468	1,041	2,765	3,294
Food, Drink, and Tobacco	26,259	23,845	1,760	6,552	4,412	21,328	23,860	1,183	3,671	3,232
Woodworking, etc.	25,989	22,672	1,004	3,343	3,358	3,847	3,377	432	1,423	866
Paper, Printing, etc.	18,602	15,995	552	3,013	2,196	11,471	10,291	391	1,049	1,043
Building and Contracting	256,863	214,164	8,225	33,528	28,740	343	423	117	273	247
Other Manufactures	8,362	6,195	29	3,378	3,543	5,799	3,833	29	1,277	1,442
Gas, Water, and Electricity	17,531	15,016	569	2,304	1,898	197	207	51	468	202
Transport and Communications	115,195	101,152	5,667	21,967	20,342	1,762	2,000	562	5,794	2,814
Distributive Trades	126,493	116,774	4,887	17,228	14,495	47,277	50,323	3,270	11,336	8,907
Commerce, Banking, Finance and Insurance	8,571	8,581	446	1,882	1,954	1,095	1,436	288	4,981	1,498
Miscellaneous Trades and Services	144,399	136,729	12,350	36,596	35,579	52,852	67,278	7,882	19,693	20,037
GRAND TOTAL (in thousands) (*a*)	1,410	1,084	81	292	213	438	316	39	100	68

B. 1948–58, Males

	1948	1949	1950	1951	1952	1953	1954	1955	1956	1957	1958
Agriculture and Forestry	8,225	8,511	8,283	6,776	6,830	9,260	8,456	8,271	8,299	9,785	12,621
Fishing	1,382	3,069	5,634	3,233	3,258	3,875	3,852	2,797	3,343	2,942	3,094
Mining and Quarrying	2,904	2,361	2,750	2,434	2,145	2,491	2,194	1,518	2,007	2,623	5,151
Bricks and Fireclay Goods	1,086	857	851	522	806	958	802	765	695	999	1,968
Pottery and Earthenware	388	425	405	204	997	607	373	311	678	960	1,025
Glass	767	751	771	441	1,042	659	459	444	558	715	1,043
Other Non-Metalliferous Mining Products	1,112	1,029	1,057	658	960	1,181	929	727	822	1,128	1,733
Chemicals, etc.	4,934	3,811	3,586	2,246	3,506	3,195	2,705	1,969	2,148	2,810	4,225
Metal Manufacture	5,740	4,812	4,520	4,068	4,431	9,984	5,238	4,931	4,152	5,188	20,433
Engineering, Shipbuilding, and Electrical Goods	27,824	27,166	23,337	14,797	18,987	21,423	15,756	13,129	13,079	16,625	32,907
Vehicles	9,774	7,495	6,460	3,507	6,061	6,355	4,409	3,756	13,715	8,855	10,589
Metal Goods not elsewhere specified	5,277	4,429	3,888	2,252	3,682	5,023	2,846	2,214	2,497	3,890	6,101
Precision Instruments, Jewellery, etc.	948	895	767	521	1,046	817	555	368	457	564	966
Textiles	4,784	4,538	3,820	2,770	48,733	6,221	4,551	9,101	6,896	6,759	19,665
Leather, Leather Goods, and Fur	996	778	672	336	1,585	611	478	353	374	520	1,011
Clothing	4,714	2,340	5,564	2,990	8,100	4,506	4,277	3,146	2,924	2,771	6,834
Food, Drink, and Tobacco	5,666	5,571	6,164	4,109	5,796	6,780	5,811	4,525	5,021	6,893	10,279
Wood and Cork Manufactures	4,157	3,501	6,127	2,681	8,271	5,120	3,603	5,543	4,602	4,186	7,170
Paper and Printing	1,870	1,723	1,640	1,161	3,298	2,158	1,453	1,146	1,471	2,224	2,562
Other Manufacturing Industries	2,834	3,675	2,239	1,299	2,977	2,244	1,680	1,258	2,016	2,230	3,472
Building and Contracting	40,959	36,862	37,245	22,749	33,291	39,537	30,909	23,989	26,091	38,382	53,344
Gas, Water, and Electricity	1,986	1,892	2,162	1,505	2,285	2,603	2,179	1,658	1,727	2,258	3,231
Transport and Communications	24,879	21,902	22,212	15,680	20,112	20,423	18,363	15,390	15,327	18,759	26,417
Distributive Trades	15,323	15,804	16,290	10,867	15,330	16,876	14,402	12,192	12,410	16,858	26,091
Insurance, Banking, and Finance	1,422	1,329	1,391	917	1,280	1,481	1,329	1,171	1,237	1,510	2,147
Public Administration, etc.	19,366	16,735	17,058	12,500	16,650	16,150	13,609	11,086	10,974	14,242	18,007
Professional Services	3,350	3,431	3,381	2,735	3,662	3,837	3,412	2,747	2,735	3,607	4,704
Miscellaneous Services	14,433	16,225	16,889	11,372	14,119	15,333	13,264	10,158	10,397	13,043	18,463
GRAND TOTAL (in thousands) (*a*)	236	219	222	144	249	220	177	153	166	205	327

See p. 136 for footnotes.

Labour Force 12. *continued*

C. 1948–58, Females

	1948	1949	1950	1951	1952	1953	1954	1955	1956	1957	1958
Agriculture and Forestry	909	1,460	1,415	1,288	1,521	1,900	1,546	1,275	1,219	1,295	1,548
Fishing	10	16	21	18	16	18	7	11	9	6	10
Mining and Quarrying	118	106	119	102	172	233	134	171	149	114	157
Bricks and Fireclay Goods	111	132	148	101	224	246	197	196	158	222	353
Pottery and Earthenware	94	114	121	89	2,079	642	260	475	1,580	1,118	964
Glass	421	339	404	262	930	587	419	282	367	379	394
Other Non-Metalliferous Mining Products	157	124	143	96	245	212	145	108	120	118	161
Chemicals, etc.	2,344	1,552	1,598	1,197	2,725	2,270	1,740	1,602	1,222	1,556	2,248
Metal Manufacture	1,604	864	802	584	1,055	1,811	914	697	703	912	1,397
Engineering, Shipbuilding and Electrical Goods	6,055	4,726	4,304	3,204	8,178	5,995	4,269	4,177	5,244	4,496	7,063
Vehicles	1,236	1,009	1,004	721	1,734	1,440	1,058	798	2,787	1,694	2,179
Metal Goods not elsewhere specified	2,709	2,019	2,434	1,723	4,703	3,936	2,105	1,755	1,792	2,405	3,143
Precision Instruments, Jewellery, etc.	473	339	610	347	1,127	626	440	411	467	593	1,257
Textiles	3,624	5,932	4,609	4,072	104,505	10,216	7,784	18,355	12,641	8,436	34,905
Leather, Leather Goods and Fur	461	335	341	236	987	446	378	314	397	324	599
Clothing	4,837	2,845	5,698	3,780	18,824	6,558	7,065	6,119	4,992	7,642	11,452
Food, Drink, and Tobacco	3,876	4,493	6,832	5,136	9,768	8,431	7,328	5,932	5,465	6,473	8,468
Wood and Cork Manufactures	779	613	952	598	1,937	1,083	861	978	916	816	1,299
Paper and Printing	846	958	1,116	853	5,137	2,243	1,455	1,175	1,275	1,631	2,204
Other Manufacturing Industries	1,848	1,596	1,770	1,116	3,874	2,106	1,690	1,298	1,433	1,497	2,381
Building and Contracting	305	273	300	236	360	338	307	240	207	292	344
Gas, Water, and Electricity	93	78	94	101	134	153	125	103	111	101	150
Transport and Communications	1,685	1,472	1,627	1,249	2,275	2,096	1,853	1,407	1,506	1,583	1,951
Distributive Trades	7,283	8,117	10,232	8,498	15,488	13,843	11,873	10,133	9,554	11,235	15,812
Insurance, Banking, and Finance	832	585	593	448	677	732	594	479	418	511	651
Public Administration, etc.	4,248	3,786	4,854	3,466	4,882	4,527	2,999	2,241	1,924	2,558	3,006
Professional Services	3,462	3,825	5,122	4,659	7,199	6,421	5,427	4,367	3,965	4,817	6,011
Miscellaneous Services	15,423	18,801	23,228	19,343	29,304	26,877	21,206	17,136	15,637	17,762	22,499
GRAND TOTAL (in thousands) (*a*)	72	72	86	71	240	114	92	90	84	92	146

D. 1959–80 Males (*cont.*)

	1959	1960	1961	1962	1963	1964	1965	1966	1967	1968	1969(*b*)	1970
Agriculture and Forestry	12,663	10,274	9,186	9,840	12,046	9,629	8,714	8,340	10,794	11,252	10,697	10,359
Fishing	3,369	3,574	2,871	3,175	3,449	2,611	2,567	2,345	2,973	3,289	3,261	3,483
Mining and Quarrying	8,115	6,303	4,342	6,417	9,537	6,821	5,949	5,949	9,142	20,059	25,194	24,311
Bricks, Fireclay, and Refractory Goods	1,948	1,147	941	1,574	1,924	1,160	1,000	999	2,029	1,913	1,918	2,373
Pottery	1,094	613	469	712	918	622	458	776	984	814	834	1,030
Glass	1,214	871	733	938	1,358	850	680	654	1,329	1,457	1,490	1,828
Other Non-Metalliferous Mining Products	1,423	1,088	875	1,385	1,700	1,101	1,069	1,071	2,092	2,395	2,200	2,875
Chemicals etc.	4,597	3,388	3,127	4,681	5,760	4,816	4,586	3,881	6,770	7,611	7,287	8,111
Metal Manufacture	16,782	5,069	7,083	14,512	14,298	5,740	4,360	6,742	19,248	13,129	10,740	13,796
Engineering and Electrical Goods	17,320	10,256	10,277	16,454	24,026	13,597	11,567	11,558	29,092	31,368	27,598	30,873
Shipbuilding and Marine Engineering	16,479	13,064	12,118	13,368	18,453	11,598	5,840	4,887	10,043	10,119	8,415	8,371
Vehicles	6,036	3,653	4,258	7,781	8,959	5,040	5,765	5,580	16,075	13,286	17,747	19,933
Metal Goods not elsewhere specified	5,921	3,669	3,528	6,837	8,332	4,553	3,811	3,959	11,476	11,364	10,158	12,864
Textiles	9,822	7,124	5,519	10,351	10,569	5,824	5,235	4,833	11,996	9,500	8,884	11,862
Leather, Leather Goods, and Fur	771	611	484	893	980	603	462	458	1,006	915	968	1,205
Clothing	2,968	1,964	1,537	2,524	3,634	1,873	1,614	1,334	3,565	2,884	2,859	3,213
Food, Drink, and Tobacco	9,258	6,807	5,863	8,352	10,392	7,267	6,088	6,364	11,457	12,992	13,539	15,103
Timber, Furniture, etc.	4,839	4,331	2,975	5,008	5,464	3,392	2,980	3,116	6,655	5,961	6,948	7,287
Paper, Printing, and Publishing	2,801	1,809	1,823	2,551	3,418	2,312	2,190	2,252	4,914	5,388	5,395	6,793
Other Manufacturing Industries	2,969	2,172	2,247	3,157	4,029	2,805	2,302	2,370	4,943	5,056	5,461	9,682
Construction	62,432	46,417	39,320	61,543	75,121	51,386	45,604	43,846	93,214	103,657	96,604	101,791
Gas, Water, and Electricity	3,170	2,557	2,288	3,010	3,676	2,830	2,385	2,442	4,095	5,344	5,598	7,449
Transport and Communications	26,137	21,185	19,236	24,274	28,120	21,746	21,720	22,170	32,219	32,857	32,302	33,121
Distributive Trades	30,595	23,647	19,978	28,176	37,454	26,204	22,211	21,358	38,611	42,457	38,743	40,554
Insurance, Banking, and Finance	2,839	2,943	3,165	4,227	5,126	5,495	5,872	6,212	7,937	8,805	9,512	11,080
Public Administration, etc.	18,208	15,633	14,028	17,551	20,890	17,057	14,371	13,626	20,909	23,953	22,959	23,818
Professional and Scientific Services	4,980	3,889	3,514	4,599	5,873	4,574	4,239	4,305	6,935	8,072	8,369	9,346
Miscellaneous Services	25,405	19,387	16,942	22,710	29,647	22,099	19,876	19,051	33,195	36,240	33,795	35,378
GRAND TOTAL (in thousands) (*a*)	324	242	217	319	386	267	233	229	431	466	456	495

Labour Force 12. *continued*

D. 1959–80 Males (*cont.*)

	1971	1972	1972	1973	1974	1975	1976	1977	1978	1979	1980
Agriculture and Forestry	12,470	12,712	12,662	8,234	7,723	12,920	17,705	19,657	19,215	16,823	17,403
Fishing	3,678	3,645	2,614	1,857	1,990	2,536	2,841	3,114	3,179	3,196	3,406
Mining and Quarrying	21,566	19,330	19,322	17,546	15,360	15,476	16,986	16,474	22,022	23,166	24,556
Bricks, Fireclay, and Refractory Goods	2,998	2,953	2,920	1,650	1,495	2,909	3,203	3,014	2,799	2,279	2,615
Pottery	1,255	1,313	1,290	672	560	1,174	1,745	1,513	1,429	1,535	1,905
Glass	2,462	2,607	2,594	1,881	1,611	2,817	3,797	2,996	2,842	2,510	3,293
Other Non-Metalliferous Mining Products	4,056	3,809	3,798	2,291	1,937	3,259	4,157	3,811	3,266	2,904	3,141
Chemicals etc.	10,647	13,367	13,351	9,646	8,094	11,192	14,372	14,608	14,260	13,029	15,390
Metal Manufacture	28,538	27,826	23,397	12,932	10,775	17,677	24,737	21,780	25,680	23,444	32,794
Engineering and Electrical Goods	57,642	59,993	55,281	31,274	26,736	47,163	59,684	54,271	52,587	48,113	59,617
Shipbuilding and Marine Engineering	9,947	18,614	11,111	7,581	5,853	7,089	8,946	8,978	9,171	10,098	13,521
Vehicles	28,637	22,585	19,133	10,439	9,074	19,051	26,050	18,769	17,747	17,340	20,134
Metal Goods not elsewhere specified	21,050	23,977	22,325	12,570	11,768	23,526	30,471	27,054	26,682	25,116	30,182
Textiles	19,549	18,194	17,355	10,436	8,577	15,746	19,501	19,046	18,555	16,158	22,923
Leather, Leather Goods, and Fur	1,416	1,644	1,639	1,061	996	1,656	2,562	2,213	2,018	1,911	2,314
Clothing	3,830	4,637	4,498	2,852	2,475	4,503	7,364	6,632	6,433	5,505	7,935
Food, Drink, and Tobacco	21,301	21,251	21,186	14,908	14,206	23,004	28,515	29,319	31,398	27,818	31,180
Timber, Furniture, etc.	9,093	8,941	8,674	5,597	5,882	9,939	12,487	13,055	11,856	10,701	13,695
Paper, Printing, and Publishing	10,819	10,716	10,662	6,954	7,234	10,838	13,503	13,319	11,992	11,044	12,041
Other Manufacturing Industries	9,618	9,797	9,634	6,252	5,832	11,311	13,431	14,219	12,944	12,795	15,217
Construction	126,684	130,536	130,379	90,206	99,772	158,090	209,449	214,861	197,646	171,143	200,161
Gas, Water, and Electricity	8,801	9,660	9,640	6,459	5,424	5,894	8,022	8,350	7,638	6,718	6,379
Transport and Communications	40,131	44,869	44,733	35,952	29,977	43,425	54,628	54,849	53,083	48,847	56,105
Distributive Trades	51,688	57,765	57,584	39,235	36,014	58,928	81,342	82,604	80,581	72,632	83,176
Insurance, Banking, and Finance	13,116	14,142	14,139	12,087	12,177	16,188	18,808	18,942	18,274	17,664	21,070
Public Administration, etc.	27,500	30,838	30,791	29,961	28,760	36,197	46,414	55,373	60,714	55,906	57,185
Professional and Scientific Services	12,375	14,188	14,149	12,329	12,217	16,565	22,599	24,629	26,439	25,207	26,799
Miscellaneous Services	42,191	50,026	49,957	37,105	35,829	56,458	80,501	86,937	86,104	79,747	91,751
GRAND TOTAL (in thousands) (*a*)	652	702	683(*c*)	489(*c*)	466(*c*)	717(*c*)	1,009	994	1,001	922	1,049

E. 1959–80 Females

	1959	1960	1961	1962	1963	1964	1965	1966	1967	1968	1969	1970
Agriculture and Forestry	1,649	1,280	1,117	1,230	1,478	1,206	1,081	904	1,189	1,326	1,099	1,032
Fishing	8	16	12	10	8	11	16	16	22	18	15	13
Mining and Quarrying	314	227	152	180	242	172	144	127	172	185	199	161
Bricks, Fireclay, and Refractory Goods	300	212	126	232	247	141	117	106	182	105	113	95
Pottery	809	322	334	385	702	362	225	276	624	256	242	326
Glass	607	394	298	381	478	264	246	201	284	236	154	202
Other Non-Metalliferous Mining Products	156	119	96	151	148	95	96	62	164	119	96	116
Chemicals etc.	2,071	1,453	1,202	1,581	1,893	1,383	1,001	812	1,466	1,104	1,020	1,183
Metal Manufacture	1,521	702	572	901	1,063	621	531	469	949	733	589	752
Engineering and Electrical Goods	6,497	4,487	4,054	5,835	7,339	5,008	4,331	3,713	7,864	5,576	4,977	5,532
Shipbuilding and Marine Engineering	328	303	242	255	350	260	178	141	236	160	141	122
Vehicles	1,184	786	1,124	1,257	1,196	755	654	562	1,377	905	1,150	1,347
Metal Goods not elsewhere specified	2,925	1,916	1,822	3,022	3,356	1,799	1,417	1,289	2,693	1,942	1,707	2,115
Textiles	14,310	9,398	7,598	13,499	11,205	5,722	4,552	3,377	10,812	4,904	3,661	4,976
Leather, Leather Goods, and Fur	431	285	256	382	612	238	197	159	393	228	237	255
Clothing	6,476	4,089	4,443	6,556	8,895	4,503	3,588	2,762	9,212	4,179	3,927	4,190
Food, Drink, and Tobacco	8,230	5,789	5,243	6,682	8,236	5,555	4,229	3,373	5,469	4,479	4,134	4,293
Timber, Furniture, etc.	988	771	467	812	1,008	568	511	411	761	575	582	540
Paper, Printing, and Publishing	2,178	1,485	1,398	2,142	2,835	1,859	1,405	1,225	1,954	1,527	1,492	1,699
Other Manufacturing Industries	2,129	1,390	1,328	2,034	2,470	1,737	1,214	1,120	1,994	1,439	1,356	1,457
Construction	559	390	337	468	583	464	475	393	693	613	600	704
Gas, Water, and Electricity	239	172	173	166	219	198	198	169	236	242	251	272
Transport and Communications	2,430	1,721	1,510	1,895	2,412	1,673	1,498	1,341	1,997	1,847	1,663	1,708
Distributive Trades	18,342	13,969	11,914	16,326	21,206	14,389	11,995	10,212	17,246	15,376	13,373	14,033
Insurance, Banking, and Finance	745	613	570	766	977	808	755	846	1,116	1,110	1,410	1,811
Public Administration, etc.	2,735	2,206	1,893	2,293	2,878	2,379	2,089	2,021	2,909	3,119	2,941	3,128
Professional and Scientific Services	6,593	5,245	4,514	5,831	7,168	5,330	4,598	4,285	6,286	6,143	5,960	6,337
Miscellaneous Services	22,897	16,981	14,301	17,346	21,729	15,701	13,342	11,319	17,211	15,473	13,178	12,978
GRAND TOTAL (in thousands) (*a*)	125	93	82	113	130	87	72	62	109	87	78	83

See p. 136 for footnotes.

Labour Force 12. *continued*

E. 1959–80 Females (*cont.*)

	1971	1972	1972	1973	1974	1975	1976	1977	1978	1979	1980
Agriculture and Forestry	1,322	1,334	1,305	903	851	1,398	2,471	3,046	3,491	3,476	3,705
Fishing	9	5	5	4	3	14	37	35	38	61	59
Mining and Quarrying	162	189	188	151	133	157	243	326	344	388	519
Bricks, Fireclay, and Refractory Goods	151	126	118	86	79	147	264	215	203	204	251
Pottery	322	362	346	172	159	425	734	691	816	970	1,316
Glass	248	320	319	228	184	413	766	698	706	767	1,138
Other Non-Metalliferous Mining Products	176	183	175	109	87	201	339	400	320	304	389
Chemicals etc.	1,690	2,024	2,018	1,404	1,315	2,264	3,805	4,316	4,505	4,730	6,208
Metal Manufacture	1,072	1,388	1,314	714	542	1,064	1,901	1,959	2,021	2,142	3,106
Engineering and Electrical Goods	8,657	9,197	8,883	5,522	4,693	11,951	17,724	17,255	17,548	17,926	23,128
Shipbuilding and Marine Engineering	155	364	198	135	131	182	337	362	364	403	558
Vehicles	1,812	1,558	1,440	810	673	1,657	2,774	2,514	2,410	2,689	3,750
Metal Goods not elsewhere specified	2,940	3,742	3,408	2,147	1,841	4,846	6,667	6,734	7,058	7,004	9,402
Textiles	7,800	7,360	6,645	3,730	2,829	6,492	9,745	10,394	11,754	11,250	15,344
Leather, Leather Goods, and Fur	333	425	417	284	244	478	937	975	1,054	977	1,355
Clothing	5,029	7,748	7,459	4,855	3,911	8,852	15,085	15,845	18,217	16,759	24,146
Food, Drink, and Tobacco	6,203	7,093	7,015	4,560	3,796	7,390	11,479	13,292	14,844	14,713	18,570
Timber, Furniture, etc.	800	909	874	625	587	1,150	1,764	2,060	2,004	1,898	2,861
Paper, Printing, and Publishing	2,629	2,912	2,901	1,956	1,632	3,257	5,172	5,708	5,761	5,682	7,227
Other Manufacturing Industries	2,232	2,338	2,309	1,447	1,292	3,283	4,741	5,407	5,754	5,454	7,955
Construction	919	1,113	1,113	783	707	1,510	2,622	3,662	3,644	3,513	4,113
Gas, Water, and Electricity	369	489	489	346	314	527	855	1,019	1,195	1,236	1,453
Transport and Communications	2,154	2,807	2,805	1,965	1,808	3,068	5,572	6,639	7,135	7,261	9,249
Distributive Trades	18,017	22,533	22,264	14,757	13,236	26,057	46,291	54,099	57,363	55,281	69,391
Insurance, Banking, and Finance	2,261	3,268	3,265	2,363	2,437	5,018	8,718	10,554	10,566	10,835	14,225
Public Administration, etc.	3,481	4,360	4,347	3,794	3,863	6,538	11,673	16,785	19,667	20,408	23,878
Professional and Scientific Services	7,693	9,283	9,259	7,680	7,061	11,366	20,280	26,031	30,564	31,730	37,910
Miscellaneous Services	15,411	18,845	18,809	13,712	12,413	22,828	41,050	51,318	54,788	52,107	62,726
GRAND TOTAL (in thousands) (*a*)	110	132	130(*c*)	93(*c*)	83(*c*)	163(*c*)	322	347	386	377	461

(*a*) This includes some unspecified workers (eg. those in government training schemes) not included in individual categories.

(*b*) There were minor differences in the composition of some categories with the adoption of a new Standard Industrial Classification.

(*c*) Adjusted totals, taking into account changes notified within four days of the count, are available a follows:-

	Males	Females
1972	677	129
1973	484	92
1974	461	82
1975	709	161

Labour Force 13. Numbers and Membership of Trade Unions with Headquarters in Great Britain and Northern Ireland – 1892–1980

NOTE

[1] SOURCES: Department of Employment and Productivity, *British Labour Statistics: Historical Abstract* (London, 1971), with subsequent data and some revisions from *Abstract*.

[2] The statistics relate to all organisations of employees which are known to include in their objects that of negotiating with employers with a view to regulating the remuneration or working conditions of their members.

[3] A small number of members in branches overseas, notably in Ireland, is included.

[4] The subdivision of the total membership by sexes is partly estimated as some unions cannot make precise returns.

	Total Unions	Members (in thousands) Total	Males	Females
1892	1,233	1,576	...	...
1893	1,279	1,559	...	...
1894	1,314	1,530	...	...
1895	1,340	1,504	...	...
1896	1,358	1,608	1,466	142
1897	1,353	1,731	1,583	147
1898	1,326	1,752	1,608	144
1899	1,325	1,911	1,761	150
1900	1,323	2,022	1,868	154
1901	1,322	2,025	1,873	152
1902	1,297	2,013	1,857	156
1903	1,285	1,994	1,838	156
1904	1,256	1,967	1,802	165
1905	1,244	1,997	1,817	180
1906	1,282	2,210	1,999	211
1907	1,283	2,513	2,263	250
1908	1,268	2,485	2,230	255
1909	1,260	2,477	2,214	263
1910	1,269	2,565	2,287	278
1911	1,290	3,139	2,804	335
1912	1,252	3,416	3,026	390
1913	1,269	4,135	3,702	433
1914	1,260	4,145	3,708	437
1915	1,229	4,359	3,868	491
1916	1,225	4,644	4,018	626
1917	1,241	5,499	4,621	878
1918	1,264	6,533	5,324	1,209
1919	1,360	7,926	6,600	1,326
1920	1,384	8,348	7,006	1,342
1921	1,275	6,633	5,628	1,005
1922	1,232	5,625	4,753	872
1923	1,192	5,429	4,607	822
1924	1,194	5,544	4,730	814
1925	1,176	5,506	4,671	835
1926	1,164	5,219	4,407	812
1927	1,159	4,919	4,125	794
1928	1,142	4,806	4,011	795
1929	1,133	4,858	4,056	802
1930	1,121	4,842	4,049	793
1931	1,118	4,624	3,859	765
1932	1,081	4,444	3,698	746
1933	1,081	4,392	3,661	731
1934	1,063	4,590	3,854	736
1935	1,049	4,867	4,106	761
1936	1,036	5,295	4,495	800
1937	1,032	5,842	4,947	895
1938	1,024	6,053	5,127	926
1939	1,019	6,298	5,288	1,010
1940	1,004	6,613	5,494	1,119
1941	996	7,165	5,753	1,412
1942	991	7,867	6,151	1,716
1943	987	8,174	6,258	1,916
1944	963	8,087	6,239	1,848
1945	781	7,875	6,237	1,638
1946	757	8,803	7,186	1,617
1947	734	9,145	7,483	1,662
1948	749	9,362	7,677	1,685
1949	742	9,318	7,644	1,674
1950	732	9,289	7,605	1,684
1951	735	9,535	7,745	1,790
1952	723	9,588	7,797	1,792
1953	720	9,527	7,749	1,778
1954	711	9,566	7,756	1,810
1955	704	9,741	7,874	1,867
1956	685	9,778	7,871	1,907
1957	685	9,829	7,935	1,894
1958	675	9,639	7,789	1,850
1959	668	9,623	7,756	1,868
1960	664	9,835	7,884	1,951
1961	655	9,916	7,911	2,005
1962	649	10,014	7,960	2,054
1963	643	10,067	7,963	2,104
1964	641	10,218	8,043	2,174
1965	630	10,325	8,084	2,241
1966	622	10,259	8,003	2,256
1967	606	10,194	7,908	2,286
1968	586	10,200	7,836	2,364
1969	565	10,471	7,972	2,507
1970	543	11,187	8,444	2,743
1971	525	11,135	8,382	2,753
1972	507	11,359	8,452	2,907
1973	519	11,456	8,450	3,006
1974	507	11,764	8,586	3,178
1975	501	12,193	8,729	3,464
1976	473	12,386	8,825	3,561
1977	481	12,846	9,071	3,775
1978	462	13,112	9,238	3,874
1979	456	13,477	9,544	3,902
1980	438	12,952	9,162	3,790

Labour Force 14. Numbers and Membership of Trade Unions with Headquarters in the Republic of Ireland – 1923–80

NOTE
SOURCE: *Statistical Abstract of Ireland*.

	Total Unions	Members (thousands)		Total Unions	Members (thousands)		Total Unions	Members (thousands)
1923	...	131	1943	...	115	1962	101	300
1924	...	127	1944	...	134	1963	90	298
1925	...	99	1945	...	143	1964	95	302
1926	...	95	1946	...	160	1965	92	307
1927	...	89	1947	...	185	1966	88	302
1928	...	88	1948	...	205	1967	77	305
1929	...	87	1949	...	224	1968	84	316
1930	...	87	1950	...	243	1969	93	338
1931	...	87	1951	...	257	1970	91	338
1932	...	87	1952	...	259	1971	85	328
1933	...	92	1953	...	264	1972	85	326
1934	...	98	1954	97	267	1973	85	327
1935	...	97	1955	98	272	1974	89	367
1936	...	101	1956	97	271	1975	91	359
1937	...	118	1957	101	265	1976	90	367
1938	...	122	1958	99	264	1977	91	382
1939	...	135	1959	97	272	1978	90	369
1940	...	128	1960	104	283	1979	90	397
1941	...	104	1961	104	291	1980	91	394
1942	...	113						

Labour Force 15. Financial Summary of 100 Principal Trade Unions – Great Britain 1892–1932

NOTE
SOURCES: 1892–1910 – 1st to 17th *Abstract of Labour Statistics*, or annual *Report on Trade Unions* (both in sessional papers), whichever provides the latest figure for any year; 1911–32 – 18th–21st *Abstract of Labour Statistics*.

	Members (in thousands)	Income (£000)	Expenditure (in £000) Unemployment Benefit (a)	Dispute Benefit	Provident Benefits	Management and Other Expenses	Funds at end of Year (£000)
1892	903	1,462	325	398	377	333	1,574
1893	909	1,614	458	574	413	380	1,352
1894	924	1,617	447	168	415	396	1,546
1895	907	1,542	417	197	461	302	1,712
1896	988	1,652	261	168	448	335	2,151
1897	1,107	1,968	330	646	480	432	2,221
1898	1,084	1,902	237	328	505	410	2,644
1899	1,164	1,835	187	120	551	395	3,226
1900	1,210	1,950	263	140	587	453	3,733
1901	1,219	2,050	328	210	619	488	4,139
1902	1,217	2,094	433	221	653	500	4,426
1903	1,206	2,109	517	176	695	535	4,612
1904	1,203	2,124	660	118	749	528	4,680
1905	1,220	2,228	529	214	787	549	4,830
1906	1,307	2,364	429	154	820	570	5,222
1907	1,471	2,518	469	138	866	600	5,668
1908	1,451	2,767	1,026	606	929	672	5,201
1909	1,437	2,585	952	156	923	675	5,079
1910	1,472	2,716	702	352	926	662	5,153
	----	----	---	---	---	---	----
1911 (b)	2,218	3,386	448	590	994	733	5,669
1912	2,429	3,535	591	1,672	1,054	871	4,828
1913	3,023	4,132	490	373	1,199	1,012	5,675
1914	3,023	4,494	993	588	1,197	1,055	6,146
1915	3,233	4,403	382	91	1,182	1,138	7,546
1916	3,477	4,532	151	113	1,172	1,181	9,248
1917	4,174	5,211	250	132	1,233	1,393	11,200
1918	5,000	6,304	224	231	1,422	1,879	13,351
1919	6,046	8,721	1,081	2,064	1,479	2,605	14,081
1920	6,335	11,583	1,835	2,792	1,646	3,807	14,645
1921	4,922	19,351	14,925	3,131	1,911	3,833	9,452
1922	4,103	13,842	7,701	1,409	1,853	3,226	8,470
1923	3,952	10,293	3,507	676	1,786	2,793	9,378
1924	4,073	9,993	2,927	1,149	1,896	2,836	9,987
1925	4,050	10,831	4,225	265	1,947	2,789	11,081
1926	3,774	12,599	6,181	5,104	2,079	2,744	7,040
1927	3,509	9,066	2,866	156	2,006	2,532	8,172
1928	3,402	8,704	2,898	183	2,023	2,458	8,932
1929	3,440	8,825	2,557	556	2,094	2,483	9,631
1930	3,428	10,023	4,770	243	2,036	2,493	9,758
1931	3,240	12,223	7,157	375	2,119	2,517	9,389
1932	3,074	11,217	5,962	607	2,113	2,396	9,169

(*a*) Includes travelling and emigration benefits.

(*b*) The revised figures for 1911 published in the 18th *Abstract of Labour Statistics* differ considerably from those in the 17th *Abstract* – e.g. the number of members is stated to be 608,000 more in the 18th than in the 17th. It therefore seems reasonable to suppose that there is a break in all series between 1910 and 1911.

Labour Force 16. Financial Summary of Registered Trade Unions – Great Britain 1910–70

NOTE
SOURCES: 1910–21 – 18th *Abstract of Labour Statistics*; 1922–39 – *Report of the Chief Registrar of Friendly Societies*, annually.

	Number of Unions	Members (thousands)	Income (£000)	Expenditure (£000): Unemployment Benefit (*a*)	Dispute Benefit	Provident Benefits	from Political Fund	Working Expenses	Other Outgoings	Funds at End of Year (£000)
1910	548	1,982	3,149	677 (*b*)	530	1,096	—	682		5,871
1911	542	2,321	3,646	478 (*b*)	603	1,141	—	737		6,294
1912	539	2,547	3,824	630 (*b*)	1,655	1,172	—	912		5,589

1913	546	3,205	4,516	507	446	1,373	7	1,120		6,471
1914	540	3,199	4,830	881	661	1,371	21	1,179		6,969
1915	539	3,389	4,766	291	91	1,306	38	1,269		8,552
1916	528	3,649	4,932	117	90	1,284	32	1,329		10,472
1917	522	4,361	5,815	267	137	1,348	43	1,582		12,712
1918	527	5,259	7,068	283	295	1,591	133	2,121		14,948
1919	544	6,516	9,560	967	2,132	1,642	113	3,036		15,956
1920	557	6,929	12,872	1,718	3,219	1,756	185	4,275		15,861
1921	524	5,454	21,065	15,150	3,427	2,150	160	4,401		10,815
1922	514	4,506	15,301	8,359	1,428	2,030	267	3,527	714	9,861
1923	490	4,369	11,267	3,733	721	1,989	228	3,072	550	10,752
1924	484	4,458	11,223	3,139	1,188	2,110	215	3,105	795	11,434
1925	488	4,448	11,834	4,527	313	2,160	114	3,076	473	12,556
1926	485	4,148	13,821	6,377	5,617	2,250	108	2,956	621	8,478
1927	487	3,903	10,072	3,131	187	2,231	134	2,783	364	9,710
1928	481	3,765	9,715	3,234	128	2,242	118	2,707	394	10,602
1929	472	3,779	9,682	2,853	398	2,333	178	2,719	429	11,361
1930	474	3,764	11,374	5,350	319	2,269	95	3,134		11,651
1931	469	3,577	13,807	8,340	169	2,343	167	3,175		11,285
1932	464	3,405	12,538	6,941	257	2,320	88	3,024		11,192
1933	458	3,347	10,989	5,017	190	2,329	94	2,526	271	11,760
1934	449	3,513	10,171	3,633	104	2,253	100	2,548	392	12,893
1935	448	3,795	9,434	2,504	232	2,307	168	2,633	311	14,167
1936	441	4,214	8,673	1,882	195	2,430	102	2,808	680	16,032
1937	433	4,695	9,097	1,708	336	2,535	126	3,086	442	18,105
1938	426	4,867	9,581	3,202	148	2,568	117	3,303	535	20,014

1939	424	5,019	9,702	746 (*b*)	163	2,659	118	3,408	451	22,183
1940	416	5,363	9,918	797	55	2,797	102	3,486	469	24,708
1941	417	5,928	10,243	198	18	2,769	124	3,781	530	27,525
1942	423	6,530	11,416	84	18	2,772	111	4,099	551	31,318
1943	418	6,839	12,113	59	15	2,988	117	4,531	617	35,110
1944	421	6,756	12,548	59	29	3,083	137	4,805	638	38,950
1945	427	6,536	12,881	108	43	3,253	346	5,093	632	42,417
1946	428	7,475	14,617	273	75	3,544	201	5,996	583	46,211
1947	417	7,758	16,663	437	57	3,747	313	6,803	1,350	50,081
1948	416	7,917	17,155	180	250	3,765	375	7,535	810	54,398
1949	417	7,884	17,681	159	74	4,299	517	7,945	1,103	58,119
		----(*c*)	----(*c*)						----(*c*)	
1950	416	7,948	17,624	163	244	4,130	451	8,226	812	62,150
1951	413	8,287	18,248	133	178	4,480	555	9,094	1,400	64,825
1952	406	8,377	19,451	358	351	4,713	357	9,913	1,235	67,607
1953	410	8,323	20,354	172	258	5,046	389	10,338	1,111	70,709
1954	411	8,357	20,898	128	483	5,079	394	10,540	1,129	73,887

For 1910–21 and 1930–32 a single figure is printed spanning the Working Expenses and Other Outgoings columns.

Labour Force 16. *continued*

	Number of Unions	Members (thousands)	Income (£000)	Expenditure (£000): Unemployment Benefit (*a*)	Dispute Benefit	Provident Benefits	from Political Fund	Working Expenses	Other Outgoings	Funds at E of Year (£000)
1955	405	8,517	22,093	136	649	5,278	611	11,319	1,397	76,565
1956	400	8,549	23,424	184	819	5,539	399	12,129	1,362	79,495
1957	400	8,593	25,707	186	2,971	5,976	516	13,032	1,702	80,796
1958	401	8,405	27,056	328	1,383	6,191	678	13,619	1,414	84,275
1959	398	8,352	27,431	287	2,681	6,532	868	13,905	1,401	86,180
1960	398	8,532	28,631	196	456	6,620	524	14,881	2,033	90,267
1961	393	8,545	30,910	178	539	6,810	605	15,870	2,078	95,134
1962	388	8,532	33,583	309	697	7,183	606	16,981	2,109	100,839
1963	372	8,524	34,753	464	462	7,509	1,063	17,988	1,881	106,179
1964	369	8,620	36,853	209	489	7,527	975	19,199	2,798	111,324
1965	356	8,683	39,069	216	649	8,171	658	20,619	2,539	117,572
1966	351	8,584	41,863	251	919	9,663	1,155	22,486	2,989	121,882
1967	345	8,472	43,382	521	730	10,278	700	23,768	2,462	127,249
1968	337	8,529	44,322	478	1,162	10,453	712	25,412	3,424	129,762
1969	328	8,753	45,782	427	1,619	10,393	718	27,384	2,696	132,746
1970	326	9,277	52,226	533	3,583	10,804	1,566	30,222	3,694	134,599

(*a*) Includes travelling and emigration benefits.
(*b*) Except in these years, money issued as unemployment benefit from government sources is included as well as that direct from trade union funds.

(*c*) From 1950 these columns are adjusted to eliminate duplications in respe registered trade unions that are affiliated to a registered federation.

Labour Force 17. Industrial Disputes – United Kingdom 1888–1980

NOTES

[1] SOURCES: 1888–1936 – *Abstract of Labour Statistics*; 1937–80 – *Abstract*.

[2] For the years before 1910 there were revisions in each successive *Abstract of Labour Statistics*. The last figure to be published has been used here. The final figure for totals back to 1893 was given in the 21st issue and for the industry groups back to 1910 in the 18th issue.

[3] Totals for Great Britain and Northern Ireland are given back to 1893 in the 21st *Abstract of Labour Statistics*, but are not shown here beyond 1910.

[4] The number of working days recorded as lost includes those lost by workers at the establishments where disputes occurred, though they themselves were not parties to the dispute. It does not include days lost at other establishments.

A. U.K. (G.B. and Ireland) 1888–1913

Number of Disputes beginning in Year

	Total	Building	Mining and Quarrying	Metal, Engineering and Shipbuilding	Textiles	Clothing	Transport
1888	517	21	139	138	186	7	9
1889	1,211	86	131	339	241	66	184
1890	1,040	113	104	203	241	78	163
1891	906	125	132	164	220	63	61
1892	700	142	109	131	143	48	38
1893 (*a*)	615	131	127	117	79	65	31
1894	929	162	232	161	178	65	48
1895	745	146	187	160	124	39	27
1896	926	171	171	266	153	48	25
1897	864	193	127	229	108	56	48
1898	711	183	129	152	99	53	22
1899	719	180	109	140	124	37	47
1900	648	146	136	111	96	38	50
1901	642	104	210	103	96	39	20
1902	442	39	168	71	82	23	14
1903	387	44	125	87	55	25	15
1904	355	37	113	75	52	26	10
1905	358	31	106	70	67	29	11
1906	486	19	96	125	124	42	19
1907	601	22	112	134	153	64	29
1908	399	19	145	62	69	32	21
1909	436	15	207	62	56	29	19
1910	531	17	224	97	90	40	19
1911	903	27	179	255	133	46	99
1912	857	58	155	234	136	68	73
1913	1,497	198	192	392	243	75	123

B. U.K. (G.B. and Northern Ireland) 1910–80

	Total	Building	Mining and Quarrying	Metal, Engineering and Shipbuilding	Textiles	Clothing	Transport
1910	521	17	221	96	89	40	17
1911	872	14	179	253	133	44	91
1912	834	53	154	231	135	66	68
1913	1,459	192	192	391	240	73	115
1914	972	177	176	232	97	50	53
1915	672	63	85	189	67	40	75
1916	532	73	75	105	74	44	44
1917	730	51	148	225	70	55	32
1918	1,165	107	173	420	75	67	48
1919	1,352	134	250	335	65	77	113
1920 (*b*)	1,607	268	250	340	126	68	150
1921	763	158	173	151	28	29	42
1922	576	77	169	115	21	23	56
1923	628	65	197	103	35	24	61
1924	710	66	204	136	50	31	81

See p. 146 for footnotes.

Labour Force 17. *continued*

B. U.K. (G.B. and Northern Ireland) 1910–80 (*cont.*)

Number of Disputes beginning in Year

	Total	Building	Mining and Quarrying	Metal, Engineering and Shipbuilding	Textiles	Clothing	Transport
1925	603	58	175	94	59	31	54
1926 (*c*)	323	43	69	62	33	12	42
1927	308	34	115	69	27	10	16
1928	302	38	100	51	33	9	16
1929	431	40	162	80	58	17	21
1930	422	47	158	76	44	21	22
1931	420	57	155	61	38	21	17
1932	389	29	115	46	105	24	25
1933	357	20	117	68	43	20	30
1934	471	44	150	81	57	25	31
1935	553	46	233	73	64	28	36
1936	818	77	290	148	79	27	66
1937	1,129	98	470	220	84	33	50
1938	875	110	374	138	42	36	49
1939	940	122	417	181	73	25	34
1940	922	81	386	229	60	34	36
1941	1,251	77	482	472	42	20	58
1942	1,303	66	555	476	47	13	51
1943	1,785	71	862	612	52	23	68
1944	2,194	48	1,275	610	48	30	82
1945	2,293	36	1,319	591	41	29	156
1946	2,205	77	1,339	449	36	37	105
1947	1,721	35	1,066	291	25	22	119
1948	1,759	36	1,125	266	40	26	111
1949	1,426	59	879	250	27	20	85
1950	1,339	71	861	227	15	11	68
1951	1,719	95	1,067	318	14	11	91
1952	1,714	94	1,226	215	6	11	55
1953	1,746	80	1,313	194	7	17	73
1954	1,989	75	1,466	207	15	16	125
1955	2,419	96	1,784	302	12	12	118
1956	2,648	114	2,078	249	25	7	102
1957	2,859	126	2,226	268	27	9	121
1958	2,629	178	1,964	301	18	11	83
1959	2,093	171	1,311	396	14	11	88
1960	2,832	215	1,669	551	26	15	179
1961	2,686	286	1,466	547	28	13	138
1962	2,449	316	1,207	583	32	14	134
1963	2,068	168	993	568	38	8	133
1964	2,524	222	1,063	766	38	19	180
1965	2,354	261	743	854	30	14	179
1966	1,937	265	556	701	21	9	178
1967	2,116	256	399	910	41	19	208
1968	2,378	276	227	1,103	54	15	342
1969	3,116	285	193	1,430	72	24	540
1970	3,906	337	165	1,921	96	27	584
1971	2,228	234	138	1,107	70	27	269
1972	2,497	243	229	1,249	66	31	236
1973	2,873	217	305	1,342	92	31	298
1974	2,922	203	196	1,326	94	31	305

See p. 146 for footnotes.

B. U.K. (G.B. and Northern Ireland) 1910–80 (*cont.*)

Number of Disputes beginning in Year

	Total	Building	Mining and Quarrying	Metal, Engineering and Shipbuilding	Textiles	Clothing	Transport
1975	2,282	208	217	1,045	72	45	189
1976	2,016	244	283	800	49	31	193
1977	2,703	248	272	1,124	77	38	247
1978	2,471	185	351	975	67	36	209
1979	2,080	170	309	848	42	27	180
1980	1,330	103	310	380	25	10	158

A. U.K. (G.B. and Ireland) 1888–1913

Number of Working Days lost through Disputes (in thousands)

	Total	Building	Mining and Quarrying	Metal, Engineering and Shipbuilding	Textiles	Clothing	Transport
1888	...	...	...	...	...	...	...
1889	...	...	...	...	...	...	...
1890	...	...	...	...	...	...	...
1891	6,809	1,577	584	1,536	1,067	601	757
1892	17,382	1,478	5,376	1,865	6,952	692	362
1893 (*a*)	30,468	469	24,408	701	3,918	185	335
1894	9,529	378	6,639	1,274	748	100	267
1895	5,725	383	1,086	1,369	1,077	1,617	35
1896	3,746	1,060	1,012	863	520	99	23
1897	10,346	353	1,446	7,141	678	301	76
1898	15,289	379	12,876	1,371	274	70	47
1899	2,516	854	504	421	552	42	62
1900	3,153	727	553	349	411	60	304
1901	4,142	575	2,086	602	276	87	38
1902	3,479	116	2,550	420	238	54	10
1903	2,339	114	1,398	481	117	136	27
1904	1,484	346	657	185	122	13	42
1905	2,470	413	1,256	468	126	71	67
1906	3,029	56	922	1,118	763	92	10
1907	2,162	23	569	468	642	278	85
1908	10,834	74	1,351	3,836	5,365	69	52
1909	2,774	19	2,229	180	178	19	95
1910	9,895	35	5,524	3,147	918	59	71
1911	10,320	75	4,101	1,322	1,434	94	2,730
1912	40,915	107	31,594	1,369	3,698	601	2,985
1913	11,631	824	1,656	2,988	2,028	174	1,245

B. U.K. (G.B and Northern Ireland) 1910–80

	Total	Building	Mining and Quarrying	Metal, Engineering and Shipbuilding	Textiles	Clothing	Transport
1910	9,867	35	5,524	3,147	913	59	67
1911	10,155	72	4,101	1,265	1,434	88	2,656
1912	40,890	106	31,594	1,357	3,698	601	2,980
1913	11,631	814	1,656	2,985	2,019	173	1,184
1914	9,878	3,184	3,777	1,308	765	79	87
1915	2,953	130	1,657	357	369	28	152
1916	2,446	103	326	305	1,161	156	103
1917	5,647	68	1,183	3,063	710	142	184
1918	5,875	186	1,263	1,499	1,704	298	277
1919	34,969	391	7,713	12,248	8,160	239	4,200

See p. 146 for footnotes.

B. U.K. (G.B. and Northern Ireland) 1910–80 (*cont.*)

Number of Working Days lost through Disputes (in thousands)

	Total	Building	Mining and Quarrying	Metal, Engineering and Shipbuilding	Textiles	Clothing	Transport
1920	26,568	789	17,508	3,414	1,443	727	549
1921	85,872	557	72,962	4,420	6,939	81	296
1922	19,850	179	1,387	17,484	68	46	107
1923	10,672	394	1,212	5,997	1,228	28	1,031
1924	8,424	3,145	1,628	1,400	200	45	1,543
1925	7,952	85	3,740	184	3,173	38	73
1926 (*b*)	162,233	38	146,456	221	188	8	167
1927	1,174	129	695	81	36	199	7
1928	1,388	84	461	60	695	25	11
1929	8,287	28	666	768	6,752	11	13
1930	4,399	46	671	92	3,392	10	25
1931	6,983	145	2,859	99	3,717	16	13
1932	6,488	36	292	48	5,811	32	194
1933	1,072	9	455	112	85	6	272
1934	959	172	373	160	88	36	44
1935	1,955	37	1,385	93	106	44	82
1936	1,829	44	969	206	97	155	86
1937	3,413	39	1,501	778	156	72	748
1938	1,334	115	701	243	84	33	40
1939	1,356	131	612	332	100	13	56
1940	940	73	508	163	77	40	13
1941	1,079	36	338	556	36	16	54
1942	1,527	29	862	526	26	19	35
1943	1,808	25	889	635	17	7	181
1944	3,714	7	2,495	1,048	47	5	85
1945	2,835	5	644	528	10	68	1,491
1946	2,158	24	424	1,084	43	111	161
1947	2,433	24	915	579	13	15	627
1948	1,944	27	473	898	56	26	347
1949	1,807	32	755	285	68	10	533
1950 (*a*)	1,389	64	431	294	44	3	188
1951	1,694	83	351	514	8	8	601
1952	1,792	157	662	791	2	3	32
1953	2,184	101	394	1,525	19	8	69
1954	2,457	233	468	741	3	9	919
1955	3,781	71	1,112	669	15	8	1,687
1956	2,083	78	503	1,017	28	1	35
1957	8,412	84	514	6,592	37	7	998
1958	3,462	151	450	609	10	10	2,116
1959	5,270	138	370	962	54	2	95
1960 (*a*)	3,024	110	495	1,450	16	9	636
1961	3,046	285	740	1,464	18	5	230
1962	5,798	222	308	4,559	31	6	431
1963	1,755	356	326	854	23	2	72
1964	2,277	125	309	1,338	27	7	312
1965	2,925	135	413	1,763	46	6	305
1966	2,398	145	118	871	10	1	1,069
1967	2,787	201	108	1,422	25	6	823
1968	4,690	233	57	3,363	34	7	559
1969	6,846	278	1,041	3,739	120	19	786

See p. 146 for footnotes.

B. U.K. (G.B. and Northern Ireland) 1910–80 (*cont.*)

Number of Working Days lost through Disputes (in thousands)

	Total	Building	Mining and Quarrying	Metal, Engineering and Shipbuilding	Textiles	Clothing	Transport
1970	10,980	242	1,092	4,540	192	192	1,313
1971	13,551	255	65	6,035	58	13	6,539
1972	23,909	4,188	10,800	6,636	236	38	876
1973	7,197	176	91	4,800	140	53	331
1974	14,750	252	5,628	5,837	236	19	705
1975	6,012	247	56	3,932	257	93	422
1976	3,284	570	78	1,977	39	26	132
1977	10,142	297	97	6,133	208	56	301
1978	9,405	416	201	5,985	131	47	360
1979	29,474	834	128	20,390	72	38	1,419
1980	11,964	281	166	10,155	36	8	253

(*a*) The latest *Abstract of Labour Statistics* to show figures for 1892 (the 4th) also published figures for 1893 which differed very much in some respects from later revisions. The main differences were: (i) the 4th issue showed a larger number of disputes in every group of industries; and (ii) the 4th issue showed a larger number of days lost in some groups, but a smaller number in others. By far the most important variation of this latter kind was in textiles, where the 4th *Abstract* gave only 424,000 days lost in 1893 as against 3,918,000 in later revisions. The other major variation is in the building trades, where the 4th *Abstract* gave 813,000 days lost, compared with 469,000 in later issues. A further break between 1892 and 1893 is caused by the omission from 1893 onwards of stoppage involving less than ten workers, or lasting less than one day except when the number of working days lost exceeded one hundred.

(*b*) The General Strike is included in the totals but not the industry group figures.

Labour Force 18. Industrial Disputes – Republic of Ireland 1923–80

NOTE
SOURCE: *Statistical Abstract of Ireland*.

	Number of Disputes beginning in Year	Working Days Lost (in thousands)		Number of Disputes beginning in Year	Working Days Lost (in thousands)		Number of Disputes beginning in Year	Working Days Lost (in thousands)
1923	131	1,209	1942	69	115	1961	96	377
1924	104	302	1943	81	62	1962	60	104
1925	86	294	1944	84	38	1963	70	234
1926	57	85	1945	87	244	1964	87	545
1927	53	64	1946	105	150	1965	89	552
1928	52	54	1947	194	449	1966	112	784
1929	53	101	1948	147	258	1967	79	183
1930	83	77	1949	153	273	1968	126	406
1931	60	310	1950	154	217	1969	134	936
1932	70	42	1951	138	545	1970	134	1,008
1933	88	200	1952	82	529	1971	133	274
1934	99	180	1953	75	82	1972	131	207
1935	99	288	1954	81	67	1973	182	207
1936	107	186	1955	96	236	1974	219	552
1937	145	1,755	1956	67	48	1975	151	296
1938	137	209	1957	45	92	1976	134	777
1939	99	106	1958	51	126	1977	175	442
1940	89	152	1959	58	124	1978	152	613
1941	71	77	1960	49	80	1979	140	1,465
						1980	130	412

Labour Force 19. Hours Worked – United Kingdom 1856–1973

NOTE
SOURCE: R. C. O. Matthews, C. H. Feinstein, and J. C. Odling-Smee, *British Economic Growth, 1856–1973* (Oxford, 1982), Appendix D.

	Average Full-time Hours per Week	Average(*a*) Hours per Week	Average(*b*) Hours per Year		Average Full-time Hours per Week	Average(*a*) Hours per Week	Average(*b*) Hours per Year
1856	65·00	65·00	3,185	1955	45·88	44·32	2,051
1873	56·00	56·00	2,744	1960	44·75	42·69	1,969
1913	56·40	56·40	2,753	1964	43·85	41·24	1,904
1924	47·00	46·60	2,219	1968	42·16	39·31	1,804
1937	48·60	48·20	2,293	1973	41·40	38·06	1,715
1951	45·63	44·59	2,071				

(*a*) after allowing for part-time workers.
(*b*) after allowing for holidays, sickness, and strikes.

Labour Force 20. Indices of Normal Weekly Hours of Work of Manual Workers – United Kingdom 1920–80 (January 1956 = 100)

NOTES

[1] SOURCES: Department of Employment and Productivity, *British Labour Statistics: Historical Abstract, 1868–1968* (London, 1971), table 20, and *Department of Employment Gazette*.

[2] The index numbers are derived from the five separate series, based on 1924, 1934, 1947, 1956 and 1972. Completely accurate comparisons between the periods covered by each of these separate series is not possible because of changes in scope and methodology. Hours are shown in footnotes at the beginning and end of each series.

[3] The figures are for December each year.

Year	Index	Year	Index	Year	Index	Year	Index
1920	106·9 (*a*)	1936	108·1	1951	100·2	1966	91·0
1921	106·9	1937	107·8	1952	100·1	1967	90·8
1922	107·3	1938	107·7	1953	100·1	1968	90·7
1923	107·3	1939	107·7	1954	100·0	1969	90·6
1924	107·5	1940	107·7	1955	100·0	1970	90·4
1925	107·3	1941	107·7	1956	100·0 (*d*)	1971	90·1
1926	108·6	1942	107·7	1957	99·7	1972	89·9
1927	108·6	1943	107·7	1058	99·6	1973	89·6
1928	108·6	1944	107·7	1959	99·5	1974	89·6
1929	108·0	1945	107·6	1960	97·1	1975	89·5
1930	108·1	1946	105·6	1961	95·4	1976	89·5
1931	108·3	1947	100·7 (*c*)	1962	95·1	1977	89·5
1932	108·3	1948	100·4	1963	94·9	1978	89·5
1933	108·3	1949	100·2	1964	93·9	1979	89·4
1934	108·2 (*b*)	1950	100·2	1965	92·0	1980	89·1
1935	108·2						

(*a*) 46·7 hours.
(*b*) 47·3 hours.
(*c*) 102·0 = 44·6 hours in June; 101·5 = 45·5 hours in July.
(*d*) 44·6 hours.

Labour Force 21. Indices of Average Wages – United Kingdom 1790–1980

NOTES TO PART A

[1] SOURCE: Phyllis Deane and W. A. Cole, *British Economic Growth, 1688–1955* (Cambridge University Press, 1962).

[2] The authors say: 'The index for Great Britain is a weighted average of Wood's general unweighted index of average money wages in towns in the United Kingdom (*E.J.*, 1899) and Bowley's indices of average agricultural earnings in England and Wales, and Scotland respectively (combined according to his weights, *J.R.S.S.*, 1899). No attempt has been made to extract the Irish components from Wood's U.K. index in constructing our G.B. index because they were not sufficiently different or weighty to affect the result. The index for Ireland is an average of Wood's index of average money wages in Dublin and Bowley's index of average agricultural earnings (allowing for unemployment) in Ireland. The average is again weighted in accordance with our estimates of the proportions employed in agricultural and non-agricultural occupations'.

[3] The authors suggest that the Irish index must 'be treated with considerable reserve', but 'for all its crudeness . . . it offers a more acceptable estimate . . . than any index of British or United Kingdom wages as a whole'.

A. At Intervals 1790–1860 for Great Britain and Ireland, (1840 = 100)

	Great Britain	Ireland		Great Britain	Ireland
1790	70	107	1824	105	120
1795	82	115	1831	101	114
1800	95	125	1840	100	100
1805	109	139	1845	98	100
1810	124	139	1850	100	100
1816	117	136	1855	117	129
1820	110	122	1860	115	134

NOTES TO PART B

[1] SOURCE: G. H. Wood, 'Real Wages and the Standard of Comfort since 1850', *J.R.S.S.* (1909).

[2] Column 1 was continued by A. L. Bowley in *Wages and Income since 1860* (Cambridge, 1937), p. 6, from information supplied by Wood, as follows:

1903	176	1905	175	1907	190	1909	184
1904	176	1906	181	1908	187	1910	187

[3] The index of retail prices was described by Wood as 'experimental' and should not be used for purposes other than that for which it was computed.

B. Wages and Earnings, 1850–1902, United Kingdom (1850 = 100)

	Average Money Wages		Average Real Wages		
	Not Allowing for Unemployment	Allowing for Unemployment	Not Allowing for Unemployment	Allowing for Unemployment	Average Retail Prices
1850	100	100	100	100	100
1851	100	100	102	102	97
1852	100	98	102	100	97
1853	110	113	105	107	106
1854	114	115	96	97	122
1855	116	114	95	94	126
1856	116	115	96	95	126
1857	112	109	96	94	119
1858	110	101	102	94	109
1859	112	111	104	104	107
1860	114	116	103	105	111
1861	114	112	100	99	114
1862	116	110	105	100	111
1863	117	115	109	107	107
1864	124	126	117	118	106
1865	126	129	117	120	107
1866	132	133	116	117	114
1867	131	126	109	105	121
1868	130	124	110	105	119
1869	130	126	115	111	113
1870	133	133	118	118	113
1871	138	141	121	125	113
1872	146	150	122	126	120
1873	155	159	128	132	122
1874	156	159	133	136	117
1875	154	156	135	138	113
1876	152	153	137	136	110
1877	151	150	133	132	113
1878	148	143	132	128	110
1879	146	134	137	126	103

B. Wages and Earnings, 1850–1902, United Kingdom (1850 = 100) (*cont.*)

	Average Money Wages		Average Real Wages		
	Not Allowing for Unemployment	Allowing for Unemployment	Not Allowing for Unemployment	Allowing for Unemployment	Average Retail Prices
1880	147	144	134	132	107
1881	147	147	136	136	105
1882	147	149	135	138	106
1883	149	151	139	142	102
1884	150	144	144	138	100
1885	149	141	148	140	96
1886	148	138	151	142	92
1887	149	143	155	149	89
1888	151	149	157	155	89
1889	156	158	159	161	91
1890	163	166	166	169	91
1891	163	164	164	166	92
1892	162	158	163	159	92
1893	162	156	167	161	89
1894	162	157	170	165	87
1895	162	158	174	170	84
1896	163	164	176	177	83
1897	166	167	176	176	86
1898	167	169	174	176	87
1899	172	174	180	183	86
1900	179	180	183	184	89
1901	179	179	181	181	90
1902	176	175	177	176	91

NOTES TO PART C

[1] SOURCE: A. L. Bowley, *Wages and Income since 1860* (Cambridge University Press, 1937), p. 30.

[2] Bowley heads column 3 'quotient' rather than real wages, 'because of the numerous qualifications with which it must be used'. He suggests the figures should be treated as ± 5.

[3] The index is carried back for five years in the period 1860–80, as follows, but the margin of error is much greater:

	Money Wages	Cost of Living	Quotient
1860	58	113	51
1866	66	114	58
1870	66	110	60
1874	80	115	70
1877	77	110	70

[4] As well as the link provided here between 1914 and 1924, Bowley produced another different one, together with figures for the intervening years associated with each link. The problems associated with all these statistics are exhaustively discussed in J. A. Dowie, "1919–20 is in Need of Attention", *E.H.R.*, second series XXVIII, 3 (1975), who concludes that neither series is satisfactory. For what they are worth, the two indices are shown here, along with an index of average *earnings* derived from C. H. Feinstein, *National Income, Expenditure and Output of the United Kingdom, 1855–1965* (Cambridge, 1972), table 65, which Dowie regards as preferable but still not ideal. Bowley I is derived from A. L. Bowley, *Prices and Wages in the United Kingdom, 1914–1920* (Oxford, 1921) continued in the L.C.E.S. *Bulletin* from 1923, and Bowley II comes from A. L. Bowley, "Index-Numbers of Wage Rates and Cost of Living", *J.R.S.S.*, series A, XCV (1952).

	Money Wages in July		Weekly Average Earnings
	Bowley I	Bowley II	
1914	100	100	100
1915	107·5	109	116
1916	117·5	121	132
1917	137·5	144	168
1918	177·5	189	209
1919	212·5	230	239
1920	263	285	275
1921	253	274	257
1922	194	210	207
1923	174	188	191
1924	179	194	194

[5] This cost of living index is discussed in *Wages and Income since 1860*, appendix D. It should not be used for purposes other than those for which it was computed.

C. Wages, United Kingdom (as constituted at each date), 1880–1936, (1914 = 100)

	Money Wages	Cost of Living	Real Wages
1880	72	105	69
1881	72	103	71
1882	75	102	73
1883	75	102	73
1884	75	97	77
1885	73	91	81
1886	72	89	81
1887	73	88	84
1888	75	88	86
1889	80	89	90
1890	83	89	93
1891	83	89	92
1892	83	90	92
1893	83	89	94
1894	83	85	98
1895	83	83	100
1896	83	83	100
1897	84	85	98
1898	87	88	99
1899	89	86	104

C. Wages, United Kingdom (as constituted at each date), 1880–1936, (1914 = 100) (*cont.*)

	Money Wages	Cost of Living	Real Wages		Money Wages	Cost of Living	Real Wages
1900	94	91	103	1924	194	175	111
1901	93	90	102	1925	196	175	112
1902	91	90	101	1926	195	172	113
1903	91	91	99	1927	196	167	117
1904	89	92	97	1928	194	166	117
1905	89	92	97	1929	193	164	118
1906	91	93	98	1930	191	157	122
1907	96	95	101	1931	189	147	129
1908	94	93	101	1932	185	143	129
1909	94	94	100	1933	183	140	131
1910	94	96	98				
1911	95	97	97				
1912	98	100	97	1934	183	141	130
1913	99	102	97	1935	185	143	130
1914	100	100	100	1936	190	147	129

NOTES TO PARTS D and E

[1] SOURCES: Department of Employment and Productivity, *British Labour Statistics, Historical Abstract, 1886–1968* (London, 1971), tables 11 and 13; *Abstract*.

[2] The index numbers in part D relate to the unweighted mean of indices representing wage movements in building, coal mining, engineering, textile trades, and agriculture.

[3] The index numbers in part E are derived from five separate series based on 1924, 1939, 1947, 1956, and 1972. Completely accurate comparisons between the periods covered by each of these separate series is not possible because of charges in scope and methodology.

[4] The figures in part E are means of June and December index numbers to 19 and of twelve monthly numbers subsequently.

[5] The Department of Employment and Productivity (*op. cit.* in note 1 abov table 12) give the following estimates of the average percentage increase in week wages at the end of each year compared with July 1914:

1914	1 to 2	1917	55 to 60	1919	115 to 120
1915	10 to 15	1918	95 to 100	1920	170 to 180
1916	20 to 25				

D. Weekly Wage Rates of Manual Workers, United Kingdom, 1874–1914, (1900 = 100)

1874	91·7	1885	83·8	1895	89·2	1905	97·3
1875	90·3	1886	83·1	1896	90·1	1906	98·7
1876	89·4	1887	83·3	1897	91·0	1907	102·2
1877	88·3	1888	85·0	1898	93·2	1908	101·6
1878	85·1	1889	87·6	1899	95·6	1909	100·4
1879	83·4	1890	90·6	1900	100·0	1910	100·8
1880	83·1	1891	91·7	1901	99·1	1911	101·1
1881	84·6	1892	90·3	1902	97·9	1912	103·7
1882	85·8	1893	90·5	1903	97·4	1913	106·8
1883	85·9	1894	89·7	1904	96·9	1914	107·9
1884	85·2						

E. Basic Weekly Wage Rates, United Kingdom, 1920–80 (January 1956 = 100)

1920	55·2	1936	35·8	1951	76·9	1966	153·5
1921	48·6	1937	37·0	1952	83·2	1967	159·3
1922	37·6	1938	38·1	1953	87·1	1968	169·9
1923	35·9	1939	38·5	1954	90·8	1969	178·8
1924	37·0	1940	42·8	1955	97·0	1970	196·7
1925	37·2	1941	46·5	1956	104·7	1971	222·1
1926	37·2	1942	50·1	1957	110·0	1972	252·8
1927	36·7	1943	52·7	1958	113·9	1973	287·4
1928	36·3	1944	55·1	1959	117·0	1974	344·3
1929	36·2	1945	57·5	1960	120·1	1975	445·9
1930	36·0	1946	62·1	1961	125·0	1976	531·9
1931	35·3	1947	64·6	1962	129·6	1977	567·1
1932	34·7	1948	67·8	1963	134·3	1978	647·0
1933	34·5	1949	69·6	1964	140·6	1979	743·8
1934	34·6	1950	70·9	1965	146·7	1980	877·7
1935	35·0						

Labour Force 22. Trends in Full-time Earnings – England 1755–1851

NOTES

[1] SOURCE: Peter H. Lindert and Jeffrey G. Williamson, "English Workers' Living Standards during the Industrial Revolution: A New Look", *E.H.R.*, Second Series XXXVI, 1 (1983), but using their modified cost-of-living index as reproduced on p. 737 below.

[2] The original cost-of-living index was subject to criticism by N. F. R. Crafts in *J.E.H.*, XLV, 1 (1985).

[3] The statistics relate to adult males.

1851 = 100

	Farm Labourers		"Middle Group"		Artisans		All Blue Collar Workers		White Collar Workers		All Workers	
	Nominal Earnings	Real Earnings	Nominal Earnings	Real Earnings	Nominal Earnings	Real Earnings	Nominal Earnings	Real Earnings	Nominal Earnings	Real Earnings	Nominal Earnings	Real Earnings
1755	59·16	65·46	42·95	47·54	50·86	56·29	51·05	56·50	21·62	23·93	38·62	42.74
1781	72·62	59·67	54·88	49·40	57·38	51·65	59·64	53·68	26·42	23·78	46·62	41·96
1797	103·41	78·34	72·92	55·24	64·86	49·14	74·42	56·38	32·55	24·66	58·97	44·67
1805	139·12	78·38	98·89	55·72	79·44	44·75	96·58	54·41	38·88	21·90	75·87	42·74
1810	144·76	69·90	110·95	53·57	92·03	44·44	107·81	52·06	43·01	20·77	84·89	40·99
1815	137·88	83·92	105·55	64·24	95·28	57·99	106·18	64·63	46·55	28·33	85·30	51·92
1819	134·47	80·71	99·41	59·67	91·92	55·17	101·84	61·13	50·77	30·47	84·37	50·64
1827	106·89	81·04	98·89	74·97	93·55	70·92	97·59	73·99	55·09	41·77	83·11	63·01
1835	103·41	94·52	96·98	88·65	88·68	81·06	94·11	86·02	75·03	68·58	88·77	81·14
1851	100.00	100·00	100·00	100·00	100·00	100·00	100·00	100·00	100·00	100·00	100·00	100·00

Labour Force 23. Nominal Annual Earnings – England and Wales, 1710–1911

NOTES

[1] SOURCE: Jeffrey G. Williamson, "The Structure of Pay in Britain, 1710–1911", *Research in Economic History*, 7 (1982).

[2] The statistics relate to adult males.

(in current £)

	1710	1737	1755	1781	1797	1805	1810	1815	1819
Agricultural Labourers	17·78	17·18	17·18	21·09	30·03	40·40	42·04	40·04	39·05
General Labourers	19·22	20·15	20·75	23·13	25·09	36·87	43·94	43·94	41·74
Messengers and Porters (exc. govt.)	31·15	34·75	33·99	33·54	57·66	69·43	76·01	80·69	81·35
Government low-wage	21·58	28·79	28·62	46·02	46·77	52·48	57·17	60·22	60·60
Police, Guards, Watchmen	13·28	26·05	25·76	48·08	47·04	51·26	67·89	69·34	69·18
Miners	22·46	27·72	22·94	24·37	47·79	64·99	63·22	57·82	53·37
Government high-wage	62·88	84·04	78·91	104·55	133·73	151·09	176·86	195·16	219·25
Skilled in Shipbuilding	36·26	37·00	38·82	45·26	51·71	51·32	55·25	59·20	57·23
Skilled in Engineering	40·73	41·56	43·60	50·83	58·08	75·88	88·23	94·91	92·71
Skilled in Building Trades	28·50	29·08	30·51	35·57	40·64	55·30	66·35	66·35	63·02
Skilled in Textiles	33·59	34·28	35·96	41·93	47·90	65·18	78·21	67·60	67·60
Skilled in Printing Trades	43·29	44·17	46·34	54·03	66·61	71·11	79·22	79·22	71·14
Clergymen	99·66	96·84	91·90	182·65	238·50	266·42	283·89	272·53	266·55
Solicitors and Barristers	113·16	178·18	231·00	242·67	165·00	340·00	447·50	447·50	447·50
Clerks (exc. govt.)	43·64	68·29	63·62	101·57	135·26	150·44	178·11	200·79	229·64
Surgeons, Medical Officers	51·72	56·85	62·02	88·35	174·95	217·60	217·60	217·60	217·60
Teachers	15·78	15·03	15·97	16·53	43·21	43·21	51·10	51·10	69·35
Engineers, Surveyors	131·09	122·37	137·51	170·00	190·00	291·43	305·00	337·00	326·43

	1827	1835	1851	1861	1871	1881	1891	1901	1911
Agricultural Labourers	31·04	30·03	29·04	36·04	41·05	41·52	41·94	46·12	46·96
General Labourers	43·65	39·29	44·83	44·18	51·44	55·88	62·68	68·90	74·04
Messengers and Porters (exc. govt.)	84·39	87·20	88·88	82·21	87·34	97·05	89·51	110·97	85·91
Government low-wage	59·01	58·70	66·45	67·15	63·72	74·65	70·40	72·20	67·95
Police, Guards, Watchmen	62·95	63·33	53·62	53·94	55·86	76·73	72·33	68·69	70·62
Miners	54·61	56·41	55·44	62·89	66·20	59·58	82·75	89·37	83·63
Government high-wage	222·95	276·42	234·87	251·33	281·02	275·29	215·01	159·63	161·61
Skilled in Shipbuilding	62·22	62·74	64·12	69·11	76·83	81·38	87·80	92·51	102·34
Skilled in Engineering	80·69	77·26	84·05	88·77	94·38	96·68	107·06	116·20	125·21
Skilled in Building Trades	66·35	59·72	66·35	72·90	83·33	87·18	91·52	103.35	105·14
Skilled in Textiles	58·50	64·56	58·64	63·26	82·55	85·77	93·60	101·40	108·50
Skilled in Printing Trades	70·23	70·23	74·72	74·72	79·92	86·42	90·04	92·66	97·29
Clergymen	254·60	258·76	267·09	272·30	293·84	315·37	336·90	238·00	206·00
Solicitors and Barristers	522·50	1,166·67	1,837·50	1,600·00	1,326·67	1,280·00	1,342·60	1,500·00	1,343·50
Clerks (exc. govt.)	240·29	269·11	235·81	248·47	268·63	286·65	268·06	286·86	229·89
Surgeons, Medical Officers	175·20	200·92	200·92	343·00	645·40	520·29	475·47	265·39	272·75
Teachers	69·35	81·89	81·11	93·76	97·02	120·80	133·90	147·50	176·15
Engineers, Surveyors	365·71	398·89	479·00	529·15	579·13	312·97	380·61	333·99	287·37

Labour Force 24. Indices of Wages of Labourers in London and Lancashire – 1700–1796

NOTES

[1] SOURCE: Elizabeth W. Gilboy, "The Cost of Living and Real Wages in Eighteenth Century England", *Review of Economic Statistics* (1936).

[2] The years referred to are those *beginning* at Michaelmas.

[3] The cost-of-living index is derived mainly from contract prices, and must be regarded as very rough. It relates principally to London and southern England, but was nevertheless used to estimate Lancashire real wages.

[4] All wage indices relate to the weekly wages of men in full employment.

(1700 = 100)

		London Wages		Lancashire Wages	
	Cost of Living	Money	Real	Money	Real
1700	100	100	100	100	100
1701	100	99	99	95	95
1702	91	99	109	89	98
1703	99	109	110	89	90
1704	88	114	130	89	101
1705	95	109	115	105	111
1706	86	109	127	105	122
1707	94	109	116	105	112
1708	116	109	94	105	90
1709	135	111	82	89	66
1710	147	109	74	105	71
1711	104	110	106	105	101
1712	98	110	112	105	107
1713	108	110	102	100	93
1714	105	109	104	111	106
1715	100	109	109	111	111
1716	92	109	118	111	121
1717	92	109	118	89	97
1718	92	109	118	111	121
1719	106	109	103	111	105
1720	102	110	108	133	130
1721	91	110	121	123	135
1722	86	110	128	123	143
1723	97	110	113	123	127
1724	99	110	111	123	124
1725	105	110	105	111	106
1726	100	110	110	111	111
1727	106	110	104	133	126
1728	112	105	94	111	99
1729	102	110	108	133	130
1730	89	109	122	133	149
1731	88	114	130	123	140
1732	81	114	141	133	164
1733	89	114	128	133	149
1734	91	114	125	133	146
1735	88	118	134	133	151
1736	93	116	125	133	143
1737	94	118	126	133	141
1738	91	116	127	133	146
1739	109	118	108	133	122
1740	119	116	97	133	112
1741	103	116	113	133	129
1742	98	118	120	133	136
1743	82	115	140	133	162
1744	83	118	142	133	160
1745	94	118	126	133	141
1746	92	118	128	128	139
1747	95	118	124	128	135
1748	100	118	118	133	133
1749	98	118	120	133	136

Labour Force 24. *continued*

		(1700 = 100) London Wages		Lancashire Wages	
	Cost of Living	Money	Real	Money	Real
1750	93	120	129	133	143
1751	98	118	120	133	136
1752	94	118	126	133	141
1753	95	118	124	133	140
1754	92	118	128	133	145
1755	98	118	120	133	136
1756	125	118	94	133	106
1757	118	118	100	111	94
1758	108	118	109	111	103
1759	99	118	119	133	134
1760	97	118	122	123	127
1761	99	118	119	123	124
1762	109	118	108	123	113
1763	110	121	110	177	161
1764	115	121	105	156	136
1765	117	121	103	156	133
1766	124	121	98	156	126
1767	123	121	98	156	127
1768	109	121	111	200	183
1769	108	121	112	200	185
1770	118	121	103	200	169
1771	130	121	93	177	136
1772	136	121	89	200	147
1773	131	121	92	200	153
1774	129	121	94	200	155
1775	128	118	92	200	156
1776	120	118	98	200	167
1777	131	118	90	200	153
1778	123	118	96	200	163
1779	117	123	105	200	171
1780	125	123	98	200	160
1781	125	123	98	200	160
1782	144	123	85	211	147
1783	139	123	88	200	144
1784	129	123	95	189	146
1785	132	123	93	205	155
1786	128	123	96	223	174
1787	130	123	95	211	162
1788	127	...	...	228	180
1789	134	...	...	228	170
1790	133	...	...	233	175
1791	131	...	...	223	170
1792	140	...	...	200	143
1793	148	...	...	267	180
1794	168	...	...	233	133
1795	179	...	...	233	130
1796	153	...	...	233	152

Labour Force 25. Bowley & Wood's Indices of Average Wages in a Normal Week in Certain Industries – United Kingdom 1770–1914

NOTES

[1] SOURCES: Articles by A. L. Bowley and G. H. Wood (separately and together) in the *J.R.S.S.* 1898 and 1899 for Agriculture (up to 1879), 1899 for Compositors, 1900–1 for Building (up to 1879), 1905–6 for Shipbuilding and Engineering and 1910 for Cotton (up to 1879); A. L. Bowley, *Wages and Income since 1860* for all remaining figures, these being in many cases revisions of the earlier articles. The figures in this book for shipbuilding and engineering simply repeat the series for agriculture. Since there must have been a transcription error, they are not shown here.

[2] In the article on Shipbuilding and Engineering, Bowley and Wood say of possible errors: 'We are making a liberal allowance for these if we affix a ±5 to our earlier index numbers. We may, indeed, depend on them to ±3, or less than a shilling in the average wage' (*J.R.S.S.*, 1906, p. 185). This almost certainly applies to all the figures except the very early Shipbuilding and Engineering ones which are in brackets, and possibly to some of the Agriculture series. What Bowley called the pivot years in the latter – i.e. years for which there is definite information – are printed in bold type. The remaining indices for for agriculture are interpolations.

[3] For the West Riding woollen and worsted industries, Bowley produced the following indices 'expressing the average wage of all adults' (*J.R.S.S.*, 1902, p. 125):

1795	80	1860	90	1883	105
1815	115	1866	100	1886	100
1840	75	1874–7	120	1891	100

[4] These index numbers allow for the changing importance of the different occupations within each industry.

[5] The separate index numbers for wages in agriculture continue after 1880 as follows:

	E. & W.	Scot.		E. & W.	Scot.
1880	103	98	1889	98	99
1881	100	94	1890	99	100
1882	97	94	1891	100	100
1883	97	95	1892	102	101
1884	96	96	1893	101	...
1885	94	97	1894	101	...
1886	92	98	1895	100	...
1887	92	98	1896	98	...
1888	97	98			

[6] G. H. Wood ('Real Wages and the Standard of Comfort since 1850', in the *J.R.S.S.*, 1909, p. 93) gives the following index numbers of average wages in three other trades, and a slightly different index for coal-mining, for 1850–1906:

	Coal-mining	Puddling	Gas	Furniture
1850	67	92	70	70
1855	94	124	71	72
1860	76	92	73	76
1866	100	117	76	83
1871	80	108	83	86
1874	108	143	90	97
1877	76	107	93	99
1880	72	113	91	98
1883	77	97	91	98
1886	72	89	91	97
1891	100	100	100	100
1896	87	90	101	101
1900	108	139	104	106
1906	97	108	106	106

1891 = 100

	Agriculture					Cotton	
	England & Wales	Scotland	Compositors	Building	Shipbuilding and Engineering	Factory Workers	All Workers
1770	...	**18**	....	...	...	...	...
1770–88	**51**	...	...	...	...	...	...
1777–85	...	...	60	...	...	...	...
1786	...	...	62	...	...	...	...
1789	52	...	...	...	...	...	...
1790	53	**31**	...	...	...	...	...
1791	55	31	62	...	...	...	...
1792	57	32	62	...	...	...	...
1793	59	32	{74}	...	(40)	...	...
1794	61	**33**		...	{52}	...	...
1795	**67**	35	...			...	...
1796	73	37	...		...	...	...
1797	76	38	...	near 44	...	...	...
1798	79	39	...		...	...	...
1799	81	40	...		...	...	...
1800	83	41	...		(56)	...	...
1801	85	42	74		...	...	...
1802	86	43	74		(56)	...	...
1803	87	44	74		...	...	...
1804	94	49	...	rising to	...	...	...
1805	100	54	79	about 63	(65)	...	...
1806	105	58	...		...	59	98
1807	105	58	...		...	...	87
1808	105	58	...		...	...	72
1809	105	58	83		...	...	75

Labour Force 25. *continued*

1891 = 100

	Agriculture					Cotton	
	England & Wales	Scotland	Compositors	Building	Shipbuilding and Engineering	Factory Workers	All Workers
1810	105	58				62	76
1811	105	58			(71)	62	69
1812	105	58				62	76
1813	104	55	88			62	79
1814	103	53			(72)	62	92
1815	102	51				62	73
1816	101	51			72	62	61
1817	100	49	85			61	55
1818	98	48	80	near	71	61	53
1819	97	47	...	63	73	61	53
1820	95	46	78			61	53
1821	88	42	...			60	53
1822	77	39			71	60	53
1823	77	37				58	52
1824	72	37				58	53
1825	78	37			71	58	53
1826	78	38		...	71	58	50
1827	78	38	78			...	50
1828	78	38		near		...	49
1829	78	38		59	71	...	49
1830	76	38				...	45
1831	78	38		59		...	44
1832	80	39		59		56	45
1833	81	39		59		56	45
1834	79	38	78	59		...	49
1835	76	41		59		...	47
1836	77	43	81	60	73	57	48
1837	78	46	81	61		...	49
1838	80	48	81	62		...	49
1839	82	52	83	63		55	49
1840	82	54		63	75	55	49
1841	82	57		63	75	55	50
1842	82	59		63	75	55	50
1843	82	62		63	75	54	50
1844	77	62	83	63	75	55	51
1845	71	61		63	75	58	50
1846	77	61		63	75	58	50
1847	77	61	83	63	75	...	51
1848	72	61		64	74	...	51
1849	72	61		64	73	54	51
1850	72	61	83	64	73	54	52
1851	72	61	83	64	74	55	53
1852	72	61		64	75	56	54
1853	83	69	83	64	77	59	57
1854	93	77		68	82	58	56
1855	96	79	83	70	82	59	57
1856	96	79	83	72	82	62	60
1857	91	76	83	73	82	62	61
1858	84	72	83	73	80	62	61

Labour Force 25. *continued*

1891 = 100

	Agriculture					Cotton		
	England & Wales	Scotland	Compositors	Building	Shipbuilding and Engineering	Factory Workers	All Workers	Coalmining
1859	85	72		73	80	64	63	...
1860	89	75		76	79	68	68	...
1861	90	75	83	76	80	68	68	...
1862	90	75		76	81	67	67	...
1863	90	75		76	81	66		...
1864	90	75	83	76	82	66		...
1865	90	75	83	79	84	71		...
1866	90	75		83	85	77		...
1867	92	76	84	83	83	77		...
1868	94	77	84	83	83	79		...
1869	95	82		83	83	78		...
1870	96	85	85	84	84	81		...
1871	104	88	88	86	85	85		...
1872	113	94	88	88	89	87		...
1873	117	100	88	89	92	89		...
1874	122	106	93	93	94	90		...
1875	117	112	94	98	94	90		...
1876	117	112	95	100	94	92		...
1877	117	112	96	100	95	94		...
1878	114	112	96	98	94	88		...
1879	107	103		97	89	84		...
1880	100			96	90	87		71
1881	99		96	96	92	90		73
1882	97			96	95	90		78
1883	96		96	96	95	91		79
1884	94		96	96	94	91		76
1885	93			96	92	90		73
1886	91		96	96	90	89		70
1887	94			97	91	90		70
1888	96		96	97	95	94		74
1889	97			99	98	95		87
1890	100		98	100	100	96		99
1891	100		100	100	100	100		100
1892	100			101	99	101		91
1893	99		101	103	98	101		93
1894	99			103	98	101		88
1895	97			104	98	101		84
1896	97			105	101	102		83
1897	99		101	107	103	102		84
1898	101			108	105	103		91
1899	103		101	109	108	104		96
1900	109		...	111	108	107		116
1901	110		...	111	108	108		109
1902	110		...	111	108	107		101
1903	110		...	111	106	107		98
1904	110		...	111	106	108		95
1905	110		...	111	106	110		94
1906	110		...	111	...	115		96
1907	110		...	111	...	...		111

Labour Force 25. *continued*

1891 = 100

	Agriculture				Cotton		
	England & Wales	Scotland	Compositors	Building	Factory Workers	All Workers	Coalmining
1908	110		...	111	...		108
1909	110		...	111	...		103
1910	110		...	111	...		104
1911	112		...	111	...		102
1912	114		...	112	...		108
1913	118		...	114	...		116
1914	122		...	118	...		113

Labour Force 26. Indices of Weekly Wage Rates in Certain Industry Groups – United Kingdom 1914–80

NOTES

[1] SOURCES: Part A – A. L. Bowley, *Prices and Wages in the United Kingdom, 1914–1920* (Oxford, 1921), Part B to 1938 – E. C. Ramsbottom, "The Course of Wage Rates in the United Kingdom, 1921–34", *J.R.S.S.*, XCVIII (1935) and similar articles for 1934–7 and 1938 in *ibid.*, XCXI and XCXII (1938 and 1939). Part B from 1938, Part C, and Part B to 1958 – kindly supplied by the Department of Employment and Productivity in 1970. Remainder – Department of Employment [and Productivity] *Gazette*.

[2] The user's attention is drawn to the critique of the methodology used for Part A in J. A. Dowie, "1919–20 is in Need of Attention", *E.H.R.*, second series XXVIII, 3 (1975).

A. 1914–20. July 1914 = 100

	Agriculture (E. & W.)	Coal-mining	Engineering Fitters	Engineering Labourers	Shipbuilding Platers	Cotton Operatives	Woollen & Worsted Operatives	Compositors	Bricklayers	Bricklayers' Labourers	Dock Labourers	Railwaymen
July 1914	100	100	100	100	100	100	100	100	100	100	100	100
July 1915	112	113	110	...	...	103	115	100	102	103	111	110
July 1916	...	129	111	...	...	107	126	105	108	115	130	120
July 1917	...	136	134	154	130	119	144	120	122	134	150	155
July 1918	189	187	173	213	169	157	164	156	157	185	193	195
Jan. 1919	189	222	197	255	...	205	195	185	172	208	212	227
July 1919	226	224	199	255	193	202	196	196	185	224	209	225
Dec. 1919	227	222	216	281	...	235	222	217	198	248	208	227
July 1920	270	260	231	309	223	259	239	246	235	300	266	280
Dec. 1920	277	274	229	310	...	302	296	287	238	306	264	288

B. 1920–47: 1924 = 100

	Agriculture E. & W.	Agriculture Scot.	Coal-Mining	Iron and Steel	Engineering (*a*)	Shipbuilding and Repairing (*b*)	Cotton	Woollen and Worsted	Printing and Bookbinding	Furniture	Building	Gas Supply	Railway Service
1920	160·5	142·5	187	202·5	152	175	162	147·5	117	134·5	145·5	140	127·5
1921	158	142·5	163·5	181·5	147	162·5	137·5	139	118	126·5	137	136	125
1922	115	118	95	104	121	118·5	109	105	108	106·5	105·5	111	108
1923	100	100	94	95	100	96·5	100	100	101	100	96	100	101·5
1924	100	100	100	100	100	100	100	100	100	100	100	100	100
1925	109	99	98·5	99	101	106	100	100	101	101	103	103	100
1926	113	98	98	95	102	106	100	100	101	100·5	103	104	100
1927	113	98	94	95	102·5	106	100	100	101	100	103	104	100
1928	113	97	88	91·5	104	106·5	100	100	101	101	101·5	104	98
1929	113	95·5	87	91·5	104	108	98·5	100	101	100	101	104	96
1930	113	94	87	92·5	104	109·5	94	93	101	100	99·5	104	98
1931	113	94	84	91	103	110	94	89·5	101	99	97	104	95
1932	111	94	84	89	101	108	92	85	101	94·5	94·5	102	94
1933	109	89	84	90	101	108	86	83	101	92	92·5	101	94
1934	110	87	84	91	101	108	86	82	101	92	92	101	94
1935	113	88	84	92	103	109	85·5	82	100	92·5	92·5	102	95
1936	114	90	89	95	105	111	85	84	100	96	96	103	95
1937	118	95	96	104	109·5	117	91	89	100	100	99	107	97
1938	123	100	97·5	116·5	113	124	92	89	100	101	101·5	109	99
1939	124	103	99	117	115	126	93	90·5	100	102	103	109	100·5
1940	156	127	113	130·5	125	137·5	110	107·5	102·5	110	110·5	116·5	112·5
1941	178	145·5	130	142	133	145·5	120·5	115	107	117·5	119	124·5	121
1942	214·5	181·5	150	143	141	154	124	119·5	113	120	123	132	130·5
1943	216	181·5	160·5	152	150·5	165·5	134	123·5	116	124	127	139	140·5
1944	232	192·5	166·5	157·5	157	172	143·5	128	124	131	129·5	147·5	148·5
1945	247	208·5	166·5	163·5	166	179	153·5	134	124	133	137·5	152	158
1946	268	219·5	166·5	170·5	176	190·5	169·5	141	137·5	140·5	161·5	168	165
1947	300·5	250	166·5	175	178	193	170	147·5	148·5	145	165	172·5	171·5

See p. 162 for footnotes.

Labour Force 26. *continued*

C. 1948–55: June 1947 = 100

	Agriculture, Forestry, and Fishing	Mining and Quarrying	Treatment of Non-Metalliferous Mining Products Other than Coal	Chemicals and Allied Trades	Metals	Textiles	Leather, Leather Goods, and Fur	Clothing	Food, Drink, and Tobacco
1948	112·5	105·5	102	106	102	107	102	108	105·5
1949	117	106	105	109	105·5	112	105	111·5	110
1950	119	106·5	106	112	107	115·5	107	112	112·5
1951	127·5	114	116	123	117	128·5	118·5	120	120·5
1952	138	124	126·5	134·5	127	135	127·5	126	131·5
1953	144·5	127	132	140	133	140	135·5	134·5	138·5
1954	150	132·5	138	145·5	139	145	140·5	143	144·5
1955	159	144·5	147·5	155·5	149	151·5	149	150·5	153·5

	Manufactures of Wood and Cork	Paper and Printing	Other Manufactures	Building and Contracting	Public Utilities	Transport and Communication	Distributive Trades	Public Administration and Professional Services	Miscellaneous Services
1948	105	108	102·5	109·5	105	106·5	110	103·5	105
1949	109	111	106	112	108·5	107·5	111	106·5	109·5
1950	112·5	115	107	115·5	111·5	108	116·5	107·5	112
1951	123	127·5	118	125·5	120	118·5	123	115	117·5
1952	137	143·5	127·5	137	130	126	133	125·5	124·5
1953	142·5	150	131	144·5	136·5	130·5	141	131	131·5
1954	147	152·5	137·5	152	143	138	146·5	136·5	135
1955	155	160	146	161·5	155·5	149	154·5	147	142

D. 1956–72: January 1956 = 100 and 1972–80: July 1972 = 100

	Agriculture, Forestry, and Fishing	Mining and Quarrying	Treatment of Non-Metalliferous Mining Products Other than Coal(*c*)	Chemicals and Allied Trades	Metals	Textiles	Leather, Leather Goods, and Fur	Clothing(*d*)	Food, Drink, and Tobacco
1956	102	107	104	100	106	102	103	104	105
1957	107	112	111	106	112	117	109	111	111
1958	113	115	112	109	114	110	114	116	116
1959	117	118	115	112	117	112	118	118	119
1960	120	119	120	115	119	116	121	123	123
1961	127	126	126	118	125	121	122	124	128
1962	132	129	131	124	127	124	126	132	132
1963	138	135	138	131	139	128	131	135	138
1964	143	139	146	139	136	133	135	144	144
1965	152	145	155	144	140	139	142	151	150
1966	158	152	161	149	147	145	148	157	156
1967	163	156	165	152	155	148	150	161	161
1968	173	163	172	158	170	152	157	167	169
1969	185	172	182	166	181	156	164	171	177
1970	198	191	210	198	196	181	180	181	197
1971	226	229	241	253	213	212	210	218	224
1972	247	282	273	285	244	238	232	245	251
	---(*h*)	---(*h*)	---(*h*)	---(*h*)	---(*h*)	---(*h*)	---(*h*)	---(*h*)	---(*h*)
1972	100	100	110	96	104	97	95	100	100
1973	116	106	112	106	119	110	108	111	112
1974	149	143	133	124	137	136	136	129	136
1975	186	190	171	165	179	176	171	167	177
1976	232	211	203	199	214	211	200	213	209
1977	247	225	218	218	218	232	220	232	228
1978	273	247	242	240	271	254	243	255	250
1979	310	276	276	265	314	288	280	300	285
1980	371	334	347	324	369	330	318	355	325

See p. 162 for footnotes.

Labour Force 26. *continued*

D. 1956–72: January 1956 = 100 and 1972–80: July 1972 = 100

	Manufactures of Wood and Cork(*e*)	Paper and Printing(*f*)	Other Manufactures	Building and Contracting(*g*)	Public Utilities	Transport and Communication	Distributive Trades	Public Administration and Professional Services	Miscellaneous Services
1956	105	106	101	106	101	103	104	106	104
1957	111	111	105	112	105	109	109	112	109
1958	116	116	109	117	109	112	115	116	114
1959	118	118	112	120	112	115	117	119	118
1960	122	122	115	122	115	121	121	123	120
1961	126	126	120	125	120	125	128	129	125
1962	134	133	128	133	125	129	132	134	132
1963	138	137	135	138	132	135	138	140	137
1964	143	143	142	144	141	144	143	148	143
1965	149	152	146	148	156	153	150	156	147
1966	156	160	151	154	164	159	158	162	159
1967	160	162	155	161	169	164	164	170	161
1968	171	170	177	172	175	177	171	179	172
1969	178	177	183	176	188	188	179	191	177
1970	194	198	195	195	211	212	193	209	188
1971	235	223	213	216	236	240	217	242	207
1972	270	252	238	245	257	266	243	268	235
	---(*h*)	---(*h*)	---(*h*)	---(*h*)	---(*h*)	---(*h*)	---(*h*)	---(*h*)	---(*h*)
1972	100	98	99	109	102	97	101	100	97
1973	113	105	109	139	111	107	114	114	105
1974	138	126	130	162	135	131	138	145	128
1975	171	160	158	215	170	169	181	182	163
1976	199	198	183	247	199	199	217	214	212
1977	213	209	207	268	214	213	243	230	233
1978	248	232	...	290	261	232	272	252	253
1979	279	270	...	321	301	266	320	281	319
1980	335	310	...	374	384	318	380	329	386

(*a*) Including railway engineering workshops.
(*b*) This covers time workers only. The available information for pieceworkers is insufficient to provide a basis for index numbers.
(*c*) Described from 1959 as "Bricks, Cement, Pottery, Glass, etc."
(*d*) Described from 1959 as "Clothing and Footwear."
(*e*) Described from 1959 as "Timber, Furniture, etc."
(*f*) Described from 1959 as "Paper, Printing, and Publishing."
(*g*) Described from 1959 as "Construction."
(*h*) The second line for 1972 is on the basis July 1972 = 100.

Labour Force 27. Indices of Hourly Wages in Industrial Occupations – Republic of Ireland, 1931–80

NOTE
SOURCE: *Statistical Abstract of Ireland*.

1953 = 100

1931	44·5	1944	54·1	1957	110·8	1969	221·1
1932	44·0	1945	55·3	1958	112·7	1970	252·9
1933	43·9	1946	57·0	1959	116·6	1971	294·6
1934	43·9	1947	68·3	1960	124·4	1972	337·0
1935	44·0	1948	74·5	1961	126·4	1973	380·7
1936	44·1	1949	81·1	1962	145·3	1974	439·3
1937	44·4	1950	81·3	1963	147·5	1975	515·3
1938	47·1	1951	81·7	1964	166·8	1976	602·2
1939	47·9	1952	91·7	1965	169·9	1977	696·0
1940	48·1	1953	100	1966	173·3	1978	811·2
1941	49·6	1954	100·3	1967	191·0	1979	879·3
1942	49·6	1955	100·4	1968	197·2	1980	1,017·3
1943	51·8	1956	108·4				

Labour Force 28. Wages in Agriculture – England and Wales, 1850–1980

NOTES

[1] SOURCES: Department of Employment and Productivity, *British Labour Statistics: Historical Abstract, 1886–1968* (London, 1981), tables 7 and 8; P. J. Lund *et al.*, *Wages and Employment in Agriculture: England and Wales, 1960–80* (Government Economics Service Working Paper No. 52, March 1982).

[2] Allowances in kind are not included.

A. Average Weekly Cash Wages of Ordinary Labourers, 1850–1914 (*a*)

	s.	d.		s.	d.		s.	d.		s.	d.
1850	9	3½	1865	11	3	1880	13	7½	1895	13	8½
1851	9	2½	1866	11	6	1881	13	7½	1896	13	9
1852	9	3	1867	11	11	1882	13	7½	1897	13	10½
1853	9	11	1868	12	0	1883	13	8	1898	14	1½
1854	10	8	1869	11	8½	1884	13	7½	1899	14	4
1855	10	11½	1870	11	10½	1885	13	5½	1900	14	10
1856	11	0½	1871	12	1	1886	13	4	1901	14	11
1857	10	11½	1872	12	8½	1887	13	2½	1902	14	11½
1858	10	9½	1873	13	4	1888	13	2½	1903	14	11½
1859	10	8½	1874	13	11½	1889	13	4	1904	14	11½
1860	10	11	1875	14	0	1890	13	6	1905	15	0
1861	11	1	1876	14	1½	1891	13	9½	1906	15	1
1862	11	1	1877	14	1½	1892	13	10	1910	15	4
1863	11	0	1878	14	0½	1893	13	9	1914 (July)	16	9
1864	11	0½	1879	13	8½	1894	13	8			

B. Average Minimum Wages for Basic Hours, 1914–80 (*b*)

	Minimum Wage		Basic Hours		Minimum Wage		Basic Hours		Minimum Wage		Basic Hours
	s.	d.			s.	d.			s.	d.	
1914	16	9	approx. 58	1938/9	34	8	50·2	1959/60	158	5	46·4
1918/9(*c*)	30	6	52	1939/40	39	5½	50·2	1960/1	166	8½	46·0
1919/20(*d*)	37	10½	...	1940/1	48	5	50·2	1961/2	172	7	46·0
1920 (*e*)	43	0½	...	1941/2	57	10	50·2	1962/3	181	9	46·0
1920/1 (*f*)	46	10½	...	1942/3	60	0	49·9	1963/4	189	1	45·1
1921/2 (*g*)	33	9½	49·9	1943/4	63	11½	49·4	1964/5	198	10½	45·0
1922/3	28	0	50·7	1944/5	67	10½	49·4	1965/6	207	11½	44·3
1923/4	28	0	50·7	1945/6	72	2	48·4	1966/7	213	11	44·0
1924/5	30	1	51·0	1946/7	80	10	48·0	1967/8	225	10	44·0
1925/6	31	6	50·1	1947/8	90	0	48·0	1968 (*i*)	231	0	44·0
1926/7	31	8	49·9	1948/9	92	2½	47·5	1969	248	0	44·0
1927/8	31	8	50·2	1949/50	94	0	47·0	1970	263	0	43·1
1928/9	31	8	50·2	1950/1	99	4	47·0	1971	296	0	42·0
									£	p.	
1929/30	31	8	50·6	1951/2	108	1½	47·0	1972(*j*)	16	20	42·0
1930/1	31	7½	50·4	1952/3	113	9½	47·0	1973	19	50	42·0
1931/2	31	3	51·0	1953/4	120	0	47·0	1974	21	80	40·1
1932/3	30	9	51·1	1954/5	124	10	47·0	1975	28	50	40·0
1933/4	30	8	50·4	1955/6	132	8	47·0	1976	36	50	40·0
1934/5	31	5½	50·1	1956/7	141	0	47·0	1977	39	00	40·0
1935/6	32	0	50·6	1957/8	149	4	47·0	1978	43	00	40·0
1936/7	32	9	50·3	1958/9	155	7	47·0	1979	48	50	40·0
1937/8	34	2	50·2					1980	58	00	40·0

(*a*) Cash wages exclude extra payments for piecework, hay and corn harvests, overtime, and the value of allowances in kind.

(*b*) District/local county (national minimum wages under Corn Production Acts (1917 and 1920), the Corn Production (Repeal) Act (1921), and Agricultural Wages (Regulation) Acts (1924 and 1940).

(*c*) July/May.

(*d*) May/April.

(*e*) April/August.

(*f*) August/August.

(*g*) October/September subsequently to 1967/8, except in 1939/40.

(*h*) October/July.

(*i*) Calendar years subsequently.

(*j*) Subsequently the statutory minimum for "ordinary" hired regular whole-time men.

Labour Force 29. Indices of Average Weekly Wages in Agriculture – Republic of Ireland, 1931–80

NOTE
SOURCE: *Statistical Abstract of Ireland*

1953 = 100

1931	29·8	1944	49·4	1957	118·7	1969	283·7
1932	28·8	1945	49·4	1958	118·7	1970	320·9
1933	27·3	1946	55·5	1959	126·1	1971	399·3
1934	25·8	1947	62·9	1960	131·0	1972	436·1
1935	26·1	1948	69·0	1961	134·7	1973	486·0
1936	26·7	1949	75·1	1962	150·3	1974	608·8
1937	27·0	1950	75·1	1963	150·3	1975	746·5
1938	33·4	1951	84·3	1964	178·2	1976	811·5
1939	33·7	1952	90·8	1965	197·2	1977	946·5
1940	37·1	1953	100	1966	212·9	1978	1,044·7
1941	37·1	1954	104·9	1967	221·5	1979	1,225·5
1942	40·8	1955	104·9	1968	240·2	1980	1,514·4
1943	44·5	1956	118·7				

Labour Force 30. Money Wage Rates of Building Craftsmen and Labourers – Southern England, 1264–1954

NOTES

[1] SOURCE: Henry Phelps Brown and Sheila V. Hopkins, "Seven Centuries of Building Wages", *Economica* 22 (1955).
[2] The figures are per day to 1846 and per 10 hours subsequently.

(in old pence)

	Craftsmen		Labourers		Craftsmen		Labourers		Craftsmen	Labourers
1264–1300	3			1773–76	24 to 29	1773–76	16 to 19	1919	170	140
1300–04	3 to 3½			1776–91	29	1776–91	19	1920	240	210
1304–08	3½	1301–50	1½ or 2	1791–96	29 to 36	1791–93	19 to 22	1921	205	165
1308–11	3½ to 4			1796–1802	36	1793–98	22	1922–23	165	125
1311–37	4					1799–1802	23	1924–29	180	138
1337–40	4 to 3			1802–06	36 to 43	1802–06	23 to 29	1930	175	133
1340–50	3			1806–09	43	1806–09	29	1931–32	170	128
1350–60	3 to 5	1350–71	1½ or 2 to 3	1810–46	48	1810–46	32	1933–34	165	125
1360–1402	5	1371–1402	3	1847–52	49	1847–52	33	1935	175	133
1402–12	5 to 6	1402–12	3 to 4	1853–60	54	1853–65	34	1936	180	135
1412–1532	6	1412–1545	4	1861–64	56			1937	185	140
1532–48	6 to 7			1864–66	56 to 64	1866	36	1938	190	143
1548–52	7 to 8	1545–51	4 to 6	1866–71	64	1867–71	38	1939	195	148
1552–61	8 to 10			1871–73	64 to 72	1872	42	1940	210	163
1561–73	10	1551–80	6 to 8	1873–92	72	1873–82	46	1941	220	173
1573–80	10 to 12					1883–86	48	1942	225	178
1580–1629	12	1580–1626	8			1887	46	1943	235	185
1629–42	12 to 16	1626–39	8 to 10			1888–93	48	1944	245	193
1642–55	16 to 18	1639–46	10 to 12	1893–98	75	1894–1905	50	1945	255	205
1655–87	18	1646–93	12	1898–1913	80	1906–12	55	1946	295	238
1687–1701	18 to 20	1693–1701	12 to 14	1914	85	1913–14	60	1947	325	260
1701–10	20 to 22	1701–10	14 to 15	1915	90	1915	65	1948	330	265
1710–30	22	1710–30	15	1916	93	1916	73	1949	335	275
1730–36	22 to 24	1730–36	15 to 16	1917	103	1917	83	1950	340	285
1736–73	24	1736–73	16	1918	120	1918	95	1951	370	315
								1952	400	345
								1953	420	365
								1954	445	390

Labour Force 31. Indices of Prices and Real Wages of Building Craftsmen – Southern England, 1264–1954

NOTES

[1] SOURCE: Henry Phelps Brown and Sheila V. Hopkins, "Seven Centuries of the Prices of Consumables, compared with Builders' Wage-rates", *Economica* 23 (1956), Appendix B (reprinted in *ibid.*, *A Perspective of Wages and Prices*, London, 1981).

[2] The price index relates to a "composite unit of consumables" and the wage index to the money wage expressed in terms of that "composite physical unit".

(average of 1451–75 = 100)

	Prices	Real Wages		Prices	Real Wages		Prices	Real Wages		Prices	Real Wages
1264	83	60	1314	112	60	1364	151	55	1414	108	93
1265	80	63	1315	132	51	1365	143	58	1415	115	87
1266	83	60	1316	216	31	1366	121	69	1416	124	81
1267	...	...	1317	215	31	1367	137	61	1417	129	78
1268	70	71	1318	154	44	1368	139	60	1418	114	88
1269	83	60	1319	119	56	1369	150	55	1419	95	105
1270	...	...	1320	106	63	1370	184	45	1420	102	98
1271	98	51	1321	121	55	1371	164	51	1421	93	108
1272	130	38	1322	141	48	1372	132	63	1422	97	103
1273	98	51	1323	165	41	1373	131	63	1423	108	93
1274	95	53	1324	137	49	1374	125	66	1424	103	97
1275	100	50	1325	127	53	1375	125	66	1425	109	92
1276	96	52	1326	124	54	1376	146	57	1426	103	97
1277	97	52	1327	96	70	1377	112	74	1427	96	104
1278	103	49	1328	96	70	1378	95	87	1428	99	101
1279	94	53	1329	119	56	1379	94	88	1429	127	79
1280	94	53	1330	120	56	1380	106	78	1430	138	72
1281	93	54	1331	134	50	1381	119	70	1431	115	87
1282	104	48	1332	131	51	1382	111	75	1432	102	98
1283	111	45	1333	111	60	1383	108	77	1433	112	89
1284	120	42	1334	99	68	1384	116	72	1434	109	92
1285	83	60	1335	96	70	1385	112	74	1435	105	95
1286	91	55	1336	101	66	1386	104	80	1436	95	105
1287	91	55	1337	111	60	1387	100	83	1437	93	108
1288	72	69	1338	85	...	1388	102	81	1438	128	78
1289	69	72	1339	79	...	1389	100	83	1439	154	65
1290	80	63	1340	96	52	1390	106	78	1440	140	71
1291	106	47	1341	86	58	1391	133	62	1441	93	108
1292	96	52	1342	85	59	1392	104	80	1442	85	118
1293	93	54	1343	84	60	1393	100	83	1443	97	103
1294	110	45	1344	97	52	1394	101	82	1444	102	98
1295	131	38	1345	98	51	1395	93	89	1445	87	115
1296	104	48	1346	88	57	1396	99	84	1446	95	105
1297	93	54	1347	109	46	1397	116	72	1447	100	100
1298	106	47	1348	116	43	1398	121	69	1448	102	98
1299	96	52	1349	97	52	1399	113	73	1449	106	94
1300	113	44	1350	102	49	1400	104	80	1450	102	98
1301	89	...	1351	134	...	1401	130	64	1451	109	92
1302	93	...	1352	160	...	1402	127	65	1452	97	103
1303	89	...	1353	138	...	1403	119	...	1453	97	103
1304	94	62	1354	117	...	1404	99	...	1454	105	95
1305	97	60	1355	115	...	1405	99	...	1455	94	106
1306	100	58	1356	121	...	1406	100	...	1456	101	99
1307	94	62	1357	133	...	1407	99	...	1457	93	108
1308	105	55	1358	139	...	1408	107	...	1458	99	101
1309	119	...	1359	126	...	1409	120	...	1459	95	105
1310	135	...	1360	135	61	1410	130	...	1460	97	103
1311	123	54	1361	131	63	1411	106	...	1461	117	85
1312	108	62	1362	153	54	1412	103	97	1462	115	87
1313	101	66	1363	155	54	1413	108	93	1463	88	114

Labour Force 31. *continued*

(average of 1451–75 = 100)

	Prices	Real Wages		Prices	Real Wages		Prices	Real Wages		Prices	Real Wages
1464	86	116	1519	129	78	1574	374	...	1629	510	39
1465	108	93	1520	137	73	1575	...	...	1630	595	...
1466	109	92	1521	167	60	1576	309	...	1631	682	...
1467	108	93	1522	160	63	1577	363	...	1632	580	...
1468	106	94	1523	136	74	1578	351	...	1633	565	...
1469	107	93	1524	133	75	1579	326	...	1634	611	...
1470	102	98	1525	129	78	1580	342	58	1635	597	...
1471	103	97	1526	133	75	1581	347	58	1636	593	...
1472	104	96	1527	147	68	1582	343	58	1637	621	...
1473	97	103	1528	179	56	1583	324	62	1638	707	...
1474	95	105	1529	159	63	1584	333	60	1639	607	...
1475	90	111	1530	169	59	1585	338	59	1640	546	...
1476	85	118	1531	154	65	1586	352	57	1641	586	...
1477	81	123	1532	179	56	1587	491	41	1642	557	48
1478	89	112	1533	169	...	1588	346	58	1643	553	...
1479	97	103	1534	145	...	1589	354	56	1644	531	...
1480	103	97	1535	131	...	1590	396	51	1645	574	...
1481	115	87	1536	164	...	1591	459	44	1646	569	...
1482	145	69	1537	155	...	1592	370	54	1647	667	...
1483	162	62	1538	138	...	1593	356	56	1648	770	...
1484	128	78	1539	147	...	1594	381	52	1649	821	...
1485	99	101	1540	158	...	1595	515	39	1650	839	...
1486	86	116	1541	165	...	1596	505	40	1651	704	...
1487	103	97	1542	172	...	1597	685	29	1652	648	...
1488	110	90	1543	171	...	1598	579	35	1653	579	...
1489	109	92	1544	178	...	1599	474	42	1654	543	...
1490	106	94	1545	191	...	1600	459	44	1655	531	56
1491	112	89	1546	248	...	1601	536	37	1656	559	54
1492	103	97	1547	231	...	1602	471	42	1657	612	49
1493	117	85	1548	193	61	1603	448	45	1658	646	46
1494	96	104	1549	214	...	1604	404	50	1659	700	43
1495	99	112	1550	262	...	1605	448	45	1660	684	44
1496	94	106	1551	285	...	1606	468	43	1661	648	46
1497	101	99	1552	276	48	1607	449	45	1662	769	39
1498	96	104	1553	259	...	1608	507	39	1663	675	44
1499	99	101	1554	276	...	1609	559	36	1664	657	46
1500	94	106	1555	270	...	1610	503	40	1665	616	49
1501	107	93	1556	370	...	1611	463	43	1666	664	45
1502	122	82	1557	409	...	1612	524	38	1667	577	52
1503	114	88	1558	230	...	1613	549	36	1668	602	50
1504	107	93	1559	225	...	1614	567	35	1669	572	52
1505	103	97	1560	265	...	1615	561	36	1670	577	52
1506	106	94	1561	283	59	1616	562	36	1671	595	50
1507	98	102	1562	266	63	1617	537	37	1672	557	54
1508	100	100	1563	...	...	1618	524	38	1673	585	51
1509	92	109	1564	...	...	1619	494	40	1674	650	46
1510	103	97	1565	290	58	1620	485	41	1675	691	43
1511	97	103	1566	287	58	1621	461	43	1676	526	46
1512	101	99	1567	282	59	1622	523	38	1677	592	51
1513	120	83	1568	281	59	1623	588	34	1678	633	47
1514	118	85	1569	276	61	1624	543	37	1679	614	49
1515	107	93	1570	300	56	1625	534	37	1680	568	53
1516	110	90	1571	265	63	1626	552	36	1681	567	53
1517	111	90	1572	270	62	1627	496	40	1682	600	50
1518	116	86	1573	274	61	1628	466	43	1683	587	51

Labour Force 31. *continued*

(average of 1451–75 = 100)

	Prices	Real Wages		Prices	Real Wages		Prices	Real Wages		Prices	Real Wages
1684	570	53	1739	547	73	1794	978	...	1849	1,035	79
1685	651	46	1740	644	62	1795	1,091	...	1850	969	84
1686	559	54	1741	712	56	1796	1,161	52	1851	961	85
1687	580	52	1742	631	63	1797	1,045	57	1852	979	84
1688	551	...	1743	579	69	1798	1,022	59	1853	1,135	79
1689	535	...	1744	518	77	1799	1,148	52	1854	1,265	71
1690	513	...	1745	528	76	1800	1,567	38	1855	1,274	71
1691	493	...	1746	594	67	1801	1,751	34	1856	1,264	71
1692	542	...	1747	574	70	1802	1,348	45	1857	1,287	70
1693	652	...	1748	599	67	1803	1,268	...	1858	1,190	76
1694	693	...	1749	609	66	1804	1,309	...	1859	1,214	74
1695	645	...	1750	590	68	1805	1,521	...	1860	1,314	68
1696	697	...	1751	574	70	1806	1,454	49	1861	1,302	72
1697	693	...	1752	601	67	1807	1,427	50	1862	1,290	72
1698	767	...	1753	585	68	1808	1,476	49	1863	1,144	82
1699	773	...	1754	615	65	1809	1,619	44	1864	1,200	78
1700	671	...	1755	578	69	1810	1,670	48	1865	1,238	...
1701	586	57	1756	602	66	1811	1,622	49	1866	1,296	82
1702	582	...	1757	633	55	1812	1,836	44	1867	1,346	79
1703	551	...	1758	731	55	1813	1,881	43	1868	1,291	82
1704	587	...	1759	673	59	1814	1,642	49	1869	1,244	86
1705	548	...	1760	643	62	1815	1,467	55	1870	1,241	86
1706	583	...	1761	614	65	1816	1,344	60	1871	1,320	81
1707	531	...	1762	638	63	1817	1,526	52	1872	1,378	...
1708	571	...	1763	655	61	1818	1,530	52	1873	1,437	84
1709	697	...	1764	713	56	1819	1,492	54	1874	1,423	84
1710	798	46	1765	738	54	1820	1,353	59	1875	1,310	92
1711	889	41	1766	747	54	1821	1,190	67	1876	1,370	88
1712	638	58	1767	790	51	1822	1,029	78	1877	1,330	90
1713	594	62	1768	781	51	1823	1,099	73	1878	1,281	94
1714	635	58	1769	717	56	1824	1,193	67	1879	1,210	99
1715	646	57	1770	714	56	1825	1,400	57	1880	1,174	102
1716	645	57	1771	775	52	1826	1,323	60	1881	1,213	99
1717	602	61	1772	858	47	1827	1,237	65	1882	1,140	105
1718	575	64	1773	855	47	1828	1,201	67	1883	1,182	102
1719	609	60	1774	863	...	1829	1,189	67	1884	1,071	112
1720	635	58	1775	815	...	1830	1,146	70	1885	1,026	117
1721	604	61	1776	797	61	1831	1,260	63	1886	931	129
1722	554	66	1777	794	61	1832	1,167	69	1887	955	126
1723	525	70	1778	826	58	1833	1,096	73	1888	950	126
1724	589	62	1779	756	64	1834	1,011	79	1889	948	127
1725	610	60	1780	730	66	1835	1,028	78	1890	947	127
1726	637	58	1781	760	64	1836	1,141	70	1891	998	120
1727	596	62	1782	776	62	1837	1,169	68	1892	996	120
1728	649	57	1783	869	56	1838	1,177	68	1893	914	137
1729	681	54	1784	874	55	1839	1,263	63	1894	982	127
1730	599	61	1785	839	58	1840	1,286	62	1895	968	129
1731	553	...	1786	839	58	1841	1,256	64	1896	947	132
1732	557	...	1787	834	58	1842	1,161	69	1897	963	130
1733	544	...	1788	867	56	1843	1,030	78	1898	982	127
1734	518	...	1789	856	56	1844	1,029	78	1899	950	140
1735	529	...	1790	871	55	1845	1,079	74	1900	994	134
1736	539	74	1791	870	55	1846	1,122	71	1901	986	135
1737	581	69	1792	883	...	1847	1,257	65	1902	963	138
1738	563	71	1793	908	...	1848	1,105	74	1903	1,004	133

Labour Force 31. *continued*

(average of 1451–75 = 100)

	Prices	Real Wages		Prices	Real Wages		Prices	Real Wages		Prices	Real Wages
1904	985	135	1919	2,254	126	1934	1,097	251	1949	3,145	178
1905	989	135	1920	2,591	154	1935	1,149	254	1950	3,155	180
1906	1,016	131	1921	2,048	167	1936	1,211	248	1951	3,656	170
1907	1,031	129	1922	1,672	164	1937	1,275	242	1952	3,987	167
1908	1,043	128	1923	1,726	159	1938	1,274	249	1953	3,735	187
1909	1,058	126	1924	1,740	172	1939	1,209	269	1954	3,825	194
1910	994	134	1925	1,708	176	1940	1,574	222			
1911	984	135	1926	1,577	190	1941	1,784	206			
1912	999	133	1927	1,496	201	1942	2,130	176			
1913	1,021	131	1928	1,485	202	1943	2,145	183			
1914	1,147	124	1929	1,511	199	1944	2,216	184			
1915	1,317	114	1930	1,275	229	1945	2,282	186			
1916	1,652	94	1931	1,146	247	1946	2,364	208			
1917	1,965	87	1932	1,065	251	1947	2,580	210			
1918	2,497	80	1933	1,107	254	1948	2,781	198			

Labour Force 32. Indices of Shift Earnings of Coal Hewers on Piecework – United Kingdom, 1800–1914

NOTES

[1] SOURCE: B. R. Mitchell, *The Economic Development of the British Coal Industry, 1800–1914* (Cambridge, 1984), pp. 194–5 and 202–3.

[2] The index numbers are representative of normal earnings per shift, but it must be remembered that the range of actual earnings was wide.

[3] The figures are weighted averages of index numbers for the main individual coalfields.

1886 = 100

1800/2	65	1843	69	1861	97	1879	97	1897	123
1813/14	73	1844	73	1862	99	1880	97	1898	127
1819	64	1845	80	1863	99	1881	101	1899	138
1822	69	1846	90	1864	106	1882	105	1900	157
1825	86	1847	89	1865	111	1883	106	1901	167
1829	72	1848	75	1866	119	1884	103	1902	154
1830	74	1849	75	1867	108	1885	102	1903	151
1831	80	1850	76	1868	97	1886	100	1904	146
1832	78	1851	76	1869	97	1887	99	1905	142
1833	77	1852	78	1870	101	1888	100	1906	143
1834	79	1853	84	1871	110	1889	112	1907	158
1835	81	1854	96	1872	138	1890	132	1908	169
1836	86	1855	103	1873	166	1891	141	1909	159
1837	87	1856	107	1874	146	1892	137	1910	158
1838	85	1857	97	1875	125	1893	130	1911	159
1839	86	1858	90	1876	116	1894	132	1912	163
1840	82	1859	90	1877	109	1895	124	1913	178
1841	77	1860	94	1878	101	1896	121	1914	180
1842	72								

Labour Force 33. Indices of Average Weekly Wage Rates of Skilled Engineering Workers – Great Britain, 1850–1927

NOTE

SOURCE: R. S. Spicer, *British Engineering Wages* (London, 1928), p. 34.

1900 = 100

1850	73·08	1870	83·12	1890	92·68	1909	101·32
1851	74·27	1871	84·31	1891	93·31	1910	102·03
1852	74·66	1872	88·65	1892	93·31	1911	103·26
1853	76·40	1873	90·47	1893	92·60	1912	104·24
1854	77·59	1874	91·66	1894	92·56	1913	105·00
1855	79·01	1875	92·60	1895	93·18	1914	105·40
1856	79·56	1876	92·20	1896	96·75	1915	108·10
1857	80·20	1877	92·04	1897	98·18	1916	126·60
1858	78·22	1878	90·23	1898	99·19	1917	178·20
1859	78·78	1879	87·86	1899	99·61	1918	203·30
1860	79·01	1880	88·05	1900	100·00	1919	218·20
1861	79·18	1881	89·36	1901	100·29	1920	242·50
1862	79·80	1882	89·94	1902	100·29	1921	204·20
1863	80·35	1883	90·09	1903	99·93	1922	152·40
1864	80·98	1884	89·99	1904	99·93	1923	152·40
1865	81·94	1885	89·96	1905	100·05	1924	152·40
1866	83·37	1886	89·60	1906	100·83	1925	152·40
1867	82·97	1887	90·29	1907	102·00	1926	152·40
1868	82·72	1888	91·29	1908	101·68	1927	157·70
1869	82·34	1889	91·72				

Labour Force 34. Indices of Average Incomes of Wage-earners by Industry Groups – United Kingdom 1920–38

NOTES

[1] Source: Agatha Chapman and Rose Knight, *Wages and Salaries in the United Kingdom, 1920–1938* (Cambridge University Press, 1953). The indices are constructed from the tables on pp. 18, 22 and 98–103, together with (for Part B) the cost of living index on p. 30.

[2] United Kingdom here refers to Great Britain and Northern Ireland for the whole period.

[3] For a full definition of the concept of average income as used here the original source must be consulted. Briefly, it represents the average income per man-year of employment, rather than per person employed, i.e. it is the average income of a man in normal full-time employment, including periods of sickness and recognised holidays, but not periods of unemployment. So far as possible, short-time was treated as partial employment in making the estimates of numbers employed, whilst overtime was regarded as varying average earnings rather than the level of employment.

[4] Most of the headings are self-explanatory, but the following seem to require a little elaboration: *Iron and Steel* – covers workers in blast furnaces, smelting and rolling mills, foundries, tube manufacture and tinplate works; *Shipbuilding* – includes ship repairing, but does not cover workers in naval dockyards; *Engineering* – combines mechanical and electrical engineering, other than in ordnance factories; *Printing, etc.* – covers printing, bookbinding and kindred trades, stationery and cardboard box manufacture, and newspaper publication; *Professional Services* – covers wage-earning assistants in the professions, other than those employed by local authorities; *Miscellaneous Services* – comprises wage-earning assistants in entertainment and sport.

A. Index of Average Money Incomes (1924 = 100)

	Agriculture and Forestry	Fishing	Mining and Quarrying	Manufacturing: Total	Iron and Steel	Shipbuilding	Engineering	Cotton	Woollen and Worsted	Printing, etc.	Furniture
1920	146	132	159	145	176	175	153	162	142	116	133
1921	154	102	129	137	167	163	147	137	139	118	126
1922	110	91	93	110	106	119	120	109	105	108	106
1923	99	88	94	100	96	97	100	100	100	101	100
1924	100	100	100	100	100	100	100	100	100	100	100
1925	109	98	99	101	100	106	101	100	100	101	100
1926	111	93	83	101	97	106	101	100	100	101	100
1927	111	94	96	101	97	107	102	100	100	101	100
1928	111	98	88	101	95	107	103	100	100	100	100
1929	111	104	88	102	94	108	105	98	99	100	100
1930	112	102	89	100	94	110	105	91	93	100	98
1931	112	97	89	98	94	110	103	92	90	100	97
1932	111	94	90	96	92	109	101	92	85	100	94
1933	109	93	89	96	92	106	101	88	87	100	91
1934	108	99	89	98	95	105	103	89	86	103	91
1935	111	103	89	100	96	103	107	89	91	104	92
1936	115	106	96	101	97	105	109	88	92	104	96
1937	118	109	101	105	105	108	112	94	95	104	99
1938	127	113	106	109	114	115	114	95	95	104	100

B. Index of Average Real Incomes (1924 = 100)

	Agriculture and Forestry	Fishing	Mining and Quarrying	Manufacturing: Total	Iron and Steel	Shipbuilding	Engineering	Cotton	Woollen and Worsted	Printing, etc.	Furniture
1920	103	92	115	102	124	123	108	114	100	82	94
1921	119	79	100	106	129	126	114	106	108	91	98
1922	105	87	89	105	101	114	115	104	100	103	101
1923	100	89	95	100	97	98	101	101	101	102	101
1924	100	100	100	100	100	100	100	100	100	100	100
1925	108	97	98	101	100	105	100	100	100	100	100
1926	113	95	85	103	99	108	103	102	102	103	102
1927	116	98	100	106	101	112	107	104	104	105	104
1928	117	104	93	106	100	113	109	105	105	105	105
1929	119	111	94	109	100	115	112	105	106	107	107
1930	124	113	98	111	104	122	116	101	103	111	109
1931	133	115	106	116	112	130	122	109	107	119	115
1932	135	115	109	117	112	133	123	112	103	122	114
1933	136	117	111	120	115	133	126	110	109	125	114
1934	135	123	111	122	118	130	128	111	107	128	113
1935	135	125	109	122	118	126	131	109	111	127	113
1936	137	126	114	121	116	125	130	105	110	124	114
1937	134	123	114	119	119	123	127	107	108	118	113
1938	142	126	119	122	128	129	128	107	107	117	112

Labour Force 34. *continued*

A. Index of Average Money Incomes (*continued*) (1924 = 100)

	Building and Contracting	Gas, Water and Electricity Supply	Transport and Communications	Distributive Trades	Insurance, Banking and Finance	Local Govt. Service	Professional Services	Miscellaneous Services	Grand Total All Wage-earners
1920	148	129	119	126	146	138	145	144	142
1921	136	123	118	125	140	136	138	138	133
1922	107	107	106	111	108	116	106	107	106
1923	97	99	98	102	96	103	98	99	99
1924	100	100	100	100	100	100	100	100	100
1925	102	102	100	100	100	102	100	101	101
1926	103	102	96	100	99	103	100	101	98
1927	103	103	99	101	101	102	99	99	100
1928	101	103	99	101	99	101	97	98	99
1929	101	101	99	100	98	101	97	98	99
1930	102	100	98	101	97	101	95	96	99
1931	99	97	95	101	97	100	93	93	97
1932	96	94	93	102	95	99	91	92	95
1933	95	94	92	103	92	98	90	90	94
1934	95	95	94	104	94	99	90	91	95
1935	97	96	95	106	95	99	91	91	97
1936	97	97	97	109	96	100	93	94	99
1937	100	97	99	111	101	103	97	94	102
1938	102	102	100	114	102	106	99	100	106

B. Index of Average Real Incomes (*continued*) (1924 = 100)

	Building and Contracting	Gas, Water and Electricity Supply	Transport and Communications	Distributive Trades	Insurance, Banking and Finance	Local Govt. Service	Professional Services	Miscellaneous Services	Grand Total All Wage-earners
1920	104	91	84	88	102	97	102	101	100
1921	106	96	91	97	109	105	107	107	103
1922	102	102	101	106	103	111	102	102	102
1923	98	99	99	103	97	103	98	99	99
1924	100	100	100	100	100	100	100	100	100
1925	102	102	100	99	99	102	100	100	100
1926	105	104	98	102	101	105	102	102	100
1927	107	108	104	105	105	107	104	104	105
1928	107	108	104	106	105	106	103	103	104
1929	108	107	106	107	104	108	104	104	106
1930	113	111	108	111	107	112	106	106	109
1931	118	115	112	120	115	119	110	111	114
1932	117	112	113	124	116	120	111	111	115
1933	118	118	115	129	115	122	112	113	117
1934	118	118	117	129	117	123	111	112	118
1935	118	118	117	130	116	121	111	112	118
1936	116	116	116	130	114	119	110	111	118
1937	113	110	112	126	114	117	110	107	115
1938	114	114	112	128	114	119	111	112	118

Labour Force 35. Average Weekly Earnings and Hours of Manual Workers in Certain Industries – United Kingdom 1938–80

NOTES

[1] SOURCES: Department of Employment and Productivity, *British Labour Statistics: Historical Abstract, 1886–1968* (London, 1971), tables 40–45; *Ministry of Labour/Dept. of Employment [and Productivity] Gazette*.

[2] The figures apply to one week in October in each year, except for 1940–45 when the month was July, and 1948 in part A, when it was April.

[3] The figures relate to full-time.

A. 1938–48

(earnings in £)

	Non-metalliferous Mining Products		Bricks, Pottery, Glass		Chemicals, Paint, etc.		Metal, Engineering, and Shipbuilding		Textiles		Leather, Leather Goods, and Fur		Clothing		Food, Drink, & Tobacco		Woodworking	
Males	Earnings	Hours	Earnings	Hours	Earnings	Hours	Earnings	Hours	Earnings	Hours	Earnings	Hours	Earnings	Hours	Earnings	Hours	Earnings	Hours
1938	3·32	49·8	3·16	48·7	3·46	48·4	3·75	48·0	2·86	47·7	3·20	47·4	3·25	44·2	3·26	49·4	3·31	46·9
1940	4·24	...	3·89	...	4·39	...	5·12	...	3·79	...	3·84	...	3·63	...	3·82	...	3·82	...
1941	4·72	...	4·43	...	4·92	...	5·61	...	4·08	...	4·30	...	4·24	...	4·37	...	4·33	...
1942	5·18	...	4·83	...	5·40	...	6·40	...	4·52	...	4·75	...	4·63	...	4·65	...	4·78	...
1943	5·47	52·1	5·21	50·8	5·81	52·4	6·91	54·1	4·58	51·4	5·01	49·7	4·99	46·7	5·08	51·9	5·11	49·8
1944	5·63	51·1	5·40	49·9	6·02	52·4	6·95	51·3	5·09	51·0	5·24	48·9	5·33	46·2	5·33	51·3	5·37	49·2
1945	5·82	51·1	5·55	49·6	6·14	51·6	6·65	49·3	5·23	50·1	5·38	48·8	5·61	45·6	5·52	51·1	5·53	48·1
1946	6·16	49·5	6·00	48·3	6·00	48·3	6·64	48·0	5·50	48·2	5·93	47·4	5·81	44·0	5·63	48·7	5·95	45·1
1947	6·24	49·7	6·50	48·0	6·36	46·4	7·01	46·0	5·96	47·2	6·30	45·7	6·11	43·7	6·06	48·1	6·33	45·1
1948	6·99	49·5	6·74	47·3	6·70	46·2	7·20	46·3	6·33	47·4	6·40	45·0	6·38	43·5	6·20	47·3	6·48	45·0
Females																		
1938	1·48	45·5	1·39	42·6	1·63	44·0	1·67	44·2	1·59	44·5	1·75	45·7	1·70	41·7	1·65	45·8	1·68	44·3
1940	1·95	...	1·65	...	1·86	...	2·19	...	2·02	...	1·79	...	1·87	...	1·77	...	1·93	...
1941	2·25	...	1·93	...	2·25	...	2·40	...	2·10	...	2·00	...	2·11	...	2·01	...	2·14	...
1942	2·65	...	2·22	...	2·82	...	3·03	...	2·42	...	2·36	...	2·45	...	2·30	...	2·58	...
1943	2·95	44·7	2·47	44·5	3·18	44·6	3·49	46·9	2·65	46·6	2·54	44·7	2·58	43·7	2·54	45·4	2·84	44·2
1944	3·09	44·9	2·53	43·9	3·25	44·3	3·55	45·1	2·78	45·7	2·65	43·3	2·74	42·5	2·70	44·6	2·95	42·5
1945	3·15	44·2	2·59	43·3	3·14	44·2	3·45	43·4	2·91	44·7	2·73	42·8	2·83	41·8	2·83	43·8	3·12	42·2
1946	3·37	43·4	2·90	43·1	3·19	42·8	3·53	42·8	3·18	43·9	3·28	42·6	3·26	40·6	3·00	43·4	3·39	41·8
1947	3·47	41·1	3·32	42·1	3·39	41·6	3·68	41·1	3·40	42·5	3·57	40·9	3·53	40·1	3·25	42·5	3·60	41·2
1948	3·63	42·1	3·48	41·6	3·56	41·6	3·76	41·1	3·70	42·7	3·54	41·0	3·68	40·1	3·40	42·4	3·68	40·9

Labour Force 35. *continued*

A. 1938–48 (*cont.*)

(earnings in £)

	Printing, etc.		All Manufacturing (*a*)		Mining & Quarrying (except coal)		Building, etc.		Transport		Public Utilities		Government Industrial Establishments		All Industries Covered	
Males	Earnings	Hours	Earnings	Hours	Earnings	Hours	Earnings	Hours	Earnings	Hours	Earnings	Hours	Earnings	Hours	Earnings	Hours
1938	4·21	46·1	3·55	47·8	3·00	45·9	3·30	46·3	3·50	48·9	3·15	49·0	3·76	49·5	3·45	47·7
1940	4·20	...	4·65	...	3·74	...	4·25	...	4·26	...	3·53	...	5·30	...	4·45	...
1941	4·85	...	5·20	...	4·18	...	4·85	...	4·61	...	3·87	...	5·54	...	4·97	...
1942	5·28	...	5·93	...	4·42	...	5·10	...	4·95	...	4·18	...	6·10	...	5·57	...
1943	5·63	48·5	6·43	53·1	4·90	49·1	5·42	53·4	5·21	51·8	4·43	50·3	6·61	55·1	6·06	52·9
1944	6·03	48·6	6·54	51·0	4·95	47·9	5·40	52·1	5·71	52·3	4·73	50·6	6·93	53·6	6·22	51·2
1945	6·15	48·3	6·34	49·4	5·18	48·0	5·57	50·3	5·74	51·7	4·93	49·5	6·35	50·2	6·07	49·7
1946	6·33	46·0	6·33	47·7	5·63	47·6	5·53	45·5	5·76	50·0	5·30	47·9	5·83	48·4	6·04	47·6
1947	6·86	45·0	6·71	46·2	6·16	46·8	5·85	47·1	6·18	48·6	5·58	47·0	6·03	46·0	6·40	46·6
1948	7·19	45·2	6·93	46·3	6·55	46·6	6·40	46·6	6·60	48·9	5·83	46·8	6·26	45·8	6·70	46·5
Females																
1938	1·70	44·4	1·65	44·3	...	...	...	...	1·75	45·7	1·38	32·8	2·24	44·9	1·63	43·5
1940	1·76	...	1·98	...	...	...	...	...	2·18	...	1·73	...	2·65	...	1·95	...
1941	1·98	...	2·20	...	...	...	...	...	2·98	...	1·86	...	2·70	...	2·20	...
1942	2·25	...	2·71	...	...	...	2·58	...	3·37	...	2·13	...	3·34	...	2·71	...
1943	2·56	44·7	3·12	46·2	...	...	3·07	46·5	3·57	46·3	2·39	41·5	4·05	45·6	3·11	45·9
1944	2·69	43·9	3·22	44·7	...	...	3·10	43·4	3·95	45·7	2·51	40·5	4·26	45·1	3·21	44·6
1945	2·73	43·3	3·16	43·5	...	...	3·02	42·0	4·08	45·8	2·57	38·8	4·05	42·4	3·16	43·3
1946	3·03	42·9	3·28	42·7	...	...	3·07	40·7	4·22	45·3	2·80	39·2	3·77	44·9	3·25	42·5
1947	3·34	42·0	3·50	41·5	3·21	41·4	3·33	40·9	4·44	44·2	3·09	39·3	3·89	43·1	3·47	41·4
1948	3·61	42·0	3·67	41·5	3·55	42·3	3·39	40·4	4·88	43·9	3·18	39·8	3·98	43·0	3·65	41·5

See p. 178 for footnotes.

B. 1948–80

Males	Non-metalliferous Mining Products (except coal) (b)		Chemicals and Allied Trades (c)		Metal Manufacture		Engineering and Electrical Goods (a)		Electrical Engineering		Shipbuilding and Marine Engineering		Vehicles		Textiles		Leather, Leather Goods, and Fur		Clothing (e)	
	Earnings	Hours	Earnings	Hours	Earnings	Hours	Earnings	Hours	Earnings	Hours	Earnings	Hours	Earnings	Hours	Earnings	Hours	Earnings	Hours	Earnings	Hours
1948	6·96	48·1	6·89	46·8	7·84	47·2	7·30	46·6	...	...	...	...	7·76	45·7	6·45	47·2	6·63	45·6	6·64	43·8
1949	7·30	48·0	7·23	47·1	8·11	47·2	7·37	46·5	...	...	...	...	7·87	45·5	6·95	47·4	6·96	46·3	6·98	44·0
1950	7·72	49·0	7·62	48·0	8·55	48·0	7·82	47·8	...	...	...	...	8·33	46·4	7·34	48·0	7·41	46·3	7·33	44·3
1951	8·66	49·4	8·45	47·8	9·35	48·1	8·61	48·3	...	...	...	...	9·00	46·9	8·14	47·3	7·88	45·9	7·58	43·4
1952	9·17	49·0	8·81	47·0	10·10	47·8	9·41	48·4	...	...	...	...	9·65	46·8	8·57	47·6	8·50	46·9	8·30	44·7
1953	9·80	49·5	9·64	48·1	10·51	47·8	9·93	48·2	...	...	...	...	10·40	47·2	9·23	48·4	9·00	46·9	8·75	44·6
1954	10·49	50·0	10·30	48·5	11·43	48·5	10·78	49·0	...	...	...	...	11·29	47·7	9·84	48·6	9·56	47·2	9·21	44·5
1955	11·38	50·4	11·30	48·9	12·48	48·8	11·79	49·3	...	...	...	...	12·29	47·8	10·38	48·4	10·35	47·4	9·84	44·9
1956	12·05	50·0	12·03	48·4	13·40	48·4	12·67	49·0	...	...	...	...	12·58	46·5	10·94	48·3	10·99	47·0	10·64	44·6
1957	12·49	49·6	12·81	48·4	14·33	47·9	13·36	48·5	...	...	...	...	13·88	47·1	11·54	47·9	11·48	46·7	11·02	44·3
1958	12·91	49·4	13·19	47·9	14·02	46·3	13·47	47·6	...	...	...	...	14·03	46·1	11·62	47·3	11·78	47·0	11·38	44·3
	13·60	50·3	13·74	48·3	15·17	47·8	13·98	48·3					15·23	47·5	12·40	48·7	12·51	47·7	11·80	44·5
1959	---(b)	---(b)	---(i)	---(i)	---(i)	---(i)	---(d)	---(d)	...	...	13·37	47·4	---(i)	---(i)	---(i)	---(i)	---(i)	---(i)	---(e)	---(e)
	13·64	50·3	13·79	48·4	15·18	47·8	14·11	48·3					16·62	47·5	12·42	48·6	12·48	47·8	12·09	44·5
1960	14·62	50·2	15·00	47·3	16·14	47·3	15·26	47·6	...	...	14·39	46·6	16·98	44·8	13·32	48·0	13·22	47·7	12·99	44·3
1961	15·62	49·3	15·65	46·8	16·45	46·0	16·11	47·3	...	...	15·22	46·2	17·69	44·9	13·97	46·6	13·74	46·7	13·60	43·7
1962	16·18	48·8	16·19	46·3	16·91	45·3	16·28	46·3	...	...	15·43	45·6	18·33	44·4	14·43	46·4	14·36	46·2	14·09	43·0
1963	17·21	49·4	17·41	46·7	17·93	46·5	16·89	46·7	...	...	16·18	46·4	19·83	45·4	15·36	47·0	15·33	47·2	14·85	43·7
1964	18·60	49·4	18·93	46·9	19·51	46·6	18·36	47·1	...	...	17·84	47·3	21·04	45·0	16·37	46·9	16·18	46·1	15·79	43·7
1965	20·03	48·7	20·38	46·0	21·16	46·0	19·80	46·0	...	...	19·79	46·1	22·43	43·6	17·86	46·7	17·36	46·1	17·23	43·0
1966	20·86	47·8	21·23	45·1	21·47	44·9	20·58	45·2	...	...	21·29	45·9	21·97	41·3	18·53	45·7	17·64	44·1	17·79	41·5
1967	21·94	48·0	22·24	45·4	22·38	44·9	21·39	45·0	...	...	21·88	45·4	24·42	43·4	19·56	45·5	18·71	44·7	18·76	41·8
1968	23·38	47·9	23·65	45·9	24·4	45·9	23·08	45·6	...	...	23·93	45·7	26·45	43·9	21·33	46·1	20·42	45·6	20·27	42·4
	24·90	47·9	25·64	45·8	26·56	45·7	25·07	45·5			26·13	45·3	28·67	43·6	22·85	45·9	21·44	45·1	21·44	41·9
1969	---(i)	---(i)	---(c)	---(c)	---(i)	---(i)	---(d)	---(d)	24·70	45·2	---(i)	---(i)	---(i)	---(i)	---(i)	---(i)	---(i)	---(i)	---(i)	---(i)
	24·86	47·8	25·27	46·1	26·56	45·8	25·33	45·9			26·15	45·3	28·71	43·6	22·95	45·8	21·40	45·1	21·45	41·9
1970	28·72	46·9	29·23	44·9	29·98	45·1	28·43	44·9	27·69	44·4	29·59	45·3	32·43	42·4	25·29	46·7	24·23	45·0	24·12	41·5
1971	31·95	46·3	32·73	44·0	31·67	43·3	29·84	43·0	30·12	43·4	33·13	43·8	35·21	41·2	28·02	44·1	26·56	44·5	26·00	41·2
1972	37·25	46·5	36·77	44·2	37·97	44·6	34·73	43·5	34·48	43·4	34·98	43·5	41·63	42·3	32·05	44·7	30·03	44·2	29·52	41·5
1973	42·59	47·1	41·31	44·6	43·85	45·1	40·51	44·6	39·14	44·0	41·60	44·0	45·74	43·0	36·75	44·9	34·53	44·5	33·90	42·0
1974	50·40	46·1	51·29	44·2	51·76	44·8	48·49	44·2	46·18	43·4	50·40	43·5	52·73	42·3	43·74	43·6	41·39	44·2	40·37	41·1
1975	61·07	44·5	63·10	42·7	62·50	41·9	58·86	42·6	56·79	42·2	67·53	43·9	62·52	41·4	53·65	42·4	50·76	43·7	48·16	40·5
1976	68·82	45·3	71·72	44·1	73·72	44·0	66·11	42·9	63·48	42·3	72·09	43·4	72·48	42·6	61·19	43·4	55·89	43·1	53·30	40·9
1977	75·15	45·7	77·80	44·4	79·40	43·8	73·38	43·3	69·13	42·6	76·37	43·7	75·59	42·2	65·32	43·1	61·91	42·9	61·61	41·3
1978	87·48	45·4	90·78	44·6	91·93	43·7	85·39	43·0	80·35	42·9	88·64	43·8	84·88	41·4	75·96	43·6	71·20	43·4	67·50	41·3
	102·32	45·0	107·95	44·5	103·58	43·0	96·39	42·5	92·34	42·3	95·46	43·7	98·01	41·5	87·35	43·1	80·82	43·0	80·37	41·0
1979	---(j)	---(j)	---(j)	---(j)	---(j)	---(j)	---(j)	---(j)	---(j)	---(j)	---(j)	---(j)	---(j)	---(j)	---(j)	---(j)	---(j)	---(j)	---(j)	---(j)
1980	114·47	43·2	123·36	42·9	118·20	41·6	109·34	41·5	107·41	41·6	109·63	41·8	109·41	40·1	97·90	42·2	92·74	42·5	90·62	40·1

See p. 178 for footnotes.

Labour Force 35. *continued*

B. 1940–80 (*cont.*)

(earnings in £)

	Food, Drink, & Tobacco		Manufacturers of Wood and Cork (*f*)		Paper and Printing (*g*)		All Manufacturing (*a*)		Mining and Quarrying (except coal)		Building and Contracting (*h*)		Gas, Water, and Electricity		Transport and Communication		Public Administration		All Industries Covered	
Males	Earnings	Hours	Earnings	Hours	Earnings	Hours	Earnings	Hours	Earnings	Hours	Earnings	Hours	Earnings	Hours	Earnings	Hours	Earnings	Hours	Earnings	Hours
1948	6·38	47·9	6·63	45·5	7·33	45·1	7·17	46·5	6·52	46·3	6·53	47·1	6·51	46·6	6·55	48·1	5·65	45·1	6·90	46·7
1949	6·62	47·8	7·08	45·9	7·91	46·3	7·40	46·6	6·80	46·1	6·85	47·1	6·79	47·3	6·83	48·8	5·75	44·9	7·13	46·8
1950	6·95	48·5	7·53	47·0	8·25	46·4	7·83	47·5	7·25	47·7	7·25	47·8	7·08	47·8	7·01	49·7	5·88	45·2	7·52	47·6
1951	7·73	48·7	8·15	45·8	9·37	46·7	8·60	47·6	8·26	48·4	8·05	48·2	7·81	48·3	7·86	49·9	6·60	45·5	8·30	47·8
1952	8·17	48·5	8·86	46·4	9·82	45·6	9·24	47·6	8·69	48·4	8·73	48·1	8·49	47·8	8·35	49·2	7·05	45·4	8·93	47·7
1953	8·62	48·7	9·40	46·9	10·66	47·4	9·83	47·9	9·09	48·2	9·18	48·2	8·73	47·7	8·73	49·6	7·37	45·4	9·46	47·9
1954	9·28	49·4	10·14	47·5	11·38	48·0	10·61	48·5	9·72	48·9	9·93	48·8	9·37	48·5	9·45	50·8	7·87	45·6	10·22	48·5
1955	10·11	49·4	10·81	47·5	12·35	48·1	11·55	48·7	10·67	50·0	10·78	49·5	10·28	48·8	10·58	51·5	8·55	45·7	11·15	48·9
1956	10·91	49·4	11·39	47·5	13·69	47·2	12·28	48·2	11·34	49·7	11·73	49·8	11·00	48·2	11·37	51·0	9·19	45·6	11·90	48·5
1957	11·60	49·2	11·93	46·7	14·18	47·0	13·06	48·0	11·68	48·8	12·05	49·0	11·69	48·3	12·11	50·8	9·67	46·1	12·58	48·2
1958	12·02	49·1	12·60	47·4	14·82	46·8	13·27	47·3	12·07	49·0	12·46	49·0	12·11	48·4	12·35	50·2	10·03	45·5	12·83	47·7
	12·42	49·1	13·27	48·0	16·13	47·7	14·06	48·2	12·75	50·4	12·96	49·7	12·52	48·9	13·09	51·0	10·33	45·8	13·54	48·5
1959	----(*i*)	----(*i*)	----(*f*)	----(*f*)	----(*g*)	----(*g*)	----(*i*)	----(*i*)	----(*i*)	----(*i*)	----(*h*)	----(*h*)	----(*i*)	----(*i*)	----(*i*)	----(*i*)	----(*i*)	----(*i*)	----(*i*)	----(*i*)
	12·48	49·1	13·34	48·1	16·20	47·7	14·21	48·2	12·83	50·6	13·03	49·8	12·52	48·9	13·22	50·7	10·33	45·8	13·55	48·5
1960	13·57	49·1	13·91	47·0	16·95	47·5	15·11	47·4	13·95	51·5	13·95	50·3	13·90	47·7	14·33	50·9	10·88	45·6	14·53	48·0
1961	14·49	48·5	14·90	46·7	17·87	46·7	15·89	46·8	14·76	50·2	15·25	49·4	14·08	47·9	14·96	50·3	11·73	44·4	15·34	47·4
1962	15·06	47·9	15·56	46·3	18·66	45·9	16·34	46·2	15·50	50·8	16·10	49·5	15·02	48·5	15·25	49·4	12·25	44·6	15·86	47·0
1963	15·91	48·2	16·52	47·2	19·50	46·4	17·29	46·8	16·40	51·4	16·63	49·8	16·28	49·2	16·61	50·5	12·88	44·8	16·75	47·6
1964	17·13	48·0	17·69	46·9	21·19	46·8	18·67	46·9	17·66	51·2	18·20	49·8	17·66	48·7	17·66	50·5	13·93	44·8	18·11	47·7
1965	18·68	47·7	18·98	46·5	22·83	46·5	20·16	46·1	19·07	50·8	19·77	49·8	18·40	43·8	19·77	50·6	15·03	44·9	19·59	47·0
1966	19·73	47·3	19·50	45·3	23·85	45·5	20·78	45·0	20·03	50·8	20·56	48·5	19·12	43·8	20·88	50·3	15·64	43·7	20·30	46·0
1967	20·84	47·5	20·81	45·9	24·76	45·8	21·89	45·3	21·25	50·9	21·68	48·3	19·89	43·7	21·66	50·0	16·76	43·7	21·38	46·2
1968	22·10	47·6	22·15	45·9	26·95	46·2	23·62	45·8	22·68	51·1	22·87	47·8	20·70	43·9	24·20	50·4	17·47	43·7	23·00	46·4
	24·14	47·6	23·33	45·7	29·12	46·1	25·54	45·7	24·85	51·9	24·43	48·2	22·60	44·5	25·92	50·7	18·46	43·8	24·80	46·5
1969	---(*i*)	---(*i*)	---(*i*)	---(*i*)	---(*i*)	---(*i*)	---(*i*)	---(*i*)	---(*i*)	---(*i*)	---(*i*)	---(*i*)	---(*i*)	---(*i*)	---(*i*)	---(*i*)	---(*i*)	---(*i*)	---(*i*)	---(*i*)
	24·08	47·6	23·34	45·8	29·40	46·1	25·54	45·7	24·74	51·5	24·46	48·2	22·51	44·1	25·88	50·9	18·46	43·8	24·85	46·5
1970	28·00	46·8	26·06	45·6	33·68	45·3	28·91	44·9	28·86	51·8	26·85	47·5	26·02	44·0	29·68	49·2	21·60	43·7	28·05	45·7
1971	31·60	46·4	29·25	44·7	36·04	44·4	31·37	43·6	31·05	49·3	30·11	47·2	30·74	43·7	33·73	48·0	24·51	43·5	30·93	44·7
1972	35·75	46·4	34·06	45·0	41·21	44·7	36·20	46·1	35·12	49·0	36·59	47·0	35·29	43·1	37·97	48·5	26·93	43·5	35·82	45·0
1973	40·24	47·1	39·36	45·1	48·69	45·1	41·52	44·7	39·86	48·8	41·41	47·2	39·78	43·8	43·31	49·6	31·32	43·9	40·92	45·6
1974	47·97	46·6	45·61	43·8	54·96	43·9	49·12	44·0	48·46	48·0	48·75	46·8	47·71	44·0	52·06	49·5	37·87	43·7	48·63	45·1
1975	60·29	46·2	55·83	43·1	65·17	42·4	59·74	42·7	59·82	47·2	60·38	45·2	60·45	42·3	63·81	47·3	49·88	43·2	59·58	43·6
1976	66·81	45·9	61·48	42·8	73·88	43·6	67·83	43·5	66·36	46·4	65·80	44·3	68·42	42·8	71·22	47·5	53·97	42·7	66·97	44·0
1977	72·46	46·4	67·66	43·0	82·09	44·5	73·56	43·6	74·96	47·2	72·91	44·7	72·72	42·4	76·96	48·0	59·04	42·9	72·89	44·2
1978	83·91	46·2	77·85	43·0	96·79	44·6	84·77	43·5	84·52	47·2	81·77	44·9	87·78	42·8	88·03	48·8	67·15	43·2	83·50	44·2
1979	99·79	46·3	91·05	43·2	114·88	43·8	98·28	43·2	99·82	46·8	94·06	44·9	104·30	43·4	103·30	48·6	76·92	43·1	96·94	44·0
	---(*j*)	---(*j*)	---(*j*)	---(*j*)	---(*j*)	---(*j*)	---(*j*)	---(*j*)	---(*j*)	---(*j*)	---(*j*)	---(*j*)	---(*j*)	---(*j*)	---(*j*)	---(*j*)	---(*j*)	---(*j*)	---(*j*)	---(*j*)
1980	115·61	45·5	101·16	41·7	137·73	42·5	111·64	41·9	116·58	47·9	113·36	44·0	126·12	42·2	123·77	47·1	96·60	42·7	113·06	43·0

Females	Non-metalliferous Mining Products (except coal) (b)		Chemicals and Allied Trades (c)		Metal Manufacture		Engineering and Electrical Goods (d)		Electrical Engineering		Shipbuilding and Marine Engineering		Vehicles		Textiles		Leather, Leather Goods, and Fur		Clothing (e)	
	Earnings	Hours	Earnings	Hours	Earnings	Hours	Earnings	Hours	Earnings	Hours	Earnings	Hours	Earnings	Hours	Earnings	Hours	Earnings	Hours	Earnings	Hours
1948	3·61	42·0	3·60	41·5	3·82	41·1	3·80	41·5	...	...	...	...	4·17	41·2	3·75	42·2	3·66	40·8	3·79	40·0
1949	3·79	41·0	3·84	42·1	4·02	41·4	4·06	41·8	...	...	...	...	4·43	41·3	4·03	42·0	3·78	40·9	3·98	40·1
1950	3·97	41·4	4·03	42·5	4·19	41·7	4·22	42·3	...	...	...	...	4·71	41·8	4·25	42·3	4·10	41·6	4·14	40·1
1951	4·32	41·4	4·40	42·1	4·60	41·3	4·52	41·8	...	...	...	...	4·98	41·6	4·78	41·8	4·26	40·9	4·26	38·6
1952	4·59	41·3	4·34	42·5	4·97	41·2	5·04	41·9	...	...	...	...	5·44	41·8	4·91	42·0	4·57	41·3	4·63	40·2
1953	4·85	41·4	5·13	42·4	5·23	41·4	5·41	42·3	...	...	...	...	5·86	42·0	5·32	42·4	4·87	41·3	4·93	39·9
1954	5·13	41·2	5·31	42·4	5·72	41·4	5·80	42·5	...	...	...	...	6·22	42·1	5·60	42·1	5·13	41·0	5·17	39·8
1955	5·45	40·9	5·75	42·4	6·13	41·0	6·18	42·1	...	...	...	...	6·69	41·9	5·82	41·7	5·47	41·3	5·51	39·8
1956	5·73	40·6	6·13	42·1	6·47	40·9	6·64	41·9	...	...	...	...	6·87	41·4	6·15	41·7	5·89	40·9	5·91	39·5
1957	6·07	40·5	6·38	41·7	6·93	41·0	7·01	41·8	...	...	...	...	7·49	41·7	6·50	41·4	6·14	40·3	6·15	39·1
1958	6·26	40·6	6·63	41·7	7·15	40·8	7·36	42·0	...	...	...	...	7·70	40·5	6·57	40·9	6·39	40·8	6·33	39·0
	6·59	40·9	6·88	42·0	7·40	41·5	7·60	42·4					8·24	42·0	6·96	41·8	6·80	41·0	6·67	39·4
1959	---(b)	---(b)	---(i)	---(i)	---(i)	---(i)	---(d)	---(d)	...	...	7·33	43·5	---(i)	---(i)	---(i)	---(i)	---(i)	---(i)	---(e)	---(e)
	6·59	41·1	6·86	42·2	7·32	41·3	7·65	42·6					8·48	41·7	6·93	41·7	6·78	41·2	6·73	39·7
1960	6·93	39·6	7·26	40·7	7·51	39·6	7·85	40·6	...	...	7·50	41·4	8·57	39·8	7·40	41·2	7·10	40·6	7·16	39·2
1961	7·27	38·8	7·51	39·9	7·85	39·3	8·23	40·3	...	...	7·69	40·2	8·90	39·5	7·63	39·5	7·15	38·9	7·42	38·5
1962	7·61	38·5	7·82	40·1	8·03	38·8	8·53	40·0	...	...	7·83	40·0	9·44	39·9	7·85	39·3	7·66	39·3	7·76	38·1
1963	8·00	38·7	8·23	40·1	8·32	39·1	8·80	40·2	...	...	8·18	40·2	9·95	39·9	8·33	39·8	8·09	39·4	8·08	38·4
1964	8·54	38·7	8·68	39·3	9·02	38·9	9·33	39·7	...	...	8·63	39·3	10·52	39·5	8·83	39·3	8·35	38·5	8·69	38·4
1965	9·25	38·1	9·35	38·9	9·53	37·6	9·90	38·5	...	...	10·00	39·5	11·22	38·5	9·46	39·1	9·14	38·4	9·36	37·9
1966	9·74	37·7	9·82	38·6	9·91	37·4	10·43	38·1	...	...	10·22	38·4	11·23	38·1	9·94	38·4	9·48	37·6	9·88	37·0
1967	10·27	37·3	10·37	38·7	10·32	37·4	11·09	38·5	...	...	10·16	37·9	12·28	38·6	10·35	37·9	10·00	38·1	10·16	37·0
1968	10·85	37·4	11·00	38·5	11·18	38·1	11·84	38·4	...	...	10·75	38·0	13·33	38·6	11·17	38·1	10·42	37·9	10·98	37·3
	11·90	37·2	12·08	39·0	12·19	38·1	12·74	38·2			11·50	37·2	14·64	38·2	11·88	37·7	10·85	37·2	11·51	37·0
1969	----(i)	----(i)	----(c)	----(c)	----(i)	----(i)	----(d)	----(d)	12·68	38·0	----(i)	----(i)	----(i)	----(i)	----(i)	----(i)	----(i)	----(i)	----(i)	----(i)
	11·92	37·2	11·97	38·9	12·16	38·0	13·15	38·4			11·51	37·2	14·70	38·1	11·93	37·7	10·78	37·2	11·50	37·0
1970	13·88	36·9	14·29	38·7	13·63	37·4	15·31	38·1	14·56	37·7	14·17	38·4	17·06	37·9	13·40	37·3	12·08	37·3	13·15	37·2
1971	15·64	36·5	16·41	38·4	15·18	37·3	17·18	37·9	16·55	37·7	17·23	37·6	19·70	37·7	15·09	37·3	13·64	37·0	14·53	36·8
1972	18·32	36·8	18·55	38·7	18·80	38·3	20·43	38·4	19·32	37·8	18·29	38·2	23·81	38·2	17·28	37·6	15·41	37·5	16·60	36·7
1973	21·16	36·5	21·47	38·5	21·08	37·7	23·52	38·1	22·36	37·4	24·09	40·0	26·18	37·7	19·89	37·3	17·94	36·7	19·03	36·4
1974	27·54	36·3	28·73	38·4	27·38	37·5	30·02	38·0	28·21	37·2	28·01	36·7	33·48	37·9	25·52	37·2	22·38	36·1	24·04	36·1
1975	35·20	35·9	37·40	37·9	35·41	36·7	38·94	37·5	36·38	37·1	39·19	37·0	42·33	37·5	31·76	36·1	28·13	36·5	28·70	35·5
1976	42·22	36·7	44·11	38·4	43·58	37·7	46·77	38·0	43·54	37·6	46·08	37·4	50·43	37·8	37·93	36·7	32·61	36·4	33·59	36·0
1977	45·59	36·8	48·64	38·2	47·21	37·3	51·14	37·8	47·04	37·8	49·55	38·1	53·68	38·0	40·95	36·4	36·90	36·2	38·08	36·1
1978	52·12	36·7	54·85	38·2	54·33	37·8	56·79	37·9	53·96	37·9	56·59	37·9	60·50	37·4	46·02	36·7	42·03	36·7	41·94	36·0
1979	60·06	36·8	64·44	38·5	63·27	38·0	64·02	37·6	62·55	37·6	61·00	39·5	69·52	37·6	52·44	36·4	49·62	36·7	50·43	36·0
	----(j)	----(j)	----(j)	----(j)	----(j)	----(j)	----(j)	----(j)	----(j)	----(j)	----(j)	----(j)	----(j)	----(j)	----(j)	----(j)	----(j)	----(j)	----(j)	----(j)
1980	71·01	37·3	77·68	38·9	73·64	38·0	75·29	37·8	73·98	37·7	71·57	35·6	80·71	37·7	61·06	37·1	61·02	37·4	58·62	36·4

See p. 178 for footnotes.

Labour Force 35. *continued*

B. 1948–80 *(continued)*

(earnings in £)

	Food, Drink, & Tobacco		Manufacturers of Wood and Cork (*f*)		Paper and Printing (*g*)		All Manufacturing (*a*)		Mining and Quarrying (except coal)		Building and Contracting (*h*)		Gas, Water, and Electricity		Transport and Communication		Public Administration		All Industries Covered	
Females	Earnings	Hours	Earnings	Hours	Earnings	Hours	Earnings	Hours	Earnings	Hours	Earnings	Hours	Earnings	Hours	Earnings	Hours	Earnings	Hours	Earnings	Hours
1948	3·48	42·6	3·76	40·9	3·69	41·9	3·92	41·4	3·59	42·4	3·50	40·5	3·99	39·2	4·77	42·9	3·18	38·3	3·71	41·4
1949	3·66	42·5	4·01	41·1	3·80	42·5	3·95	41·5	4·12	42·8	3·69	41·6	3·86	40·0	5·02	43·4	3·59	39·6	3·93	41·5
1950	3·87	43·1	4·27	41·8	3·98	42·5	4·14	41·8	4·30	42·7	3·76	41·7	3·90	40·9	5·13	44·2	3·75	40·7	4·12	41·8
1951	4·27	43·0	4·59	40·4	4·64	42·6	4·50	41·2	4·46	42·3	4·05	40·9	4·50	40·7	5·93	44·5	4·13	41·2	4·49	41·3
1952	4·54	43·0	5·14	41·9	4·97	42·1	4·77	41·6	4·92	43·7	4·33	40·1	4·96	41·1	6·44	44·6	4·43	40·8	4·81	41·7
1953	4·75	42·8	5·38	41·9	5·29	43·2	5·15	41·8	5·40	43·6	4·54	40·7	5·33	41·6	6·58	45·1	4·69	40·9	5·12	41·8
1954	4·99	42·7	5·71	41·7	5·48	43·3	5·43	41·8	5·54	43·0	4·78	41·2	5·48	40·3	7·04	45·7	4·93	40·5	5·41	41·8
1955	5·45	42·9	6·24	41·4	5·78	42·6	5·78	41·5	5·93	42·4	5·21	40·5	5·83	40·3	7·75	45·8	5·41	41·1	5·77	41·6
1956	5·83	42·6	6·50	40·6	6·50	42·3	6·17	41·3	6·42	42·4	5·65	41·0	6·41	39·5	8·38	45·4	5·87	40·8	6·16	41·3
1957	6·14	42·3	6·91	40·4	6·64	41·7	6·49	41·0	6·62	41·2	5·93	40·6	6·80	39·0	9·31	45·6	6·18	40·2	6·49	41·0
1958	6·43	42·3	7·26	41·2	7·01	42·2	6·70	40·9	6·93	41·6	6·09	39·5	7·00	38·6	9·15	44·9	6·49	39·5	6·70	41·0
	6·66	42·4	7·56	41·0	7·53	42·4	7·05	41·4	6·98	41·6	6·14	38·4	7·21	38·9	9·48	45·3	6·64	40·1	7·03	41·4
1959	----(*i*)	----(*i*)	----(*f*)	----(*f*)	----(*g*)	----(*g*)	----(*i*)	----(*i*)	----(*i*)	----(*i*)	----(*h*)	----(*h*)	----(*i*)	----(*i*)	----(*i*)	----(*i*)	----(*i*)	----(*i*)	----(*i*)	----(*i*)
	6·69	42·7	7·70	41·3	7·52	42·5	7·07	41·4	7·18	42·0	6·16	37·9	7·21	39·8	9·55	45·3	6·64	39·5	7·05	41·4
1960	7·12	41·4	7·86	39·5	7·67	41·6	7·41	40·4	7·43	40·4	6·64	39·8	7·80	38·6	10·36	44·5	7·48	41·1	7·42	40·5
1961	7·47	40·7	8·31	39·4	8·12	40·4	7·71	39·6	7·66	40·5	7·12	39·4	7·53	37·9	10·92	43·9	8·06	40·7	7·73	39·7
1962	7·79	40·2	8·73	38·9	8·52	39·6	8·03	39·3	7·43	38·1	7·54	39·1	8·44	39·1	11·15	43·7	8·22	40·0	8·04	39·4
1963	8·23	40·4	9·23	39·7	8·82	39·5	8·41	39·6	8·53	40·1	7·82	38·8	8·73	38·0	11·57	44·0	8·82	40·8	8·41	39·7
1964	8·70	40·4	9·76	39·0	9·37	39·8	8·95	39·3	9·07	40·7	8·06	38·2	9·67	38·2	12·43	43·8	9·34	40·8	8·95	39·4
1965	9·38	39·1	10·36	38·4	10·15	39·4	9·60	38·6	9·03	38·9	8·42	37·7	10·85	37·6	13·35	43·7	9·66	40·3	9·60	38·7
1966	9·81	38·8	10·65	37·4	10·73	39·0	10·06	38·0	9·74	39·3	8·95	37·4	11·20	37·2	14·00	43·0	10·12	39·8	10·07	38·1
1967	10·23	38·8	11·51	38·1	10·95	39·1	10·54	38·0	9·91	39·0	9·87	39·0	11·55	37·4	14·54	42·7	10·48	40·1	10·56	38·2
1968	10·95	39·0	12·20	37·9	11·69	39·3	11·31	39·0	11·04	40·4	10·05	39·0	11·88	37·2	15·59	43·7	11·22	39·8	11·30	38·3
	11·93	38·6	12·86	37·4	12·57	39·3	12·12	38·6	10·88	37·8	11·39	38·0	12·42	37·7	16·87	44·2	11·86	40·2	12·10	38·1
1969	----(*i*)	----(*i*)	----(*i*)	----(*i*)	----(*i*)	----(*i*)	----(*i*)	----(*i*)	----(*i*)	----(*i*)	----(*i*)	----(*i*)	----(*i*)	----(*i*)	----(*i*)	----(*i*)	----(*i*)	----(*i*)	----(*i*)	----(*i*)
	11·87	38·6	12·88	37·5	12·61	39·3	11·87	38·6	10·77	36·9	11·39	38·0	12·73	37·6	16·88	44·2	11·86	40·1	12·10	38·1
1970	14·34	38·5	14·43	37·4	15·51	38·9	14·34	38·5	13·05	37·6	12·83	38·1	14·45	36·1	19·30	42·8	15·39	39·7	13·99	37·9
1971	16·65	38·2	17·06	37·7	17·10	38·7	15·80	37·5	15·65	37·9	13·42	37·1	16·88	35·9	22·32	43·3	17·57	39·6	15·80	37·9
1972	19·40	38·2	19·68	38·1	19·86	38·9	19·40	38·2	...	...	15·20	36·8	19·59	37·1	24·95	42·8	18·52	40·0	18·30	37·7
1973	22·68	38·6	22·93	37·5	22·79	38·6	22·68	38·6	...	...	18·96	37·2	23·04	37·3	28·84	43·0	23·37	40·3	21·16	37·9
1974	28·75	38·0	28·86	37·7	30·09	38·7	27·05	37·2	...	...	23·92	38·1	29·89	36·7	34·58	42·4	29·18	39·5	27·01	37·7
1975	37·28	37·7	36·77	37·0	38·51	37·9	34·23	36·8	...	...	30·45	37·5	38·76	35·4	44·07	41·5	38·64	40·3	34·19	37·4
1976	43·69	37·9	42·14	37·3	45·20	38·4	40·71	37·2	...	...	36·11	38·3	43·43	36·4	50·23	41·6	43·62	39·9	40·61	37·0
1977	47·51	38·1	46·20	37·2	48·87	38·5	44·45	37·2	...	...	39·14	37·9	47·94	36·0	53·25	41·3	46·41	39·4	44·31	37·4
1978	53·85	37·9	53·62	37·5	55·33	38·1	50·08	37·2	...	...	42·97	38·5	58·10	36·8	63·79	43·5	52·98	40·3	50·03	37·4
1979	62·86	38·1	61·84	36·7	67·15	38·3	58·44	37·2	...	...	48·23	37·2	70·29	37·6	72·38	43·3	57·04	40·5	58·24	37·4
	----(*j*)	----(*j*)	----(*j*)	----(*j*)	----(*j*)	----(*j*)	----(*j*)	----(*j*)			----(*j*)	----(*j*)	----(*j*)	----(*j*)	----(*j*)	----(*j*)	----(*j*)	----(*j*)	----(*j*)	----(*j*)
1980	74·60	37·9	74·01	36·8	82·15	38·2	68·40	37·3	...	...	61·45	38·5	81·75	37·0	92·14	42·3	76·18	39·8	68·73	37·5

(*a*) Including small groups not shown separately.
(*b*) Described as "Bricks, Pottery, Glass, Cement, etc", from 1959 (2nd line).
(*c*) Excluding coal and petroleum products from 1969 (2nd line).
(*d*) Shipbuilding and marine engineering are included to 1959 (1st line). From 1969 (2nd line), these columns relate to mechanical engineering only, electrical engineering being shown separately, and instrument engineering being excluded.
(*e*) Described as "Clothing and Footwear" from 1959 (2nd line).
(*f*) Described as "Timber, Furniture, etc." from 1959 (2nd line).
(*g*) Described as "Paper, Printing, and Publishing" from 1959 (2nd line).
(*h*) Described as "Construction" from 1959 (2nd line).
(*i*) There were minor changes in coverage consequent on the adoption of new Standard Industrial Classifications.
(*j*) The 1980 figures are for full-time workers on adult rates of pay.

Labour Force 36. Average Earnings in Coal Mines – Great Britain 1920–78

NOTE
SOURCES: Annual Report of the Department of Mines, Ministry of (Fuel and) Power, *Statistical Digest*, and Department of Trade and Industry, *Digest of United Kingdom Energy Statistics*.

(in £)

	Quarterly		Weekly		Weekly
1920	55·84	1938	2·90	1959	15·01
1921	48·05 (*a*)	1939	3·09	1960	15·58
1922	31·28	1940	3·56	1961	16·58
1923	33·57	1941	4·14	1962	17·27
1924	34·55	1942	4·71	1963	18·30 (*d*)
1925	32·92	1943	5·16	1964	19·13
1926	34·66 (*b*)	1944	5·65	1965	20·35
	30·64	1945	5·85	1966	21·50
1927	---- (*c*)	1946	6·16	1967	22·65
	31·94	1947	6·94	1968	23·85
1928	29·66				
1929	30·80	1948	8·19	1969	25·45
		1949	8·73	1970	28·95
1930	29·70	1950	9·12	1971	33·01
1931	29·05	1951	10·18	1972	38·19
1932	28·54	1952	11·25	1973	40·09
1933	28·74				
1934	30·08	1953	11·60	1974	60·53
		1954	12·30	1975	78·30
1935	30·80				---- (*e*)
1936	34·07	1955	13·05	1976	81·23
		1956	14·23	1977	90·12
1937	37·38	1957	15·25	1978	108·30
1938	37·74	1958	15·01		

(*a*) Excluding the second quarter.
(*b*) First quarter only.
(*c*) Allowances in kind are included subsequently.
(*d*) This figure is for the 15 months ended 31 March 1964, and subsequent figures are for years beginning 1 April.
(*e*) Holidays were not treated uniformly throughout the coalfields prior to 1976.

CHAPTER III

AGRICULTURE

TABLES

'The demand for accurate arithmetical information about farming and its net output is of long standing, and the details necessary for administrative purposes were envisaged nearly three hundred years ago', wrote Fussell in the mid 1940s.[1] But the necessary centralised government machinery did not exist until well into the nineteenth century, as was shown by the failure of various official attempts to get crop statistics during the early years of the struggle with Napoleon.[2] Arthur Young's works, it is true, contain a good deal of statistical information; but it is scattered and unsystematic, and not in a form which can be used

[1] G. E. Fussell, 'The Collection of Agricultural Statistics in Great Britain: Its Origin and Evolution', *Agricultural History*, 18 (1944).

[2] The results of these attempts are summarised and assessed in W. E. Minchinton, 'Agricultural Returns and the Government during the Napoleonic Wars', *Agricultural History Review*, 1 (1953).

here.[3] A century before Arthur Young, Gregory King had made estimates of agricultural production, which, though no more than guesses, are generally agreed to have been acceptable.[4] And contemporaneously with Arthur Young, Charles Smith made elaborate estimates of the production and consumption of corn.[5] But these, like subsequent estimates, including those of Deane and Cole, were essentially based on assumptions that were necessarily arbitrary about relations between population and consumption per head.[6] However, Deane and Cole were prepared to 'take these estimates of corn production... as an index of the progress of agricultural production as a whole',[7] despite their discussion of the different behaviour of some of the livestock products. Their procedures were criticised by Crafts,[8] who produced better estimates of the value of farm output (which are included in table 8 of chapter XVI), though none in terms of physical quantities. However, these, too, are the result of necessarily arbitrary assumptions, notably that the income elasticity of demand for agricultural products was 0.7 and constant, and they need to be treated with some caution.

In the two or three decades after the end of the Napoleonic Wars there were a number of attempts made to get agricultural statistics, mainly about particular areas, but these were not very successful.[9] By the 1850s, however, government interest in the subject was growing. Collection of Irish crop and livestock statistics had begun at least partly as a consequence of the Famine, in 1847 – though there had earlier been questions about livestock and agricultural holdings in the census of 1841. And in 1854 an attempt was made to collect them in Great Britain.[10] But though this was successful so far as Scotland was concerned, where the Highland and Agricultural Society conducted the survey, it failed in England and Wales, largely because of the agency used – the Boards of Guardians under the Poor Law. The Scottish effort was repeated for a few years, but complaints about its cost led to discontinuation after 1857.[11] Nevertheless, Sir James Caird and others persisted in their agitation for collection of official agricultural statistics, and he and others, such as Lawes and

[3] See especially *A Six Weeks' Tour through the Southern Counties of England and Wales* (London, 1768); *A Six Months' Tour through the North of England* (4 vols., London, 1770); and *The Farmer's Tour through the East of England* (4 vols., London, 1771). Estimates of wheat production in the eighteenth century partly based on this material are given in G. E. Fussell, 'Population and Wheat Production in the Eighteenth Century', *History Teacher's Miscellany*, VII (1929).

[4] George E. Barnett (ed.), *Two Tracts by Gregory King* (Baltimore, 1936).

[5] C. Smith, *Three Tracts on the Corn Trade* (London, 1766).

[6] Phyllis Deane and W. A. Cole, *British Economic Growth, 1688–1959* (Cambridge, 1962), pp. 62–75.

[7] *Ibid.*, p. 74.

[8] N. F. R. Crafts, 'Income Elasticities of Demand and the Release of Labour by Agriculture during the British Industrial Revolution', *Journal of European Economic History*, 9 (1980). The criticisms were largely accepted by W. A. Cole in his contribution to Roderick Floud and Donald McCloskey (eds.), *The Economic History of Britain since 1700*, vol. 1 (Cambridge, 1981).

[9] Examples can be found in the *Journal of the Statistical Society* (1834, 1835, and 1843). A useful survey of these and similar studies is D. B. Grigg, 'The Changing Agricultural Geography of England', *Transactions and Papers of the Institute of British Geographers*, 41 (1967).

[10] An earlier small-scale experiment in 1844 was judged a failure.

[11] For these Scottish statistics see *S.P.* 1854–5 XLVII; *S.P.* 1856 LIX; *S.P.* 1857 (Sess. 1) XV; and *S.P.* 1857–8 LVI.

Gilbert, made their own estimates; and the first proper Agricultural Census of Great Britain was taken in 1865. And though it, too, was not fully successful,[12] the returns of 1867 did at last constitute the beginning of a continuous acreage and livestock series, which was followed in a few years by the yield and production returns. As Fussell said: 'These details are still, with the modifications that experience has shown to be necessary, the backbone of agricultural statistics.'[13]

The British acreage and livestock figures shown in summary form here in tables 1 and 6 are based on returns from farmers, whereas the Irish ones, shown in tables 2 and 7, were collected by the police. For several years after 1867 the Board of Trade statisticians continued to report the reluctance of some farmers in Britain to send in their returns. Indeed, it was not until about the end of the next decade that their response could be regarded as satisfactory, though it has been reckoned that most omissions had been eliminated by 1875.[14] In part this was a result of placing a lower limit, in 1869, of a quarter of an acre on the size of holdings about which information was required – though it may be worth noting that farmers appear to have been most cooperative in Scotland and least so on some of the large estates of southern and eastern England. (In 1893 this limit was raised to one acre, the figure which had always applied in Ireland, but the effect was negligible.)[15]

Whilst it may be that the overall figures need to be treated with less caution after 1875, it is clear that, as J. T. Coppock once pointed out in a very useful assessment of continuity of the agricultural statistics,[16] 'differences of interpretation by farmers were frequent'. The most obvious possibility for differences and changes in interpretation over the years were in the allocation to the categories rotation grasses, permanent pasture, and rough grazing.[17] According to the report of the 1925 census, 'the main difficulty in connection with the collection of these annual statistics was in ensuring that all holdings are enumerated. The frequent changes in occupation, especially in recent years, the combination or division of farms, and the withdrawal of land for building or other purposes, make the task of seeing that all the agricultural land in the country is accounted for a very serious one. A proportion of the holdings do, in fact, escape enumeration, especially in the case of the smaller occupations under five acres, though the total area omitted from the returns in this way is a very small proportion of the agricultural area of the country.'[18]

It is perhaps worth pointing out here that the questions of the annual census all relate to the actual position on farms at a given date in each year. For the first decade of the British

[12] The first returns were for 1866, but they were for farms of five acres and over, and the livestock returns were taken at the end of the winter, not, as later, in the middle of the summer. For these and other reasons, the 1866 returns are not comparable with later ones, and they are omitted here.

[13] *loc. cit.*

[14] *A Century of Agricultural Statistics: Great Britain 1866–1966* (H.M.S.O., 1968), p. 7.

[15] The estimated reduction in total returned acreage in 1893 was 0.1 per cent.

[16] J. T. Coppock, 'The Statistical Assessment of British Agriculture', *Agricultural History Review*, IV (1956).

[17] Figures for rough grazing are not shown here since they are not available in comparable form for England and Wales and for Scotland.

[18] *S.P.* 1927 XXV – *The Agricultural Output of England and Wales, 1925*, p. 2.

statistics this was 25 June. Subsequently it has been 4 June. The Irish returns for 1847–57 were compiled in August and September. Subsequently they have been for a date in June, though for a long time this was unspecified.

Unlike the British statistics in their earlier years, the Irish ones have always been regarded as 'tolerably accurate' throughout, with the possible exception of the yield and production data in their earliest years.[19] But even these have been defended by the only modern historian to discuss them in detail.[20]

Turning to the significance of the livestock statistics, attention must be drawn to the fact that they show stocks rather than flows, and in so far as there have been changes in the rate of turnover caused by changes in the age to which animals have been kept, these figures will not serve as accurate proxies for output series. There clearly have been such changes over the period of more than a century which the statistics cover; and though it is known that the average age to which animals are kept has declined, with changes in both the purposes for which they are kept and in the speed of fattening, there is no way to assess exactly when the changes have taken place.

Official estimates of the annual yield and production of each crop in Great Britain date from 1884, though in Ireland they were started at the same time as the acreage and livestock returns. For Britain, there are unofficial estimates for wheat by Lawes and Gilbert, and their yield figures (along with modern estimates back to 1815) are shown in table 3. These were described by Vigor as 'untrustworthy',[21] though this may be too harsh a judgment. It is true that they are based on yields on different plots at just one location, Rothamsted Experimental Station; but Lawes and Gilbert made rather elaborate attempts to allow for regional variations from that location in different kinds of years, their efforts seem to have been well received by their contemporaries,[22] and another authority, Venn, thought they were 'reliable'.[23] Both Venn's and Vigor's epithets came in the course of a vigorous controversy between them on the validity of the official crop estimates, and are probably too extreme. The series certainly cannot be regarded as unquestionably accurate; but agricultural historians have generally taken them to be usable.[24]

The official crop statistics are based on the evidence of crop reporters who are 'for the most part land agents, valuers and others with considerable local experience who estimate the yield per acre of the principal crops parish by parish'.[25] In the late 1920s, Venn attacked their estimates as being consistently too conservative, a bias towards underestimation, he alleged,

[19] Cormac Ó Gráda, 'Supply Responsiveness in Irish Agriculture during the Nineteenth Century', *Economic History Review*, second series XXVIII, 2 (1975).

[20] P. M. A. Bourke, 'The Average Yields of Food Crops in Ireland on the Eve of the Great Famine', *Journal of the Department of Agriculture*, LXVI (1968), p. 4.

[21] H. D. Vigor, 'Official Crop Estimates in England', *Journal of the Royal Statistical Society*, XCI (1928).

[22] See the discussions after the Lawes and Gilbert paper cited in note 1 of table 3.

[23] J. A. Venn, 'An Inquiry into British Methods of Crop Estimating', *Economic Journal* XXXVI (1926).

[24] See, for example, Susan Fairlie, 'The Corn Laws and British Wheat Production', *Economic History Review*, second series XXII, 1 (1969), pp. 109–10.

[25] *S.P.* 1927 XXV – *The Agricultural Output of England and Wales, 1925*, p. 2.

having been built in from the early days. Vigor put up a strong defence, and, as Venn eventually accepted, the truth probably lay between their two positions. It is possible that the crop reporters' skills improved through time, though unlikely that any such improvements would be noticeable after 1900 or thereabouts. It is likely that year-to-year fluctuations in yields have been underestimated as a result of failures of reporters' judgment. And there seems to be a fair amount of evidence that they overestimate yields in bad harvests and underestimate in the good years.

Data on the output of livestock products became available rather later than those for crops. Indeed, the first full census of agricultural production, undertaken in 1908, provides the first certain information. However, the Ministry of Agriculture made estimates of meat and milk production back to 1900/1 which have been generally accepted as having only a small margin of error;[26] and a few earlier estimates can be found in contributions to the *Journal of the Royal Statistical Society*.[27] Official statistics for the Republic of Ireland were rather late in being organised, not beginning until at least 1930. But for Ireland, too, there are scattered estimates for earlier periods, and these are most easily found in R. D. Crotty, *Irish Agricultural Production*.[28]

The last 'production' series, table 10, shows the statistics of both the British and the Irish fisheries, which were (and are) collected at all ports where fish are landed, and seem to be very firmly based.

Estimates of the overall value of the agricultural output of Britain and of the value of inputs of factors of production were not included in the agricultural census until the Second World War, but they have been reconstructed by modern researchers for periods back to the middle of the nineteenth century or earlier. Two sets of such estimates – those by Feinstein and those by Ojala – are shown here in tables 11 and 12, together with later, official estimates. (Those for the Republic of Ireland are shown in table 13.) The related series, which Feinstein produced, of estimated farm incomes, is shown in table 15.

Statistics of the numbers employed in agriculture are available, in one form or another, from the census of 1811 (see chapter II, tables 2 and 3 above); but it is difficult to make a consistent series from them until fairly recently, though this can be attempted from 1851.[29] Since 1921, however, the annual agricultural returns have enumerated farm workers on a uniform basis, with the exception that farmers' wives were not completely excluded in the earlier years, as had been the intention. The summary totals are shown in table 14. A much more detailed breakdown by different categories is available in the original source.

The quantity statistics of external trade in corn, of meat imports, and, for the Irish Republic, of meat and butter exports have been included in this chapter, though the value

[26] See *S.P.* 1924–5 XIII – Report of the Royal Commission on Food Prices, para. 184.

[27] Vols. LXV (1902) and LXVII (1904) contain reports by the Society's committee on the subject, and vol. LX (1892) has estimates in an article by R. H. Rew. A modern discussion of dairying is D. Taylor, 'The English Dairy Industry, 1860–1930', *Economic History Review*, second series, XXIX, 4 (1976).

[28] (Cork, 1966).

[29] See F. D. W. Taylor, 'United Kingdom: Numbers in Agriculture', *The Farm Economist*, VII, 4 (1955).

figures are to be found in chapter XIX. Table 16, dealing with the corn trade of Britain during the eighteenth and early nineteenth centuries, links up to some extent with table 17, showing the United Kingdom trade from the end of the eighteenth century. But the link is by no means exact, since British imports from Ireland were substantial. Moreover, the British statistics treat grain and meal or flour separately, whilst the earlier United Kingdom ones take them together. The long overlap between the two sets of figures should help, however, in making comparisons. For information about the statistics of Irish overseas trade in the eighteenth century, only a small part of which has yet been extracted from the ledgers, the reader should consult Crotty's book, cited above.

Finally, in table 21, there is a small amount of the vast mass of detailed statistical information which exists on Parliamentary enclosure. The intention has been to reproduce only the most up-to-date summary figures, and the reader who requires more detail must go to the source cited in note 1 to the table, or to the many other sources mentioned there or in Turner's Economic History Society/Macmillan pamphlet.[30]

[30] Michael Turner, *Enclosures in Britain 1750–1830* (London, 1984).

Agriculture 1. Acreage of Crops – Great Britain 1867–1980

NOTES

[1] SOURCE: *Agricultural Statistics* and *A Century of Agricultural Statistics: Great Britain 1866–1966* (London, 1968).

[2] To maintain comparability, vegetables for human consumption have been included throughout under the appropriate headings.

[3] The returns are made in June.

[4] Total arable acreage in 1866 was 17,531 thousand acres.

(in thousands of acres)

	Wheat	Barley	Oats	Other Corn (*a*)	Potatoes	Turnips and Swedes	Mangold	Cabbage Kohl-rabi and Rape	Other Green Crops	Bare Fallow	Rotation Grasses for Hay	Rotation Grasses for Grazing	Permanent Pasture for Hay	Permanent Pasture for Grazing	Small Fruit	Orchards	Hops	Total Arable
1867	3,368	2,259	2,750	907	492	2,174	258	134	440	923	3,003		11,136		...	...	64	17,760
1868	3,652	2,151	2,757	873	542	2,165	249	115	333	958	2,920		12,136		...	...	64	17,820
1869	3,688	2,251	2,783	1,035	585	2,172	293	145	401	739(*b*)	2,637(*b*)		12,736(*b*)		...	...	62	17,603
1870	3,501	2,372	2,763	912	588	2,211	307	144	361	611	2,069	2,436	3,067	9,006	...	...	61	18,335
1871	3,572	2,386	2,716	1,002	628	2,164	361	179	424	543	2,165	2,205	3,490	8,946	...	207	60	18,403
1872	3,599	2,316	2,706	953	564	2,084	329	178	476	648	2,300	2,214	3,578	8,997	...	170	62	18,429
1873	3,490	2,336	2,676	957	515	2,122	326	175	455	706	2,139	2,228	3,415	9,501	...	148	63	18,187
1874	3,630	2,288	2,596	917	520	2,133	323	169	445	660	2,046	2,295	3,279	9,899	...	151	66	18,089
1875	3,342	2,510	2,664	935	523	2,143	362	190	454	558	2,109	2,245	3,611	9,702	...	155	69	18,104
1876	2,996	2,533	2,798	867	503	2,146	348	179	404	651	2,241	2,299	3,621	9,895	...	157	70	18,036
1877	3,169	2,418	2,754	870	512	2,073	358	183	465	616	2,176	2,318	3,759	9,970	...	163	71	17,984
1878	3,218	2,470	2,699	781	508	2,032	343	172	443	632	2,308	2,265	3,840	10,071	...	165	72	17,943
1879	2,890	2,667	2,657	771	541	2,017	364	168	473	721	4,473		14,167		...	175	68	17,809
1880	2,909	2,467	2,797	702	551	2,024	343	162	406	813	4,434		14,427		...	180	67	17,675
1881	2,806	2,442	2,901	699	579	2,036	349	143	411	796	4,342		14,646		...	185	65	17,568
1882	3,004	2,255	2,834	741	541	2,024	334	150	431	784	4,327		14,822		...	188	66	17,492
1883	2,613	2,292	2,975	738	543	2,029	330	146	410	778	4,396		15,065		...	191	68	17,320
1884	2,677	2,169	2,915	724	565	2,028	327	147	423	750	4,381		15,291		...	195	69	17,175
1885	2,478	2,257	2,940	716	549	2,015	355	153	453	560	2,159	2,495	4,024	11,319	...	198	71	17,202
1886	2,286	2,241	3,082	651	554	2,003	349	152	426	553	2,252	2,438	4,418	11,117	...	200	70	17,056
1887	2,317	2,085	3,088	656	560	1,972	361	154	421	486	2,325	2,456	4,562	11,109	...	202	64	16,944
1888	2,564	2,086	2,882	656	590	1,944	361	159	419	457	2,292	2,432	4,777	10,969	37	199	58	16,938
1889	2,449	2,122	2,889	615	579	1,921	326	147	329	513	2,477	2,401	4,987	10,878	42	200	58	16,867
1890	2,386	2,111	2,903	632	530	1,948	331	160	331	508	2,292	2,517	4,779	11,239	46	202	54	16,751
1891	2,307	2,113	2,899	606	533	1,919	355	157	337	429	2,130	2,586	4,503	11,931	59	210	56	16,485
1892	2,220	2,037	2,998	553	525	1,937	361	151	296	457	2,135	2,537	4,490	11,869	62	209	56	16,327
1893	1,898	2,075	3,172	511	528	1,975	347	156	282	515	2,047	2,523	4,270	12,222	65	212	58	16,151
1894	1,928	2,096	3,253	578	504	1,957	354	177	311	376	2,122	2,382	4,852	11,613	68	214	60	16,165
1895	1,417	2,166	3,296	521	541	1,916	335	153	283	476	2,303	2,426	4,761	11,850	75	218	59	15,967
1896	1,694	2,105	3,095	523	564	1,883	338	162	314	432	2,172	2,424	4,638	12,089	76	221	54	15,836
1897	1,889	2,036	3,036	496	505	1,833	355	167	331	385	2,286	2,568	4,510	12,003	70	224	51	16,007
1898	2,102	1,904	2,918	477	525	1,772	352	166	319	352	2,382	2,530	4,536	12,023	70	226	50	15,918
1899	2,001	1,982	2,960	464	548	1,741	374	173	313	339	2,215	2,593	4,339	12,292	72	229	52	15,826
1900	1,845	1,990	3,026	474	561	1,689	414	196	320	308	2,202	2,557	4,373	12,356	74	232	51	15,708
1901	1,701	1,972	2,996	464	577	1,665	399	180	309	344	2,356	2,500	4,350	12,477	75	235	51	15,590

See p. 189 for footnotes.

(in thousands of acres)

	Wheat	Barley	Oats	Other Corn(*a*)	Potatoes	Turnips and Swedes	Man-gold	Sugar Beet	Cabbage Kohl-rabi and Rape	Other Green Crops	Bare Fallow	Rotation Grasses for Hay	Rotation Grasses for Grazing	Permanent Pasture for Hay	Permanent Pasture for Grazing	Small Fruit	Orch-ards	Hops	Total Arable
1902	1,726	1,909	3,057	491	574	1,609	441	...	193	332	293	2,364	2,468	4,581	12,226	75	237	48	15,581
1903	1,582	1,858	3,140	481	564	1,603	402	...	183	313	351	2,412	2,395	4,755	12,180	76	239	48	15,409
1904	1,375	1,841	3,253	485	570	1,604	399	...	178	286	433	2,323	2,349	4,765	12,333	78	243	48	15,220
1905	1,797	1,714	3,051	492	608	1,589	404	...	179	296	349	2,189	2,288	4,689	12,512	79	244	49	15,086
1906	1,756	1,751	3,043	508	566	1,591	431	...	182	312	315	2,192	2,249	4,785	12,460	80	248	47	15,022
1907	1,625	1,712	3,123	537	549	1,563	450	...	187	339	261	2,250	2,241	4,937	12,341	82	250	45	14,966
1908	1,627	1,667	3,109	512	562	1,551	428	...	173	306	315	2,232	2,189	4,950	12,466	85	250	39	14,796
1909	1,823	1,664	2,982	554	575	1,556	456	...	172	324	289	2,036	2,179	4,777	12,675	87	251	33	14,731
1910	1,809	1,729	3,021	487	540	1,565	443	...	159	289	354	2,075	2,082	5,005	12,472	84	251	33	14,669
1911	1,906	1,598	3,011	526	572	1,563	452	...	157	295	329	2,075	2,045	5,003	12,444	84	251	33	14,648
1912	1,926	1,648	3,029	549	613	1,513	488	...	174	329	281	1,979	2,013	5,108	12,227	85	247	35	14,660
				---						---									
1913	1,756	1,757	2,913	496(*c*)	591	1,486	421	...	150	305(*c*)	396	2,116	1,854	5,227	12,340	84	245	36	14,360
1914	1,868	1,699	2,849	529	614	1,476	434	...	152	340	348	1,963	1,900	4,942	12,664	85	245	37	14,294
1915	2,247	1,381	3,071	454	608	1,353	416	...	145	322	317	1,928	1,898	4,806	12,773	81	250	35	14,256
1916	1,975	1,502	3,075	414	558	1,352	380	...	145	340	430	2,183	1,888	4,985	12,510	80	253	31	14,355
1917	1,979	1,619	3,300	409	656	1,387	391	...	126	295	361	2,103	1,884	4,954	12,297	79	261	17	14,607
		----	----	---															
1918	2,636	1,654(*d*)	4,024(*d*)	662(*d*)	803	1,308	404	1	119	293	414	1,836	1,614	4,447	11,449	72	265	16	15,852
1919	2,301	1,683	3,675	711	630	1,410	399	--	169	339	657	1,895	1,766	4,318	11,464	65	234	17	15,717
1920	1,929	1,842	3,304	681	707	1,417	388	3	192	393	573	2,100	1,786	4,547	11,299	65	222	21	15,400
1921	2,041	1,606	3,161	616	712	1,306	377	8	170	327	514	2,168	1,858	4,195	11,711	79	...	25	14,967
1922	2,032	1,521	3,152	680	719	1,225	425	8	180	374	411	1,959	1,854	4,558	11,545	82	...	26	14,649
1923	1,799	1,486	2,946	579	604	1,272	405	17	181	346	443	2,229	1,876	4,510	11,679	71	233(*e*)	25	14,479
1924	1,594	1,466	2,993	618	591	1,238	391	23	179	372	363	2,167	1,895	4,656	11,734	80	241	26	14,202
1925	1,548	1,471	2,794	507	635	1,202	360	56	167	313	472	2,125	1,951	4,468	12,081	76	239	26	13,911
1926	1,646	1,270	2,804	506	641	1,158	340	129	178	349	424	1,991	1,996	4,525	12,102	77	242	26	13,742
1927	1,703	1,166	2,649	474	661	1,093	307	233	172	318	430	1,986	1,971	4,485	12,308	77	250	23	13,479
1928	1,454	1,296	2,641	442	633	1,100	300	178	169	298	474	1,969	1,974	4,666	12,262	73	249	24	13,242
1929	1,381	1,221	2,743	472	664	1,071	301	231	170	287	331	1,932	1,937	4,864	12,174	73	249	24	13,053
1930	1,400	1,127	2,640	493	548	1,044	289	349	180	303	300	2,006	1,917	5,222	11,895	74	248	20	12,905
1931	1,247	1,117	2,487	454	575	982	272	234	177	305	364	2,149	1,967	4,943	12,338	70	246	20	12,634
1932	1,340	1,029	2,448	426	653	929	231	256	156	278	440	1,935	1,987	4,709	12,707	67	248	17	12,413
1933	1,739	811	2,351	422	671	907	239	366	165	283	465	1,653	1,899	4,783	12,671	69	251	17	12,280
1934	1,857	957	2,219	416	628	874	248	404	190	288	353	1,683	1,806	5,003	12,386	71	256	18	12,241
1935	1,873	868	2,246	410	594	850	253	375	224	304	302	1,785	1,969	4,821	12,353	69	264	18	12,381
1936	1,798	891	2,249	407	590	795	249	355	236	270	348	1,736	1,794	4,839	12,531	65	262	18	12,096
1937	1,832	904	2,042	332	591	772	211	314	199	230	550	1,878	1,788	4,857	12,479	62	260	18	12,016

See p. 189 for footnotes.

Agriculture 1. *continued*

(in thousands of acres)

	Wheat	Barley	Oats	Other Corn(*a*)	Potatoes	Turnips and Swedes	Mangold	Sugar Beet	Cabbage Kohl-rabi and Rape	Bare Fallow	Rotation Grasses for Hay	Rotation Grasses for Grazing	Permanent Pasture for Hay	Permanent Pasture for Grazing	Small Fruit	Orchards	Hops	Total Arable
1938	1,923	984	2,098	386	610	746	218	336	210	370	1,571	1,788	4,402	13,007	58	253	18	11,861
1939	1,763	1,010	2,135	381	589	705	215	345	215	374	1,689	1,838	4,786	12,545	56	256	19	11,870
1940	1,797	1,321	3,002	518	695	739	229	329	265	306	1,698	1,678	4,398	11,497	51	258	19	13,203
1941	2,247	1,457	3,501	990	966	820	265	351	365	219	1,547	1,528	3,883	10,184	45	271	18	14,991
1942	2,504	1,513	3,658	1,053	1,116	846	268	425	407	280	1,858	1,478	3,343	9,409	43	266	18	16,175
											----(*f*)	----(*f*)						
1943	3,451	1,771	3,210	1,094	1,193	823	285	417	426	240	2,095	1,633	2,811	8,609	38	267	19	17,387
1944	3,215	1,957	3,215	1,087	1,219	818	307	431	468	231	2,266	1,962	2,433	8,376	40	264	20	17,936
1945	2,272	2,201	3,305	1,002	1,207	807	307	417	464	347	2,589	2,213	2,524	8,369	36	260	20	17,866
1946	2,060	2,203	3,154	988	1,230	751	303	436	441	294	2,640	2,436	2,421	8,641	38	272	21	17,675
1947	2,161	2,053	2,927	913	1,149	722	271	395	400	508	2,684	2,345	2,716	8,662	42	272	22	17,275
1948	2,275	2,077	2,945	1,067	1,338	661	280	413	405	245	2,477	2,411	2,778	8,618	48	268	23	17,393
1949	1,961	2,054	2,878	1,162	1,121	641	274	421	433	309	2,712	2,437	2,760	8,885	57	270	22	17,152
											----(*f*)	----(*f*)						
1950	2,476	1,774	2,760	1,312	1,056	596	276	429	477	269	2,501	2,426	2,891	8,794	61	274	22	17,159
1951	2,130	1,906	2,541	1,218	906	593	263	425	481	384	2,746	2,444	2,949	9,041	57	278	22	16,868
1952	2,028	2,275	2,580	1,247	854	590	223	408	481	305	2,745	2,410	3,036	8,833	55	279	22	16,571
1953	2,215	2,220	2,552	1,265	846	588	214	415	524	225	2,621	2,520	2,996	8,724	51	274	22	17,062
1954	2,455	2,058	2,320	1,026	815	569	205	437	535	281	2,655	2,722	2,890	9,095	50	268	20	16,868
1955	1,947	2,290	2,330	822	757	566	182	424	547	349	2,774	2,811	3,023	9,261	48	264	20	16,571
1956	2,290	2,317	2,309	779	796	526	176	426	556	217	2,637	2,825	3,075	9,173	47	259	20	16,617
1957	2,109	2,609	2,109	646	709	511	153	430	565	314	2,819	2,900	3,005	9,266	48	250	20	16,603
1958	2,204	2,739	1,999	595	722	496	147	439	559	255	2,907	2,838	3,202	9,045	49	244	21	16,635
						--(*g*)												
1959	1,927	3,032	1,833	504	719	483	132	434	529	366	2,960	3,253	3,001	8,975	50	241	20	16,855
																		-----(*h*)
1960	2,099	3,313	1,771	488	742	455	133	436	552	193	2,924	3,285	3,158	8,522	50	235	20	17,096
1961	1,822	3,717	1,550	390	628	421	110	427	510	305	3,129	3,387	2,970	8,660	48	228	20	17,073
1962	2,252	3,858	1,357	370	660	395	105	424	489	178	3,074	3,378	2,970	8,549	48	221	20	17,210
1963	1,925	4,565	1,149	347	687	370	89	423	432	225	3,130	3,297	2,912	8,497	49	216	21	17,300
1964	2,203	4,867	1,000	336	706	359	72	443	392	199	3,123	3,083	3,018	8,284	49	198	21	17,381
1965	2,531	5,211	918	337	680	335	59	455	375	167	2,840	3,063	2,865	8,253	47	195	21	17,544
1966	2,235	5,958	825	346	612	306	42	446	341	262	2,631	2,970	2,791	8,325	45	189	20	17,519
1967	2,302	5,874	929	421	651	294	36	457	323	229	2,549	2,792	2,762	8,410	44	180	19	17,417

	Wheat	Barley	Oats	Other Corn(*a*)	Potatoes	Turnips and Swedes	Mangold	Sugar Beet	Cabbage Kohl-rabi and Rape	Bare Fallow	Rotation Grasses for Hay	Rotation Grasses for Grazing	Permanent Pasture for Hay	Permanent Pasture for Grazing	Small Fruit	Orchards	Hops	Total Arable
									--- (*i*)									
1968	2,415	5,794	872	436	640	275	31	465	319	199	2,525	2,814	2,627	8,324	44	172	18	17,420
1969	2,056	5,826	887	450	571	268	25	457	330	414	2,468	2,772	2,640	8,374	44	157	17	17,220
1970	2,492	5,418	884	459	621	255	24	463	293	241	2,574	2,597	2,700	8,204	44	154	17	17,045
1971	2,707	5,515	858	517	592	253	22	471	293	184	2,584	2,621	2,747	8,083	44	147	18	17,135
1972	2,783	5,527	748	514	548	247	20	468	290	197	2,536	2,562	2,771	8,191	44	139	17	17,154
1973	2,829	5,484	670	545	521	250	18	480	243	151	2,529	2,764	2,524	8,243	44	135	17	17,037
1974	3,045	5,350	602	579	501	258	18	482	282	151	2,447	2,776	2,431	8,326	43	130	16	17,025
1975	2,555	5,672	552	532	477	272	17	488	366	318	2,359	2,200	2,464	8,914	42	126	16	16,307
1976	3,041	5,268	564	540	513	263	16	510	370	160	2,573	2,045	2,662	8,694	40		15	16,370
						---(*g*)	---(*g*)											
1977	2,658	5,802	466	548	528	250	18	501	380	172	2,393	2,160	2,549	8,603	39		14	16,399
1978	3,105	5,663	432	501	494	233	16	518	379	168	4,386		11,150		41		15	16,409
1979	3,386	5,661	325	502	467	223	15	529	381	180	4,060		11,416		46		14	16,199
1980	3,559	5,630	355	...	470	...	...	525	...	145	4,172		...		47		14	16,405

(*a*) This comprises mixed corn, rye, peas, and beans.
(*b*) Changes in the official classification of land between 1868 and 1869 affect the comparability of these series.
(*c*) From 1913 onwards, the Scottish component of the acreage of beans was no longer included wholly with *Other Corn* since beans for fodder were included with *Other Green Crops*.
(*d*) In 1918 there was a new heading in the *Returns* – mixed corn. This included items previously included with oats and barley.
(*e*) Prior to 1923 the area of orchards was also shown under the crop grass, or fallow beneath the trees.
(*f*) From 1943 to 1950 lucerne is included with rotation grasses.
(*g*) Fodder beet is included with turnips from 1959 to 1976 and with mangold subsequently.
(*h*) From 1960 tillage grass under 7 years old is included in the Scottish component.
(*i*) Rape for oil seed was included from 1968.

Agriculture 2. Acreage of Crops – Ireland 1847–1980

NOTES

[1] SOURCES: 1847–1917 – *Agricultural Statistics (Ireland)*, annually; 1918–80 – Eire Department of Industry and Commerce: *Agricultural Statistics, 1847–1926* (Dublin, 1928); *Agricultural Statistics, 1927–1933* (Dublin, 1935), and *Statistical Abstract of Ireland* and *Report upon the Agricultural Statistics of Northern Ireland*.

[2] Before 1857 the returns were obtained during August and September, but from that date they were made in June.

A. Ireland 1847–1922

(in thousands of acres)

	Wheat	Barley	Oats	Other Corn(*a*)	Potatoes	Turnips and Swedes	Man-gold(*b*)	Other Green Crops(*c*)	Flax	Hay	Pasture	Total Arable
1847	744	333	2,201	36	284	370	14	60	58	1,139	...	4,100
1848	...	...	...	...	...	...	...	...	...	...	...	...
1849	688	352	2,061	74	719	360	19	70	60	1,141	...	4,402
1850	605	321	2,143	81	875	347	20	74	91	1,200	...	4,558
1851	504	336	2,190	69	869	384	26	95	141	1,246	...	4,613
1852	354	290	2,283	49	877	357	31	91	137	1,271	...	4,468
1853	327	301	2,158	48	899	399	33	87	175	1,271	9,381	4,426
1854	411	253	2,045	34	990	329	21	77	151	1,258	9,501	4,313
1855	446	238	2,119	40	982	367	22	73	97	1,315	9,558	4,374
1856	529	189	2,037	29	1,105	354	22	78	106	1,303	9,545	4,451
1857	560	217	1,981	29	1,147	350	21	87	98	1,370	9,316	4,480
1858	547	196	1,981	24	1,160	338	30	90	92	1,424	9,354	4,458
1859	464	182	1,983	24	1,200	322	27	87	136	1,437	9,491	4,425
1860	466	184	1,966	23	1,172	319	32	85	129	1,595	9,484	4,376
1861	401	202	1,999	23	1,134	334	23	81	148	1,546	9,534	4,344
1862	356	195	1,978	24	1,018	377	23	79	150	1,553	9,700	4,201
1863	260	175	1,954	21	1,023	351	16	87	214	1,561	9,758	4,102
1864	276	176	1,815	22	1,040	337	14	85	302	1,610	9,694	4,067
1865	267	180	1,745	24	1,066	334	14	87	251	1,678	9,823	3,970
1866	299	153	1,700	23	1,050	317	20	94	264	1,601	10,004	3,944
1867	261	173	1,661	21	1,002	336	19	76	253	1,658	10,061	3,827
1868	285	188	1,702	18	1,035	320	19	83	206	1,692	9,999	3,880
1869	280	224	1,685	19	1,042	322	21	84	229	1,671	10,041	3,927
1870	260	244	1,650	20	1,044	339	25	91	195	1,774	9,967	3,886
1871	244	223	1,636	21	1,058	327	32	94	157	1,829	10,071	3,815
1872	225	220	1,625	21	992	347	35	101	122	1,800	10,246	3,605
1873	168	231	1,511	21	903	348	38	83	129	1,838	10,414	3,446
1874	188	212	1,481	20	892	334	38	89	107	1,907	10,472	3,374
1875	159	235	1,502	21	901	333	43	94	101	1,945	10,409	3,399
1876	120	221	1,487	21	881	345	49	90	133	1,861	10,507	3,356
1877	139	227	1,476	20	873	334	49	98	123	1,925	10,145	3,357
1878	154	244	1,413	20	847	330	45	96	112	1,943	10,116	3,278
1879	158	255	1,330	19	843	315	51	86	128	1,937	10,211	3,201
1880	149	219	1,382	17	821	303	42	82	158	1,910	10,259	3,187
1881	154	211	1,393	19	855	295	45	75	147	2,001	10,075	3,214
1882	153	188	1,397	19	838	294	36	81	113	1,962	10,110	3,141
1883	95	184	1,382	18	806	307	38	79	96	1,932	10,192	3,029
1884	68	167	1,348	16	799	304	35	84	89	1,962	10,347	2,934
1885	71	180	1,329	16	797	297	37	88	108	2,035	10,251	2,941
1886	70	182	1,322	17	800	299	37	85	128	2,094	10,163	2,957
1887	67	162	1,315	18	797	300	42	90	130	2,144	10,050	2,935
1888	99	171	1,281	20	805	294	46	90	114	2,222	9,905	2,934
1889	90	186	1,239	20	787	298	44	91	114	2,188	9,998	2,881
1890	92	182	1,221	19	781	295	46	92	97	2,094	10,212	2,839
1891	81	178	1,215	18	753	300	52	86	75	2,060	10,299	2,780
1892	75	176	1,226	18	740	300	52	83	71	2,143	10,254	2,764
1893	55	169	1,248	17	724	303	47	80	67	2,167	10,321	2,732
1894	49	165	1,255	15	717	311	52	83	101	2,183	10,214	2,768
1895	37	172	1,216	14	710	313	53	75	95	2,194	10,280	2,694
1896	38	173	1,194	16	706	308	54	79	72	2,202	10,334	2,659

See p. 194 for footnotes.

A. Ireland 1847–1922 (*cont.*)

(in thousands of acres)

	Wheat	Barley	Oats	Other Corn(*a*)	Potatoes	Turnips and Swedes	Man-gold(*b*)	Other Green Crops(*c*)	Flax	Hay	Pasture	Total Arable
1897	47	171	1,175	15	677	309	55	75	46	2,176	10,462	2,589
1898	53	158	1,165	15	665	307	56	77	34	2,174	10,470	2,547
1899	52	170	1,136	15	663	301	63	75	35	2,119	10,575	2,522
1900	54	174	1,105	14	654	298	69	78	47	2,166	10,563	2,506
1901	43	162	1,099	14	635	290	77	77	55	2,179	10,577	2,463
1902	44	168	1,062	12	629	289	77	75	50	2,168	10,635	2,436
1903	38	159	1,098	12	620	288	76	76	45	2,224	10,598	2,420
1904	31	158	1,079	11	619	286	76	70	44	2,260	10,586	2,383
1905	38	155	1,067	12	617	282	73	73	46	2,295	10,598(*d*)	2,371
											- - - - -	
1906	44	177	1,076	13	616	278	67	72	55	2,330	10,063	2,411
1907	38	170	1,075	11	591	275	67	70	60	2,281	9,979	2,369
1908	37	155	1,060	10	587	279	72	70	47	2,299	10,037	2,330
1909	44	163	1,036	9	580	277	73	71	38	2,279	9,997	2,304
1910	48	168	1,074	11	593	275	75	69	46	2,422	9,868	2,371
1911	45	158	1,040	11	591	271	78	74	67	2,512	9,847	2,349
1912	45	165	1,046	9	595	272	82	73	55	2,487	9,828	2,358
1913	34	173	1,049	8	582	277	79	72	59	2,482	9,861	2,348
1914	37	172	1,029	9	583	277	82	74	49	2,488	9,928	2,328
1915	87	142	1,089	9	594	265	83	68	53	2,496	9,819	2,404
1916	76	150	1,072	8	586	263	80	58	91	2,406	9,908	2,400
1917	124	177	1,464	9	709	293	93	43	108	2,533	8,784	3,038
1918	157	185	1,580	11	702	295	98	51	143	2,470	8,683	3,239
1919	70	187	1,442	7	589	273	75	48	96	2,520	...	2,806
1920(*e*)	50	207	1,332	7	584	276	77	51	121	2,518	...	2,733
1921(*e*)	43	176	1,254	8	568	266	78	59	38	2,370	...	2,510
1922(*e*)	41	170	1,213	9	569	248	84	56	32	2,545	...	2,443

B. Northern Ireland 1923–80

(in thousands of acres)

	Wheat	Barley	Oats	Other(*f*) Corn	Potatoes	Turnips	Mangold	Flax	Rotation Grasses	Permanent Grasses	Total Arable
1923	7·0	2·1	352	1·4	163	49	1·9	28	593	1,208	1,230
1924	5·0	2·4	333	1·4	157	51	1·7	43	638	1,215	1,249
1925	3·6	2·3	322	1·4	154	46	1·0	38	660	1,217	1,243
1926	6·1	1·7	320	1·7	153	46	1·2	31	692	1,195	1,266
1927	6·0	1·5	310	1·8	153	42	1·2	26	648	1,250	1,202
1928	4·9	2·0	307	1·6	156	43	1·4	37	666	1,214	1,232
1929	3·6	1·9	314	1·5	152	42	1·3	34	673	1,222	1,216
1930	4·5	2·1	307	1·8	136	40	1·1	28	704	1,198	1,249
1931	3·0	1·5	286	1·3	134	36	0·9	7·4	722	1,254	1,205
1932	3·3	1·1	286	1·3	142	37	0·9	6·1	672	1,293	1,162
1933	6·2	1·5	288	1·1	139	36	0·9	9·8	674	1,291	1,169
1934	8·7	2·4	280	1·0	137	36	1·1	16	634	1,336	1,129
1935	9·1	3·1	273	0·9	129	33	1·0	28	618	1,362	1,107
1936	6·9	2·8	265	0·8	132	31	1·2	25	646	1,353	1,123
1937	4·4	2·8	257	0·7	125	29	1·1	19	622	1,404	1,072
1938	5·5	3·4	297	0·7	123	26	1·0	21	607	1,388	1,096
1939	2·9	3·5	291	1·0	115	23	1·1	21	565	1,442	1,036
1940	12·0	17·7	397	6·1	137	26	1·7	46	483	1,188	1,143
1941	17·6	17·6	449	18·0	157	29	2·0	90	451	1,047	1,249
1942	12·3	15·3	475	19·4	187	26	1·6	73	495	955	1,323

See p. 194 for footnotes.

B. Northern Ireland 1923–80 (*cont.*) (in thousands of acres)

	Wheat	Barley	Oats	Other(*f*) Corn	Potatoes	Turnips	Mangold	Flax	Rotation Grasses	Permanent Grasses	Total Arable
1943	13·8	14·4	470	17·9	197	24	1·4	93	491	910	1,341
1944	5·0	16·1	441	12·0	198	22	1·1	125	497	926	1,337
1945	1·8	14·3	448	9·7	190	21	1·1	80	532	947	1,318
1946	2·5	7·8	413	8·4	193	20	1·2	36	604	969	1,305
1947	1·8	6·5	381	7·2	182	17	1·0	17	623	1,026	1,256
1948	4·4	5·8	390	9·2	210	15·5	0·9	21	595	1,002	1,271
1949	2·0	5·7	374	7·8	188	13·8	0·8	30	577	1,042	1,217
1950	2·1	3·8	345	7·6	179	12·4	0·8	22	604	1,085	1,196
1951	1·3	2·9	316	5·4	144	11·6	0·9(*g*)	21	606	1,143	1,129

1952	1·9	5·4	302	6·1	137	10·7	2·4	23	582	1,190	1,089
1953	2·3	6·3	288	6·6	139	11·1	1·9	18	552	1,233	1,045
1954	2·1	5·1	268	5·6	130	11·0	1·8	11	543	1,228	996
1955	1·3	5·0	251	4·6	116	10·0	1·1	9	553	1,248	971
1956	2·7	6·3	256	4·5	125	8·6	1·1	9	561	1,224	993
1957	3·8	13·0	238	5·4	103	7·6	0·9	3	527	1,231	922
1958	3·9	16	218	5·3	99	7·1	0·8	1	511	1,238	881
1959	2·4	27	199	4·9	96	5·6	0·5	--	551	1,137	905
1960	3·5	59	202	4·2	87	4·6	0·4	--	578	1,129	955
											---- (*h*)
1961	4·9	111	183	2·8	75	3·9	0·3	--	486	1,048	882
1962	4·1	128	162	...	77	3·8	0·3	--	497	1,037	890
1963	2·5	148	146	...	81	2·9	0·2	--	515	1,023	912
1964	3·1	165	125	...	72	2·7	0·2	--	617	1,002	1,001
1965	3·8	184	96	...	61	2·1	0·2	--	615	1,020	979
1966	2·9	172	82	...	57	1·7	0·1	--	633	1,083	965
1967	2·7	153	182	...	58	1·8	0·1	...	593	1,156	908
1968	2·1	139	73	...	50	1·5	0·1	...	535	1,244	821
1969	2·6	136	58	...	43	1·3	0·1	...	459	1,333	723
1970	3·0	124	45	...	48	1·3	...	...	492	1,313	743
1971	2·5	140	38	...	42	1·2	...	...	474	1,342	722
1972	2·3	126	29	...	36	1·1	...	...	473	1,379	692
1973	1·6	119	24	...	35	1·1	...	...	464	1,376	666
1974	1·6	121	22	...	31	1·3	...	...	457	1,400	652
1975	1·4	123	22	...	27	1·6	...	...	690	1,160	884
1976	1·4	123	17	...	35	1·6	...	...	669	1,199	865
1977	1·1	129	15	...	47	1·7	...	...	654	1,211	865
									---(*i*)	---(*i*)	
1978	1·5	138	13	...	35	1·8	...	...	684	1,210	891
1979	1·3	129	10	...	35	1·8	...	...	643	1,254	841
1980	1·1	128	10	...	37	...	...	...	684	...	882

C. Republic of Ireland 1923–1980 (in thousands of acres)

	Wheat	Barley	Oats	Other Corn	Potatoes	Turnips	Mangold	Sugar Beet	Flax	Hay	Pasture	Total Arable
1923	36	146	729	8·7	399	198	84	—	8·0	2,177	...	1,669
1924	33	156	689	9·2	393	202	84	—	10	2,288	...	1,632
1925	22	146	671	8·5	380	199	79	—	11	2,265	8,411	1,571
1926	29	141	647	7·3	375	195	81	9·5	6·8	2,288	8,416	1,551
1927	35	121	645	6·7	365	183	80	18	6·0	2,183	8,469	1,511
1928	31	129	649	5·5	364	189	85	17	8·0	2,155	8,432	1,529
1929	29	118	666	4·6	363	188	83	13	6·3	2,334	8,204	1,521
1930	27	116	644	3·9	347	179	80	14	4·0	2,296	8,082	1,458
1931	21	116	623	3·9	346	182	84	5·0	0·6	2,313	7,989	1,425
1932	21	103	632	3·3	348	177	81	14	0·5	2,282	7,957	1,424

See p. 194 for footnotes.

C. Republic of Ireland 1923–1980 (*cont.*) (in thousands of acres)

	Wheat	Barley	Oats	Other Corn	Potatoes	Turnips	Mangold	Sugar Beet	Flax	Hay	Pasture	Total Arable
1933	50	117	635	3·3	341	170	80	15	0·9	2,244	8,004	1,455
1934	94	143	583	2·5	343	159	83	46	2·2	2,147	8,053	1,497
1935	163	139	614	2·6	336	152	84	57	4·8	2,083	7,925	1,591
1936	255	130	559	2·6	334	150	85	61	5·1	2,050	7,936	1,621
1937	220	131	573	2·2	327	149	86	62	4·2	2,087	7,951	1,592
1938	230	118	570	2·2	327	143	86	51	3·9	2,037	8,040	1,568
1939	255	74	537	2·1	317	141	86	42	4·1	2,062	8,052	1,492
1940	305	132	681	3·4	367	151	93	63	10	2,126	7,616	1,846
1941	463	163	782	4·4	428	157	96	78	16	2,004	7,336	2,236
1942	574	186	878	7·2	426	146	84	55	19	1,960	7,178	2,425
1943	509	209	936	9·2	408	143	84	83	28	1,958	7,142	2,459
1944	642	168	945	12	412	144	84	82	30	1,898	7,092	2,567
1945	662	170	834	13	388	152	87	85	33	1,950	7,130	2,474
1946	643	144	831	12	391	151	88	79	26	1,935	7,217	2,413
1947	580	146	826	9·5	383	159	84	62	18	2,011	7,242	2,314
1948	518	120	880	9·3	385	153	82	66	21	2,021	7,268	2,285
1949	363	157	686	7·1	350	138	78	59	15	2,000	7,680	1,904
1950	366	123	614	5·5	337	128	78	60	10	1,990	7,826	1,769
1951	282	167	620	4·9	321	129	76	60	12	1,936	7,935	1,717
1952	254	225	611	5·5	310	127	73	54	11	1,932	7,938	1,720
1953	354	188	570	5·7	310	125	66	65	4·2	1,902	7,945	1,753
1954	486	163	533	5·1	292	120	64	74	2·0	1,878	7,929	1,808
1955	358	213	545	4·9	286	129	63	55	1·9	1,889	8,008	1,728
1956	340	236	525	4·9	283	119	62	59	1·2	1,897	8,028	1,707
1957	406	306	461	4·4	266	109	57	71	0·4	1,962	7,997	1,757
1958	419	310	457	6·2	263	105	54	85	0·2	1,929	7,948	1,778
1959	282	333	462	6·8	260	105	53	69	0·2	1,881	8,118	1,654
											----(*j*)	
1960	366	328	426	6·9	234	103	[66](*k*)	68	...	1,981	7,578	1,675
1961	345	362	368	6·7	213	97	[62](*k*)	79	...	1,889	7,780	1,599
1962	314	406	346	8·2	209	97	49	78	...	1,853	7,964	1,588
1963	233	429	332	11	205	97	...	88	...	1,918	7,982	1,513
1964	214	454	289	8·5	182	99	...	80	...	1,932	8,147	1,438
1965	182	464	284	8·5	174	107	...	66	...	1,971	8,270	1,395
1966	131	462	243	5·4	168	108	...	54	...	2,020	8,465	1,262
1967	189	451	238	6·2	160	109	...	64	...	2,059	8,458	1,302

See p. 194 for footnotes.

Agriculture 2. *continued*

C. Republic of Ireland 1923–1980 (*cont.*) (in thousands of acres)

	Wheat	Barley	Oats	Other Corn	Potatoes	Turnips	Mangold	Sugar Beet	Hay	Pasture	Total Arable
1968	224	454	218	8·5	147	108	29	64	2,095	8,467	1,306
									----(*l*)	----(*l*)	
1969	204	490	189	10	136	99	27	62	2,203	8,428	1,272
1970	234	530	168	11	140	95	23	64	2,270	8,263	1,315
1971	225	581	148	10	128	87	21	74	2,426	8,176	1,322
1972	168	622	129	7·4	109	76	17	84	2,418	8,255	1,260
1973	145	600	123	7·6	118	69	14	75	2,511	8,263	1,196
1974	141	609	117	8·1	104	63	13	63	2,561	8,259	1,165
1975	110	606	121	9·1	100	55	11	82	2,632	7,821	1,136
1976	125	639	100	...	117	...	...	85	...	...	1,175
1977	120	715	85	...	132	...	...	87	...	...	...
1978	122	759	76	...	102	...	...	90	...	...	...
1979	121	800	70	...	100	...	...	86	...	...	...
1980	131	905	61	6·6	103	34	4·5	81	2,997	7,238	1,370

(*a*) Rye, beans and peas.
(*b*) This generally includes fodder beet, of which the area grown has always been very small.
(*c*) Including sugar beet.
(*d*) More careful compilation of returns was demanded from 1906 onwards, and this resulted in some transfers from pasture to mountain and bog land.
(*e*) The figures for these years are approximations, since the police compiled the returns, not individual farmers.
(*f*) Beans, peas, ryes, and dredge corn.
(*g*) Subsequently includes fodder beet which has not been collected separately previously. In 1952 the fodder beet acreage amounted to 1·7 thousand acres.
(*h*) There was a change in the method of estimation.
(*i*) Subsequently grasses under 5 years old and grasses over 5 years old.
(*j*) The practice of adjusting the reported figures was subsequently discontinued.
(*k*) Including fodder beet, which occupied 14 thousand acres in 1959 and 1962.
(*l*) Grass for silage, which had been previously split between hay and pasture was transferred wholly to hay in subsequent years.

Agriculture 3. Estimated Wheat Yields – England 1815–84

NOTES

[1] SOURCES: Part A – M. J. R. Healy and E. L. Jones, "Wheat Yields in England, 1815–59", *J.R.S.S.*, series A LXXV (1962). Part B – Sir John B. Lawes and Sir J. Henry Gilbert, "Home Produce, Imports, Consumption, and Price of Wheat, over Forty Harvest-Years, 1852–3 to 1891–2", *Journal of the Royal Agricultural Society of England*, 3rd series, IV (1893).

[2] The statistics in part A relate to estimates made by agents of Liverpool corn merchants covering an area bounded by Liverpool, York, Norwich, Tonbridge, and Hereford. It is believed that they represent farms of above-average quality, but that yearly changes for the county as a whole are accurately represented.

[3] The statistics in part B are estimates made on the basis of yields at Rothamsted. Their reliability is discussed in the introduction to this chapter. They were made on the basis of weight and converted to bushels by the authors on the assumption that one bushel equalled 60lb.

A. 1815–59

(in bushels per acre)

1815	37·0	1830	33·6	1845	44·9
1816	25·3	1831	30·3	1846	45·7
1817	33·4	1832	35·7	1847	46·4
1818	32·6	1833	34·3	1848	44·1
1819	27·7	1834	41·5	1849	57·0
1820	37·3	1835	32·8	1850	41·8
1821	30·9	1836	36·7	1851	48·9
1822	30·9	1837	34·0	1852	45·0
1823	25·8	1838	33·1	1853	37·9
1824	29·0	1839	31·2	1854	57·3
1825	34·9	1840	45·1	1855	46·3
1826	35·3	1841	39·7	1856	52·7
1827	34·7	1842	54·8	1857	57·3
1828	27·1	1843	50·0	1858	57·9
1829	27·7	1844	54·5	1859	55·1

B. 1852–84 (*a*)

1852	23·2	1863	39·4	1874	29·7
1853	21·2	1864	35·9	1875	23·2
1854	35·4	1865	31·1	1876	25·4
1855	27·9	1866	25·5	1877	27·0
1856	27·5	1867	21·4	1878	30·5
1857	33·6	1868	34·6	1879	15·7
1858	32·0	1869	27·5	1880	24·9
1859	26·5	1870	30·5	1881	24·4
1860	22·5	1871	24·4	1882	26·0
1861	25·6	1872	24·4	1883	28·5
1862	29·7	1873	22·9	1884	29·9

(*a*) The figures are given in fractions in the original. They have been rounded down here – i.e. ¼ = 0·2, ¾ = 0·7, etc.

Agriculture 4. Agricultural Production – Great Britain 1884–1980

NOTES

[1] SOURCES: *Agricultural Statistics* and *A Century of Agricultural Statistics: Great Britain 1866–1966* (London, 1968).

[2] Cereal production was at one time recorded only in bushels, but the retrospective data in terms of weight, published by the Ministry of Agriculture in 1968, has extended the series back to all except the first year of collection, 1884. Figures in thousands of bushels for that year are as follows: wheat 80,216; barley 73,913; oats 109,397.

(in thousands of tons, except hops, which are in thousands of hundredweights)

	Wheat	Barley	Oats	Potatoes	Turnips and Swedes(*a*)	Mangold	Sugar Beet	Rotation Hay(*b*)(*c*)	Pasture Hay(*c*)	Hops
1884	...	...	...	3,743	27,073	5,558	—	...		...
1885	2,145	1,900	1,925	3,199	20,511	5,470	—	8,731		509
1886	1,699	1,728	2,072	3,168	29,983	7,280	—	3,311	5,763	776
1887	2,055	1,565	1,907	3,565	19,748	5,423	—	3,169	4,724	458
1888	1,989	1,642	1,908	3,059	24,675	6,239	—	3,214	6,738	281
1889	2,024	1,616	2,016	3,588	28,097	6,119	—	4,147	7,284	498
1890	2,028	1,772	2,137	2,812	27,747	6,046	—	3,494	6,378	284
1891	1,994	1,729	1,996	3,053	25,392	6,751	—	3,039	5,289	437
1892	1,619	1,689	2,065	3,049	27,348	6,681	—	2,725	4,290	413
1893	1,361	1,427	2,007	3,476	26,262	4,457	—	1,918	2,681	415
1894	1,636	1,733	2,404	2,789	26,398	6,552	—	3,448	6,942	637
1895	1,028	1,646	2,169	3,593	24,730	5,549	—	3,117	4,559	553
1896	1,577	1,697	2,027	3,562	23,254	5,092	—	2,624	4,060	453
1897	1,519	1,601	2,075	2,608	25,652	6,628	—	3,319	5,635	411
1898	2,019	1,631	2,111	3,283	21,337	6,218	—	4,007	6,632	357
1899	1,812	1,623	2,037	3,077	16,061	6,538	—	3,044	4,979	661
1900	1,455	1,493	2,039	2,735	23,960	8,463	—	3,188	5,340	348
1901	1,450	1,464	1,957	3,671	20,414	7,774	—	3,002	3,616	649
1902	1,567	1,594	2,313	3,194	24,169	9,347	—	3,846	6,223	311
1903	1,317	1,425	2,213	2,914	19,927	7,188	—	3,671	6,082	421
1904	1,019	1,371	2,261	3,588	23,036	7,481	—	3,497	5,876	282
1905	1,628	1,393	2,068	3,763	21,841	8,213	—	3,143	5,088	696
1906	1,659	1,471	2,247	3,429	22,628	8,538	—	3,201	5,384	246
1907	1,518	1,435	2,394	2,977	22,086	8,937	—	3,710	6,719	374
1908	1,449	1,307	2,189	3,918	23,768	8,995	—	3,507	6,213	471
1909	1,673	1,443	2,166	3,674	25,124	9,571	—	2,936	5,432	214
1910	1,502	1,339	2,161	3,477	25,695	9,353	—	3,264	6,252	303
1911	1,776	1,259	2,072	3,825	16,397	7,480	—	2,613	4,569	328
1912	1,496	1,195	1,863	3,180	20,279	8,837	—	2,675	6,343	373
1913	1,541	1,408	1,986	3,865	20,125	7,648	—	3,397	6,602	256
1914	1,706	1,367	2,033	4,031	19,762	7,961	—	2,746	5,389	507
1915	1,961	986	2,168	3,830	19,340	7,890	—	2,831	4,521	255
1916	1,559	1,110	2,100	3,036	18,882	7,382	—	3,659	6,214	308
1917	1,634	1,189	2,730	4,451	20,217	8,535	—	3,061	5,399	221
1918	2,428	1,299	2,965	5,360	17,532	8,280	...	2,692	4,912	130
1919	1,848	1,202	2,343	3,565	18,305	6,337	...	2,290	3,608	189
1920	1,515	1,391	2,215	4,388	21,885	7,336	...	3,278	5,875	281
1921	2,027	1,171	2,142	3,998	13,740	6,287	65	2,725	3,400	224
1922	1,742	1,096	1,932	5,203	17,788	8,595	55	2,410	4,281	301
1923	1,586	1,099	2,045	3,579	17,440	6,989	104	3,484	5,113	229
1924	1,412	1,143	2,200	3,541	18,290	7,846	184	3,507	5,466	444
1925	1,414	1,153	2,095	4,209	16,0[illegible]3	7,151	428	3,209	4,783	355
1926	1,360	1,025	2,240	3,662	17,876	7,143	1,117	3,071	5,050	332
1927	1,488	956	1,964	3,854	14,567	5,468	1,503	2,755	4,424	255
1928	1,328	1,122	2,147	4,545	16,613	5,777	1,370	2,769	4,533	242
1929	1,329	1,099	2,277	4,74[illegible]	14,909	5,712	2,004	2,429	3,857	359
1930	1,127	832	1,988	3,6[illegible]3	13,753	5,463	3,060	2,980	5,843	253

Agriculture 4. *continued*

(in thousands of tons, except hops, which are in thousands of hundredweights)

	Wheat	Barley	Oats	Potatoes	Turnips and Swedes(*a*)	Mangold	Sugar Beet	Rotation Hay(*b*)(*c*)	Pasture Hay(*c*)	Hops
1931	1,010	847	1,861	3,154	12,416	4,549	1,667	3,336	5,582	169
1932	1,165	833	1,967	4,450	13,322	4,358	2,232	2,836	4,919	188
1933	1,666	688	1,920	4,555	10,957	4,168	3,298	2,175	4,406	216
1934	1,859	817	1,761	4,464	9,206	4,769	4,095	2,229	4,424	259
1935	1,743	732	1,819	3,765	10,301	4,618	3,404	2,482	5,104	248
1936	1,473	729	1,722	3,804	11,507	4,756	3,448	2,252	4,976	252
1937	1,505	655	1,604	4,048	10,161	3,749	2,583	2,846	5,252	236
1938	1,959	901	1,702	4,404	10,605	3,689	2,191	1,913	3,389	258
1939	1,642	889	1,733	4,354	9,930	4,050	3,529	2,273	4,783	288
1940	1,628	1,089	2,514	5,375	10,632	4,229	3,176	2,315	3,898	270
1941	2,000	1,127	2,815	6,783	11,780	5,090	3,226	2,139	3,786	262
1942	2,556	1,432	3,125	8,162	13,035	5,404	3,923	2,669	3,233	262
								----(b)		
1943	3,435	1,632	2,670	8,537	11,980	5,785	3,760	3,038	2,844	286
1944	3,134	1,737	2,574	8,026	12,070	5,543	3,267	2,894	2,093	254
1945	2,174	2,096	2,862	8,702	12,156	6,508	3,886	3,843	2,659	282
1946	1,965	1,956	2,527	8,614	10,951	6,264	4,522	3,705	2,369	282
1947	1,666	1,614	2,244	6,742	9,220	4,328	2,960	3,654	2,673	290
1948	2,356	2,021	2,571	10,132	9,676	5,901	4,319	3,570	2,873	274
1949	2,202	2,123	2,641	7,605	9,220	5,308	3,962	4,039	2,776	250
								----(b)(c)	----(c)	
1950	2,604	1,707	2,384	8,164	9,230	6,486	5,218	3,113	2,553	368
1951	2,315	1,936	2,321	7,087	9,932	6,068	4,534	3,643	2,823	322
1952	2,305	2,328	2,483	6,775	9,708	4,808	4,236	3,814	2,994	282
1953	2,662	2,514	2,549	7,135	10,789	5,498	5,275	3,615	3,036	272
1954	2,781	2,238	2,201	6,413	9,906	4,498	4,521	3,329	2,584	246
1955	2,598	2,930	2,485	5,521	8,208	3,788	4,556	3,834	3,236	256
1956	2,842	2,793	2,237	6,659	9,034	4,286	5,169	3,161	2,876	184
1957	2,679	2,942	1,941	5,030	8,628	3,549	4,539	3,645	2,929	268
1958	2,707	3,152	1,956	4,982	8,704	3,570	5,742	3,860	3,391	302
					----(a)					
1959	2,782	3,982	2,000	6,194	7,279	2,669	5,510	7,071		224
1960	2,988	4,168	1,870	6,455	8,760	3,585	7,215	7,402		250
1961	2,568	4,879	1,681	5,638	7,782	2,714	5,936	8,061		204
1962	3,905	5,598	1,585	6,012	7,725	2,655	5,313	7,727		266
1963	2,995	6,430	1,303	5,929	6,874	2,148	5,254	7,822		276
1964	3,729	7,196	1,206	6,411	6,862	1,666	6,218	8,851		252
1965	4,099	7,830	1,124	6,955	6,619	1,508	6,705	7,755		259
1966	3,415	8,392	1,031	6,008	5,885	1,038	6,495	7,819		226
1967	3,836	8,870	1,286	6,568	5,782	896	6,775	7,899		214
1968	3,411	7,944	1,131	6,302	5,524	801	7,006	7,638		199
1969	3,307	8,347	1,230	5,728	5,586	...	5,939	7,749		209
1970	4,164	7,253	1,156	6,964	5,677	...	6,311	7,110		236
1971	4,735	8,228	1,300	6,910	5,324	...	7,745	8,797		225
1972	4,700	8,927	1,200	6,124	5,007	...	6,118	8,542		175
1973	4,921	8,691	1,037	6,394	5,654	...	7,310	8,074		206
1974	6,030	8,795	916	6,391	6,240	...	4,515	7,066		200
1975	4,415	8,194	759	4,240	6,057	...	4,787	6,199		163
1976	4,662	7,358	735	4,388	4,854	...	6,255	7,428		159
1977	5,189	10,151	761	6,059	5,961	...	6,281	7,824		142
1978	6,506	9,476	681	6,871	5,624	...	6,969	7,316		146
1979	7,053	9,397	522	6,041	...	...	7,538	6,628		140
1980	8,330	9,966	580	6,602	...	...	7,263	6,293		140

(*a*) Including fodder beet in England and Wales from 1959.
(*b*) Excluding hay from lucerne, except in 1943–1949 in England & Wales.
(*c*) Including grass mown for silage drying or seed up to 1949.

Agriculture 5. Agricultural Production – Ireland 1847–1980

NOTE

SOURCES: 1847–1917 – *Agricultural Statistics (Ireland)*, 1918–30 – Department of Industry and Commerce: *Agricultural Statistics, 1847–1926* (Dublin, 1928), *Agricultural Statistics, 1927–1933* (Dublin, 1935), and *Statistical Abstract of Ireland*; and *Report upon the Agricultural Statistics of Northern Ireland*, and *Annual General Reports* of the Northern Ireland Ministry of Agriculture and its successors. The 1978–80 figures for wheat, barley, oats, potatoes, and sugar beet for the Republic of Ireland are from the United Nations, *Statistical Yearbook, 1982*.

A. Ireland 1847–1922

(in thousands of the stated unit)

	Wheat cwt.	Barley cwt.	Oats cwt.	Potatoes tons	Turnips and Swedes tons	Mangold(a) tons	Hay tons
1847	12,291	5,827	32,258	2,048	5,735	252	2,164
1848	...	...	...	...	...	...	...
1849	9,103	5,874	27,542	4,014	5,796	352	2,282
1850	6,510	5,647	28,956	3,946	5,448	358	2,400
1851	6,272	5,851	30,158	4,441	6,106	468	2,492
1852	4,847	5,255	32,793	4,256	5,676	561	2,669
1853	4,761	5,526	29,933	5,742	6,544	584	2,542
1854	6,160	4,651	31,617	5,062	5,198	361	2,390
1855	6,387	4,137	28,744	6,235	6,092	396	2,630
1856	6,845	2,836	25,862	4,409	4,567	286	2,476
1857	6,984	3,153	24,905	3,509	4,360	299	2,567
1858	7,335	2,972	25,068	4,892	4,365	404	2,701
1859	6,167	2,562	22,877	4,330	3,462	308	2,322
1860	5,340	2,752	24,756	2,741	2,628	290	3,206
1861	3,578	2,513	22,526	1,858	3,393	236	2,810
1862	2,869	2,425	20,392	2,148	3,793	222	2,782
1863	3,519	2,782	24,999	3,446	4,184	185	2,762
1864	3,675	2,795	21,872	4,312	3,468	147	2,607
1865	3,470	2,684	21,406	3,866	3,302	192	3,069
1866	3,381	2,397	20,359	3,069	3,786	250	2,879
1867	3,046	2,708	20,780	3,147	3,910	239	3,070
1868	3,969	3,224	21,320	4,062	3,514	246	2,871
1869	3,341	3,745	19,488	3,372	3,965	264	3,040
1870	3,165	3,768	21,126	4,218	3,941	322	3,387
1871	2,962	3,385	20,711	2,794	4,246	432	3,316
1872	2,559	3,154	18,597	1,806	3,963	432	3,496
1873	1,970	3,679	19,319	2,683	4,430	517	3,306
1874	2,886	4,086	20,007	3,552	4,408	542	3,461
1875	2,318	4,255	22,926	3,513	5,293	717	4,355
1876	2,023	3,891	21,415	4,155	4,541	699	3,458
1877	1,901	3,518	17,847	1,757	3,564	600	4,331
1878	2,308	3,928	19,045	2,527	4,686	685	4,417
1879	1,799	3,268	15,533	1,114	2,058	409	3,599
1880	2,228	3,453	19,558	2,986	4,340	604	3,795
1881	2,297	3,334	19,703	3,434	3,821	602	3,990
1882	2,075	2,758	18,286	1,994	3,392	433	4,115
1883	1,297	2,826	18,851	3,452	4,292	526	3,937
1884	992	2,681	18,109	3,040	3,508	439	3,823
1885	1,097	2,889	18,134	3,176	3,552	500	4,156
1886	1,007	2,776	18,379	2,668	3,974	506	4,429
1887	1,019	2,075	15,149	3,569	2,719	455	3,599
1888	1,367	2,707	17,631	2,523	3,327	590	5,181
1889	1,436	3,249	17,633	2,848	3,910	622	4,854
1890	1,414	3,062	17,796	1,810	4,255	663	4,594
1891	1,401	3,315	18,834	3,037	4,349	807	4,343
1892	1,186	2,881	18,068	2,585	4,071	747	4,501
1893	892	2,773	19,396	3,064	4,848	769	4,483
1894	820	2,815	19,291	1,873	4,279	758	5,309
1895	594	2,847	18,221	3,472	4,491	828	4,562
1896	640	3,147	17,008	2,701	4,783	783	4,731

See p. 201 for footnotes.

A. Ireland 1847–1922 (*cont.*)

(in thousands of the stated unit)

	Wheat cwt.	Barley cwt.	Oats cwt.	Potatoes tons	Turnips and Swedes tons	Mangold(*a*) tons	Hay tons
1897	726	2,589	16,265	1,498	4,134	751	5,088
1898	995	2,982	18,684	2,942	5,163	1,010	5,278
1899	927	3,043	17,896	2,760	4,309	1,066	4,876
1900	901	2,782	17,512	1,842	4,426	1,187	5,214
1901	788	2,918	17,783	3,372	4,884	1,452	4,740
1902	858	3,547	18,734	2,726	4,947	1,463	5,177
1903	630	2,605	16,805	2,363	3,596	1,024	5,202
1904	557	2,348	17,183	2,642	4,997	1,332	5,487
1905	766	3,078	17,358	3,423	4,722	1,280	5,323
1906	818	3,092	17,929	2,661	4,956	1,343	4,927
1907	710	3,001	17,166	2,246	4,096	1,182	5,174
1908	747	3,057	18,240	3,200	5,417	1,579	4,917
1909	940	3,574	19,400	3,203	4,970	1,442	4,576
1910	919	2,934	18,791	2,871	4,624	1,466	5,778
1911	887	3,042	16,916	3,695	5,273	1,735	4,475
1912	838	3,111	19,105	2,547	3,783	1,301	5,006
1913	694	3,430	18,887	3,739	5,189	1,629	5,396
1914	758	3,460	18,082	3,446	4,433	1,562	4,269
1915	1,734	2,522	19,601	3,710	5,091	1,807	5,097
1916	1,514	2,802	17,815	2,433	4,436	1,628	5,325
1917	2,450	3,374	27,046	4,153	4,625	1,834	4,702
1918	3,040	3,580	28,980	3,863	5,303	2,041	4,728
1919	1,320	3,480	24,440	2,747	4,487	1,432	4,810(*b*)
1920(*b*)	776	3,189	17,831	1,986	4,107	1,246	5,547
1921(*b*)	826	2,488	15,086	2,556	3,882	1,510	3,258
1922(*b*)	829	2,986	16,300	3,431	3,438	1,330	4,626

B. Northern Ireland, 1923–80

(in thousand tons)

	Wheat	Barley	Oats	Potatoes	Turnips and Swedes	Mangold(*a*)	Hay
1923	6·2	1·8	275	917	855	30	834
1924	4·2	2·0	268	829	475	14	1,081
1925	3·4	2·2	274	1,168	859	16	1,055
1926	6·1	1·5	293	1,069	876	23	1,096
1927	5·8	1·4	276	1,057	709	19	945
1928	4·9	1·9	277	1,154	766	22	795
1929	3·8	1·8	287	1,124	843	23	811
1930	4·6	2·1	277	856	753	21	836
1931	2·8	1·3	226	698	543	13	901
1932	3·3	1·1	289	1,126	641	14	784
1933	6·1	1·5	263	949	597	15	842
1934	9·7	2·5	274	923	518	18	805
1935	9·7	3·2	260	887	578	18	785
1936	7·3	2·8	259	785	496	19	731
1937	4·4	2·6	243	868	482	17	833
1938	5·7	3·3	290	711	320	16·2	825
1939	3·0	3·1	270	864	385	18·5	734
1940	12·8	15·0	378	1,030	448	28·7	798
1941	18·2	17·2	432	1,221	466	30·0	704
1942	11·4	13·9	428	1,231	380	22·1	758
1943	12·1	12·9	394	1,285	336	19·7	787
1944	4·4	14·8	379	1,070	318	16·7	703
1945	1·5	12·5	383	1,089	324	16·1	690
1946	2·2	7·4	376	1,552	303	17·6	754
1947	1·4	4·5	265	1,024	240	13·6	904

See p. 201 for footnotes.

B. Northern Ireland 1923–80 (*cont.*)

(in thousand tons)

	Wheat	Barley	Oats	Potatoes	Turnips and Swedes	Mangold(*a*)	Hay
1948	4·7	6·5	392	1,666	262	16·9	784
1949	2·1	6·4	354	1,430	226	13·1	690
1950	2·0	4·0	308	1,343	174	11·5	592
1951	1·4	3·3	295	1,197	178	14·7	746
1952	2·2	6·5	289	1,073	164	9·5	723
1953	2·5	7·1	272	1,125	179	10·8	667
1954	2·1	5·9	239	912	165	14·9	737
1955	1·3	5·8	224	757	174	11·9	716
1956	3·2	7·4	249	874	151	12·1	709
1957	4·4	14·7	204	659	129	10·5	702
1958	4·3	17·8	182	574	110	8·4	766
							--- (*c*)
1959	2·9	33	187	722	87	5·8	583
1960	4·3	73	188	703	72	6·3	629
1961	5·5	95	141	623	59	5·0	649
1962	5·8	175	162	641	60	5·5	618
1963	3·3	168	135	647	46	4·4	602
1964	4·3	207	119	541	43	3·6	732
1965	5·7	232	90	503	35	3·1	712
1966	4·2	194	72	468	28	2·3	737
1967	4·2	199	78	519	25	1·9	739
1968	3·5	196	74	462	22	1·6	757
1969	4·1	180	57	389	20	1·5	781
1970	5·1	157	42	400	18	—	753
1971	4·4	195	39	369	17	—	741
1972	3·9	172	29	299	13	—	682
1973	2·7	174	26	306	14	—	674
1974	2·9	194	24	292	18	—	633
1975	2·6	184	23	239	29	—	570
1976	2·4	169	17	326	28	—	746
1977	2·0	214	18	459	33	—	672
1978	2·8	217	14	345	39	—	665
1979	2·3	172	12	343	38	—	615
1980	2·1	193	12	390	37	—	542

C. Republic of Ireland, 1923–80

(in thousand tons)

	Wheat	Barley	Oats	Potatoes	Turnips and Swedes	Mangold	Sugar Beet	Hay
1923	32	115	467	1,476	2,810	1,208	—	3,919
1924	28	123	482	1,492	2,672	1,000	—	4,576
1925	20	132	586	2,138	3,299	1,319	—	4,280
1926	31	143	639	1,932	3,735	1,685	86	5,234
1927	38	135	668	2,443	3,478	1,618	134	4,993
1928	32	132	637	2,246	3,534	1,600	140	4,720
1929	32	128	689	3,007	3,681	1,758	141	5,088
1930	29	118	632	2,337	3,176	1,577	158	4,787
1931	21	105	521	1,932	3,303	1,540	34	5,116
1932	22	107	627	3,015	3,384	1,638	149	4,842
1933	53	120	624	2,497	3,075	1,572	202	4,635
1934	102	145	561	2,545	2,793	1,617	484	4,336
1935	179	156	616	2,577	2,793	1,629	594	4,358
1936	210	122	517	2,421	2,663	1,605	630	4,374
1937	187	118	573	2,706	2,736	1,661	583	4,744

Agriculture 5. *continued*

C. Republic of Ireland, 1923–80 (*cont.*)

(in thousand tons)

	Wheat	Barley	Oats	Potatoes	Turnips and Swedes	Mangold	Sugar Beet	Hay
1938	198	110	559	2,461	2,506	1,544	416	4,593
1939	255	74	540	2,998	2,580	1,692	410	4,182
1940	313	139	724	3,118	2,441	1,700	660	4,663
1941	435	143	684	3,690	2,632	1,760	720	4,224
1942	512	172	768	3,120	2,100	1,386	399	4,072
1943	435	188	796	3,093	2,259	1,418	732	4,248
1944	546	153	780	3,007	2,197	1,364	630	3,915
1945	573	150	726	2,984	2,554	1,557	735	4,313
1946	463	121	689	3,227	2,264	1,350	529	4,170
1947	313	88	653	2,600	2,367	1,247	480	4,468
1948	410	101	792	3,275	2,461	1,375	611	4,547
1949	361	159	559	2,692	1,985	1,439	643	4,422
1950	328	119	528	2,874	2,006	1,317	588	4,468
1951	248	176	577	2,766	2,210	1,359	575	4,452
1952	262	249	578	2,676	1,988	1,230	570	4,523
1953	411	225	567	2,717	2,107	1,235	822	4,508
1954	489	176	475	2,248	2,165	1,233	674	4,489
1955	399	246	567	2,114	2,247	1,260	597	4,242
1956	426	314	536	2,607	2,256	1,278	630	4,083
1957	514	384	431	2,339	2,135	1,172	795	4,080
1958	345	330	448	1,850	1,733	983	785	4,105
1959	364	452	475	2,592	1,924	1,172	928	3,708
1960	462	435	419	1,800	2,158	1,254	936	4,239
1961	462	507	375	2,111	2,080	1,091	878	4,052
1962	432	594	340	2,084	2,117	1,142	916	3,642
1963	296	580	362	1,938	2,092	1,016	937	4,249
1964	267	542	308	1,502	2,072	912	879	4,283
1965	229	606	319	1,622	2,235	886	747	4,284
1966	182	628	278	1,652	2,378	780	693	4,325
1967	293	666	289	1,720	2,366	747	941	4,574
1968	406	741	281	1,591	2,409	769	1,076	4,823
1969	357	776	248	1,430	1,976	661	903	5,213
1970	375	591	203	1,445	1,908	562	967	4,124
1971	374	976	204	1,406	1,869	535	1,199	4,622
1972	266	966	176	1,053	1,368	359	1,095	4,358
1973	225	890	160	1,311	1,414	337	1,300	4,278
1974	241	1,021	155	1,094	1,252	315	911	3,726
1975	192	1,003	162	1,002	1,020	253	1,406	3,661
1976	197	907	128	1,161	920	226	1,448	4,469
1977	246	1,422	133	1,498	...	...	1,376	...
1978	249	1,374	116	1,079	...	...	1,427	...
1979	241	1,416	103	1,123	...	...	1,301	...
1980	235	1,227	89	965	797	131	1,343	4,000

(*a*) This usually includes fodder beet, of which the production was very small.
(*b*) The figures for 1920–2, and the figure for hay in 1919, are approximations, the returns being made by the police and not by individual farmers.
(*c*) Subsequently excluding grass for silage.

Agriculture 6. Numbers of Livestock – Great Britain 1867–1980

NOTES
[1] SOURCE: *Agricultural Statistics*.
[2] The changes in the size of the lower limit of holdings making returns, and the level of that limit (referred to in the introduction), are of particular importance for pigs and poultry.

(in thousands at 25th June 1867–76 and 4th June 1877–1980)

	Cattle			Sheep					
	Cows and Heifers	Other Cattle	Total	One Year and Above	Under One Year Old	Total	Pigs	Horses	Poultry
1867	2,038	2,955	4,993	18,449	10,470	28,919	2,967	...	...
1868	2,144	3,280	5,424	19,708	11,004	30,711	2,309	...	...
1869	2,135	3,178	5,313	18,986	10,553	29,538	1,930	...	...
1870	2,162	3,242	5,403	18,410	9,987	28,398	2,171	1,267	...
1871	2,091	3,246	5,338	17,572	9,548	27,120	2,500	1,254	...
1872	2,165	3,460	5,625	17,961	9,961	27,922	2,772	1,258	...
1873	2,238	3,727	5,965	18,778	10,650	29,428	2,500	1,276	...
1874	2,274	3,852	6,125	19,449	10,865	30,314	2,423	1,312	
1875	2,253	3,760	6,013	18,775	10,393	29,167	2,230	1,340	...
1876	2,226	3,618	5,844	18,258	9,925	28,183	2,294	1,375	...
1877	2,207	3,491	5,698	18,016	10,016	28,161	2,499	1,389	...
1878	2,208	3,530	5,738	18,055	10,351	28,406	2,483	1,413	...
1879	2,255	3,601	5,856	18,172	9,985	28,157	2,092	1,433	...
1880	2,242	3,670	5,912	17,186	9,433	26,619	2,001	1,421	...
1881	2,270	3,641	5,912	16,143	8,438	24,581	2,048	1,425	...
1882	2,267	3,540	5,807	15,574	8,746	24,320	2,510	1,414	...
1883	2,306	3,657	5,963	15,949	9,120	25,068	2,618	1,411	...
1884	2,391	3,878	6,269	16,385	9,683	26,068	2,584	1,414	...
1885	2,530	4,068	6,598	16,538	9,997	26,535	2,403	1,409	...
1886	2,538	4,109	6,647	16,176	9,345	25,521	2,221	1,425	...
1887	2,536	3,905	6,441	16,146	9,813	25,959	2,299	1,428	...
1888	2,450	3,679	6,129	15,727	9,530	25,257	2,404	1,420	...
1889	2,444	3,706	6,140	15,862	9,770	25,632	2,511	1,421	...
1890	2,538	3,971	6,509	16,757	10,516	27,272	2,774	1,433	...
1891	2,657	4,196	6,853	17,787	10,946	28,733	2,889	1,488	...
1892	2,651	4,294	6,945	17,957	10,778	28,735	2,138	1,518	...
				Ewes kept for Breeding	Other Sheep				
1893	2,555	4,146	6,701	10,129	17,152	27,280	2,114	1,525	...
1894	2,460	3,887	6,347	9,668	16,193	25,862	2,390	1,529	...
1895	2,486	3,869	6,354	9,663	16,129	25,792	2,884	1,545	...
1896	2,512	3,982	6,494	9,926	16,780	26,705	2,879	1,553	...
1897	2,532	3,968	6,500	10,007	16,334	26,340	2,342	1,526	...
1898	2,587	4,035	6,622	10,138	16,605	26,743	2,452	1,517	...
1899	2,671	4,124	6,796	10,461	16,778	27,239	2,624	1,517	...
1900	2,621	4,184	6,805	10,350	16,242	26,592	2,382	1,500	...
1901	2,602	4,162	6,764	10,162	16,215	26,377	2,180	1,511	...
1902	2,556	4,000	6,556	9,999	15,767	25,766	2,300	1,505	...
1903	2,588	4,116	6,705	9,879	15,761	25,640	2,687	1,537	...
1904	2,679	4,180	6,858	9,881	15,326	25,207	2,862	1,560	...
1905	2,707	4,280	6,987	9,936	15,321	25,257	2,425	1,572	...
1906	2,738	4,272	7,011	10,061	15,359	25,420	2,323	1,569	...
1907	2,759	4,153	6,912	10,277	15,838	26,115	2,637	1,556	...
1908	2,764	4,141	6,905	10,569	16,551	27,120	2,823	1,546	...
1909	2,794	4,227	7,021	10,810	16,808	27,618	2,381	1,553	...
1910	2,768	4,270	7,037	10,666	16,437	27,103	2,350	1,545	...
1911	2,825	4,289	7,114	10,443	16,052	26,495	2,822	1,481	...
1912	2,784	4,242	7,026	10,120	14,938	25,058	2,656	1,441/1,611(*a*)	...

See p. 204 for footnote.

Agriculture 6. *continued*

(in thousands at 25th June 1867–76 and 4th June 1877–1980)

	Cattle			Sheep					
	Cows and Heifers	Other Cattle	Total	Ewes kept for Breeding	Other Sheep	Total	Pigs	Horses	Poultry
1913	2,695	4,268	6,964	9,613	14,318	23,931	2,234	1,324/1,607	...
1914	2,938	4,155	7,093	9,813	14,472	24,286	2,634	1,296/1,609	...
1915	2,884	4,404	7,288	9,877	14,722	24,598	2,579	1,213/1,487	...
1916	2,870	4,572	7,442	10,066	14,941	25,007	2,314	1,293/1,567	...
1917	2,907	4,530	7,437	9,899	14,144	24,043	2,051	1,324/1,583	...
1918	3,030	4,380	7,410	9,501	13,852	23,353	1,825	1,337/1,586	...
1919	3,009	4,415	7,424	8,590	12,944	21,534	1,936	1,338/1,600	...
1920	2,787	3,925	6,713	7,865	11,879	19,744	2,122	1,312/1,580	...
1921	2,944	3,715	6,660	8,151	12,339	20,490	2,651	1,340/1,601	...
1922	2,974	3,895	6,869	8,301	11,821	20,122	2,450	1,308/1,552	...
1923	3,070	3,946	7,017	8,409	12,213	20,621	2,798	1,253/1,485	...
1924	3,112	3,947	7,059	8,986	12,744	21,729	3,427	1,190/1,426	...
1925	3,164	4,205	7,368	9,453	13,641	23,094	2,799	1,131/1,350	...
1926	3,207	4,244	7,451	9,870	14,192	24,062	2,345	1,307	...
1927	3,251	4,235	7,486	10,201	14,406	24,608	2,888	1,249	49,221
1928	3,183	4,058	7,240	10,112	13,856	23,968	3,167	1,204	49,399
1929	3,166	4,024	7,191	9,998	13,663	23,661	2,509	1,160	52,283
1930	3,128	3,958	7,086	10,136	13,829	23,965	2,454	1,118	58,219
1931	3,244	4,030	7,274	10,678	14,903	25,580	2,945	1,091	63,562
1932	3,337	4,254	7,591	11,077	15,345	26,412	3,350	1,067	69,297
1933	3,439	4,475	7,914	11,154	14,747	25,901	3,236	1,052	73,835
1934	3,491	4,482	7,973	10,663	13,520	24,183	3,526	1,034	73,642
1935	3,548	4,311	7,860	10,466	13,778	24,243	4,074	1,021	70,256
1936	3,571	4,282	7,853	10,548	13,657	24,205	4,040	1,013	70,005
1937	3,563	4,346	7,909	10,606	14,106	24,712	3,883	1,005	63,704

				Sheep						
	Cows and Heifers	Other Cattle	Total	Shearling Ewes	Ewes for Breeding	Other Sheep	Total	Pigs	Horses	Poultry
1938	3,576	4,454	8,030	2,254	10,406	13,222	25,882	3,822	1,002	64,053
1939	3,615	4,504	8,119	2,240	10,572	13,181	25,993	3,767	987	64,137
1940	3,698	4,662	8,361	2,216	10,309	12,941	25,465	3,631	959	62,121
1941	3,708	4,446	8,153	1,859	8,865	10,722	21,445	2,207	962	49,126
1942	3,883	4,365	8,248	1,769	8,520	10,475	20,764	1,872	917	43,212
1943	3,999	4,428	8,428	1,977	7,899	9,823	19,700	1,571	871	35,299
1944	4,035	4,580	8,616	2,112	7,820	9,503	19,435	1,631	829	38,481
1945	3,996	4,702	8,697	2,071	7,916	9,508	19,496	1,903	796	44,665
1946	4,066	4,649	8,716	2,084	8,018	9,617	19,718	1,644	756	47,276
1947	4,009	4,623	8,633	1,847	6,904	7,436	16,186	1,294	703	48,977
1948	4,108	4,733	8,840	1,554	7,292	8,742	17,589	1,816	635	61,138
1949	4,224	5,038	9,263	1,888	7,473	9,485	18,847	2,364	557	71,257
1950	4,265	5,366	9,630	2,004	7,780	9,929	19,714	2,463	494	75,385
1951	4,145	5,368	9,512	2,046	7,813	9,453	19,311	3,306	432	76,506
1952	4,159	5,144	9,303	1,936	8,183	10,741	20,860	4,287	374	78,519
1953	4,208	5,300	9,508	2,096	8,375	11,089	21,560	4,406	333	77,511
1954	4,255	5,521	9,777	2,120	8,561	11,261	21,943	5,431	300	72,258
1955	4,202	5,563	9,764	2,127	8,840	11,111	22,078	5,157	274	75,585
1956	4,370	5,620	9,989	2,113	9,225	11,384	22,721	4,821	233	80,928
1957	4,417	5,491	9,909	2,192	9,451	12,226	23,868	5,232	208	83,131

Agriculture 6. *continued*

(in thousands at 25th June 1867–76 and 4th June 1877–1980)

	Cattle			Sheep						
	Cows and Heifers	Other Cattle	Total	Shear-ling Ewes	Ewes for Breeding	Other Sheep	Total	Pigs	Horses	Poultry
1958	4,345	5,631	9,976	2,501	9,903	12,721	25,125	5,695	189	87,474
1959	4,367	5,960	10,328	2,626	10,310	13,665	26,601	5,135	...	94,718
1960	4,506	6,266	10,772	2,467	10,764	13,541	26,772	4,739	157	92,612
1961	4,624	6,237	10,861	2,390	11,001	14,393	27,784	5,009	...	104,075
1962	4,702	6,048	10,749	2,447	11,318	14,523	28,289	5,540	...	99,436
1963	4,632	5,974	10,605	2,410	11,375	14,418	28,204	5,670	...	102,891
1964	4,549	5,966	10,515	2,384	11,475	14,704	28,563	6,227	...	107,820
1965	4,574	6,253	10,826	2,508	11,517	14,812	28,837	6,731	147	107,746
1966	4,605	6,413	11,017	2,478	11,592	14,833	28,903	6,276	...	108,076
1967	4,742	6,364	11,106	2,383	11,339	14,152	27,874	6,131	...	113,680
1968	4,771	6,172	10,944	2,381	11,017	13,644	27,042	6,375	...	115,400
1969	4,854	6,276	11,131	2,288	10,556	12,825	25,669	6,750	138	113,571
1970	4,912	6,349	11,261	2,182	10,146	12,785	25,114	7,020	...	129,464
1971	4,911	6,509	11,420	2,181	10,027	12,795	25,006	7,567	...	124,352
1972	5,166	6,874	12,040	2,355	10,260	13,258	25,873	7,572	...	125,175
1973	5,461	7,448	12,910	2,654	10,524	13,801	26,979	7,965	...	131,386
1974	5,667	7,917	13,583	2,593	10,799	14,170	27,562	7,705	...	127,854
1975	5,404	7,687	13,091	2,392	10,882	14,061	27,336	6,886	165	124,515
1976	5,312	7,210	12,522	2,293	10,896	14,150	27,339	7,249	...	130,113
1977	5,162	7,079	12,434	2,407	10,845	13,987	27,239	7,132	...	123,860
1978	5,120	7,001	12,122	2,638	11,064	15,097	28,798	7,045	...	126,037
1979	5,106	6,942	12,048	2,780	11,286	14,880	28,946	7,142	...	124,460
1980	4,971	6,847	11,918	2,654	11,730	16,001	30,385	7,123	...	123,716

(*a*) Where two figures are shown for this and subsequent years, the first is comparable with earlier years and the second with later years. The first is of horses used solely in agriculture (including brood mares and unbroken horses); the second is of all horses on agricultural holdings.

Agriculture 7. Numbers of Livestock – Ireland 1841–1980

NOTES

[1] SOURCES: 1847–1917 – *Agricultural Statistics (Ireland)*, annually; 1918–39 – Eire Department of Industry and Commerce; *Agricultural Statistics, 1847–1926* (Dublin, 1928), *Agricultural Statistics, 1927–1933* (Dublin, 1935), and *Statistical Abstract of Ireland*; and *Report upon the Agricultural Statistics of Northern Ireland*, and *Annual General Reports* of the Ministry of Agriculture (and its successors). The 1978–9 figures are from F.A.O., *Production Yearbook*.

[2] Before 1857 the returns were obtained during August and September, but from that date they were made in June.

A. Ireland 1841–1922

(in thousands)

	Cattle			Sheep				Horses		
	Cows and Heifers	Other Cattle	Total	One Year and Above	Under One Year Old	Total	Pigs	for Agricultural Purposes	Total (a)	Poultry
1841	...	...	1,863	...	...	2,106	1,413	...	...	8,459
1847	...	...	2,591	1,676	510	2,186	622	...	558	5,691
1848	...	...	...	...	...	...	...	...	...	...
1849	...	...	2,771	1,403	374	1,777	795	...	526	6,328
1850	...	...	2,918	1,393	483	1,876	928	...	527	6,945
1851	...	...	2,967	1,544	578	2,122	1,085	...	522	7,471
1852	...	...	3,095	1,929	685	2,614	1,073	...	525	8,176
1853	...	...	3,383	2,192	951	3,143	1,145	...	540	8,661
				Ewes (b)	Other Sheep					
1854	1,518	1,980	3,498	1,777	1,945	3,722	1,343	388	546	8,630
1855	1,561	2,003	3,564	1,734	1,868	3,602	1,178	393	556	8,367
1856	1,580	2,008	3,588	1,655	2,039	3,694	919	407	573	8,908
1857	1,605	2,016	3,621	1,538	1,914	3,452	1,255	424	600	9,491
1858	1,635	2,032	3,667	1,522	1,973	3,495	1,410	432	611	9,563
1859	1,690	2,126	3,816	1,564	2,029	3,593	1,266	444	629	10,252
1860	1,626	1,980	3,606	1,567	1,975	3,542	1,271	441	620	10,061
1861	1,545	1,927	3,472	1,528	2,028	3,556	1,102	445	614	10,371
1862	1,487	1,768	3,255	1,495	1,962	3,456	1,154	449	603	9,917
1863	1,397	1,747	3,144	1,420	1,888	3,308	1,067	440	580	9,649
1864	1,349	1,913	3,262	1,435	1,932	3,367	1,058	431	562	10,424
1865	1,387	2,111	3,498	1,579	2,115	3,694	1,306	420	548	10,682
1866	1,483	2,263	3,746	1,799	2,475	4,274	1,497	408	536	10,890
1867	1,521	2,187	3,708	2,034	2,802	4,836	1,235	399	524	10,335
1868	1,476	2,171	3,647	2,052	2,849	4,901	870	394	525	10,603
1869	1,506	2,228	3,734	1,938	2,713	4,651	1,082	392	528	10,802
1870	1,529	2,271	3,800	1,807	2,529	4,337	1,461	389	533	11,159
1871	1,546	2,430	3,976	1,752	2,481	4,233	1,621	385	538	11,717
1872	1,552	2,507	4,059	1,742	2,521	4,263	1,389	384	541	11,738
1873	1,528	2,619	4,147	1,822	2,662	4,485	1,044	377	532	11,863
1874	1,491	2,634	4,125	1,818	2,624	4,442	1,099	367	527	12,068
1875	1,530	2,585	4,115	1,750	2,504	4,254	1,252	360	526	12,139
1876	1,533	2,584	4,117	1,639	2,371	4,009	1,425	361	535	13,619
1877	1,523	2,475	3,998	1,629	2,359	3,988	1,469	366	553	13,566
1878	1,484	2,501	3,985	1,654	2,441	4,095	1,269	373	562	13,711
1879	1,465	2,603	4,068	1,625	2,393	4,018	1,072	379	572	13,783
1880	1,398	2,524	3,922	1,440	2,123	3,562	850	378	557	13,430
1881	1,392	2,565	3,957	1,338	1,918	3,256	1,096	375	548	13,972
1882	1,399	2,588	3,987	1,261	1,811	3,072	1,430	372	539	13,999
1883	1,402	2,695	4,097	1,330	1,889	3,219	1,348	368	534	13,382
1884	1,357	2,756	4,113	1,333	1,913	3,245	1,307	363	535	12,747
1885	1,417	2,812	4,229	1,421	2,056	3,478	1,269	363	547	13,851
1886	1,419	2,765	4,184	1,386	1,980	3,366	1,263	363	549	13,910
1887	1,394	2,763	4,157	1,382	1,995	3,378	1,408	365	557	14,461
1888	1,385	2,714	4,099	1,485	2,142	3,627	1,398	362	565	14,486

See p. 209 for footnotes.

A. Ireland 1841–1922 (*cont.*)

(in thousands)

	Cattle			Sheep				Horses		
	Cows and Heifers	Other Cattle	Total	Ewes (*b*)	Other Sheep	Total	Pigs	for Agricultural Purposes	Total (*a*)	Poultry
1889	1,364	2,730	4,094	1,542	2,247	3,789	1,381	368	574	14,857
1890	1,401	2,839	4,240	1,752	2,571	4,323	1,570	367	585	15,408
1891	1,442	3,007	4,449	1,922	2,801	4,723	1,368	363	593	15,276
1892	1,451	3,080	4,531	1,970	2,858	4,828	1,113	364	606	15,336
1893	1,441	3,023	4,464	1,822	2,599	4,421	1,152	368	614	16,097
1894	1,447	2,945	4,392	1,686	2,419	4,105	1,389	376	623	16,181
1895	1,434	2,924	4,358	1,603	2,310	3,913	1,338	387	630	16,370
1896	1,430	2,978	4,408	1,656	2,425	4,081	1,405	388	629	17,538
1897	1,435	3,030	4,465	1,703	2,454	4,158	1,327	386	610	17,777
1898	1,431	3,056	4,487	1,746	2,542	4,288	1,254	382	591	17,687
1899	1,444	3,063	4,507	1,785	2,580	4,365	1,363	379	580	18,234
1900	1,458	3,151	4,609	1,798	2,589	4,387	1,269	370	567	18,547
1901	1,482	3,191	4,673	1,692(*b*)	2,687(*b*)	4,379	1,219	355	565	18,811
1902	1,511	3,271	4,782	1,653	2,563	4,216	1,328	358	580	18,504
1903	1,495	3,169	4,664	1,576	2,369	3,945	1,384	365	596	18,154
1904	1,498	3,179	4,677	1,525	2,303	3,828	1,315	369	605	18,257
1905	1,487	3,158	4,645	1,506	2,243	3,749	1,164	373	609	18,549
1906	1,496	3,143	4,639	1,480	2,235	3,715	1,244	371	604	18,977 (*c*)
1907	1,561	3,115	4,676	1,522	2,295	3,817	1,317	366	596	24,327
1908	1,587	3,205	4,792	1,635	2,443	4,126	1,218	375	605	24,031
1909	1,549	3,151	4,700	1,638	2,446	4,133	1,149	373	599	24,105
1910	1,558	3,131	4,689	1,581	2,351	3,980	1,200	377	613	24,339
1911	1,566	3,146	4,712	1,523	2,334	3,907	1,415	382	616	25,448
1912	1,599	3,249	4,848	1,515	2,265	3,829	1,324	382	618	25,526
1913	1,606	3,327	4,933	1,412	2,165	3,621	1,060	388	614	25,701
1914	1,639	3,413	5,052	1,408	2,146	3,601	1,306	394	619	26,919
1915	1,593	3,251	4,844	1,432	2,123	3,600	1,205	360	561	26,089
1916	1,611	3,359	4,970	1,504	2,213	3,764	1,290	382	599	26,473
1917	1,592	3,317	4,909	1,511	2,185	3,744	947	390	598	22,245
1918	1,557	3,306	4,863	1,449	2,178	3,627	974	414	619	24,424
1919	1,562	3,467	5,029	1,407	2,061	3,513	978	408	625	...
1920	1,578	3,445	5,023	1,424	2,114	3,586	982	400	624	...
1921	1,631	3,566	5,197	1,138	2,570	3,708	977	425	...	...
1922	1,633	3,523	5,157	1,325	2,242	3,567	1,037	433	...	...

B. Northern Ireland 1923–80

(in thousands)

	Cattle			Sheep				Horses		
	Cows and Heifers	Other Cattle	Total	Ewes for Breeding	Other Sheep	Total	Pigs	for Agricultural Purposes	Total	Poultry
1923	280	469	748	206	258	464	196	100	122	6,682
1924	271	465	736	226	284	509	140	96	117	6,614
1925	250	417	667	216	268	484	112	93	112	6,733
1926	260	407	666	234	295	529	158	91	109	7,916
1927	271	426	697	264	336	600	236	89	107	7,897
1928	275	464	738	277	347	624	229	87	105	7,980
1929	264	436	700	289	364	654	192	86	104	8,309
1930	256	417	673	310	394	703	216	87	104	8,808
1931	260	421	681	349	445	794	236	86	103	8,691
1932	268	447	715	355	437	792	220	87	104	9,371

See p. 209 for footnotes.

B. Northern Ireland 1923–80 (*cont.*)

(in thousands)

	Cattle			Sheep				Horses		
	Cows and Heifers	Other Cattle	Total	Ewes for Breeding	Other Sheep	Total	Pigs	for Agricultural Purposes	Total	Poultry
1933	271	464	734	335	415	750	271	86	102	10,150
1934	283	486	769	350	412	761	380	85	101	10,292
1935	279	520	799	367	451	818	458	83	100	10,085
1936	275	495	770	382	454	835	522	81	99	10,570
1937	270	460	730	377	453	829	570	81	98	10,182
1938	259	473	732	402	491	893	561	80	99	10,193
1939	270	483	753	403	492	895	627	76	97	10,220
1940	259	473	732	379	476	854	475	77	97	9,122
1941	281	506	787	364	448	812	351	80	97	12,933
1942	316	511	827	332	410	742	271	80	95	14,601
1943	325	507	832	301	382	683	257	77	90	15,430
1944	339	546	886	300	371	672	237	75	88	16,646
1945	347	573	919	295	359	654	249	72	85	17,471
1946	356	557	913	324	316	640	312	65	77	19,841
1947	373	561	934	278	249	527	334	65	75	21,029
1948	383	583	966	290	285	575	335	60	68	24,234
1949	375	604	980	321	324	645	458	54	61	24,242
1950	364	626	990	346	371	717	523	49	55	20,724
1951	331	630	961	335	337	672	585	40	45	17,838
1952	314	627	941	372	423	795	676	35	40	16,456
1953	302	634	936	398	496	895	759	33	37	14,608
1954	305	637	942	425	505	930	820	30	...	11,386
1955	288	616	904	437	433	870	686	28	...	11,272
1956	299	619	918	451	423	873	653	24	...	11,536
1957	309	663	972	472	457	929	742	21	...	11,737
1958	303	678	980	504	476	980	790	19	...	12,250
1959	298	666	964	514	497	1,011	848	16	...	11,886
1960	331	667	998	561	538	1,099	985	13	...	10,393
1961	357	718	1,075	586	597	1,183	1,033	11	...	10,214
1962	370	739	1,109	597	612	1,209	1,182	8.6 ----(d) 7·9	...	9,595
1963	372	738	1,110	537	603	1,140	1,190	6·5	...	9,283
1964	374	737	1,112	520	574	1,094	1,152	5·3	...	10,557
1965	391	724	1,115	518	557	1,074	1,248	4·1	...	10,394
1966	413	776	1,189	516	538	1,054	1,057	3·9	...	10,864
1967	430	806	1,235	501	510	1,012	975	2·6	...	11,944
1968	433	773	1,207	398	564	961	1,012	1·8	...	12,059
1969	453	790	1,243	390	545	935	1,033	1·8	...	12,942
1970	494	825	1,320	398	569	966	1,069	1·0	6·2	13,966
1971	531	852	1,384	395	581	975	1,157	0·9	6·9	14,664
1972	589	855	1,444	408	596	1,004	1,047	0·8	8·1	14,870
1973	641	895	1,536	397	567	964	1,015	0·6	8·3	12,693
1974	655	964	1,620	393	543	937	839	0·5	8·1	11,818
1975	639	986	1,626	397	537	934	645	0·5	8·3	12,056
1976	619	928	1,548	401	525	926	698	0·5	8·9	12,109
1977	619	946	1,565	402	549	951	625	0·5	8·8	11,070
1978	600	948	1,548	412	562	974	683	0·5	9·3	11,936
1979	593	947	1,541	423	577	1,000	722	0·5	9·4	11,884
1980	574	934	1,507	448	613	1,061	691	...	...	11,389

See p. 209 for footnotes.

Agriculture 7. *continued*

C. Republic of Ireland 1923–80

(in thousands)

	Cattle			Sheep					
	Cows and Heifers	Other Cattle	Total	Ewes for Breeding	Other Sheep	Total	Pigs	Horses	Poultry
1923	1,377	2,900	4,278	1,182	1,484	2,666	1,286	473	17,278
1924	1,365	2,903	4,268	1,236	1,489	2,726	987	460	16,982
1925	1,264	2,727	3,991	1,224	1,589	2,813	732	434	17,279
1926	1,282	2,664	3,947	1,284	1,719	3,003	884	424	21,367
1927	1,331	2,716	4,047	1,344	1,776	3,120	1,178	429	21,584
1928	1,314	2,810	4,125	1,392	1,871	3,263	1,183	433	21,714
1929	1,307	2,830	4,137	1,423	1,953	3,375	945	436	22,089
1930	1,311	2,727	4,038	1,490	2,025	3,515	1,052	448	22,900
1931	1,300	2,729	4,029	1,507	2,068	3,575	1,227	450	22,782
1932	1,298	2,727	4,025	1,500	1,961	3,461	1,108	446	22,536
1933	1,338	2,798	4,137	1,459	1,946	3,405	931	441	22,505
1934	1,384	2,702	4,086	1,310	1,620	2,931	968	429	19,984
1935	1,400	2,619	4,019	1,309	1,733	3,042	1,088	420	19,485
1936	1,411	2,603	4,014	1,320	1,741	3,062	1,017	424	20,312
1937	1,362	2,593	3,955	1,286	1,713	3,000	934	429	19,491
1938	1,346	2,710	4,056	1,321	1,875	3,197	959	442	19,630
1939	1,344	2,713	4,057	1,298	1,750	3,048	931	445	19,551
1940	1,314	2,709	4,023	1,300	1,770	3,071	1,049	459	19,975
1941	1,309	2,841	4,150	1,232	1,678	2,909	764	459	17,393
1942	1,300	2,784	4,084	1,121	1,572	2,693	519	452	17,365
1943	1,305	2,831	4,136	1,043	1,418	2,560	434	454	17,097
1944	1,325	2,920	4,246	1,079	1,584	2,663	380	459	18,330
1945	1,318	2,892	4,211	1,058	1,523	2,581	426	465	18,314
1946	1,309	2,838	4,146	1,001	1,422	2,423	479	452	18,276
1947	1,240	2,710	3,950	903	1,191	2,094	457	438	17,304
1948	1,262	2,659	3,921	877	1,181	2,058	457	421	20,044
1949	1,299	2,827	4,127	909	1,283	2,192	675	402	21,495
1950	1,322	2,999	4,322	990	1,395	2,385	645	391	20,908
1951	1,269	3,107	4,376	1,080	1,536	2,615	558	367	18,734
1952	1,248	3,061	4,309	1,164	1,592	2,857	719	342	19,297
1953	1,273	3,123	4,397	1,209	1,721	2,930	882	329	19,046
1954	1,303	3,201	4,504	1,281	1,832	3,113	958	313	16,062
1955	1,285	3,198	4,483	1,356	1,912	3,269	799	296	16,076
1956	1,296	3,240	4,537	1,446	1,993	3,439	747	276	16,362
1957	1,351	3,066	4,417	1,575	2,145	3,720	900	258	14,502
1958	1,391	3,076	4,606	1,772	2,402	4,174	948	244	14,078
1959	1,409	3,074	4,684	1,864	2,548	4,412	852	234	13,904
1960	1,405	3,335	4,741	1,837	2,477	4,314	951	224	13,047
1961	1,418	3,296	4,713	1,927	2,601	4,528	1,056	207	12,843
1962	1,451	3,290	4,742	2,041	2,629	4,671	1,111	196	11,870
1963	1,482	3,378	4,860	2,085	2,605	4,691	1,102	190	11,888
1964	1,602	3,360	4,962	2,200	2,749	4,950	1,108	180	11,627
1965	1,741	3,619	5,359	2,197	2,816	5,014	1,266	172	11,405
1966	1,748	3,842	5,590	2,084	2,580	4,664	1,014	158	10,793
1967	1,745	3,840	5,586	1,936	2,303	4,239	985	143	10,593
1968	1,790	3,782	5,572	1,882	2,195	4,077	1,063	134	10,492
1969	1,836	3,852	5,688	1,853	2,153	4,006	1,116	125	10,335
1970	1,909	4,047	5,956	1,844	2,239	4,082	1,192	124	11,231
1971	2,025	4,152	6,177	1,879	2,285	4,163	1,323	117	11,777
1972	2,177	4,359	6,527	1,855	2,353	4,208	1,199	112	11,734

C. Republic of Ireland 1923–80 (*cont.*)

(in thousands)

	Cattle			Sheep					
	Cows and Heifers	Other Cattle	Total	Ewes for Breeding	Other Sheep	Total	Pigs	Horses	Poultry
1973	2,401	4,712	7,113	1,845	2,339	4,184	1,108	103	11,339
1974	2,435	4,979	7,413	1,768	2,193	3,962	923	98	10,707
1975	2,336	4,832	7,168	1,688	1,995	3,683	796	89	9,536
1976	2,285	4,669	6,954	1,603	1,872	3,475	925	83	9,532
1977	2,317	4,808	7,124	1,614	1,920	3,534	939	80	9,336
1978	...	...	7,125	...	...	3,385	1,056	76	9,557
1979	...	...	7,178	...	...	3,376	1,154	78	9,358
1980	2,308	4,600	6,909	1,547	1,744	3,292	1,030	68	9,903

(*a*) To 1920, this column covers all horses in the country, not solely those on agricultural holdings.
(*b*) From 1901, only ewes kept for breeding purposes were included under the heading *Ewes*.
(*c*) From 1907, much better returns were obtained of young birds.
(*d*) Subsequently excluding unbroken horses.

Agriculture 8. Production of Meat – United Kingdom 1901–80 and Republic of Ireland 1935–80

NOTES

[1] Sources: U.K. to 1921 (1st line) – Report of the Royal Commission on Food Prices (*S.P.* 1924–5 XIII), Annex IV; U.K. 1921 (2nd line) to 1938 (1st line) – based on L.C.E.S. *Bulletin*; U.K. 1938 (2nd line) to 1980 – Abstract; Republic of Ireland – *Statistical Abstract of Ireland*.

[2] The *Statistical Year Book of the League of Nations* for 1938/9 and 1939/40 gives the following figures for meat production; converted to thousands of Imperial tons:

	G.B.		G.B.	Republic of Ireland
1929	1,202	1933	1,254	...
1930	1,136	1934	1,296	156
1931	1,139	1935	1,361	161
1932	1,197	1936	1,380	154
		1937	1,339	147
		1938	...	150

[3] Except as indicated in the headings, the statistics relate to meat from home-fed cattle, sheep, and pigs, but with meat from Irish livestock shipped to the U.K. excluded from 1946 (2nd line).

(in thousand tons)

	U.K.(*a*)		U.K.	Republic of Ireland(*e*)		U.K.	U.K. Poultry	Republic of Ireland
1901	1,452	1928	1,125	...	1955	1,370	...	180
1902	1,473	1929	1,147	...	1956	1,493	...	167
1903	1,425	1930	1,077	...	1957	1,533	...	199
1904	1,452	1931	1,019	...	1958	1,556	...	215
1905	1,474	1932	1,072	...	1959	1,523	...	220
1906	1,439	1933	1,125	...	1960	1,613	...	243
1907	1,420	1934	1,193	...	1961	1,753	328	284
1908	1,425	1935	1,214	156	1962	1,810	345	280
1909	1,521	1936	1,304	160	1963	1,852	352	288
1910	1,482	1937	1,271	154	1964	1,827	366	276
1911	1,442	1938	1,211 ----(*c*) 1,145	146	1965	1,842	398	292
1912	1,572	1939	1,180	152	1966	1,883	432	305
1913	1,516	1940	1,072	163	1967	1,874	452	371
1914	1,355	1941	902	190	1968	1,859	519	354
1915	1,537	1942	772	176	1969	1,798	550	380
1916	1,440	1943	754	143	1970	1,911	583	394
1917	1,497	1944	783	141 ---(*e*)	1971	1,958	579	430
1918	1,289	1945	812	...	1972	1,889	650	404
1919	1,147	1946	847 ----(*d*) 838	159	1973	1,876	654	388
1920	1,225	1947	721	150	1974	2,139	642	510
1921	1,169 ----(*a*)(*b*) 869	1948	723	133	1975	2,180	642	556
1922	925	1949	794	138	1976	2,036	684	481
1923	946	1950	941	144	1977	1,986	706	543
1924	993	1951	974	151	1978	2,002	716	558
1925	1,137	1952	1,030	174	1979	2,091	739	570
1926	1,040	1953	1,127	187	1980	2,191	742	634
1927	1,013	1954	1,463	212				

(*a*) Years ending 31 May to 1921 (1st line).
(*b*) Subsequently excluding Southern Ireland.
(*c*) This break occurs on a change of source. See note 1 above.
(*d*) See note 3 above.
(*e*) Years ending 31 May to 1944.

Agriculture 9. Production of Dairy Produce – United Kingdom 1900–80 and Republic of Ireland 1926–80

NOTES

[1] SOURCES: U.K. to 1937 – L.C.E.S., *Key Statistics* (estimates to 1924 being based on E. M. Ojala, *Agriculture and Economic Progress* (London, 1952) and including Southern Ireland); U.K. 1937–80 – Abstract; Republic of Ireland – *Statistical Abstract of Ireland*.

[2] Data relate to cows' milk only and do not include milk fed to livestock.

	(milk in million gallons)					(in thousands of tons)				
	Liquid Milk for Consumption		Milk for Factory Production		Milk Used in Farm Butter	Creamery Butter		Farm Butter	Margarine	Cheese
	U.K.(*b*)	Ireland(*c*)	U.K.	Ireland(*c*)	Ireland(*c*)	U.K.	Ireland	Ireland(*c*)	U.K.	U.K.
1900	1,605	...	(*a*)	...	...	...	...	...	...	...
1901	1,608	...	(*a*)	...	...	...	...	...	...	...
1902	1,594	...	(*a*)	...	...	...	...	...	...	...
1903	1,599	...	(*a*)	...	...	...	...	...	...	...
1904	1,719	...	(*a*)	...	...	...	...	...	...	...
1905	1,733	...	(*a*)	...	...	...	...	...	...	...
1906	1,736	...	(*a*)	...	...	...	...	...	...	...
1907	1,727	...	(*a*)	...	...	...	...	...	...	...
1908	1,743	...	(*a*)	...	...	...	...	...	...	...
1909	1,746	...	(*a*)	...	...	...	...	...	...	...
1910	1,790	...	(*a*)	...	...	...	...	...	...	...
1911	1,805	...	(*a*)	...	...	...	...	...	...	...
1912	1,813	...	(*a*)	...	...	...	...	...	...	...
1913	1,816	...	(*a*)	...	...	...	...	...	...	...
1914	1,859	...	(*a*)	...	...	...	...	...	...	...
1915	1,861	...	(*a*)	...	...	...	...	...	...	...
1916	1,862	...	(*a*)	...	...	...	...	...	...	...
1917	1,862	...	(*a*)	...	...	...	...	...	...	...
1918	1,899	...	(*a*)	...	...	...	...	...	...	...
1919	1,892	...	(*a*)	...	...	...	...	...	...	...
1920	1,807	...	(*a*)	...	...	...	...	...	...	...
1921	1,894	...	(*a*)	...	...	...	...	...	...	...
1922	1,907	...	(*a*)	...	...	...	...	...	...	...
1923	1,928	...	(*a*)	...	...	...	...	...	...	...
1924	1,965	...	(*a*)	...	...	...	...	...	...	...
	---- (*b*)									
1925	1,152	...	(*a*)	...	...	...	...	...	...	...
1926	1,186	82	(*a*)	168	191	...	...	...	...	...
1927	1,212	...	(*a*)	...	...	...	...	...	...	...
1928	1,224	...	(*a*)	...	...	...	33	...	...	...
1929	1,235	82	(*a*)	197	170	...	35	...	...	...
1930	1,255	...	(*a*)	...	...	7	35	...	202	57
1931	1,249	...	(*a*)	...	...	...	31	...	...	...
1932	1,248	...	(*a*)	...	...	...	31	...	...	...
1933	1,255	...	(*a*)	...	...	...	34	...	173	...
1934	1,255	88	(*a*)	217	138	12	38	...	165	50
1935	1,277	88	(*a*)	224	133	21	41	...	176	57
1936	1,331	88	(*a*)	220	127	27	42	...	180	55
1937	1,336 ---- (*d*) 802	92	(*a*) --- (*d*) 358	202	135	19	38	22	184	38
1938	860	92	389	197	135	20	38	22	208	43
1939	863	92	436	203	143	21	36	24	226	43

See p. 212 for footnotes.

Agriculture 9. *continued*

	(milk in million gallons)							(in thousands of tons)		
	Liquid Milk for Consumption		Milk for Factory Production		Milk Used in Farm Butter	Creamery Butter		Farm Butter	Margarine	Cheese
	U.K.(*b*)	Ireland(*c*)	U.K.	Ireland(*c*)	Ireland(*c*)	U.K.	Ireland	Ireland(*c*)	U.K.	U.K.
1940	937	91	290	187	131	16	33	22	359	32
1941	1,064	95	159	188	136	8	33	23	419	30
1942	1,114	95	155	182	130	10	31	22	406	20
1943	1,169	96	175	180	139	9	30	23	392	22
1944	1,205	97	173	173	145	10	29	24	399	18
		--- (*c*)		--- (*c*)	--- (*c*)			--- (*c*)		
1945	1,243	99	181	181	141	8	30	24	406	22
1946	1,304	97	190	166	141	11	28	24	330	25
1947	1,305	98	145	157	124	7	26	21	353	13
1948	1,417	102	201	170	122	8	29	21	407	27
1949	1,514	102	221	209	116	11	34	20	420	33
1950	1,557	107	326	230	108	16	37	18	372	55
1951	1,567	106	223	214	96	6	33	16	447	44
1952	1,545	104	271	212	96	6	33	16	445	55
1953	1,518	113	419	233	80	13	35	14	406	88
1954	1,515	119	463	241	79	20	39	13	360	82
1955	1,516	122	427	236	78	15	38	13	366	63
1956	1,521	122	609	263	77	27	43	13	365	99
1957	1,504	124	697	290	75	36	49	13	351	114
1958	1,518	123	624	276	74	31	47	13	329	95
1959	1,537	125	531	245	73	15	39	12	358	87
1960	1,559	127	724	281	72	40	46	12	368	109
1961	1,583	129	805	305	69	51	49	12	330	112
1962	1,606	130	853	324	70	60	49	12	330	112
1963	1,621	130	766	336	59	43	50	10	337	104
1964	1,641	131	698	362	50	23	55	9	340	109
1965	1,643	133	794	391	38	36	58	7	314	113
1966	1,651	133	762	413	34	30	60	6	311	107
1967	1,660	134	838	467	29	37	67	5	304	120
1968	1,653	133	912	516	23	51	73	4	298	118
1969	1,647	133	947	521	17	56	73	3	313	122
1970	1,641	134	1,005	509	14	63	70	2	309	132
1971	1,622	135	1,098	527	12	65	72	2	339	160
1972	1,629	137	1,278	561	11	93	74	2	362	181
1973	1,655	137	1,308	574	9	95	82	1	336	179
1974	1,693	136	1,188	569	7	53	71	1	294	215
1975	1,729	137	1,159	624	6	47	83	1	293	231
1976	1,707	139	1,289	680	5	88	97	1	337	201
1977	1,646	139	1,522	744	4	132	100	1	373	203
1978	1,624	139	1,697	860	3	161	117	...	362	213
1979	1,607	141	1,718	878	2	158	120	...	353	230
1980	1,583	142	1,757	863	2	167	109	...	377	234

(*a*) Included in liquid milk for consumption.
(*b*) See note 1 above.
(*c*) Data to 1944 are for years beginning 1 June.
(*d*) Subsequent statistics relate to sales.

Agriculture 10. Landings of Fish – Great Britain 1887–1980, Ireland 1888–1980

NOTES

[1] SOURCES: *Abstract* and *Statistical Abstract of Ireland*.

[2] Shellfish are not included until 1957 (2nd line) for Britain and 1971 (2nd line) for the Republic of Ireland. Ireland fish landings are not included throughout.

(thousand tons)

	G.B.	Ireland
1887	553	...
1888	549	34
1889	602	40
1890	598	40
1891	570	31
1892	596	30
1893	639	39
1894	661	42
1895	669	40
1896	635	51
1897	647	48
1898	732	60
1899	688	60
1900	698	35
1901	752	41
1902	867	32
1903	886	42
1904	966	48
1905	958	50
1906	989	38
1907	1,150	35
1908	1,096	37
1909	1,069	50
1910	1,081	50
1911	1,197	49
1912	1,160	45
1913	1,199	34
1914	878	30
1915	405	28
1916	383	28
1917	357	33
1918	400	38

	G.B.	Northern Ireland	Republic of Ireland
1919	814	40	
1920	1,046	34	
1921	819	24	
1922	888	21	
1923	847	2·3	13
1924	1,042	2·8	16
1925	963	5·0	24
1926	948	7·1	28
1927	1,000	4·8	32
1928	1,002	3·4	23
1929	1,053	3·1	16
1930	1,094	2·6	12
1931	989	2·9	11
1932	975	2·3	7·7
1933	935	2·7	7·8
1934	931	1·4	6·2
1935	993	3·0	8·2
1936	1,044	3·0	8·3
1937	1,087		9·2
1938	1,046		8·6
1939	785	3·3	9·4
1940	314		11
1941	245		14
1942	305		13
1943	309		14
1944	324		15
1945	492		19
1946	900		16
1947	994		16
1948	1,042		19
1949	1,002	5·9	12

(1919–1922: figures for Northern Ireland and Republic of Ireland combined.)

	G.B.	Northern Ireland	Republic of Ireland
1950	883	4·0	11
1951	944	5·2	9·4
1952	990	5·3	10
1953	980	5·7	11
1954	932	6·7	13
1955	953	7·1	15
1956	928	5·2	19
1957	865 ... (a) 886	7·1	27
1958	881	8·7	27
1959	875	9·2	30
1960	823	6·8	34
1961	767	6·1	26
1962	807	7·4	22
1963	831	5·8	20
1964	836	7·5	24
1965	902	8·4	28
1966	928	5·1	31
1967	881	7·0	42
1968	889	6·3	42
1969	930	5·7	54
1970	948	8·3	65
1971	949	7·8	60 ... (a) 69
1972	927	8·2	85
1973	982	11	84
1974	939	12	83
1975	842	9·6	75
1976	903	11	79
1977	890	8·1	81
1978	930	6·7	92
1979	814	7·9	84
1980	736	10	133

(a) See note 2 above.

Agriculture 11. Index of Output at Constant Factor Cost – United Kingdom 1855–1965

NOTES

[1] SOURCE: C. H. Feinstein, *National Income, Expenditure and Output of the U.K., 1855–1965* (Cambridge, 1972), Appendix table 8.

[2] The index actually covers forestry and fishing, as well as agriculture.

[3] An index of eighteenth-century agricultural output was given in Phyllis Deane & W. A. Cole, *British Economic Growth, 1688–1959* (Cambridge, 1962), p. 78, but this has been criticised cogently by N. F. R. Crafts, *British Economic Growth during the Industrial Revolution*, pp. 38 *et seq*. Crafts gives the following estimates of the rate of growth of agricultural output in that period (in per cent per year):

1700–60	0·60
1760–80	0·13
1780–1801	0·75

[4] An index for the output at constant prices of agriculture, forestry and fishing in the first half of the nineteenth century may be constructed from Deane and Cole, *op. cit.*, p. 166 and the Rousseaux price index for agricultural products (see below, pp. 722–4). It is as follows, on the base 1861 = 100:

1801	35	1821	59	1841	75
1811	62	1831	62	1851	112

1913 = 100

1855	99·3	1878	102·9	1900	95·8	1922	73·7	1944	...
1856	99·3	1879	82·8	1901	97·2	1923	74·9	1945	...
1857	100·0	1880	100·0	1902	100·7	1924	72·6	1946	94·9
1858	100·0	1881	100·0	1903	92·2	1925	78·2	1947	91·0
1859	100·7	1882	95·0	1904	97·2	1926	80·5	1948	97·9
1860	100·7	1883	101·5	1905	98·7	1927	80·7	1949	105·2
1861	101·5	1884	103·6	1906	92·2	1928	85·4	1950	107·7
1862	101·5	1885	100·7	1907	100·0	1929	85·6	1951	110·1
1863	102·1	1886	104·3	1908	102·9	1930	87·7	1952	112·6
1864	102·1	1887	97·9	1909	105·0	1931	79·9	1953	115·0
1865	102·9	1888	100·0	1910	103·6	1932	83·7	1954	117·4
1866	103·6	1889	102·1	1911	101·5	1933	89·7	1955	116·2
1867	100·7	1890	103·6	1912	100·0	1934	90·8	1956	122·4
1868	107·8	1891	106·4	1913	100·0	1935	88·5	1957	124·8
1869	103·6	1892	102·9	1914	...	1936	87·1	1958	122·4
1870	107·2	1893	98·7	1915	...	1937	86·7	1959	127·2
1871	104·3	1894	100·7	1916	...	1938	85·7	1960	135·8
1872	99·3	1895	99·3	1917	...	1939	...	1961	135·8
1873	102·1	1896	99·3	1918	...	1940	...	1962	140·7
1874	110·0	1897	96·4	1919	...	1941	...	1963	145·5
1875	110·7	1898	100·7	1920	93·0 ---- (a) 71·5	1942	...	1964	154·1
1876	104·3	1899	97·9	1921	72·8	1943	...	1965	157·9
1877	95·0								

(a) Subsequently excluding Southern Ireland.

Agriculture 12. Inputs and Outputs of Agriculture – United Kingdom 1867/9 to 1980

NOTES

[1] SOURCES: Part A – E. M. Ojala, *Agriculture and Economic Progress* (London, 1952); Part B – *A Century of Agricultural Statistics: Great Britain 1866–1966* (London, 1968) and *Abstract*; Part C – *Abstract*.

[2] Statistics in Parts A and B relate to crop-years ending 31 May.

[3] The basis of estimating inputs and income to 1968/9 is the assumption that the notional farm was wholly tenanted, hence labour, rent and interest, and depreciation of machinery are counted as part of total expenses. From 1969, the assumption is that the notional farm is wholly owner-occupied, hence labour, depreciation, and rent and interest are not counted as part of total expenses. From the last date farm net income, which had previously been total revenue less expenses, became the income of farmers and their wives after providing for depreciation, interest, and net rent.

A. 1867–9 to 1935–9 (*a*)

(in £ million)

	Crops	Livestock	Livestock Products	Total Gross Revenue	Feeding-stuffs	Fertilisers	Imported Livestock	Seeds	Machinery	Total Expenses (*b*)	Agricultural Incomes (*c*)
1867–9	104·17	80·96	44·70	229·83	25·1	5·9	3·7	3·1	1·5	52·6	194
1870–6	94·99	100·17	52·02	247·18	33·2	7·4	4·4	3·3	1·7	64·1	201
1877–85	75·99	95·20	48·01	219·20	35·9	4·8	4·9	3·0	1·4	61·5	174
1886–93	56·75	85·04	46·00	187·80	30·2	3·9	5·2	2·9	1·2	53·2	148
1894–1903	49·77	86·11	46·90	182·78	34·9	4·8	5·7	3·4	1·4	59·7	135
1904–10	50·68	91·71	58·36	200·75	38·3	5·7	5·6	3·4	1·6	65·7	149
1911–3	56·23	98·84	67·05	222·12	44·4	7·1	5·4	3·8	1·9	75·0	162
1920–2	126·97	190·32	172·68	489·97	81·0	18·5	11·2	8·4	12·4	157·0	377
1924–9	72·06	112·87	93·74	279·67	67·8	10·1	16·6	4·6	8·7	122·3	173
1930–4	59·93	91·93	84·61	236·46	53·3	8·4	14·5	3·7	6·8	96·9	159
1935–9	66·40	84·42	93·72	244·53	70·0	10·0	14·5	4·0	11·0	120·5	185

See p. 217 for footnotes.

Agriculture 12. *continued*

B. 1937/8 to 1965/6

(in £ million)

	Farm Crops	Horti-cultural Crops	Live-stock	Milk & its Products	Eggs	Other Products	Pro-duction Grants, etc.	Total Gross Revenue (d)	Feeding -stuffs	Ferti-lisers	Machinery: Depreci-ation	Machinery: Other	Labour	Rent & Interest	Total Expenses (b)	Farm Net Income
1937/8	43·5	34	96·5	80	31·5	10	5	306·5	78	8	7·5	16	66	43	250·5	56
1938/9	46·5	32	93	85	31	7·5	6	299·5	68·5	9·5	7·5	16	66	44	246·5	53
1939/40	52·5	43·5	107·5	91	43·5	9·5	8	376·5	66·5	12·5		28.5	72·5	45	266	110·5
1940/1	76	55	136	114	57·5	11·5	11·5	493	61	17		41.5	99·5	46	307·5	185·5
1941/2	118·5	84	99·5	129	48	10·5	14·5	537	41	22		50.5	120	47	332·5	204·5
1942/3	156	95	110·5	145·5	36·5	12·5	15·5	587	28·5	27		59.5	142	46	366·5	220·5
1943/4	175	102	105	156	35·5	15	17	629	31	30·5		65.5	154·5	46·5	396	233
1944/5	163	96·5	114·5	163	37·5	12·5	17·5	614	32	30		69.5	168	47	416	198
1945/6	158	97·5	128	175	45·5	21	16·5	656	42	30		75	179	47	443·5	212·5
1946/7	149	109	137·5	189	50·5	12·5	18·5	673	34	30·5		82	207	39·5	476·5	196·5
1947/8	147	123	142·5	208	62·5	13·5	21	762	43·5	36·5	26	71	222	51	530·5	231·5
1948/9	189·5	113	178	240·5	79	24	31	883	61·5	40·5	27	76	233	53·5	582	301
1949/50	175	115·5	213	272·5	103	19	36·5	978	113·5	46·5	32	84	234·5	57	661.5	316·5
1950/1	196·5	95·5	255·5	281·5	107·5	19·5	34	1,023·5	142·5	55·5	41·5	100	237·5	60·5	743	280·5
1951/2	199·5	111	312·5	297·5	117·5	33·5	38·5	1,159	177·5	54	48·5	113	248	64	820·5	338·5
1952/3	187	121·5	367	316	133·5	28	55	1,232	187	70	56	121·5	257	68	882·5	349·5
1953/4	255	114	396	335·5	129·5	26	64	1,348	276	73	58·5	121·5	266	71·5	1,001	347
1954/5	238	129	468	328	131·5	27	60·5	1,385·5	334	71·5	59	119·5	265·5	74·5	1,071·5	314
1955/6	253	142	425·5	339	143·5	30	74	1,448	324	91	61·5	125·5	275·5	77·5	1,097·5	350·5
1956/7	246·5	129·5	478·5	348·5	148·5	37·5	86	1,507	347·5	93·5	64·5	130·5	284·5	81·5	1,166	341
1957/8	264	148	504·0	345	159	43	92·5	1,566	327·5	102·5	70·5	134	293	86·5	1,189·5	376·5
1958/9	268	132·5	509·5	334	162·5	43	93·5	1,575	359	100	73	138	305	87·5	1,242	333·5
1959/60	265	145	500·5	340·5	164	51	113·5	1,617	355	118	78	137·5	300·5	93·5	1,254·5	362·5
1960/1	277	141·5	503·5	349·5	170	54	119	1,654·5	354	111	76	132	299·5	95·5	1,262·5	392
1961/2	288	172·5	567·5	359·5	165	51	120·5	1,760·5	381·5	120·5	79·5	139·5	298	95	1,334·5	426
1962/3	335	163·5	591·5	360	171	50	117·5	1,812	404	108·5	80	139·5	307	117	1,364·5	447·5
1963/4	299	164	613·5	370·5	166·5	48	113·5	1,816	401	120	81	139	312·5	124·5	1,406·5	409·5
1964/5	338·5	181	632	397·5	167·5	52	112·5	1,934	444·5	122	84·5	140	307	135	1,457	477
1965/6	360·5	176	652·5	410·5	180	42	108·5	1,978	478	120	90	142	312·5	142·5	1,513·5	464·5

C. 1964/5 to 1980

(in £ million)

	Farm Crops	Horti-cultural Crops	Live-stock	Live-stock Products	Pro-duction Grants, etc.	Total Gross Output	Feeding -stuffs	Fertili-lisers	Machinery: Depreci-ation	Machinery: Other	Labour	Rent & Interest	Total Expen-diture	Farm Net Income
1964/5	364	212	652	585	125	1,979	465	122	96	136	314	69	1,016	462
1965/6	382	208	673	610	110	2,035	499	120	101	136	322	72	1,054	455
1966/7	401	219	678	612	120	2,074	463	132	110	137	322	77	1,047	479
1967/8	409	231	725	636	148	2,196	499	144	112	145	324	83	1,124	520
1968/9	388	253	747	655	129	2,237	513	150	121	154	333	88	1,174	481
	----(e)	----(e)	----(e)	----(e)	----(e)	----(e)	----(e)	----(e)	----(e)	----(e)	----(e)	----(e)	----(e)	----(e)
1969	419	289	778	685	123	2,317	527	148	129	154	338	[49](f)	1,173	[582](g)
1970	463	286	878	712	128	2,475	596	172	144	164	349	79	1,299	605
1971	451	305	957	788	143	2,713	620	173	159	187	394	77	1,384	636
1972	480	348	1,083	828	143	2,949	661	203	180	199	437	82	1,508	682
1973	726	416	1,385	1,022	121	3,774	977	213	200	224	510	113	1,909	952
1974	890	506	1,543	1,184	129	4,278	1,157	296	261	278	616	144	2,329	803
1975	1,115	570	1,918	1,388	192	5,013	1,180	325	350	330	758	148	2,578	1,004
1976	1,464	641	2,202	1,692	151	6,133	1,567	376	422	380	882	171	3,189	1,293
1977	1,387	768	2,476	1,940	124	6,890	1,827	426	511	453	981	195	3,717	1,269
1978	1,525	753	2,754	2,065	121	7,298	1,774	490	581	493	1,100	245	3,858	1,252
1979	1,895	858	3,043	2,276	113	8,181	2,089	548	658	593	1,257	389	4,462	1,141
1980	2,126	902	3,288	2,500	163	8,996	2,188	651	716	668	1,445	540	4,840	1,027

(a) Southern Ireland is excluded from 1923.
(b) Includes miscellaneous expenses not shown separately, but does not include rates and land tax.
(c) Includes allowances for the retail value of food consumed on farms.
(d) Includes the increase in value at cost of farm stocks and work in progress.
(e) The size of holding covered was subsequently lowered, and the changes referred to in note 3 above occurred.
(f) Interest only.
(g) Net rent was not excluded.

Agriculture 13. Inputs and Outputs of Agriculture – Republic of Ireland 1926/7 to 1980

NOTES
[1] SOURCE: *Statistical Abstract of Ireland*.
[2] Statistics to 1944/5 relate to years ending 31 May for livestock and its products, 30 June for potatoes, and 30 September for other crops.

(in £ million)

	Crops	Livestock	Livestock Products	Turf	Total Gross Output (*a*)	Total Inputs
1926/7	7·7	27·3	19·3	3·3	57·8	8·5
1929/30	6·5	30·5	20·9	3·3	61·4	9·9
1934/5	7·6	14·8	13·5	2·8	38·8	6·7
1935/6	8·4	16·3	14·1	3·1	42·0	6·3
1936/7	9·6	18·7	14·6	3·4	46·4	6·8
1937/8	8·7	20·0	16·2	3·5	48·4	7·8
1938/9	9·2	23·1	16·2	3·7	52·2 ----(*a*) 51·9	8·7
1939/40	10·1	28·0	18·1	3·8	60·5	9·4
1940/1	14·0	28·2	20·3	5·3	69·1	12·9
1941/2	15·9	30·4	22·0	7·6	74·2	5·6
1942/3	20·3	33·4	24·4	8·2	87·3	2·6
1943/4	23·3	34·9	27·9	8·7	98·2	4·7
1944/5	23·8	36·1	30·4	8·6	99·2	5·2
1945	25·7	39·1	31·3	8·5	104·9	5·2
1946	23·2	41·4	30·6	8·1	101·1	8·8
1947	22·7	45·6	34·7	9·0	104·4	11·9
1948	26·5	47·5	39·2	7·0	121·5	16·2
1949	26·8	53·2	41·2	7·2	133·0	18·5
1950	25·9	57·4	45·7	5·9	132·5	22·4
1951	26·8	64·0	47·6	8·2	142·5	23·6
1952	27·8	74·8	48·8	8·2	161·0	23·7
1953	34·0 ---- (*b*) 33·4	87·2 ---- (*b*) 77·2	55·3 ---- (*b*) 53·9	7·4	177·9	29·5
1954	33·4	86·7	52·4	5·2	174·4	33·0
1955	35·1	85·7	53·6	7·1	186·9	32·7
1956	35·2	78·5	54·5	7·3	175·1	32·3
1957	38·8	88·8	55·9	6·7	190·2	33·9
1958	32·7	88·2	52·2	4·9	181·5	35·8
1959	38·3	85·3	49·9	6·8	191·2	34·2
1960	37·2	92·8	55·6	5·9	193·1	32·3
1961	40·2	106·5	57·4	5·4	206·5	37·1
1962	43·5	100·2	59·6	5·7	213·1	41·2
1963	38·6	104·8	62·4	5·6	215·0	43·5
1964	39·4	117·7	68·2	5·1	240·2	45·5
1965	40·0	115·9	71·5	5·1	252·5	53·8
1966	40·8	120·9	75·8	5·0	248·9	53·8
1967	46·1	138·0	83·3	4·8	266·1	57·4
1968	54·6	149·8	89·8	5·0	303·9	66·8
1969	57·0	160·5	90·2	4·8	318·9	73·3
1970	60·8	173·1	91·6	5·0	344·2	81·6
1971	65·5	208·3	102·1	5·5	387·8	95·3
1972	67·7	243·7	124·2	5·8	487·7	102·1
1973	82·7	303·5	167·0	5·8	623·5	144·9
1974	93·5	355·1	190·5	7·3	648·7	175·2
1975	133·0	510·9	254·3	9·8	859·1	196·9
1976	160·2	526·3	312·3	10·1	1,023·1	262·5
1977	222·0	700·3	444·7	11·3	1,365·9	341·6
1978	222·2	831·4	541·5	11·5	1,593·1	451·4
1979	254·0	814·8	570·8	12·2	1,677·5	526·7
1980	250·3	960·8	567·9	14·2	1,667·3	502·8

(*a*) Including change in the value of livestock from 1938/9 (2nd line).

(*b*) There was a change in the basis of valuation.

Agriculture 14. Numbers of Agricultural Workers – Great Britain 1921–80, Republic of Ireland 1927–80

NOTES

[1] SOURCES: G.B. – *A Century of Agricultural Statistics: Great Britain 1866–1966* (London, 1968) and *Abstract*; Ireland – *Statistical Abstract of Ireland*.

[2] The Irish statistics relate to the numbers in farm work. Those for Britain exclude farmers, partners, directors and their wives.

(in thousands)

	Great Britain		Republic of Ireland		Great Britain		Republic of Ireland		Great Britain		Republic of Ireland
	Total	of which regular full-time	Males		Total	of which regular full-time	Males		Total	of which regular full-time	Males
1921	996	789	...	1941	759	602	556	1961	617	449	380
1922	...	...	...	1942	824	640	541	1962	589	430	361
1923	892	726	...	1943	843	644	536	1963	569	416	355
1924	924	745	...	1944	863	690	526	1964	544	389	344
1925	925	742	...	1945	887	712	522	1965	514	365	330
1926	921	757	...	1946	889	739	520	1966	488	342	320
1927	894	751	597	1947	891	739	508	1967	451	323	308
1928	890	751	603	1948	849	682	500	1968	418	303	299
1929	888	745	566	1949	855	685	482	1969	402	288	288
									---(a)	---(a)	
1930	857	729	562	1950	843	670	470	1970	395	251	274
1931	829	714	563	1951	812	642	453	1971	391	246	265
1932	809	694	559	1952	804	618	441	1972	381	238	258
										---(a)	
1933	828	692	551	1953	780	600	421	1973	385	233	251
1934	801	673	579	1954	755	583	421	1974	368	221	245
1935	787	665	574	1955	732	554	418	1975	354	211	242
1936	751	643	560	1956	700	528	409	1976	348	203	234
									---(a)	---(a)	
1937	742	631	555	1957	696	520	399	1977	350	194	227
1938	697	604	537	1958	679	503	395	1978	345	183	220
1939	711	601	531	1959	669	493	389	1979	330	179	212
1940	712	588	544	1960	645	473	383	1980	326	172	207

(a) There was an expansion of the workers covered in 1970, and changes in the definition of whole-time workers in 1970 and 1973. Changes were also probably brought about by changes in the wording of the census questions in 1977.

Agriculture 15. Farm Incomes – United Kingdom, 1855–1980

NOTE
SOURCES: Part A – C. H. Feinstein, *National Income, Expenditure and Output of the U.K., 1855–1965* (Cambridge, 1972), table 23; Part B – *Abstract*.

A.

(in £ million)

	Wages	Rent (*a*)	Farmers' Income (*b*)		Wages	Rent (*a*)	Farmers' Income (*b*)		Wages	Rent (*a*)	Farmers' Income (*b*)
1855	61	45	40	1886	54	49	24	1916	64	45	127
1856	60	47	42	1887	54	48	22	1917	78	46	155
1857	57	49	49	1888	54	48	23	1918	87	46	173
1858	56	49	41	1889	54	48	24	1919	122	47	176
1859	57	49	37	1890	55	48	30	1920	150 ---(*c*) 105	48 ---(*c*) 40	197 ---(*c*) 161
1860	56	49	37	1891	54	48	37	1921	106	41	124
1861	56	50	48	1892	54	47	29	1922	73	42	99
1862	56	50	49	1893	54	46	25	1923	65	42	78
1863	55	50	53	1894	54	45	22	1924	67	42	70
1864	55	50	43	1895	54	44	24	1925	71	42	61
1865	56	49	46	1896	54	43	27	1926	74	42	59
1866	56	50	50	1897	54	42	31	1927	74	41	43
1867	55	51	54	1898	54	41	28	1928	74	40	48
1868	55	52	49	1899	55	41	34	1929	73	40	49
1869	53	53	34	1900	56	41	33	1930	70	40	60
1870	57	53	46	1901	56	41	33	1931	67	39	47
1871	56	54	49	1902	56	42	40	1932	65	38	47
1872	62	55	44	1903	56	41	30	1933	64	36	69
1873	61	56	55	1904	56	41	30	1934	63	35	82
1874	61	56	47	1905	56	41	34	1935	65	34	75
1875	62	57	44	1906	57	42	40	1936	65	35	86
1876	61	57	43	1907	57	42	41	1937	64	35	61
1877	61	58	35	1908	56	43	46	1938	66	35	69
1878	60	56	30	1909	56	43	37	1939	70	35	104
1879	58	55	13	1910	57	43	35	1940	88	35	174
1880	58	53	21	1911	58	43	51	1941	111	35	218
1881	58	53	24	1912	59	43	46	1942	132	35	236
1882	57	55	29	1913	60	43	39	1943	149	35	251
1883	57	55	24	1914	62	44	67	1944	162	35	235
1884	56	53	24	1915	65	44	79	1945	175	35	227
1885	55	51	21					1946	197	35	233

(*a*) Gross rent of farm land excluding the payment for dwellings.
(*b*) Before providing for depreciation and stock appreciation.
(*c*) Subsequently excluding Southern Ireland.

B. Ministry of Agriculture series, Farming Income 1938–80 (*a*)

(in £ million)

1938	56	1947	196·5	1956	350·5	1965	477 ---(*b*) 462	1973	952
1939	53	1948	231·5	1957	341	1966	455 ---(*a*)	1974	803
1940	110·5	1949	301	1958	376·5	1967	479 ---(*b*) 509	1975	1,004
1941	185·5	1950	316·5	1959	333·5	1968	520	1976	1,293
1942	204·5	1951	280·5	1960	362·5	1969	481 ---(*b*) 582	1977	1,269
1943	220·5	1952	338·5	1961	392	1970	605	1978	1,252
1944	233	1953	349·5	1962	426	1971	636	1979	1,141
1945	198	1954	347	1963	447·5	1972	682	1980	1,027
1946	212·5	1955	314	1964	409·5				

(*a*) i.e. income of farmers and their wives net of stock appreciation and after charging depreciation, payment of interest, and net rent for tenants. Data to 1966 are for years ending May.
(*b*) These breaks results from changes in the basis of collection of data.

Agriculture 16. The Overseas Corn Trade – Great Britain 1697–1842

A. Trade in Wheat and Wheaten Flour, 1697–1842, Distinguishing Imports from Ireland from 1800

NOTE
SOURCE: *S.P.* 1843, LIII.

(in thousands of quarters)

	Imports	Exports
1697(*a*)	..	15
1698(*b*)	2	7
1699	..	1
1700	..	49
1701	..	98
1702	—	90
1703	..	107
1704	..	90
1705	—	96
1706	..	188
1707	—	174
1708	..	84
1709	2	72
1710	..	17
1711	—	81
1712	—	149
1713	—	180
1714	..	181
1715	—	173
1716	—	76
1717	—	26
1718	—	74
1719	..	131
1720	—	84
1721	—	83
1722	—	179
1723	—	158
1724	..	247
1725	..	211
1726	—	144
1727	—	31
1728	75	4
1729	40	19
1730	..	95
1731	..	131
1732	—	203
1733	..	427
1734	..	499
1735	..	155
1736	..	118
1737	..	466
1738	..	588
1739	..	285
1740	5	54
1741	8	45
1742	..	296
1743	..	376
1744	..	234
1745	..	325

	Imports	Exports
1746	—	131
1747	—	270
1748	..	545
1749	..	631
1750	..	950
1751	..	663
1752	—	430
1753	—	301
1754	..	357
1755	—	237
1756	..	103
1757	142	12
1758	20	9
1759	..	228
1760	..	394
1761	—	442
1762	..	295
1763	..	430
1764	..	397
1765	765	167
1766	11	165
1767	498	5
1768	349	7
1769	4	50
1770	..	75
1771	3	10
1772	25	7
1773	57	8
1774	289	16
1775	561	91
1776	21	211
1777	233	88
1778	106	141
1779	5	222
1780	4	224
1781	160	103
1782	81	145
1783	584	52
1784	217	89
1785	111	133
1786	51	205
1787	59	121
1788	149	83
1789	113	140
1790	223	31
1791	469	71
1792	22	300
1793	490	77
1794	328	155

	Imports	Imports from Ireland	Exports
1795	314	...	19
1796	879	...	25
1797	462	...	55
1798	397	...	60
1799	463	...	39
1800	1,265	1	22
1801	1,425	..	28
1802	648	109	149
1803	374	61	77
1804	461	70	63
1805	921	84	78
1806	310	102	30
1807	405	45	25
1808	85	43	98
1809	456	67	31
1810	1,567	126	76
1811	336	147	98
1812	291	158	46
1813	559	217	...
1814	853	225	111
1815	384	190	228
1816	332	122	122
1817	1,090	55	318
1818	1,694	105	59
1819	626	154	45
1820	996	403	95
1821	707	570	200
1822	511	463	160
1823	424	400	146
1824	442	356	62
1825	788	396	39
1826	897	314	20
1827	712	405	57
1828	1,410	653	76
1829	2,190	519	75
1830	2,206	530	37
1831	2,868	557	66
1832	1,254	790	290
1833	1,166	844	96
1834	981	780	159
1835	751	662	134
1836	861	599	257
1837	1,109	534	308
1838	1,923	543	159
1839	3,111	258	43
1840	2,527	174	87
1841	2,910	219	30
1842	3,111	202	68

(*a*) Year ended Michaelmas.

(*b*) Fifteen months ended 25th December. Subsequent figures are for years ended on that date.

B. Trade in Barley, Oats and Malt, 1697–1818

NOTE

SOURCES: 1697–1764 – C. Smith, *Three Tracts on the Corn Trade* (London, 1776); 1770–1800 – *S.P.* 1804, VII; 1801–4 – *S.P.* 1814–5, X; 1815 – *S.P.* 1816, XIV; 1816–17 – *S.P.* 1818 XIV; 1818 – *S.P.* 1819, XVI.

(in thousands of quarters)

	Barley		Oats		Malt
	Imports	Exports	Imports	Exports	Exports
Average of:					
1697–9	..(*a*)	21(*a*)	1(*a*)	...	37(*a*)
1700–4	—	33	..	...	77
1705–9	..	21	..	...	125
1710–14	..	22	..	...	170
1715–19	—	24	..	...	248
1720–4	..	22	12	...	301
1725–9	6	10	51	...	239
1730–4	1	30	25	...	191
1735–9	—	43	1	...	180
1740–4	3	20	17	...	180
1745–9	..	97	..	...	315
1750–4	—	96	11	...	294
1755–9	3	18	12	...	162
1760–4	2	62	71	...	231
1765–9	...	...	...	...	...
1770–4	28	3	218	18	42
1775–9	40	9	329	26	96
1780–4	28	33	166	17	86
1785–9	39	82	408	19	115
1790–4	97	11	787	16	20
1795–9	52	8	592	13	10
1800–4	57	32	566	14	5(*b*)
1805–9	28	8	687	20	...
1810–14	56	42(*b*)	524	30(*b*)	...
1815–18	248(*b*)	31(*b*)	1,125(*b*)	29(*b*)	...

(*a*) The period Michaelmas 1696 to 25th December 1698 has been counted as two years in computing the averages for 1697–9. All other figures are for years ended 25th December.

(*b*) Average of four years only. The malt statistics end in 1803 and the others in 1818, while the export statistics for 1813 were destroyed in the Customs House fire of that year.

C. Imports of Barley, Oats and Oatmeal from Ireland 1800–42

NOTE
SOURCE: *S.P.* 1843, LIII.

(in thousands of quarters)

	Barley and Bear	Oats and Oatmeal		Barley and Bear	Oats and Oatmeal
1800	..	2	1822	23	569
1801	—	..	1823	19	1,102
1802	7	341	1824	45	1,225
1803	13	266	1825	154	1,630
1804	3	240	1826	65	1,304
1805	16	203	1827	68	1,343
1806	3	357	1828	84	2,076
1807	23	390	1829	97	1,674
1808	31	580	1830	190	1,471
1809	17	846	1831	185	1,656
1810	8	493	1832	124	2,052
1811	3	276	1833	102	1,763
1812	43	391	1834	218	1,770
1813	64	691	1835	156	1,823
1814	17	564	1836	184	2,132
1815	27	598	1837	187	2,275
1816	62	684	1838	156	2,743
1817	27	611	1839	62	1,905
1818	25	1,069	1840	96	2,038
1819	20	790	1841	76	2,539
1820	87	916	1842	50	2,261
1821	83	1,162			

Agriculture 17. The Overseas Corn Trade – United Kingdom 1792–1980

NOTES

[1] SOURCES: Part A – *S.P.* 1849, L: Part B – *Annual Statement of Trade and Overseas Trade Statistics of the United Kingdom*.

[2] The proportion of meal included with barley was negligible, whilst that included with oats was not more than 5 per cent, and usually less.

[3] Conversion factors from bushels to hundredweights are not directly available for the period to 1839. The 1840 ratio for barley and oats can probably be used without much concern for earlier years, but the considerable and variable imports of wheaten flour make such a proceeding much less accurate for wheat.

A. Imports and Re-exports, 1792–1840

(in thousands of quarters)

	Wheat and Wheaten Flour		Barley and Barley Meal		Oats and Oatmeal	
	Imports	Re-exports	Imports	Re-exports	Imports	Re-exports
1792	24	29	112	..	451	10
1793	477	44	142	..	430	3
1794	340	68	111	1	485	1
1795	299	2	18	—	105	—
1796	879	1	40	—	460	2
1797	421	18	51	..	274	2
1798	379	21	66	2	411	6
1799	456	6	19	..	170	5
1800	293	4	131	—	543	..
1801	1,427	7	114	..	583	1
1802	542	131	8	1	242	3
1803	314	54	1	..	255	2
1804	391	32	9	..	500	4
1805	838	57	28	3	274	—
1806	208	9	2	..	183	1
1807	364	6	3	..	426	—
1808	42	16	4	..	34	1
1809	395	3	13	1	296	..
1810	1,440	63	18	4	116	1
1811	189	71	40	23	12	2
1812	132	18	40	29	15	5
1813	340	...	20	...	60	...
1814	624	23	29	9	248	1
1815	192	56	2	1	120	..
1816	210	20	15	..	75	2
1817	1,064	44	134	4	484	1
1818	1,594	18	696	..	987	..
1819	472	23	373	3	586	2
1820	585	88	29	5	682	4
1821	130	193	14	9	101	14
1822	43	148	19	5	56	15
1823	16	120	..	5	28	13
1824	83	54	27	3	488	11
1825	385	33	426	4	206	12
1826	577	14	278	5	1,125	9
1827	304	49	208	19	1,741	1
1828	741	74	166	4	165	7
1829	1,663	72	277	10	540	59
1830	1,662	35	139	1	506	26
1831	2,304	63	377	1	623	6
1832	447	288	96	8	29	84
1833	298	94	85	3	23	20
1834	176	159	89	10	175	13
1835	67	132	68	44	113	31
1836	242	255	83	18	131	57
1837	560	308	88	11	419	49
1838	1,372	156	2	20	56	56
1839	2,875	39	579	1	671	40
1840	2,433	84	625	4	546	37

Agriculture 17. *continued*

B. Imports of the Main Grains, and Exports and Re-exports of Wheat, 1840–1980

(in thousands of hundredweights)

	Imports					
	Wheat	Wheat Meal and Flour	Barley	Oats	Maize	Exports and Re-exports of Wheat, Wheat Meal and Flour
1840	8,638	1,538	2,234	1,487	100	...
1841	10,442	1,263	945	336	18	95
1842	11,776	1,130	262	828	153	267
1843	4,074	437	640	232	2	273
1844	4,763	981	3,641	824	159	322
1845	3,777	946	1,316	1,624	242	278
1846	6,208	3,190	1,324	2,171	3,025	592
1847	11,511	6,329	2,760	4,691	15,464	1,381
1848	11,184	1,754	3,765	2,659	6,752	46
1849	16,663	3,350	4,932	3,485	9,533	26
1850	16,202	3,819	3,700	3,175	5,473	56
1851	16,519	5,314	2,963	3,296	7,747	304
1852	13,261	3,865	2,234	2,721	6,305	279
1853	21,300	4,622	2,943	2,828	6,619	739
1854	14,869	3,647	1,975	2,791	5,784	633
1855	11,560	1,904	1,247	2,843	5,209	792
1856	17,649	3,970	2,612	3,154	7,619	1,111
1857	14,898	2,178	6,077	4,703	4,932	958
1858	18,381	3,856	5,934	5,105	7,504	94
1859	17,337	3,328	6,171	4,613	5,633	258
1860	25,484	5,086	7,546	6,300	7,936	78
1861	29,956	6,153	5,001	5,114	13,244	2,929
1862	41,034	7,207	6,625	4,427	11,695	142
1863	24,364	5,219	7,384	6,496	12,737	317
1864	23,197	4,512	4,921	5,563	6,286	153
1865	20,963	3,904	7,818	7,714	7,096	116
1866	23,156	4,972	8,434	8,845	14,323	309
1867	34,646	3,593	5,684	9,407	8,540	597
1868	32,640	3,093	7,476	8,113	11,472	509
1869	37,696	5,402	8,054	7,917	17,664	154
1870	30,901	4,804	7,217	10,831	16,757	2,590
1871	39,390	3,978	8,569	10,912	16,820	4,935
1872	42,128	4,388	15,047	11,537	24,533	795
1873	43,863	6,214	9,241	11,908	18,823	2,264
1874	41,528	6,236	11,335	11,388	17,694	1,271
1875	51,877	6,136	11,049	12,436	20,438	211
1876	44,455	5,960	9,773	11,211	39,963	1,325
1877	54,270	7,377	12,960	12,910	30,478	1,184
1878	49,906	7,828	14,157	12,774	41,674	1,652
1879	59,592	10,782	11,546	13,472	36,148	1,330
1880	55,262	10,558	11,705	13,827	37,225	1,845
1881	57,148	11,357	9,806	10,324	33,481	1,422
1882	64,241	13,057	15,540	13,638	18,276	1,598
1883	64,139	16,329	16,461	15,138	31,739	867
1884	47,306	15,095	12,953	12,922	24,780	1,466
1885	61,499	15,833	15,366	13,057	31,527	1,008
1886	47,436	14,690	13,714	13,485	31,012	1,481
1887	55,803	18,063	14,240	14,463	31,167	1,009
1888	57,261	16,910	21,305	18,771	25,370	835
1889	58,552	14,672	17,401	15,991	36,192	857

B. Imports of the Main Grains, and Exports and Re-exports of Wheat, 1840–1980 (*cont.*)

(in thousands of hundredweights)

	Imports					
	Wheat	Wheat Meal and Flour	Barley	Oats	Maize	Exports and Re-exports of Wheat, Wheat Meal and Flour
1890	60,474	15,773	16,678	12,727	43,438	852
1891	66,313	16,723	17,466	16,600	26,826	1,049
1892	64,902	22,106	14,277	15,661	35,381	1,321
1893	65,462	20,408	22,845	13,955	32,903	1,156
1894	70,126	19,135	31,241	14,979	35,365	828
1895	81,750	18,368	23,619	15,528	33,944	833
1896	70,026	21,320	22,477	17,587	51,772	1,001
1897	62,740	18,681	18,959	16,117	53,785	907
1898	65,228	21,017	24,457	15,578	57,169	1,471
1899	66,636	22,946	17,189	15,627	62,741	1,820
1900	68,669	21,548	17,055	20,110	54,152	1,408
1901	69,709	22,576	21,873	22,471	51,373	1,523
1902	81,002	19,386	25,211	15,857	44,493	981
1903	88,131	20,601	26,575	16,284	50,099	841
1904	97,783	14,723	27,173	14,098	42,898	1,043
1905	97,623	11,955	21,427	17,095	42,101	1,541
1906	92,967	14,190	19,935	15,287	48,685	1,638
1907	97,168	13,297	19,628	10,485	53,380	2,031
1908	91,131	12,970	18,137	14,269	33,841	2,927
1909	97,854	11,053	21,556	17,836	39,363	1,896
1910	105,223	9,960	18,282	17,495	37,021	2,281
1911	98,068	10,065	24,545	18,273	38,602	2,442
1912	109,573	10,189	20,126	18,300	43,877	2,856
1913	105,878	11,978	22,439	18,163	49,155	2,517
1914	103,927	10,060	16,044	14,157	39,041	2,931
1915	88,668	10,482	12,292	15,640	48,581	2,248
1916	100,070	9,960	15,820	12,504	34,159	1,341
1917	91,435	14,340	9,139	12,622	25,009	810
1918	57,948	26,360	5,025	10,983	14,490	417
1919	71,443	17,711	16,644	6,711	16,861	406
1920	109,328	11,970	12,668	6,102	33,840	447
1921	80,479	15,841	15,813	8,357	36,757	4,629
1922	96,380	13,475	12,703	9,357	37,200	2,677
1923(*a*)	100,467	11,718	18,129	9,759	34,490	4,878
1924	117,421	11,046	21,656	10,316	37,667	7,598
1925	96,854	9,113	15,779	8,366	27,585	8,826
1926	96,256	10,661	11,570	7,640	31,784	4,797
1927	110,436	10,961	16,419	5,907	41,928	4,829
1928	103,577	8,927	12,975	7,447	33,016	5,317
1929	111,767	9,703	11,986	6,930	34,909	5,389
1930	104,775	11,728	15,208	9,631	34,165	5,408
1931	119,419	10,747	15,423	8,753	53,261	4,861
1932	105,637	8,530	10,178	6,472	52,746	5,963
1933	112,375	9,843	15,985	5,620	51,316	3,780
1934	102,625	9,447	15,476	3,210	61,350	4,006

See p. 228 for footnotes.

B. Imports of the Main Grains, and Exports and Re-exports of Wheat, 1840–1980 (*cont.*)

(in thousands of hundredweights)

	Imports					
	Wheat	Wheat Meal and Flour	Barley	Oats	Maize	Exports and Re-exports of Wheat, Wheat Meal and Flour
1935	101,226	7,981	17,097	3,554	59,456	3,314
1936	100,772	8,367	18,294	2,161	73,293	3,202
1937	96,859	8,540	18,176	1,208	71,671	3,369
1938	101,626	7,677	19,876	1,576	57,581	3,448
1939	106,074	7,333	13,740	1,468	46,399	2,339
1940	115,081	11,547	9,146	1,634	41,581	473
1941	107,864	14,158	1,277	2	13,458	164
1942	69,744	7,488	—	1	2,623	166
1943	65,126	14,351	—	—	1,299	110

Agriculture 17. *continued*

B. Imports of the Main Grains, and Exports and Re-exports of Wheat, 1840–1980 (*cont.*)

(in thousands of hundredweights)

	Imports					Exports and Re-exports of Wheat, Wheat Meal and Flour	Exports of Barley
	Wheat	Wheat Meal and Flour	Barley	Oats	Maize		
1944	56,474	15,831	—	—	2,341	711	719
1945	71,035	10,857	2,037	2,088	10,207	5,135	715
1946	67,443	10,705	2,195	2,096	2,387	1,334	3,282
1947	83,879	17,876	2,257	2,118	9,540	217	522
1948	84,616	16,217	15,618	5,878	26,599	204	720
1949	95,682	11,783	9,223	1,304	14,014	206	217
						...(*b*)	
1950	65,327	8,616	15,289	1,794	19,514	258	699
1951	81,055	10,285	24,270	2,114	20,460	291	1
1952	78,073	9,989	22,641	2,696	27,435	250	2,288
1953	80,407	9,605	28,702	2,184	27,588	246	2
1954	69,262	7,214	18,602	453	26,094	276	1,986
1955	89,821	6,891	18,554	1,032	29,951	286	1,800
1956	95,626	7,211	16,215	459	30,736	328	2,792
1957	90,599	6,767	20,168	1,004	32,480	230	172
1958	90,343	7,437	26,504	3,358	46,036	329	2,589
1959	85,500	7,528	19,924	2,399	58,569	118	4,893
1960	82,076	7,325	14,083	525	61,688	104	4,411
1961	78,412	7,733	19,474	776	63,126	214	2,710
1962	78,432	7,698	7,003	1,299	91,203	308	6,096
						...(*b*)	
1963	78,713	6,419	6,978	679	68,605	2,821	3,063
1964	75,740	5,518	6,772	492	68,015	329	1,759
1965	86,799	4,677	5,616	411	64,031	342	3,919
1966	80,124	3,924	2,510	589	64,779	324	19,605
1967	75,314	1,856	4,362	416	73,204	351	18,295
1968	80,677	1,497	1,417	42	74,505	396	11,819
1969	93,234	1,567	12,806	603	61,988	353	197
1970	98,098	1,653	23,729	170	61,349	376	2,203
1971	90,664	1,454	21,357	381	58,219	317	1,413
1972	82,498	1,295	14,574	500	61,888	345	1,020
1973	74,391	362	5,737	157	66,722	515	5,290
1974	56,227	122	15,960	502	64,049	753	3,215
1975	71,446	72	9,881	568	59,623	4,798	21,022
1976	74,846	71	12,725	1,053	74,050	2,309	3,898
1977	75,697	152	18,035	860	80,923	4,103	9,229
1978	60,792	167	6,887	408	65,668	6,609	40,077
1979	51,194	58	5,886	1,305	61,857	3,409	16,382
1980	44,497	50	4,069	486	55,363	22,345	32,253

(*a*) As from 1st April 1923, Southern Ireland was treated as foreign territory.
(*b*) Domestic exports of wheat were not distinguished between 1950 and 1962 and cannot therefore be included.

Agriculture 18. Principal Sources of Imports of Wheat – United Kingdom 1828–1980

NOTES

[1] SOURCES: 1828–39 – *S.P.* 1842, XL and *S.P.* 1843, LIII; 1840–53 – *Abstract*; 1854–1980 – *Annual Statement of Trade* and *Overseas Trade Statistics of the United Kingdom*.

[2] Figures have not been included for some countries during periods when imports from them were not of much significance.

[3] The main sources of wheat meal and wheaten flour (not shown here) were Canada and the U.S.A., though on some occasions substantial amounts came from Russia and from Australia.

(in thousands of hundredweights)

	Russia	Prussia	Germany	Canada	U.S.A.
1828(*a*)	80	1,109	...	62	—
1829(*a*)	1,485	1,565	...	18	4
1830(*a*)	1,039	2,290	...	261	27
1831(*a*)	2,055	1,322	...	844	190
1832(*a*)	402	526	...	398	27
1833(*a*)	84	389	...	349	—
1834(*a*)	—	133	...	199	—
1835(*a*)	—	13	...	62	—
1836(*a*)	4	442	...	—	—
1837(*a*)	49	1,392	...	—	—
1838(*a*)	181	2,435	...	—	4
1839(*a*)	1,644	3,271	...	—	18
1840	1,162	3,469	...	35	320
1841	432	3,822	...	305	46
1842	1,247	3,197	...	145	70
1843	146	2,851	...	88	—
1844	453	2,387	...	157	10
1845	146	1,836	...	167	101
1846	888	1,560	...	297	742
1847	3,654	2,125	...	385	1,837
1848	2,264	2,262	...	118	339
1849	2,573	2,665	...	45	469
1850	2,766	3,609	...	38	436
1851	3,030	3,017	...	94	877
1852	3,179	1,958	...	150	2,095
1853	4,641	4,960	...	366	3,090
1854	2,196	2,916	...	79	1,810
1855	—	2,323	...	63	1,079
1856	3,291	965	...	485	5,543
1857	3,061	(3,754)(*b*)	5,388	497	2,820
1858	2,653	(2,713)	3,986	437	2,577
1859	3,837	(3,344)	4,256	29	160
1860	5,638	(4,981)	6,543	795	6,497
1861	4,513	(4,454)	6,270	2,381	10,867
1862	5,751	(6,285)	7,588	3,733	16,141

Agriculture 18. *continued*

(in thousands of hundredweights)

	Russia	Prussia	Germany	Canada	U.S.A.	Argentine	India	Australia
1863	4,534	(4,410)	5,297	2,094	8,704	...	...	...
1864	5,119	(4,935)	6,364	1,226	7,895	...	...	...
1865	8,094	(5,404)	6,817	307	1,178	...	...	...
1866	8,937	(4,401)	6,261	9	635	...	...	...
1867	14,025	(5,572)	7,103	683	4,188	...	...	...
1868	10,054	(4,585)	6,043	557	5,908	...	...	...
1869	9,158	(4,635)	6,149	2,723	13,182	...	...	...
1870	10,269	...	3,348	2,838	12,372	...	...	...
1871	15,654	...	3,050	3,278	13,386	...	...	...
1872	17,886	...	3,891	1,735	8,720	...	157	501
1873	9,596	...	2,155	3,762	19,796	...	741	1,801
1874	5,726	...	3,063	3,812	23,090	...	1,074	907
1875	10,005	...	5,613	3,622	23,523	...	1,334	1,157
1876	8,781	...	2,324	2,423	19,323	...	3,287	2,606
1877	10,828	...	5,455	2,952	21,387	...	6,105	426
1878	9,022	...	5,118	2,621	29,061	...	1,821	1,454
1879	8,005	...	3,614	4,782	36,042	...	887	2,248
1880	2,880	...	1,599	3,888	36,191	...	3,229	4,246
1881	4,047	...	1,361	2,876	36,083	...	7,335	2,969
1882	9,576	...	3,080	2,689	35,137	...	8,461	2,475
1883	13,347	...	2,871	1,799	26,129	...	11,249	2,684
1884	5,402	...	1,090	1,757	22,641	...	7,981	5,091
1885	11,976	...	1,980	1,745	24,273	...	12,170	5,279
1886	3,721	...	1,317	3,081	24,649	269	11,024	739
1887	5,501	...	1,552	3,969	30,530	1,014	8,512	1,347
1888	21,450	...	3,279	1,090	14,644	1,752	8,166	2,316
1889	21,310	...	2,538	1,171	17,009	38	9,218	1,406
1890	19,389	...	1,101	1,128	17,201	2,810	9,112	3,058
1891	14,553	...	714	3,174	24,195	2,748	13,006	2,086
1892	4,363	...	606	3,875	33,887	3,466	12,495	2,017
1893	10,062	...	362	3,157	32,263	7,846	6,196	2,590
1894	16,776	...	715	2,829	24,658	13,272	5,349	3,877
1895	23,017	...	753	1,845	27,084	11,400	8,803	3,487
1896	17,242	...	1,033	3,618	30,695	4,928	2,113	7
1897	15,050	...	1,333	4,821	34,603	933	573	—
1898	6,233	...	711	5,012	37,855	3,983	9,538	212
1899	2,518	...	466	5,257	34,651	11,369	8,192	3,703
1900	4,478	...	1,828	6,338	32,588	18,524	6	3,788
1901	2,542	...	595	6,692	40,466	8,080	3,342	6,821
1902	6,540	...	...	9,528	43,313	4,315	8,842	4,331

Agriculture 18. *continued*

(in thousands of hundredweights)

	Russia	Canada	U.S.A.	Argentine	India	Australia
1903	17,176	10,802	24,198	14,120	17,058	—
1904	23,530	6,195	7,052	21,440	25,493	10,631
1905	24,703	6,522	6,635	23,236	22,807	10,405
	....	....	....	....	....	....
1905(*c*)	25,561	6,618	6,539	23,259	22,808	10,405
1906	16,058	11,246	22,554	19,177	12,636	7,865
1907	11,430	13,221	19,946	21,901	18,270	8,328
1908	5,147	15,797	25,769	31,691	2,949	5,518
1909	17,845	16,616	15,504	20,038	14,633	10,402
1910	28,942	16,449	10,949	15,132	17,917	13,748
1911	18,106	14,374	12,939	14,749	20,162	14,641
1912	9,005	21,551	19,974	18,784	25,379	12,193
1913	5,011	21,788	34,068	14,756	18,766	10,183
1914	7,235	31,457	34,220	6,498	10,709	12,122
1915	796	19,725	41,649	12,156	13,957	180
1916	13	21,551	64,544	4,496	5,612	3,730
1917	111	18,408	54,208	6,701	2,745	9,247
1918	—	15,969	24,758	14,389	621	2,014
1919	—	17,865	31,769	6,819	—	14,953
1920	2	10,189	45,422	30,831	20	19,971
1921	—	14,589	36,065	4,186	2,660	20,109
1922	—	22,910	37,262	18,804	488	16,682
1923	151	28,487	31,462	21,026	12,523	4,702
1924	753	38,769	30,321	24,022	9,816	10,871
1925	1,265	29,677	26,,509	11,960	7,324	16,306
1926	2,268	35,670	31,183	11,899	2,695	9,186
1927	2,459	32,181	35,619	19,452	5,014	14,839
1928	82	41,005	23,662	24,399	1,546	10,268
1929	—	27,191	22,266	45,378	141	12,897
1930	18,717	26,179	21,036	15,189	3,342	12,733
1931	28,931	27,098	11,242	20,734	482	23,300
1932	3,275	46,853	4,636	20,616	—	24,121
1933	5,754	45,570	5	24,702	—	29,656
1934	2,095	35,703	131	35,081	166	21,658
1935	6,910	36,894	593	22,752	159	17,684
1936	167	57,813	46	957	3,249	23,270
1937	8,123	34,257	3,492	15,472	6,274	22,389
1938	9,543	28,831	15,805	5,811	4,397	30,995
1939	—	35,157	13,561	24,962	1	13,464
1940	—	55,734	4,587	30,537	184	17,324
1941	—	87,326	614	13,075	103	6,746

Agriculture 18. *continued*

(in thousands of hundredweights)

	Russia	Canada	France	U.S.A.	Argentine	Australia
1942	—	56,885	—	29	6,225	6,605
1943	—	61,736	—	—	1,476	1,913
1944	—	49,665	—	215	6,595	—
1945	—	65,290	—	—	5,745	—
1946	—	57,688	—	7,525	2,231	—
1947	—	68,761	—	6,930	7,741	—
1948	—	66,542	359	183	2,099	15,420
1949	—	73,179	342	5,548	—	16,321
1950	—	49,217	982	8,955	—	5,989
1951	—	44,987	642	21,257	1,686	11,339
1952	3,919	55,360	426	9,071	—	8,932
1953	41	55,796	356	8,907	3,653	9,301
1954	1,168	39,223	6,649	7,473	6,566	6,150
1955	708	45,079	12,876	9,454	7,668	9,919
1956	122	52,661	3,684	18,759	6,328	12,031
1957	258	42,589	6,550	16,737	9,045	12,793
1958	1,829	47,991	10,428	13,801	7,499	5,154
1959	2,744	45,824	1,019	9,511	8,100	9,838
1960	3,848	42,598	1,857	11,230	5,932	13,620
1961	6,259	41,784	1,925	7,941	3,447	12,459
1962	6,861	38,948	3,241	6,909	8,811	10,951
1963	5,896	41,594	5,137	4,787	3,676	11,133
1964	—	39,887	9,503	6,710	3,973	10,843
1965	—	40,620	5,990	6,332	10,022	12,260
1966	—	33,894	3,964	11,871	3,572	10,427
1967	586	32,320	3,384	8,748	4,039	7,669
1968	4,868	29,624	7,554	3,060	993	6,888
1969	7,378	24,998	15,558	833	2,319	16,457
1970	3,683	30,205	7,804	13,480	317	23,198
1971	4,905	26,961	5,141	17,089	—	27,024
1972	5,072	25,337	16,497	15,494	—	11,282
1973	—	29,079	21,256	10,157	—	4,711
1974	—	21,714	14,032	7,039	—	—
1975	—	19,110	13,383	6,115	—	—
1976	—	24,977	25,142	1,680	—	—
1977	—	26,857	32,467	1,294	—	—
1978	—	30,756	17,670	5,142	—	—
1979	—	25,723	7,038	11,186	—	—
1980	—	30,261	4,297	4,892	—	—

(*a*) The statistics for 1828–39 were in quarters in the original source. They have been converted into hundredweights using the ratio 1·81 bushels equals one hundredweight. This ratio represents the average of British experience from 1910–39, and whilst it cannot be exactly correct for most years the margin of error cannot be large.

(*b*) The Prussian figures from 1857 onwards are included in Germany. They have been shown here for as long as they can be separately distinguished, but in brackets.

(*c*) The first figure for 1905 is comparable with earlier years, and shows imports according to port of origin. The second figure is comparable with later years, and is according to country of consignment.

Agriculture 19. Imports of Meat – United Kingdom 1840–1980

NOTE
SOURCES: 1840–54 *Abstract*; 1855–1980 *Annual Statement of Trade* and *Overseas Trade Statistics of the United Kingdom*.

(in thousands of hundredweights)

Year		Year		Year	
1840	65	1885	6,712 ----(b)	1930	31,672
1841	93	1886	6,811	1931	34,849
1842	93	1887	6,691	1932	33,795
1843	95	1888	6,834	1933	31,351
1844	144	1889	8,593	1934	30,654
1845	133	1890	10,068	1935	29,549
1846	264	1891	9,894	1936	29,162
1847	460	1892	10,608	1937	30,813
1848	595	1893	9,408	1938	30,963
1849	895	1894	10,719	1939	31,285
1850	699	1895	12,098	1940	29,245
1851	454	1896	13,518	1941	30,569
1852	302	1897	15,005	1942	32,627
1853	542	1898	16,445	1943	33,577
1854	677	1899	17,658	1944	35,730
1855	----(a) 679	1900	17,912	1945	23,338
1856	742	1901	18,764	1946	27,141
1857	613	1902	16,971	1947	28,046
1858	456	1903	17,498	1948	22,627
1859	495	1904	17,517	1949	23,420
1860	783	1905	18,680	1950	25,279
1861	807	1906	19,255	1951	20,283
1862	1,765	1907	19,444	1952	21,308
1863	2,440	1908	19,654	1953	26,057
1864	1,647	1909	19,398	1954	24,125
1865	1,192	1910	19,983	1955	26,966
1866	1,228	1911	21,581	1956	28,063
1867	1,048	1912	21,360	1957	29,456
1868	1,093	1913	----(c) 23,557	1958	28,338
1869	1,240	1914	23,811	1959	28,137
1870	1,159	1915	25,432	1960	29,608
1871	1,989	1916	23,485	1961	27,750
1872	2,848	1917	19,702	1962	28,634
1873	3,878	1918	25,263	1963	27,843
1874	3,511	1919	25,694	1964	28,594
1875	3,437	1920	----(d) 24,661	1965	27,935
1876	4,349	1921	27,241	1966	26,642
1877	4,402	1922	26,631	1967	27,403
1878	6,000	1923	31,443	1968	27,513
1879	6,892	1924	30,463	1969	27,924
1880	7,567	1925	30,907	1970	26,022
1881	6,831	1926	30,726	1971	26,253
1882	4,649	1927	31,176	1972	26,285
1883	6,050	1928	30,716	1973	23,583
1884	5,819	1929	29,691	1974	20,527
				1975	20,490
				1976	21,041
				1977	22,074
				1978	24,312
				1979	23,833
				1980	21,948

(*a*) Unenumerated and preserved meat is not included before 1855, when it amounted to 3 thousand cwt.
(*b*) Rabbit meat is not included before 1886, when it amounted to 104 thousand cwt.
(*c*) Poultry is not included before 1913, when it amounted to 278 thousand cwt.
(*d*) Game is not included before 1920, when it amounted to 17 thousand cwt.

Agriculture 20. Exports of Meat and Butter – Republic of Ireland, 1924–80

NOTE
SOURCES: *Statistical Abstract of Ireland*.

(in thousands of hundredweights)

	Meat	of which bacon & hams (*a*)	Butter
1924	1,090	613	457
1925	826	466	402
1926	822	442	501
1927	1,001	459	586
1928	1,247	574	559
1929	1,055	497	560
1930	868	345	525
1931	907	311	378
1932	647	218	330
1933	665	232	404
1934	743	402	508
1935	857	501	531
1936	895	541	518
1937	842	532	380
1938	820	557	377
1939	794	477	262
1940	1,139	564	263
1941	1,523	233	128
1942	870	8·7	4·5
1943	545	—	2·8
1944	523	..	0·6
1945	621	...	...
1946	532	...	...
1947	322	...	...
1948	375	..	...
1949	520	33	13
1950	748	55	62
1951	973	9·5	4·5
1952	1,233	9·4	1·2
1953	1,707	115	5·8
1954	2,124	253	67
1955	1,259	57	27
1956	1,052	95	14
1957	1,347	303	316
1958	1,671	576	330
1959	1,238	381	26
1960	1,720	457	150
1961	2,677	566	303
1962	2,599	521	320
1963	2,661	524	385
1964	2,447	555	362
1965	2,700	547	405
1966	2,888	562	467
1967	4,237	473	559
1968	3,813	559	742
1969	4,077	556	832
1970	4,276	537	902
1971	4,741	550	633
1972	2,449	590	741
1973	4,267	486	959
1974	5,414	373	775
1975	6,503	192	1,125
1976	4,900	289	1,327
1977	6,903	421	1,004
1978	6,997	393	1,642
1979	7,061	454	2,337
1980	8,955	557	1,781

(*a*) Excluding tinned ham.

Agriculture 21. Acreage Enclosed by Parliamentary Act – England

NOTES

[1] SOURCE: Michael Turner, *English Parliamentary Enclosure* (Folkestone, 1980), tables 2, 3, and 8.

[2] The difference between the sum of the third and fourth columns and the total given in the first column represents enclosure under General Acts of Enclosure.

	Total Acreage Enclosed	Percentage of County Area	Acreage Enclosed by Acts for Common and Waste only	Acreage containing some Arable Enclosed by Private Act	Percentage of All Parliamentary Enclosure which was for Open-field Arable Land			
					pre-1793	1793–1815	1816–29	post-1829
	000		000					
Bedfordshire	146	49·3	3	129	16·1	64·7	3·2	12·4
Berkshire	155	34·1	6	128	19·6	55·3	5·7	13·6
Buckinghamshire	164	34·9	3	148	35·3	40·7	6·1	13·0
Cambridgeshire	292	53·4	42	234	2·1	52·2	3·4	27·3
Cheshire	29	4·1	27	..	—	0·4	—	—
Cornwall	11	1·2	4	—	—	—	—	—
Cumberland	270	27·7	220	7	0·7	1·7	0·2	1·9
Derbyshire	149	23·2	45	101	25·4	38·7	3·5	0·4
Devonshire	42	2·5	30	—	—	—	—	—
Dorsetshire	94	15·0	27	49	9·8	30·6	7·2	7·5
Durham	107	15·3	103	2	1·6	0·7	—	..
Essex	42	4·2	15	15	—	28·1	4·6	20·5
Gloucestershire	213	26·3	12	181	36·1	41·7	4·9	9·9
Hampshire	157	16·8	47	77	24·1	19·7	4·1	4·4
Isle of Wight	3	3·4	3	—	—	—	—	15·3
Herefordshire	33	6·1	6	23	—	69·7	—	3·6
Hertfordhsire	61	15·5	11	34	6·3	44·1	2·5	26·5
Huntingdonshire	116	50·5	1	107	27·9	57·4	2·6	11·6
Kent	8	0·8	6	—	—	—	—	—
Lancashire	85	7·0	73	—	—	—	—	—
Leicestershire	238	46·6	20	218	78·1	11·8	0·8	0·8
Lincolnshire	667	38·7	149	494	43·2	29·4	2·0	1·3
Middlesex	50	28·0	13	35	4·7	60·7	4·8	3·5
Monmouthshire	16	4·7	12	1	4·8	—	—	3·2
Norfolk	420	31·1	93	313	14·7	52·4	6·2	2·9
Northamptonshire	336	53·0	14	316	61·7	23·2	5·3	5·4
Northumberland	222	18·0	157	25	4·7	6·0	—	0·6
Nottinghamshire	193	36·4	17	164	49·3	31·1	4·2	3·6
Oxfordshire	254	54·3	10	201	37·9	31·8	4·9	19·5
Rutland	41	44·6	—	38	42·4	42·0	4·8	10·8
Shropshire	63	7·4	48	4	2·4	2·2	2·4	—
Somerset	171	16·4	119	37	—	18·6	2·2	1·7
Staffordshire	94	12·9	57	24	10·1	11·3	0·7	3·4
Suffolk	95	10·0	20	69	3·5	54·5	10·5	7·8
Surrey	69	14·4	20	33	..	45·2	1·9	4·4
Sussex	41	4·4	9	20	—	31·1	8·1	13·3
Warwickshire	179	31·7	11	157	65·1	18·5	3·6	6·2
Westmoreland	106	20·9	76	..	—	0·2	0·1	—
Wiltshire	255	29·4	16	220	33·8	43·0	8·9	5·9
Worcestershire	85	18·4	16	63	39·4	31·0	2·0	5·9
Yorkshire E.	335	45·2	21	302	57·5	27·6	3·7	4·7
Yorkshire N.	255	19·1	127	85	19·5	13·7	—	1·0
Yorkshire W.	432	24·3	170	193	17·4	21·8	5·1	2·2
England	6,794	20·9	1,880	4,248	27·3	29·2	3·5	6·0

CHAPTER IV

FUEL AND ENERGY

TABLES

The coal industry possesses two attributes which make it especially suitable for relatively extensive treatment – first, it is an old-established industry in Britain, and, moreover, one which concerned government from early days; and second, its product is relatively homogeneous, and consequently comparisons over time are not so bedevilled by differences in definition as is the case with some industries.[1] Official statistics for the coal industry as a whole were not collected until 1854, when *Mineral Statistics* first appeared.[2] But for a long period before that a considerable amount of official material is available about the Northumberland and Durham coalfield, which, at any rate until the end of the eighteeenth

[1] Some differences in the product occurred through the introduction and development of screening and washing plant – but they represent improvements in the product, not complete alterations in its nature.

[2] Originally compiled by Robert Hunt and published by the Geological Survey, but subsequently as Blue Books.

century, dominated the industry. These, and other more scattered material, have been used by Pollard and by Flinn to make estimates of total coal output going back to the beginning of the eighteenth century. It may well be, however, that these will require modification in the light of later work.

Until well into the nineteenth century, 'the coal trade' meant the industry of producing coal from the Northumberland and Durham coalfield, and shipping it to London and other places. In this trade English government officials had long shown a considerable interest, for, apart from the fact that much of it took place under their noses, it was an important source of revenue, yielding in the 1770s, for example, upwards of £250,000. As a result of this interest there are several statistical series, going back in some cases to the seventeenth century and beyond, connected with shipments from the north-east coast to London. In the absence of more complete, country-wide figures, these have come to be used as indicators of the overall level of output. Reasonably connected series of shipments from the North-East go back to 1655, and are shown in table 1, whilst table 2 shows the imports into London back to 1700.[3] Both these tables may be regarded as indicators of total British output until towards the end of the eighteenth century. But with the development of canals, and the increasing use of coal for industrial purposes, Northumberland and Durham gradually lost their absolute dominance in the British coal industry, and for this reason table 1 is not continued beyond 1832. Table 2 has been carried on much longer, but with a different purpose – namely, to show the growth in importance of the railways as carriers of coal.

The official output statistics beginning in 1854 are shown in table 3, together with the earlier estimates already referred to. As indicated in the notes to this table, the output figures before 1873 are, in some cases at any rate, to be regarded with suspicion. In general they give a reasonable indication of trend, but are less reliable as evidence of year-to-year fluctuations.

Table 5 needs little or no explanation or warnings beyond those given in the footnotes. For the methods by which Part A was estimated, the original source must be consulted; and there is also discussion there of the lack of reliability of the pre-1873 figures in Part B. It is perhaps worth pointing out that, apart from their primary significance, the statistics of employment can be used in conjunction with those of output to arrive at output per man-year, which may be used (with caution) as a crude indicator of trends in productivity, though fluctuations are wider than they are in the preferred measure of productivity, output per man-shift, during the period when they can be compared.[4]

The statistics of exports in table 7 suffer from the breaks in continuity common to practically all statistics of external trade. In the case of coal, however, the various eighteenth- and nineteenth-century series do not overlap in time, so that there is no exact indication of the size of the breaks. Indeed, there is a gap between 1808 and 1816 when not only are there no published statistics, but the definition of exports changed with the exclusion of the Irish

[3] A few earlier figures, back to 1377 and 1580 respectively, can be found in J. U. Nef, *The Rise of the British Coal Industry* (2 vols., London, 1932), appendix D.

[4] See B. R. Mitchell, *The Economic Development of the British Coal Industry, 1800–1914* (Cambridge, 1984), pp. 311–12 for discussion of the validity of this.

trade – something that was restored again so far as southern Ireland was concerned in April 1922.

Table 8 shows the development of various markets for coal since the early nineteenth century, though the statistics are of varying degrees of reliability. Those for 1869 and 1903 are probably the best prior to the beginning of the continuous official series in 1913.[5] Of these earlier figures, it is clear that those for the consumption of coal in the various specific uses are always more reliable than the residual categories, 'domestic' and 'general manufacturing'. However, even the most detailed of these, the ones for coal used in blast furnaces (shown separately as table 9), are, in a sense, notional ones, for they are arrived at by applying a changing, but estimated, co-efficient to the known output of pig iron.

The final table for coal, table 10, covers a topic which has at various times received a good deal of attention from critics of British industrialists, though my own analysis does not support them.[6] This is the speed of adoption of the mechanisation of the central process of coalmining, namely the getting of the coal. The same sources as are used for this table also give some indicators of the spread of mechanical conveying from the coalface, though these are not included here.

The next five tables are concerned with sales and generation of electricity. These were not collected officially in Great Britain before 1920, and about a decade later in Ireland, and the only continuously available source of data, a private publication run by Emil Garcke, which is the source of table 11, had to rely on information supplied voluntarily. As a result there were various omissions, which were roughly allowed for in compiling this table, though the result is probably very approximate until about 1900. Moreover, the accounting years of the different undertakings varied to some extent, so that figures could not be obtained for uniform periods. To complicate matters still further, there were changes in these accounting years for some of the undertakings from time to time, notably when a municipality took over from a private company. However, despite all these drawbacks to the accuracy and even to the precision of meaning of the statistics in table 11, they are not without use as an indicator of the early stages of the growth of electricity supply in Britain. It is worth noting, though, that both these figures and those which were collected officially from 1920 onwards relate only to authorised – or, latterly, nationalised – undertakings. In other words, they do not include electricity which was generated by undertakings which did not produce for direct commercial sale. The main electricity works of this type were those of the railways, and since they are excluded throughout, the trend indicated by the figures is probably not very much affected by the limitation of coverage. However, up to and including the 1920s, and to a less extent in the 1930s and even later, there was certainly some decline in private generation other than by the railways, and this served to increase the sales of the authorised undertakings.

[5] See *ibid.*, p. 14 for discussion of this.

[6] See *ibid.*, pp. 83 *et seq.*, where some of the contemporary critics are quoted. A modern example is D. H. Aldcroft, 'The Entrepreneur and the British Economy, 1870–1914', *Economic History Review*, second series XVII, 1 (1964), p. 117.

Very much the same sort of qualification has to be made to the gas sales statistics in table 16, though there was probably much less private production of gas by the 1880s, when the figures begin, than there was private generation of electricity up to the 1930s. Nevertheless, private production of gas by iron and steel works was not negligible at any time.

The final tables in this chapter, those for external trade in oil, natural gas, and (for Ireland) coal, are reasonably straightforward, and do not call for any particular comment.

Fuel and Energy 1. Shipments of Coal from Newcastle and Sunderland – 1655–1832

NOTES

[1] SOURCES: 1655–1709 (except 1691–4) and 1733 – J. U. Nef, *The Rise of the British Coal Industry* (2 vols., Routledge, London, 1932), vol. II, appendix D; 1691–4 and (for Newcastle) 1710–66 and 1784–6 – F. W. Dendy (editor), *Records of the Company of Hostmen* (Surtees Society Transactions, vol. 105, 1901); 1767–79 (for Newcastle) and 1748–71 and 1800 (for Sunderland) – T. S. Ashton and J. Sykes, *The Coal Industry of the Eighteenth Century* (Manchester University Press, 1929); 1780–93 (for Newcastle) and 1772–99 (for Sunderland) – *Report of the Select Committee on the Coal Trade* (1800); *P.P.* x, appendices; 1794–1832 (for Newcastle) – *Report of the Commissioners on Municipal Corporations, Newcastle-upon-Tyne, S.P.* 1835, xxv; 1801–32 (for Sunderland) – G. R. Porter, *The Progress of the Nation* (London, 1847 edition), p. 278.

[2] The following conversion factors from Newcastle chaldrons to tons are suggested by Nef (*op. cit.* appendix C(1)):

1636–60	1 chaldron = 52 cwt.
1661–86	1 chaldron = 52½ cwt.
after 1686	1 chaldron = 53 cwt.

[3] M. W. Flinn, *The History of the British Coal Industry*, vol. 2 (Oxford, 1984), table 7.3 gives the following figures of total coastwise shipments from Newcastle Sunderland, and Blyth:

(annual averages in thousand tons)

1720–4	895	1760–4	1,173	1800–4	2,250
1725–9	956	1765–9	1,351	1805–9	2,456
1730–4	960	1770–4	1,458	1810–4	2,729
1735–9	1,037	1775–9	1,478	1815–9	2,838
1740–4	...	1780–4	1,493	1820–4	3,175
1745–9	1,030	1785–9	1,785	1825–9	3,445
1750–4	1,132	1790–4	1,852		
1755–9	1,108	1795–9	1,983		

(in thousands of chaldrons)

	from Newcastle		from Sunderland		from Newcastle and Sunderland	
	coastwise	oversea	coastwise	oversea	oversea	total
1655	147	...	...	...	...	...
1658(*a*)	132	6	26	2	8	167
1659(*a*)	187	16	43	3	19	250
1660(*a*)	167	11	39	11	22	228
1661	167	10	...	1	12	...
1662	194	...	...	...	...	...
1663	179	...	...	...	...	...
1664	198	...	...	...	...	...
1665	124	...	...	...	...	...
1666	84	3	...	--	3	...
1667	106	4	...	1	4	...
1668	188	...	...	...	...	...
1669	176	...	...	...	...	...
1670	185	...	...	...	...	...
1671	189	...	...	...	...	...
1672	150	...	...	...	...	...
1673	156	...	...	...	...	...
1674	170	14	44	3	17	231
1675	194	...	...	...	...	...
1676	195	10	40	4	15	249
1677	194	15	...	5	19	...
1678	218	12	54	3	15	287
1679	195	...	47	...	...	...
1680	202	16	...	5	21	...
1681	219	...	...	...	...	...
1682	190	...	...	...	...	...
1683	211	...	...	...	...	...
1684	205	...	...	...	...	...
1685	214	21	54	8	29	297
1686	178	...	...	...	...	...
1687	199	...	...	...	...	...
1688	231	...	...	...	...	...
1689	168	...	...	...	...	...
1690	137	...	...	...	...	...
1691	177	...	...	...	...	...
1692	156	...	...	...	...	...
1693	180	...	...	...	...	...
1694	160	...	...	...	...	...
1695	171	...	...	...	...	...
1696	151	...	...	...	...	...

Fuel and Energy 1. *continued*

(in thousands of chaldrons)

	from Newcastle		from Sunderland		from Newcastle and Sunderland	
	coastwise	oversea	coastwise	oversea	oversea	total
1697	181	...	...	...	...	...
1698	211	...	...	...	...	...
1699	221	...	...	...	...	...
1700	205	...	...	...	...	...
1701	245	...	...	...	...	...
1702	153	...	...	...	...	...
1703	170	...	...	...	...	...
1704	198	...	...	...	...	...
1705	182	...	...	...	...	...
1706	163	...	...	...	...	...
1707	151	...	...	...	...	...
1708	193	...	...	...	...	...
1709	211	...	...	...	...	...
1710	168	...	...	...	...	...
1723	262		...	...	...	...
1724	253		...	...	...	...
1725	266		...	...	...	...
1726	286		...	...	...	...
1727	276		...	...	...	...
1728	247		...	...	...	...
1729	293		...	...	...	...
1730	277		...	...	...	...
1731	311		...	...	...	...
1732	269		...	...	...	...
1733	275	16	104	20	36	414
1734	274		...	...	...	...
1735	282		...	...	...	...
1736	297		...	...	...	...
1737	276		...	...	...	...
1738	271		...	...	...	...
1739	288		...	...	...	...
1740	321		...	...	...	...
1741	263		...	...	...	...
1742	270		...	...	...	...
1743	298		...	...	...	...
1744	273		...	...	...	...
1745	295		...	...	...	...
1746	303		...	...	...	...
1747	259		...	...	...	...
1748	271		147		...	418
1749	299		135		...	434
1750	288		162		...	450
1751	343		129		...	472
1752	308		177		...	485
1753	301		167		...	468
1754	305		166		...	471
1755	294		174		...	468
1756	311		175		...	486
1757	274		179		...	453
1758	240		187		...	427

Fuel and Energy 1. *continued*

(in thousands of chaldrons)

	from Newcastle		from Sunderland		from Newcastle and Sunderland	
	coastwise	oversea	coastwise	oversea	oversea	total
1759	302		187		...	489
1760	285		180		...	465
1761	328		170		...	498
1762	294		172		...	466
1763	293		182		...	475
1764	349		205		...	554
1765	349		204		...	553
1766	353		206		...	559
1767	359		196		...	555
1768	...		203		...	...
1769	...		215		...	...
1770	372		213		...	585
1771	...		220		...	...
1772	352		257		...	509
1773	...		241		...	...
1774	...		245		...	...
1775	...		244		...	...
1776	...		262		...	...
1777	...		253		...	...
1778	366		233		...	599
1779	...		215		...	...
1780	366		225		...	591
1781	335		210		...	546
1782	364		212		...	576
1783	413		238		...	652
1784	459		244		...	703
1785	450		266		...	716
1786	429		259		...	688
1787	411		275		...	686
1788	446		279		...	725
1789	490		256	39	...	785
1790	420		236	47	...	704
1791	445		239	54	...	737
1792	499		260	54	...	813
1793	497		248	50	...	795
1794	389	40	240	39	79	708
1795	465	40	283	6	46	789
1796	441	43	247	6	49	737
1797	461	38	267	6	45	773
1798	396	45	264	5	50	710
1799	452	43	284	4	47	783
1800	538	47	322		...	817
1801	452	50	231	4	55	738
1802	494	44	305	31	75	875
1803	505	44	299	10	54	859
1804	580	53	300	4	57	936
1805	553	50	313	6	56	922
1806	588	47	306	3	49	944
1807	530	27	293	4	32	854
1808	619	16	349	2	18	986

Fuel and Energy 1. *continued*

(in thousands of chaldrons)

	from Newcastle		from Sunderland		from Newcastle and Sunderland	
	coastwise	oversea	coastwise	oversea	oversea	total
1809	539	14	324	1	15	878
1810	632	17	371	2	20	1,022
1811	633	18	331	2	20	984
1812	631	25	339	3	28	998
1813	584	15	347	2	17	948
1814	649	32	373	11	43	1,065
1815	650	42	338	17	59	1,048
1816	678	44	388	16	60	1,126
1817	623	52	364	12	63	1,050
1818	672	48	392	16	64	1,127
1819	640	40	378	15	54	1,074
1820	757	45	416	14	59	1,232
1821	692	48	395	14	62	1,151
1822	655	54	397	16	71	1,123
1823	739	46	497	16	61	1,297
1824	688	49	491	16	65	1,244
1825	687	51	522	16	67	1,276
1826	792	63	549	14	67	1,419
1827	684	65	523	15	80	1,288
1828	725	59	510	23	82	1,317
1829	738	62	565		...	1,365
1830	818	74	524		...	1,416
1831	773	61	474		...	1,308
1832	683	74	452		...	1,211

(*a*) Year ended 24th June. All other figures are for Year ended 25th December.

Fuel and Energy 2. Coal Imported into London by Sea and Rail – 1700–1879

NOTES

[1] SOURCES: 1700–99 – T. S. Ashton and J. Sykes, *The Coal Industry of the Eighteenth Century*, appendix E; 1800–79 – returns published in *Sessional Papers* annually.

[2] The figures are quoted as in the sources. One London chaldron equalled 25½ cwt.

(in thousands of tons or thousands of London chaldrons)

	By Sea 000 chaldrons
1700	335
1701	400
1702	243
1703	301
1708	361
1710	328
1713	346
1714	414
1715	388
1716	412
1717	440
1718	412
1719	420
1720	425
1721	459
1722	460
1723	458
1724	451
1725	471
1726	508
1727	496
1728	453
1729	494
1730	455
1731	475
1732	451
1733	496
1734	448
1735	503
1736	512
1737	476
1738	491
1739	442
1740	563
1741	453
1742	457
1743	478
1744	468

	By Sea 000 chaldrons
1745	471
1746	487
1747	469
1748	450
1749	504
1750	458
1751	539
1752	508
1753	508
1754	527
1755	479
1756	550
1757	503
1758	452
1759	552
1760	499
1761	505
1762	530
1763	603
1764	597
1765	588
1766	639
1767	599
1768	614
1769	642
1770	613
1771	678
1772	711
1773	645
1774	615
1775 (*a*)	664
1776	690
1777	685
1778	640
1779	589
1780	657
1781	651
1782	661
1783	695
1784	725
1785	733

	By Sea 000 chaldrons
1786	730
1787	653
1788	771
1789	811
1790	753
1791	822
1792	850
1793	801
1794	783
1795	910
1796	783
1797	890
1798	775
1799	880
1800	1,011
1801	833
1802	928
1803	916
1804	976
1805 (*b*)	964
1806	986
1807	911
1808	1,092
1809	974
1810	1,099
1811	1,095
1812	1,065
1813	1,019
1814	1,118
1815	1,143
1816	1,218
1817	1,151
1818	1,204
1819	1,170
1820	1,321
1821	1,292
1822	1,235
1823	1,434
1824	1,467
1825	1,423
1826	1,558

Fuel and Energy 2. *continued*

(in thousands of tons or thousands of London chaldrons)

	By Sea			By Rail
	000 chaldrons		000 tons	000 tons
1827	1,476	or	1,882	—
1828	1,538		1,961	—
1829	1,584		2,019	—
1830	1,631		2,079	—
1831	1,604		2,045	—
1832	1,678		2,139	—
1833			2,010	—
1834			2,079	—
1835			2,299	—
1836			2,398	—
1837			2,627	—
1838			2,581	—
1839			2,625	—
1840			2,567	—
1841			2,909	—
1842			2,723	—
1843			2,629	—
1844			2,491	—
1845			3,403	8
1846			2,954	12
1847			3,280	19
1848			3,418	38
1849			3,339	20
1850			3,553	55
1851			3,237	248
1852			3,330	378
1853			3,373	630
1854			3,400	945
1855			3,017	1,138
1856			3,120	1,246
1857			3,133	1,207
1858			3,266	1,191
1859			3,299	1,191
1860			3,573	1,478
1861			3,567	1,643
1862			3,442	1,513
1863			3,335	1,776
1864			3,117	2,342
1865			3,162	2,733
1866			3,033	2,970
1867			3,016	3,296
1868			2,918	2,979
1869			2,874	3,342
1870			2,994	3,758
1871			2,763	4,449
1872			3,549	4,999
1873			2,666	5,147
1874			2,728	4,690
1875			3,135	5,065
1876			3,272	5,173
1877			3,171	5,416
1878			3,198	5,593
1879			3,509	6,547

(*a*) For the period 1775–1800 slightly different figures are to be found in other sources. The Ashton and Sykes series has been shown here, since it is the longest. The others are shown overleaf.

(*b*) From 1805 onwards negligible amounts were also brought to London by canal. The most in any one year was 72,000 tons in 1844; in most years it was much less.

Fuel and Energy 2. *continued*

(*a*) *continued*

(in thousands of London chaldrons)

	Customs	Orphans	Metage	City Due	Gillespy	Martindale
1775	...	...	...	640	664	...
1776	...	...	...	703	701	...
1777	...	...	...	693	699	...
1778	...	...	...	669	645	...
1779	...	664	...	639	592	...
1780	657	636	668	624	670	...
1781	660	701	641	646	643	...
1782	676	661	695	622	697	...
1783	662	727	674	690	710	...
1784	720	729	724	732	719	719
1785	740	754	739	712	734	737
1786	750	744	744	763	739	739
1787	740	758	759	738	753	753
1788	797	807	764	785	760	760
1789	786	750	800	773	795	795
1790	745	794	754	794	747	747
1791	805	843	832	794	825	824
1792	877	812	848	853	841	841
1793	818	784	807	801	801	801
1794	790	894	796	823	789	789
1795	879	818	895	830	888	888
1796	836	866	848	853	819	859
1797	851	782	872	828	864	864
1798	795	863	792	856	786	786
1799	872	...	868	839	828	862
1800	1,019	...	...	940	1,005	...

Customs = *Select Committee on the Coal Trade* (1800), *P.P.* x, appendix 45 D – figures 'taken at the Custom House'. Years ended 1st December.

Orphans = *ibid.* appendix 57 – figures derived from the yield of the Orphans' Duty of 1od per chaldron. Years ended 5th January in the year following that for which the figures are shown, according to the source, but it seems possible that they were mistakenly given for the year previous to that to which they apply.

Metage = *ibid.* appendix 58 – figures derived from the yield of the metage due of 4d per chaldron. Calendar years.

City Due = *Select Committee on the Coal Trade (Port of London) Bill* (*S.P.* 1837–8, xv) – figures derived from the yield of the city due of 1od per chaldron. Years ended 5th July.

Gillespy = *Epitome of the Coal Trade in the Port of London*, by Thomas Gillespy, printed as appendix 15 to the *Report of the Royal Commission on the Coal Supply* (*Committee E*), *S.P.* 1871 XVIII.

Martindale = *Select Committee on the Coal Trade* (1800), *P.P.* x, appendix 19 – figures given by John Martindale of the Customs House, Sunderland.

Fuel and Energy 3. Output of Coal in the United Kingdom and its Main Coalfields – 1750–1945

NOTES

[1] Sources: Part A – Sidney Pollard, "A New Estimate of British Coal Production, 1750–1850", *E.H.R.*, second series, XXXIII, 2 (1980); Part B – 1854–72 – *Mineral Statistics*; 1873–81 – *Reports of H.M. Inspectors of Mines*; 1882–1921 – *Mineral Statistics*; 1922–38 – *Annual Report of the Department of Mines*; 1939–45 – Ministry of Fuel and Power, *Statistical Digest*, and its *Supplement*.

[2] M. W. Flinn, *The History of the British Coal Industry*, vol. 2 (Oxford, 1984), table 1.2 gives the following estimates (in thousand tons) to 1830, and these are continued in Roy Church, *ibid.*, vol. 3 (Oxford, 1986), table 1.1, in quinquennial averages (in million tons):

	1700	1750	1775	1800	1815	1830	1830–4	1835–9	1840–4	1845–9	1850–4	1855–9	1860–4	1865–9	1870–4
Scotland	450	715	1,000	2,000	2,500	3,000	3·2	3·8	4·6	6·1	8·1	9·9	12·0	13·9	15·9
Cumberland	25	350	450	500	520	560	0·6	0·7	0·8	0·8	0·9	0·9	1·3	1·4	1·2
Lancashire & Cheshire	80	350	900	1,400	2,800	4,000	4·2	4·9	6·0	7·5	9·6	11·2	12·8	13·7	15·8
North Wales	25	80	110	150	350	600	0·6	0·7	0·7	1·0	1·4	1·6	1·8	2·2	2·5
South Wales	80	140	650	1,700	2,750	4,400	4·8	6·0	7·1	8·7	10·6	13·2	14·3	15·1	16·5
South-West	150	180	250	445	610	800	0·8	0·9	1·0	1·1	1·4	1·3	1·8	2·0	2·0
East Midlands	75	140	250	750	1,400	1,700	1·8	2·0	2·4	2·9	3·4	4·4	6·0	7·2	9·7
West Midlands	510	820	1,400	2,550	3,990	5,600	5·9	6·9	7·8	9·2	10·9	11·5	13·0	15·2	16·8
Yorkshire	300	500	850	1,100	1,950	2,800	3·0	3·5	4·4	5·4	6·7	8·5	9·2	9·9	13·6
North-East	1,290	1,955	2,990	4,450	5,395	6,915	7·1	8·4	10·0	12·0	15·2	17·4	20·9	25·8	35·2
Total	2,985	5,230	8,850	15,045	22,265	30,861	32·0	37·8	44·7	55·9	68·4	80·0	92·5	106·4	123·3

Part A. Decennial and Quinquennial Estimates, 1750–1850

(in thousand tons)

	North-East (*a*)	Yorkshire	Midland (*b*)	Lancashire (*c*)	Staffordshire (*d*)	South Wales	Scotland	G.B. Total
1750–5	1,564	500	180	200	250	80	900	4,230
1756–60	1,568							4,520
1761–5	1,718	600	200	240	350	100	1,100	4,950
1766–70	1,861							5,520
1771–5	2,019	750	250	325	500	200	1,300	6,120
1776–80	2,092							6,750
1781–5	2,232	850	290	500	650	500	1,500	7,550
1786–90	2,526							8,570
1791–5	2,817	950	450	800	850	800	1,700	9,570
1796–1800	2,863							10,960
1801–05	3,177	1,500	760	1,400	1,600	1,200	2,200	12,960
1806–10	3,438							14,790
1811–5	3,702	1,800	1,180	1,600	2,400	1,800	2,500	16,590
1816–20	4,104				3,400			18,900
1821–5	4,512	2,400	1,500	2,400	4,000	2,500	2,900	20,900
1826–30	5,208			4,500				24,800
1831–5	6,056	3,600	2,200	4,500	4,000	4,000	4,000	29,560
1836–40	7,833							35,270
1841–5	9,696	4,500	2,700	6,000	4,800	5,000	5,300	41,706
1846–50	12,588	5,500	3,250	7,500	5,600	6,500	6,000	50,968

Part B. Annual Statistics, 1854–1945

(Output in millions of tons and value in £ million)

	North-East (*a*)	Yorkshire	Midland (*b*)	Lancashire (*c*)	Staffordshire (*d*)	South Wales	Scotland	U.K. Total Output	U.K. Total Value
1854	15·4	7·3	3·9	9·9	7·5	8·5	7·4	64·7	16·2
1855	15·4	7·7	3·8	9·7	7·3	8·6	7·3	64·5	16·1
1856	15·5	9·1	4·3	9·7	7·3	8·9	7·5	66·6	16·7
1857	15·8	8·9	4·8	9·3	7·2	7·1	8·2	65·4	16·3
1858	15·9	8·3	5·1	8·7	6·7	7·5	8·9	65·0	16·3
1859	16·0	8·4	5·4	11·4	6·1	9·6	10·3	72·0	17·2
1860	18·2	9·3	6·2	12·1	7·6	...	10·9	80·0	20·0
1861	19·1	9·4	6·5	13·0	7·3	...	11·1	83·6	20·9
1862	19·4	9·3	6·6	11·4	7·5	10·5	11·1	81·6	20·4
1863	22·2	9·4	6·8	11·7	7·9	11·0	11·1	86·3	21·6
1864	23·3	8·8	6·9	12·4	11·5(*e*)	11·0	12·4	92·8	23·2
1865	25·0	9·4	7·5	12·8	12·2	12·0	12·7	98·2	24·5
1866	25·2	9·7	8·0	13·2	12·3	13·8	12·6	101·6	25·4
1867	24·9	9·8	8·2	13·8	12·5	13·7	14·1	104·5	26·1
1868	24·4	9·7	7·7	13·7	12·3	13·2	14·7	103·1	25·8

Part B. Annual Statistics, 1854–1945 (*cont.*)

(Output in millions of tons and value in £ million)

	North-East (*a*)	Yorkshire	Midland (*b*)	Lancashire (*c*)	Staffordshire (*d*)	South Wales	Scotland	U.K. Total Output	U.K. Total Value
1869	25·8	10·8	8·6	15·0	12·7	13·5	14·4	107·4	26·9
1870	27·6	10·6	8·5	14·7	13·2	13·7	14·9	110·4	27·6

1871	29·2	12·8	9·3	14·8	14·3	14·0	15·4	117·4	35·2(*f*)
1872	28·6	14·6	10·7	18·4	14·6	15·2	15·4	123·5	46·3
	---	---	---	---	---	---	---	----	----
1873(*g*)	29·7	15·3	11·5	18·4	15·2	16·2	16·9	128·7	47·6
1874	30·6	14·8	12·2	18·7	13·0	16·5	16·8	126·6	45·8
1875	32·3	15·9	12·4	21·0	14·5	14·2	18·6	133·3	46·2
1876	32·3	15·1	12·3	20·6	13·9	17·0	18·7	134·1	46·7
1877	31·4	15·8	12·9	20·9	13·7	16·3	18·3	134·2	47·1
1878	30·2	15·6	13·4	21·0	13·1	17·9	17·8	132·6	46·4
1879	28·8	16·2	14·0	21·5	13·3	17·8	17·5	133·7	46·9
1880	34·9	17·5	14·5	22·2	13·7	21·2	18·3	147·0	62·4
1881	35·6	18·3	15·5	21·9	14·9	21·5	20·8	154·2	65·5

1882	36·3	18·5	15·6	23·0	15·0	22·2	20·5	156·5	44·2(*h*)
1883	37·4	19·6	16·6	23·9	15·2	24·1	21·3	163·7	46·1
1884	36·1	19·2	16·1	23·4	14·4	24·8	20·4	160·8	43·4
1885	35·1	18·5	17·0	23·6	14·7	24·3	21·3	159·4	41·1
1886	34·8	19·4	16·8	23·8	13·3	24·8	20·4	157·5	38·1
1887	34·5	20·1	17·2	24·2	13·7	25·4	21·5	162·1	39·1
1888	37·6	20·6	18·1	23·9	14·5	28·2	22·3	169·9	43·0
1889	39·1	22·0	19·7	24·6	14·8	28·1	23·2	176·9	56·2
1890	39·7	22·3	20·5	25·8	14·7	29·4	24·3	181·6	75·0
1891	39·1	22·8	21·6	26·0	15·3	30·0	25·4	185·5	74·1
1892	32·4(*l*)	23·2	21·6	26·0	15·0	31·3	27·2	181·8	66·1
1893	39·9	16·0(*l*)	16·0(*l*)	18·1(*l*)	13·9(*l*)	30·2(*l*)	25·5	164·3(*l*)	55·8(*l*)
1894	42·1	23·4	21·7	27·1	14·1	33·4	21·6(*l*)	188·3	62·7
1895	39·8	22·8	21·5	25·6	13·3	33·0	28·8	189·7	57·2
1896	41·8	23·9	22·4	25·5	13·9	34·0	28·3	195·4	57·2
1897	43·6	24·0	23·8	25·7	14·3	35·5	29·1	202·1	59·7
1898	45·3	25·6	25·8	27·5	14·6	26·7(*l*)	30·2	202·1	64·2
1899	46·1	26·9	27·6	27·6	14·7	39·9	31·1	220·1	83·5
1900	46·3	28·2	28·9	28·7	15·0	39·3	33·1	225·2	121·7
1901	45·2	27·0	28·2	26·8	14·9	39·2	32·8	219·0	102·5
1902	46·4	28·0	29·6	27·6	15·1	41·3	34·1	227·1	93·5
1903	47·9	28·5	29·4	27·7	13·8	42·2	35·0	230·3	88·2
1904	48·4	28·8	29·7	27·1	13·4	43·7	35·5	232·4	83·9
1905	50·1	29·9	31·0	27·1	13·6	43·2	35·8	236·1	82·0
1906	52·1	32·5	33·2	28·4	14·1	47·1	39·2	251·1	91·5
1907	54·0	35·2	37·2	30·0	15·3	50·0	40·1	267·8	120·5
1908	53·9	34·9	35·2	27·9	14·4	50·2	39·2	261·5	116·6
1909	55·3	35·9	35·1	27·3	14·2	50·4	39·8	263·8	106·3
1910	52·6	38·3	35·9	27·2	14·7	46·7	41·3	264·4	108·4
1911	56·4	39·1	36·5	27·4	14·7	50·2	41·7	271·9	110·8
1912	51.3(*l*)	38·3(*l*)	35·1(*l*)	26·3(*l*)	14·2(*l*)	50·1(*l*)	39·5(*l*)	260·4(*l*)	117·9(*l*)
1913	56·4	43·7	38·8	28·1	14·9	56·8	42·5	287·4	145·5
1914	50·0	39·5	39·4	26·2	14·5	53·8	38·8	265·7	132·6
1915	44·8	40·3	36·7	21·7	14·0	50·5	35·6	253·2	157·8
1916	45·0	40·2	37·5	21·7	14·2	52·1	36·1	256·4	200·0
1917	41·1	40·9	38·9	22·1	14·3	48·5	34·2	248·5	207·8
1918	38·3	35·6	34·2	19·9	12·7	46·7	31·9	227·7	238·2

Part B. Annual Statistics, 1854–1945 (*cont.*)

(Output in millions of tons and value in £ million)

	North-East (*a*)	Yorkshire	Midland (*b*)	Lancashire (*c*)	Staffordshire (*d*)	South Wales	Scotland	U.K. Total Output	U.K. Total Value
1919	42·0	32·8	33·7	19·9	13·0	47·5	32·5	229·8	314·1
1920	42·0	36·2	33·6	19·0	12·6	46·2	31·5	229·5	396·9
1921	29·8(*l*)	28·5(*l*)	24·4(*l*)	13·1(*l*)	8·8(*l*)	30·6(*l*)	22·5(*l*)	163·3(*l*)	213·7(*l*)
								----	----
1922	48·1	42·1	35·5	17·8	12·0	50·3	35·4	249·6(*i*)	220·0(*i*)
1923	52·5	46·5	40·2	20·2	14·2	54·3	38·5	276·0	259·7
1924	50·4	46·6	39·3	19·8	14·3	51·1	36·2	267·1	251·7
1925	43·4	45·3	37·5	17·4	13·2	44·6	33·0	243·2	199·0
1926	20·3(*l*)	21·6(*l*)	24·4(*l*)	9·2(*l*)	8·9(*l*)	20·3(*l*)	16·8(*l*)	126·3(*l*)	123·4(*l*)
1927	48·1	45·9	36·4	17·1	13·3	46·3	34·6	251·2	183·5
1928	47·7	43·4	34·5	15·1	11·9	43·3	32·4	237·5	152·5
1929	53·5	46·4	37·5	15·7	12·8	48·2	34·2	257·9	173·2
1930	49·0	44·6	36·9	15·0	12·1	45·1	31·7	243·9	165·7
1931	42·7	40·6	35·3	14·1	11·6	37·1	29·1	219·5	147·7
1932	40·0	38·1	33·4	13·2	11·6	34·9	28·8	208·7	138·4
1933	40·1	37·3	32·5	13·2	11·7	34·4	29·2	207·1	134·6
1934	44·4	39·9	34·3	13·8	12·7	35·2	31·3	220·7	142·1
1935	44·3	40·7	34·6	14·1	13·2	35·0	31·3	222·3	144·5
1936	45·8	42·5	36·7	14·7	13·9	33·9	32·0	228·5	160·1
1937	47·7	45·1	39·6	15·1	13·9	37·8	32·2	240·4	182·7
1938	44·7	42·4	37·8	14·3	13·4	35·3	30·3	227·0	188·8
	----(*j*)	----(*j*)	----(*j*)	----(*j*)	----(*j*)	----(*j*)	----(*j*)	----(*j*)	
1939	43·5	44·4	40·5	14·3	14·0	35·3	30·5	231·3	...
1940	38·7	45·2	43·0	13·6	13·6	32·4	29·7	224·3	...
1941	35·4	42·8	42·4	12·2	12·3	27·4	26·6	206·3	...
								----(*j*)	
1942	36·3	41·1	42·8	11·7	11·9	26·7	26·2	204·9	...
1943	35·0	38·9(*k*)	41·4(*k*)	11·1	11·5	25·1	24·7	198·9	...
		--- 40·3	--- 40·1						
1944	33·4	37·9	38·8	10·8	11·0	22·4	23·4	192·7	...
1945	31·6	36·7	37·1	10·5	10·8	20·5	21·4	182·8	...

(*a*) Northumberland and Durham.
(*b*) Derbyshire, Leicestershire, Nottinghamshire, and Warwickshire.
(*c*) Lancashire and Cheshire.
(*d*) North and South Staffordshire, and Worcestershire.
(*e*) It is clear that the Staffordshire figures become progressively more unreliable from 1854–64, at which date there was probably a more comprehensive survey of the output of the very many small mines of the area than had been undertaken since 1854.
(*f*) The value figures up to 1870 are purely notional, being based on a constant assumption of five shillings per ton as the pitmouth price.
(*g*) The figures for output in 1854–72 were calculated by the Office of Mining Records on the basis of voluntary returns from a large number of collieries. Those from 1873 onwards were based on compulsory returns to the Inspectors of Mines. Where the two sets of statistics overlap (for the years 1873–9) the compulsory returns have been preferred. The latter are about 1½ million tons higher for Lancashire in 1873–8, and it is clear that for some years before 1873 the output of this area was underestimated by the Office of Mining Records. Differences are small for other areas. Prior to 1873, estimates were made by some Inspectors, and for the year 1872 these have been preferred to those in *Mineral Statistics* for Lancashire, South Wales and the North-East.
(*h*) The value figures from 1870–81 are of doubtful value in view of the sudden drop in 1882, in which year adequate methods of obtaining this series were first adopted. (See the preface to *Mineral Statistics*, 1882.)
(*i*) Output in southern Ireland is excluded after 1921. In 1913 it had amounted to about 90,000 tons valued at £50,000.
(*j*) Coal mined from quarries is included prior to 1938 in all figures, but thereafter it is not included in the district figures. In 1942–5 it is included in the totals. Opencast coal mined in those years was as follows:

1942 1,311,000 tons, 1944 8,651,000 tons,
1943 4,427,000 tons, 1945 8,118,000 tons

(*k*) In 1943 the boundary between the Yorkshire and Midland districts was redefined. For that date two figures are shown the first on the old basis, the second on the new.
(*l*) These figures were affected by major strikes.

Addendum

Roy Church, *The History of the British Coal Industry*, vol. 3 (Oxford, 1986), which appeared after the preparation of this book, makes the following estimates (on p. 86) of U.K. output in million tons, which seem preferable to those given above:

1830	30·5	1838	39·3	1845	51·1	1852	68·3	1859	82·8	1866	104·9
1831	31·5	1839	40·8	1846	53·1	1853	71·2	1860	87·9	1867	106·4
1832	32·1	1840	42·6	1847	54·0	1854	75·1	1861	89·2	1868	108·2
1833	32·9	1841	43·8	1848	56·6	1855	76·4	1862	91·1	1869	110·9
1834	33·8	1842	44·2	1849	59·3	1856	79·0	1863	95·7	1870	115·5
1835	35·2	1843	46·0	1850	62·5	1857	81·9	1864	99·1	1871	121·4
1836	36·4	1844	47·6	1851	65·2	1858	80·3	1865	102·3	1872	125·1
1837	37·8										

Fuel and Energy 4. Output of Coal in the United Kingdom and in National Coal Board Divisions – 1938–80

NOTE

SOURCES: Ministry of Fuel and Power (later Ministry of Power) *Statistical Digest* and its *Supplement* for 1945, later issued by the Ministry of Technology, the Department of Trade (and Industry), and the Ministry of Energy as *Digest of Energy Statistics*. The Division figures for 1946 were not published in these sources and have been obtained from the *Annual Report* of the National Coal Board for 1947 (*S.P.* 1947–8, x) and the *Coal Mining Industry: Annual Statistical Statement for the Year 1946* (*S.P.* 1946–7, xv).

(in millions of tons)

	Scottish	Northern	Durham	North-Eastern/ Yorkshire	North-Western	East Midlands	West Midlands	South-Western	South-Eastern	Opencast	U.K. Total
1938	30·3	14·9	31·4	43·8	17·0	30·8	19·7	37·4	1·8	—	227·0
1939	30·5	14·4	30·6	45·9	17·0	33·2	20·5	37·4	1·9	—	231·3
1940	29·7	13·6	26·7	46·8	16·0	36·0	19·7	34·3	1·6	—	224·3
1941	26·6	12·0	24·6	44·4	14·4	36·1	17·7	29·2	1·4	—	206·3
1942	26·2	12·0	25·3	42·8	13·8	36·5	17·2	28·5	1·3	1·3	204·9
1943	24·7	11·7	24·3	40·3	13·1	35·5	16·5	26·8	1·4	4·4	198·9
1944	23·4	11·3	23·2	37·9	12·8	34·3	16·0	24·0	1·3	8·7	192·7
1945	21·4	10·5	22·1	36·7	12·4	32·8	15·7	22·0	1·2	8·1	182·8
1946	22·5	11·3	23·2	37·6	12·8	32·7	16·4	22·1	1·3	8·8	190·1(*a*)
1947	22·8	11·8	24·3	38·2	13·4	35·1	17·0	22·6	1·4	10·2	197·4
1948	23·5	12·3	25·6	40·1	14·1	37·2	17·7	23·7	1·5	11·7	209·4
1949	23·8	12·8	26·4	42·1	14·4	39·1	18·3	24·2	1·6	12·4	215·1
1950	23·3	13·3	26·5	42·6	14·7	40·1	17·6	24·3	1·7	12·2	216·3
1951	23·6	13·4	27·2	44·4	15·3	43·0	18·0	24·7	1·8	11·0	222·9
1952	22·9	13·2	26·5	44·9	15·5	44·0	18·2	25·0	1·7	12·1	226·4
1953	22·8	13·4	25·9	44·9	15·6	44·5	18·1	25·0	1·7	11·7	224·2
										---(*b*)	---(*b*)
1954	22·6	13·5	25·9	45·6	15·6	45·6	18·0	25·1	1·7	10·1	224·1
1955	22·0	13·5	25·6	43·9	15·6	46·1	17·7	24·2	1·5	11·4	221·6
1956	21·5	13·7	25·6	43·6	15·7	46·3	17·7	24·1	1·7	12·1	----(*c*)
											222·0
1957	21·3	13·5	25·2	43·7	15·5	46·9	17·9	24·3	1·7	13·6	223·6
1958	19·5	13·2	24·0	42·7	15·0	45·7	16·9	22·8	1·6	14·3	215·8
1959	18·9	12·8	23·5	42·3	14·2	44·9	16·0	21·2	1·6	10·8	206·1
	---(*d*)	---(*d*)	---(*d*)	---(*d*)	---(*d*)	---(*d*)	---(*d*)	---(*d*)			
	18·5	12·7	23·3	41·9	14·0	44·6	15·4	20·5			
1960	17·7	12·0	22·8	40·4	12·9	43·7	13·8	19·1	1·5	7·6	193·6
1961	17·2	11·8	22·3	39·4	11·7	44·1	13·8	17·9	1·4	8·5	190·5
1962	17·5	11·9	22·8	42·3	12·3	46·3	14·3	18·8	1·5	8·1	197·4
		---(*f*)			---(*f*)						
1963(*e*)	17·1	11·0	23·0	42·6	13·2	46·8	14·6	18·8	1·5	7·3	197·7
1964(*e*)	16·5	11·0	21·5	43·1	12·7	46·7	14·7	19·5	1·6	6·1	195·2

Fuel and Energy 4. *continued*

(in millions of tons)

Year ending 31 March	Scottish North	Scottish South	Northumberland	North Durham	South Durham	North Yorkshire	Doncaster	Barnsley	South Yorkshire	North Western	Staffordshire
1964	7·5	9·0	11·0	9·4	12·1	10·4	9·8	11·8	11·2	12·8	10·9
1965	6·8	8·7	10·8	8·8	11·6	10·0	10·3	12·0	11·3	12·4	10·4
1966	6·3	8·5	10·6	8·4	10·7	9·7	9·8	11·0	10·9	11·6	10·2
1967	6·1	8·4	9·3	7·9	10·1	9·5	8·6	9·8	11·0	9·7	10·0
1968	5·5	8·2	8·6	7·7	9·8	9·8	9·3	9·7	11·3	9·6	9·8
1969	5·1	7·5	8·0	6·5	8·7	9·7	9·6	9·3	11·6	7·9	9·0
1970	5·0	6·4	6·9	5·4	8·3	9·2	8·5	8·1	10·1	7·0	8·6
1971	5·3	6·0	6·3	5·1	7·6	9·5	8·0	7·8	9·5	6·1	8·3
1972	5·0	5·4	5·1	4·1	6·2	8·4	6·8	6·7	7·6	4·4	6·4
1973	5·3	5·9	6·2	4·5	6·9	9·9	8·7	8·1	9·4	5·5	7·3
1974	8·8		5·0	3·3	5·3	7·2	6·5	6·1	7·6	4·0	6·0
1975	10·0			14·6		8·3	8·3	7·6	8·1	12·6	
1976	9·7			14·4		8·3	7·9	7·4	7·8	11·9	
1977	9·0			12·9		8·1	7·7	7·2	7·7	11·2	
1978	8·3			12·6		8·0	7·4	7·4	7·5	10·6	
1979	8·0			12·7		8·1	6·8	7·3	7·5	10·8	
1980	8·0			13·9		8·0	7·4	7·9	7·5	11·0	

Year ending 31 March	North Nottingham	South Nottingham	North Derbyshire	East Wales	West Wales	South Midlands	Kent	Opencast	U.K. Total
1964	11·1	14·0	14·6	11·9	7·6	11·1	1·6	6·1	187·6
1965	11·4	13·6	14·4	11·3	7·6	11·3	1·5	7·0	184·1
1966	11·2	13·4	13·0	10·3	6·7	10·6	1·5	7·1	174·4
1967	10·8	12·4	12·6	10·4	6·4	10·4	1·5	7·1	164·8
1968	10·9	12·1	12·4	9·8	6·0	10·7	1·4	7·1	162·7
1969	11·7	11·1	11·6	8·9	5·6	9·8	1·4	6·6	153·1
1970	11·8	11·2	10·6	7·7	5·1	9·3	1·1	6·6	140·0
1971	12·1	10·6	9·8	6·9	4·8	8·9	1·0	8·3	133·4
1972	9·6	8·4	7·6	5·7	4·0	6·9	0·8	10·4	109·2
1973	11·8	9·9	8·3	10·8		7·7	0·9	10·5	127·0
1974	9·0	7·8	6·3	7·4		6·1	0·7	9·4	97·1
1975	10·8	9·7	7·7	8·7		7·8	0·8	9·5	115·0
1976	10·6	9·6	7·8	8·3		8·9		10·5	112·6
1977	10·5	8·9	7·2	7·7		8·7		11·5	106·7
1978	10·9	8·8	7·3	7·3		8·4		13·8	104·6
1979	10·8	8·5	7·3	7·6		8·4		13·6	103·7
1980	11·7	8·5	7·6	7·5		8·4		13·2	107·4

(*a*) This is the latest available figure given in the Ministry of Power *Statistical Digest*. The figure of U.K. total output given in the National Coal Board *Annual Report* for 1947 was 188·6 million tons.

(*b*) Losses of 2 per cent in screening opencast coal were excluded after 1953.

(*c*) After 1955 there was a change to a 52-week period instead of the calendar year.

(*d*) Subsequent district figures apply to mines operated by the National Coal Board only.

(*e*) Years ending 31 March.

(*f*) Cumberland was transferred from Northern to North-Western.

Fuel and Energy 5. Numbers Employed in Coal Mines in the United Kingdom and its Main Coalfields – 1801–1938

NOTE

SOURCES: Part A – B. R. Mitchell, *Economic Development of the British Coal Industry, 1800–1914* (Cambridge, 1984); Part B – 1864–96 – *Reports* of H. M. Inspectors of Mines; 1897–1920 – *Mineral Statistics*; 1921–38 – *Annual Report of the Department of Mines*.

Part A. Census-based Statistics, 1801–71

(in thousands)

	Durham & Northum-berland	Cumber-land	Yorkshire	North Derby-shire & Nottingham-shire	South Derby-shire & Leicester-shire	Warwick-shire	Lanca-shire & Cheshire	North Wales	West Midlands	Somerset & Glou-cestershire	South Wales	Scotland	Total
1801	14·2	1·4	7·1	3·0	0·6	0·6	9·6	2·7	10·4	3·8	7·2	8·9	69·6
1811	16·6	1·8	8·2	3·5	0·7	0·6	11·6	3·0	13·1	4·3	10·7	11·0	84·0
1821	18·8	2·0	9·0	4·0	0·9	0·8	13·7	3·8	15·3	4·5	13·0	12·4	99·2
1831	21·0	2·0	10·1	4·6	1·0	0·9	16·0	4·1	18·5	6·5	16·8	13·6	115·1
1841	24·6	2·1	12·2	5·4	1·2	1·0	18·7	4·8	23·5	7·6	25·8	17·5	141·5
1851	38·0	3·5	20·5	8·3	2·3	1·4	31·0	5·1	32·5	8·2	30·9	32·6	214·1
1861	47·7	4·2	31·1	16·0	3·6	1·8	43·9	6·4	38·8	9·3	37·9	35·4	276·5
1871	59·6	4·9	38·6	23·0	4·9	2·2	52·3	10·2	44·2	11·1	50·6	50·6	351·4

B. Official Statistics, 1864–1938

(in thousands)

	Northern (*a*)	Yorkshire	Midland (*b*)	North Wales and Lanca-shire (*c*)	South Wales	Scotland	Total U.K.
1864	57·5	34·5	26·6	47·8	29·1	39·2	307·5
1865	59·0	35·0	27·1	51·1	29·1	39·5	315·5
1866	61·4	35·5	27·1	55·4	29·2	41·2	320·7
1867	63·3	37·0	27·0	56·8	29·3	50·1	333·1
1868	69·0	37·0	28·0	58·4	29·3	50·2	346·8
1869	69·8	36·0	28·5	58·6	29·0	48·0	354·4
1870	75·1	36·5	28·8	58·5	29·0	47·0	350·9
1871	79·0	38·6	31·1	58·3	38·0	47·0	370·9
1872	84·3	51·1	39·3	62·7	38·4	50·7	418·1
	- - -	- - -	- - -	- - -	- - -	- - -	- - -
1873(*d*)	100·5	57·5	47·0	64·2	45·5	58·6	514·1
1874	104·8	62·5	52·4	79·3	73·3	76·1	538·8
1875	108·6	62·2	52·5	80·9	72·6	71·7	535·8
1876	107·1	61·0	52·4	75·2	57·5	69·9	514·5
1877	104·4	60·6	50·3	72·2	65·3	67·8	494·4
1878	98·3	59·8	49·4	71·2	63·7	66·4	475·3
1879	95·4	60·1	51·0	72·6	66·5	67·0	476·8
1880	100·7	60·5	49·4	72·9	69·2	68·2	484·9
1881	102·2	60·5	50·1	73·9	72·9	69·3	495·5
1882	104·8	61·5	49·9	74·8	74·9	67·9	504·0
1883	105·9	63·2	52·2	76·6	80·7	68·4	514·9
1884	108·9	64·0	53·4	76·3	83·9	69·4	520·4
1885	108·8	63·6	55·2	75·6	85·2	70·0	520·6
1886	108·5	65·7	55·1	76·4	85·1	63·1	520·0
1887	108·5	66·9	55·8	77·3	86·9	71·2	526·3
1888	110·5	67·0	58·0	78·3	91·4	70·5	549·2
1889	115·4	69·9	61·3	81·4	99·4	74·1	581·8
1890	123·9	76·8	66·5	88·8	109·9	81·1	623·4
1891	131·2	82·0	71·6	93·7	116·6	85·1	668·0
1892	131·7	86·6	74·7	96·7	116·7	89·0	683·6
1893	138·5	88·6	76·3	99·3	118·0	90·8	683·0
1894	144·6	91·0	80·1	100·7	124·7	93·8	705·2
1895	143·3	88·7	80·0	99·5	126·1	94·1	700·3
1896	144·9	89·6	79·6	95·3	125·2	88·8	692·7
1897	145·9	89·6	80·3	96·1	126·8	89·0	695·2
1898	147·9	91·2	82·3	94·9	128·8	92·0	706·9

B. Official Statistics, 1864–1938 (*cont.*)

(in thousands)

	Northern (*a*)	Yorkshire	Midland (*b*)	North Wales and Lancashire (*c*)	South Wales	Scotland	Total U.K.
1899	153·3	94·9	85·8	95·4	132·7	95·9	729·0
1900	161·1	100·8	90·4	100·6	147·6	103·8	780·1
1901	164·0	105·3	95·8	106·2	150·4	108·0	806·7
1902	167·9	107·7	99·6	106·7	154·6	109·0	824·8
1903	169·8	109·8	102·2	108·5	159·2	111·1	842·1
1904	174·4	112·0	102·4	106·9	163·0	112·8	847·6
1905	179·0	112·6	103·4	106·6	165·6	114·3	858·4
1906	186·1	115·5	106·6	105·4	174·7	115·7	882·3
1907	195·9	123·9	112·6	109·9	190·3	124·8	940·6
1908	203·7	135·2	116·5	115·5	201·8	132·1	987·8
1909	210·5	141·0	119·4	118·7	205·0	133·6	1,014·0
1910	222·9	146·9	121·2	119·8	213·3	137·9	1,049·4
1911	227·3	148·0	124·3	119·4	220·9	138·4	1,067·2
1912	229·6	152·8	126·0	121·5	225·5	143·3	1,089·1
1913	237·8	161·2	130·6	123·9	233·1	147·5	1,127·9
1914	239·0	164·3	130·6	124·0	234·1	146·2	1,133·7
1915	184·1	140·8	. . . (*e*)	105·7	202·7	121·9	953·6
1916	191·3	146·2	. . . (*e*)	111.1	214·1	127·1	998·1
1917	195·2	148·7	. . . (*e*)	114·0	219·7	130·0	1,021·3
1918	196·2	145·5	. . . (*e*)	112·8	218·9	124·5	1,008·9
1919	246·2	166·6	148·2	129·4	257·6	147·0	1,191·3
1920	258·2	173·5	. . . (*e*)	136·0	271·5	154·5	1,248·2
1921(*f*)	228·7	175·6	149·2	123·5	232·0	133·8	1,131·6
1922	234·2	178·3	151·0	122·5	243·0	134·0	1,148·5 (*g*)
1923	250·0	187·4	156·7	124·6	252·6	143·3	1,203·3
1924	251·7	195·3	160·2	124·7	250·1	141·8	1,213·7
1925	207·5	192·0	154·8	116·7	217·8	126·0	1,102·4
Mar. 1926(*h*)	216·7	193·7	155·3	116·7	217·8	127·5	1,115·6
Dec. 1926(*h*)	178·3	177·8	149·1	103·9	156·4	98·9	943·6
1927	192·9	188·7	150·8	106·1	194·1	109·0	1,023·9
1928	187·6	176·2	138·7	96·2	168·3	96·5	939·0
1929	198·1	172·7	138·0	94·5	178·3	100·0	956·7
1930	190·4	171·6	137·4	90·2	172·9	96·6	931·4
1931	167·4	164·3	134·1	86·3	158·2	88·0	867·9
1932	155·4	155·4	129·8	80·9	145·7	82·4	819·3
1933	151·1	144·5	122·2	76·9	142·9	81·6	789·1
1934	158·2	143·4	121·0	72·9	139·8	83·1	788·2
1935	157·7	140·3	117·8	69·4	131·7	83·5	769·5
1936	158·5	140·4	116·9	69·9	126·2	86·6	767·1
1937	167·6	143·2	116·9	70·0	135·9	90·6	791·7
1938	167·8	144·7	118·1	68·1	136·0	90·0	790·9

(*a*) Northumberland, Durham and Cumberland.
(*b*) Derbyshire, Leicestershire, Nottinghamshire, and Warwickshire.
(*c*) Lancashire, Cheshire, Denbighshire, and Flintshire.
(*d*) The figures for 1864–72 were calculated by the Inspectors of Mines on the basis of voluntary returns from a large number of collieries. After 1873 they were based on compulsory returns. The compulsory returns for 1873 itself were incomplete and were supplemented by estimates.
(*e*) The figures for Leicestershire and Warwickshire were not given separately for 1915–18 (owing to wartime staff shortage) and for 1920 (owing to the transfer of responsibility to the Department of Mines).
(*f*) Prior to 1921 the statistics relate to mines under the Coal Mines Act, and thus include a small number of men working minerals other than coal, principally in Scotland, where there were about 6,000. From 1921 only coal mines were covered. Prior to 1925 owners were asked to state the number 'ordinarily employed'. From that date an average of four selected dates in each year was taken. It is not thought that this change made a noticeable difference.
(*g*) Southern Ireland is excluded from the total after 1921.
(*h*) The two figures shown for 1926 are for the months immediately before and after the strike.

Fuel and Energy 6. Average Number of Wage-Earners on Colliery Books in the United Kingdom and in National Coal Board Divisions – 1938–80

NOTE
SOURCES: as for table 4.

(in thousands)

	Scottish	Northern	Durham	North-Eastern	North-Western	East Midlands	West Midlands	South-Western	South-Eastern	U.K. Total
1938	89·9	51·7	114·5	145·8	68·0	94·8	66·8	143·4	6·6	781·7
1939	88·3	50·9	111·2	145·3	65·7	94·9	66·5	137·1	6·4	766·3
1940	86·4	49·1	105·4	145·4	61·3	95·2	64·5	136·4	5·7	749·2
1941	82·9	45·9	93·0	141·5	56·6	93·2	60·4	119·2	5·0	697·6
1942	83·7	45·6	98·8	142·4	57·4	94·0	60·2	121·8	5·3	709·3
1943	82·8	45·4	100·0	140·8	58·0	93·6	59·6	122·0	5·5	707·8
1944	81·7	45·6	102·0	141·4	58·7	95·0	60·0	120·0	5·8	710·2
1945	80·3	45·6	103·5	141·5	58·8	95·0	60·6	117·6	6·0	708·9
1946	79·1	150·3		137·5	58·1	91·8	58·9	114·9	6·0	696·7
1947	81·1	47·1	108·9	138·5	59·8	94·6	59·5	115·5	6·4	711·4
1948	82·4	48·2	111·0	141·5	61·1	98·2	59·9	115·4	6·3	724·0
1949	82·7	48·5	110·7	140·5	60·1	98·0	59·9	113·0	6·1	719·5
1950	81·5	48·6	108·2	135·5	57·5	95·7	56·2	107·8	6·0	697·0
1951	82·2	49·3	107·1	136·3	57·8	96·6	55·2	107·9	6·2	698·6
1952	84·8	49·9	107·1	140·1	60·6	99·3	57·4	110·0	6·4	715·6
1953	85·2	48·9	105·2	141·1	60·9	100·8	58·3	110·1	6·4	716·9
(a)	---	---	---	---	---	---	---	---	---	---
	84·2	47·9	103·7	141·1	60·1	100·5	58·6	110·4	6·4	712·9
1954	83·5	47·1	102·4	140·1	59·5	100·8	58·2	109·1	6·5	707·2
1955	83·7	47·1	102·1	139·3	58·9	101·8	57·4	107·1	6·7	704·1
1956	84·8	47·4	102·3	137·8	58·9	102·2	57·2	105·7	7·1	703·4
1957	86·7	47·6	101·8	138·4	58·4	103·7	59·6	106·7	7·2	710·1
1958	85·8	46·7	100·0	137·0	56·8	103·1	58·0	104·2	7·2	698·8
1959	81·0	44·0	96·1	132·7	52·4	100·4	53·9	97·1	6·9	664·5
(b)	---	---	---	---	---	---	---	---	---	---
	79·9	43·7	95·6	132·1	51·9	100·1	53·1	94·9	6·9	658·2
1960	72·2	39·7	90·1	121·9	45·4	94·4	45·5	87·0	5·9	602·1
1961	69·4	37·1	85·3	116·5	41·8	91·3	41·8	81·6	5·7	570·5
1962	63·8	35·2	81·1	115·3	40·0	90·1	40·3	79·6	5·5	550·9
1963	55·8	33·7	75·0	112·8	36·8	88·6	38·4	77·5	5·2	523·8

	Scottish										
	North	South	Northumberland	North Durham	South Durham	North Yorkshire	Doncaster	Barnsley	South Yorkshire	North Western	Staffordshire
1964(c)	24·3	30·3	29·6	33·4	40·2	24·9	25·7	30·5	30·8	39·8	27·9
1965	22·4	28·4	28·3	30·4	38·2	24·2	24·8	29·6	29·8	37·6	26·4
1966	20·5	26·5	26·5	27·3	34·7	23·3	23·1	28·2	28·5	35·1	24·2
1967	18·5	24·5	24·0	24·0	31·2	22·2	22·1	25·9	27·0	31·4	22·6
1968	16·5	22·8	21·9	22·3	27·6	21·7	21·2	24·0	26·2	28·6	21·3
1969	13·7	19·3	18·1	17·8	22·5	19·0	19·0	21·0	23·9	21·0	17·9
1970	13·3	17·3	14·7	14·9	21·0	18·0	17·9	19·5	21·8	17·8	15·7
1971	13·2	16·5	13·9	13·9	20·0	17·0	17·4	18·2	20·6	16·5	14·9
1972	13·2	16·2	13·7	14·0	19·9	16·9	17·1	17·7	20·0	15·4	14·5
1973	12·6	14·9	12·9	12·8	18·5	16·2	16·8	17·2	18·9	14·7	14·1
1974	25·2		12·0	11·4	17·2	15·1	16·5	16·4	18·2	13·4	13·5
1975	24·4		37·7			14·4	16·8	16·6	17·9	25·8	
1976	24·2		36·6			15·4	17·2	16·7	18·0	25·7	
1977	23·1		35·4			15·3	17·1	16·5	17·8	25·0	
1978	22·1		34·9			15·5	17·2	16·5	17·8	24·3	
1979	21·1		34·4			15·6	16·6	15·9	17·3	23·6	
1980	21·0		33·5			15·8	16·7	15·8	17·1	23·0	

Fuel and Energy. *continued*

	North Nottingham	South Nottingham	North Derbyshire	East Wales	West Wales	South Midlands	Kent	U.K. Total
1964(*c*)	20·7	24·2	31·0	43·9	32·6	22·0	5·2	517·0
1965	20·2	23·5	29·4	41·3	30·7	20·8	5·0	491·0
1966	19·6	22·8	26·7	37·4	27·2	19·3	4·8	455·7
1967	19·0	22·2	24·3	34·4	23·3	18·1	4·7	419·4
1968	19·1	21·1	22·3	32·4	21·0	17·2	4·7	391·9
1969	19·1	17·9	19·7	29·3	18·3	14·5	4·3	336·3
1970	18·8	16·9	17·5	26·1	16·5	13·5	3·9	305·1
1971	18·6	16·6	14·7	23·4	15·2	13·0	3·6	287·2
1972	18·8	16·4	14·1	22·4	14·8	12·9	3·5	281·5
1973	18·5	15·9	13·6	35·0		12·2	3·3	268·1
1974	17·6	15·4	13·2	32·3		11·7	3·0	252·0
1975	17·4	15·4	12·6	31·4		12·1	3·0	246·0
1976	17·7	15·8	12·6	31·1		16·1		247·1
1977	17·6	15·7	12·4	30·1		16·0		242·0
1978	17·8	16·1	12·5	29·5		16·3		240·5
1979	18·0	15·9	12·3	28·0		16·2		234·9
1980	18·1	15·9	12·1	27·0		16·5		232·5

(*a*) There was a change in the definition used in 1954. The second line of figures for 1953 is on the new basis.

(*b*) From 1960 the figures relate to mines operated by the National Coal Board only. The second line of figures for 1959 is on this basis.

(*c*) Subsequent statistics are for years ended 31 March.

Fuel and Energy 7. Coal Exports – England & Wales 1697–1791, Great Britain 1792–1808 and United Kingdom 1816–1980

NOTES

[1] SOURCES: Parts A and B – Elizabeth B. Schumpeter, *English Overseas Trade Statistics, 1697–1808* (Oxford University Press, 1960) tables VIII and IX (converted to tons); Part C – 1816–29 – *S.P.* 1830–1, x; 1830–2 – *Report of the Royal Commission on the Coal Supply* (*S.P.* 1871, XVIII), appendix 60 to the report of committee E; 1833–70 – returns in sessional papers annually; 1871–1918 – *Report of the Coal Industry Commission* (*S.P.* 1919, XII), appendix 21; 1919–20 – *Mineral Statistics*; 1921–38 – *Annual Report of the Department of Mines*; 1939–80 – Ministry of (Fuel and) Power, *Statistical Digest* and Ministry of Technology (later Department of Trade and Industry and then Department of Energy); *Digest of Energy Statistics*.

[2] In converting the original figures to tons, one Newcastle chaldron has been taken to equal 53 cwt. (see table 1, note 2) and one Winton chaldron has been assumed to equal half a Newcastle chaldron, since the valuation rates were respectively 48 shillings and 24 shillings.

[3] In Parts A and B the very small quantities of 'kennel' coal have not been included.

[4] In Parts A and B exports to Ireland are included.

A. England & Wales, 1697–1791

(in thousands of tons)

1697	37	1729	127	1761	189
1698	66	1730	89	1762	189
1699	56	1731	120	1763	203
1700	68	1732	131	1764	217
1701	75	1733	124	1765	312
1702	55	1734	136	1766	481
1703	46	1735	138	1767	464
1704	50	1736	145	1768	366
1705	...	1737	135	1769	339
1706	47	1738	135	1770	289
1707	57	1739	156	1771	374
1708	60	1740	179	1772	370
1709	69	1741	142	1773	347
1710	64	1742	131	1774	396
1711	67	1743	151	1775	392
1712	...	1744	136	1776	415
1713	81	1745	139	1777	425
1714	103	1746	147	1778	366
1715	98	1747	126	1779	336
1716	100	1748	151	1780	346
1717	87	1749	175	1781	272
1718	95	1750	164	1782	281
1719	103	1751	216	1783	424
1720	92	1752	201	1784	419
1721	104	1753	205	1785	549
1722	105	1754	190	1786	508
1723	107	1755	182	1787	457
1724	165	1756	181	1788	612
1725	100	1757	156	1789	584
1726	122	1758	158	1790	605
1727	132	1759	150	1791	632
1728	99	1760	150		

B. Great Britain, 1792–1808

1792	667	1798	512	1804	587
1793	689	1799	527	1805	580
1794	605	1800	579	1806	619
1795	514	1801	515	1807	524
1796	590	1802	590	1808	581
1797	513	1803	589		

Fuel and Energy 7. *continued*

C. United Kingdom, 1816–1938

(in thousands of tons)

Year		Year		Year		Year	
1816	238	1857	6,483	1898	35,058	1939	36,917
1817	253	1858	6,292	1899	41,180	1940	19,646
1818	272	1859	6,784	1900	44,089	1941	5,084
1819	238	1860	7,050	1901	41,877	1942	3,574
1820	251	1861	7,561	1902	43,159	1943	3,625
1821	263	1862	8,011	1903	44,950	1944	2,606
1822	287	1863	8,005	1904	46,256	1945	3,325
1823	254	1864	8,537	1905	47,477	1946	4,455
1824	282	1865	8,861	1906	55,600	1947	1,057
1825	313	1866	9,635	1907	63,601	1948	10,505
1826	348	1867	10,053	1908	62,547	1949	13,916
1827	369	1868	10,498	1909	63,077	1950	13,551
1828	358	1869	10,233	1910	62,085	1951	7,807
1829	371	1870	11,162	1911	64,599	1952	11,751
1830	504	1871	12,208	1912	64,444	1953	13,972
1831	511	1872	12,712	1913	73,400	1954	13,716
1832	588	1873	12,078	1914	59,040	1955	12,233

1833(*a*)	629	1874	13,381	1915	43,535	1956	8,542
1834	610	1875	13,979	1916	38,352	1957	7,027
1835	729	1876	15,690	1917	34,996	1958	4,223
1836	911	1877	14,881	1918	31,753	1959	3,479
1837	1,106	1878	14,999	1919	35,250	1960	5,143
1838	1,303	1879	15,740	1920	24,932	1961	5,597
1839	1,432	1880	17,891	1921	24,661	1962	4,711
1840	1,592	1881	18,760	1922(*b*)	64,198	1963	7,876
1841	1,832	1882	19,926	1923	79,459	1964	5,870
1842	1,975	1883	21,671	1924	61,651	1965	3,795
1843	1,820	1884	22,354	1925	50,817	1966	2,769
1844	1,698	1885	22,710	1926	20,596	1967	1,850
1845	2,443	1886	22,107	1927	51,149	1968	2,662
1846	2,390	1887	23,259	1928	50,051	1969	3,396
1847	1,996	1888	25,632	1929	60,267	1970	3,309
1848	2,699	1889	27,505	1930	54,874	1971	2,652
1849	2,731	1890	28,738	1931	42,750	1972	1,721
1850	3,212	1891	29,497	1932	38,899	1973	2,651
1851	3,300	1892	29,048	1933	39,068	1974	1,865
1852	3,479	1893	27,708	1934	39,660	1975	2,182
1853	3,758	1894	31,756	1935	38,714	1976	1,436
1854	4,120	1895	31,715	1936	34,519	1977	1,910
1855	4,763	1896	32,948	1937	40,338	1978	2,230
1856	5,638	1897	35,354	1938	35,856	1979	2,302
						1980	3,978

(*a*) Prior to 1833 the small quantity of coke exported is included (without conversion to coal equivalent).

(*b*) Shipments to southern Ireland are counted as exports from April 1922.

Fuel and Energy 8. Consumption of Coal in the United Kingdom according to Use – 1816–1980

NOTES

[1] SOURCES: Part A – B. R. Mitchell, *Economic Development of the British Coal Industry 1800–1914* (Cambridge, 1984); Part B – Ministry of (Fuel and) Power, *Statistical Digest* and Ministry of Technology (later Department of Trade and Industry, then Department of Energy), *Digest of Energy Statistics* (with ships 1959–62 from *The Colliery Year Book and Coal Trades Directory*).

[2] The substantially different figures for ships in 1913 in Parts A and B result from different treatment of bunker coal taken on at overseas stations.

A. 1816–1913

(in millions of tons)

	Domestic	General Manufacture	Iron and Steel	Gasworks	Electricity	Railways	Ships	Mines
1816	9·3	4·9	1·9	..	—	—	—	0·9
1830	10·7	7·0	3·6	0·5	—	..	0·2	1·2
1840	11·5	9·7	7·1	1·0	—	0·3	0·6	2·0
1855	15·0	18·0	15·5	2·7	—	1·4	1·6	4·2
1869	19·5	30·0	26·5	6·3	—	3·2	3·3	7·6
1887	28	46	27	10	—	6	9	11
1903	32	62	28	15	3	13	13	15
1913	35	68	37	18	5	15	17	18

B. 1913–80

(in millions of tons)

	Coke Ovens	Domestic	Electricity	Gasworks	Industry	Mines	Railways	Ships
1913	19·7	...	4·9	17·8	...	18·0	14·3	23·4
1914	17·1	...	5·6	17·5	...	18·0(*a*)	13·9	20·9
1915	18·2	...	5·5	17·4	...	18·0(*a*)	14·2	15·6
1916	20·2	...	6·0	17·4	...	18·0(*a*)	14·4	14·7
1917	20·5	...	6·6	18·8		18·0(*a*)	13·6	11·5
1918	19·7	...	7·1	18·5	...	17·0(*a*)	13·3	9·8
1919	17·6	...	7·7	17·7	...	17·0(*a*)	13·5	13·3
1920	18·9	...	7·4	18·6	...	17·2	14·5	15·6
1921	6·9	...	6·3	16·7	...	13·7	11·5	12·1
1922	13·3	...	6·8	16·6	...	16·3	13·3	19·9
	---		---	---		---	---	---
1923(*a*)	19·8	...	7·2	17·2	...	16·9	14·0	19·5
1924	18·9	...	7·7	18·1	...	16·6	14·2	19·2
1925	16·4	...	8·1	17·8	...	15·4	14·1	17·9
1926	7·1	...	8·3	17·3	...	7·6(*a*)	12·1	8·5
1927	17·4	...	9·0	18·5	...	14·6	14·3	18·2
1928	17·4	...	9·3	18·3	...	13·5	13·8	18·1
1929	20·0	...	9·8	18·6	...	13·7	14·1	18·0
1930	17·2	...	9·7	18·4	...	13·5	13·6	17·1
1931	12·7	...	9·6	18·1	...	12·6	13·0	15·9
1932	12·7	...	9·8	17·7	...	12·0	12·4	15·5
1933	13·1	...	10·3	17·4	...	11·6	12·4	14·7
1934	16·9	...	11·2	17·9	...	11·7	12·9	14·9
1935	17·4	...	12·2	18·0	...	11·6	13·0	13·9
1936	20·1	...	13·6	19·1	...	11·8	13·5	13·4
1937	21·9	...	14·8	19·4	...	12·2	13·8	13·1
1938	19·1	...	14·9	19·1	...	11·9	13·2	11·8
1939	20·4	...	15·9	18·9	...	12·1	12·9	10·8
1940	22·3	...	18·1	17·8	...	12·3	13·5	8·2
1941	21·1	...	20·4	19·1	...	12·1	13·8	5·6
1942	21·6	...	22·3	20·7	...	12·0	14·5	4·8
1943	20·9	42·4	22·6	20·8	39·0	11·6	14·8	4·4
1944	20·1	39·6	24·1	20·7	37·0	11·1	15·0	3·6
1945	20·1	36·4	23·5	21·0	35·0	10·5	14·6	4·1
1946	20·1	35·3	26·2	22·7	38·0	10·6	14·8	5·7
1947	19·8	35·8	27·1	22·7	36·0	11·0	14·3	5·4

B. 1913–80 (*cont.*)

(in millions of tons)

	Coke Ovens	Domestic	Electricity	Gasworks	Industry	Mines	Railways	Ships
1948	22·3	36·4	28·8	24·6	38·0	11·2	14·3	6·3
1949	22·6	36·0	30·0	25·3	38·3	10·8	14·4	6·0
1950	22·6	37·3	32·9	26·2	40·1	10·7	14·2	4·9
1951	23·4	37·1	35·4	27·4	40·9	10·6	14·1	4·6
1952	25·1	36·8	35·5	27·7	38·9	10·3	13·9	4·1
1953	25·9	37·1	36·7	27·1	39·4	9·9	13·4	3·7
1954	26·6	38·2	39·6	27·3	40·8	9·5	13·0	3·2
1955	27·0	37·1	42·9	27·9	40·7	8·7	12·2	2·8
1956	29·3	37·5	45·6	27·8	39·5	7·9	12·1	2·2
1957	30·7	35·6	46·4	26·4	37·5	7·2	11·4	1·7
1958	27·8	36·2	46·1	24·8	33·7	6·5	10·3	1·3
1959	25·7	33·4	46·0	22·5	31·7	5·6	9·5	1·1
1960	28·5	34·4	51·1	22·3	31·3	5·0	8·9	0·6
1961	26·8	32·4	54·7	22·2	29·2	4·5	7·7	0·4
1962	23·5	32·7	60·4	22·1	27·4	4·2	6·1	0·3
1963	23·5	32·0	66·8	22·1	25·9	3·9	4·9	...
1964	25·5	27·9	67·4	20·2	24·7	3·7	3·8	...
1965	25·7	27·3	69·3	18·0	24·1	3·4	2·8	...
1966	24·3	25·5	67·9	16·7	22·2	3·1	1·7	...
1967	23·1	23·0	66·6	14·4	20·1	2·9	0·8	...
1968	24·9	22·3	72·5	10·6	22·2	2·4	0·2	...
1969	25·4	20·8	75·2	6·8	21·1	2·0	0·2	...
1970	24·9	19·0	75·5	4·2	19·0	1·9	0·1	...
1971	23·2	16·2	71·1	1·8	15·3	1·6	0·1	...
1972	20·2	13·7	65·0	0·6	11·3	1·4	0·1	...
1973	21·5	13·5	75·2	0·5	11·7	1·4	0·1	...
1974	18·2	12·5	65·5	0·1	10·7	1·2	0·1	...
1975	18·8	10·6	73·1	--	9·4	1·2	0·1	...
1976	19·1	9·9	76·3	--	8·7	1·1	0·1	...
1977	17·1	10·1	78·2	...	8·7	1·1	0·1	...
1978	14·7	9·2	78·9	...	8·5	1·0	0·1	...
1979	14·9	9·5	86·9	...	9·1	0·8	0·1	...
1980	11·4	8·0	87·6	...	7·7	0·7	0·1	...

(*a*) Irish consumption is excluded after 1922, shipments to southern Ireland being regarded as exports, and those to Northern Ireland being separately recorded.

Fuel and Energy 9. Solid Fuel Used in Pig Iron Manufacture – Great Britain 1867–1980

NOTES

[1] SOURCES: Part A – 1867–72 – *Report of the Select Committee on the Dearness and Scarcity of Coal* (*S.P.* 1873, x), p. 314; 1873–82 – *S.P.* 1884, LXXXV, p. 606; 1883–1920 – *Mineral Statistics*; 1921–7 – *Annual Report of the Department of Mines*; Part B – British Iron and Steel Federation (and its successors), *Annual Statistics*.

[2] The figures in Part A are derived from those of pig iron output by applying estimates made annually of the amount of coal required to make a ton of pig iron. After 1871 these estimates were made for each county, but there was still a considerable element of guesswork involved, especially in the 1870s.

[3] Fuel used in the production of blast furnace ferro-alloys is included.

A. 1867–1927

(in thousands of tons)

	Coal		Coal	Coke
1867	14,283	1898	17,196	
1868	14,911	1899	19,061	
1869	16,337	1900	18,742	
1870	17,891	1901	16,274	
1871	19,882	1902	17,649	
	---(*a*)			
1872	17,211	1903	18,302	
1873	16,719	1904	17,535	
1874	15,292	1905	19,256	
1875	15,646	1906	20,837	
1876	15,598	1907	21,120	
1877	15,342	1908	18,742	
1878	14,112	1909	19,463	
1879	13,117	1910	20,486	
1880	16,983	1911	19,218	
1881	17,485	1912	17,998	
1882	17,796	1913	21,224	
1883	17,775	1914	18,381	
1884	16,078	1915	2,509	9,747
1885	15,288	1916	2,613	10,301
1886	15,304	1917	2,816	10,962
1887	14,250	1918	2,607	11,287
1888	16,131	1919	2,310	9,384
1889	16,767	1920	2,062	10,036
1890	16,169	1921	651	3,076
1891	15,374	1922	948	5,819
1892	13,860	1923	1,834	8,633
1893	13,806	1924	1,376	8,609
1894	14,885	1925	886	7,466
1895	15,225	1926	282	2,956
1896	17,114	1927	1,093	8,404
1897	17,552			

B. 1927–80

(in thousands of tons of coke equivalent)

1927	9,060·2	1954	11,877·1
1928	8,205·0	1955	12,250·2
1929	9,450·3	1956	12,983·1
1930	7,676·8	1957	13,529·6
1931	4,665·7	1958	11,628·6
1932	4,300·8	1959	10,538·6
1933	4,804·5	1960	12,998·4
1934	6,848·3	1961	12,058·8
1935	7,168·9	1962	10,596·2
1936	8,659·8	1963	10,488·9
1937	9,721·4	1964	12,050·1
1938	7,621·6	1965	11,875·5
1939	8,759·8	1966	10,586·2
1940	9,611·3	1967	9,949·8
1941	9,134·5	1968	10,776·4
1942	9,582·2	1969	10,653·0
1943	8,752·2	1970	10,873·8
1944	8,201·6	1971	9,396·6
1945	8,174·7	1972	8,890·2
1946	8,564·5	1973	9,713·9
1947	8,562·9	1974	8,292·7
1948	9,974·4	1975	7,265·0
1949	9,984·5	1976	8,248·6
1950	9,897·8	1977	7,239·7
1951	10,281·8	1978	6,600·9
1952	11,478·9	1979	7,382·7
1953	11,834·1	1980	3,654·6

(*a*) The figures up to 1871 are very rough guesses, made by multiplying pig iron output by a factor of three.

Fuel and Energy 10. Percentage of Coal Output Cut Mechanically and Power-Loaded – United Kingdom 1900–78

NOTES

[1] SOURCES: 1900–20 – *Mineral Statistics*; 1921–38 – *Annual Report of the Department of Mines*; 1939–80 – Ministry of (Fuel and) Power, *Statistical Digest* and Ministry of Technology (later Department of Trade & Industry then Department of Energy), *Digest of Energy Statistics*.

[2] Statistics relate to coal got by both coal-cutters and mechanical picks.

	Mechanically Cut		Mechanically Cut	Power-loaded (a)		Mechanically Cut	Power-loaded (a)
1900	1	1927	23	...	1954	84	7·4
1901	1	1928	26	...	1955	87	9·9
1902	2	1929	28	...	1956	87	15·5
1903	2	1930	31	...	1957	88	23·1
							---(b)
1904	2	1931	35	...	1958	90	27·8
1905	3	1932	38	...	1959	90	31·3
1906	4	1933	42	...	1960	92	37·5
1907	5	1934	47	...	1961	...	47·7
1908	5	1935	51	...	1962	...	58·8
							---(c)
1909	5	1936	55	...	1963	...	68·4
1910	6	1937	57	...	1964	...	75·0
1911	7	1938	59	...	1965	...	80·7
1912	8	1939	61	...	1966	...	85·7
1913	8	1940	64	...	1967	...	89·7
1914	9	1941	66	...	1968	...	91·8
1915	10	1942	66	...	1969	...	92·3
1916	10	1943	69	...	1970	...	92·2
1917	11	1944	72	...	1971	...	92·2
1918	12	1945	72	...	1972	...	93·0
1919	12	1946	74	...	1973	...	93·5
1920	13	1947	75	2·4	1974	...	93·5
1921	14	1948	76	2·5	1975	...	93·6
1922	15	1949	78	3·2	1976	...	93·8
1923	17	1950	79	3·8	1977	...	93·6
1924	19	1951	81	4·2	1978	...	93·5
1925	20	1952	82	4·9			
1926	20	1953	83	6·0			

(*a*) Relates to National Coal Board mines only.

(*b*) Prior to 1958 figures relate to pithead rather than saleable output.

(*c*) Subsequent figures are for years ended on 31 March following that shown.

Fuel and Energy 11. Sales of Electricity – United Kingdom 1895–1920

NOTES

[1] SOURCES: Garcke's *Manual of Electricity Undertakings* (annually from 1896).

[2] The figures relate to authorised undertakings only.

[3] The figures are not of actual sales within the calandar year, but relate to various accounting years ending during a twelve-month period centred on 31 December of the year shown.

(in gigaWatt hours)

1895	20	1910	1,097
1896	30	1911	1,236
1897	43	1912	1,318
1898	60	1913	1,635
1899	85	1914	1,694
1900	125	1915	2,001
1901	196	1916	2,367
1902	247	1917	2,716
1903	345	1918	3,079
1904	448	1919	3,086
1905	554	1920	3,677
1906	713		
1907	817		
1908	955		
1909	1,027		

Fuel and Energy 12. Sales of Electricity according to Type of Consumer – Great Britain 1920–80

NOTES

[1] SOURCE: Ministry of Fuel and Power (later Ministry of Power) *Statistical Digest*, and Ministry of Technology (later Department of Trade & Industry then Department of Energy), *Digest of Energy Statistics*.

[2] The figures apply to authorised undertakings prior to 1948 and to nationalised ones subsequently.

(in gigaWatt hours)

	Domestic and Farms	Shops, Offices, etc.	Industry	Public Lighting	Traction	Total
1920	297	398	2,545	48	419	3,707
1921	316	403	2,081	51	391	3,242
1922	370	460	2,456	58	415	3,759
1923	453	543	2,989	67	443	4,495
1924	543	626	3,435	78	486	5,168
1925	635	699	3,709	90	519	5,652
1926	754	812	3,592	96	563	5,817
1927	921	923	4,375	113	649	6,981
1928	1,098	1,042	4,762	126	716	7,744
1929	1,311	1,191	5,318	144	782	8,746
1930	1,532	1,314	5,355	162	806	9,169
1931	1,776	1,439	5,282	181	822	9,500
1932	2,027	1,577	5,518	199	855	10,176
1933	2,296	1,741	6,073	216	947	11,273
1934	2,647	1,963	7,060	240	982	12,892
1935	3,227	2,257	7,853	268	1,036	14,641
1936	3,964	2,619	8,914	298	1,096	16,891
1937	4,687	2,944	10,019	339	1,180	19,169
1938	5,361	3,107	10,320	367	1,249	20,404
1939	5,936	3,117	11,672	248	1,261	22,234
1940	6,228	2,997	13,874	17	1,147	24,263
1941	6,637	3,266	16,244	18	1,143	27,308
1942	6,720	3,256	19,142	20	1,148	30,286
1943	6,709	3,062	20,516	20	1,142	31,449
1944	7,835	3,510	19,976	29	1,169	32,519
1945	8,805	3,482	17,679	161	1,236	31,363
1946	11,663	3,892	17,632	242	1,369	34,798
1947	12,728	3,973	17,606	190	1,361	35,858
1948	13,576	4,469	19,121	257	1,398	38,821
1949	13,657	5,035	20,445	335	1,447	40,919
1950	14,911	5,765	22,920	415	1,463	45,474
1951	16,939	6,354	25,350	441	1,429	50,513
1952	16,869	7,115	26,068	479	1,401	51,950
1953	17,691	7,948	28,000	528	1,401	55,568
1954	19,075	8,746	31,553	576	1,451	61,401
1955	21,146	9,545	34,635	627	1,470	67,423
1956	23,755	10,337	37,224	692	1,512	73,520
1957	24,850	10,733	39,348	742	1,545	77,218
1958	28,227	12,057	41,241	793	1,551	83,869
1959	30,487	12,837	44,695	855	1,630	90,504
1960	35,270	14,526	49,991	922	1,654	102,363
1961	39,968	15,809	51,740	994	1,721	110,232
1962	47,628	18,284	53,529	1,060	1,856	122,357
1963	54,475	20,263	56,106	1,127	1,879	133,850
1964	54,411	21,321	61,604	1,191	1,847	140,374
1965	59,421	23,427	65,040	1,260	1,923	151,071
1966	61,961	24,796	66,732	1,328	2,114	156,931
1967	64,365	26,254	67,446	1,379	2,220	161,604
1968	68,810	28,687	72,724	1,452	2,252	173,925
1969	74,256	31,002	76,304	1,573	2,288	185,423
1970	78,989	32,628	78,300	1,682	2,308	193,907

Fuel and Energy 12. *continued*

(in gigaWatt hours)

	Domestic and Farms	Shops, Offices, etc.	Industry	Public Lighting	Traction	Total
1971	82,692	33,815	78,840	1,764	2,331	199,442
1972	88,821	34,997	78,486	1,822	2,244	206,370
1973	93,279	37,773	85,412	1,946	2,181	220,591
1974	94,545	34,470	80,734	1,826	2,327	213,902
1975	90,817	37,471	80,656	2,073	2,482	213,499
1976	86,737	38,808	86,132	2,150	2,455	216,282
1977	87,720	40,654	87,855	2,163	2,512	220,904
1978	87,662	42,956	90,002	2,177	2,549	225,346
1979	91,506	45,449	93,976	2,160	2,553	235,644
1980	87,907	45,822	86,453	2,252	2,619	225,053

Fuel and Energy 13. Sales of Electricity – Republic of Ireland 1929–80

NOTES
[1] SOURCE: *Statistical Abstract of Ireland.*
[2] The figures apply to the Republic of Ireland Electricity Supply Board.
[3] Statistics are for years beginning 1 April.

(in gigaWatt hours)

	Domestic	Commercial	Industry	Total
1929				43
1930				86
1931				111
1932				120
1933				139
1934				157
1935				187
1936				219
1937				244
1938				295
1939				319
1940				345
1941				357
1942				328
1943				347
1944				319
1945				379
1946	169	113	173	454
1947	189	122	180	492
1948	222	141	206	569
1949	246	152	228	626
1950	326	187	257	770
1951	351	210	275	835
1952	384	235	300	930
1953	428	274	349	1,052
1954	479	311	401	1,192
1955	531	345	430	1,307
1956	568	352	433	1,353
1957	611	372	442	1,425
1958	670	402	476	1,549
1959	703	421	566	1,692
1960	769	455	640	1,864
1961	822	499	684	2,005
1962	933	571	735	2,239
1963	994	592	790	2,376
1964	1,132	669	882	2,683
	---(a)	---(a)	---(a)	
1965	1,325	716	912	2,953
1966	1,452	777	1,009	3,238
1967	1,581	842	1,147	3,570
1968	1,791	918	1,303	4,012
1969	1,965	1,033	1,414	4,412
1970	2,206	1,083	1,573	4,862
1971	2,374	1,155	1,743	5,272
1972	2,533	1,231	1,941	5,705
1973	2,693	1,259	2,200	6,152
1974	2,650	1,279	2,225	6,153
1975	2,706	1,309	2,244	6,259
1976	2,906	1,384	2,493	6,783
1977	3,091	1,491	2,748	7,330
1978	3,404	1,623	2,938	7,965
1979	3,600	1,722	3,238	8,560
1980	3,515	1,774	3,076	8,365

(a) There were minor rearrangements of categories in 1965. 72 gWh were added to domestic consumption, 65 gWh being from the industry category.

Fuel and Energy 14. Electricity Generated according to Type of Plant – Great Britain 1920–80

NOTES

[1] SOURCE: As for table 12.

[2] The figures relate to authorised undertakings prior to 1948 and nationalised ones thereafter.

[3] Thermal electricity generated by nuclear stations is included below as follows (gross to 1966 (1st line), net thereafter):

1956	58	1965	14,145	1973	23,658
1957	409	1966	18,894 17,848	1974	29,395
1958	305	1967	21,279	1975	26,518
1959	1,201	1968	24,056	1976	32,419
1960	2,079	1969	25,271	1977	36,417
1961	2,399	1970	21,870	1978	33,339
1962	3,477	1971	23,209	1979	34,604
1963	5,949	1972	25,304	1980	33,462
1964	7,629				

(in gigaWatt hours)

	Thermal	Hydro	Total		Thermal	Hydro	Total
1920(*a*)	4,263	12	4,275	1951	58,434	1,142	59,576
1921	3,880	10	3,890	1952	60,723	1,268	61,991
1922	4,531	10	4,541	1953	64,232	1,284	65,516
1923	5,276	13	5,289	1954	71,137	1,759	72,896
1924	6,007	15	6,022	1955	79,001	1,147	80,148
1925	6,604	15	6,619	1956	85,494	1,667	87,161
1926	6,977	15	6,992	1957	88,868	2,098	90,966
1927	8,421	31	8,452	1958	96,389	2,109	98,498
1928	9,216	108	9,324	1959	102,994	2,175	105,169
1929	10,265	136	10,401	1960	116,309	2,539	118,484
1930	10,597	320	10,917	1961	124,393	3,196	127,589
1931	11,001	416	11,417	1962	138,328	3,252	141,580
1932	11,894	354	12,248	1963	150,698	3,074	153,772
1933	13,228	330	13,558	1964	158,758	3,420	162,178
1934	14,998	464	15,462	1965	170,743	3,931	174,674
1935	16,944	625	17,569	1966	177,294	3,879	181,173
1936	19,554	668	20,222	1967	182,855	5,046	187,901
1937	22,150	755	22,905	1968	197,092	3,848	200,940
1938	23,384	988	24,372	1969	210,563	3,929	214,492
1939	25,427	982	26,409	1970	219,006	4,981	223,987
1940	27,973	800	28,773	1971	227,480	3,754	231,234
1941	31,529	831	32,360	1972	234,076	3,737	237,813
1942	34,557	1,097	35,654	1973	249,411	3,903	253,314
1943	35,622	1,329	36,951	1974	241,029	4,231	245,260
1944	37,187	1,176	38,363	1975	241,722	4,354	246,076
1945	36,140	1,144	37,284	1976	245,050	4,519	249,569
1946	40,114	1,139	41,253	1977	251,910	4,643	256,553
1947	41,452	1,128	42,580	1978	256,593	4,571	261,164
1948	45,148	881	46,029	1979	269,702	4,803	273,505
1949	47,886	719	48,605	1980	256,213	4,497	260,710
1950	53,486	1,035	54,521				

(*a*) The only reliable figure for an earlier date is contained in the 1907 Census of Production, which gave the public supply as 1,432 million kWh.

Fuel and Energy 15. Electricity Generated according to Type of Plant – Republic of Ireland 1931–80

NOTES

[1] SOURCE: *Statistical Abstract of Ireland*.

[2] The figures relate to the Republic of Ireland Electricity Supply Board.

[3] Statistics from 1947 are for years beginning 1 April.

(in gigaWatt hours)

	Hydro	Total		Hydro	Total		Hydro	Total
1931		149	1948	343	709	1965	940	3,538
1932		163	1949	312	782	1966	851	3,845
1933		179	1950	467	969	1967	797	4,242
1934		200	1951	457	1,029	1968	770	4,745
1935		229	1952	361	1,161	1969	593	5,242
1936		273	1953	532	1,292	1970	704	5,915
1937		309	1954	780	1,458	1971	525	6,293
1938		354	1955	488	1,570	1972	653	6,746
1939		401	1956	689	1,644	1973	746	7,287
1940		428	1957	702	1,771	1974	712	7,616
1941		444	1958	782	1,894	1975	486	7,850
1942		421	1959	756	2,094	1976	662	8,647
1943		432	1960	932	2,260	1977	741	9,278
1944		408	1961	738	2,452	1978	628	10,159
1945		463	1962	659	2,709	1979	889	10,767
1946		552	1963	657	2,894	1980	827	10,574
		...(*a*)						
1947	422	618	1964	793	3,231			

(*a*) See note 3 above.

Fuel and Energy 16. Gas Sold to Consumers – Great Britain 1881–1980

NOTES

[1] Sources: 1881–1920 – *Returns* published annually in Parliamentary Papers; 1921–80 – Ministry of Fuel and Power (later Ministry of Power) *Statistical Digest*, and Ministry of Technology (later Department of Trade & Industry, then Department of Energy), *Digest of Energy Statistics*.

[2] The figures apply to statutory undertakings prior to 1943, and to undertakings later vested in the Gas Boards thereafter, together with a few small transport gasworks until 1954.

[3] The local authority accounting year ended in March or May, and these figures have been attributed to the previous calendar year.

A. in million cubic feet

1881	61,616(*a*)	1896	113,940	1911	184,412
1882	64,830	1897	119,099	1912	194,084
1883	68,269	1898	124,123	1913	201,594
				...	
1884	71,639	1899	132,326	1919	222,883
1885	75,260	1900	136,856	1920	235,403
1886	78,478	1901	140,421	1921	229,077
1887	81,416	1902	143,990	1922	232,603
1888	84,712	1903	147,702	1923	241,627
1889	87,908	1904	155,141	1924	256,892
1890	92,242	1905	157,322	1925	265,757
1891	97,350	1906	163,800	1926	276,569
1892	100,186	1907	168,630	1927	280,202
1893	99,212	1908	169,706	1928	282,429
1894	102,436	1909	173,340	1929	292,598
1895	108,564	1910	178,279	1930	289,991

B. in million therms

1923	1,153	1948	2,178	1965	3,484
...		1949	2,241	1966	3,755
1925	1,268	1950	2,337	1967	4,199
...		1951	2,449	1968	4,664
1930	1,383	1952	2,453	1969	5,235
1931	1,390	1953	2,436	1970	6,133
1932	1,373	1954	2,527	1971	7,992
1933	1,366	1955	2,583	1972	10,179
	---(*b*)	1956	2,591	1973	11,487
1934	1,383	1957	2,537	1974	12,932
1935	1,405		---(*d*)		
				1975	13,454
1936	1,465	1958	2,551	1976	13,837
1937	1,496	1959	2,540	1977	15,172
1938	1,500	1960	2,612	1978	15,934
1939	1,499	1961	2,683	1979	16,736
1940	1,443	1962	2,867		
				1980	16,386
1941	1,523	1963	2,924		
1942	1,636	1964	3,169		
	---(*c*)				
1943	1,691				
1944	1,770				
1945	1,821				
1946	2,002				
1947	2,094				

(*a*) Includes an estimated figure of 3,750 for Scotland.

(*b*) From 1934 includes gas 'supplied separately for industrial purposes only' through a separate main, which amounted to 11·4 million therms in that year.

(*c*) See note 2 above.

(*d*) Years beginning 1 April subsequently.

Fuel and Energy 17. Production of Crude Petroleum and Natural Gas – Great Britain 1939–80

NOTES

[1] SOURCES: As for table 12.

[2] Shale oil is not included in these statistics.

	Crude Petroleum (thousand tons)		Crude Petroleum (thousand tons)	Natural Gas (million therms)		Crude Petroleum (thousand tons)	Natural Gas (million therms)
1939	4	1953	55	...	1967	87	166·64
1940	17	1954	59	...	1968	80	746·83
							(million cubic metres)
1941	30	1955	54	...	1969	76	5,060
1942	82	1956	66	...	1970	82	11,101
1943	113	1957	82	...	1971	82	18,462
1944	95	1958	80	...	1972	82	26,565
1945	72	1959	83	...	1973	87	28,903
1946	55	1960	86	0·50	1974	87	34,825
1947	47	1961	106	1·16	1975	1,204	36,257
1948	44	1962	111	1·39	1976	11,446	38,419
1949	46	1963	123	2·23	1977	36,829	40,307
1950	46	1964	127	2·09	1978	52,096	38,501
1951	45	1965	82	4·53	1979	75,386	39,232
1952	55	1966	77	1·24	1980	77,671	37,294

Fuel and Energy 18. Imports and Re-exports of Petroleum – United Kingdom 1863–1922 and Great Britain 1920–80

NOTES

[1] SOURCES: 1863–1922 *Annual Statement of Trade*; 1920–80 Ministry of Fuel and Power (later Ministry of Power) *Statistical Digest*, and Ministry of Technology (later Department of Trade & Industry, then Department of Energy), *Digest of Energy Statistics*.

[2] Figures of imports before 1863 are given in the *Annual Statement of Trade* in cwt., and are as follows:

1854	1	1859	11,264
1855	120	1860	35
1856	5,543	1861	25,839
1857	56,544	1862	398,872
1858	65,281		

One cwt. equals approximately 12½ gallons.

A. United Kingdom, in million gallons

	Imports	Re-exports		Imports	Re-exports
1863	7·4	1·0	1893	155·1	1·6
1864	4·4	1·0	1894	163·0	1·9
1865	3·0	0·4	1895	177·1	1·8
1866	6·5	0·6	1896	190·0	2·6
1867	4·7	0·6	1897	185·7	1·8
1868	4·3	0·4	1898	219·3	1·4
1869	5·4	0·3	1899	240·1	1·8
1870	6·9	0·7	1900	255·0	2·0
1871	9·0	0·4	1901	253·8	3·6
1872	6·4	0·1	1902	284·9	4·1
1873	16·7	0·3	1903	285·9	8·7
1874	21·5	0·2	1904	302·1	8·1
1875	19·4	0·1	1905	300·1	7·9
1876	25·2	0·4	1906	299·2	6·9
1877	33·9	0·4	1907	304·1	5·0
1878	30·3	0·8	1908	343·6	5·5
1879	43·3	0·3	1909	358·1	4·5
1880	38·8	0·4	1910	345·5	5·8
1881	59·2	0·4	1911	365·6	7·1
1882	59·7	0·8	1912	414·3	6·7
1883	70·5	0·8	1913	488·1	4·2
1884	53·0	0·8	1914	646·7	5·2
1885	73·9	1·1	1915	588·5	11·6
1886	71·1	0·6	1916	451·6	7·0
1887	77·4	0·5	1917	826·9	5·2
1888	94·4	0·8	1918	1,324·5	1·8
1889	102·9	0·9	1919	713·8	28·2
1890	105·1	1·0	1920	879·4	64·1
1891	130·6	1·2	1921	1,161·0	26·4
1892	130·2	2·4	1922	1,213·3	89·7

B. Great Britain, in thousands of tons

	Crude and Process Oils		Refined Products	
	Imports	Exports and Re-exports	Imports	Exports and Re-exports
1920	17	1	3,382	252
1921	406	..	4,046	107
1922	869	..	3,760	345
1923	1,339	8	3,738	468
1924	1,858	..	4,157	624
1925	2,276	..	3,904	858
1926	2,150	..	5,103	599
1927	2,659	2	5,167	619
1928	1,992	1	5,943	622
1929	1,949	..	6,241	792
1930	1,844	..	7,088	657

B. Great Britain, in thousands of tons (*cont.*)

	Crude and Process Oils		Refined Products	
	Imports	Exports and re-exports	Imports	Exports and re-exports
1931	1,378	..	6,785	512
1932	1,474	..	6,831	513
1933	1,571	1	7,444	512
1934	1,904	17	8,274	610
1935	1,954	22	8,368	702
1936	2,047	12	8,724	657
1937	2,109	—	9,132	760
1938	2,272	—	9,390	592
1939	2,166	—	8,733	532
1940	1,564	—	10,001	218
1941	976	—	12,081	53
1942	591	—	9,785	66
1943	527	—	14,452	37
1944	684	—	19,577	79
1945	949	—	14,818	168
1946	2,179	..	12,232	404
1947	2,474	—	10,592	644
1948	4,641	—	13,196	342
1949	6,048	—	11,453	500
1950	9,246	—	9,896	1,193
	---(*a*)		---(*a*)	
1951	16,702	—	9,786	3,412
1952	22,829	—	5,961	5,441
1953	25,750	15	6,016	7,391
1954	28,075	24	6,612	7,829
1955	27,854	68	8,515	6,274
1956	28,608	69	9,420	7,714
1957	27,967	21	10,829	6,287
1958	33,747	6	11,014	8,390
1959	39,238	121	12,752	8,221
1960	44,615	65	13,802	9,069
1961	48,958	110	11,807	7,701
1962	52,349	991	15,694	9,737
1963	53,868	1,415	18,219	9,724
1964	59,396	396	18,615	9,086
1965	65,653	268	20,207	10,626
1966	70,153	125	21,884	11,819
1967	73,236	758	24,105	11,394
1968	81,277	428	22,188	13,988
1969	92,866	551	20,368	13,988
1970	101,349	1,334	20,549	16,809
1971	107,639	1,746	19,726	16,355
1972	105,346	3,270	19,943	15,826
1973	113,478	2,833	20,237	16,736
1974	111,454	996	15,627	14,932
1975	87,117	1,037	14,427	13,803
1976	87,321	3,344	14,148	16,248
	---(*a*)	---(*a*)	---(*b*)	---(*b*)
	85,579	3,262	15,838	16,331
1977	67,479	15,012	16,013	14,989
1978	64,425	22,774	14,448	14,051
1979	56,976	38,178	15,747	14,154
1980	44,076	37,856	13,884	15,800

(*a*) After 1950 refinery feedstock was transferred from refined to crude. From 1976 (2nd line) it was excluded.

(*b*) The reason for this break is not known.

Fuel and Energy 19. Imports of Coal and Petroleum – Republic of Ireland 1923–80

NOTES

SOURCES: *Statistical Abstract of Ireland* and *Trade Statistics of Ireland*.

(Coal in thousands of tons; petroleum in millions of gallons to 1972 (1st line) then thousands of tons)

	Coal	Petroleum & Products		Coal	Petroleum & Products		Coal	Petroleum & Products
1923			1943	1,015	26·0	1962	1,464	517
1924	2,481	29·6	1944	735	30·4	1963	1,435	552
1925	2,239	33·1	1945	921	34·2	1964	1,286	607
1926	1,756	37·6	1946	1,277	67·1	1965	1,269	708
1927	2,497	42·7	1947	1,506	114	1966	1,309	691
1928	2,405	47·2	1948	1,697	135	1967	1,238	955
1929	2,461	46·3	1949	1,632	148	1968	1,201	905
1930	2,500	54·2	1950	1,829	163	1969	1,121	1,025
1931	2,413	66·9	1951	2,036	207	1970	1,198	1,215
1932	2,304	64·6	1952	1,699	207	1971	1,022	1,450
						1972	877	1,302
								---(a)
1933	2,265	59·6	1953	1,639	199			5,178
1934	2,338	63·4	1954	1,708	241	1973	794	5,711
1935	2,245	64·1	1955	1,801	290	1974	878	5,774
1936	2,477	65·2	1956	1,413	350	1975	679	5,352
1937	2,563	70·5	1957	1,202	284	1976	617	5,239
1938	2,484	72·7	1958	1,354	340	1977	854	5,687
1939	2,876	71·5	1959	1,574	399	1978	825	5,632
1940	2,757	62·6	1960	1,650	473	1979	1,197	6,051
1941	1,488	38·3	1961	1,772	473	1980	1,186	5,953
1942	1,049	31·3						

(*a*) Categories of products are included subsequently which were always measured by weight and so could not be included previously.

CHAPTER V

METALS

TABLES

The iron industry had been established in Britain for a long time before the Industrial Revolution. But in comparison with textiles it was of very modest size; and unlike coal and, especially, copper and tin, it was widely scattered and there was no dominant producing district or overwhelmingly important market to attract the attention of governments on the look-out for easily collected taxes. In conseqence, there were few statistics, other than those of external trade, until *Mineral Statistics* began in 1854.[1] Indeed, the estimates of pig iron production back to 1720, given in Parts A and B of table 2, are the only reasonably connected series that we have.[2] The first of these – Riden's overall national estimates – though making no claim to perfect accuracy, especially before 1790, is a major improvement on the earlier totals which can be derived from Meade's 1882 compilation, and which were subjected to

[1] Originally published as part of the records of the Geological Survey, subsequently as Blue Books.

[2] More scattered statistics relating to numbers of furnaces or forges are available in various places – see especially George Hammersley, 'The Charcoal Iron Industry and its Fuel, 1540–1750', *Economic History Review*, second series XXVI, 4 (1973); M. W. Flinn, 'The Growth of the English Iron Industry, 1660–1760', *Economic History Review*, second series XI, 1 (1958); Alan Birch, *The Economic History of the British Iron and Steel Industry, 1784–1879* (London, 1967); and C. K. Hyde, *Technological Change and the British Iron Industry, 1700–1870* (Princeton, 1977). Others relating especially to forge output can be found in E. W. Hulme, 'Statistical History of the Iron Trade of England and Wales, 1717–1750', *Transactions of the Newcomen Society*, IX (1928–9).

severe criticism by Ashton and Flinn amongst others.[3] Meade's district estimates, however, are still useful in showing the approximate relative importance of different districts.

Regional statistics of iron ore production are available in the sources from which table 1 is drawn, but they are probably of interest only to the specialist, and only the overall national output is shown here, along with the imports, which became of major importance during the 1870s. Unfortunately neither series takes any account of variations in the metal content of the ores, which may have changed quite substantially over time as the relative importance of different producing districts changed. The underlying trend for domestic production was downwards, especially when the Jurassic limestone ores were taking over as the main source in the 1850s to 1870s. The content of imported ores, on the other hand, has risen during the twentieth century – from about 50 per cent to nearly 60 per cent – though there is no way of knowing what was its trend earlier.[4]

Part C of table 2 shows the returns of total pig iron output published in *Mineral Statistics* (and its successors) from 1854 onwards, with the breakdown by quality, which was collected from 1891, shown in table 3, and steel output as given by the British Iron and Steel Federation from 1871, in table 4. These statistics are believed to be essentially complete and reliable, though it is possible that the figures for the 1850s and 1860s may be slight underestimates. Statistics of puddled iron output could be given from 1881 onwards, but it was already being replaced in most uses by that time by cheap steel, and later statistics are not of much general interest. Clapham estimated that it came to 1.25 million tons at most in 1855, 1.75 million tons in 1865, and probably did not reach three million tons even in the boom of 1872.[5] In 1881–3 it averaged 2.8 million tons, and thereafter declined steadily, the most convenient source for these later statistics is the B.I.S.F.'s *Statistical Year Book* (and its successors).

Unlike the coal mines, where the Inspectors made estimates of the numbers employed from soon after the middle of the nineteenth century, and there were official returns from the early 1870s under the Mines Regulation Acts, no attempt was made to find out the number of workers in the iron and steel industries, except through the censuses, until after the First World War. At that time there was the beginning of the National Insurance statistics, and the B.I.S.F. began to publish its own estimates based on returns from a large proportion of works. The latter are presumed to be the most complete, and are shown here in table 5. As with the insurance statistics, however, there are, unfortunately, several changes in the basis on which they were collected.

The external trade statistics for iron and steel in tables 6 to 9 exhibit the usual problems of breaks in continuity associated with all such statistics, with perhaps rather more minor breaks than usual, because of small but fairly frequent readjustments in the allocation of items amongst categories. In all cases the principal constituent items are given as well as total

[3] T. S. Ashton, *Iron and Steel in the Industrial Revolution* (Manchester, 1924), p. 235, and M. W. Flinn, *loc. cit.*, pp. 144–53.

[4] Dr R. Robson of the Iron and Steel Board kindly supplied information on this last point in the late 1950s.

[5] J. H. Clapham, *An Economic History of Modern Britain*, vol. II (Cambridge, 1932), p. 52.

trade in iron and steel. From these it is possible to get a good idea of the change in the importance of the various branches of the industry. Statistics of the value of imports and exports have not been given in this chapter, but can be found, at a rather high level of aggregation, in chapter IX. It should be noted that the import and export figures given in the B.I.S.F. publications differ in certain respects from those derived from the *Trade and Navigation Accounts* because of differences in classification.

In the early nineteenth century, the changes in the trade records associated with the absorption of Ireland in the United Kingdom had virtually no effect on iron imports, since the great majority was intended for further processing, and Ireland had no iron industry. The effect on exports at this period was considerable, but since it can be eliminated in the figures from 1805 onwards, the resulting overlap with Elizabeth Schumpeter's figures going up to 1808 at least tells us the exact size of the change. The exclusion of southern Ireland after 1 April 1923 had a proportionately rather larger effect on iron and steel imports and a rather smaller effect on exports than had the nineteenth-century political change. But in relation to the total remaining British trade it was only about 2 per cent in each case. Only for re-exported iron and steel was there any substantial change. The increase in re-exports resulting from the treatment of southern Ireland as external was about 10 per cent.

The remainder of this chapter is concerned with the main non-ferrous metals mined or manufactured in the United Kingdom, and table 10, relating to the tin mines of Cornwall, provides us with our longest and almost our earliest statistical series, going back, admittedly with large gaps in the thirteenth and fourteenth centuries, to 1198. The statistics relate only to tin actually coined, and perhaps 'can only be regarded as a rough guide to production in view of the time-lag between the actual mining of the tin and its coining', and because some 'tin-stuff and smelted tin were smuggled out of the country without coining'.[6] However, the most recent writer on the industry's history believes that the series 'enable trends in output to be charted with considerable accuracy and continuity from the late thirteenth century'.[7] The significance of British tin-mining, or course, became progressively less during the nineteenth century; but such as it was, it can be traced in table 12.

In comparison with tin, the statistics of copper-mining in the South-West are of quite recent origin, copper production not being of much significance until the end of the seventeenth century. The earliest figure is for 1726, and even then it was not complete for Cornwall and Devon, which were themselves not the only producing district in Britain. The first point is probably not of much importance until well into the nineteenth century, for it seems clear that by far the greatest proportion of British copper was sold at public ticketings, and for a long period this proportion was fairly constant. When exactly things began to change is not at all certain; but the eventual extent of the change was very considerable. In 1854–6, when Hunt's *Mineral Statistics* enables us to speak with confidence,[8] the propor-

[6] John Rowe, *Cornwall in the Age of the Industrial Revolution* (Liverpool, 1953), p. 327.

[7] John Hatcher, *English Tin Production and Trade before 1550* (Oxford, 1973), p. 5.

[8] The fact that Hunt's sources seem to have been mainly on the smelting side of the industry should help to make his figures more certain on this point.

tion of the entire British output which was sold by private contract was not far short of one-third.

The South-West's output of copper is not a good guide to national output for the whole of that period when its statistics are the only ones available. According to Hoffman, the South-West produced about 85 per cent of national output at the beginning of the eighteenth century and 80 per cent in 1770; and by the 1850s (and almost certainly a good deal earlier) the proportion was virtually back to that level. But the period after 1770 had seen the rise and fall of the easily won Anglesey mines, for which no returns of output were ever published. Various contemporary estimates give a rough picture of their contribution, as follows:[9]

approximate date	output of fine copper in tons	approximate date	output of fine copper in tons
1778	1,200	1975	1,900
1784	3,000	1798	1,700
1785	2,300	1812	600
1787	4,000	1823–7	737

In terms of ore the proportion of output derived from Anglesey during its brief heyday was much larger than it was in terms of metal content, since the ores were only about half as rich as those of Cornwall.[10]

The other main metallic ores mined in Britain were lead and zinc, though of these there is little statistical record until the mid nineteenth century. Such as there is is discussed in an article by Burt,[11] but it is not sufficiently comprehensive to provide statistics which can be included here.

With the beginning of Hunt's zealous collection of data on mining, a continuous record of British production of metals is available, and the main national series are shown in table 12, together with, in table 13, a selection relating to the metal refining industries which, until fairly recent years, is based on the work of Schmitz, cited in note 1 to the table.

Finally, the last two tables in this chapter give the main statistics of external trade in non-ferrous metals from the time when they first become available in regular form, or when they first achieved even modest significance.

Additional, more detailed information, for example on production by county, on prices, or on the direction of trade, is available in the original sources cited in the tables. There is also a

[9] Sources: 1778 and 1785 – R. Hunt, *British Mining* (London, 1884), p. 105; 1784, 1795, and 1798 – *House of Commons Reports* X, p. 671; 1787 – quoted in H. Hamilton, *English Brass and Copper Industries to 1800* (London, 1926), p. 180; 1812 – A. H. Dodd, *Industrial Revolution in North Wales* (Cardiff, 1933), p. 161; and 1823–27 – J. R. McCulloch, *Statistical Account of the British Empire* (London, 1854), p. 615.

[10] J. Mawe, *Mineralogy of Derbyshire* (London, 1801), p. 168, stated the metal content of Anglesey ore to be 7.5 per cent. R. Hunt, *op. cit.*, p. 828, gives the Anglesey ore output in 1784 as 64,500 tons, which represents approximately 5 per cent.

[11] Roger Burt, 'Lead Production in England and Wales, 1700–1770', *Economic History Review*, second series XXII, 2 (1969).

certain amount of statistical material on trade in finished manufactures of non-ferrous metals, though there is nothing on their production until quite recently, except in the Censuses of Production. Some summary figures on the values of the main aggregates of external trade in non-ferrous metals can also be found in chapter IX.

Metals 1. Output and Imports of Iron Ore – United Kingdom 1855–1980

NOTES

[1] SOURCES: Output – 1854–1920 – *Mineral Statistics* (corrected for arithmetical and other errors); 1921–38 – *Annual Report of the Department of Mines*; 1939–80 – British Iron & Steel Trades Federation (and its successors), *Statistical Year Book* (later *Annual Statistics*). Imports – *Annual Statement of Trade* and *Overseas Trade Statistics of the United Kingdom*.

[2] *Mineral Statistics* were first published as part of the *Memoirs of the Geological Survey*, and were based entirely on information supplied voluntarily to Robert Hunt, Keeper of Mining Records. Compulsory returns of output to H.M. Mines Inspectors were required after 1872, and Hunt used those under the Metaliferous Mines Act. But he continued to rely on voluntary returns supplemented by estimates for iron mines which came under the Coal Mines Act, since he regarded these as superior to the incomplete Inspectors' returns (except in the case of Scotland, where he used the latter without alteration). That they *were* superior in general seems to have been accepted by later compilers of *Mineral Statistics* (which became wholly official in 1882 and were published in Parliamentary Papers). No breaks have been indicated in the series shown here up to 1881, because there is, in fact, no clearly identifiable break. Improvements in the quality of the estimates obviously occurred from time to time.

(in thousands of tons)

	Output	Imports		Output	Imports		Output	Imports
1855	9,554	11	1897	13,788	5,969	1939	14,486	5,308
1856	10,483	..	1898	14,177	5,468	1940	17,702	4,562
1857	9,623	17	1899	14,461	7,055	1941	18,974	2,295
1858	8,041	29	1900	14,028	6,298	1942	19,906	1,922
1859	7,880	29	1901	12,275	5,549	1943	18,494	1,894
1860	8,024	23	1902	13,426	6,440	1944	15,472	2,172
1861	7,216	23	1903	13,716	6,314	1945	14,175	4,071
1862	7,562	36	1904	13,774	6,101	1946	12,173	6,601
1863	8,614	62	1905	14,591	7,345	1947	11,091	6,845
1864	10,065	74	1906	15,500	7,823	1948	13,089	8,736
1865	9,910	77	1907	15,732	7,642	1949	13,397	8,693
1866	9,665	57	1908	15,031	6,058	1950	12,963	8,392
1867	10,021	87	1909	14,804	6,329	1951	14,777	8,747
1868	10,169	114	1910	15,226	7,021	1952	16,232	9,691
1869	11,509	131	1911	15,519	6,347	1953	15,818	10,981
1870	14,371	208	1912	13,790	6,602	1954	15,557	11,611
1871	16,635	324	1913	15,997	7,442	1955	16,175	12,859
1872	15,835	802	1914	14,868	5,705	1956	16,245	14,330
1873	15,583	968	1915	14,235	6,197	1957	16,902	15,912
1874	14,845(*a*)	754	1916	13,495	6,934	1958	14,612	12,899
1875	15,821	459	1917	14,846	6,190	1959	14,870	13,350
1876	16,730	672	1918	14,613	6,582	1960	17,087	17,969
1877	16,697	1,141	1919	12,254	5,201	1961	16,518	14,966
1878	15,726	1,173	1920	12,707	6,500	1962	15,277	12,897
1879	14,380	1,085	1921	3,478	1,888	1963	14,912	14,324
1880	18,026	2,633	1922	6,868	3,473	1964	16,326	18,598
1881	17,446	2,451	1923	10,875(*c*)	5,860	1965	15,415	18,857
	---(*b*)							
1882	18,032	3,285	1924	11,051(*c*)	5,927	1966	13,658	15,943
1883	17,383	3,191	1925	10,143(*c*)	4,382	1967	12,739	16,075
1884	16,138	2,731	1926	4,094	2,088	1968	13,716	17,590
1885	15,418	2,823	1927	11,207	5,164	1969	12,104	18,170
1886	14,110	2,878	1928	11,262	4,440	1970	11,828	19,855
1887	13,098	3,766	1929	13,215	5,689	1971	10,067	17,180
1888	14,591	3,562	1930	11,627	4,138	1972	8,906	17,087
1889	14,546	4,031	1931	7,626	2,119	1973	6,993	22,507
1890	13,781	4,472	1932	7,328	1,795	1974	3,545	19,637
1891	12,778	3,181	1933	7,462	2,708	1975	4,419	15,533
1892	11,313	3,781	1934	10,587	4,359	1976	4,510	18,285
1893	11,203	4,066	1935	10,895	4,547	1977	3,686	15,297
1894	12,367	4,414	1936	12,701	5,961	1978	4,172	15,209
1895	12,615	4,450	1937	14,215	7,039	1979	4,202	17,560
1896	13,701	5,438	1938	11,859	5,164	1980	901	8,395

(*a*) Estimates for mines in South Staffordshire which did not make returns were not added to the total in 1874. In 1873 they had come to 350 thousand tons.

(*b*) See note 2 above.

(*c*) B.I.S.F., *Statistics of the Iron and Steel Industries* gives slightly different figures for these years.

Metals 2. Output of Pig Iron – Great Britain 1720–1980

NOTES

[1] Sources: Part A – Philip Riden, "The Output of the British Iron Industry before 1870", *E.H.R.*, second series XXX, 3 (1977); Part B – R. Meade, *The Coal and Iron Industries of the United Kingdom* (London, 1882), pp. 829 *et seq.*, where the original authorities are given, except for the total for 1720, which comes from T. S. Ashton, *Iron and Steel in the Industrial Revolution* (Manchester University Press, 1924), p. 235. The latter's authority is used for the attribution of the first estimates to 1720 instead of 1740, as given in Meade. Part C – 1854–1920 – *Mineral Statistics* (with corrections of arithmetical errors); 1921–80 – British Iron and Steel Federation (and its successors), *Statistical Year Book* (later *Annual Statistics*).

[2] The B.I.S.F. *Statistical Year Book* during the 1920's gave the estimates shown in Part B together with the following additional ones of total output:

1818	325,000 tons	1835	1,000,000 tons
1820	368,000 tons	1841	1,500,000 tons
1825	581,367 tons	1842	1,099,138 tons
1827	690,500 tons	1844	1,999,608 tons
1828	703,184 tons	1845	1,512,500 tons
1833	700,000 tons	1850	2,249,000 tons

[3] C. K. Hyde, *Technological Change and the British Iron Industry, 1700–1870* (Princeton, 1977), Appendix C, gives the following figures for years not shown in part B (in thousand tons):

	Shropshire	Staffordshire	South Wales	Other Districts
1805	55	49·5	78	...
1810	70	100	100	...
1812	60	110	115	...
1815	50	125	140	80
1816	100		110	50
1817	120		125	40
1818	160		125	50
1819	160		125	60
1820	180		150	70
1821	180		170	70
1822	175		165	70

A. Riden's estimates of total output, 1720–1853

(in thousand tons)

1720–4	27	1745–9	27	1770–4	40		
1725–9	29	1750–4	28	1775–9	48		
1730–4	28	1755–9	31	1780–4	62		
1735–9	27	1760–4	34	1785–9	80		
1740–4	26	1765–9	40				
1790	90	1806	270	1822	360	1838	1,120
1791	100	1807	290	1823	450	1839	1,250
1792	100	1808	300	1824	550	1840	1,400
1793	110	1809	350	1825	580	1841	1,330
1794	110	1810	400	1826	520	1842	1,080
1795	120	1811	360	1827	690	1843	1,220
1796	120	1812	360	1828	700	1844	1,560
1797	140	1813	370	1829	690	1845	2,200
1798	160	1814	400	1830	680	1846	2,210
1799	170	1815	340	1831	600	1847	2,000
1800	180	1816	270	1832	630	1848	2,090
1801	200	1817	260	1833	780	1849	2,170
1802	220	1818	280	1834	790	1850	2,250
1803	230	1819	280	1835	930	1851	2,500
1804	240	1820	320	1836	970	1852	2,700
1805	250	1821	390	1837	1,030	1853	2,900

B. District Estimates, 1720–1852

(in tons)

	Total	Derbyshire	Hampshire	Shropshire	North Staffordshire	South Staffordshire	Sussex	North Wales	Yorkshire	Scotland	Durham and Northum-berland	South Wales
1720	25,000(*a*)	(500)	(1,350)	(2,100)	(1,700)	(1,000)	(1,400)	(400)	(1,400)	...	...	(4,850)
1788	68,300	4,500	...	24,900	4,500	2,400	300	400	5,100	7,000	...	12,500
1796	125,080	9,656	...	32,970	1,959	13,211	173	1,144	10,398	16,086	...	34,101
1806	243,851	9,074	...	54,966	50,002		...	2,981	27,646	22,840	...	71,107
1823	455,166	14,038	...	57,923	133,590		...	13,100	27,311	24,500	2,379	182,325
1830	677,417	17,999	...	73,418	211,604		...	25,000	28,926	37,500	5,327	277,643
1839	1,248,781	34,372	...	80,940	18,200	346,213	...	33,800	52,416	196,560	13,000	453,880
1840	1,396,400	31,000	...	82,750	20,500	407,150	...	26,500	56,000	241,000	...	505,000
1843	1,215,350	25,750	...	76,200	21,750	300,250	...	19,750	42,000	238,550	...	457,350
1847	1,999,608	95,160	...	88,400	65,520	320,320	...	16,120	67,600	539,968	...	706,680
1852	2,701,000	(incl. with Yorkshire)	...	120,000	90,000	725,000	...	30,000	150,000 (incl. Derby)	775,000	145,000	666,000

C. Returns, 1854–1980

(in thousand tons)

	Total	Durham and Northum-berland	North Yorkshire	West Yorkshire	Cumber-land	Lanca-shire and North Wales	Notts and Derby-shire	Shrop-shire	North Staffs	South Staffs	Northants	Leicester-shire and Lincs	South Wales	Scotland
1854	3,070	174	101	73	53		128	125	104	744	—	—	750	797
1855	3,218	214	85	91	48		117	122	102	754	—	—	840	828
1856	3,586	331	179	96	74		107	110	131	777	—	—	877	881
1857	3,659	348	180	117	31	38	112	117	134	657	12	—	971	918
1858	3,456	310	189	86	26	31	132	101	135	598	10	—	886	926
1859	3,713	402	216	85	50	...	139	149	144	475	13	—	985	961
1860	3,827	410	249	98	88	130	126	145	147	470	8	—	969	937
1861	3,712	385	235	143	55	156	130	141	188	396	8	—	886	950
1862	3,943	384	283	112	103	171	131	126	184	610	13	—	893	1,080
1863	4,510	509	315	105	106	215	170	136	177	691	15	—	848	1,160
1864	4,768	522	409	102	141	246	175	131	218	629	13	10	938	1,159
1865	4,805	526	486	123	107	257	189	117	206	693	15	11	845	1,163
1866	4,524	349	546	120	136	295	200	121	210	533	19	14	927	994
1867	4,761	509	641	109	110	352	160	124	202	516	25	26	886	1,031
1868	4,970	517	699	100	117	362	159	145	230	532	36	34	894	1,068
1869	5,446	674	766	106	129	476	188	197	232	570	42	34	801	1,150
1870	5,963	711	917	78	255	466	180	112	303	589	43	32	979	1,206
1871	6,627	793	1,030	115	337	562	270	129	268	726	61	30	1,046	1,169
1872	6,742	799	1,122	149	441	565	283	133	276	673	59	37	1,003	1,090
1873	6,566	844	1,156	152	457	572	296	135	283	673	58	52	818	993

Metals 2. *continued*

C. Returns, 1854–1980 (*cont.*)

(in thousand tons)

	Total	Durham and Northumberland	North Yorkshire	West Yorkshire	Cumberland	Lancashire and North Wales	Notts and Derbyshire	Shropshire	North Staffs	South Staffs	Northants	Leicestershire and Lincs	South Wales	Scotland
1874	5,991	862	1,158	164	391	541	302	126	274	452	54	67	715	806
1875	6,365	809	1,240	267	486	614	272	121	241	475	81	112	542	1,050
1876	6,556	823	1,261	235	437	586	301	107	214	466	85	125	756	1,103
1877	6,609	734	1,375	229	538	711	328	102	255	428	107	117	711	982
1878	6,381	660	1,358	220	543	639	306	81	232	393	138	125	741	902
1879	5,995	557	1,210	219	532	650	291	61	210	326	165	132	670	932
1880	7,749	750	1,666	307	790	809	367	88	225	385	179	208	890	1,049
1881	8,144	842	1,792	256	925	739	368	79	274	374	190	188	911	1,176
1882	8,587	909	1,804	321	1,001	844	446	80	276	398	192	202	934	1,126
1883	8,529	912	1,867	304	876	836	422	78	268	430	217	237	906	1,129
1884	7,812	779	1,726	248	846	749	438	53	296	357	196	259	851	988
1885	7,415	730	1,748	166	688	736	444	45	269	344	190	235	793	1,004
1886	7,010	701	1,736	137	715	730	346	41	234	294	198	242	667	936
1887	7,560	683	1,841	178	945	793	296	52	260	293	236	252	767	932
1888	7,999	775	1,856	191	854	779	363	61	279	366	237	299	871	1,028
1889	8,323	867	1,915	229	900	830	470	52	276	373	231	336	826	978
1890	7,904	876	1,961	249	833	802	464	43	256	327	225	268	825	737
1891	7,406	862	1,769	228	725	769	471	48	232	350	194	285	761	674
1892	6,709	611	1,334	262	605	639	481	50	241	338	178	263	684	972
1893	6,977	770	1,943	155	713	615	343	40	199	330	144	217	680	793
1894	7,427	886	2,088	225	689	637	377	40	210	333	223	344	709	642
1895	7,703	868	2,058	195	649	581	413	49	194	338	255	349	705	1,049
1896	8,660	1,003	2,209	289	771	729	455	47	236	389	274	361	780	1,114
1897	8,796	1,063	2,135	295	819	760	488	39	243	400	250	363	805	1,137
1898	8,610	1,103	2,095	297	886	792	529	42	268	406	251	382	495	1,063
1899	9,421	1,040	2,211	306	955	811	572	41	283	415	279	409	929	1,171
1900	8,960	973	2,137	291	857	729(*b*)	562	39	273	398	248	389	908(*b*)	1,157
1901	7,929	961	1,859	247	790	642(*b*)	458	41	225	341	206	322	700(*b*)	1,136
1902	8,679	987	1,974	284	863	677(*b*)	519	41	249	380	247	386	800(*b*)	1,272
1903	8,935	1,041	2,067	298	797	689(*b*)	547	47	246	397	254	386	876(*b*)	1,291
1904	8,694	1,009	2,115	263	696	579	551	287		394	267	377	805	1,351
1905	9,608	1,039	2,447	293	872	649	568	304		430	273	443	912	1,375
1906	10,184	1,072	2,557	336	887	754	640	349		452	290	497	900	1,451
1907	10,114	1,144	2,538	333	857	654	676	356		470	289	482	929	1,389
1908	9,057	931	2,458	282	670	492	638	323		449	296	492	866	1,225

	Total	Durham and Northumberland	North Yorkshire	West Yorkshire	Cumberland	Lancashire and North Wales	Notts and Derbyshire	Shropshire	North Staffs	South Staffs	Northants	Leicestershire and Lincs	South Wales	Scotland
1909	9,532	1,113	2,437	292	723	593	646	335	482		315	475	743	1,377
1910	10,012	1,128	2,551	313	749	640	687	354	495		366	512	788	1,428
1911	9,526	1,107	2,435	284	598	598	666	356	473		386	496	718	1,409
1912	8,751	1,074	2,184	265	548	559	586	350	442		351	450	756	1,186
1913	10,260	1,230	2,639	303	697	667	699	383	467		386	531	889	1,369
1914	8,924	994	2,313	264	564	705	641	339	420		339	472	753	1,126
1915	8,724(c)	946	2,061	285	623	567	558	345	426		295	533	829	1,109
1916	8,919(c)	1,033	2,064	293	720	762	499	339	410		285	533	656	1,125
1917	9,338(c)	1,134	2,096	307	782	788	544	368	433		300	649	779	1,157
1918	9,107(c)	1,004	1,988	282	797	759	567	372	413		314	639	881	1,091
1919	7,417(c)	878	1,629	239	591	663	482	335	319		244	535	599	903
1920	8,035	2,639		260	622	719	563		697		283	657	692	903

	Total	North Yorkshire and Durham	West Yorkshire, South Lancashire and North Wales	North-West Coast (Cumberland and Furness)	Derbyshire Essex, Leicestershire, Northants and Notts	Staffordshire, Shropshire, Worcestershire and Warwickshire	Lincolnshire	South Wales	Scotland
1921	2,616	1,054	219	284	348	194	107	121	289
1922	4,902	1,495	416	560	698	394	383	596	361
1923	7,441	2,127	597	871	1,034	533	702	808	769
1924	7,307	2,247	571	716	1,103	482	657	865	668
1925	6,262	1,905	529	633	1,010	417	549	789	430
1926	2,458	821	167	261	356	167	215	284	189
1927	7,293	2,298	516	879	995	460	714	739	692
1928	6,610	1,940	400	699	1,040	408	721	853	550
1929	7,589	2,349	472	755	1,174	440	865	927	607
1930	6,192	1,861	387	686	1,120	376	754	542	466
1931	3,773	1,137	205	404	979	202	412	280	154
1932	3,574	878	235	346	872	282	463	354	144
1933	4,136	1,063	222	513	750	307	609	451	220
1934	5,969	1,684	388	674	1,104	385	850	492	392
1935	6,424	1,721	398	673	1,441	405	862	513	413
1936	7,721	2,117	460	767	1,699	434	1,023	751	471
1937	8,493	2,429	477	825	1,938	470	1,043	815	497
1938	6,761	1,833	349	722	1,598	317	868	665	409
1939	7,980	1,983	365	661	1,827	432	1,130	1,101	481
1940	8,205	1,934	401	705	1,787	447	1,308	962	659

See p. 285 for footnotes.

Metals 2. *continued*

C. Returns, 1854–1980 (*cont.*)

	Total	North Yorkshire and Durham	West Yorkshire, South Lancashire and North Wales	North-West Coast (Cumberland and Furness)	Derbyshire Essex, Leicestershire, Northants and Notts	Staffordshire, Shropshire, Worcestershire and Warwickshire	Lincolnshire	South Wales	Scotland
1941	7,393	1,678	396	552	1,790	409	1,252	805	511
1942	7,726	1,799	423	595	1,909	372	1,303	829	496
1943	7,187	1,683	379	526	1,781	347	1,180	804	487
1944	6,737	1,606	323	538	1,681	317	982	778	513
1945	7,107	1,664	349	613	1,697	339	1,039	864	542
1946	7,761	1,902	354	696	1,783	343	1,071	1,011	603
1947	7,785	1,934	364	703	1,832	287	1,048	1,024	592
1948	9,276	2,410	420	750	2,019	491	1,248	1,173	766
1949	9,499	2,369	414	790	2,108	540	1,306	1,203	769
1950	9,633	2,402	437	824	2,209	551	1,239	1,232	739
1951	9,669	2,338	448	792	2,150	543	1,259	1,351	790
1952	10,728	2,601	472	933	2,262	523	1,505	1,545	886
1953	11,175	2,646	783	930	2,267	474	1,559	1,653	863
1954	11,883	2,811	873	954	2,276	482	1,647	1,894	947
1955	12,470	2,824	992	964	2,342	567	1,880	1,975	927
1956	13,170	2,761	1,176	1,116	2,581	605	1,804	2,195	931
1957	14,283	3,113	1,272	1,077	2,506	609	2,120	2,526	1,060
1958	12,975	2,848	1,272	801	2,080	438	2,048	2,511	976
1959	12,583	2,474	1,219	782	2,131	372	2,105	2,682	816
1960	15,763	3,412	1,407	1,028	2,633	553	2,290	3,141	1,299
1961	14,747	3,025	1,463	895	2,308	525	2,334	2,961	1,236
1962	13,692	2,397	1,628	744	1,887	439	2,303	3,428	866
1963	14,591	2,668	1,466	630	1,819	518	2,395	4,207	888
1964	17,274	3,561	1,646	764	2,084	540	2,723	4,420	1,535
1965	17,460	3,434	1,686	695	1,971	585	2,697	4,718	1,675
1966	15,710	2,784	1,693	559	1,634	595	2,521	4,611	1,313
1967	15,153	2,647	1,722	465	1,505	579	2,401	4,583	1,251
1968	16,432	2,896	1,660	581	1,508	648	2,685	4,712	1,744
1969	16,390	3,109	1,527	572	1,611	685	2,945	4,034	1,908

	Total	Northern	Yorkshire & Humberside	North-West	East Midlands	West Midlands	South-East	Wales	Scotland
1970	17,393	3,682	3,338	359	1,449	649	304	5,797	1,664
1971	15,173	3,048	2,789	312	1,150	499	279	5,458	1,638
1972	15,074	3,110	2,757	—	1,102	523	282	5,753	1,547
1973	16,572								
1974	13,683	3,056	3,266	—	423	563	241	4,600	1,535
1975	11,939	2,939	3,212	—	633	460	233	3,478	985
1976	13,616	3,121	3,454	—	750	428	134	4,459	1,270
1977	12,039	2,534	3,083	—	665	343	230	3,995	1,188
1978	11,253	2,441	3,082	—	706	78	80	3,833	1,033
1979	12,694	2,964	3,226	—	700	—	—	4,597	1,207
1980	6,216	1,911	1,808	—	3	—	—	1,584	910

(*a*) This figure is regarded as a better estimate than the sum of the district estimates, which is 17,350 tons.
(*b*) The output of North Wales for these years is included with South Wales and cannot be separately distinguished.

(*c*) The B.I.S.F.'s *Statistics of the Iron and Steel Industries* gives the following figures for these years

1915 8,794 1917 9,322 1919 7,398
1916 9,048 1918 9,086

Metals 3. Output of Pig Iron according to Quality – Great Britain 1891–1980

NOTE
SOURCE: British Iron and Steel Federation (and its successors), *Statistical Year Book* (later *Annual Statistics*).

(in thousands of tons)

	Hematite	Basic	Foundry	Forge	Blast Furnace Ferro-Alloys	Total (incl. direct castings)
1891	2,992	232	3,990		192	7,406
1892	2,710	262	3,585		152	6,709
1893	3,088	179	3,531		179	6,977
1894	3,165	93	4,011		159	7,427
1895	3,266	278	4,003		156	7,703
1896	3,648	760	4,055		197	8,660
1897	3,651	705	4,212		229	8,796
1898	3,597	780	4,029		204	8,610
1899	4,206	861	4,105		249	9,421
1900	3,865	925	3,866		303	8,960
1901	3,515	795	3,387		232	7,929
1902	3,750	922	3,742		266	8,679
1903	3,698	992	3,940		305	8,935
1904	3,472	1,192	3,815		214	8,694
1905	4,039	1,058	4,232		279	9,608
1906	4,103	1,263	4,447		371	10,184
1907	4,023	1,406	4,352		333	10,114
1908	3,413	1,819	3,576		249	9,057
1909	3,567	1,449	4,214		302	9,532
1910	3,874	1,875	3,939		324	10,012
1911	3,526	1,917	3,813		270	9,526
1912	3,472	1,772	3,252		256	8,751
1913	3,605	2,530	3,802		324	10,260
1914	3,225	2,003	3,370		326	8,924
1915	3,564	2,273	2,598		256	8,794
1916	4,042	2,291	2,318		292	9,048
1917	3,922	2,723	2,379(*a*)		298	9,322
1918	3,557	2,987	2,302(*a*)		241	9,086
1919	2,782	2,374	1,435(*a*)	610	197	7,398
1920	2,942	2,662	1,550	605	244	8,035
1921	842	700	773	240	52	2,616
1922	1,571	1,570	1,202	278	228	4,902
1923	2,431	2,422	1,787	423	285	7,441
1924	2,343	2,445	1,858	376	191	7,307
1925	1,909	2,065	1,704	296	185	6,262
1926	815	759	690	105	46	2,458
1927	2,453	2,359	1,933	277	182	7,293
1928	2,139	2,432	1,570	269	148	6,610
1929	2,348	3,197	1,511	275	179	7,589
1930	1,841	2,408	1,458	283	133	6,192
1931	879	1,436	1,162	175	68	3,773
1932	794	1,550	1,025	134	47	3,574
1933	1,108	1,911	945	101	49	4,136
1934	1,517	2,953	1,295	103	95	5,969
1935	1,466	3,383	1,344	116	111	6,424
1936	1,728	4,343	1,346	147	149	7,721
1937	1,866	4,689	1,607	176	147	8,493
1938	1,484	3,763	1,230	151	130	6,761
1939	1,396	5,108	1,204	167	102	7,980
1940	1,428	5,453	1,062	119	141	8,205

Metals 3. *continued*

(in thousands of tons)

	Hematite	Basic	Foundry	Forge	Blast Furnace Ferro-Alloys	Total (incl. direct castings)
1941	906	5,182	1,082	101	120	7,393
1942	964	5,553	963	69	175	7,726
1943	927	5,070	1,025	40	124	7,187
1944	1,009	4,792	740	35	160	6,737
1945	1,076	4,884	964	52	131	7,107
1946	1,121	5,288	1,135	66	150	7,761
1947	1,117	5,183	1,282	70	132	7,785
1948	1,366	6,256	1,396	93	164	9,276
1949	1,437	6,248	1,555	87	168	9,499
1950	1,477	6,478	1,467	61	148	9,633
1951	1,333	6,675	1,417	70	172	9,669
1952	1,426	7,528	1,522	74	176	10,728
1953	1,392	8,070	1,466	52	194	11,175
1954	1,436	8,772	1,441	45	187	11,883
1955	1,415	9,296	1,509	57	193	12,470
1956	1,547(*b*)	9,982	1,412	45	183	13,170
1957	1,571(*b*)	11,265	1,259	29	158	14,283
1958	1,237	10,315	1,229	20	174	12,975
1959	1,021	10,285	1,089	39	148	12,583
1960	1,187	13,072	1,293	5	205	15,763
1961	1,137	12,256	1,196		158	14,747
1962	876	11,568	1,054		194	13,692
1963	817	12,644	1,006		124	14,591
1964	957	15,069	1,079		168	17,274
1965	877	15,377	1,012		193	17,460
1966	678	13,945	927		160	15,710
1967	642	13,681	679		152	15,153
1968	888	14,925	454		165	16,432
1969	863	14,777	596		154	16,390
1970	937	15,589	699		168	17,393
1971	815	13,743	464		151	15,173
1972	770	13,924	231		150	15,074
1973	...	15,580	835		157	16,572
1974	...	12,869	724		90	13,683
1975	...	11,087	768		84	11,939
1976	...	12,916	580		120	13,616
1977	...	11,351	592		95	12,039
1978	...	10,769	416		68	11,253
1979	...	12,236	324		134	12,694
1980	...	6,003	162		51	6,216

(*a*) Including direct castings, which amounted to 105,000 tons in 1916 and 32,000 tons in 1920.

(*b*) Includes special hematite low silicon iron for basic steelmaking.

Metals 4. Output of Steel Ingots and Castings by Process – United Kingdom 1871–1980

NOTE

SOURCES: British Iron Trades Association, *Annual Report* and British Iron and Steel Federation (and its successors), *Statistical Year Book* (later called *Annual Statistics*). Some additional figures were supplied by the British Iron and Steel Federation.

(in thousands of tons)

		Open Hearth		Bessemer	
	Total	Acid	Basic	Acid	Basic
1868	110	—		110	
1869	160	—		160	
1870	240	25		215	
1871	357	28		329	
1872	450	40		410	
1873	573	77		496	
1874	630	90		540	
1875	708	88		620	
1876	828	128		700	
1877	887	137		750	
1878	982	175		806	
1879	1,009	175		834	
1880	1,295	251		1,044	
1881	1,778	338		1,440	
1882	2,109	436		1,673	
1883	2,008	455		1,553	
1884	1,774	475		1,299	
1885	1,887	584		1,304	
1886	2,264	694		1,570	
1887	3,044	981		2,064	
1888	3,304	1,292		2,012	
1889	3,571	1,356	72	1,719	422
1890	3,579	1,463	101	1,613	402
1891	3,157	1,415	100	1,306	336
1892	2,920	1,311	108	1,202	299
1893	2,950	1,378	79	1,231	262
1894	3,111	1,470	105	1,140	396
1895	3,260	1,564	160	1,094	442
1896	4,132	2,145	172	1,358	457
1897	4,486	2,394	208	1,374	510
1898	4,566	2,591	216	1,255	504
1899	4,855	2,735	295	1,308	517
1900	4,901	2,863	293	1,254	491
1901	4,904	2,946	351	1,116	491
1902	4,909	2,677	407	1,157	668
1903	5,034	2,613	511	1,317	593
1904	5,027	2,583	662	1,129	652
1905	5,812	3,043	795	1,396	578
1906	6,462	3,379	1,176	1,307	600
1907	6,523	3,385	1,279	1,280	579
1908	5,296	2,579	1,238	906	572
1909	5,882	2,763	1,385	1,111	622
1910	6,374	3,017	1,579	1,138	641
1911	6,462	3,131	1,869	888	573
1912	6,796	3,366	1,908	981	542
1913	7,664	3,811	2,252	1,049	552
1914	7,835	3,681	2,875	797	482

Metals 4. *continued*

(in thousands of tons)

	Total	Open Hearth		Bessemer		Electric		Other
		Acid	Basic	Acid	Basic	Arc	Induction	
1915	8,550	4,091(*a*)	2,959(*a*)	821(*a*)	480(*a*)	22		177(*a*)
1916	8,992	4,356(*a*)	2,979(*a*)	914(*a*)	542(*a*)	47		154(*a*)
1917	9,717	4,545(*a*)	3,356(*a*)	916(*a*)	585(*a*)	99		216(*a*)
1918	9,539	3,881(*a*)	3,986(*a*)	755(*a*)	551(*a*)	126		241(*a*)
1919	7,894	2,960(*a*)	3,935(*a*)	493(*a*)	296(*a*)	77		133(*a*)
		....	...	....	...			...
1920	9,067	3,380	4,580	587	376	89		57
1921	3,703	1,170	2,217	209	54	27		28
1922	5,881	1,709	3,626	289	196	39		22
1923	8,482	2,568	5,284	387	137	64		43
1924	8,201	2,410	5,125	437	109	65		55
1925	7,385	2,016	4,750	477	28	64		51
1926	3,596	1,055	2,265	174	—	61		41
1927	9,097	2,571	5,929	475	—	75		48
1928	8,520	2,219	5,669	503	—	79		50
1929	9,636	2,451	6,488	559	—	87		51
1930	7,326	1,805	5,099	279	—	76		66
1931	5,203	1,182	3,785	129	—	54		53
1932	5,261	1,123	3,912	125	—	55		46
1933	7,024	1,552	5,140	203	—	75		54
1934	8,850	1,751	6,678	239	—	97		84
1935	9,859	1,858	7,361	199	224	106		110
1936	11,785	2,159	8,772	239	324	153		138
1937	12,984	2,276	9,673	255	418	216		147
1938	10,398	1,721	7,743	164	431	223		117
1939	13,221	2,157	9,705	233	702	292		133
1940	12,975	2,174	9,274	176	738	435		179
1941	12,312	1,808	8,945	98	696	573		193
1942	12,942	1,605	9,394	96	726	860		261
1943	13,031	1,409	9,555	72	731	992		272
1944	12,142	1,173	9,096	85	709	795		284
1945	11,824	1,159	9,026	171	687	542		240
1946	12,695	1,229	9,901	210	724	479		153
1947	12,725	1,229	9,870	208	678	576		164
1948	14,877	1,398	11,589	218	786	707		178
1949	15,553	1,367	12,230	226	819	740		171
1950	16,293	1,311	12,981	248	846	736		171
1951	15,639	1,259	12,277	241	862	819		179
1952	16,418	1,239	12,923	246	887	816	114	193
1953	17,609	1,133	14,298	263	798	822	107	188
1954	18,520	995	15,249	265	909	818	112	172
1955	19,791	1,000	16,252	252	1,032	972	127	156
1956	20,659	986	17,018	230	1,078	1,067	131	150
1957	21,699	961	18,075	250	1,058	1,078	133	143
1958	19,566	762	16,385	229	945	1,011	115	119
1959	20,186	616	16,708	215	1,196	1,225	123	103
1960	24,305	658	19,875	294	1,681	1,540	146	112

Metals 4. *continued*

(in thousands of tons)

		Open Hearth		Bessemer		Electric			
	Total	Acid	Basic	Acid	Basic	Arc	Induction	Oxygen	Other
1961	22,051	611	17,767	254	1,629	1,507	141	70	106
1962	20,491	445	16,274	193	1,583	1,371	109	431	84
1963	22,519	384	16,725	214	1,537	1,955	121	1,504	79
1964	26,222	419	18,064	290	1,441	2,789	148	2,990	80
1965	26,988	392	16,817	258	1,333	3,286	155	4,682	70
1966	24,296	256	14,111	175	798	3,194	148	5,552	62
1967	23,874	132	13,513	183	767	3,284	133	5,821	42
1968	25,840	154	14,024	206	795	4,028	121	6,469	43
1969	26,398	166	13,782	257	357	4,729	130	6,925	51
1970	27,844	160	12,999	279	—	5,276	151	8,942	38
1971	23,772	137	9,877	233	—	4,154	139	9,198	35
1972	24,894	60	9,149	220	—	4,709	124	10,597	35
1973	26,174	31	8,288	232	—	5,065	145	12,379	33
1974	21,970	20	6,071	137	—	5,018	157	10,538	30
1975	19,781	14	4,362	—	—	5,327	147	9,905	26
1976	21,922	—	3,962	—	—	6,505	144	11,289	21
1977	20,089	—	3,227	—	—	6,026	145	10,671	20
1978	19,990	—	1,736	—	—	6,935	152	11,157	11
1979	21,125	—	1,144	—	—	7,134	134	12,690	22
1980	11,099	—	—	—	—	4,373	133	6,583	9

(*a*) Bessemer and Open Hearth castings included in 'Other', ingots only being under their proper heading.

Metals 5. Numbers Employed in the Iron and Steel Industries – United Kingdom 1920–80

NOTES

[1] SOURCES: British Iron and Steel Federation (and its successors), *Statistical Year Book* (later called *Annual Statistics*).

[2] Statistics to 1946 are annual averages of quarterly or monthly figures, except in 1920 and 1921, which are for June and March respectively, in 1926, which is for April, and in 1930 and 1931, which are for July. Statistics for 1947–49 are for a date in July, and subsequent ones are for a date in December.

[3] Except as indicated in footnote (*b*), the figures to 1938 relate to all workers employed at blast furnaces, steel furnaces, rolling mills etc, but do not cover tinplate, galvanised sheet, and wrought iron workers. From 1940 they include workers at iron mines and quarries, steel foundries and in tinplate, and some maintenance and clerical workers not covered previously. Workers in iron foundries are available and are shown separately from 1942. There is a slight increase in coverage from 1950, and a decrease from 1963.

[4] Two part-time female workers are counted as one full-time worker.

(in thousands)

			General Works	Iron Foundries		General Works	Iron Foundries
1920	168(*a*)	1941	310	...	1961	318	127
1921	121(*a*)	1942	329	114	1962	304	121
						---(*c*)	
1922	114	1943	336	113	1963	290	120
			---(*d*)	---(*d*)			
1923	143	1944	316	106	1964	305	124
1924	146	1945	289	101	1965	305	123
1925	132	1946	275	119	1966	291	117
			---(*a*)	---(*a*)			
1926	130(*a*)	1947	269	137	1967	282	110
1927	129	1948	278	147	1968	283	110
1928	122	1949	282	146	1969	279	112
			---(*a*)(*c*)	---(*a*)			
1929	124	1950	296	150	1970	281	109
1930	90(*a*)	1951	296	154	1971	260	93
1931	75(*a*)	1952	304	150	1972	252	87
1932	82	1953	300	141	1973	249	88
1933	91	1954	300	142	1974	250	87
1934	113	1955	309	146	1975	240	80
1935	116	1956	319	140	1976	236	76
	---(*b*)						
1936	140	1957	321	137	1977	238	77
1937	155	1958	299	125	1978	221	74
1938	139	1959	309	127	1979	209	72
1939	...	1960	326	131	1980	154	63
	---(*c*)						
1940	306						

(*a*) See note 2 above.

(*b*) Workers at coke ovens attached to blast furnaces are excluded from 1936.

(*c*) See note 3 above.

(*d*) Workers temporarily absent are excluded from 1944.

Metals 6. Iron Imports – England & Wales 1700–91, and Great Britain 1792–1814

NOTES

[1] Sources: 1700–1808 – Elizabeth B. Schumpeter, *English Overseas Trade Statistics, 1697–1808* (Oxford University Press, 1960), tables XVI and XVII (converted to tons); 1809–14 – Returns printed in sessional papers at irregular intervals.

[2] The figures are for years ended on 5th January in the year following that for which they are shown.

[3] Bar iron re-exports for the period 1805–19 were as follows:

1805	2·0	1810	8·3
1806	3·0	1811	4·7
1807	3·3	1812	5·4
1808	3·5	1813	...
1809	4·9	1814	8·8

A. England & Wales, 1700–91

(in thousands of tons)

	Bar Iron	Total Iron		Bar Iron	Total Iron
1700	16·9	17·3	1746	21·9	25·3
1701	17·8	18·1	1747	19·7	23·0
1702	12·6	12·8	1748	26·0	31·0
1703	18·9	19·1	1749	22·7	26·7
1704	16·0	16·2	1750	35·1	40·3
1705	...	...	1751	26·5	31·6
1706	18·1	18·4	1752	24·9	30·1
1707	13·7	14·1	1753	28·8	33·5
1708	17·6	17·9	1754	31·1	36·1
1709	12·8	13·2	1755	29·4	34·9
1710	17·4	17·8	1756	26·2	31·8
1711	14·6	15·1	1757	26·7	32·5
1712	...	...	1758	30·7	38·9
1713	14·1	15·3	1759	33·1	39·3
1714	21·8	22·9	1760	27·7	33·7
1715	17·3	18·2	1761	42·3	47·3
1716	14·9	15·9	1762	32·2	35·5
1717	7·1	7·8	1763	37·6	41·7
1718	17·1	18·5	1764	43·9	48·6
1719	21·1	22·5	1765	51·4	57·0
1720	22·3	23·6	1766	32·4	37·2
1721	15·9	17·0	1767	36·5	42·5
1722	22·6	23·5	1768	44·7	49·8
1723	18·9	19·7	1769	48·6	55·0
1724	20·9	22·5	1770	46·0	53·7
1725	18·2	19·7	1771	46·0	53·8
				...	...
1726	21·2	22·7	1772	51·9(*a*)	57·8(*a*)
1727	15·7	17·5	1773	46·5	51·4
1728	21·8	24·3	1774	45·4	50·1
1729	19·3	21·8	1775	41·9	47·1
1730	21·8	25·0	1776	50·2	53·0
1731	24·4	27·9	1777	43·1	45·9
1732	23·3	27·0	1778	31·5	33·9
1733	24·2	28·1	1779	42·1	44·0
1734	24·9	29·0	1780	37·2	39·1
1735	26·3	30·5	1781	51·7	52·1
1736	24·0	27·6	1782	39·9	40·8
1737	29·6	33·2	1783	44·0	45·7
1738	28·3	32·5	1784	48·8	50·6
1739	28·5	32·0	1785	40·4	42·7
1740	23·0	26·4	1786	44·3	47·2
1741	23·1	28·0	1787	42·4	47·0
1742	19·8	23·1	1788	46·9	51·4
1743	15·4	19·4	1789	46·5	51·4
1744	24·1	26·9	1790	43·8	49·9
1745	29·3	32·7	1791	51·6	57·3

(*a*) The size of the break occasioned by the change in original source can be judged from the following figures from the old source for 1775 and 1780:

	Bar Iron	Total Iron
1775	32·3	37·5
1780	36·4	38·5

Metals 6. *continued*

B. Great Britain, 1792–1814

	Bar Iron	Total Iron		Bar Iron	Total Iron
1792	57·7	64·2	1804	22·5	23·0
1793	59·0	64·5	1805	27·3	27·8
1794	42·5	46·7	1806	32·1	33·0
1795	49·3	51·0	1807	23·7	24·0
1796	53·2	54·8	1808	21·0	21·1
1797	36·9	37·7	1809	24·5	...
1798	51·9	52·6	1810	20·1	...
1799	48·3	49·4	1811	28·0	...
1800	38·2	38·9	1812	17·4	...
1801	33·4	34·8	1813	...	...
1802	52·9	57·7	1814	21·9	...
1803	43·5	44·7			

Metals 7. Iron and Steel Imports and Re-exports – United Kingdom 1815–1980

NOTES

[1] SOURCES: 1815–39 – Returns printed in sessional papers annually from 1817; 1840–54 *Abstract*; 1855–1980 – *Annual Statement of Trade* and *Overseas Trade Statistics of the United Kingdom*.

[2] The figures up to 1854 are for years ended on 5th January in the year following that for which they are shown.

A. Bar Iron, 1815–61 (in thousands of tons)

	Imports	Re-exports		Imports	Re-exports		Imports	Re-exports
1815	21·3	13·1	1831	17·4	4·3	1847	33·3	5·1
1816	8·5	8·2	1832	19·2	3·5	1848	23·9	3·4
1817	10·1	3·0	1833	17·9	2·0	1849	29·4	5·0
1818	16·6	3·8	1834	16·2	2·9	1850	34·1	6·0
1819	14·0	3·8	1835	19·8	2·6	1851	40·3	4·8
1820	9·9	3·2	1836	25·0	4·8	1852	33·4	5·8
1821	10·2	3·2	1837	19·3	2·6	1853	44·8	5·5
1822	12·7	3·4	1838	23·0	4·4	1854	41·7	4·3
1823	13·4	2·9	1839	20·8	4·5	1855	37·4	3·2
1824	14·2	3·5	1840	18·9	5·7	1856	51·9	6·6
1825	23·2	6·7	1841	23·8	3·6	1857	50·2	6·3
1826	13·0	2·3	1842	18·7	2·2	1858	25·5	5·9
1827	18·5	3·5	1843	12·8	4·0	1859	42·7	9·3
1828	15·1	3·0	1844	24·5	5·9	1860	54·1	7·6
1829	15·1	3·0	1845	33·4	2·6	1861	35·5	6·8
1830	14·9	3·0	1846	34·6	4·1			

B. Iron and Steel, 1862–1914

	Imports			Re-exports	
	Pig and Puddled Iron	Bar Iron	Total Iron and Steel	Bar Iron	Other Iron and Steel
1862	14·4	49·7	79	14·6	..
1863	11·3	46·6	70	12·9	..
1864	20·1	53·9	100	12·9	..
1865	11·4	51·5	94	9·6	..
1866	13·4	64·2	92	14·8	..
1867	21·6	71·7	121	23·1	2·8
1868	21·3	64·7	113	21·8	3·8
1869	19·9	68·5	121	21·1	5·4
1870	35·9	74·1	150	21·3	4·5
1871	55·6	74·3	160	20·3	4·9
1872	100·6	82·4	230	16·7	8·4
1873	74·8	74·7	190	16·3	9·4
1874	56·9	73·5	190	24·4	11·8
1875	47·6	89·8	203	34·3	12·8
1876	31·4	85·4	196	36·1	12·7
1877	44·0	91·8	225	42·2	24·5
1878	27·7	102·8	241	60·3	22·8
1879	26·3	95·5	239	49·0	27·4
1880	66·9	120·0	348	69·4	48·5
1881	55·8	111·5	349	62·1	66·0

B. Iron and Steel (including simple manufactures), 1862–1914 (*cont.*)

(in thousands of tons)

	Imports					Re-exports	
	Pig and Puddled Iron	Bar Iron	Part-wrought and Unwrought Steel	Wrought Iron, Steel, and Manufactures	Total Iron and Steel	Bar Iron	Wrought Iron, Steel, and Manufactures
1882	44·4	139·2	5·9	172·2	362	74·1	68·9
1883	38·9	122·9	4·5	194·0	360	67·4	61·7
1884	37·1	115·5	6·7	185·1	344	62·7	48·5
1885	38·6	122·6	11·2	173·7	346	77·4	47·7
1886	45·2	105·5	12·1	176·9	340	73·5	51·7
1887	38·6	113·0	14·7	198·4	365	85·0	53·5
1888	37·2	113·2	12·1	226·6	389	82·8	52·5
1889	70·3	111·8	10·9	230·4	423	75·4	40·0
1890	61·8	92·9	8·1	222·8	386	65·2	25·3
1891	61·9	77·4	8·4	229·1	377	56·1	27·2
1892	56·5	75·9	6·5	218·4	357	46·5	35·1
1893	35·4	65·8	8·9	216·7	327	28·1	45·6
1894	62·0	63·2	8·6	224·4	358	18·4	34·0
1895	93·1	67·7	10·9	234·4	406	22·8	34·2
1896	106·4	71·1	17·5	264·6	460	16·6	36·7
				...	...		...
1897	158·0	68·2	40·0	249·7(*b*)	516(*b*)	21·5	27·2(*b*)
1898	159·5	69·2	40·2	322·4	591	26·5	27·5
1899	171·4	73·2	77·3	323·1	645	18·8	26·9
1900	181·2	80·1	179·3	359·0	800	10·9	24·4
1901	198·5	98·1	182·9	444·1	924	12·4	28·2
1902	226·8	171·9	281·0	451·0	1,131	8·4	24·1
1903	136·6	186·6	274·1	706·5	1,304	8·9	51·3
1904	133·7	104·2	522·7	531·3	1,292	7·0	29·1
1905	129·0	106·0	603·9	517·1	1,356	6·4	19·7
1906	90·9	107·7	486·0	531·1	1,216	6·7	20·8
				...			...
1907	104·8	80·4	327·2	423·1(*c*)	935	6·8	24·8(*c*)
1908	68·8	82·9	560·5	407·2	1,119	4·6	17·7
1909	109·9	93·7	550·4	439·4	1,193	2·9	18·3
1910	172·5	96·7	559·0	539·0	1,367	7·4	26·3
1911	175·9	117·1	827·3	641·7	1,762	5·2	45·1
1912	218·1	164·4	873·2	741·0	1,997	2·4	23·5
1913	217·8	200·0	904·7	897·9	2,220	3·5	28·7
1914	223·5	129·9	597·9	666·6	1,618	2·6	20·4

See p. 297 for footnotes.

Metals 7. *continued*

C. Iron and Steel (including simple manufactures), 1910–39

(in thousands of tons)

	Imports			
	Pig Iron and Ferro-Alloys	Steel Blooms, Billets and Slabs (except Alloys)	Total Iron and Steel (*d*)	Re-exports of Iron and Steel
1910	172	329	1,379	34
1911	175	481	1,775	51
1912	217	564	2,012	27
1913	217	514	2,231	33
1914	223	299	1,627	29
1915	194	428	1,182	46
1916	159	146	776	48
1917	155	58	497	17
1918	129	20	337	30
1919	163	71	509	42
		---(*e*)		
1920	230	251	1,108	25
1921	679	172	1,640	16
1922	164	171	881	4·5
	---	---	---	---
1923	110(*f*)	418(*f*)	1,322	7·7(*f*)
	---	---	---	---
1924	308	705	2,429	9·1
1925	286	650	2,720	8·7
1926	492	845	3,738	14
1927	609	926	4,406	13
1928	119	616	2,897	8·3
1929	153	573	2,822	8·9
1930	312	566	2,912	12
1931	307	531	2,844	7·1
1932	153	360	1,593	3·4
1933	121	230	971	2·0
1934	163	331	1,366	2·8
1935	128	262	1,152	3·2
1936	311	453	1,483	7·0
1937	716	437	2,033	7·1
1938	443	317	1,342	30
1939	427	372	1,811	2·8

D. Iron and Steel, 1938–80 (*g*)

(in thousands of tons)

	Imports				Imports		
	Pig Iron and Ferro-Alloys	Ingots, Blooms, Billets and Slabs	Total Iron and Steel		Pig Iron and Ferro-Alloys	Ingots, Blooms, Billets and Slabs	Total Iron and Steel
1938	443	338	1,271	1960	441	270	1,682
1939	427	399	1,754	1961	239	107	694
1940	770	1,826	3,629	1962	314	157	1,085
1941	1,071	2,166	4,124	1963	409	257	1,603
1942	424	1,571	2,474	1964	611	457	2,162
1943	497	1,435	2,795	1965	632	30	1,200
1944	341	997	1,735	1966	659	103	1,556
1945	155	117	304	1967	530	280	2,159
1946	64	374	497	1968	503	468	2,647
1947	89	316	507	1969	511	1,004	2,744
1948	146	193	553	1970	442	1,009	2,670
1949	346	309	1,234	1971	429	400	2,451
1950	284	161	742	1972	500	307	3,143
1951	403	105	850	1973	464	126	3,231
1952	866	756	2,396	1974	491	134	4,294
1953	785	540	1,702	1975	407	219	4,140
1954	395	104	764	1976	601	396	4,680
1955	801	476	2,316	1977	485	241	4,210
1956	716	384	2,122	1978	446	254	4,157
1957	540	254	1,282	1979	500	336	4,313
1958	272	88	730	1980	390	353	5,037
1959	250	4·1	627				

(*a*) New items included under this heading, making a difference of 500 tons in this year.

(*b*) Cycles and machinery no longer included under this heading.

(*c*) Old rails included under this heading henceforward.

(*d*) The difference between totals in Parts B and C results from the inclusion of holloware and the exclusion of old rails.

(*e*) Alloy steels, of which very small quantities were imported, *were* included prior to this date. Also prior to this date, 'Iron Bars, Rods' etc.' included iron ingots and billets.

(*f*) Southern Ireland was treated as foreign from 1st April 1923.

(*g*) Manufactures (other than railway axles, tyres, and wheels) are not included in this part.

Metals 8. Iron and Steel Exports – England & Wales 1697–1791 and Great Britain 1792–1808

NOTES

[1] SOURCE: Elizabeth B. Schumpeter, *English Overseas Trade Statistics, 1697–1808* (Oxford University Press, 1960), tables VIII and IX (converted to tons where necessary).

[2] The figures are for years ended on 5th January of the years following that for which they are shown.

[3] Exports to Ireland are included throughout.

A. England & Wales, 1697–1791

(in tons)

	Wrought Iron (*b*)	Total Iron	Total Steel
1697	1,459	1,776	20
1698	1,019	1,844	33
1699	1,040	1,837	39
1700	1,085	1,980	19
1701	1,020	2,177	31
1702	707	1,263	21
1703	935	1,676	30
1704	902	1,567	20
1705	...	...	...
1706	703	1,009	25
1707	893	1,468	24
1708	865	1,518	31
1709	876	1,463	19
1710	967	1,450	34
1711	977	1,411	80
1712	...	...	...
1713	1,359	2,014	50
1714	1,628	2,399	59
1715	1,576	2,543	46
1716	1,358	2,193	19
1717	1,623	2,806	56
1718	1,292	1,997	34
1719	1,389	2,386	44
1720	1,283	1,906	26
1721	1,400	2,029	25
1722	1,632	2,726	47
1723	1,575	2,513	52
1724	1,942	3,126	67
1725	2,101	3,063	86
1726	1,828	2,972	50
1727	1,886	2,834	31
1728	2,168	3,602	26
1729	2,572	3,424	29
1730	2,460	3,694	61
1731	2,323	3,509	76
1732	2,367	3,386	47
1733	2,285	3,300	113
1734	2,221	3,381	113
1735	2,855	4,014	167
1736	2,971	4,376	172
1737	2,983	4,677	215
1738	3,278	5,023	151
1739	2,938	4,549	226
1740	3,743	5,851	351
1741	4,361	6,750	269
1742	3,852	5,834	140
1743	3,810	5,701	96
1744	3,238	5,147	341
1745	2,676	4,121	224
1746	5,500	8,463	831
1747	4,127	6,369	454
1748	4,800	7,392	372
1749	6,477	8,998	481
1750	6,126	9,272	436
1751	5,952	9,285	544
1752	5,455	8,590	532
1753	6,530	9,863	661
1754	6,162	8,864	686
1755	6,052	8,750	797
1756	5,266	7,012	386
1757	6,474	8,199	548
1758	6,588	8,514	536
1759	7,316	8,975	406
1760	8,153	10,779	590
1761	7,198	8,806	522
1762	6,788	8,370	610
1763	7,948	10,328	623
1764	9,294	12,612	965
1765	8,532	11,484	1,031
1766	9,974	14,691	839
1767	10,568	17,927	1,357
1768	10,940	16,841	1,403
1769	10,376	12,194	1,443
1770	10,918	16,891	1,381
1771	13,702	21,316	1,675
	---	---	---
1772	13,644(*a*)	15,761(*a*)	1,266(*a*)
1773	11,643	14,251	1,309
1774	11,561	13,479	873
1775	12,243	14,256	1,317
1776	9,311	10,871	1,001
1777	8,233	9,644	1,206
1778	7,565	9,019	2,026
1779	5,967	7,185	1,300
1780	7,406	8,997	1,733
1781	6,458	7,867	728
1782	8,894	10,477	1,933
1783	9,512	11,033	870
1784	11,498	13,165	1,109
1785	10,543	12,391	1,175
1786	10,987	14,818	2,414
1787	12,450	17,783	1,868
1788	12,201	13,773	2,066
1789	13,792	16,082	2,337
1790	15,232	17,884	2,324
1791	19,655	22,647	2,502

Metals 8. *continued*

B. Great Britain, 1792–1808

(in tons)

	Wrought Iron	Iron in Bars or Unwrought	Steel	Total Iron and Steel
1792	23,386	332	3,008	32,156
1793	16,997	180	3,624	25,032
1794	17,248	104	2,883	25,640
1795	16,167	220	2,937	24,019
1796	19,686	408	3,135	28,972
1797	17,672	1,318	2,516	26,530
1798	17,750	1,889	2,007	25,903
1799	23,109	2,676	6,308	38,261
1800	24,372	2,845	4,267	37,846
1801	21,489	3,001	4,769	35,906
1802	23,791	5,459	4,348	41,087
1803	16,948	3,575	4,225	31,414
1804	17,964	6,065	654	30,190
1805	16,397	6,595	498	37,423
1806	20,167	8,124	381	37,306
1807	21,830	10,863	394	42,116
1808	18,902	14,924	492	42,197

(*a*) The size of this break, caused by the change in original source, can be judged by the following figures from the old source for 1775 and 1780:

	Wrought Iron	Total Iron	Total Steel
1775	11,639	13,319	1,305
1780	7,049	8,531	1,733

(*b*) Includes hardware and, presumably, other goods which were not wrought (in the technical sense), but cast.

Metals 9. Iron and Steel Exports – Great Britain 1805–14, and United Kingdom 1815–1980

NOTES

[1] SOURCES: 1805–14 – *S.P.* 1814–5, x; 1815–18 – *S.P.* 1819, xvi; 1819–20 – *S.P.* 1821, xviii; 1821–4 – *S.P.* 1825, xxi; 1825–8 – *S.P.* 1829, xvii; 1829–48 – Returns printed in *Sessional Papers* annually; 1849–1908 – *Abstract*; 1906–80 – *Abstract* and *Annual Statement of Trade* and *Overseas Trade Statistics of the United Kingdom*.

[2] The figures up to and including 1854 are for years ended on 5th January of the year following that for which they are shown.

A. 1805–1907

(in thousands of tons)

	Pig and Puddled Iron	Iron in Bars or Unwrought & Railway Material	Total Iron and Steel		Pig and Puddled Iron	Iron in Bars or Unwrought & Railway Material	Total Iron and Steel.
1805	--	3	20	1831	12	70	124
1806	--	4	27	1832	18	81	148
1807	--	5	24	1833	23	83	163
1808	--	9	26	1834	22	80	158
1809	...	...	...	1835	33	108	199
1810	...	...	...	1836	34	98	192
1811	...	...	...	1837	44	96	194
1812	--	13	32	1838	49	142	257
1813	...	...	...	1839	43	136	248
1814	--	15	37	1840	50	145	269
1815	--	25	49	1841	86	189	360
1816	1	27	52	1842	94	191	369
1817	4	39	67	1843	155	199	450
1818	3	48	79	1844	100	250	459
1819	1	27	52	1845	77	164	351
1820	3	42	67	1846	159	158	433
1821	4	39	65	1847	176	228	550
1822	5	39	70	1848	176	339	626
1823	8	41	65	1849	162	402	709
1824	2	30	59	1850	142	469	783
1825	3	30	61	1851	201	538	919
1826	7	40	76	1852	240	568	1,036
1827	7	53	93	1853	334	654	1,261
1828	8	59	101	1854	293	617	1,197
1829	9	63	108	1855	292	541	1,093
1830	12	68	118	1856	357	760	1,439

A. 1805–1907 (*cont.*)

(in thousands of tons)

	Pig and Puddled Iron	Iron in Bars or Unwrought	Railway Material	Total Iron and Steel (*a*)		Pig and Puddled Iron	Iron in Bars or Unwrought	Railway Material	Total Iron and Steel
1857	422	302	458	1,593	1883	1,564	288	971	4,043
1858	363	254	433	1,404	1884	1,270	296	729	3,497
1859	316	301	529	1,526	1885	961	264	714	3,131
1860	343	311	453	1,503	1886	1,045	243	740	3,388
1861	388	258	378	1,359	1887	1,126	295	1,012	4,143
				----(*b*)					
1862	445	308	401	1,557	1888	1,036	298	1,020	3,967
1863	466	331	446	1,703	1889	1,190	252	1,090	4,186
1864	466	280	408	1,559	1890	1,145	223	1,035	4,001
1865	548	254	434	1,687	1891	840	217	702	3,240
1866	501	269	498	1,762	1892	767	173	468	2,739
1867	566	301	581	1,968	1893	840	149	558	2,857
1868	553	303	583	2,042	1894	831	129	425	2,650
1869	711	359	888	2,675	1895	867	144	458	2,836
1870	753	321	1,059	2,826	1896	1,060	178	748	3,550
1871	1,057	349	981	3,169	1897	1,201	168	782	3,686
1872	1,331	314	945	3,383	1898	1,043	150	609	3,244
1873	1,142	287	785	2,958	1899	1,380	160	591	3,717
1874	776	259	783	2,488	1900	1,428	157	464	3,541
1875	948	276	546	2,458	1901	839	118	573	2,898
1876	910	228	415	2,224	1902	1,103	125	716	3,576
1877	882	248	498	2,346	1903	1,065	128	723	3,707
1878	923	224	439	2,297	1904	811	116	654	3,426
1879	1,223	231	464	2,883	1905	983	134	706	3,870
1880	1,632	304	694	3,793	1906	1,666	151	614	4,860
1881	1,482	294	821	3,820	1907	1,944	159	586	5,312
1882	1,758	314	933	4,354					

B. 1907–38

(in thousands of tons)

	Pig Iron and Ferro-Alloys	Railway Material (*c*)	Total Iron and Steel (*d*)		Pig Iron and Ferro-Alloys	Railway Material	Total Iron and Steel
1907	1,942	655	5,168	1923	893(*e*)	493(*e*)	4,318(*e*)
					---	---	---
1908	1,294	640	4,115	1924	600	370	3,851
1909	1,135	774	4,238	1925	560	421	3,731
1910	1,205	656	4,622	1926	313	306	2,988
1911	1,203	545	4,552	1927	331	729	4,196
1912	1,262	651	4,844	1928	455	610	4,261
1913	1,124	775	4,969	1929	545	487	4,380
1914	781	654	3,910	1930	317	389	3,160
1915	611	399	3,209	1931	202	206	1,979
1916	917	127	3,308	1932	128	105	1,887
1917	734	85	2,338	1933	112	110	1,922
1918	482	81	1,613	1934	133	190	2,251
1919	357	218	2,233	1935	157	217	2,369
1920	580	311	3,251	1936	112	241	2,234
1921	136	340	1,697	1937	167	241	2,607
1922	794	477	3,397	1938	101	202	1,960
	---	---	---				

Metals 9. *continued*

C. 1938–80

(in thousands of tons)

	Pig Iron and Ferro-Alloys	Ingots, Blooms, Billets & Slabs	Total Iron and Steel (*f*)		Pig Iron and Ferro-Alloys	Ingots, Blooms, Billets & Slabs	Total Iron and Steel
1938	101	10	1,625	1960	158	27	3,361
1939	78	4·7	1,362	1961	151	105	3,441
1940	25	7·8	960	1962	226	88	3,390
1941	21	0·3	402	1963	112	39	3,549
1942	5·4	0·4	193	1964	73	98	3,855
1943	5·0	1·9	95	1965	127	102	4,122
1944	3·4	0·9	176	1966	86	106	3,717
1945	34	0·7	543	1967	173	333	4,097
1946	92	6·0	1,916	1968	113	226	4,490
1947	53	6·1	1,448	1969	120	114	4,124
1948	6·6	8·6	1,621	1970	102	133	4,297
1949	21	7·2	1,957	1971	55	179	5,056
1950	41	10	2,596	1972	48	237	4,691
1951	19	14	2,127	1973	44	195	4,341
1952	8·0	7·5	2,065	1974	81	218	3,494
1953	9·2	6·3	2,200	1975	59	250	3,338
1954	55	7·3	2,407	1976	103	255	3,808
1955	55	6·6	2,792	1977	86	409	4,503
1956	149	7·0	2,895	1978	75	349	4,483
1957	133	13	3,293	1979	71	380	4,640
1958	156	29	2,896	1980	73	233	2,864
1959	169	84	3,178				

(*a*) Now including tinplates.
(*b*) Certain manufactures of iron and steel combined were included from 1862 (in which year they amounted to 6 thousand tons).
(*c*) Now including tyres and axles, but excluding old rails.
(*d*) Now excluding scrap and old iron, but including some manufactures not covered previously.
(*e*) Southern Ireland was treated as foreign from 1 April 1923.
(*f*) Now excluding all manufactures of iron and steel except railway axles, tyres, and wheels.

Metals 10. Output of Tin – England, 1198–1837

NOTES

[1] SOURCES: to 1549 – John Hatcher, *English Tin Production and Trade before 1550* (Oxford, 1973), Appendix A; 1553–1749 – G. R. Lewis, *The Stannaries* (Cambridge, Mass., 1908), appendix J.; 1750–1837 – R. Hunt, *British Mining* (London, 1884), p. 887.

[2] An alternative source for 1750–1837 is "Statistics of the Tin Mines in Cornwall and of the Consumption of Tin in Great Britain", by J. Carne, in *J.S.S.* II, p. 261. For the period 1801–11 Carne's figures differ slightly from Hunt's.

[3] The statistics relate to "white tin", i.e. the metal content of ore mined in Cornwall and Devon.

[4] The figures for the years up to 1749 are for years ending Michaelmas.

A. Tin Paying Coinage Dues, 1199–1837

(in thousandweight) (*a*)

1198	869	1201	808	1207 } 1208 }	1,229	1209	612	1212	1,003
1199	901	1204	712			1211	815	1214	1,199
1200	807	1206	607						

(in tons of 2,240 lb.)

1301	279	1395	599	1460	335	1546	805	1600	571
1303	390	1396	592	1462	346	1547	801	1601	644
1304	[346] (*b*)	1397	643	1463	341	1549	549	1602	738
1305	[380] (*b*)	1398	638	1464	337	1553	866	1603	589
1306	[385] (*b*)	1400	715	1465	386	1554	800	1604	617
1309	[365] (*b*)	1407	633	1466	485	1555	753	1605	593
1313 }	[737] (*b*)	1412	639	1467	485	1556	750	1606	561
1314 }		1413	621	1469	463	1561	715	1607	550
1315	[359] (*b*)	1414	709	1470	496	1563	596	1608	580
1316	[330] (*b*)	1415	691	1471	464	1564	679	1609	557
1317	[238] (*b*)	1416	650	1472	510	1565	648	1610	547
1324	[442] (*b*)	1418	499	1477	462	1566	671	1611	587
1332	[734] (*b*)	1423	570	1478	475	1567	749	1612	582
1333	[637] (*b*)	1424	523	1487	492	1568	522	1613	610
1334	[582] (*b*)	1425	564	1494	607	1569	747	1614	622
1335	[666] (*b*)	1426	522	1495	571	1570	571	1625	751
1336	[665] (*b*)	1427	516	1503	591	1571	515	1638	536
1337	[616] (*b*)	1428	452	1504	587	1572	509	1639	539
1338	[548] (*b*)	1429	536	1515	803	1573	549	1640	537
1339 }	[939] (*b*)	1430	512	1516	790	1574	530	1641	513
1340 }									
		1431	539	1517	791	1575	584	1642	543
1341 }	[1,034] (*b*)	1432	464	1518	777	1576	642	1643	363
1342 }		1433	450	1519	798	1577	659	1644	122
1351	[106] (*b*)	1434	494	1520	801	1578	573	1645	316
1352	[155] (*b*)	1435	413	1521	900	1579	634	1646	157
1353	[170] (*b*)								
		1436	445	1522	690	1580	734	1647	193
1354	[189] (*b*)	1437	366	1523	788	1581	683	1648	4
1355	[222] (*b*)	1438	428	1524	855	1582	673	1667	911
1356	[235] (*b*)	1439	420	1525	852	1583	...	1668	...
1357	[241] (*b*)	1440	377	1526	831	1584	651	1669	706
1361	[255] (*b*)								
		1441	405	1527	876	1585	666	1670	778
1362	[168] (*b*)	1442	344	1528	858	1586	656	1671	890
1366	[227] (*b*)	1443	385	1529	828	1587	639	1672	793
1368	[292] (*b*)	1445	380	1530	792	1588	665	1673	956
1375	[215] (*b*)	1446	376	1531	794	1589	615	1674	635
1377	[307] (*b*)								
		1447	432	1532	793	1590	632	1675	1,155
1378	[360] (*b*)	1448	408	1533	785	1591	686	1676	1,122
1379	410	1449	429	1534	814	1592	708	1677	1,344
1383	441	1450	417	1535	782	1593	634	1678	1,308
1384	467	1451	388	1536	673	1594	686	1679	1,061
1385	484								
		1452	385	1537	690	1595	727	1680	1,161
1386	582	1453	378	1539	782	1596	658	1681	1,181
1387	606	1454	377	1542	818	1597	560	1682	1,364
1392 }	1,102	1455	368	1543	694	1598	476	1683	1,407
1393 }		1456	367	1544	752	1599	541	1684	1,212
1394	592								

Metals 10. *continued*

A. Tin Paying Coinage Dues, 1199–1837 (*cont.*)

(in tons)

1685	1,370	1715	1,189	1745	1,735	1775	2,619	1805	2,742
1686	1,543	1716	1,086	1746	1,917	1776	2,652	1806	2,855
1687	1,460	1717	1,655	1747	1,843	1777	2,770	1807	2,426
1688	1,400	1718	1,631	1748	2,004	1778	2,515	1808	2,330
1689	1,493	1719	...	1749	1,154	1779	2,678	1809	2,508
1690	1,268	1720	1,477	1750	2,876	1780	2,926	1810	2,006
1691	1,309	1721	1,145	1751	2,273	1781	2,610	1811	2,384
1692	1,233	1722	1,396	1752	2,550	1782	2,546	1812	2,373
1693	1,268	1723	1,379	1753	2,516	1783	2,570	1813	2,324
1694	1,197	1724	1,603	1754	2,724	1784	2,685	1814	2,611
1695	1,259	1725	1,663	1755	2,757	1785	2,885	1815	2,941
1696	1,195	1726	1,515	1756	2,774	1786	3,309	1816	3,348
1697	1,068	1727	1,593	1757	2,752	1787	3,204	1817	4,120
1698	1,258	1728	1,462	1758	2,720	1788	3,352	1818	4,066
1699	1,433	1729	1,585	1759	2,637	1789	3,405	1819	3,315
1700	1,428	1730	1,546	1760	2,717	1790	3,193	1820	2,990
1701	1,376	1731	...	1761	2,395	1791	3,470	1821	3,373
1702	1,114	1732	1,861	1762	2,584	1792	3,809	1822	3,278
1703	1,610	1733	1,628	1763	2,736	1793	3,202	1823	4,213
1704	1,490	1734	1,837	1764	2,618	1794	3,351	1824	5,005
1705	1,407	1735	1,760	1765	2,757	1795	3,440	1825	4,358
1706	1,484	1736	1,547	1766	3,055	1796	3,061	1826	4,603
1707	1,464	1737	1,686	1767	2,850	1797	3,240	1827	5,555
1708	1,454	1738	1,351	1768	2,667	1798	2,820	1828	4,931
1709	1,428	1739	1,784	1769	2,898	1799	2,862	1829	4,434
1710	2,176	1740	1,694	1770	2,977	1800	2,522	1830	4,444
1711	1,437	1741	1,546	1771	2,823	1801	2,328	1831	4,300
1712	1,439	1742	1,784	1772	3,159	1802	2,627	1832	4,323
1713	1,356	1743	1,890	1773	2,852	1803	2,914	1833	4,065
1714	1,112	1744	1,872	1774	2,458	1804	2,993	1834	3,989
								1835	4,228
								1836	4,054
								1837	4,790

(*a*) The thousandweight contained 1,000 lbs in Cornwall and 1,200 lb in Devon.

(*b*) Cornwall only. In 1303 the Cornish contribution to the total was 342 and in 1379 it was 371.

Metals 11. Sales of Copper Mined in Cornwall and Devon, 1726–1860

NOTE

Sources: 1726–71 (including decennial averages of value 1726–75) – W. Pryce, *Mineralogia Cornubiensis* (London, 1772), p. xv; 1771–1837 – Sir Charles Lemon, 'The Statistics of the Copper Mines of Cornwall', in *J.S.S.*, vol. 1, p. 70; 1838–52 (except value) – R. Hunt, *British Mining* (London, 1884), p. 892; 1845–47 (value) – *Memoirs of the Geological Survey*, vol. II, part 2, p. 703; 1848–52 (value) – *Records of the School of Mines*, vol. I, part IV; 1853–60 – *Mineral Statistics*.

(in thousands of tons and £000)

	Copper Ore Sold at Public Ticketings in Cornwall and Devon	Value of Copper Ore Sold Publicly in Cornwall and Devon	Metallic Copper from Ore Sold Publicly in Cornwall and Devon
1726	5·0		...
1727	6·7		...
1728	6·8		...
1729	6·9		...
1730	6·9		...
		474	...
1731	7·0		...
1732	7·3		...
1733	7·0		...
1734	6·0		...
1735	5·2		...
1736	8·0		...
1737	9·0		...
1738	10·0		...
1739	11·0		...
1740	5·0		...
		560	...
1741	5·5		...
1742	6·1		...
1743	7·0		...
1744	7·2		...
1745	6·7		...
1746	7·0		...
1747	4·9		...
1748	6·0		...
1749	7·2		...
1750	9·4		...
		731	...
1751	11·0		...
1752	12·1		...
1753	13·0		...
1754	14·0		...
1755	14·2		...
1756	16·0		...
1757	17·0		...
1758	15·0		...
1759	16·7		...
1760	15·8		...
		1,243	...
1761	17·0		...
1762	16·1		...
1763	17·9		...
1764	21·5		...
1765	16·8		...
1766	21·3	...	...
1767	18·5	...	...
1768	23·7	...	...
1769	26·7	...	...
1770	30·8	...	...
		1,778	
1771	27·9	190	3·3
1772	27·7	190	3·4
1773	27·8	148	3·3
1774	30·3	162	3·6
1775	30·0	192	3·6

Metals 11. *continued*

(in thousands of tons and £000)

	Copper Ore Sold at Public Ticketings in Cornwall and Devon	Value of Copper Ore Sold Publicly in Cornwall and Devon	Metallic Copper from Ore Sold Publicly in Cornwall and Devon
1776	29·4	192	3·5
1777	28·2	177	3·4
1778	24·7	141	3·0
1779	31·1	181	3·7
1780	24·4	171	2·9
1781	28·7	179	3·5
1782	28·1	152	3·4
1783	35·8	220	4·3
1784	36·6	209	4·4
1785	37·0	205	4·4
1786	39·9	237	4·8
1787	38·0	191	...
1788	31·5	150	...
1789	33·3	184	...
1790	...	...	...
1791	...	...	...
1792	...	...	...
1793	...	...	...
1794	42·8	321	...
1795	43·6	326	...
1796	43·3	357	5·0
1797	47·9	378	5·2
1798	51·4	423	5·6
1799	51·3	470	4·9
1800	56·0	551	5·2
1801	56·6	476	5·3
1802	53·9	445	5·2
1803	60·6	534	5·6
1804	64·6	508	5·4
1805	78·5	862	6·2
1806	79·3	731	6·9
1807	71·7	609	6·7
1808	67·9	495	6·8
1809	76·2	770	6·8
1810	66·0	570	5·7
1811	66·8	557	6·1
1812	71·5	550	6·7
1813	74·0	594	6·9
1814	74·3	628	6·4
1815	78·5	553	6·5
1816	77·3	448	6·7
1817	76·7	494	6·5
1818	86·2	686	6·8
1819	88·7	624	6·8
1820	91·5	602	7·5
1821	98·4	606	8·5
1822	104·5	663	9·1
1823	95·8	608	7·9
1824	99·7	587	7·8
1825	107·5	726	8·2

Metals 11. *continued*

(in thousands of tons and £000)

	Copper Ore Sold at Public Ticketings in Cornwall and Devon	Value of Copper Ore Sold Publicly in Cornwall and Devon	Metallic Copper from Ore Sold Publicly in Cornwall and Devon
1826	117·3	789	9·0
1827	126·7	745	10·3
1828	130·4	756	9·9
1829	124·5	717	9·7
1830	135·7	784	10·9
1831	146·5	818	12·2
1832	139·1	836	12·1
1833	138·3	859	11·2
1834	143·3	888	11·2
1835	150·6	896	12·3
1836	141·0	958	11·6
1837	140·8	909	10·8
1838	145·7	...	11·5
1839	159·6	...	12·5
1840	147·3	...	11·0
1841	147·8	...	10·0
1842	154·2	...	9·9
1843	153·7	...	10·9
1844	152·7	...	11·2
1845	162·6	920	12·9
1846	150·4	796	11·9
1847	148·7	889	12·0
1848	155·6	720	12·9
1849	145·0	764	12·1
1850	150·9	840	11·8
1851	154·3	783	12·2
1852	152·8	976	11·7
1853	180·1	1,155	11·8
1854	184·9	1,193	12·0
1855	195·2	1,264	12·6
1856	206·2	1,242	13·5
1857	192·1	1,201	12·2
1858	183·4	1,058	12·1
1859	183·5	1,096	12·2
1860	182·5	1,065	12·2

Metals 12. Mineral Content of Main Non-ferrous Metals Mined – United Kingdom, 1845–1980

NOTES

[1] SOURCES: 1845–52 (or 3) – R. Hunt, *British Mining* (London, 1884) for tin, and *Memoirs of the Geological Survey of Great Britain*, vol. II, part II and *Records of the School of Mines*, vol. I, part IV for lead; 1853 (or 4)–1921 and 1965–80 – *Mineral Statistics*, 1922–38 – *Annual Report* of the Department of Mines; 1939–64 *Abstract* (except for lead 1962–4 which is estimated from the dressed ore output given in *Mineral Statistics*, 1975).

[2] The output of the Isle of Man is included.

[3] The exclusion of southern Ireland after 1921 made little difference to the zinc series and none to any other.

[4] R. Hunt, *op. cit.* above, gives the following figures for production of tin ore in 1848–53 (in thousands of tons):

1848	10·2	1850	10·4	1852	9·7
1849	10·7	1851	9·5	1853	8·9

(in thousands of tons)

	Copper	Lead	Tin	Zinc		Copper	Lead	Tin	Zinc
1845		52·7			1885	2·8	37·7	9·3	9·8
1846		50·2			1886	1·5	39·5	9·3	9·0
1847		55·7			1887	0·9	37·9	9·3	9·8
1848		54·9			1888	1·5	37·6	9·2	10·0
1849		58·7			1889	0·9	35·6	8·9	9·4
1850		64·5			1890	0·9	33·6	9·6	8·6
1851		65·1			1891	0·7	32·2	9·4	8·9
1852		65·0			1892	0·5	29·5	9·3	9·3
1853		61·0	5·8		1893	0·4	29·7	8·8	9·3
1854	19·9	64·0	6·0		1894	0·4	29·7	8·3	8·1
1855	21·3	65·5	6·0		1895	0·6	29·0	6·6	6·7
1856	24·3	73·1	6·2		1896	0·6	30·8	4·8	7·1
1857	17·4	67·4	6·6		1897	0·5	26·6	4·5	7·0
1858	14·5	68·3	6·9	3·5	1898	0·6	25·4	4·6	8·6
1859	15·8	63·2	7·1	3·7	1899	0·6	23·6	4·0	8·7
1860	16·0	63·3	6·7	4·4	1900	0·8	24·4	4·3	9·1
1861	15·3	65·6	7·4	4·4	1901	0·5	20·0	4·6	8·4
1862	14·8	69·0	8·5	2·2	1902	0·5	17·7	4·4	9·1
1863	14·2	68·2	10·0	3·8	1903	0·5	20·0	4·3	9·3
1864	13·3	67·1	10·1	4·0	1904	0·5	19·8	4·1	10·3
1865	11·9	67·2	10·0	4·5	1905	0·7	20·6	4·5	8·9
1866	11·2	67·4	10·0	3·2	1906	0·7	22·3	4·5	8·5
1867	10·2	68·4	8·7	3·8	1907	0·7	24·5	4·4	7·6
1868	9·8	71·0	9·3	3·7	1908	0·6	21·0	5·1	5·8
1869	8·3	73·3	9·8	4·5	1909	0·4	22·5	5·2	3·8
1870	7·2	73·4	10·2	3·9	1910	0·4	21·5	4·8	4·2
1871	6·3	69·1	10·9	5·0	1911	0·4	18·0	4·9	6·1
1872	5·7	60·4	9·6	5·2	1912	0·3	19·2	5·3	6·1
1873	5·2	54·2	10·0	4·5	1913	0·4	18·1	5·3	5·8
1874	4·9	58·8	9·9	4·5	1914	0·3	19·4	5·1	5·2
1875	4·6	57·4	9·6	6·7	1915	0·2	15·5	5·0	4·1
1876	4·7	58·7	8·5	6·6	1916	0·3	12·6	4·7	3·0
1877	4·5	61.4	9·5	6·3	1917	0·2	11·3	3·9	2·7
1878	4·0	58·0	10·1	6·3	1918	0·2	10·9	4·0	3·2
1879	3·5	51·6	9·5	5·6	1919	0·1	10·3	3·3	2·4
1880	3·7	56·9	8·9	7·2	1920	0·1	11·0	3·1	1·7
1881	3·9	48·6	8·6	14·9	1921	0·1	5·2	0·7	0·3
1882	3·5	50·3	9·2	16·1	1922	0·1	8·4	0·4	0·6
1883	2·6	43·4	9·3	13·6	1923	0·1	9·5	1·0	0·7
1884	3·4	40·1	9·6	9·9	1924	0·1	10·9	2·0	0·8

Metals 12. *continued*

(in thousands of tons)

	Copper	Lead	Tin	Zinc		Copper	Lead	Tin	Zinc
1925	0·1	11·8	2·3	0·6	1953	—	6·6	1·1	2·8
1926	0·1	14·5	2·3	0·7	1954	—	6·9	0·9	3·5
1927	0·2	15·5	2·6	1·0	1955	—	6·1	1·0	2·8
1928	0·1	14·1	2·8	0·6	1956	—	7·5	1·0	1·4
1929	0·1	17·7	3·3	0·7	1957	—	8·1	1·0	1·0
1930	..	19·3	2·5	0·5	1958	—	4·3	1·1	0·3
1931	0·1	22·4	0·6	0·2	1959	—	2·4	1·3	—
1932	0·1	31·3	1·3	..	1960	—	1·4	1·2	—
1933	—	37·7	1·5	..	1961	—	1·5	1·2	—
1934	—	51·1	2·0	0·3	1962	—	0·8	1·2	—
1935	—	39·2	2·0	0·9	1963	—	1·0	1·2	—
1936	—	29·0	2·1	3·3	1964	—	1·4	1·2	—
1937	—	25·1	2·0	6·2	1965	—	2·4	1·3	—
1938	—	28·3	2·0	9·0	1966	—	3·0	1·3	—
1939	—	16·6	1·6	...	1967	—	3·2	1·5	—
1940	—	13·6	1·6	...	1968	—	3·5	1·8	—
1941	—	8·0	1·5	8·4	1969	—	3·6	1·6	—
1942	—	5·4	1·4	6·8	1970	—	4·0	1·7	—
1943	—	4·2	1·4	12·8	1971	—	4·9	1·8	—
1944	—	4·0	1·2	15·8	1972	0·2	4·4	3·3	1·2
1945	—	2·9	1·2	6·8	1973	0·5	3·6	3·6	2·9
1946	—	2·6	0·8	0·1	1974	0·4	3·7	3·2	2·8
1947	—	2·8	0·9	—	1975	0·6	6·3	3·3	3·9
1948	—	2·3	0·9	—	1976	0·5	6·9	3·3	4·7
1949	—	2·1	0·9	—	1977	0·4	8·0	3·8	7·4
1950	—	3·0	0·9	0·2	1978	0·1	4·5	2·8	2·7
1951	—	4·1	0·8	0·2	1979	—	4·6	2·4	0·6
1952	—	4·7	0·9	1·7	1980	0·2	3·5	3·0	4·4

Metals 13. Output of Main Refined Non-ferrous Metals – United Kingdom 1850–1980

NOTES

[1] SOURCES: 1850–1941 – based on Christopher J. Schmitz, *World Non-Ferrous Metal Production and Prices, 1700–1976* (London, 1979); 1942–80 – *Abstract* (except "other refined lead", which is from Schmitz, *op. cit.*, to 1964 and *Mineral Statistics*, subsequently).

[2] Schmitz notes that the copper statistics given in *Mineral Statistics* for 1880–1914 underestimate total smelter production owing to the exclusion of copper from imported pyrites. His estimates are preferred here.

(in thousands of tons)

	Copper	Lead	Zinc		Copper	Lead	Zinc
1850	23·8	65·6	...	1865	23·4	71·2	...
1851	22·8	67·2	...	1866	22·3	74·6	...
1852	20·5	65·5	...	1867	30·3	74·8	...
1853	22·3	61·5	...	1868	38·1	79·4	...
1854	23·1	64·8	...	1869	43·2	81·6	...
1855	26·1	66·1	...	1870	34·2	82·1	15·8
1856	29·6	73·6	...	1871	30·0	83·6	...
1857	17·4	70·0	...	1872	27·4	69·9	14·8
1858	31·6	69·9	...	1873	32·0	62·6	20·0
1859	32·7	65·8	...	1874	32·9	69·3	13·0
1860	29·7	63·8	...	1875	33·8	65·8	15·0
1861	30·9	67·2	...	1876	40·9	67·4	11·5
1862	28·8	71·2	...	1877	58·1	70·5	...
1863	34·6	68·8	...	1878	62·0	68·9	...
1864	28·4	69·3	...	1879	54·5	64·1	...

(in thousands of tons)

	Aluminium	Copper	Lead	Tin	Zinc		Aluminium	Copper	Lead	Tin	Zinc
1880	—	59·9	66·8	9·1	22·1	1910	4·9	69·9	29·2	17·6	62·1
1881	—	57·9	59·2	8·8	24·4	1911	4·9	66·6	25·3	18·5	65·9
1882	—	61·9	60·7	9·4	26·1	1912	9·8	62·1	28·8	18·6	56·3
1883	—	66·2	54·8	9·9	29·2	1913	7·4	51·8	30·1	22·3	65·2
1884	—	73·0	59·1	10·0	29·8	1914	7·3	50·9	39·2	21·0	49·8
1885	—	84·4	58·7	9·7	24·3	1915	7·0	34·2	26·7	27·0	51·6
1886	—	66·5	50·2	9·6	21·2	1916	7·6	38·9	21·2	21·5	51·8
1887	—	74·8	49·2	9·9	19·8	1917	7·0	28·8	12·0	24·2	51·1
1888	—	92·4	49·2	10·4	26·8	1918	8·2	25·4	12·1	19·8	38·4
1889	—	96·4	46·8	9·9	30·8	1919	8·0	14·9	13·5	22·5	37·6
1890	..	88·0	47·7	10·9	29·1	1920	8·0	26·0	12·5	21·0	24·6
1891	0·1	93·3	47·4	10·4	29·4	1921	5·0	11·9	2·9	13·1	5·7
1892	..	99·0	42·1	11·0	30·3	1922	7·0	18·3	5·0	23·6	32·8
1893	...	89·3	35·7	10·3	28·3	1923	9·0	18·3	6·7	29·3	42·6
1894	...	68·5	39·1	10·5	32·1	1924	8·0	17·0	5·3	34·3	47·6
1895	...	77·0	44·8	9·1	29·5	1925	9·6	10·5	4·7	41·3	41·9
1896	0·1	74·8	56·3	7·2	24·9	1926	8·0	13·1	4·2	39·8	16·9
1897	0·3	73·8	39·7	7·3	23·5	1927	9·6	12·9	6·0	40·4	41·9
1898	0·3	68·2	49·2	7·6	28·0	1928	9·6	21·1	8·5	48·0	55·4
1899	0·5	77·7	41·3	7·2	31·7	1929	8·0	21·9	10·6	56·9	58·3
1900	0·6	78·4	35·0	7·8	29·8	1930	13·0	44·3	10·2	50·6	48·6
1901	0·6	78·6	35·1	10·1	30·0	1931	14·0	54·1	10·5	35·2	21·2
1902	0·6	65·0	50·5	10·3	39·6	1932	10·0	59·1	7·0	27·3	26·9
1903	0·7	69·2	42·3	10·5	43·4	1933	10·8	78·7	5·5	26·5	45·0
1904	0·7	64·0	24·4	11·4	45·5	1934	12·7	113·2	9·9	24·7	54·0
1905	1·0	66·8	23·1	12·8	50·1	1935	14·9	118·1	22·1	31·8	63·0
1906	1·0	71·6	23·9	13·7	51·8	1936	16·0	108·3	13·6	33·8	65·0
1907	1·8	69·8	27·4	14·3	54·7	1937	19·0	127·9	10·1	37·5	62·0
1908	2·0	70·3	29·4	16·4	53·6	1938	23·0	137·8	9·8	32·1	55·0
1909	2·8	65·4	28·0	16·9	58·4						

Metals 13. *continued*

(in thousands of tons)

	Virgin Aluminium	Secondary Aluminium	Virgin Copper	Secondary Copper	English Refined Lead (*a*)	Other Refined Lead (*b*)	Refined Nickel (*c*)	Virgin Tin	Slab Zinc
1939	25·0	...	...	...	12·9	...	...	37·3	51·0
1940	19·0	38·1	161·5	...	10·2	...	...	46·7	55·6
1941	22·7	53·2	146·1	...	10·1	...	...	41·3	67·5
1942	46·8	78·8	183·0	48·5	5·4	10·6	20·3	37·3	72·6
1943	55·7	93·5	171·4 ----(*d*) 183·3	46·7	4·8	11·2	15·4	31·6	69·4
1944	35·5	104·5	154·5	48·4	3·3	10·3	15·0	28·6	71·0
1945	31·9	81·0	93·2	51·5	2·7	10·8	13·4	27·5	62·0
1946	31·5	74·9	107·1	73·8	2·6	22·4	11·3	29·1	65·4
1947	28·9	97·6	112·5	73·1	2·8	26·7	14·3	28·1	68·3
1948	30·0	80·2	124·9	67·6	36·2		17·1	31·0	69·4
1949	30·3	75·2	105·1	72·5	35·8		21·6	28·4	64·1
1950	29·5	79·9	119·3	70·9	73·1		20·9	28·5	70·3
1951	27·7	71·4	132·1	73·8	73·6		23·3	27·7	69·7
1952	28·0	73·1	146·4	78·9	86·1		23·8	29·5	68·7
1953	30·9	80·5	97·0	88·2	77·4		23·9	29·4	72·7
1954	31·6	84·1	136·5	82·6	82·1		23·9	28·0	81·2
1955	24·4	95·6	123·5	103·7	82·9		24·3	27·7	81·3
1956	27·6	96·2	113·7	102·7	94·5		24·2	26·8	81·5
1957	29·4	97·2	112·3	89·0	85·7	49·8	23·9	34·5	76·9
1958	26·4	99·0	98·3	94·9	79·8	53·7	23·1	33·0	74·6
1959	24·5	107·3	95·5	96·7	86·7	49·9	24·9	27·6	73·0
1960	28·9	129·8	110·9	104·5	91·1	51·3	33·8	27·6	74·3
1961	32·3	131·0	129·0	105·3	86·3	46·4	37·4	26·4	92·9
1962	34·0	141·3	117·0	111·1	88·6	46·8	37·7	19·9	97·3
1963	30·6	161·1	90·0	107·4	95·1	61·6	37·5	18·7	99·0
1964	31·7	183·1	110·7	110·6	120·8	56·8	37·4	19·3	109·3
1965	35·6	185·8	101·2	122·9	125·4	43·9	39·8	18·4	105·1
1966	36·5	195·2	43·1	133·9	110·8	61·1	36·9	18·8	99·7
1967	38·4	188·2	35·4	131·3	123·9	64·8	38·0	25·9	102·7
1968	37·6	197·1	48·9	145·7	141·4	90·6	41·0	27·6	140·6
1969	33·3	223·5	48·5	146·5	139·4	117·0	29·2	28·3	157·5
1970	39·0	211·0	48·6	154·3	144·4	138·1	36·1	24·1	144·3
1971	117·1	186·1	48·7	126·1	140·5	118·9	38·1	24·8	114·7
1972	168·7	194·3	58·7	100·9	147·2	119·1	31·4	25·9	72·6
1973	247·6	206·3	74·7	93·5	142·7	118·2	36·2	22·7	82·5
1974	288·5	203·3	68·0	89·6	137·7	134·8	35·1	15·2	83·1
1975	303·4	173·4	74·3	74·8	192·4	116·0	36·7	14·8	52·6
1976	329·2	202·6	50·8	84·3	206·4	130·1	32·6	13·5	40·9
1977	344·2	197·6	43·7	76·6	208·1	137·5	22·8	13·7	80·2
1978	340·7	190·6	45·5	78·1	219·4	120·9	21·1	11·0	72·4
1979	353·8	173·9	47·7	72·0	240·3	122·1	18·6	11·2	75·5
1980	368·5	159·5	67·2	91·5	208·1	111·6	19·0	11·2	85·3

(*a*) Smelter production of primary lead.
(*b*) Including secondary lead.
(*c*) Including cupronickel.
(*d*) Subsequently including scrap refined on private account.

Metals 14. Main Imports and Re-exports of Non-ferrous Metals – United Kingdom 1820–1980

NOTES

[1] SOURCES: 1820–86 – annual returns in *Sessional Papers*, supplemented by *Annual Statement of Trade*; 1887–1980 – *Annual Statement of Trade* and *Overseas Trade Statistics of the United Kingdom*. A few earlier statistics are available, but the amounts involved are negligible.

[2] Up to and including 1854, the figures are for years beginning 6 January.

[3] Up to and including 1841 most imported copper ore was smelted in bond and re-exported, the quantities retained being insignificant. In 1842, when import duty was abolished, 16 thousand tons were retained, and thenceforward almost all imported ores were retained.

(in thousands of tons)

	Imports					Re-exports		
	Copper Ore (a)	Unmanufactured Copper	Pig and Sheet Lead	Unmanufactured Tin	Unmanufactured Zinc	Unmanufactured Copper	Pig and Sheet Lead	Unmanufactured Tin
1820	—	0·1	..	0·1	...	...	..	0·2
1821	—	0·4	..	0·1	...	...	—	..
1822	—	0·6	0·1	0·1	...	...	0·1	0·1
1823	—	2·0	0·4	0·3	...	...	0·3	0·3
1824	..	0·1	0·7	0·3	...	...	0·8	0·2
1825	..	0·6	6·2	0·2	...	...	3·7	0·2
1826	..	0·8	0·9	0·2	...	...	1·8	0·3
1827	..	0·5	2·2	0·1	6·0	0·6	2·3	0·1
1828	..	0·2	2·5	0·2	4·6	0·1	1·8	0·2
1829	1	0·5	1·5	0·1	4·2	0·7	1·7	0·1
1830	1	0·1	0·6	0·8	4·4	0·1	0·9	0·5
1831	2	..	1·2	0·4	3·8	0·1	1·2	0·6
1832	4	..	1·1	1·5	3·4	..	1·0	1·1
1833	6	0·1	0·8	1·8	3·3	0·2	0·9	2·0
1834	7	0·6	1·0	2·3	2·8	0·6	0·9	2·3
1835	14	0·3	1·3	1·0	7·1	0·4	1·3	1·2
1836	18	0·4	1·9	1·2	8·9	0·2	0·9	0·9
1837	19	0·3	1·8	1·5	2·5	0·6	1·5	1·5
1838	27	0·1	3·4	1·5	1·6	0·1	3·4	1·5
1839	30	0·7	3·6	0·9	2·6	0·6	3·7	1·1
1840	42	0·4	1·6	0·5	5·1	0·3	2·5	0·3
1841	49	0·5	1·2	1·4	6·6	0·6	0·9	1·3
1842	50	0·3	2·5	0·6	6·1	0·3	1·8	0·6
1843	56	0·2	2·8	1·6	10·2	0·2	2·4	0·7
1844	60	1·5	3·1	0·6	10·4	1·3	3·2	1·0
1845	57	0·1	5·2	1·3	12·9	0·3	3·2	0·9
1846	52	0·6	7·9	1·0	7·2	0·5	4·7	1·1
1847	41	0·8	3·9	1·2	12·8	0·7	3·5	0·6
1848	50	1·6	3·8	0·3	13·5	0·3	3·7	0·4
1849	47	2·6	7·2	1·8	15·9	0·6	5·2	0·4

(in thousands of tons)

	Imports								Re-exports		
	Copper Ore (a)	Unmanufactured Copper	Lead Ore	Pig and Sheet Lead	Tin Ore	Unmanufactured Tin	Zinc Ore	Unmanufactured Zinc	Unmanufactured Copper	Pig and Sheet Lead	Unmanufactured Tin
1850	46	4·9	...	11·9	...	1·7	...	18·6	0·8	3·2	0·2
1851	42	5·0	...	14·6	...	2·6	...	23·0	1·3	4·3	0·2
1852	43	5·2	...	13·3	...	2·4	...	18·5	1·0	3·0	0·4
1853	50	5·2	...	7·6	...	2·5	...	23·4	1·6	1·4	1·1
1854	57	3·2	...	11·9	...	2·3	...	19·6	1·8	0·2	0·7
1855	67	8·0	...	7·2	--	1·6	...	17·9	1·0	0·1	0·3
1856	83	3·8	...	10·3	1	3·5	...	18·2	1·3	...	0·2
1857	95	6·4	...	12·8	1	2·7	...	18·0	2·1	...	0·4
1958	97	6·4	...	14·1	1	3·0	...	23·7	2·3	...	0·3
1859	85	10·9	2	23·6	1	2·7	...	30·2	2·4	...	0·4
1860	97	11·8	1	22·2	1	2·9	—	23·5	3·7	--	0·5
1861	95	15·8	2	23·1	1	3·7	6	24·9	3·9	--	1·0
1862	117	13·4	3	23·7	1	4·4	1	23·7	8·7	0·4	1·1
1863	102	12·2	1	28·6	1	2·7	2	34·6	6·3	0·6	1·1
1864	93	24·9	3	30·6	1	4·9	2	31·3	9·0	1·2	1·4
1865	122	21·7	6	34·9	1	5·7	5	30·7	9·3	0·4	2·0
1866	130	21·0	10	36·9	--	5·5	14	29·2	14·1	0·9	1·1
1867	103	29·7	9	45·2	--	5·4	12	33·8 ---(b) 35·9	14·2	0·4	1·3
1868	114	35·2	12	49·5	--	5·7	40	33·9	20·9	0·5	1·1
1869	111	31·5	12	52·7	1	5·4	42	32·7	12·1	0·9	1·1
1870	107	29·5	12	58·6	--	4·7	45	31·1	14·5	2·3	1·1
1871	76	32·2	21	64·9	--	8·6	29	29·7	17·3	0·6	2·1
1872	72	47·7	15	69·8	1	8·3	33	28·1	12·4	0·7	2·4
1873	79	34·5	12	62·6	6	7·8	30	32·5	20·4	0·3	1·4
1874	76	37·8	15	62·0	4	9·2	21	34·8	24·3	4·9	2·4
1875	87	39·7	12	79·8	--	16·8	22	37·9	14·7	3·2	4·2
1876	103	39·2	13	80·6	--	15·2	12	44·0	17·3	6·8	5·3
1877	149	40·2	13	94·5	--	13·8	19	51·4	14·2	5·4	3·9
1878	137	39·6	15	100·1	1	16·6	24	48·9	12·7	2·1	6·6
1879	134	46·9	18	102·1	--	16·8	28	49·4	17·8	3·7	9·0

See p. 317 for footnotes.

Metals 14. *continued*

(in thousands of tons)

	Imports								Re-exports		
	Copper Ore (*a*)	Unmanufactured Copper	Lead Ore	Pig and Sheet Lead	Tin Ore	Unmanufactured Tin	Zinc Ore	Unmanufactured Zinc	Unmanufactured Copper	Pig and Sheet Lead	Unmanufactured Tin
1880	146	36·6	14	95·0	. .	19·5	43	50·0	14·9	4·8	8·7
1881	147	32·2	15	93·6	1	20·3	34	65·4	13·8	5·4	10·0
1882	152	35·2	15	87·9	1	24·3	34	60·1	12·8	2·6	12·4
1883	164	35·7	20	101·7	1	26·1	46	61·1	11·2	3·5	14·2
1884	187	39·8	30	109·0	1	26·1	35	67·7	10·8	3·1	14·7
1885	190	41·9	27	108·0	1	25·5	21	79·8	6·4	2·9	12·1
1886	152	43·1	35	107·9	1	24·1	14	72·3	8·6	7·5	14·4
1887	170	29·3	18	114·5	1	25·9	18	76·8	15·4	6·2	12·0
1888	230	43·7	17	132·9	2	28·1	24	78·3	32·8	10·5	18·6
1889	251	38·8	14	145·2	2	30·1	24	75·6	14·6	13·2	17·5
1890	216	49·5	19	158·6	3	27·0	36	73·8	17·0	15·7	14·8
1891	212	44·2	21	169·7	2	28·2	37	78·7	11·8	16·0	14·6
1892	226	35·1	18	182·8	3	29·5	33	71·8	11·2	15·6	16·4
1893	200	42·0	10	188·2	3	33·6	35	75·4	12·8	18·8	19·1
1894	162	57·1	16	161·9	4	39·1	46	71·4	6·5	13·8	21·5
1895	191	42·5	32	162·9	5	41·6	37	81·9	8·0	17·7	20·7
1896	178	61·2	56	167·8	5	38·4	21	97·6	9·7	12·3	18·7
1897	171	61·1	32	167·4	5	26·8	25	91·9	10·0	6·9	14·8
1898	165	68·9	24	194·5	6	20·3	53	98·7	13·2	16·2	15·6
1899	207	59·6	32	198·4	6	27·2	38	91·1	24·1	16·7	16·9
1900	188	71·1	31	195·4	7	33·1	42	91·3	18·9	13·2	19·8
1901	193	67·7	44	218·1	11	35·4	35	88·9	23·2	12·9	20·9
1902	162	90·9	39	231·8	12	35·2	45	109·7	21·5	9·3	23·0
1903	161	63·6	17	229·3	12	35·5	40	108·0	9·4	11·0	23·8
1904	146	89·3	9	246·5	15	39·3	54	111·1	7·3	20·9	27·2
1905	162	70·2	9	229·5	18	39·8	56	112·0	14·3	18·9	29·2
1906	171	74·3	9	208·3	21	43·6	63	113·1	14·8	13·5	32·3
1907	176	82·7	13	204·7	21	43·8	65	109·1	17·1	13·3	26·8
1908	180	120·0	23	237·5	25	47·7	61	108·5	19·6	10·2	32·8
1909	154	131·7	16	207·7	24	41·7	74	121·6	23·1	7·9	30·2

1910	167	87·9	18	218·9	26	46·3	93	139·3	31·1	13·5	31·5
1911	151	99·5	17	213·7	29	45·9	74	134·3	22·3	18·0	34·0
1912	150	95·0	16	205·4	29	43·2	67	157·6	14·4	11·7	32·7
1913	133	106·9	18	204·1	35	45·7	65	163·8	19·4	13·6	30·2
1914	114	150·5	28	224·9	32	41·0	144	128·3	10·8	15·1	30·8
1915	76	180·4	14	256·0	45	38·9	114	82·5	7·3	27·8	23·4
1916	78	111·4	11	158·4	34	33·6	78	57·0	7·3	5·8	17·5
1917	45	142·8	9	147·1	41	27·1	87	80·2	3·1	0·1	18·1
1918	36	203·9	2	207·9	32	12·6	93	67·1	0·7	—	4·2
1919	31	115·0	4	217·6	36	22·9	79	98·9	7·9	10·8	9·9

(in thousands of tons)

	Imports											Re-exports		
	Bauxite	Aluminium and Alloys	Copper Ore (a)	Unmanufactured Copper	Pig and Sheet Lead	Nickel Ore and Matte	Unmanufactured Nickel and Alloys	Tin Ore	Unmanufactured Tin	Zinc Ore	Unmanufactured Zinc	Unmanufactured Copper	Pig and Sheet Lead	Unmanufactured Tin
1920	32	8·0	31	111·9	162·8	3	0·1	34	28·7	40	116·9	16·9	27·1	13·6
1921	8	1·5	24	85·6	132·6	5	0·5	22	21·0	12	81·9	15·9	11·8	15·0
1922	44	2·3	33	69·2	181·7	..	0·3	39	24·7	96	85·8	9·9	11·6	15·5
	- - -	- - -	- - -	- - -	- - -	- - -	- - -	- - -	- - -	- - -	- - -	- - -	- - -	- - -
1923	64(c)	5·6(c)	42(c)	119·0(c)	205·2(c)	.. (c)	0·5(c)	52(c)	14·2(c)	61(c)	144·4(c)	8·1(c)	7·5(c)	8·8(c)
	- - -	- - -	- - -	- - -	- - -	- - -	- - -	- - -	- - -	- - -	- - -	- - -	- - -	- - -
1924	78	12·8	39	151·5	240·1	..	0·7	59	16·9	121	139·3	5·0	12·1	11·0
1925	75	13·2	37	164·4	275·1	2	1·2	64	15·9	122	152·0	7·1	14·6	9·5
1926	63	15·5	35	130·9	269·2	..	1·3	63	13·8	104	164·3	7·9	7·1	8·8
1927	89	19·5	40	148·1	290·2	..	2·6	64	14·0	134	159·2	4·6	8·3	4·7
1928	110	18·7	46	167·3	261·7	—	2·6	81	16·4	169	154·6	6·7	18·8	7·7
1929	121	28·9	39	172·0	297·3	..	1·9	93	14·7	132	162·2	6·5	27·3	11·9
1930	140	24·3	47	173·5	335·3	..	1·7	76	11·8	157	157·0	5·3	41·2	7·5
1931	88	22·7	36	161·7	309·7	—	1·4	61	12·2	77	167·8	4·4	15·4	5·3
1932	122	9·5	33	165·7	265·6	—	1·6	47	4·2	114	100·6	3·8	14·1	2·0
1933	115	14·7	32	161·9	285·0	—	2·0	27	3·4	132	97·5	4·2	5·4	0·9
1934	161	18·3	41	277·7	315·8	—	5·1	39	10·2	90	148·8	7·5	4·6	2·8
1935	194	20·9	31	317·1	318·9	—	9·0	45	15·1	152	160·2	29·9	23·0	6·8
1936	231	28·2	31	309·0	358·0	—	12·4	52	12·0	129	180·5	70·3	23·6	6·8
1937	219	36·7	(d)	411·2	375·2	28	23·1	51	21·5	151	185·8	98·5	37·1	13·2
1938	250	51·8		374·0	409·5	30	22·9	55	11·8	157	173·1	96·3	25·0	4·4
				- - -										
1939	302	67·7		378·2 346·8	341·0	32	11·2	54	4·5	175	175·2	18·8	5·2	2·1

See p. 317 for footnotes.

Metals 14. *continued*

(in thousands of tons)

	Imports											Re-exports		
	Bauxite	Aluminium and Alloys	*Lead Ore* (*e*)	Unmanufactured Copper	Pig and Sheet Lead	Nickel Ore and Matte	Unmanufactured Nickel and Alloys	Tin Ore	Unmanufactured Tin	Zinc Ore	Unmanufactured Zinc	Unmanufactured Copper	Pig and Sheet Lead	Unmanufactured Tin
1940	112	77.1		513.1	336.8	33	11.7	84	1.5	226	207.4	0.8	0.3	1.1
1941	87	142.3		477.6	139.4	28	8.6	66	—	201	209.8	2.0	..	..
1942	48	140.7		459.2	235.7	26	5.4	44	—	143	211.7	..	0.2	—
1943	242	238.3		518.9	226.5	20	4.9	52	0.6	97	187.6	—	..	0.3
1944	172	189.2		465.3	224.9	22	3.5	33	—	179	119.4	9.5	—	—
1945	163	23.2		193.2	176.3	19	1.5	45	0.1	157	97.1	49.3	11.0	—
1946	157	83.1		297.6	157.0	13	8.2	47	0.7	165	54.9	6.1	3.0	—
1947	164	96.4		378.1	198.4	22	13.4	39	0.2	130	148.7	..	..	—
1948	308	139.4		370.0	161.3	26	14.4	48	0.2	157	167.8	—	..	—
1949	327	165.6		323.1	186.4	33	3.8	47	0.5	198	143.3	—	—	—
1950	199	141.5		318.8	171.9	25	3.7	46	4.6	197	142.3	—	0.2	0.5
1951	346	179.7		356.7	175.2	34	5.6	51	10.9	180	122.9	—	..	0.9
1952	283	240.2		385.4	147.0	34	6.6	55	2.9	193	229.1	..	33.3	9.1
1953	269	179.2		336.3	179.1	34	9.1	62	1.0	165	130.2	18.1	17.7	0.7
1954	370	191.3		400.5	196.6	33	8.8	58	2.4	193	155.0	21.5	4.3	0.5
1955	328	259.7		411.5	217.8	33	11.7	61	1.2	200	161.6	11.8	1.6	0.5
1956	315	233.4		403.2	168.0	35	10.7	57	2.2	181	127.2	17.2	0.5	1.1
1957	354	192.7		468.2	158.4	36	11.5	82	9.8	207	147.9	12.9	0.4	0.3
1958	351	213.8		461.6	164.9	37	14.5	65	13.2	121	135.4	32.2	2.3	1.1
1959	328	256.7		440.0	179.8	34	14.9	61	0.7	152	174.7	22.5	4.3	3.5
1960	375	324.8		554.4	210.2	55	29.6	58	2.9	189	190.8	6.6	0.8	0.7
1961	395	257.1		504.6	181.0	63	29.2	51	1.8	206	165.0	7.0	0.6	2.4
1962	426	272.4		504.3	181.0	54	17.6	50	9.2	188	145.5	12.4	0.5	0.9
1963	331	291.5	34	497.6	180.6	62	15.6	45	8.0	212	160.7	11.9	0.8	0.2
1964	374	352.1	31	528.9	192.5	56	33.3	44	8.9	304	191.1	6.3	2.6	0.3
1965	466	340.7	22	584.4	215.6	64	28.5	45	9.3	229	193.7	3.3	5.3	0.2
1966	485	369.3	22	509.5	204.8	58	41.1	56	10.0	235	184.2	4.2	0.5	0.1
1967	451	333.1	32	451.2	181.1	59	31.1	63	8.2	255	160.2	3.4	3.3	..
1968	435	393.6	59	463.1	213.5	58	32.0	68	9.5	331	170.4	3.0	1.6	..
1969	471	398.5	70	465.3	226.9	46	24.7	75	7.1	328	160.9	7.9	0.1	0.3

(in thousands of tons)

	Imports											Re-exports		
	Bauxite	Aluminium and Alloys	Lead Ore (e)	Unmanufactured Copper	Pig and Sheet Lead	Nickel Ore and Matte	Unmanufactured Nickel and Alloys	Tin Ore	Unmanufactured Tin	Zinc Ore	Unmanufactured Zinc	Unmanufactured Copper	Pig and Sheet Lead	Unmanufactured Tin
1970	413	455·4	65	454·9	252·8	72	35·8	69	6·4	295	161·4	...	...	...
1971	439	349·2	74	405·2	228·7	74	48·6	59	7·9	287	171·4	...	...	...
1972	313	347·6	28	464·0	204·7	59	20·7	58	6·4	109	227·8	...	...	...
1973	294	375·5	38	498·7	214·6	47	26·3	50	8·2	139	225·0	...	...	...
1974	319	384·0	54	506·6	214·7	49	31·0	39	7·9	195	206·6	...	...	...
1975	291	234·2	44	468·3	200·0	66	29·1	42	6·2	106	200·7	...	...	...
1976	292	331·7	12	460·6	249·0	54	23·7	41	8·0	118	203·5	...	...	...
1977	340	323·1	45	479·3	183·4	61	24·2	44	9·4	180	203·8	...	...	...
1978	316	349·7	42	464·3	196·9	31	19·7	38	8·4	158	190·4	...	...	...
1979	279	368·4	67	473·8	204·2	27	22·2	35	8·5	179	180·0	...	...	...
1980	263	321·6	55	417·3	203·8	38	22·4	36	7·3	208	136·4	...	...	...

(a) Including regulus and precipitate.
(b) Certain semi-manufactures are included subsequently.
(c) Southern Ireland was treated as foreign from 1 April 1923.
(d) Amounts are negligible for subsequent years.
(e) Imports of lead ore were of minor significance from 1920 to 1949 and were not separately distinguished for some years thereafter.

Metals 15. Main Exports of Non-ferrous Metals – United Kingdom 1697–1980

NOTES

[1] Sources: 1697–1808 – Elizabeth B. Schumpeter, *English Overseas Trade Statistics, 1697–1808* (Oxford, 1960); 1809–39 (copper and tin), 1816–52 (lead), and 1843–52 (zinc) – returns in *Sessional Papers*; 1840–52 (copper and tin) – *Abstract*; 1853–1980 *Annual Statement of Trade* and *Overseas Trade Statistics of the United Kingdom*.

[2] Ireland was treated as a foreign country to 1815, and southern Ireland was so treated from 1 April 1923.

[3] Up to and including 1854 the figures are for years beginning 6 January.

[4] Statistics to 1791 relate to exports from England and Wales, and from 1792 to 1815 they relate to exports from Great Britain (and, in effect, this applies to tin subsequently).

(in thousands of tons)

	Brass	Wrought Copper	Lead and Shot	Unmanufactured Tin		Brass	Wrought Copper	Lead and Shot	Unmanufactured Tin
1697	--	--	8·0	0·9	1732	0·3	0·1	14·0	1·5
1698	0·1	--	13·2	1·3	1733	0·3	0·1	15·1	1·3
1699	0·1	--	11·6	1·2	1734	0·2	0·1	11·7	1·4
1700	0·1	0·1	11·6	1·4	1735	0·3	0·1	12·7	1·6
1701	0·1	0·1	12·9	1·3	1736	0·4	0·1	11·8	1·1
1702	0·1	--	9·2	0·9	1737	0·3	0·2	12·0	1·5
1703	--	0·1	11·1	1·0	1738	0·4	0·3	12·1	1·4
1704	--	--	10·2	0·9	1739	0·4	0·2	13·8	1·4
1705	...	...	...	...	1740	0·3	0·2	14·5	1·4
1706	--	--	13·0	1·2	1741	0·4	0·2	14·0	1·5
1707	--	--	14·7	0·9	1742	0·5	0·3	11·8	1·5
1708	0·2	--	14·1	1·4	1743	0·6	0·3	16·2	1·2
1709	--	--	10·6	1·1	1744	0·5	0·3	9·7	1·4
1710	--	0·1	12·9	3·4	1745	0·5	0·2	11·9	1·5
1711	0·1	--	14·1	0·5	1746	0·6	0·2	12·8	1·8
1712	...	...	...	...	1747	0·6	0·2	11·0	1·6
1713	0·1	0·1	11·6	0·7	1748	0·7	0·2	11·2	1·5
1714	0·1	0·1	17·8	1·2	1749	0·9	0·4	12·6	1·6
1715	0·1	0·1	10·8	1·3	1750	1·0	0·4	14·0	1·8
1716	0·1	0·1	12·1	0·7	1751	0·7	0·4	13·6	1·8
1717	0·1	0·1	13·6	1·1	1752	0·7	0·4	10·9	1·9
1718	0·1	0·1	8·3	1·1	1753	0·9	0·6	15·8	1·6
1719	0·1	0·1	10·7	1·8	1754	0·9	0·4	13·6	1·8
1720	0·1	0·1	7·4	1·0	1755	0·7	0·4	12·4	1·7
1721	0·1	--	10·0	1·0	1756	0·7	0·5	14·9	1·6
1722	0·1	0·1	10·6	0·9	1757	0·7	0·5	13·0	1·6
1723	0·1	0·1	9·1	1·3	1758	0·7	0·4	12·0	1·6
1724	0·1	0·1	9·9	1·2	1759	0·9	0·4	12·3	1·7
1725	0·2	0·1	9·4	0·8	1760	1·0	0·6	12·0	1·9
1726	0·2	0·1	10·2	1·3	1761	1·0	0·8	10·8	1·4
1727	0·2	0·1	12·5	1·4	1762	0·9	1·0	13·6	1·5
1728	0·2	0·1	10·6	1·2	1763	1·2	0·9	14·1	2·2
1729	0·2	0·1	12·3	1·3	1764	1·5	1·1	17·4	1·7
1730	0·3	0·2	11·4	1·4	1765	1·4	1·0	17·4	2·1
1731	0·3	0·1	12·5	1·2	1766	1·1	0·9	17·2	2·0

Metals 15. *continued*

(in thousands of tons)

	Brass	Unwrought Copper	Wrought Copper	Lead and Shot	Unmanufactured Tin
1767	1·6	...	1·1	15·9	2·0
1768	1·5	...	1·1	19·3	1·8
1769	1·5	...	1·3	18·0	2·0
1770	1·6	...	1·2	17·8	1·8
1771	1·9	...	1·2	13·0	2·0
	---(*a*)		---(*a*)		
1772	1·8	—	1·3	15·8	1·3
1773	1·8	—	1·4	15·7	1·5
1774	1·6	—	1·3	15·8	2·1
1775	1·7	0·3	1·6	13·1	1·7
1776	1·4	0·2	1·3	13·7	2·3
1777	1·1	--	1·0	15·7	2·5
1778	1·2	--	1·3	12·2	1·3
1779	0·7	0·8	1·1	12·4	2·0
1780	0·6	0·6	1·7	15·3	2·7
1781	0·5	0·3	1·1	11·7	1·7
1782	1·5	0·7	3·0	14·3	1·8
1783	1·1	0·4	2·3	11·9	1·8
1784	1·2	0·4	1·4	15·8	1·7
1785	1·0	0·7	1·5	15·6	2·0
1786	1·1	0·7	2·0	18·7	2·4
1787	1·1	0·6	1·9	14·6	2·5
1788	1·3	0·9	2·8	12·4	2·3
1789	1·6	0·4	2·4	19·0	2·2
1790	2·0	0·2	3·0	18·4	2·9
1791	2·4	0·3	3·0	12·9	1·9
	---(*b*)	---(*b*)	---(*b*) (*c*)	---(*b*)	---(*b*)
1792	3·2	2·7	4·1	14·2	2·9
1793	3·6	0·5	4·4	11·0	2·0
1794	3·1	0·2	4·5	14·1	2·3
1795	3·1	0·2	4·1	14·2	2·5
1796	3·2	2·0	4·4	11·5	2·8
1797	2·5	1·0	3·7	11·7	1·8
1798	2·4	0·4	3·9	12·2	2·2
1799	3·9	0·1	4·9	12·8	1·7
1800	4·7	—	4·8	10·7	1·8
1801	4·1	—	4·8	12·4	1·7

	Brass	Unwrought Copper	Wrought Copper (*c*)	Lead and Shot	Unmanufactured Tin
1802	4·6	—	6·3	11·8	1·8
1803	3·6	—	4·6	9·9	1·5
1804	1·3	—	2·9	11·2	1·9
1805	1·0	—	3·0	8·4	2·1
1806	0·8	—	2·3	9·4	1·1
1807	0·6	—	3·4	9·2	1·6
1808	0·4	—	3·0	7·7	1·3
1809	...	—	3·3	...	...
1810	...	—	2·8	...	...
1811	...	—	2·3	...	...
1812	...	...	...	...	...
1813	...	...	...	...	...
1814	...	...	...	...	...
1815	...	...	...	...	1·2
	---(*b*)	---(*b*)	---(*b*)	---(*b*)	---(*b*)
1816	...	0·9	4·2	17·4	1·7
1817	...	1·2	5·4	17·7	2·4
1818	...	1·0	5·0	13·0	1·7
1819	...	1·9	2·9	14·1	1·4
1820	...	2·1	3·1	18·3	1·3
1821	...	1·7	3·2	15·6	1·4
1822	...	1·3	4·4	13·8	1·8
1823	...	1·2	3·9	11·0	1·1
1824	...	1·0	4·0	10·8	1·8
1825	...	—	3·6	8·6	1·6
1826	...	0·1	4·7	10·2	2·2
1827	...	1·3	5·8	13·3	2·5
1828	...	1·1	5·1	10·0	2·1
1829	...	2·7	5·3	6·8	1·7
1830	...	3·2	6·2	7·4	1·5
1831	...	3·7	5·2	6·8	1·1
1832	...	4·6	5·9	12·2	1·6
1833	...	4·0	5·4	9·0	1·2
1834	...	5·3	4·9	8·7	0·5
1835	...	5·9	5·9	11·1	0·4
1836	...	3·9	6·1	9·8	0·6

See p. 323 for footnotes.

Metals 15. *continued*

(in thousands of tons)

	Brass	Unwrought Copper	Wrought Copper (*c*)	Lead and Shot	Unmanufactured Tin	Unmanufactured Zinc
1837	...	6·8	5·5	7·9	0·9	--
1838	...	7·4	5·6	7·4	1·3	--
1839	...	6·5	6·9	10·5	1·5	--
1840	0·4	8·7	6·5	13·2	1·8	--
1841	0·3	10·5	5·5	12·7	1·2	--
1842	0·4	12·4	7·0	20·2	3·1	0·3
1843	0·4	8·7	9·1	15·0	1·8	1·4
1844	0·6	8·7	10·1	15·7	1·1	1·6
1845	0·6	9·8	8·3	11·5	0·6	1·1
1846	0·5	7·3	8·4	7·4	1·2	1·2
1847	0·7	5·8	9·3	9·4	1·7	0·9
1848	0·7	4·3	9·2	6·1	1·8	0·6
1849	1·2	7·4	13·1	17·0	1·8	0·9
1850	1·3	7·7	13·6	21·9	1·6	1·2
1851	1·0	5·6	11·9	19·5	1·0	1·3
1852	0·9	5·9	11·0	20·6	0·9	1·3
1853	0·9	4·8	10·9	16·2	1·3	3·2
1854	0·9	3·0	10·6	19·6	1·4	3·0
1855	0·8	5·1	11·5	22·2	1·3	2·5
1856	1·0	6·1	15·8	23·1	1·9	3·2
				---(*d*)		
1857	1·1	7·1	17·0	19·3	2·2	3·1
1858	1·3	6·7	18·1	17·6	2·3	4·0
1859	1·3	6·3	16·4	18·4	2·8	4·9
1860	1·8	7·0	19·1	22·0	2·7	5·3
1861	1·0	4·4	17·4	17·5	2·8	4·4
1862	1·9	5·1	22·8	34·0	4·1	5·1
1863	2·4	12·8	30·3	33·6	4·4	5·3
1864	2·1	6·0	30·9	33·6	4·4	5·2
1865	2·2	5·6	26·0	24·8	5·2	4·5
1866	2·1	6·0	22·5	27·4	4·3	5·5
1867	2·3	9·6	28·1	26·7	4·2	7·3
1868	2·1	8·2	30·0	41·6	4·0	8·5
1869	2·7	12·1	30·5	48·4	5·1	10·1
1870	2·9	10·7	27·7	47·8	5·1	7·3
1871	3·5	14·2	25·4	44·5	5·7	6·5
1872	3·5	14·8	19·6	44·3	5·7	5·0
1873	4·2	13·0	22·0	32·0	5·8	3·4
1874	5·2	10·7	24·6	36·7	7·7	3·8
1875	4·5	11·1	25·6	35·4	5·2	4·9
1876	4·7	11·9	23·6	35·9	5·0	5·7
1877	4·6	11·6	28·3	42·5	6·1	5·8
1878	4·9	17·4	27·0	34·4	6·2	6·7

See p. 323 for footnotes.

Metals 15. *continued*

(in thousands of tons)

	Brass	Unwrought Copper	Wrought Copper (*c*)	Unmanufactured Lead	Unmanufactured Tin	Unmanufactured Zinc
1879	4·0	16·8	31·9	36·8	6·2	6·7
1880	3·8	15·4	33·5	33·6	4·4	8·0
1881	4·7	18·7	32·6	43·0	4·8	7·8
1882	5·0	12·7	33·8	37·4	5·5	8·6
1883	4·8	16·9	35·8	39·3	5·4	7·1
1884	5·3	17·9	40·0	33·6	5·5	7·4
1885	4·6	18·8	42·0	38·5	4·7	7·7
1886	4·3	19·0	37·8	42·4	4·7	8·4
1887	4·5	21·4	36·2	44·3	4·9	10·5
1888	3·8	25·2	14·4	48·6	6·0	5·6
1889	5·4	32·5	30·8	52·0	5·4	6·6
1890	5·3	45·0	31·1	55·6	5·1	8·2
1891	5·7	35·4	30·2	48·2	5·2	7·7
1892	5·4	42·3	30·9	58·1	5·6	9·8
1893	5·8	28·3	31·5	48·9	6·7	9·7
1894	5·5	19·5	31·2	47·1	5·9	9·2
1895	5·4	29·5	30·6	41·7	5·7	9·9
1896	6·0	23·3	26·6	41·2	6·2	9·5
1897	5·6	20·9	26·0	40·3	5·0	7·9
1898	5·3	26·7	23·8	38·1	5·5	8·7
1899	5·7	31·9	18·0	40·3	4·7	6·6
1900	6·0	18·0	19·4	36·0	5·6	8·2
1901	5·8	26·6	20·1	37·6	5·5	8·6
1902	6·3	21·3	27·0	33·0	6·1	8·0
1903	7·5	23·3	30·9	35·6	6·2	7·3
1904	8·7	14·5	34·7	35·0	5·9	7·9
1905	12·3	20·9	31·6	41·5	7·6	7·3
1906	13·4	19·4	23·0	44·9	8·5	7·8
1907	11·5	25·2	24·3	43·4	8·7	6·6
1908	10·2	14·6	34·8	49·4	9·3	8·4
1909	10·3	12·3	28·2	45·7	11·2	8·5
1910	12·9	11·9	38·3	46·8	12·4	9·1
1911	13·0	11·2	39·1	44·0	11·6	9·6
1912	14·1	13·1	30·0	47·0	12·0	10·5
1913	13·9	16·8	36·4	48·4	11·5	11·1
1914	10·5	8·8	31·3	35·8	13·4	7·4
1915	11·1	7·9	17·7	40·4	14·2	2·4
1916	11·7	10·7	9·6	28·4	18·0	3·5
1917	5·0	6·3	3·9	9·4	19·3	7·8
1918	3·9	4·6	2·7	4·9	15·2	1·4
1919	11·7	11·1	22·8	25·7	14·6	6·5
	- - -(*e*)	- - -(*e*)				
	19·2	26·1				

See p. 323 for footnotes.

Metals 15. *continued*

(in thousands of tons)

	Aluminium and Alloys	Brass	Copper	Unmanufactured Lead	Nickel and Alloys	Unmanufactured Tin	Unmanufactured Zinc
1920	6·5	49·2	40·3	34·1	4·6	13·3	10·1
1921	4·2	19·2	29·3	16·0	1·9	9·9	7·2
1922	6·4	26·3	34·6	24·4	3·6	12·6	4·3
	---	---	---	---	---	---	---
1923	6·0(*e*)	27·3(*e*)	39·4(*e*)	18·4(*e*)	4·9(*e*)	20·0(*e*)	5·5(*e*)
	---	---	---	---	---	---	---
1924	4·5	31·8	32·8	17·1	6·6	18·1	7·7
1925	6·0	26·6	25·2	13·9	5·6	25·8	5·1
1926	6·7	22·8	38·6	13·3	6·2	27·4	4·4
1927	9·2	21·8	36·6	12·4	8·7	27·1	7·4
1928	9·7	23·5	30·3	12·3	9·3	23·5	7·6
1929	9·4	21·6	35·1	11·5	9·1	30·4	6·3
1930	7·9	16·6	27·9	11·4	5·3	22·9	5·3
1931	6·0	12·1	19·4	9·3	4·7	12·1	6·2
1932	5·9	16·0	18·3	8·8	3·7	12·8	6·2
1933	7·1	20·3	23·0	10·8	5·3	29·2	5·6
1934	5·9	26·2	36·9	12·1	7·8	16·9	6·5
1935	6·8	22·8	39·0	12·0	10·7	23·0	8·1
1936	5·5	17·7	36·2	10·1	11·6	15·4	5·9
1937	8·9	21·6	37·9	16·9	13·5	14·8	6·6
1938	5·4	21·8 ---(*f*) 15·0	32·4 ---(*f*) 28·5	17·6 ---(*f*) 12·1	13·8	12·3	5·2
1939	5·3	13·7	25·4	10·7	9·7	18·5	5·3
1940	1·7	7·7	18·7	5·8	7·0	13·7	3·1
1941	0·2	5·9	19·0	2·5	1·6	6·6	2·5
1942	0·2	5·3	8·5	2·9	1·3	10·2	0·7
1943	0·1	3·3	4·8	4·8	1·5	12·3	2·3
1944	0·1	3·5	4·6	3·4	1·7	3·1	0·7
1945	6·3	10·1	18·8	10·2	4·7	9·8	3·4
1946	24·5	67·9	70·5	2·4	6·2	20·6	6·2
1947	31·7	42·6	66·6	1·7	7·1	3·9	2·9
1948	57·5	47·1	70·1	2·8	8·4	2·2	4·0
1949	62·4	56·8	87·3	2·4	13·2	4·2	3·9
1950	49·6	47·5	71·6	2·9	11·0	15·5	3·8

Metals 15. *continued*

(in thousands of tons)

	Aluminium and Alloys	Brass and Copper Alloys	Copper	Unmanufactured Lead	Nickel and Alloys	Unmanufactured Tin	Unmanufactured Zinc
1951	44·4	20·7	28·4	3·5	9·0	4·9	2·1
1952	38·1	22·8	29·5	11·4	12·4	12·6	1·7
1953	58·2	39·0	40·0	10·2	15·8	13·8	9·3
1954	44·1	25·0	58·0	11·0	18·0	8·1	4·6
1955	49·0	30·9	72·3	7·6	16·1	8·5	4·2
1956	61·4	44·3	120·5	10·9	14·4	7·3	4·2
1957	48·9	48·9	136·2	14·9	14·7	7·3	4·1
1958	37·5	57·2	182·2	17·9	16·7	9·2	7·5
1959	53·2	57·1	133·7	14·7	24·0	29·4	6·6
1960	53·1	57·1	113·4	21·1	26·7	7·8	10·2
1961	58·6	72·3	109·5	31·5	27·7	9·8	8·1
1962	64·6	73·7	144·3	37·7	20·7	7·2	14·3
1963	63·3	141·0		44·3	23·7	8·5	13·1
1964	53·8	133·5		41·4	33·3	6·4	11·4
1965	68·7	153·7		44·2	33·7	6·7	7·4
1966	73·4	173·5		44·7	33·4	6·0	6·1
1967	59·6	196·0		73·1	39·7	9·4	15·3
1968	60·4	174·5		103·0	45·1	10·5	26·9
	61·6	188·6		143·1	35·0	13·6	22·9
1969	---(g)	---(g)		---(g)	---(g)	---(g)	---(g)
	65·2	196·8		143·2	42·0	16·4(h)	23·0
1970	67·4	186·8		153·0	44·3	15·5	22·1
1971	73·7	171·1		151·8	42·9	11·7	17·2
1972	118·8	158·5		147·4	44·8	15·3	22·9
1973	137·1	236·3		147·9	50·2	18·4	37·5
1974	161·1	180·6		139·6	53·6	12·6	22·7
1975	140·7	163·4		108·0	41·2	9·4	21·7
1976	221·1	132·8		104·4	39·2	10·0	16·5
1977	209·4	177·9		127·2	36·2	8·6	26·7
1978	220·2	169·0		122·4	30·0	8·4	26·6
1979	276·5	164·4		139·6	27·6	7·3	24·7
1980	295·8	177·6		145·9	19·8	8·1	39·1

(*a*) The change in original source from the *Inspector General's Ledgers* to the *States of Navigation and Commerce* results in a break in these series. At the level of rounding used here the break is negligible.
(*b*) See note 4 above.
(*c*) Part-wrought copper is included from 1792.
(*d*) Shot was not included subsequently. At this period it amounted to about 2 thousand tons per year.
(*e*) See note 2 above.
(*f*) Certain manufactured articles are excluded subsequently. In the case of brass, other copper alloys, except those with nickel, are included subsequently.
(*g*) Re-exports are included from 1969 (2nd line).
(*h*) Alloys are included from 1969 (2nd line), to which they contributed 2·6 thousand tons.

CHAPTER VI

TEXTILES

TABLES

As Britain's leading industries for so long, it might be expected that the textile trades would be well endowed with historical statistics. This is so, but only to a relative extent. Wool, as the major British manufacturing industry, until it was overtaken by cotton in the early nineteenth century, was the subject of innumerable Parliamentary reports and pamphlets during the eighteenth century and earlier. At the same time the external trade figures for textiles were recorded in considerable detail, as, indeed, they had been earlier, in the period covered by the Enrolled Customs Accounts from the thirteenth to the fifteenth centuries. Moreover, government regulation of the Yorkshire woollen industry and of the Scottish linen industry gives us two output series for the eighteenth century which, though admittedly incomplete, are nevertheless useful. Furthermore, in the nineteenth century the factory inspectors were concerned primarily with textile mills for many decades.

But there remain gaps, of which the main one is, perhaps, the lack of consistent overall output series, such as we have for some of the mineral industries. This is less serious in the cases of cotton and silk, perhaps, since the whole of their raw material originates abroad. It should be noted, however, that imports are not the sole source of waste silk, which, from constituting only about 3 per cent of the raw material in the 1820s, represented over three-quarters by 1900. It should also be noted that the raw material tended to constitute a lower proportion of the value of the final product through time, and hence using input statistics as an indicator of output growth tends to a degree of understatement. This may be quite considerable at certain periods.

The tables in this chapter have been arranged in five groups, dealing respectively with imports and production of raw materials, production of finished products, exports, mechanical equipment, and labour employed. These will be discussed in turn, except that it is convenient to treat those pertaining to external trade together.

The first of these in point of time is table 17, showing wool and woollen cloth exports from the thirteenth to the sixteenth centuries. It is not without hesitation that these are included, since they have several deficiencies. They are based on summing the figures for the various individual ports where the king's officials collected dues, which were extracted by Carus-Wilson and Coleman. These did not normally include Cornwall or the north-western counties, Cheshire, Cumberland, and Lancashire. This is probably of little significance, since little wool and less cloth seems to have been exported from those parts. More serious, however, is the fact that accounts are quite frequently missing for some of the remaining ports, including some important ones, either through mishap or because certain ports' Customs were farmed at some periods. This was especially the case up to 1406. A consequence of this is that year-to-year fluctuations in the statistics in this earlier period may be misleading, reflecting merely differences in the coverage. Variations in the periods covered by individual figures for the different ports may have a similar effect.

Aside from these problems, and the obvious additional one of the smuggling of taxed commodities, it should be noted that the statistics of cloth exports apply only to woollen cloths, and do not include worsteds. However, the latter do not seem to have been of much significance, except for a short period in the middle of the fourteenth century.

When all that needs to be said about the deficiencies of the statistics has been said, however, it is fair to quote the verdict of those who compiled the port series from the ledgers: 'Sufficient reliance could be placed upon the customs accounts for the period ... to warrant their use as a firm and indeed indispensable bearing for the study of English commerce at this time.'[1]

Apart from table 4, showing rather rough estimates of the domestic wool clip, the first nine tables are all concerned with imports and re-exports of raw materials since the present Customs regime was established in 1696. So, largely, is table 10, but estimates of domestic production of flax have been incorporated. The textile export statistics for the same period are in tables 16 and 18 to 23. These figures, up to the early nineteenth century (other than those for raw cotton) are based on the work of Elizabeth Schumpeter, which is referred to in the introduction to chapter IX. The cotton series come from the same basic ledgers, of course, but they were compiled at a rather earlier date by Wadsworth and Mann, Baines, and Ellison. It was the latter who, from his great knowledge of the cotton trade, first refined them into genuine consumption statistics by allowing for changes in stocks. These, along with later continuations, are shown in table 2.

Trade figures from 1840 onwards come from the *Statistical Abstract* or the *Annual Statement of Trade*; but for the period between 1808 and 1840 we must rely on a variety of returns in *Sessional Papers*, including some included in the annual *Finance Accounts*, together with data published in Porter's *Tables of Revenue, Population and Commerce*.[2] There are many problems in trying to establish comparability during this early nineteenth-century period between the earlier and the later statistics. These problems almost all spring either from the Union with Ireland, or from changes in the system of entering various products, mainly cloth exports. Ireland was treated as a foreign country in the Customs ledgers until well into the second decade of the nineteenth century, and trade with Ireland continued to be recorded separately until 1826. It is possible, therefore, to continue Mrs Schumpeter's series into the 1820s. This provides an overlap in most cases with the trade statistics for the United Kingdom, which were issued retrospectively in the late 1820s and the 1830s for the few years preceding the combination of the British and Irish Customs. In this way, though the problem of comparability is not solved, the size of the break is at least

[1] E. M. Carus-Wilson and Olive Coleman, *England's Export Trade, 1275–1547* (Oxford, 1963), p. 18.

[2] Published in *Sessional Papers* in 1833 and annually from 1835 until shortly after the *Statistical Abstract* was begun.

indicated. And, in fact, it is not very large, except in the case of linen, where, unfortunately, no overlap exists. The difference in that trade can, however, be shown fairly well from the re-export figures of Irish linen.[3] Statistics of Irish linen exports prior to the Union, nearly all of which came to Great Britain, have not been given here.[4]

The problem of changes in methods of entering cloth is less easily circumvented, though it affects only the exports. In the eighteenth century both cotton and wool goods were entered in a variety of different ways according to the kind of cloth – by number, by weight, by length, or by the piece. As it has proved impossible to combine these into a single unit, eighteenth-century exports of these commodities are shown only at their total official (i.e. virtually constant) values. These can be found in table 8 of chapter IX. More detailed statistics, including those in varied units for different types of cloth, are available in Elizabeth Schumpeter's work.[5]

From 1815 onwards, when figures expressed in a single unit of quantity are available, these have been shown. In the case of linen the variety of units used in the ledgers was less, and it has been possible to get a single figure of exports expressed in yards, which is accurate to within 2 or 3 per cent. This is some compensation for the lack of overlap between British and United Kingdom statistics. For silk manufactures the problem of quantities does not arise until 1826, and then it is insoluble; but in the intervening period the returns give them in a mixture of pieces, yards, and pounds weight, and Porter's *Tables* gives only their declared value.

Statistics relating to the output of the textile industries are, as has been indicated, of only a partial nature until the early years of the twentieth century. The excise duty on printed fabrics provides one such series, relating to the more valuable sorts of English cotton, linen, and mixtures cloths over the period of its imposition. This is given in table 11. There follow the two series resulting from government regulation mentioned earlier – those of broad and narrow cloths milled (i.e. passing through fulling mills) in the West Riding of Yorkshire, and those of Scottish linen stamped for sale. Both are incomplete records in a number of respects. Most importantly, the Yorkshire statistics apply only to woollen, not worsted, cloth; and not even all kinds of woollens were included: Kerseymeres, for example, were exempt. Moreover, evasion and incompetence will also have affected the figures. It is certain that, prior to 1765, the broad cloth statistics were more defective than those of narrow cloth, and there is evidence that the width of cloth was liable to vary through time to an unknown extent. There is an extended discussion of these problems in Heaton's book, from which the figures reproduced here are taken, and he concluded that 'the figures ... were probably always too low'.[6] However, he also said that 'they embrace

[3] See note 2 to table 21.
[4] They can be found in C. Gill, *The Rise of the Irisn Linen Industry* (Oxford, 1925), pp. 341–3.
[5] Elizabeth B. Schumpeter, *English Overseas Trade Statistics, 1697–1808* (Oxford, 1960), tables X, XI, XII, and XIII.
[6] H. Heaton, *The Yorkshire Woollen and Worsted Industries* (Oxford, 1920), pp. 408–17.

the great staple kinds of cloth and furnish a reliable indication as to the progress of the industry'.[7]

The Scottish statistics have not been so thoroughly assessed, and Warden, the source cited in table 13, appears to accept them without question. One way in which they are certainly incomplete is that linen produced for home consumption rather than for sale is omitted, and sailcloth and vitries were also exempt.

For statistics of the mechanical equipment of the textile industries in the nineteenth century we have to rely almost entirely on the periodic irregular returns made by the factory inspectors in their *Reports*. These were subjected to some criticism towards the end of that century, notably by Ellison.[8] But if any figure is better than none – which is usually the case provided one knows and accepts its limitations – we are better off for the nineteenth century than for the twentieth, except for the cotton industry and, to a much less extent, wool. In both these cases, trade associations have published data, though only since 1938 has it been at all regular for the wool industry. For linen and silk there is virtually nothing, except in the Censuses of Production.

The factory inspectors' figures did not distinguish between different sorts of spindles or looms, but this has been a matter of considerable interest to historians of the cotton industry and, more generally, for the light that it has been supposed to throw on entrepreneurial qualities in late nineteenth-century Britain.[9] Even partial statistical information is of use in this context, and it was therefore decided to include, as table 26, Saxonhouse and Wright's figures of orders of mule and ring spindles to six major manufacturers.

Our statistics of the numbers employed in textiles in the nineteenth century are also largely drawn from the *Reports* of the factory inspectors. So far as they go they are no doubt reasonably accurate; but since they are for single years at irregular intervals (except for a period in the 1890s), they give a picture of change which is inevitably distorted by the workings of the trade cycle. Moreover, they cover only workers in factories, omitting outworkers, who remained important, on Wood's estimate (table 31), until the middle of the century, in the cotton industry. We may safely say that this was true until much later in wool and linen.

For the period since 1923 there are the annual statistics of insured employees (monthly in the source, the Ministry of Labour *Gazette*), which are at least as comprehensive as the inspectors' figures. These illustrate well the decline of the cotton, wool, and linen industries, but the picture is confused in the case of silk in the interwar period by the inclusion of rayon. (Indeed, man-made fibres complicate the output statistics given in tables 14 and 15 as well.) Occupation statistics from the decennial censuses, available in some detail from 1841, have not been given here because of the virtual impossibility of disentangling a comparable series

[7] *ibid*., p. 279.

[8] T. Ellison, *The Cotton Trade of Great Britain* (London, 1886), p. 325.

[9] See Gary R. Saxonhouse and Gavin Wright, 'New Evidence on the Stubborn English Mule and the Cotton Industry, 1878–1920', *Economic History Review*, second series XXXVII, 4 (1984) for references to the earlier literature.

from the differing classifications of successive censuses, at least without undertaking a major research project. The figures in tables 2 and 3 of Chapter II are at a very aggregate level, but may be of some use in this respect.

Some information on prices of raw cotton and wool and of cotton cloth is given in chapter XIV.

Textiles 1. Raw Cotton Imports and Re-exports – Great Britain 1697–1819

NOTES

[1] SOURCES: 1697–1780 – A. P. Wadsworth and Julia de L. Mann, *The Cotton Trade and Industrial Lancashire, 1600–1780* (Manchester University Press, 1931), pp. 520–1; 1781–1819 – E. Baines, *History of the Cotton Manufacture* (London, 1835), p. 347.

[2] The figure for 1697–8 is for the year ended Michaelmas 1698. Other figures are for the years ended 25th December, or 5th January following.

(in thousand lb.)

	Imports	Re-exports		Imports	Re-exports
1697–8	1,266	404	1738	2,537	169
1699	1,349	60	1739	2,246	82
1700	1,396	313	1740	1,546	82
1701	1,976	208	1741	1,680	109
1702	1,505	125	1742	1,933	169
1703	757	173	1743	1,268	65
1704	1,446	420	1744	2,032	17
1705	...	...	1745	1,635	86
1706	461	95	1746	2,408	33
1707	499	27	1747	2,325	35
1708	2,800	16	1748	5,258	385
1709	907	35	1749	1,837	357
1710	714	51	1750	2,318	64
1711	675	62	1751	2,977	74
1712	...	...	1752	3,496	86
1713	1,798	849	1753	4,278	176
1714	1,755	471	1754	3,181	145
1715	1,762	101	1755	3,820	155
1716	2,161	205	1756	3,089	375
1717	2,034	320	1757	2,706	888
1718	2,082	125	1758	2,225	237
1719	1,489	147	1759	2,552	343
1720	1,968	159	1760	2,359	618
1721	1,513	71	1761	2,996	369
1722	2,103	98	1762	3,519	646
1723	2,144	102	1763	2,707	250
1724	977	76	1764	3,870	223
1725	1,841	103	1765	3,777	78
1726	1,523	115	1766	6,918	65
1727	...	...	1767	3,623	198
1728	1,561	87	1768	4,131	186
1729	1,182	94	1769	4,406	361
1730	1,545	77	1770	3,612	366
1731	1,473	172	1771	2,547	219
1732	1,605	199	1772	5,307	356
1733	1,918	134	1773	2,906	518
1734	1,478	170	1774	5,707	307
1735	2,189	168	1775	6,694	617
1736	2,296	460	1776	6,216	372
1737	1,679	153	1777	7,037	665

Textiles 1. *continued*

(in thousand lb.)

	Imports	Re-exports		Imports	Re-exports
1778	6,569	673	1799	43,379	845
1779	5,861	393	1800	56,011	4,417
1780	6,877	324	1801	56,004	1,861
1781	5,199	97	1802	60,346	3,730
1782	11,828	421	1803	53,812	1,561
1783	9,736	178	1804	61,867	503
1784	11,482	202	1805	59,682	804
1785	18,400	407	1806	58,176	652
1786	19,475	323	1807	74,925	2,177
1787	23,250	1,073	1808	43,606	1,645
1788	20,467	853	1809	92,812	4,351
1789	32,576	298	1810	132,489	8,787
1790	31,448	844	1811	91,577	1,267
1791	28,707	363	1812	63,026	1,741
1792	34,907	1,485	1813	50,966	...
1793	19,041	1,172	1814	60,060	6,282
1794	24,359	1,350	1815	99,306	6,780
1795	26,401	1,194	1816	93,920	7,105
1796	32,126	695	1817	124,913	8,155
1797	23,354	609	1818	177,282	15,159
1798	31,881	601	1819	149,740	16,623

Textiles 2. Raw Cotton Consumption – United Kingdom 1800–1980

NOTE

Sources: 1800–10 – T. Ellison, *A Handbook of the Cotton Trade* (London, 1858); 1811–65 – T. Ellison, *The Cotton Trade of Great Britain* (London, 1886); 1866–1936 – Liverpool Cotton Association, *Annual Circular* (using the editions from 1926 to 1937); 1937–80 – *Abstract*.

(in million lb.)

1800	52	1847	441	1894	1,603
1801	54	1848	577	1895	1,664
1802	56	1849	630	1896	1,637
1803	52	1850	588	1897	1,618
1804	61	1851	659	1898	1,761
1805	59	1852	740	1899	1,762
1806	57	1853	761	1900(*c*)	1,737
1807	73	1854	776	1901	1,569
1808	42	1855	839	1902	1,633
1809	88	1856	891	1903	1,617
1810	124	1857	826	1904	1,486

1811	89(*a*)	1858	906	1905	1,813
1812	73	1859	977	1906	1,855
1813	78	1860	1,084	1907	1,985
1814	74	1861	1,007	1908	1,917
1815	81	1862	452	1909	1,824
1816	89	1863	508	1910	1,632
1817	107	1864	554	1911	1,892
1818	110	1865	723	1912	2,142
1819	109	1866	881	1913	2,178
1820	120	1867	967	1914	2,077
1821	129	1868	992	1915(*c*)	1,931
1822	145	1869	939	1916	1,972
1823	154	1870	1,078(*b*)	1917	1,800
1824	165	1871	1,207	1918	1,499
1825	167	1872	1,181(*b*)	1919	1,526
1826	150	1873	1,245	1920	1,726
1827	197	1874	1,277(*b*)	1921	1,066
1828	218	1875	1,229	1922	1,409
1829	219	1876	1,280(*b*)	1923	1,362
1830	248	1877	1,230(*b*)	1924	1,369
1831	263	1878	1,192(*b*)	1925	1,609
1832	277	1879	1,150(*b*)	1926	1,509
1833	287	1880	1,361(*b*)	1927	1,557
1834	303	1881	1,430(*b*)	1928	1,520
1835	318	1882	1,458(*b*)	1929	1,498
1836	347	1883	1,526(*b*)	1930	1,272
1837	366	1884	1,481(*b*)	1931	985
1838	417	1885	1,298	1932	1,257
1839	382	1886	1,450	1933	1,177
1840	459	1887	1,499	1934	1,322
1841	438	1888	1,525	1935	1,262
1842	435	1889	1,564	1936	1,391
1843	518	1890	1,664	1937(*c*)	1,431
1844	544	1891	1,666	1938	1,109
1845	607	1892	1,548	1939	1,317
1846	614	1893	1,434	1940	1,389

Textiles 2. *continued*

(in million lb.)

1941	965	1955	780	1968	394
1942	939	1956	728	1969	388
1943	885	1957	759	1970	379
1944	804	1958	643	1971	329
1945	717	1959	636	1972	304
1946	813	1960	614	1973	293
1947	815	1961	551	1974	240
1948	977	1962	488	1975	234
1949	979	1963	497	1976	265
1950	1,017	1964	522	1977	227
1951	1,024	1965	506	1978	203
1952	685	1966	468	1979	212
1953	831	1967	399	1980	152
1954	892				

(*a*) Figures prior to 1811 are simply exports less re-exports, taking no account of changes in stocks.

(*b*) Ellison's figures continue up to 1885, and are slightly different from those given here.

(*c*) Prior to 1900 the figures are for calendar years. From 1900 to 1914 they are for years ended 31st August, and from 1915 to 1936 for years ended 31st July. Subsequently they are for periods of 52 weeks corresponding as closely to the calendar year as possible.

Textiles 3. Raw Cotton Imports in Total and from the U.S.A., and Re-exports – United Kingdom 1815–1980

NOTES

[1] SOURCES: 1815–39 (Imports) – *S.P.* 1847–8, LVIII; 1820–39 (Re-exports) – *Porter's Tables*; 1840–1920 – *Abstract*; 1921–80 – *Annual Statement of Trade* and *Overseas Trade Statistics of the United Kingdom*.

[2] Statistics to 1854 are for years beginning 6 January.

(in million lb.)

	Total Imports	Imports from U.S.A.	Re-exports		Total Imports	Imports from U.S.A.	Re-exports
1815	101	54	...	1855	892	682	124
1816	95	51	...	1856	1,024	780	147
1817	126	61	...	1857	969	655	132
1818	179	68	...	1858	1,034	833	150
1819	151	62	...	1859	1,226	962	175
1820	152	90	6	1860	1,391	1,116	250
1821	133	93	15	1861	1,257	820	298
1822	143	101	18	1862	524	14	215
1823	191	143	9	1863	670	6	241
1824	149	92	13	1864	893	14	245
1825	228	140	18	1865	978	136	303
1826	178	131	24	1866	1,377	520	389
1827	272	217	18	1867	1,263	528	351
1828	228	152	17	1868	1,328	574	323
1829	223	157	30	1869	1,221	457	273
1830	264	211	9	1870	1,339	716	238
1831	289	219	22	1871	1,778	1,039	362
1832	287	220	18	1872	1,409	626	273
1833	304	238	17	1873	1,528	833	220
1834	327	269	...	1874	1,567	875	259
1835	364	284	...	1875	1,492	841	263
1836	407	290	...	1876	1,488	933	203
1837	407	321	...	1877	1,355	912	169
1838	508	431	...	1878	1,340	1,026	147
1839	389	312	...	1879	1,469	1,082	188
1840	592	488	39	1880	1,629	1,224	225
1841	488	358	38	1881	1,679	1,211	208
1842	532	414	45	1882	1,784	1,155	265
1843	673	575	40	1883	1,734	1,239	247
1844	646	517	47	1884	1,749	1,212	252
1845	772	627	43	1885	1,426	1,051	206
1846	468	402	66	1886	1,715	1,293	198
1847	475	365	75	1887	1,791	1,257	293
1848	713	600	74	1888	1,732	1,349	275
1849	755	635	99	1889	1,937	1,424	278
1850	664	493	102	1890	1,793	1,317	215
1851	757	597	112	1891	1,995	1,618	182
1852	930	766	112	1892	1,775	1,406	233
1853	895	658	149	1893	1,417	1,056	225
1854	887	722	123	1894	1,788	1,393	240

Textiles 3. *continued*

(in million lb.)

	Total Imports	Imports from U.S.A.	Re-exports
1895	1,757	1,395	203
1896	1,755	1,394	184
1897	1,724	1,380	225
1898	2,129	1,805	203
1899	1,626	1,234	284
1900	1,760	1,365	216
1901	1,830	1,481	207
1902	1,817	1,364	275
1903	1,793	1,361	305
1904	1,955	1,491	254
1905	2,204	1,734	283
1906	2,007	1,488	245
1907	2,387	1,756	330
1908	2,061	1,589	291
1909	2,189	1,640	269
1910	1,973	1,470	256
1911	2,207	1,682	291
1912	2,806	2,165	324
1913	2,174	1,585	258
1914	1,864	1,284	216
1915	2,648	2,022	344
1916	2,171	1,647	237
1917	1,623	1,186	111
1918	1,489	976	..
1919	1,958	1,371	121
1920	1,949	1,417	256
1921	1,204	815	250
1922	1,490	943	88
	- - -	- - -	- - -
1923	1,357(*a*)	693(*a*)	112(*a*)
	- - -	- - -	- - -
1924	1,633	971	144
1925	1,960	1,254	141
1926	1,802	1,097	148
1927	1,637	974	134
1928	1,570	897	71
1929	1,609	866	80
1930	1,276	611	74
1931	1,154	464	42
1932	1,326	766	54
1933	1,487	803	56
1934	1,353	510	65
1935	1,376	625	75
1936	1,658	637	63
1937	1,800	794	64
1938	1,324	469	49
1939	1,434	560	44
1940	1,587	785	13
1941	888	307	..
1942	1,329	348	..
1943	1,118	585	..
1944	913	256	—
1945	1,020	239	44
1946	910	120	49
1947	897	249	35
1948	956	239	6
1949	1,130	456	3
1950	1,200	333	6
1951	1,166	290	2
1952	719	264	9
1953	871	195	8
1954	1,003	298	8
1955	849	236	14
1956	926	322	25
1957	988	569	13
1958	739	324	7
1959	825	218	14
1960	819	325	12
1961	677	260	13
1962	667	151	13
1963	701	175	13
1964	736	250	20
1965	614	139	11
1966	643	129	10
1967	525	99	5
1968	594	87	6
1969	519	47	4
1970	529	56	15
1971	452	79	32
1972	449	58	28
1973	551	80	30
1974	335	50	41
1975	352	29	27
1976	392	22	37
1977	346	37	43
1978	351	38	41
1979	361	46	41
1980	276	39	40

(*a*) Southern Ireland was treated as foreign from 1 April 1923.

Textiles 4. Estimated Domestic Wool Clip of the United Kingdom – 1755–1980

NOTES

[1] Sources: 1775 to 1860–4 and 1909–13 to 1927 – Committee on Industry and Trade (Balfour Committee); *Survey of Textile Industries*, p. 275; 1865–1908 – *S.P.* 1900, CII, quoting Messrs Schwartze's estimates; 1909–11 – *Textile Mercury Wool Year Book, 1922*, also quoting Messrs Schwartze's estimates, which were discontinued in 1911; 1928–38 (1st line) – League of Nations, *Statistical Yearbook*; 1938 (2nd line) to 1980 – *Abstract*.

[2] Statistics to 1938 (1st line) relate to greasy weight. Later figures are estimates of clean weight.

(in million lb.)
yearly figures or annual averages

1775	80	1883	128	1919–23	106	1953	64
1776–99	90	1884	132	1924	105	1954	71
1800–19	100	1885	136	1925	110	1955	67
1820–4	110	1886	136	1926	115	1956	69
1825–9	115	1887	134	1927	119	1957	74
1830–4	120	1888	134	1928	114	1958	78
1835–9	120	1889	133	1929	112	1959	83
1840–4	125	1890	138	1930	111	1960	78
1845–9	130	1891	148	1931	113	1961	86
1850–4	135	1892	153	1932	119	1962	86
1855–9	140	1893	151	1933	120	1963	82
1860–4	145	1894	142	1934	115	1964	84
1865	150	1895	135	1935	109	1965	86
1866	145	1896	136	1936	108	1966	85
1867	163	1897	139	1937	107	1967	80
1868	172	1898	139		111	1968	69
1869	165	1899	140	1938	---(*a*)	1969	68
870	158	1900	141		68	1970	68
1871	152	1901	138	1939	69	1971	68
1872	156	1902	136	1940	91	1972	68
				1941	80		
1873	165	1903	133	1942	72	1973	71
1874	167	1904	132			1974	73
1875	162	1905	131	1943	62	1975	73
1876	156	1906	130	1944	59	1976	71
1877	152	1907	131	1945	58	1977	66
				1946	61		
1878	152	1908	134	1947	50	1978	71
1879	153	1909	142			1979	71
1880	149	1910	143	1948	50	1980	75
1881	139	1911	136	1949	56		
1882	129	1909–13	102	1950	58		
				1951	56		
				1952	62		

(*a*) See note 2 above.

Textiles 5. Raw Wool Imports – England & Wales 1700–80

NOTES

[1] SOURCE: Elizabeth B. Schumpeter, *English Overseas Trade Statistics, 1697–1808* (Oxford University Press, 1960), table XVI.

[2] The equivalent modern weight of a great stone or a bag is uncertain. Indeed, comparison of the figures for 1775 and 1780 in this table and the next suggests that the weight of a bag varied greatly.

	Irish Wool (great stones)	Spanish Wool (bags)
1700	304,160	5,778
1701	289,981	8,740
1702	303,862	4,605
1703	352,343	34
1704	333,762	356
1705	...	...
1706	278,569	4,037
1707	247,839	2,970
1708	217,395	404
1709	224,280	3,626
1710	269,799	2,522
1711	268,209	7,695
1712	...	...
1713	157,439	5,712
1714	210,586	4,076
1715	145,525	3,771
1716	207,801	5,984
1717	144,390	4,749
1718	144,188	3,606
1719	75,369	1,588
1720	79,074	4,701
1721	139,404	2,766
1722	129,582	3,266
1723	98,499	4,188
1724	113,290	4,220
1725	75,621	5,961
1726	51,371	6,395
1727	58,179	2,624
1728	49,784	3,700
1729	38,667	3,755
1730	19,824	6,859
1731	13,027	4,455
1732	9,734	5,594
1733	64,677	4,996
1734	88,153	3,815
1735	96,713	4,777
1736	68,013	4,680
1737	61,436	4,986
1738	55,103	5,356
1739	45,131	2,157
1740	31,309	2,828
1741	39,608	49
1742	35,627	7,148
1743	20,780	7,630
1744	13,518	1,184
1745	21,601	4,769
1746	71,412	4,395
1747	187,661	2,387
1748	42,837	6,675
1749	43,208	3,312
1750	45,439	5,269
1751	73,037	4,891
1752	71,556	4,139
1753	15,342	3,653
1754	6,622	6,114
1755	5,518	5,100
1756	4,260	6,656
1757	5,975	5,701
1758	4,472	6,422
1759	1,880	4,532
1760	5,366	5,655
1761	1,729	9,742
1762	3,675	3,609
1763	7,207	10,922
1764	13,196	8,598
1765	22,264	8,569
1766	51,182	7,524
1767	49,268	6,674
1768	4,389	5,183
1769	2,079	9,731
1770	678	11,370
1771	1,668	8,582
1775	258	9,507
1780	653	9,576

Textiles 6. Raw Wool Imports – England & Wales 1772–91, and Great Britain 1792–1824

NOTE

SOURCES: Columns 1 and 2, 1772–1808 – Elizabeth B. Schumpeter, *English Overseas Trade Statistics, 1697–1808* (Oxford University Press, 1960), table XVII; Column 1, 1809–20 – *S.P.* 1821, XVII; Column 1, 1821–2 – *S.P.* 1823, XIII; Column 1, 1823–4 – *S.P.* 1825 XXI; Column 3, 1796–1801 – *S.P.* 1806, XII; Column 3, 1802–11 – *S.P.* 1812, X; Column 3, 1812 – *S.P.* 1813–14, XII; Column 3, 1814 – *S.P.* 1814–15, X; Column 3, 1815–18 – *S.P.* 1819, XVI; Column 3, 1819–24 – *S.P.* 1825, XXI.

(in thousand lb.)

	Total	'Spanish'	From Spain, Portugal and Gibraltar
1772	1,571	1,537	...
1773	1,479	1,477	...
1774	2,136	2,058	...
1775	1,487	1,481	...
1776	1,917	1,909	...
1777	2,887	2,852	...
1778	478	453	...
1779	574	520	...
1780	1,813	1,801	...
1781	2,487	2,478	...
1782	997	992	...
1783	2,637	2,630	...
1784	1,603	1,603	...
1785	3,135	3,135	...
1786	1,557	1,555	...
1787	4,212	4,188	...
1788	4,195	4,174	...
1789	2,713	2,694	...
1790	3,245	3,133	...
1791	2,776	2,645	...
1792	4,514	4,351	...
1793	1,891	1,750	...
1794	4,486	4,424	...
1795	4,903	4,764	...
1796	3,454	3,400	3,413
1797	4,654	4,603	4,367
1798	2,398	2,362	2,141
1799	5,152	5,010	4,106
1800	8,418	8,131	7,828
1801	7,387	6,539	6,298
1802	7,702	6,493	6,167
1803	6,006	4,702	4,694
1804	8,151	7,209	7,311
1805	8,542	7,042	7,100
1806	7,334	5,598	5,772
1807	11,769	10,484	10,595
1808	2,354	1,982	2,070
1809	6,846	...	5,541
1810	10,936	...	9,360
1811	4,740	...	4,582
1812	7,015	...	6,793
1813	...	...	...
1814	15,713	...	9,254
1815	14,992	...	8,089
1816	8,118	...	3,477
1817	14,716	...	7,031
1818	26,405	...	10,201
1819	16,190	...	7,352
1820	10,044	...	3,635
1821	16,680	...	7,091
1822	19,333	...	6,121
1823	20,651	...	5,451
1824	23,859	...	5,513

Textiles 7. Raw Wool Trade – United Kingdom 1816–1980

NOTES

[1] Sources: 1816–39 – *S.P.* 1844, XLV and *Porter's Tables*; 1840–1920 – *Abstract*; 1921–80 – *Annual Statement of Trade* and *Overseas Trade Statistics of the United Kingdom*.

Germany (excluding Prussia)			
1816	2.8	1825	28.8
1817	4.8	1826	10.5
1818	8.4	1827	21.2
1819	4.5	1828	22.0
1820	5.1	1829	14.1
1821	8.6	1830	26.1
1822	11.1	1831	22.4
1823	12.6	1832	19.8
1824	15.4	1833	25.4

Germany (excluding Prussia)			
1834	22.6	1843	16.8
1835	23.8	1844	21.8
1836	31.8	1845	18.5
1837	19.7	1846	15.8
1838	27.5	1847	12.7
1839	23.8	1848	14.4
1840	21.8	1849	12.9
1841	21.0	1850	9.2
1842	15.6		

[2] This table includes alpaca, vicuna, and llama wool, except as indicated in footnote (*c*).

[3] At various times sources of supply other than Australasia have been important. These are shown (in million lb.) for the more interesting periods below:

Spain, Portugal, and Gibraltar			
1816	3.5	1829	3.8
1817	7.0	1830	2.1
1818	10.2	1831	3.9
1819	7.4	1832	2.8
1820	3.6	1833	4.0
1821	7.1	1834	4.3
1822	6.1	1835	2.8
1823	5.5	1836	6.4
1824	5.5	1837	3.4
1825	9.2	1838	2.6
1826	2.2	1839	3.9
1827	4.4	1840	1.9
1828	4.1		

British South Africa			
1860	16.6	1910	104.3
1870	32.8	1922	146.9
1880	51.4	1930	158.2
1890	87.2	1939	84.4
1900	32.2		

South America			
1860	9.0	1910	69.6
1870	12.7	1922	103.7
1880	10.3	1930	126.5
1890	11.2	1939	141.0
1900	35.6		

(in million lb.)

	Imports			
	Total	from Australasia	Re-exports	Exports (*a*)
1816	7.5	..	...	...
1817	14.1	—	...	...
1818	24.7	0.1	...	...
1819	16.1	0.1	...	...
1820	9.8	0.1	0.1	...
1821	16.6	0.2	0.3	...
1822	19.1	0.1	0.2	...
1823	19.4	0.5	0.2	...
1824	22.6	0.4	0.4	...
1825	43.8	0.3	0.7	...
1826	16.0	1.1	0.9	0.1
1827	29.1	0.5	0.8	0.3
1828	30.2	1.6	0.9	1.7
1829	21.5	1.8	0.4	1.3
1830	32.3	2.0	0.7	3.0
1831	31.7	2.5	1.0	3.5
1832	28.1	2.4	0.6	4.2
1833	38.0	3.5	0.4	5.0
1834	46.5	3.6	0.8	2.3
1835	42.2	4.2	4.1	4.6
1836	64.2	5.0	0.6	3.9
1837	48.4	7.1	2.8	2.6
1838	52.6	7.8	1.9	5.9
1839	57.4	10.1	0.7	4.6
1840	49.4	9.7	1.0	4.8
1841	56.2	12.4	2.6	8.5
1842	45.9	13.0	3.6	8.6
1843	49.2	17.4	3.0	8.2
1844	65.7	17.6	2.0	8.9
1845	76.8	24.2	2.7	9.1
1846	65.3	21.8	3.0	5.9
1847	62.6	26.1	4.8	5.6
1848	70.9	30.0	6.6	4.0
1849	76.8	35.9	12.5	11.2
1850	74.3	39.0	14.4	12.0
1851	83.3	41.8	13.7	8.6
1852	93.8	43.2	11.3	13.9
1853	119.4	47.1	11.7	6.7
1854	106.1	47.5	24.5	12.9
1855	99.3	49.1	29.5	16.2

Textiles 7. *continued*

(in million lb.)

	Imports		Re-exports	Exports (*a*)
	Total	from Australasia		
1856	116·2	52·1	26·7	14·4
1857	129·8	49·2	36·5	15·1
1858	126·7	51·1	26·7	13·5
1859	133·3	53·7	29·1	9·1
1860	148·4	59·2	30·8	11·3
1861	147·2	68·5	54·4	15·7
1862	171·9	71·3	48·1	10·2
1863	177·4	77·2	63·9	8·2
1864	206·5	99·0	55·9	7·3
1865	212·2	109·7	82·4	9·1
1866	239·4	113·8	66·6	9·7
1867	283·7	133·1	90·8	8·9
1868	252·7	155·7	105·1	9·5
1869	258·5	158·5	116·6	12·4
1870	263·3	175·1	92·5	9·1
1871	323·0	182·7	134·9	12·0
1872	306·4	173·2	137·5	7·6
1873	318·0	186·7	123·2	7·0
1874	344·5	225·4	144·3	10·1
1875	365·1	238·6	172·1	10·5
1876	390·1	263·9	173·0	9·8
1877	409·9	281·2	187·4	9·5
1878	399·4	276·2	199·3	6·6
1879	417·1	287·8	243·4	15·7
1880	463·5	300·6	237·4	17·2
1881	450·1	329·7	265·6	14·1
1882	489·0	345·8	264·0	13·8
1883	495·9	351·7	277·2	19·4
1884	526·5	381·4	276·9	18·1
1885	505·7	356·1	267·5	23·5
1886	596·5	401·4	312·0	22·2

Textiles 7. *continued*

(in million lb.)

	Imports				
	Total	from Australia	from New Zealand	Re-exports	Exports
1887	577·9	292·5	91·1	319·2	19·6
1888	639·3	343·7	84·2	339·1	23·6
1889	700·9	338·9	92·1	363·6	21·8
1890	633·0	323·1	95·6	340·7	19·5(*b*)
1891	720·0	372·9	104·8	384·2	16·7
1892	743·0	408·7	104·7	430·8	17·9
1893	677·9	355·3	117·0	346·4	16·1
1894	705·5	377·2	124·8	345·9	13·0
1895	775·4	417·2	124·2	404·9	21·7
1896	718·5	360·0	117·6	334·7	18·0
1897	740·7	363·6	127·7	371·5	40·1
1898	699·6	311·7	135·9	283·3	12·3
1899	668·8	295·9	131·2	292·9	22·6
1900	559·0	250·1	136·2	196·2	24·9
1901	692·4	334·4	139·5	294·2	20·2
1902	643·3	269·2	148·2	285·4	37·2
1903	605·0	223·4	155·1	285·5	36·0
1904	566·7	222·6	133·8	252·3	37·9
1905	620·4	253·7	139·3	277·9	35·3
1906	645·2	253·3	146·8	267·1	29·8
1907	764·3	321·5	158·4	313·5	31·0
1908	723·8	321·1	159·7	326·3	37·8
1909	808·7	312·7	176·5	390·7	62·3
1910	803·3	314·5	189·7	335·2	37·0
1911	799·9	324·0	174·1	304·5	30·8
1912	810·5	285·1	184·2	337·9	47·1
1913	806·4	265·1	181·2	306·8	28·7
1914	717·1	239·2	184·6	295·5	38·5
1915	934·5	426·2	200·0	123·0	32·0
1916	624·8	241·7	157·9	45·4	13·1
1917	628·8	338·2	142·1	30·7	7·0
1918	420·6	204·8	89·3	20·5	2·3
1919	1,046·7	587·6	254·2	169·5	18·5
1920	876·9	508·6	154·2	220·4	22·0
1921	763·1	311·1	148·3	335·0	35·4
1922	1,111·5	457·9	304·7	449·0	61·3
1923	745·6	276·3	181·1	414·5	57·8
1924	767·0	228·8	178·6	361·1	52·3
1925	732·4	225·1	172·5	341·4	53·8
1926	816·6	304·4	184·2	340·6	54·4
1927	828·4	237·6	192·4	347·8	62·0
1928	784·1	222·9	182·3	339·8	48·0
1929	818·7	269·9	194·0	332·6	52·0
1930	786·5	257·0	174·7	290·1	32·7
1931	852·6	290·0	188·4	265·3	35·8
1932	921·9	302·0	201·1	319·5	41·9
1933	956·8	308·7	243·7	352·2	69·4
1934	793·6	255·5	216·5	261·2	54·8
1935	868·4	364·5	172·2	261·1	80·3
1936	917·5	347·8	233·6	266·0	58·5
1937	785·8	301·0	180·5	221·2	45·5

Textiles 7. *continued*

(in million lb.)

	Imports				
	Total	from Australia	from New Zealand	Re-exports	Domestic (*a*) Exports
1938	883·8	365·5	198·0	257·0	42·4
1939	904·2	355·1	223·8	197·3	33·9
1940	1,814·1	675·0	222·5	70·2	15·2
1941	331·7	93·8	158·2	0·6	21·1
1942	412·8	139·0	156·7	—	5·4
1943	270·4	101·3	98·0	—	0·7
1944	508·6	292·7	157·6	—	1·1
1945	505·1	350·5	64·9	76·3	14·2
1946	481·6	229·7	185·7	91·1	41·2
1947	624·1	292·9	211·4	152·5	25·6
1948	678·1	331·9	226·1	153·0	21·8
1949	818·8	472·5	209·4	136·7	32·5
1950	708·5	383·6	180·1	115·7	45·6
1951	507·9	255·9	138·5	75·1	27·6
1952	698·5	320·6	190·0	72·3	42·4
1953	831·5	364·9	191·8	69·0	40·2
1954	686·3	291·7	186·4	65·4	46·3
1955	748·0	346·8	185·4	69·1	48·5
1956	725·2	310·6	163·6	71·7	50·5
1957	700·6	315·3	166·1	63·3	43·1
1958	677·0	292·4	168·2	49·6	45·9
1959	779·9	333·5	170·9	52·2	53·7
1960	670·0	265·2	161·0	51·2	54·8
1961	659·6	224·8	161·1	49·9	63·1
1962	641·4	237·5	163·2	40·5	61·0
1963	654·0	241·5	156·8	29·5	70·5
1964	573·5	217·9	139·4	19·9	57·0
1965	560·7	181·6	135·3	21·0	61·5
1966	523·4	138·8	135·9	15·9	59·0
1967	518·0	169·4	109·9	15·2	54·5
1968	546·8	145·7	141·6	10·4	63·7
1969	519·3 ---(*c*) 516·5	144·5	148·4	6·9	59·7
1970	452·9	129·7	137·0	55·8	
1971	343·5	73·4	128·7	58·2	
1972	457·6	99·0	156·7	60·9	
1973	332·5	59·8	94·2	58·7	
1974	266·6	42·8	104·4	53·4	
1975	292·0	46·4	84·5	63·9	
1976	357·2	75·1	90·1	68·6	
1977	301·2	39·2	95·6	68·5	
1978	327·7	41·3	103·6	60·7	
1979	267·9	38·0	79·2	71·8	
1980	211·6	35·2	61·9	67·4	

(*a*) Includes wool from imported skins and foreign wool treated (e.g. carbonised) in the United Kingdom.

(*b*) A very small amount of wool waste had been included under this heading previously.

(*c*) Subsequently excluding alpaca, vicuna, and llama wool.

Textiles 8. Imports and Re-exports of Raw and Thrown Silk – England & Wales 1700–91, and Great Britain 1792–1825

NOTE

SOURCES: 1700–1808 (Imports) – Elizabeth B. Schumpeter, *English Overseas Trade Statistics, 1697–1808* (Oxford University Press, 1960), tables XVI and XVII; 1786–1805 (Re-exports) – *S.P.* 1806, XIII; 1806–16 (Re-exports) and 1809–16 (Imports) – *S.P.* 1817, XIV; 1817–25 – returns printed in sessional papers in most years.

(in thousand lb.)

	Imports	
	Raw Silk	Thrown Silk
1700	358	83
1701	462	36
1702	293	80
1703	413	55
1704	696	147
1705	...	...
1706	328	138
1707	149	145
1708	367	165
1709	507	69
1710	43	54
1711	517	176
1712	...	...
1713	516	156
1714	242	181
1715	409	169
1716	276	282
1717	525	253
1718	550	193
1719	183	184
1720	487	288
1721	53	254
1722	414	281
1723	458	295
1724	430	302
1725	396	340
1726	360	294
1727	554	292
1728	463	266
1729	294	226
1730	397	267
1731	343	242
1732	242	269
1733	516	287
1734	499	305
1735	381	284
1736	369	176
1737	347	265
1738	412	279
1739	371	194
1740	169	240
1741	546	224
1742	155	213
1743	332	267
1744	216	191
1745	441	192
1746	204	151

	Imports		Re-exports	
	Raw Silk	Thrown Silk	Raw Silk	Thrown Silk
1747	406	325	...	...
1748	373	242	...	...
1749	357	280	...	...
1750	233	75	...	...
1751	355	258	...	...
1752	396	335	...	...
1753	508	288	...	...
1754	357	294	...	...
1755	399	344	...	...
1756	331	169	...	...
1757	549	346	...	...
1758	279	411	...	...
1759	491	281	...	...
1760	371	303	...	...
1761	548	515	...	...
1762	307	217	...	...
1763	446	522	...	...
1764	488	451	...	...
1765	502	379	...	...
1766	556	421	...	...
1767	584	311	...	...
1768	567	380	...	...
1769	698	497	...	...
1770	535	448	...	...
1771	591	488	...	...
	---	---		
1772	587(*a*)	436(*a*)	...	...
1773	346	235		
1774	468	429	...	...
1775	436	412	...	...
1776	867	454	...	...
1777	760	397	...	...
1778	658	187	...	...
1779	386	383	...	...
1780	598	488	...	...
1781	1,040	443	...	...
1782	245	332	...	...
1783	730	495	...	...
1784	1,115	406	...	...
1785	730	344	...	...
1786	473	361	45	25
1787	771	390	120	13
1788	812	307	116	47
1789	843	393	107	23
1790	745	508	70	20
1791	977	470	67	22
	---	---	---	---
1792	932(*b*)	437(*b*)	35(*b*)	11(*b*)
1793	1,020	242	29	3

See p. 344 for footnotes.

Textiles 8. *continued*

(in thousand lb.)

	Imports		Re-exports			Imports		Re-exports	
	Raw Silk	Thrown Silk	Raw Silk	Thrown Silk		Raw Silk	Thrown Silk	Raw Silk	Thrown Silk
1794	683	331	84	24	1810	1,341	451	23	50
1795	731	337	55	27	1811	602	20	29	31
1796	488	399	89	39	1812	1,312	618	40	86
1797	266	402	64	18	1813	...	...	...	...
1798	731	403	43	52	1814	1,634	646	33	61
1799	1,241	468	80	39	1815	1,443	358	94	52
1800	834	335	30	31	1816	946	92	300	52
1801	739	275	34	27	1817	932	274	75	21
1802	560	396	33	36	1818	1,645	457	110	35
1803	804	385	24	19	1819	...	...	...	...
1804	1,032	449	53	74	1820	...	...	...	...
1805	1,190	433	26	69	1821	2,119	339	49	22
1806	803	515	19	52	1822	2,053	493	51	11
1807	778	346	30	59	1823	2,452	360	46	25
1808	328	415	33	22	1824	3,048	335	...	...
1809	698	502	21	48	1825	2,854	770	290	71

(*a*) This break, caused by a change in the original source, is negligible.

(*b*) For the period 1786–91 there is no difference between Mrs Schumpeter's figures of English imports and those of British imports given in *S.P.* 1806, XIII. It is probable, therefore, that there is no break at all here.

Textiles 9. Imports and Re-exports of Raw Silk and Silk Yarn – United Kingdom 1814–1980

NOTE

SOURCES: 1814–30 – *Report of the Select Committee on the Silk Trade* (*S.P.* 1831–2, XIX), p. 10; 1831–9 – *Tables of Revenue, Population, Commerce, etc.*; 1840–1920 – *Abstract* (except for waste silk re-exports, 1851–76, which are only available in the *Trade and Navigation Accounts*); 1921–80 – *Annual Statement of Trade* and *Overseas Trade Statistics of the United Kingdom*.

(in thousand lb.)

	Imports		Re-exports			Imports		Re-exports	
	Raw Silk, Knubs and Waste	Thrown and Spun Silk	Raw Silk, Knubs and Waste	Thrown and Spun Silk		Raw Silk, Knubs and Waste	Thrown and Spun Silk	Raw Silk, Knubs and Waste	Thrown and Spun Silk
1814	1,663	646	10	2	1859	12,251	327	2,321	254
1815	1,474	360	75	..	1860	11,132	224	3,323	427
1816	948	195	269	5	1861	12,029	125	4,191	83
1817	981	248	55	2	1862	13,524	62	5,206	138
1818	1,745	461	80	4	1863	12,798	59	3,975	217
1819	1,555	293	29	3	1864	8,441	73	4,017	334
1820	2,308	334	8	5	1865	11,476	60	3,273	307
1821	2,201	341	8	..	1866	8,301	67	3,360	72
1822	2,178	503	16	..	1867	8,429	196	2,420	16
1823	2,512	368	9	5	1868	10,458	327	3,051	58
1824	3,136	342	2	1	1869	8,843	260	3,860	36
1825	3,117	778	129	25	1870	9,820	284	3,111	40
1826	2,488	177	257	22	1871	12,619	177	3,866	41
1827	3,147	464	35	15	1872	11,095	63	3,608	41
1828	4,256	509	23	9	1873	10,008	109	3,103	21
1829	3,595	211	221	33	1874	9,848	115	3,199	22
1830	3,904	414	59	13	1875	8,272	110	2,750	88
1831	3,993	629	26	25	1876	9,339	164	3,537	50
1832	4,048	177	64	29	1877	7,162	114	2,487	18
1833	3,435	229	66	6	1878	7,854	40	2,739	40
1834	4,656	192	207	21	1879	8,172	117	1,939	24
1835	5,159	216	120	17	1880	9,834	204	1,982	8
1836	6,061	397	201	24	1881	8,966	132	1,411	6
1837	5,090	231	367	30	1882	8,336	294	1,693	6
1838	4,404	265	167	31	1883	10,130	292	1,108	6
1839	9,789	225	103	13	1884	12,054	324	1,109	51
1840	4,458	289	147(*a*)	13	1885	8,023	230	1,105	76
1841	4,735	231	189(*a*)	4	1886	9,850	253	1,609	130
1842	5,388	397	165(*a*)	4	1887	9,872	454	912	59
1843	4,964	384	166(*a*)	12	1888	12,414	559	1,000	63
1844	5,899	401	228(*a*)	22	1889	12,020	608	1,768	31
1845	5,817	512	296(*a*)	28	1890	9,872	585	1,515	124
1846	5,303	432	317(*a*)	40	1891	11,121	582	877	29
1847	5,286	313	436(*a*)	55	1892	6,699	503	992	33
1848	5,518	1,071	291(*a*)	44	1893	8,639	345	910	39
1849	6,420	615	473(*a*)	133	1894	7,986	398	643	31
1850	6,689	470	557(*a*)	75	1895	7,907	460	762	45
1851	6,184	413	550	155	1896	8,745	573	708	74
1852	7,589	426	706	242	1897	7,941	412	648	54
1853	8,608	828	456	253	1898	10,071	424	558	13
1854	9,717	1,022	1,189	525	1899	10,922	378	586	30
1855	7,975	930	2,305	402	1900	8,214	665	861	36
1856	9,399	853	1,502	283	1901	6,726	625	846	49
1857	14,394	641	1,812	239	1902	7,501	803	842	96
1858	8,156	358	2,587	365	1903	8,590	663	1,269	82

Textiles 9. *continued*

(in thousand lb.)

	Imports		Re-exports			Imports		Re-exports	
	Raw Silk, and Waste	Thrown and Spun Silk	Raw Silk, and Waste	Thrown and Spun Silk		Raw Silk, and Waste	Thrown and Spun Silk	Raw Silk, and Waste	Thrown and Spun Silk
1904	9,340	769	1,211	44	1943	2,024	..	—	—
1905	9,230	879	1,703	54	1944	1,605	1	—	—
1906	8,467	924	455	57	1945	1,557	..	—	—
1907	8,620	938	642	47	1946	630	4	234	..
1908	8,353	810	314	44	1947	2,243	112	259	1
1909	8,675	831	555	54	1948	2,054	55	270	6
1910	9,736	956	958	55	1949	1,651	96	73	4
1911	10,339	1,086	1,527	61	1950	2,046	49	15	5
1912	9,724	1,213	724	51	1951	2,051	16	11	6
1913	8,328	1,054	971	43	1952	318	6	122	..
1914	6,875	716	516	34	1953	894	17	4	5
1915	8,045	762	215	18	1954	977	25	2	7
1916	7,304	819	272	3	1955	869	56	6	8
1917	6,347	621	13	1	1956	1,090	56	4	5
1918	7,819	623	532	7	1957	1,077	37	4	7
1919	6,401	533	303	26	1958	742	25	1	3
1920	5,787	796	187	12	1959	1,140	39	40	8
1921	1,797	373	169	11	1960	1,110	53	21	—
1922	5,226	676	144	12	1961	1,048	50	24	..
1923	3,497(*b*)	687(*b*)	165(*b*)	13(*b*)	1962	867	64	5	2
1924	5,242	714	279	18	1963	986	60	6	—
1925	4,761	1,299	237	10	1964	931	67	5	..
1926	4,152	564	80	14	1965	884	63	10	..
1927	3,662	809	238	8	1966	802	81	47	..
1928	3,924	810	176	9	1967	707	59	24	6
1929	4,683	774	49	12	1968	803	95	23	..
1930	3,977	1,034	58	18	1969	481	124	16	3
1931	3,413	952	81	9	1970	595	147	...	...
1932	4,724	472	35	8	1971	367	122	...	...
1933	5,548	261	29	3	1972	446	114	...	...
1934	7,605	203	454	30	1973	480	168	...	...
1935	6,356	204	84	8	1974	286	157	...	...
1936	6,824	162	28	6	1975	384	207	...	...
1937	7,510	194	69	9	1976	553	434	...	...
1938	6,837	126	77	15	1977	661	941	...	...
1939	5,414	148	103	9	1978	966	172	...	...
1940	7,391	24	3	2	1979	679	106	...	...
1941	3,895	6	—	..	1980	741	196	...	...
1942	1,716	17	—	..					

(*a*) These figures are of raw silk only. Exports of waste etc. were, however, very small at this period.

(*b*) Southern Ireland was treated as foreign from 1st April 1923.

Textiles 10. Flax, Hemp, and Jute Consumption – United Kingdom 1700–1980

NOTES

[1] SOURCES: Flax to 1935 – based on 1913 net imports and domestic output (from *Annual Statement of Trade* and *Agricultural Statistics* respectively) and the index in the endpapers of W. G. Hoffman, *British Industry, 1700–1950* (Oxford, 1955); Hemp to 1800 – E. B. Schumpeter, *English Overseas Trade Statistics, 1697–1808* (Oxford, 1960); Hemp 1800–52 – *Returns relating to Flax and Hemp*, printed in *Sessional Papers* at intervals to 1854; Flax output from 1936 – *Agricultural Statistics*; Flax trade from 1936, and hemp and jute from 1853 – *Annual Statement of Trade* and *Overseas Trade Statistics of the United Kingdom*.

[2] The figure for any year cannot be regarded as precisely applicable to that year owing to wastage and to changes in stocks. Prior to 1840, the small quantities of hemp exported are not taken into account.

[3] Statistics to 1771 relate to England and Wales. From 1772 to 1800 they relate to Great Britain.

(in thousands of tons)

	Hemp		Flax	Hemp		Flax	Hemp
1700	4	1735	...	7	1770	28	18
1701	7	1736	...	8	1771	32	25
							----(a)
1702	5	1737	...	11	1772	28	14
1703	9	1738	...	9	1773	25	17
1704	13	1739	...	12	1774	25	21
1705	...	1740	...	9	1775	28	15
1706	2	1741	...	11	1776	29	16
1707	7	1742	...	11	1777	29	17
1708	9	1743	...	6	1778	30	17
1709	8	1744	...	12	1779	27	26
1710	5	1745	...	12	1780	27	19
1711	8	1746	...	11	1781	27	21
1712	...	1747	...	12	1782	33	25
1713	4	1748	...	16	1783	29	12
1714	3	1749	...	8	1784	33	18
1715	10	1750	...	15	1785	32	15
1716	8	1751	...	7	1786	35	13
1717	9	1752	...	15	1787	37	17
1718	7	1753	...	11	1788	38	27
1719	5	1754	...	12	1789	38	22
1720	7	1755	...	21	1790	38	27
1721	7	1756	...	23	1791	39	17
1722	4	1757	...	13	1792	41	31
1723	5	1758	...	10	1793	41	28
1724	7	1759	...	27	1794	41	29
1725	8	1760	22	3	1795	42	29
1726	8	1761	21	14	1796	44	31
1727	8	1762	24	14	1797	40	24
1728	8	1763	25	14	1798	42	32
1729	8	1764	24	17	1799	46	38
1730	9	1765	23	17	1800	47	30
							---(a)
1731	4	1766	26	10	1801	46	27
1732	7	1767	28	8	1802	47	25
1733	10	1768	27	13	1803	50	38
1734	8	1769	26	17	1804	55	37

Textiles 10. *continued*

(in thousands of tons)

	Flax	Hemp		Flax	Hemp	Jute		Flax	Hemp	Jute
1805	53	32	1845	109	46	...	1885	104	53	187
1806	50	37	1846	93	44	...	1886	85	45	173
1807	52	39	1847	87	40	...	1887	94	52	221
1808	55	13	1848	112	42	...	1888	114	58	211
1809	51	43	1849	134	51	...	1889	112	59	268
1810	50	48	1850	135	52	...	1890	111	57	260
1811	49	23	1851	97	57	6	1891	97	49	235
1812	49	43	1852	110	42	10	1892	95	48	168
1813	49	...	1853	119	48	13	1893	89	53	171
1814	56	28	1854	90	35	24	1894	96	63	226
1815	61	38	1855	92	36	26	1895	126	74	274
1816	59	19	1856	114	37	36	1896	100	54	239
1817	68	24	1857	123	38	31	1897	99	60	226
1818	67	34	1858	89	41	36	1898	102	63	246
1819	57	25	1859	94	52	52	1899	101	44	188
1820	59	21	1860	105	36	39	1900	78	60	173
1821	66	13	1861	94	37	41	1901	80	63	199
1822	68	31	1862	118	44	42	1902	75	61	292
1823	71	33	1863	99	47	53	1903	97	63	160
1824	69	29	1864	119	46	88	1904	79	79	203
1825	72	30	1865	123	45	85	1905	99	66	227
1826	60	24	1866	103	42	60	1906	91	62	231
1827	72	29	1867	102	40	61	1907	109	74	225
1828	71	25	1868	118	48	88	1908	99	71	249
1829	73	19	1869	101	47	103	1909	89	72	199
1830	76	25	1870	146	51	98	1910	87	78	201
1831	74	27	1871	152	57	144	1911	82	85	191
1832	78	30	1872	126	47	164	1912	110	89	245
1833	87	26	1873	141	55	192	1913	107	86	221
1834	69	34	1874	146	55	178	1914	89	77	158
1835	65	34	1875	111	59	118	1915	83	93	295
1836	113	29	1876	97	50	145	1916	85	101	160
1837	81	39	1877	134	52	134	1917	76	85	82
1838	119	37	1878	102	54	161	1918	40	97	203
1839	95	50	1879	106	50	182	1919	13	71	204
		---(*b*)								
1840	97	32	1880	120	49	178	1920	37	96	180
1841	103	30	1881	114	56	182	1921	20	33	184
1842	91	28	1882	120	54	225	1922	34	50	141
1843	109	36	1883	94	59	276	1923	32	65	127
1844	118	45	1884	95	53	171	1924	45	78	170

Textiles 10. *continued*

(in thousands of tons)

	Flax	Hemp	Jute		Flax	Hemp	Jute
1925	37	66	185	1953	37	85	173
1926	58	52	115	1954	32	92	124
							--- (*c*)
1927	53	74	234	1955	32	108	129
1928	38	68	194	1956	38	89	123
1929	52	67	202	1957	38	99	149
1930	42	63	127	1958	24	92	133
1931	40	66	139	1959	32	96	150
1932	36	56	129	1960	30	101	137
1933	28	65	158	1961	27	84	95
1934	41	82	173	1962	29	95	151
1935	38	80	152	1963	28	96	133
1936	50	85	166	1964	26	96	118
1937	44	93	170	1965	29	79	113
1939	41	76	160	1966	22	74	108
1939	50	96	142	1967	15	72	116
1940	29	149	192	1968	20	64	112
1941	25	101	95	1969	14 --- (*d*) 33	69	85
1942	27	88	106	1970	31	71	75
1943	40	68	103	1971	20	61	51
1944	43	95	80	1972	26	54	90
1945	41	68	87	1973	23	54	68
1946	28	67	74	1974	17	40	75
1947	33	83	64	1975	13	25	29
1948	32	93	93	1976	16	23	58
1949	31	60	96	1977	69	26	53
1950	39	86	113	1978	12	20	42
1951	35	102	114	1979	12	22	51
1952	35	81	100	1980	9	15	26

(*a*) See note 3 above.
(*b*) See note 2 above.

(*c*) Subsequently including a small amount of waste jute imports.
(*d*) Subsequently including flax tow and waste.

Textiles 11. Printed Goods Charged with Duty – England & Wales 1713–1829

NOTES

[1] SOURCE: *Excise Revenue Accounts* in the Customs and Excise Library.

[2] This table covers silks, linens, calicoes and stuffs, but not stained paper.

(in thousand yards)

Year		Year		Year	
1713 (*a*)	2,028	1753 (*b*)	4,230	1793	21,142
1714	2,580	1754	4,388	1794	20,502
1715	1,840	1755	4,932	1795	24,054
1716	2,503	1756	4,206	1796	30,058
1717	2,654	1757	4,184	1797	27,205
1718	2,689	1758	5,143	1798	28,294
1719	2,841	1759	5,698	1799	32,178
1720	1,669	1760	6,359	1800	34,134
1721	1,048	1761	6,880	1801	38,727
1722	1,535	1762	5,617	1802	39,496
1723	3,064	1763	5,892	1803	43,344
1724	2,886	1764	6,631	1804	43,667
1725	2,760	1765	6,425	1805	48,342
1726	2,898	1766	7,159	1806	43,543
1727	2,861	1767	7,167	1807	52,907
1728	2,216	1768	7,691	1808	46,963
1729	2,684	1769	9,350	1809	58,068
1730	2,279	1770	8,723	1810	67,539
1731	2,123	1771	8,736	1811	47,271
1732	2,427	1772	9,168	1812	49,969
1733	2,925	1773	7,528	1813	58,553
1734	2,793	1774	8,201	1814	69,759
1735	3,005	1775	8,160	1815	69,790
1736	2,630	1776	8,244	1816	68,744
1737	3,057	1777	9,024	1817	59,490
1738	3,150	1778	8,246	1818	86,003
1739	3,224	1779	7,803	1819	80,374
1740	3,125	1780	8,326	1820	75,516
1741	3,027	1781	10,156	1821	93,335
1742	2,766	1782	9,605	1822	90,386
1743	3,064	1783	10,081	1823	96,044
1744	3,037	1784	11,179	1824	108,580
1745	2,629	1785	14,113	1825	114,636
1746	2,729	1786	13,528	1826 (*c*)	(56,077)
1747	3,527	1787	15,131	1827 (*d*)	81,030 (*e*)
1748	3,220	1788	14,603	1828	117,013
1749	3,997	1789	14,154	1829	103,961
1750	4,417	1790	16,777		
1751	4,224	1791	19,645		
1752	4,208	1792	21,720		

(*a*) Years ended 24th June henceforth to 1752.
(*b*) Years ended 5th July, henceforth to 1826.
(*c*) Half-year ended 5th January.
(*d*) Years ended 5th January henceforth.
(*e*) The duty on silks was repealed from 5th April, 1826. In the full year ended 5th January, 1826, 969,000 yards of printed silks had been charged with duty.

Textiles 12. Broad and Narrow Cloth Milled in the West Riding of Yorkshire – 1726–1820

NOTES

[1] SOURCES: 1727–1805 – *Report of the Select Committee on the Woollen Manufacture* (*S.P.* 1806, III), p. 25; 1806–20 – *S.P.* 1820, XII.

[2] Figures of broad cloth pieces are for years ended 25th March up to and including 1752, and for years ended 5th April thereafter. The narrow cloth pieces statistics are for years ended 20th January up to and including 1752, and for years ended 31st January thereafter. For both cloths in yards the figures are for years ended at the Easter Sessions.

[3] The width as well as the length of cloths was subject to variation. A fair average seems to have been 54 inches for broad and 27 inches for narrow cloths. (The legal minimum for broad cloth was 49½ inches until its abolition in 1765.)

	Broad Cloth		Narrow Cloth	
	thousand pieces	thousand yards	thousand pieces	thousand yards
1727	29·0			
1728	25·2			
1729	29·6			
1730	31·6			
1731	35·6			
1732	35·5			
1733	34·6			
1734	31·1			
1735	31·7			
1736	38·9			
1737	42·3			
1738	42·4			
1739	43·1		58·8	
1740	41·4		58·6	
1741	46·4		61·2	
1742	45·0		62·8	
1743	45·2		63·5	
1744	54·6		63·1	
1745	50·5		63·4	
1746	56·6		68·8	
1747	62·5		68·4	
1748	60·8		68·1	
1749	60·7		68·9	
1750	60·4		78·1	
1751	61·0		74·0	
1752	60·7		72·4	
1753	55·4		71·6	
1754	56·1		72·4	
1755	57·1		76·3	
1756	33·6		79·3	
1757	55·8		77·1	
1758	60·4		66·4	
1759	51·9		65·5	
1760	49·4		69·6	
1761	48·9		75·5	
1762	48·6		72·9	
1763	48·0		72·1	
1764	54·9		79·5	
1765	54·7		77·4	
	...			
1766	72·6 (*a*)		78·9	
1767	102·4		78·8	
1768	90·0		74·5	
1769	92·5	2,772	87·8	2,144
1770	93·1	2,717	85·4	2,256
1771	92·8	2,966	89·9	2,236
1772	112·4	3,224	95·5	2,378
1773	120·2	3,636	89·9	2,306

	Broad Cloth		Narrow Cloth	
	thousand pieces	thousand yards	thousand pieces	thousand yards
1774	87·2	2,587	88·3	2,134
1775	95·9	2,841	96·8	2,441
1776	99·7	2,975	99·6	2,488
1777	107·8	3,154	95·8	2,602
1778	132·5	3,796	101·6	2,747
1779	110·9	3,427	93·1	2,660
1780	94·6	2,803	87·3	2,571
1781	102·0	2,099	98·7	2,671
1782	112·5	4,458	96·7	2,599
1783	131·1	4,563	108·6	3,292
1784	138·0	4,094	115·5	3,357
1785	157·3	4,845	116·0	3,409
1786	158·8	4,935	123·0	3,537
1787	155·7	4,851	128·1	4,058
1788	139·4	4,244	132·1	4,208
1789	154·1	4,716	145·5	4,410
1790	172·6	5,152	140·4	4,582
1791	187·6	5,815	154·4	4,798
1792	214·9	6,761	190·5	5,532
1793	190·3	6,055	150·7	4,784
1794	191·0	6,067	130·4	4,634
1795	251·0	7,760	155·1	5,173
1796	246·8	7,831	151·6	5,246
1797	229·3	7,235	156·7	5,504
1798	224·2	7,134	148·6	5,180
1799	272·8	8,807	180·2	6,377
1800	285·9	9,264	169·3	6,014
1801	264·1	8,699	137·2	4,834
1802	265·7	8,686	137·1	5,024
1803	266·8	8,943	139·6	5,024
1804	298·2	9,987	150·0	5,440
1805	300·2	10,079	165·8	6,193
1806	290·3	9,561	175·3	6,430
1807	262·0	8,422	161·8	5,931
1808	279·9	9,051	144·6	5,309
1809	311·2	9,826	151·9	5,952
1810	273·7	8,671	158·3	6,181
1811	269·9	8,536	141·8	5,716
1812	316·4	9,949	136·9	5,117
1813	369·9	11,703	142·9	5,616
1814	338·9	10,656	147·5	6,045
1815	330·3	10,394	162·4	6,650
1816	325·4	10,135	120·9	5,651
1817	351·1	10,974	132·6	5,234
1818	324·5	10,246	140·3	5,721
1819	363·3	8,406	119·7	4,889
1820	286·7	9,186	129·3	5,226

(*a*) The increase in the number of broad cloths after 1765 is partly explained by more stringent inspection. (See H. Heaton, *The Yorkshire Woollen and Worsted Industries* (Oxford, 1920, pp. 414–416.)

Textiles 13. Linen Stamped for Sale – Scotland 1728–1822

NOTE
SOURCE: A. J. Warden, *The Linen Trade, Ancient and Modern* (London, 1867), p. 480. Also given in John Horner, *The Linen Trade of Europe during the Spinning Wheel Period* (Belfast, 1920), p. 299.

	Million Yards	£ thousand		Million Yards	£ thousand
1728	2·2	103	1776	13·6	639
1729	3·2	114	1777	14·8	711
1730	3·8	131	1778	13·3	592
1731	3·9	146	1779	12·9	551
1732	4·4	168	1780	13·4	622
1733	4·7	183	1781	15·2	738
1734	4·9	185	1782	15·3	775
1735	4·9	177	1783	17·1	867
1736	4·5	168	1784	19·1	933
1737	4·7	184	1785	17·3	835
1738	4·7	185	1786	17·5	823
1739	4·8	196	1787	19·4	844
1740	4·6	189	1788	20·5	855
1741	4·9	188	1789	20·0	780
1742	4·4	192	1790	18·1	723
1743	5·1	216	1791	18·7	756
1744	5·5	229	1792	21·1	843
1745	5·5	224	1793	20·7	757
1746	5·5	223	1794	20·5	797
1747	6·7	263	1795	21·4	827
1748	7·4	294	1796	23·1	906
1749	7·4	322	1797	19·5	735
1750	7·6	362	1798	21·3	850
1751	7·9	367	1799	24·5	1,116
1752	8·8	409	1800	24·2	1,048
1753	9·4	445	1801	25·3	1,019
1754	8·9	407	1802	23·8	915
1755	8·1	345	1803	15·9	688
1756	8·5	368	1804	15·2	749
1757	9·8	402	1805	19·4	936
1758	10·6	424	1806	21·5	973
1759	10·8	451	1807	20·8	957
1760	11·7	523	1808	19·4	1,015
1761	12·0	516	1809	22·5	1,172
1762	11·3	475	1810	26·5	1,266
1763	12·4	552	1811	21·5	999
1764	12·8	573	1812	19·0	1,020
1765	12·7	579	1813	19·8	977
1766	13·2	637	1814	26·1	1,254
1767	12·8	634	1815	32·1	1,404
1768	11·8	600	1816	26·1	1,027
1769	13·4	690	1817	28·8	1,093
1770	13·0	634	1818	31·3	1,254
1771	13·5	620	1819	29·3	1,158
1772	13·1	580	1820	26·3	1,039
1773	10·7	463	1821	30·5	1,232
1774	11·4	492	1822	36·3	1,396
1775	12·1	562			

Textiles 14. Output of Man-made Fibres and Yarns of Cotton, Wool, and Man-made Fibres – United Kingdom 1901–80

NOTES

[1] SOURCES: Cotton 1901–11 – *Ellison's Annual Review of the Cotton Trade*; cotton 1912–34 and man-made fibres to 1929 – London & Cambridge Economic Service, *Bulletin*; man-made fibre 1930–4 – League of Nations, *Statistical Year Book*; wool to 1935 – Census of Production; others – *Abstract*.

[2] Except as indicated in footnote (*a*), yarns of mixed fibres are included with that which constitutes the main one.

[3] Except for worsted in 1947, wool yarn figures after 1935 are of the wool content of yarn. The worsted figures are of deliveries.

(in million lb.)

	Cotton (*a*)	Continuous Filament	Staple Fibre	Woollen	Worsted
1901	1,549	...		...	...
1902	1,539	...		...	...
1903	1,463	...		...	...
1904	1,485	...		...	...
1905	1,752	...		...	...
1906	1,790	...		...	...
1907	1,854	...		...	...
1908	1,603	...		...	...
1909	1,749	...		...	...
1910	1,541	...		...	...
1911	1,845	...		...	...
1912	...	7		...	...
1913	1,922	...		...	...
1919	...	5		...	...
1920	1,512	6		...	...
1921	971	9		...	...
1922	1,368	15		...	...
1923	1,230	17		...	...
1924	1,352	25		313	214
1925	1,492	30		...	...
1926	1,296	26		...	...
1927	1,433	39		...	...
1928	1,297	52		...	...
1929	1,241	53		...	...
1930	955	45	1	200	162
1931	986	51	2	...	...
1932	1,037	67	2	...	...
1933	1,093	77	4	283	223
1934	1,124	85	4	290	214
1935	1,118	108	11	299	227
1936	1,196	112	27	...	...
1937	1,234	115	35	...	241
1938	952	102	32	...	...
1939	1,092	111	59	...	...

Textiles 14. *continued*

(in million lb.)

	Cotton (*a*)	Cotton Waste Yarn	Continuous Filament	Staple Fibre	Spun Yarn of Man-made Fibres	Woollen	Worsted
1940	1,191	...	111	58	...	...	...
1941	821	81	79	57	...	...	...
1942	733 --- (*a*) 744	69	73	48	24	...	152
1943	723	74	72	52	26	...	131
1944	673	74	78	55	23	...	123
1945	605	71	85	53	20	...	127
1946	669	84	108	71	28	260	146
1947	670	84	119	84	34	277	[163] (*b*)
1948	817	100	148	86	46	307	194
1949	831	103	172	117	55	320	208
1950	868	109	198	173	76	329	227
1951	884	110	217	167	84	302	199
1952	611	89	156	127	71	277	178
1953	731	108	217	202	114	314	221
1954	779	110	220	228	108	313	226
1955	684	108	233	239	87	317	222
1956	738	112	227	256	99	297	232
1957	661	113	233	263	103	304	234
1958	565	112	192	231	106	288	206
1959	545	107	236	279	107	313	232
1960	528	111	269	323	112	303	245
1961	486	106	262	306	95	281	246
1962	422	107	291	336	83	290	229
1963	428	100	330	389	88	313	240
1964	445	102	378	447	107	326	233
1965	426	100	396	466	101	322	228
1966	406	97	411	470	90	315	221
1967	340	84	438	517	85	304	198
1968	343	82	533	656	101	324	216
1969	343	82	557	665	103	313	222
1970	328	80	568	754	111	284	215
1971	295	86	609	742	115	289	205
1972	282	60	582	799	106	289	224
1973	283	58	674	938	116	298	220
1974	257	54	597	786	105	271	192
1975	237	49	543	697	90	247	166
1976	260	43	597	767	100	238	178
1977	246	41	528	689	99	234	179
1978	233	38	530	808	96	234	171
1979	235	35	508	806	92	231	152
1980	176	29	358	633	69	179	132

(*a*) Pure cotton yarns only to 1942 (1st line).

(*b*) See note 3 above.

Textiles 15. Output of Cloth of Cotton, Wool, and Man-made Fibres – United Kingdom 1907–80

NOTES

[1] SOURCES: 1907–30 – Censuses of Production; 1933–80 – *Abstract*.

[2] Except as indicated in footnote (*a*), fabrics of mixed fibres are included with that which constitutes the main one.

(in million linear yards or, for wool, million square yards)

	Cotton (*a*)	Man-made Fibres (*a*)	Wool (*b*)
1907	7,088	—	640
1913	8,050	...	722
1924	5,589	40	471
1930	3,179	151	344
1933	3,183	300	413
1934	3,116	322	421
1935	3,068	380	439
1936	...	...	...
1937	3,640	484	475
1938	...	...	...
1939	...	...	...
1940	...	...	...
1941	2,150	302	...
1942	1,772 ---- (*a*) 1,816	282 --- (*a*) 239	...
1943	1,830	250	366
1944	1,678	261	301
1945	1,569	278	299
1946	1,662	312	346
1947	1,669	442	359
1948	1,996	444	415
1949	2,077	519	439
1950	2,207	623	450
1951	2,294	666	418
1952	1,766	526	378
1953	1,973	660	412

	Cotton	Man-made Fibres	Wool
1954	2,109	667	414
1955	1,876	604	410
1956	1,709	605	397
1957	1,728	560	394
1958	1,515	515	349
1959	1,421	507	365
1960	1,380	531	367
1961	1,315	528	352
1962	1,119	493	328
1963	1,083	491	325
1964	1,104	541	325
1965	1,090	550	323
1966	986	545	302
1967	818	557	294
1968	820	465	295
1969	826	485	286
1970	780	435	257
1971	720	416	222
1972	670	405	219
1973	620	426	230
1974	573	427	209
1975	557	436	181
1976	527	422	171
1977	514	433	180
1978	504	413	172
1979	488	422	165
1980	399	327	141

(*a*) All mixed cloth is included under man-made fibres to 1942 (1st line).

(*b*) Deliveries rather than production statistics.

Textiles 16. Exports of Cotton Manufactures – United Kingdom 1815–1980

NOTE

SOURCES: 1815–39 – *S.P.* 1847–8, LVIII; 1840–1920 – *Abstract*; 1921–80 – *Annual Statement of Trade* and *Overseas Trade Statistics of the United Kingdom.*

	Piece Goods (million yd.)	Thread (million lb.)	Twist & Yarn (million lb.)
1815	253	0·2	9
1816	189	0·2	16
1817	237	0·3	13
1818	255	0·3	15
1819	203	0·3	18
1820	251	0·4	23
1821	266	0·5	22
1822	304	0·6	27
1823	302	0·6	27
1824	345	0·6	34
1825	336	0·7	33
1826	267	0·8	42
1827	365	1·3	45
1828	363	1·3	51
1829	403	1·1	61
1830	445	1·2	65
1831	421	1·5	64
1832	461	1·7	76
1833	496	1·9	71
1834	556	2·3	76
1835	558	2·3	83
1836	638	2·2	88
1837	531	2·2	103
1838	690	2·5	115
1839	731	3·0	106
1840	791	2·8	118
1841	751	2·8	123
1842	734	2·5	137
1843	919	2·8	140
1844	1,047	3·2	139
1845	1,092	2·9	135
1846	1,065	2·8	162
1847	943	3·5	120
1848	1,097	3·7	136
1849	1,338	5·0	150
1850	1,358	4·4	131
1851	1,543	4·4	144
1852	1,524	4·6	145
1853	1,595	4·9	148
1854	1,693	4·6	147
1855	1,938	4·9	165
1856	2,035	5·4	181
1857	1,979	4·4	177
1858	2,324	4·5	200
1859	2,563	5·4	192
1860	2,776	6·3	197
1861	2,563	5·1	178
1862	1,681	4·6	93
1863	1,711	4·4	74
1864	1,752	4·4	76

	Piece Goods (million yd.)	Thread (million lb.)	Twist & Yarn (million lb.)
1865	2,014	4·6	104
1866	2,576	6·4	139
1867	2,832	6·5	169
1868	2,977	6·6	174
1869	2,866	6·9	170
1870	3,267	7·3	186
1871	3,417	7·5	194
1872	3,538	8·0	212
1873	3,484	8·3	215
1874	3,607	9·0	221
1875	3,562	10·4	216
1876	3,669	9·6	233
1877	3,838	11·2	228
1878	3,619	12·2	251
1879	3,725	11·7	236
1880	4,496	13·1	216
1881	4,777	15·5	255
1882	4,349	15·5	238
1883	4,539	14·4	265
	- - - -		
1884	4,417 (*a*)	14·7	271
1885	4,375	15·0	246
1886	4,850	17·3	254
1887	4,904	20·4	251
1888	5,038	21·7	256
1889	5,001	17·3	252
1890	5,125	18·1	258
1891	4,912	18·1	245
1892	4,873	16·2	233
1893	4,652	17·2	207
1894	5,312	17·1	236
1895	5,033	23·8	252
1896	5,218	25·9	246
1897	4,792	26·4	253
1898	5,216	27·1	247
1899	5,439	30·7	213
1900	5,032	34·5	158
1901	5,365	31·1	170
1902	5,332	32·4	166
1903	5,157	34·3	151
1904	5,592	24·3	164
1905	0,197	23·4	205
1906	6,261	26·5	207
1907	6,298	31·7	241
1908	5,531	27·8	215
1909	5,722	29·7	215
1910	6,018	24·4	192
1911	6,654	23·0	224
1912	6,913	22·6	244
1913	7,075	20·7	210
1914	5,736	19·2	178

Textiles 16. *continued*

	Piece Goods (million yd.)	Thread (million lb.)	Twist & Yarn (million lb.)
1915	4,748	20·9	188
1916	5,254	24·7	172
1917	4,978	22·3	133
1918	3,699	17·1	102
1919	3,524	19·6	163
1920	... (*b*)	22·2	147
1921	3,038	15·0	146
1922	4,313	17·6	202
	----	---	---
1923	4,324 (*c*)	17·9 (*c*)	145 (*c*)
	----	---	---
1924	4,585	18·1	163
1925	4,637	18·4	190
1926	3,923	19·0	169
1927	4,189	18·2	200
1928	3,968	18·5	169
1929	3,765	18·1	167
1930	2,491	16·1	137
1931	1,790	13·6	134
1932	2,303	15·6	141
1933	2,117	15·8	135
1934	2,060	16·7	130
1935	2,013	17·2	142
1936	1,993	16·0	151
1937	2,023	16·0	159
1938	1,448	13·5	123
1939	1,462	14·3	114
1940	1,045	14·6	67
1941	846	13·6	29
1942	531	14·2	19
1943	399	13·3	19
1944	466	12·0	20
1945	469	13·8	16
1946	562	14·9	19
1947	577	10·8	27
1948	817	12·2	59
1949	957	13·9	82

	Piece Goods (million yd.)	Thread (million lb.)	Twist & Yarn (million lb.)
1950	867	13·4	71
1951	900	14·4	65
1952	748	9·4	36
1953	747	10·5	42
1954	669	11·4	40
1955	587	11·1	36
1956	510	11·1	36
1957	491	10·0	38
1958	404	8·0	27
1959	370	7·9	23
1960	344	8·6	21
1961	301	8·3	14
	million sq. yds		
1961	287		
1962	235	6·5	15
1963	223	6·7	14
1964	209	6·3	15
1965	205	5·0	10
1966	167	4·8	12
1967	148	4·8	12
1968	153	3·9	14
1969	143	3·4	16
1970	... (*d*)	18	
1971	146	17	
1972	128	21	
1973	155	19	
1974	... (*d*)	27	
1975	... (*d*)	22	
1976	140	29	
1977	141	23	
1978	147	23	
1979	160	23	
1980	172	21	

(*a*) It was stated that up to 1883 'large quantities of piece goods of mixed materials in which wool predominated were erroneously entered as cotton manufactures'.

(*b*) Exports of piece goods in 1920 were not recorded in linear yards, only in square yards. At 4,435 million square yards they would have amounted to 4,643 linear yards if the proportion between units had been the same as in 1921.

(*c*) Southern Ireland was treated as foreign from 1st April, 1923.

(*d*) Available in weight only, viz. 1970 19·7, 1974 21·6, and 1975 17·6 thousand tons. The 1976 figure in weight was 22·5 thousand tons.

Textiles 17. Exports of Wool and Cloth – England 1280–1544

NOTES

[1] SOURCE: E. M. Carus-Wilson and Olive Coleman, *England's Export Trade, 1275–1547* (Oxford, 1963).

[2] Except as indicated in footnotes, the figures are in principle for years ended Michaelmas, though statistics for minor ports sometimes covered both longer and shorter periods. It is unlikely that the series is much affected at this level of rounding, and attention is drawn here to the more significant omissions and variations only.

[3] The statistics are derived from national customs accounts, and do not generally cover Cheshire, Cornwall, Cumberland, and Lancashire, where the King's officials did not collect for most of this period. The exports of wool and cloth from these areas is believed to have been slight.

[4] The sack of wool had a standard weight of 364 lb. Wool fells have been converted into sacks at the rate of 240 to the sack. The standard cloth, in which exports were expressed, was approximately 24 yards by 1½ to 2 yards. It is probable that the figures of the late 15th and early 16th centuries are undervalued owing to failure to convert 'long' cloths, of as much as 40 yards, properly. Prior to 1388, and for parts of the next two years, kerseys were not recorded. Worsteds are not included at any time.

(wool in thousands of sacks, cloth in thousands)

	Wool		Wool			Wool	Cloth
1280 (*a*)	24·0	1325	26·7		1367	30·0	[17·5] (*i*)
1281 (*b*)	25·8	1326	18·8		1368	23·7	[11·0] (*i*)
1282 (*b*)	24·8	1327	25·8		1369	27·9	[13·4] (*i*)
1283 (*b*)	25·2	1328	19·5		1370	17·5	[12·6] (*h*) (*i*)
1284 (*b*)	30·5	1329	31·5		1371	28·1	13·2
1285 (*b*)	27·2	1330	29·3		1372	25·4	[10·1] (*h*) (*i*)
1286 (*b*)	23·9	1331	34·0		1373	26·2	. . .
1287 (*b*)	23·6	1332	37·1		1374	23·6	. . .
1288 (*b*)	26·6	1333	28·4		1375	27·6	. . .
1289 (*b*)	29·5	1334	34·6		1376	21·0	. . .
1290 (*b*)	31·3	1335	34·1		1377	14·2	. . .
1291 (*b*)	. . .	1336	[18·3] (*f*)		1378	29·9	[9·4] (*h*) (*i*)
1292 (*b*)	. . .	1337	4·3		1379	16·5	[9·1] (*h*) (*i*)
1293 (*b*)	. . .	1338	19·5		1380	19·3	[11·1] (*h*) (*i*) (*j*)
1294 (*b*)	. . .	1339	41·8		1381	18·4	[12·7] (*h*) (*i*) (*j*)
1295 (*c*)	[16·7] (*d*)	1340	19·9		1382	18·0	[16·4] (*h*) (*i*) (*j*)
1296	[14·9] (*d*)	1341	18·6		1383	14·0	[13·5] (*h*) (*i*) (*j*)
1297	[21·3] (*d*)	1342	22·8		1384	22·3	[20·4] (*h*) (*i*) (*j*)
1298	[26·2] (*e*)	1343	[13·4]		1385	12·7	[30·5] (*h*) (*i*) (*j*)
1299	[21·2] (*e*)	1344	. . .		1386	16·5	[19·0] (*h*) (*i*) (*j*)
1300	[31·6] (*e*)	1345	. . .		1387	23·5	[11·6] (*h*) (*i*) (*j*)
1301	[34·6] (*e*)	1346	. . .		1388	17·6	[15·6] (*h*) (*i*) (*j*)
1302	[16·8] (*e*)				1389	16·3	[16·9] (*h*) (*i*) (*j*)
1303	31·4				1390	26·5	[22·2] (*h*) (*i*) (*j*)
1304	32·5				1391	13·0	[21·3] (*h*) (*i*) (*j*)
			Wool	Cloth			
1305	46·4	1347	. . .	. . .	1392	16·1	[19·3] (*h*) (*i*) (*j*)
1306	41·4	1348	. . .	4·4	1393	22·5	[15·4] (*i*)
1307	41·6	1349	. . .	1·8	1394	19·8	[17·2] (*i*)
1308	36·8	1350	. . .	1·3	1395	19·3	[22·3] (*j*)
1309	40·4	1351	35·9	0·7	1396	18·5	[24·1] (*j*)
1310	34·9	1352	23·2	1·3	1397	17·5	[18·6] (*i*)
1311	37·7	1353	16·8	1·1	1398	16·9	[22·5] (*i*)
1312	38·6	1354	44·9	3·7	1399	15·8	[26·8] (*i*)
1313	37·0	1355	32·9	2·8	1400	15·3	[21·0] (*i*)
1314	[19·3] (*e*)	1356	27·8	5·4	1401	13·6	[23·3] (*i*)
1315	[32·5] (*e*)	1357	37·9	10·3	1402	16·4	[33·5] (*d*) (*j*)
1316	[20·9] (*e*)	1358	34·2	10·0	1403	10·2	[24·6] (*j*)
1317	27·9	1359	29·9	10·6	1404	12·1	[31·4] (*j*)
1318	27·4	1360	33·6	11·9	1405	12·0	[17·8] (*i*) (*j*)
1319	21·6	1361	26·2	10·0	1406	16·6	[30·1] (*i*)
1320	31·5	1362	42·7	10·5	1407	12·5	29·5
1321	29·9	1363	28·8	[12·5] (*i*)	1408	14·6	26·0
1322	18·4	1364	19·2	[9·3] (*i*)	1409	17·4	33·2
1323	30·1	1365	33·6	[14·7] (*i*)	1410	13·6	34·4
1324	23·0	1366	32·8	[10·9] (*i*)	1411	11·2	26·2

Textiles 17. *continued*

(wool in thousands of sacks, cloth in thousands)

	Wool	Cloth		Wool	Cloth		Wool	Cloth
1412	12·0	21·4	1457	5·1	27·8	1502	9·5	86·4
1413	16·4	32·6	1458	9·6	40·6	1503	8·9	75·1
1414	14·4	22·1	1459	8·1	37·0	1504	6·1	75·2
1415	13·9	33·6	1460	2·1	26·2	1505	7·6	68·3
1416	13·7	26·4	1461	8·9	30·8	1506	4·7	78·0
1417	14·2	28·0	1462	3·3	39·0	1507	7·1	83·4
1418	16·0	28·3	1463	5·5	25·5	1508	8·6	93·8
1419	15·6	28·0	1464	8·4	34·9	1509	7·8	90·5
1420	12·2	28·0	1465	7·3	15·8	1510	8·4	76·1
1421	12·5	28·1	1466	8·0	33·9	1511	8·4	85·5
1422	13·0	31·9	1467	9·9	41·9	1512	6·1	74·8
1423	17·1	51·8	1468	9·4	39·1	1513	5·6	84·3
1424	16·5	40·9	1469	9·7	42·9	1514	7·4	94·4
1425	13·0	48·4	1470	9·6	28·4	1515	6·6	91·0
1426	13·2	40·0	1471	1·6	27·5	1516	7·5	81·8
1427	17·6	34·8	1472	12·3	34·1	1517	7·1	87·3
1428	16·9	38·2	1473	7·4	35·2	1518	6·7	91·8
1429	11·7	46·8	1474	10·0	[43·5] (*e*)	1519	10·2	91·2
1430	7·3	42·7	1475	8·9	[31·2] (*e*)	1520	9·6	98·3
1431	11·9	42·0	1476	14·4	[33·0] (*e*)	1521	7·8	75·6
1432	10·0	38·1	1477	3·0	[46·0] (*e*)	1522	4·8	60·8
1433	9·0	38·4	1478	8·7	39·0	1523	5·0	86·1
1434	1·7	43·3	1479	10·6	67·3	1524	4·6	90·3
1435	13·0	39·1	1480	8·7	56·6	1525	3·4	96·2
1436	3·9	25·2	1481	11·4	64·1	1526	4·6	91·4
1437	1·6	40·5	1482	9·0	67·0	1527	6·8	91·1
1438	1·5	57·1	1483	4·7	35·0	1528	5·2	99·6
1439	1·6	52·5	1484	6·6	50·8	1529	3·1	...
1440	18·2	59·8	1485	6·0	46·7	1530	4·5	90·4
1441	7·4	57·0	1486	9·2	57·3	1531	2·7	86·6
1442	2·4	58·2	1487	9·5	33·5	1532	3·0	81·8
1443	14·2	56·7	1488	10·1	47·4	1533	2·0	100·0
1444	13·2	53·0	1489	9·8	53·5	1534	3·6	110·1
1445	2·9	56·8	1490	10·5	58·4	1535	3·7	91·6
1446	16·8	48·3	1491	3·5	56·1	1536	4·6	108·3
1447	2·3	53·9	1492	4·1	54·7	1537	3·3	103·0
1448	13·2	55·6	1493	6·9	55·3	1538	2·9	103·8
1449	1·9	35·6	1494	8·0	59·5	1539	4·2	113·9
1450	15·6	34·6	1495	11·3	[21·9] (*k*)	1540	4·7	117·5
1451	7·2	40·2	1496	12·6	[19·8] (*k*)	1541	4·6	130·9
1452	9·3	32·2	1497	8·8	56·8	1542	5·4	111·9
1453	6·7	44·6	1498	9·8	62·2	1543	3·7	89·1
1454	4·9	31·1	1499	6·3	54·6	1544	...	137·3
1455	12·4	30·1	1500	6·7	70·2			
1456	4·3	52·0	1501	7·4	82·5			

(*a*) Year ended 19 May.
(*b*) Period ended Easter.
(*c*) Period ended Michaelmas.
(*d*) Excluding Southampton.
(*e*) Excluding Bristol.
(*f*) Excluding Hull.
(*g*) to a date in July only, whereafter all ports were farmed until 23 September 1350.
(*h*) Excluding Exeter.
(*i*) Excluding Yarmouth.
(*j*) Excluding Lynn.
(*k*) Excluding London.

Textiles 18. Exports of Wool Manufactures – Great Britain 1815–19, and United Kingdom 1820–1980

NOTES

[1] SOURCES: 1815–19 – *S.P.* 1821, XVII; 1820–5 – *S.P.* 1833, XXXIII, and (for yarn) *S.P.* 1828, XIX; 1826–40 – *S.P.* 1844, XLV; 1840–1920 – *Abstract*; 1921–80 – *Annual Statement of Trade* and *Overseas Trade Statistics of the United Kingdom*.

[2] Exports to Ireland have been excluded from the British figures for 1815–19.

[3] It is impossible to bridge completely the break caused by the adoption of a new classification of exports in 1890. Total manufactures including carpets (but excluding blankets which were only recorded by number from 1890) amounted to 233,962,000 yards in 1890, and to 178,175,000 yards in 1909. Thereafter carpets were included with rugs, and recorded by the square yard.

[4] It is impossible to continue the series for *Total Manufactures* after 1919 since several items were thereafter recorded in units other than the square yard.

	Woollen and Worsted Yarn (thousand lb.)	Wool Goods Entered by the Piece (thousand pieces)	Wool Goods Entered by the Yard (thousand yd.)
1815	—	1,483	12,173
1816	—	1,285	7,112
1817	—	1,400	6,614
1818	—	1,626	8,997
1819	14	1,231	6,488
	--	----	----
1820	11	1,293	4,791
1821	18	1,610	6,322
1822	31	1,706	8,436
1823	18	1,656	8,140
1824	20	1,857	7,338
1825	77	1,743	7,804
1826	131	1,619	4,941
1827	256	1,852	6,461
1828	437	1,821	6,816
1829	590	1,773	5,298
1830	1,108	1,747	5,562
1831	1,592	1,997	5,798
1832	2,204	2,297	6,011
1833	2,107	2,384	7,456
1834	1,862	1,910	6,689
1835	2,357	2,390	7,907
1836	2,546	2,225	9,100
1837	2,514	1,519	5,923
1838	3,086	2,052	6,912
1839	3,320	2,144	8,171
1840	3,797	2,014	8,164

Textiles 18. *continued*

	Woollen and Worsted Yarn (million lb.)	Total Manufactures (*a*) of Wool (million yards)		Woollen and Worsted Yarn (million lb.)	Total Manufactures (*a*) of Wool (million yards)
1840	3·8	69	1865	31·7	279
1841	4·9	78	1866	27·4	282
1842	6·0	75	1867	37·4	249
1843	7·4	96	1868	43·7	269
1844	8·3	112	1869	38·8	303
1845	9·4	107	1870	35·5	293
1846	8·6	88	1871	43·7	368
1847	10·1	99	1872	39·7	413
1848	8·4	85	1873	34·7	346
1849	11·8	124	1874	35·0	327
1850	13·8	151	1875	31·7	318
1851	14·7	151	1876	30·9	282
1852	14·2	166	1877	27·0	261
1853	14·0	169	1878	31·2	258
1854	15·7	153	1879	33·4	251
1855	20·4	133	1880	26·5	262
1856	27·3	156	1881	29·7	273
1857	24·7	177	1882	31·8	265
1858	24·1	166	1883	33·5	256
					--- (*b*)
1859	22·8	194	1884	39·3	290
1860	27·5	190	1885	43·5	268
1861	27·5	164	1886	45·7	274
1862	27·8	167	1887	40·2	283
1863	32·5	217	1888	42·6	266
1864	31·8	241	1889	45·4	270

Textiles 18. *continued*

	Woollen and Worsted Yarn (million lb.)	Noils (million lb.)	Tops (million lb.)	Woollen Tissues (million yd.)	Worsted Tissues (million yd.)	Total Wool Manufactures (except carpets and blankets) (million yd.)
1890	41·1	10·2	9·0	56	153	223
1891	41·4	10·6	6·4	56	145	212
1892	44·8	11·1	9·6	51	143	203
1893	50·1	11·2	11·1	47	130	185
1894	53·0	9·0	11·6	41	111	161
1895	61·1	13·8	14·3	58	164	233
1896	62·2	11·2	18·2	60	137	210
1897	57·1	11·6	25·5	50	130	190
1898	58·8	11·9	24·1	46	95	152
1899	63·7	13·0	29·9	49	103	162
1900	57·1	7·9	28·0	51	102	164
1901	48·5	9·9	27·1	45	94	149
1902	52·7	11·9	40·7	47	103	158
1903	59·8	13·0	42·5	51	106	166
1904	54·4	9·3	37·4	67	104	181
1905	49·6	11·6	35·4	72	107	188
1906	55·3	11·5	38·6	80	99	188
1907	58·1	12·7	35·8	85	99	193
1908	50·9	13·2	34·7	76	74	157
1909	58·3	16·1	40·7	79	85	171
1910	67·9	17·2	42·1	95	95	199
1911	65·4	17·1	38·0	98	78	184
1912	63·0	19·6	44·8	101	72	180
1913	54·7	20·0	43·6	106	62	176
1914	36·7	14·3	36·8	82	70	160
1915	16·6	12·1	16·2	92	56	155
1916	28·0	12·9	22·6	132	52	200
1917	21·0	11·5	14·4	124	43	177
1918	15·2	5·1	15·1	67	31	102
1919	28·7	13·3	14·9	131	32	168
				(million sq. yds)	(million sq. yds)	
1920	31·0	10·8	23·8	187	77	...
1921	29·5	15·6	34·7	77	41	...
1922	52·6	20·3	41·6	122	62	...
	---	---	---	---	---	
1923	44·1 (*c*)	20·4 (*c*)	39·0 (*c*)	149 (*c*)	63 (*c*)	...
	---	---	---	---	---	
1924	53·9	20·8	41·1	165	57	...
				---	---	
1925	44·7	15·1	32·0	132 (*d*)	47 (*d*)	...
1926	37·2	13·8	33·6	119	43	...
1927	51·9	18·8	42·0	131	40	...
1928	49·0	20·5	34·4	128	42	...
1929	46·7	17·1	32·7	108	47	...
1930	37·3	12·8	28·8	79	35	...
1931	34·9	10·5	28·0	56	30	...
1932	38·0	12·1	41·8	54	28	...
1933	43·4	15·0	45·8	61	33	...
1934	42·9	10·5	41·7	69	33	...
1935	40·9	16·7	55·9	71	38	...
1936	37·1	17·6	52·1	78	40	...
1937	32·3	12·7	40·2	80	43	...
1938	27·8	11·8	32·5	59	32	...
					--- (*e*)	
					29	...

Textiles 18. *continued*

	Woollen and Worsted Yarn (million lb.)	Noils (million lb.)	Tops (million lb.)	Woollen Tissues (million sq. yards)	Worsted Tissues (million sq. yards)
1939	26·3	8·6	33·8	59	32
1940	17·7	6·7	28·2	45	36
1941	13·2	4·8	16·2	58	28
1942	10·2	1·9	11·7	48	25
1943	9·0	0·4	8·2	28	16
1944	8·7	0·4	5·0	23	11
1945	9·0	0·3	16·1	27	13
1946	15·4	1·1	29·0	51	21
1947	14·5	5·2	38·5	52	23
1948	20·9	13·1	59·6	70	33
1949	29·0	12·3	60·0	70	36
				--- (f)	--- (f)
1950	35·2	16·9	72·9	77	40
1951	26·6	13·1	49·4	70	39
1952	25·3	13·4	54·0	58	34
1953	28·9	15·7	70·2	62	34
1954	25·5	17·0	67·1	59	32
				--- (f)	--- (f)
1955	26·4	19·9	76·6	68	34
1956	28·9	17·8	81·5	71	33
1957	29·9	19·1	83·3	70	34
1958	25·3	20·8	88·9	60	31
1959	31·1	21·6	96·4	64	34
1960	32·8	22·4	91·1	59	33
1961	29·1	26·2	92·1	54	32
1962	29·5	20·8	78·2	52	31
1963	33·9	23·6	96·0	52	31
1964	32·1	21·6	75·1	54	30
1965	30·1	20·3	63·9	53	30
1966	29·5	17·1	58·4	51	26
1967	27·7	16·9	51·5	52	24
1968	31·6	19·0	56·0	57	24
1969	35·4	14·0	57·3	58	25
1970	34·9	. . .	46·5	(g)	
1971	35·0	. . .	41·1	65	
1972	40·0	. . .	45·2	68	
1973	40·3	. . .	47·1	73	
1974	34·3	. . .	28·5	64	
1975	30·5	. . .	35·7	52	
1976	37·6	. . .	35·6	54	
1977	39·8	. . .	37·6	62	
1978	35·5	. . .	23·4	63	
1979	36·5	. . .	22·2	58	
1980	37·0	. . .	21·1	55	

(a) Including carpets.

(b) It was stated that prior to 1884 'large quantities of piece goods of mixed materials in which wool predominated were erroneously entered as cotton manufactures'.

(c) Southern Ireland was treated as foreign from 1st April 1923.

(d) Prior to 1925 woollen and worsted tissues included manufactures of pure alpaca, mohair, and cashmere. The size of this break is probably very small, particularly for woollens.

(e) Subsequently excluding knitted, netted, and crocheted goods, linings, and lastings. There is no break in the woollens series at this level of rounding.

(f) From 1950 to 1954 cut lengths containing less than 25 square yards were recorded under a heading which did not discriminate between woollens and worsteds. They are not included in either column here. They amounted to the following (in sq. yd.):

1950	2·7	1953	2·1
1951	2·4	1954	2·2
1952	1·6		

(g) The 1970 figure was given by weight. It was 44·2 million lb.

Textiles 19. Exports of British Silk Manufactures – England & Wales 1697–1791, and Great Britain 1792–1823

NOTE

SOURCES: 1697–1807 – Elizabeth B. Schumpeter, *English Overseas Trade Statistics, 1697–1808* (Oxford University Press, 1960), tables XI and XIV; 1814–23 – returns printed in *Sessional Papers* from time to time.

(in thousand lb.)

1697	41	1738	47	1799	61
1698	55	1739	49	1780	95
1699	48	1740	40	1781	86
1700	38	1741	58	1782	60
1701	39	1742	62	1783	105
1702	28	1743	71	1784	146
1703	33	1744	46	1785	78
1704	32	1745	40	1786	78
1705	...	1746	50	1787	88
1706	42	1747	56	1788	82
1707	44	1748	54	1789	80
1708	52	1749	60	1790	98
1709	57	1750	63	1791	120
1710	54	1751	23	1792	121 (*b*)
1711	46	1752	92	1793	95
1712	...	1753	90	1794	113
1713	44	1754	85	1795	121
1714	52	1755	91	1796	146
1715	58	1756	89	1797	118
1716	47	1757	93	1798	87
1717	62	1758	118	1799	119
1718	71	1759	173	1800	112
1719	40	1760	198	1801	97
1720	41	1761	144	1802	78
1721	38	1762	137	1803	54
1722	43	1763	86	1804	51
1723	44	1764	127	1805	52
1724	49	1765	97	1806	60
1725	86	1766	72	1807	51
1726	50	1767	80		...
1727	37	1768	74		
1728	45	1769	53	1814 (*c*)	242
1729	43	1770	54	1815	269
1730	58	1771	103	1816	205
1731	42	1772	91 (*a*)	1817	203
1732	47	1773	65	1818	241
1733	45	1774	85	1819	...
1734	36	1775	41	1820	...
1735	45	1776	48	1821	276
1736	47	1777	61	1822	287
1737	46	1778	47	1823	225

(*a*) There was no break on the change in original source at this time.

(*b*) There being no silk industry in Scotland, the inclusion of that country at this time makes no break in the series.

(*c*) The figures for 1697–1807 relate to piece goods only. It is not clear whether those for 1814–23 include sewing silk or not, but it seems probable that there was some difference in definition.

Textiles 20. Exports of Silk Manufactures – United Kingdom 1840–1980

NOTE

SOURCES: 1840–1920 – *Abstract*; 1921–80 – *Annual Statement of Trade* and *Overseas Trade Statistics of the United Kingdom*.

A. Silk Manufactures, in thousand lb.

1840	622	1848	411	1856	1,164
1841	638	1849	818	1857	1,196
1842	369	1850	1,186	1858	964
1843	398	1851	1,181	1859	1,184
1844	488	1852	1,131	1860	1,307
1845	470	1853	1,377	1861	1,060
1846	470	1854	1,000		
1847	620	1855	835		

B. Silk Broad Piece Goods, in thousand yards

1862	2,603	1882	7,662	1902	9,585
1863	2,828	1883	7,688	1903	9,778
1864	2,771	1884	6,810	1904	10,085
1865	2,873	1885	6,016	1905	11,451
1866	3,067	1886	7,266	1906	13,464
1867	2,377	1887	6,592	1907	13,018
1868	2,926	1888	8,345	1908	8,518
1869	2,900	1889	9,619	1909	10,074
1870	3,854	1890	9,507	1910	11,612
1871	5,160	1891	6,455	1911	11,740
1872	4,417	1892	5,952	1912	11,953
1873	2,984	1893	6,036	1913	11,841
1874	4,025	1894	5,535	1914	10,221
1875	3,655	1895	6,830	1915	9,556
1876	3,944	1896	7,611	1916	10,070
1877	4,356	1897	7,477	1917	7,760
1878	4,819	1898	8,999	1918	6,385
1879	4,724	1899	9,737	1919	8,615
1880	6,219	1900	10,247	1920	8,241
1881	7,051	1901	9,290		

C. Silk Tissues (except ribbons) in thousand square yards

1921	3,224	1941	945	1961	909
1922	5,142	1942	656	1962	992
1923	5,001	1943	100	1963	1,040
1924	5,308	1944	82	1964	831
1925	4,728	1945	244	1965	940
1926	5,240	1946	3,995	1966	885
1927	8,127	1947	1,691	1967	847
1928	7,841	1948	902	1968	705
1929	6,502	1949	704	1969	986
1930	5,292	1950	899	1970	(*a*)
1931	4,705	1951	765	1971	908
1932	4,270	1952	420	1972	789
1933	2,596	1953	562	1973	1,103
1934	2,484	1954	751	1974	(*a*)
1935	3,072	1955	708	1975	(*a*)
1936	2,996	1956	792	1976	819
1937	3,475	1957	725	1977	1,021
1938	2,698	1958	551	1978	1,024
1939	3,005	1959	755	1979	994
1940	1,735	1960	887	1980	1,060

(*a*) Recorded by weight, or mainly by weight, in these years.

Textiles 21. Exports of Linen Piece Goods of English Manufacture from England & Wales 1697–1791, and of British Manufacture from Great Britain 1792–1825

NOTES

[1] Sources: 1697–1807 – Elizabeth B. Schumpeter, *English Overseas Trade Statistics, 1697–1808* (Oxford University Press, 1960), tables x and xi (converted to yards) with British linens exported with bounty from 1743 to 1764 added from J. Horner, *The Linen Trade of Europe during the Spinning Wheel Period* (Belfast, 1920), pp. 231–232; 1808–9 *S.P.* 1812–3, xiii; 1810–25 – Returns printed in *Sessional Papers* annually from 1821 to 1826.

[2] Ireland is treated as a foreign country throughout this table, and re-exports of Irish linen from Great Britain, even though made with bounty, are not included here.

(in thousand yards)

1697	145	1740	1,523	1783	9,690
1698	285	1741	2,201	1784	8,426
1699	245	1742	2,120	1785	6,397
1700	181	1743	1,690	1786	6,581
1701	141	1744	1,354	1787	9,097
1702	138	1745	1,423	1788	10,029
1703	145	1746	3,031	1789	8,670
1704	147	1747	2,667	1790	7,806
1705	...	1748	2,990	1791	9,045

1706	139	1749	4,068	1792	13,248(*b*)
1707	171	1750	4,029	1793	12,083
1708	323	1751	3,868	1794	16,075
1709	348	1752	4,025	1795	12,903
1710	304	1753	5,004	1796	15,616
1711	427	1754	4,802	1797	12,936
1712	...	1755	3,324	1798	18,983
1713	287	1756	4,528	1799	19,466
1714	293	1757	5,982	1800	13,678
1715	363	1758	7,116	1801	17,778
1716	324	1759	8,389	1802	15,706
1717	381	1760	10,494	1803	9,853
1718	576	1761	7,858	1804	13,005
1719	448	1762	7,746	1805	11,392
1720	412	1763	7,605	1806	13,793
1721	497	1764	8,507	1807	13,456

1722	601	1765	7,463	1808	15,858(*c*)
1723	451	1766	8,592	1809	20,507

1724	471	1767	8,043	1810	17,926(*d*)
1725	672	1768	9,037	1811	12,695
1726	575	1769	7,474	1812	15,275
1727	632	1770	7,618	1813	...
1728	742	1771	10,308	1814	18,752

1729	810	1772	11,619(*a*)	1815	17,183
1730	741	1773	8,804	1816	17,541
1731	748	1774	11,318	1817	24,595
1732	707	1775	8,224	1818	28,131
1733	610	1776	6,379	1819	20,591
1734	645	1777	6,639	1820	24,099
1735	955	1778	4,905	1821	28,239
1736	1,040	1779	4,892	1822	33,806
1737	778	1780	7,178	1823	34,716
1738	1,176	1781	3,475	1824	43,978
1739	1,238	1782	5,680	1825	33,765

(*a*) This break, caused by the change in original source, was not significant.

(*b*) The inclusion of Scotland in 1792 must have had a considerable bearing on the increase in that and subsequent years.

(*c*) The figure for 1807 in *S.P.* 1812–13, xiii differs from that derived from Mrs Schumpeter by about 3 per cent. It may therefore be presumed that there is a slight break between 1807 and 1808 when the source is changed.

(*d*) Prior to 1810 there is no official record of the total yardage of linen exports. Some classes of linen were entered by the yard, others by the ell or by the piece. For this table, these latter entries have been converted to yards on the assumption that each piece was 35 yards long. (This assumption is based on the rates of valuation, which for some types of linen were 35 shillings per piece, *or* 15 pence per ell, *or* one shilling per yard.) For the period 1810–12, when official yardage figures are available as well as the older type of entries, yardage figures based on our assumption differ from the official figures by only 2 or 3 per cent.

Textiles 22. Exports of Linen – United Kingdom 1826–1980

NOTES

[1] SOURCES: 1826–39 – Returns printed in *Sessional Papers* annually; 1840–1920 – *Abstract*; 1921–80 – *Annual Statement of Trade* and *Overseas Trade Statistics of the United Kingdom*.

[2] The following table of exports from Great Britain of Irish linen (in thousand yards) will assist comparison with the previous table:

1814	7,226	1817	9,477	1820	9,422	1823	13,889
1815	9,562	1818	9,385	1821	11,630	1824	15,174
1816	8,801	1819	6,138	1822	12,854	1825	13,801

Exports from Britain to Ireland and from Ireland to foreign parts were not very large, and probably cancelled each other.

	Piece Goods (thousand yd.)	Thread (thousand lb.)	Yarn (thousand lb.)
1826	37,791	...	...
1827	55,132	...	...
1828	60,287	...	...
1829	57,698	...	...
1830	61,920	...	...
1831	69,234	...	...
1832	49,531	...	110
1833	63,253	...	936
1834	67,834	...	1,533
1835	77,977	...	2,611
1836	82,089	...	4,575
1837	58,426	...	8,373
1838	77,196	...	14,923
1839	85,257	...	16,315
1840	89,373	959	17,734
1841	90,322	1,378	25,220
1842	69,233	1,161	29,491
1843	84,173	1,527	23,358
1844	91,284	2,154	25,971
1845	88,402	1,969	23,289
1846	84,799	1,752	19,484
1847	89,329	1,877	12,689
1848	89,002	1,992	11,722
1849	111,259	2,874	17,264
1850	122,343	3,360	18,221
1851	129,107	2,740	18,841
1852	133,193	3,852	23,929
1853	134,165	4,349	22,894
1854	111,649	3,190	17,697
1855	118,040	3,069	18,177
1856	146,410	4,163	25,118
1857	133,840	3,361	28,848
1858	121,940	3,176	32,047
1859	138,120	2,886	27,290
1860	143,997	3,230	31,211
1861	116,322	2,390	27,981
1862	156,895	3,909	32,559
1863	181,637	4,257	38,452
1864	210,469	3,978	40,177
1865	247,006	3,935	36,797
1866	255,469	3,785	33,608
1867	211,275	2,754	34,002
1868	210,050	2,677	32,779
1869	214,715	2,188	34,566
1870	226,471	2,379	37,239
1871	220,467	2,902	36,236
1872	245,019	2,642	31,187
1873	208,123	2,302	28,734
1874	194,682	2,690	27,155
1875	204,573	2,758	27,888

	Piece Goods (thousand yd.)	Thread (thousand lb.)	Yarn (thousand lb.)
1876	162,969	2,638	22,278
1877	177,767	2,447	19,216
1878	160,802	2,395	18,474
1879	160,311	2,829	17,429
1880	164,967	2,878	16,478
1881	174,011	2,590	18,250
1882	176,451	2,796	18,156
1883	162,256	2,253	17,678
1884	155,317	2,581	19,534
1885	149,469	2,633	16,600
1886	163,756	2,691	15,892
1887	163,930	2,818	16,381
1888	176,718	2,806	14,711
1889	180,630	2,800	13,945
1890	184,040	2,949	15,313
1891	159,458	2,474	14,860
1892	171,303	2,458	15,461
1893	158,335	2,397	16,259
1894	156,254	2,094	15,540
1895	203,588	2,402	17,046
1896	174,208	2,240	18,462
1897	164,583	2,019	18,366
1898	148,005	1,870	17,355
1899	174,279	2,038	18,152
1900	154,708	1,838	16,347
1901	150,215	1,721	12,971
1902	163,129	1,835	14,370
1903	154,947	1,908	14,090
1904	161,763	1,889	14,751
1905	183,446	2,262	14,694
1906	190,958	2,181	14,978
1907	184,999	2,382	16,442
1908	151,894	2,234	13,706
1909	223,935	2,264	15,533
1910	220,568	2,739	18,549
1911	193,829	2,597	18,012
1912	213,085	2,667	17,685
1913	193,681	2,646	16,307
1914	178,893	2,493	12,445
1915	128,776	3,627	6,418
1916	144,064	4,238	9,585
1917	103,538	3,568	18,144
1918	70,204	936	1,669
1919	76,864	3,217	13,238
	(thousand sq. yd.)		
1920	93,045	3,114	6,380
1921	39,962	1,499	4,496
1922	77,436	2,211	7,486
1923	89,666	2,586	7,517
1924	110,786	2,656	10,700

Textiles 22. *continued*

	Piece Goods (thous. sq. yd.)	Thread (thousand lb.)	Yarn (thousand lb.)
1925	83,694	2,752	8,970
1926	75,283	2,596	7,301
1927	73,911	2,494	11,523
1928	66,135	2,465	10,186
1929	71,540	2,355	10,101
1930	61,451	1,968	8,201
1931	65,342	1,718	6,491
1932	65,890	1,812	6,928
1933	76,860	1,898	10,344
1934	77,597	1,900	9,907
1935	77,163	2,114	9,643
1936	88,728	2,020	10,904
1937	83,115	2,283	10,411
1938	51,790	1,822	8,378
1939	77,414	1,890	7,119
1940	45,392	1,895	3,144
1941	27,799	1,546	1,058
1942	22,605	1,778	607
1943	10,528	948	416
1944	6,182	1,473	387
1945	8,814	1,821	772
1946	39,448	2,795	2,084
1947	46,066	2,317	2,763
1948	44,433	1,836	3,091
1949	38,521	1,592	4,461
1950	49,358	1,846	6,324
1951	49,667	2,147	6,579
1952	38,743	1,387	7,279
1953	47,131	1,596	5,429
1954	47,166	1,797	6,313

	Piece Goods (thous. sq. yd.)	Thread (thousand lb.)	Yarn (thousand lb.)
1955	45,849	1,855	6,192
1956	46,054	1,774	6,896
1957	40,621	1,783	9,178
1958	34,516	1,593	7,730
1959	37,206	1,666	7,183
1960	36,757	1,681	6,280
1961	30,553	1,782	6,144
1962	33,510	1,586	7,008
1963	32,743	1,611	7,242
1964	33,058	1,740	7,732
1965	30,929	1,309	6,021
1966	29,081	1,507	5,843
1967	26,270	1,440	3,486
1968	26,751	1,559	5,524
1969	25,988	1,792	5,582
1970	20,932	8,530	
1971	19,487	7,657	
1972	18,972	8,609	
1973	20,811	8,249	
1974	13,988	6,622	
1975	9,204	5,974	
1976	8,938	5,811	
1977	7,813	5,463	
1978	7,144	4,411	
1979	6,380	4,850	
1980	5,873	5,108	

Textiles 23. Exports of Man-made Fibre Manufactures – United Kingdom 1920–80

NOTE
SOURCES: *Annual Statement of Trade* and *Overseas Trade Statistics of the United Kingdom*.

	Yarn (million lb.)	Tissues (a) (million lb.)		Yarn (million lb.)	Tissues (a) (million sq. yards)		Yarn (million lb.)	Tissues (a) (million sq. yards)
1920	1·0	...	1941	20·2	90·5	1961	53·5	48·9
1921	1·6	...	1942	16·3	116·3	1962	67·8	55·0
1922	2·4	...	1943	13·8	75·9	1963	81·5	80·4
1923	4·8	...	1944	15·6	91·2	1964	96·7	115·4
1924	6·4	...	1945	14·2	94·6	1965	90·9	94·5
1925	7·2	...	1946	16·6	113·2	1966	95·4	65·1
1926	5·8	11·4	1947	15·3	112·6	1967	105·5	63·7
1927	8·4	13·2	1948	23·5	157·3	1968	130·5	74·5
1928	9·5	17·7	1949	21·5	184·5	1969	150·1	95·2
1929	8·2	15·4	1950	28·4	215·7	1970	180·2	... (b)
1930		11·9						
		(million sq. yds)						
1930	6·4	65·5	1951	28·2	219·2	1971	212·4	127·5
1931	4·7	43·3	1952	20·9	152·1	1972	245·5	177·1
1932	6·8	55·5	1953	31·5	176·8	1973	298·6	203·5
1933	6·7	54·2	1954	32·3	175·3	1974	300·3	198·8
1934	11·1	65·3	1955	30·8	133·7	1975	224·8	189·8
1935	9·8	51·8	1956	36·2	120·8	1976	278·4	245·9
1936	8·0	66·8	1957	44·1	111·3	1977	264·6	273·0
1937	14·1	80·2	1958	37·7	84·1	1978	287·7	266·5
1938	8·0	62·6	1959	45·1	63·7	1979	297·8	270·4
1939	6·9	74·8	1960	48·5	54·3	1980	287·6	283·0
1940	15·0	85·4						

(a) Excluding ribbon, lace, etc., but including tyre cord fabric.

(b) Recorded by weight only.

Textiles 24. Spindles, Power Looms, and Power Employed in Cotton Factories – United Kingdom 1835–1980

NOTES TO PART A

[1] SOURCE: *Reports of H.M. Inspectors of Factories* published in sessional papers.

[2] It is not always clear whether the figures relate to all machines in place or merely to those in use. The returns for 1870 and 1874 include all machines, but Ellison, in criticising the figures for 1885, suggested that they (and possibly those for 1878 also) related only to machines in use. (*The Cotton Trade of Great Britain* (London, 1886), p. 325. Ellison states quite categorically that 'the figures for 1885 are wrong'.)

A. Spindles, Power Looms and Power, at intervals 1835–1903, in thousands

	Spindles		Power Looms	Horsepower Used	
	Spinning	Doubling		Steam	Water
1835	...		110	...	...
1838	...		...	46	12
1850	20,977		250	71	11
1856	28,010		299	87	9
				---- (a)	---- (a)
1861	30,387		400	281	12
1867	32,000	2,215	379	190	12
1870	33,995	3,724	441	299	8
1874	37,516	4,366	463	...	...
1878	39,528	4,679	515	...	...
1885	40,120	4,228	561	...	...
1890	40,512	3,993	616	...	...
1903	43,905	3,952	684	...	...

(*a*) Between 1856 and 1861 the unit changed from 'nominal' to 'indicated' horsepower.

B. Spinning Spindles in Place, 1906–39, in millions

NOTES TO PART B

[1] SOURCE: *International Cotton Bulletin*, 1922–39.

[2] Figures refer to 31st August to 1921, 31st January in 1939 and 31st July in other years.

	Total		Mules	Rings		Mules	Rings
1906	48·8	1922	44·0	12·6	1931	41·2	13·0
1907	50·7	1923	44·0	12·5	1932	39·2	12·7
1908	52·8	1924	43·6	13·1	1933	37·0	12·0
1909	53·3	1925	43·7	13·5	1934	34·1	11·8
1910	53·4	1926	43·9	13·4	1935	31·7	11·0
1911	54·5	1927	43·8	13·5	1936	30·4	11·0
1912	55·3	1928	44·1	13·1	1937	28·0	10·8
1913	55·7	1929	42·8	13·1	1938	26·4	10·5
1921	56·1	1930	42·1	13·1	1939	25·8	10·5

C. Spinning Spindles and Looms Running in Cotton Factories, 1941–80

NOTES TO PART C

[1] SOURCES: *Cotton Board Trade Letter Statistical Supplement*, and its successor from 1952, the *Cotton Board Quarterly Statistical Review*, and *Abstract*.

[2] Doubling and waste-spinning spindles are not included in this table.

[3] The statistics of looms cover those working on man-made fibres as well as cotton.

[4] Statistics of spindles in place, in continuation of part B, are available for 1941 and 1945–53, and are given in B. R. Mitchell & H. G. Jones, *Second Abstract of British Historical Statistics* (Cambridge, 1971). The 1941 figures are 23·4 million mules and 10·4 million rings.

[5] The Report of the Cotton Board Committee to enquire into Post-War Problems (Jan. 1944) gave the following figures of looms in place for 1938–41 (in thousands): 1938 – 495; 1939–41 – 490.

	Mules (millions)	Rings (millions)	Looms (thousands)		Mules (millions)	Rings (millions)	Looms (thousands)
1941	10·49	6·00	293	1961	2·56	6·24	150
1942	10·27	5·92	228	1962	1·80	5·54	132
1943	9·69	5·68	225	1963	1·20	5·01	119
1944	9·24	5·36	228	1964	0·76	4·37	117
1945	9·24	5·20	216	1965	0·6	4·1	113
1946	11·91	5·64	224	1966	0·4	3·5	106
1947	12·93	5·88	241	1967	0·3	3·5	87
1948	14·56	7·04	271	1968	0·3	3·3	79
1949	15·23	7·70	289	1969	0·3	3·3	75
1950	15·22	8·16	304	1970	0·2	3·1	68
1951	15·01	8·55	312	1971	0·1	2·8	58
1952	10·33	7·18	250	1972	0·1	2·5	52
1953	11·25	8·40	271	1973	2·5 (mules and rings)		50
1954	11·77	8·78	281	1974	2·5 (mules and rings)		49
1955	9·68	8·33	253	1975	2·3 (mules and rings)		43
1956	8·52	8·13	229	1976	2·2 (mules and rings)		39
1957	8·12	8·24	223	1977	2·2 (mules and rings)		38
1958	5·98	7·49	192	1978	2·0 (mules and rings)		34
1959	4·90	7·05	172	1979	1·9 (mules and rings)		33
1960	2·83	6·22	149	1980	1·5 (mules and rings)		26

Textiles 25. Spindles and Power Looms in Cotton Factories – Lancashire 1882–1939

NOTES

[1] SOURCE: *The Lancashire Textile Industry* (J. Worrall Ltd., Oldham, 1959).

[2] These figures include waste spinning and doubling spindles.

	Million Spindles	Thousand Looms		Million Spindles	Thousand Looms
1882	38·4	485	1912	58·1	759
1883	...	...	1913	58·5	786
1884	40·5	534	1914	59·3	805
1885	41·3	546	1915	59·9	808
1886–7	41·0	550	1916	59·8	809
1887–8	40·9	583	1917	61·0	808
1889	41·3	597	1918	59·5	788
1890	41·4	607	1919	59·2	791
1891	42·4	611	1920	60·1	798
1892	43·1	616	1921	60·1	790
1893–4	43·0	603	1922	59·8	799
1894–5	43·2	628	1923	59·8	795
1896	42·7	638	1924	59·5	792
1897	42·1	642	1925	59·9	788
1898	41·8	630	1926	60·3	786
1899	42·2	639	1927	60·5	768
1900	42·6	649	1928	60·0	755
1901	43·1	651	1929	59·1	740
1902	44·6	648	1930	57·7	704
1903	44·6	647	1931	57·6	658
1904	45·2	653	1932	55·4	625
1905	46·0	652	1933	53·6	602
1906	48·3	685	1934	49·2	560
1907	52·6	725	1935	47·1	516
1908	55·2	736	1936	44·6	500
1909	57·0	739	1937	43·1	471
1910	57·7	741	1938	40·9	461
1911	58·0	741	1939	39·1	453

Textiles 26. Spindles Ordered by English Firms from Six Major Producers – 1878–1920

NOTES

[1] SOURCE: Gary R. Saxenhouse and Gavin Wright, "New Evidence on the Stubborn English Mule and the Cotton Industry, 1878–1920", *E.H.R.*, 2nd series XXXVII, 4 (1984).

[2] The six firms from whose records this series is drawn produced nearly 80 per cent of total English output of spindles.

(in thousands)

	Mules	Rings		Mules	Rings		Mules	Rings
1878	49	0	1893	828	91	1907	1,963	393
1879	209	0	1894	667	8	1908	1,379	279
1880	809	20	1895	605	56	1909	1,064	352
1881	847	46	1896	391	145	1910	686	333
1882	921	46	1897	288	272	1911	1,137	352
1883	1,396	40	1898	993	142	1912	1,680	668
1884	2,076	211	1899	1,342	172	1913	933	496
1885	1,325	130	1900	1,041	98	1914	1,212	392
1886	917	63	1901	1,956	164	1915	261	315
1887	753	37	1902	1,541	116	1916	281	153
1888	835	58	1903	1,504	203	1917	22	60
1889	940	91	1904	840	417	1918	192	160
1890	1,373	49	1905	2,509	703	1919	162	496
1891	880	81	1906	2,927	801	1920	419	411
1892	1,162	65						

Textiles 27. Spindles, Power Looms, and Power Employed in Wool Factories – United Kingdom 1835–1980

NOTES TO PART A

[1] SOURCES: 1835–1904 – Returns made by the Factory Inspectors, in sessional papers from 1836; 1918 (first row), Skinner's directory, *The World's Wool, 1930*, quoting the Wool Control Board; 1918 (second row) – Committee on Industry and Trade, *Survey of Textile Industries* (1928), p. 273 for power looms, and the Bradford Chamber of Commerce, *Statistics relating to the Worsted, Woollen and Artificial Silk Trades* for spindles; 1938 – Working Party Reports, *Wool* (1947).

[2] This table covers woollen, worsted and shoddy factories.

[3] It is not always clear whether the Inspectors' returns relate to all machines in place or merely to those in use. The 1871 and 1874 returns specifically include all machines, but later returns may not have done. See note 2 to table 7 for Ellison's remarks on the cotton industry figures, which probably apply to wool also. The 1871 returns for wool received particular criticism from Bradford, and 'are, to say the least, strongly suspect'. (Eric M. Sigsworth, *Black Dyke Mills* (Liverpool, 1958), p. 78 note.)

A. Spindles, Power Looms, and Power, at intervals, 1835–1938

(in thousands)

	Spindles			Horsepower Used	
	Spinning	Doubling	Power Looms	Steam	Water
1835	...		5	...	...
1838	...		...	17	10
1850	2,471		42	23	10
1856	3,112		53	31	9
1861	3,472		65	53	11
1867	6,456	520	119	85	12
1871	4,486	472	115	103	12
1874	5,449	559	140	...	...
1878	5,518	784	146	...	...
1885	5,375	769	140	...	...
1890	5,605	970	132	...	...
1904	5,625	1,059	105	...	...
1918	8,023		121	...	...
1918 (*a*)	6,459	1,337	115	...	...
1938	5,493	1,469	78	...	...

NOTES TO PART B

[1] SOURCE: Commonwealth Economic Committee, *Wool Intelligence* (supplement to June or July issue in each year from 1949) (later called *Wool Statistics*).

[2] Doubling and twisting spindles and carpet looms are not included in this table.

[3] The statistics are of spindles and looms installed and capable of operating.

B. Spinning Spindles and Looms, 1938–80

(in thousands)

	Spinning Spindles				Spinning Spindles		
	Worsted	Woollen	Looms		Worsted	Woollen	Looms
1938	2,283	3,210	78	1966	2,067	1,500	34
				1967	1,906	1,334	32
1943	2,309	3,311	73 (*a*)	1968	1,771	1,288	30
				1969	1,696	1,237	28
1951	2,949	2,229	64	1970	1,526	1,121	26
1952	2,937	2,305	63				
1953	2,916	2,180	61	1971	1,372	1,020	22
1954	2,899	2,120	60	1972	1,286	980	20
1955	2,876	2,095	59	1973	1,254	884	19
				1974	1,169	813	17
1956	2,838	2,050	57	1975	970	786	15
1957	2,844	2,010	56				
1958	2,782	1,995	52	1976	913	720	13
1959	2,726	1,909	49	1977	850	610	12
1960	2,719	1,895	47	1978	810	580	11
				1979	659	560	9
1961	2,631	1,776	44	1980	559	540	8
1962	2,570	1,750	43				
1963	2,416	1,620	40				
1964	2,303	1,570	38				
1965	2,177	1,520	36				

(*a*) The first row of figures for 1918 is for Great Britain and the whole of Ireland, and is comparable with earlier years. The second row is for Great Britain and Northern Ireland so far as power looms are concerned, and compares with later years. The second row of spindle figures for 1918, however, is for Great Britain alone, and does not compare exactly with later years, when Northern Ireland was included.

Textiles 28. Spindles, Power Looms, and Power Employed in Silk Factories – United Kingdom 1835–90

NOTES

[1] SOURCE: *Reports of H.M. Inspectors of Factories*, published in sessional papers.

[2] It is not always clear from the *Reports* whether they relate to all machines or merely those in use. The returns for 1870 and 1874 include all machines, but later ones may not have done so.

(in thousands)

	Spindles			Horsepower Used	
	Spinning	Doubling	Power Looms	Steam	Water
1835	...		2	...	...
1838	...		...	2	1
1850	1,226		6	3	1
1856	1,094		9	4	1
1861	1,339		11	6	1
1867	978	182	15	6	1
1870	940	190	12	8	1
1874	1,115	222	10	...	...
1878	843	176	13	...	...
1885	888	175	12	...	...
1890	847	183	11	...	...

Textiles 29. Spindles, Power Looms, and Power Employed in Flax, Jute, Hemp, and China Grass Factories – United Kingdom 1835–1905

NOTES

[1] SOURCE: *Reports of H.M. Inspectors of Factories*, published in sessional papers.

[2] It is not always clear whether the *Reports* relate to all machines in place or merely to those in use. The returns for 1870 and 1874 include all machines, but later returns may not have done so. See note 2 to table 7 for Ellison's remarks on the cotton industry, which probably applied to linen also.

(in thousands)

	Spindles			Horsepower Used	
	Spinning	Doubling	Power Looms	Steam	Water
1835	...		0.3 ...	...	
1838	...		...	7	4
1850	965		4	11	3
1856	1,288		8	14	4
1861	1,252		15	32	4
1867	1,679	59	35	42	5
1871	1,620	77	40	52	5
1874	1,712	96	52	...	...
1878	1,499	76	56	...	...
1885	1,447	84	61	...	...
1890	1,445	85	63	...	...
1905	1,321	79	68	...	...

Textiles 30. Numbers Employed in the Cotton Industry: Estimates by G. H. Wood – United Kingdom 1806–62

NOTES

[1] SOURCE: *J.R.S.S.* (1910), pp. 598–9.

[2] Wood's estimates are based on T. Ellison, *The Cotton Trade of Great Britain* (London, 1886), E. Baines, *History of the Cotton Manufacture* (London, 1835), and G. R. Porter, *The Progress of the Nation* (London, 2nd edition, 1847), and the returns of H.M. Factory Inspectors, published from time to time in sessional papers.

[3] All increases or decreases between known years were assumed to be uniform and gradual, though allowance was made for the great increase in factories in 1823–5 and 1832–4. Wood says that 'in criticising these numbers it should be borne in mind that they are not intended so much for definite estimates of the numbers employed in the cotton industry as for proportions between factory workers and handloom weavers'.

[4] No account is taken of hand spinners, of winders and warpers for the hand looms, or of those engaged in the finishing trades.

(in thousands)

	Factory Workers	Handloom Weavers		Factory Workers	Handloom Weavers
1806	90	184	1835	220	188
1807	93	188	1836	230	174
1808	95	192	1837	240	160
1809	97	196	1838	250	147
1810	100	200	1839	259	135
1811	102	204	1840	262	123
1812	105	208	1841	264	110
1813	107	212	1842	267	97
1814	110	216	1843	269	85
1815	114	220	1844	271	72
1816	117	224	1845	273	60
1817	121	228	1846	275	57
1818	123	232	1847	277	53
1819	125	236	1848	295	50
1820	126	240	1849	313	47
1821	129	240	1850	331	43
1822	132	240	1851	339	40
1823	135	240	1852	347	37
1824	167	240	1853	355	33
1825	173	240	1854	363	30
1826	175	240	1855	371	27
1827	177	240	1856	379	23
1828	180	240	1857	391	20
1829	182	240	1858	403	17
1830	185	240	1859	415	13
1831	187	240	1860	427	10
1832	196	227	1861	439	7
1833	208	213	1862	452	3
1834	215	200			

Textiles 31. Numbers Employed in Textile Factories – United Kingdom 1835–1907

NOTES

[1] Returns by the Factory Inspectors, in *Sessional Papers* at intervals from 1836.

[2] The Inspectors' returns were incomplete owing to the failure of some employers to send information; but it seems clear that the omissions were of little significance, even in the earlier years.

A. Cotton Factories

(in thousands)

	Children under 13		Children 13–18		All Ages		Grand Total
	Males	Females	Males	Females	Males	Females	
1835	15 (*a*)	14 (*a*)	28	38	100	119	219
1838	7 (*a*)	5 (*a*)	40	55	113	146	259
1847	11	7	37	57	134	182	316
1850	9	6	37	...	142	189	331
1856	14	10	39	...	157	222	379
1861	22	18	41	...	183	269	452
1867	22	19	34	...	161	240	401
1870	23	20	38	...	178	272	450
1874	34	33	39	...	188	292	480
	Children under 14 Working Half-Time		Persons under 18 Working Full Time				
1878	29	33	35	...	185	297	483
1885	24	26	40	...	196	308	504
1890	23	25	44	...	208	321	529
1895	14	17	42	82	205	334	539
1896	13	16	41	80	204	329	533
1897	12	15	40	80	200	328	527
1898	12	14	39	80	198	328	526
1901	10	11	37	78	194	329	523
1904	8	10	37	72	196	327	523
1907	9	10	46	86	218	359	577

B. Woollen, Worsted, and Shoddy Factories

(in thousands)

	Children under 13		Children Aged 13–18		All Ages		Grand Total
	Males	Females	Males	Females	Males	Females	
1835	7 (*a*)	7 (*a*)	12	11	32	23	55
1838	5 (*a*)	5 (*a*)	14	19	42	45	87
1847	8	7	16	21	59	66	126
1850	8	9	20	...	72	82	154
1856	9	9	18	...	76	91	167
1861	10	10	18	...	81	92	173
1867	15	17	23	...	110	152	262
1870	12	12	24	...	108	130	239
1874	19	19	25	...	125	155	280
	Children under 14 Working Half-Time		Persons under 18 Working Full Time				
1878	15	16	22	...	116	154	270
1885	12	12	24	...	125	158	282
1890	11	12	26	...	132	170	302
1895	7	7	23	37	121	161	282
1896	6	7	23	37	121	163	284
1897	5	6	21	35	111	154	266
1898	4	5	20	34	106	150	256
1901	4	4	19	35	107	153	260
1904	4	4	19	32	109	153	262
1907	4	4	19	34	109	152	261

Textiles 31. *continued*

C. Silk Factories

(in thousands)

	Children under 13		Children Aged 13–18		All Ages		Grand Total
	Males	Females	Males	Females	Males	Females	
1835	3·4 (*a*)	5·6 (*a*)	2·6	6·9	10	21	31
1838	3·4 (*a*)	5·2 (*a*)	3·2	8·5	11	23	34
1847	3·0	4·8	3·7	9·6	14	31	45
1850	2·4	4·8	3·2	...	13	30	43
1856	2·7	5·4	4·1	...	17	39	56
1861	2·1	4·9	3·2	...	16	37	52
1867	1·3	3·6	2·5	...	12	29	41
1870	2·3	4·7	2·7	...	14	34	48
1874	2·3	4·5	2·4	...	13	32	46
	Children under 14 Working Half-Time		Persons under 18 Working Full Time				
1878	1·4	2·8	2·2	...	12	29	41
1885	1·2	2·0	2·2	...	13	30	43
1890	1·2	1·7	2·5	...	13	28	41
1895	0·5	0·8	2·1	6·1	11	24	36
1896	0·4	0·8	2·0	6·3	11	25	36
1897	0·3	0·8	2·0	6·7	11	26	37
1898	0·3	0·6	1·9	6·2	10	25	35
1901	0·3	0·4	1·7	5·1	9	23	32
1904	0·2	0·5	1·5	4·7	9	21	30
1907	0·3	0·5	1·7	4·8	9	20	29

D. Linen, Hemp, Jute, and China Grass Factories

(in thousands)

	Children under 13		Children Aged 13–18		All Ages		Grand Total
	Males	Females	Males	Females	Males	Females	
1835	2·4 (*a*)	2·9 (*a*)	3·5	8·5	10	23	33
1838	0·8 (*a*)	0·7 (*a*)	5·7	12·4	13	31	42
1847	1·0	1·1	6·8	13·0	18	40	58
1850	0·8	0·8	8	...	21	48	68
1856	0·9	1·0	9	...	23	57	80
1861	1·5	2·2	9	...	27	67	94
1867	1·8	2·9	11	...	40	96	135
1870	2·0	3·6	14	...	44	102	146
1874	5·2	6·3	15	...	52	120	172
	Children under 14 Working Half-Time		Persons under 18 Working Full Time				
1878	5·0	7·0	11	...	45	105	150
1885	6·0	7·8	12	...	50	113	163
1890	5·2	6·4	13	...	52	111	163
1895	4·0	4·7	12	20	51	110	161
1896	4·2	4·8	12	20	52	111	162
1897	4·1	4·8	12	20	50	109	159
1898	3·9	4·6	11	20	49	108	157
1901	3·0	4·1	10	19	46	105	150
1904	1·9	2·7	10	18	45	103	148
1907	1·9	2·7	10	21	46	105	151

(*a*) The numbers of children under 10 years old in 1835 and 1838 were as follows:

	1835		1838	
	Males	Females	Males	Females
Cotton	372	331	1,046	686
Wool	384	280	1,154	1,018
Silk	905	1,353	1,131	1,463
Linen	86	65	117	93

Textiles 32. Numbers of Insured Employees in Textile Industries – United Kingdom 1923–78

NOTES

[1] SOURCES: 1923–36 – *Abstract of Labour Statistics*, 1937–9 and 1945–78 *Ministry of Labour Gazette* and its successors; 1940–4 – *Abstract*.

[2] The figures relate to a date in July in 1947, to June in 1948 and from 1962, and in May from 1949 to 1961.

[3] Coverage was changed from time to time as indicated in footnotes.

(in thousands)

	Cotton			Wool			Silk & Man-made Fibres			Silk and Weaving of Man-made Fibres			Man-made Fibre Production			Linen		
	Males	Females	Total	Males	Females	Total	Males	Females	Total	Males	Females	Total	Males	Females	Total	Males	Females	Total
1923	206	362	568	117	152	269	14	23	37							26	56	82
1924	205	367	572	111	151	262	16	26	41							26	58	83
1925	208	366	573	107	149	256	18	28	47							27	59	87
1926	209	366	575	105	148	254	21	30	51							28	62	90
	208	362	570	104	145	249	23	32	55							26	59	85
1927	--- (a)	--- (a)	--- (a)	--- (a)	--- (a)	--- (a)	--- (a)	--- (a)	--- (a)							--- (a)	--- (a)	--- (a)
	202	360	562	96	143	240	22	32	54							25	57	83
1928	198	356	554	98	144	243	31	39	70							25	56	81
1929	201	354	555	96	143	239	33	41	74							25	55	80
1930	197	367	564	96	145	240				18	32	49	15	13	29	25	56	81
1931	191	359	550	96	143	239				16	29	45	14	13	27	24	54	78
1932	187	332	518	96	137	234				15	28	44	15	12	26	23	51	75
1933	180	320	500	96	135	231				16	29	45	14	11	25	23	50	73
1934	170	298	467	95	134	230				17	31	48	15	10	25	23	51	75
1935	162	280	442	93	129	222				18	31	49	19	11	29	23	51	74
1936	150	270	421	94	130	223				19	31	50	19	11	30	23	51	74
1937	144	264	409	93	131	224				20	32	52	18	11	29	23	53	76
1938	137	256	393	90	126	216				20	32	52	17	9	26	22	52	74
1939	130	248	378	91	123	214				19	31	50	16	9	24	21	51	72
	--- (b)	--- (b)	--- (b)	--- (b)	--- (b)	--- (b)				--- (b)	--- (b)	--- (b)	--- (b)	--- (b)	--- (b)	--- (b)	--- (b)	--- (b)(c)
			395			228						53			26			99
1940	...	...	383	...	...	231				...	...	54	...	...	26	...	...	105
1941	...	...	297	...	...	204				...	...	39	...	...	21	...	...	89
1942	...	...	236	...	...	163				...	...	30	...	...	20	...	...	77

See p. 381 for footnotes.

Textiles 32. *continued*

(in thousands)

	Cotton			Wool			Silk and Weaving of Man-made Fibres			Man-made Fibre Production					
	Males	Females	Total	Males	Females	Total	Males	Females	Total	Males	Females	Total	Males	Females	Total
1943	...	...	224	...	...	142	...	...	27	...	...	19	...	...	73
1944	...	...	214	...	...	127	...	...	26	...	...	18	...	...	69
															73
1945	63	146	209	51	77	128	9	17	27	11	8	19	18	36	--- (c)
															54
1946	81	160	240	66	81	147	13	22	35	13	8	21	20	38	58
1947	88	163	251	77	87	164	10	17	27	22	15	37	20	38	58
	--- (d)	--- (d)	--- (d)	--- (d)	--- (d)	--- (d)	--- (d)	--- (d)	--- (d)	--- (d)	--- (d)	--- (d)	--- (d)	--- (d)	--- (d)
1948	101	193	293	93	116	209	19	29	48	27	14	41	23	43	65
1949	106	201	307	97	119	216	20	32	52	30	14	44	23	43	66
1950	111	206	316	99	123	222	23	35	58	33	14	47	23	43	66
1951	109	212	322	97	121	218	24	37	61	33	13	45	22	44	67
1952	98	189	287	87	108	195	20	31	51	27	10	38	22	41	64
1953	98	189	287	94	119	213	21	31	52	29	11	40	22	40	62
1954	101	194	295	94	121	215	22	32	54	29	11	40	20	38	58
1955	94	181	274	92	117	209	22	32	54	30	11	41	19	36	56
1956	88	158	246	91	119	210	23	32	54	31	11	42	19	34	52
1957	87	168	256	95	120	214	23	30	53	31	11	42	18	32	50
1958	84	155	239	92	111	203	22	28	50	28	9	37	15	26	42

	Spinning of Cotton, Flax, and Man-made Fibres			Weaving of Cotton, Linen and Man-made Fibres			Wool			Man-made Fibre Production		
	Males	Females	Total	Males	Females	Total	Males	Females	Total	Males	Females	Total
1959	55	101	157	54	88	142	93	109	202	30	10	40
1960	52	96	148	53	83	137	93	110	204	34	10	44
1961	49	91	140	52	79	131	94	109	204	35	10	45
1962	46	77	123	51	71	122	91	103	193	35	10	45
1963	44	73	118	49	64	113	91	102	193	36	10	45
1964	47	73	119	47	61	109	90	99	189	39	10	48
1965	46	70	116	47	60	107	86	94	180	41	10	51
1966	44	65	109	46	56	103	86	90	176	42	9	51
1967	42	56	98	43	48	91	82	82	165	40	9	49
1968	43	53	95	40	44	84	80	77	157	40	8	47
1969	45	50	95	39	37	76	83	76	159	45	8	53
1970	48	48	96	37	35	72	79	68	147	48	9	57
1971	47	42	89	36	30	66	70	57	127	47	8	55
	--- (*e*)	--- (*e*)	--- (*e*)	--- (*e*)	--- (*e*)	--- (*e*)	--- (*e*)	--- (*e*)	--- (*e*)	--- (*e*)	--- (*e*)	--- (*e*)
	42	37	79	33	27	60	62	53	114	41	6	47
1972	38	32	70	30	24	54	59	49	108	38	6	44
1973	37	32	69	30	24	54	59	49	108	38	6	44
1974	36	31	67	29	23	52	56	46	102	41	6	48
1975	32	26	59	27	21	48	49	40	89	38	5	43
1976	32	25	57	26	18	44	46	36	82	38	6	44
1977	31	25	56	25	18	44	44	37	83	35	5	40
1978	28	22	50	24	18	42	31	35	79	33	5	38

(*a*) From 1927 (2nd line) the figures relate to male employees aged 16–64 and female employees aged 16–60.
(*b*) From 1939 (2nd line) workers aged 14 and 15 are included.
(*c*) From 1939 (2nd line) to 1945 (1st line) workers in rope, net, and twine are included.
(*d*) As a consequence of the National Insurance Act there was an increase in the number of insured employees in all industries. Figures on the old basis were collected in 1948 for Great Britain but not for the United Kingdom. These indicate that the increase was from 10 to 15 per cent.
(*e*) Figures from 1971 (2nd line) are derived from the Census of Employment, and relate to people in employment only.

CHAPTER VII

BUILDING

TABLES

Although it obviously has been one of the most important industries for a long time, building has of necessity been scattered over the country, and its organisation has been very fragmented. Until comparatively recently, therefore, it has escaped official attention, more particularly since by its nature it could not enter into external trade. Our first statistical series relating solely to building – other than those of builders' wages given in chapter II – is that of the output of bricks as recorded by the excise officials, though the glass statistics, similarly generated and shown in the next chapter, have a major link to the building industry, and go back nearly forty years earlier. The import statistics for timber, shown in tables 7 and 10 of chapter IX, also relate very largely to building.

The general question of the reliability of the excise statistics is discussed in the introduction to the next chapter. The brick series itself was, of course, the subject of lengthy analysis in Shannon's well-known article,[1] and is also mentioned by Lewis.[2] It is enough here to say that it is probably the most reliable of the excise statistics, since the tax was relatively light, and the conditions of manufacture were not conducive to evasion. With the ending of the tax, in 1849, there is a gap in our statistical information on the output of building materials until modern times, until 1935 in fact. These latterday statistics for the two most important materials, bricks and cement, are shown in table 2.

Table 3 gives the most important statistics which can be derived from the records of the Inhabited House Duty which was imposed in 1851 on *dwelling* house of £20 annual value and

[1] H. A. Shannon, 'Bricks – A Trade Index, 1785–1849', *Economica*, I, 3 (1934).
[2] J. Parry Lewis, *Building Cycles and Britain's Growth* (London, 1965), chapter 2.

over. The complete lack of information prior to 1875 about houses exempt from duty robs the early part of this table of much of its potential usefulness. Even after that date there are deficiencies, of which two may be singled out for special mention.[3] In the first place the figures are of net quantities, offsetting much demolition against new building, and it seems probable that demolition was nothing like constant from year to year. Secondly, the value figures for England and Wales were not reassessed annually, and in the years of reassessment there was an upward bias to the series, whilst in other years the tendency was in the opposite direction. The numbers of houses in different categories were also affected by this factor, though not the total, of course. An earlier series of Inhabited House Duty returns is available for 1821–4 (rents of £5 being exempt) and 1825–33 (rents of under £10 exempt). These returns give a detailed distribution by rent groups and distinguish England and Wales from Scotland.[4]

A rough indication of the increase in the stock of houses over a longer period than the Inhabited House Duty statistics is given by the numbers of houses enumerated at the decennial censuses. These are shown in national summary in table 4, but a good deal of regional information is available in the original sources. The two main difficulties in using these statistics are the changes which have taken place in definitions and the likely omissions of many uninhabited houses.[5] However, according to Marion Bowley, 'as far as historical research is concerned with broad trends, the difficulties created by the imperfect definitions and classifications of the earlier censuses are not very important. It was, however, a piece of great good fortune in connection with the assessment of interwar housing problems that the 1911 census contained enough improvements to make its data reasonably useful and capable of comparison with those of the 1921 and 1931 censuses.'[6]

It is only since 1920 that official statistics of new housing built have become available, and these are shown, with the breakdown between local authority and private building, in table 7, along with the Irish figures from 1923 in table 6. But there are useful estimates for earlier years – Weber's back to 1856, which are given in table 5, and Lewis's index, which used and added very substantially to Weber's work, and is shown here as table 5A. Both of these used local authority sources which had not been tapped previously.[7] The provenance and reliability of these statistics – as also of table 8, giving Maywald's index of building costs – is perhaps best judged by reference to the original sources. Much detailed calculation, and several assumptions, were required, and it would be impertinent to attempt a summary judgment here. It should perhaps be pointed out, however, that Maywald's index is one of input costs rather than of selling prices.

[3] There is an extended discussion in J. C. Stamp, *British Incomes and Property* (London, 1916), pp. 107–37.
[4] *S.P.*, 1833 XLI.
[5] J. C. Stamp, *op. cit.*, p. 126.
[6] Marion Bowley, 'The Housing Statistics of Great Britain', *Journal of the Royal Statistical Society*, XCXXIII (1950).
[7] A useful regional study is A. G. Kenwood, 'Residential Building Activity in North-Eastern England, 1853–1913', *Manchester School*, XXXI (1963).

One series of statistics which has not been included is perhaps best referred to here. This is the annual series of government expenditure on harbours covering the period 1800–75.[8] The amount of money involved was never very large, but the timing of the expenditure is interesting.

[8] *S.P.* 1876 XIV.

Building 1. Bricks Charged with Duty – England & Wales 1785–1849

NOTE
SOURCE: H. A. Shannon, 'Bricks – A Trade Index, 1785–1849', *Economica*, 1, 2 (1934), pp. 300 *et seq.* The original source is an MS account in the Customs and Excise Library.

(in millions)

Years ended 5th July				Years ended 5th January			
1785	358·8	1801	674·4	1816	673·0	1833	1,011·3
1786	495·7	1802	698·6	1817	701·7	1834	1,152·4
1787	635·8	1803	842·1	1818	952·1	1835	1,349·3
1788	668·2	1804	795·7	1819	1,101·6	1836	1,606·1
1789	590·3	1805	845·5	1820	949·2	1837	1,478·2
1790	711·2	1806	933·2	1821	899·2	1838	1,427·0
1791	749·9	1807	831·3	1822	1,019·5	1839	1,568·7
1792	808·0	1808	841·6	1823	1,244·7	1840	1,677·8
1793	908·9	1809	779·3	1824	1,463·2	1841	1,423·8
1794	787·7	1810	874·4	1825	1,948·8	1842	1,271·9
1795	559·3	1811	950·6	1826	1,350·2	1843	1,158·9
1796	633·0	1812	939·6	1827	1,103·3	1844	1,420·7
1797	517·7	1813	912·0	1828	1,078·8	1845	1,820·7
1798	516·8	1814	758·1	1829	1,109·6	1846	2,039·7
1799	421·3	1815	778·4	1830	1,091·3	1847	2,193·8
1800	543·1			1831	1,125·4	1848	1,461·0
				1832	971·9	1849	1,462·7

Building 2. Production of Bricks and Cement, 1935–80

NOTES
[1] SOURCE: *Abstract*.
[2] The brick series is for Great Britain, the cement series for the United Kingdom.

	Bricks (millions)	Cement (million tons)		Bricks (millions)	Cement (million tons)		Bricks (millions)	Cement (million tons)
1935	7,294	5·9	1955	7,163	12·5	1968	7,465	17·7
			1956	7,131	12·8	1969	6,734	17·2
1938	7,800	7·7	1957	6,914	12·0	1970	6,062	16·9
			1958	6,440	11·7	1971	6,541	17·4
1945	1,227	4·1	1959	6,967	12·6	1972	6,938	17·8
1946	3,450	6·6						
1947	4,535	7·0	1960	7,283	13·3	1973	7,183	19·7
1948	4,600	8·5	1961	7,414	14·1	1974	5,575	17·5
1949	5,227	9·2	1962	7,289	14·0	1975	5,046	16·6
			1963	7,139	13·8	1976	5,406	15·5
1950	5,921	9·8	1964	7,954	16·7	1977	5,067	15·2
1951	6,080	10·2						
1952	6,621	11·1	1965	7,868	16·7	1978	4,842	15·7
1953	7,195	11·2	1966	7,072	16·5	1979	4,887	15·9
1954	7,247	12·0	1967	7,208	17·3	1980	4,562	14·6

Building 3. Inhabited House Duty – Great Britain 1851–1924

NOTES TO BOTH PARTS

[1] SOURCES: 1852–68 – *S.P.* 1870, XX; 1869–84 – *S.P.* 1884–5, XXII; 1884–1924 – *Report of the Commissioners of Inland Revenue*, in sessional papers annually.

[2] Private dwelling houses of under £20 annual value (i.e. exempt) were not separately distinguished from residential shops of like value. The latter are therefore included under the heading *Dwelling Houses Exempt from Duty*.

[3] Exempt farmhouses and farm buildings, and exempt buildings belonging to railways and mines are not included under any heading.

[4] New assessments came into force in the following years: Metropolitan area – 1871, 1877, 1882, 1887, 1892, 1897, 1902, 1907, 1912; Rest of England & Wales (including metropolitan area up to 1871) – 1852, 1854, 1858, 1862, 1865, 1868, 1871, 1874, 1877, 1880, 1883, 1886, 1889, 1894, 1899, 1904, 1911.

A. Numbers of Houses, 1851–1915

(in thousands)

Years ended 5th April or 31st March	Dwelling Houses						All Premises					
	Charged with Duty			Exempt from Duty			Charged with Duty			Exempt from Duty		
	England & Wales	Scotland	Great Britain	England & Wales	Scotland	Great Britain	England & Wales	Scotland	Great Britain	England & Wales	Scotland	Great Britain
1852	251	24	276	...	...	...	434	31	465	...	...	...
1853	253	24	277	...	...	...	436	30	466	...	...	...
1854	257	25	282	...	...	...	441	30	471	...	...	...
1855	266	25	291	...	...	...	454	31	485	...	...	...
1856	270	25	295	...	...	...	458	31	489	...	...	...
1857	274	26	300	...	...	...	464	31	495	...	...	...
1858	281	26	308	...	...	...	474	32	506	...	...	...
1859	290	28	317	...	...	...	486	33	519	...	...	...
1860	299	29	328	...	...	...	498	35	533	...	...	...
1861	307	30	336	...	...	...	509	35	544	...	...	...
1862	316	30	346	...	...	...	520	36	556	...	...	...
1863	332	31	363	...	...	...	540	37	578	...	...	...
1864	343	32	375	...	...	...	556	38	594	...	...	...
1865	357	33	389	...	...	...	576	39	615	...	...	...
1866	378	34	412	...	...	...	608	40	648	...	...	...
1867	390	35	424	...	...	...	623	41	664	...	...	...
1868	415	36	451	...	...	...	658	42	701	...	...	...
1869	435	37	472	...	...	...	687	44	731	...	...	...
1870	448	39	486	...	...	...	708	46	754	...	...	...
1871	481	40	521	...	...	...	749	48	796	...	...	...
1872	486	41	527	...	...	...	757	49	806	...	...	...
1873	494	43	537	...	...	...	767	50	818	...	...	...
1874	513	45	558	...	...	...	797	53	851	...	...	...
1875	523	47	569	3,401	521	3,922	809	56	865	3,667	612	4,280
1876	535	48	583	3,462	533	3,995	824	57	881	3,753	627	4,380
1877	576	52	629	3,487	557	4,045	883	62	945	3,788	656	4,444
1878	596	55	651	3,566	575	4,142	907	66	973	3,827	676	4,503
1879	617	58	675	3,629	589	4,218	932	69	1,002	3,898	701	4,599
1880	653	61	713	3,679	592	4,271	983	72	1,056	3,956	701	4,657
1881	673	61	734	3,732	600	4,332	1,008	73	1,081	4,018	711	4,729
1882	701	62	764	3,768	608	4,376	1,037	74	1,111	4,059	719	4,779
1883	730	64	794	3,836	622	4,458	1,078	76	1,154	4,110	731	4,841
1884	745	64	809	3,896	628	4,524	1,095	76	1,171	4,177	740	4,916
1885	752	65	817	3,952	636	4,589	1,100	77	1,176	4,238	748	4,987
1886	773	66	839	3,979	648	4,627	1,127	78	1,205	4,275	761	5,037
1887	785	67	851	4,029	659	4,688	1,136	78	1,214	4,334	768	5,103
1888	789	68	857	4,089	665	4,753	1,140	79	1,219	4,404	775	5,179
1889	805	69	875	4,144	671	4,815	1,162	81	1,242	4,467	779	5,247
1890	812	70	882	4,213	678	4,891	1,167	82	1,248	4,548	787	5,333
1891	807	71	878	4,264	685	4,950	1,175	83	1,257	4,605	796	5,402

Building 3. *continued*

A. Numbers of Houses, 1851–1915 (*cont.*)

(in thousands)

Years ended 5th April or 31st March	Dwelling Houses: Charged with Duty: England & Wales	Scot-land	Great Britain	Dwelling Houses: Exempt from Duty: England & Wales	Scot-land	Great Britain	All Premises: Charged with Duty: England & Wales	Scot-land	Great Britain	All Premises: Exempt from Duty: England & Wales	Scot-land	Great Britain
1892	817	73	890	4,333	690	5,023	1,186	84	1,270	4,682	800	5,482
1893	827	74	901	4,378	695	5,073	1,197	85	1,283	4,743	808	5,551
1894	869	77	946	4,370	697	5,066	1,253	89	1,342	4,379	813	5,551
1895	881	79	960	4,422	704	5,126	1,266	91	1,357	4,801	825	5,625
1896	897	82	979	4,491	713	5,204	1,287	94	1,380	4,879	836	5,716
1897	927	85	1,012	4,558	725	5,284	1,320	97	1,417	4,957	854	5,811
1898	947	88	1,036	4,627	737	5,364	1,344	100	1,445	5,031	864	5,895
1899	1,024	93	1,117	4,656	740	5,396	1,447	105	1,553	5,067	880	5,947
1900	1,055	97	1,152	4,753	757	5,510	1,480	110	1,590	5,183	900	6,083
1901	1,087	101	1,188	4,843	770	5,613	1,517	114	1,630	5,288	916	6,204
1902	1,128	103	1,231	4,919	784	5,704	1,560	116	1,676	5,375	929	6,304
1903	1,158	107	1,265	4,997	795	5,792	1,593	120	1,712	5,456	941	6,396
1904	1,240	111	1,350	5,034	799	5,834	1,692	124	1,816	5,498	957	6,454
1905	1,267	115	1,382	5,122	813	5,935	1,721	128	1,848	5,601	971	6,571
1906	1,297	117	1,414	5,222	826	6,048	1,746	130	1,876	5,726	987	6,713
1907	1,327	120	1,446	5,294	834	6,128	1,774	132	1,906	5,812	1,000	6,812
1908(*a*)	(1,345)	(123)	(1,468)	(5,365)	(143)	(6,208)	(1,792)	(135)	(1,927)	(5,894)	(1,013)	(6,907)
1909	1,366	126	1,492	5,440	841	6,281	1,812	138	1,951	5,985	1,010	6,995
1910	1,380	127	1,507	5,522	846	6,368	1,825	139	1,964	6,081	1,015	7,096
1911	1,404	128	1,533	5,528	851	6,379	1,857	141	1,998	6,085	1,027	7,112
1912	1,415	130	1,545	5,607	852	6,459	1,866	143	2,009	6,188	1,028	7,216
1913	1,427	132	1,559	5,652	853	6,506	1,874	144	2,018	6,249	1,031	7,280
1914	1,441	134	1,574	5,698	851	6,549	1,886	146	2,032	6,310	1,031	7,340
1915	1,455	137	1,592	5,751	850	6,601	1,898	149	2,047	6,377	1,031	7,408

(*a*) The figures for 1908 are estimates. Those originally compiled were incomplete owing to a necessary change in practice following legislation.

B. Value of Houses, 1851–1924

(in £ thousand)

Years	Dwelling Houses: Charged with Duty: England & Wales	Scot-land	Great Britain	Dwelling Houses: Exempt from Duty: England & Wales	Scot-land	Great Britain	All Premises: Charged with Duty: England & Wales	Scot-land	Great Britain	All Premises: Exempt from Duty: England & Wales	Scot-land	Great Britain
1852	12,368	1,029	13,397	...	...	...	20,463	1,241	21,703	...	...	...
1853	12,381	1,024	13,405	...	...	...	20,495	1,220	21,715	...	...	...
1854	12,568	1,051	13,619	...	...	...	20,699	1,249	21,948	...	...	...
1855	12,979	1,077	14,055	...	...	...	21,282	1,271	22,553	...	...	...
1856	13,207	1,091	14,297	...	...	...	21,573	1,280	22,852	...	...	...
1857	13,432	1,119	14,551	...	...	...	21,837	1,302	23,140	...	...	...
1858	13,896	1,168	15,064	...	...	...	22,485	1,352	23,836	...	...	...
1859	14,377	1,212	15,588	...	...	...	23,223	1,399	24,622	...	...	...
1860	14,804	1,260	16,064	...	...	...	23,704	1,459	25,162	...	...	...
1861	15,203	1,297	16,499	...	...	...	24,199	1,500	25,698	...	...	...
1862	15,676	1,348	17,024	...	...	...	24,878	1,558	26,436	...	...	...
1863	16,516	1,391	17,907	...	...	...	26,102	1,606	27,708	...	...	...
1864	17,090	1,426	18,516	...	...	...	26,853	1,645	28,498	...	...	...
1865	17,882	1,473	19,355	...	...	...	27,917	1,695	29,612	...	...	...
1866	19,306	1,520	20,826	...	...	...	30,032	1,747	31,779	...	...	...
1867	20,077	1,579	21,655	...	...	...	30,973	1,815	32,788	...	...	...
1868	21,605	1,662	23,267	...	...	...	33,160	1,904	35,064	...	...	...
1869	23,031	1,702	24,733	...	...	...	35,210	1,955	37,165	...	...	...
1870	23,678	1,783	25,461	...	...	...	35,962	2,047	38,009	...	...	...
1871	25,672	1,876	27,549	...	...	...	38,859	2,156	41,015	...	...	...

B. Value of Houses, 1851–1924 *(cont.)*

(in £ thousand)

Years ended 5th April or 31st March	Dwelling Houses: Charged with Duty: England & Wales	Scotland	Great Britain	Dwelling Houses: Exempt from Duty: England & Wales	Scotland	Great Britain	All Premises: Charged with Duty: England & Wales	Scotland	Great Britain	All Premises: Exempt from Duty: England & Wales	Scotland	Great Britain
1872	26,014	1,922	27,936	...	...	...	39,194	2,223	41,417	...	...	...
1873	26,464	1,992	28,456	...	...	...	39,726	2,298	42,024	...	...	...
1874	27,635	2,092	29,727	...	...	...	41,481	2,422	43,903	...	...	...
1875	28,272	2,186	30,458	25,429	3,179	28,608	42,256	2,526	44,782	40,275	6,558	46,834
1876	28,938	2,263	31,201	26,082	3,286	29,368	43,087	2,611	45,698	41,446	6,848	48,293
1877	31,850	2,513	34,363	27,248	3,578	30,826	47,476	2,911	50,387	43,744	7,525	51,229
1878	32,835	2,652	35,487	28,095	3,751	31,846	48,751	3,079	51,830	45,080	7,816	52,896
1879	33,834	2,776	36,610	28,821	3,871	32,692	50,008	3,228	53,236	46,304	8,132	54,436
1880	34,859	2,917	37,776	29,562	3,986	33,558	51,735	3,422	55,157	49,091	8,410	57,511
1881	35,791	2,941	38,732	30,286	4,057	34,345	52,905	3,447	56,351	50,264	8,459	58,723
1882	36,864	2,981	39,845	30,778	4,149	34,927	54,166	3,492	57,658	52,202	8,573	60,775
1883	38,226	3,046	41,271	31,573	4,181	35,755	56,273	3,588	59,861	53,852	8,529	62,383
1884	39,029	3,069	42,098	32,282	4,236	36,520	57,205	3,607	60,812	55,103	8,596	63,698
1885	39,372	3,093	42,465	32,973	4,303	37,276	57,372	3,622	60,994	56,156	8,733	64,889
1886	40,136	3,144	43,280	33,718	4,379	38,097	58,495	3,672	62,167	57,679	8,959	66,638
1887	40,771	3,158	43,929	34,304	4,474	38,779	59,088	3,684	62,773	58,831	9,005	67,836
1888	40,922	3,191	44,113	35,090	4,537	39,827	59,230	3,711	62,941	60,025	9,080	69,105
1889	41,494	3,242	44,736	35,760	4,611	40,371	60,142	3,769	63,911	61,100	9,213	70,313
1890	41,791	3,281	45,072	36,522	4,687	41,209	60,337	3,798	64,135	62,297	9,304	71,601
1891	41,526	3,300	44,825	37,104	4,784	41,888	60,943	3,826	64,769	63,502	9,496	72,999
1892	41,780	3,340	45,120	37,859	4,856	42,715	61,617	3,876	65,493	65,054	9,626	74,680
1893	42,026	3,395	45,422	38,493	4,909	43,402	61,985	3,946	65,931	66,285	9,774	76,059
1894	43,726	3,498	47,224	39,086	5,025	44,111	64,679	4,065	68,744	67,929	10,024	77,953
1895	44,041	3,566	47,606	39,809	5,125	44,934	65,083	4,135	69,218	69,169	10,249	79,419
1896	44,590	3,659	48,249	40,691	5,223	45,914	65,925	4,241	70,166	70,744	10,435	81,179
1897	45,748	3,776	49,524	41,547	5,365	46,912	67,779	4,365	72,144	72,631	10,715	83,346
1898	46,344	3,892	50,236	42,440	5,516	47,955	68,826	4,491	73,317	74,040	11,008	85,048
1899	49,213	4,071	53,284	43,600	5,682	49,282	73,665	4,696	78,361	76,748	11,490	88,238
1900	50,234	4,201	54,435	44,858	5,906	50,764	74,894	4,854	79,749	79,076	11,890	90,966
1901	51,401	4,338	55,739	46,058	6,073	52,131	76,372	5,010	81,381	81,567	12,289	93,856
1902	53,208	4,434	57,642	47,095	6,225	53,320	78,689	5,115	83,804	84,360	12,626	96,986
1903	54,227	4,556	58,783	48,283	6,402	54,684	79,846	5,237	85,084	86,564	12,921	99,486
1904	57,547	4,710	62,257	49,582	6,642	56,224	84,709	5,404	90,113	90,749	13,231	103,981
1905	58,308	4,835	63,143	50,764	6,780	57,544	85,417	5,534	90,951	93,048	13,623	106,671
1906	59,189	4,935	64,124	52,040	6,941	58,981	85,900	5,627	91,527	96,052	13,930	109,982
1907	60,649	5,032	65,682	53,003	7,058	60,061	87,229	5,721	92,950	99,022	14,294	113,316
1908	61,168	5,125	66,293	54,099	7,171	61,270	87,619	5,820	93,439	101,465	14,455	115,920
1909	61,863	5,214	67,078	55,158	7,216	62,375	88,100	5,907	94,007	103,774	14,637	118,412
1910	62,350	5,255	67,605	56,203	7,288	63,491	88,291	5,949	94,240	105,724	14,710	120,434
1911	63,408	5,354	68,761	55,867	7,357	63,224	90,135	6,026	96,161	106,863	14,826	121,689
1912	63,409	5,375	68,784	56,888	7,401	64,289	89,111	6,030	95,141	109,341	14,925	124,266
1913	63,506	5,384	68,890	57,569	7,447	65,016	88,630	6,027	94,657	111,820	15,038	126,858
1914	63,882	5,429	69,311	58,216	7,480	65,696	88,767	6,065	94,833	114,062	15,221	129,283
1915	64,048	5,518	69,567	58,906	7,500	66,405	88,690	6,154	94,844	116,384	15,670	132,054
1916	64,075	5,571	69,646	...	...	...	88,519	6,199	94,718	...	...	...

Building 3. *continued*

B. Value of Houses, 1851–1924 (*cont.*)

(in £ thousand)

Years ended 5th April or 31st March	Dwelling Houses						All Premises					
	Charged with Duty			Exempt from Duty			Charged with Duty			Exempt from Duty		
	England & Wales	Scotland	Great Britain	England & Wales	Scotland	Great Britain	England & Wales	Scotland	Great Britain	England & Wales	Scotland	Great Britain
1917	63,887	5,523	69,410	...	...	...	87,834	6,133	93,968	...	...	...
1918	63,149	5,535	68,684	...	...	...	86,734	6,128	92,862	...	...	...
1919	63,246	5,539	68,785	...	...	...	86,536	6,110	92,645	...	...	...
1920	63,256	5,614	68,870	...	...	...	86,460	6,185	92,645	...	...	...
1921	63,228	5,630	68,858	...	...	...	86,554	6,208	92,762	...	...	...
1922	65,158	5,739	70,897	...	...	...	89,582	6,312	95,894	...	...	...
1923	69,556	5,990	75,546	...	...	...	93,597	6,550	100,147	...	...	...
1924	72,281	6,680	78,961	...	...	...	99,677	7,241	106,918	...	...	...

Building 4. Number of Houses at Censuses – United Kingdom 1851–1981

NOTES

[1] Source: *Abstract*, based on the *Census Reports*.

[2] The definition of the term 'house' has changed slightly from time to time. Details can be found in *Guides to Official Sources*, no. 2, and in the general explanatory notes to the housing tables of the censuses.

(in thousands)

	England & Wales	Scotland	Ireland	Northern Ireland
1851	3,432	...	1,111	267
1861	3,924	...	1,036	269
1871	4,520	...	993	267
1881	5,218	799	972	273
1891	5,824	869	940	274
1901	6,710	986	932	291
1911	7,550	1,102	931	291
1921	7,979	1,109		
			Southern Ireland	...
1926	...	...	631	285
1931	9,400	1,197	...	...
1936/7	...	...	648	322
1951	12,389	1,442	680(1946)	346
1961	14,646	1,627	676	387
1966	15,449	1,691	...	419
1971	16,455	1,717	705	455
1981	18,147	1,885	876	...

Building 5. Houses Built – Great Britain 1856–1980

NOTE

SOURCES: 1856–1950 – B. Weber, 'A New Index of Residential Construction 1838–1950', *Scottish Journal of Political Economy*, II, 2 (1955); 1950–80 – *Abstract*, which is used by Weber for 1924–50. For the methods of estimation for 1856–1923 the original source must be consulted.

(in thousands)

1856	52·6	1881	79·1	1906	130·6	1931	210·0	1956	300·6
1857	47·5	1882	81·9	1907	121·3	1932	218·1	1957	300·1
1858	50·9	1883	81·9	1908	100·9	1933	275·2	1958	273·7
1859	44·6	1884	82·4	1909	98·8	1934	336·7	1959	276·7
1860	45·2	1885	76·7	1910	86·0	1935	350·5	1960	297·8
1861	45·2	1886	75·1	1911	67·5	1936	365·0	1961	296·1
1862	58·1	1887	78·7	1912	53·4	1937	362·2	1962	305·4
1863	64·4	1888	79·9	1913	54·2	1938	359·1	1963	298·9
1864	60·9	1889	79·5	1914	48·3	1939	255·6	1964	373·7
1865	53·6	1890	75·8	1915	30·8	1940	95·1	1965	382·3
1866	55·2	1891	79·1	1916	17·0	1941	23·4	1966	385·5
1867	65·3	1892	84·0	1917	...	1942	12·9	1967	404·4
1868	70·4	1893	85·9	1918	...	1943	9·5	1968	413·7
1869	77·0	1894	91·2	1919	...	1944	8·1	1969	366·8
1870	85·9	1895	89·8	1920	29·7	1945	13·8	1970	350·4
1871	90·4	1896	107·1	1921	76·1	1946	138·5	1971	350·6
1872	93·8	1897	130·4	1922	84·5	1947	186·0	1972	319·3
1873	81·7	1898	157·7	1923	66·1	1948	245·9	1973	294·1
1874	90·9	1899	156·2	1924	131·2	1949	197·7	1974	269·5
1875	120·3	1900	139·7	1925	174·2	1950	198·2	1975	313·0
1876	130·8	1901	139·7	1926	222·3	1951	194·8	1976	315·2
1877	124·1	1902	153·8	1927	254·9	1952	239·9	1977	303·3
1878	106·5	1903	156·9	1928	206·8	1953	318·8	1978	279·8
1879	86·0	1904	136·6	1929	212·2	1954	347·8	1979	244·4
1880	83·1	1905	127·4	1930	202·4	1955	317·4	1980	233·7

Building 5a. Parry Lewis's Index of House-building Activity, 1856–1913

NOTES

[1] SOURCE: J. Parry Lewis, *Building Cycles and Britain's Growth* (London, 1965), pp. 316–7.

[2] This index is based on more towns than Weber's estimates shown in table 5 above.

average of 1901–10 = 100

1856	37·2	1868	64·1	1880	75·9	1892	68·0	1903	124·2
1857	33·7	1869	70·1	1881	76·8	1893	76·5	1904	112·0
1858	37·1	1870	75·2	1882	73·1	1894	77·8	1905	112·5
1859	38·8	1871	77·1	1883	74·5	1895	79·9	1906	99·3
1860	37·9	1872	82·0	1884	74·2	1896	94·6	1907	92·2
1861	39·3	1873	75·0	1885	68·3	1897	107·8	1908	81·0
1862	47·6	1874	86·5	1886	65·4	1898	129·8	1909	80·0
1863	52·1	1875	108·0	1887	68·6	1899	129·6	1910	71·3
1864	54·9	1876	123·0	1888	67·3	1900	118·7	1911	60·0
1865	48·7	1877	115·9	1889	66·9	1901	115·7	1912	48·4
1866	51·4	1878	99·4	1890	62·9	1902	121·5	1913	43·1
1867	57·7	1879	80·2	1891	63·6				

Building 6. Houses Built – Ireland 1923–80

NOTES

[1] SOURCES: *Abstract* and *Statistical Abstract of Ireland*.

[2] Statistics for the Republic of Ireland relate to houses built and reconstructed under state-aided schemes.

(in thousands)

	Northern Ireland (*a*)	Republic of Ireland (*a*)		Northern Ireland (*a*)	Republic of Ireland (*a*)		Northern Ireland (*a*)	Republic of Ireland (*a*)
1922		..	1942	—	3·7	1962	8·2	16·8
1923		0·4	1943	..	2·5	1963	8·8	17·5
				... (*a*)				
1924		1·5	1944	...	1·7	1964	9·5	18·3
1925		3·4	1945	0·1	1·3	1965	8·9	19·6
1926		3·7	1946	0·6	1·8	1966	10·5	19·2
1927		2·1	1947	1·2	2·1	1967	11·1	21·9
1928		2·7	1948	4·8	4·2	1968	12·1	22·3
1929		3·4	1949	7·6	9·4	1969	11·5	21·8
1930		3·0	1950	7·3	15·4	1970	11·8	21·7
1931		5·2	1951	7·0	15·0	1971	13·9	23·9
1932		2·2	1952	8·4	16·6	1972	11·7	30·5
1933	...	7·0	1953	8·0	15·4	1973	10·6	33·9
1934	1·4	13·3	1954	6·3	15·4	1974	10·1	[24·2](*a*)
1935	4·2	14·3	1955	7·0	16·3	1975	8·9	35·9
1936	5·5	14·4	1956	7·0	19·1	1976	9·6	36·8
1937	0·7	14·3	1957	6·5	14·6	1977	10·8	28·9
1938	1·3	17·0	1958	4·9	12·1	1978	8·8	35·4
1939	0·4	12·2	1959	4·9	14·2	1979	7·3	44·2
1940	0·4	8·4	1960	6·4	15·5	1980	6·5	35·6
1941	..	6·3	1961	7·1	14·6			

(*a*) Statistics are for years beginning 1 April to 1944 for Northern Ireland and to 1973 for Republic of Ireland. The 1974 figure for the latter is for the 9 months ending 31 December.

Building 7. Local Authority and Private House-Building – United Kingdom 1920–80

NOTES

[1] SOURCE: *Abstract*.

[2] The following categories of houses are not covered by this table: (i) Private houses having a rateable value exceeding £78 (£105 in the Metropolitan Police District) up to 1945; (ii) houses built for government departments; (iii) war-destroyed houses rebuilt; and (iv) temporary houses.

[3] In the *Abstract* before World War II the series were headed 'Built by Local Authorities' and 'Built by Private Enterprise'. These are apparently equivalent to the postwar headings used here.

	Houses Built in England & Wales		Houses Built in Scotland		Houses Built in Northern Ireland	
1 April–31 March	For Local Authorities	For Private Owners	For Local Authorities	For Private Owners	For Local Authorities	For Private Owners
1919/20	576	...	—	...	—	...
1920/1	15,585	...	1,201	...	—	...
1921/2	80,783	...	5,796	...	—	...
1922/3	57,535	...	9,527	...	—	...
1923/4	14,353	71,857	5,233	...	—	...
1924/5	20,624	116,265	3,238	3,638	73	...
1925/6	44,218	129,208	5,290	5,639	882	...
1926/7	74,093	143,536	9,621	7,496	123	...
1927/8	104,034	134,880	16,460	6,137	91	...
1928/9	55,723	113,809	13,954	5,024	198	...
1929/30	60,245	141,815	13,023	5,011	300	...
	---- (*a*)					
1930/1	55,874	127,933	8,122	4,571	144	...
1931/2	70,061	130,751	8,952	4,766	37	...
1932/3	55,991	144,505	12,165	6,596	15	...
1933/4	55,840	210,782	16,503	10,760	20	...
1934/5	41,593	287,513	15,733	6,096	50	1,392
			---- (*b*)		---- (*b*)	
1935/6	52,357	272,503	18,814	7,086	20	4,132
1936/7	71,740	274,313	16,044	7,757	213	5,239
1937/8	77,970	259,632	13,341	8,187	350	355
1938/9	101,744	230,616	19,162	7,311	1,126	207
1939/40	50,452	145,510	19,118	6,411	(169) (*c*)	(96) (*c*)
1940/1	15,408	27,090	10,474	3,732	400	—
1941/2	2,913	5,601	4,714	692	206	—
1942/3	1,378	2,494	3,072	224	—	—
1943/4	2,539	1,079	2,717	92	—	—
1944/5	2,432	1,852	2,383	170	—	10
Calendar Years						
1945	(508) (*d*)	(937) (*d*)	1,428	141	—	21
1946	21,202	29,720	3,811	499	232	347
1947	86,567	39,626	10,773	1,354	688	507
1948	170,821	31,210	19,547	1,541	3,180	1,639
1949	141,766	24,688	24,180	1,102	4,860	2,667
1950	139,356	26,576	24,314	782	4,247	2,882
1951	141,587	21,406	20,997	1,145	3,899	2,934
1952	165,637	32,078	27,623	2,242	5,917	2,350
1953	202,891	60,528	35,992	2,393	6,033	1,946
1954	199,642	88,028	35,331	2,608	4,345	1,787
1955	162,525	109,934	29,278	3,523	4,221	2,636
1956	139,977	119,585	26,290	4,576	4,443	2,270
1957	137,584	122,942	28,326	3,513	3,719	2,329
1958	113,146	124,087	27,373	4,061	2,764	2,072
1959	99,456	146,476	22,709	4,232	2,380	2,458
1960	103,235	162,100	21,503	6,529	3,478	2,776
1961	92,880	170,366	19,541	7,147	3,697	3,214
1962	105,302	167,016	18,788	7,784	4,487	3,411
1963	97,015	168,242	21,164	6,622	5,724	2,923

Building 7. *continued*

Calendar years	Houses Built in England & Wales: For Local Authorities	Houses Built in England & Wales: For Private Owners	Houses Built in Scotland: For Local Authorities	Houses Built in Scotland: For Private Owners	Houses Built in Northern Ireland: For Local Authorities	Houses Built in Northern Ireland: For Private Owners
1964	119,468	210,432	29,156	7,662	6,130	3,170
1965	133,024	206,246	26,584	7,553	5,349	3,363
1966	142,430	197,502	27,515	7,870	6,926	3,275
1967	159,347	192,940	33,222	7,498	7,180	3,770
1968	148,049	213,273	32,011	8,719	7,924	4,075
1969	139,850	173,377	33,932	8,327	7,176	4,213
1970	134,874	162,084	34,360	8,220	7,692	4,038
1971	117,215	179,998	28,577	11,614	9,102	4,701
1972	93,635	184,622	19,593	11,835	7,203	4,298
1973	79,289	174,413	17,349	12,215	5,966	4,452
1974	99,423	129,626	16,182	11,239	5,412	4,312
1975	122,857	140,381	22,784	10,371	4,885	3,776
1976	124,152	138,477	21,154	13,704	6,518	3,048
1977	121,246	128,688	14,328	12,132	7,676	3,085
1978	96,752	134,578	9,907	14,443	5,681	3,145
1979	77,192	125,306	7,853	15,069	3,436	3,574
1980	78,261	114,761	7,448	12,187	2,513	3,568

(*a*) Figures up to this point exclude a small number of houses built by local authorities without state assistance.
(*b*) Subsequent figures are for the calendar year indicated first in the stub.
(*c*) Houses built from 1 April to 31 December 1939.
(*d*) Houses built from 1 April to 31 December 1945.

Building 8. Index of Building Costs – United Kingdom 1845–1938

NOTES

[1] Source: K. Maywald, 'An Index of Building Costs in the United Kingdom', in *E.H.R.* (second series) VII, 2 (1954).

[2] Of the two indices presented in Dr Maywald's article, the one shown here is the more complete one, which includes materials used in roofing, installations and painting.

1930 = 100

	Wages	Materials	Total		Wages	Materials	Total
1845	24·7	78·6	51·7	1892	41·6	56·2	48·9
1846	24·7	83·0	53·9	1893	42·2	54·0	48·1
1847	24·7	80·2	52·5	1894	42·4	52·7	47·5
1848	25·0	75·4	50·2	1895	42·5	51·3	46·9
1849	25·2	70·8	48·0	1896	43·0	52·1	47·5
1850	25·2	69·1	47·2	1897	43·7	53·9	48·8
1851	25·2	68·0	46·6	1898	45·0	57·1	51·1
1852	25·2	69·4	47·3	1899	45·9	61·5	53·7
1853	25·2	80·5	52·9	1900	46·4	67·2	56·8
1854	26·1	82·6	54·3	1901	46·6	65·0	55·8
1855	26·1	81·3	53·7	1902	46·6	58·9	52·7
1856	26·1	75·3	50·7	1903	46·5	55·9	51·2
1857	26·1	77·1	51·6	1904	46·5	53·9	50·2
1858	26·1	74·5	50·3	1905	46·5	53·3	49·9
1859	26·9	72·8	49·8	1906	46·5	56·0	51·2
1860	27·4	72·6	50·0	1907	46·5	59·5	53·0
1861	27·4	70·6	49·0	1908	46·6	55·6	51·1
1862	27·4	69·9	48·6	1909	46·5	54·6	50·6
1863	28·2	71·2	49·7	1910	46·5	57·5	52·0
1864	28·2	72·8	50·5	1911	46·6	61·1	53·9
1865	28·4	71·1	49·7	1912	47·2	65·1	56·2
1866	29·8	73·3	51·6	1913	48·6	66·9	57·8
1867	30·8	70·9	50·8	1914	49·9	67·1	58·5
1868	32·0	68·3	50·1	1915	51·7	89·0	70·4
1869	33·6	68·0	50·8	1916	55·5	108·8	82·2
1870	33·9	69·3	51·6	1917	66·3	122·9	94·6
1871	33·9	71·0	52·4	1918	89·7	145·2	117·5
1872	33·9	80·9	57·4	1919	112·8	179·1	146·0
1873	35·5	90·4	63·0	1920	146·8	196·8	171·8
1874	37·2	84·9	61·0	1921	127·6	153·3	140·5
1875	37·4	76·8	57·1	1922	103·4	123·7	113·6
1876	38·1	73·2	55·7	1923	98·8	114·9	106·9
1877	38·1	71·5	54·8	1924	104·3	117·4	110·9
1878	38·1	66·2	52·2	1925	104·7	117·4	111·1
1879	38·1	63·2	50·7	1926	105·2	110·4	107·8
1880	39·7	67·7	53·7	1927	105·4	106·3	105·9
1881	39·8	64·3	52·0	1928	102·8	100·6	101·7
1882	39·7	65·5	52·6	1929	102·6	101·8	102·2
1883	39·5	63·2	51·4	1930	100·0	100·0	100·0
1884	39·5	59·4	49·4	1931	97·7	94·7	96·2
1885	39·4	58·7	49·1	1932	95·0	88·7	91·8
1886	39·5	56·6	48·0	1933	92·4	87·5	90·0
1887	39·5	55·0	47·3	1934	92·5	87·8	90·2
1888	39·5	55·4	47·4	1935	95·0	89·9	92·0
1889	39·6	58·2	48·9	1936	97·9	93·3	95·6
1890	40·4	60·7	50·6	1937	100·2	100·6	100·4
1891	41·0	58·0	49·5	1938	103·3	101·3	102·3

Building 9. Indices of Construction Costs – Great Britain 1939–80

NOTES

[1] SOURCES: Part A – Building Research Station, *Collection of Construction Statistics* (2nd edition, 1971). Part B – Department of the Environment, *Housing and Construction Statistics*.

[2] In Part B, indices with differing base years have been crudely spliced together.

Part A

(1958–60 = 100)

1939	29	1949	67	1959	99
1940	33	1950	69	1960	101
1941	38	1951	80	1961	106
1942	41	1952	88	1962	110
1943	42	1953	86	1963	113
1944	44	1954	88	1964	118
1945	50	1955	92	1965	124
1946	56	1956	97	1966	130
1947	61	1957	99	1967	136
1948	65	1958	100	1968	142

Part B

(1980 = 100)

1967	17	1972	26	1977	58
1968	18	1973	33	1978	65
1969	19	1974	42	1979	80
1970	20	1975	50	1980	100
1971	22	1976	54		

CHAPTER VIII

MISCELLANEOUS INDUSTRIAL STATISTICS

TABLES

As its title implies, the statistics presented in this chapter are a heterogeneous mixture. Roughly half of the tables are derived from excise duties, with the rest consisting of various indicators of industrial production, together with summary statistics of patents and related matters.

The excise statistics come from the records made by the officials of the quantities of the various commodities concerned which were charged with duty. They were, with the exception of certain allowances for wastage, intended to be records of production; but, of course, there was a premium on evasion, so that they undoubtedly understate the output of all excisable goods. The amount of understatement is, however, undeterminable. It depended on the proportion of tax to price, on the ease of concealment of production, and on the efficiency of the excisemen. It has been possible, however, to make some qualitative assessments of the importance of evasion, largely thanks to the kindness of Selma Fine Goldsmith in placing at our disposal her unpublished thesis.

The efficiency of the excisemen seems to have been exceptionally high in the eighteenth century by the standards of the bureaucracy of that day, and this probably accounts for the particular hatred felt for him by the general public.[1] But the contemporary standards were so low that this statement tells us little about the absolute efficiency of the excise. From 1708 to 1788 none of the officials received an increase in salary, and 'the temptation to accept bribes in order to eke out their existence was strengthened by the increasing inadequacy of their incomes . . .'.[2] Nevertheless, 'the fall in management costs . . . indicates that, despite the low salaries which must have discouraged the employment of honest and skilful officers, a steady improvement in the organization and efficiency of the department took place during the eighteenth century'.[3] Writing of the period 1774–92, Binney says that 'the system of check and counter-check must have gone far to ensure that the duties were accurately assessed'.[4] So far as the surveillance of brewing was concerned, efficiency became high in London early in the eighteenth century, but 'as one moved away from the range of the central organisation, so the standards of conscientiousness and the bonds of discipline relaxed . . .'.[5] There seems to be no reason to suppose that what was true of brewing gaugers was not true of the other excisemen, though perhaps this did not apply in the case of printed cloth. It is likely to have been of particular importance, though, in the case of soap, which was primarily, though not entirely, a London industry until into the second half of the eighteenth century.

The conditions of manufacture prevented much evasion of duty on some of the other excisable goods. This was true of glass,[6] bricks, and, because of the concentration of growing areas, of hops to some extent, though thefts by pickers must have affected this commodity. It may also have been true of printed goods, for only small printers with no regular place of

[1] Selma E. Fine, *Production and Excise in England 1643–1825* (unpublished Radcliffe College thesis), p. 142, says: 'The regulation and close inspection of the excise officers was to be seen on all sides and the excise-gauger became an object of scorn and derision.'

[2] *Ibid.*, p. 158. Increases in 1788 did something to alleviate the trouble, and the large increases of 1800 finally cured it.

[3] *Ibid.*, p. 163.

[4] J. E. D. Binney, *British Public Finance and Administration, 1774–92* (Oxford, 1958), pp. 37–8.

[5] P. Mathias, *The Brewing Industry in England 1700–1830* (Cambridge, 1959), pp. 343–4.

[6] Selma E. Fine, *loc. cit.*, p. 203, says, however, that 'in the early years of the tax . . . there was said to have been a good deal of clandestine manufacture . . . As time progressed the excise regulations were more strictly enforced and the amount of glass which escaped the tax decreased.'

business could easily evade duty.[7] It was certainly true of paper, in the sense that papermakers' equipment was too bulky to avoid the exciseman's eye; but in this case, evasion took a different form. The variety of rates of duty on different types of paper encouraged the makers to classify their products in more lowly rated categories than was strictly correct. By following Coleman's methods, however, it is hoped to avoid this defect in the official published statistics.[8]

The proportion of tax to price was, for most commodities, relatively high, and in nearly all cases it increased during the eighteenth century, as wars had to be paid for. This naturally raised the premium on evasion, but it seems likely that this was counterbalanced by the increasing efficiency of the officials.[9] The only commodity on which the tax was so light that evasion was scarcely worthwhile was bricks, shown in table 1 of chapter VII.

The conditions of manufacture were not always a hindrance to tax-evasion, however, and in the case of candles, starch, and malt they were virtually an incentive to fraud. These three commodities, together with spirits, seem to have been the ones for which evasion of duty was most common, though it was also appreciable for soap. The processes of manufacture of candles and of starch were both short,[10] and the rates of duty were relatively high. Both series definitely understate the true output, but the degree of understatement for candles at least appears to have been fairly constant, and, according to Fine, 'we can safely use the series for candles as an indication of the movements of the production of that commodity, though the actual output may have been very much larger'.[11] For starch, however, the series does not reflect output accurately, at least for the period 1714–40, when the downward trend is partially explained by an increase in illicit manufacture.[12]

The process of manufacture of malt was not particularly short, but this industry was carried on almost entirely in the countryside, where supervision was difficult, and Mathias notes that 'the reported annual production of malt in the British Isles may underestimate the actual quantities ... by as much as a quarter, even at the end of the eighteenth century'.[13] English production of spirits was mainly concentrated in London, where close supervision no doubt limited the opportunities for evasion. But in Scotland and Ireland the stills were scattered throughout the country, so that opportunities were generally good. Moreover, the inclination to outwit the exciseman was much stronger in these disaffected regions. We have no means of knowing how successful the people of these parts were in the eighteenth century; but judged by the enormous increase in the quantity charged with duty which accompanied

[7] This is implied in A. P. Wadsworth and Julia de L. Mann, *The Cotton Trade and Industrial Lancashire 1600–1780* (Manchester, 1931), pp. 135–44. It is confirmed, but with important qualification, by Selma E. Fine, *loc. cit.*, p. 212, where she writes: 'Not many printing firms escaped the excise, but there is evidence that certain printers were able to defraud the revenue by failing to report the true amount of the material they had printed.'

[8] D. C. Coleman, *The British Paper Industry 1495–1860* (Oxford, 1958), p. 346.

[9] P. Mathias, *op. cit.*, p. 370.

[10] Selma E. Fine, *loc. cit.*, pp. 216–17 and 225.

[11] *Ibid.*, p. 219.

[12] *Ibid.*, p. 225.

[13] P. Mathias, *op. cit.*, p. 343.

the reduction in rates in 1823, illicit manufacture must have been very great, and can scarcely have been much less than half the total output.[14]

The earliest supposedly comprehensive production statistics not directly related to taxation were those of shipbuilding, which are shown as tables 15 and 16. These began with an Act of 1786. They are not wholly complete, though the series for the British Empire as a whole is only lacking the years 1812 and 1813, when records were lost in the Customs House fire. However, it should be noted that they are not a full record of shipbuilding, since vessels sold to foreigners and not put on the British register were not included. It is doubtful if this was of much significance. The main problem in using the shipbuilding statistics is caused by changes in the method of reckoning tonnage. This is discussed fully in the introduction to chapter X. It is perhaps needless to say that the value of ships built is not necessarily reflected in the tonnage figures.

The modern production series, shown in tables 13, 14, 17, and 18 do not call for any particular comment. They are, of course, only a very small selection from what is available in official publications.

Tables 19 and 20 summarise the principal aggregate statistics of the Censuses of Production of the United Kingdom and the Republic of Ireland respectively. The Census reports themselves give a very great deal more detail, of course, including figures of numbers employed and of power used, as well as many more disaggregated statistics of gross and net value of output. The main problem in using them is that of comparability between them, at least in the earlier years. The compilers did generally try to overcome this to some extent by revaluing each census in terms of the categories etc. used in its successor; but some difficulties remain, nevertheless, and these are mentioned in the notes to the tables.

There follow in table 21 various composite indices of industrial production which require comment. The Hoffman aggregate index, which is given here for its entire period, is well known and has been subjected to much criticism.[15] This seemed to be so cogent, especially so far as the eighteenth century was concerned, that, when the first version of this volume was produced, the values of the index prior to 1800 were omitted. However, it now appears that the index is no less subject to criticism so far as the nineteenth century is concerned; and, indeed, it may be doubted whether it can be used safely at all. Apart from criticisms of its coverage, the fact that so many of its components relate to raw materials inputs rather than

[14] In 1823 the rates were reduced by 2*s*. 4¾*d*. per gallon from 5*s*. 7½*d*. in Ireland and 6*s*. 2*d*. in Scotland, and this reduction was followed by a campaign to suppress illicit distilling, which, in Scotland at least, was almost entirely successful. The increase in the quantity charged with duty is easily apparent in table 5. Taking averages of the years ended 5 January 1819–1823 and 1825–1829, it rose by 132 per cent in Scotland and 134 per cent in Ireland, and these compare with 33 per cent in England. If McCulloch (*Dictionary of Commerce* (London, 1847), vol. II, p. 1168) was right in saying that 'consumption ... was not in any degree increased ...', then the proportion evading duty before 1823 must have been well over half. Even allowing for some increase in demand resulting from the fall in price of legally distilled spirits, the proportion was evidently very high.

[15] See, for example, the reviews by Phyllis Deane in *Economic Journal*, LXVI (1956), pp. 25–48; by J. R. Meyer in *Explorations in Entrepreneurial History*, VII (1956), pp. 172–6; and by J. F. Wright in *Journal of Economic History*, XVI (1956), pp. 356–64; and also W. A. Cole, 'The Measurement of Industrial Growth', *Economic History Review*, second series XI, 2 (1958), pp. 309–15.

to outputs implies that a great deal of the growth of industrial production is omitted when such growth takes the form of increasing value added per unit of input. This clearly happened in the nineteenth century as well as the eighteenth; probably, indeed, to an increasing extent as the century went on. So the Hoffman index is shown here rather as an historical curiosity than as one which ought now to be used. It has featured in so many works published since the mid 1950s, however, that it seemed worthwhile to reproduce it for its historiographical significance.

For the period since 1855 the Feinstein index (which is a refinement of earlier indices by Lomax and by Lewis,[16] as well as Hoffman's) is available. This is designed to avoid the inadequacies of Hoffman's index, so far as that is possible: allowance is made, for example, for improvements in the quality (or value-added) of industrial output. This index may be readily spliced on to subsequent official indices. Prior to 1855, however, there is no satisfactory substitute for Hoffman. Instead, a range of more limited indicators of the growth of industrial production is shown – indicators which relate to individual benchmark years rather than forming a continuous series. Clearly, they must be regarded as tentative and provisional.

The statistics of patents granted, given in table 23, together with those for the Republic of Ireland in table 25, and the associated figures of trade marks and designs, are not production series, but seem to fit more appropriately into this chapter than anywhere else. Table 23 is divided into two parts by the major break in 1852, when the change in the law resulted in a quadrupling of the numbers, and when the statistics of applications become available. The change effected by the Act of 1883 was, however, very nearly as startling. With the exception of these two breaks, the statistics of patents provide a series which permits comparisons over long periods. It must be remembered, however, that the number of patents granted by most of the Stuart monarchs bore more relation to their financial needs than to the progress of invention. In fact it is probably true to say that this series has little significance for economic history until about the middle of the eighteenth century.

[16] K. S. Lomax, 'Production and Productivity Movements in the United Kingdom since 1900', *Journal of the Royal Statistical Society*, CXXII (1959). Lewis's index was not published except in mimeograph form.

Miscellaneous Industrial Statistics 1. Malt Charged with Duty – England & Wales 1702–1880, Scotland 1770–1880, and Ireland 1785–1880

NOTE
SOURCES: 1702–1869 – *S.P.* 1870, XX; 1870–80 – *S.P.*, 1884–5, XXII.

(in million Imperial bushels)
England & Wales

1702 (*a*)	12·2	1725	27·3	1748	26·4
1703	26·8	1726	27·0	1749	25·0
1704	19·8	1727	25·4	1750	29·3
1705	27·1	1728	21·0	1751	27·0
1706	23·1	1729	23·0	1752	24·3
1707	25·0	1730	28·4	1753 (*b*)	25·2
1708	23·2	1731	25·8	1754	27·3
1709	20·3	1732	27·0	1755	27·9
1710	19·7	1733	29·8	1756	24·1
1711	22·3	1734	27·1	1757	17·6
1712	22·3	1735	25·5	1758	25·0
1713	25·1	1736	23·7	1759	28·1
1714	20·0	1737	24·5	1760	27·8
1715	24·5	1738	26·1	1761	28·9
1716	26·6	1739	26·7	1762	26·0
1717	28·9	1740	22·1	1763	19·6
1718	26·9	1741	20·1	1764	26·3
1719	28·2	1742	25·9	1765	25·6
1720	25·6	1743	26·3	1766	20·8
1721	28·6	1744	31·8	1767	21·9
1722	33·0	1745	24·9	1768	27·1
1723	30·7	1746	24·0	1769	26·5
1724	24·2	1747	24·9		

	England & Wales	Scotland	Ireland		England & Wales	Scotland	Ireland
1770	24·5	1·8	...	1795	24·0	1·7	4·7
1771	22·0	1·7	...	1796	27·3	1·2	5·0
1772	27·5	1·7	...	1797	30·0	2·1	4·7
1773	21·5	1·5	...	1798	26·1	1·9	4·4
1774	24·0	1·4	...	1799	30·8	2·4	3·3
1775	25·0	1·4	...	1800	14·1	0·9	0·7
1776	23·3	1·6	...	1801	18·0	0·6	1·0
1777	25·8	1·8	...	1802	29·4	1·7	3·6
1778	26·3	1·9	...	1803	29·6	1·6	3·6
1779	26·3	2·0	...	1804	21·9	1·1	2·8
1780	30·8	2·2	...	1805	21·7	1·1	2·8
1781	26·7	1·9	...	1806	26·7	1·2	2·8
1782	27·2	2·0	...	1807	24·2	1·3	2·4
1783	16·7	1·1	...	1808	21·7	1·0	2·6
1784	25·8	1·8	...	1809	22·1	0·8	3·0
1785	26·3	1·7	4·4	1810	23·5	0·8	2·5
1786	22·1	1·6	3·5	1811	26·0	1·0	2·7
1787	26·4	1·7	3·7	1812	18·1	0·9	2·2
1788	26·0	1·7	3·9	1813	21·7	0·7	3·0
1789	23·5	1·6	3·6	1814	25·3	1·3	3·2
1790	22·0	1·5	4·6	1815	26·2	1·3	2·7
1791	27·1	1·7	4·8	1816	21·2	1·2	1·9
1792	27·8	2·0	4·7	1817	20·9	1·1	1·4
1793	23·7	1·7	5·6	1818	24·6	1·4	1·8
1794	24·8	1·7	4·9	1819	22·6	1·5	1·7

Miscellaneous Industrial Statistics 1. *continued*

(in million Imperial bushels)

	England & Wales	Scotland	Ireland		England & Wales	Scotland	Ireland
1820	23·9	1·2	1·8	1850	34·4	4·6	1·7
1821	26·1	1·3	1·9	1851	34·6	4·1	1·6
1822	26·7	1·4	1·8	1852	35·5	3·9	1·7
1823	24·8	1·6	1·7	1853	36·2	4·2	1·6
1824	27·6	2·8	2·1	1855(*d*)	30·6	3·2	1·4
					---	--	--
1825	29·6	3·9	2·7	1856	30·7 (*e*)	1·6 (*e*)	1·2 (*e*)
1826(*c*)	27·3	2·7	2·4	1857	36·3	1·1	1·7
1827	25·1	2·7	1·8	1858	38·0	1·3	1·8
1828	30·5	3·9	2·4	1859	39·1	1·5	2·2
1829	23·4	3·7	2·0	1860	40·7	1·6	2·2
1830	26·9	4·1	2·0	1861	33·7	1·6	2·1
1831	33·0	4·2	2·1	1862	41·3	1·7	2·5
1832	31·7	3·7	2·0	1863	37·4	1·7	1·9
1833	33·8	4·3	2·0	1864	43·6	2·0	2·4
1834	34·5	4·5	2·2	1865	44·0	2·1	2·5
1835	36·1	4·5	2·4	1866	45·2	2·5	2·5
1836	37·2	4·9	2·3	1867	46·0	2·5	2·4
1837	33·7	4·6	2·3	1868	43·6	2·4	2·5
1838	33·8	4·4	2·3	1869	44·4	2·4	2·8
1839	33·8	4·4	1·7	1870	45·4	2·4	3·0
1840	36·7	4·4	1·4	1871	47·1	2·7	3·2
1841	30·8	4·1	1·2	1872	46·3	2·8	2·9
1842	30·8	3·8	1·3	1873	51·5	3·0	2·7
1843	30·9	3·6	1·2	1874	52·9	3·2	3·4
1844	31·9	3·9	1·4	1875	53·7	2·8	3·2
1845	30·5	4·4	1·7	1876	52·9	2·8	3·3
1846	35·7	4·6	1·8	1877	54·2	3·0	3·3
1847	30·3	3·7	1·4	1878	52·2	2·9	3·1
1848	31·8	4·0	1·7	1879	51·6	3·1	3·4
1849	33·2	4·2	1·6	1880	44·9	2·6	2·9

(*a*) The date for the years' end is not given in the source, but from accounts in the Customs and Excise Library it appears that it was 24th June up to 1752.
(*b*) Years ended 5th July henceforth to 1825. Mr R. C. Jarvis of H.M. Customs and Excise Library points out that our source is defective in not noting this change.
(*c*) Years ended on 5th January of the year following that stated henceforth to 1853.
(*d*) Years ended 31st March henceforth.
(*e*) From August 1855 malt for distillery purposes was not charged with duty. This change had virtually no effect in England & Wales, but was of great importance in Scotland, and moderately important in Ireland.

Miscellaneous Industrial Statistics 2. Hops Charged with Duty – England 1712–1862

NOTE
SOURCE: *S.P.* 1870, xx.

(in million lb.)

Year		Year		Year	
1712 (*a*)	12·1	1763	19·0	1813	6·4
1713	7·3	1764	21·2	1814	27·4
1714	5·5	1765	4·1	1815	29·3
1715	3·5	1766	17·8	1816	25·9
1716	10·8	1767	28·0	1817	9·7
1717	4·9	1768	6·2	1818	13·9
1718	13·1	1769	27·4	1819	41·6
1719	3·6	1770	3·9	1820	50·5
1720	21·7	1771	24·3	1821	28·9
1721	9·2	1772	8·0	1822	31·8
1722	14·8	1773	24·6	1823	42·5
1723	11·9	1774	11·0	1824	5·4
1724	7·3	1775	33·3	1825	31·2
1725	14·7	1776	10·0	1826 (*c*)	(5·1)
1726	1·6	1777	30·2	1827	57·2
1727	20·4	1778	10·5	1828	29·4
1728	16·7	1779	38·4	1829	35·9
1729	10·0	1780	12·7	1830	8·0
1730	11·6	1781	27·9	1831	18·5
1731	10·6	1782	25·9	1832	36·5
1732	5·6	1783	3·1	1833	29·0
1733	8·4	1784	15·8	1834	32·7
1734	16·9	1785	19·7	1835	39·6
1735	9·0	1786	23·5	1836	49·1
1736	10·3	1787	20·0	1837	41·9
1737	11·1	1788	8·8	1838	37·3
1738	13·6	1789	30·0	1839	35·8
1739	21·0	1790	21·2	1840	42·9
1740	17·0	1791	22·3	1841	7·1
1741	9·1	1792	18·9	1842	30·5
1742	18·0	1793	33·9	1843	35·4
1743	10·9	1794	5·0	1844	27·9
1744	15·3	1795	42·5	1845	29·3
1745	11·2	1796	17·2	1846	33·0
1746	8·3	1797	15·7	1847	50·7
1747	22·1	1798	32·9	1848	45·1
1748	15·2	1799	11·8	1849	44·3
1749	21·0	1800	15·3	1850	16·7
1750	8·7	1801	15·2	1851	48·5
1751	17·3	1802	50·4	1852	27·0
1752	17·8	1803	3·2	1853	51·1
1753	19·7 (*b*)	1804	41·3	1854	31·8
1754	21·9	1805	37·1	1855	9·9
1755	27·0	1806	6·9	1856	83·2
1756	19·8	1807	32·0	1857	55·9
1757	11·5	1808	20·9	1858	47·7
1758	16·7	1809	52·6	1859	53·1
1759	17·5	1810	13·4	1860	68·5
1760	10·1	1811	15·3	1861	11·2
1761	28·4	1812	32·8	1862	24·0
1762	19·6				

(*a*) Years ended 24th June henceforth to 1752. The figure for 1712 is for the period beginning 1st June 1711.
(*b*) Years ended 5th July henceforth to 1825. R. C. Jarvis of H.M. Customs and Excise Library pointed out that our source is defective in not noting this change.
(*c*) Years ended 5th January henceforth. The figure for 1826 is for 6 months only.

Miscellaneous Industrial Statistics 3. Beer Charged with Duty – England & Wales 1684–1830, and Scotland 1787–1830

NOTES

[1] Sources: 1684–1828 – MS. Account in the Customs and Excise Library; 1829–30 – *S.P.* 1830, XXII.

[2] The barrel was reckoned at 36 gallons for strong and small beer and 32 gallons for ale in London. Elsewhere it was 34 gallons for all malt liquor.

[3] Various allowances were made for wastage before 5th January 1826, at which time they amounted to one-twelfth of output. For a full account of these, see P. Mathias, *The Brewing Industry in England, 1700–1830* (Cambridge, 1959).

[4] From 1825 the following small amounts of intermediate beer were charged with duty in England (in thousand barrels):

Year ended 5 July 1825	10	Year ended 5 Jan. 1828	17
Year ended 5 July 1826	6	Year ended 5 Jan. 1829	63
Year ended 5 Jan. 1826	6	Year ended 5 Jan. 1830	55
Year ended 5 Jan. 1827	8		

A. England & Wales

(in thousand barrels)

	Strong Beer	Small Beer		Strong Beer	Small Beer		Strong Beer	Small Beer
1684 (*a*)	4,384	1,934	1717	3,596	2,085	1750	3,736	2,056
1685	4,655	2,102	1718	3,716	2,165	1751	3,773	2,060
1686	4,780	2,255	1719	3,801	2,256	1752	3,771	1,966
1687	5,044	2,435	1720	3,788	2,277	1753 (*b*)	3,762	1,948
1688	4,989	2,544	1721	3,736	2,180	1754	3,733	1,934
1689	5,134	2,708	1722	3,795	2,196	1755	3,694	1,915
1690	4,691	2,646	1723	3,853	2,252	1756	3,780	1,976
1691	4,070	2,375	1724	3,874	2,313	1757	3,497	1,937
1692	3,797	2,379	1725	3,797	2,187	1758	3,717	1,877
1693	3,529	2,386	1726	3,642	2,205	1759	3,908	1,834
1694	3,505	2,466	1727	3,704	2,213	1760	4,137	1,992
1695	3,344	2,212	1728	3,443	2,166	1761	4,062	1,973
1696	3,680	2,389	1729	3,310	2,044	1762	3,805	1,972
1697	3,258	2,162	1730	3,533	2,081	1763	3,759	1,848
1698	3,097	2,007	1731	3,645	2,112	1764	3,824	1,796
1699	2,973	1,921	1732	3,704	2,184	1765	3,690	1,746
1700	3,152	1,971	1733	3,690	2,181	1766	3,682	1,800
1701	3,364	2,082	1734	3,679	2,153	1767	3,625	1,745
1702	3,721	2,319	1735	3,525	2,104	1768	3,731	1,741
1703	3,649	2,278	1736	3,552	2,111	1769	3,791	1,690
1704	3,763	2,335	1737	3,613	2,073	1770	3,783	1,702
1705	3,807	2,333	1738	3,531	2,015	1771	3,767	1,733
1706	3,630	2,214	1739	3,604	2,080	1772	3,791	1,695
1707	3,654	2,225	1740	3,515	2,085	1773	3,804	1,717
1708	3,566	2,155	1741	3,295	1,985	1774	3,601	1,676
1709	3,357	2,066	1742	3,458	2,083	1775	3,863	1,616
1710	3,217	1,984	1743	3,469	2,021	1776	3,959	1,677
1711	3,154	1,972	1744	3,601	2,042	1777	4,107	1,625
1712	3,143	1,926	1745	3,479	1,972	1778	4,130	1,709
1713	3,300	1,938	1746	3,416	2,035	1779	4,197	1,798
1714	3,415	2,001	1747	3,580	2,009	1780	4,355	1,881
1715	3,434	2,035	1748	3,621	2,086	1781	4,343	1,825
1716	3,486	2,013	1749	3,707	2,011	1782	4,525	1,908

A. England & Wales (*cont.*)

(in thousand barrels)

	Strong Beer	Small Beer	Table Beer		Strong Beer	Table Beer
1783	3,914	1,325	452	1808	5,571	1,710
1784	4,336	1,306	468	1809	5,513	1,683
1785	4,329	1,244	447	1810	5,753	1,636
1786	4,147	1,276	462	1811	5,903	1,650
1787	4,426	1,342	486	1812	5,861	1,593
1788	4,305	1,335	524	1813	5,383	1,456
1789	4,438	1,244	515	1814	5,624	1,433
1790	4,526	1,282	546	1815	6,151	1,518
1791	4,755	1,347	580	1816	5,982	1,515
1792	5,082	1,402	625	1817	5,236	1,454
1793	5,168	1,414	620	1818	5,364	1,435
1794	5,011	1,447	587	1819	5,629	1,460
1795	5,038	1,453	576	1820	5,297	1,444
1796	5,504	1,479	566	1821	5,576	1,440
1797	5,840	1,519	584	1822	5,713	1,492
1798	5,784	1,548	622	1823	6,177	1,420
1799	5,774	1,597	611	1824	6,188	1,401
1800	4,824	1,361	575	1825	6,501	1,486
1801	4,736	1,192	500	1826	6,641	1,572
1802	5,346	977	392	1826 (*d*)	7,008	1,607
1703	5,583	...	(1,661)(*c*)	1827	6,690	1,605
1804	5,266	...	1,780	1828	6,395	1,532
1805	5,412	...	1,777	1829	6,559	1,531
1806	5,444	...	1,772	1830	5,949	1,380
1807	5,577	...	1,733			

B. Scotland

	Strong Beer	Small Beer	Table Beer	Twopenny Ale		Strong Beer	Small Beer	Table Beer	Twopenny Ale
1787 (*b*)	24	108	...	114	1810	127	...	227	...
1788	23	115	...	119	1811	120	...	230	...
1789	34	121	...	116	1812	121	...	222	...
1790	43	136	...	122	1813	116	...	199	...
1791	43	139	...	124	1814	133	...	206	...
1792	47	160	...	145	1815	135	...	222	...
1793	48	172	...	158	1816	127	...	222	...
1794	40	154	...	139	1817	111	...	206	...
1795	40	156	...	139	1818	109	...	192	...
1796	78	178	...	150	1819	124	...	209	...
1797	88	168	...	165	1820	116	...	207	...
1798	77	179	...	171	1821	123	...	206	...
1799	84	184	...	169	1822	125	...	224	...
1800	75	161	...	150	1823	124	...	222	...
1801	73	162	...	102	1824	114	...	229	...
1802	94	95	41	87	1825	124	...	244	...
1803	106	...	249	...	1826	132	...	275	...
1804	93	...	230	...	1826 (*d*)	134	...	264	...
1805	105	...	221	...	1827	122	...	271	...
1806	119	...	230	...	1828	112	...	241	...
1807	121	...	234	...	1829	119	...	247	...
1808	114	...	234	...	1830	111	...	229	...
1809	118	...	221	...					

(*a*) Years ended 24th June henceforth to 1752.
(*b*) Years ended 5th July henceforth to 1825.
(*c*) Small beer merged with table beer.
(*d*) Years ended 5th January in the year following that shown henceforth.

Miscellaneous Industrial Statistics 4. Beer Charged with Duty – United Kingdom, 1881–1980 and Republic of Ireland 1923–80

NOTES

[1] SOURCES: to 1903 – *Annual Report of the Commissioners of Inland Revenue*; from 1904 – *Annual Report of the Commissioners of Customs and Excise*, and *Annual Report of the Revenue Commissioners of Saorstat Eirean*.

[2] The figures relate to 'standard' barrels to 1900 (1st line) and to 'bulk' barrels less 6% allowance for wastage subsequently. The figures for Ireland are in 'standard' barrels throughout. The 'standard' barrel represented the amount in 'bulk' (or liquid) barrels which would have been produced if it had been at a standard gravity of 1057° initially and 1055° from the mid-1880s.

[3] Except as indicated in footnotes (*a*) and (*e*), the figures are for years beginning 1 April.

(in million barrels of 36 gallons)

	U.K.		U.K.	Republic of Ireland		U.K.	Republic of Ireland
1880	[14·0] (*a*)	1914	36·3	...	1948	27·0	1·6
1881	27·9	1915	37·6	...	1949	26·5	1·8
1882	27·1	1916	30·2	...	1950	24·9	1·8
1883	27·8	1917	19·1	...	1951	25·2	1·9
1884	28·0	1918	23·3	...	1952	24·9	1·8
1885	27·2	1919	35·0	...	1953	24·6	1·8
1886	27·9	1920	34·5	...	1954	23·9	1·9
1887	28·2	1921	30·2 --- (*c*)	...	1955	24·6	2·0
1888	28·6	1922	23·9	2·4	1956	24·5	2·0
1889	30·9	1923	25·4	2·4	1957	24·6	1·9
1890	31·9	1924	26·8	2·4	1958	23·8	1·9
1891	32·2	1925	26·8	2·3	1959	26·1	2·0
1892	32·1	1926	25·2	2·2	1960	27·1	2·0
1893	32·2	1927	25·4	2·1	1961	27·5	2·1
1894	31·7	1928	24·6	[2·0] (*d*)	1962	27·8	2·0
1895	33·8	1929	25·1	2·3	1963	29·0	2·0
1896	34·2	1930	23·9	2·1	1964	29·5	2·1
1897	35·6	1931	20·8	1·9	1965	30·0	2·0
1898	36·5	1932	18·0	1·7	1966	30·4	2·0
1899	37·1	1933	20·2	1·8	1967	30·5	2·1
1900	36·4 --- (*b*) 39·6	1934	20·9	1·8	1968	31·6	2·2
1901	36·9	1935	22·0	1·9	1969	32·9	2·2
1902	37·2	1936	22·7	1·8	1970	34·4	2·3
1903	36·3	1937	24·2	1·7	1971	35·0	2·5
1904	35·4	1938	24·7	1·4	1972	35·3	2·4
1905	35·1	1939	25·4	1·4	1973	37·9	2·7
1906	35·4	1940	26·2	1·3	1974	38·2	[2·0] (*e*)
1907	35·4	1941	29·9	1·5	1975	39·1	2·6
1908	34·4	1942	29·3	1·3	1976	39·6	2·5
1909	34·3	1943	30·5	1·2	1977	39·2	2·5
1910	34·9	1944	31·3	1·5	1978	38·8	2·6
1911	36·5	1945	32·7	1·7	1979	39·1	2·7
1912	34·9	1946	29·3	1·5	1980	37·3	2·7
1913	36·5	1947	30·4	1·5			

(*a*) Six months beginning 1 October.
(*b*) See note 2 above.
(*c*) Subsequently excluding southern Ireland.
(*d*) Owing to a reduction in the period of credit, 13 months are included in this figure.
(*e*) April–December only. Subsequent figures are for calendar years.

Miscellaneous Industrial Statistics 5. Home-produced Spirits Charged with Duty for Consumption – 1684–1980

NOTES

[1] SOURCES: United Kingdom – *S.P.* 1870, xx, *S.P.* 1884–5, xxii, and subsequent *Annual Report of the Commissioners of Inland Revenue* and *Annual Report of the Commissioners of Customs and Excise*. The country figures for 1961–5 were kindly supplied by the Statistical Office of the Board of Customs and Excise, Republic of Ireland – *Annual Report of the Revenue Commissioners of Saorstat Eirean*.

[2] This account refers to potable spirits, and relates to the amounts released for consumption in each country.

[3] Spirits granted rebate for medical or scientific use are included, but spirits delivered for redistillation, methylation, use in art or manufacture, or in fortifying wines are not.

(in thousand proof gallons)

	England & Wales	Scotland	Ireland		England & Wales	Scotland	Ireland
1684 (*a*)	527	...	...	1734	6,075	204	209
1685	594	...	...	1735	6,440	225	196
1686	468	...	...	1736	6,116	524	229
1687	516	...	...	1737	4,250	538	217
1688	559	...	...	1738	5,439	412	211
1689	570	...	...	1739	5,763	411	240
1690	544	...	...	1740	6,651	261	248
1691	659	...	...	1741	7,439	352	272
1692	849	...	...	1742	7,955	404	354
1693	948	...	...	1743	8,203	360	402
1694	810	...	...	1744	6,627	591	452
1695	968	...	...	1745	7,200	598	334
1696	1,104	...	...	1746	6,865	512	402
1697	828	...	...	1747	7,310	522	531
1698	846	...	...	1748	7,082	569	565
1699	877	...	...	1749	6,671	575	599
1700	1,233	...	...	1750	6,613	776	598
1701	1,271	...	...	1751	7,050	849	596
1702	1,073	...	...	1752	4,483	839	623
1703	1,146	...	...	1754(*b*)	4,869	731	561
1704	1,375	...	...	1755	5,051	653	498
1705	1,438	...	...	1756	4,652	674	480
1706	1,675	...	...	1757	4,679	459	404
1707	1,974	...	...	1758	3,714	105	400
1708	1,717	...	...	1759	1,849	68	108
1709	1,738	...	...	1760	1,819	55	225
1710	2,201	...	...	1761	2,323	75	432
1711	2,233	...	...	1762	3,181	59	693
1712	2,067	...	...	1763	2,296	48	668
1713	2,049	...	...	1764	2,272	51	661
1714	1,951	...	...	1765	2,220	54	715
1715	2,266	...	...	1766	2,227	54	649
1716	2,381	...	...	1767	2,431	54	355
1717	2,596	...	...	1768	2,043	70	658
1718	2,418	...	174	1769	2,207	83	831
1719	2,464	...	136	1770	2,549	70	801
1720	2,483	...	131	1771	2,570	69	734
1721	2,793	...	125	1772	2,495	76	759
1722	3,380	...	134	1773	2,583	73	960
1723	3,703	...	133	1774	2,224	70	1,026
1724	3,564	146	134	1775	2,010	72	980
1725	3,926	221	169	1776	2,515	72	1,160
1726	3,981	275	219	1777	2,519	73	1,115
1727	4,612	252	155	1778	2,507	106	1,127
1728	4,793	191	129	1779	2,956	144	1,094
1729	4,728	186	135	1780	2,639	189	1,229
1730	3,778	209	175	1781	2,292	194	1,753
1731	4,334	213	184	1782	2,114	196	2,037
1732	4,374	227	226	1783	1,942	337	1,738
1733	4,824	237	268	1784	1,228	171	1,409

See p. 410 for footnotes.

Miscellaneous Industrial Statistics 5. *continued*

(in thousand proof gallons)

	England & Wales	Scotland	Ireland		England & Wales	Scotland	Ireland
1785	1,338	239	1,423	1840	8,187	6,189	10,816
1786	2,743	489	1,814	1841	8,278	6,180	7,401
1787	3,695	825	1,923	1842	8,167	5,990	6,485
1788	3,561	...	2,187	1843	7,956	5,595	5,291
1789	3,670	...	2,748	1844	7,724	5,594	5,546
1790	3,909	...	2,871	1845	8,234	5,923	6,451
1791	3,858	...	3,442	1846	9,076	6,441	7,605
1792	4,073	...	3,417	1847	9,180	6,975	7,952
1793	4,545	...	3,344	1848	8,409	6,193	6,037
1794	4,244	...	3,834	1849	8,581	6,548	7,073
1795	4,595	...	4,154	1850	9,054	6,935	6,973
1796	4,712	...	3,612	1851	9,332	7,123	7,408
1797	301	...	3,788	1852	9,595	6,831	7,551
1798	2,809	...	4,694	1853	9,821	7,172	8,208
1799	3,631	...	4,173	1854	10,350	6,535	8,136
1800	4,115	1,670	3,554	1855 (*c*)	10,852	6,009	8,037
1801	4,353	1,278	1,331	1856	10,123	5,637	6,509
1802	2,556	296	355	1857	11,386	5,368	6,807
1803	3,981	1,159	4,715	1858	11,634	5,575	6,783
1804	5,370	2,022	4,343	1859	11,860	5,325	5,418
1805	3,691	1,190	3,544	1860	12,904	5,581	5,950
1806	4,933	1,626	3,686	1861	11,198	4,250	4,192
1807	4,095	1,812	3,858	1862	10,728	4,417	4,190
1808	4,747	2,653	5,597	1863	10,482	4,511	3,892
1809	5,391	2,683	3,575	1864	10,721	4,769	3,934
1810	4,036	1,315	1,360	1865	11,197	5,030	4,157
1811	4,788	1,748	4,729	1866	11,258	5,203	4,518
1812	4,776	1,951	6,378	1867	11,591	5,452	5,103
1813	5,242	1,688	4,009	1868	11,562	4,781	4,677
1814	4,292	1,234	3,159	1869	11,239	5,027	4,842
1815	4,957	1,474	5,394	1870	11,592	5,364	5,025
1816	5,469	1,591	4,324	1871	12,191	5,557	5,213
1817	4,745	919	3,557	1872	13,036	5,802	5,750
1818	4,133	1,907	3,587	1873	14,856	6,610	6,091
1819	5,260	2,067	4,284	1874	16,222	6,910	6,177
1820	4,147	2,125	3,677	1875	16,737	6,990	6,094
1821	4,285	1,864	3,300	1876	16,749	6,856	6,697
1822	4,126	2,385	3,311	1877	16,415	7,006	6,381
1823	4,694	2,225	2,910	1878	17,027	7,142	6,115
1824	3,803	2,303	3,590	1879	16,518	6,409	6,008
1825	4,393	4,350	6,690	1880	16,125	6,086	5,075
1826	3,684	5,982	9,263	1881	17,200	6,394	5,185
1827	7,407	3,989	6,834	1882	16,950	6,542	5,132
1828	6,672	4,752	8,261	1883	16,656	6,496	5,377
1829	7,760	5,716	9,938	1884	16,536	6,708	5,304
1830	7,701	5,777	9,212	1885	16,323	6,629	5,069
1831	7,732	6,008	9,005	1886	15,291	6,297	4,755
1832	7,434	5,701	8,711	1887	14,702	6,122	4,927
1833	7,282	5,407	8,658	1888	15,139	6,024	4,954
1834	7,717	5,989	8,169		----	----	----
				1889	15,843 (*d*)	5,769 (*d*)	4,224 (*d*)
1835	7,644	6,045	9,708				
1836	7,315	6,014	11,381	1890	16,854	6,264	4,711
1837	7,876	6,621	12,249	1891	18,459	6,550	4,821
1838	7,134	6,124	11,236		----	----	---
1839	7,930	6,260	12,296	1892	20,127 (*d*)	6,938 (*d*)	4,405 (*d*)

See p. 410 for footnotes.

(in thousand proof gallons)

	England & Wales	Scotland	Ireland		England & Wales	Scotland	Ireland
1893	19,935	6,446	4,280	1908	21,916	6,956	3,635
1894	19,765	6,422	4,265	1909	21,827	6,661	3,563
1895	19,232	6,019	4,040	1910	14,537	4,559	2,351
1896	20,376	6,490	4,222	1911	17,485	5,053	2,776
1897	21,297	6,622	4,207	1912	17,106	5,539	2,729
1898	21,982	6,760	4,157	1913	16,935	5,709	2,643
1899	23,146	7,079	4,110	1914	17,891	6,173	2,731
1900	25,623	8,380	4,713	1915	18,834	6,107	2,871
1901	24,994	7,471	4,238	1916	19,666	6,108	3,176
1902	22,827	7,115	3,807	1917	12,849	3,912	2,035
1903	23,357	7,399	4,009	1918	6,646	2,448	1,230
1904	22,975	7,192	3,936	1919	8,107	2,445	1,338
1905	22,661	6,786	3,738	1920	12,548	3,546	1,731
1906	22,140	6,711	3,636	1921	10,759	3,355	1,350
1907	22,027	6,852	3,633	1922	10,107	3,068	1,372

	England & Wales	Scotland	Northern Ireland	Republic of Ireland
1923	9,723	2,757	379	
1924	9,942	2,641	314	
1925	9,473	2,532	281	752
1926	9,350	2,454	251	657
1927	8,398	2,099	215	663
1928	9,135	2,314	229	642
1929	8,869	2,180	223	664
1930	8,303	2,122	205	635
1931	8,039	1,958	191	609
1932	7,011	1,684	159	577
1933	7,187	1,483	152	542
1934	7,098	1,342	148	491
1935	6,660	1,543	141	470
1936	7,184	1,623	163	483
1937	7,425	1,692	173	499
1938	7,344	1,733	163	495
1939	7,282	1,728	167	494
1940	7,468	2,001	196	480
1941	5,555	1,923	185	455
1942	5,318	1,499	182	504
1943	5,608	1,952	173	520
1944	5,975	1,803	161	547
1945	5,214	1,418	133	596
1946	5,353	1,425	134	651
1947	5,344	1,493	121	632
1948	4,024	1,078	96	657
1949	3,908	895	90	698
1950	4,783	1,226	90	748
1951	6,223	1,413	115	787
1952	5,506	1,287	101	770
1953	5,953	1,459	104	566
1954	6,243	1,802	121	654
1955	6,939	1,948	142	677
1956	7,620	1,952	147	669
1957	7,769	2,195	152	612

See p. 410 for footnotes.

Miscellaneous Industrial Statistics 5. *continued*

(in thousand proof gallons)

	England & Wales	Scotland	Northern Ireland	Republic of Ireland
1958	8,073	2,254	166	562
1959	7,888	2,497	176	589
1960	8,672	2,475	215	595
1961	7,415	4,925	193	605
1962	7,027	5,191	202	708
1963	7,139	5,354	233	611
1964	7,875	6,158	251	684
1965	7,731	6,721	258	811
1966		13,632		829
1967		14,027		836
1968		15,029		823
1969		13,758		948
1970		14,054		1,074
1971		15,356		1,121
1972		16,672		1,242
1973		18,106		1,365
1974		24,023		1,566
				--- (*e*)
1975		24,947		1,492
1976		24,874		1,523
1977		27,598		1,682
1978		25,294		1,876
1979		31,732		1,862
1980		33,435		

(*a*) Years ended 25th December henceforth to 1754.
(*b*) Years ended 5th January henceforth to 1854.
(*c*) Years ended 31st March henceforth.
(*d*) New systems of accounting for removals from bonded warehouses showed that the previous statistics were somewhat inaccurate in their respective proportions.
(*e*) Subsequent figures are for calendar years.

Miscellaneous Industrial Statistics 6. British Spirits Distilled – United Kingdom 1850–1981

NOTES

[1] SOURCES: *S.P.* 1870, xx, *S.P.* 1884–5, xxii, and subsequent *Annual Report of the Commissioners of Inland Revenue* and *Annual Report of the Commissioners of Customs and Excise*.

[2] This account relates to all spirits, whether potable or not.

[3] Figures to 1854 are for years ended 5 January, and later ones are for years ending 31 March.

(in million proof gallons)

Year		Year		Year		Year	
1850	24·8	1883	38·4	1916	49·1	1949	67·5
1851	25·8	1884	40·4	1917	51·8	1950	76·8
1852	24·5	1885	41·0	1918	37·1	1951	98·4
1853	24·4	1886	39·0	1919	27·7	1952	88·9
1854	26·4	1887	37·7	1920	40·1	1953	70·7
1855	25·0	1888	39·0	1921	47·5	1954	77·2
1856	27·5	1889	39·1	1922	36·6	1955	96·7
					---- (*a*)		
1857	29·7	1890	41·0	1923	36·1	1956	105·7
1858	31·4	1891	44·6	1924	37·3	1957	112·3
1859	27·2	1892	46·2	1925	38·0	1958	115·2
1860	28·3	1893	44·4	1926	37·8	1959	105·7
1861	23·2	1894	44·9	1927	27·3	1960	115·9
1862	24·8	1895	44·9	1928	31·4	1961	136·1
1863	25·0	1896	49·3	1929	34·8	1962	139·2
1864	26·2	1897	54·6	1930	40·7	1963	146·9
1865	27·8	1898	60·7	1931	35·4	1964	169·2
1866	26·5	1899	63·4	1932	28·4	1965	196·5
1867	24·8	1900	59·2	1933	28·1	1966	208·3
1868	23·9	1901	57·0	1934	43·5	1967	200·7
1869	25·4	1902	55·2	1935	47·6	1968	180·4
1870	27·7	1903	49·7	1936	55·6	1969	187·4
1871	31·0	1904	51·8	1937	64·7	1970	210·9
1872	31·4	1905	49·1	1938	78·4	1971	223·4
1873	35·9	1906	49·2	1939	78·5	1972	226·3
1874	37·0	1907	50·3	1940	74·6	1973	255·7
1875	35·3	1908	47·8	1941	60·1	1974	283·8
1876	38·2	1909	49·5	1942	57·0	1975	304·4
1877	39·3	1910	43·8	1943	32·2	1976	244·3
1878	40·1	1911	41·2	1944	23·0	1977	259·8
1879	39·3	1912	45·7	1945	58·0	1978	288·0
1880	37·4	1913	46·7	1946	52·7	1979	311·7
1881	36·3	1914	51·8	1947	47·4	1980	318·0
1882	39·3	1915	50·1	1948	65·9	1981	218·9

Miscellaneous Industrial Statistics 7. Tallow Candles Charged with Duty – England & Wales 1711–1830

NOTES

[1] SOURCES: 1711–1828 – MS. Accounts in the Customs and Excise Library; 1829–30 – *Returns Relating to Candles*, in sessional papers.

[2] Figures of the much smaller amounts of wax candles are available but have not been included here.

(in million lb.)

Year		Year		Year	
1711 (*a*)	31·4	1751	37·2	1791	54·4
1712	27·2	1752	37·6	1792	54·9
1713	31·6	1753 (*b*)	38·6	1793	59·1
1714	29·2	1754	36·9	1794	59·4
1715	30·2	1755	34·9	1795	58·1
1716	30·6	1756	37·8	1796	56·1
1717	30·8	1757	37·1	1797	58·7
1718	31·7	1758	36·3	1798	61·1
1719	33·1	1759	38·2	1799	64·4
1720	32·3	1760	40·3	1800	61·7
1721	33·3	1761	41·4	1801	62·9
1722	34·2	1762	43·2	1802	64·8
1723	36·0	1763	42·7	1803	69·0
1724	35·6	1764	43·3	1804	68·4
1725	35·0	1765	42·3	1805	73·7
1726	35·5	1766	40·2	1806	71·1
1727	36·0	1767	40·1	1807	75·6
1728	33·9	1768	41·8	1808	73·5
1729	32·0	1769	41·8	1809	59·6
1730	31·2	1770	43·2	1810	71·1
1731	32·7	1771	42·7	1811	73·2
1732	33·7	1772	42·1	1812	75·4
1733	34·3	1773	42·2	1813	69·1
1734	36·0	1774	43·0	1814	73·3
1735	37·6	1775	44·1	1815	77·8
1736	38·1	1776	46·3	1816	81·1
1737	36·9	1777	47·3	1817	77·9
1738	37·2	1778	47·9	1818	77·3
1739	37·2	1779	46·8	1819	80·8
1740	34·4	1780	50·5	1820	82·5
1741	29·2	1781	49·8	1821	87·4
1742	29·2	1782	50·8	1822	89·3
1743	30·1	1783	48·4	1823	97·2
1744	32·1	1784	49·6	1824	100·6
1745	32·7	1785	46·1	1825	105·3
1746	33·5	1786	47·9	1826 (*c*)	(59·3)
1747	34·7	1787	47·7	1827	103·8
1748	35·0	1788	50·5	1828	108·9
1749	34·7	1789	51·5	1829	111·4
1750	35·5	1790	52·0	1830	109·4

(*a*) Years ended 24th June henceforth to 1752.
(*b*) Years ended 5th July henceforth to 1825.
(*c*) Years ended 5th January henceforth. The figure for 1826 is for 6 months only.

Miscellaneous Industrial Statistics 8. Paper Charged with Duty – England & Wales, 1713–1861, and Scotland 1737–1861

NOTES

[1] SOURCES: 1713–1828 (England & Wales) – MS. Account in Customs and Excise Library; all other figures – *S.P.* 1870, xx. Conversion to tonnage figures has been made by the method described in D. C. Coleman, *The British Paper Industry, 1495–1860* (Oxford, 1958), p. 346. In using this method on the Scottish statistics, it has been assumed that the units in which paper charged *ad valorem* was recorded were pounds sterling, though this is not specifically stated in *S.P.* 1870, xx.

[2] Figures of pasteboard charged with duty are included throughout.

(in tons)

	England & Wales	Scotland		England & Wales	Scotland		England & Wales	Scotland
1713 (*a*)	2,583	...	1756	4,706	115	1799	11,599	1,070
1714	2,764	...	1757	4,815	106	1800	12,394	1,189
1715	2,503	...	1758	5,199	125	1801	14,161	1,468
1716	2,634	...	1759	5,234	151	1802	11,575	1,029
1717	2,987	...	1760	5,209	175	1803	14,219	1,354
1718	3,118	...	1761	5,354	213	1804	13,053	1,265
1719	3,027	...	1762	5,329	219	1805	15,126	1,423
1720	2,911	...	1763	5,340	239	1806	14,857	1,490
1721	2,825	...	1764	5,970	281	1807	15,152	1,495
1722	2,726	...	1765	6,084	273	1808	16,213	1,426
1723	2,903	...	1766	6,000	305	1809	15,984	1,498
1724	3,006	...	1767	6,253	306	1810	16,988	1,684
1725	3,038	...	1768	6,339	295	1811	17,228	1,693
1726	3,012	...	1769	6,536	363	1812	17,807	1,681
1727	2,850	...	1770	6,406	374	1813	17,093	1,655
1728	2,867	...	1771	6,286	417	1814	17,513	1,676
1729	2,763	...	1772	6,667	397	1815	18,715	1,820
1730	2,878	...	1773	6,939	411	1816	17,400	1,781
1731	2,815	...	1774	6,684	351	1817	17,173	1,931
1732	2,588	...	1775	6,740	334	1818	19,870	2,018
1733	2,868	...	1776	6,454	311	1819	19,296	1,964
1734	2,967	...	1777	6,770	333	1820	18,913	2,008
1735	2,997	...	1778	6,866	310	1821	20,443	2,274
1736	2,956	...	1779	6,287	285	1822	21,614	2,427
1737	3,034	86	1780	5,943	261	1823	22,005	2,598
1738	3,087	94	1781	6,914	40	1824	23,597	2,681
				---- (*c*)	-- (*c*)			
1739	3,059	86	1782	9,044	305	1825	25,500	3,129
1740	2,989	76	1783	9,223	355	1826	(12,183)(*d*)	...
1741	3,199	88	1784	8,918	473	1827 (*e*)	20,362	2,449
1742	3,294	69	1785	9,950	495	1828	24,744	3,146
1743	3,425	72	1786	9,745	384	1829	26,569	3,682
1744	3,509	86	1787	10,976	515	1830	24,464	3,577
1745	3,480	76	1788	10,908	763	1831	25,443	4,238
1746	3,302	62	1789	10,159	869	1832	25,514	4,081
1747	3,496	59	1790	11,086	948	1833	25,839	4,301
1748	3,639	59	1791	10,993	1,122	1834	27,294	4,486
1749	4,024	65	1792	11,183	1,191	1835	28,258	4,674
1750	4,115	84	1793	11,437	1,209	1836	28,973	5,364
1751	4,105	84	1794	11,613	1,309	1837	29,918	5,449
1752	4,493	97	1795	11,133	1,004	1838	32,108	6,152
1753 (*b*)	4,626	83	1796	12,494	1,301	1839	32,949	7,190
1754	4,610	85	1797	11,548	1,246	1840	34,369	7,677
1755	4,577	111	1798	11,719	1,113	1841	34,277	7,530

Miscellaneous Industrial Statistics 8. *continued*

(in tons)

	England & Wales	Scotland		England & Wales	Scotland		England & Wales	Scotland
1842	34,059	7,510	1849	40,820	11,072	1856	57,547	16,769
1843	33,738	7,619	1850	44,159	12,028	1857	64,013	18,303
1844	35,329	8,888	1851	47,193	12,768	1858	62,032	18,098
1845	37,594	9,253	1852	50,088	14,162	1859	65,442	19,881
1846	42,440	10,500	1853	51,126	14,542	1860	71,022	20,800
1847	43,550	10,721	1854	59,143	16,573	1861	76,307	21,906
1848	41,451	10,448	1855 (*f*)	56,511	16,454			

(*a*) Years ended 24th June henceforth to 1752.
(*b*) Years ended 5th July henceforth to 1825.
(*c*) With the improvements in the methods of assessing paper and in the efficiency of collection, it is obvious that a great deal of paper had escaped duty before 1782. Dr Coleman's method of conversion to tonnage statistics reduces the size of the break, since it compensates for evasion by assessment *ad valorem*, but it cannot cover avoidance of duty.
(*d*) Six months ended 5th January.
(*e*) Years ended 5th January henceforth to 1854.
(*f*) Years ended 31st March henceforth.

Miscellaneous Industrial Statistics 9. Starch Charged with Duty – England & Wales 1713–1828

NOTE
SOURCE: MS. Account in the Customs and Excise Library.

(in million lb.)

1713 (*a*)	2·7	1742	1·5	1771	2·8	1800	2·9
1714	2·5	1743	1·6	1772	3·5	1801	0·3
1715	2·7	1744	1·6	1773	3·7	1802	2·5
1716	2·5	1745	1·5	1774	5·4	1803	4·9
1717	2·9	1746	1·5	1775	4·9	1804	3·8
1718	2·8	1747	1·7	1776	5·6	1805	3·4
1719	3·1	1748	1·9	1777	4·9	1806	3·7
1720	2·9	1749	2·0	1778	4·7	1807	4·2
1721	2·6	1750	2·3	1779	6·6	1808	4·1
1722	2·7	1751	2·3	1780	6·4	1809	3·1
1723	2·5	1752	2·4	1781	4·9	1810	3·7
1724	2·5	1753 (*b*)	2·6	1782	6·9	1811	4·0
1725	2·3	1754	2·9	1783	5·4	1812	3·2
1726	2·0	1755	3·3	1784	6·7	1813	1·8
1727	2·4	1756	3·2	1785	6·3	1814	3·9
1728	1·9	1757	2·2	1786	6·6	1815	4·1
1729	1·7	1758	3·4	1787	6·0	1816	2·9
1730	1·8	1759	4·1	1788	6·1	1817	2·4
1731	1·8	1760	3·8	1789	6·4	1818	3·4
1732	2·0	1761	3·5	1790	7·0	1819	4·2
1733	1·9	1762	3·6	1791	7·8	1820	4·4
1734	1·7	1763	3·6	1792	8·5	1821	4·4
1735	1·4	1764	4·0	1793	7·3	1822	5·0
1736	1·4	1765	3·6	1794	7·9	1823	5·9
1737	1·5	1766	3·8	1795	8·6	1824	4·8
1738	1·4	1767	3·6	1796	1·9	1825	5·5
1739	1·4	1768	3·6	1797	3·1	1826 (*c*)	(3·1)
1740	1·1	1769	4·1	1798	7·3	1827	5·7
1741	0·9	1770	3·9	1799	5·9	1828	6·8

(*a*) Years ended 24th June henceforth to 1752.
(*b*) Years ended 5th July henceforth to 1825.
(*c*) Years ended 5th January henceforth. The figure for 1826 is for 6 months only.

Miscellaneous Industrial Statistics 10. Soap Charged with Duty – England & Wales 1713–1852

NOTE

SOURCES: 1713–1828 – MS. Accounts in the Customs and Excise Library; 1829–52 – *Returns relating to Soap*.

(in million lb.)

						Hard	Soft
1713 (*a*)	24·4	1760	29·4		1806	58·7	3·1
1714	24·7	1761	29·3		1807	61·0	3·1
1715	24·6	1762	29·4		1808	64·7	3·6
1716	23·9	1763	29·6		1809	53·6	3·6
1717	24·9	1764	29·9		1810	63·3	4·3
1718	25·1	1765	29·9		1811	61·0	3·3
1719	25·7	1766	30·0		1812	62·0	4·0
1720	26·2	1767	29·5		1813	60·2	3·8
1721	25·4	1768	30·2		1814	61·3	3·9
1722	26·3	1769	30·6		1815	68·7	4·5
1723	27·3	1770	30·8		1816	70·5	4·5
1724	27·8	1771	31·1		1817	64·7	3·8
1725	26·9	1772	30·6		1818	68·0	4·4
1726	27·0	1773	31·7		1819	69·2	4·7
1727	26·7	1774	30·8		1820	74·3	5·3
1728	25·9	1775	31·2		1821	78·9	5·6
1729	24·9	1776	34·8		1822	80·9	5·8
1730	25·0	1777	33·7		1823	88·4	6·5
1731	26·5	1778	33·7		1824	86·6	6·7
1732	26·6	1779	34·2		1825	92·2	7·4
1733	27·7	1780	37·1		1826 (*c*)	(50·1)	(2·8)
1734	26·7	1781	36·8		1827	88·2	5·1
1735	27·5	1782	40·9		1828	94·6	7·3
1736	27·7		Hard	Soft	1829	98·1	7·3
1737	27·7	1783	28·4	2·3	1830	93·3	6·7
1738	27·3	1784	33·0	2·9	1831	107·0	7·5
1739	27·5	1785	33·1	2·8	1832	99·9	7·3
						- - -	- -
1740	26·2	1786	34·0	2·8	1833	109·1 (*d*)	7·5 (*d*)
1741	24·3	1787	32·0	2·9	1834	126·4	8·3
1742	24·7	1788	34·8	2·7	1835	132·0	7·1
1743	25·3	1789	36·0	2·5	1836	137·8	8·6
1744	26·5	1790	37·3	2·8	1837	135·8	9·7
1745	26·2	1791	38·9	3·0	1838	130·8	8·4
1746	26·5	1792	40·1	2·8	1839	146·8	9·6
1747	27·2	1793	40·4	2·6	1840	144·1	10·0
1748	27·0	1794	44·8	2·5	1841	148·8	8·9
1749	27·6	1795	44·1	2·7	1842	144·7	9·8
1750	28·4	1796	43·5	2·8	1843	144·6	8·1
1751	30·0	1797	43·6	2·6	1844	153·5	10·7
1752	29·8	1798	47·6	2·5	1845	158·9	12·2
1753 (*b*)	29·8	1799	48·0	2·6	1846	161·4	10·8
1754	29·1	1800	46·9	2·3	1847	156·7	9·5
1755	28·9	1801	45·7	1·9	1848	148·3	8·8
1756	28·5	1802	46·5	2·4	1849	159·2	9·7
1757	28·1	1803	53·2	3·0	1850	164·2	11·1
1758	27·9	1804	51·4	2·6	1851	168·9	12·3
1759	27·9	1805	56·8	3·1	1852	170·8	11·9

(*a*) Years ended 24th June henceforth to 1752.
(*b*) Years ended 5th July henceforth to 1825.
(*c*) Years ended 5th January henceforth. The figures for 1826 are for 6 months only.
(*d*) Prior to 1833 manufacturers were allowed to deduct 10 per cent before paying duty.

Miscellaneous Industrial Statistics 11. Hides and Skins Charged with Duty – England & Wales 1722–1828

NOTES

[1] Sources: 1722–1825 – MS. Account in Customs and Excise Library; 1826–8 – *Returns relating to Hides and Skins*.

[2] This is not an exhaustive account of all hides and skins charged with duty. The less homogeneous group which was measured in dozens, namely goat skins, horse and cow hides, vellum and parchment, has been omitted.

(Tanned, Tawed, or Dressed in Oil, measured in million lb.)

1722 (*a*)	29·4	1749	28·7	1776	32·2	1803	39·4
1723	29·0	1750	29·5	1777	33·3	1804	39·2
1724	28·5	1751	28·8	1778	33·6	1805	41·8
1725	29·2	1752	30·4	1779	32·8	1806	44·3
1726	29·8	1753 (*b*)	30·1	1780	32·7	1807	45·0
1727	29·5	1754	29·1	1781	33·5	1808	44·7
1728	28·5	1755	29·2	1782	34·5	1809	47·3
1729	27·4	1756	30·1	1783	35·1	1810	48·5
1730	28·4	1757	29·5	1784	34·3	1811	48·9
1731	27·8	1758	30·1	1785	35·3	1812	52·1
1732	28·1	1759	31·1	1786	34·9	1813	48·0
1733	28·0	1760	30·2	1787	35·3	1814	48·9
1734	28·4	1761	31·3	1788	35·9	1815	49·4
1735	29·5	1762	32·4	1789	34·1	1816	43·9
1736	31·3	1763	31·7	1790	37·0	1817	43·8
1737	31·3	1764	34·7	1791	37·5	1818	45·5
1738	30·3	1765	32·9	1792	37·4	1819	47·2
1739	30·7	1766	31·6	1793	38·7	1820	45·0
1740	28·1	1767	31·0	1794	39·7	1821	44·6
1741	28·5	1768	30·2	1795	39·0	1822	42·5
1742	27·9	1769	30·9	1796	41·8	1823	51·6
1743	26·7	1770	31·1	1797	38·7	1824	54·9
1744	26·3	1771	32·0	1798	38·7	1825	57·3
1745	25·7	1772	32·9	1799	37·3	1826 (*c*)	(28·0)
1746	26·7	1773	33·7	1800	38·9	1827	46·3
1747	27·9	1774	33·1	1801	40·0	1828	48·3
1748	27·3	1775	32·8	1802	39·9		

(*a*) Years ended 24th June henceforth to 1752.
(*b*) Years ended 5th July henceforth to 1825.
(*c*) Years ended 5th January henceforth. The figure for 1826 is for 6 months only.

Miscellaneous Industrial Statistics 12. Glass Charged with Duty – England & Wales 1747–1845

NOTES

[1] Sources: 1747–1828 – MS. Accounts in the Customs and Excise Library; 1829–45 – *Returns relating to Glass*.

[2] The term *White Glass* covers all types other than common green bottle glass – namely, flint, plate, crown, German sheet, and broad glass.

(in thousand tons)

	White Glass	Common Bottles, etc.		White Glass	Common Bottles, etc.
1747 (*a*)	1·4	9·2	1797	7·9	11·5
1748	2·2	8·6	1798	6·9	8·3
1749	2·5	9·3	1799	7·4	10·0
1750	3·1	11·0	1800	8·2	11·3
1751	3·1	12·8	1801	8·5	12·4
1752	3·4	13·4	1802	9·0	13·1
1753 (*b*)	3·6	12·2	1803	9·8	14·0
1754	4·1	13·6	1804	8·6	13·0
1755	3·8	13·0	1805	9·9	13·6
1756	3·9	11·6	1806	9·1	13·5
1757	3·9	10·6	1807	9·3	15·7
1758	4·5	9·0	1808	9·1	16·7
1759	4·1	8·3	1809	9·1	16·0
1760	4·6	9·5	1810	9·1	16·5
1761	4·6	10·4	1811	9·3	16·6
1762	5·0	10·7	1812	7·9	15·0
1763	4·9	11·6	1813	6·2	10·7
1764	5·4	13·3	1814	7·0	11·7
1765	5·9	12·9	1815	7·7	13·9
1766	5·9	13·1	1816	6·9	15·4
1767	6·5	12·2	1817	5·9	14·0
1768	6·9	12·1	1818	7·4	15·5
1769	6·6	11·8	1819	8·4	16·7
1770	6·4	11·0	1820	6·7	12·8
1771	6·3	11·2	1821	7·1	11·7
1772	7·0	12·0	1822	7·3	12·4
1773	6·7	11·6	1823	8·3	13·3
1774	6·6	11·5	1824	9·1	15·5
1775	6·7	11·3	1825	10·2	15·9
1776	6·7	11·8	1826 (*c*)	(7·1)	(8·7)
1777	7·2	12·4	1827	12·3	16·6
1778	6·4	11·3	1828	12·5	16·6
1779	6·6	8·5	1829	10·2	17·1
1780	5·6	6·9	1830	9·1	15·1
1781	5·5	8·3	1831	8·1	13·7
1782	5·7	8·3	1832	8·8	12·2
1783	5·7	8·5	1833	9·0	12·9
1784	5·8	8·5	1834	10·8	13·4
1785	6·2	9·5	1835	11·7	14·1
1786	6·2	9·7	1836	12·6	15·3
1787	6·6	10·4	1837	13·8	17·7
1788	7·3	10·4	1838	13·2	17·5
1789	8·4	10·9	1839	12·7	17·2
1790	8·2	12·3	1840	12·9	18·3
1791	8·1	12·6	1841	13·7	20·4
1792	8·5	12·8	1842	12·6	18·9
1793	8·5	13·6	1843	10·7	14·6
1794	9·1	12·2	1844	11·2	12·7
1795	6·6	11·8	1845	12·3	17·3
1796	7·5	11·8			

(*a*) Years ended 24th June henceforth to 1752.
(*b*) Years ended 5th July henceforth to 1825.

(*c*) Years ended 5th January henceforth. The figures for 1826 are for 6 months only.

Miscellaneous Industrial Statistics 13. Production of Paper – United Kingdom 1939–80

NOTE
SOURCE: *Abstract*.

(in thousand tons)

	News-print	Other Paper & Board		News-print	Other Paper & Board		News-print	Other Paper & Board		News-print	Other Paper & Board
1939	800	1,831	1950	544	2,070	1961	712	3,314	1971	566	3,732
1940	296	1,498	1951	527	2,193	1962	655	3,296	1972	460	3,845
1941	150	1,234	1952	537	1,804	1963	672	3,452	1973	435	4,198
1942	140	1,148	1953	603	2,084	1964	750	3,654	1974	375	4,178
1943	129	1,032	1954	612	2,467	1965	768	3,773	1975	310	3,290
1944	151	1,073	1955	620	2,676	1966	737	3,790	1976	321	3,801
1945	162	1,139	1956	643	2,640	1967	703	3,699	1977	296	3,784
1946	295	1,441	1957	653	2,721	1968	724	3,904	1978	314	3,816
1947	258	1,477	1958	626	2,876	1969	777	4,115	1979	358	3,828
1948	298	1,596	1959	669	2,986	1970	745	4,118	1980	357	3,400
1949	473	1,823	1960	741	3,332						

Miscellaneous Industrial Statistics 14. Production of Motor Vehicles – United Kingdom, 1923–80

NOTES
[1] SOURCES: 1923–39 – League of Nations, *Statistical Year Book*; 1940–80 – *Abstract*.
[2] The figures relate to the production of complete vehicles other than motor cycles.
[3] Data to 1939 are for years ended 30 September.

(in thousands)

	Passenger Cars	Commercial Vehicles		Passenger Cars	Commercial Vehicles		Passenger Cars	Commercial Vehicles
1923	71	24	1943	2	148	1962	1,249	425
1924	117	30	1944	2	131	1963	1,607	404
1925	132	35	1945	17	122	1964	1,868	465
1926	154	44	1946	219	146	1965	1,722	455
1927	165	47	1947	287	155	1966	1,604	438
1928	165	47	1948	335	173	1967	1,552	385
1929	182	57	1949	412	216	1968	1,816	409
1930	170	67	1950	523	261	1969	1,717	466
1931	159	67	1951	476	258	1970	1,641	458
1932	171	61	1952	448	242	1971	1,742	456
1933	221	66	1953	595	239	1972	1,921	408
1934	257	86	1954	769	269	1973	1,747	417
1935	338	92	1955	898	340	1974	1,534	403
1936	354	114	1956	708	297	1975	1,268	381
1937	390	114	1957	861	288	1976	1,333	372
1938	341	104	1958	1,052	313	1977	1,316 --- (a) 1,304	398 --- (a) 410
1939	305	97	1959	1,190	370	1978	1,223	385
1940	2	132	1960	1,353	458	1979	1,070	408
1941	5	140	1961	1,004	460	1980	924	389
1942	5	155						

(*a*) Estate vehicles of 1·6 to 2·8 litres were transferred between categories.

Miscellaneous Industrial Statistics 15. Ships Built and First Registered in the British Empire and in Great Britain, 1787–1818, and in the United Kingdom, 1814–70; and all Ships Built in the United Kingdom for British Citizens and Companies 1870–1980

NOTES

[1] SOURCES: 1787–1800 – *Navigation Reports* in the Public Record Office; 1801–18 (Empire) – *Finance Accounts* (Trade and Navigation section); 1804–5 (G.B.) – *S.P.* 1806, XIII; 1814–18 (G.B.) – *S.P.* 1821 XVII; 1814–38 (all ships) – *S.P.* 1852, XLIX; 1814–26 (sail/steam breakdown) – *S.P.* 1826–7, XVIII; 1827–38 (sail/steam breakdown) – G. R. Porter, *The Progress of the Nation* (London, 2nd edition, 1847); p. 318; 1840–1980 – *Abstract*.

[2] Tonnage figures are net in Parts A and B, gross in Part C.

[3] The Isle of Man and the Channel Islands are included as part of Great Britain in Part A, but they are excluded from the United Kingdom in Parts B and C.

[4] Vessels exported from 1957 onwards were as follows:

	Number	000 GRT		Number	000 GRT		Number	000 GRT
1957	65	375	1965	33	150	1973	26	327
1958	46	314	1966	38	287	1974	31	235
1959	47	173	1967	58	611	1975	41	365
1960	37	119	1968	39	590	1976	43	589
1961	41	296	1969	38	315	1977	25	410
1962	44	188	1970	25	260	1978	27	396
1963	41	280	1971	38	357	1979	27	243
1964	39	120	1972	30	398	1980	33	232

A. British Empire and Great Britain, 1787–1818

	All Ships, Britain and Empire		All Ships, Britain Alone	
	Number	thousand tons	Number	thousand tons
1787	1,427	118·3	943	91·7
1788	1,327	103·3	848	73·5
1789	827	71·1	627	58·0
1790	725	68·7	577	57·1
1791	766	68·9	624	58·8
1792	821	78·1	655	67·0
1793	800	75·1	652	65·6
1794	714	66·0	555	55·6
1795	719	72·2	540	63·2
1796	823	95·0	628	84·9
1797	756	86·2	630	78·3
1798	833	89·3	702	79·9
1799	858	98·0	689	83·7
1800	1,041	134·2	845	115·3
1801	1,065	122·6	918	110·2
1802	1,281	137·5	967	104·8
1803	1,407	135·7		
1804	991	96·0	715	79·9
1805	1,001	89·6	714	71·4
1806	772	69·2		
1807	770	68·0	...	...
1808	568	57·1	...	...
1809	596	61·4	...	...
1810	685	84·9	...	...
1811	870	115·6	...	...
1812	...	...	...	...
1813	...	...	...	...
1814	818	96·0	660	84·1
1815	864	97·9	877	101·0
1816	1,183	128·5	810	82·7
1817	1,274	117·4	656	78·1
1818	1,082	104·4	704	84·7

Miscellaneous Industrial Statistics 15. *continued*

B. United Kingdom, 1814–1938

	Sailing Ships		Steamships (*a*)		All Ships	
	Number	thousand tons	Number	thousand tons	Number	thousand tons
1814	701	85·8	5	0·3	706	86·1
1815	904	102·1	9	0·8	913	102·9
1816	843	84·1	8	0·6	851	84·7
1817	751	80·8	7	0·4	758	81·3
1818	746	85·4	6	1·3	752	86·7
1819	773	88·7	4	0·3	777	89·1
1820	611	66·0	8	0·7	619	66·7
1821	563	55·1	22	3·0	585	58·1
1822	537	48·5	27	2·4	564	50·9
1823	575	60·7	19	2·5	594	63·2
1824	782	88·8	17	2·2	799	91·1
1825	951	119·5	24	3·0	975	122·5
1826	1,043	109·7	72	8·6	1,115	118·4
1827	866	89·8	28	3·4	894	93·1
1828	812	86·6	30	2·0	842	88·7
1829	702	74·9	16	1·8	718	76·6
1830	712	73·8	18	1·7	730	75·5
1831	711	81·1	31	2·7	742	83·9
1832	700	87·3	33	2·9	733	90·2
1833	678	86·3	33	2·9	711	89·2
1834	744	95·2	36	5·1	780	100·4
1835	774	105·7	86	10·1	860	116·6
1836	616	77·8	63	8·8	679	86·5
1837	858	119·5	78	11·7	936	131·2
1838	1,005	147·7	84	9·5	1,089	157·3
1839	1,155	175·2	62	6·1	1,217	181·3
1840	1,296	201·1	74	10·2	1,370	211·3
1841	1,063	148·2	48	11·4	1,111	159·6
1842	856	116·2	58	13·7	914	129·9
1843	652	77·0	46	6·1	698	83·1
1844	624	88·9	65	6·1	689	95·0
1845	788	112·3	65	10·9	853	123·2
1846	732	109·4	77	16·0	809	125·4
1847	830	129·7	103	16·2	933	145·8
1848	733	107·2	114	15·3	847	122·6
1849	662	105·5	68	12·5	730	118·0
1850	621	119·1	68	14·6	689	133·7
1851	594	126·9	78	22·7	672	149·6
1852	608	136·7	104	30·7	712	167·5
1853	645	155·0	153	48·2	798	203·2
1854	628	132·7	174	64·3	802	196·9
1855	865	242·2	233	81·0	1,098	323·2
1856	921	187·0	229	57·6	1,150	244·6
1857	1,050	197·6	228	52·9	1,278	250·5
1858	847	154·9	153	53·2	1,000	208·1
1859	789	148·0	150	38·0	939	186·0
1860	818	158·2	198	53·8	1,016	212·0
1861	774	130·0	201	70·9	975	200·8
1862	827	164·1	221	77·3	1,048	241·4
1863	881	253·0	279	108·0	1,160	361·0
1864	867	272·5	374	159·4	1,241	431·9
1865	922	235·6	382	179·6	1,304	415·2
1866	969	207·7	354	133·5	1,323	341·2
1867	879	174·5	279	94·6	1,158	269·1
1868	787	237·7	232	78·5	1,019	316·2

Miscellaneous Industrial Statistics 15. *continued*

B. United Kingdom, 1814–1938 (*cont.*)

	Sailing Ships		Steamships (*a*)		All Ships	
	Number	thousand tons	Number	thousand tons	Number	thousand tons
1869	688	230·8	283	123·5	971	354·3
1870	541	117·0	433	225·7	974	342·7
	...	....	...	....	...	....
1871	472	56·5	470	297·8	942	354·4
1872	408	55·0	503	338·0	911	393·0
1873	418	88·5	396	282·1	814	370·7
1874	499	187·3	482	333·9	981	521·2
1875	566	241·6	357	178·9	923	420·6
1876	687	236·9	320	123·5	1,007	360·4
1877	703	212·3	389	221·3	1,092	433·7
1878	585	141·2	499	287·1	1,084	428·2
1879	395	59·1	412	297·7	807	356·8
1880	348	57·5	474	346·4	822	403·8
1881	359	92·4	486	408·8	845	501·2
1882	362	145·7	610	521·6	972	667·3
1883	368	146·8	806	621·8	1,174	768·6
1884	431	162·2	570	335·2	1,001	497·4
1885	459	208·4	393	197·0	852	405·4
1886	363	138·4	308	154·6	671	293·0
1887	258	81·3	322	225·4	580	306·7
1888	269	75·7	465	407·4	734	483·1
1889	277	117·5	582	554·0	859	671·5
1890	277	123·2	581	528·8	858	652·0
1891	308	191·9	622	478·7	930	670·6
1892	322	258·7	521	434·1	843	692·8
1893	333	114·9	448	380·4	781	495·3
1894	363	89·2	524	485·5	887	574·6
1895	319	54·2	541	465·5	860	519·6
1896	389	57·5	542	462·5	931	520·0
1897	518	66·7	536	415·5	1,054	482·3
1898	665	41·8	705	654·2	1,370	696·0
1899	570	45·5	675	703·9	1,245	749·4
1900	504	38·6	667	698·3	1,171	736·9
1901	567	55·0	637	720·7	1,204	775·7
1902	650	64·8	645	735·6	1,295	800·4
1903	468	42·3	695	568·8	1,163	629·1
1904	363	33·7	680	701·6	1,043	735·4
1905	286	30·4	713	821·1	999	851·4
1906	334	31·9	819	890·3	1,153	922·2
1907	337	24·3	929	716·5	1,266	740·8
1908	301	26·6	593	386·4	894	413·1
1909	254	26·6	570	484·3	824	510·9
1910	262	20·5	604	580·5	866	601·0
1911	286	26·9	790	887·7	1,076	914·7
1912	289	43·1	721	857·2	1,010	900·3
1913	290	25·2	755	950·0	1,045	975·2
1914	256	26·3	754	812·4	1,010	838·6
1915	149	12·5	373	361·9	522	374·4
1916	114	14·3	365	372·0	479	386·3
1917	58	6·6	339	745·5	397	752·1
1918	11	5·7	309	815·2	320	820·9

Miscellaneous Industrial Statistics 15. *continued*

B. United Kingdom, 1814–1938 (*cont.*)

	Sailing Ships		Steamships (*a*)		All Ships	
	Number	thousand tons	Number	thousand tons	Number	thousand tons
1919	186	44·4	571	892·1	757	936·5
1920	270	33·5	543	773·0	813	806·5
1921	205	19·6	427	658·6	632	678·2
1922	150	15·8	289	486·5	439	502·2
	---	---	---	---	----	----
1923	269 (*b*)	26·1 (*b*)	313 (*b*)	375·7 (*b*)	582 (*b*)	401·8 (*b*)
1924	238	22·8	476	760·4	714	783·2
1925	324	36·4	438	563·7	762	600·1
1926	183	18·4	280	337·6	463	356·0
1927	205	17·3	481	647·3	686	664·5
1928	170	14·4	550	766·8	720	781·3
1929	171	13·0	611	785·0	782	798·0
1930	232	18·7	544	526·3	776	545·0
1931	104	10·7	283	206·7	387	217·4
1932	92	7·3	191	94·9	283	102·2
1933	111	9·6	284	74·0	395	83·6
1934	188	14·5	421	254·3	609	268·9
1935	266	17·2	480	287·8	746	305·0
1936	298	24·0	608	473·4	906	497·3
1937	203	18·2	564	499·9	767	518·0
1938	147	20·8	454	489·5	601	510·3

Miscellaneous Industrial Statistics 15. *continued*

C. United Kingdom, 1938–80

	Numbers of Vessels				Thousand Gross Tons			
	All Vessels	Tankers	Passenger and Cargo	Other Vessels	All Vessels	Tankers	Passenger and Cargo	Other Vessels
1938	267	...	...	...	1,030	...	...	...
1939	201	...	...	...	630	...	...	...
1940	172	5	132	35	801	32	731	38
1941	235	41	148	46	1,158	274	816	68
1942	258	44	144	70	1,302	318	930	54
1943	237	36	146	55	1,201	217	939	45
1944	269	79	138	52	1,013	200	769	44
1945	238	37	128	73	743	193	504	46
1946	283	53	130	100	987	326	582	79
1947	293	15	168	110	949	119	772	58
1948	332	24	183	125	1,221	203	947	71
1949	332	42	167	123	1,361	380	885	96
1950	302	58	129	115	1,376	564	694	118
1951	240	69	78	93	1,343	782	485	76
1952	234	58	99	77	1,271	658	520	93
1953	220	61	86	73	1,223	696	449	78
1954	232	61	108	63	1,493	770	673	50
1955	260	46	100	114	1,282	598	611	73
1956	279	36	127	116	1,426	527	842	57
1957	264	30	126	108	1,442	507	870	65
	--- (*c*)	-- (*c*)	--- (*c*)	--- (*c*)	---- (*c*)	--- (*c*)	--- (*c*)	-- (*c*)
1957	299	35	132	132	1,448	510	884	54
1958	298	40	128	130	1,453	554	853	46
1959	292	44	101	147	1,388	646	691	51
1960	282	33	89	160	1,303	483	765	55
1961	279	33	81	165	1,390	548	763	79
1962	249	19	75	155	1,022	342	618	62
1963	208	21	77	110	1,127	469	608	50
1964	193	26	50	117	848	403	378	66
1965	202	20	69	113	1,204	479	662	63
1966	211	19	58	134	1,130	401	630	99
1967	199	17	59	123	1,192	155	891	146
1968	152	13	49	90	1,046	239	757	51
1969	138	13	53	72	814	47	723	44
1970	144	21	54	69	1,297	519	741	37
1971	134	15	53	66	1,259	469	734	57
1972	139	19	56	64	1,208	412	747	50
1973	137	9	50	78	1,069	221	804	44
1974	134	10	35	89	1,189	457	673	59
1975	144	12	38	94	1,203	592	573	39
1976	140	14	44	82	1,460	720	691	49
1977	104	8	40	56	1,007	426	540	42
1978	96	11	45	40	1,135	649	474	12.
1979	95	10	45	40	707	331	353	22
1980	88	10	42	36	431	87	320	22

(*a*) Including motor ships throughout.
(*b*) Ships built in southern Ireland are not included after 1922.

(*c*) Non-propelled vessels are subsequently included, and there was also some rearrangement of categories at this time.

Miscellaneous Industrial Statistics 16. Ships Built and First Registered in the United Kingdom or Built in the United Kingdom for British Citizens or Companies, according to Type and Material – 1850–1908

NOTES
[1] SOURCES: 1850–2 – *Shipping Returns*; 1853–1908 – *Annual Statement of Trade*.
[2] All tonnage figures are net.
[3] Ships built in the Isle of Man and the Channel Islands are not included.

	Sailing Ships						Steamships					
	Wood		Iron		Steel		Wood		Iron		Steel	
	Number	thousand tons	Number	thousand tons	Number	thousand tons	Number	thousand tons	Number	thousand tons	Number	thousand tons
1850	610	117·0	11	2·1			18	3·9	50	10·7		
1851	587	124·9	7	2·0			30	8·9	48	13·8		
1852	605	134·7	3	2·1			45	4·8	59	26·0		
1853	635	146·4	10	8·6			36	3·3	117	44·9		
1854	592	115·8	36	16·9			22	2·1	152	62·2		
1855	818	211·9	47	30·3			38	3·1	195	77·9		
1856	888	175·4	33	11·6			54	2·8	175	54·8		
1857	1,012	184·2	38	13·4			73	3·0	155	49·9		
1858	822	140·4	25	14·5			41	3·6	112	49·5		
1859	755	128·3	34	19·7			44	1·8	106	36·2		
1860	786	144·6	32	13·6			49	2·7	149	51·1		
1861	731	107·2	43	22·7			42	2·5	159	68·4		
1862	758	120·0	69	44·0			40	1·0	181	76·3		
1863	739	146·0	142	107·1			39	2·1	240	105·8		
1864	713	146·8	154	125·7			32	2·4	342	157·0		
1865	806	150·5	116	85·1			38	2·3	344	177·4		
	---	---	---	---			--	--	---	---		
1866	815(*a*)	112·0(*a*)	112(*a*)	69·5(*a*)			50(*a*)	3·0(*a*)	299(*a*)	129·7(*a*)		
1867	744	97·2	99	59·0			51	3·2	224	90·8		
1868	596	87·2	162	131·7			39	1·1	188	75·1		
1869	499	71·2	157	138·4			35	2·1	238	118·4		
1870	450	56·1	63	48·8			49	2·5	382	222·9		
1871	435	38·5	30	16·7			51	2·1	416	295·1		
1872	386	39·2	18	15·1			55	2·1	446	335·8		
1873	369	40·4	49	48·1			56	2·5	335	279·1		
1874	382	43·9	116	143·2			78	2·6	393	328·1		
1875	372	41·6	193	198·8			56	1·7	291	175·8		
1876	466	45·2	218	190·7			31	1·1	288	122·3		
1877	532	42·5	174	169·7			29	0·4	355	220·0		
1878	480	37·5	110	103·7			64	1·0	431	285·4		
			---	---					---	---		
1879	352	22·1	44(*b*)	36·8(*b*)	1(*b*)	under 50(*b*)	35	0·7	351(*b*)	275·9(*b*)	24(*b*)	21·0(*b*)
1880	288	17·8	39	37·3	5	1·8	33	1·3	396	309·8	40	34·8
1881	259	16·5	87	72·4	4	3·1	30	0·9	415	361·5	37	46·3
1882	232	13·4	120	118·5	10	13·9	37	0·7	467	440·2	101	80·3
	---	---					---	---				
1883	247(*a*)	13·9(*a*)	96	114·1	23	18·7	54(*a*)	1·2(*a*)	613	508·6	137	111·8
1884	297	17·4	107	128·3	23	16·3	57	2·1	369	239·9	139	93·1
1885	265	17·3	154	155·5	32	34·5	51	0·9	182	87·8	159	108·3
1886	227	13·9	93	92·3	39	31·8	29	0·5	122	44·9	155	109·3
1887	179	9·4	44	46·6	34	25·2	18	0·6	76	18·9	227	205·9
1888	176	9·1	55	21·0	38	45·6	24	1·9	91	26·2	350	379·4
1889	191	9·1	24	15·1	62	93·3	23	0·6	113	35·4	445	518·1

Miscellaneous Industrial Statistics 16. *continued*

	Sailing Ships						Steamships					
	Wood		Iron		Steel		Wood		Iron		Steel	
	Number	thousand tons	Number	thousand tons	Number	thousand tons	Number	thousand tons	Number	thousand tons	Number	thousand tons
1890	182	9·3	25	12·7	70	101·3	32	0·7	125	32·8	424	495·3
1891	167	8·0	25	6·6	116	177·3	22	0·6	181	16·0	419	462·1
1892	156	8·2	28	9·0	138	241·5	23	1·0	88	9·4	410	423·7
1893	184	8·8	50	3·4	99	102·7	35	0·7	85	7·3	328	372·4
1894	178	8·9	46	4·5	139	75·8	20	0·3	87	8·2	417	477·0
1895	180	8·1	46	5·0	93	41·0	37	1·0	79	5·6	425	458·8
1896	209	10·1	51	5·0	129	42·4	21	0·3	89	6·7	432	455·5
1897	256	11·7	90	8·8	172	46·2	56	1·1	65	4·0	415	410·4
1898	297	14·0	113	8·0	255	19·9	21	0·5	93	5·0	591	648·6
1899	273	12·7	75	5·6	222	27·2	31	0·7	71	4·6	573	698·6
1900	250	13·0	52	3·9	202	21·6	75	2·3	84	5·7	508	690·4
1901	259	13·3	66	5·0	242	36·7	98	3·1	24	2·7	515	714·9
1902	289	14·6	49	3·5	312	46·6	80	2·4	38	2·5	527	730·7
1903	262	13·2	6	0·4	200	28·7	89	2·6	15	0·8	591	583·4
1904	240	12·1	5	0·4	118	21·3	63	1·6	2	--	615	700·0
1905	180	11·2	20	1·2	86	18·0	41	0·8	2	0·1	670	820·1
1906	171	8·5	8	0·8	155	22·5	119	2·7	3	0·3	697	887·3
1907	195	11·1	3	0·2	139	12·9	210	4·4	2	5·1	717	707·1
1908	152	7·8	8	0·6	141	18·1	120	3·4	—	—	473	383·0

(*a*) From 1866–82 composite ships were separately distinguished. Prior to 1866 they were included in either wood or iron, and after 1882 they were included with wood. The following are the details for 1866–82:

	Sailing Ships		Steamships	
	Number	thousand tons	Number	thousand tons
1866	42	26·1	5	0·8
1867	36	18·3	4	0·5
1868	29	18·8	5	2·3
1869	32	21·2	10	3·0
1870	28	12·1	2	0·3
1871	7	1·4	3	0·6
1872	4	0·6	2	0·1
1873	—	—	5	0·5
1874	1	0·2	11	3·1
1875	1	1·3	10	1·4
1876	3	1·0	1	0·1
1877	—	—	—	—
1878	—	—	4	0·7
1879	3	0·1	2	0·1
1880	21	0·7	5	0·5
1881	9	0·4	4	0·1
1882	—	—	5	0·5

(*b*) Prior to 1878 steel ships were included with iron.

Miscellaneous Industrial Statistics 17. Production of Sulphuric Acid – United Kingdom 1865–1980

NOTES

[1] SOURCES: 1865–1900 – L. F. Haber, *The Chemical Industry during the Nineteenth Century* (Oxford, 1952); 1913–34 – League of Nations, *Statistical Year Book*; 1935–80 – *Abstract*.

[2] It is not clear whether the estimates to 1900 are in Imperial tons or metric tons, but in view of their tentative nature it is not of much concern. Considerably lower estimates are given in T. J. Kreps, *The Economics of the Sulphuric Acid Industry* (Stanford, 1938) for 1867 and 1878, *viz*. 155 and 600 thousand tons respectively.

(in thousand tons)

1865	380	1933	760	1949	1,660	1965	3,305
1870	590	1934	850	1950	1,803	1966	3,118
1875	730	1935	936	1951	1,606	1967	3,183
1880	900	1936	1,043	1952	1,506	1968	3,282
1885	890	1937	1,100	1953	1,875	1969	3,235
1890	870	1938	995	1954	2,043	1970	3,299
1895	770	1939	1,120	1955	2,097	1971	3,404
1900	1,010	1940	1,196	1956	2,251	1972	3,395
1913	1,065	1941	1,200	1957	2,336	1973	3,824
1925	835	1942	1,284	1958	2,241	1974	3,794
1927	847	1943	1,250	1959	2,429	1975	3,116
1928	886	1944	1,268	1960	2,701	1976	3,220
1929	915	1945	1,216	1961	2,662	1977	3,351
1930	800	1946	1,328	1962	2,732	1978	3,399
1931	671	1947	1,333	1963	2,881	1979	3,443
1932	751	1948	1,552	1964	3,135	1980	3,327

Miscellaneous Industrial Statistics 18. Consumption of Rubber – United Kingdom 1935–80

NOTES

[1] SOURCE: *Abstract*.

[2] Total consumption includes that of reclaimed rubber.

(in thousand tons)

	Total	of which synthetic		Total	of which synthetic		Total	of which synthetic
1935	102	—	1951	271	4	1966	382	180
1936	107	—	1952	230	5	1967	381	186
1937	125	—	1953	241	5	1968	425	214
1938	114	—	1954	284	9	1969	439	236
1939	133	—	1955	301 (*a*)	21 (*a*)	1970	450	253
1940	...	—	1956	269	41 (*a*)	1971	452	257
1941	165	—	1957	278	59	1972	432	252
1942	121	...	1958	281	65	1973	437	260
1943	106	4	1959	300	80	1974	424	252
1944	115	42	1960	332	116	1975	389	218
1945	137	64	1961	323	121	1976	429	255
1946	152	30	1962	333	133	1977	430	261
1947	178	3	1963	348	143	1978	376	230
1948	219	3	1964	363	156	1979	363	222
1949	206	2	1965	378	170	1980	333	198
1950	247	3						

(*a*) Including estimates of the amounts by which the returns were incomplete.

Miscellaneous Industrial Statistics 19. Output at the Censuses of Production – United Kingdom 1907–79

NOTES

[1] SOURCES: *Final Report* of the first (1907) and fourth (1930) Censuses of Production and *Abstract*.

[2] There is no exact comparability from one Census to the next, at least until 1970s, for a variety of reasons and the 'break' lines where two figures are shown for one year should not be taken to mean that these are the only significant failures of continuity.

[3] The headings from 1935 correspond to the various Standard Industrial Classifications. Data for earlier years has been reallocated to the 1948 S.I.C. so far as possible, but output which cannot be so allocated – namely that of local authorities; railway, tramway, canal, dock, and harbour companies; and government departments – has been collected under two separate headings.

[4] The Censuses relate to the United Kingdom as constituted at the time at which each took place, except that the figures for mining and quarrying from 1948 onwards do not cover Northern Ireland.

[5] The 1907 Census covered all industrial businesses. In the 1930 and 1935 censuses, firms employing ten people or less (five in Northern Ireland) were not included, and in the source used here, the 1924 figures were adjusted to this basis so far as Great Britain was concerned.

[6] For years prior to 1958, the value of goods for merchanting and canteen supplies were not included, and for years prior to 1963 the value of services rendered to other organisations was not included.

Gross Output

(in £ million)

	Food, Drink, and Tobacco	Chemicals and Allied Industries	Metal Manufacture	Engineering and Allied Industries	Textiles, Leather, and Clothing	Other Manufactures	All Manufacturing Industries	Mining and Quarrying	Construction	Gas, Electricity, and Water	Public Utilities not included elsewhere, and Government Departments	All Census Industries
1907	283(*a*)	90(*a*)(*e*)	147(*f*)(*g*)	287(*f*)(*g*)	458	143(*e*)		134	88	51	72	1,765
1924	670(*a*)	220(*a*)(*e*)	280(*g*)	526(*g*)	987	341(*e*)		273	160	124	161	3,747
1930	662(*a*)(*b*)	199(*a*)(*e*)	214(*g*)	613(*g*)	647	372(*e*)		187	191	152	162	3,371
									214			
1935	665(*b*)	206	245	710	656	413	2,900	167	---- (*h*)	181	...	3,543
									295			
1948	2,632	762	970	3,055	1,968	1,367	10,754	509	1,216	482	...	12,961
1951	3,227	1,283	1,479	4,408	3,339	2,174	15,909	617	1,600	607	...	18,733
	3,819	1,687	1,879	5,644	2,934	2,297	18,259	775	2,053	810	...	21,897
1954 (*c*)	----	----	----	----	----	----	----	----	----	----		----
	3,235	1,663	1,778	5,297	2,892	2,305	17,170	746	1,997	795		20,709
1958	4,285	2,319	2,325	7,433	2,763	2,914	22,039	988	2,780	1,173	...	26,980
	5,195	2,957	2,597	9,845	3,236	3,999	27,819	1,051	3,866	1,732	...	34,467
1963 (*d*)	----	----	----	----	----	----	----	----	----			----
	5,347	2,900	2,602	9,770	3,204	3,949	27,772	1,049	3,903			34,456

Miscellaneous Industrial Statistics 19. *continued*

Gross Output

(in £ million)

	Food, Drink, and Tobacco	Chemicals and Allied Industries	Metal Manufacture	Engineering and Allied Industries	Textiles, Leather, and Clothing	Other Manufactures	All Manufacturing Industries	Mining and Quarrying	Construction	Gas, Electricity, and Water	Public Utilities not included elsewhere, and Government Departments	All Census Industries
1968	7,568	4,353	3,524	13,517	3,933	5,802	38,697	1,040	5,935	2,544	...	48,216
1970	9,157	5,158	4,404	17,096	4,420	7,124	47,360	1,202	...	2,841	...	[51,402](*i*)
1971	9,745	5,731	3,935	18,348	4,643	7,922	50,324	1,205	...	3,192	...	[54,721](*i*)
1972	10,346	6,170	4,236	19,102	4,987	8,919	53,760	1,452	...	3,559	...	[58,771](*i*)
1973	11,806	7,683	5,270	22,171	5,920	10,490	63,340	1,443	...	3,726	...	[68,509](*i*)
1974	14,537	13,634	7,094	27,670	7,072	13,146	83,153	2,053	12,932	4,856	...	102,994
1975	17,173	14,390	7,005	32,575	7,414	14,491	93,048	2,719	14,899	6,238	...	116,994
1976	20,947	18,444	8,861	38,247	8,867	17,803	113,170	3,133	15,779	7,219	...	139,300
1977	25,098	21,027	9,736	45,291	10,080	20,799	132,030	3,556	16,784	8,503	...	160,872
1978	26,969	21,215	9,993	50,864	10,889	23,049	142,980	4,122	19,658	9,625	...	176,385
1979	30,579	27,624	10,953	57,183	12,093	26,718	165,090	4,691	23,403	10,968	...	204,152

Net Output

(in £ million)

1907	87	27	45(f)	112(f)	141	74		115	43	32	36	712
1924	172	73	78	253	308	191		226	79	69	96	1,548
1930	187(a)(b)	77(a)(e)	69(g)	290(g)	236	206(e)		155	93	94	97	1,504
									99			
1935	203(b)	89	88	357	249	237	1,226	136	---(h)	128	...	1,640
1948	525	269	323	1,534	733	693	4,077	407	631	261	...	5,377
1951	608	372	443	1,989	935	924	5,271	471	770	327	...	6,838
1954 (c)	742	529	519	2,622	968	1,058	6,438	577	983	437	...	8,435
	----	----	----	----	----	----	----	----	----	----		----
	645	538	533	2,489	964	1,066	6,234	575	933	438	...	8,180
1958	917	736	689	3,227	967	1,313	7,848	723	1,245	621	...	10,438
1963 (d)	1,269	1,058	830	4,493	1,245	1,956	10,851	772	1,819	982	...	14,423
	----	----	----	----	----	----	----	----	----			----
	1,292	1,068	883	4,457	1,236	1,933	10,820	771	1,834			14,406
1968	1,841	1,516	1,069	6,411	1,614	2,838	15,289	727	2,969	1,572	...	20,284
1970 (j)	2,347	1,933	1,464	7,553	1,796	3,440	18,532	802	...	1,664	...	[20,998](i)
	----	----	----	----	----	----	----	----		----		----
	2,485	2,031	1,552	7,698	1,838	3,651	19,256	892		1,669		[21,817](i)
1971	2,730	2,187	1,350	8,265	1,981	4,090	20,624	868	...	1,883	...	[23,375](i)
1972	3,067	2,377	1,480	9,043	2,150	4,670	22,786	1,068	...	2,134	...	[25,988](i)
1973	3,431	2,807	1,887	10,479	2,565	5,431	26,600	989	...	1,996	...	[29,584](i)
1974	4,114	3,955	2,528	13,087	2,915	6,449	33,048	1,549	5,624	2,478	...	42,698
1975	4,772	4,367	2,352	15,080	3,209	7,168	36,948	2,056	6,704	3,336	...	49,043
1976	5,828	5,283	2,904	17,859	3,745	8,816	44,434	2,344	7,127	4,114	...	58,020
1977	6,576	6,312	2,899	20,983	4,050	10,043	50,862	2,580	7,512	4,652	...	65,607
1978	7,418	6,390	3,215	23,781	4,557	11,473	56,834	3,032	8,725	5,037	...	73,628
1979	8,359	9,084	3,330	27,129	5,131	13,318	66,351	3,464	10,057	5,490	...	85,362

(a) Starch cannot be distinguished from polishes and is included in Chemicals and Allied Industries instead of Food, Drink, and Tobacco.
(b) Includes the subsidy on home-grown sugar.
(c) The first line is on the 1948 S.I.C., the second on the 1958 S.I.C.
(d) The first line is on the 1958 S.I.C., the second on the 1968 S.I.C.
(e) Manufactured fuel cannot be distinguished from coke and is included in Chemicals and Allied Trades instead of Other Manufacturing Industries.
(f) Manufactures of non-ferrous metals other than copper, brass, gold, and silver are included in metal manufacture instead of Other Manufacturing Industries.
(g) The small output of metals in Northern Ireland is included in Engineering and Allied Industries.
(h) Private firms only are covered to 1935 (1st line).
(i) Construction was not included in the Censuses in these years.
(j) Net output from 1970 (2nd line) does not include provision for the deduction of amounts payable to other organisations for the transport of goods within the United Kingdom.

Miscellaneous Industrial Statistics 20. Value of Industrial Production – Republic of Ireland 1926–78

NOTES
[1] SOURCE: *Statistical Abstract of Ireland*.
[2] The figures relate to "transportable goods", including gas, electricity, and water from 1953 (2nd line).
[3] A new basis was adopted from 1979.

(in £ million)

	Gross Output	Net Output		Gross Output	Net Output		Gross Output	Net Output
1926	49·4	16·4	1948	176·1	54·9	1964	665·4	228·6
			1949	201·7	61·5	1965	711·2	247·4
1929	53·7	18·4	1950	235·5	68·6	1966	755·4	274·5
			1951	271·9	74·5	1967	856·3	316·0
1931	44·1	18·2	1952	295·7	77·7	1968	975·1	363·6
				328·9	89·2			
1936	68·0	24·9	1953	--- (*a*)	--- (*a*)	1969	1,106·6	425·8
				346·6	98·6			
1937	73·7	25·4	1954	350·7	102·9	1970	1,226·9	480·4
1938	73·1	25·3	1955	362·7	108·5	1971	1,369·1	548·9
1939	78·3	27·7	1956	357·4	111·9	1972	1,624·7	635·6
							2,091·1	810·1
1940	92·8	28·9	1957	373·0	113·4	1973	--- (*a*)	--- (*a*)
							2,120·5	811·8
1941	90·0	30·6	1958	394·2	122·3	1974	2,758·4	1,010·2
1942	85·8	30·3	1959	430·5	136·8	1975	3,303·5	1,203·6
1943	97·9	32·6	1960	468·8	147·4	1976	4,110·0	1,532·2
1944	105·7	33·5	1961	517·6	168·2	1977	5,250·2	1,819·5
1945	120·1	37·8	1962	560·6	187·5	1978	6,177·6	2,202·4
1946	134·0	42·8	1963	605·2	203·5			
1947	156·9	49·8						

(*a*) New definitions were adopted in these years. (See also note 2 above.)

Miscellaneous Industrial Statistics 21. Indices of Industrial Production – United Kingdom 1700–1980

A. The Hoffman Index, 1700–1913

NOTES TO PART A

[1] SOURCE: W. G. Hoffman, *British Industry, 1700–1950* (Oxford, 1955).

[2] For a review of the critical comments on this index see above, pp. 399–400.

[3] The index including building is a 10-year moving average.

1913 = 100

	excluding building	including building		excluding building	including building		excluding building	including building
1700	1·19	1·59	1745	1·71	2·25	1790	4·07	4·79
1701	1·46	1·57	1746	1·83	2·29	1791	4·13	4·94
1702	1·00	1·56	1747	1·89	2·33	1792	4·47	5·09
1703	1·22	1·55	1748	2·06	2·36	1793	3·83	5·23
1704	1·25	1·55	1749	1·84	2·40	1794	3·95	5·37
1705	1·32	1·56	1750	2·03	2·43	1795	4·18	5·53
1706	1·07	1·57	1751	2·05	2·46	1796	4·49	5·69
1707	1·10	1·58	1752	2·04	2·48	1797	4·12	5·86
1708	1·75	1·60	1753	2·07	2·49	1798	4·51	6·05
1709	1·26	1·62	1754	2·05	2·49	1799	5·35	6·25
1710	1·19	1·64	1755	2·07	2·49	1800	5·65	6·45
1711	1·19	1·66	1756	1·88	2·48	1801	5·35	6·64
1712	1·19	1·69	1757	1·94	2·48	1802	5·65	6·85
1713	1·31	1·73	1758	1·93	2·48	1803	5·70	7·06
1714	1·37	1·78	1759	1·89	2·48	1804	5·89	7·27
1715	1·46	1·82	1760	1·86	2·50	1805	6·02	7·42
1716	1·60	1·87	1761	1·94	2·52	1806	6·07	7·64
1717	1·68	1·90	1762	1·94	2·54	1807	6·31	7·80
1718	1·66	1·94	1763	1·88	2·58	1808	6·00	7·94
1719	1·55	1·97	1764	2·05	2·62	1809	6·15	8·08
1720	1·61	1·99	1765	2·01	2·67	1810	6·69	8·22
1721	1·58	2·01	1766	2·32	2·72	1811	7·03	8·36
1722	1·80	2·03	1767	2·35	2·77	1812	6·61	8·49
1723	1·77	2·03	1768	2·27	2·82	1813	6·67	8·63
1724	1·43	2·03	1769	2·38	2·86	1814	6·78	8·80
1725	1·69	2·03	1770	2·33	2·90	1815	7·37	8·99
1726	1·64	2·03	1771	2·34	2·94	1816	7·20	9·24
1727	1·61	2·02	1772	2·55	2·97	1817	7·87	9·51
1728	1·49	2·02	1773	2·41	2·99	1818	8·19	9·81
1729	1·51	2·02	1774	2·23	3·01	1819	7·92	10·13
1730	1·62	2·03	1775	2·36	3·04	1820	8·13	10·46
1731	1·55	2·04	1776	2·41	3·07	1821	8·47	10·83
1732	1·58	2·05	1777	2·47	3·11	1822	8·93	11·25
1733	1·77	2·06	1778	2·56	3·17	1823	9·41	11·66
1734	1·56	2·07	1779	2·38	3·22	1824	9·91	12·08
1735	1·74	2·07	1780	2·43	3·30	1825	10·82	12·50
1736	1·72	2·08	1781	2·34	3·40	1826	9·88	12·89
1737	1·60	2·09	1782	2·81	3·52	1827	11·23	13·30
1738	1·86	2·10	1783	2·73	3·65	1828	11·94	13·71
1739	1·76	2·11	1784	2·80	3·80	1829	11·55	14·14
1740	1·61	2·12	1785	3·27	3·96	1830	12·6	14·6
1741	1·48	2·13	1786	3·42	4·13	1831	12·8	15·1
1742	1·63	2·15	1787	3·57	4·29	1832	12·7	15·6
1743	1·56	2·18	1788	3·46	4·46	1833	13·4	16·1
1744	1·79	2·21	1789	4·13	4·62	1834	14·2	16·7

A. The Hoffman Index, 1700–1913 (*cont.*)

1913 = 100

	excluding building	including building		excluding building	including building		excluding building	including building
1835	14·7	17·3	1862	31·6	40·8	1888	61·9	71·6
1836	16·2	17·9	1863	33·3	42·0	1889	65·9	72·9
1837	15·4	18·5	1864	34·6	43·4	1890	65·5	74·2
1838	16·8	19·1	1865	36·9	44·7	1891	65·8	75·6
1839	18·2	19·8	1866	38·4	46·1	1892	62·9	77·1
1840	17·8	20·4	1867	37·8	47·5	1893	61·3	78·8
1841	18·1	21·0	1868	39·9	49·0	1894	65·1	80·6
1842	17·2	21·6	1869	40·6	50·5	1895	67·3	82·6
1843	18·2	22·2	1870	43·4	52·0	1896	70·8	84·6
1844	20·5	22·9	1871	46·1	53·4	1897	71·3	86·5
1845	21·7	23·8	1872	47·5	54·8	1898	73·9	88·5
1846	21·6	24·4	1873	49·1	56·2	1899	77·3	90·2
1847	21·0	25·2	1874	50·1	57·5	1900	77·1	91·7
1848	23·0	26·0	1875	49·3	58·3	1901	75·8	93·1
1849	23·3	26·9	1876	49·9	60·0	1902	77·2	94·4
1850	23·3	27·8	1877	51·2	61·1	1903	77·2	95·5
1851	24·3	28·8	1878	48·5	62·0	1904	76·8	96·5
1852	25·8	29·9	1879	46·3	63·0	1905	82·0	97·6
1853	28·0	31·0	1880	54·2	64·0	1906	85·1	98·5
1854	28·4	32·0	1881	54·6	64·9	1907	86·8	99·2
1855	27·8	33·0	1882	58·3	65·9	1908	82·1	99·7
1856	30·6	34·1	1883	59·8	66·7	1909	83·4	100·1
1857	31·9	35·2	1884	57·9	67·5	1910	86·5	100·5
1858	29·8	36·3	1885	56·1	68·4	1911	89·6	100·8
1859	32·6	37·4	1886	54·9	69·2	1912	90·9	100·5
1860	34·2	38·6	1887	57·6	70·3	1913	100	100
1861	33·6	39·7						

B. Various Indices of the Growth of Industrial Production at Intervals – Britain, 1700–1841

NOTE TO PART B

SOURCES: Phyllis Deane and W. A. Cole, *British Economic Growth, 1688–1959* (Cambridge, 1962), p. 78; C. Knick Harley, "British Industrialization before 1841: Evidence of Slower Growth during the Industrial Revolution", *J.E.H.* XLII, 2 (1982) p. 276; N. F. R. Crafts, *British Economic Growth during the Industrial Revolution* (Oxford, 1985), p. 26.

	Deane & Cole 1700 = 100		
	Export Industries	Home Industries	Total Industry & Commerce
1700	100	100	100
1710	108	98	104
1720	125	108	118
1730	142	105	127
1740	148	105	131
1750	176	107	148
1760	222	114	179
1770	256	114	199
1780	246	123	197
1790	383	137	285
1800	544	152	387

	Harley's 'divisia' Indices and Industrial Percentage Growth Rates	
	Index	Growth Rate
1770	100	1·5–1·6
1815	198–209	
1815	100	3·0–3·2
1841	219–228	

	Crafts's Industrial Percentage Growth Rates
1700–60	0·71
1760–70	1·23
1770–80	1·79
1780–90	1·60
	... (*a*)
1780–90	2·40
1790–1801	1·83
1801–11	2·72
1811–21	2·63
1821–31	3·65

Misellaneous Industrial Statistics 21. *continued*

C. The Feinstein Index, 1855–1965

NOTES TO PART C

[1] SOURCE: C. H. Feinstein, *National Income, Expenditure and Output of the United Kingdom, 1855–1965* (Cambridge, 1972), table 51.

[2] The classification follows the 1948 Standard Industrial Classification for 1913–48 and the 1958 S.I.C. subsequently. Differences between them are minor. The classification used prior to 1913 is broadly comparable.

1913 = 100

	All Industries	Manufacturing Industries	Chemicals & Allied Industries	Metal Manufacture	Engineering & Allied Industries	Textiles, Leather, and Clothing	Food, Drink, and Tobacco	Other Manufacturing Industries	Mining and Quarrying	Building and Contracting	Gas, Electricity, and Water
1855	26.3	26.7	12.1	22.0	15.5	39.4	40.4	15.4	22.8	37.2	5.2
1856	28.1	28.9	13.4	24.6	16.6	42.9	43.8	15.9	24.7	38.5	5.5
1857	29.1	30.3	14.1	24.4	17.1	45.2	47.0	15.9	24.2	37.5	5.7
1858	28.5	28.9	13.4	24.1	16.0	40.7	47.8	17.4	24.0	44.3	6.0
1859	30.0	30.5	13.3	24.6	16.7	45.6	46.3	18.2	26.3	44.7	6.4
1860	31.7	31.9	14.7	25.9	17.2	48.0	47.7	19.6	29.1	47.2	7.0
1861	31.7	31.2	14.1	25.6	17.3	44.5	48.5	20.8	30.4	50.6	7.2
1862	32.4	29.4	14.0	27.9	18.6	32.2	53.8	23.3	30.0	59.7	7.6
1863	32.5	30.7	15.6	29.7	21.0	33.6	53.7	23.9	31.8	61.7	7.8
1864	35.0	32.7	15.9	30.7	23.4	36.4	53.7	26.7	34.2	71.0	8.7
1865	37.3	34.8	16.9	32.2	23.7	41.7	53.3	29.2	36.1	78.5	9.3
1866	38.7	35.8	16.1	31.0	21.9	45.7	54.7	31.1	37.1	84.5	10.1
1867	36.4	34.9	15.9	31.4	21.5	46.0	55.1	24.4	38.0	60.5	10.5
1868	36.4	36.4	17.4	32.8	22.5	49.0	59.1	21.3	37.6	47.1	10.7
1869	35.8	35.7	17.7	35.7	23.6	44.8	59.7	20.5	39.2	42.4	11.2
1870	40.2	39.5	19.8	38.4	25.4	53.0	58.9	25.4	40.4	61.4	11.8
1871	43.5	43.0	21.8	40.5	28.6	59.3	58.9	28.2	43.2	70.5	12.6
1872	44.8	44.0	22.3	41.1	31.4	58.0	61.6	29.8	45.0	72.7	12.9
1873	45.3	44.9	22.5	40.6	30.4	61.5	64.0	29.0	46.3	64.4	13.6
1874	46.4	45.9	20.8	38.3	30.3	62.6	67.9	31.2	45.4	72.6	14.1
1875	46.7	45.3	21.8	40.8	30.2	58.6	67.5	33.6	47.6	75.9	14.7
1876	47.5	45.5	23.5	42.2	29.8	60.0	65.1	34.6	48.4	81.2	15.4
1877	47.4	46.4	23.2	44.7	31.1	60.3	68.2	32.5	48.8	71.8	16.0
1878	47.3	45.4	21.3	43.5	30.2	57.3	69.0	34.1	48.2	80.4	16.8
1879	45.6	42.9	21.6	41.8	28.6	53.5	63.0	34.8	48.5	79.1	17.5
1880	50.3	49.8	26.7	52.2	35.1	65.0	66.8	36.0	53.1	76.6	19.7
1881	53.5	51.7	28.4	55.8	40.1	63.1	67.9	39.5	55.4	84.7	20.6
1882	55.7	55.0	30.8	60.2	45.2	66.8	69.8	39.9	56.3	81.3	21.5
1883	56.5	55.4	29.9	60.2	45.1	66.6	70.8	42.4	58.9	81.3	22.8
1884	54.4	52.6	27.5	56.7	37.6	66.1	69.5	42.5	57.8	80.5	23.9
1885	52.1	50.2	27.0	56.9	35.5	60.0	71.6	40.1	57.2	73.1	25.1
1886	51.0	49.8	28.3	54.5	35.1	62.7	67.1	38.3	56.4	65.1	26.2
1887	55.1	54.5	33.0	61.3	42.1	65.8	71.6	40.8	57.9	71.1	27.2
1888	58.3	58.2	36.6	68.0	48.3	68.9	72.2	43.0	60.7	73.2	28.2
1889	62.4	62.5	39.8	71.8	54.8	73.2	74.1	46.4	62.9	79.1	29.2
1890	63.3	63.0	39.2	69.2	53.0	74.4	77.0	49.5	64.6	82.6	30.7
1891	64.1	63.5	37.8	65.6	48.9	77.9	80.7	52.0	65.8	85.8	32.5
1892	61.0	59.5	36.0	61.7	45.3	69.0	79.8	52.3	64.4	84.7	33.6
1893	60.0	59.4	37.9	61.4	44.9	69.3	78.8	52.6	58.4	83.7	33.6
1894	63.5	61.4	43.1	60.6	45.0	73.6	80.2	54.2	66.5	84.7	34.9
1895	66.5	65.3	45.0	65.8	50.3	78.7	81.5	56.5	66.8	93.5	37.2
1896	71.4	70.8	51.5	74.8	60.0	78.8	84.5	64.9	68.5	104.0	38.9
1897	73.4	71.2	52.8	76.5	59.9	76.7	83.6	71.6	70.7	118.8	41.1
1898	77.0	75.2	53.6	76.3	63.2	82.5	88.2	76.1	70.7	128.2	43.1
1899	80.1	78.2	58.0	82.3	67.1	83.1	90.3	81.1	76.8	126.0	46.1

Miscellaneous Industrial Statistics 21. *continued*

C. The Feinstein Index, 1855–1965 (*cont.*)

1913 = 100

	All Industries	Manufacturing Industries	Chemicals & Allied Industries	Metal Manufacture	Engineering & Allied Industries	Textiles, Leather, and Clothing	Food, Drink, and Tobacco	Other Manufacturing Industries	Mining and Quarrying	Building and Contracting	Gas, Electricity, and Water
1900	80·1	77·4	58·8	80·4	67·0	80·9	89·3	81·7	78·5	125·4	48·1
1901	80·3	77·2	59·4	80·7	67·2	77·7	89·7	85·7	76·3	135·4	50·2
1902	81·7	77·4	61·0	77·4	66·0	77·5	91·8	88·3	79·2	145·0	52·3
1903	80·0	75·5	62·7	79·7	62·9	74·4	91·9	85·7	80·3	135·3	54·5
1904	81·0	76·0	65·6	77·8	65·6	71·4	92·1	89·6	81·0	138·6	57·2
1905	85·7	82·6	73·8	86·9	74·1	81·6	93·0	90·4	82·3	135·3	60·6
1906	89·3	86·4	80·8	93·8	81·5	84·3	93·2	90·7	87·5	130·0	64·4
1907	91·0	88·8	85·2	94·3	81·6	91·1	93·7	90·9	93·2	119·6	68·4
1908	83·7	81·2	75·5	82·2	66·0	88·8	92·5	83·8	91·1	97·8	71·2
1909	84·3	82·2	83·1	87·9	70·2	85·5	94·5	81·7	91·6	92·7	75·1
1910	85·5	83·1	92·6	93·3	69·3	83·7	95·7	85·9	92·0	92·8	79·8
1911	91·5	90·2	92·1	91·4	85·3	90·5	98·7	88·2	94·6	100·5	85·4
1912	93·9	93·9	94·9	89·2	86·3	100·0	99·4	92·1	90·6	101·4	92·5
1913	100	100	100	100	100	100	100	100	100	100	100
1914	93·7	93·2	96·2	93·5	...	88·9	98·3	...	92·9	90·6	107·1
1915	95·5	98·0	98·1	94·7	...	108·5	97·1	...	88·0	70·3	109·5
1916	90·4	91·8	101·9	91·9	...	95·9	95·3	...	88·2	...	...
1917	84·4	85·0	102·6	94·9	...	87·2	81·0	...	85·7	...	...
1918	81·5	82·5	103·7	96·7	...	75·9	77·3	...	79·3	...	...
1919	89·8	92·2	104·6	83·9	...	93·8	97·4	...	79·9	...	...
1920 (*a*)	99·8	101·5	112·6	92·3	110·8	83·4	107·5	110·9	81·0	103·4	128·2
	97·9	99·7	112·0	92·0	110·1	82·6	100·8	109·0	80·9	101·1	126·3
1921	79·7	77·6	80·6	44·8	84·4	62·5	93·1	78·6	57·9	140·1	115·5
1922	92·2	90·3	95·4	64·6	86·4	83·0	93·0	93·2	86·2	116·0	118·5
1923	97·6	96·7	104·1	91·1	102·2	74·1	97·2	113·4	95·9	96·4	128·3
1924	108·4	106·5	110·5	98·4	115·4	83·4	99·7	121·3	94·0	152·9	139·5
1925	112·7	109·8	106·8	91·2	124·2	83·7	102·3	129·3	86·6	195·1	147·0
1926	106·6	106·3	98·4	63·2	120·6	81·7	102·9	130·9	48·1	226·9	152·8
1927	122·8	117·5	112·6	106·8	133·5	86·7	106·4	145·4	90·1	249·7	163·6
1928	119·5	117·2	118·1	99·7	134·5	83·6	109·5	142·0	85·7	201·1	172·5
1929	125·5	122·0	124·1	104·7	141·9	84·0	112·4	152·8	93·1	217·3	182·8
1930	120·1	116·8	117·8	94·4	134·1	77·2	113·4	149·9	88·5	200·7	186·2
1931	112·3	108·8	113·1	73·4	113·0	79·6	110·3	145·8	79·8	189·6	191·0
1932	111·9	109·4	120·6	75·2	107·4	83·9	110·1	147·4	75·7	178·8	195·9
1933	119·3	117·5	126·3	88·1	113·1	90·2	113·8	158·2	75·8	207·8	207·4
1934	131·2	128·2	136·3	108·3	135·7	92·5	120·6	170·2	81·4	234·4	222·9
1935	141·2	139·8	148·1	119·4	158·6	95·9	128·9	179·4	82·2	239·9	243·3
1936	153·9	152·8	154·3	134·0	182·6	103·2	134·6	192·3	85·0	262·7	268·6
1937	163·1	162·1	164·4	150·4	200·9	104·0	142·2	198·9	89·6	273·8	291·2
1938	158·7	157·4	155·9	125·0	201·6	96·7	146·2	193·2	85·2	262·5	301·8
1946	162·6	164·7	234·1	154·8	241·5	71·4	161·4	173·9	66·3	201·6	404·4
1947	171·3	174·2	237·9	164·8	256·0	76·7	164·3	189·3	68·2	210·2	419·2
1948	186·0	190·0	257·6	184·0	278·0	86·3	168·3	210·5	7[illegible]·3	229·1	445·7
1949	196·8	202·1	266·3	184·9	297·9	93·1	174·8	230·1	74·7	239·6	476·5
1950	208·0	216·0	302·1	194·3	317·7	99·6	173·4	255·5	75·5	239·9	519·7
1951	214·8	225·2	317·3	206·1	337·6	97·8	179·3	270·7	78·0	230·8	552·1
1952	210·0	217·0	301·6	211·9	339·7	84·3	182·4	241·2	79·1	237·7	569·1
1953	222·0	230·5	337·8	207·0	351·1	97·3	189·6	263·6	78·7	254·3	597·6
1954	235·6	246·0	379·2	221·1	376·0	98·8	192·5	294·9	79·7	264·3	646·2
1955	247·6	261·7	402·3	239·7	413·2	98·2	197·6	312·6	78·8	264·9	680·9

C. The Feinstein Index, 1855–1965 (*cont.*)

1913 = 100

	All Industries	Manufacturing Industries	Chemicals & Allied Industries	Metal Manufacture	Engineering & Allied Industries	Textiles, Leather, and Clothing	Food, Drink, and Tobacco	Other Manufacturing Industries	Mining and Quarrying	Building and Contracting	Gas, Electricity, and Water
1956	248·6	260·4	419·3	243·2	406·0	97·8	203·1	304·3	79·0	279·6	712·5
1957	253·1	266·2	435·9	246·2	419·5	97·7	205·8	309·5	78·5	278·7	737·9
1958	250·3	262·8	435·9	223·6	422·5	90·2	210·6	310·5	75·1	277·4	771·1
1959	263·1	278·6	482·5	233·6	442·8	96·9	218·2	334·7	73·1	292·9	791·2
1960	281·6	301·2	534·4	271·0	475·7	101·9	224·8	367·6	70·5	309·3	852·1
1961	285·1	301·7	543·5	254·9	479·5	100·5	232·1	370·4	69·5	331·4	891·4
1962	288·1	303·0	564·0	241·0	485·0	97·9	236·4	374·1	71·4	334·8	962·3
1963	297·9	315·4	605·4	252·0	502·8	101·4	242·2	389·3	71·3	335·6	1,025·6
1964	320·9	340·3	660·8	285·9	539·9	107·0	249·2	430·6	71·5	375·3	1,059·5
1965	330·2	351·6	690·9	298·7	560·2	109·1	254·9	440·2	68·9	383·0	1,120·4

(*a*) Southern Ireland is included to 1920 (1st line) and excluded thereafter.

D. Official Indices, 1950–80

NOTES TO PART D

[1] Source: *Abstract.*

[2] The weights are shown in italics for the years that follow up to the next line of weights.

	All Industries	Manufacturing Industries	Bricks, Pottery, Glass, Cement, etc.	Chemicals	Metals: Ferrous	Metals: Non-ferrous	Engineering (excl.) ships)	Shipbuilding and Marine Engineering	Vehicles	Metal Goods n.e.s.
1954 = 100	*1,000*	*760*	*30*	*63*	*54*	*15*	*164*	*22*	*78*	*42*
1950	88·3	87·8	88·8	79·7	88·0	87·4	84·5	93·5	76·4	95·0
1951	91·3	91·6	93·7	83·7	91·8	98·4	90·5	96·2	79·9	101·2
1952	89·2	88·2	92·3	79·6	95·4	97·5	92·4	99·2	79·5	97·5
1953	94·3	93·7	96·9	89·1	96·1	84·8	93·6	105·1	90·4	91·8
1954	100	100	100	100	100	100	100	100	100	100
1955	105·1	99·0	103·9	106·2	107·8	110·6	107·4	108·5	114·6	111·6
1956	105·6	99·2	102·4	110·6	110·8	107·5	107·0	117·4	107·2	108·1
1957	107·5	98·5	99·3	115·0	112·7	106·5	111·0	107·9	114·9	108·6
1958	106·3	94·3	98·0	115·0	99·9	105·5	111·5	108·8	118·4	106·0
1958 = 100	*1,000*	*748*	*28*	*68*	*55*	*13*	*167*	*22*	*79*	*42*
1958	100	100	100	100	100	100	100	100	100	100
1959	105·1	106·0	106·4	110·7	103·8	107·3	105·4	93·6	109·3	99·8
1960	112·5	114·6	118·4	122·6	120·8	122·6	113·7	84·8	118·0	112·2
1961	113·9	114·8	123·5	124·7	113·5	116·4	121·2	85·7	109·8	104·7
1962	115·1	115·3	125·6	129·4	106·3	113·6	123·2	86·6	112·0	101·1
1963	119·0	120·0	129·6	138·8	111·3	118·7	126·1	77·4	121·0	108·3
1964	128·2	129·5	148·4	151·6	127·1	131·5	137·2	74·9	126·4	120·6
1965	131·9	133·8	150·6	158·5	133·7	133·3	144·1	74·0	129·3	123·5
1966	133·4	135·6	151·2	164·5	125·1	126·7	152·1	73·9	131·2	114·8
1970 = 100	*1,000*	*745*	*27*	*58*	*43*	*14*	*182*	*16*	*72*	*48*
1966	90·6	89·2	94·1	78·9	97·9	96·7	84·7	92·1	96·3	94·1
1967	91·7	89·8	97·7	82·7	91·4	94·0	87·5	93·0	94·5	90·2
1968	97·2	96·0	103·7	89·3	96·8	101·5	91·2	95·0	102·6	98·3
1969	99·8	99·6	104·1	94·7	100·4	99·8	97·1	94·8	106·6	104·1
1970	100	100	100	100	100	100	100	100	100	100
1971	100·4	99·6	108·1	102·2	89·8	95·8	100·8	96·6	99·4	93·6
1972	102·7	102·4	115·2	107·5	89·4	97·3	100·4	91·8	103·7	95·7
1973	110·2	110·8	127·1	120·0	97·3	108·5	111·3	95·1	105·1	103·1

Miscellaneous Industrial Statistics 21. *continued*

D. Official Indices, 1950–80 (*cont.*)

	All Industries	Manufacturing Industries	Bricks, Pottery, Glass, Cement, etc.	Chemicals	Metals: Ferrous	Metals: Non-ferrous	Engineering (excl.) ships)	Shipbuilding and Marine Engineering	Vehicles	Metal Goods n.e.s.
1975 = 100	*1,000*	*697*	*28*	*66*	*35*	*12*	*170*	*14*	*68*	*46*
1973	109·4	108·4	113·6	107·3	129·5	117·0	98·4	95·4	113·3	110·4
1974	105·1	106·6	107·2	110·4	116·2	113·3	102·3	98·9	108·9	109·1
1975	100	100	100	100	100	100	100	100	100	100
1976	102·1	101·4	100·6	111·2	104·7	105·4	96·6	96·5	99·2	99·0
1977	106·1	103·0	99·6	114·2	103·1	108·3	97·5	93·5	101·6	103·8
1978	110·3	104·0	101·4	115·0	102·3	106·9	99·4	86·4	102·0	102·2
1979	113·1	104·4	100·9	117·4	104·4	105·3	101·2	78·1	99·0	98·5
1980	105·9	95·5	90·8	107·7	67·1	97·3	98·4	69·2	94·1	83·6

	Textiles	Leather	Clothing	Food, Drink, and Tobacco	Paper and Printing	Timber	Other Manufactures	Mining and Quarrying	Construction	Gas, Electricity and Water
1954 = 100	*77*	*5*	*33*	*81*	*53*	*22*	*22*	*72*	*120*	*48*
1950	100·1	110·1	101·2	90·1	86·5	84·1	86·8	94·8	90·8	80·4
1951	99·8	106·8	95·7	93·1	91·3	90·6	91·6	98·0	87·3	85·5
1952	81·9	94·2	91·7	94·7	76·7	80·2	81·9	99·3	90·0	88·1
1953	97·4	101·5	100·3	98·5	85·7	89·0	88·3	98·8	96·3	92·5
1954	100	100	100	100	100	100	100	100	100	100
1955	97·5	99·7	103·7	102·7	107·7	100·1	110·8	99·0	100·3	105·4
1956	96·4	93·5	105·8	105·5	106·3	94·0	105·6	99·2	105·8	110·2
1957	96·5	93·3	105·1	106·9	109·1	96·0	111·9	98·5	105·5	114·3
1958	87·1	88·0	101·5	109·4	111·2	93·6	112·6	94·3	105·0	119·4
1958 = 100	*58*	*4*	*30*	*86*	*55*	*20*	*22*	*72*	*126*	*54*
1958	100	100	100	100	100	100	100	100	100	100
1959	105·6	103·3	111·5	103·6	107·0	111·9	108·2	97·4	105·6	102·6
1960	110·4	101·6	119·6	106·7	119·4	114·0	120·1	93·9	111·5	110·5
1961	106·6	102·4	121·9	110·2	119·7	115·8	116·0	92·6	119·5	115·6
1962	104·6	96·8	118·1	112·2	122·1	111·1	118·2	95·1	120·7	124·8
1963	109·6	98·8	120·0	115·0	127·8	112·6	125·8	95·0	121·0	133·0
1964	116·2	101·9	125·6	118·3	138·5	127·8	136·7	95·3	135·3	137·4
1965	118·1	103·2	129·3	121·0	141·7	127·4	144·1	91·8	138·1	145·3
1966	117·3	100·7	127·5	124·0	144·1	121·2	151·8	86·5	139·4	151·3
1970 = 100	*49*	*3*	*24*	*84*	*64*	*22*	*31*	*37*	*146*	*72*
1966	85·9	107·7	100·9	91·3	92·8	95·9	81·9	115·3	96·7	83·0
1967	84·1	96·7	97·8	93·0	92·5	98·8	85·2	114·5	100·4	86·0
1968	97·2	104·4	101·8	95·5	96·2	106·5	95·7	111·2	102·6	91·6
1969	100·2	103·0	100·4	98·5	99·3	99·7	99·5	104·0	101·9	96·2
1970	100	100	100	100	100	100	100	100	100	100
1971	100·7	103·0	105·4	100·6	97·3	103·0	99·7	100·0	103·0	103·9
1972	103·0	104·5	107·8	104·9	102·6	113·5	104·2	84·1	104·8	111·2
1973	108·6	101·0	114·6	109·3	112·1	132·6	116·5	92·6	107·3	118·1
1975 = 100	*40*	*3*	*24*	*77*	*58*	*25*	*31*	*41*	*182*	*80*
1973	116·5	107·1	102·1	103·1	115·2	120·2	110·3	110·3	117·8	98·6
1974	105·8	98·7	100·2	102·5	115·2	102·3	106·8	89·7	105·6	98·5
1975	100	100	100	100	100	100	100	100	100	100
1976	102·8	102·4	97·1	102·5	102·4	103·3	108·7	127·9	98·6	102·3
1977	100·8	97·1	103·2	104·0	106·7	96·8	114·7	193·5	98·2	106·4
1978	99·0	97·3	105·6	106·2	109·1	101·3	118·0	241·1	104·9	109·7
1979	96·0	92·3	107·5	107·6	112·4	102·8	117·9	307·3	101·3	116·1
1980	79·3	72·3	93·7	106·6	105·4	88·9	107·5	312·9	95·9	113·0

Miscellaneous Industrial Statistics 22. Index of Industrial Production – Republic of Ireland 1926–80

NOTES
[1] Source: *Statistical Abstract of Ireland*.
[2] The index relates to transportable industrial goods.

1953 = 100

1926	35·2	1944	46·8	1957	104·5	1969	234·8
		1945	53·5	1958	106·5	1970	242·7
1929	38·4	1946	60·8	1959	117·5	1971	252·5
		1947	65·2	1960	126·0	1972	263·1
1931	37·6	1948	71·3	1961	137·4	1973	291·1
1936	54·0	1949	80·6	1962	146·2	1974	296·4
1937	54·9	1950	91·4	1963	153·5	1975	277·4
1938	53·6	1951	94·0	1964	165·4	1976	302·3
1939	56·2	1952	91·6	1965	172·2	1977	341·2
1940	56·0	1953	100	1966	180·4	1978	364·2
1941	52·2	1954	103·3	1967	195·7	1979	386·9
1942	43·0	1955	107·5	1968	217·5	1980	383·1
1943	44·1	1956	105·3				

Miscellaneous Industrial Statistics 23. Patents – England 1617–1852 and United Kingdom 1852–1980

NOTE TO PART A

SOURCE: *Titles of Patents of Inventions* (2 vols., 1854).

A. English Patents Sealed, 1617–1852

Year	Patents	Year	Patents	Year	Patents	Year	Patents
1617(*a*)	(4)	1688	4	1743	7	1798	77
1618	6	1689	1	1744	17	1799	82
1619	5	1690	3	1745	4	1800	96
1620	2	1691	20	1746	4	1801	104
1621	2	1692	25	1747	8	1802	107
1622	3	1693	19	1748	11	1803	73
1623	5	1694	9	1749	13	1804	60
1624	3	1695	8	1750	7	1805	95
1625	2	1696	3	1751	8	1806	99
1626	3	1697	3	1752	7	1807	94
1627	6	1698	7	1753	13	1808	95
1628	3	1699	5	1754	9	1809	101
1629	4	1700	2	1755	12	1810	108
1630	5	1701	1	1756	3	1811	115
1631	2	1702	1	1757	9	1812	118
1632	6	1703	1	1758	14	1813	131
1633	4	1704	4	1759	10	1814	96
1634	12	1705	1	1760	14	1815	102
1635	11	1706	5	1761	9	1816	118
1636	11	1707	2	1762	17	1817	103
1637	15	1708	2	1763	20	1818	132
1638	8	1709	3	1764	18	1819	101
1639	1	1710	—	1765	14	1820	97
1640	3	1711	3	1766	31	1821	109
1641	—	1712	3	1767	23	1822	113
1642	1	1713	2	1768	23	1823	138
1643–59	—	1714	3	1769	36	1824	180
1660	3	1715	4	1770	30	1825	250
1661	4	1716	9	1771	22	1826	141
1662	6	1717	6	1772	29	1827	150
1663	2	1718	6	1773	29	1828	154
1664	4	1719	2	1774	35	1829	130
1665	2	1720	7	1775	20	1830	180
1666	2	1721	8	1776	29	1831	151
1667	5	1722	13	1777	33	1832	147
1668	3	1723	7	1778	30	1833	180
1669	—	1724	14	1779	37	1834	207
1670	2	1725	9	1780	33	1835	231
1671	4	1726	5	1781	34	1836	296
1672	3	1727	7	1782	39	1837	256
1673	4	1728	11	1783	64	1838	394
1674	5	1729	8	1784	46	1839	411
1675	11	1730	12	1785	61	1840	440
1676	4	1731	9	1786	60	1841	440
1677	7	1732	3	1787	55	1842	371
1678	7	1733	5	1788	42	1843	420
1679	3	1734	8	1789	43	1844	450
1680	1	1735	1	1790	68	1845	572
1681	5	1736	5	1791	57	1846	493
1682	8	1737	4	1792	85	1847	493
1683	7	1738	6	1793	43	1848	388
1684	13	1739	3	1794	55	1849	514
1685	5	1740	4	1795	51	1850	513
1686	3	1741	8	1796	75	1851	455
1687	6	1742	6	1797	54	1852 (*b*)	(470)

(*a*) From 2nd March only.

(*b*) To 30th September only.

NOTE TO PART B

SOURCES: 1852–75 – *Report of the Commissioners of Patents for Inventions* (S.P. 1876, XXVII); 1876–1938 – *Abstract*; 1939–80 – *Report of the Comptroller General of Patents, Designs and Trade Marks*.

B. United Kingdom Patents Applied for and Sealed, 1852–1980

	Applications	Patents Sealed
1852 (a)	(1,211)	(914)
1853	3,045	2,187
1854	2,764	1,878
1855	2,958	2,046
1856	3,106	2,094
1857	3,200	2,028
1858	3,007	1,954
1859	3,000	1,977
1860	3,196	2,063
1861	3,276	2,047
1862	3,490	2,191
1863	3,309	2,094
1864	3,260	2,024
1865	3,386	2,186
1866	3,453	2,124
1867	3,723	2,284
1868	3,991	2,490
1869	3,786	2,407
1870	3,405	2,180
1871	3,529	2,376
1872	3,970	2,771
1873	4,294	2,974
1874	4,492	3,162
1875	4,561	3,112
1876	5,069	3,435
1877	4,949	3,317
1878	5,343	3,509
1879	5,338	3,524
1880	5,517	3,741
1881	5,751	3,950
1882	6,241	4,337
1883	5,993	3,962
	---	---
1884	17,100 (b)	2,345 (b)
1885	16,101	9,308
1886	17,176	8,923
1887	18,051	9,226
1888	19,103	9,309
1889	21,008	10,081
1890	21,307	10,646
1891	22,888	10,643
1892	24,169	11,164
1893	25,123	11,530
1894	25,386	11,699
1895	25,962	12,191

	Applications	Patents Sealed
1896	30,193	12,473
1897	30,952	14,210
1898	27,649	14,063
1899	25,800	14,160
1900	23,924	13,170
1901	26,788	13,062
1902	28,976	13,764
1903	28,832	15,718
1904	29,678	15,089
1905	27,577	14,786
1906	30,030	14,707
1907	28,915	16,272
1908	28,598	16,284
1909	30,603	15,065
1910	30,388	16,269
1911	29,353	17,164
1912	30,089	15,814
1913	30,077	16,599
1914	24,820	15,036
1915	18,191	11,457
1916	18,602	8,424
1917	19,285	9,347
1918	21,839	10,809
1919	32,853	12,301
1920	36,672	14,191
1921	35,132	17,697
1922	35,494	17,366
1923	32,621	17,073
1924	31,370	16,839
1925	33,003	17,199
1926	33,080	17,333
1927	35,469	17,624
1928	38,556	17,695
1929	39,898	18,937
1930	39,359	20,765
1931	36,117	21,949
1932	37,052	21,150
1933	36,734	16,568
1934	37,409	16,890
1935	36,116	17,675
1936	35,867	17,819
1937	36,266	17,614
1938	37,973	19,314
1939	33,109	17,605

	Applications	Patents Sealed
1940	18,254	11,453
1941	16,847	11,179
1942	18,624	7,969
1943	21,944	7,945
1944	26,200	7,712
1945	35,332	7,465
1946	38,181	8,971
1947	35,378	11,727
1948	33,626	15,558
1949	33,347	20,703
	--- (c)	--- (c)
1950	31,686	13,509
1951	30,513	13,761
1952	33,142	21,380
1953	36,401	17,882
1954	37,871	17,985
1955	37,551	20,630
1956	39,730	19,938
1957	40,498	25,205
1958	42,277	18,531
1959	44,495	18,157
1960	44,914	26,775
1961	46,811	28,871
1962	49,187	27,721
1963	51,468	30,148
1964	53,104	32,619
1965	55,507	33,864
1966	58,471	37,272
1967	59,290	38,999
1968	61,995	43,038
1969	63,614	37,127
1970	62,101	40,004
1971	61,078	38,989
1972	60,281	41,609
1973	60,312	40,440
1974	56,250	35,883
1975	53,400	39,019
1976	54,561	41,755
1977	54,423	35,442
	--- (d)	
1978	51,305	40,148 (d)
1979	75,067	28,149 (d)
1980	68,081	22,263 (d)

(*a*) October to December.

(*b*) The Act of 1883 greatly increased the numbers of both applications and grants. under the new Act, the number sealed in each year was given instead of, as previously, the number sealed in respect of applications during the year. This accounts for the low numbers sealed in 1884, since most of the applications under the new Act were sealed in 1885.

(*c*) Under the Patents Act of 1949 and application claiming two or more Convention priorities is now filed as a single application with additional fees, whereas, prior to 1950, the former Acts required a separate application in respect of each Convention priority.

(*d*) Subsequent statistics are of Requests for Grant under the 1977 Patents Act, the European Patent Convention and Article 10 of the Patent Cooperation Treaty, as well as of applications under the 1949 Patents Act. The figures of patents sealed, however, continue to relate to the 1949 Act alone.

Miscellaneous Industrial Statistics 24. Designs and Trade Marks – United Kingdom 1884–1980

NOTE
SOURCE: *Reports of the Comptroller General of Patents, Designs and Trade Marks.*

	Designs		Trade Marks			Designs		Trade Marks	
	Applications	Registered	Applications	Registered		Applications	Registered	Applications	Registered
1884	19,753	19,687	7,104	4,523	1934	20,681	17,830	10,016	5,533
1885	20,725	20,602	8,026	4,332	1935	21,229	18,269	9,169	5,783
1886	24,041	23,838	10,677	4,725	1936	20,292	17,523	9,163	5,337
1887	26,043	25,314	10,586	4,740	1937	19,343	16,831	8,836	5,027
1888	26,239	25,135	13,315	5,520	1938	16,118	16,544	8,493	5,265
1889	24,705	23,989	11,316	5,053	1939	11,588	10,595	6,690	4,643
1890	22,553	21,107	10,258	6,014	1940	4,473	4,632	3,507	2,529
1891	21,950	20,880	10,787	4,225	1941	3,118	2,576	3,726	2,090
1892	19,527	18,501	9,101	3,649	1942	2,301	2,254	4,082	2,386
1893	19,480	18,338	8,675	3,522	1943	2,824	2,049	5,471	2,739
1894	22,255	20,847	8,013	2,905	1944	3,525	2,436	6,943	3,340
1895	21,417	20,192	8,272	2,821	1945	4,755	3,103	9,341	3,341
1896	22,849	21,727	9,466	2,917	1946	6,524	4,285	11,690	4,167
1897	20,417	19,301	10,624	3,358	1947	5,463	5,196	10,365	4,476
1898	20,049	18,830	9,767	3,437	1948	5,725	5,060	10,326	7,397
1899	19,495	18,470	8,927	3,777	1949	6,631	4,800	9,362	8,006
1900	16,952	16,282	7,937	3,223	1950	7,327	5,362	9,791	7,777
1901	16,934	16,217	8,775	3,246	1951	9,155	8,412	8,649	7,828
1902	17,825	17,106	8,899	3,377	1952	9,671	8,447	9,913	6,846
1903	21,104	20,426	9,467	3,748	1953	8,270	7,435	11,734	7,261
1904	23,531	22,604	9,972	3,842	1954	9,215	7,316	12,384	8,285
1905	23,938	23,138	10,521	4,261	1955	9,792	8,121	11,793	7,884
1906	22,001	21,212	11,414	4,731	1956	9,964	7,821	11,356	7,737
1907	24,928	24,039	10,796	6,255	1957	10,512	8,320	11,756	8,217
1908	24,907	24,389	10,645	5,965	1958	10,891	8,680	12,938	7,250
1909	26,412	25,754	10,880	6,112	1959	9,098	7,893	14,166	6,987
1910	32,745	32,212	10,623	5,722	1960	9,237	7,840	16,128	9,894
1911	43,057	41,581	9,743	4,868	1961	9,427	8,361	13,997	10,841
1912	43,015	42,077	10,014	4,942	1962	7,780	7,431	14,210	9,754
1913	40,429	39,275	9,689	5,071	1963	7,915	6,722	15,024	10,121
1914	34,354	33,362	8,317	4,408	1964	8,327	6,866	15,388	11,462
1915	18,130	17,390	6,057	3,241	1965	8,105	6,800	14,995	9,814
1916	15,399	14,766	5,837	2,878	1966	8,477	5,568	14,868	9,927
1917	13,208	12,729	5,502	2,744	1967	8,299	6,792	15,495	10,429
1918	10,019	9,597	6,968	3,055	1968	7,096	5,567	16,820	10,907
1919	14,094	13,049	12,479	4,837	1969	6,692	5,859	17,139	10,005
1920	13,669	13,071	14,064	7,122	1970	6,306	5,135	16,511	9,372
1921	13,387	12,313	11,959	7,518	1971	6,788	5,517	15,735	12,023
1922	15,736	14,419	12,397	7,099	1972	5,805	5,119	18,703	11,695
1923	19,085	17,807	12,571	7,694	1973	4,541	4,259	18,694	11,266
1924	22,155	20,155	12,597	7,968	1974	4,183	4,016	17,613	10,626
1925	23,801	22,308	12,387	7,464	1975	4,730	3,019	16,659	11,440
1926	23,206	21,874	13,007	7,734	1976	4,623	3,700	15,607	12,195
1927	22,707	21,009	12,381	7,543	1977	4,492	4,325	16,236	10,093
1928	24,746	23,899	12,684	6,818	1978	5,147	4,748	18,150	10,643
1929	23,648	22,072	11,753	7,455	1979	5,111	5,273	19,328	10,036
1930	21,463	20,169	10,830	6,728	1980	5,329	4,965	20,102	6,708
1931	18,886	17,685	9,870	6,016					
1932	22,374	19,887	10,322	6,060					
1933	25,015	20,767	9,845	5,472					

Miscellaneous Industrial Statistics 25. Patents, Designs, and Trade Marks – Republic of Ireland 1927–80

NOTES
[1] SOURCE: *Statistical Abstract of Ireland*.
[2] The figures relate to applications.
[3] The 1929 figures are for the period from 1 August 1927 to 31 March 1929. Subsequent figures to 1974 are for years ended 31 March. From 1975 they relate to calendar years.

	Patents	Designs	Trade Marks
1929 (*a*)	968	129	1,594
1930	1,017	58	777
1931	829	65	1,386
1932	687	113	994
1933	487	81	979
1934	550	46	651
1935	587	57	524
1936	546	48	483
1937	642	40	531
1938	613	41	531
1939	663	19	477
1940	492	28	322
1941	320	9	244
1942	308	14	112
1943	385	40	269
1944	330	22	498
1945	390	14	703
1946	573	36	789
1947	864	49	982
1948	1,044	74	1,048
1949	769	39	922
1950	626	85	907
1951	598	39	845
1952	646	30	920
1953	687	65	919
1954	709	53	1,067
1955	734	68	1,013
1956	711	76	1,208
1957	685	58	1,045
1958	675	67	1,058
1959	776	61	1,155
1960	867	49	1,271
1961	959	107	1,383
1962	1,084	80	1,413
1963	1,100	81	1,664
1964	1,361	121	1,733
1965	1,317	130	1,890
1966	1,370	144	1,893
1967	1,530	103	1,999
1968	1,613	117	2,024
1969	1,668	109	2,290
1970	1,682	140	2,208
1971	1,691	136	2,173
1972	1,675	113	2,553
1973	1,891	181	3,236
1974	2,536	180	3,180
1975 (*a*)	2,844	230	3,554
1976	2,865	200	3,189
1977	2,667	247	3,319
1978	2,583	256	3,182
1979	2,533	299	3,574
1980	2,749	315	3,823

(*a*) See note 3 above.

CHAPTER IX

EXTERNAL TRADE

TABLES

According to Clark, whose systematic study of the early English external trade figures is an indispensable guide to this subject: 'The real beginnings of commercial statistics belong to the sixteenth and early seventeenth centuries.'[1] For it was not until the late sixteenth century that the Customs figures began to be used to measure the balance of trade and thus to guide policy. In earlier periods the purpose of the statistics was merely fiscal, and although medieval statistics exist for the chief commodities subject to tax – and, indeed, some of the quantity data are shown in table 17 of chapter VI above – overall statistics of values are not available.

Regular and complete central records of English external trade – complete in the sense of covering all ports – date from the establishment of the office of Inspector-General of Imports and Exports in 1696. For Scotland they are available from 1755. No series of statistics for Irish trade in the seventeenth and eighteenth centuries has been published, but Cullen gives a few for individual years, and he has rather more for the main commodities.[2] The basic source of these statistics for the eighteenth century and on into the early years of the nineteenth is the Inspector-General's manuscript ledgers, though aggregates and some details have been transcribed from them (often inaccurately), and there are various Parliamentary returns and secondary sources derived from them. So many inaccurate or incomplete published versions of these eighteenth-century statistics had appeared by the 1950s that the publication of Elizabeth Schumpeter's carefully transcribed extracts from the ledgers, edited for publication by T. S. Ashton, who contributed a very useful introduction, were of great value to students of British commerce at this period.[3]

The eighteenth-century trade records have inherent defects, however, and one historian in the 1950s went so far as to call them 'a snare'.[4] This probably goes too far; but they must certainly not be used without full awareness of the problems.

One important defect is that most of the rates at which the various commodities were valued by the Customs officials ossified within a few years of the beginning of the ledgers, in 1696. They did not remain unaltered from the start, as has sometimes been stated, following the early lead given by Macpherson;[5] but what changes there were almost all took place in the first few years. This, together with the fact that some goods (especially from Asia, and some new commodities) continued to be entered at a declared (i.e. fluctuating) rate, means that the unadjusted figures of the 'official' values of trade are a true index neither of volume nor of value. Nevertheless, two points may be made in mitigation. First, as the leading modern student of the subject, Ralph Davis, pointed out, the difference between official and real values was 'of minor importance during much of the eighteenth century but becoming very serious towards its end'.[6] He regarded his own estimates of current values from 1784–6

[1] G. N. Clark, *Guide to English Commercial Statistics, 1696–1782* (London, 1938), p. x.
[2] L. M. Cullen, *Anglo-Irish Trade 1660–1800* (Manchester, 1968), chapters II and III.
[3] Elizabeth B. Schumpeter, *English Overseas Trade Statistics 1697–1808* (Oxford, 1960).
[4] G. D. Ramsay, *English Overseas Trade During the Centuries of Emergence* (London, 1957), p. 260.
[5] D. Macpherson, *Annals of Commerce* (4 vols., London, 1805), II, p. 340.
[6] Ralph Davis, *The Industrial Revolution and British Overseas Trade* (Leicester, 1979), p. 77.

onwards (table 2A) as essentially continuing an 'official' series acceptable up to then. Second, by applying constant valuation rates to the quantity figures, as Mrs Schumpeter largely did to the export figures up to 1771 using the rates of 1703, the ledgers can be made to supply a good volume index. Except towards the end of the century, when re-exports are exaggerated because some prices, especially those of coffee and tea, fell below the official rates, this weighting of the series with the early-eighteenth-century prices produces surprisingly little distortion, as is shown by comparing them with an index based on late-eighteenth-century prices.[7]

What is possibly a more serious defect of the external trade statistics is that which springs from the importance of smuggling in eighteenth-century Britain. Probably Davis is right to say that 'we cannot go behind these figures . . . and must accept them as subject to this type of error, probably not very important in relation to the total, but considerable at times for trade in particular commodities and with particular countries'. Clearly, smuggling activity varied at different times, and, as Cole showed, there seem to have been two peaks – one in the 1730s and early 1740s, and another during the American War of Independence.[8] But illicit trade was not seriously restricted until the younger Pitt's reforms of the 1780s, and its total disappearance had to wait until free trade rendered it superfluous. At its high point during the War of Independence, Cole estimated that smuggled imports may have been between two and three million pounds sterling, or up to 25 per cent of the official value of legal imports. This points a very obvious warning that the official figures of imports and re-exports cannot be taken as an *exact* guide to the volume of trade.[9]

Overall figures at official values of first English and then British external trade in the eighteenth century have long been available, though it was not until the 1960s that a series was published distinguishing re-exports of foreign and colonial produce from exports of British goods, which is reproduced here as table 1. This also includes the statistics of trade with Ireland, which were collected by W. A. Cole and made available by his kindness. The Union with Ireland led eventually to the unification of the British and Irish Customs, and in consequence to the substitution of United Kingdom for British statistics. These are given in table 2 for the period, up to 1853, when official values were still employed. Apart from the elimination (or incorporation) of Irish trade it is directly comparable with table 1. But it also includes Imlah's estimates of values at current prices of imports and re-exports, which link up, practically without break, with table 3, which gives the external trade aggregates at

[7] Phyllis Deane and W. A. Cole, *British Economic Growth, 1688–1959* (Cambridge, 1962).

[8] W. A. Cole, 'Trends in Eighteenth Century Smuggling', *Economic History Review*, second series X, 3 (1958). See also the discussion in G. D. Ramsay, *op. cit.*, pp. 166–206.

[9] Hoh-Cheung and Lorna H. Mui, '"Trends in Eighteenth Century Smuggling" Reconsidered', *Economic History Review*, second series XXVIII, 1 (1975), suggested that Cole's figures for smuggled tea were approximately a third too high. If correct – and Cole's rejoinder, in the same journal issue, accepts that it *may* be, though he thinks that it probably is not – this would reduce Cole's estimates by perhaps as much as a fifth. The point about the uncertainty of the series which results from smuggling is not affected, of course.

current prices down to 1980 (with the Republic of Ireland statistics in table 4).[10] The increasing artificiality of the official values in the nineteenth century is well brought out by table 2.

Davis carried Imlah's current value estimates of imports and re-exports back to 1784, and provided similar figures for exports as well, though because of the great labour involved these figures are for three years in each decade (up to the 1850s) and not for every year. These figures also lead on to the current price data in table 3. As he said of these estimates – and it applies also to the more detailed figures derived from his book in tables 5, 10, 12, and 16 – 'It can properly be said that even a study of the long-term would be better for taking its sample years all from the same point of successive trade cycles, rather than an arbitrarily chosen group of dates identical within each decade. There were, however, some difficulties in doing this during the first half of the period because of peculiar irregularities caused by the war; and the block of years before 1813 for which data are missing further restricted the choice of method.'[11]

Tables 5 to 13 give a certain amount of detail about external trade by commodity groups and some individual commodities. Following on from Davis's figures in Part A of table 5, there are Schlote's reworking of the data in the *Annual Statement of Trade* from 1854 to 1899, whereafter officially provided figures became available. Similar figures for the Republic of Ireland are in table 6. Tables 7 and 8 depend heavily on the work of Mrs Schumpeter. Nearly all the figures up to 1808 are taken from her worksheets, which T. S. Ashton, in the 1950s, kindly allowed us to photograph and use. One peculiarity of these must be noted: whereas in her summary totals prize goods were included throughout, this was not done in the detailed tables in the period 1772–99, and only partially in 1800.

The later figures, together with the whole of table 9, are taken for the most part from the *Trade and Navigation Accounts*.[12] In constructing these tables two main difficulties have been encountered – the provision of links between official and current price values, and between the British and the United Kingdom figures. For this purpose an overlap has been provided for the differing series, together with an indication, where possible, of the exact size of the break caused by the change. The overlap is generally three years, though for the official and current price values of exports, for which it is a simple matter to make it longer, it is fifteen years.

It is perhaps unnecessary to stress again the unreality of the official rates of valuation by

[10] In the same way, there is no serious break on the change in 1871 from computed real values of imports and re-exports to declared values. Computations of real values were also made for 1805–9 for the Bullion Committee (*S.P.* 1810 III, Appendix pp. 228–9), and for 1840 and 1852 in a Board of Trade report (*S.P.* 1863 LXVI).

[11] Ralph Davis, *op. cit.*, p. 11. An earlier attempt to provide an annual series at current values by John J. McCusker, 'Current Values of English Exports 1697–1800', *William and Mary Quarterly* (1971) is flawed because it simply applies the Schumpeter-Gilboy price index (see chapter XIV, table 1) to the official values. That index is both inappropriate and too crude.

[12] Prior to 1854 these were published as a section of the annual *Finance Accounts* in *Sessional Papers*. Subsequently they appeared as separate Blue Books, and, from 1921, as non-Parliamentary official papers, entitled the *Annual Statement of Trade*, and more recently, *Trade Statistics of the United Kingdom*.

the later years of the eighteenth century. But the dangers of taking the official statistics as anything other than volume indicators by then – and rather inexact ones at that[13] – are so great that a further warning is justified. This is particularly so in relation to the official value series for the United Kingdom, since by 1826 the rates for many, perhaps most, articles bore little relation to their prices, and in the following thirty years the situation became worse. This deterioration was most prominent in export values, as the cost of many manufactured goods fell, and these are not given here beyond 1829. In any event, a better volume index has been compiled for the period after 1796 by Imlah, and this is shown in table 18, where it is continued from modern sources.

The remaining commodity tables are fairly straightforward, and the main general problems they raise are of continuity or definition of the various commodity groups. These are dealt with in the notes. A full discussion of the problems of valuation, measurement, and classification of the trade statistics is given in an article by Maizels, which the interested user should consult.[14] In selecting the groups to be shown, the main principle followed has been to take those which bulked largest in each branch of trade for some considerable part of the period. Some commodities which were important only for a short time (e.g. guano in the mid nineteenth century) have been omitted, and others (e.g. tobacco and hemp) have been continued, though no longer of major importance, for the sake of comparison with other periods when they were pre-eminent. Still other goods (e.g. silk) have been included, though they were never in the first rank of traded commodities, because of the interest which historians have shown in them.

Tables 14 to 17 show the breakdown of external trade on a geographical basis, the first two of these giving the official values up to 1822, and the last two the current price values from the earliest date for which they are available (including Davis's figures, already referred to). Unfortunately, the source of the annual figures in table 14, Moreau, follows the practice of his period in not distinguishing exports from re-exports. However, the distinction has been made for certain years by Deane and Cole, and these are shown in table 15.

The constitution of the regions adopted in these two tables and in the early part of table 16 is that used in the early nineteenth century by writers such as Moreau and Porter[15] (though modified somewhat for Davis's figures). These regions are appropriate for the period for which they are used, but would become less so if their use were continued further into the nineteenth century. It should be noted that until 1904 the geographical analysis was given in the trade returns by country of shipment. After that date the basis of analysis was country of

[13] Referring to the first half of the nineteenth century, A. W. Flux wrote: 'The official values appear to give a much better indication on the movements in the volume of trade than one could have expected' (*Transactions of the Manchester Statistical Society* (1898–9), p. 81). For many purposes the official values provide a good enough guide to volume, and the stress laid on their inexactness here should not be taken to mean that they are useless.

[14] A. Maizels, 'The Overseas Trade Statistics of the United Kingdom', *Journal of the Royal Statistical Society*, XCXII (1949).

[15] César Moreau, *State of the Trade of Great Britain with All Parts of the World* (London 1822); G. R. Porter, *The Progress of the Nation* (London, 2nd edition, 1847).

consignment until 1936, when it became country of origin or consumption. These changes had most effect on the figures of trade with western Europe.[16]

Reference has already been made to Imlah's index of the volume of external trade, which is given as part A of table 18. It is carried on beyond 1913 in the other two parts of the table. A more detailed breakdown of the volume of trade by different categories of goods was made by Schlote up to 1933, and a selection from his work is given as table 19. Unfortunately there is then a gap until the post-1947 indices kindly made available to me by my colleague John Wells.

Modern concern about the international position of British manufacturing industry has led to much attention to the decline of Britain's share of world trade in manufactures. Table 21 shows the summary results of three such studies. They do not call for much comment here except to note that whilst figures for British exports may be reasonably complete and accurate, those for the world as a whole are inevitably less so. These statistics must, therefore, be seen as guides to trends rather than precise.

Finally, there are two tables concerned with Britain's terms of trade since the start of continuous external trade statistics. Since the eighteenth-century data are primarily volume indicators, as has been explained, the terms of trade for that period are gross barter only. Later periods are covered by the estimates of first Imlah and subsequently the Board of Trade (and its successors) for the net barter terms of trade. These are given alongside the price indices (or, as Kindleberger more accurately describes them, unit-value indices)[17] on which they are based. Gross barter terms have not been shown after the eighteenth century, but they are easily estimated from the volume indices in table 18.

Other data on the volume of external trade in certain commodities can be found in other chapters – on certain foodstuffs in chapter III, on fuels in chapter IV, on metals in chapter V, and on textiles in chapter VI. In addition, balance of payments estimates have been included in chapter XVI with other national accounts statistics.

[16] Stephen Bourne, *Trade, Population and Food* (London, 1880), pp. 35–6 gives examples of traffic flowing through intermediate ports in the nineteenth century. Much German trade, for example, was routed through Dutch ports and attributed in the returns to the Netherlands. For a more recent discussion of this problem see A. Maizels, cited in footnote 14 above.

[17] C. P. Kindleberger, *The Terms of Trade* (New York, 1956). He gives a further series for the terms of trade from 1870 to 1952.

External Trade 1. Official Values of External Trade – England & Wales 1697–1791, and Great Britain, 1772–1804

NOTES

[1] SOURCE: Phyllis Deane and W. A. Cole, *British Economic Growth, 1688–1959* (Cambridge University Press, 1962).

[2] Prize goods are included throughout, except as indicated in footnote (c).

[3] Bullion and specie are definitely excluded from 1706 onwards, and they have been excluded so far as possible in earlier years.

A. England & Wales 1697–1791

(in £ thousand)

	Total Trade			Trade with Ireland		
	Imports	Domestic Exports	Re-exports	Imports	Domestic Exports	Re-exports
1697	3,344	2,295 (a)	1,096	...	...	...
1698	4,608	3,582 (a)	1,608	...	...	...
1699	5,621	3,655 (a)	1,570	417	131 (a)	139
1700	5,840	3,731 (a)	2,081	234	131 (a)	141
1701	5,796	4,049 (a)	2,192	285	142 (a)	164
1702	4,088	3,130 (a)	1,144	258	106 (a)	113
1703	4,450	3,888 (a)	1,622	324	108 (a)	159
1704	5,329	3,723 (a)	1,804	321	92 (a)	125
1705	...	...	...	...	...	...
1706	4,064	4,142 (a)	1,447	266	95 (a)	103
1707	4,267	4,173 (a)	1,602	306	109 (a)	154
1708	4,699	4,404 (a)	1,495	275	107 (a)	145
1709	4,511	4,406	1,507	276	108	144
1710	4,011	4,279	1,566	311	102	184
1711	4,686	4,088	1,875	297	112	149
1712	...	...	...	...	...	...
1713	5,811	4,490	2,402	296	148	159
1714	5,929	5,564	2,440	326	140	257
1715	5,641	5,015	1,908	389	171	249
1716	5,800	4,807	2,243	562	163	182
1717	6,347	5,384	2,613	470	209	221
1718	6,669	4,381	1,980	326	169	165
1719	5,367	4,514	2,321	380	217	171
1720	6,090	4,611	2,300	283	182	147
1721	5,908	4,512	2,689	333	175	196
1722	6,378	5,293	2,972	356	279	210
1723	6,506	4,725	2,671	361	292	262
1724	7,394	5,107	2,494	368	279	190
1725	7,095	5,667	2,814	334	204	271
1726	6,678	5,001	2,692	333	321	249
1727	6,799	4,605	2,670	307	273	163
1728	7,569	4,910	3,797	318	229	247
1729	7,541	4,940	3,299	288	254	264
1730	7,780	5,326	3,223	294	240	293
1731	6,992	5,081	2,782	309	272	347
1732	7,088	5,675	3,196	294	279	336
1733	8,017	5,823	3,015	386	318	277
1734	7,096	5,403	2,897	401	279	348
1735	8,160	5,927	3,402	417	369	400
1736	7,308	6,118	3,585	447	301	419
1737	7,074	6,668	3,414	346	329	402
1738	7,439	6,982	3,214	381	276	420
1739	7,829	5,572	3,272	412	289	385
1740	6,704	5,111	3,086	391	242	387
1741	7,936	5,995	3,575	405	265	434

External Trade 1. *continued*

A. England & Wales 1697–1791 (*cont.*)

(in £ thousand)

	Total Trade			Trade with Ireland		
	Imports	Domestic Exports	Re-exports	Imports	Domestic Exports	Re-exports
1742	6,867	6,095	3,480	347	318	457
1743	7,802	6,868	4,442	817	349	511
1744	6,363	5,411	3,780	391	281	454
1745	7,847	5,739	3,333	(1,441) (*b*)	578	333
1746	6,206	7,201	3,566	533	466	330
1747	7,117	6,744	3,031	541	318	431
1748	8,136	7,317	3,824	464	417	489
1749	7,918	9,081	3,598	568	472	534
1750	7,772	9,474	3,225	613	666	651
1751	7,943	8,775	3,644	664	658	516
1752	7,889	8,226	3,469	564	694	447
1753	8,625	8,732	3,511	561	689	461
1754	8,093	8,318	3,470	610	732	441
1755	8,773	7,915	3,150	643	616	454
1756	8,962	8,632	3,089	828	593	519
1757	9,253	8,584	3,755	687	520	441
1758	8,415	8,763	3,855	1,050	513	414
1759	8,923	10,079	3,869	832	519	413
1760	9,833	10,981	3,714	904	692	358
1761	8,544	10,804	4,069	855	883	593
1762	8,870	9,400	4,351	889	830	699
1763	11,199	9,522	5,146	769	809	831
1764	10,391	11,536	4,725	777	794	840
1765	10,981	10,122	4,451	1,071	800	967
1766	11,513	9,890	4,193	1,154	933	987
1767	12,074	9,492	4,375	1,103	791	1,089
1768	11,879	9,695	5,425	1,226	901	1,348
1769	11,909	8,984	4,454	1,265	998	967
1770	12,217	9,503	4,764	1,214	1,003	1,122
1771	12,822	11,219	5,905	1,381	771	1,213
1772	13,305	10,503	5,656	1,242	893	1,071
1773	11,560	8,976	5,944	1,253	850	1,069
1774	13,098	10,049	5,868	1,447	1,036	1,070
1775	13,550	9,723	5,478	1,550	1,133	1,037
1776	11,703	9,275	4,454	1,517	1,221	958
1777	11,842	8,750	3,903	1,503	1,077	(855) (*c*)
1778	10,293	7,754	3,797	1,361	796	675
1779	10,660	7,113	5,588	1,384	705	663
1780	10,812	8,033	4,564	1,549	890	1,040
1781	11,919	7,043	3,526	1,434	930	840
1782	(9,533) (*d*)	8,605	(3,750) (*d*)	1,349	829	887
1783	12,115	10,096	4,116	1,499	999	1,020
1784	14,119	10,497	3,675	1,523	621	789
1785	14,900	10,315	4,795	1,694	740	1,142
1786	14,610	11,191	4,200	1,905	872	849
1787	16,335	11,310	4,445	1,884	958	1,066
1788	16,551	11,937	4,346	1,862	1,245	852
1789	16,408	12,970	5,201	2,069	1,079	964
1790	17,443	14,057	4,828	2,203	1,114	823
1791	17,688	15,896	5,539	2,102	1,295	907

See p. 450 for footnotes.

External Trade 1. *continued*

B. Great Britain, 1772–1804

(in £ thousand)

	Total Trade			Trade with Ireland		
	Imports	Domestic Exports	Re-exports	Imports	Domestic Exports	Re-exports
1772	14,515	10,974	6,746	1,382	981	1,188
1773	12,676	9,418	7,114	1,379	954	1,273
1774	14,300	10,557	6,732	1,602	1,133	1,205
1775	14,817	10,072	6,253	1,688	1,229	1,224
1776	12,449	9,705	5,051	1,654	1,372	1,086
1777	12,644	9,300	4,191	1,653	1,214	(987) (*c*)
1778	10,976	8,208	4,046	1,482	958	858
1779	11,435	7,648	5,890	1,547	843	802
1780	11,715	8,814	4,785	1,743	1,063	1,152
1781	12,724	7,622	3,710	1,630	1,119	956
1782	(10,342) (*d*)	9,110	(3,900) (*d*)	1,498	964	953
1783	13,122	10,710	4,327	1,612	1,156	1,147
1784	15,273	11,274	3,827	1,778	772	862
1785	16,279	10,975	5,143	2,012	890	1,278
1786	15,786	11,830	4,476	2,171	1,023	939
1787	17,804	12,054	4,816	2,222	1,136	1,206
1788	18,027	12,725	4,748	2,185	1,422	1,003
1789	17,821	13,780	5,561	2,405	1,243	1,072
1790	19,131	14,921	5,199	2,574	1,328	937
1791	19,670	16,810	5,922	2,479	1,471	1,000
1792	19,659	18,337	6,568	2,623	1,513	860
1793	19,257	13,892	6,498	2,285	1,055	888
1794	22,289	16,725	10,024	2,750	1,281	1,199
1795	22,737	16,527	10,785	2,637	1,612	1,185
1796	23,187	19,102	11,417	2,765	1,782	1,115
1797	21,014	16,903	12,014	3,114	1,311	1,126
1798	27,858	19,673	13,919	2,736	1,658	1,316
1799	26,837	24,084	11,907	2,771	2,406	1,681
1800	30,571	24,304	18,848	2,313	1,788	1,954
1801	32,796	25,700	16,602	2,360	1,577	1,373
1802	31,442	26,993	19,128	3,134	2,117	1,423
1803	27,992	22,112	11,540	2,888	2,281	1,083
1804	29,201	23,936	13,532	2,747	2,199	1,182

(*a*) In arriving at the export figures for 1697–1708, the original values of woollen goods have not been used, but they have been replaced by figures computed at the 1709 rates of valuation.

(*b*) The figure of imports from Ireland is as given in the Inspector-General's Ledgers. The principal component was exceptionally heavy shipments of linen yarn. But from the Irish export figures given in C. Gill's *The Rise of the Irish Linen Industry* (Oxford, 1925), p. 341, it seems that there must have been an error in the English ledgers.

(*c*) Excluding prize goods.

(*d*) The accounts for this year are defective. These figures are partly based on returns quoted in D. Macpherson, *Annals of Commerce* ... (4 vols, London, 1805).

External Trade 2. Official Values and Values at Current Prices of External Trade – United Kingdom 1796–1853

NOTE

SOURCES: Computed value of imports and re-exports – A. H. Imlah, *Economic Elements in the Pax Britannica* (Cambridge, Mass., Harvard University Press, 1958), pp. 37–8; declared values of exports and all official values – *S.P.* 1898, LXXXV.

(in £ million)

	Computed or Declared Values			Official Values		
	Imports	Domestic Exports	Re-exports	Imports	Domestic Exports	Re-exports
1796	39·6	30·1 (*a*)	8·5	...	...	...
1797	34·4	27·5 (*a*)	9·3	...	...	...
1798	49·6	32·2 (*b*)	11·3	...	...	...
1799	50·9	36·8 (*b*)	9·4	...	...	...
1800	62·3	37·7 (*b*)	14·7	...	...	...
1801	68·7	40·6 (*b*)	12·9	31·8	24·9	10·4
1802	54·7	45·9 (*b*)	12·9	29·8	25·6	12·8
1803	53·9	36·9 (*b*)	9·1	26·6	20·5	8·1
1804	57·3	38·2 (*b*)	11·0	27·8	22·7	9·0
1805	61·0	38·1	10·0	28·6	23·4	7·7
1806	53·3	40·9	9·2	26·9	25·9	7·8
1807	53·8	37·2	8·3	26·7	23·4	7·7
1808	51·5	37·3	6·5	26·8	24·6	5·8
1809	73·7	47·4	14·3	31·8	33·5	12·8
1810	88·5	48·4	12·5	39·3	34·1	9·5
1811	50·7	32·9	6·7	26·5	22·7	6·2
1812	56·0	41·7	9·1	26·2	29·5	9·7
1813	...	...	...	...	...	...
1814	80·8	45·5	24·8	33·8	34·2	19·4
1815	71·3	51·6	16·8	33·0	42·9	15·7
1816	50·2	41·7	12·6	27·4	35·7	13·5
1817	61·0	41·8	10·1	30·8	40·1	10·3
1818	80·7	46·5	12·3	36·9	42·7	10·9
1819	56·0	35·2	10·2	30·8	33·5	9·9
1820	54·2	36·4	10·4	32·4	38·4	10·6
1821	45·6	36·7	9·5	30·8	40·8	10·6
1822	44·6	37·0	7·8	30·5	44·2	9·2
1823	52·0	35·4	7·2	35·8	43·8	8·6
1824	51·2	38·4	7·5	37·5	48·7	10·2
1825	73·6	38·9	8·2	44·2	47·2	9·2
1826	50·4	31·5	7·3	37·8	41·0	10·1
1827	58·8	37·2	6·8	44·9	52·2	9·8
1828	57·3	36·8	6·5	45·2	52·8	9·9
1829	54·1	35·8	6·6	44·0	56·2	10·6
1830	55·9	38·3	5·6	46·3	61·2	8·5
1831	62·0	37·2	6·7	49·7	60·7	10·7
1832	52·5	36·5	7·3	44·6	65·0	11·0
1833	58·9	39·7	6·9	45·9	70·0	9·8
1834	64·7	41·6	8·0	49·4	73·8	11·6
1835	68·0	47·4	9·2	49·0	78·4	12·8
1836	84·4	53·3	9·3	57·3	85·2	12·4
1837	70·1	42·1	9·0	54·8	72·5	13·2
1838	80·1	50·1	9·2	61·3	95·5	12·7
1839	90·8	53·2	10·2	62·0	97·4	12·8
1840	91·2	51·4	10·0	67·5	102·7	13·8

External Trade 2. *continued*

(in £ million)

	Computed or Declared Values			Official Values		
	Imports	Domestic Exports	Re-exports	Imports	Domestic Exports	Re-exports
1841	83·9	51·6	9·9	64·4	102·2	14·7
1842	76·4	47·4	8·4	65·3	100·3	13·6
1843	71·0	52·3	7·8	70·2	117·9	14·0
1844	78·9	58·6	8·0	75·4	131·6	14·4
1845	88·4	60·1	9·3	85·3	134·6	16·3
1846	87·3	57·8	9·2	75·9	132·3	16·3
1847	112·1	58·8	11·7	90·9	126·1	20·0
1848	88·2	52·8	8·4	93·5	132·6	18·4
1849	101·4	63·6	12·1	105·9	164·5	25·6
1850	103·0	71·4	12·0	100·5	175·4	21·9
1851	109·5	74·4	12·5	110·5	190·7	23·7
1852	110·0	78·1	13·0	109·3	196·2	23·3
1853	148·5	98·9	16·8	123·1	214·3	27·7

(*a*) Imlah's estimates based on British and Irish trade.

(*b*) Declared values of British trade plus Imlah's estimates of the market value of Irish exports. (See Imlah, *op. cit.* p. 20 *et seq.*)

External Trade 2a. Computed Values at Current Prices of External Trade – Great Britain 1784–6 to 1854–6

NOTES

[1] Source: Ralph Davis, *The Industrial Revolution and British Overseas Trade* (Leicester, 1979), Appendix, table 37.

[2] After 1825, British trade with Ireland was not recorded. Before 1826, therefore, British trade with Ireland is included, and afterwards it is excluded in the first column for each category. The second column is a computation excluding trade with Ireland.

[3] Figures for 1784–6 are for years ended 30 September, and subsequently they are for years beginning 6 January.

[4] Imports are valued c.i.f. and exports and re-exports are valued f.o.b.

(annual averages in £ million)

	British Trade			British Trade excluding with Ireland		
	Imports	Exports	Re-exports	Imports	Exports	Re-exports
1784–6	22·8	13·6	3·6	20·4	12·7	2·7
1794–6	37·9	24·0	8·3	34·3	21·8	6·9
1804–6	55·6	41·2	9·8	50·6	37·5	8·3
1814–6	71·8	48·0	17·7	64·7	44·5	16·1
1824–6	66·4	39·9	9·6	57·0	35·3	8·1
1834–6	70·3	46·2	10·2	70·3	46·2	10·2
1844–6	82·0	58·4	10·8	82·0	58·4	10·8
1854–6	151·6	102·5	21·0	151·6	102·5	21·0

External Trade 3. Values at Current Prices of External Trade – United Kingdom 1854–1980

NOTES

[1] SOURCE: *Annual Statement of Trade*, *Overseas Trade Statistics of the United Kingdom*, and *Abstract*.

[2] Imports are valued c.i.f., exports and re-exports f.o.b.

[3] The value of bullion, specie, and diamonds is excluded throughout.

(in £ million)

	Imports	Domestic Exports	Re-exports
1854	152·4	97·2	18·6
1855	143·5	95·7	21·0
1856	172·5	115·8	23·4
1857	187·8	122·1	24·1
1858	164·6	116·6	23·2
1859	179·2	130·4	25·3
1860	210·5	135·9	28·6
1861	217·5	125·1	34·5
1862	225·7	124·0	42·2
1863	248·9	146·6	50·3
1864	275·0	160·4	52·2
1865	271·1	165·8	53·0
1866	295·3	188·9	50·0
1867	275·2	181·0	44·8
1868	294·7	179·7	48·1
1869	295·5	190·0	47·1
1870	303·3	199·6	44·5
	- - -		- - -
1871	331·0 (*a*)	223·1	60·5 (*a*)
1872	354·7	256·3	58·3
1873	371·3	255·2	55·8
1874	370·1	239·6	58·1
1875	373·9	223·5	58·1
1876	375·2	200·6	56·1
1877	394·4	198·9	53·5
1878	368·8	192·8	52·6
1879	363·0	191·5	57·3
1880	411·2	223·1	63·4
1881	397·0	234·0	63·1
1882	413·0	241·5	65·2
1883	426·9	239·8	65·6
1884	390·0	233·0	62·9
1885	371·0	213·1	58·4
1886	349·9	212·7	56·2
1887	362·2	221·9	59·3
1888	387·6	234·5	64·0
1889	427·6	248·9	66·7
1890	420·7	263·5	64·7
1891	435·4	247·2	61·9
		- - -	- - -
1892	423·8	227·2 (*b*)	64·4 (*b*)
1893	404·7	218·3	58·9
1894	408·3	216·0	57·8
1895	416·7	226·1	59·7
1896	441·8	240·1	56·2
1897	451·0	234·2	60·0
1898	470·5	233·4	60·7
		- - -	
1899	485·0	264·5 (*c*)	65·0
1900	523·1	291·2	63·2
1901	522·0	280·0	67·8

	Imports	Domestic Exports	Re-exports
1902	528·4	283·4	65·8
1903	542·6	290·8	69·6
1904	551·0	300·7	70·3
1905	565·0	329·8	77·8
1906	607·9	375·6	85·1
1907	645·8	426·0	91·9
1908	593·0	377·1	79·6
1909	624·7	378·2	91·3
1910	678·3	430·4	103·8
1911	680·2	454·1	102·8
1912	744·6	487·2	111·7
1913	768·7	525·2	109·6
1914	696·6	430·7	95·5
1915	851·9	384·9	99·1
1916	948·5	506·3	97·6
1917	1,064·2	527·1	69·7
1918	1,316·2	501·4	30·9
1919	1,626·2	798·6	164·7
1920	1,932·6	1,334·5	222·8
1921	1,085·5	703·4	106·9
1922	1,003·1	719·5	103·7
	- - - -	- - -	- - -
1923	1,096·2 (*d*)	767·3 (*d*)	118·5 (*d*)
	- - - -	- - - -	- - - -
1924	1,277·4	801·0	140·0
1925	1,320·7	773·4	154·0
1926	1,241·4	653·0	125·5
1927	1,218·3	709·1	123·0
1928	1,195·6	723·6	120·3
1929	1,220·8	729·3	109·7
1930	1,044·0	570·8	86·8
1931	861·3	390·6	63·9
1932	701·7	365·0	51·0
1933	675·0	367·9	49·1
1934	731·4	396·0	51·2
1935	756·0	425·8	55·3
1936	847·8	440·6	60·8
1937	1,027·8	521·4	75·1
1938	919·5	470·8	61·5
1939	885·5	439·5	46·0
1940	1,152·1 (*e*)	411·2 (*e*)	26·0 (*e*)
1941	1,145·1 (*e*)	365·4 (*e*)	12·7 (*e*)
1942	1,206·2 (*e*)	391·1 (*e*)	10·6 (*e*)
1943	1,885·4 (*e*)	337·1 (*e*)	13·4 (*e*)
1944	2,359·8 (*e*)	327·1 (*e*)	18·2 (*e*)
1945	1,516·9 (*e*)	434·5 (*e*)	51·1 (*e*)
1946	1,301·0	914·7	50·3
	1,794·5	1,138·3	
1947	- - - - (*f*)	- - - - (*f*)	59·8
	1,798·4	1,141·8	
1948	2,075·4	1,578·3	64·7
1949	2,277·5	1,787·4	58·6
1950	2,606·6	2,174·2	84·7

See p. 454 for footnotes.

External Trade 3. *continued*

(in £ million)

	Imports	Domestic Exports	Re-exports
1951	3,901·9	2,581·6	127·0
	---- (*g*)	---- (*g*)	
	3,892·1	2,566·4	
1952	3,464·8	2,566·7	142·0
1953	3,328·1	2,558·0	103·1
1954	3,359·2	2,649·9	98·3
1955	3,860·8	2,876·7	116·4
1956	3,861·5	3,143·3	143·7
1957	4,043·7	3,295·0	129·8
1958	3,747·5	3,176·2	141·2
1959	3,983·4	3,330·1	130·9
1960	4,540·7	3,554·8	141·2
1961	4,395·1	3,681·5	158·6
1962	4,487·0	3,791·0	157·6
1963	4,812·7	4,081·0	153·8
1964	5,506·7	4,253·4	153·4

	Imports	Domestic Exports	Re-exports
1965	5,751·1	4,728·0	172·8
		———————— (*h*)	
1966	5,969·4	5,255·3	
1967	6,436·7	5,229·6	
1968	7,897·5	6,433·9	
1969	8,315·0	7,339·4	
1970	9,036·8	8,061·1	
	---- (*i*)	---- (*i*)	
	9,112·7	8,095·7	
1971	9,798·9	9,071·1	
1972	11,072·9	9,602·3	
1973	15,723·5	12,087·0	
1974	23,138·9	16,309·2	
1975	24,046·4	19,606·9	
1976	31,084·1	25,276·6	
1977	36,219·1	31,990·1	
1978	39,533·0	35,380·3	
1979	46,924·9	40,637·0	
1980	49,772·9	47,357·1	

(*a*) Up to 1870 the values of imports and re-exports were computed by the Board of Trade. All other values were declared by shippers.

(*b*) From 1892 tobacco manufactured in bond was transferred from re-exports to exports. The effect of this change was very slight.

(*c*) The value of new ships (with their machinery) sold abroad was included in exports for the first time in 1899, when it came to £9·2 million.

(*d*) Southern Ireland was treated as foreign from 1st April 1923.

(*e*) These figures include munitions. If these are excluded the series are as follows:

	Imports	Exports	Re-exports
1940	1,082·1	392·6	25·9
1941	986·1	323·8	8·3
1942	996·7	271·3	4·5
1943	1,233·9	233·5	6·0
1944	1,309·3	266·3	15·6
1945	1,103·7	399·3	51·0

(*f*) This break is apparently caused by a revaluation of non-ferrous metal ores and manufactures. Revised figures back to 1949 were published in the 1953 *Annual Statement* and back to 1947 in the 1954 *Abstract*.

(*g*) This break is caused by, firstly, a new system of valuing the parcel post, and secondly, the subsequent treatment of Channel Islands trade as part of the internal trade of the United Kingdom. Revised figures back to 1951 were published in the 1960 *Abstract* and have been used here.

(*h*) The separate recording of re-exports ceased at the end of 1969, but it has not been continued here beyond 1965 because revised figures of total exports, but not of domestic exports and re-exports separately, were published later for 1966–69. The re-export figures given in each *Annual Statement* for that period are as follows:

1966	194·4	1968	219·6
1967	184·8	1969	259·5

(*i*) This break is caused by various changes in the categories excluded from the trade statistics during the 1970s. Revised figures back to 1970 on a basis comparable with 1980 were published in the 1978 *Annual Statement* and the 1982 *Abstract* and have been used here.

External Trade 4. Values at Current Prices of External Trade – Republic of Ireland 1924–80

NOTES

[1] SOURCE: *Statistical Abstract of Ireland*.

[2] Imports are valued c.i.f., exports and re-exports f.o.b.

[3] The value of bullion and specie is excluded throughout.

(in £ million)

	Imports	Exports	Re-exports		Imports	Exports	Re-exports
1924	68·9	49·7	1·3	1953	182·5	111·5	2·6
1925	63·0	42·7	1·0	1954	179·9	111·8	3·6
1926	61·3	40·5	0·8	1955	204·3 --- (a) 207·7	106·7 --- (a) 107·2	3·7
1927	60·8	43·6	0·7	1956	182·8	104·3	3·9
1928	59·9	45·0	0·7	1957	184·2	127·1	4·3
1929	61·3	46·2	1·1	1958	199·0	126·0	4·7
1930	56·8	43·8	1·2	1959	212·6	126·6	4·0
1931	50·5	35·5	0·8	1960	226·2	147·8	4·9
1932	42·6	25·2	1·1	1961	261·4	175·2	5·3
1933	35·8	18·4	0·6	1962	273·7	168·9	5·5
1934	39·1	17·6	0·4	1963	307·7	191·9	4·6
1935	37·3	19·6	0·3	1964	349·3 --- (b) 360·8	217·0 --- (b) 230·8	5·0 --- (b) 3·1
1936	39·9	22·0	0·5	1965	387·8	237·4	3·8
1937	44·1	22·2	0·6	1966	396·7	267·6	5·8
1938	41·4	23·9	0·4	1967	414·7	308·8	5·7
1939	43·4	26·5	0·4	1968	516·1	358·2	5·5
1940	46·8	32·7	0·3	1969	613·6	395·2	9·0
1941	29·5	31·7	0·1	1970	676·7	455·5	11·2
1942	34·6	32·6	0·1	1971	754·9	527·9	10·8
1943	26·4	27·7	0·1	1972	838·1	635·5	12·0
1944	28·5	29·8	0·1	1973	1,137·2	869·2	
1945	41·1	35·2	0·3	1974	1,626·3	1,134·3	
1946	72·0	38·6	0·4	1975	1,704·1	1,447·4	
1947	131·3	38·6	0·9	1976	2,337·9	1,859·1	
1948	136·3	47·9	1·5	1977	3,090·9	2,518·2	
1949	130·2	59·0	1·6	1978	3,713·1	2,963·2	
1950	159·4	70·5	1·9	1979	4,827·9	3,477·7	
1951	204·6	79·8	1·7	1980	5,420·7	4,082·5	
1952	172·3	99·2	2·4				

(a) This break results from new valuations for parcel post.

(b) Trade of Shannon Free Airport is included subsequently.

External Trade 5. Imports and Exports by Categories – Great Britain 1784–6 to 1854–6, and United Kingdom 1854–1980

NOTES

[1] SOURCES: Part A – Ralph Davis, *The Industrial Revolution and British Overseas Trade* (Leicester, 1979), Appendix tables 38 and 40; Part B – Werner Schlote, *British Overseas Trade from 1700 to the 1930s* (Oxford, 1952), Appendix tables 4 and 5; Part C – *Annual Statement of Trade, Overseas Trade Statistics of the United Kingdom*, and *Abstract*.

[2] Imports are valued c.i.f., exports f.o.b. In Part A the values are computed ones, the method of calculation being described in the source. Trade with Ireland is excluded throughout this Part.

[3] Exports include re-exports from 1968 (2nd line), but not previously.

[4] The figures for 1784–6 are for years ended 30 September. Others are for calendar years or years beginning 6 January to 1853.

[5] Classifications have changed from time to time, though, in principle, those used in Parts A and B are uniform throughout each part. The main general changes in the twentieth century were in 1920 and 1948. Substantial breaks in continuity are indicated by giving figures comparable with earlier and later years.

A. Great Britain, 1784–6 to 1854–6 (annual averages)

(in £ thousand)

	Foodstuffs, etc.		Raw Materials and Mainly Unmanufactured Goods		Manufactures	
	Imports	Exports	Imports	Exports	Imports	Exports
1784–6	8,657	1,165	9,585	867	2,144	10,658
1794–6	16,520	1,926	15,356	801	2,450	19,043
1804–6	21,444	2,663	27,446	1,097	1,729	33,775
1814–6	27,602	4,995	36,408	1,460	731	38,019
1824–6	20,563	1,639	35,520	1,040	892	32,619
1834–6	20,680	1,571	47,659	2,539	1,926	42,083
1844–6	27,386	1,809	51,033	5,177	3,544	51,434
1854–6	54,469	5,764	89,432	13,646	7,680	83,091

B. United Kingdom, 1854–1899

(in £ million)

	Foodstuffs and Livestock		Raw Materials and Mainly Unmanufactured Goods		Finished Manufactures	
	Imports	Exports	Imports	Exports	Imports	Exports
1854	60·5	5·3	80·3	6·6	11·6	85·3
1855	56·6	7·2	77·6	7·2	9·4	81·3
1856	66·0	8·6	94·0	8·2	12·6	99·0
1857	67·3	7·1	108·8	9·3	11·8	105·7
1858	59·4	6·4	94·9	8·0	10·3	102·2
1859	58·8	7·5	107·6	8·0	12·9	115·0
1860	80·9	7·0	114·4	8·6	15·3	120·3
1861	86·4	7·7	112·3	8·8	18·9	108·7
1862	92·8	7·1	111·1	9·6	21·9	107·3
1863	85·5	7·5	140·1	10·5	23·4	128·5
1864	84·3	7·4	165·3	10·4	25·3	142·7
1865	85·1	7·2	159·9	11·0	26·1	147·7
1866	96·4	7·9	169·8	12·0	29·0	169·0
1867	105·5	7·4	139·1	12·4	30·6	161·2
1868	110·5	7·7	151·2	12·7	33·0	159·2
1869	112·5	7·5	149·4	14·3	33·5	168·2
1870	108·6	9·5	156·4	14·7	38·2	175·4
1871	127·4	12·5	167·7	17·8	36·0	192·7
1872	144·5	9·6	169·8	26·0	40·3	220·7
1873	152·2	10·8	176·4	28·3	42·7	216·1
1874	149·6	10·5	173·4	23·7	47·1	205·3
1875	161·2	9·9	163·3	20·9	49·4	192·6
1876	162·1	10·1	161·1	19·4	51·9	171·1
1877	180·8	10·6	160·8	18·4	52·9	169·9
1878	169·7	10·5	144·8	17·6	54·2	164·8
1879	173·4	10·1	139·0	19·4	50·6	162·0
1880	186·4	11·3	166·1	24·3	58·8	187·4
1881	178·8	11·5	162·4	24·6	55·8	197·9
1882	178·3	12·4	175·6	26·6	59·2	202·5
1883	192·0	12·4	175·0	26·0	60·0	201·4

B. United Kingdom, 1854–1899 (*cont.*)

(in £ million)

	Foodstuffs and Livestock		Raw Materials and Mainly Unmanufactured Goods		Finished Manufactures	
	Imports	Exports	Imports	Exports	Imports	Exports
1884	161·5	11·9	169·0	24·6	59·6	196·6
1885	160·4	11·5	151·2	22·7	59·4	178·9
1886	144·8	10·9	144·8	22·8	60·3	178·7
1887	150·9	11·0	150·0	24·9	61·3	185·5
1888	159·1	11·8	163·8	27·2	64·7	195·6
1889	174·1	12·6	182·0	31·2	71·5	205·2
1890	176·2	12·6	174·0	37·4	70·5	213·5
1891	187·2	12·0	176·3	34·6	72·0	200·6
1892	187·5	11·7	164·0	32·3	72·3	183·2
1893	178·6	11·8	154·1	29·2	71·9	177·3
1894	176·6	11·9	156·4	30·6	75·3	173·5
1895	178·4	12·1	155·8	29·6	82·5	184·4
1896	186·6	12·6	166·1	29·3	89·2	198·3
1897	193·4	12·6	165·6	32·8	92·1	188·4
1898	207·7	13·0	168·6	33·9	94·2	185·9
1899	208·6	13·9	177·3	44·1	99·1	206·5

C. United Kingdom, 1899–1980

(in £ million)

	Food, Drink & Tobacco (*a*)		Raw Materials and Mainly Unmanufactured Goods		Mainly Manufactured Goods	
	Imports	Exports	Imports	Exports	Imports	Exports
1899	210·3	12·7	150·5	29·5	121·7	218·8
1900	220·0	14·0	172·0	45·0	128·4	228·3
1901	224·0	15·5	167·1	36·9	128·3	223·2
1902	223·6	17·0	168·9	35·3	133·4	226·8
1903	231·5	16·1	173·3	36·2	135·6	234·0
1904	230·6	16·6	181·9	36·5	136·3	243·1
1905	231·3	19·1	187·9	36·7	143·6	268·6
1906	238·2	20·6	211·1	43·8	156·2	305·0
1907	247·3	22·4	241·2	55·6	154·9	341·4
1908	244·1	21·7	203·5	52·8	143·1	296·6
1909	254·3	23·3	220·1	51·2	147·7	296·8
1910	257·7	26·1	261·2	53·3	156·8	342·9
1911	264·0	29·0	248·2	53·7	165·6	362·2
1912	280·6	32·7	275·7	59·4	185·5	385·0
1913	290·2	32·6	281·8	69·9	193·6	411·4
1914	297·0	26·9	236·5	56·7	160·5	338·6
1915	380·9	25·1	286·6	52·4	181·5	292·9
1916	419·2	29·5	336·8	64·3	189·2	393·4
1917	454·7	16·3	384·8	67·2	218·6	423·6
1918	569·9	12·0	458·5	61·0	280·1	406·6
1919	707·3 --- (*b*) 719·1	33·3 --- (*b*) 33·8	646·0 --- (*b*) 606·8	121·3 --- (*b*) 111·3	266·6 --- (*b*) 296·0	632·0 --- (*b*) 641·5
1920	765·8	50·9	710·4	145·5	453·4	1,119·7
1921	567·0 --- (*b*) 566·8	37·4 --- (*b*) 36·5	270·8	63·6	244·5 --- (*b*) 244·6	588·9 --- (*b*) 589·8
1922	471·8	35·3	298·3	102·0	229·8	569·5
1923	[508·8] (*c*)	[43·3] (*c*)	[324·9] (*c*)	[130·8] (*c*)	[257·1] (*c*)	[581·0] (*c*)

C. United Kingdom, 1899–1980 (*cont.*)

(in £ million)

	Food, Drink & Tobacco (*a*)		Raw Materials and Mainly Unmanufactured Goods		Mainly Manufactured Goods	
	Imports	Exports	Imports	Exports	Imports	Exports
1924	571·0	55·9	400·0 --- (*b*) 401·1	106·5	299·9 --- (*b*) 298·8	619·9
1925	570·0	53·9	425·8	84·4	318·7	617·6
1926	529·7	49·5	393·0	47·2	314·0	540·2
1927	538·4	51·2	352·6	76·4	321·7	565·0
1928	530·8	53·3	335·5	70·2	317·1	579·8
1929	535·4	54·7	340·5	78·9	333·5	574·7
1930	475·0	47·3	251·1	63·8	306·8	440·9
1931	416·7	34·8	173·6	47·1	261·3	292·8
1932	372·9	31·5	165·0	43·6	157·4	276·3
1933	339·9	27·8	180·9	46·0	150·4	281·7
1934	346·6	30·5	210·0	48·3	170·9	304·8
1935	355·1	31·6	212·3	52·8	184·5	328·8
1936	381·6	35·6	247·9	51·3	212·7	340·8
1937	431·1	38·8	315·2	64·6	274·9	404·7
1938	430·1	35·9	248·2	56·9	233·5	365·2
1939	398·4	35·7	241·0	54·4	239·0	338·2
1940	420·2	33·4	338·8	36·2	387·0	334·1
1941	422·0	27·8	227·4	15·7	487·7	316·1
1942	435·3	18·4	237·0	10·2	310·8	236·6
1943	513·3	19·0	263·9	9·4	441·3	201·4
1944	521·2	22·9	280·0	8·1	477·7	229·9
1945	489·9	55·7	294·4	15·1	300·1	306·8
1946	637·5	63·7	390·5	33·0	244·9	789·1
1947	803·5	64·8	566·6	34·2	398·9	1,000·1
1948	883·2	93·9	684·3	67·5	486·0	1,376·7

External Trade 5. *continued*

C. United Kingdom, 1899–1980 (*cont.*)

(in £ million)

	Food, Drink & Tobacco (*a*)		Fuels, Lubricants, etc.		Other Crude Materials including Oils, Fats, etc.		Manufactured Goods	
	Imports	Exports	Imports	Exports	Imports	Exports	Imports	Exports
1948	876·2	92·4	158·6	52·5	646·7	45·0	371·7	1,344·6
1949	966·6	95·8	149·1	70·0	727·3	50·2	414·7	1,526·4
1950	1,026·2	132·9	197·0	77·0	910·7	89·3	458·9	1,827·4
	1,291·6	158·3		69·8	1,522·5	108·5	759·8	2,195·6
1951	---- (*b*)	---- (*b*)	315·7	---- (*b*)	---- (*b*)	---- (*b*)	---- (*b*)	---- (*b*)
	1,282·1	154·9		68·7	1,512·5	108·4	767·1	2,187·0
1952	1,196·2	151·9	338·6	124·0	1,135·3	82·0	775·8	2,133·9
1953	1,303·4	146·5	313·5	146·1	1,044·3	96·8	650·0	2,085·1
1954	1,314·4	154·3	328·9	150·5	1,015·2	101·0	686·6	2,158·7
	1,426·5	167·7			1,107·9	111·2	903·9	2,370·9
1955	---- (*b*)	---- (*b*)	408·2	139·4	---- (*b*)	---- (*b*)	---- (*b*)	---- (*b*)
	1,424·3	172·5			1,121·4	113·3	895·2	2,312·0
1956	1,434·2	182·5	413·7	159·6	1,099·2	117·8	903·9	2,554·7
							923·8	2,696·0
1957	1,477·8	206·2	465·7	150·4	1,165·4	125·0	---- (*d*)	---- (*d*)
							1,011·6	2,774·8
1958	1,489·5	194·2	438·9	130·8	905·7	110·8	977·0	2,714·3
1959	1,519·2	195·0	467·1	119·0	945·7	132·0	1,127·1	2,874·9
1960	1,540·1	201·9	480·3	132·6	1,079·5	127·4	1,522·2	3,059·3
1961	1,484·4	213·6	482·1	123·5	1,009·1	136·3	1,530·9	3,198·7
1962	1,569·4	220·3	532·7	146·2	924·8	146·9	1,556·4	3,270·3
1963	1,675·9	245·8	557·8	164·7	990·4	160·9	1,701·7	3,498·8
1964	1,771·1	283·0	583·6	138·6	1,128·5	158·2	2,160·8	3,694·7
1965	1,707·9	298·0	609·2	133·4	1,109·3	151·0	2,253·0	3,997·5
1966	1,711·6	327·3	624·8	134·2	1,060·6	154·6	2,470·6	4,278·6
1967	1,762·4	330·6	729·0	128·6	1,012·1	152·7	2,843·7	4,273·3
		398·4		166·4		179·0		5,278·4
1968	1,900·0	---- (*e*)	901·5	---- (*e*)	1,207·4	---- (*e*)	3,772·3	---- (*e*)
		430·2		167·8		232·3		5,412·7
1969	1,929·6	453·7	906·5	173·0	1,252·6	249·5	4,137·3	6,256·2
			944·9	206·8	1,362·0	272·8	4,572·1	6,806·4
1970	2,047·3	514·1	---- (*b*)	---- (*b*)	---- (*b*)	---- (*b*)	---- (*b*)	---- (*b*)
			950·4	210·3	1,361·7	252·7	4,672·5	6,913·3
					1,278·0		5,119·9	7,936·6
1971	2,175·8	587·7	1,253·3	239·4	---- (*b*)	263·2	---- (*b*)	---- (*b*)
					1,295·6		4,921·1	7,717·7
1972	2,355·9	659·9	1,247·0	241·5	1,342·4	302·4	5,983·2	8,113·9
1973	3,093·8	875·6	1,732·9	374·0	1,990·9	397·9	8,697·7	10,067·3
1974	3,762·4	1,063·3	4,643·9	781·6	2,589·9	552·5	11,693·2	13,306·4
1975	4,334·8	1,427·6	4,316·3	826·6	2,246·5	530·1	12,605·7	16,063·0
1976	4,983·3	1,692·5	5,668·7	1,264·7	3,392·9	764·8	15,577·7	20,700·7
1977	5,937·0	2,216·4	5,254·8	2,092·0	3,820·0	902·1	20,702·5	25,823·6
1978	6,141·3	2,911·5	4,805·2	2,374·6	3,594·6	997·4	24,421·4	28,028·6
1979	6,516·9	2,940·5	5,782·2	4,323·6	4,179·9	1,281·0	29,688·7	30,869·5
1980	6,122·6	3,256·7	6,875·4	6,428·8	4,049·4	1,449·5	31,177·0	34,811·2

(*a*) Including live animals of types chiefly for food.
(*b*) This break results from a change in classification.
(*c*) Southern Ireland was treated as foreign from 1 April 1923.
(*d*) Subsequently including precious stones and pearls.
(*e*) See note 3 above.

External Trade 6. Imports and Exports by Categories – Republic of Ireland 1924–1980

NOTES

[1] SOURCE: *Trade Statistics of Ireland.*

[2] Imports are valued c.i.f., exports f.o.b.

[3] Classifications have changed from time to time. Breaks in continuity which have any substance are indicated by footnotes and the giving of two figures comparable with earlier and later years.

[4] Export figures relate to domestic exports to 1972 (1st line).

(in £ million)

	Food, Drink & Tobacco (*a*)		Raw Materials and Simply-Prepared Articles		Manufactured Goods and Prepared Articles	
	Imports	Exports	Imports	Exports	Imports	Exports
1924	30·3	43·4	7·0	2·5	28·5	2·6
1925	27·9	37·6	6·4	2·1	26·7	2·2
1926	26·2	36·8	6·5	1·7	26·6	1·8
1927	25·6	39·0	7·1	2·4	26·4	1·8
1928	24·6	40·4	6·4	2·4	27·5	2·9
1929	24·4	40·2	6·5	2·3	29·3	3·5
1930	21·4	38·4	6·6	1·4	27·9	4·1
1931	18·8	32·7	5·9	1·0	25·0	1·9
1932	15·9	22·3	5·3	0·9	20·9	1·5
1933	11·0	16·4	4·8	1·1	19·6	0·7
1934	12·0	15·5	5·5	1·1	21·3	0·7
1935	10·3	17·4	5·5	1·3	21·2	0·7
1936	11·3	19·4	6·7	1·7	21·6	0·6
1937	13·0	19·3	7·9	2·0	22·2	0·7
1938	12·9	21·8	7·1	1·2	20·5	0·6
1939	12·5	24·0	8·0	1·6	21·9	0·7
1940	14·3	29·3	9·5	1·9	22·1	1·2
1941	5·5	28·0	5·5	2·2	18·0	1·3
1942	12·2	29·8	4·6	2·1	17·8	0·6
1943	8·1	24·0	5·4	2·2	12·5	1·3
1944	10·7	25·5	4·8	2·6	12·8	1·6
1945	13·7	29·8	5·8	2·9	21·0	2·3
1946	17·8	32·6	9·3	3·1	43·9	2·3
1947	33·2	32·8	18·6	2·8	76·9	2·5
1948	39·2	38·6	16·7	3·5	77·7	5·3
1949	31·7	49·1	18·1	3·9	78·1	3·9
1950	41·9	58·7	24·3	6·0	90·5	5·2

External Trade 6. *continued*

(in £ million)

	Food, Drink & Tobacco (*a*)		Fuel, Lubricants, etc.		Other Crude Materials including Oils, Fats, etc.		Manufactured Goods	
	Imports	Exports	Imports	Exports	Imports	Exports	Imports	Exports
1950	41·9	58·7	17·2	--	16·6	6·0	82·2	4·8
1951	52·0	64·3	24·4	--	23·7	5·9	102·2	7·8
1952	43·2	83·2	23·2	--	19·4	6·6	81·1	5·8
1953	50·4	92·5	22·2	0·2	18·3	7·2	85·3	7·1
1954	36·8	88·6	23·5	0·1	19·2	6·8	93·6	11·1
1955	46·0	79·3	27·9	0·1	20·6	9·5	101·5	13·1
1956	30·8	77·6	28·9	0·2	20·0	8·9	93·9	12·3
1957	39·6	94·3	28·4	0·3	18·4	8·0	88·6	17·2
1958	43·0	93·0	25·3	0·2	16·8	6·9	101·6	17·5
1959	46·4	82·8	26·1	1·6	19·9	9·7	107·6	23·7
1960	42·8	96·0	26·1	4·2	23·1	10·6	120·4	28·4
1961	54·1	118·1	27·3	3·7	23·0	11·5	140·5	31·0
1962	53·6	110·8	26·8	2·8	23·3	10·2	154·2	34·5
1963	60·5	124·9	27·9	3·2	25·8	10·9	175·1	41·3
1964	63·9	139·5 ----- (*b*) 137·5	29·6	2·6	29·4	10·4	208·4	54·3
1965	72·3	129·9	31·4	3·3	27·9	12·3	222·0	57·3
1966	69·3	139·1	32·2	1·9	28·6	16·7	225·0	67·4
1967	68·9	163·0	37·5	6·3	30·4	16·5	235·7	78·5
1968	81·8	175·8	40·9	3·5	39·1	22·7	308·2	107·2
1969	83·7	183·1	44·6	5·0	41·2	33·2	398·1	123·3
1970	89·9	206·9	53·3	6·3 ---- (*b*) 6·1	43·5	34·7 ---- (*b*) 34·5	440·2 ---- (*b*) 439·9	151·2
1971	93·6	251·6	68·3	6·3	44·7	32·2	497·7	183·8
1972	111·9 ---- (*b*) 114·3	290·1 ---- (*b*)(*c*) 294·6	63·6	5·5 ---- (*c*) 6·4	48·8	38·9 ---- (*c*) 39·0	562·7 ---- (*b*) 574·7	243·9 ---- (*b*)(*c*) 264·3
1973	144·0	375·9	77·5	6·7	83·3	53·4	789·6	379·6
1974	197·3	447·6	226·5	14·9	119·3	72·9	1,033·9	536·4
1975	226·8	674·0	243·7	19·1	79·9	67·1	1,101·9	610·9
1976	288·6	773·1	313·0	12·3	123·2	86·1	1,537·1	890.1
1977	394·7	999·2	388·8	16·7	147·7	106·5	2,063·4	1,263·8
1978	433·3	1,192·9	376·2	12·2	146·7	130·9	2,658·0	1,484·5
1979	552·2	1,276·4	586·8	16·7	190·8	181·9	3,396·6	1,852·9
1980	639·7	1,452·7	803·2	26·7	194·1	190·8	3,658·4	2,250·3

(*a*) Including live animals and animal feeding stuffs.
(*b*) See note 3 above.
(*c*) See note 4 above.

External Trade 7. Official Values of Principal Imports – England & Wales 1700–91, Great Britain 1792–1829, and United Kingdom 1826–56

NOTE

SOURCES: 1700–1807 (except last three columns) – Elizabeth B. Schumpeter, *English Overseas Trade Statistics, 1697–1808* (Oxford University Press, 1960), tables XV and XVII; 1808–56 (including the whole of the last three columns) – *Trade and Navigation Accounts*. Certain figures for 1812 are taken from various returns of specific imports given in *Sessional Papers* from 1818 to 1822.

A. England & Wales 1700–1791

(in £ thousand)

	Corn	Coffee	Sugar	Tea	Wine	Timber (*a*)	Raw Wool	Raw, Thrown and Waste Silk	Tobacco	Iron	Flax	Hemp	Linen Yarn
1700	--	36	668	14	647	119	220	377	315	182	110	71	46
1701	--	38	599	6	513	97	251	388	236	185	52	118	94
1702	--	47	358	3	382	95	199	334	272	131	47	93	90
1703	--	26	565	9	290	113	161	316	148	197	63	150	62
1704	--	75	436	20	371	130	159	682	255	164	65	227	59
1705	...	...	...	...	...	...	...	...	...	...	...	...	...
1706	--	5	459	70	258	111	178	423	145	185	63	35	66
1707	--	5	533	28	310	140	152	204	205	142	44	124	99
1708	--	52	521	116	392	125	106	543	212	179	59	152	57
1709	3	71	546	12	367	100	154	494	252	131	39	146	98
1710	6	23	697	37	379	95	189	213	186	177	75	78	68
1711	--	81	505	49	394	66	255	640	264	150	55	131	63
1712	...	...	...	...	...	...	...	...	...	...	...	...	...
1713	--	100	700	170	383	138	166	621	115	144	71	69	125
1714	--	124	708	136	500	121	190	410	274	223	76	48	127
1715	--	48	854	42	582	138	266	534	167	176	71	168	104
1716	--	24	939	5	489	97	385	556	265	157	90	134	140
1717	--	41	1,057	87	537	115	278	720	278	78	77	147	139
1718	--	72	784	158	587	133	133	644	299	181	67	124	123
1719	--	64	756	142	501	131	63	360	316	218	78	84	219
1720	--	38	980	33	464	167	109	742	324	227	65	117	111
1721	--	55	691	134	619	133	117	344	350	162	64	119	140
1722	--	133	859	133	615	144	119	684	268	228	89	62	124
1723	--	121	919	83	544	127	108	715	275	191	66	93	138
1724	38	130	1,011	132	564	169	117	681	250	215	108	123	134
1725	1	105	1,182	13	596	170	115	708	197	187	88	134	107
1726	--	51	928	73	461	140	103	633	303	216	104	141	151
1727	--	88	897	28	516	138	65	782	406	165	61	139	101
1728	239	35	1,349	35	729	154	75	659	399	223	103	131	97
1729	388	75	1,379	143	621	118	69	496	375	198	92	134	85
1730	64	146	1,446	170	468	133	90	610	329	224	107	155	102
1731	14	37	1,029	182	583	123	66	557	272	251	127	65	120
1732	10	86	1,246	156	513	160	76	484	290	239	128	120	114
1733	--	67	1,393	82	513	147	105	729	376	249	100	172	136
1734	--	71	956	71	509	150	102	747	227	255	141	130	156
1735	3	76	1,255	59	586	141	126	609	376	270	100	127	126
1736	--	72	1,220	65	498	148	101	491	355	245	120	128	33
1737	--	80	764	166	636	144	99	290	471	302	181	186	111
1738	--	88	1,200	105	528	135	97	645	376	290	152	151	123
1739	--	94	1,320	199	446	101	58	500	438	289	136	202	145
1740	9	81	981	151	358	118	53	395	338	235	122	160	118
1741	101	93	1,229	127	530	145	26	687	558	238	133	194	128
1742	1	44	1,014	179	492	157	110	356	408	204	168	195	105
1743	--	5	1,242	168	203	149	107	580	532	160	99	94	131
1744	--	52	1,115	75	251	120	25	376	389	245	91	207	167

A. England & Wales 1700–1791 (*cont.*)

(in £ thousand)

	Corn	Coffee	Sugar	Tea	Wine	Timber (*a*)	Raw Cotton	Raw Wool	Raw, Thrown and Waste Silk	Tobacco	Iron	Flax	Hemp	Linen Yarn
1745	--	190	1,095	90	397	141	...	73	568	385	298	130	203	(1,210)(*b*)
1746	--	29	1,098	218	304	155	...	98	344	376	224	110	181	169
1747	---	103	1,060	544	361	125	...	140	705	481	202	171	206	190
1748	2	81	1,435	376	369	156	...	107	587	476	267	209	266	142
1749	--	66	1,300	239	521	135	...	142	625	419	234	148	144	156
1750	1	75	1,270	484	368	171	...	97	276	481	359	218	254	182
1751	1	75	1,147	292	353	152	...	109	583	431	273	178	116	150
1752	--	2	1,161	318	330	168	...	94	678	537	258	141	252	203
1753	--	77	1,551	333	451	166	...	55	732	588	297	206	180	197
1754	33	79	1,178	352	356	165	...	81	656	553	318	209	204	126
1755	1	139	1,636	401	393	191	...	69	699	461	303	199	354	205
1756	31	94	1,513	427	288	181	...	86	460	153	271	179	388	174
1757	244	406	755	384	345	157	...	80	757	396	280	161	220	215
1758	67	246	1,661	166	383	156	...	83	735	413	325	189	176	180
1759	1	207	1,814	287	370	178	...	61	728	326	342	295	463	223
1760	--	257	1,799	969	371	147	...	91	626	491	289	128	58	232
1761	1	313	2,126	291	346	183	...	138	1,056	442	433	198	243	231
1762	13	541	1,996	645	402	158	...	50	691	414	329	179	232	326
1763	138	490	2,422	419	405	214	...	142	984	611	383	275	235	247
1764	85	150	1,978	678	393	195	...	114	913	512	448	288	293	191
1765	198	193	1,652	691	437	245	...	146	862	454	523	211	286	75
1766	144	234	2,052	1,018	444	251	...	124	917	407	334	225	176	301
1767	987	242	2,103	933	411	197	...	110	779	367	379	215	130	273
1768	623	257	2,203	413	450	210	...	67	825	336	456	255	226	315
1769	51	283	2,025	703	445	224	...	122	1,088	318	499	241	290	285
1770	66	218	2,436	1,093	401	220	...	141	917	395	476	213	307	391
1771	126	345	1,977	896	405	271	...	108	1,027	546	472	331	427	339
1772 (*c*)	89	457	2,429	1,279	376	277	160	79	927	484	489	245	230	326
1773	317	440	1,963	881	402	250	93	86	511	543	473	113	291	229
1774	812	411	2,704	385	445	217	178	125	817	526	503	208	356	307
1775	1,175	451	2,664	215	438	256	204	86	791	526	428	296	254	361
1776	295	363	2,298	337	434	244	194	117	1,123	69	508	199	268	371
1777	684	341	1,837	562	455	249	218	163	969	9	438	259	296	423
1778	395	272	1,933	340	407	255	187	28	614	20	321	216	291	352
1779	256	187	1,983	251	313	238	138	31	697	43	426	218	441	383
1780	144	146	1,813	187	502	225	211	110	956	70	361	255	320	450
1781	324	98	1,411	1,142	326	221	159	151	1,167	55	505	179	356	437
1782	166	201	1,799	403	240	232	357	61	576	45	392	165	427	404
1783	1,104	184	2,061	415	333	360	300	160	1,050	152	433	205	210	389
1784	476	303	2,451	767	352	242	349	98	1,169	378	481	197	302	324
1785	433	304	2,855	1,337	367	226	543	191	869	323	400	338	259	360
1786	403	348	2,072	2,144	371	308	568	94	745	357	439	277	225	404
1787	366	213	2,474	2,000	523	340	665	254	933	298	423	289	297	387
1788	415	225	2,620	1,788	573	331	589	255	866	368	465	262	455	380
1789	386	243	2,488	1,779	590	314	917	164	988	446	463	140	380	380
1790	770	390	2,402	1,777	656	376	875	193	928	443	440	254	468	391
1791	1,133	317	2,304	2,218	736	366	783	163	991	362	513	301	281	368

See p. 467 for footnotes.

External Trade 7. *continued*

B. Great Britain 1792–1829 (Principal Imports)

(in £ thousand)

	Corn	Coffee	Sugar	Tea	Wine	Timber (*a*)	Raw Cotton	Raw Wool	Raw, Thrown and Waste Silk
1792	777	482	2,721	1,303	863	543	1,129	269	962
1793	1,410	651	2,955	1,589	524	450	632	110	705
1794	1,088	1,396	3,348	2,365	724	413	780	269	661
1795	728	2,214	2,901	2,693	839	477	859	291	712
1796	2,174	2,302	3,057	617	535	690	1,027	207	684
1797	1,175	2,297	2,885	1,624	371	552	768	280	599
1798	1,215	2,748	3,663	4,487	541	431	1,049	144	801
1799	1,108	2,678	4,637	1,508	803	433	1,430	307	1,123
1800	2,673	3,988	4,301	1,510	732	582	1,848	500	739
1801	3,031	4,608	5,436	2,980	932	682	1,629	417	653
1802	1,401	3,169	5,878	2,736	735	527	2,088	423	756
1803	935	1,498	4,356	3,085	914	626	1,871	317	824
1804	1,201	3,513	4,440	2,668	459	627	2,156	460	981
1805	1,835	2,394	4,337	2,854	795	674	2,081	463	1,010
1806	814	3,608	5,205	2,216	854	511	2,034	382	987
1807	1,124	2,821	4,972	1,260	952	714	2,610	666	743
	----	----	----	----	---	---	----	---	---
1808 (*d*)	146	4,899	5,128	3,568	1,122	410	1,471	128	246
1809	1,137	4,711	5,451	2,164	1,174	484	3,117	350	947
1810	2,701	5,330	6,558	1,961	1,130	808	4,555	564	1,175
1811	466	3,765	5,346	2,121	499	799	3,148	271	266
1812	379	(2,574)(*e*)	(5,033)(*e*)	1,826	839	578	2,131	412	1,288
1813	...	...	...	...	...	...	...	...	...
1814	1,210	6,448	5,493	2,611	766	338	2,031	745	1,478
1815	396	5,340	5,440	2,560	768	602	3,336	655	1,031
		----			---		----		
1816	406	3,325(*f*)	5,141	3,623	445(*f*)	439	3,152(*f*)	316	596
1817	2,196	3,520	5,189	3,147	680	457	4,158	617	693
1818	3,914	2,804	5,418	2,007	892	565	5,764	1,017	1,249
1819	1,613	2,451	5,568	2,375	576	652	4,869	692	967
1820	1,388	2,974	5,553	3,015	558	591	4,934	375	1,384
1821	273	2,771	5,739	3,073	594	602	4,347	672	1,342
1822	116	2,672	4,977	2,736	676	609	4,735	696	1,535
1823	41	2,755	5,477	2,905	748	672	6,242	679	1,499
1824	456	3,109	5,733	3,168	725	768	4,865	763	1,875
1825	1,128	3,238	5,056	2,935	1,179	979	7,406	1,437	2,366
1826	2,117	2,569	5,603	2,984	786	738	5,727	478	1,272
1827	1,994	2,945	5,328	3,975	868	658	8,964	884	2,080
1828	1,673	2,503	6,312	3,268	1,016	634	7,483	913	2,745
1829	3,500	2,373	6,280	3,054	790	657	7,289	678	1,800

See p. 467 for footnotes.

External Trade 7. *continued*

B. Great Britain 1792–1829 (Principal Imports, *continued*)

(in £ thousand)

	Tobacco	Iron	Flax	Hemp	Linen Yarn	Oils, Seeds and Nuts for Expressing Oil, Gums and Tallow (*a*)	Hides and Skins	Dyewoods and Dyestuffs (*a*)
1792	424	577	479	522	465	...	...	...
1793	241	589	528	471	438	...	...	...
1794	313	428	682	495	379	...	...	...
1795	216	489	447	486	415	...	...	...
1796	224	526	640	526	404	...	...	...
1797	255	363	410	415	360	...	...	...
1798	389	510	766	551	441	...	...	...
1799	354	480	828	640	525	...	...	...
1800	357	375	795	507	506	...	...	...
1801	423	331	530	636	423	...	...	...
1802	254	531	530	415	418	...	...	...
1803	346	429	575	620	375	...	...	...
1804	217	222	714	618	463	...	...	...
1805	173	268	914	519	540	992	630	1,316
1806	228	317	699	620	501	1,127	499	798
1807	244	233	830	643	325	941	401	1,355
	---	---	---	---	---	---	---	----
1808	78	205	403	219	35	644	406	1,155
1809	276	240	968	722	234	941	507	673
1810	499	197	945	752	287	1,195	943	1,762
1811	321	273	431	388	12	852	751	1,322
1812	146	171	675	629	12	(907)(*e*)	272	1,155
1813	...	...	...	...	...	...	...	...
1814	54	214	948	464	273	1,542	576	1,833
1815	416	208	633	620	251	1,272	581	1,413
						----		----
1816	290	83	435	313	52	1,036(*f*)	411	1,609(*f*)
1817	186	99	818	389	127	1,020	305	1,047
1818	419	162	844	561	256	1,516	564	1,945
1819	259	137	795	402	130	1,323	434	1,011
1820	342	96	763	355	111	1,676	454	1,226
1821	214	99	1,013	205	134	1,514	613	1,400
1822	329	124	1,197	509	229	1,720	769	1,261
1823	328	131	1,083	543	317	1,878	935	2,000
1824	201	139	1,456	465	336	1,812	1,161	1,778
1825	372	227	2,079	491	326	2,333	1,212	2,008
1826	242	127	1,347	396	143	1,931	801	1,734
1827	309	180	1,786	463	182	2,417	738	1,693
1828	231	147	1,737	401	162	2,295	1,055	2,460
1829	205	148	1,846	288	166	2,326	1,219	1,811

See p. 467 for footnotes.

C. United Kingdom 1826–1856 (Principal Imports)

(in £ thousand)

	Corn	Coffee	Sugar	Tea	Wine	Timber (*a*)	Raw Cotton	Raw Wool
1826	...	...	6,061	2,984	879	1,026	5,823	478
1827	...	...	5,772	3,975	938	823	9,086	884
1828	...	...	6,822	3,268	1,122	836	7,551	913
1829	3,511	2,396	6,808	3,054	894	896	7,344	679
1830	3,280	2,560	6,857	3,190	792	772	8,786	883
1831	4,726	2,669	7,534	3,165	813	875	9,612	930
1832	899	3,131	6,784	3,171	681	898	9,483	803
1833	654	2,110	6,627	3,206	845	870	10,019	1,095
1834	619	2,588	6,650	3,364	1,117	858	10,897	1,292
1835	334	1,762	6,214	4,433	1,044	1,011	12,071	1,138
1836	746	2,100	6,519	4,880	1,078	1,009	13,352	1,792
1837	1,501	2,262	6,286	4,876	926	1,029	13,483	1,323
1838	2,388	2,470	7,040	4,001	980	1,059	16,656	1,420
1839	6,060	2,505	6,618	3,817	1,132	1,190	12,705	1,602
1840	5,156	4,316	5,698	2,802	1,046	1,228(*h*)	19,500	1,332
1841	5,238	2,686	6,845	3,079	872	1,147	15,948	1,486
1842	5,511	2,577	6,738	4,074	827	820	17,244	1,206
1843	2,049	2,419	7,139	4,534	769	1,032	22,279	1,289
1844	3,631	2,898	6,929	5,315	973	1,128	21,239	1,797
1845	2,799	3,138	8,762	5,106	953	1,587	23,950	2,062
1846	6,101	3,234	8,150	5,477	868	1,740	15,376	1,775
1847	16,042	3,450	11,742	5,562	890	1,442	15,377	1,656
1848	9,491	3,553	10,185	4,777	852	1,375	23,405	1,813
1849	14,233	3,956	10,521	5,346	893	1,202	24,901	1,996
1850	12,290	3,172	9,787	5,051	1,038	1,265	21,532	1,953
1851	14,178	3,318	12,276	7,147	1,012	1,653(*i*)	24,582	2,204
1852	11,272	3,427	10,448	6,636	749	1,447	30,326	2,463
1853	14,835	3,471	11,043	7,074	1,246	1,801	28,883	3,114
1854	10,139	4,155	13,764	8,579	1,231	1,879	28,657	2,723
1855	8,003	3,996	11,350	8,326	1,012	1,389	28,588	2,533
1856	12,224	3,552	11,297	8,620	1,074	1,706	32,953	3,011

External Trade 7. *continued*

C. United Kingdom 1826–1856 (Principal Imports, *continued*)

(in £ thousand)

	Raw, Thrown and Waste Silk	Tobacco	Flax	Hemp	Oils, Seeds and Nuts for Expressing Oil, Gums and Tallow (*a*)	Hides and Skins	Dyewoods and Dyestuffs (*a*)
1826	1,272	252	1,377	414	2,001	816	1,791
1827	2,080	331	1,827	485	2,522	750	1,730
1828	2,745	243	1,781	425	2,418	1,071	2,590
					- - - -		
1829	1,803	226	1,876	302	2,542(*g*)	1,240	1,850
1830	2,145	283	1,912	394	2,620	1,335	2,113
1831	2,315	330	1,898	449	2,929	1,225	2,284
1832	1,839	197	2,039	501	2,635	944	2,348
1833	1,729	214	2,313	447	2,891	1,290	2,156
1834	1,920	373	1,680	568	3,206	1,903	2,460
1835	2,131	244	1,532	582	2,637	1,534	2,269
1836	2,651	497	3,210	495	3,176	1,566	3,005
1837	2,109	263	2,034	653	3,174	1,439	2,795
1838	2,026	299	3,354	618	3,183	1,495	2,727
1839	2,163	353	2,481	841	3,593	1,666	3,152
1840	2,298	350	2,625	579	3,320	1,487	3,717
1841	2,032	441	2,811	551	3,188	2,135	3,757
1842	2,565	341	2,418	496	3,010	2,102	3,922
1843	2,302	424	2,988	621	3,517	2,279	3,645
1844	2,631	334	3,277	773	3,550	2,194	4,151
1845	2,677	348	2,965	783	3,951	2,560	4,488
1846	2,500	518	2,356	749	3,276	1,961	4,179
1847	2,245	341	2,168	696	3,144	2,154	4,051
1848	3,376	343	3,027	736	4,004	1,963	4,586
1849	3,023	417	3,730	926	4,078	2,355	5,135
1850	2,914	355	3,776	960	4,317	2,187	5,570
1851	2,687	292	2,457	1,143	4,363	2,439	6,215
1852	3,280	312	2,955	940	3,971	2,060	5,850
1853	4,269	382	4,034	1,173	4,531	2,834	4,874
1854	4,734	305	2,773	1,098	3,711	2,296	5,584
1855	3,992	346	2,716	1,245	4,395	2,260	6,257
1856	4,587	425	3,518	1,380	5,218	2,443	6,224

(*a*) Only the main items of these commodities are included, since the minor ones were not separately distinguished. The heading *Timber* does not include furniture woods.

(*b*) See footnote (*b*) to table 1, p. 450.

(*c*) The break occasioned by the change in basic source in 1772 from the *Inspector-General's Ledgers* to the *States of Navigation and Commerce* is not of much significance for most goods. Mrs Schumpeter collected figures from the former source for 1775 and 1780 for the sake of comparison with the latter. Only in the cases of iron (in 1775) and of coffee (in 1780) are the differences large – namely, 333 in the *Ledgers* as against 428 in the *States etc.* for iron in 1775, and 259 in the *Ledgers* compared with 187 in the *States etc.* for coffee in 1780.

(*d*) From 1808 onwards imports of Irish and Manx products into Great Britain are no longer included. The figures of these imports for 1808 can be deduced by subtracting the statistics in the *Trade and Navigation Accounts* from those given by Mrs Schumpeter. These are shown below, together with the imports from Ireland and the Isle of Man in 1814–18, given in the *Trade and Navigation Accounts*.

Main Items of Irish and Manx Produce Imported into Great Britain

	Corn	Wool	Flax	Hides and Skins	Linen Yarn
1808	338	2	76	...	203
1814	716	9	49	21	83
1815	688	34	47	35	75
1816	660	15	67	39	90
1817	481	17	79	68	122
1818	824	42	64	47	83

(*e*) These figures are incomplete to a minor degree because of the non-publication of the accounts of goods imported from Asia – a result of the Customs House fire of 1813.

(*f*) From 1816 onwards imports of foreign and colonial produce to Great Britain via Ireland are no longer included. The resulting break is extremely slight, and is confined to these commodities.

(*g*) Tallow is the only item in this column for which Irish statistics are available before 1829.

(*h*) Some very minor items, previously separately distinguished, cannot be included any longer.

(*i*) Firewood is included from this date. The resulting break is very slight.

External Trade 8. Official Values of Principal Domestic Exports – England & Wales 1697–1791, and Great Britain 1792–1829

NOTE

SOURCES: 1697–1807 (except Wool Official Value 1697–1771) – Elizabeth B. Schumpeter, *English Overseas Trade Statistics, 1697–1808* (Oxford University Press, 1960), tables VII, IX, X, XI, XII and XIII; 1808–29 – *Trade and Navigation Accounts*. Wool Official Values: 1697–1717 and 1725–37 – [Sir Joseph Banks], *The Propriety of Allowing a Qualified Exportation of Wool* (London, 1782), p. 83; 1718–24 and 1738–53 – J. Smith, *Memoirs of Wool* (2 vols, London, 1757), vol. II, pp. 210 and 280; 1754–71 – J. Bischoff, *A Comprehensive History of the Woollen and Worsted Manufacture* ... (2 vols, London, 1842), vol. II, appendix table VI. The value of British linen exported with bounty from 1743 to 1764 was omitted by Mrs Schumpeter, and is added here, the amounts being taken from J. Horner, *The Linen Trade of Europe* (Belfast, 1920), pp. 231–2.

A. England & Wales 1697–1791

(in £ thousand)

	Coal	Iron and Steel	Non-ferrous Metals and Manufactures	Cotton Yarn and Manufactures	Woollen and Worsted Yarn and Manufactures (*a*) (Official Values)	Woollen and Worsted Yarn and Manufactures (*a*) (Mrs Schumpeter's Values)	Linen Yarn and Manufactures	Silk Yarn and Manufactures
1697	33	98	171	11	1,481	1,871	8	72
1698	59	83	274	22	2,455	3,168	14	96
1699	51	91	253	14	2,446	2,908	12	85
1700	62	86	264	28	2,542	2,989	9	69
1701	68	90	263	24	2,697	3,238	7	69
1702	50	54	186	16	2,193	2,617	7	50
1703	41	75	211	6	2,760	3,359	8	57
1704	46	70	189	7	2,740	3,327	7	58
1705	...	...	...	...	2,508	...	...	...
1706	43	51	247	7	2,902	3,503	7	74
1707	52	71	237	13	2,912	3,595	10	78
---	---	---	---	---	----	----	---	---
1708 (*b*)	54	72	279	11	3,257	3,875	16	93
1709	62	71	216	7	3,342	3,916	17	100
1710	58	72	411	6	3,543	4,271	15	96
1711	61	71	222	4	2,933	3,663	21	82
1712	...	...	...	...	3,514	4,181	...	...
1713	73	97	213	10	2,858	3,391	14	77
1714	94	116	321	10	3,650	4,361	16	92
1715	89	119	359	8	3,359	4,053	19	108
1716	90	103	221	8	3,254	3,765	19	83
1717	79	122	275	10	3,706	4,589	20	108
1718	86	96	208	10	2,674	3,262	30	125
1719	93	108	281	9	2,730	3,132	23	71
1720	83	94	192	16	3,059	3,493	21	71
1721	94	100	214	20	2,903	3,427	25	66
1722	95	125	217	27	3,385	3,919	33	75
1723	97	118	235	27	2,921	3,418	24	80
1724	150	142	248	14	3,068	3,570	24	86
1725	91	151	225	14	3,513	4,000	34	164
1726	111	134	255	11	3,038	3,284	29	88
1727	120	136	289	7	2,877	3,250	32	64
1728	90	157	284	15	3,193	3,521	38	79
1729	115	171	327	10	3,199	3,633	45	76
1730	80	172	308	14	3,468	3,840	40	104
1731	109	168	320	12	3,166	3,477	40	75
1732	119	165	343	13	3,567	4,078	39	84
1733	112	164	324	14	3,427	4,440	33	80
1734	123	161	292	9	3,033	3,762	35	64
1735	125	199	356	17	3,713	4,222	51	81
1736	131	208	324	21	4,008	4,468	58	84

See p. 471 for footnotes.

A. England & Wales 1697–1791 (*cont.*)

(in £ thousand)

	Coal	Iron and Steel	Non-ferrous Metals and Manufactures	Cotton Yarn and Manufactures	Woollen and Worsted Yarn and Manufactures (*a*) (Official Values)	Woollen and Worsted Yarn and Manufactures (*a*) (Mrs Schumpeter's Values)	Linen Yarn and Manufactures	Silk Yarn and Manufactures
1737	122	213	394	18	4,047	4,628	50	81
1738	122	233	356	13	4,159	4,735	69	85
1739	141	211	358	15	3,218	3,835	72	88
1740	162	265	401	14	3,057	3,827	83	70
1741	128	306	454	20	3,670	4,192	117	103
1742	119	271	447	15	3,359	3,793	111	110
1743	137	266	541	9	3,542	3,967	89	125
1744	123	237	415	10	2,763	3,332	72	81
1745	125	195	376	8	2,947	3,503	76	73
1746	133	397	406	8	3,647	4,519	165	89
1747	114	297	398	8	3,554	4,224	150	101
1748	136	338	373	8	3,514	4,471	174	97
1749	158	439	459	9	4,478	5,666	234	110
1750	148	431	489	20	4,320	5,350	225	115
1751	196	428	450	44	4,207	5,282	217	46
1752	182	394	421	73	3,718	4,609	226	166
1753	186	466	489	115	4,223	5,267	273	163
1754	172	422	458	85	3,625	4,605	265	153
1755	165	417	413	65	3,575	4,506	186	171
1756	164	351	441	101	4,934	5,715	256	159
1757	141	426	412	124	4,758	5,660	333	166
1758	143	433	409	116	4,673	5,734	393	208
1759	135	472	431	113	5,352	6,341	446	306
1760	136	539	494	167	5,453	6,445	557	348
1761	171	466	450	151	4,344	5,927	435	254
1762	172	440	496	183	3,905	4,638	425	242
1763	184	515	576	399	3,971	4,908	414	155
1764	197	613	626	200	5,171	6,216	473	224
1765	283	569	624	249	4,475	5,467	413	213
1766	436	656	580	224	4,629	5,669	477	164
1767	421	738	635	273	4,277	5,242	448	189
1768	331	743	656	213	4,359	5,252	498	179
1769	307	664	681	212	3,897	4,705	413	127
1770	261	742	671	199	4,114	5,064	432	132
1771	339	945	679	311	4,960	6,135	559	250
1772 (*c*)	334	875	646	245	4,570	5,552	625	212
1773	315	746	666	181	3,840	4,723	491	153
1774	358	706	674	258	4,438	5,449	632	203
1775	354	742	680	252	4,298	5,144	427	98
1776	376	582	640	289	3,944	4,742	332	103
1777	387	520	602	246	3,772	4,018	371	140
1778	331	511	512	191	3,237	3,918	271	103
1779	292	398	522	303	2,737	3,485	269	131
1780	313	493	670	306	2,614	3,140	354	220
1781	246	409	473	296	2,843	3,314	234	170

See p. 471 for footnotes.

External Trade 8. *continued*

A. England & Wales 1697–1791 (*cont.*)

(in £ thousand)

	Coal	Iron and Steel	Non-ferrous Metals and Manufactures	Cotton Yarn and Manufactures	Woollen and Worsted Yarn and Manufactures (*a*) (Official Values)	(Mrs Schumpeter's Values)	Linen Yarn and Manufactures	Silk Yarn and Manufactures
1782	255	594	841	405	3,067	3,562	342	128
1783	384	577	694	746	3,560	4,288	554	231
1784	383	671	669	848	3,556	4,635	473	322
1785	497	656	679	826	3,814	4,504	361	209
1786	460	748	792	872	3,578	4,298	373	174
1787	414	811	757	1,025	3,805	4,598	504	211
1788	554	765	855	1,150	4,064	4,864	629	201
1789	528	869	884	1,089	4,280	5,297	573	203
1790	548	955	1,002	1,456	5,093	6,208	544	223
1791	574	1,259	1,048	1,637	5,408	6,085	605	268

B. Great Britain 1792–1829

(in £ thousand)

	Coal	Iron and Steel	Hardwares and Cutlery	Machinery	Non-ferrous Metals and Manufactures	Cotton Yarn and Manufactures	Woollen and Worsted Yarn and Manufactures (*a*) (Official Values)	(Mrs Schumpeter's Values)	Linen Yarn and Manufactures	Silk Yarn and Manufactures
1792	590	1,465	...	...	1,271	1,922	5,154(*d*)	6,472	959	285
1793	605	1,134	...	...	1,183	1,653	3,547	4,482	818	237
1794	535	1,121	...	...	1,206	2,280	4,126	5,153	1,017	284
1795	452	1,044	...	...	1,208	2,309	5,096	6,296	810	316
1796	522	1,277	...	...	1,243	3,061	5,677	7,001	955	373
1797	453	1,152	...	...	1,011	2,464	4,625	6,775	757	296
1798	455	1,145	...	...	1,079	3,622	6,177	7,559	1,103	225
1799	467	1,596	...	...	1,346	5,859	6,435	7,578	1,115	306
1800	510	1,605	...	...	1,414	5,851	6,918	8,099	808	297
1801	465	1,466	...	...	1,349	6,941	7,321	8,463	1,009	280
1802	521	1,610	...	...	1,557	7,667	6,687	7,808	895	232
1803	511	1,197	...	...	1,185	7,143	5,303	6,070	561	155
1804	514	1,102	...	...	874	8,792	5,694	6,533	727	187
1805	509	1,008	...	...	842	9,653	6,006	6,714	657	200
1806	543	1,260	...	...	693	10,482	6,248	7,109	800	218
1807	471	1,394	...	...	818	10,287	5,373	6,050	766	198
	---					----				
1808	527(*e*)	1,193	...	...	682	13,411(*e*)	4,854	5,070	874	129
1809	406	1,392	...	...	700	19,732	5,416	...	1,157	190
1810	510	1,578	...	...	717	19,109	5,774	...	1,018	190
1811	524	1,245	...	...	491	12,261	4,376	...	703	137
1812	617	1,446	...	...	737	16,939	5,085	...	840	166
1813	...	...	...	...	...	...	...	...	...	...
	---	---	---		---	---	---		---	---
1814 (*f*)	675	1,095	355	...	750	17,869	5,629	...	1,543	219
1815	698	1,127	871	...	1,150	22,555	7,480	...	1,619	258
		----	---		----	----	----		----	---
1816 (*g*)	200	938	740	...	1,212	17,564	5,586	...	1,559	162
1817	214	1,065	439	...	1,343	21,259	5,675	...	1,943	153
1818	230	1,288	580	...	1,231	22,589	6,344	...	2,158	168
1819	201	961	443	...	959	18,282	4,602	...	1,547	127
1820	213	1,025	343	...	1,135	22,532	4,364	...	1,935	118
1821	223	1,059	455	...	1,129	23,542	5,501	...	2,303	136

B. Great Britain 1792–1829 (*cont.*)

(in £ thousand)

	Coal	Iron and Steel	Hard-wares and Cutlery	Machinery	Non-ferrous Metals and Manu-factures	Cotton Yarn and Manu-factures)	Woollen and Worsted Yarn and Manufactures (*a*) (Official Values)	(Mrs Schum-peter's Values)	Linen Yarn and Manu-factures	Silk Yarn and Manu-factures
1822	241	1,140	535	116	1,084	26,911	5,944	...	2,595	141
1823	217	1,204	527	158	999	26,545	5,540	...	2,654	140
1824	235	1,125	612	130	1,042	30,156	6,147	...	3,283	160
1825	266	1,107	630	212	822	29,495	5,929	...	2,710	151
1826	298	1,330	563	229	1,033	25,194	5,042	...	2,057	107
1827	314	1,581	714	202	1,399	33,183	5,980	...	2,808	173
1828	302	1,687	711	262	1,196	33,476	5,720	...	3,118	179
1829	313	1,745	766	250	1,286	37,269	5,362	...	2,857	220

(*a*) The official values of wool manufactures exported before 1709 appear to have been revised in accordance with the rates adopted in that year, and Mrs Schumpeter's valuations are also constant.

(*b*) Prior to 1708 the small amounts of exports by sea to Scotland are included.

(*c*) The break in 1772 resulting from the change in basic source from the *Inspectors-General's Ledgers* to the *States of Navigation and Commerce* is insignificant for the items listed here.

(*d*) Both series of wool manufactures include woollen hats up to 1791. Thereafter the value of woollen hats has been subtracted from the official values series in order to facilitate comparison with later years. If they were included this series for 1792–1807 would read as follows:

1792	5,520	1796	6,011	1800	7,316	1804	5,951
1793	3,807	1797	4,936	1801	7,665	1805	6,237
1794	4,391	1798	6,499	1802	7,054	1806	6,545
1795	5,363	1799	6,871	1803	5,562	1807	5,594

(*e*) There are presumed to be slight breaks in these series since the figures in the *Trade and Navigation Accounts* differ to some degree from those given by Mrs Schumpeter.

(*f*) Prior to 1813 the figures relate to British produce exported, thus excluding Irish linens (so described) which went via Britain. After 1813 the statistics relate to British and Irish produce exported from Britain. The extent of the break this change produced cannot be stated, but except in linens it cannot have been significant.

(*g*) From 1816 onwards British exports to Ireland and the Isle of Man are no longer included. The extent of the break can be gauged from the following figures for 1816 including the Irish and Manx trade:

	Coal	Iron and Steel	Hardwares and Cutlery	Machinery	Non-ferrous Metals and Manufactures	Cotton Yarns and Manufactures	Woollen and Worsted Yarns and Manufactures	Linen Yarns and Manufactures	Silk Yarns and Manufactures
1816	681	1,074	783	...	1,240	17,771	5,862	1,561	196

External Trade 9. Official Values of Principal Re-Exports – Great Britain 1805–29, and United Kingdom 1826–56

NOTE
SOURCE: *Trade and Navigation Accounts.*

A. Great Britain 1805–29

(in £ thousand)

	Coffee	Sugar	Tea	Raw Cotton	Tobacco	Dyewoods and Dyestuffs (*a*)
1805	2,472	1,060	600	41	195	473
1806	3,027	688	515	26	162	685
1807	3,143	1,539	610	78	176	503
1808	1,848	784	715	60	124	512
1809	5,845	1,713	704	156	202	850
1810	1,455	1,472	569	344	165	876
1811	1,418	1,215	631	48	150	495
1812	4,383	1,570	664	58	218	519
1813	...	...	...	...	...	...
1814	8,072	2,394	1,548	366	212	1,356
1815	6,074	1,984	891	398	256	1,042
	----	----	---	---	---	----
1816 (*b*)	4,977	1,255	141	321	220	1,020
1817	3,363	898	122	663	174	596
1818	3,145	770	155	1,124	92	766
1819	2,671	593	124	1,016	361	767
1820	2,755	981	93	371	288	994
1821	2,598	839	91	1,092	329	700
1822	2,217	613	74	1,279	156	605
1823	1,871	728	75	707	197	720
1824	2,464	918	94	904	159	786

B. United Kingdom 1826–56

	Coffee	Sugar	Tea	Raw Cotton	Tobacco	Dyewoods and Dyestuffs (*a*)
1825	1,709	606	68	1,160	55	954
1826	1,988	752	42	1,663	191	1,020
1827	1,841	645	38	1,518	241	862
1828	1,486	928	39	1,401	203	1,155
1829	1,439	744	38	2,216	140	1,102
1830	1,437	744	38	2,216	138	1,102
1826	1,988	752	42	1,663	194	1,020
1827	1,841	645	38	1,518	247	862
1828	1,486	928	39	1,401	209	1,155
1830	1,255	779	36	718	186	1,104
1831	1,405	1,050	35	1,626	176	1,115
1832	1,608	907	40	1,390	131	1,252
1833	959	914	38	1,255	156	970
1834	953	1,490	177	1,515	248	1,156
1835	834	927	324	2,200	254	1,284
1836	667	695	640	2,708	241	1,267
1837	503	1,115	707	2,853	246	1,152
1838	706	936	387	2,094	232	1,444
1839	797	964	498	2,016	197	1,502
1840	794	573	358	2,617	251	1,928
1841	892	1,058	673	2,643	205	2,006
1842	594	1,004	856	2,928	243	1,732
1843	793	1,434	687	2,474	178	1,560
1844	394	983	725	3,036	166	2,102
1845	1,199	1,932	608	2,740	190	1,769
1846	733	683	530	4,209	270	1,974
1847	835	2,156	708	4,785	241	2,433
1848	1,503	1,116	533	4,725	210	2,625
1849	2,178	1,933	727	6,312	311	3,313
1850	761	1,178	752	6,539	165	2,491

B. United Kindgom 1826–56 (*cont.*)

(in £ thousand)

	Coffee	Sugar	Tea	Raw Cotton	Tobacco	Dyewoods and Dyestuffs (*a*)
1851	1,420	919	679	7,144	245	3,230
1852	809	1,117	920	7,138	190	2,613
1853	1,665	777	725	9,479	172	2,720
1854	2,036	1,165	1,298	7,870	212	2,947
1855	1,798	687	2,044	7,934	164	3,173
1856	1,725	2,024	858	9,357	197	3,206

(*a*) Includes only the principal items, which are alone separately listed in the source. These items are fewer in number than those listed as imports.

(*b*) From 1816 onwards re-exports to Ireland and the Isle of Man are no longer included. In that year they were as follows:

	Coffee	Sugar	Tea	Cotton	Tobacco	Dyewoods & Dyestuffs
1816	7	340	406	23	39	30

External Trade 10. Values (c.i.f.) at Current Prices of Principal Imports – Great Britain 1784–6 to 1854–6, and United Kingdom 1854–1980

NOTES

[1] SOURCES: Part A – Ralph Davis, *The Industrial Revolution and British Overseas Trade* (Leicester, 1979), Appendix table 57; Parts B and C – *Annual Statement of Trade*, *Overseas Trade Statistics of the United Kingdom*, and *Abstract*.

[2] Trade with Ireland is excluded in Part A.

[3] The figures for 1784–6 are for years ended 30 September. Others are for calendar years or years beginning 6 January to 1853.

[4] Not all the very minor breaks in continuity are indicated, but it is believed that all significant ones have been noted.

A. Computed Values, Great Britain, 1784–6 to 1854–6 (annual averages)

(in £ thousand)

	Butter & Cheese	Coffee	Corn	Fruit	Meat	Spices	Sugar	Tea	Wine & Spirits	Tobacco	Raw Cotton	Raw Silk
1784–6	3	158	534	134	1	214	2,614	2,587	1,519	541	1,814	1,218
1794–6	172	1,337	2,013	198	14	242	5,943	2,794	2,835	371	2,736	1,161
1804–6	602	2,451	2,227	401	69	247	6,878	3,957	3,188	600	5,603	1,802
1814–6	688	2,766	1,359	459	45	1,160	11,128	4,616	3,758	855	8,525	2,556
1824–6	1,069	1,022	1,244	462	100	516	6,695	4,121	3,862	597	7,444	3,483
1834–6	1,191	1,026	805	559	55	603	7,070	3,846	3,992	742	14,494	4,383
1844–6	1,929	897	5,685	1,166	788	456	8,084	2,908	3,184	695	11,306	4,002
1854–6	3,295	1,588	18,240	1,762	1,734	690	10,944	5,305	5,672	1,700	22,486	6,964

	Raw Wool	Flax, Hemp, & Jute	Iron & Iron Ore	Main oils, Seeds & Tallow	Hides & Skins	Dyestuffs	Timber	European Silk Goods	Asian Cotton & Silk Goods	Linens
1784–6	268	938	702	897	309	1,078	917	2	1,344	672
1794–6	642	1,846	852	1,256	636	1,973	1,625	–	1,687	685
1804–6	1,764	3,286	442	2,811	1,845	3,232	3,189	65	823	755
1814–6	3,911	2,501	258	3,315	3,132	4,217	3,773	4	515	113
1824–6	4,168	2,712	333	2,662	1,248	5,187	3,959	110	363	42
1834–6	6,718	3,335	314	4,312	1,999	3,279	3,832	585	347	91
1844–6	5,408	3,498	426	5,036	2,822	4,736	6,694	1,096	478	58
1854–6	6,990	5,416	665	9,714	3,394	4,934	9,711	2,054	481	95

B. Computed Values, United Kingdom, 1854–70

(in £ million)

	Grain and Flour (*a*)	Coffee	Sugar: Refined	Sugar: Un-refined	Tea	Wine	Meat and Animals (*b*)	Butter and Margar-ine	Timber (*c*)	Raw Cotton (*d*)	Raw Wool (*e*)	Silk Yarn and Goods	Tobacco
1854	21·8	1·6	0·6	9·6	5·5	3·6	3·3	2·2	11·8	20·2	6·5	3·5	1·3
1855	17·5	1·7	0·7	9·6	5·2	3·1	3·2	2·1	8·5	20·8	6·5	3·1	1·6
1856	23·0	1·5	0·3	11·4	5·2	3·7	3·3	1·8	10·2	26·4	8·7	3·8	2·2
1857	19·4	1·7	0·8	14·7	4·7	4·1	... 3·5(*b*)	2·1	9·7 ... 9·8 (*c*)	29·3	9·7	3·2	2·2
1858	20·2	1·7	0·8	12·3	5·2	2·0	2·4	1·8	8·0	30·1	9·0	2·6	2·5
1859	18·0	2·0	0·5	11·8	5·8	2·8	2·8	2·1	10·3	34·6	9·9	3·3	1·8
1860	31·7	2·5	0·6	11·8	6·9	4·2	4·0	4·1	11·4	35·8	11·2	3·7	1·8
1861	34·9	2·6	0·4	12·2	6·9	3·9	4·2	4·9	11·9	38·7	10·1	6·1	2·2
1862	37·8	3·3	0·5	10·9	9·2	3·6	5·2	4·9	11·5	31·1	12·2	6·7	2·4
1863	26·0	4·2	0·5	11·5	10·7	4·5	6·2	4·5	12·6	56·3	12·4	6·7	3·0
1864	19·9	3·6	1·7	14·4	9·4	5·0	7·5	5·7	13·1	78·2	16·1	8·0	3·4
1865	20·7	4·6	1·3	11·3	10·0	3·9	8·5	5·9	14·0	66·0	15·5	8·6	3·3
1866	30·1	4·1	1·0	10·8	11·2	4·7	8·1	6·0	12·8	77·5	18·1	9·6	2·6
1867	41·4	4·4	1·3	11·5	10·1	4·8	6·9	5·9	11·1	52·0	16·6	9·5	2·4
1868	39·4	4·9	1·2	13·3	12·4	5·4	5·6	6·3	12·1	55·2	15·5	11·8	2·3
1869	37·4	4·9	1·8	13·5	10·3	5·3	8·9	6·9	12·1	56·8	15·1	12·5	2·3
1870	34·2	4·9	2·7	14·4	10·1	4·8	7·8	6·8	13·3	53·5	16·2	15·8	2·4

See p. 480 for footnotes.

B. Computed Values 1854–70

(in £ million)

	Oils, Oil-seed, Gums, Resins, Tallow etc. (*f*)	Iron and Steel (*g*)	Un-dressed Hides, Skins, and Furs	Dye-woods and Dye-stuffs	Rubber	Non-ferrous Metals and Manufac-tures (*j*)	Paper-making Materials	Petrol-eum	Mach-inery
1854	10·4	0·6	2·3	3·8	0·3	1·6	0·3	...	...
1855	12·0	0·6	2·5	3·8	0·3	2·1	0·2	...	...
1856	12·6	0·8	3·6	5·0	0·2	1·7	0·2	...	...
	...		...	...		...			
1857	13·8(*h*)	0·7	5·1(*h*)	5·5(*h*)	0·1	2·1(*h*)	0·3	...	...
1858	12·4	0·3	3·2	4·9	0·1	2·0	0·2	...	...
1859	13·0	0·6	4·2	4·9	0·2	3·0	0·3	...	...
1860	14·9	0·7	4·0	5·5	0·5	2·9	0·3	...	...
1861	13·0	0·6	3·4	5·7	0·4	3·2	0·3	...	...
1862	12·3	0·8	3·6	5·2	0·5	2·9	0·4	...	...
1863	15·0	0·8	3·8	5·3	0·5	3·0	0·6	...	...
1864	14·0	1·0	3·5	5·0	0·5	4·9	0·7	...	...
1865	15·8	1·0	3·4	4·7	0·5	4·3	0·7	...	...
1866	15·8	1·3	4·0	5·5	0·7	4·0	0·8	...	...
1867	14·8	1·3	3·7	5·8	0·7	4·6	0·6	...	...
1868	16·6	1·1	4·2	7·2	1·2	5·1	0·9	...	...
1869	15·8	1·1	4·0	6·4	1·1	4·9	0·9	...	...
1870	17·7	1·3 ... 1·6(*g*)	6·2	6·2	1·6	4·7	1·2	...	...

C. Declared Values, United Kingdom, 1871–1980

(in £ million)

	Grain and Flour (*a*)	Coffee	Sugar: Refined	Sugar: Un-refined	Tea	Wine	Meat and Animals (*b*)	Butter and Margar-ine	Timber (*c*)	Raw Cotton (*d*)	Raw Wool (*e*)	Silk Yarn and Goods	Tobacco
1871	42·7	5·4	3·0	15·2	11·6	7·1	10·4	6·9	12·3	55·9	18·4	8·6	3·3
1872	51·2	5·3	3·1	18·0	12·9	7·7	10·7	6·0	14·2	53·4	19·1	9·5	2·7
1873	51·7	7·2	3·8	17·1	11·4	8·3	13·8	7·0	19·1	54·7	20·0	10·3	3·9
1874	51·1	7·1	4·2	15·8	11·5	6·9	13·4	9·1	22·3	50·7	21·7	12·1	4·0
1875	53·1	7·5	4·3	17·2	13·8	6·8	16·4	8·5	15·8	46·3	24·0	12·4	3·0
1876	51·8	6·4	4·1	16·3	12·7	7·0	18·9	9·7	19·6	40·2	24·3	12·0	4·0
1877	63·5	7·8	5·8	21·4	12·5	7·1	17·3	9·5	20·7	35·4	25·3	13·0	3·5
1878	59·1	5·9	4·8	16·0	13·0	6·0	20·5	10·0	14·4	33·5	23·9	12·8	3·7
1879	61·3	7·1	4·1	17·9	11·3	5·4	21·0	10·4	11·2	36·2	24·2	13·0	2·0
1880	62·9	6·9	4·4	18·5	11·6	6·5	26·9	12·1	17·3	42·8	27·2	13·6	2·9
1881	60·9	4·8	4·0	20·3	11·2	5·7	25·1	10·9	15·7	43·8	26·8	11·9	2·6
1882	63·5	5·2	4·0	20·9	11·0	5·5	22·2	11·4	17·9	46·7	25·8	11·5	2·6
1883	67·6	4·9	4·5	20·5	11·5	5·5	28·7	11·8	18·0	45·0	25·7	10·8	2·9
1884	48·1	3·8	4·5	15·2	10·5	5·3	26·1	12·5	15·8	44·5	27·2	11·3	2·7
1885	53·3	3·3	4·8	13·5	10·7	5·1	24·6	11·6	16·0	36·5	21·9	10·5	3·8
									...				
1886	43·5	3·3	5·3	10·5	11·3	5·1	21·6	11·1	13·0(*c*)	38·1	23·2	10·9	3·7
1887	48·3	4·2	5·5	11·0	9·8	5·5	21·2	11·9	12·5	40·2	25·1	10·8	3·4
1888	51·3	3·6	6·0	12·1	10·2	5·4	23·3	12·2	15·2	40·0	26·7	10·9	2·8
1889	51·2	4·3	8·8	13·6	10·0	5·9	29·3	13·9	20·4	45·6	29·3	12·3	3·9
1890	53·5	4·0	8·1	9·9	9·9	5·9	32·3	13·7	17·8	42·8	27·9	11·9	3·5
							...						
1891	62·0	3·4	9·4	10·5	10·7	6·0	29·9 (*b*)	15·1	15·6	46·1	28·8	11·7	3·4
1892	58·7	3·9	9·1	10·7	10·0	6·0	32·3	15·7	17·8	37·9	27·6	11·9	3·5
1893	51·2	4·0	10·6	11·5	10·1	5·3	29·3	16·4	16·1	30·7	25·4	12·0	3·5
1894	48·2	3·5	10·8	8·3	9·8	5·0	32·3	16·5	17·8	32·9	25·7	13·1	3·5
1895	49·7	3·8	9·4	8·3	10·2	5·4	33·3	16·8	16·4	30·4	27·0	15·6	3·4

See p. 480 for footnotes.

C. Declared Values, United Kingdom, 1871–1980 (*cont.*)

(in £ million)

	Grain and Flour (*a*)	Coffee	Sugar: Refined	Sugar: Un-refined	Tea	Wine	Meat and Animals (*b*)	Butter and Margar-ine	Timber (*c*)	Raw Cotton (*d*)	Raw Wool (*e*)	Silk Yarn and Goods	Tobacco
1896	52·8	3·6	10·0	8·3	10·6	5·9	35·9	17·8	20·3	36·3	25·9	17·1	4·4
1897	53·6	3·6	9·7	6·2	10·4	6·4	39·5	18·4	24·6	32·2	25·3	17·2	4·1
1898	62·9	3·6	10·4	7·1	10·3	6·6	41·0	18·3	22·1	34·1	24·4	16·9	3·9
1899	58·1	3·3	11·2	6·9	10·6	5·6	42·9	19·8	24·2	27·7	24·6	16·4	5·5
1900	58·9	2·5	12·3	6·9	10·7	5·2	46·8	19·9	27·9	41·0	22·7	14·9	4·8
1901	61·2	3·3	12·9	6·4	9·4	4·9	50·4	21·9	24·6	42·0	22·3	13·6	4·7
1902	62·5	2·6	9·7	5·0	8·8	4·9	48·1	23·1	25·2	41·1	20·9	14·1	5·8
1903	66·2	3·1	10·0	5·5	9·6	4·7	50·4	23·1	27·1	44·8	21·5	13·2	4·2
1904	65·2	3·3	10·8	7·5	9·4	3·8	48·7	23·6	23·6	54·7	21·4	13·4	4·5
1905	65·4	2·6	10·9	8·6	9·3	4·1	49·4	24·3	23·3	52·2	24·8	13·1	3·7
1906	63·9	2·0	10·5	6·8	9·9	4·2	52·0	26·2	27·5	55·8	28·4	13·5	4·7
1907	70·8	2·4	11·8	7·3	10·7	4·0	51·9	24·6	27·1	70·5	34·0	13·3	4·2
1908	68·3	2·2	12·2	7·8	10·7	3·5	49·4	26·2	24·3	55·8	29·1	12·3	5·2
1909	79·0	2·1	12·6	9·1	11·6	3·7	47·6	24·7	23·6	60·3	33·1	12·5	5·0
1910	72·6	2·3	13·1	11·4	11·4	4·2	48·9	27·4	26·2	71·7	35·4	13·3	4·6
1911	71·7	2·5	14·4	12·2	13·0	4·2	49·7	27·1	25·9	71·2	34·5	13·2	5·3
1912	83·4	2·5	13·4	11·8	13·1	4·3	49·1	27·9	28·4	80·2	34·4	14·0	6·4
1913	80·9	2·9	12·4	10·7	13·8	4·1	56·7	28·0	33·8	70·6	35·6	14·7	8·0
1914	75·0	3·5	15·6	16·5	14·2	3·6	63·2	28·0	25·3	55·4	32·4	13·1	7·5
1915	103·7	4·9	12·7	19·1	19·6	2·9	86·8	32·8	32·8	64·7	43·2	14·6	8·6
1916	123·0	4·7	12·5	24·9	17·7	3·5	94·1	27·9	40·2	84·7	38·8	13·1	7·4
1917	161·7	1·9	6·4	30·3	14·7	2·4	102·4	26·7	25·6	110·6	51·1	11·4	3·9
1918	140·1	0·7	0·8	33·6	29·0	7·3	173·7	21·3	29·2	150·3	38·7	17·2	18·2
1919	144·0	6·0	19·2	34·7	33·1	18·2	175·4	22·1	72·3	190·2	100·5	22·9	41·7
1920	223·3	4·5	7·7	65·5	27·0	12·8	141·5	30·0	82·1	256·7	90·6	36·9	34·9
1921	130·2	2·4	14·9	20·4	23·1	5·3	135·7	47·6	30·0	73·3	41·9	18·9	22·8
1922	99·9	4·4	11·0	22·4	26·0	5·6	104·9	41·2	37·3	87·3	59·9	20·9	18·6
1923	93·1	2·1	11·6	29·6	33·5	5·7	125·4	48·7	47·7	93·4	47·9	22·5	16·4
1924	116·4	3·3	15·9	28·0	40·4	6·9	128·6	54·4	51·1	121·6	71·9	24·9	17·3
1925	107·1	4·7	13·7	19·5	37·5	7·0	140·0	58·1	46·5	125·8	73·6	22·6	17·0
1926	95·9	3·4	11·2	14·8	38·6	7·3	131·2	53·0	39·3	84·4	63·9	16·7	17·7
1927	107·9	4·8	8·7	18·4	41·6	7·0	119·0	52·3	49·7	67·8	61·0	16·0	19·2
1928	94·7	4·5	3·6	23·4	35·7	5·7	125·3	55·6	42·6	80·8	61·6	14·3	17·5
1929	93·3	3·8	0·7	22·7	37·6	6·2	130·0	57·4	45·8	77·4	61·1	13·0	18·5
1930	70·6	4·8	0·6	16·4	34·1	5·3	129·8	49·3	42·8	45·0	43·5	11·0	15·7
1931	53·9	4·0	0·5	14·3	29·6	5·2	109·9	41·3	29·1	27·2	33·5	8·2	11·4
1932	56·0	3·5	0·3	18·0	25·4	3·7	91·8	34·4	25·6	31·2	32·9	•	10·1
1933	53·6	2·9	0·3	15·0	24·9	4·7	84·6	33·3	29·9	36·8	36·1		11·8
1934	52·8	2·5	0·4	13·3	27·9	5·0	86·8	39·4	39·5	36·1	37·6		17·0
1935	55·1	1·8	0·4	12·2	25·9	5·5	83·3	44·4	35·5	37·3	36·0		17·6
1936	67·7	1·6	0·2	14·8	26·4	6·3	86·0	44·5	43·5	45·8	44·6		18·5
1937	89·3	1·3	0·4	20·0	29·6	6·1	94·2	47·5	61·8	48·7	50·8		18·0
1938	72·6	1·4	0·3	18·9	30·8	5·3	99·9	51·0	42·9	29·6	41·6		23·3
1939	53·2	2·0	22·0		24·4	5·5	104·3	48·5	37·1	34·2	39·4		13·6
1940	91·1	3·5	23·7		27·5	4·7	108·1	33·0	37·9	50·3	66·3		8·8
1941	84·0	0·4	26·0		30·3	0·8	125·8	27·8	24·8	35·8	21·3		18·0
1942	51·8	1·7	15·1		23·5	0·4	161·9	17·8	20·4	52·7	27·3		20·6
1943	61·6	3·0	29·4		36·0	0·5	178·4	20·8	32·6	53·8	18·8		42·2
1944	64·0	3·4	23·8		35·1	0·9	179·5	21·2	36·0	42·0	35·5		32·7
1945	80·6	4·2	24·1		33·4	2·9	126·3	31·7	45·8	48·8	35·6		53·4

External Trade 10. *continued*

C. Declared Values, United Kingdom, 1871–1980 (*cont.*)

(in £ million)

	Grain and Flour (*a*)	Coffee	Sugar: Refined	Sugar: Un-refined	Tea	Wine	Meat and Animals (*b*)	Butter and Margar-ine	Timber (*c*)	Raw Cotton (*d*)	Raw Wool (*e*)	Tobacco
1946	90·0	3·3	37·1		35·2	7·3	151·5	37·3	55·1	46·4	38·5	68·1
1947	139·9	5·7	59·2		44·8	10·3	159·3	42·9	113·6	58·8	60·7	47·4
1948	196·4	6·0	58·3		55·7	10·6	137·7	67·8	93·9	106·7	87·3	42·6
1949	179·3	5·6	65·7		66·3	8·3	171·1	86·9	99·4 ---- (*c*) 94·1	121·5	128·3 ---- (*e*) 132·1	52·5
1950	155·2	11·0	80·1		57·4	9·5	223·6	91·4	86·8	160·6	196·2	64·6
1951	238·2	13·9	105·7		76·2	12·2	214·8	90·5	209·2	258·8	250·0	81·4
1952	254·4	14·1	93·3		79·4	9·7	244·5	82·4	155·6	128·3	179·4	51·9
1953	231·8	10·9	119·1		83·0	10·3	288·0	94·9	159·3	107·2	245·1	77·8
1954	177·2	14·2	96·7		127·2	11·9	286·1	101·4	155·2	125·9	196·8	76·2
1955	219·5	12·7	95·3		125·8	13·5	325·5	112·0	192·5	98·6	191·5	86·5
1956	227·7	15·5	100·7		114·5	14·0	320·3	120·6	159·9	104·2	187·4	80·6
1957	216·2	16·1	146·5		134·2	16·4	347·8	101·5	173·5	108·4	205·3	85·6
1958	219·8	14·7	95·6		127·5	15·7	346·2	97·8	140·5	71·6	145·3	86·9
1959	223·4	14·2	80·8		112·3	18·1	339·9	134·7	142·4	67·9	168·3	84·7
1960	212·1	12·5	75·8		116·1	21·7	371·7	122·5	186·4	73·5	149·3	103·6
1961	207·2	12·7	70·0		115·3	25·6	350·0	106·3	177·1	62·2	144·4	100·6
1962	233·1	14·4	56·7		115·5	24·7	350·1	117·8	156·7	59·7	136·8	80·8
1963	213·1	17·2	164·6		114·2	28·1	354·6	135·8	170·4	60·1	159·7	99·5
1964	214·5	23·5	134·9		109·0	31·4	419·3	157·7	218·0	65·1	160·7	91·1
1965	222·1	14·8	94·6		107·5	29·6	405·7	148·0	220·2	53·7	128·4	84·0
1966	211·2	22·5	97·8		99·0	30·8	414·3	141·4	194·2	53·5	123·8	84·6
1967	214·9	22·7	93·1		105·6	35·4	415·2	148·0	191·8	43·5	111·7	89·3
1968	227·7	31·2	93·9		112·1	44·0	445·9	136·9	231·1	57·7	114·2	116·6
1969	247·8 ---(*a*) 251·6	34·1	101·9		82·8	39·4	476·4 ---(*b*) 477·0	127·6	217·4	49·7	118·3	114·6
1970	280·5	42·4	104·0		104·6	42·9	483·2	126·5	238·6	50·3	92·6	110·4
1971	282·7	51·1	106·5		94·9	53·5	524·5	162·6	245·3	47·1	63·8	108·9
1972	257·1	47·4	132·6		82·2	69·7	596·5	170·0	253·6	50·9	109·7	121·5
1973	369·8	77·6	151·2		82·8	142·7	771·2	136·9	458·3	76·1	180·9	153·7
1974	590·9	64·0	331·6		117·4	138·9	740·3	230·1	587·2	72·0	142·6	185·4
1975	612·0	69·5	588·2		128·6	127·4	796·7	355·6	362·3	68·8	124·5	192·0
1976	747·5	155·5	377·8		166·5	148·8	953·1	350·5	585·2	109·6	235·1	236·6
1977	820·4	283·8	367·9		335·2	192·7	1,057·2	319·5	632·6	120·7	236·4	256·1
1978	674·6	212·7	378·6		192·0	233·5	1,252·2	365·3	599·6	96·8	277·1	454·0
1979	668·4	268·0	314·9		197·7	316·2	1,320·1	323·8	743·0	102·2	245·2	350·9
1980	603·2	195·2	303·9		199·1	284·8	1,295·5	299·7	683·1	72·8	197·9	235·0

See p. 480 for footnotes.

C. Declared Values, United Kingdom, 1871–1980

(in £ million)

	Oils, Oil-seed, Gums, Resins, Tallow etc. (f)	Iron and Steel (g)	Undressed Hides, Skins, and Furs	Dye-woods and Dye-stuffs	Rubber	Non-ferrous Metals and Manufactures	Paper-making Materials	Petroleum	Machinery	Road (o) Vehicles and Aircraft
1871	18·6(f)	1·8	6·1(i)	7·0	1·7	5·9	1·8	0·6(f)	...	
1872	17·8	2·9	7·8(i)	6·8	1·8	8·4	1·3	0·4	...	
1873	17·6	2·7	7·5(i)	6·3	1·7	7·1	1·3	1·0	...	
1874	16·7	2·9	7·2(i)	6·0	1·3	7·5	1·4	1·0		
1875	18·4	3·2	7·0(i)	5·9	1·6	8·6	1·5	0·8	...	
1876	18·3	2·9	5·7	6·0	1·5	7·7	1·4	1·4	...	
1877	18·5	2·8	5·7	5·4	1·5	7·7	1·7	1·8		
1878	16·4	3·0	5·4	5·2	1·3	7·1	1·4	1·2	...	
1879	15·4	2·8	5·1	5·1	1·6	7·5	1·6	1·4	...	
1880	16·9	4·0	6·7	5·5	2·4	7·6	2·1	1·3	...	
1881	16·4	4·1	5·9	5·8	2·3	7·4	2·0	2·0	...	
1882	17·5	4·2	6·7	6·2	2·8	8·3	2·1	1·7	...	
1883	18·3	4·4	6·7	6·3	3·7	8·1	2·3	2·2	...	
1884	16·6	4·1	7·2	6·4	2·3	7·7	2·1	1·7	...	
1885	15·9	3·9	6·8	5·7	2·0	7·5	2·3	2·3	...	
1886	13·7	3·5	6·5	5·4	2·2	7·6	2·2	2·1	...	
1887	13·4	3·6	6·1	5·1	2·7	7·8	2·3	2·1	...	
1888	14·6	4·0	6·0	5·2	2·6	11·4	2·8	2·6	...	
1889	15·8	4·4	6·8	5·5	2·6	9·4	2·5	2·6	...	
1890	14·4	4·5	6·0	5·3	3·3	10·3	2·5	2·4	...	
1891	15·9	4·4	6·4	4·4	3·4	10·1	2·5	2·7	...	
1892	15·0	4·0	6·1	4·6	3·0	9·0	2·4	2·4	...	
1893	15·9	3·8	6·6	4·5	3·3	9·1	2·5	2·5	...	
1894	16·2	4·0	6·1	4·4	3·3	8·8	2·7	2·5	...	
1895	15·1	4·4	7·4	4·8	3·8	8·6	2·8	3·4	...	
1896	15·5	5·7	6·0	4·9	5·0	10·0	2·8	3·7	...	
1897	14·0	4·5(g)	6·7	4·1	4·6	9·9	3·2	3·3	2·4	
1898	14·2	5·0	6·9	3·6	6·2	11·2	3·0	3·7	3·1	
1899	15·7	5·6	7·5	3·8	5·9	14·7	3·1	4·6	3·7	
1900	18·0	7·3	8·5	3·3	7·0	17·4	3·7	5·6	3·5	
1901	18·1	7·6	8·0	3·7	5·8	15·7	3·5	5·1	4·0	...
1902	20·0	7·9	8·0	3·8	5·2	16·0	3·4	5·2	4·8	1·1
1903	19·2	8·7	7·4	3·6	6·7	15·3	3·4	5·3	4·5	2·0
1904	19·5	8·2	6·6	3·7	7·7	18·0	3·6	5·8	4·3	2·5
1905	18·2	8·6	8·1	3·5	9·6	18·7	3·8	5·4	4·5	3·4
1906	19·8	8·4	10·7	3·6	10·0	23·8	3·9	5·8	5·1	4·5
1907	24·6	7·2(g)	10·8	4·1	10·8	24·2	4·4	6·1	5·3	4·6
1908	21·9	7·7	9·4	3·9	8·4	21·6	4·6	6·7	4·6	4·1
1909	25·0	8·0	11·6	4·1	14·1	21·5	4·5	6·1	4·4	4·4
1910	31·9	9·1	12·9	4·1	26·1	21·5	5·0	5·7	4·5	5·3
1911	29·4	11·1	11·1	3·9	18·3	24·2	4·8	5·7	5·8	6·1

See p. 480 for footnotes.

C. Declared Values, United Kingdom, 1871–1980 (*cont.*)

(in £ million)

	Oils, Oil-seed, Gums, Resins, Tallow etc. (*f*)	Iron and Steel (*g*)	Undressed Hides, Skins, and Furs	Dye-woods and Dye-stuffs	Rubber	Non-ferrous Metals and Manufactures	Paper-making Materials	Petroleum	Machinery	Road (*o*) Vehicles and Aircraft	Textiles (*p*)	Chemicals (*q*)	Footwear, (*q*) Clothing, etc.
1912	30.1	13.0	13.7	4.0	21.6	27.7	5.6	7.4	6.8	7.5 --- (*o*)			
1913	30.7	15.2	15.1	4.4	20.5	29.3	5.8	10.9	7.3	5.3			
1914	28.6	10.9	12.7	4.0	15.8	27.2	6.0	12.8	6.7	5.0			
1915	36.4	10.8	14.0	6.6	19.7	39.9	6.2	13.3	8.8	7.3			
1916	43.6	11.2	13.8	9.9	23.1	35.6	8.1	19.8	8.0	3.3			
1917	41.9	10.8	18.4	8.1	23.9	41.2	10.4	33.9	8.9	5.1			
1918	52.5	9.7	29.5	8.4	12.1	44.8	13.2	63.9	10.7	11.6			
1919	91.4	11.6	29.5	8.3	26.5	33.6	16.5	36.3	15.0	9.4	*	*	*
1920	81.9	29.0	32.0	13.9	26.7	39.1	33.3	66.6	20.0	25.4	87.5	34.3	15.7
1921	36.4	22.9	10.9	3.5	10.5	18.4	13.8	54.5	10.8	6.2	41.0	12.6	9.6
1922	33.9	10.4	14.9	3.8	7.3	18.2	9.6	39.1	8.3	6.1	48.2	11.4	14.4
1923	39.2	13.8	16.9	3.4	12.3	25.6	11.5	35.0	9.5	3.9	47.6	13.5	16.9
1924	44.2	22.4	21.3	3.8	9.6	32.7	11.6	41.4	10.9	5.2	66.3	14.6	19.6
1925	46.6	24.0	21.8	3.1	29.4	38.1	11.1	39.4	12.3	5.0	65.8	14.4	22.0
1926	36.3	29.5	19.5	3.0	33.5	37.1	11.9	46.8	12.9	6.4	55.4	15.4	18.4
1927	35.5	34.0	23.0	3.5	25.4	32.6	12.8	43.3	16.0	8.2	58.0	15.5	19.7
1928	38.8	24.1	26.1	3.7	11.8	33.0	10.2	49.2	16.8	7.6	58.0	15.4	21.5
1929	39.2	24.7	20.4	2.9	17.3	37.0	13.2	43.4	19.3	9.3	57.5	16.9	22.1
1930	29.4	23.3	16.1	3.2	10.7	29.4	12.1	46.4	18.0	5.7	50.6	13.8	21.6
1931	22.0	19.6	11.7	3.1	4.5	21.4	10.0	29.0	15.4	3.1	45.7	14.0	21.7
1932	19.2	8.7	12.1	2.5	2.4	14.7	9.8	31.2	10.5	2.8	16.8	9.5	8.0
1933	17.7	6.1	14.3	2.5	3.0	15.7	9.3	30.2	8.6	2.1	15.0	9.6	8.4
1934	17.4	9.2	14.7	2.9	12.0	22.0	11.1	31.8	11.2	3.0	14.9	11.1	8.6
1935	21.6	8.7	14.7	2.8	10.1	28.0	10.8	33.6	13.1	4.0	14.7	11.6	8.5
1936	24.5	11.7	19.5	•	4.4	33.2	11.9	37.0	18.0	4.4	16.3	12.6	10.0
1937	30.2	19.8 --- (*g*) 17.2	25.2		12.2	55.7	15.9	47.8	24.2	5.6	18.4	13.9	10.9
1938	25.4	12.3	18.2		11.5	40.8	16.0	46.0	21.8	4.0	16.5	13.3 --- (*r*) 21.6	10.8
1939	26.1	15.0	15.5		9.5	38.7	15.7	47.1	24.5	7.4	16.2	24.3	8.3
1940	39.1	45.2	15.7		23.8	59.5	13.1	72.6	41.2	43.6	22.1	28.1	2.6
1941	34.9	66.8	8.6		22.2	57.7	7.8	93.7	53.8	104.3	6.1	23.3	1.4
1942	36.0	45.1	12.5		9.1	60.9	10.5	99.4	41.7	125.4	7.3	45.2	1.1
1943	51.5	57.3	10.5		13.3	84.0	9.4	153.5	56.4	239.3	9.0	61.0	1.4
1944	49.0	31.2	11.7		25.7	66.6	8.8	222.3	55.8	459.0	16.0	50.4	5.6
1945	42.0	5.5	14.5		11.7	22.1	15.4	145.6	24.2	231.5	14.1	38.2	5.5
1946	52.2	9.1	27.3		42.3	40.8	18.8	86.6	13.5	2.3	18.7	28.5	2.4
1947	105.4	14.3	39.9		27.8	79.2	27.3	98.5	29.6 --- (*m*) 33.6	6.0	49.8	46.1	6.0
1948	112.8	18.4	34.6		30.0	88.8	52.3	154.9	49.5	12.2	70.2	46.7	5.3
1949	131.3 --- (*f*) 128.9	35.5	38.0		22.4	93.5 --- (*j*) 92.0	48.4 --- (*k*) 42.3	146.9	62.3	25.2	73.2	42.2	6.3
1950	129.2	22.9	49.2		59.9	104.1	47.1	193.5	60.6	19.6	81.2	60.3	10.9
1951	178.5	37.4	68.5		160.3	160.5	126.3	300.0 --- (*l*) 306.9	68.8	11.4	153.9	106.6	11.3

See p. 480 for footnotes.

External Trade 10. *continued*

C. Declared Values, United Kingdom, 1871–1980 (*cont.*)

(in £ million)

	Oils, Oil-seed, Gums, Resins, Tallow etc. (*f*)	Iron and Steel (*g*)	Un-dressed Hides, Skins, and Furs	Rubber	Non-ferrous Metals and Manu-factures	Paper-making Materials	Petrol-eum	Mach-inery	Road (*o*) Vehicles and Aircraft	Textiles (*p*)	Chemi-cals (*q*)	Foot-wear, (*q*) Clothing, etc.
1952	165·4	115·7	40·4	103·3	202·8	99·4	335·5	122·9	16·3	81·6	77·9	8·3
1953	127·4	61·1	50·2	56·3	154·6	67·8	310·0	107·9	47·6	48·3	77·5	8·5
1954	122·7	28·2	43·8	50·0	175·0	86·6	312·0	90·8	23·5	70·7	104·8	13·3
1955	108·7	98·4	45·7	95·8	233·2	106·7	334·3	114·0	26·3	74·2	115·5	17·8
1956	112·5	105·1	44·0	88·5	225·2	107·5	370·4	132·4	23·1	75·5	110·1	22·7
1957	117·1	79·6	48·0	84·2	199·2	105·1	440·2	148·8	27·9	89·2	117·3	25·5
1958	95·1	45·8	39·0	75·8	177·5	97·6	431·8	162·8	26·0	85·3	121·4	29·1
1959	112·5	40·1	48·7	63·8	196·2	99·9	465·7	202·2	33·6	98·0	139·3	40·1
1960	108·3	100·6	49·9	77·7	262·9	121·8	479·8	255·6	73·3	136·9	176·7	58·1
1961	99·6	49·0	46·8	72·0	226·9	117·9	481·3	315·1	34·7	147·4	169·0	64·9
1962	94·7	53·6	46·4	61·5	225·8	105·0	531·8	325·0	37·3	135·0	173·5	71·4
1963	96·2	75·0	58·8	52·7	224·5	115·1	556·5	346·3	51·9	144·7	205·8	74·3
1964	101·3	105·9	57·1	50·5	298·8	137·1	581·7	454·2	69·0	177·0	252·2	96·9
1965	113·5	78·0	55·7	47·3	347·4	139·3	598·5	496·8	80·5	151·5	283·2	75·3
1966	108·2	87·7	66·4	46·1	395·9	133·6	611·3	580·1	89·8	158·8	293·9	91·0
1967	99·4	120·1	50·8	44·5	343·4	126·2	713·8	696·1	145·8	182·0	328·7	110·1
1968	108·2	154·9	62·4	48·5	453·6	155·5	881·6	869·5	281·2	213·2	415·4	142·9
1969	111·3	174·2	78·2	60·9	514·5	164·9	885·5	948·5	326·5	238·7	464·3	160·0
1970	142·4	222·4	70·1	57·6	570·5	197·8	924·5	1,199·3	260·2	256·3	542·8	170·0
					---- (*n*)		---- (*l*)	---- (*n*)		---- (*n*)	---- (*n*)	---- (*n*)
					568·0		930·0	1,192·3		260·5	532·9	170·4
1971	147·0	206·5	73·9	52·8	436·0	161·4	1,191·2	1,274·2	401·2	329·4	548·9	232·6
1972	140·6	252·1	85·1	47·5	433·3	171·6	1,171·4	1,585·9	595·7	376·4	630·8	280·1
1973	233·4	373·3	112·5	74·8	633·2	201·0	1,687·5	2,414·5	811·7	523·0	861·6	417·1
1974	358·1	716·3	106·3	100·3	908·5	329·8	4,550·4	3,001·2	820·6	695·3	1,523·0	511·3
1975	292·4	826·4	106·7	92·8	645·9	357·8	4,175·2	3,337·9	1,085·1	690·2	1,349·6	629·0
1976	406·4	967·5	171·7	140·5	910·6	463·3	5,535·4	4,304·8	1,647·8	920·1	1,924·3	849·6
1977	579·9	984·9	210·4	166·5	1,040·9	439·6	5,088·7	5,294·8	2,458·2	1,129·7	2,360·9	981·5
1978	532·2	1,056·4	196·0	160·8	1,019·2	348·7	4,503·7	6,332·2	3,595·4	1,453·9	2,756·7	1,172·7
1979	575·0	1,215·2	224·6	185·2	1,382·6	388·8	5,228·2	7,426·6	4,998·5	1,691·1	3,402·2	1,546·6
1980	525·7	1,448·0	227·6	182·8	1,340·3	398·7	6,072·7	7,725·1	4,971·9	1,543·7	3,146·9	1,584·7

• Subsequently or previously too small to be worth showing.

(*a*) Corresponds to 'Corn' in the eighteenth-century table up to 1969 (1st line), i.e. rice, tapioca, etc. are not included. Subsequent figures are of cereals and cereal preparations.

(*b*) In principle, only food animals are included, with breeding animals excluded from 1969 (2nd line). Pigs were not included until 1891. Prior to 1857 "other meat" than beef and pigmeat was not included, but it was unimportant at that time and for some years afterwards.

(*c*) Excluding cork to 1949 (1st line) and dyewoods throughout, but including certain wood manufactures, to 1885 (1st line) and others to 1949 (1st line).

(*d*) Including unmanufactured waste.

(*e*) Including rags for use as raw material for cloth. Animal hair and wool tops are included from 1949 (2nd line).

(*f*) To 1949 (1st line), this includes all types of oil (except, from 1871, petroleum), all nuts and seeds used for expressing oil, all types of gum, resin, tallow, and stearin. From 1949 (2nd line) gums and resins are not included.

(*g*) From 1871 (2nd line) to 1896 machinery is included, old rails are included from 1907 to 1937 (1st line). From 1937 (2nd line) manufactures of steel, other than railway tyres, axles, and shafts are no longer included.

(*h*) Prior to 1857 certain minor items were not shown by value.

(*i*) Including a small amount of dressed skins.

(*j*) Base metals only. Minor metals were included from 1871 (2nd line), and some manufactures were excluded in 1949.

(*k*) Pulp and waste paper only from 1949 (2nd line).

(*l*) Subsequently including more petroleum products.

(*m*) Including heavy electrical machinery throughout, but other electrical goods are only included from 1947 (2nd line).

(*n*) The break in 1970 results from the revision of the S.I.C.

(*o*) All tyres are included to 1912; subsequently only those on complete vehicles.

(*p*) Including silks, which are shown separately until 1931. It would be possible to carry this category back further than 1920, but the main single component was silks, and the big change in classification in that year makes a convenient starting point.

(*q*) Most of this category was scattered under a variety of headings prior to the 1920 classification.

(*r*) Many related products were included from 1938 (2nd line).

External Trade 11. Values (f.o.b.) at Current Prices of Principal Exports – Great Britain 1814–1829 and United Kingdom 1826–1980

NOTES

[1] Sources: *Annual Statement of Trade*, *Overseas Trade Statistics of the United Kingdom*, and *Abstract*.

[2] The figures to 1969 (1st line) relate to domestic exports.

[3] Not all the minor breaks in continuity of series have been shown, but it is believed that all those of significance have been indicated.

[4] Figures to 1853 are for years beginning 6 January.

[5] Ralph Davis, *The Industrial Revolution and British Overseas Trade* (Leicester, 1979) Appendix, table 41, computed the following earlier estimates of current values for British exports, excluding those to Ireland:

(annual averages in £ thousand)

	Cotton Goods	Linen Goods	Wool Goods	Haberdashery, Clothing, etc.	Metals and Metalwares
1784–6	766	647	3,700	314	2,180
1794–6	3,392	867	5,194	851	4,134
1804–6	15,871	749	6,172	1,597	4,927
1814–6	18,742	1,642	7,865	1,443	4,488

A. Great Britain 1814–29 (excluding exports to Ireland)

(in £ million)

	Coal (*a*)	Iron & Steel (*b*)	Machinery (*c*)	Non-ferrous Metals and Manufactures (*d*)	Cotton Goods (*e*)	Wool Goods (*f*)	Chemicals (*g*)
1814	0·1	1·0		1·0	20·0	6·4	...
1815	0·1	1·1		1·5	20·6	9·3	...
1816	0·1	1·0		1·5	15·6	7·8	...
1817	0·1	1·1		1·6	16·0	7·2	...
1818	0·1	1·3		1·6	18·8	8·1	...
1819	0·1	0·9		1·3	14·7	6·0	...
1820	0·1	0·9		1·4	16·5	5·6	...
1821	0·1	0·9		1·3	16·1	6·5	...
1822	0·1	0·8	0·1	1·2	17·2	6·5	...
1823	0·1	0·9	0·2	1·2	16·3	5·6	...
1824	0·1	0·9	0·1	1·2	18·4	6·0	...
1825	0·1	1·0	0·2	1·1	18·3	6·2	...
1826	0·1	1·1	0·2	1·2	14·0	5·0	...
1827	0·2	1·2	0·2	1·5	17·5	5·3	...
1828	0·1	1·2	0·3	1·3	17·1	5·1	...
1829	0·1	1·2	0·3	1·3	17·4	4·7	...

B. United Kingdom 1826–1980

	Coal (*a*)	Iron & Steel (*b*)	Machinery (*c*)	Non-ferrous Metals and Manufactures (*d*)	Cotton Goods (*e*)	Wool Goods (*f*)	Chemicals (*g*)
1826	...	...	...	...	14·1	5·0	...
1827	...	...	...	...	17·6	5·3	...
1828	...	...	...	...	17·2	5·1	...
1829	0·1	1·2	0·3	1·3	17·5	4·7	...
1830	0·2	1·1	0·2	1·3	19·4	4·9	...
1831	0·2	1·1	0·1	1·2	17·3	5·4	...
1832	0·2	1·2	0·1	1·4	17·4	5·5	...
1833	0·2	1·4	0·1	1·4	18·5	6·5	...
1834	0·2	1·4	0·2	1·5	20·5	6·0	...
1835	0·2	1·6	0·3	1·7	22·1	7·2	...
1836	0·3	2·3	0·3	1·7	24·6	8·0	...
1837	0·4	2·0	0·5	1·8	20·6	5·0	...
1838	0·5	2·5	0·6	1·9	24·1	6·2	...
1839	0·5	2·7	0·7	2·0	24·5	6·7	...
1840	0·6	2·6 ---(*b*) 2·9	0·6	2·1 ---(*d*) 1·8	24·7	5·8	0·4
1841	0·7	3·2	0·6	1·9	23·5	6·3	0·3
1842	0·7	2·8	0·6	2·4	21·7	5·8	0·4
1843	0·7	3·0	0·7	2·0	23·4	7·5	0·5
1844	0·7	3·6	0·8	2·1	25·8	9·2	0·5
1845	1·0	4·1	0·9	2·0	26·1	8·8	0·6
1846	1·0	4·8	1·1	1·9	25·6	7·2	0·6
1847	1·0	5·7	1·3	1·9	25·3	7·9	0·7
1848	1·1	5·3	0·8	1·5	22·7	6·5	0·6
1849	1·1	5·7	0·7	2·3	26·8	8·4	0·9
1850	1·3	6·2	1·0	2·5	28·3	10·0	1·0

See p. 485 for footnotes.

B. United Kingdom 1826–1980 (*cont.*)

(in £ million)

	Coal (*a*)	Iron & Steel (*b*)	Machinery (*c*)	Non-ferrous Metals and Manufactures (*d*)	Cotton Goods (*e*)	Wool Goods (*f*)	Chemicals (*g*)
1851	1·3	6·8	1·2	2·1	30·1	9·9	1·0
1852	1·4	7·7	1·3	2·2	29·9	10·2	1·0
1853	1·6	12·0	2·0	2·5	32·7	11·6	1·3
1854	2·1	12·7	1·9	2·5	31·7	11·7	1·3 ---(*g*) 1·4
1855	2·4	10·7	2·2	2·8	34·8	9·7	1·5
1856	2·8	14·2	2·7	3·6 ---(*d*)	38·2	12·4	1·7
1857	3·2 ---(*a*) 3·3	14·9	3·9	4·0	39·1	13·5	1·8 ---(*g*) 1·9
1858	3·1	12·5	3·6	3·6	43·0	12·5	1·8
1859	3·3	13·8	3·7	3·5	48·2	14·9	2·2
1860	3·4	13·6	3·8	4·0	52·0	15·7	2·2
1861	3·7	11·2	4·2	3·1	46·9	14·4	1·8
1862	3·8	12·5 ---(*b*) 12·9	4·1	4·2	36·8	16·8	2·5
1863	3·8	14·8	4·4	5·6	47·6	20·4	2·5
1864	4·2	15·0	4·8	5·2	54·9	23·8	2·9
1865	4·5	15·4	5·2	4·3	57·3	25·3	3·1
1866	5·2	17·1	4·8	3·9	74·6	26·4	3·8
1867	5·5	17·4	5·0	4·4	70·8	25·9	3·9 ---(*g*) 4·7
1868	5·4	17·3	4·7	4·6	67·7	25·8	4·7
1869	5·2	21·9	5·1	5·4	67·1	28·2	4·8
1870	5·6	23·5	5·3	4·8	71·4	26·7	5·1
1871	6·2	25·5	6·0	5·0	72·8	33·3	6·2
1872	10·4	35·3	8·2	5·7	80·2	38·5	7·6
1873	13·2	37·4	10·0	5·4	77·4	30·7	7·8
1874	12·0	30·9	9·8	5·5	74·2	28·4	8·0
1875	9·7	25·6	9·1	5·1	71·8	26·8	7·8
1876	8·9	20·6	7·2	4·8	67·6	23·0	7·6
1877	7·8	20·0	6·7	5·0	69·2	21·0	7·8
1878	7·3	18·3	7·5	4·7	65·9	20·6	7·4
1879	7·2	18·6	7·3	4·5	64·0	19·6	7·7
1880	8·4	27·2	9·3	4·8	75·6	20·6	8·8

See p. 485 for footnotes.

B. United Kingdom 1826–1980 (*cont.*)

(in £ million)

	Coal (*a*)	Iron & Steel (*b*)	Machinery (*c*)	Electrical Goods (*h*)	Motor Road Vehicles & Aircraft (*i*)	Ships & Boats (*j*)	Non-ferrous Metals & Manufactures (*d*)	Cotton Goods (*e*)	Wool Goods (*f*)	Man-made Fibre Goods (*l*)	Chemicals (*g*)
1881	8·8	27·1	10·0	...	...	...	5·1	80·1	21·4	...	9·4
1882	9·6	31·1	11·9	...	...	...	5·1 / 5·4 (*d*)	75·8	22·2	...	9·8
1883	10·6	28·3	13·4	...	...	...	5·5	76·4	21·6	...	10·1
1884	10·9	24·3	13·1	...	...	...	5·5	73·2 / 72·7 (*k*)	23·5 / 24·0 (*k*)	...	10·2
1885	10·6	21·4	11·1	...	...	...	4·9	67·0	23·2	...	9·1
1886	9·8	21·4	10·1	...	...	...	4·6	68·9	24·1	...	8·6
1887	10·2	24·2	11·1	...	...	...	4·8	71·0	24·6	...	9·1
1888	11·3	26·0	12·9	...	...	...	5·4	72·0	24·0	...	9·8
1889	14·8	28·7	15·3	...	...	...	5·8	70·5	25·7	...	10·6
1890	19·0	31·1	16·4	...	...	...	7·2	74·4	24·5	...	12·0
1891	18·9	26·5	15·8	1·7	...	...	6·4	71·4	22·4	...	12·1
1892	16·8	21·4	13·9	1·1	...	...	6·3	66·0	22·0	...	11·4
1893	14·4	20·3	13·9	1·3	0·2	...	5·3	63·8	20·9	...	11·4
1894	17·4	18·5	14·2	1·6	0·2	...	4·2	66·6	18·7	...	11·1
1895	15·4	19·4	15·2	1·1	0·2	...	4·7	63·7	25·1	...	11·4
1896	15·2	23·5	17·0	1·2	0·3	...	4·6	69·4	23·9	...	11·7
1897	16·7	24·4	16·3	1·4	0·3	...	4·6	64·0	20·8	...	12·0
1898	18·1	22·4	18·4	1·5	0·2	...	5·0	64·9	18·4	...	11·6
1899	23·1	27·7	19·7	1·9	0·3	9·2	6·4	67·5	19·7	...	12·2
1900	38·6	31·6	19·6	3·3	0·3	8·6	6·0	69·8	20·2	...	13·1
											--- (*g*)
1901	30·3	25·0	17·8	3·7	0·3	9·1	6·3	73·7	17·7	...	12·1
1902	27·6	28·9	18·8	3·5	0·5	5·9	5·7	72·5	18·8	...	12·8
1903	27·3	29·4 / 30·4 (*b*)	20·1	3·5 / 2·5 (*h*)	0·7	4·3	6·4	73·6	20·1	...	13·5
1904	26·9	28·6	21·1	1·6	0·7	4·5	6·3	83·9	22·2	...	13·6
1905	26·1	32·5	23·3	2·4	1·0	5·4	8·3	92·0	23·8	...	14·5
1906	31·5	40·7	26·8	2·4	1·5	8·6	9·4	99·6	25·9	...	15·5
1907	42·1	47·4	31·7	2·5	2·1	10·0	10·9	110·4	28·2	...	17·1
1908	41·6	38·2	31·0	1·9	1·8	10·6	8·2	95·1	23·8	...	16·3
1909	37·1	39·0	28·1	2·2	2·2	5·9	7·9	93·4	25·7	...	16·8
							--- (*d*)				
1910	37·8	44·0	29·3	4·1	3·4	8·8	9·3	105·9	31·6	...	18·6
											--- (*g*)
1911	38·4	44·8	31·0	2·8	3·6	5·7	9·9	120·1	31·8	...	20·1
1912	42·6	49·7	33·2	4·3	4·4	7·0	11·1	122·2	32·0	...	21·0
1913	53·7	55·4	37·0	5·4	5·4	11·0	12·0	127·2	31·8	...	22·0
1914	42·2	42·5	31·4	3·0	5·3	6·9	9·4	103·3	26·6	...	19·5
1915	38·8	41·1	19·2	3·2	3·5	1·7	9·1	85·9	30·5	...	22·1
1916	50·7	57·5	20·2	4·1	4·7	1·3	11·9	118·3	42·8	...	27·6
1917	51·3	45·5	19·5	2·9	4·8	1·1	9·7	145·9	49·7	...	23·6
1918	52·4	37·3	16·1	2·4	4·9	1·0	8·4	180·1	46·3	...	22·7
1919	92·3	64·4	32·7	5·7	6·9	2·3	14·4	241·0 / 238·0 (*e*)	94·2	...	29·5 / 27·0 (*g*)
1920	120·3	128·9	71·0 / 70·5 (*c*)	11·7 / 11·6 (*h*)	18·2 / 13·1 (*i*)	26·6	25·8	401·4	(139·3) (*f*)	3·0	40·5

See p. 485 for footnotes.

B. United Kingdom 1826–1980 (*cont.*)

(in £ million)

	Coal (*a*)	Iron & Steel (*b*)	Machinery (*c*)	Electrical Goods (*h*)	Motor Road Vehicles & Aircraft (*i*)	Ships & Boats (*j*)	Non-ferrous Metals & Manufactures (*d*)	Cotton Goods (*e*)	Wool Goods (*f*)	Man-made Fibre Goods (*l*)	Chemicals (*g*)
1921	46·4	63·6	84·2	13·0	7·8	30·6	11·7	178·7	51·9	1·7	19·1
1922	77·7	60·9	58·0	7·3	5·1	30·0	11·5	186·9	57·4	2·6	20·3
1923	109·9	76·2	48·5	10·2	6·5	9·7	14·5	177·4	60·1	3·5	25·7
1924	78·3	74·5	47·4	10·7	10·7	5·5	15·7	199·2	64·6	4·3	25·5
1925	54·3	68·2	52·3	11·6	13·9	6·3	16·8	199·4	57·1	5·4	23·6
1926	20·5	55·1	49·1	13·4	13·3	4·6	19·5	154·3	50·2	7·1	21·7
1927	49·2	69·4	52·8	11·9	14·8	4·5	19·9	148·8	53·5	6·6	23·4
1928	42·7	66·8	58·4	11·6	15·8	15·9	16·4	145·3	54·1	10·1	25·4
1929	52·9	68·0	59·6	13·2	18·5	15·5	18·3	135·4	50·5	8·4	26·6
1930	49·2	51·3	52·0	11·9	15·5	20·1	12·0	87·6	35·5	5·9	23·4
1931	37·6	30·4	35·1	7·4	10·9	10·5	6·9	56·6	24·0	3·4	18·2
1932	34·3	28·0	30·3	5·8	10·9	3·9	6·9	62·8	21·7	3·9	18·5
1933	34·1	29·9	28·4	6·7	12·8	2·6	12·1	58·9	22·8	3·8	18·6
1934	34·6	35·1	33·8	8·0	15·7	1·8	11·9	59·1	25·9	4·8	19·6
1935	34·6	37·1	40·9	9·5	17·3	3·1	14·1	60·2	26·0	4·0	21·3
1936	32·3	36·7	43·2	10·0	19·2	3·6	12·1	61·5	27·4	4·4	21·1
1937	41·9	49·2 --- (*b*) 38·0	51·7	12·5	23·7	4·1	15·7	68·5	30·7	5·7	24·7
1938	40·7	31·1	60·7 --- (*c*) 57·9	13·4	23·5	8·5	12·3	49·7	23·6 --- (*f*) 23·7	4·2	22·1
1939	42·3	24·8	47·4	11·3	13·7	7·0	12·7	49·1	23·5	4·7	22·8
1940	27·5	24·8	36·5	13·2	19·5	1·2	12·4	49·3	24·2	7·6	27·7
1941	9·2	13·7	30·9	11·4	26·5	0·3	7·6	44·7	26·9	10·7	25·0
1942	6·8	5·8	29·9	11·2	42·2	2·2	7·0	40·1	23·1	16·0	24·0
1943	7·4	3·2	28·0	11·1	47·2	0·4	6·8	34·2	16·8	12·6	27·9
1944	5·3	5·1	41·2	12·6	39·9	1·1	4·7	37·1	14·1	16·3	29·4
1945	7·1	14·1	47·1	13·8	31·3	1·2	12·1	42·7	18·5	17·1	38·2
1946	10·1	57·1	114·7	37·4	68·6	5·7	37·6	63·2	38·7	23·8	66·1
1947	2·7	53·2	180·9	49·4	106·2	18·8	40·3	77·9	49·8	27·7	67·4
1948	43·6	69·6	254·2	72·5	150·6	39·0	54·6	131·1	79·1	37·8	83·6
1949	59·7	85·8	279·3	79·2	202·6	44·4	63·6	159·1	85·5	40·4	86·1
1950	60·5	108·9	317·3 --- (*c*) 295·1	84·0 --- (*h*) 113·6	289·6 --- (*i*) 253·6	41·6 --- (*j*) 42·0	76·9	158·4 --- (*e*) 126·7	108·4 --- (*f*) 82·8	48·5 --- (*l*) 45·7	107·5 --- (*g*) 141·2

B. United Kingdom 1826–1980 (*cont.*)

(in £ million)

	Coal (*a*)	Iron & Steel (*b*)	Machinery (*c*)	Electrical Goods (*h*)	Motor Road Vehicles & Aircraft (*i*)	Ships & Boats (*j*)	Non-ferrous Metals (*d*)	Cotton Goods (*e*)	Wool Goods (*f*)	Man-made Fibre Goods (*l*)	Chemicals (*g*)	Petroleum and Products
1951	34·1	108·4	372·7	141·1	270·8	52·9	70·5	181·4	108·6	54·4	193·5	35·7
1952	65·9	135·9	429·3	158·7	279·3	35·5	82·3 --- (*d*) 61·5	130·4	82·2	34·6	184·4	59·0
1953	70·8	141·2	426·2	150·3	263·2	39·4	71·7	117·1	87·4	39·4	177·8	76·3
1954	68·0	140·8	437·9	147·6	279·3	50·6	64·9	112·1	83·4	40·0	204·0 --- (*g*)	83·6
1955	63·9	161·9	493·3	175·7	306·1	53·4	87·5	97·7	88·0	33·9	234·3	76·9
1956	62·4	178·4	536·8	190·5	341·6	93·4	118·5	88·7	90·0	31·9	245·6	98·7
1957	61·8	221·8	596·8	197·4	378·2	79·0	111·0	88·5	95·3	33·0	268·2	90·0
1958	32·7	198·0	605·9	194·6	434·4	62·8	101·7	71·2	80·0	27·9	263·8	99·4
1959	23·9	197·3	663·8	201·8	466·8	47·6	122·3	63·2	82·9	27·1	295·3	95·1
1960	28·4	220·9	746·1	208·1	480·7	51·7	112·5	63·0	86·2	29·4	319·0	104·2
1961	29·3	215·2	853·2	228·4	418·3	88·1	116·7	56·5	81·8	31·6	327·3	94·2
1962	31·2	204·9	878·3	240·0	464·8	35·3	122·5	46·5	80·4	39·0	343·7	115·0
1963	47·8	207·7	898·2	279·4	543·1	41·8	115·6	43·7	85·2	47·9	368·0	116·4
1964	36·9	220·1	898·5	277·9	582·0	29·5	125·9	44·6	89·4	58·7	412·2	100·9
1965	25·4	238·5	975·7	287·3	647·9	30·9	155·7	42·0	88·5	58·0	441·7	107·7
1966	20·0	218·2	1,089·2	299·8	726·0	47·1	180·6	45·4	84·1	56·1	469·3	114·0
1967	14·0	231·7	1,083·1	298·0	620·2	68·2	194·9	33·6	78·0	57·4	493·4	114·4
1968	18·4	267·9	1,317·6	362·1	796·7	81·4	249·9	38·3	86·7	70·4	599·7	147·2
1969	25·0	286·8 --- (*m*) 289·0	1,472·1 --- (*m*) 1,516·4	409·3 --- (*m*) 427·7	968·5 --- (*m*) 977·1	61·3 --- (*m*) 66·6	287·4 --- (*m*) 302·4	39·3 --- (*m*) 39·9	94·4 --- (*m*) 94·6	85·3 --- (*m*) 88·4	684·3 --- (*m*) 693·4	145·7 --- (*m*) 147·3
1970	29·1	350·8	1,729·0	492·4	967·4	60·8	319·4	37·5	93·4	109·4	784·4	179·7
1971	22·3	406·4	2,053·2 --- (*n*) 2,087·1	539·5 --- (*n*) 536·5	1,150·3	64·5	269·6	38·7	86·0	121·5	884·0 --- (*n*) 872·6	215·6
1972	17·0	379·4	2,196·3	556·4	1,107·9	112·7	287·0	40·6	94·2	132·2	950·7	222·2
1973	26·7	437·0	2,583·0	686·7	1,347·2	120·8	441·5	56·4	128·4	178·5	1,256·6	344·5
1974	62·9	559·3	3,280·6	975·2	1,601·1	127·2	570·5	74·0	148·2	232·9	2,113·0	710·6
1975	83·8	691·0	4,534·0	1,248·1	2,095·4	214·4	456·8	65·5	130·0	205·1	2,144·6	733·9
1976	71·7	834·1	5,363·3	1,630·0	2,640·8	236·8	572·3	98·7	161·2	233·7	3,006·8	1,171·6
1977	79·9	1,021·8	6,288·3	2,043·9	3,165·5	362·7	635·0	121·7	228·8	238·8	3,817·1	1,979·0
1978	90·4	1,100·0	7,080·3	2,140·7	4,006·3	378·8	707·7	132·1	241·8	370·6	4,198·9	2,235·0
1979	100·7	1,269·4	7,609·8	2,191·8	4,297·2	411·7	891·6	147·6	243·0	395·7	4,910·9	4,157·5
1980	180·0	971·8	8,953·1	2,511·1	4,948·8	374·0	1,113·0	144·6	246·1	276·5	5,286·2	6,133·2

(*a*) Including coke, and from 1857 (2nd line), manufactured fuel based on coal.

(*b*) Including many manufactures of iron and steel from 1862 (2nd line) to 1937 (1st line). Tinplate is not included until 1840 (2nd line). Telegraphic wire is included from 1903 (2nd line).

(*c*) Electricity generating and furnace machinery, electric motors, and agricultural tractors are included under this heading, as are transformers from 1920 (2nd line) to 1950 (1st line). Electric powertools, magnetos, and switchgear are excluded from 1950 (2nd line).

(*d*) Brass, copper, lead, pewter, tin, and zinc to 1882 (1st line), including tinplate to 1840 (2nd line). All other non-ferrous metals except silver are included from 1882 (2nd line). Lead shot is excluded from 1857, and regulus and precipitate are excluded from 1910: All were negligible at the time of exclusion. Most manufactures are excluded from 1952 (2nd line).

(*e*) Comprising yarn, woven fabrics, knitted, netted and crocheted goods, hosiery and gloves, and finished articles such as sheets and counterpanes to 1919 (1st line). Hosiery and gloves are excluded subsequently, and knitted, netted and crocheted goods and finished articles are excluded from 1950 (2nd line). Mixtures in which cotton predominates are included.

(*f*) Comprising yarn, woven fabrics, knitted, netted and crocheted goods, hosiery and gloves (except in 1920), and finished articles such as blankets to 1938 (1st line) provided they were made of wool or mainly of wool. Hosiery and gloves are excluded from 1938 (2nd line), but goods made of angora, mohair, etc. are included. Knitted, netted and crocheted goods and finished articles are excluded from 1950 (2nd line).

(*g*) Initially comprising alkali, drugs and chemical products, and painters' colours. The following additions were made before 1867: In 1854 bleaching materials, in 1855 coal tar (negligible at the time), in 1857 manures; and in 1861 naphtha (negligible at the time). Major new classifications cause the breaks in 1919 and 1950, whilst those in 1901, 1911 and 1955 result from very minor additions to the commodities covered.

(*h*) Generating and furnace machinery, and motors are not included under this heading, nor are transformers from 1920 (2nd line) to 1950 (1st line). Electric powertools, magnetos, switchgear, and electrical equipment for vehicles are included from 1950 (2nd line).

(*i*) Including tyres to 1920 (1st line) but only those on complete vehicles subsequently. Works trucks and electrical equipment for vehicles is included to 1950 (1st line).

(*j*) New vessels only to 1950 (1st line).

(*k*) To 1884 (1st line) some piece goods of mixed materials in which wool predominated were erroneously entered as cotton goods.

(*l*) Comprising yarn, woven fabrics, knitted, netted and crocheted goods, and finished articles such as sheets to 1950 (1st line). Subsequently only yarn and woven fabrics are covered. Mixtures in which man-made fibres predominate are included.

(*m*) Statistics from 1969 (2nd line) include re-exports, which ceased to be recorded separately in 1970.

(*n*) There were minor revisions in classification in 1978 which can be carried back easily to 1971 only.

External Trade 12. Values (f.o.b.) at Current Prices of Principal Re-exports – Great Britain 1784–6 to 1854–6, United Kingdom 1854–1969

NOTES

[1] SOURCES: Part A – Ralph Davis, *The Industrial Revolution and British Overseas Trade* (Leicester, 1979), Appendix, table 50; Parts B and C – *Annual Statement of Trade*.

[2] Trade with Ireland is excluded in Part A.

[3] The figures for 1784–6 are for years ended 30 September. Others are for calendar years or years beginning 6 January to 1853.

[4] Not all the very minor breaks in continuity are indicated, but it is believed that all significant ones have been noted.

[5] Re-exports of raw silk were of some importance up to about 1880, as can be seen from the following figures (in £ million):

1854	0·8	1859	2·2	1864	4·4	1869	3·6	1874	3·0	1879	1·1
1855	1·5	1860	3·4	1865	4·1	1870	3·4	1875	1·9	1880	0·7
1856	1·4	1861	3·6	1866	2·6		...	1876	2·8	1881	0·7
1857	1·9	1862	4·9	1867	2·5	1871	4·0	1877	1·5	1882	0·7
1858	2·1	1863	3·9	1868	3·6	1872	3·9	1878	1·5	1883	0·4
						1873	3·7				

A. Computed Values, Great Britain, 1784–6 to 1854–6

(annual averages in £ thousand)

	Coffee	Sugar	Tea	Wine & Spirits	Tobacco	Raw Cotton	Raw Silk	Raw Wool	Dyestuff	Cotton & Silk Goods	Linen Goods
1784–6	133	8	61	207	504	1	28	15	181	394	181
1794–6	1,721	872	41	446	222	62	28	20	625	1,142	476
1804–6	2,337	602	73	799	244	42	6	17	1,058	777	557
1814–6	3,527	2,337	452	1,724	388	855	106	84	2,119	432	106
1824–6	649	539	79	641	156	755	155	91	2,002	429	15
1834–6	421	684	250	1,015	249	1,240	176	252	1,401	406	59
1844–6	240	821	247	877	179	840	261	218	1,689	450	20
1854–6	741	748	587	1,884	582	2,708	1,678	1,765	2,152	532	—

B. Computed Values, United Kingdom, 1854–70

(in £ million)

	Coffee	Tea	Raw Cotton (*a*)	Raw Wool (*b*)	Hides, Skins and Furs	Non-ferrous Metals and Manu-factures	Rubber
1854	0·8	0·6	2·3	1·5	...	0·4	...
1855	0·7	0·9	2·5	1·9	0·8	0·3	--
1856	0·7	0·3	3·3	1·9	1·1	0·3	0·1
1857	0·5	0·6	3·4	2·8	1·3	0·5	--
1858	0·8	0·5	4·0	1·9	1·2	0·4	0·1
1859	0·9	0·5	4·2	2·1	1·3	0·5	0·1
1860	1·4	0·7	5·4	2·3	1·4	0·6	0·1
1861	1·5	0·9	8·6	3·6	1·4	0·6	0·1
1862	2·0	2·2	13·5	3·3	1·5	1·0	0·2
1863	2·5	2·0	20·1	4·3	1·5	1·0	0·2
1864	2·6	2·1	20·9	4·4	1·3	1·4	0·2
1865	3·3	2·7	18·8	5·9	1·3	1·3	0·2
1866	3·1	2·4	19·2	5·0	1·1	1·5	0·3
1867	3·0	2·5	12·4	6·4	1·4	1·5	0·2
1868	3·7	2·8	11·9	6·4	1·4	2·0	0·3
1869	3·6	2·5	11·5	6·7	1·6	1·3	0·3
1870	3·9	2·2	8·1	5·6	1·9	1·5	0·5

C. Declared Values, 1871–1969

(in £ million)

	Coffee	Tea	Raw Cotton (*a*)	Raw Wool (*b*)	Hides, Skins and Furs	Non-ferrous Metals and Manufactures	Rubber	Petroleum
1871	4·7	3·1	11·9	7·6	1·9	1·8	0·6	...
1872	4·6	3·3	8·8	9·3	2·8	2·0	0·7	...
1873	5·8	2·6	6·5	8·9	2·4	2·5	0·6	...
1874	5·2	2·6	6·8	10·2	2·5	3·1	0·5	...
1875	5·7	2·6	6·6	12·1	2·7	2·3	0·6	...
1876	5·8	2·3	4·5	11·4	2·0	2·3	0·6	...
1877	5·3	2·4	4·0	11·9	1·9	1·8	0·7	...
1878	4·7	2·6	3·4	12·3	1·7	1·6	0·7	...
1879	5·8	2·3	4·3	14·2	1·9	2·1	1·0	...
1880	5·3	2·8	5·5	14·5	2·3	2·2	1·1	...
1881	4·1	2·5	5·0	15·9	2·1	2·3	1·2	...
1882	4·0	2·4	6·3	15·3	2·3	2·6	1·5	...
1883	3·4	2·4	5·3	16·0	2·7	2·6	1·5	...
1884	3·3	2·5	5·4	15·4	2·6	2·4	1·2	...
1885	2·4	2·2	4·5	14·1	3·2	1·9	1·0	...
1886	2·6	2·2	4·0	12·1	3·4	2·4	1·3	...
1887	2·7	1·7	5·7	13·8	2·9	2·7	1·3	--
1888	3·1	1·8	5·5	13·8	2·9	5·3	1·3	--
1889	2·7	1·7	5·9	15·4	3·1	3·2	1·4	--
1890	2·9	1·7	4·8	14·5	2·9	3·4	1·7	--
1891	2·2	1·6	3·8	15·8	2·8	2·8	1·8	0·1
1892	2·4	1·6	4·5	16·8	3·4	2·8	1·6	0·1
1893	2·3	1·5	4·6	13·3	3·6	2·9	1·6	0·1
1894	2·5	1·4	4·7	13·5	3·3	2·4	1·8	0·1
1895	2·1	1·4	3·5	15·2	4·1	2·2	2·3	0·1
1896	2·0	1·4	3·6	12·3	3·2	2·1	2·6	0·1
1897	1·9	1·5	4·3	13·4	4·1	1·9	2·8	0·1
1898	2·1	1·5	3·6	10·1	4·5	2·4	4·0	--
1899	2·3	1·4	4·8	10·2	4·8	4·5	4·3	0·1
1900	1·5	1·7	4·8	7·5	5·2	4·7	3·8	0·1
1901	2·0	1·7	5·0	10·7	4·8	4·7	3·6	0·1
1902	1·1	1·8	6·3	10·2	4·7	4·3	3·6	0·1
1903	1·7	1·7	7·4	10·4	4·1	4·0	4·9	0·2
1904	1·8	1·8	6·8	9·5	4·0	4·5	5·0	0·2
1905	2·3	1·8	6·6	11·1	5·1	5·7	6·2	0·2
1906	1·8	2·2	6·6	11·3	6·5	7·7	6·4	0·2
1907	1·3	2·1	9·5	13·5	6·3	6·9	6·0	0·2
1908	1·2	1·9	8·3	12·9	5·0	6·0	5·7	0·2
1909	1·5	2·3	7·8	16·0	7·0	5·9	9·1	0·1
1910	1·9	2·3	9·8	14·5	7·1	7·3	14·9	0·1
1911	2·1	2·4	10·7	13·1	6·3	8·4	13·5	0·2
1912	1·6	2·6	10·6	14·4	8·3	8·6	16·3	0·2
1913	1·8	2·8	9·1	13·4	8·4	8·3	14·8	0·1
1914	2·2	3·3	7·4	13·6	6·0	6·3	12·1	0·1
1915	1·9	3·4	9·6	6·8	4·8	5·9	16·0	0·4

See p. 489 for footnotes.

External Trade 12. *continued*

C. Declared Values, 1871–1969 *(cont.)*

(in £ million)

	Coffee	Tea	Raw Cotton (*a*)	Raw Wool (*b*)	Hides, Skins and Furs	Non-ferrous Metals and Manufactures	Rubber	Petroleum
1916	1·5	3·5	9·8	3·8	5·1	5·0	15·1	0·4
1917	0·4	1·0	7·7	3·6	3·8	4·8	16·5	0·4
1918	0·1	0·3	..	2·4	2·0	1·7	4·5	0·2
1919	3·9	2·7	11·4	23·4	12·3	5·0	14·2	2·0
1920	2·9	3·4	33·7	35·3	15·6	8·2	14·1	5·4
1921	2·0	2·0	8·3	19·1	7·4	4·6	4·1	1·4
1922	1·1	2·8	5·4	26·4	8·7	3·9	4·7	2·3
1923	2·6	5·4	7·3	29·8	9·8	3·1	9·9	2·7
1924	1·7	6·9	11·6	31·0	13·1	3·8	10·1	2·9
1925	1·6	7·8	11·1	32·0	14·3	4·2	22·1	3·0
1926	1·8	7·6	8·5	27·5	12·8	3·7	16·3	1·3
1927	1·9	7·7	6·8	27·3	14·5	2·5	15·1	1·1
1928	2·2	7·8	4·3	27·1	15·3	3·3	12·7	1·3
1929	1·7	7·9	4·6	24·8	12·8	4·4	5·4	3·0
1930	2·3	6·8	3·4	16·9	9·9	2·8	3·6	2·0
1931	1·9	5·9	1·2	11·0	8·4	1·5	1·8	1·2
1932	1·5	4·4	1·6	12·0	6·8	1·3	1·4	1·4
1933	1·4	4·4	1·7	13·5	7·2	0·7	0·9	1·2
1934	0·9	4·3	2·1	12·6	7·0	1·3	3·2	1·3
1935	0·7	4·6	2·4	11·5	8·3	4·0	2·9	1·5
1936	0·5	4·5	2·0	13·2	9·4	6·1	4·9	1·6
1937	0·3	4·8	2·0	14·4	11·7	13·6	4·4	1·8
1938	0·4	4·6	1·3	12·5	9·6	9·1	2·7	0·8
1939	0·2	4·0	1·2	8·6	7·8	2·7	3·6	0·8
1940	0·1	3·7	0·5	4·8	3·6	0·7	1·2	1·1
1941	..	1·2	..	0·1	0·3	1·1	1·2	0·3
1942	..	0·6	..	—	0·1	0·6	..	0·6
1943	..	0·7	..	—	0·2	0·3	0·2	0·4
1944	0·5	0·8	—	—	0·2	0·9	0·8	0·6
1945	0·6	1·7	2·3	7·2	0·3	5·4	0·9	1·5
1946	0·1	4·8	2·6	8·2	3·9	1·1	7·2	2·5
1947	0·2	1·6	3·0	18·4	3·7	0·2	13·3	3·1
1948	0·2	1·1	0·6	23·1	6·2	0·2	4·6	1·7
1949	0·5	1·6	0·4	22·0	5·8	0·2	4·0	1·3
1950	0·7	3·1	1·1	28·9	10·8	0·7	8·7	1·4
1951	0·4	3·2	0·5	34·9	16·7	1·1	28·8	2·2
1952	1·3	4·1	1·4	18·2	18·9	12·4	48·3	0·6
1953	2·4	7·2	1·1	20·2	15·5	7·1	10·0	1·4
1954	2·1	8·2	0·9	19·0	14·6	5·9	3·1	2·7
1955	1·3	9·7	2·1	16·3	19·5	4·9	11·3	2·4
1956	0·7	8·4	3·9	15·3	19·9	7·6	33·1	4·8
1957	0·7	8·2	1·6	16·1	19·0	4·2	18·5	3·5
1958	0·9	8·6	0·7	9·2	18·9	2·0	32·0	5·2
1959	0·5	10·1	1·1	10·0	21·3	9·1	11·2	5·5
1960	0·5	8·4	1·2	10·4	22·5	3·1	23·5	2·3

External Trade 12. *continued*

C. Declared Values, 1871–1969 (*cont.*)

(in £ million)

	Coffee	Tea	Raw Cotton (*a*)	Raw Wool (*b*)	Hides, Skins and Furs	Non-ferrous Metals and Manu-factures	Rubber	Petroleum
1961	1·1	8·9	1·3	9·2	22·1	7·1	29·0	1·1
1962	0·3	9·9	1·4	7·7	27·6	8·0	18·3	1·6
1963	0·2	9·6	1·3	6·5	31·5	6·6	9·9	1·9
1964	0·9	10·5	2·0	5·2	26·3	9·0	3·2	0·9
1965	0·7	11·2	1·3	4·6	29·7	11·1	1·9	0·3
1966	0·2	11·9	1·2	3·8	33·3	14·5	1·5	0·2
1967	0·2	10·3	0·5	3·0	25·2	7·7	2·0	3·8
1968	0·2	13·8	0·8	2·2	36·6	11·3	1·9	1·4
1969	0·4	15·3	0·5	1·6	34·6	15·1	1·3	1·6

(*a*) Including waste.
(*b*) Including rags for use as raw material for cloth.

External Trade 13. Values at Current Prices of Principal Imports and Exports – Republic of Ireland 1924–80

NOTES

[1] SOURCES: *Trade Statistics of Ireland* and *Statistical Abstract of Ireland*.

[2] Exports are of domestic products only to 1972 (1st line).

[3] Imports are valued c.i.f. and exports f.o.b.

(in £ million)

	Imports					Exports				
	Cereals & Feeding Stuffs	Tea	Tobacco	Coal	Petroleum & Products	Live Animals	Meat	Butter	Eggs	Beer
1924	13·4	2·4	0·8	4·2	1·4	22·2	5·3	4·0	3·1	5·8
1925	12·2 / 12·5 (a)	2·3	0·7	3·5	1·4	16·9	4·7	3·6	3·1	5·9
1926	11·4	2·5	0·5	3·4	1·4	17·5	4·7	3·8	2·8	5·0
1927	12·2	2·5	0·7	3·7	1·3	18·1	4·7	4·6	3·0	4·9
1928	11·5	2·3	0·5	3·0	1·4	19·2	5·6	4·5	3·1	4·5
1929	11·2	2·3	0·6	3·1	1·5	19·7	5·3	4·6	3·2	4·8
1930	9·1	2·2	0·8	3·2	1·6	21·1	4·1	3·3	2·7	5·3
1931	7·7	2·1	0·6	3·1	1·3	18·3	3·3	2·1	2·2	4·7
1932	7·6	1·6	0·4	2·7	1·4	11·9	2·1	1·5	1·7	4·0
1933	4·9	1·5	0·3	2·5	1·1	7·5	1·9	1·2	1·1	4·0
1934	5·0	1·6	1·2	2·4	1·0	6·1	2·2	1·3	1·0	3·6
1935	4·3	1·5	0·8	2·5	1·1	7·3	2·5	1·7	1·0	3·7
1936	4·7	1·5	1·1	3·0	1·1	9·0	2·6	1·9	1·0	3·5
1937	6·3	1·9	0·6	3·3	1·5	9·8	2·5	1·6	0·9	3·2
1938	6·0	1·7	0·9	3·3	1·4	11·9	3·1	2·2	1·2	2·2
1939	5·6	1·6	0·4	4·1	1·5	14·3	3·4	1·6	1·2	2·2
1940	7·7	1·9	0·1	5·2	2·0	14·5	6·4	1·6	2·5	2·3
1941	1·8	1·0	0·2	3·4	1·2	8·1	9·4	0·8	2·7	4·1
1942	5·3	1·3	1·5	2·3	1·2	15·7	5·6	..	2·5	3·2
1943	2·5	0·7	1·1	2·4	1·1	13·6	4·1	..	1·9	2·5
1944	6·4	0·7	1·3	1·8	1·3	14·3	4·0	..	2·2	3·0
1945	6·6	1·0	2·1	2·5	1·4	17·2	4·7	—	2·1	3·6
1946	6·0	1·8	2·3	3·6	2·4	19·9	2·5	—	2·4	3·6
1947	11·1	4·0	2·1	9·1	3·8	22·1	3·1	—	1·5	3·7
1948	17·6	4·2	2·0	7·2	5·5	22·3	4·4	..	3·6	3·9
1949	10·3	3·1	3·5	7·1	6·2	27·1	5·6	0·1	5·2	4·4
1950	16·0	4·2	4·4	8·2	7·6	29·2	8·4	1·1	5·1	4·3
1951	17·2	7·1	4·4	12·2	10·3	29·8	12·4	0·1	2·6	4·4
1952	15·1	2·6	4·0	10·1	11·7 / 12·3 (a)	32·3	20·0	0·1	3·3	5·1
1953	15·5	2·6	4·5	9·0	12·6	32·6	22·2	0·1	4·1	5·0
1954	9·9	5·4	3·5	9·4	13·5	41·6	26·5	1·2	1·4	4·9
1955	14·2	6·7	3·7	10·7	16·5	44·6	16·7	0·5	0·9	5·1
1956	9·0	2·6	2·5	9·9	18·3	45·4	13·8	0·2	0·9	5·7
1957	7·7	6·3	2·9	9·1	18·8	54·3	17·9	4·3	0·2	5·7
1958	11·2	3·9	3·8	8·2	16·7	47·3	23·4	4·0	0·2	6·1
1959	13·4	4·5	3·3	7·9	17·7	39·2	23·0	0·5	0·1	6·4
1960	10·5	4·5	4·8	8·2	17·6	44·7	27·5	2·2	0·1	6·8
1961	13·0	5·2	4·4	8·8	18·1	55·4	34·0	3·8	0·1	6·9
1962	13·7	4·6	4·7	7·9	18·4 / 18·7 (a)	47·6 / 47·5 (a)	32·2 / 32·0 (a)	4·7	..	6·7
1963	14·4	5·8	4·3	8·3	19·3	52·8	33·4	6·4	0·1	6·9

External Trade 13. *continued*

(in £ million)

	Imports					Exports				
	Cereals & Feeding Stuffs	Tea	Tobacco	Coal	Petroleum & Products	Live Animals	Meat	Butter	Eggs	Beer
1964	15·2	3·7	4·4	8·2	21·0	66·7	32·4	6·7	0·1	6·9
1965	25·6	5·3	3·6	8·1	22·9	56·3	35·0	7·0	--	7·0
1966	22·9	4·3	4·5	8·3	23·3	54·7	40·6	7·6	--	7·5
1967	19·0	4·4	4·8	7·8	29·3	53·0	58·7	9·1	0·1	7·9
1968	23·3	5·7	7·3	8·1	32·2	58·0	59·0	10·0	0·1	8·2
1969	19·7	4·5	8·5	8·1	35·6	54·7	66·5	9·6	0·1	8·0
1970	24·2	4·8	3·8	9·5	43·0	56·9	75·1	12·2	--	8·4
1971	27·5	5·2	4·7	9·2	58·1	72·1	89·2	14·7	0·1	9·6
1972	32·0	5·7	6·1 --- 8·7 (*a*)	9·0 --- 9·1 (*a*)	53·2	86·4 --- 85·1 (*a*)	96·8	18·0	--	10·2
1973	41·1	4·5	12·3	9·0	67·0	84·6	132·4	20·8	0·1	10·9
1974	69·6	6·2	15·9	16·3	207·6	72·3	179·7	21·3	0·1	10·4
1975	71·3	9·2	18·6	14·9	224·7	123·6	239·8	45·1	0·1	14·2
1976	102·9	7·4	13·5	14·6	290·5	108·3	241·6	68·8	0·2	14·9
1977	138·0	21·0	13·3	26·4	352·2	153·3	382·5	60·4	0·2	15·1
1978	136·9	14·5	13·5	28·7	337·7	179·7	428·8	116·3	0·2	15·9
1979	186·3	14·2	13·1	46·6	526·8	131·5	451·9	156·3	0·3	16·9
1980	205·2	18·9	13·3	58·4	722·0	185·5	596·8	126·4	0·6	18·7

(*a*) These breaks result from minor changes in classification.

External Trade 14. Official Values of Imports and Exports according to Regional Direction – England & Wales, 1710–58, and Great Britain 1755–1822

NOTES

[1] SOURCE: César Moreau, *State of the Trade of Great Britain with all Parts of the World* (London, 1822).

[2] The source attributes all figures to Great Britain, but a comparison of Moreau's totals with those in tables 1 and 2 indicates that they relate to England & Wales only prior to 1755 (imports) and 1759 (exports and re-exports).

[3] The heading *Exports* includes re-exports in this table.

[4] *Northern Europe* comprises the ports of Europe as far south as the Franco-Belgian frontier, and *Southern Europe* the remainder plus Turkey and its domains (including Egypt). In determining the regions on the American continent, the frontiers used were those of 1822.

A. England & Wales 1710–58

(in £ thousand)

	Northern Europe		Southern Europe		Asia		Africa		British North America		United States		British West Indies		Foreign W. Indies & South America	
	Imports	Exports	Imports	Exports	Imports	Exports	Imports	Exports	Imports	Exports	Imports	Exports	Imports	Exports	Imports	Exports
1710	1,571	3,475	722	1,776	248	126	14	69	14	13	250	294	781	205	5	34
1711	1,530	3,479	1,258	1,416	637	152	8	64	11	7	325	298	557	222	1	44
1712	1,577	3,514	882	2,207	457	142	11	38	26	12	366	310	649	265	36	69
1713	1,756	3,340	1,536	2,126	953	94	12	112	19	8	303	285	792	358	2	110
1714	1,821	4,119	1,422	2,435	1,046	77	25	63	18	12	396	333	845	333	2	176
1715	1,724	3,317	1,591	1,989	580	37	30	52	11	10	297	451	1,000	302	2	303
1716	1,588	3,243	1,520	2,303	403	106	32	98	23	8	424	402	1,104	413	19	93
1717	1,707	3,682	1,808	2,612	495	83	19	112	20	9	426	540	1,090	340	169	253
1718	1,826	3,094	1,674	1,676	1,333	74	26	93	23	10	457	425	897	347	84	263
1719	1,792	3,347	1,233	2,171	547	88	18	66	15	9	463	393	876	246	29	96
1720	1,604	3,322	1,602	2,372	931	84	25	130	26	14	468	320	1,119	220	6	83
1721	1,578	3,613	1,415	2,240	1,021	128	22	126	29	9	494	332	856	219	4	143
1722	1,780	3,667	1,929	2,216	764	123	34	187	33	14	438	425	1,019	264	11	344
1723	1,670	3,248	1,842	2,245	969	115	30	139	30	13	462	412	1,092	300	23	336
1724	2,237	3,154	1,733	2,563	165	101	47	216	26	14	463	462	1,166	384	167	206
1725	2,125	3,305	1,953	2,858	760	94	68	284	31	22	416	550	1,364	364	25	484
1726	1,957	3,303	1,688	2,597	914	75	36	148	29	16	526	553	1,128	272	47	135
1727	1,815	3,276	1,722	2,397	1,126	98	39	139	49	13	637	503	1,041	249	49	125
1728	2,187	4,499	1,972	2,808	869	116	22	187	51	17	605	518	1,501	333	17	208
1729	2,280	3,514	1,879	2,749	972	138	49	253	57	17	575	423	1,517	380	7	199
1730	2,236	3,388	1,794	2,891	1,060	135	57	261	42	24	573	537	1,572	349	134	393
1731	1,905	3,157	1,722	2,691	825	139	29	206	45	22	651	536	1,312	249	154	124
1732	2,204	3,490	1,568	3,207	981	159	50	204	69	31	519	531	1,316	240	57	346
1733	2,229	3,599	1,875	3,371	1,107	132	58	129	41	34	670	549	1,619	236	12	130
1734	2,210	3,340	1,798	3,052	768	135	69	130	41	23	611	556	1,142	217	33	169

1735	2,290	3,652	1,889	3,373	1,297	186	42	139	40	28	652	669	1,461	263	44	182
1736	2,051	3,837	1,593	3,380	929	261	54	193	42	30	700	559	1,423	295	17	212
1737	2,357	3,487	1,561	3,954	916	378	56	234	55	42	775	682	949	254	9	227
1738	2,118	3,533	1,939	4,186	743	169	62	277	45	38	620	751	1,477	238	5	175
1739	2,256	3,634	1,341	2,815	1,279	217	43	220	60	36	754	696	1,567	246	65	209
1740	2,173	5,166	1,129	2,039	871	282	63	111	55	26	718	813	1,185	343	6	320
1741	2,322	3,736	1,600	2,646	1,130	487	44	133	48	24	912	885	1,403	454	3	417
1742	2,107	3,783	1,107	2,462	1,214	374	35	130	64	43	659	800	1,210	535	4	459
1743	1,945	5,345	1,511	2,367	906	646	26	219	47	39	681	829	1,405	445	3	353
1744	2,010	4,559	956	1,726	744	476	14	95	31	27	668	641	1,157	282	1	222
1745	1,991	4,213	1,326	1,757	974	293	11	71	40	32	554	535	1,024	280	14	194
1746	1,980	4,890	892	2,061	647	894	25	117	44	41	560	755	1,148	497	2	359
1747	2,210	4,291	1,340	2,361	822	346	2	186	35	56	561	727	941	389	6	345
1748	2,196	4,839	1,332	2,739	1,099	306	18	234	57	43	717	830	1,616	442	5	352
1749	2,010	5,076	1,918	3,665	1,124	557	16	201	52	68	664	1,231	1,481	554	3	185
1750	2,262	4,249	1,315	4,476	1,104	509	29	161	46	63	815	1,313	1,516	547	1	—
1751	2,010	4,262	1,709	3,939	1,097	798	56	215	58	100	836	1,233	1,448	631	1	—
1752	2,041	4,099	1,627	3,630	1,068	628	43	236	50	70	1,004	1,148	1,433	704	4	1
1753	2,261	3,752	1,771	3,845	1,008	788	34	276	49	74	973	1,453	1,903	833	3	..
1754	2,096	3,823	1,575	3,719	1,186	844	22	235	42	70	1,008	1,176	1,467	686	1	—
1755	...	3,904	...	3,123	...	875	...	174	...	65	...	1,113	...	695	...	—
1756	...	4,047	...	3,935	...	489	...	188	...	77	...	1,352	...	733	...	1
1757	...	2,744	...	3,728	...	845	...	154	...	98	...	1,628	...	777	...	—
1758	...	3,679	...	3,050	...	922	...	168	...	119	...	1,713	...	878	...	—

B. Great Britain 1755–1822

1755	2,267	...	1,606	...	1,247	...	40	...	46	...	940	...	1,869	...	..	...
1756	2,249	...	1,355	...	796	...	39	...	30	...	659	...	1,689	...	4	...
1757	2,392	...	1,349	...	1,112	...	30	...	42	...	611	...	1,910	...	4	...
1758	2,266	...	1,534	...	223	...	44	...	46	...	671	...	1,863	...	1	...
1759	2,413	3,920	1,535	3,797	974	665	24	228	59	139	640	2,345	1,835	935	93	61
1760	2,277	4,347	1,446	3,672	1,786	1,162	39	346	36	179	832	2,713	1,907	1,300	424	120
1761	2,668	5,874	1,741	3,498	841	846	12	325	52	351	895	1,722	2,000	992	491	140
1762	2,249	5,862	1,105	1,603	973	1,067	31	273	70	214	918	1,387	1,809	989	827	460
1763	3,412	5,590	2,036	3,261	1,059	887	18	464	74	226	1,157	1,660	2,349	1,154	1,036	32
1764	2,916	5,903	2,032	4,116	1,183	1,166	86	465	85	354	1,126	2,273	2,528	984	62	7

External Trade 14. *continued*

B. Great Britain 1755–1822 (*cont.*)

(in £ thousand)

	Northern Europe		Southern Europe		Asia		Africa		British North America		United States		British West Indies		Foreign W. Indies & South America	
	Imports	Exports	Imports	Exports	Imports	Exports	Imports	Exports	Imports	Exports	Imports	Exports	Imports	Exports	Imports	Exports
1765	2,722	4,944	2,156	3,327	1,456	914	52	469	94	345	1,160	1,973	2,302	1,072	85	5
1766	2,445	4,429	2,028	3,318	1,976	784	52	497	105	457	1,048	1,844	2,688	1,195	28	5
1767	3,249	4,151	1,946	2,929	1,981	1,273	56	558	103	281	1,134	1,946	2,851	1,144	34	10
1768	3,021	4,421	1,904	3,511	1,508	1,156	67	612	95	184	1,273	2,198	3,139	1,261	54	12
1769	2,736	4,148	2,222	2,926	1,863	1,205	59	605	105	264	1,073	1,373	2,927	1,370	103	14
1770	2,803	4,288	2,012	3,034	1,942	1,082	68	571	106	374	1,095	1,955	3,342	1,339	112	11
1771	3,278	4,461	2,151	3,529	1,882	1,185	97	703	100	319	1,348	4,201	2,937	1,214	47	6
1772	2,843	4,733	2,046	3,423	2,473	941	92	866	130	354	1,265	3,091	3,405	1,440	92	9
1773	2,358	3,774	1,644	3,361	1,933	846	68	662	123	430	1,374	1,987	2,836	1,336	65	18
1774	3,588	4,981	2,009	3,286	1,387	546	57	847	136	438	1,380	2,599	3,561	1,419	35	14
1775	3,427	5,444	2,148	3,809	1,092	1,041	67	786	136	659	1,953	197	3,628	1,717	59	25
1776	3,076	4,873	2,249	3,398	1,468	726	100	471	119	830	106	56	3,301	1,605	53	20
1777	3,712	4,019	2,103	2,782	1,834	786	63	239	120	1,653	14	59	2,792	1,257	49	3
1778	2,910	4,296	1,429	2,258	1,526	1,200	82	154	132	1,030	18	38	3,011	1,151	53	7
1779	3,671	4,323	667	1,633	716	703	34	159	135	842	24	351	2,831	1,167	16	18
1780	4,278	4,270	817	922	971	1,116	22	196	120	837	20	829	2,606	1,752	34	127
1781	4,243	3,870	685	840	2,526	595	26	313	119	536	100	855	1,859	1,024	33	31
1782	3,763	4,400	717	1,262	626	1,468	68	352	223	702	38	267	2,506	1,272	100	229
1783	4,704	3,665	1,216	2,050	1,301	701	48	788	150	732	170	1,003	2,892	1,797	29	61
1784	3,753	3,826	1,964	2,433	2,997	731	119	524	180	760	749	3,679	3,405	1,370	136	31
1785	3,567	4,558	2,251	3,009	2,704	1,154	48	587	209	691	894	2,308	4,354	1,236	61	1
1786	3,326	4,258	2,228	2,886	3,157	2,242	118	889	202	791	843	1,603	3,443	1,336	113	45
1787	3,818	4,185	3,031	3,060	3,431	1,551	118	728	243	913	894	2,014	3,783	1,733	71	14
1788	3,703	4,471	2,733	3,655	3,454	1,431	90	735	250	895	1,024	1,886	4,088	1,766	315	28
1789	3,351	5,241	2,956	3,924	3,350	1,957	103	670	237	874	1,050	2,525	3,906	1,764	251	31
1790	4,313	4,913	3,350	3,314	3,150	2,386	72	929	202	841	1,191	3,432	3,891	1,986	229	39
1791	4,591	5,323	3,368	3,971	3,699	2,272	80	856	214	895	1,194	4,225	3,691	2,649	198	56
1792	4,422	6,084	3,977	4,228	2,672	2,438	83	1,368	256	1,120	1,039	4,271	4,183	2,922	280	107
1793	4,944	5,739	1,904	2,039	3,499	2,722	120	385	210	905	904	3,515	4,392	2,695	308	21
1794	4,486	9,649	2,518	2,126	4,458	2,922	49	750	241	971	626	3,860	4,783	3,633	272	54

1795	4,106	10,045	2,566	2,412	5,761	2,383	65	429	315	1,000	1,352	5,254	4,099	2,461	385	206
1796	6,805	8,317	2,072	2,457	3,737	2,377	120	614	204	815	2,081	6,054	3,967	3,223	877	1,041
1797	4,897	9,185	1,277	1,587	3,942	2,288	54	887	213	845	1,176	5,057	4,309	3,144	1,078	665
1798	6,528	10,139	1,303	1,405	7,627	1,146	70	1,291	220	1,054	1,783	5,580	5,419	5,198	1,159	1,264
1799	7,292	7,939	1,842	2,099	4,285	2,436	113	1,622	170	1,092	1,819	7,057	6,162	5,947	1,390	1,048
1800	7,026	14,325	2,403	3,404	4,942	2,860	97	1,099	393	976	2,358	7,886	7,369	4,087	1,497	479
1801	7,235	14,442	2,274	3,545	5,424	2,946	139	1,124	456	1,017	2,707	7,518	8,436	4,386	2,577	589
1802	5,916	15,015	3,242	7,752	5,795	2,930	169	1,161	368	1,351	1,924	5,329	8,531	3,926	1,658	285
1803	5,346	11,372	3,527	3,968	6,349	2,733	94	819	328	1,082	1,914	5,273	6,132	2,380	355	193
1804	6,435	12,716	2,217	3,033	5,215	1,766	164	1,173	378	1,056	1,651	6,398	7,682	4,282	346	312
1805	7,137	13,026	2,872	2,440	6,073	1,669	107	991	294	865	1,767	7,147	6,720	3,832	736	319
1806	5,805	10,533	2,392	2,678	3,755	1,937	116	1,433	330	951	2,000	8,613	8,815	4,734	1,227	1,796
1807	5,154	9,412	2,819	3,278	3,402	1,884	122	798	450	1,061	2,848	7,921	7,980	4,579	1,341	1,326
1808	2,120	4,734	2,091	6,547	3,858	1,933	143	533	827	1,125	836	3,992	8,778	5,929	2,838	4,830
1809	5,660	13,666	3,935	10,055	3,366	1,648	185	706	678	1,748	2,205	5,188	7,703	5,975	5,090	6,382
1810	7,480	11,221	4,996	8,385	4,710	1,717	257	484	885	1,845	2,614	7,813	8,258	4,790	6,961	5,970
1811	2,652	2,358	1,685	12,606	4,106	1,665	189	317	802	1,910	2,309	1,432	8,452	4,123	3,831	3,047
1812	3,213	5,460	2,952	15,528	5,602	1,779	172	444	720	1,419	1,294	4,136	7,487	4,767	2,471	4,115
1813	...	...	...	...	...	...	...	...	...	...	...	...	...	...	...	...
1814	6,399	22,922	3,443	12,348	6,304	1,698	269	422	323	4,093	23	7	8,497	6,315	6,220	4,302
1815	4,986	19,860	3,244	9,071	8,042	2,093	325	393	369	3,099	2,370	11,937	8,527	6,916	3,371	3,786
1816	2,784	18,493	2,068	9,000	8,313	2,205	240	380	493	2,208	2,386	7,800	7,547	4,608	1,974	3,284
1817	4,897	16,988	3,100	9,529	7,688	2,795	348	506	615	1,396	3,057	6,377	8,021	6,762	1,702	4,882
1818	7,875	17,181	4,944	10,141	7,343	3,196	285	479	690	1,795	3,427	8,383	8,347	5,785	2,331	5,552
1819	4,819	16,016	3,175	9,441	7,344	2,422	254	423	751	2,001	2,688	4,302	7,888	4,490	2,017	3,472
1820	4,799	18,982	3,453	10,693	7,568	3,391	174	566	841	1,676	3,651	3,921	8,011	4,353	2,326	4,450
1821	3,966	16,052	3,631	11,264	6,939	4,428	299	684	844	1,396	3,642	6,607	7,978	5,069	2,471	4,927
1822	5,095	15,358	3,824	13,932	6,123	4,101	275	682	781	1,535	4,021	7,368	7,691	4,146	2,108	5,323

External Trade 15. Official Values of Trade with Various Regions – England & Wales 1700–1 to 1772–3, and Great Britain 1772–3 to 1797–8

NOTES

[1] SOURCE: Phyllis Deane and W. A. Cole, *British Economic Growth, 1688–1955* (Cambridge University Press, 1962).

[2] All figures exclude prize goods. The totals are those given in the ledgers, no allowance being made for changes in the rates of valuation, notably that of woollen goods in 1709. The figures do not, therefore, provide an accurate index of changes in the volume of trade between 1700–1 and 1730–1.

[3] *N.W. Europe* comprises France, the Low Countries, the German states (excluding Prussia) and Belle-Isle. *The North* comprises Denmark and Norway, East Country, Poland, Prussia, Russia and Sweden. *The South* consists of Portugal, Spain, Gibraltar, Italy, Straits, Turkey and Venice (and includes Madeira, the Canaries, and the Turkish dominions). *British Islands* comprise Ireland, the Isle of Man, and the Channel Islands. *The Fisheries* include Greenland and Iceland.

(in £ thousand)

	England & Wales Imports				England & Wales Exports				England & Wales Re-exports			
	1700–1	1730–1	1750–1	1772–3	1700–1	1730–1	1750–1	1772–3	1700–1	1730–1	1750–1	1772–3
N.-W. Europe	1,387	1,424	1,120	1,086	1,941	1,475	2,458	1,461	1,333	1,800	1,790	3,009
The North	541	690	1,084	1,446	241	186	314	290	86	71	90	187
The South	1,650	1,715	1,445	1,769	1,478	2,321	3,562	2,132	233	234	248	459
British Islands	285	325	695	1,303	144	275	695	912	159	345	609	1,102
North America	372	655	877	1,442	256	351	971	2,460	106	208	384	522
West Indies	785	1,586	1,484	3,080	205	374	449	1,168	131	183	140	169
East India (*a*)	775	943	1,101	2,203	114	116	585	824	11	32	68	69
Africa	24	43	43	80	81	105	89	492	64	128	99	285
The Fisheries	—	56	7	21	—	—	—	—	—	...	—	—
TOTAL	5,819	7,386	7,855	12,432	4,461	5,203	9,125	9,739	2,136	3,002	3,428	5,800

	Great Britain Imports				Great Britain Exports				Great Britain Re-exports			
	1772–3	1780–1	1789–90	1797–8	1772–3	1780–1	1789–90	1797–8	1772–3	1780–1	1789–90	1797–8
N.-W. Europe	1,220	2,172	1,841	2,426	1,539	2,298	2,640	2,063	3,865	1,280	2,664	8,056
The North	1,629	2,092	2,572	3,304	314	364	508	820	206	117	346	914
The South	1,793	748	2,573	1,273	2,143	755	2,229	975	464	123	282	180
British Islands	1,437	1,818	2,563	3,127	1,008	1,162	1,377	1,641	1,262	1,079	1,056	1,286
North America	1,977	219	1,351	1,696	2,649	1,359	3,295	5,700	605	419	468	364
West Indies	3,222	2,322	4,045	5,982	1,226	1,295	1,690	4,612	176	217	202	489
East India (*a*)	2,203	1,749	3,256	5,785	824	821	2,096	1,640	69	35	77	75
Africa	80	29	87	62	492	165	517	650	285	90	282	437
The Fisheries	27	42	188	248	—	—	—	—	—	—	2	1
TOTAL	13,595	11,189	18,476	23,903	10,196	8,218	14,350	18,288	6,930	3,359	5,380	11,802

(*a*) i.e. Asia.

External Trade 16. Values at Current Prices of External Trade According to Regions and Principal Countries – Great Britain 1784–6 to 1854–6, and United Kingdom 1805–1980

NOTES TO PART A

[1] SOURCE: Ralph Davis, *The Industrial Revolution and British Overseas Trade* (Leicester, 1979) Appendix tables 38–40.

[2] Trade with Ireland is excluded in Part A.

[3] The figures for 1784–6 are for years ended 30 September. Others are for years beginning 6 January to 1853.

[4] *Northern Europe* comprises the Baltic states except Germany, Scandinavia, Iceland, Greenland, and Russia; *North Western Europe* comprises Netherlands, France, Germany, and the Channel Islands; *Southern Europe* comprises Spain, Portugal, and Italy; and the *Near East* comprises Turkey, the Balkans, Egypt, and Russian Black Sea Ports.

A. Computed Values of External Trade – Great Britain, 1784–6 to 1854–6

(in £ thousand)

	Ireland			Northern Europe			North Western Europe			Southern Europe		
	Imports	Exports	Re-exports	Imports	Exports	Re-exports	Imports	Exports	Re-exports	Imports	Exports	Re-exports
1784–6	2,375	924	2,668	3,808	535	193	2,247	2,335	1,471	2,871	2,478	193
1794–6	3,591	2,258	6,944	6,822	978	679	3,589	2,056	4,445	4,632	2,500	373
1804–6	4,939	3,706	8,311	13,195	7,448	3,494	3,626	2,749	2,547	6,370	3,524	508
1814–6	7,055	3,528	16,067	8,575	3,086	1,779	6,482	10,103	10,896	7,661	7,955	1,516
1824–6	9,414	4,608	8,121	7,245	1,762	1,041	9,862	6,995	4,110	6,009	5,145	980
1834–6	...	...	...	7,430	1,890	859	13,069	9,752	4,767	5,839	5,968	1,641
1844–6	...	...	...	8,826	2,590	1,017	15,499	14,754	5,350	5,869	5,907	1,070
1854–6	...	...	...	11,235	2,404	1,304	33,663	22,396	13,629	10,182	8,191	1,608

	Near East			Africa			Asia			Australasia		
	Imports	Exports	Re-exports	Imports	Exports	Re-exports	Imports	Exports	Re-exports	Imports	Exports	Re-exports
1784–6	273	64	14	148	489	160	4,952	1,813	69	—	—	—
1794–6	378	62	70	191	483	283	7,340	3,539	87	...	7	...
1804–6	241	137	33	386	1,187	208	8,011	2,703	287	8	36	4
1814–6	416	222	94	703	353	80	11,796	2,757	438	23	22	2
1824–6	1,154	650	57	681	372	133	11,019	3,676	657	177	196	50
1834–6	1,274	1,300	84	2,017	967	274	11,535	4,852	473	1,232	730	282
1844–6	1,798	3,038	228	2,898	1,368	325	14,120	9,645	815	2,494	1,176	204
1854–6	6,309	6,613	465	5,218	2,623	409	25,701	13,458	604	4,844	9,491	1,360

	Canada			U.S.A.			West Indies			Latin America		
	Imports	Exports	Re-exports	Imports	Exports	Re-exports	Imports	Exports	Re-exports	Imports	Exports	Re-exports
1784–6	350	703	214	1,156	2,838	209	4,573	1,428	144	8	7	1
1794–6	562	1,177	211	1,943	6,399	238	8,594	4,490	548	275	79	10
1804–6	940	1,223	303	4,174	10,143	274	12,398	7,260	569	1,270	1,125	84
1814–6	2,226	3,246	538	3,976	7,348	246	16,656	6,906	367	6,227	2,476	111
1824–6	3,081	1,675	234	6,061	5,695	307	8,577	4,123	280	3,109	5,009	272
1834–6	3,320	2,132	370	13,223	9,438	779	7,946	4,117	392	3,380	5,047	305
1844–6	5,559	3,280	413	14,058	7,162	547	5,937	3,866	375	4,905	5,634	450
1854–6	5,740	4,326	251	30,282	20,078	813	8,709	3,947	254	9,698	8,974	358

External Trade 16. *continued*

NOTES TO PART B

[1] Sources: Columns 1–9 – G. R. Porter, *The Progress of the Nation* (London, 1912, edited by F. W. Hurst, pp. 479–80; columns 10–16 and modifications to columns 6 and 7 for the period 1827–47 – *Porter's Tables* (published in sessional papers from 1833), and the first *Abstract*.

[2] *Northern Europe* comprise France, the Low Countries, Scandinavia, Germany, Prussia and Russia. *Southern Europe* consists of Spain, Portugal, Gibraltar, Malta, the Azores, Madeira, the Canary Islands, the Italian states, Turkey, Greece and Austria-Hungary. *Asia* includes Australia and the Pacific settlements. *Germany* comprises Prussia, as well as the other states which were not separately distinguished in contemporary summaries. Prior to 1840 *India* includes Ceylon.

[3] The year began on 6 January to 1853.

B. Declared Value of Exports – United Kingdom, 1805–1847

(in £ thousand)

	Northern Europe	Southern Europe	Africa	Asia and Australasia	U.S.A.	British North America	British West Indies	Foreign West Indies	Central and South America	Russia	Germany	Netherlands	Belgium	France	India	Australia and Pacific Settlements
1805	13,626		756	2,905	11,011	7,771				...	...	...	...	...	...	...
1806	11,364		1,164	2,938	12,389	10,878				...	...	...	...	...	...	...
1807	9,002		765	3,359	11,847	10,439				...	...	...	...	...	...	...
1808	9,016		633	3,525	5,242	16,592				...	...	...	...	...	...	...
1809	15,849		804	2,868	7,259	18,014				...	...	...	...	...	...	...
1810	15,628		595	2,977	10,921	15,640				...	...	...	...	...	...	...
1811	12,835		337	2,941	1,841	11,940				...	...	...	...	...	...	...
1812	...	...	...	...	...	...		...	...	...	...	...	...	...	...	...
1813	...	...	...	...	...	...		...	...	...	...	...	...	...	...	...
1814	14,114	12,756	372	2,340	8	11,429		1,791	2,683	...	...	...	...	...	...	...
1815	11,972	8,765	334	2,932	13,255	10,688		1,157	2,531	...	...	...	...	...	...	...
1816	11,369	7,284	352	3,071	9,557	7,016		861	2,147	...	...	...	...	...	...	...
1817	11,408	7,685	406	3,725	6,930	7,406		1,280	2,651	...	...	...	...	...	...	...
1818	11,809	7,630	391	3,877	9,451	7,790		1,170	3,996	...	...	...	...	...	...	...
1819	9,895	6,895	316	2,715	4,930	6,861		892	2,376	...	...	...	...	...	...	...
1820	11,290	7,140	393	3,810	3,875	5,757		940	2,921	...	...	...	...	...	...	...
1821	9,044	6,859	482	4,278	6,215	5,462		1,051	2,942	...	...	...	...	...	...	...
1822	8,328	8,274	385	3,985	6,865	4,779		868	3,167	...	...	...	...	...	...	...
1823	8,056	6,801	507	3,941	5,465	5,312		1,074	4,219	...	...	...	...	...	...	...
1824	7,691	8,008	418	3,692	6,090	5,779		1,171	5,573	...	...	...	...	...	...	...
1825	8,548	6,099	402	3,623	7,019	5,847		908	6,426	...	...	...	...	...	...	...
1826	7,823	6,070	296	4,322	4,659	4,601		570	3,195	...	...	...	...	...	...	...

1827	8,533	5,946	671	4,799	7,018	1,397	3,584	907	4,004	1,409	4,829	2,105		447	3,662	340
1828	8,243	5,533	717	4,892	5,810	1,691	3,290	818	5,489	1,319	4,573	2,143		499	...	446
1829	8,346	6,199	829	4,231	4,823	1,582	3,612	970	4,930	1,436	4,663	2,050		491	...	312
1830	8,377	7,234	905	4,455	6,132	1,857	2,839	940	5,189	1,490	4,582	2,022		476	...	316
1831	7,318	6,233	803	4,105	9,054	2,089	2,582	1,040	3,616	1,192	3,836	2,083		603	...	403
1832	9,897	5,687	881	4,235	5,468	2,076	2,440	1,177	4,272	1,587	5,328	2,789		675	...	468
1833	9,314	6,298	937	4,712	7,580	2,092	2,598	959	4,842	1,531	4,500	2,182	886	848	2,579	559
1834	9,506	8,501	993	4,644	6,845	1,671	2,680	1,270	5,178	1,382	4,684	2,470	750	1,117	3,193	716
1835	10,303	8,161	1,146	5,456	10,568	2,158	3,188	1,153	4,887	1,753	4,791	2,648	818	1,454	4,286	699
1836	10,000	9,011	1,468	6,751	12,426	2,732	3,787	1,239	5,955	1,742	4,624	2,510	839	1,591	3,613	836
1837	11,528	7,873	1,440	5,561	4,695	2,141	3,457	1,063	4,313	2,047	5,030	3,040	805	1,643	3,613	922
1838	12,130	10,113	1,848	6,956	7,586	1,922	3,394	1,136	4,727	1,663	5,144	3,549	1,068	2,314	3,876	1,338
1839	12,332	8,466	1,607	7,643	8,839	3,048	3,986	1,285	6,027	1,776	5,422	3,564	882	2,298	4,749	1,703
1840	12,283	9,208	1,615	9,276	5,283	2,848	3,575	1,115	6,202	1,603	5,628	3,416	880	2,378	5,213	2,052
1841	13,160	9,695	1,857	8,167	7,099	2,947	2,504	1,065	5,142	1,607	6,018	3,611	1,066	2,902	4,823	1,337
1842	14,031	9,879	1,733	7,456	3,529	2,334	2,591	854	4,975	1,886	6,579	3,573	1,099	3,194	4,433	959
1843	14,024	10,947	1,714	9,547	5,014	1,751	2,883	973	5,427	1,896	6,651	3,565	985	2,535	5,689	1,307
1844	14,327	11,294	1,616	11,274	7,938	3,044	2,478	1,174	5,440	2,129	6,657	3,132	1,471	2,656	6,919	792
1845	15,092	11,211	1,896	10,974	7,143	3,551	2,794	1,464	5,986	2,153	7,096	3,439	1,479	2,791	5,873	1,244
1846	14,696	11,431	1,803	10,190	6,830	3,308	3,506	1,445	5,578	1,725	7,151	3,576	1,158	2,716	5,773	1,495
1847	13,906	11,703	2,049	9,119	10,974	3,233	2,273	1,510	5,075	1,845	6,840	3,017	1,059	2,554	4,799	1,670

NOTES TO PART C

[1] SOURCES: *Annual Statement of Trade* and *Overseas Trade Statistics of the United Kingdom*.

[2] Exports include re-exports from 1854 (2nd line).

[3] Trade was recorded according to ports of shipment or destination to 1905 (1st line) and according to country of consignment subsequently.

C. Computed Values (Imports and Re-exports 1854–70) and Declared Values, 1846–1980 – United Kingdom

(in £ million)

	North and North-East Europe (a)		Western Europe (b)		Central and South-East Europe (c)		Southern Europe & North Africa (d)		Turkey and the Middle East (e)		The remainder of Africa (f)		Asia (g)	
	Imports	Exports	Imports	Exports	Imports	Exports	Imports	Exports	Imports	Exports	Imports	Exports	Imports	Exports
1846	...	2·4	...	7·5	...	8·1	...	5·8	...	2·5	...	1·4	...	8·7
1847	...	2·4	...	6·6	...	7·6	...	4·5	...	3·3	...	1·6	...	7·4
1848	...	2·5	...	4·7	...	6·0	...	5·6	...	3·5	...	1·6	...	7·0
1849	...	2·3	...	6·9	...	7·0	...	5·9	...	3·4	...	1·6	...	8·8
1850	...	2·3	...	7·1	...	8·4	...	5·8	...	3·5	...	2·0	...	10·3
1851	...	2·2	...	6·6	...	8·8	...	6·5	...	3·3	...	1·9	...	10·9
1852	...	2·0	...	7·9	...	8·8	...	6·3	...	3·6	...	2·1	...	10·6
1853	...	2·4	...	8·5	...	9·0	...	6·5	...	3·1	...	2·8	...	10·9
1854	10·9	1·6 --- (h) 2·2	21·0	9·2 --- (h) 16·6	17·6	9·2 --- (h) 15·0	9·0	6·4 --- (h) 7·4	5·7	4·4 --- (h) 4·9	4·8	2·5 --- (h) 2·9	23·0	12·0 --- (h) 12·6
1855	7·7	2·5	18·2	21·5	17·4	16·4	9·4	8·3	6·1	8·6	5·1	3·0	24·3	13·6
1856	17·2	6·3	20·8	22·6	12·1	18·4	10·8	10·6	8·3	7·2	6·2	3·4	29·8	16·0
1857	19·1	7·3	22·6	24·1	14·7	19·6	9·6	10·3	10·3	6·0	6·6	4·4	33·8	17·5
1858	16·6	7·1	22·6	21·7	9·6	18·6	8·4	11·0	8·9	7·5	5·6	4·0	25·5	23·3
1859	19·8	8·7	27·1	21·4	11·5	17·3	9·8	10·5	11·4	7·3	5·5	4·2	27·5	29·4
1860	23·3	7·9	30·1	26·4	16·4	20·4	12·5	13·0	13·6	7·9	5·9	4·7	28·5	27·0
1861	16·9 --- (i) 17·8	8·2 --- (i) 8·5	29·3	33·2	16·1 --- (i) 16·5	21·4 --- (i) 21·4	10·2 --- (i) 10·7	15·0 --- (i) 15·2	12·1	6·4	5·7	4·6	36·9	25·5
1862	20·3	6·3	34·4	37·0	16·9	21·6	10·3	14·4	16·6	7·1	5·0	4·6	52·1	21·6
1863	18·5	8·2	37·9	41·0	15·9	24·9	11·5	17·8	21·9	11·6	6·0	3·9	69·6	29·0
1864	21·5	9·8	43·7	43·9	16·4	26·3	11·9	16·4	25·5	13·9	5·5	4·7	74·9	30·1
1865	25·3	10·2	51·4	47·2	17·6	29·2	12·0	15·4	27·3	13·5	6·2	4·1	56·7	29·9
1866	27·5	11·1	56·7	48·2	20·9	26·4	13·4	15·7	20·8	15·8	6·9	4·1	54·5	35·7
1867	31·4	11·3	52·1	45·4	20·6	31·5	13·2	13·8	19·7	15·4	6·6	4·7	40·8	37·6
1868	28·7	11·1	53·5	48·6	21·6	34·2	14·5	13·4	23·8	14·1	7·2	4·4	49·8	36·6
1869	25·3	14·0	55·7	49·6	21·9	34·6	15·2	15·1	24·5	15·5	6·6	4·3	51·8	33·6
1870	32·2 ---	15·6 ---	63·2 ---	48·2 ---	17·6 ---	30·8 ---	14·9 ---	15·2 ---	20·8 ---	16·4 ---	6·8 ---	5·0 ---	42·9 ---	36·9 ---

1871 (j)	33·8	15·4	57·4	68·3	21·7	41·4	19·5	17·1	23·5	13·7	7·4	5·3	51·0	35·0
1872	35·0	16·7	68·1	65·7	21·2	46·0	21·1	18·5	21·9	15·6	8·8	7·4	57·2	36·4
1873	35·4	21·6	69·7	69·0	21·8	39·7	22·8	20·5	20·3	14·6	8·7	8·4	53·5	37·4
1874	36·2	21·8	76·0	63·3	21·4	37·9	19·9	20·0	16·7	11·5	8·8	8·2	52·7	41·4
1875	33·9	20·4	76·4	61·2	23·7	36·7	22·4	19·4	17·8	9·6	8·6	8·3	56·0	43·1
1876	32·4	17·7	75·8	60·5	23·2	31·6	19·9	19·7	19·2	9·3	8·3	7·7	55·8	39·5
1877	36·5	14·8	78·6	53·5	28·1	30·6	23·4	18·2	18·3	8·7	9·4	8·1	58·3	44·3
1878	31·5	15·7	75·2	52·6	26·2	31·3	18·8	16·4	11·3	10·8	8·0	8·9	51·4	39·9
1879	28·9	16·5	71·1	53·9	24·7	31·8	17·8	15·6	12·7	10·4	8·2	9·6	47·0	39·3
1880	32·3	18·4	79·1	56·6	26·2	31·1	21·2	16·5	13·5	10·8	9·5	10·5	55·2	52·0
1881	28·7	16·7	74·5	58·9	27·8 --- (k) 27·9	31·6 --- (k) 31·8	20·5	18·4	13·8 --- (k) 13·9	10·9 --- (k) 11·1	8·8	10·9	56·0	51·1
1882	38·1	16·2	79·4	61·1	32·7	32·8	22·1	18·8	13·0	10·0	10·0	12·0	65·1	47·7
1883	39·1	15·6	79·9	60·0	34·3	34·9	22·3	19·7	16·0	11·4	9·6	9·2	63·6	50·8
1884	32·1	15·5	78·5	59·4	28·8	33·3	20·1	19·4	15·5	10·6	9·3	8·9	58·0	49·7
1885	33·5	13·6	75·8	52·7	28·3	29·1	19·1	17·4	13·8	11·1	7·3	7·4	53·1	48·8
1886	28·7	13·0	76·2	47·6	25·8	28·7	17·7	16·8	11·7	9·8	7·3	6·8	52·9	48·1
1887	31·3	13·7	77·2	48·8	29·6	29·7	19·4	18·9	11·9	9·6	7·5	8·5	49·4	51·0
1888	44·6	15·5	80·6	52·2	32·5	30·0	21·2	17·1	11·9	9·0	8·1	9·7	52·7	54·1
1889	47·7	17·9	90·1	52·1	32·8	34·1	22·0	20·0	14·4	10·3	9·0	13·7	57·7	50·9
1890	43·4	18·8	88·1	54·8	32·4	33·7	22·8	21·4	13·5	11·7	9·4	14·1	51·6	55·8
1891	43·9	17·8	89·3	52·6	33·7	33·4	21·0	19·1	16·4	12·1	9·6	13·1	53·3	52·0
1892	35·0	18·2	89·4	49·8	30·0	32·7	21·4 --- (l) 21·5	17·0 --- (l) 17·1	16·3 --- (l) 16·4	10·4 --- (l) 10·5	8·7	12·7	48·7	46·6
1893	39·5	19·5	89·4	48·6	32·3	31·2	18·6	15·5	14·0	10·0	9·1	13·9	44·7	46·3
1894	45·1	21·1	88·1	46·7	32·4	32·8	18·9	16·1	14·5	11·5	8·5	13·6	43·9	47·0
1895	47·2	20·4	93·4	43·5	30·4	36·0	19·7	15·7	15·6	9·6	9·0	15·9	43·5	43·5
1896	47·2	21·7	98·6	45·3	32·4	37·7	20·4	15·3	15·2	9·7	8·9	20·5	41·8	51·9
1897	48·1	22·9	103·2	45·6	30·1	36·0	22·2	15·7	15·8	12·1	8·9	20·3	40·0	47·7
1898	45·9	26·6	101·5	47·4	32·3	37·3	23·2	16·2	14·1	11·8	10·4	19·4	42·9	49·7
1899	46·5	30·4	106·3	50·9	33·5	42·1	24·6(m)	20·5(m)	16·1(m)	11·4(m)	10·6	19·4	46·1	57·7
1900	51·6	31·4	108·5	45·7	34·0	42·5	26·6	23·2	18·6	12·2	8·4	21·6	47·0	57·2
1901	51·7	27·7	112·0	50·1	37·5	48·5	24·2	21·7	18·0	14·6	9·5	26·9	45·8	60·7
1902	56·4	26·4	112·1	48·0	43·1	37·3	24·9	21·7	20·3	13·2	10·2	34·1	47·0	56·2
1903	63·8	29·1	113·3	49·9	41·5	38·3	24·2	22·1	19·2	13·1	10·9	36·2	51·1	57·6
1904	62·9	28·2	116·3	48·1	39·9	40·8	23·1	22·8	20·5	16·8	11·3	28·0	56·5	69·2
1905 (n)	64·8 --- 66·0	29·2 --- 29·2	119·6 --- 86·0	52·6 --- 52·6	39·0 --- 61·7	47·4 --- 47·4	23·5 --- 26·6	22·8 --- 22·8	20·8 --- 20·9	15·8 --- 15·8	11·3 --- 11·8	27·4 --- 27·4	56·5 --- 57·2	80·9 --- 83·0

See p. 515 for footnotes.

External Trade 16. *continued*

C. Computed Values (Imports and Re-exports 1854–70) and Declared Values, 1846–1980 – United Kingdom (*cont.*)

(in £ million)

	North and North-East Europe (*a*)		Western Europe (*b*)		Central and South-East Europe (*c*)		Southern Europe & North Africa (*d*)		Turkey and the Middle East (*e*)		The remainder of Africa (*f*)		Asia (*g*)	
	Imports	Exports	Imports	Exports	Imports	Exports	Imports	Exports	Imports	Exports	Imports	Exports	Imports	Exports
1906	65.7	32.2	89.2	52.4	66.0	53.9	30.2	26.9	23.4	18.3	13.0	27.5	62.4	86.8
1907	69.0	38.2	88.3	71.9	68.7	48.8	32.1	30.8	28.9	19.1	16.7	26.8	71.7	93.9
1908	66.2	37.6	82.7	64.7	65.7	54.4	27.1	31.6	23.1	17.8	14.2	24.5	53.8	85.3
1909	73.2	35.0	87.2	67.1	69.0	54.4	27.4	27.3	25.4	16.6	16.9	27.5	63.8	77.3
1910	81.8	39.7	91.8	73.1	72.8	63.0	28.5	29.2	26.3	18.8	19.7	37.2	79.5	84.2
1911	82.1	41.1	91.2	76.4	79.1	67.6	29.3	30.8	27.9	21.4	19.1	37.4	83.8	97.2
1912	83.0	42.3	101.2	81.2	80.8	70.1	31.0	34.8	33.5	19.3	20.9	40.3	97.2	104.9
1913	86.0	50.2	104.4	87.2	90.2	68.8	30.6	36.7	27.6	19.2	22.9	41.8	92.6	128.3
					--- (*o*)	--- (*o*)	--- (*o*)	--- (*o*)	--- (*o*) (*p*)	--- (*o*) (*p*)				
1914	75.4	45.4	88.3	72.5	54.9	42.8	31.0	32.5	22.4	15.1	23.3 --- (*p*) 23.9	34.8 --- (*p*) 35.2	93.5	107.0
1915	77.8	56.6	71.7	116.0	0.3	1.4	40.5	38.8	24.4	10.3	33.4	34.3	130.7	77.6
1916	78.4	70.1	65.5	146.5	0.1	0.1	50.7	49.2	28.5	13.3	38.6	44.3	151.8	97.9
1917	69.6	73.3	54.4	160.0	..	0.7	42.6	54.8	34.3	17.3	39.6	39.0	148.3	98.1
1918	58.2	17.6	55.9	169.1	..	—	68.0	59.1	55.2	26.1	47.1	43.0	157.8	92.4
1919	78.8	117.7	94.3	324.6	1.5	32.6	76.9	78.9	72.2	45.4	74.4	48.2	230.4	134.8
1920	145.5	132.8	197.0	321.9	36.3	66.0	78.2	114.9	86.1	80.2	80.6	104.5	238.6	327.2
	--- (*q*)	--- (*q*)	--- (*q*)	--- (*q*)	--- (*q*)	--- (*q*)	--- (*q*)	--- (*q*)						
1921	86.7	50.3	145.3	129.4	33.1	58.9	43.9	52.9	39.4	36.6	48.5	59.2	101.5	200.4
1922	94.1	51.1	128.4	152.6	39.0	59.2	42.2	51.7	45.5	29.7	42.7	51.7	100.6	171.8
	---	---	---	---	---	---	---	---	---	---	---	---	---	---
1923 (*r*)	110.0	52.4	143.0	147.8	54.5	72.5	47.0	50.4	46.4	28.3	46.4	57.8	130.0	163.6
	---	---	---	---	---	---	---	---	---	---	---	---	---	---
1924	126.5	61.4	166.6	137.6	64.5	86.6	51.2	51.8	50.8	28.8	52.2	61.1	142.4	173.9
1925	130.0	62.1	166.6	125.3	70.1	87.2	51.1	51.6	45.3	31.7	60.2	67.9	160.5	157.1
1926	127.7	46.9	169.1	93.4	97.9	59.6	42.8	33.1	38.7	22.0	53.7	63.9	137.9	150.0
1927	134.1	47.3	169.5	102.4	83.1	86.6	47.9	42.8	40.1	23.3	56.2	68.1	142.7	150.9
1928	130.9	42.2	161.8	107.0	81.0	85.5	45.5	43.2	41.6	21.4	60.0	69.7	127.0	157.2
1929	146.6	47.5	157.1	112.4	91.6	86.7	48.0	46.8	38.1	23.7	59.0	68.1	135.7	149.7
1930	143.4	50.3	140.0	95.1	89.8	57.1	41.6	38.5	27.5	19.4	45.8	58.7	106.6	100.8

Year	Imports	Exports	Imports	Exports	Imports	Exports	Imports	Exports	Imports	Exports	Imports	Exports	Imports	Exports
1931	123·1	38·2	121·3	68·3	87·7	41·3	37·5	27·4	20·5	12·9	29·7	42·5	79·2	66·8
1932	99·7	39·1	62·7	58·5	45·9	34·3	30·9	25·4	21·2	13·8	35·0	36·4	68·4	67·6
1933	94·7	36·2	56·1	57·7	46·8	34·3	28·2	23·9	23·5	14·1	33·9	41·5	69·8	61·4
1934	98·5	45·8	60·9	55·9	49·2	34·5	28·9	27·4	22·9	15·1	32·2	48·4	89·9	65·5
1935	101·3	50·7	66·2	55·6	50·1	37·9	28·3	26·8	25·9	17·7	37·8	57·0	86·5	66·3
1936	108·5	56·7	76·3	59·3	62·2	39·7	23·6	15·5	27·6	16·9	44·0	62·7	94·7	63·6
1937	137·1	72·7	88·8	69·9	67·5	37·1	29·2	20·4	33·8	19·0	59·4	73·0	122·9	76·9
1938	122·4	66·0	79·4	55·1	57·6	42·6	25·0	22·3	27·9	22·3	46·5	63·8	108·2	68·8
1939	106·4	59·7	85·1	52·0	39·1	26·9	27·0	17·8	29·0	21·0	51·0	57·9	99·6	61·0
1940	34·3	20·4	41·5	36·6	12·2	3·0	25·5	14·3	31·7	24·2	75·4	59·6	149·1	66·0
1941	9·6	34·1	1·4	0·9	0·4	0·1	16·0	9·2	17·3	23·8	75·9	62·7	118·6	62·1
1942	10·3	80·5	1·2	1·2	0·1	..	16·8	6·2	20·2	23·3	85·8	59·1	84·1	28·7
1943	9·5	61·8	1·0	0·4	..	—	21·8	20·5	14·8	23·4	87·4	59·0	85·5	20·8
1944	13·0	58·7	3·1	12·5	..	—	29·5	18·2	24·5	19·9	102·7	60·4	86·3	28·2
1945	45·1	46·3	9·1	52·8	2·1	11·1	35·0	18·4	25·9	29·9	78·3	70·9	87·1	42·7

(in £ million)

	E.E.C. Countries (s)		E.F.T.A. Countries (t)		Eastern Europe (u)		Southern Europe & North Africa (d)		Turkey and the Middle East (e)		The Remainder of Africa (f)		Asia (g)	
	Imports	Exports	Imports	Exports	Imports	Exports	Imports	Exports	Imports	Exports	Imports	Exports	Imports	Exports
1946	66·0	140·6	72·2	114·2	5·9	38·3	55·7 --- (d) 32·6	50·4 --- (d) 29·7	50·9	78·0	95·4	130·1	130·9	135·9
1947	137·7	136·4	99·3	122·7	18·9	43·0	48·5	32·5	58·4	94·6	134·6	163·9	170·3	191·7
1948	189·0	182·6	137·2	174·1	56·6	32·7	58·6	49·3	123·0	126·4	197·3	239·7	196·3	226·3
1949	257·6	193·7	185·2	191·3	54·0	39·4	69·0	48·8	111·2	126·6	228·0	284·9	206·8	270·0
1950	331·9 --- (s)	278·2 --- (s)	223·3	258·6	74·4	37·9	71·3	54·0	159·3	136·6	271·1	286·6	265·0	276·2
1951	512·6	313·3	353·4	287·7	102·7 --- (u) 105·6	51·9 --- (u) 52·5	110·6	62·7	245·0	146·5	393·9	372·5	475·9	367·0
1952	426·2	330·9	319·8	271·4	99·9	63·4	101·1	74·9	276·4	163·9	407·8	415·5	351·4	384·3
1953	346·9	380·4	330·5	292·9	82·3	35·4	86·4	74·1	254·3	147·7	387·3	424·6	290·3	359·2
1954	390·6	391·8	332·6	308·1	81·2	42·5	89·3	77·4	239·6	130·9	403·9	417·0	335·7	350·4
1955	482·1	422·3	371·4	311·6	112·5	60·5	96·2	88·4	236·8	158·4	412·9	455·0	404·9	374·7
1956	492·8	478·3	384·9	341·5	106·3	86·7	97·8	106·4	245·5	169·7	417·3	452·7	377·8	446·9
1957	491·0	506·2	397·8	353·0	118·5	89·7	99·9	100·7	248·4	178·3	372·8	472·7	394·9	465·3
1958	534·8	462·5	365·9	331·7	115·2	87·5	94·0	97·6	295·5	186·4	339·3	465·3	386·2	420·4
1959	558·7	511·8	391·9	359·7	129·8	84·0	93·7	82·3	311·5	188·0	387·2	427·1	398·5	457·0
1960	661·7	567·1	464·0	397·3	154·4	111·8	118·6	102·2	334·7	190·5	404·4	449·9	430·4	462·6

See p. 515 for footnotes.

External Trade 16. *continued*

C. Computed Values (Imports and Re-exports 1854–70) and Declared Values, 1846–1980 – United Kingdom *(cont.)*

(in £ million)

	E.E.C. Countries (*s*)		E.F.T.A. Countries (*t*)		Eastern Europe (*u*)		Southern Europe & North Africa (*d*)		Turkey and the Middle East (*e*)		The Remainder of Africa (*f*)		Asia (*g*)	
	Imports	Exports	Imports	Exports	Imports	Exports	Imports	Exports	Imports	Exports	Imports	Exports	Imports	Exports
1961	677·1	666·1	460·5	446·9	174·9	151·6	117·4	114·9	331·2	211·6	400·9	448·5	428·3	474·6
1962	707·5	781·3	463·0	476·7	177·7	148·3	139·6	141·1	348·7	201·8	399·6	418·1	434·1	433·6
1963	768·6	892·9	506·3	516·7	186·8	151·4	153·0	157·1	350·8	223·7	449·5	477·4	437·6	467·6
1964	914·1	906·4	621·7	570·3	204·4	126·8	184·8	170·6	355·7	214·7	471·9	505·1	475·4	465·4
1965	994·7	980·3	666·9	614·3	234·5	137·3	202·9	199·4	325·4	247·7	604·7	571·1	456·5	483·1
1966	1,104	1,045	717·7	684·7	254·0	178·1	204·7	226·0	343·5	276·0	601·0	529·0	457·6	496·3
1967	1,264	1,042	811·9	708·1	269·4	197·3	219·2	210·1	385·1	256·1	594·3	542·2	483·3	492·9
1968	1,551	1,292	1,001	805·9	326·2	254·3	345·2	256·2	510·0	371·0	713·3	587·8	577·0	522·3
1969	1,608	1,526	1,074	975·3	355·6	260·8	346·5	318·7	513·2	450·2	810·6	654·7	549·2	623·7
1970	1,823	1,753	1,411	1,284	376·0	304·6	379·0	316·0	521·3	424·3	787·9	740·9	599·1	662·5
1971	2,106	1,926	1,570	1,392	361·9	315·1	397·0	376·0	708·4	485·7	720·9	909·5	981·1	760·2
1972	2,726	2,231	1,959	1,587	409·2	318·6	396·1	428·1	718·2	577·8	814·7	769·7	856·7	752·1
1973	4,201 --- (*s*) 5,215	3,075 --- (*s*) 3,827	2,502 --- (*t*) 2,370	2,075 --- (*t*) 1,746	569·7	379·5	560·5	523·9	1,105	777·1	1,100	879·0	1,288	1,018
1974	7,731	5,362	2,994	2,245	700·1	512·3	892·2	607·8	3,017	1,203	1,462	1,215	1,610	1,272
1975	8,807	6,273	3,046	2,631	697·5	678·6	702·9	783·9	2,714	1,990	1,474	1,773	1,764	1,374
1976	11,438	8,951	3,796	3,269	1,055	784·6	871·4	993·8	3,713	2,605	1,719	2,070	2,377	1,640
1977	14,064	11,622	4,562	4,328	1,296	1,010	945·2	1,272	3,463	3,386	2,149	2,461	2,923	2,063
1978	16,455	13,415	6,223	4,656	1,225	1,135	1,013	1,369	3,258	3,681	2,025	2,842	3,234	2,590
1979	20,750	17,219	7,048	5,748	1,444	1,140	1,301	1,588	3,410	3,362	1,765	2,412	3,978	3,050
1980	20,758	20,823	7,039	7,048	1,337	1,316	1,428	1,795	4,448	3,912	1,946	3,403	4,671	3,050

(in £ million)

	West Indies (v)		Central and South America (v)		Argentina		Australia		Belgium		British North America (w)		France	
	Imports	Exports	Imports	Exports	Imports	Exports	Imports	Exports	Imports	Exports	Imports	Exports	Imports	Exports
1846	...	4·0	...	5·6	...	--	...	1·4	...	1·2	...	3·3	...	2·7
1847	...	3·8	...	5·1	...	0·2	...	1·6	...	1·1	...	3·2	...	2·6
1848	...	2·5	...	5·8	...	0·4	...	1·4	...	0·8	...	2·0	...	1·0
1849	...	3·6	...	7·2	...	1·4	...	2·0	...	1·5	...	2·3	...	2·0
1850	...	4·0	...	6·8	...	0·8	...	2·5	...	1·1	...	3·2	...	2·4
1851	...	4·5	...	8·2	...	0·5	...	2·6	...	1·0	...	3·8	...	2·0
1852	...	3·9	...	8·5	...	0·8	...	4·1	...	1·1	...	3·1	...	2·7
1853	...	3·7	...	8·5	...	0·6	...	14·3	...	1·4	...	4·9	...	2·6
1854	7·6	3·8 --- (b) 4·0	11·3	8·3 --- (b) 8·7	1·3	1·3 --- (b) 1·3	4·3	11·6 --- (b) 13·1	3·6	1·4 --- (b) 3·4	7·1	6·0 --- (b) 6·3	10·4	3·2 --- (b) 6·4
1855	6·5	--- (v) 3·4	12·2	--- (v) 9·8	1·1	0·8	4·5	6·9	2·5	3·9	4·7	3·1	9·1	10·4
1856	7·0	3·4	11·5	11·0	1·0	1.0	5·6	11·3	2·9	4·0	6·9	4·4	10·4	10·5
1857	8·9	4·3	16·0	13·1	1·6	1·3	5·8	12·8	3·4	3·9	6·4	4·7	12·0	11·3
1858	8·9	4·0	13·8	10·5	1·2	1·0	5·0	11·1	3·1	4·3	4·7	3·4	13·3	9·2
1859	7·7	3·8	12·1	10·7	1·6	1·0	5·5	11·8	3·5	3·7	5·5	4·0	16·9	9·6
1860	7·9	4·1	13·0	13·7	1·1	1·8	6·0	9·9	4·1	4·0	6·8	4·0	17·8	12·7
1861	8·9	3·8	13·8	12·5	1·5	1·4	6·4	10·6	3·8	4·9	8·7	4·2	17·8	17·4
1862	9·1	5·1	16·2	9·8	1·1	0·9	6·5	11·5	4·9	4·6	8·5	4·8	21·7	21·8
1863	11·0	5·9	18·6	13·2	1·2	1·3	6·4	11·4	5·2	5·1	8·2	5·5	24·0	23·3
1864	13·9	6·7	23·1	18·5	1·2	1·8	8·9	10·9	6·4	6·0	6·9	6·3	25·6	23·8
1865	10·6	5·6	24·8	17·4	1·0	2·0	9·0	12·4	7·4	6·9	6·4	5·7	31·6	25·4
1866	8·0	6·0	20·9	20·9	1·1	2·9	9·9	12·3	7·9	6·8	6·9	6·7	37·0	26·6
1867	9·1	5·3	20·4	19·1	0·9	2·9	11·2	8·7	7·6	7·4	6·8	6·7	33·7	23·0
1868	10·0	5·5	22·4	16·6	1·5	2·0	11·1	11·2	8·3	8·4	6·8	5·6	33·9	23·5
1869	9·9	4·0	21·5	18·5	1·3	2·3	10·6	12·4	9·4	8·9	7·7	5·9	33·5	23·3
1870	10·2	6·9	21·6	18·4	1·5	2·4	11·9	9·1	11·2	8·9	8·5	7·6	37·6	22·0
	---	---	---	---	---	---	---	---	---	---	---	---	---	---
1871 (j)	8·5	6·8	22·5	20·5	2·0	2·5	12·0	9·6	13·6	12·8	9·3	9·1	29·8	33·4
1872	10·9	7·8	28·3	26·8	1·9	4·0	13·0	13·0	13·2	13·1	9·1	11·3	41·8	28·3
1873	10·2	7·2	27·7	25·9	2·6	3·8	14·1	15·6	13·1	14·2	11·3	9·4	43·3	30·2
1874	8·7	5·8	24·5	23·4	1·3	3·2	15·0	16·0	15·0	12·7	11·9	10·2	46·5	29·4
1875	9·7	6·8	25·1	19·4	1·4	2·5	17·1	17·1	14·8	13·8	10·2	9·7	46·7	27·3
1876	7·9	5·7	22·8	16·5	1·7	1·6	18·5	16·0	13·8	12·8	11·0	8·0	45·3	29·0
1877	6·6	5·8	22·7	17·9	1·7	2·2	18·0	17·9	12·9	11·8	12·0	8·3	45·8	25·7
1878	6·4	5·5	19·5	17·0	1·1	2·4	16·8	16·8	12·4	11·4	9·5	7·0	41·4	26·6
1879	8·0	5·4	19·6	15·2	0·8	2·1	17·4	14·2	10·7	11·9	10·4	6·1	38·5	26·6
1880	6·5	5·9	19·4	18·4	0·9	2·5	20·4	15·6	11·3	13·0	13·4	8·5	42·0	28·0

See p. 515 for footnotes.

External Trade 16. *continued*

C. Computed Values (Imports and Re-exports 1854–70) and Declared Values, 1846–1980 – United Kingdom (*cont.*)

(in £ million)

	West Indies		Central and South America		Argentina		Australia		Belgium		British North America		France	
	Imports	Exports	Imports	Exports	Imports	Exports	Imports	Exports	Imports	Exports	Imports	Exports	Imports	Exports
1881	5·5	5·9	18·7	21·1	0·6	3·4	21·8	19·8	11·5	13·5	11·3	9·3	40·0	30·1
1882	6·1	6·3	21·6	23·3	1·2	4·3	20·4	22·8	14·9	15·1	10·4	10·7	39·1	29·8
1883	4·6	6·6	19·2	22·5	0·9	5·1	20·1	22·5	16·2	14·8	12·3	10·1	38·6	29·4
1884	3·8	5·7	17·2	23·2	1·2	5·9	22·3	22·6	15·1	14·8	11·0	9·7	37·4	26·3
1885	3·7	5·0	15·4	17·8	1·9	4·8	18·1	23·7	15·1	13·9	10·3	8·4	35·7	23·0
1886	1·9	5·2	13·8	20·0	1·6	5·3	16·2	21·3	14·2	12·3	10·4	9·0	36·6	20·3
1887	2·1	5·4	16·0	22·9	2·2	6·4	17·6	18·9	14·7	13·2	10·6	9·2	37·1	20·5
1888	2·7	5·8	17·4	25·6	2·7	7·8	19·9	25·3	15·6	13·0	9·3	8·7	38·9	24·2
1889	2·4	6·0	15·9	30·6	2·0	10·9	20·0	22·0	17·7	13·7	12·2	9·4	45·8	22·2
1890	2·1	7·0	17·2	29·6	4·1	8·5	21·0	21·8	17·4	13·6	12·4	8·3	44·8	24·7
1891	1·8	5·9	16·7	24·2	3·5	4·4	23·1	24·5	17·3	13·3	12·6	8·3	44·8	24·3
1892	2·1	5·9	17·5	25·5	4·5	5·8	22·8	17·6	17·0	12·8	14·6	8·5	43·5	21·3
1893	2·0	5·6	18·8	24·1	4·8	5·7	21·8	13·2	16·8	13·0	13·3	8·6	43·7	19·8
1894	2·3	5·1	18·9	22·4	6·2	4·6	23·5	14·5	17·1	13·0	12·9	7·4	43·5	19·8
1895	2·1	4·7	21·1	25·0	9·1	5·5	25·0	15·9	17·5	11·9	13·4	6·6	47·5	20·3
1896	1·9	4·2	21·7	25·6	9·0	6·9	21·3	19·9	19·2	12·3	16·4	6·7	50·1	20·7
1897	1·6	3·7	17·4	20·5	5·8	5·0	20·7	19·2	20·9	12·8	19·5	6·5	53·3	19·5
1898	1·4	3·1	21·4	21·4	7·8	5·8	19·8	19·0	21·5	13·9	20·8	7·5	51·4	20·5
1899	1·6	4·7	23·4	22·2	10·9	6·5	23·6	19·8	22·9	14·6	20·7	8·8	53·0	22·3
1900	1·8	4·7	28·4	25·3	13·1	7·4	23·8	23·5	23·5	14·8	22·2	9·7	53·6	25·9
1901	2·0	4·6	26·7	22·5	12·4	7·0	24·2	23·5	24·7	12·6	20·4	9·7	51·2	23·7
1902	2·3	4·3	29·2	22·7	14·0	6·1	19·7	21·5	26·5	12·6	23·6	12·4	50·6	22·3
1903	2·0	4·9	35·9	26·0	19·1	8·6	17·1	18·1	27·8	12·7	27·3	13·2	49·3	23·1
1904	2·2	5·4	41·4	30·1	23·0	11·6	23·6	19·8	27·5	13·5	23·1	12·8	51·1	21·7
1905 (*n*)	2·2	5·6	46·1	34·3	25·0	13·4	27·0	19·5	27·8	14·8	26·2	14·3	53·1	23·2
	---	---	---	---	---	---	---	---	---	---	---	---	---	---
	3·4	5·5	49·0	34·3	25·4	13·4	27·0	19·5	16·7	13·3	26·2	14·3	46·5	23·0
1906	3·8	5·6	47·4	45·1	23·9	19·9	29·3	22·8	18·0	15·1	28·7	16·1	47·1	28·5
1907	3·6	6·6	52·7	49·4	26·7	18·3	33·8	27·1	16·2	16·9	25·8	19·7	46·3	33·2
1908	3·8	5·5	60·7	41·0	36·0	16·9	29·1	25·7	16·2	14·8	24·8	14·7	41·9	31·4
1909	3·8	5·7	61·5	43·5	32·7	19·2	32·6	27·2	17·7	16·5	25·5	18·8	44·2	31·1
1910	6·3	6·1	65·9	54·6	29·0	19·7	38·6	31·1	19·2	17·8	26·2	23·6	44·3	33·5

1911	3·8	6·6	56·6	51·7	27·3	19·3	39·1	34·5	20·8	18·6	25·3	23·4	41·6	35·5
1912	5·3	6·8	70·3	54·7	40·8	21·3	36·1	38·3	23·6	19·6	27·7	28·2	45·5	37·5
1913	6·1	6·3	73·7	56·5	42·5	23·4	38·1	37·8	23·4	20·7	31·5	28·3	46·4	40·9
1914	7·1	5·6	66·2	34·3	37·2	15·1	36·9	37·1	16·1	13·3	32·4	21·1	37·8	35·1
1915	12·6	5·4	100·1	26·4	63·9	12·1	45·2	31·9	1·6	0·2	42·2	16·5	31·4	81·2
1916	18·4	5·9	91·8	35·5	51·6	14·6	36·2	39·1	1·3	0·3	60·5	22·1	26·6	107·6
1917	24·4	4·9	91·6	36·5	48·4	13·3	64·3	24·0	0·3	0·3	85·1	18·2	22·9	128·0
1918	31·0	4·2	121·2	44·7	63·0	17·7	45·4	28·1	0·2	0·1	125·3	15·3	35·0	144·5
1919	29·4	5·0	138·7	50·9	81·7	21·7	111·4	27·8	9·2	65·5	117·8	18·6	48·5	183·3
1920	41·0	15·6	201·9	112·1	128·0	43·8	112·3	68·3	44·9	68·5	97·4	49·9	75·8	175·7
													--- (q)	--- (q)
1921	13·1	7·7	112·2	60·3	68·4	28·1	68·1	48·4	32·9	29·3	63·8	21·9	53·0	57·1
1922	15·7	7·6	98·2	54·0	56·6	23·3	64·8	65·5	23·6	35·7	56·8	28·4	48·5	66·2
	---	---	---	---	---	---	---	---	---	---	---	---	---	---
1923 (r)	16·1	9·2	107·0	65·2	64·9	28·8	49·0	61·9	27·5	35·5	55·5	31·1	58·5	68·3
	---	---	---	---	---	---	---	---	---	---	---	---	---	---
1924	21·3	8·9	128·2	67·0	79·0	27·7	59·0	65·9	36·4	32·9	67·8	32·6	66·6	59·5
1925	22·3	8·6	120·9	74·1	68·9	29·7	72·6	64·0	35·6	28·9	72·6	32·2	65·0	54·2
1926	13·3	7·4	111·5	51·7	67·5	23·6	61·0	63·8	44·9	22·4	65·6	29·9	59·2	40·6
1927	16·8	8·2	122·7	66·1	76·5	27·6	52·7	63·7	46·5	23·3	57·4	32·3	63·4	42·1
1928	22·9	8·6	122·6	73·1	76·8	31·8	54·4	57·9	43·4	27·4	59·2	38·2	60·6	43·7
1929	18·4	8·6	129·3	73·4	82·4	29·7	55·6	56·3	44·0	28·6	48·4	38·6	56·5	49·2
1930	17·3	7·3	97·4	55·6	56·7	25·7	46·4	33·1	38·0	21·6	40·4	32·1	49·3	44·2
1931	13·2	5·8	82·7	30·4	52·7	15·1	45·7	15·2	33·2	14·6	34·9	22·7	40·9	42·0
1932	18·1	6·2	75·3	25·1	50·9	10·9	46·0	20·6	16·0	12·8	45·1	18·1	19·1	26·8
1933	19·2	6·2	67·9	30·9	41·7	13·3	48·6	22·1	12·9	12·9	48·4	19·3	19·1	25·8
1934	20·2	6·6	80·1	32·7	47·0	14·9	49·9	27·0	14·6	12·9	52·8	22·0	19·2	23·5
1935	22·5	6·8	73·8	32·5	44·0	15·6	54·3	30·0	15·5	13·1	58·2	23·6	21·6	23·5
1936	27·2	7·3	79·7	33·3	45·1	15·5	61·4	33·0	18·6	14·2	77·4	25·5	25·6	25·8
1937	33·7	8·7	97·9	43·1	59·8	20·4	71·7	38·3	22·7	17·0	92·0	30·1	25·6	30·0
1938	31·5	8·1	70·7	37·0	38·5	19·7	71·8	38·9	18·6	12·7	81·3	24·6	23·6	23·3
1939	32·9	7·2	77·8	36·8	46·8	20·6	62·0	33·1	18·8	10·5	82·1	24·3	26·9	20·6
1940	44·4	7·5	108·4	37·0	61·4	17·9	96·8	46·8	9·4	3·7	153·0	34·2	14·7	22·5
1941	71·6	6·8	88·8	29·9	52·2	15·6	46·4	38·2	..	—	193·8	39·5	0·1	—
1942	49·2	6·7	83·6	26·7	49·4	13·3	40·2	64·2	..	0·4	178·4	32·7	0·1	—
1943	57·6	6·5	98·6	22·7	58·3	9·6	32·8	44·4	..	—	284·9	31·7	..	—
1944	52·6	5·6	113·4	11·3	80·8	4·1	53·8	50·6	2·8	0·9	389·5	26·6	0·1	10·9
1945	50·4	7·0	87·9	17·6	47·6	6·5	52·8	49·8	3·1	48·4	323·3	27·8	2·1	39·7

See p. 515 for footnotes.

External Trade 16. *continued*

C. Computed Values (Imports and Re-exports 1854–70) and Declared Values, 1846–1980 – United Kingdom (*cont.*)

(in £ million)

	West Indies		Central and South America		Argentina		Australia		Belgium (*x*)		Canada		France	
	Imports	Exports	Imports	Exports	Imports	Exports	Imports	Exports	Imports	Exports	Imports	Exports	Imports	Exports
1946	74·7	14·0	127·1	55·6	66·7	20·9	67·4	55·5	14·7	30·7	201·3	34·3	14·2	38·8
1947	109·4	16·5	195·6	82·7	130·6	35·0	97·1	72·4	35·3	36·8	239·1	45·9	31·4	29·2
1948	122·9	25·6	194·3	122·6	121·8	52·8	168·9	145·3	38·2	42·4	223·4	74·5	45·9	44·6
1949	101·8	29·4	159·3	139·3	77·1	51·6	212·9	189·1	37·5	40·2	225·2	81·6	75·0	42·1
1950	124·5	37·9	210·9	156·2	95·6	38·9	219·7	256·8	42·5	58·0	180·2	128·4	109·8	55·3
1951	164·6	48·8	269·8	160·9	86·2	29·0	254·4	325·7	87·7	62·8	260·5	140·1	134·8	73·2
1952	129·0	54·8	142·4	154·5	53·1	21·6	226·7	221·8	92·0	60·8	319·7	132·4	86·9	72·1
1953	134·4	52·2	211·2	115·5	99·1	15·2	294·2	214·1	58·9	60·5	305·5	161·0	82·1	76·2
1954	117·3	58·4	211·7	123·4	81·1	23·8	235·9	279·2	52·8	60·1	272·8	135·6	97·1	73·7
1955	113·1	69·9	232·4	120·2	86·7	24·0	263·9	286·4	63·6	67·2	343·7	144·7	136·5	83·0
1956	126·7	82·9	254·4	137·3	91·6	17·6	236·1	241·2	72·9	73·3	347·5	182·3	112·2	102·0
1957	156·0	91·0	308·9	169·2	108·0	33·1	248·0	237·5	60·1	81·3	320·2	199·8	110·4	101·9
1958	113·1	96·6	278·9	145·9	104·4	32·9	199·1	237·4	61·7	64·2	308·6	193·6	100·5	81·1
1959	111·6	105·4	315·4	150·5	105·6	40·4	222·9	225·1	57·5	64·6	312·0	213·6	103·7	85·9
1960	113·1	93·2	304·1	177·8	97·7	42·1	197·2	262·2	68·2	68·3	374·9	220·6	131·9	97·6
1961	100·9	83·5	278·0	173·6	75·0	50·7	174·1	203·0	64·8	81·3	349·4	228·2	142·8	124·2
1962	92·9	80·6	299·2	167·7	93·2	47·1	185·2	230·7	72·5	96·6	348·9	194·3	131·3	152·3
1963	135·0	76·2	299·6	147·7	89·0	25·2	206·1	238·0	87·0	106·0	368·5	179·5	153·5	194·4
1964	121·3	89·5	294·6	149·9	78·2	28·0	250·2	257·6	95·5	117·8	452·0	192·8	184·2	200·4
1965	98·7	98·9	289·7	160·6	71·5	27·5	219·5	284·4	121·8	173·8	458·2	208·0	190·5	193·5
1966	95·6	93·5	286·9	169·5	70·6	23·3	207·9	258·0	128·8	186·0	425·0	223·5	212·3	213·0
1967	101·4	89·0	301·2	174·6	72·1	25·3	173·8	256·3	143·1	182·5	455·9	220·3	255·0	217·9
1968	103·5	110·7	324·4	230·8	51·7	33·8	210·8	319·4	168·7	240·8	512·8	266·2	311·9	253·1
1969	96·4	129·3	366·0	251·1	78·7	47·0	236·0	321·3	182·5	288·7	505·3	309·0	324·5	312·0
1970	91·6	150·7	334·8	283·0	65·5	44·0	260·2	345·8	193·1	288·5	682·2	288·2	368·2	339·1
1971	101·4	175·9	332·4	333·6	57·0	53·5	276·8	365·0	218·9	332·0	637·3	349·0	444·9	393·5
1972	106·8	160·6	346·8	337·9	76·5	51·4	283·1	317·9	308·5	386·8	604·4	379·8	603·4	511·5
1973	132·0	160·9	491·3	358·1	106·1	41·7	340·7	404·1	446·3 --- (*x*) 454·1	612·2 --- (*x*) 620·7	735·2	413·4	978·3	678·3
1974	184·2	189·3	660·3	486·2	93·3	49·2	311·1	598·9	728·1	835·5	981·3	487·9	1,345	914·0
1975	234·9	239·7	678·9	685·4	53·5	67·8	279·3	631·7	951·3	922·6	855·0	538·3	1,622	1,164
1976	263·3	279·0	755·2	756·3	91·1	63·7	387·2	687·6	1,300	1,400	1,160	628·7	2,090	1,709
1977	236·6	358·0	828·9	987·8	120·6	130·3	347·2	763·3	1,685	1,844	1,217	702·4	2,694	2,167
1978	267·1	497·1	848·6	959·5	153·2	114·6	349·7	854·3	1,829	2,200	1,086	739·2	3,215	2,523
1979	296·4	430·2	1,053	1,021	144·2	128·4	474·6	840·8	2,320	2,467	1,252	767·2	4,056	3,070
1980	374·2	448·2	1,069	1,064	114·2	172·9	484·7	816·5	2,593	2,624	1,399	758·9	3,897	3,660

(in £ million)

	Germany (v)		India (z)		Netherlands		New Zealand		Russia (aa)		South Africa (bb)		U.S.A.	
	Imports	Exports	Imports	Exports	Imports	Exports	Imports	Exports	Imports	Exports	Imports	Exports	Imports	Exports
1846	...	7·2	...	5·8	...	3·6	...	--	...	1·7	...	0·5	...	6·8
1847	...	6·8	...	4·8	...	3·0	...	0·1	...	1·8	...	0·7	...	11·0
1848	...	5·3	...	4·6	...	2·8	...	0·1	...	1·9	...	0·6	...	9·6
1849	...	6·1	...	6·2	...	3·5	...	0·1	...	1·6	...	0·5	...	12·0
1850	...	7·5	...	7·2	...	3·5	...	0·1	...	1·5	...	0·8	...	14·9
1851	...	7·7	...	7·0	...	3·5	...	0·2	...	1·3	...	0·8	...	14·4
1852	...	7·9	...	6·5	...	4·1	...	0·1	...	1·1	...	1·1	...	16·6
1853	...	8·2	...	7·3	...	4·5	...	0·2	...	1·2	...	1·2	...	23·7
1854	16·3	8·5 --- (b) 13·1	10·7	9·1 --- (b) 9·6	6·7	4·6 --- (b) 6·9	--	0·3 --- (b) 0·3	4·3	0·1 --- (b) 0·1	0·7	0·9 --- (b) 1·0	29·8	21·4 --- (b) 22·3
1855	16·3	15·4	12·7	10·4	6·5	7·2	--	0·3	0·5	—	0·9	0·8	25·7	18·1
1856	10·5	17·0	17·3	11·0	7·4	8·2	0·1	0·4	11·6	3·4	1·5	1·4	36·0	22·6
1857	13·5	17·9	18·7	12·2	7·2	8·9	0·2	0·4	13·4	5·0	1·8	1·9	33·6	20·1
1858	9·0	16·8	15·0	17·4	6·3	8·1	0·3	0·5	11·9	5·3	1·7	1·8	34·3	15·8
1859	10·5	16·1	15·2	20·8	6·7	8·2	0·3	0·7	13·5	6·3	1·7	2·0	34·3	24·4
1860	15·4	18·7	15·1	17·7	8·3	9·8	0·4	0·7	16·2	5·4	1·7	2·2	44·7	22·9
1861	13·2 --- (i) 14·1	19·2 --- (i) 19·4	22·0	17·1	7·7	11·0	0·5	1·0	12·8	5·8	1·4	2·1	49·4	11·0
1862	15·1	20·0	34·1	15·3	7·9	10·6	0·6	1·4	15·1	3·7	1·5	2·0	27·7	19·2
1863	14·4	23·2	48·4	20·8	8·7	12·7	0·7	2·2	12·4	5·3	1·9	1·6	19·6	19·7
1864	15·2	24·8	52·3	20·8	11·7	14·1	1·1	2·1	14·7	6·1	2·0	2·4	17·9	20·2
1865	16·6	28·2	37·4	18·8	12·4	15·0	1·3	1·7	17·4	6·2	2·4	1·8	21·6	25·2
1866	19·1	25·1	36·9	20·7	11·8	14·9	1·6	2·4	19·6	6·9	2·7	1·5	46·9	31·8
1867	18·9	29·9	25·5	22·8	10·8	14·9	1·7	1·6	22·3	7·3	2·7	2·0	41·0	24·1
1868	18·2	32·3	30·1	22·3	11·4	16·7	1·5	1·9	20·1	7·2	2·7	1·7	43·1	23·8
1869	18·4	32·1	33·2	18·5	12·7	17·4	1·6	2·0	16·7	9·7	2·7	1·6	42·6	26·8
1870	15·4	28·1	25·1	20·1	14·3	17·3	2·1	1·6	20·6	10·1	2·9	2·0	49·8	31·3
	---	---	---	---	---	---	---	---	---	---	---	---	---	---
1871 (j)	19·3	38·5	30·7	19·0	14·0	22·1	2·5	1·5	23·7	9·9	2·9	2·3	61·1	38·7
1872	19·2	43·2	33·7	19·5	13·1	24·3	2·7	2·5	24·3	9·5	3·7	4·0	54·7	45·9
1873	19·9	36·1	29·9	22·3	13·3	24·6	3·2	3·6	21·2	11·5	4·1	4·6	71·5	36·7
1874	19·9	35·1	31·2	25·4	14·5	21·3	3·5	4·7	20·9	11·9	4·3	4·7	73·9	32·2
1875	21·8	34·1	30·1	25·6	14·8	20·1	3·5	4·1	20·7	11·3	4·5	5·4	69·6	25·1

See p. 515 for footnotes.

External Trade 16. *continued*

C. Computed Values (Imports and Re-exports 1854–70) and Declared Values, 1846–1980 – United Kingdom (*cont.*)

(in £ million)

	Germany (*y*)		India (*z*)		Netherlands		New Zealand		Russia (*aa*)		South Africa (*bb*)		U.S.A.	
	Imports	Exports	Imports	Exports	Imports	Exports	Imports	Exports	Imports	Exports	Imports	Exports	Imports	Exports
1876	21.1	29.7	30.0	23.7	16.6	18.7	3.5	3.5	17.6	8.6	4.2	4.7	75.9	20.2
1877	26.3	29.0	31.2	26.6	19.9	16.0	3.7	3.6	22.1	6.2	4.3	4.5	77.8	19.9
1878	23.6	29.2	27.5	24.7	21.5	14.7	4.0	4.7	17.8	9.5	4.4	5.5	89.1	17.5
1879	21.6	29.6	24.7	22.7	22.0	15.5	4.5	3.8	15.9	10.6	4.6	6.4	91.8	25.5
1880	24.4	29.1	30.1	32.0	25.9	15.7	5.2	3.2	16.0	11.0	5.6	7.2	107.1	38.0
1881	23.7	29.3	32.6	31.1	23.0	15.3	5.1	4.1	14.1	9.3	5.4	7.7	103.2	36.8
1882	25.6	30.5	39.9	30.6	25.3	16.3	4.7	4.7	21.0	8.6	6.3	8.1	88.4	38.7
1883	27.9	31.8	38.9	33.4	25.1	15.9	5.8	4.2	21.0	7.6	5.9	5.0	99.3	36.7
1884	23.6	30.8	34.4	32.1	25.9	18.2	6.0	4.1	16.3	7.6	5.9	4.5	86.3	32.7
1885	23.1	27.1	31.9	30.9	25.0	15.8	5.1	4.4	17.7	6.2	4.5	4.2	86.5	31.1
1886	21.4	26.4	32.1	32.6	25.3	15.0	4.7	3.7	13.6	6.4	4.7	3.6	81.6	37.6
1887	24.6	27.2	30.5	32.1	25.3	15.1	5.7	3.4	16.0	6.9	5.1	5.5	83.0	40.2
1888	26.7	27.4	30.8	33.9	26.1	15.0	5.9	3.3	26.3	7.7	5.6	6.4	79.8	41.2
1889	27.1	31.3	36.2	32.4	26.7	16.2	6.8	3.6	27.2	8.6	6.1	9.8	95.5	43.9
1890	26.1	30.5	32.7	35.2	25.9	16.4	8.3	3.7	24.8	8.8	6.1	9.8	97.3	46.3
1891	27.0	29.9	32.2	32.5	27.3	15.0	8.2	3.8	24.1	8.2	6.3	8.6	104.4	41.1
1892	25.7	29.6	30.5	29.0	28.8	15.6	7.8	3.9	15.1	8.9	5.5	8.6	108.2	41.4
1893	26.4	28.0	26.2	29.9	28.9	15.7	8.1	3.7	18.6	10.4	5.6	9.4	91.8	45.7
1894	26.9	29.2	27.6	30.1	27.6	13.9	8.3	3.4	23.6	11.5	5.0	9.0	89.6	30.8
1895	27.0	32.7	26.4	25.5	28.4	11.3	8.4	3.4	24.7	10.7	5.4	11.5	86.5	44.1
1896	27.6	34.0	25.3	30.8	29.3	12.3	8.1	4.4	22.7	11.4	5.3	14.9	106.3	32.0
1897	26.2	32.0	24.8	28.0	29.0	13.3	8.6	4.5	22.3	11.9	5.0	14.4	113.0	37.9
1898	28.5	33.3	27.5	30.4	28.5	13.0	9.0	4.5	19.5	14.2	6.2	13.1	126.1	28.5
1899	30.1	38.0	27.7	32.0	30.5	14.0	9.7	4.9	18.7	16.1	6.1	12.2	120.1	36.0
1900	31.2	38.5	27.4	31.0	31.4	14.9	11.6	5.9	22.0	16.4	4.0	14.0	138.8	37.3
1901	32.2	34.2	27.4	35.7	32.9	13.7	10.6	6.1	21.9	14.2	5.1	18.9	141.0	37.7
1902	33.6	33.1	28.7	33.5	34.8	13.1	10.9	6.2	25.7	13.9	5.7	26.4	127.0	43.1
1903	34.5	34.5	32.3	35.3	35.0	14.0	13.5	7.0	30.9	16.2	5.8	27.0	122.1	41.6
1904	33.9	36.4	36.5	41.5	34.7	12.9	12.7	6.9	31.4	15.3	5.5	19.1	119.2	39.3
1905(*n*)	35.8	42.7	36.1	44.4	35.5	14.5	13.4	7.0	33.4	14.9	5.5	17.8	115.6	47.3
	---	---	---	---	---	---	---	---	---	---	---	---	---	---
	53.8	42.7	36.0	44.4	15.2	14.4	13.4	7.0	34.5	14.9	5.5	18.4	114.7	47.3

See p. 515 for footnotes.

															Republic of Ireland	
															Imports	Exports
1906	55.9	48.3	37.7	46.4	16.2	16.7	15.6	8.1	31.5	15.9	6.3	17.1	131.1	53.2	...	...
1907	57.2	56.7	43.9	53.2	16.1	18.9	17.8	9.4	32.9	19.1	8.6	15.5	134.3	58.1	...	...
1908	55.0	46.4	29.6	50.8	16.6	15.7	14.7	9.5	29.7	20.5	7.4	13.8	123.9	42.5	...	...
1909	57.8	47.2	35.4	44.7	16.8	16.2	17.7	8.1	38.0	18.3	9.8	15.9	118.4	59.3	...	...
1910	61.8	54.9	42.8	47.0	18.5	17.9	20.9	9.4	43.6	21.2	10.2	21.2	117.6	62.2	...	...
1911	65.3	57.4	45.4	53.9	18.7	17.8	17.9	10.6	43.2	22.3	9.7	21.9	122.7	56.1	...	...
1912	70.0	59.6	52.1	59.8	21.4	19.4	20.3	11.2	40.5	21.7	11.3	23.3	134.6	64.6	...	...
1913	80.4	60.5	48.4	71.7	23.6	20.5	20.3	11.8	40.3	27.7	12.3	24.0	141.7	59.5	...	...
1914	47.0	36.4	43.3	63.8	24.3	20.7	23.0	10.4	28.1	21.8	10.8	20.4	138.6	64.6	...	...
1915	0.2	—	62.2	46.9	23.4	30.5	30.4	10.1	21.4	24.9	11.0	19.9	237.8	56.5	...	...
1916	0.1	—	72.4	54.4	22.1	33.0	31.6	12.9	18.3	34.3	12.0	24.8	291.8	64.5	...	...
1917	..	—	66.8	60.7	19.9	24.8	29.1	7.4	17.9	52.7	11.4	20.0	376.3	60.1	...	...
1918	..	—	88.5	49.6	7.7	15.4	24.5	8.0	6.7	0.3	11.9	23.3	515.4	26.8	...	...
1919	1.0	23.2	108.2	71.9	21.7	60.6	52.7	9.9	16.4	17.5	22.8	19.9	541.6	65.5	...	...
1920	30.3	51.1	95.7	184.0	39.3	62.1	47.5	28.0	33.5	16.8	19.1	51.7	563.3	131.1	...	...
	--- (q)	--- (q)							--- (q)	--- (q)						
1921	20.5	40.7	44.3	111.4	38.8	36.5	48.7	15.5	2.7	3.4	18.7	31.0	274.8	64.3	...	...
1922	26.5	49.1	47.7	93.4	34.1	40.6	48.5	16.8	8.1	4.6	16.0	25.6	221.8	77.3	...	...
	---	---	---	---	---	---	---	---	---	---	---	---	---	---		
1923 (r)	35.0	60.9	67.0	87.3	37.1	35.3	43.0	21.7	9.3	4.5	15.3	29.2	210.7	85.6	[32.7](cc)	[31.2](cc)
	---	---	---	---	---	---	---	---	---	---	---	---	---	---		
1924	36.9	61.5	78.9	91.7	42.7	32.5	47.0	21.4	19.8	11.1	18.0	31.9	241.2	78.6	51.1	58.5
1925	48.4	71.5	80.1	87.2	45.6	31.7	51.3	24.2	25.3	19.3	25.1	32.2	245.3	83.2	43.4	51.2
1926	72.6	47.3	57.6	83.2	50.3	22.6	46.8	21.4	24.1	14.4	18.8	33.6	228.9	75.0	40.9	45.2
1927	59.9	69.4	65.8	86.3	44.5	26.0	46.5	20.4	21.1	11.3	21.3	31.8	200.2	66.9	43.2	45.6
1928	63.7	67.3	64.5	85.1	42.9	26.6	47.3	20.1	21.6	4.8	24.1	33.1	188.4	68.7	45.1	44.7
1929	68.8	60.2	62.8	79.4	42.4	27.0	47.7	22.2	26.5	6.5	24.3	34.1	196.0	62.0	45.1	46.3
1930	65.5	44.1	51.0	54.2	39.5	23.0	44.9	18.6	34.2	9.3	20.2	27.7	153.5	39.9	43.0	44.3
1931	64.2	32.0	36.7	33.1	35.2	16.7	37.8	11.7	32.3	9.2	13.1	22.9	104.0	26.2	36.5	39.0
1932	30.5	25.4	32.3	34.7	22.0	14.5	37.0	10.6	19.6	10.6	15.4	18.6	83.6	20.8	26.5	31.9
1933	29.8	24.6	37.4	34.1	18.6	14.3	37.2	9.8	17.5	4.3	14.4	24.0	75.8	26.2	17.8	23.7
1934	30.6	22.9	42.1	37.2	20.9	14.1	40.4	11.7	17.3	7.5	11.9	30.8	82.0	23.2	17.2	24.8
1935	31.8	28.1	41.2	38.5	23.1	14.0	38.1	13.6	21.8	9.7	13.7	34.3	87.5	30.1	18.8	25.2

See p. 515 for footnotes.

External Trade 16. *continued*

C. Computed Values (Imports and Re-exports 1854–70) and Declared Values, 1846–1980 – United Kingdom (*cont.*)

(in £ million)

	Germany (*v*)		India (*z*)		Netherlands		New Zealand		Russia (*aa*)		South Africa (*bb*)		U.S.A.		Republic of Ireland	
	Imports	Exports	Imports	Exports	Imports	Exports	Imports	Exports	Imports	Exports	Imports	Exports	Imports	Exports	Imports	Exports
1936	35·3	27·9	51·9	34·6	25·1	14·3	43·6	17·6	18·9	13·3	13·6	38·2	93·2	36·8	20·4	26·0
1937	38·8	31·4	64·7 --- (*z*) 58·2	39·6 --- (*z*) 36·3	32·0	17·1	49·9	20·6	29·1	19·5	17·9	42·2	114·1	42·3	21·1	27·3
1938	31·9	28·5	49·9	34·3	29·3	14·8	46·9	19·5	19·5	17·4	14·6	40·1	118·0	28·8	23·0	26·0
1939	19·4	16·2	48·5	30·2	30·2	15·1	41·8	16·2	8·2	7·7	15·9	36·8	117·3	36·5	25·3	28·4
1940	..	—	72·9	33·7	11·8	6·9	55·8	16·7	1·3 --- (*aa*) 1·9	1·0 --- (*aa*) 1·3		38·6	275·3	37·9	31·7	28·6
1941	..	—	57·3	32·0	..	—	56·4	14·8	1·2	29·3	15·9	40·4	409·0	32·8	32·1	20·8
1942	..	—	60·2	22·3	..	—	60·3	25·0	3·2	74·5	16·6	38·2	535·6	26·3	34·0	19·5
1943	..	—	60·1	17·6	—	0·3	49·8	19·6	1·8	58·9	14·4	31·7	1,104	25·4	28·4	13·2
1944	..	—	69·5	23·6	..	0·5	57·2	17·2	2·1	56·2	18·5	28·5	1,391	22·9	30·8	13·8
1945	2·1	2·9	67·6	33·4	1·3	9·8	62·9	14·9	3·8	29·6	15·7	37·2	610·3	22·6	35·0	21·2
1946	6·4	23·7	69·0	80·3	11·6	35·7	74·4	28·0	5·0	11·1	15·3	75·5	229·6(*dd*)	39·7(*dd*)	37·1	43·5
1947	19·3	28·0	94·7	92·1	26·2	33·0	90·0	43·3	7·5	14·4	26·3	92·2	297·2	61·3	35·1	59·5
1948	29·6	31·1	107·6 --- (*z*) 96·3	114·5 --- (*z*) 96·4	44·3	48·4	108·7	52·6	27·1	7·1	31·7	120·8	183·2	70·7	43·3	79·2
1949	37·6	33·6	99·0	117·4	65·4	55·9	117·1	64·8	16·1	10·3	33·4	125·2	222·1	62·5	55·5	79·7
1950	41·6	55·6	98·3	97·2	85·8	76·4	133·9	86·7	34·2	14·2	51·7	121·5	211·4	127·3	62·5	90·2
1951	77·7 --- (*v*) 74·8	60·8 --- (*v*) 60·2	152·6	115·9	128·1	80·4	164·7	111·2	60·1	24·2	59·9	166·9	380·0	154·6	70·0	102·1
1952	90·1	63·6	114·7	113·2	102·3	78·4	165·7	115·7	58·1	37·5	64·2	145·9	314·6	181·1	90·6	93·1
1953	69·8	76·2	113·4	115·2	88·9	100·2	169·8	100·7	39·9	12·3	71·9	159·1	252·7	172·1	104·8	97·3
1954	77·6	87·4	148·4	115·2	109·6	106·3	176·0	126·6	41·8	14·7	84·3	157·4	282·4	160·8	103·3	105·3
1955	91·3	95·6	159·0	131·4	132·9	113·8	179·9	140·1	62·6	31·9	80·5	168·1	420·0	198·8	97·3	113·9
1956	109·9	111·4	141·4	169·8	137·3	127·0	197·0	127·8	55·1	55·9	90·9	155·6	408·0	259·1	89·7	108·8
1957	124·6	123·8	157·5	177·6	131·8	122·6	183·1	140·6	70·5	51·7	92·7	174·3	482·5	258·9	109·4	110·4
1958	136·0	140·7	139·4	161·8	159·3	105·4	160·5	129·0	59·5	52·0	90·4	187·5	351·7	293·6	108·8	116·4
1959	144·3	162·8	142·6	172·7	160·0	120·9	182·9	98·4	63·1	34·8	89·3	150·8	370·7	382·1	103·8	114·8
1960	181·5	184·1	148·5	151·8	180·3	123·0	183·0	121·6	74·9	53·3	96·4	155·9	565·8	342·7	121·9	118·3

See p. 515 for footnotes.

1961	194·3	193·0	144·9	152·9	172·5	144·1	159·6	124·7	85·0	69·5	103·3	148·7	484·4	298·1	145·8	139·5
1962	193·6	224·9	135·9	118·2	197·1	158·2	160·4	107·9	84·2	57·5	103·1	148·4	476·4	347·5	138·8	142·0
1963	208·3	240·3	140·7	138·0	208·7	175·4	173·1	116·0	90·8	63·9	115·0	197·8	498·4	360·5	151·8	156·5
1964	265·8	245·7	140·7	128·3	235·0	199·8	207·8	117·8	90·1	39·7	126·6	224·4	639·1	378·7	170·4	173·8
1965	265·4	285·4	128·3	116·4	270·8	203·0	208·2	126·1	118·8	47·4	191·4	265·3	671·4	514·7	170·4	185·7
1966	301·9	289·0	119·1	96·7	291·1	207·1	187·0	127·6	125·4	50·4	180·9	246·7	720·2	646·8	186·1	189·4
1967	338·9	276·7	125·7	83·3	328·7	205·6	185·9	100·0	123·5	64·2	219·6	261·5	803·0	634·9	223·6	196·6
1968	435·8	362·7	135·0	72·8	393·0	255·5	196·6	103·8	158·1	104·7	271·7	264·9	1,055	902·7	268·7	272·9
1969	466·1	415·6	107·0	66·4	408·0	297·3	215·7	121·3	196·2	95·2	302·2	290·8	1,124	897·3	293·4	329·6
1970	549·0	502·8	105·3	72·9	458·7	377·1	203·2	129·0	210·5	102·4	258·4	332·2	1,170	933·3	341·4	381·1
1971	647·0	534·3	111·2	138·4	508·1	409·4	227·5	146·1	199·5	88·8	241·1	395·0	1,091	1,082	507·2	501·2
1972	840·6	589·1	112·2	140·9	614·3	451·4	251·6	146·6	218·6	90·3	291·6	308·3	1,171	1,208	444·7	469·4
1973	1,351	785·2	147·5	132·9	910·8	603·7	276·1	167·2	327·0	97·4	399·2	374·3	1,610	1,513	526·9	625·5
1974	1,894	1,010	201·8	126·8	1,631	981·7	242·3	255·5	388·1	109·7	466·0	525·0	2,234	1,756	806·8	819·9
1975	2,001	1,303	235·4	164·7	1,861	1,114	266·8	253·6	391·2	210·7	630·5	684·3	2,329	1,776	922·1	907·0
1976	2,755	1,834	355·1	206·8	2,425	1,499	320·9	251·2	645·1	240·2	612·4	645·3	3,043	2,448	1,006	1,246
1977	3,609	2,527	387·0	277·9	2,524	2,178	383·8	289·9	787·6	347·1	881·0	586·1	3,710	3,095	1,300	1,648
1978	4,511	3,103	322·1	348·4	2,523	2,255	434·1	267·8	692·2	422·9	764·3	666·2	4,220	3,524	1,605	2,042
1979	5,801	4,235	365·5	455·8	3,445	3,064	415·9	312·1	828·7	416·2	533·3	717·6	4,914	4,049	1,686	2,554
1980	5,689	5,109	318·0	529·2	3,398	3,842	409·0	251·1	787·4	452·1	756·6	1,002	6,029	4,687	1,780	2,662

See p. 515 for footnotes.

External Trade 16. *continued*

C. Computed Values (Imports and Re-exports 1854–70) and Declared values, 1846–1980 – United Kingdom (*cont.*)

(in £ million)

	Iran		Italy		Japan		Saudi Arabia	
	Imports	Exports	Imports	Exports	Imports	Exports	Imports	Exports
1946	21·0	12·0	19·1	11·2	0·1	--	...	...
1947	16·0	16·0	25·1	9·2	5·2	0·1	1·4	0·8
1948	36·1	24·6	30·2	15·7	5·3	0·4	5·3	1·6
1949	34·5	31·0	37·5	21·3	10·8	1·2	6·8	3·5
1950	47·8	30·3	51·3	32·6	7·9	2·9	8·2	2·9
1951	33·0	19·5	83·1	36·0	17·7	9·8	37·3	3·7
1952	3·0	5·6	45·5	54·6	29·0	9·4	35·6	7·4
1953	2·6	4·7	43·0	66·0	9·3	18·3	2·2	6·0
1954	3·3	8·3	52·4	63·3	15·5	12·0	1·8	5·7
1955	16·8	18·1	55·3	62·4	23·9	14·4	3·2	4·9
1956	34·1	26·7	57·4	64·1	24·2	23·9	5·0	9·1
1957	35·5	35·9	62·7	76·2	24·2	29·0	5·5	7·6
1958	56·2	38·9	76·9	70·7	35·3	20·2	7·5	8·0
1959	56·9	38·5	92·8	77·3	43·1	33·2	5·4	7·0
1960	48·6	36·6	98·7	93·7	42·0	29·2	9·8	6·3
1961	48·9	33·8	102·1	122·9	39·2	43·1	13·1	6·8
1962	35·4	28·7	112·6	148·5	53·2	44·9	20·5	8·9
1963	34·5	28·3	109·9	175·3	52·7	51·2	13·2	9·7
1964	39·7	27·9	131·9	139·9	73·2	58·3	12·2	13·9
1965	38·2	39·6	166·2	148·0	77·1	69·0	39·7	20·9
1966	41·0	38·3	144·6	123·1	78·2	52·9	26·1	12·8
1967	136·7	43·3	195·1	157·6	91·0	87·4	62·5	16·2
1968	90·7	61·0	235·8	177·9	115·2	98·4	68·7	47·0
1969	73·2	71·6	222·5	209·6	104·5	128·5	85·4	56·9
1970	76·3	66·2	249·0	240·0	134·6	147·8	104·8	35·3
1971	109·5	78·5	282·2	249·2	201·5	156·5	174·0	39·0
1972	124·2	116·9	353·1	283·9	315·0	171·5	183·7	45·2
1973	236·3	169·4	506·6	386·0	443·4	272·6	317·7	58·5
1974	511·6	279·1	721·6	509·7	569·7	319·0	1,184	119·6
1975	701·2	494·7	807·1	563·0	672·8	309·5	857·0	199·7
1976	1,047	513·1	1,104	825·4	795·8	359·5	977·8	399·5
1977	789·0	659·0	1,544	986·6	1,061	470·9	1,132	601·1
1978	527·8	752·0	1,931	1,123	1,283	541·8	870·5	785·7
1979	242·8	231·8	2,485	1,469	1,488	606·2	1,115	893·0
1980	107·2	392·7	2,299	1,900	1,710	598·0	1,915	1,049

(*a*) Comprises Denmark, the Faroe Islands, Iceland, Norway, Russia, and Sweden initially, and later, Finland and the Baltic republics.

(*b*) Comprises Belgium, France and the Netherlands initially, and Luxembourg and Switzerland when the consignments series begins.

(*c*) Comprises the German states, Austria-Hungary, and Wallachia and Moldavia, initially, and later, states created out of these territories. Changes in composition are noted in (*i*), (*k*), and (*o*) below.

(*d*) Comprises Algeria, Gibraltar, Greece, the Ionian Islands, the Italian States, Malta, Morocco, Portugal, Spain, Tripoli, and Tunis, initially. From 1946 (2nd line) Italy and Portugal are no longer included, but the Canary Isles are. Other changes in composition are noted in (*i*), (*l*), (*m*), and (*o*) below.

(*e*) Comprises Aden, Persia, and all Turkish territories except Wallachia and Moldavia, initially (including Serbia and Egypt but not the remainder of North Africa); and later, states created out of these territories, other than those noted in (*k*) below. Other changes in composition are noted in (*f*), (*l*), (*m*) and (*o*) below.

(*f*) Comprises the whole of Africa other than the Mediterranean coastal states and Morocco, together with islands off the African Coast from Cape Verde southwards and in the Indian Ocean.

(*g*) Comprises Asia east of Iran. Islands in the Pacific Ocean east of Okinawa, the Philippines, and Indonesia are not included.

(*h*) See note 2 above.

(*i*) Schleswig-Holstein is recorded with Germany rather than Denmark, and hence with Central and South-East Europe, from 1861 (2nd line), and Venetia is recorded with Italy rather than Austria-Hungary, and hence with Southern Europe and North Africa from the same time.

(*j*) Imports and re-exports are recorded at official computed rather than declared values prior to 1871.

(*k*) Bulgaria, Montenegro, and Serbia were recorded separately from Turkey, and are included in Central and South-East Europe from 1881 (2nd line).

(*l*) Cyprus was recorded separately from Turkey and is included in Central and South-East Europe from 1892 (2nd line).

(*m*) Crete was recorded separately from Turkey and is included in Central and South-East Europe from 1899 (2nd line).

(*n*) See note 3 above.

(*o*) In 1913 all the Balkan states were enlarged and Albania was created out of Turkish territory. There resulted some small but unascertainable transfer of trade to both Central and South-East Europe and to Southern Europe and North Africa.

(*p*) Sudan was recorded separately from Egypt and is transferred from Turkey and the Middle East to the Remainder of Africa from 1914 (2nd line).

(*q*) The boundary changes following the First World War were used in the British trade statistics from 1921.

(*r*) Southern Irish trade is excluded from 1 April 1923.

(*s*) Comprises Belgium, France, Germany, Italy, Luxembourg, and the Netherlands initially. East Germany is excluded from 1951. Denmark, the Faroe Islands, and the Republic of Ireland are included from 1973 (2nd line). Greece is not included.

(*t*) Comprises Austria, Denmark (including the Faroe Islands and Greenland), Liechtenstein, Norway (including Spitzbergen), Portugal (including Azores and Madeira), Sweden, and Switzerland, initially. Denmark and its possessions are excluded from 1973 (2nd line).

(*u*) Comprises Albania, Bulgaria, Czechoslovakia, Hungary, Poland, Romania, the Soviet Union, Yugoslavia, and from 1951 (2nd line) East Germany.

(*v*) Exports to British Guiana and British Honduras are included in West Indies to 1854 and in Central and South America subsequently.

(*w*) i.e. modern Canada, including Labrador and Newfoundland.

(*x*) Including Luxembourg from 1973 (2nd line).

(*y*) The states which formed the German Empire initially. Statistics from 1951 (2nd line) relate to West Germany only.

(*z*) British India to 1948 (1st line), including Burma to 1937 (1st line). Pakistan is not included.

(*aa*) The Russian Empire followed by the Soviet Union. The Baltic republics and Bessarabia are included from 1940 (2nd line).

(*bb*) Cape Province and Natal until the consignments series begins. South-West Africa is not included.

(*cc*) April–December only.

(*dd*) Alaska and Hawaii are included from 1946.

External Trade 17. Values at Current Prices of External Trade According to Principal Countries – Republic of Ireland 1924–80

NOTES

[1] SOURCES: *Statistical Abstract of Ireland*.

[2] Exports include re-exports.

[3] Imports were recorded by country of consignment to 1936 (1st line) and by country of origin subsequently.

(in £ million)

	Belgium		Canada		France		Germany		Great Britain		Netherlands		Northern Ireland		U.S.A.	
	Imports	Exports	Imports	Exports	Imports	Exports	Imports	Exports	Imports	Exports	Imports	Exports	Imports	Exports	Imports	Exports
1924	0·6	0·2	1·4		0·4	0·1	0·7	0·1	48·0	43·1	0·8	..	7·9	7·5	3·7	0·2
1925	0·5	0·2	1·4		0·4	0·1	0·9	0·1	44·2	36·7	0·7	0·1	6·8	6·5	3·2	0·3
1926	1·0	0·1	1·2		0·5	0·1	2·3	0·2	39·9	34·9	0·9	0·1	6·5	5·7	5·0	0·3
1927	0·7	0·1	1·2		0·4	0·1	1·5	0·4	40·6	37·8	0·7	0·1	6·4	5·1	4·7	0·5
1928	0·7	0·2	1·0	0·1	0·4	0·1	1·8	0·3	40·5	39·2	0·7	0·1	6·2	5·3	3·8	0·3
1929	0·7	0·2	0·8	0·1	0·4	0·2	1·6	0·7	41·8	38·9	0·6	0·1	6·1	5·2	4·8	1·0
1930	0·7	0·1	0·8	0·1	0·4	0·2	1·3	0·7	39·7	36·2	0·6	0·1	5·8	4·8	3·9	1·2
1931	0·7	0·1	0·7	..	0·4	0·1	1·2	0·1	35·7	31·1	0·4	0·1	5·0	3·9	2·0	0·4
1932	0·7	0·2	0·8	..	0·2	0·1	1·3	0·1	28·9	22·3	0·4	..	3·8	3·0	1·3	0·1
1933	0·9	0·2	1·1	..	0·2	0·1	1·8	0·2	22·9	15·6	0·5	..	2·1	2·2	1·1	0·2
1934	1·1	0·3	1·1	..	0·3	0·1	2·3	0·2	24·1	14·5	0·8	..	2·0	2·3	1·9	0·1
1935	1·1	0·2	0·9	..	0·3	0·1	1·3	0·5	25·3	16·2	0·6	0·1	1·8	2·0	1·4	0·2
	1·3		1·1		0·3		1·3		26·6		0·7		1·6		1·9	
1936	--- (a)	0·2	--- (a)	..	--- (a)	..	--- (a)	0·6	--- (a)	18·3	--- (a)	0·1	--- (a)	2·3	--- (a)	0·3
	1·2		1·6		0·5		1·4		20·7		0·5		0·5		3·1	
1937	1·2	0·2	1·9	0·1	0·4	..	1·4	0·8	21·5	18·6	0·5	0·1	0·6	2·2	2·9	0·2
1938	1·0	0·1	1·6	..	0·6	0·1	1·5	0·9	20·3	19·9	0·5	0·1	0·6	2·5	4·7	0·1
1939	0·5	0·1	1·5	0·1	0·7	..	1·0	0·6	23·4	22·5	0·5	0·1	0·8	2·7	3·6	0·3
1940	0·5	0·2	3·3	0·2	0·4	0·1	..	—	24·2	28·3	0·3	0·2	0·6	3·4	4·1	0·5
1941	0·3	—	1·6	0·1	..	—	..	—	20·6	27·5	..	—	0·6	3·4	2·3	0·7
1942	..	—	4·6	0·1	..	—	..	—	18·8	27·1	..	—	1·0	5·1	3·0	0·3
1943	..	—	2·6	..	..	—	..	—	12·9	22·6	..	—	0·5	4·9	3·6	0·3
1944	..	—	5·0	..	..	—	..	—	12·6	23·8	..	—	0·8	5·7	3·0	0·3
1945	..	0·2	5·5	..	0·1	0·1	..	—	18·6	27·9	..	—	0·9	6·9	4·0	0·4
1946	0·9	0·5	2·9	..	0·9	0·2	0·1	..	36·0	28·9	0·7	0·8	1·6	7·2	8·5	0·6
1947	2·9	1·8	5·7	..	2·1	0·2	..	..	52·3	27·4	2·9	1·0	7·5	7·5	29·3	0·3
1948	2·6	1·5	2·9	..	1·1	0·2	0·2	0·1	71·2	35·5	2·2	1·8	2·2	7·6	11·4	0·4
							--- (b)	--- (b)								
1949	2·0	1·3	3·0	0·1	1·8	0·2	0·5	0·4	72·3	46·1	3·2	1·4	2·3	8·4	18·5	0·5
1950	2·3	0·5	6·0	0·1	2·5	0·6	1·9	1·5	82·0	54·3	2·9	2·0	2·4	8·5	20·8	1·3
1951	4·5	1·1	8·8	0·4	3·0	0·9	4·6	1·2	93·0	57·7	5·1	1·2	2·7	10·8	25·5	3·2
1952	3·7	1·5	10·9	0·3	2·1	1·4	5·4	0·9	85·1	73·2	6·4	1·7	2·6	14·3	18·5	3·2
1953	3·6	1·2	5·7	0·4	3·3	0·5	5·3	0·9	90·1	86·1	8·7	0·6	2·4	17·3	16·5	2·4

1954	3·0	1·5	3·9	0·6	3·4	0·4	7·3	1·8	97·4	85·6	5·3	0·7	2·7	16·6	12·2	2·2
1955	3·8	1·6	6·8	0·3	3·1	0·8	9·6	1·5	107·5	81·4	5·3	0·6	3·1	15·3	17·8	3·0
1956	3·0	1·9	4·6	0·4	2·4	3·5	8·0	2·3	101·4	67·6	4·8	1·8	3·4	14·8	13·7	3·2
1957	3·6	1·6	3·8	0·8	3·1	1·9	7·0	3·3	96·0	79·0	4·6	1·0	8·6	22·3	10·7	4·0
1958	3·5	1·0	5·9	0·9	3·2	1·0	8·0	2·8	103·5	79·8	5·7	0·7	8·4	21·1	14·0	7·5
1959	3·9	0·9	5·6	1·3	3·5	1·2	10·5	3·5	100·8	77·4	6·3	1·1	8·9	19·0	14·0	9·8
1960	4·5	1·2	4·7	1·2	4·6	1·2	12·0	3·7	104·6	92·3	6·0	1·1	7·4	20·3	18·6	11·2
1961	5·6	1·4	6·3	1·6	5·5	1·2	14·5	5·6	118·7	110·8	6·9	2·1	13·7	23·1	20·0	13·0
1962	5·9	1·0	6·0	1·7	7·0	1·5	18·6	5·3	125·2	104·8	8·1	1·8	11·2	22·7	20·9	14·1
1963	5·7	1·4	7·4	3·2	7·4	2·9	20·2	5·8	141·8	111·4	10·1	2·0	14·3	29·6	18·4	14·0
1964	7·6	3·6	7·6	1·7	7·5	4·4	23·8	9·0	161·8	129·1	10·7	5·0	16·0	29·4	26·8	10·0
1965	7·1	2·0	9·7	2·3	10·7	5·7	24·0	11·8	173·5	127·3	10·1	6·9	14·6	26·5	29·8	8·8
1966	5·3	3·9	9·8	2·2	8·2	7·2	22·0	9·5	179·2	140·8	9·9	4·9	13·9	28·5	34·5	17·0
			9·0	3·1					179·4	170·4					31·6	26·1
1967	5·8	4·3	--- (c)	--- (c)	9·2	6·7	24·8	6·9	--- (c)	--- (c)	12·0	4·9	17·5	35·1	--- (c)	---(c)
			9·0	4·0					182·6	177·0					33·8	42·9
1968	6·7	5·2	9·4	5·0	15·1	10·0	36·3	8·1	236·7	194·9	14·7	4·6	20·9	43·0	38·3	49·0
1969	7·6	5·1	9·0	5·4	16·8	13·3	43·4	10·8	289·2	200·6	14·2	7·3	25·4	50·1	54·7	56·8
1970	9·6	7·1	10·5	6·9	21·1	13·5	46·0	12·7	322·4	235·3	17·5	9·6	30·2	57·2	48·9	60·0
1971	9·9	5·9	10·1	7·1	22·1	12·8	55·3	14·1	347·9	289·4	20·9	8·0	25·8	65·8	65·5	59·9
1972	11·8	17·0	10·3	8·4	28·5	26·0	63·7	29·8	396·6	327·1	25·2	17·3	30·9	66·9	62·5	61·1
1973	20·2	27·8	12·4	11·3	52·3	45·5	93·1	54·0	534·1	393·1	36·7	37·8	42·6	82·2	78·2	86·1
1974	35·1	36·5	24·4	16·4	87·5	35·7	126·2	66·5	706·0	529·7	55·6	46·3	51·7	104·7	105·1	109·3
1975	30·7	53·0	17·6	16·8	85·9	63·5	119·6	114·5	768·3	628·1	54·8	85·6	64·4	153·5	122·4	90·8
1976	45·4	83·1	30·1	20·9	109·9	94·7	160·8	161·0	1,067·1	743·1	74·4	109·9	84·1	161·9	199·8	139·0
1977	59·6	112·6	35·7	26·2	148·3	186·8	202·0	216·4	1,362·7	992·5	94·6	143·3	126·2	190·3	274·9	156·5
1978	69·9	150·8	32·6	31·5	189·9	263·9	265·5	247·6	1,673·8	1,151·4	101·6	149·5	161·6	248·3	312·4	182·6
1979	103·5	204·5	46·6	35·7	248·2	282·7	360·9	304·9	2,202·2	1,358·7	150·9	185·8	212·1	266·5	411·0	166·8
1980	108·1	207·8	73·6	52·9	283·7	319·6	374·3	398·9	2,531·2	1,463·4	151·9	225·3	223·5	300·4	474·2	216·5

(a) See note 3 above.
(b) Subsequent statistics relate to West Germany only.

(c) Trade through Shannon Free Airport is included from 1968. Comparable figures for 1967 are shown for those countries for which the changes were made retrospectively.

External Trade 18. Indices of the Volume of External Trade – United Kingdom 1796–1980

NOTE TO PART A

SOURCE: A. H. Imlah, *Economic Elements in the Pax Britannica* (Cambridge, Mass., Harvard University Press, 1958), pp. 94–8 and 205–7. The original figures have been rounded.

A. Imlah's Index, 1796–1913. (1880 = 100)

	Total Imports	Re-exports	Net Imports	Exports
1796	6	9	5	4
1797	5	9	4	4
1798	7	10	6	4
1799	7	9	7	5
1800	8	14	7	5
1801	8	12	8	5
1802	8	15	7	5
1803	7	9	7	4
1804	8	10	7	5
1805	8	9	8	5
1806	7	9	7	5
1807	7	8	7	5
1808	7	6	7	4
1809	8	13	7	6
1810	10	12	10	6
1811	7	7	7	4
1812	7	10	6	5
1813	...	...	...	...
1814	8	19	6	6
1815	9	16	7	8
1816	10	14	6	7
1817	8	10	8	7
1818	10	11	10	8
1819	9	11	8	6
1820	9	11	8	7
1821	8	12	8	7
1822	8	10	8	8
1823	10	10	10	8
1824	10	11	10	9
1825	13	11	13	8
1826	11	12	11	8
1827	12	11	13	10
1828	13	11	13	10
1829	12	12	13	10
1830	13	11	14	11
1831	14	12	15	11
1832	12	14	12	12
1833	13	12	13	13
1834	14	14	14	13
1835	14	16	14	14
1836	17	15	17	15
1837	16	16	15	13
1838	17	16	18	16
1839	18	15	19	17
1840	19	16	19	18
1841	19	18	19	19
1842	18	15	18	19
1843	18	16	18	21
1844	20	17	21	23
1845	22	19	23	23
1846	22	18	22	22
1847	27	22	28	22
1848	25	20	26	22
1849	29	28	29	28
1850	28	24	29	32
1851	30	25	31	34
1852	29	26	30	36
1853	35	30	35	41
1854	33	32	34	40
1855	31	35	30	40
1856	36	35	36	48
1857	36	33	37	49
1858	37	36	37	48
1859	39	39	39	52
1860	45	43	45	55
1861	47	51	46	51
1862	48	50	48	48
1863	49	54	48	51
1864	49	55	48	51
1865	52	61	50	55
1866	56	60	56	61
1867	56	60	55	62
1868	60	67	58	66
1869	62	66	61	70
1870	65	67	64	76
1871	75	89	72	85
1872	75	82	74	88
1873	78	78	79	85
1874	80	82	80	84
1875	85	87	84	84
1876	87	86	88	81
1877	90	82	91	84
1878	90	85	91	84
1879	93	94	93	89
1880	100	100	100	100
1881	98	103	97	110
1882	103	109	102	111
1883	109	114	108	114
1884	105	115	103	115
1885	106	111	105	109
1886	107	118	105	114
1887	112	120	111	119
1888	118	133	115	127
1889	128	137	126	132
1890	127	132	127	134
1891	131	127	132	127

A. Imlah's Index, 1796–1913. (1880 = 100) (*cont.*)

	Total Imports	Re-exports	Net Imports	Exports
1892	133	139	132	122
1893	130	126	130	117
1894	140	131	142	122
1895	148	139	149	133
1896	155	129	160	140
1897	159	140	163	138
1898	164	139	169	137
1899	166	143	170	146(*a*)
1900	166	128	173	140
1901	171	141	177	141
1902	175	138	182	150
1903	177	142	184	154
1904	179	141	186	157
1905	182	152	188	173
1906	187	153	193	186
1907	190	161	196	201
1908	182	148	189	185
1909	189	163	194	193
1910	193	166	198	210
1911	199	171	204	218
1912	214	183	219	230
1913	220	183	227	239

(*a*) New ships included from 1900 onwards. In constructing the index the estimated value of new ships in 1880 was added to the recorded export volume of that base year.

NOTE TO PART B

SOURCE: This index was supplied by the statistician of the London and Cambridge Economic Service. It is based on statistics of volume appearing in the *Board of Trade Journal*.

B. L.C.E.S. Index 1913–47 (1938 = 100)

	Total Imports	Re-exports	Net Imports	Exports
1913	87	165	81	173
1919	77	129	73	95
1920	77	148	72	123
1921	65	129	60	86
1922	74	133	70	119
1923	81	141	77	129
1924	90	159	86	132
1925	93	155	89	130
1926	96	135	93	117
1927	99	141	96	134
1928	96	137	93	137
1929	101	132	99	141
1930	98	126	96	115
1931	100	120	99	88
1932	88	106	86	88
1933	88	99	87	89
1934	92	90	92	95
1935	93	103	92	102
1936	99	102	99	104
1937	105	106	105	113
1938	100	100	100	100
1946	67	40	69	99
1947	75	45	77	108

NOTES TO PART C

[1] SOURCE: *Abstract*.

[2] The export figures relate to domestic exports up to and including the index based on 1961.

[3] All indices are base year weighted, except the 1938 = 100 one, which is weighted by 1947 values.

C. Official Indices 1938–80

	Imports	Exports
1938 = 100		
1938	100	100
1947	70	99
1950 = 100		
1947	89	62
1948	93	78
1949	100	86
1950	100	100
1951	112	101
1954 = 100		
1950	89	101
1951	100	100
1952	92	94
1953	99	96
1954	100	100
1955	111	107
1956	110	113
1957	114	116
1961 = 100		
1956	81	92
1957	84	93
1958	84	90
1959	90	93
1960	102	98
1961	100	100
1962	103	102
1963	107	108
1964	119	111
1965	120	117
1966	122	121
1967	132	119
1968	146	136
1969	149	150
1970	156	155
1971	162	164
1975 = 100		
1970	84·1	79·5
1971	87·2	85·0
1972	95·8	86·0
1973	109·0	97·2
1974	109·4	102·3
1975	100	100
1976	106·5	108·6
1977	108·4	117·7
1978	115·6	121·0
1979	126·7	123·8
1980	121·3	126·0

External Trade 19. Import and Export Volumes by Category – United Kingdom 1814–1933

NOTES

[1] SOURCE: Werner Schlote, *British Overseas Trade from 1700 to the 1930s* (Oxford, 1952). Appendix tables 8, 9, 10, 12, and 15.

[2] Though expressed in terms of 1913 prices, the calculations were based on a number of comparatively short base periods, so allowing the weights to be changed. (See the source pp. 28 *et seq.* for a detailed account of the methodology).

(in £ million at 1913 prices)

	Imports					Exports					
	Foodstuffs and Live-stock (*a*)	Raw Materials		Finished Manufactures	Total	Foodstuffs and Live-stock (*a*)	Raw Materials	Finished Manufactures		Total	Re-exports Total
		for Textiles	Total					Textiles	Total		
1814	13·6	...	16·1	3·8	33·5	3·5	0·6	...	13·1	17·2	14·3
1815	11·5	...	19·7	3·6	34·8	3·5	0·7	...	17·3	21·5	11·6
1816	8·8	...	15·0	2·5	26·4	3·1	1·2	...	14·9	19·2	10·8
1817	11·1	...	17·2	2·9	31·2	3·6	1·1	...	15·7	20·4	7·5
1818	15·3	...	25·3	3·9	44·5	3·3	0·9	...	17·3	21·5	8·2
1819	10·6	...	20·6	3·0	34·2	2·6	0·8	...	13·5	16·9	8·0
1820	11·1	8·6	22·0	3·1	36·3	2·6	1·0	...	14·4	18·1	8·5
1821	9·8	8·4	20·9	3·1	33·8	2·6	0·9	...	16·2	19·7	8·7
1822	8·9	10·0	23·9	3·1	36·0	2·8	1·0	...	18·4	22·2	7·0
1823	9·9	11·5	27·8	3·9	41·5	2·9	0·8	...	18·3	21·9	6·8
1824	11·3	11·5	28·3	3·9	43·4	2·7	0·8	...	20·5	23·9	7·5
1825	13·6	15·8	36·6	4·6	54·8	2·5	0·8	...	19·6	22·9	6·9
1826	13·8	10·9	26·6	3·5	43·8	2·3	1·0	...	17·6	20·9	7·5
1827	14·8	15·7	34·2	4·1	53·2	2·7	1·1	16·6	22·0	25·8	7·6
1828	15·3	15·3	33·3	4·6	53·1	2·8	1·1	17·1	22·7	26·6	7·5
1829	15·9	13·8	31·6	3·7	51·3	2·9	1·2	18·1	23·7	27·8	7·7
1830	15·4	15·9	34·5	4·2	54·1	3·3	1·5	19·3	25·0	29·7	7·1
1831	18·6	16·4	35·2	4·6	58·4	2·8	1·5	19·8	25·9	30·3	8·3
1832	12·2	16·5	34·9	3·5	50·6	2·6	2·0	21·3	28·0	32·5	8·4
1833	12·7	17·4	36·7	3·3	52·7	2·3	1·8	22·7	29·9	33·9	8·2
1834	13·8	18·7	40·5	3·7	58·0	2·8	1·8	22·9	29·9	34·4	9·4
1835	12·3	19·7	39·0	3·3	54·6	2·6	2·4	25·2	33·7	38·7	9·2
1836	15·1	24·7	46·2	3·8	65·1	2·3	2·4	27·1	35·5	40·2	8·3
1837	15·2	22·2	43·5	3·9	62·6	2·1	2·5	23·0	30·7	35·3	9·7
1838	16·9	26·3	48·0	4·0	69·0	2·4	2·1	29·2	38·5	44·0	9·7
1839	22·0	23·2	46·0	4·2	72·2	2·3	3·1	30·6	40·9	46·3	10·4
1840	20·9	28·0	50·8	4·3	76·0	2·7 / 2·8 (*a*)	3·7	32·4	40·8	47·2	11·0
1841	21·2	25·8	49·0	3·9	74·2	2·5	4·5	32·9	42·0	49·1	10·8
1842	20·8	25·8	46·6	3·9	71·3	2·4	5·2	32·1	41·2	48·8	10·3
1843	16·6	30·5	56·1	4·3	77·0	2·6	4·8	37·8	48·2	55·6	10·6
1844	19·9	32·7	59·3	4·6	83·8	2·5	4·5	41·9	53·7	60·7	10·3
1845	21·1	35·3	66·4	5·9	93·4	2·6	4·9	42·2	53·4	60·9	11·4
1846	25·5	26·8	54·4	6·5	86·4	2·4	4·6	41·5	52·5	59·6	11·6
1847	40·1	26·1	52·3	6·1	98·6	3·0	4·7	38·6	51·0	58·7	13·1
1848	32·7	34·5	62·5	8·5	103·7	2·6	4·5	40·5	52·8	59·8	12·7
1849	39·6	38·2	67·6	8·4	115·7	3·0	5·8	51·1	66·4	75·3	19·2
1850	37·0	35·7	65·1	7·9	109·9	3·2	6·8	55·4	73·3	83·3	16·0
1851	39·5	40·1	72·3	7·0	118·8	3·8	6·5	59·9	79·1	89·3	16·9
1852	33·7 / 36·2 (*a*)	43·7	74·8	7·1	118·0	4·4	7·3	61·2	81·5	93·2	16·8
1853	46·4	47·4	80·4	10·7	137·6	6·1	7·6	68·5	92·7	106·5	20·0

See p. 522 for footnotes.

External Trade 19. *continued*

(in £ million at 1913 prices)

	Imports					Exports					
	Foodstuffs and Live-stock (*a*)	Raw Materials		Finished Manufactures	Total	Foodstuffs and Live-stock (*a*)	Raw Materials	Finished Manufactures		Total	Re-exports Total
		for Textiles	Total					Textiles	Total		
1854	45·6	45·0	79·6	11·2	136·4	5·8	8·3	66·2	90·5	104·6	21·1
1855	39·8	44·2	76·9	9·7	126·4	7·6	9·3	67·6	88·8	105·7	22·2
1856	46·7	51·2	88·5	11·6	146·8	8·9	10·4	79·0	106·2	125·6	23·1
1857	44·5	55·5	95·8	10·5	150·8	7·8	11·6	79·0	109·6	128·9	21·7
1858	47·6	50·5	88·9	9·3	145·8	7·0	10·9	81·2	109·2	127·1	24·4
1859	45·6	60·9	102·3	11·3	159·2	8·3	10·8	88·4	121·3	140·4	26·4
1860	59·7	67·2	110·7	13·5	183·9	7·6	11·8	92·8	126·5	145·9	29·9
1861	66·5	61·8	102·3	15·6	184·4	7·8	12·5	84·7	115·8	136·1	33·9
1862	75·2	35·6	73·1	17·8	166·0	7·4	13·5	66·1	99·4	120·3	32·9
1863	75·0	40·6	81·7	20·2	176·9	8·1	14·5	68·3	103·2	125·9	36·2
1864	70·9	49·4	91·9	22·4	185·2	7·9	13·8	70·5	104·0	125·7	35·9
1865	72·3	54·4	100·5	23·2	196·0	7·7	14·6	79·4	114·3	136·6	40·1
1866	77·9	68·8	117·8	24·7	220·4	8·0	15·5	93·5	128·6	152·1	41·4
1867	77·8	63·9	112·6	25·4	215·9	7·6	16·2	98·0	135·5	159·3	41·7
1868	81·7	69·0	123·5	29·2	234·3	8·0	17·2	103·2	144·0	169·1	43·9
1869	91·3	63·9	116·8	30·1	238·3	7·8	19·7	103·5	150·5	178·0	42·4
1870	89·5	70·0	126·8	36·9	253·3	10·6	20·6	111·3	161·2	192·4	43·3
1871	100·9	90·5	154·0	32·9	287·9	13·4	24·7	123·6	175·9	213·9	59·7
1872	110·7	77·1	142·0	35·3	288·1	10·1	24·0	133·2	184·6	218·7	53·9
1873	116·5	81·3	148·7	36·4	301·7	10·9	20·8	127·3	179·2	210·9	50·4
1874	114·8	83·7	153·0	41·8	309·5	10·9	21·2	127·4	179·5	211·6	53·5
1875	128·1	79·4	149·4	43·8	321·3	10·6	23·4	124·7	177·4	211·4	56·2
1876	133·1	81·5	153·2	46·4	332·8	11·0	25·0	122·1	171·3	207·2	55·4
1877	138·2	79·6	158·9	50·6	347·7	10·9	25·6	124·2	176·7	213·2	53·7
1878	143·2	77·3	152·3	51·0	346·5	11·3	26·3	124·3	178·2	215·8	55·4
1879	153·4	83·0	153·9	47·7	354·9	10·8	31·2	125·4	184·3	226·3	61·9
1880	159·3	91·4	172·1	52·6	384·0	12·4	35·7	139·6	204·5	252·6	67·5
1881	151·6	91·0	171·2	50·4	373·1	12·4	37·9	152·6	226·3	276·6	68·1
1882	150·0	98·2	187·2	55·2	392·4	12·5	40·9	147·9	229·1	282·6	71·1
1883	168·0	97·0	191·4	56·0	415·3	13·1	40·5	148·5	233·2	286·8	76·1
1884	153·1	98·1	189·5	56·3	398·9	13·3	39·7	150·8	235·5	288·5	76·1
1885	164·2	85·6	181·2	59·3	404·7	13·1	38·1	144·6	224·2	275·5	72·3
1886	156·6	97·5	187·2	60·8	404·6	13·1	39·7	155·4	233·7	286·6	77·1
1887	165·4	101·8	193·9	64·3	423·6	13·4	43·2	159·0	245·0	301·6	81·0
1888	171·0	104·9	203·0	66·7	440·7	13·9	44·5	160·3	254·1	312·6	87·6
1889	183·4	115·4	223·9	72·9	480·3	14·1	44·7	159·9	261·0	319·7	89·4
1890	192·5	106·1	214·3	71·6	478·4	14·4	44·8	159·3	260·6	319·9	87·4
1891	192·1	116·6	224·7	73·1	489·9	13·7	43·0	152·0	244·4	301·1	83·6
1892	201·1	107·4	219·4	74·8	495·3	14·1	43·5	148·7	233·3	290·9	92·8
1893	194·6	93·1	205·8	78·1	478·4	14·0	42·3	141·2	227·4	283·7	86·2
1894	214·0	106·5	226·1	85·6	525·7	14·9	42·9	146·9	234·2	292·0	84·1
1895	223·3	112·8	234·8	93·8	551·9	15·2	45·2	158·8	255·6	316·0	89·0
1896	235·2	107·9	234·9	101·5	571·5	16·3	46·9	160·7	267·9	331·1	83·6
1897	241·0	108·5	236·9	107·5	585·4	16·1	51·7	150·5	257·2	325·0	91·0
1898	241·7	120·3	251·2	111·1	614·0	17·0	49·6	151·0	258·6	325·2	93·6
1899	259·1	102·3	241·5	115·7	616·3	15·8	56·9	157·0	272·5	345·2	96·1
1900	260·6	99·2	241·0	115·9	617·5	16·9	54·6	147·6	256·8	328·3	88·2
1901	266·9	109·6	248·5	118·3	633·6	18·4	53·7	149·3	257·5	329·6	93·5
1902	260·3	108·7	258·0	124·3	642·6	20·0	59·1	153·3	272·0	351·1	92·3
1903	270·7	102·6	245·6	126·0	642·3	19·3	61·2	153·5	275·0	355·5	93·3

See p. 522 for footnotes.

External Trade 19. *continued*

(in £ million at 1913 prices)

	Imports					Exports					
	Foodstuffs and Livestock (*a*)	Raw Materials for Textiles	Raw Materials Total	Finished Manufactures	Total	Foodstuffs and Livestock (*a*)	Raw Materials	Finished Manufactures Textiles	Finished Manufactures Total	Total	Re-exports Total
1904	270·6	107·8	255·0	121·7	647·3	21·0	61·4	158·4	279·5	362·0	92·5
1905	264·4	119·2	268·1	124·1	656·6	22·4	66·1	170·5	305·3	393·9	98·5
1906	270·5	114·9	273·3	131·7	675·6	23·6	75·5	176·2	325·1	424·2	100·4
1907	269·2	133·8	292·4	125·7	687·2	25·2	83·2	183·9	344·8	453·2	104·6
1908	258·9	119·4	279·6	116·9	655·4	24·6	81·1	158·4	307·6	413·3	95·8
1909	264·2	126·2	291·9	122·4	678·4	25·2	87·2	169·8	316·3	428·7	104·2
1910	264·8	119·5	292·9	129·3	687·0	28·9	87·3	181·8	352·8	469·0	104·1
1911	272·2	126·7	296·3	135·8	704·2	30·4	88·8	190·2	364·1	483·2	104·6
1912	273·8	151·0	332·2	150·6	756·6	32·8	91·3	197·6	383·8	508·0	111·3
1913	285·0	128·6	328·3	155·4	768·7	32·0	96·6	195·8	396·7	525·2	109·6
1914	275·0	109·8	292·3	124·4	691·7	25·5	79·3	162·0	330·2	435·0	102·5
1915	285·9	148·4	341·3	122·6	749·8	21·9	59·6	139·3	274·9	356·4	105·6
1916	268·7	114·7	269·4	101·3	639·4	19·0	58·1	158·4	292·9	369·9	85·9
1917	218·9	92·7	225·2	90·6	534·7	9·8	48·5	140·4	251·0	309·2	53·0
1918	232·2	79·7	216·9	102·1	551·2	4·4	37·6	100·3	170·8	212·9	20·0
1919	270·3	123·2	301·5	97·3	669·1	15·6	49·0	116·3	209·3	273·9	88·7
1920	258·6	114·9	298·0	115·0	671·6	19·1	49·1	148·4	294·1	362·2	97·1
1921	267·2	80·2	240·5	77·4	585·1	17·0	42·6	88·6	198·7	258·3	85·3
1922	287·7	110·3	283·3	101·2	672·2	16·4	88·8	129·1	257·0	362·3	92·5
	--- (*b*)	--- (*b*)	--- (*b*)	--- (*b*)	--- (*b*)	--- (*b*)	--- (*b*)	--- (*b*)	--- (*b*)	--- (*b*)	--- (*b*)
1923	329·3	87·8	288·0	123·1	740·4	22·2	98·1	135·2	286·0	406·3	102·0
1924	364·1	100·0	323·4	140·9	828·5	28·4	85·5	145·4	308·0	421·9	112·2
1925	352·5	107·1	334·9	165·6	853·0	26·5	78·6	143·2	313·2	418·2	112·7
1926	346·4	104·9	380·8	151·4	878·6	24·5	53·8	133·6	297·3	375·7	87·3
1927	361·6	103·7	360·9	172·3	894·8	25·6	82·5	145·6	332·0	440·1	95·9
1928	362·7	97·8	340·6	175·2	878·5	26·2	82·3	144·8	347·5	456·0	100·5
1929	371·2	101·4	362·2	185·8	919·3	28·5	94·3	136·8	346·3	469·0	85·2
1930	371·5	87·2	345·1	181·2	907·8	25·9	80·1	101·0	279·6	385·5	75·9
1931	410·6	87·2	328·0	183·4	922·0	21·9	63·6	80·0	208·8	294·3	66·6
1932	390·1	95·3	321·0	107·8	819·0	21·5	62·1	92·4	215·6	299·3	62·7
1933	378·9	103·7	340·7	106·1	825·7	18·9	68·5	93·6	221·6	308·9	54·3

(*a*) Livestock are not included until 1840 (2nd line).

(*b*) Southern Ireland was subsequently treated as foreign.

External Trade 20. Indices of Import and Export Volumes by Category – United Kingdom 1947–83

NOTE
SOURCE: Unpublished work by J. R. Wells.

(1963 = 100)

	Imports					Exports	
	Food, Drink & Tobacco	Basic Materials	Fuel	Manufactures	Total	Manufactures	Total
1947	71	82	24	32	55	48	45
1948	71	84	30	34	57	59	57
1949	77	91	30	38	62	66	63
1950	74	96	33	36	62	75	73
1951	82	100	44	46	69	77	74
1952	74	88	43	46	64	71	69
1953	83	99	46	42	69	71	71
1954	81	98	51	46	69	74	74
1955	87	103	62	57	77	80	79
1956	88	100	59	57	76	85	83
1957	92	104	58	59	79	87	86
1958	96	92	64	60	79	83	82
1959	96	99	73	68	84	86	86
1960	98	107	80	92	96	91	90
1961	98	99	84	89	93	93	92
1962	102	95	94	92	96	94	94
1963	100	100	100	100	100	100	100
1964	102	107	108	121	111	104	103
1965	100	106	118	122	112	109	107
1966	98	101	129	130	114	113	112
1967	101	101	140	149	123	112	112
1968	104	110	148	174	135	128	126
1969	100	108	158	185	137	144	140
1970	100	110	170	199	144	145	143
1971	99	100	186	217	149	158	153
1972	101	101	185	254	164	158	155
1973	102	114	191	309	187	180	175
1974	99	101	179	328	187	189	184
1975	99	84	146	306	171	183	180
1976	101	103	146	334	183	200	195
1977	101	100	121	365	186	215	212
1978	100	104	116	407	198	213	218
1979	102	109	114	469	217	213	223
1980	95	94	96	463	208	215	227
1981	98	89	79	453	200	202	224
1982	103	87	72	490	208	204	230
1983	103	98	64	550	224	200	232

External Trade 21. United Kingdom Share of World Exports of Manufactures 1850–1982

NOTES:

[1] SOURCES: Part A – Based on table 5 above and the estimates of world exports of manufactures by W. Arthur Lewis in Sven Grassman and Erik Lundberg (eds), *The World Economic Order* (London, 1981), appendix to chapter 1; Part B – Based on Alfred Maizels, *Growth and Trade* (Cambridge, 1970), table A3; Part C – Unpublished work kindly made available by J. R. Wells, based on United Nations sources.

[2] The statistics in Part B relate to the U.K. share of exports of manufactures from "industrial" countries plus India.

A. 1850–1913

(in per cent)

1850	43	1863	43	1876	42	1889	37	1902	30
1851	43	1864	43	1877	39	1890	37	1903	30
1852	42	1865	44	1878	39	1891	36	1904	29
1853	41	1866	46	1879	37	1892	35	1905	29
1854	42	1867	46	1880	39	1893	34	1906	30
1855	40	1868	44	1881	39	1894	34	1907	31
1856	42	1869	45	1882	39	1895	33	1908	30
1857	42	1870	46	1883	39	1896	33	1909	28
1858	44	1871	45	1884	38	1897	32	1910	29
1859	44	1872	46	1885	38	1898	30	1911	28
1860	43	1873	45	1886	37	1899	32	1912	28
1861	43	1874	44	1887	38	1900	31	1913	28
1862	41	1875	43	1888	38	1901	31		

B. 1899–1957

1899	33·2	1929	23·0	1937	20·9	1955	19·5
1913	30·2	1929(*a*)	22·4	1950	24·6	1957	17·7

C. 1953–82

1953	16·2	1959	13·5	1965	10·4	1971	8·3	1977	6·7
1954	16·2	1960	12·6	1966	10·0	1972	7·5	1978	6·6
1955	15·9	1961	12·5	1967	9·3	1973	6·8	1979	6·7
1956	14·2	1962	11·8	1968	8·7	1974	6·4	1980	7·1
1957	13·7	1963	11·6	1969	8·5	1975	6·9	1981	6·3
1958	13·9	1964	10·7	1970	8·1	1976	6·4	1982	6·1

(*a*) Previous figures exclude Dutch exports.

External Trade 22. Gross Barter Terms of Trade – England & Wales 1697–1774, and Great Britain 1772–1804

NOTES

[1] SOURCE: Phyllis Deane and W. A. Cole, *British Economic Growth 1688–1955* (Cambridge University Press, 1962). The official values of imports, which were based on first cost in the country of origin, were used by the authors to construct a table of imports c.i.f. The latter, less re-exports f.o.b., was used in compiling this table, together with the official values of exports f.o.b.

[2] Three-yearly moving averages are employed to eliminate random fluctuations caused by the comparatively slow pace of ocean shipping in the eighteenth century.

(Three-yearly Moving Averages)

E. & W.

Year	Index	Year	Index	Year	Index	Year	Index
1698	103	1720	133	1742	150	1764	153
1699	102	1721	133	1743	164	1765	149
1700	100	1722	133	1744	159	1766	129
1701	105	1723	122	1745	178	1767	126
1702	117	1724	118	1746	175	1768	123
1703	115	1725	119	1747	175	1769	123
1704	119	1726	120	1748	170	1770	126
1705	129	1727	116	1749	179	1771	127
1706	157	1728	112	1750	190	1772	129
1707	154	1729	112	1751	183	1773	125
1708	147	1730	110	1752	173		
1709	159	1731	119	1753	166		
1710	158	1732	120	1754	153		
1711	168	1733	123	1755	154		
1712	140	1734	118	1756	137		
1713	148	1735	129	1757	149		
1714	145	1736	140	1758	155		
1715	145	1737	154	1759	168		
1716	140	1738	142	1760	171		
1717	126	1739	133	1761	171		
1718	129	1740	124	1762	166		
1719	121	1741	140	1763	166		

G.B.

Year	Index	Year	Index
1773	125	1783	117
1774	121	1784	105
1775	119	1785	100
1776	113	1786	97
1777	113	1787	97
1778	112	1788	100
1779	116	1789	105
1780	106	1790	114
1781	111	1791	123
1782	112	1792	122
		1793	121
		1794	114
		1795	127
		1796	137
		1797	134
		1798	134
		1799	137
		1800	141
		1801	147
		1802	140
		1803	138

External Trade 23. Terms of Trade – United Kingdom 1796–1980

NOTE TO PART A

SOURCE: Albert H. Imlah, *Economic Elements in the Pax Britannica* (Cambridge, Mass., Harvard University Press, 1958), pp. 94–8.

1880=100

A. 1796–1913.

	Merchandise Price Indices				Merchandise Price Indices		
	Exports	Net Retained Imports	Net Barter Terms		Exports	Net Retained Imports	Net Barter Terms
1796	323·7	175·7	184·2	1843	112·0	99·1	113·0
1797	348·1	174·3	199·7	1844	114·9	99·0	116·1
1798	370·1	178·5	207·3	1845	118·3	98·9	119·6
1799	353·8	180·4	196·1	1846	116·3	101·0	115·1
1800	359·0	203·4	176·5	1847	118·1	105·0	112·5
1801	362·5	214·6	168·9	1848	105·8	86·9	121·7
1802	406·2	177·9	228·3	1849	100·8	87·5	115·2
1803	388·4	185·1	209·8	1850	100·8	90·7	111·1
1804	378·2	188·2	201·0	1851	99·1	90·1	110·0
1805	373·5	195·4	191·1	1852	98·1	93·5	104·9
1806	365·2	183·8	198·7	1853	108·1	107·2	100·8
1807	372·0	180·6	206·0	1854	108·7	114·9	94·6
1808	376·8	199·1	189·3	1855	106·1	118·7	89·4
1809	353·7	236·7	149·4	1856	108·4	118·4	91·6
1810	353·3	222·9	158·5	1857	111·7	128·3	87·1
1811	361·5	180·3	200·5	1858	109·1	111·3	98·0
1812	353·4	211·3	167·2	1859	111·5	113·5	98·2
1813	...	...	...	1860	110·6	116·5	94·9
1814	329·7	254·5	129·5	1861	111·1	113·3	98·1
1815	300·0	217·1	138·2	1862	116·9	110·5	105·8
1816	283·7	185·2	153·2	1863	128·8	120·1	107·2
1817	259·4	186·4	139·2	1864	141·3	134·9	104·7
1818	271·9	191·6	141·9	1865	134·6	125·8	107·0
1819	258·8	158·5	163·3	1866	139·1	126·5	110·0
1820	234·8	150·0	156·5	1867	130·9	121·4	107·8
1821	223·8	136·7	163·7	1868	122·2	121·8	100·3
1822	205·6	132·4	155·3	1869	121·4	117·7	103·1
1823	198·9	133·3	149·2	1870	118·5	115·8	102·3
1824	193·9	125·2	154·9	1871	118·0	107·9	109·4
1825	210·3	143·1	147·0	1872	130·6	115·6	113·0
1826	185·3	117·8	157·3	1873	135·2	115·4	117·2
1827	174·6	119·0	146·7	1874	127·7	112·8	113·2
1828	170·4	113·9	149·6	1875	120·0	107·5	111·6
1829	154·3	109·4	141·0	1876	110·5	104·8	105·4
1830	158·2	107·0	149·8	1877	106·2	107·8	98·5
1831	151·8	109·9	138·1	1878	102·3	99·9	102·4
1832	139·3	108·9	127·9	1879	96·4	94·8	101·7
1833	141·8	115·0	122·3	1880	100·0	100·0	100·0
1834	146·0	117·1	124·7	1881	95·8	99·1	96·7
1835	152·9	124·9	122·4	1882	97·7	98·1	99·6
1836	160·1	128·6	124·5	1883	94·4	95·8	98·5
1837	147·2	114·4	129·6	1884	90·9	91·0	99·9
1838	139·2	116·4	119·6	1885	87·4	85·3	102·5
1839	137·7	122·7	111·8	1886	83·6	80·1	104·4
1840	128·5	122·3	105·1	1887	83·4	78·4	106·4
1841	124·3	113·3	109·7	1888	82·9	81·0	102·3
1842	114·2	108·3	105·4	1889	84·6	82·1	103·0

1880=100

A. 1796–1913 (*cont.*)

	Merchandise Price Indices		
	Exports	Net Retained Imports	Net Barter Terms
1890	88·3	80·9	109·1
1891	87·5	81·5	107·4
1892	83·6	78·1	107·0
1893	83·4	76·3	109·3
1894	79·2	71·1	111·4
1895	76·2	68·8	110·8
1896	76·9	69·4	110·8
1897	76·0	69·1	110·0
1898	76·2	69·7	109·3
1899	79·8	71·1	112·2
1900	91·7	76·4	120·0
1901	87·3	73·9	118·1
1902	83·3	73·0	114·1
1903	83·2	74·0	112·4
1904	84·2	74·3	113·3
1905	84·0	74·6	112·6
1906	89·0	77·8	114·4
1907	93·4	81·3	114·9
1908	89·8	78·3	114·7
1909	86·5	79·1	109·4
1910	90·2	83·6	107·9
1911	91·8	81·5	112·6
1912	93·4	83·0	112·5
1913	96·9	83·4	116·2

NOTES TO PART B

[1] SOURCES: 1938=100 indices – *Board of Trade Journal* (4 August 1951); others – *Abstract*.

[2] The export statistics relate to domestic exports, except for that based on 1975.

B. 1913–1980

	Index of Average Value		
	Imports	Exports	Net Terms of Trade
1938 = 100			
1913	97	68	70
1919	233	189	81
1920	277	245	88
1921	185	184	99
1922	148	136	92
1923	145	130	90
1924	150	129	86
1925	151	126	83
1926	138	118	86
1927	132	112	85
1928	133	110	83
1929	130	108	83
1930	114	103	90
1931	92	92	100
1932	86	86	100
1933	83	86	104
1934	87	87	100
1935	89	88	99
1936	93	90	97
1937	107	98	92
1938	100	100	100
1946	211	196	93
1947	258	223	86
1950 = 100			
1938	30	38	127
1947	77	84	109
1948	86	92	107
1949	87	95	109
1950	100	100	100
1951	133	117	88
1954 = 100			
1950	85	85	100
1951	113	100	88
1952	111	105	95
1953	101	101	100
1954	100	100	100
1955	103	102	99
1956	105	106	101
1957	107	111	104
1961 = 100			
1956	110	95	87
1957	111	100	89
1958	103	99	96
1959	102	98	96
1960	102	100	97
1961	100	100	100
1962	99	101	102
1963	103	104	101
1964	107	106	99
1965	107	108	102

External Trade 23. *continued*

B. 1913–80 (*cont.*)

	Index of Average Value		
	Imports	Exports	Net Terms of Trade
1961 = 100			
1966	109	112	103
1967	109	114	105
1968	121	123	102
1969	126	127	101
1970	132	136	103
1975 = 100			
1970	43·7	50·7	116
1971	45·8	53·6	117
1972	47·8	56·7	119
1973	60·8	64·0	105
1974	88·0	81·6	93
1975	100	100	100
1976	122·7	119·7	98
1977	141·1	141·6	100
1978	145·0	155·2	107
1979	159·5	171·5	108
1980	182·2	192·7	106

CHAPTER X

TRANSPORT AND COMMUNICATIONS

TABLES

British shipping was a matter of close concern to our ancestors, and as a result there are fairly plentiful statistics on the subject, though, as usual, there is little that is continuous until the eighteenth century. The railways, too, were under Parliamentary surveillance from their beginning, and the record of this remains. The Post Office is less useful to us, until near the middle of the nineteenth century, at any rate. And continuous and consistent statistics relating to road transport are of fairly recent origin, though both the eighteenth and nineteenth century recorded certain figures of expenditure on roads which will be referred to later. Air traffic and broadcasting, being modern inventions, are quite well covered by statistics from an early stage.

Early sources of shipping statistics are numerous and difficult to interpret without specialised knowledge of the circumstances of collection.[1] From time to time the government called for lists of the merchant ships belonging to various ports. Willan, who reproduces figures of coasting vessels belonging to the English ports at each of seven dates in the period 1709–51, comments on the 'suspicious uniformity of some of the figures'.[2] A register of

[1] Some of the early sources are discussed by R. C. Jarvis, 'Sources for the History of Ships and Shipping', *Journal of Transport History* (1958). Much the fullest treatment, though, is Ralph Davis, *The Rise of the English Shipping Industry* (London, 1962).

[2] T. S. Willan, *The English Coasting Trade 1600–1750* (Manchester, 1938), p. 220.

British shipping engaged in the plantation trade was started in 1698,[3] but the figures do not seem to have survived. The port books recorded figures of tonnage of arrivals and departures, and these were returned to the Commissioners of Customs, but according to Clark the tonnages were 'mere estimates, formed by multiplying the numbers of ships by conventional, standardised, figures of average tonnages for each trade'.[4] Hence, when the port books overlap with the statutory register records, the tonnages recorded in these two sources do not agree.

For all the weaknesses of these pre-1787 statistics, however, some of them are shown here as table 1, namely those collated by Davis. After an extended discussion of their difficulties, and particularly of those from 1751 onwards, he had this to say: '... there are many reasons for doubting the accuracy of this, the most comprehensive series of shipping statistics available before registration. Nevertheless, they have considerable value; it is unlikely that there are major inconsistencies within the series itself at least before its last decade so for comparisons of progress over the period 1751 to 1786 they may be safely used'.[5] For this reason his statistics are included here, even though his judgment may be a somewhat too favourable one for the period after 1773, because, as he himself points out, 'measured tons' were increasingly used instead of the older 'tons burden' following the Act of that year, and the figures lose precision of meaning. The implication of Davis's appendix A, incidentally, is that the scattered figures up to 1702 are individually more reliable than the mid-eighteenth-century series.

It was not until the Act of 1786 that registration was statutorily enforced. Table 2 gives the statistics which have resulted from that and subsequent Acts. The main problem in using them – and it applies, too, to the shipbuilding figures given in tables 15 and 16 of chapter VIII – is caused by the change in the method of reckoning tonnage which came about between 1836 and 1855. Both systems of measurement used during the period covered by these tables were intended to record cargo-carrying capacity. The original system established by the Tonnage Act of 1773 was based on length and breadth, and thus encouraged the building of deep vessels. In 1836 a new law provided for measurement to be based on cubic capacity, but it was optional. Old ships did not have to be remeasured, and the new Act did not even have to be adopted for new ones. Not until 1855 was the new system made compulsory and rigorously enforced. How great was the change in tonnages recorded as a result of the new system, and when the change came, are two questions which it is not possible to answer with any certainty. Graham implied that the greater part of the change took place in 1855.[6] If this was indeed so, the conclusion to be drawn from the statistics is

[3] G. N. Clark, *Guide to English Commercial Statistics 1696–1782* (London, 1938), p. 47.
[4] *Ibid.*, p. 51.
[5] Ralph Davis, *op. cit.*, p. 405.
[6] G. S. Graham, 'The Ascendancy of the Sailing Ship 1850–85', *Economic History Review*, second series IX, 1 (1956), where he writes: 'although lengths were somewhat increased after 1836, the same general type of ship continued to be built until the new measurement law came into force in 1855' – i.e. ships of great depth, whose cargo-carrying capacity was understated by the old system.

that the adoption of the new system may have led to a slight increase in the tonnage recorded; but that the only certain thing is that the change was not large.

Until the beginning of the twentieth century the question of shipping freight rates received little attention from compilers of statistics, though the firm of Angier Brothers issued yearly reports from 1870.[7] These form part of the material used by Isserlis in compiling his index of rates included here as table 4. Since average rates were not available, that index had to be based on the mean of the highest and lowest rates for each year. Isserlis admitted the dangers of this method, but believed it gave reasonable results except for years when the rates changed very greatly, such as 1915 and 1920.[8] For a full description of his methods, the reader must consult the original source. Suffice it to say here that it is a chain index, comparing one year with the preceding one, since, as Isserlis says, 'it is clearly impossible to compare directly the freight in 1869 paid to a sailing vessel carrying grain from Odessa to the United Kingdom with a freight in 1936 payable to a modern motor ship for carrying grain from Montreal or New York to Liverpool'.

The official post-Second World War index of freight rates began in 1948, and no attempt has been made to formulate a bridge between that and the Isserlis index. The question was discussed by Kendall, and he concluded that 'a comparison of 1948 with 1938 really conveys very little because of some important alterations in the nature of sea transport'.[9] However, his conclusion seems to be excessively cautious, and it is worth noting here that on the base 1938 = 100, he had calculated an index figure for tramp shipping freights in 1948 of 330.

For the first quarter of the nineteenth century, iron railway construction was limited to small-scale, localised railroads operated by horses or by stationary engines. The opening of the Stockton and Darlington Railway in 1825 represented the beginning of the steam railway era. Since all railways that went beyond the bounds of a private estate required an Act of Parliament, the records of these legal proceedings provide records of the railways concerned. There were also company reports issued for the individual railway companies. From these and other sources a variety of contemporary lists of mileages, capital raised, etc., aggregated by years, have been compiled,[10] but the aggregates tend to vary according to the source of the data – bill, Act, or company report, for example. These, along with their original sources, have been used by modern writers to extend backwards in time various of the statistical series which were started with the official *Railway Returns* from 1843. The length of railways open is one such series, which is shown here in table 5.

[7] Collected in E. A. V. Angier, 'Fifty Years of Freight 1869–1919', *Fairplay* (1920), continued in subsequent issues of that journal.

[8] L. Isserlis, 'Tramp Shipping Cargoes and Freight 1869–1919', *Journal of the Royal Statistical Society*, XCXI (1938). It is perhaps worth pointing out that there is a certain amount of relevant material for an earlier period in Douglass C. North, 'Sources of Productivity Change in Ocean Shipping, 1600–1850', *Journal of Political Economy*, XXVI (1968).

[9] M. G. Kendall, 'The U.K. Mercantile Marine and its Contribution to the Balance of Payments', *Journal of the Royal Statistical Society* XCXXIII (series A 1950).

[10] Lists are given in a number of the old railway histories, the most useful of which are J. Francis, *History of the English Railway, 1820–1845* (2 vols., London, 1851); H. Scrivenor, *The Railways of the United Kingdom*

Official attention to the operating statistics of the railways actually began with the *Report* of the Select Committee on the State of Communication by Railway,[11] and five years later the regular *Returns* were begun. Major additions were made in 1848 and 1852. The principal series are summarised here in tables 7 and 8. These are reasonably reliable up to 1869, though there are a few, mainly trivial, omissions. There is no question about them for subsequent periods, though long-term comparisons are impaired by the changes which took place in the basis on which the statistics were collected in 1869 itself, in 1913, 1928, 1933, and 1948, with other minor reorganisations at various times. The original sources give very much more detail than is shown here, of course.

Amongst the statistics which were published in the *Railway Returns* were ones dealing with paid-up capital. These are shown as part of table 6, along with Reed's estimates for earlier years, based on the sources already mentioned. That table also includes my own estimates of capital formation in railways in the United Kingdom. Kenwood produced a similar series for Great Britain up to 1875 which differs only marginally from the (unpublished) Great Britain component of my statistics.[12]

Roads, of course, existed long before railways; but connected and exactly comparable figures for their mileage only go back to the administrative reorganisation of responsibilities for them in the early 1920s. But because expenditure on roads has always been very largely carried out by some branch or other of government, there is a good deal of information on that aspect for much of the nineteenth century, and a certain amount for the eighteenth. However, apart from the local authority outlays from 1883, provided by the annual *Local Taxation Returns*, and summarised in various tables in chapter XI, this information is to be found scattered through a variety of different kinds of Blue Book – *Highway Returns*, *Turnpike Trust Abstracts*, the returns of the country treasurers' expenditures on bridges, various reports by bodies such as the Metropolitan Board of Works, Commissioners of Sewers of the City of London, Town Improvement Commissioners, Urban Sanitary Authorities, the Commissioners of Highland Roads and Bridges, etc. In view of the scattered and unorganised character of this information, no attempt has been made to include any of it here.

Operating statistics for road transport are inevitably less complete than for railways, and it has not seemed worthwhile to include any of the partial data which are available. The same applies to statistics on charges made, though it is worth mentioning in this connection the lists of these which Jackman provided for the period 1750 to 1830, and much useful material for individual turnpikes in the more modern work by Albert. There are also some in

(London, 1849): and F. Wishaw, *The Railways of Great Britain and Ireland* (London, 1840). See also G. R. Porter, *The Progress of the Nation* (London, 2nd edition 1847), pp. 323–32.

[11] *S.P.* 1839 X.

[12] A. G. Kenwood, 'Railway Investment in Britain 1825–1875', *Economica*, XXXII (1965). Differences between the (unpublished) England and Wales components are discussed in G. R. Hawke, *Railways and Economic Growth in England and Wales 1840–1870* (Oxford, 1970), pp. 198–204, which itself contains many useful railway statistics. I have preferred to include my own series rather than Kenwood's because it covers a longer period as well as the whole United Kingdom. For some purposes, however, Kenwood's will be preferable.

Copeland's book.[13] However, there are good statistics of motor vehicles in use covering all the period when they have been of any significance, and these appear in tables 10 and 11.

Because, like the railways, most air traffic is organised by comparatively few operators and has almost from the beginning been subject to close regulation, it has been more susceptible to easy measurement than road or waterway traffic. Summary statistics for as far back as there are any, 1937, are given in table 12 for the United Kingdom and table 13 for the Republic of Ireland. It seems correct to assume that these are practically complete. Note, though, that the statistics relate to the operations of British (or Irish) registered undertakings, and not to traffic through the countries' airports.

It will be noted that no statistics are shown for inland waterways. This is because they do not exist in any systematic or extended form. How little of any sort is available may be seen from J. R. Ward, *The Finance of Canal Building in Eighteenth-century England*,[14] a careful work with a good bibliography, but only scattered statistics, mostly for individual canals.

Financial statistics for the Post Office, in summary form back to 1688, are included in the first two tables in Chapter XI, and continued in the next two. They are also available in a bit more detail back to 1724 in J. C. Hemmeon, *The History of the British Post Office*.[15] But statistics of the volume of mail only date back to the reorganisation of the Post Office under Rowland Hill in 1839–40. A selection of these showing the main aggregates is given in table 14, with telegraph and telephone statistics in table 15 (and the modern Irish figures in table 16). The first of these tables contradicts rather well the widespread belief that the statistical information available to us on all subjects continually increases and improves all the time. On the contrary, it provides some evidence for another widely held view, namely that the efficiency of the Post Office has declined during the twentieth century.

[13] W. T. Jackman, *The Development of Transportation in Modern England* (2 vols., Cambridge, 1916, reissued in one volume, London, 1962); William Albert, *The Turnpike Road System in England 1663–1840* (Cambridge, 1972); and John Copeland, *Roads and their Traffic, 1750–1850* (Newton Abbot, 1968).

[14] (Oxford, 1974).

[15] (Cambridge, Mass., 1912).

Transport and Communications 1. English Shipping Tonnage – 1572–1786

NOTES

[1] SOURCE: Ralph Davis, *The Rise of the English Shipping Industry* (London, 1962).

[2] The figures relate to tons burden almost invariably to 1773, but measured tons began to be used more commonly thereafter, and were universal after 1786.

(in thousands)

	Total Tonnage	Outport Tonnage		Total Tonnage	Outport Tonnage		Total Tonnage	Outport Tonnage
1572	50	...	1752	449	318	1769	574	446
1582	67	...	1753	468	336	1770	594	444
1629	115	...	1754	458	338	1771	577	444
1686	340	190	1755	473	342	1772	584	451
1702	323	183	1763	496	357	1773	581	445
1716	...	215	1764	523	388	1774	588	455
1723	...	219	1765	543	409	1775	608	465
1730	...	235	1766	562	429	1786	752	566
1737	...	248	1767	557	418			
1751	421	302	1768	549	426			

Transport and Communications 2. Shipping Registered in the United Kingdom 1788–1980

NOTES

[1] SOURCES: 1788–1800 – *Navigation Reports* in the Public Record Office; 1801–39 (all ships) – *Finance Accounts* (Trade and Navigation section); 1814–39 (steamships) – G. R. Porter, *The Progress of the Nation* (London, 2nd edition, 1847), p. 319; 1814–39 (sailing ships) – by inference; 1840–1948 – *Abstract*; 1948–80 – *Lloyd's Register of Shipping Statistical Tables*.

[2] The Isle of Man and the Channel Islands are included in this table.

[3] Statistics from 1948 (2nd line) relate only to vessels of 100 GRT and over.

at 30th September in each year until 1824 and subsequently at 31st December

	All Ships	
	Number	thousand net tons
1788	12,464	1,278
1789	12,801	1,308
1790	13,557	1,383
1791	13,960	1,415
1792	14,334	1,437
1793	14,440	1,453
1794	14,590	1,456
1795	14,317	1,426
1796	14,458	1,361
1797	14,405	1,454
1798	14,631	1,494
1799	14,883	1,551
1800	15,734	1,699
1801	16,552	1,797
1802	17,207	1,901
1803	18,068	1,986
1804	18,870	2,077
1805	19,027	2,093
1806	19,315	2,080
1807	19,373	2,097
1808	19,580	2,130
1809	19,882	2,167
1810	20,253	2,211
1811	20,478	2,247
1812	20,637	2,263
1813	20,951	2,349

	Sailing Ships		Steamships	
	Number	thousand net tons	Number	thousand net tons
1814	21,449	2,414	1	..
1815	21,861	2,477	8	1
1816	22,014	2,503	12	1
1817	21,761	2,420	14	1
1818	22,005	2,450	19	2
1819	21,973	2,449	24	3
1820	21,935	2,436	34	3
1821	21,593	2,350	59	6
1822	21,153	2,307	85	9
1823	20,941	2,293	101	10
1824	21,164	2,338	116	12
1825	20,442	2,313	153	16
1826	20,738	2,387	230	24
	---(a)	---(a)	---(a)	---(a)
1827	19,269	2,154	255	27
1828	19,372	2,165	274	28
1829	18,821	2,170	289	30
1830	18,876	2,168	298	30
1831	19,126	2,192	324	33
1832	19,312	2,226	352	36
1833	19,302	2,233	387	39
1834	19,545	2,268	430	44
1835	19,797	2,307	503	53
1836	19,827	2,289	561	60
1837	19,912	2,264	624	70

See p. 538 for footnotes.

Transport and Communications 2. *continued*

	Sailing Ships			Steamships		
	Number	thousand net tons	thousand gross tons	Number	thousand net tons	thousand gross
1838	20,234	2,346	...	678	75	...
1839	20,947	2,491	...	723	80	...
1840	21,883	2,680	...	771	88	...
1841	22,668	2,839	...	793	96	...
1842	23,121	2,933	...	833	108	...
1843	23,040	2,898	...	858	110	...
1844	23,116	2,931	...	900	114	...
1845	23,471	3,004	...	917	119	...
1846	23,808	3,069	...	963	131	...
1847	24,167	3,167	...	1,033	141	...
1848	24,520	3,249	...	1,118	151	...
1849	24,753	3,326	...	1,149	160	...
1850	24,797	3,397	...	1,187	168	...
1851	24,816	3,476	...	1,227	187	...
1852	24,814	3,550	...	1,272	209	...
1853	25,224	3,780	...	1,385	250	...
1854	25,335	3,943	...	1,524	306	...
1855	24,274	3,969	...	1,674	381	...
1856	24,480	3,980	...	1,697	387	...
1857	25,273	4,141	...	1,824	417	...
1858	25,615	4,205	...	1,926	452	...
1859	25,784	4,226	...	1,918	437	...
1860	25,663	4,204	...	2,000	454	...
1861	25,905	4,301	...	2,133	506	
1862	26,212	4,396	...	2,228	538	...
1863	26,339	4,731	...	2,298	597	...
1864	26,142	4,930	...	2,490	697	...
1865	26,069	4,937	...	2,718	823	...
1866	26,140	4,904	...	2,831	876	...
1867	25,842	4,853	...	2,931	901	...
1868	25,500	4,878	...	2,944	902	...
1869	24,187	4,765	...	2,972	948	...
1870	23,189	4,578	...	3,178	1,113	...
1871	22,510	4,374	...	3,382	1,320	...
1872	22,103	4,213	...	3,673	1,538	...
1873	21,698	4,091	...	3,863	1,714	...
1874	21,464	4,108	...	4,033	1,871	...
1875	21,291	4,207	...	4,170	1,946	...
1876	21,144	4,258	...	4,335	2,005	...
1877	21,169	4,261	...	4,564	2,139	...
1878	21,058	4,239	...	4,826	2,316	...
1879	20,538	4,069	...	5,027	2,511	...
1880	19,938	3,851	...	5,247	2,724	...
1881	19,325	3,688	...	5,505	3,004	...
1882	18,892	3,622	...	5,814	3,335	...
1883	18,415	3,514	...	6,260	3,728	...
1884	18,053	3,465	...	6,601	3,944	...
1885	17,018	3,457	...	6,644	3,973	6,322
1886	16,179	3,397	3,513	6,653	3,965	6,524
1887	15,473	3,250	3,363	6,663	4,085	6,951

Transport and Communications 2. *continued*

	Sailing Ships			Steamships*		
	Number	thousand net tons	thousand gross tons	Number	thousand net tons	thousand gross tons
1888	15,025	3,114	3,224	6,871	4,350	7,555
1889	14,640	3,041	3,152	7,139	4,718	8,095
1890	14,181	2,936	3,055	7,410	5,043	8,545
1891	13,823	2,972	3,108	7,720	5,307	8,975
1892	13,578	3,080	3,233	7,950	5,565	9,278
1893	13,239	3,038	3,202	8,088	5,740	9,671
1894	12,943	2,987	3,159	8,263	5,969	9,952
1895	12,617	2,867	3,040	8,386	6,122	10,238
1896	12,274	2,736	2,909	8,522	6,284	10,401
1897	11,911	2,590	2,758	8,590	6,364	10,830
1898	11,566	2,388	2,551	8,838	6,614	10,830
1899	11,167	2,247	2,405	9,029	6,917	11,342
1900	10,773	2,096	2,247	9,209	7,208	11,817
1901	10,572	1,991	2,135	9,484	7,618	12,473
1902	10,455	1,951	2,093	9,803	8,104	13,264
1903	10,330	1,869	2,007	10,122	8,400	13,771
1904	10,210	1,803	1,937	10,370	8,752	14,359
1905	10,059	1,671	1,797	10,522	9,065	14,884
1906	9,857	1,555	1,675	10,907	9,612	15,784
1907	9,648	1,461	1,576	11,394	10,024	16,514
1908	9,542	1,403	1,516	11,626	10,139	16,736
1909	9,392	1,301	1,407	11,797	10,285	16,995
1910	9,090	1,113	1,205	12,000	10,443	17,264
1911	8,830	981	1,065	12,242	10,718	17,744
1912	8,510	903	982	12,382	10,992	18,197
1913	8,336	847	922	12,602	11,273	18,683
				---(*b*)	---(*b*)	---(*b*)
1914	8,203	794	865	12,862	11,622	19,145
1915	8,019	779	845	12,771	11,650	19,166
1916	7,669	715	777	12,405	11,037	18,186
1917	7,186	625	680	11,534	9,608	15,880
1918	6,856	604	655	11,334	9,497	15,709
1919	6,555	593	643	11,791	10,335	17,160
1920	6,309	584	632	12,307	10,777	17,966
1921	6,272	610	657	12,660	10,932	18,289
1922	6,184	574	619	12,787	11,223	18,834
	---	---	---	---	---	---
1923 (*c*)	5,962	551	592	12,437	11,160	18,753
1924	5,842	522	561	12,513	11,195	18,883
1925	5,785	520	559	12,491	11,464	19,334
1926	5,678	517	555	12,432	11,389	19,229
1927	5,609	507	543	12,372	11,347	19,175
1928	5,408	496	531	12,640	11,763	19,889
1929	5,249	480	514	12,795	11,889	20,132
1930	5,098	468	500	12,966	11,986	20,332
1931	4,960	462	493	13,012	11,812	20,092
1932	4,773	472	512	12,898	11,391	19,420
1933	4,632	466	505	12,763	10,704	18,320
1934	4,435	432	459	12,790	10,313	17,705
1935	4,351	414	440	12,800	10,072	17,298
1936	4,288	419	445	12,920	10,171	17,520
1937	4,185	415	441	12,996	10,138	17,449

* including motorships.

See p. 538 for footnotes.

Transport and Communications 2. *continued*

	Steamships and Motorships		
	Number	thousand net tons	thousand gross tons
1938	13,229	10,314	17,733
	---(*d*)	---(*d*)	---(*d*)
1939	13,303	10,511	18,046
1940	13,254	10,412	17,889
1941	12,822	9,674	16,577
1942	12,185	9,000	15,424
1943	12,169	9,119	15,635
1944	12,525	9,994	17,088
1945	12,700	10,341	17,702
1946	12,581	10,315	17,705
1947	12,481	10,371	17,817
1948	12,795	10,461	18,074
	---(*d*)	---(*d*)	---(*d*)
	6,025	...	18,025
1949	6,077	...	18,093
1950	6,060	...	18,219
1951	5,983	...	18,550
1952	5,912	...	18,624
1953	5,784	...	18,584
1954	5,740	...	19,014
1955	5,632	...	19,357
1956	5,508	...	19,546
1957	5,427	...	19,857

	Steamships and Motorships		
	Number	thousand net tons	thousand gross tons
1958	5,417	...	20,286
1959	5,395	...	20,757
1960	5,246	...	21,131
1961	5,182	...	21,465
1962	5,009	...	21,658
1963	4,751	...	21,565
1964	4,538	...	21,490
1965	4,437	...	21,531
1966	4,303	...	21,542
1967	4,156	...	21,716
1968	4,020	...	21,921
1969	3,858	...	23,844
1970	3,822	...	25,825
1971	3,785	...	27,335
1972	3,700	...	28,625
1973	3,628	...	30,160
1974	3,603	...	31,566
1975	3,622	...	33,157
1976	3,549	...	32,923
1977	3,432	...	31,646
1978	3,359	...	30,897
1979	3,211	...	27,951
1980	3,181	...	27,135

(*a*) A new Registry Act in 1827 resulted in the exclusion of many ships that had been lost, but which had been continued on the old register because no evidence of loss had been produced.

(*b*) The coming into force of a new Registration Act in 1914 caused some increase in the number of steamships recorded.

(*c*) As from 1923 ships registered in the ports of southern Ireland were no longer included on the United Kingdom register.

(*d*) From 1939 to 1948 (1st line), figures include vessels registered overseas which were on a bareboat charter to, or requisitioned by, the United Kingdom. See also note 3 above.

Transport and Communications 3. Shipping Registered in the Republic of Ireland 1926–80

NOTE
SOURCE: *Statistical Abstract of Ireland.*

(at 31 December)

	Sailing Ships		Steamships and Motorships			Sailing Ships		Steamships and Motorships	
	Number	thousand net tons	Number	thousand net tons		Number	thousand net tons	Number	thousand net tons
1926	166	8·7	384	56·3	1954	41	4·2	449	45·5
1927	160	8·5	396	55·7	1955	40	4·2	457	46·3
1928	151	6·8	403	56·0	1956	39	4·2	463	55·2
1929	142	6·7	402	56·4	1957	39	4·2	463	66·1
1930	116	5·9	401	54·0	1958	39	4·2	472	78·1
1931	110	5·6	406	47·7	1959	37	4·1	496	83·1
1932	105	5·4	412	47·9	1960	37	4·1	484	76·3
1933	100	5·3	461	46·8	1961	37	4·1	496	83·0
1934	95	4·9	476	57·4	1962	34	3·1	520	96·6
1935	90	4·6	472	68·7	1963	30	3·0	553	102·4
1936	88	4·5	470	68·1	1964	30	2·9	584	102·6
1937	92	5·0	493	69·1	1965	32	3·1	606	85·5
1938	93	5·5	501	110·7	1966	33	3·1	649	86·2
1939	92	5·5	468	35·2	1967	33	3·1	699	82·4
1940	85	5·3	447	24·9	1968	34	3·3	793	88·0
1941	73	4·9	432	32·3	1969	34	3·4	875	88·5
1942	66	4·8	433	46·5	1970	35	3·4	958	107·7
1943	61	4·6	415	40·6	1971	35	3·4	1,065	108·2
1944	58	4·5	408	40·2	1972	35	3·4	1,148	106·2
1945	54	4·5	392	42·0	1973	34	3·4	1,223	143·8
1946	50	4·4	389	33·9	1974	24	0·7	1,320	144·1
1947	49	4·4	384	31·2	1975	26	0·7	1,387	144·1
1948	50	4·4	398	41·8	1976	26	0·7	1,471	135·6
1949	46	4·3	402	38·6	1977	33	0·7	1,569	155·2
1950	47	4·4	422	41·9	1978	33	0·7	1,646	154·1
1951	47	4·4	439	42·5	1979	44	0·7	1,701	147·3
1952	43	4·3	444	43·4	1980	68	1·8	1,779	148·9
1953	42	4·3	445	45·5					

Transport and Communications 4. Indices of Tramp Shipping Freights, 1869–1969

NOTES

[1] SOURCES: L. Isserlis, 'Tramp Shipping Cargoes and Freights', *J.R.S.S.* (1938) to 1936; *Abstract* subsequently.

[2] The indices from 1948 apply to voyage charter rates.

1869 = 100

1869	100	1886	59	1903	49	1920	374
1870	103	1887	65	1904	49	1921	166
1871	102	1888	76	1905	51	1922	130
1872	103	1889	75	1906	52	1923	123
1873	117	1890	64	1907	54	1924	121
1874	108	1891	63	1908	45	1925	110
1875	99	1892	55	1909	46	1926	133
1876	98	1893	60	1910	50	1927	122
1877	99	1894	58	1911	58	1928	112
1878	91	1895	56	1912	78	1929	115
1879	85	1896	56	1913	68	1930	93
1880	87	1897	56	1914	67	1931	90
1881	87	1898	68	1915	199	1932	88
1882	81	1899	65	1916	365	1933	85
1883	75	1900	76	1917	695	1934	85
1884	64	1901	57	1918	751	1935	88
1885	63	1902	49	1919	490	1936	103

1948 = 100

1948	100	1956	157·0	1962	89·1
1949	82·3	1957	112·7	1963	109·0
1950	84·0	1958	67·1	1964	112·1
1951	173·7	1959	71·9	1965	126·5
1952	110·6	1960	74·2	1966	113·5

1952 = 100

1952	100
1953	77·5
1954	86·1
1955	127·7

1960 = 100

1960	100	1967	120·5
1961	106·8	1968	123·8
		1969	117·5

Transport and Communications 5. Railway Length in Miles – British Isles 1825–1980

NOTES

[1] SOURCES: 1825–43 – H. G. Lewin, *Early British Railways* (London, 1925); 1844–1980 – *Railway Returns*, *Abstract*, and *Statistical Abstract of Ireland*.

[2] Statistics relate to route length, irrespective of the number of tracks, at 31 December (except as indicated).

[3] Narrow gauge lines are not included.

<table>
<tr><th></th><th>Great Britain</th><th>Ireland</th></tr>
<tr><td>1825</td><td colspan="2">26·75</td></tr>
<tr><td>1826</td><td colspan="2">38</td></tr>
<tr><td>1827</td><td colspan="2">40·75</td></tr>
<tr><td>1828</td><td colspan="2">44·75</td></tr>
<tr><td>1829</td><td colspan="2">51</td></tr>
<tr><td>1830</td><td colspan="2">97·5</td></tr>
<tr><td>1831</td><td colspan="2">140</td></tr>
<tr><td>1832</td><td colspan="2">166</td></tr>
<tr><td>1833</td><td colspan="2">208·25</td></tr>
<tr><td>1834</td><td colspan="2">298</td></tr>
<tr><td>1835</td><td colspan="2">337·75</td></tr>
<tr><td>1836</td><td colspan="2">403·25</td></tr>
<tr><td>1837</td><td colspan="2">540·25</td></tr>
<tr><td>1838</td><td colspan="2">742·5</td></tr>
<tr><td>1839</td><td colspan="2">969·75</td></tr>
<tr><td>1840</td><td colspan="2">1,497·75</td></tr>
<tr><td>1841</td><td colspan="2">1,775</td></tr>
<tr><td>1842</td><td colspan="2">1,938·75</td></tr>
<tr><td>1843</td><td colspan="2">2,043·75</td></tr>
<tr><td>1844</td><td colspan="2">2,148 (a)</td></tr>
<tr><td>1845</td><td colspan="2">2,441 (a)</td></tr>
<tr><td>1846</td><td colspan="2">3,036 (a)</td></tr>
<tr><td>1847</td><td colspan="2">3,945 (a)</td></tr>
<tr><td>1848</td><td>4,982</td><td>363</td></tr>
<tr><td>1849</td><td>5,538</td><td>494</td></tr>
<tr><td>1850</td><td>6,084</td><td>537</td></tr>
<tr><td>1851</td><td>6,266</td><td>624</td></tr>
<tr><td>1852</td><td>6,628</td><td>708</td></tr>
<tr><td>1853</td><td>6,805</td><td>834</td></tr>
<tr><td>1854</td><td>7,157</td><td>897</td></tr>
<tr><td>1855</td><td>7,293</td><td>987</td></tr>
<tr><td>1856</td><td>7,650</td><td>1,057</td></tr>
<tr><td>1857</td><td>8,023</td><td>1,071</td></tr>
<tr><td>1858</td><td>8,354</td><td>1,188</td></tr>
<tr><td>1859</td><td>8,737</td><td>1,265</td></tr>
<tr><td>1860</td><td>9,069</td><td>1,364</td></tr>
<tr><td>1861</td><td>9,446</td><td>1,423</td></tr>
<tr><td>1862</td><td>9,953</td><td>1,598</td></tr>
<tr><td>1863</td><td>10,581</td><td>1,741</td></tr>
<tr><td>1864</td><td>10,995</td><td>1,794</td></tr>
<tr><td>1865</td><td>11,451</td><td>1,838</td></tr>
<tr><td>1866</td><td>11,945</td><td>1,909</td></tr>
<tr><td>1867</td><td>12,319</td><td>1,928</td></tr>
<tr><td>1868</td><td>...</td><td>...</td></tr>
<tr><td>1869</td><td>[13,170](b)</td><td>[1,975](b)</td></tr>
</table>

	Great Britain	Ireland
1870	[13,562](b)	[1,975](b)
1871	13,388	1,988
1872	13,723	2,091
1873	13,981	2,101
1874	14,322	2,127
1875	14,510	2,148
1876	14,715	2,157
1877	14,874	2,203
1878	15,074	2,259
1879	15,411	2,285
1880	15,563	2,370
1881	15,734	2,441
1882	15,992	2,465
1883	16,179	2,502
1884	16,339	2,525
1885	16,594	2,575
1886	16,700	2,632
1887	16,904	2,674
1888	17,079	2,733
1889	17,152	2,791
1890	17,281	2,792
1891	17,328	2,863
1892	17,430	2,895
1893	17,655	2,991
1894	17,864	3,044
1895	18,001	3,173
1896	18,099	3,178
1897	18,265	3,168
1898	18,483	3,176
1899	18,524	3,176
1900	18,680	3,183
1901	18,870	3,208
1902	18,938	3,214
1903	19,165	3,270
1904	19,338	3,296
1905	19,535	3,312
1906	19,700	3,363
1907	19,746	3,362
1908	19,842	3,363
1909	19,889	3,391
1910	19,986	3,401
1911	20,015	3,402
1912	20,038	3,403
	----(c)	
1913	20,266	3,410
1914	...	...

See p. 542 for footnotes.

Transport and Communications 5. *continued*

	Great Britain	Northern Ireland	Republic of Ireland
1915	...	...	...
1916	...	...	...
1917	...	...	...
1918	...	...	...
1919	20,309	3,444	
1920	20,312	3,444	
1921	20,302	3,444	
1922	20,318	765	2,677
1923	20,334	765	2,677
1924	20,349	765	2,668
1925	20,400	765	2,674
1926	20,405	765	2,674
1927	20,412	765	2,674
1928	20,398 ---(*d*) 20,271	754	2,674
1929	20,271	754	2,674
1930	20,265	754	2,668
1931	20,269	754	2,671
1932	20,248	754	2,670
1933	20,233	754	2,654
1934	20,216	754	2,643
1935	20,152	754	2,556
1936	20,121	754	2,537
1937	20,080	754	2,511
1938	20,007	741	2,511
1939	19,982	741	2,511
1940	19,931	741	2,493
1941	19,904	717	2,492
1942	19,892	717	2,492
1943	19,890	717	2,493
1944	19,880	672	2,493
1945	19,863	672	2,481
1946	19,861	672	2,481
1947	19,853 ---(*e*)	672	2,440
1948	19,598	672	2,440
1949	19,573	672	2,440 ---(*f*)
1950	19,471	645	2,440
1951	19,357	645	2,440
1952	19,276	633	2,376
1953	19,222	633	2,348
1954	19,151	633	2,263
1955	19,061	549	2,259
1956	19,025	549	2,259
1957	18,965	498	2,221
1958	18,848	377	2,197
1959	18,484	340	2,193
1960	18,369	297	1,808
1961	17,903	297	1,747
1962	17,481	297	1,655
1963	16,982	297	1,462
1964	15,991	297	1,458
1965	14,920	203	1,458
1966	13,721	203	1,455
1967	13,172	203	1,334
1968	12,447	203	1,334
1969	12,098	203	1,333
1970	11,799	203	1,333
1971	11,643	203	1,361
1972	11,441	203	1,360
1973	11,357	203	1,361 ---(*f*)
1974	11,289	203	1,360
1975	11,258	203	1,247
1976	11,189	204	1,248
1977	11,168	206	1,246
1978	11,123	206	1,247
1979	11,020	206	1,236
1980	10,964	206	1,236

(*a*) at 30 June.
(*b*) mileage constructed rather than mileage open.
(*c*) Subsequently excluding line belonging to the Manchester Ship Canal.
(*d*) Subsequently excluding line transferred to the London Passenger Transport Board.
(*e*) Subsequent figures relate to the nationalised undertaking only.
(*f*) at 31 March from 1950 to 1973.

Transport and Communications 6. Railway Capital – United Kingdom 1825–1913

NOTES

[1] SOURCES: Paid-up capital – M. C. Reed, *Investment in Railways in Britain, 1820–1844* (Oxford, 1975), pp. 35–37 to 1844; *Railway Returns* subsequently. Capital formation – B. R. Mitchell, "The Coming of the Railway and United Kingdom Economic Growth", *J.E.H.*, xxiv, 3 (1964).

[2] Part of the paid-up capital represented nominal additions. This was reported in *Railway Returns* from 1890, but can be ascertained from the companies accounts for earlier years. It was never as much as £1 million prior to 1874, and was always negligible for Irish companies. Amounts for Great Britain from 1874 are as follows (in £ million at 31 December):

1874	1.1	1881	27.3	1888	42.2	1895	88.2	1902	189.1	1908	196.1
1875	2.9	1882	28.6	1889	46.7	1896	105.9	1903	190.9	1909	196.5
1876	10.6	1883	29.4	1890	57.0	1897	152.0	1904	193.1	1910	196.9
1877	10.9	1884	29.3	1891	64.1	1898	183.0	1905	194.0	1911	197.9
1878	20.5	1885	29.8	1892	67.9	1899	184.3	1906	195.0	1912	198.2
1879	23.8	1886	29.8	1893	77.7	1900	186.5	1907	195.7	1913	199.3
1880	23.9	1887	34.6	1894	80.7	1901	187.1				

[3] Railways later forming part of the London Underground system are included.

(in £ million)

	Paid-up Share and Loan Capital at 31 December		U.K. Gross Capital Formation			
	Great Britain	Ireland	Way and Works	Rolling Stock	Land	Total (*a*)
1825	0.20	—	0.0	0.03	...	...
1826	0.40	—	0.03	0.03	...	...
1827	0.65	—	0.03	0.03	...	...
1828	1.03	—	0.04	0.03	...	...
1829	1.42	—	0.03	0.03	...	...
1830	1.83	—	0.03	0.03	...	...
1831	2.40	0.01	0.17	0.03	0.04	0.26
1832	2.98	0.01	0.26	0.04	0.06	0.38
1833	3.92	0.10	0.53	0.08	0.12	0.79
1834	5.19	0.16	0.72	0.11	0.16	1.06
1835	7.27	0.20	1.17	0.17	0.25	1.64
1836	12.87	0.25	2.45	0.34	0.50	3.31
1837	17.17	0.34	4.51	0.61	0.86	6.02
1838	26.79	0.46	7.88	1.08	1.69	10.67
1839	37.03	0.51	8.60	1.12	1.30	11.04
1840	47.56	0.58	7.68	0.99	0.96	9.67
1841	54.64	0.69	5.28	0.69	0.51	6.53
1842	61.60	0.83	4.28	0.57	0.48	5.37
1843	66.49	1.04	3.47	0.51	0.74	4.75
1844	72.52	1.37	3.67	0.54	0.73	4.98
1845	88.5		10.42	0.78	1.84	13.06
1846	126.3		23.15	2.47	4.36	30.03
1847	167.3		31.87	4.78	7.10	43.87
1848	195.6	8.8	25.15	2.71	4.97	33.09
1849	224.6	9.8	18.66	2.34	3.78	24.83
1850	234.9	10.9	9.85	1.35	1.85	13.08
1851	241.8	11.2	6.68	1.66	1.51	9.92
1852	256.8	11.9	6.85	1.28	1.40	9.70
1853	265.2	13.2	6.94	1.85	1.35	10.20
1854	271.7	14.4	8.49	2.98	1.19	12.73
1855	282.4	15.2	7.68	2.27	1.25	11.31
1856	291.6	16.0	6.12	1.55	1.19	8.98
1857	298.3	16.9	6.76	1.44	1.26	9.64
1858	307.6	17.8	6.51	1.20	1.38	9.31
1859	315.2	19.1	7.13	1.37	1.29	9.92
1860	327.5	20.6	6.91	2.09	1.79	10.94
1861	340.4	21.9	10.31	2.51	1.44	14.43
1862	361.9	23.3	10.76	2.61	2.52	16.13
1863	380.7	23.5	14.33	2.15	3.27	19.95
1864	400.6	25.1	15.43	3.83	3.44	22.98

See p. 544 for footnotes.

Transport and Communications 6. *continued*

(on £ million)

	Paid-up Share and Loan Capital at 31 December		U.K. Gross Capital Formation			
	Great Britain	Ireland	Way and Works	Rolling Stock	Land	Total (*a*)
1865	429·8	25·7	18·74	4·11	5·00	28·24
1866	455·3	26·6	15·93	4·29	4·92	25·56
1867	464·9	27·4	10·57	2·90	3·76	17·43
1868	...	...	7·43	1·95	3·60	13·17
	--- (*b*)	--- (*b*)				
1869	491·9	26·9	6·32	1·67	3·32	11·50
1870	502·7	27·2	5·85	2·47	3·74	12·30
1871	525·7	27·0	7·44	3·33	3·21	14·23
1872	536·4	28·7	8·86	3·86	2·87	16·00
1873	559·1	29·2	10·50	4·80	3·33	19·17
1874	580·1	29·8	13·52	4·79	4·48	23·41
1875	600·0	30·2	14·08	4·51	4·18	23·58
1876	627·5	30·7	14·05	3·63	4·28	22·55
1877	642·8	31·3	12·78	3·03	4·12	20·41
1878	666·6	32·0	12·11	2·16	4·09	19·18
1879	683·9	33·2	9·61	2·05	2·89	15·25
1880	694·6	33·7	9·05	2·71	2·45	14·91
1881	711·3	34·3	10·70	3·06	2·66	17·22
1882	733·9	35·0	10·47	3·23	3·82	18·86
1883	749·5	35·4	10·88	4·42	3·92	20·46
1884	765·7	35·8	13·80	3·63	3·53	21·95
1885	780·3	35·6	10·57	3·34	2·58	17·18
1886	792·4	36·0	9·30	2·17	2·17	14·26
1887	809·5	36·5	8·08	2·36	1·90	12·99
1888	828·2	36·6	7·66	2·71	1·77	12·78
1889	839·6	37·0	7·90	3·36	2·37	14·33
1890	860·2	37·3	8·74	4·27	2·27	16·03
1891	881·6	37·8	10·45	5·10	2·65	18·78
1892	905·9	38·5	10·35	4·73	2·33	17·93
1893	932·6	38·8	10·01	3·56	1·85	15·93
1894	946·2	39·2	10·25	3·22	2·18	16·33
1895	961·8	39·3	11·17	3·18	2·37	17·20
1896	989·8	39·7	11·39	3·91	2·55	18·52
1897	1,050·3	39·5	12·07	4·72	2·85	20·52
1898	1,095·1	39·4	13·98	4·88	2·87	22·82
1899	1,112·2	40·1	13·47	7·15	3·68	25·49
1900	1,136·2	39·8	14·19	6·83	4·00	26·78
1901	1,155·3	40·3	13·54	6·32	3·48	24·84
1902	1,176·3	40·6	13·09	4·83	2·48	22·05
1903	1,192·3	43·3	14·96	4·28	3·88	25·01
1904	1,214·5	43·8	14·97	3·74	2·13	22·63
1905	1,228·8	43·9	12·53	4·70	2·10	21·09
1906	1,242·5	44·4	12·12	5·02	1·71	20·45
1907	1,249·5	44·6	9·47	5·12	1·62	17·73
1908	1,265·5	45·0	7·38	3·48	1·13	13·28
1909	1,269·2	45·2	6·18	3·18	0·93	11·11
1910	1,273·2	45·3	5·91	2·88	0·62	10·52
1911	1,279·0	45·0	5·96	3·29	0·90	10·95
1912	1,289·6	45·3	6·01	4·54	0·75	12·11
	--- (*c*)					
1913	1,282·0		8·47	5·22	1·14	15·82

(*a*) Including expenditure on ancillary businesses.
(*b*) There was a small change in the basis on which some companies made their returns and an improvement in coverage.
(*c*) The Manchester Ship Canal was excluded subsequently, and there was a further small change in the basis of the returns.

Transport and Communications 7. Railway Operating Statistics – Great Britain 1838–1980

NOTE

SOURCES: 1838 – *S.P.* 1839 x; 1843–1938 and later physical statistics – *Railway Returns*, *Transport Statistics Great Britain*, and *Abstract*, whichever provides the latest revisions; financial statistics 1839–47 – 77*Estimates of the Pooled Revenue Receipts and Expenses of the Controlled Undertakings* (in Parliamentary Papers); financial statistics from 1948 – *Annual Report and Accounts* of the British Transport Commission and, from 1963, the British Railways Board.

	Passenger Journeys (million)		Freight Loaded (million tons)	Train Mileage (million miles) (*b*)		Receipts (£ million)			Total Working Expenses (£ million)	Net Working Receipts (£ million)
	Ordinary	Total (*a*)		Passenger	Goods	Passenger Train	Goods Train	Total Working		
1838	5·4	...	...	...	...	...	...	...	...	...
1843 (*c*)	21·7	...	...	...	...	3·1	1·4	4·5	...	...
1844 (*c*)	25·2	...	...	...	...	3·4	1·6	5·0	...	...
1845 (*c*)	30·4	...	...	...	...	3·9	2·2	6·1	...	...
1846 (*c*)	40·2	...	...	...	...	4·6	2·8	7·5	...	...
1847 (*c*)	47·9	...	...	...	...	5·0	3·3	8·4	...	...
1848 (*c*)	54·4	...	...	...	...	5·6	4·2	9·8	...	...
1849	57·8	...	...	...	...	6·0	5·4	11·4	...	...
1850	67·4	...	...	...	...	6·5	6·2	12·7	...	...
1851	79·7	...	...	...	...	7·6	6·9	14·4	...	...
1852	82·8	...	...	33·3	24·5	7·3	7·7	15·0	...	...
1853	95·2	...	...	34·6	29·7	8·0	9·2	17·2	...	...
1854	104	...	...	36·0	33·3	9·6(*d*)	9·7(*d*)	19·3	8·8	10·5
1855	111	...	...	36·9	33·4	10·0	10·5	20·5	9·9	10·6
1856	121	...	63·7	38·3	35·5	10·6	11·4	22·0	10·4	11·6
1857	131	...	70·2	41·6	37·6	11·1	11·9	23·0	10·8	12·2
1858	131	...	71·9	43·7	38·7	10·9	11·9	22·8	11·2	11·6
1859	140	...	77·3	46·1	42·4	11·7	12·8	24·4	...	...
1860	153	...	88·4	48·8	48·0	12·2	14·2	26·4	12·6	13·8
1861	163	...	92·6	49·6	49·5	12·4	14·7	27·1	13·6	14·1
1862	170	...	91·9	52·8	48·8	13·0	14·7	27·7	13·6	14·1
1863	192	...	98·8	56·1	53·8	13·6	16·1	29·6	14·3	15·4
1864	217	...	109	61·4	60·6	14·7	17·7	32·3	15·3	17·1
1865	239	...	113	65·8	66·3	15·5	18·7	34·0	16·3	17·7
1866	261	...	122	67·8	67·2	16·4	20·1	36·4	17·9	18·5

See p. 550 for footnotes.

Transport and Communications 7. *continued*

	Passenger Journeys (million)		Freight Loaded (million tons)	Train Mileage (million miles) (*b*)		Receipts (£ million)			Total Working Expenses (£ million)	Net Working Receipts (£ million)
	Ordinary	Total (*a*)		Passenger	Goods	Passenger Train	Goods Train	Total Working		
1867	274	...	133	69·4	71·4	16·8	20·8	37·6	18·9	18·7
1868	...	...	...	...	...	...	...	...	...	...
	--- (*e*)	--- (*e*)	--- (*e*)	--- (*e*)	--- (*e*)	--- (*e*)	--- (*e*)	--- (*e*)	--- (*e*)	--- (*e*)
1869	299	...	...	75·4	74·1	17·6	21·4	40·7	19·8	20·9
1870	322	...	...	80·8	80·0	18·1	23·2	42·9	20·6	22·3
1871	360	...	166	83·8	86·6	19·4	25·5	46·6	22·0	24·6
				--- (*b*)	--- (*b*)					
1872	407	...	176	87·3	92·0	21·0	28·0	50·8	25·0	25·8
1873	439	...	188	89·0	96·5	22·4	30·7	55·2	29·3	25·8
1874	461	...	185	91·3	97·5	23·5	30·9	56·7	31·1	25·5
1875	490	...	196	95·4	102	24·3	32·1	58·6	31·8	26·8
1876	517	...	202	99·9	103	24·7	32·5	59·4	32·1	27·4
1877	532	...	208	103	104	25·1	32·8	60·2	32·4	27·8
1878	547	...	203	107	103	25·4	32·3	60·1	31·7	28·4
1879	546	...	209	109	105	24·6	32·3	59·2	30·6	28·6
1880	597	...	232	116	112	25·8	34·5	62·8	32·1	30·7
1881	608	...	241	119	116	26·3	35·6	64·5	33·4	31·1
1882	636	...	252	125	120	27·3	36·5	66·6	34·6	31·8
1883	664	...	262	131	124	28·0	37·4	68·2	35·8	32·4
1884	675	...	256	136	123	28·5	36·4	67·7	35·6	32·1
1885	678	...	254	138	122	28·3	35·6	66·8	35·2	31·5
1886	707	...	251	141	122	28·8	35·1	66·8	35·0	31·8
1887	714	...	265	144	125	29·1	36·1	68·1	35·5	32·6
1888	723	...	278	147	129	29·4	37·5	70·0	36·2	33·8
1889	754	...	293	153	135	31·0	39·7	74·0	38·4	35·5
1890	796	...	299	158	139	32·7	40·8	76·8	41·4	35·4
1891	823	...	306	163	144	33·4	41·8	78·7	43·4	35·3
1892	842	...	305	167	144	34·0	41·4	78·9	44·0	34·9
1893	849	...	288	168	137	34·1	39·5	77·4	43·9	33·5
1894	887	...	320	171	145	34·7	41·8	80·9	45·4	35·6
1895	904	...	329	175	146	35·5	42·5	82·4	46·0	36·4
				--- (*b*)	--- (*b*)					
1896	954	...	352	184	153	37·3	44·6	86·6	48·3	38·4

1897	1,005	...	369	192	159	38·7	46·2	90·2	51·1	39·1
1898	1,036	...	373	199	164	39·9	47·6	92·7	53·9	38·8
1899	1,079	...	408	206	172	41·8	50·4	98·0	58·0	40·0
1900	1,115	1,186	420	210	175	43·3	51·8	101·0	62·5	38·5
1901	1,146	1,222	411	213	164	44·6	51·3	102·7	65·1	37·6
1902	1,160	1,257	432	217	164	45·3	52·9	105·4	65·4	40·0
1903	1,167	1,277	438	221	154	45·8	53·3	106·8	66·1	40·7
1904	1,170	1,292	444	229	150	46·2	53·5	107·7	66·6	41·1
1905	1,170	1,302	455	233	150	46·6	54·6	109·4	67·5	41·9
1906	1,211	1,352	483	242	154	47·7	56·5	113·0	70·2	42·8
1907	1,230	1,378	510	250	159	48·7	59·3	117·2	74·0	43·2
1908	1,249	1,397	487	252	152	49·5	56·9	115·6	73·7	41·9
1909	1,235	1,390	494	252	149	49·0	57·5	115·8	72·4	43·5
1910	1,276	1,435	508	255	149	50·5	59·4	119·5	73·8	45·6
1911	1,296	1,464	517	259	151	51·7	61·2	122·7	75·8	46·9
1912	1,265	1,442	514	247	147	52·0	61·9	124·0	78·4	45·6
1913	1,423	...	562	...	...	54·6	64·4	...	...	...
	--- (f)	--- (f)	--- (f)	--- (f)	--- (f)	--- (f)	--- (f)	--- (f)	--- (f)	--- (f)
1913	1,199	1,550	364	261	155	54·5	64·3	119·8	75·7	44·1
1914	...	...	...	...	...	...	...	...	...	...
1915	...	...	...	...	...	...	...	...	...	...
1916	...	...	...	...	...	...	...	...	...	...
1917	...	...	...	...	...	...	...	...	...	...
1918	...	...	...	...	...	...	...	...	...	...

See p. 550 for footnotes.

Transport and Communications 7. *continued*

	Passenger Journeys (million)		Passenger -Miles (million)	Freight Loaded (million tons)	Freight Net Ton-miles (million)	Trains mileage (million miles)		Receipts (£ million)			Total Working Expenses (£ million)	Net Working Receipts (£ million)
	Ordinary	Total (*a*)				Passenger	Goods	Passenger Train	Goods Train	Total Working		
1919	1,523	2,064	...	305	...	195	139	104·2	72·1	178·2	164·6	13·5
1920	1,579	2,186	...	318	19,173	219	145	109·4	129·9	238·9	232·0	7·0
1921	1,229	1,787	...	268	13,289	205	110	105·9	109·6	217·8	226·8	−9·0
1922	1,195	1,749	...	302	16,799	239	132	101·8	115·6	219·3	174·8	44·5
1923	1,236	1,772	...	343	18,961	252	143	94·1	109·8	205·8	166·0	39·8
1924	1,236	1,747	...	335	19,063	255	144	95·1	106·4	203·4	166·9	36·5
1925	1,233	1,743	...	316	18,332	262	141	94·1	103·7	199·7	165·0	34·6
1926	1,069	1,542	...	216	14,042	234	113	85·1	85·0	171·9	154·0	17·9
1927	1,175	1,651	...	322	18,874	269	144	89·5	109·6	200·8	161·0	39·8
	--- (*g*)	--- (*g*)		--- (*g*)	--- (*g*)	--- (*g*)	--- (*g*)	--- (*g*)	--- (*g*)	--- (*g*)	--- (*g*)	--- (*g*)
1928	847	1,250	...	306	17,725	251	139	82·0	103·1	186·9	149·1	37·7
1929	870	1,268	...	330	18,846	257	144	80·0	106·5	188·2	146·9	41·3
1930	844	1,238	...	304	17,784	258	139	76·8	99·3	177·7	143·3	34·4
1931	795	1,172	...	268	16,314	254	131	71·3	90·3	163·1	132·6	30·5
1932	777	1,141	...	250	14,934	254	123	67·1	81·2	149·6	125·2	24·4
1933	799	1,159	...	251	15,018	258	123	67·4	80·8	149·6	123·1	26·5
1934	830	1,200	...	270	16,210	267	129	68·6	85·5	155·6	126·8	28·8
1935	856	1,231	...	271	16,402	273	130	70·0	86·2	157·7	127·4	30·3
1936	876	1,257	...	281	17,430	279	136	72·2	90·2	164·0	130·6	33·4
1937	906	1,295	...	297	18,384	283	140	75·2	94·6	171·4	136·1	35·3
1938	850	1,237	18,993	266	16,266	288	134	75·3	87·8	164·7	137·7	27·1
1939	845	1,226	...	288	...	257	139	...	...	...	...	...
1940	691	967	...	294	...	201	155	[104·8](*h*)	[140·5](*h*)	[248·0](*h*)	[203·5](*h*)	[44·5](*h*)
1941	778	1,023	...	287	...	202	152	[132·1](*h*)	[158·8](*h*)	[293·8](*h*)	[226·6](*h*)	[67·2](*h*)
1942	944	1,218	...	295	23,822	203	156	[163·5](*h*)	[176·7](*h*)	[343·5](*h*)	[251·7](*h*)	[91·8](*h*)
1943	1,037	1,335	32,273	301	24,358	204	156	[186·3](*h*)	[190·9](*h*)	[381·7](*h*)	[272·2](*h*)	[109·4](*h*)
1944	1,039	1,345	32,052	293	24,444	202	155	[194·6](*h*)	[196·1](*h*)	[394·4](*h*)	[301·2](*h*)	[93·2](*h*)
1945	1,056	1,372	35,248	266	22,023	216	143	[210·6](*h*)	[169·7](*h*)	[383·9](*h*)	[317·0](*h*)	[66·9](*h*)
1946	901	1,266	29,231	262	20,639	237	137	[202·2](*h*)	[155·1](*h*)	[360·7](*h*)	[325·2](*h*)	[35·5](*h*)
1947	769	1,140	23,015	257	20,190	223	131	[195·7](*h*)	[156·6](*h*)	[355·6](*h*)	[367·2](*h*)	[−11·6](*h*)
	--- (*i*)	--- (*i*)	--- (*i*)	--- (*i*)	--- (*i*)	--- (*i*)	--- (*i*)	--- (*i*)	--- (*i*)	--- (*i*)	--- (*i*)	--- (*i*)
1948	700	996	21,259	273	21,662	228	137	151·9	180·5	336·1	328·5	26·3
1949	711	993	21,138	280	22,010	241	140	142·7	178·9	325·5	327·8	12·7
1950	704	982	20,177	281	22,135	243	141	137·3	198·9	340·1	324·8	26·3

1951	720	1,001	20,793	285	22,902	235	142	140·1	227·9	372·7	349·9	35·0
1952	711	989	20,459	285	22,391	236	141	147·9	250·5	403·4	384·8	39·6
1953	711	985	20,578	289	22,766	238	142	153·3	263·1	421·4	407·6	35·1
1954	745	1,020	20,712	284	22,089	238	140	157·4	272·8	435·5	416·4	16·6
1955	730	994	20,308	274	21,353	230	133	160·1	274·2	440·0	434·1	2·1
									--- (l)			
									284·1	465·5	481·5	−16·3
1956	740	1,029	21,133	277	21,473	241	135	175·1	--- (m)	--- (m)	--- (m)	--- (m)
									300·0	479·3	497·5	−16·5
1957	788	1,101	22,591	274	20,880	247	135	190·3	301·9	499·6	528·6	−27·1
1958	777	1,090	22,150	243	18,426	250	126	189·9	274·5	469·8	519·7	−48·1
1959	749	1,069	22,270	234	17,711	250	121	198·3	254·2	455·6	499·4	−42·0
1960	721	1,037	21,547	248	18,650	253	122	206·7	261·4	476·7	546·2	−67·7
1961	708	1,025	21,061	238	17,591	253	119	213·8	250·4	472·6	561·6	−86·9
						248	111			462·7	571·4	−108·7
1962	670	965	19,728	228	16,104	--- (k)	--- (k)	218·6(l)	235·7(l)	--- (o)	--- (o)	--- (o)
						239	96·2			462·4	569·1	−104·0
1963	647	938	19,230	235	15,398	233	91·6	219·3	235·4	463·1	550·2	−87·1
1964	629	928	19,874	240	16,052	226	87·6	225·8	233·0	468·3	541·6	−73·3
								231·3				
1965	580	865	18,713	228	15,429	213	77·5	--- (n)	225·5	466·2	545·7	−79·5
								231·6				
1966	547	835	18,453	214	14,790	208	68·0	237·7	216·9	463·8	542·1	−78·3
1967	537	837	18,089	201	13,609	203	61·0	235·2	194·8	438·7	536·1	−97·4
1968	532	831	17,835	207	14,693	198	60·3	243·2	204·3	456·5	547·1	−90·6
								--- (m)	--- (m)	--- (m)	--- (m)	--- (m)
1969	517	805	18,400	207	15,458	195	61·3	263·7	197·1	471·6	491·7	−20·1
1970	526	824	18,895	205	16,394	196	62·7	290·2	208·2	509·8	532·0	−22·2
1971	499	816	18,720	195	14,848	198	57·0	326·0	193·9	532·1	578·0	−45·9
1972	446	754	18,082	176	14,284	196	52·9	342·7	183·3	564·2	625·1	−60·9
1973	428	728	18,517	195	15,603	195	53·9	371·1	198·5	581·5	687·1	−105·6
1974	436	733	19,200	175	14,780	198	51·1	404·1	205·5	621·5	882·9	−261·4
								--- (m)	--- (m)	--- (m)	--- (m)	--- (m)
1975	433	730	18,828	174	14,356	204	47·2	516·5	244·8	774·2	1,151	−376·7
1976	404	701	17,709	175	14,129	202	43·3	603·3	307·0	924·6	1,256	−331·1
					13,944							
1977	408	702	18,206	169	--- (j)	206	40·5	703·0	348·2	1,067	1,400	−332·6
					12,415							
1978	430	724	19,076	169	12,220	208	37·5	821·2	384·5	1,220	1,635	−417·9
1979	439	748	19,884	168	12,166	207	36·0	930·5	432·1	1,383	1,889	−505·8
1980	439	760	19,076	152	10,788	214	32·5	1,095	459·8	1,573	2,250	−677·1

See p. 550 for footnotes.

(*a*) Including season ticket holders.

(*b*) Mixed trains were classified separately from 1872 to 1912, though the majority was distributed amongst the other classes from 1896. Their train mileage in this period was as follows (in million miles):

1872	2·2	1879	2·1	1886	2·2	1893	2·6	1900	0·4	1907	0·3
1873	2·3	1880	2·1	1887	2·2	1894	2·6	1901	0·4	1908	0·3
1874	2·2	1881	2·2	1888	2·2	1895	2·7	1902	0·4	1909	0·4
1875	2·5	1882	2·1	1889	2·2	1896	0·4	1903	0·4	1910	0·4
1876	2·8	1883	2·1	1890	2·3	1897	0·4	1904	0·4	1911	0·5
1877	2·0	1884	2·6	1891	2·4	1898	0·3	1905	0·4	1912	0·5
1878	2·2	1885	2·1	1892	2·5	1899	0·4	1906	0·3		

(*c*) Years ended 30 June.

(*d*) Prior to 1854 passengers' luggage etc., and mails were counted as goods, whereas subsequently they contributed to passenger train receipts.

(*e*) Returns were not always made by all companies prior to 1869 though (except in 1868) the defaulters were unimportant. A more serious defect of the statistics before 1869 is that the companies did not make returns on the same basis. This affects comparisons before and after that date, most particularly so in the case of passenger journeys. After 1868 children were treated as units, whereas some companies had reckoned them as half-passengers previously – a practice which had been standard until at least 1850. Also prior to 1869, the receipts and expenses of ancillary businesses were not included in the last three columns.

(*f*) Statistics were collected on a new basis in 1913, and in addition the properties of the Manchester Ship Canal Company were no longer included.

(*g*) Another fresh basis of collecting the statistics was adopted in 1928, and in 1933 the properties transferred to the London Passenger Transport Board were excluded. Revised figures for the whole period 1928–33 are given here. The figures for 1928 on the new basis but including the L.P.T.B. are as follows:

	Passenger Journeys	Freight Loaded	Train Mileage		Receipts				
			Passenger	Goods	Passenger Train	Goods Train	Total Working	Total Working Expenses	Net Working Receipts
1928	1,195·9	306·1	277·2	139·6	88·9	103·3	194·0	153·5	40·5

(*h*) From the estimates of pooled receipts and expenses of the controlled undertakings, which included the L.P.T.B.

(*i*) British Rail(ways) only from 1948.

(*j*) There was a change in the method of estimation.

(*k*) Subsequently loaded train mileage.

(*l*) Subsequently including receipts from road freight services, though these were partly transferred to passenger train receipts in 1962.

(*m*) Major changes in the classification of receipts and expenses were made in 1957, but they did not affect the series for passenger train receipts. Other changes occurred in 1969 and 1975.

(*n*) Subsequently including Pullman car supplements.

(*o*) Subsequently excluding receipts and expenses of the ancillary activities of Rail Catering, commerical advertising, letting of sites, etc.

Transport and Communications 8. Railway Operating Statistics – Ireland 1843–1980

NOTE TO PART A

SOURCE: *Railway Returns* and *Abstract*, whichever provides the latest revisions.

A. Ireland 1843–1921

	Passenger Journeys (million) (*a*)	Freight Loaded (million tons)	Train Mileage (million miles)			Receipts (£ million)			Total Working Expenses (£ million)	Net Working Receipts (£ million)
			Passenger	Goods	Mixed	Passenger Train	Goods Train	Total Working		
1843 (*b*)	2·1	...	...	...	...	0·06	0·01	0·06	...	...
1844 (*b*)	2·6	...	...	...	...	0·06	0·01	0·07	...	...
1845 (*b*)	3·4	...	...	...	...	0·10	0·01	0·11	...	...
1846 (*b*)	3·6	...	...	...	...	0·11	0·02	0·12	...	...
1847 (*b*)	3·8	...	...	...	...	0·15	0·04	0·18	...	...
1848 (*b*)	3·8	...	...	...	...	0·21	0·07	0·28	...	...
1849	6·1	...	...	...	...	0·29	0·13	0·42	...	...
1850	5·5	...	...	...	...	0·34	0·18	0·51	...	...
1851	5·6	...	...	...	...	0·37	0·20	0·54	...	...
1852	6·2	...	2·4	0·5	—	0·44	0·24	0·68	...	...
1853	7·1	...	2·6	0·7	—	0·54	0·29	0·83	...	...
						--- (*c*)	--- (*c*)			
1854	6·9	...	2·8	0·7	—	0·62	0·26	0·88	...	...
1855	7·2	...	3·0	0·8	—	0·69	0·31	1·0	0·41	0·59
1856	7·9	1·0	3·2	1·0	—	0·76	0·35	1·1	0·41	0·71
1857	8·4	1·1	3·3	1·1	—	0·78	0·36	1·1	0·44	0·71
1858	8·4	1·2	3·3	1·2	—	0·78	0·39	1·2	0·46	0·72
1859	9·4	1·4	3·6	1·4	—	0·85	0·45	1·3	...	...
1860	10·0	1·5	4·1	1·4	—	0·88	0·49	1·4	0·62	0·75
1861	10·7	1·7	4·4	1·6	—	0·91	0·54	1·4	0·64	0·81
1862	10·4	1·7	4·7	1·7	—	0·88	0·57	1·4	0·70	0·75
1863	11·5	1·7	4·9	1·7	—	0·94	0·58	1·5	0·75	0·77
1864	11·9	1·8	5·1	2·0	—	0·99	0·59	1·6	0·75	0·83
1865	13·2	2·0	5·4	2·0	—	1·1	0·66	1·7	0·81	0·90
1866	13·1	2·3	5·6	2·3	—	1·0	0·72	1·8	0·90	0·86
1867	14·0	2·5	5·5	2·3	—	1·1	0·77	1·9	0·98	0·89
1868	...	...	...	...	...	...	...	...	...	...
	--- (*d*)	--- (*d*)	--- (*d*)	--- (*d*)	--- (*d*)	--- (*d*)	--- (*d*)	--- (*d*)	--- (*d*)	--- (*d*)
1869	13·3	...	5·7	2·2	—	1·2	0·82	2·0	1·0	1·0
1870	14·3	...	5·8	2·4	—	1·2	0·88	2·1	1·1	1·0
1871	15·5	2·9	6·2	2·5	—	1·3	0·97	2·3	1·2	1·1
1872	16·3	3·1	5·7	2·7	0·8	1·3	1·1	2·4	1·3	1·1
1873	16·3	3·2	5·9	2·8	0·8	1·4	1·1	2·6	1·4	1·2
1874	16·5	3·1	5·4	2·5	1·5	1·4	1·1	2·6	1·4	1·1
1875	16·9	3·4	5·4	2·5	1·7	1·4	1·2	2·7	1·5	1·2
1876	17·4	3·5	6·0	2·8	0·9	1·4	1·3	2·8	1·5	1·3
1877	17·3	3·7	6·2	3·0	0·8	1·4	1·3	2·8	1·5	1·3
1878	17·9	3·6	6·4	3·1	0·9	1·5	1·3	2·8	1·5	1·3
1879	16·4	3·6	6·5	3·1	0·9	1·4	1·2	2·6	1·5	1·1
1880	17·3	3·6	6·8	3·3	0·9	1·4	1·2	2·7	1·5	1·2
1881	17·6	3·6	7·3	3·6	0·4	1·4	1·2	2·6	1·5	1·2
1882	18·7	3·8	7·4	3·5	0·6	1·5	1·3	2·8	1·5	1·3
1883	19·3	4·0	7·5	3·6	0·6	1·5	1·3	2·9	1·6	1·3
1884	19·6	3·8	7·6	3·8	0·4	1·5	1·3	2·8	1·6	1·3
1885	19·1	3·7	8·0	3·9	0·4	1·5	1·2	2·8	1·6	1·3
1886	18·7	3·6	8·1	3·6	0·7	1·5	1·3	2·8	1·5	1·3
1887	19·5	3·8	8·1	3·9	0·5	1·5	1·3	2·8	1·5	1·3

See p. 554 for footnotes.

Transport and Communications 8. *continued*

A. Ireland 1843–1921 (*cont.*)

	Passenger Journeys (million) (*a*)	Freight Loaded (million tons)	Train Mileage (million miles)			Receipts (£ million)			Total Working Expenses (£ million)	Net Working Receipts (£ million)
			Passenger	Goods	Mixed	Passenger Train	Goods Train	Total Working		
1888	19·9	3·8	8·3	3·9	0·7	1·5	1·3	2·9	1·5	1·4
1889	21·0	4·2	8·4	4·1	0·9	1·6	1·4	3·0	1·7	1·4
1890	21·4	4·3	8·5	4·3	0·9	1·7	1·4	3·1	1·8	1·4
1891	22·2	4·4	8·6	4·4	0·9	1·7	1·5	3·2	1·7	1·5
1892	22·6	4·3	8·8	4·5	0·9	1·7	1·4	3·2	1·7	1·4
1893	23·7	4·2	9·1	4·4	1·1	1·7	1·5	3·2	1·8	1·5
1894	24·5	4·6	9·3	4·8	1·1	1·8	1·6	3·4	1·8	1·6
1895	26·2	4·8	9·4	4·7	1·6	1·8	1·6	3·5	1·9	1·6
1896	26·6	4·7	9·8	4·9	1·6	1·9	1·6	3·5	1·9	1·6
1897	25·9	5·0	9·8	4·9	1·7	1·9	1·6	3·5	2·0	1·6
1898	26·6	5·1	10·1	5·0	1·7	1·9	1·6	3·6	2·1	1·5
1899	27·4	5·2	10·4	5·1	1·6	2·0	1·7	3·7	2·1	1·6
1900	27·7	5·2	10·5	5·2	1·6	2·0	1·7	3·8	2·3	1·5
1901	26·9	5·1	10·8	5·4	1·3	2·0	1·7	3·8	2·4	1·4
1902	28·2	5·3	11·0	5·3	1·4	2·1	1·8	4·0	2·4	1·6
1903	28·6	5·6	11·1	5·5	1·5	2·1	1·8	4·1	2·5	1·6
1904	29·0	5·7	11·3	5·2	1·4	2·1	1·9	4·1	2·6	1·6
1905	29·0	5·7	11·3	5·0	1·4	2·1	1·8	4·1	2·5	1·6
1906	29·2	5·8	11·6	5·1	1·5	2·2	1·9	4·2	2·5	1·6
1907	29·7	6·1	12·2	5·4	1·1	2·2	1·9	4·3	2·6	1·7
1908	29·0	6·0	12·1	5·3	1·2	2·2	1·9	4·3	2·7	1·6
1909	29·6	6·2	12·0	5·3	1·2	2·2	2·0	4·3	2·7	1·7
1910	30·7	6·5	11·8	5·3	1·4	2·3	2·1	4·5	2·7	1·7
1911	30·8	6·6	11·7	5·4	1·4	2·3	2·1	4·5	2·8	1·7
1912	29·2	6·7	5·4	11·4	1·4	2·3	2·1	4·5	2·8	1·7
	--- (*e*)	--- (*e*)	--- (*e*)	--- (*e*)	--- (*e*)	--- (*e*)	--- (*e*)	--- (*e*)	--- (*e*)	--- (*e*)
1913	31·3	6·7	12·2	6·3	—	2·4	2·3	4·9	3·0	1·9
1919	28·5	6·0	8·5	5·4	—	3·7	2·8	7·3	7·3	—
1920	25·3	6·5(*f*)	8·4	6·0	—	4·2	4·8	9·1	9·4	−0·4
1921	22·6	4·8(*f*)	8·1	5·0	—	4·6	4·9	9·5	10·0	−0·4

See p. 554 for footnotes.

NOTES TO PART B

[1] SOURCES: *Railway Returns* and *Statistical Abstract of Ireland*.

[2] Prior to 1958 the statistics include the traffic in Northern Ireland of those companies which operated on both sides of the border. Similar statistics are available for Northern Ireland, but are not given here since the element of double-counting would be substantial.

B. Republic of Ireland 1922–80

	Passenger Journeys (million) (*a*)	Freight Loaded (million tons) (*g*)	Train Mileage (million miles)		Receipts (£ million)			Total Expenses (£ million)	Net Receipts (£ million)
			Passenger	Goods	Passenger Train (*h*)	Goods Train (*h*)	Total		
1922	21·8	4·1	...	...	...	...	6·9	6·5	0·4
1923	24·1	4·2	...	...	...	...	7·4	6·1	1·3
1924	24·6	4·6	...	...	...	...	7·4	6·5	0·9
1925	25·0	4·2	...	...	...	...	6·5	5·9	0·6
1926	24·2	3·1	...	...	2·7	3·1	6·2	5·6	0·6
1927	23·1	3·7	9·0	4·7	2·5	3·3	6·3	5·3	0·9
1928	22·3	3·7	9·1	4·8	2·3	3·3	6·0	5·0	1·0
1929	23·3	3·7	9·4	4·8	2·2	3·2	5·9	4·9	1·1
1930	21·6	3·4	9·3	4·7	2·1	3·1	5·7	4·8	0·9
1931	20·7	3·4	9·1	4·6	1·9	2·9	5·3	4·5	0·8
1932	19·8	2·9	8·8	4·3	1·9	2·3	4·7	4·3	0·4
1933	18·2	2·6	7·6	3·9	1·6	2·0	4·1	3·9	0·2
1934	20·2	3·1	8·5	4·3	1·8	2·2	5·2	4·8	0·4
1935	23·1	3·3	8·5	4·5	1·8	2·4	5·6	5·0	0·6
1936	21·1	3·3	8·5	4·6	1·9	2·4	5·8	5·2	0·6
1937	20·6	3·2	8·6	4·5	1·9	2·4	5·8	5·3	0·5
1938	19·9	3·0	8·5	4·4	1·9	2·4	5·7	5·4	0·3
1939	20·4	3·3	8·5	4·5	1·9	2·6	6·1	5·6	0·5
1940	20·4	3·5	8·3	4·6	1·8	2·9	6·3	5·9	0·4
1941	25·8	3·9	7·3	4·7	2·5	3·6	7·8	6·7	1·2

See p. 554 for footnotes.

Transport and Communications 8. *continued*

	Passenger Journeys (million)	Passenger-Miles (million)	Freight Loaded (million tons)	Freight Ton-Miles (million) (*g*)	Train Mileage (million miles) Passenger	Train Mileage (million miles) Goods	Receipts (£ million) Passenger Train (*h*)	Receipts (£ million) Goods Train (*h*)	Receipts (£ million) Total	Total Expenses (£ million)	Net Receipts (£ million)
1942	24·8	...	4·0	...	5·1	5·3	2·6	3·8	8·5	7·2	1·2
1943	27·7	...	4·3	...	5·4	5·4	3·2	4·2	9·6	8·3	1·3
1944	27·7	...	4·5	...	4·9	5·1	3·1	4·7	10·5	9·1	1·5
1945	27·7	...	4·4	...	5·7	4·6	3·2	4·8	12·6	11·0	1·6
1946	25·5	...	4·1	...	6·7	4·7	3·2	4·5	12·5	11·8	0·7
1947	24·9	...	3·9	...	6·0	4·1	3·1	4·5	12·6	12·9	−0·3
1948	23·1	...	3·6	...	7·0	4·1	3·5	4·7	13·9	14·9	−0·9
1949	21·3	...	3·6	...	7·3	4·1	3·5	4·6	14·4	15·0	−0·7
1950	18·1	...	3·6	...	7·2	4·1	[3·5](*i*)	[5·4](*i*)	[16·8](*i*)	[18·1](*i*)	[−1·3](*i*)
1951	18·1	...	3·5	...	7·4	4·3	3·3	5·1	15·9	17·9	−2·1
1952	17·2	...	3·1	...	7·5	4·0	3·6	5·2	16·8	19·0	−2·2
1953	16·9	...	3·3	...	7·7	4·0	[3·4](*j*)	[5·1](*j*)	[18·3](*j*)	[19·3](*j*)	[−0·9](*j*)
1954	16·4	...	3·1	...	7·9	4·0	4·0	5·8	18·7	19·1	−0·4
1955	17·2	...	3·2	...	8·0	4·0	4·0	5·5	18·9	20·2	−1·3
1956	16·2	...	2·8	...	7·9	3·7	4·2	5·3	19·1	20·2	−1·1
1957	16·9	...	2·5	...	8·1	3·6	4·4	5·3	18·9	20·1	−1·3
	--- (*k*)	--- (*k*)	--- (*k*)	--- (*k*)	--- (*k*)	--- (*k*)	--- (*k*)	--- (*k*)	--- (*k*)	--- (*k*)	--- (*k*)
1958	11·7	326	2·2	187	5·9	2·8	3·4	4·1	7·6	8·9	−1·3
1959	12·3	344	2·4	194	5·8	2·9	3·5	4·3	7·9	8·7	−0·8
1960	11·1	352	2·5	207	5·4	3·0	3·7	4·6	8·4	8·9	−0·5
1961	10·2	344	2·4	202	5·0	2·9	3·7	4·6	8·4	10·0	−1·6
1962	9·8	337	2·5	206	5·0	2·7	3·9	4·6	8·6	10·0	−1·4
1963	9·8	331	2·5	208	4·7	2·7	3·9	4·7	8·7	9·6	−0·9
1964	9·3	333	2·4	204	4·6	2·8	4·1	5·1	9·3	10·5	−1·2
1965	9·0	337	2·4	230	4·5	2·9	4·1	5·1	9·3	11·1	−1·8
1966	9·3	346	2·6	252	4·4	3·0	4·4	5·4	9·8	11·7	−1·9
1967	8·9	339	2·9	294	4·3	3·2	4·5	5·6	10·2	12·4	−2·2
1968	9·5	354	3·2	319	4·5	3·2	5·2	6·1	11·4	13·5	−2·1
1969	10·0	360	3·1	298	4·7	3·2	5·6	6·2	11·9	15·0	−3·1
1970	10·3	469	3·3	324	4·8	3·3	5·9	6·6	12·7	17·4	−4·8
1971	11·0	486	3·6	343	4·9	3·3	6·9	7·6	14·6	20·0	−5·4
1972	11·9	524	3·6	340	5·0	3·2	7·2	7·7	15·0	21·2	−6·2
1973	12·7	544	3·7	346	5·8	2·9	8·9	8·1	17·1	25·2	−8·1
1974	[11·4](*k*)	[432](*k*)	[2·7](*k*)	[274](*k*)	...	...	[7·9](*k*)	[6·1](*k*)	[14·1](*k*)	[23·5](*k*)	[−9·4](*k*)
1975	13·9	558	3·3	342	4·7	2·5	9·7	8·4	20·3	38·4	−18·1
1976	13·6	490	3·5	364	4·3	2·5	10·7	10·0	23·3	45·0	−21·7
1977	14·7	544	3·5	365	4·4	2·6	12·5	10·3	25·6	49·9	−24·3
1978	15·9	600	3·8	385	5·3	3·0	15·1	10·9	29·5	57·2	−27·7
1979	17·9	691	3·7	385	5·5	3·1	19·4	11·0	34·4	70·3	−25·8
1980	16·7	642	3·6	389	5·4	3·2	22·9	12·5	40·7	85·9	−45·2

(*a*) Excluding season ticket-holders.
(*b*) Years ended 30 June.
(*c*) Prior to 1854 passengers' luggage etc., and mails were counted as goods, whereas subsequently they contributed to passenger train receipts.
(*d*) Returns were not always made by all companies prior to 1869, though (except in 1868) the defaulters were unimportant. A more serious defect of the statistics before 1869 is that the different companies did not make returns on the same basis. This affects comparisons before and after that date, most particularly so in the case of passenger journeys. After 1868 children were treated as units, whereas some companies had reckoned them as half-passengers previously – a practice which had been standard until at least 1850. Also prior to 1869 the receipts and expenses of ancillary businesses were not included in the last three columns.
(*e*) Statistics were collected on a new basis in 1913, though there is probably no significant break in the series given here.
(*f*) Net ton-mileage figures are available for these years, as follows (in millions):
1920 380 1921 275
(*g*) Net ton mileage figures are available for 1922–26 as follows (in millions):
1922 277 1923 245 1924 256 1925 240 1926 232
They are also available for 1949–57 for the Great Southern and Great Northern Railway systems, as follows (in millions):
1949 247 1951 250 1953 233 1955 235 1957 213
1950 253 1952 218 1954 226 1956 199
(*h*) Prior to 1958 these columns cover only the Great Southern and Great Northern Railway systems.
(*i*) The Great Southern Railway (which had become the state system) component was for the 15 months ended 31 March 1951. It was subsequently for years ended 31 March following until the 1958 reorganisation.
(*j*) The Great Northern Railway component was for the 9 months ended 31 August, and it was subsequently for periods ended 30 September until the 1958 reorganisation.
(*k*) Subsequent statistics relate solely to traffic in the Republic of Ireland, and are for years beginning 1 April until 1973. The 1974 figures are for the period 1 April–31 December.

Transport and Communications 9. Mileage of Roads – Great Britain 1922–80

NOTES

[1] Sources: 1922–7 – *Annual Reports of the Road Fund*; 1928–80 – British Road Federation, *Basic Road Statistics* and *Abstract*.

[2] The figures relate to 31 March in the year indicated, or in Scotland, prior to 1976, to 16 May.

	Trunk Roads	Class I	Class II	Class III	Unclassified	Total
1922	—	22,189	14,400	—	140,717	177,306
1923	—	22,756	14,646	—	139,907	177,309
1924	—	23,230	14,739	—	139,352	177,321
1925	—	24,048	14,638	—	138,996	177,682
1926	—	24,329	14,930	—	138,947	178,206
1927	—	24,552	15,625	—	138,185	178,362
1928	—	25,121	15,683	—	137,933	178,737
1929	—	25,528	15,747	—	137,820	179,095
1930	—	25,996	15,805	—	137,485	179,286
					---(*a*)	---(*a*)
1931	—	26,417	15,924	—	134,915	177,256
					---(*a*)	---(*a*)
1932	—	26,513	16,482	—	133,796	176,791
1933	—	26,585	16,644	—	134,118	177,347
1934	—	26,663	16,774	—	134,385	177,822
1935	—	26,779	16,837	—	134,891	178,507
					---(*a*)	---(*a*)
1936	—	27,015	16,855	—	134,233	178,103
1937	—	27,142	16,930	—	134,832	178,904
1938	2,854	24,405	17,037	—	132,334	179,630
1939	4,456	23,089	17,634	—	135,348	180,527
1940	4,456	23,176	17,715	—	...	...
1941	4,463	23,176	17,715	—	...	...
1942	4,459	23,180	17,729	—	...	...
1943	4,459	23,180	17,729	—	...	...
1944	4,457	23,180	17,731	—	...	...
1945	4,457	23,195	17,750	—	...	...
1946	4,455	23,194	17,748	—	137,666	183,063
1947	8,190	19,517	17,708	48,323	89,313	183,051
1948	8,189	19,538	17,715	48,351	89,684	183,477
1949	8,189	19,583	17,694	48,584	89,608	183,658
1950	8,176	19,599	17,697	48,614	89,735	183,821
1951	8,249	19,533	17,697	48,682	90,676	184,837
1952	8,248	19,563	17,691	48,678	91,343	185,523
1953	8,254	19,551	17,700	48,693	92,063	186,261
1954	8,270	19,585	17,690	48,721	92,774	187,040
1955	8,270	19,606	17,696	48,781	93,742	188,095
1956	8,270	19,670	17,646	48,818	94,633	189,837
1957	8,271	19,736	17,605	48,849	95,690	190,151
1958	8,309	19,706	17,603	48,853	96,675	191,146
1959	8,334(*b*)	19,735	17,595	48,875	98,533	193,072
1960	8,438(*b*)	19,738	17,606	48,913	99,485	194,180
1961	8,468(*b*)	19,747(*c*)	17,620	48,927	100,455	195,217
1962	8,484(*b*)	19,758(*c*)	17,615	48,955	101,323	196,135
1963	8,541(*b*)	19,797(*c*)	17,608	48,982	103,527	198,455
1964	8,628(*b*)	19,823(*c*)	17,627	48,987	104,678	199,743

See p. 556 for footnotes.

Transport and Communications 9. *continued*

	Motorways	Trunk Roads	Principal Roads	Unclassified	Total
1964	292	8,342	19,817	171,292	199,743
1965	355	8,344	19,845	172,478	201,022
1966	392	8,336	19,908	173,428	202,064
1967	473	8,334	20,207	173,658 --- (*d*) 167,092	202,672 --- (*d*) 196,106
1968	563	8,376	20,187	168,277	197,403
1969	599	8,384	20,204	169,847	199,034
1970	657	8,352	20,225	171,149	200,382
1971	789	8,343	20,320	172,281	201,734
1972	1,037	8,351	20,359	173,880	203,627
1973	1,076	8,296	20,353	173,547	203,272
1974	1,161	8,291	20,359	174,617	204,428
1975	1,224	8,305	20,403	175,096	205,027
1976	1,343	8,357	20,595	176,549	206,844
1977	1,395	8,135	20,820	177,622	207,972
1978	1,482	7,794	21,186	178,462	208,924
1979	1,523	7,745	21,329	179,330	209,926
1980	1,588	7,701	21,252	180,382	210,922

(*a*) The reductions between 1930 and 1931, 1931 and 1932, and 1935 and 1936 result from discrepancies discovered by County Councils on transfer of highway functions over the Local Government Act, 1929.

(*b*) Including the following mileage of motorway:

1959	8	1963	194
1960	95	1964	292
1961	130		
1962	145		

(*c*) Including 6 miles of motorway from 1961 to 1964.

(*d*) Subsequently excluding unsurfaced roads.

Transport and Communications 10. Vehicles in Use – Great Britain 1904–80

NOTES

[1] SOURCES: British Road Federation, *Basic Road Statistics*. Original sources given as: 1904–20 (except trams) – Society of Motor Manufacturers and Traders, *The Motor Industry of Great Britain 1935*; 1921–5 (except trams) – *Return of Motor Taxation*; 1926–38 (including trams from 1933) – *Annual Vehicle Census*; 1904–32 (trams) – *Annual Return of Tramway and Light Railway (Street and Road) Undertakings*.

[2] Vehicles exempt from road duty are included in "Others".

(in thousands)

March	Private Cars	Motor Cycles	'Buses and Coaches	Taxis	Goods Vehicles	Others (*a*) (except trams)	Total (except trams)	Tramcars
1904	8	...	5		4	...	...	7
1905	16	...	7		9	...	...	8
1906	23	...	10		12	...	...	9
1907	32	...	12		14	...	...	10
1908	41	...	15		18	...	...	10
1909	48	...	16		22	...	...	11
1910	53	36	24		30	...	144	11
1911	72	48	33		40	...	193	11
1912	88	70	35		53	...	245	12
1913	106	98	39		64	...	306	12
1914	132	124	51		82	...	389	13
1915	139	138	44		85	...	407	...
1916	142	153	51		82	...	428	...
1917	110	119	48		64	...	341	...
1918	78	69	42		41	...	229	...
1919	110	115	44		62	...	331	13
1920	187	288	75		101	...	650	13
Aug. (March for tramcars)								
1921	243	373	83		128	19(*a*)	846(*a*)	14
1922	315	378	78		151	31	952	14
1923	384	430	86		173	32	1,105	14
1924	474	496	94		203	33	1,300	14
1925	580	572	99		224	35	1,510	14
Sept. (March for tramcars)								
1926	684	637	40	61	257	37	1,715	14
1927	787	681	42	53	283	39	1,886	14
1928	885	713	46	49	306	40	2,039	14
1929	981	731	50	48	330	42	2,182	14
1930	1,056	724	53	48	348	44	2,274	14
1931	1,083	627	49	38	361	43	2,201	13
1932	1,128	600	47	38	370	44	2,227	13
Sept. (for tramcars)								
1933	1,203	563	46	39	387	47	2,285	12
1934	1,308	548	46	39	413	50	2,405	12
1935	1,477	517	47	38	435	56	2,570	11
1936	1,643	506	49	37	459	64	2,758	10
1937	1,798	488	51	35	479	78	2,929	10

Transport and Communications 10. *continued*

(in thousands)

	Private Cars	Motor Cycles	'Buses and Coaches	Taxis	Goods Vehicles	Others (*a*) (except trams)	Total (except trams)	Tramcars
September								
1938	1,944	462	53	35	495	96	3,085	9·0
August								
1939	2,034	418	90		488	118	3,149	7·9
1940	1,423	278	81		444	98	2,325	6·9
1941	1,503	317	85		450	123	2,478	6·5
1942	858	306	85		453	139	1,840	6·4
1943	718	124	87		449	160	1,537	6·3
1944	755	124	90		448	175	1,593	6·3
1945	1,487	309	99		473	185	2,553	6·2
1946	1,770	462	57	48	560	210	3,107	6·1
September								
1947	1,944	528	62	52	670	259	3,515	5·7
1948	1,961	559	68	59	769	312	3,728	5·6
1949	2,131	654	74	60	844	346	4,108	5·3
1950	2,258	752	78	59	895	368	4,409	4·6
1951	2,380	848	79	57	934	379	4,678	4·2
1952	2,508	949	80	53	964	405	4,957	3·6
1953	2,762	1,037	80	36	996	430	5,340	3·0
1954	3,100	1,139	79	28	1,033	447	5,825	2·6
1955	3,526	1,256	78	24	1,109	472	6,465	2·3
1956	3,888	1,326	79	21	1,173	489	6,976	2·0
1957	4,187	1,471	79	19	1,215	513	7,483	1·6
1958	4,549	1,520	79	17	1,268	527	7,959	1·3
1959	4,966	1,733	77	15	1,326	545	8,662	1·1
1960	5,526	1,861	79	15	1,397	562	9,439	0·7
1961	5,979	1,869	78	13	1,451	576	9,965	0·4
1962	6,556	1,866	79	14	1,470	579	10,563	0·3
1963	7,375	1,847	82	14	1,529	599	11,446	0·1
1964	8,247	1,835	82	15	1,576	615	12,370	0·1
1965	8,917	1,707	82	15	1,602	618	12,938	0·1
1966	9,513	1,498	79	15	1,568	615	13,286	0·1
1967	10,303	1,443	79	15	1,618	638	14,096	0·1
1968	10,816	1,325	79	20	1,565	641	14,447	0·1
1969	11,228	1,223	79	23	1,564	636	14,751	0·1
1970	11,515	1,142	78	25	1,617	575	14,950	0·1
1971	12,062	1,118	78	28	1,618	574	15,478	0·1
1972	12,717	1,082	77	28	1,645	569	16,117	0·1
1973	13,497	1,111	77	29	1,722	578	17,014	0·1
1974	13,639	1,145	79	28	1,762	601	17,252	0·1
1975	13,747	1,269	80	32	1,775	597	17,501	0·1
1976	14,047	1,333	79	34	1,756	582	17,832	0·1
1977	...	...	...	...	...	...	...	...
	--- (*b*)	--- (*b*)	--- (*b*)	--- (*b*)	--- (*b*)	--- (*b*)	--- (*b*)	--- (*b*)
1978	14,070	1,297	73	37	1,702	620	17,772	0·1
1979	14,568	1,391	74	37	1,778	777	18,625	0·1
1980	15,073	1,465	71	39	1,761	795	19,210	0·1

(*a*) Includes invalid carriages and exempt vehicles, and agricultural tractors licensed to go on roads. These vehicles, however, were not counted before 1921.

(*b*) Owing to a change in the method by which the count was taken, there are no figures for 1977, and subsequent statistics are not strictly comparable with earlier ones.

Transport and Communications 11. Vehicles in Use – Ireland 1921–80

NOTES
[1] SOURCES: *Abstract* and *Statistical Abstract of Ireland*.
[2] The data relate to September in each year, except as indicated in footnote (*e*).
[3] Trams are not included.

(in thousands)

	Private Cars		Motor Cycles		Public Service Vehicles		Goods Vehicles		Total (*a*)	
	Northern Ireland	Republic of Ireland	Northern Ireland	Republic of Ireland	Northern Ireland	Republic of Ireland (*b*)	Northern Ireland	Republic of Ireland	Northern Ireland	Republic of Ireland (*c*)
1921	3·4	...	5·1	...	1·6	...	1·5	...	12	...
1922	4·5	...	6·4	...	2·1	...	2·2	...	16	...
1923	6·2	9·2	7·9	...	2·8	5·6	2·7	3·5	21	18
1924	8·1	13	8·8	...	3·3	7·8	3·4	4·5	24	25
1925	10	16	9·7	...	3·8	8·2	4·1	5·1 --- (*d*) 5·0	29	29
1926	12	20	9·3	...	3·8	8·0	4·5	5·5	30	33
1927	14	22	9·3	...	3·1	7·3	5·1	6·0	31	35
1928	16	26	8·8	...	2·0	6·4	5·7	6·5	33	39
1929	18	29	8·3	...	1·7	6·3	6·3	7·3	34	43
1930	19	33	8·4	...	1·6	5·9	6·5	7·7	36	47
1931	20	36	6·6	...	1·7	5·4	6·8	8·3	36	50
1932	22	36	6·2	...	1·8	5·2	7·0	8·3	37	50
1933	23	37	5·4	...	1·7	4·9	7·3	8·4	38	50
1934	25	35	5·0	...	1·8	4·5	7·5	8·3	40	48
1935	28	38	4·6	...	1·9	4·8	7·5	8·7	42	51
1936	32	41	4·5	...	1·8	4·9	8·4	9·4	48	55
1937	36	44	4·1	...	1·8	5·1	8·8	9·9	52	59
1938	40	49	3·9	...	1·7	5·2	9·2	10	56	65
1939	43	52	3·4	...	1·7	5·1	9·6	11	60	68
1940	31	50	3·0	...	1·6	5·0	8·5	11	49	66
1941	36	32	3·5	...	1·8	4·6	9·9	11	56	48
1942	25	8·0	3·7	...	2·0	4·7	9·8	12	48	24
1943	18	6·2	1·2	...	2·2	4·7	11	9·0	41	20
1944	18	6·6	1·1	...	2·3	4·7	11	9·0	43	20
1945	34	7·8	3·6	...	2·3	5·0	11	9·8	62	23
1946	37	44	4·7	...	2·2	5·6	12	15	67	64
1947	40	52	5·4	...	2·4	6·2	15	19	74	77
1948	42	60	6·2	...	2·9	7·7	16	23	82	91
1949	48	72	8·1	5·3	3·0	8·2	18	24	95	104
1950	50	85	9·8	5·8	3·2	8·0	20	25	102	118
1951	53	97	11	6·4	3·0	8·1	21	27	109	133
1952	57	105	13	8·0	3·0	7·9	22	28	117	141
1953	63	109	16	11	2·7	6·9	23	33	128	149
1954	73	118	18	15	2·6	6·6	24	37	142	162
1955	84	128	21	21	2·5	6·3	25	40	158	175
1956	93	136	23	27	2·3	5·8	27	42	172	184
1957	96	136	26	29	2·2	6·6	29	43	181	186
1958	102	144	26	31	2·1	6·2	30	43	190	194
1959	115	155	31	34	2·0	5·8	33	44	213	204
1960	125	170	33	41	2·1	5·5	36	44	227	219
1961	135	187	33	46	2·1	5·3	39	44	242	236
1962	150	208	32	48	2·2	5·3	41	45	260	258
1963	172	230	31	50	2·2	5·2	43	45	284	281
1964	189	255	31	52	2·1	5·0	44	47	303	307
1965	214	282	28	52	2·1	5·0	44	48	324	335

See p. 560 for footnotes.

Transport and Communications 11. *continued*

	Private Cars		Motor Cycles		Public Service Vehicles		Goods Vehicles		Total (*a*)	
	Northern Ireland	Republic of Ireland	Northern Ireland	Republic of Ireland	Northern Ireland	Republic of Ireland (*b*)	Northern Ireland	Republic of Ireland	Northern Ireland	Republic of Ireland (*c*)
1966	234	297	23	47	2·2	5·2	43	47	335	349
1967	251	315	21	46	2·3	5·9	44	46	352	367
1968	262	349	19	44	2·2	6·3	42	48	358	403
1969	276	376	16	42	2·3	6·3	41	49	369	432
1970	287	390	14	41	2·4	6·1	42	49	372	445
1971	299	414	12	40	2·4	6·1	42	45	383	465
1972	304	440	11	39	2·2	6·1	41	45	381	491
1973	...	477	...	39	...	8·1	...	49	...	534
1974	309	489	11	38	2·1	6·1	39	53	379	548
1975	314	512	12	37	1·9	6·2	38	53	384	571
1976	326	553	15	36	2·4	6·7	40	54	403	614
1977	338	574	17	34	2·3	6·3	39	54	416	634
1978	347	641	17	31	1·9	5·5	40	60	429	706
1979	358 (*e*)	685	15 (*e*)	29	2·1	5·4	42	62	439	752
1980	365	736	15	28	2·3	5·2	39	65	442	807

(*a*) Including vehicles exempt from duty.
(*b*) Excluding taxis.
(*c*) Excluding motor cycles.
(*d*) Previously including tractors.
(*e*) In December.

Transport and Communications 12. Airway Mileage and Traffic – United Kingdom 1937–80

NOTES

[1] SOURCE: *Abstract*.

[2] This table covers the United Kingdom Airway Corporations and private companies, but not the associates and overseas subsidiaries of the Corporations.

	Aircraft Stage Flights (thousands)	Aircraft Miles Flown (millions)	Average Length of Flight (miles)	Passengers Carried: Domestic Services (thousands)	Passengers Carried: International Services (thousands)	Passenger-Miles Flown(*a*) (millions)	Cargo Carried (thousand short-tons): Domestic Freight	Cargo Carried: International Freight	Cargo Carried: Domestic Mail	Cargo Carried: International Mail	Freight short-ton Miles Flown(*a*) (millions)
1937	87·0	10·6	120	162	82	49	1·0	1·6	0·4	1·3	0·9
1938	91·4	13·2	140	148	72	53	0·7	2·1	0·7	2·9	1·1
1939	80·5	11·5	140	132	70	56	0·8	1·4	0·6	1·8	0·9
1940	26·6	5·8	220	44	23	42	0·3	0·6	0·5	0·5	1·0
1941	28·8	7·6	260	57	26	57	0·1	0·9	0·6	1·0	2·0
1942	33·9	10·7	320	64	45	102	0·2	2·4	0·7	1·3	5·7
1943	38·4	13·2	340	72	61	125	0·2	4·4	0·7	1·5	9·0
1944	45·7	19·5	430	76	93	179	0·2	7·2	0·7	2·2	15·8
1945	65·6	28·0	430	117	134	302	0·5	7·5	0·6	2·2	19·0
1946	89·6	33·0	369	229	194	363	0·9	3·7	0·6	2·4	8·8
1947	114	39·5	346	342	244	441	1·1	4·6	0·8	2·6	11·4
1948	102	44·2	433	381	333	555	1·2	7·8	1·3	3·5	17·4
1949	114	44·3	388	453	468	615	2·0	13·9	1·4	4·6	20·3
1950	131	48·3	368	486	671	794	2·6	19·1	1·6	5·7	24·6
1951	139	52·5	378	528	887	1,065	2·9	34·5	2·4	6·5	31·1
1952	159	58·1	366	669	1,064	1,243	2·7	32·1	2·4	7·1	30·6
1953	178	61·7	347	833	1,327	1,434	3·5	59·4	2·4	7·4	34·0
1954	180	59·6	330	1,002	1,441	1,515	4·3	69·2	2·7	7·6	35·5
1955	203	69·1	341	1,212	1,782	1,801	8·9	101·2	3·4	8·2	48·2
1956	226	78·1	346	1,402	2,050	2,102	12·8	88·8	2·8	8·7	49·9
1957	234	85·1	363	1,588	2,386	2,422	12·7	99·7	2·9	8·8	56·5
1958	234	87·0	372	1,463	2,522	2,571	8·4	130·7	2·6	9·1	58·4
1959	251	91·9	366	1,738	2,967	3,091	11·5	183·0	2·7	9·3	69·7
1960	284	107	375	2,240	3,640	3,959	16·2	223·8	3·0	10·9	80·9
1961	310	116	375	2,841	4,010	4,531	19·3	233·4	3·5	11·4	91·6
1962	317	118	373	3,260	4,439	4,870	24·2	270·0	6·2	10·8	113
1963	314	118	376	3,673	4,974	5,447	31·3	269·5	6·8	12·2	134
1964	330	127	386	4,216	5,539	6,424	40·7	260·6	7·0	13·7	163
1965	330	137	415	4,669	6,199	7,417	52·4	252·0	7·5	14·5	208
1966	350	144	412	5,123	6,935	8,302	76·6	283·3	8·5	16·4	264
1967	349	153	438	5,314	7,004	8,742	74·3	245·2	7·2	15·7	274
1968	336	154	457	5,041	7,143	8,758	80·2	223·8	7·1	17·0	289
1969	359	168	468	5,159	8,056	10,104	79·4	233·3	7·4	18·8	364
1970	359	182	508	5,365	8,480	10,832	63·1	204·3	8·2	21·5	338
1971	364	190	523	5,367	9,095	11,597	57·5	191·1	7·0	20·3	371
1972	369	193	521	5,890	9,878	13,775	71·3	222·3	8·4	24·4	466
							--- (*b*)	--- (*b*)			
1973	391	209	533	6,513	10,852	16,272	87·3	265·0	(*b*)	(*b*)	545
1974	380	193	507	6,062	10,333	15,781	75·3	261·9	...	...	538
1975	351	178	507	5,755	10,567	17,115	51·5	219·4	...	...	496
1976	365	187	513	6,147	11,323	19,311	50·8	222·2	...	...	531
1977	363	187	513	5,484	11,663	19,804	45·7	237·3	...	...	590
1978	411	215	524	6,429	13,907	25,129	49·2	257·3	...	...	677
1979	442	232	525	7,240	15,072	29,257	43·4	281·1	...	...	733
1980	441	239	542	7,199	14,964	31,170	34·2	290·7	...	...	832

(*a*) Earlier figures from League of Nations sources are as follows (in million passenger-kilometres and thousand tonne-kilometres):

	PKM	*TKM*		*PKM*	*TKM*
1925	4·3	...	1931	11·3	328
1926	6·0	...	1932	25·8	413
1927	6·9	...	1933	34·8	534
1928	10·4	292	1934	47	744
1929	11·5	358	1935	68	1,200
1930	9·7	321	1936	66	1,074

(*b*) Mail is included with freight from 1973.

Transport and Communications 13. Air Traffic – Republic of Ireland 1949–80

NOTE
SOURCE: *Statistical Abstract of Ireland.*

(in thousands or thousand tons)

	Passengers		Freight		Mail	
	Inward	Outward	Inward	Outward	Inward	Outward
1949	112	114	1·2	1·0	0·1	0·1
1950	129	131	2·0	1·1	0·1	0·1
1951	141	142	2·5	1·8	0·5	0·6
1952	158	159	2·7	1·6	0·7	0·7
1953	162	165	3·5	1·8	0·8	0·7
1954	184	187	4·2	2·3	0·8	0·8
1955	211	213	4·5	2·4	0·9	0·8
1956	245	252	4·3	3·1	0·8	0·9
1957	266	280	4·7	2·9	0·9	0·9
1958	305	315	5·8	3·0	0·8	0·8
1959	343	349	6·8	3·5	0·8	0·8
1960	441	444	10·3	5·5	0·9	0·8
1961	519	522	10·6	6·7	0·9	0·9
1962	555	559	10·4	6·0	0·9	0·9
1963	628	639	13·4	11·6	1·1	1·1
1964	727	736	15·1	12·8	1·1	1·1
1965	797	805	17·7	12·4	1·2	1·2
1966	916	919	22·2	14·3	1·4	1·4
1967	928	943	19·9	12·2	1·3	1·2
1968	982	981	23·1	14·9	1·1	1·0
1969	1,065	1,063	26·3	17·3	1·2	1·0
1970	1,176	1,172	27·1	16·8	1·5	0·9
1971	1,265	1,264	26·8	17·7	1·3	0·9
1972	1,212	1,218	29·2	20·9	1·7	1·0
1973	1,295	1,299	33·9	23·1	1·6	1·0
1974	1,270	1,281	35·1	24·5	1·5	0·9
1975	1,332	1,340	28·7	31·5	1·5	1·0
1976	1,353	1,368	29·3	27·7	1·7	1·2
1977	1,409	1,426	31·2	26·5	1·9	1·4
1978	1,574	1,576	27·6	23·6	1·8	1·1
1979	1,699	1,715	35·4	21·5	1·1	0·8
1980	1,608	1,619	32·2	19·9	2·0	1·2

Transport and Communications 14. Post Office Mail Traffic – United Kingdom 1839–1980

NOTES

[1] SOURCES: 1839–1916 – *Annual Reports of the Postmaster General* (in *Sessional Papers* from 1854–5 annually); 1920–80 – *Abstract* (except for letter-post breakdown for 1925–34, which comes from *The Post Office* (G.P.O., 1934)).

[2] Figures from 1878 are for years ended 31 March. Earlier they are for calendar years.

[3] Statistics relate to mail and parcels delivered to 1939 and 1929 respectively. Subsequently they are of mail posted and parcels handled. See footnotes (*b*) and (*c*).

(in millions)

Calendar years	Letters			Postcards			Newspapers, Packets, etc.		
	E. & W.	Scot.	Ireland	E. & W.	Scot.	Ireland	E. & W.	Scot.	Ireland
1839 (*a*)	65	8	9	...	...	...	...	...	...
1840	132	19	18	...	...	...	...	...	...
1841	154	21	21	...	...	...	...	...	...
1842	164	22	22	...	...	...	...	...	...
1843	173	23	23	...	...	...	...	...	...
1844	190	27	26	...	...	...	...	...	...
1845	214	29	29	...	...	...	...	...	...
1846	236	31	33	...	...	...	...	...	...
1847	253	33	35	...	...	...	...	...	...
1848	260	34	35	...	...	...	...	...	...
1849	267	35	36	...	...	...	...	...	...
1850	276	35	35	...	...	...	...	...	...
1851	288	37	36	...	...	...	...	...	...
1852	304	38	37	...	...	...	...	...	...
1853	330	41	40	...	...	...	...	...	...
1854	358	44	41	...	...	...	...	...	...
1855	369	46	42	...	...	...	...	...	...
1856	388	48	42	...	...	...	51	11	12
1857	410	52	43	...	...	...	54	11	12
1858	428	51	44	...	...	...	56	11	12
1859	446	52	47	...	...	...	59	11	12
1860	462	54	48	...	...	...	60	10	12
1861	487	56	50	...	...	...	62	11	12
1862	497	57	51	...	...	...	63	11	13
1863	529	61	52	...	...	...	66	11	12
1864	560	64	55	...	...	...	72	11	13
1865	597	67	56	...	...	...	73	11	13
1866	623	70	57	...	...	...	75	11	13
1867	640	76	59	...	...	...	78	11	13
1868	670	78	60	...	...	...	81	12	13
1869	683	79	62	...	...	...	83	12	14
1870	704	79	64	...	...	...	102	14	15
1871	721	80	66	...	...	...	160	21	21
1872	737	82	66	64	8	4	177	25	21
1873	756	84	67	60	8	4	204	28	22
1874	802	90	70	66	9	4	206	29	23
1875	847	91	71	73	9	5	227	30	23
1876	856	91	72	78	10	5	242	33	24
Years ended 31 March									
1878	884	100	74	86	11	5	256	36	26
1879	922	99	76	94	12	5	265	36	27
1880	950	102	76	97	12	6	281	37	27
1881	981	105	79	104	13	6	307	39	28
1882	1,037	110	82	114	15	6	338	43	31
1883	1,078	117	86	121	16	7	353	45	31
1884	1,112	122	88	129	17	8	359	48	30

Transport and Communications 14. *continued*

(in millions)

Years ended 31 March	Letters			Postcards			Newspapers, Packets, etc.			Parcels		
	E. & W.	Scot.	Ireland	E. & W.	Scot.	Ireland	E. & W.	Scot.	Ireland	E. & W.	Scot.	Ireland
1885	1,148	123	89	134	18	8	380	51	33	19	2	1
1886	1,187	126	90	144	20	8	402	54	34	22	3	2
1887	1,240	129	91	151	20	8	429	56	35	27	3	2
1888	1,287	132	93	159	21	9	451	56	35	30	4	2
1889	1,327	136	96	170	22	9	471	57	36	33	4	3
1890	1,413	140	97	184	23	10	505	59	38	35	5	3
1891	1,463	143	100	195	24	11	540	61	41	38	5	3
1892	1,516	147	105	205	25	11	554	62	42	41	5	3
1893	1,532	152	106	206	27	11	584	69	45	43	6	4
1894	1,549	154	109	209	27	12	620	74	46	45	6	4
1895	1,502	156	113	272	29	13	640	78	48	47	6	4
1896	1,559	163	113	268	32	14	682	88	51	50	7	4
1897	1,607	169	118	287	34	15	700	93	56	53	7	4
1898	1,711	177	124	309	36	15	730	94	54	56	7	4
1899	1,860	191	137	327	39	16	709	93	54	60	8	5
1900	1,909	197	141	343	41	17	720	94	52	62	8	5
1901	1,977	202	144	359	42	18	747	97	56	67	9	5
1902	2,085	218	149	380	46	19	784	96	56	72	9	6
1903	2,208	222	150	416	54	20	820	108	58	75	10	6
1904	2,218	226	153	517	72	24	827	108	61	78	10	6
1905	2,239	230	156	617	87	31	848	113	62	81	10	6
1906	2,313	238	156	677	91	33	897	119	61	84	11	7
1907	2,398	248	158	705	92	35	936	125	62	87	11	7
1908	2,444	256	165	729	92	37	950	127	63	91	12	7
1909	2,483	256	168	732	91	37	962	127	66	94	12	7
1910	2,517	257	173	746	85	37	975	128	70	98	13	7
1911	2,606	265	177	748	87	37	1,034	135	72	101	13	8
1912	2,730	274	183	780	88	38	1,058	135	73	104	13	8
1913	2,827	284	188	776	86	37	1,069	136	76	108	14	8
1914	2,986	296	196	801	88	37	1,160	141	78	113	15	9
1915	2,926	291	192	763	82	35	1,028	130	73	121	15	9
1916–19	...	...	...	...	...	...	...	...	...	...	...	...
1920	3,290	333	209	503	53	25	1,099	142	76	120	15	10
1921	2,976	300	184	507	49	21	1,300	165	77	113	15	9
1922	2,814	285	176	415	39	17	1,249	160	76	104	14	9
			Northern Ireland			Northern Ireland			Northern Ireland			Northern Ireland
1923	2,959	289	52	432	38	5	1,478	175	27	104	14	2·3
1924	2,991	297	52	427	38	5	1,553	194	28	109	15	2·4
1925	3,135	311	54	422	38	5	1,640	205	30	119	16	2·6
1926		3,575			460			2,025		125	17	2·6
1927		3,560			400			1,840		122	16	2·4
1928		3,630			23			2,147			140·0	
1929		3,642			421			2,167			151·5 ...(b)	
1930		3,700			420			2,280			160·5	
1931		3,745			430			2,300			161·9	
1932		3,750			410			2,380			158·1	
1933		3,810			405			2,425			151·7	
1934		3,890			410			2,453			153·3	

Transport and Communications 14. *continued*

	United Kingdom	
	Letters, Postcards, Packets, etc. Years ended 31 March	Parcels
1935	6,935	149·7
1936	7,345	162·2
1937	7,690	174·4
1938	7,990	179·5
1939	8,150	184·8
	--- (*c*)	
1940	7,460	192·7
1941	6,310	187·6
1942	6,150	198·2
1943	6,390	204·7
1944	6,480	235·3
1945	6,600	284·0
1946	6,550	257·3
1947	7,300	238·7
1948	7,600	243·5
1949	8,050	239·6
1950	8,350	243·3
1951	8,500	232·7
1952	8,750	223·6
1953	8,800	243·2
1954	9,100	241·6
1955	9,500	242·8
1956	9,700	237·6
1957	9,700	249·0

	United Kingdom	
	Letters, Postcards, Packets, etc. (in thousand million)	Parcels (in millions)
1958	9·6	247·4
1959	9·7	243·3
1960	10·2	234·7
1961	10·6	248·2
1962	10·5	233·4
1963	10·6	224·2
1964	11·0	229·9
1965	11·2	216·0
1966	11·3	235·3
1967	11·4	222·3
1968	11·5	216·6
1969	11·3	212·3
1970	11·4	207·6
1971	10·5	180·8
1972	10·55	188·6
1973	10·79	194·3
1974	11·01	194·9
1975	10·88	200·5
1976	9·90	169·8
1977	9·38	162·5
1978	9·48	159·9
1979	9·96	171·5
1980	10·21	180·2

(*a*) This is an estimate based on one week in November, and applies to the year ended 5 December. It includes franked letters.

(*b*) Subsequent figures refer to parcels handled, not parcels delivered. Figures of parcels handled for 1928 and 1929 were 153·1 and 154·5 respectively.

(*c*) Subsequent figures refer to mail posted in the United Kingdom, not mail delivered. Figures for mail posted for 1938 and 1939 were 8,080 and 8,240 respectively. Figures of mail delivered for 1940–6 were as follows:

1940	7,360	1942	6,105	1944	6,270	1946	6,230
1941	6,250	1943	6,270	1945	6,250		

Transport and Communications 15. Telegraph and Telephone Services – United Kingdom 1870–1980

NOTES

[1] SOURCES: 1870–1916 – *Annual Reports of the Postmaster General* (in *Sessional Papers* from 1854–5 annually); 1917–80 – *Abstract*.

[2] Figures from 1878 are for years ended 31 March. Earlier they are for calendar years.

(millions, except telephone stations)

Calendar years	Telegrams Sent			Telephone Calls Made U.K. (*a*)		Number of Telephone Stations (*b*) (thousands)
	E. & W.	Scot.	Ireland	Trunk	Local	
1870 (*b*)	7·1	1·0	0·5	...	...	...
1871	9·7	1·3	0·8	...	...	...
1872	12·1	1·7	1·1	...	...	...
1873	14·1	1·9	1·3	...	...	...
1874	15·6	2·1	1·4	...	...	...
1875	17·1	2·3	1·4	...	...	...
1876	17·7	2·4	1·5	...	...	...
Years ended 31 March						
1878	18·1	2·5	1·6	...	...	...
1879	20·4	2·5	1·6	...	...	...
1880	22·2	2·7	1·6	...	...	...
1881	25·2	3·0	1·7	...	...	...
1882	26·3	3·2	1·9	...	...	...
1883	26·9	3·2	1·9	...	...	...
1884	27·6	3·2	1·9	...	...	...
1885	28·1	3·3	1·9	...	...	...
1886	33·1	3·8	2·2	...	...	...
1887	42·3	5·1	2·8	...	...	...
1888	44·9	5·4	3·0	...	...	...
1889	48·5	6·0	3·2	...	...	...
1890	52·4	6·5	3·4	...	...	...
1891	55·7	7·1	3·7	...	...	...
1892	58·8	7·2	3·8	...	...	...
1893	58·9	7·1	3·9	...	...	...
1894	59·6	7·3	4·0	...	...	...
1895	60·2	7·3	4·0	...	...	1·8
1896	66·4	8·1	4·3	...	...	1·9
1897	67·0	8·1	4·4	...	...	2·0
1898	70·0	8·5	4·6	5·9	...	2·0
1899	73·2	9·1	4·7	7·1	...	2·1
1900	76·1	9·4	4·9	8·1	...	2·2
1901	75·4	9·3	4·9	9·0	...	2·7
1902	75·8	9·7	4·9	10·1	...	3·9
1903	77·8	9·6	5·1	11·6	...	14
1904	75·6	9·3	5·1	13·5	...	22
1905	74·8	9·1	5·1	15·5	...	33
1906	75·1	9·1	5·2	18·1	...	45
1907	75·0	9·2	5·3	19·9	...	54
1908	71·6	9·0	5·4	22·1	...	79
1909	70·8	8·7	5·3	23·6	...	87
1910	72·7	8·7	5·5	26·7	...	98
1911	72·5	8·7	5·5	30·2	...	122
1912	74·3	9·0	5·9	33·7	...	701
1913	73·6	9·2	5·7	36·0	797	731
1914	72·3	9·1	5·7	38·2	834	775
1915	75·8	9·3	6·1	40·7	815	796
1916	70·0	8·8	5·4	40·4	776	787

Transport and Communications 15. *continued*

(millions, except telephone stations)

Years ended 31 March	Telegrams Sent, U.K.	Telephone Calls Made, U.K. (*a*)		Number of Telephone Stations (*b*) (thousands)
		Trunk	Local	
1917	79	38·8	701	774
1918	80	43·7	700	779
1919	89	46·5	716	797
1920	101	54·2	848	888
1921	88	57·8	843	980 ---(*b*) 988
1922	83 ---(*c*)	52·4 ---(*c*)	682 ---(*c*)	1,005
1923	80	59·5	730	1,061 ---(*c*)
1924	78	70·3	832	1,169
1925	79	77·7	852	1,285
1926	77	86·5	930	1,402
1927	75	95·3	1,006	1,521
1928	74	103	1,071	1,644
1929	72	111	1,155	1,768
1930	71	118	1,205	1,896
1931	66	123	1,248	1,996
1932	61	126	1,305	2,069
1933	57	130	1,361	2,137
1934	58	141 ---(*d*) 76·6	1,440 ---(*d*) 1,504	2,225
1935	55	85·9	1,595	2,388
1936	65	99·2 ---(*e*) 89·8	1,725 ---(*e*) 1,734	2,579
1937	72	101	1,882	2,827
1938	71 ---(*f*) 57	107	2,060	3,050
1939	58	113	2,124	3,235
1940	63	117	2,098	3,339
1941	61	118	1,974	3,311
1942	67	134	1,901	3,316
1943	76	161	1,942	3,536
1944	71	181	1,970	3,764
1945	71	189	2,039	3,889
1946	74	193	2,175	3,937
1947	63	205	2,509	4,319
1948	58	217	2,681	4,653

	Telegrams Sent, U.K.	Telephone Calls Made, U.K. (*a*)		Number of Telephone Stations (*b*) (thousands)
		Trunk	Local	
1949	54	227	2,820	4,919
1950	52	235	2,940	5,171
1951	65	250	3,076	5,426
1952	62	262	3,230	5,715
1953	58	264	3,165	5,873
1954	56	278	3,370	6,094
1955	48	306	3,615	6,436
1956	43	333	3,865	6,830
1957	39	321	3,743	7,167
1958	37	327	3,671	7,300
1959	35	343	3,700	7,469
1960	35	387	3,900	7,790
1961	35	426	4,300	8,208
1962	34	477	4,500	8,544
1963	33	545	4,750	8,841
1964	31	624	5,100	9,272
1965	32	736	5,600	9,883
1966	32	842	6,050	10,621
1967	31	932	6,450	11,289
1968	31	1,069	6,880	12,009
1969	29	1,207	7,420	12,805
1970	29	1,352	8,270	13,844
1971	26	1,517	9,230	14,858
1972	27	1,699	10,330	16,025
1973	27	1,944	10,200	17,441
1974	28	2,138	11,100	18,955
1975	26	2,313	12,000	20,191
1976	21	2,356	12,800	20,884
1977	19	2,456	13,500	21,516
1978	17	2,703	14,600	23,016
1979	17	3,022	16,100	24,760
1980	16	3,257	16,600	26,807

(*a*) Inland calls only.

(*b*) A station, since 1921, is a telephone directly or indirectly connected with the public exchange system. Previously private network instruments were wholly excluded.

(*c*) Subsequently excluding southern Ireland.

(*d*) Subsequently all calls of value fourpence or under are counted as local, instead of twopence and under as previously.

(*e*) Some calls were subsequently reallocated.

(*f*) Subsequently excluding telegrams sent via private cable companies.

Transport and Communications 16. Mail and Telecommunications Statistics – Republic of Ireland 1924–80

NOTES
[1] SOURCE: *Statistical Abstract of Ireland.*
[2] Figures are for years ended 31 March to 1974.
[3] Mail figures are of deliveries, telegrams of despatches.

(millions, except as indicated)

	Letters	Postcards	Newspapers and Packets	Parcels	Telegrams (thousands)	Telephone Calls Made: Trunk	Telephone Calls Made: Local	Radio Licences (thousands)	Television Licences (thousands)
1924	135	10	59	6	3,760	16		1·0	—
1925	130	9	59	5	3,506	18		1·5	—
1926	130	9	62	5	3,283	19		7·7	—
1927	124	9	64	5	3,083	20		19	—
1928	128	11	65	5	2,999	21		24	—
1929	125	11	66	5	2,472	21		26	—
1930	125	11	66	5	2,131	22		26	—
1931	125	10	71	5	1,998	22		26	—
1932	125	10	71	5	1,778	23		29	—
1933	120	8	65	5	1,675	25		33	—
1934	117	9	65	5	1,552	26		51	—
1935	...	...	...	5	1,481	27		66	—
1936	131	9	67	5	1,502	29		88	—
1937	139	10	70	5	1,531	31		105	—
1938	...	...	...	...	1,513	35		140	—
1939	141	10	74	6	1,508	37		155	—
1940	138	10	73	5	1,502	39		170	—
1941	...	...	...	...	1,441	41		184	—
						---(*a*)			
1942	124	8	54	6	1,672	44		176	—
1943	...	...	...	...	1,876	45		171	—
1944	...	...	...	...	2,061	48		173	—
1945	151	11	67	8	2,167	53		173	—
1946	...	...	...	...	2,494	58		176	—
1947	...	...	...	...	2,814	62		179	—
1948	...	...	...	...	2,895	8	56	195	—
1949	178	7	87	10	2,648	8	60	271	—
1950	180	7	89	9	2,611	9	65	289	—
1951	181	7	88	9	2,705	10	72	311	—
1952	182	7	97	9	2,587	10	76	374	—
1953	177	8	107	9	2,447	11	78	400	—
1954	193	8	117	9	2,367	12	81	399	—
1955	196	9	127	9	2,323	13	83	431	—
1956	...	...	...	...	1,919	14	87	462	—
1957	192	9	113	8	1,441	14	92	473	—
1958	194	8	124	8	1,331	15	98	474	—
1959	...	...	...	...	1,235	16	107	487	—
1960	...	...	...	...	1,174	14	121	493	—
1961	216	8	128	8	1,110	13	136	490	—
1962	...	...	...	...	1,100	15	144	419	93
1963	222	8	130	8	1,048	17	153	363	150
1964	218	7	125	8	1,022	18	164	314	222
1965	220	7	130	7	911	21	178	269	255
1966	216	7	135	7	847	23	198	240	288
1967	220	8	136	7	812	25	212	217	308
1968	225	8	139	7	792	28	234	197	376

Transport and Communications 16. *continued*

(millions, except as indicated)

	Letters	Postcards	Newspapers and Packets	Parcels	Telegrams (thousands)	Telephone Calls Made		Radio Licences (thousands)	Television Licences (thousands)
						Trunk	Local.		
1969	215	13	150	9	812	33	260	172	394
1970	220	13	154	9	804	38	263	150	416
1971	218	13	152	9	747	42	287	130	433
1972	218	13	152	9	710	47	320	115	476
						54	351	—	496
1973	219	13	133	9	726	--- (*c*) 623		—	496
1974	226	13	143	9	730	711		—	527
1975	236(*b*)	12(*b*)	139(*b*)	8(*b*)	671(*b*)	809(*b*)		—	565(*b*)
1976	239	12	139	8	614	863		—	590
1977	250	11	147	8	561	1,023		—	617
1978	250	8	148	8	573	1,161		—	616
1979	144	6	92	4	354	1,467		—	693
1980	246	12	146	6	523	1,657		—	667

(*a*) Subsequently excluding inward international calls.
(*b*) See note 2 above.
(*c*) Revised total figures only available back to 1973.

Transport and Communications 17. Broadcast Receiving Licences – United Kingdom 1923–1980

NOTES
[1] SOURCE: *Abstract*.
[2] The figures are of licences current at 31 March.

(in thousands)

	Sound		Sound	Television		Sound	Television
1923	125	1943	9,242		1962	3,538	11,834
1924	748	1944	9,555		1963	3,256	12,443
1925	1,350	1945	9,711		1964	2,999	12,885
1926	1,960	1946	10,396		1965	2,794	13,253
1927	2,270	1947	10,763	15	1966	2,611	13,567
1928	2,483	1948	11,134	46	1967	2,506	14,267
1929	2,730	1949	11,621	127	1968	2,557	15,089
1930	3,091	1950	11,876	344	1969	2,464	15,496
1931	3,647	1951	11,605	764	1970	2,301	15,883
1932	4,620	1952	11,304	1,449	1971	—	15,943
1933	5,497	1953	10,750	2,142	1972	—	16,658
1934	6,260	1954	10,188	3,249	1973	—	17,125
1935	7,012	1955	9,477	4,504	1974	—	17,325
1936	7,618	1956	8,522	5,740	1975	—	17,701
1937	8,131	1957	7,559	6,966	1976	—	17,788
1938	8,589	1958	6,556	8,090	1977	—	18,056
1939	8,968	1959	5,481	9,255	1978	—	18,149
1940	8,951	1960	4,535	10,470	1979	—	18,381
1941	8,752	1961	3,909	11,268	1980	—	18,285
1942	8,683						

CHAPTER XI

PUBLIC FINANCE

TABLES

Men of affairs in Britain have no doubt always been concerned about its governmental finances, but until these came completely under the control of Parliament, no regular and detailed statistics about them seem to have been kept. Certainly they were not published. Before the Revolution of 1688 it was common practice to farm out to private contractors the task of collecting the principal taxes. Not until 1674 were the collectors of the excise obliged by their contracts to give full accounts, and not until 1679 was a similar stipulation involved in the contract for the farm of the hearth money.

As far as contemporaries were concerned, published statistics remained deficient until the early nineteenth century. Sir John Sinclair, for example, wrote in 1804 that 'since the reign of Queen Anne the national accounts are far from being distinguished for their regularity and precision; no complete statement has ever been made of the total income and expenditure of the country'.[1] No balanced annual accounts were made available to Parliament or the public until 1823. Up to then, contemporaries had to depend for their information on the Parliamentary votes on supplies and on ways and means, and similar incomplete statements which appeared in the *House of Commons Journals*. These were the sources of Whitworth's and other contemporary compilations of public income, wealth and expenditure.[2]

The fact that we now have balanced income and expenditure accounts dating from 1688 is due to the twelve years' research in Treasury records carried out by a Chief Clerk of the Exchequer in the middle of the nineteenth century and published in 1869.[3] Whether even so they are absolutely complete is unclear, and probably unknowable. Binney noted that it was not until after 31 March 1857 that 'at last, every item of receipt and every item of expenditure was consolidated into the account submitted to Parliament';[4] but whether that implies that the historical volume may have omitted some items is not clear. Unfortunately, the series then published involved a major break, in 1801–2, when the publication of gross accounts was begun. In the historical volume the net accounts end in 1801, and no overlap is provided with the gross accounts beginning in 1802. Reference to the original *Finance Accounts* for this period shows that, in order to maintain long-period comparability, the compilers of the historical volume altered the contents of most categories. As a result, an overlap could be provided from these original sources only with immense labour – if at all. In this volume, therefore, the break in 1801–2 is left, and one pair of tables (1 and 2) cover Great Britain in the eighteenth century, and another pair (3 and 4) cover the United Kingdom subsequently – with the Republic of Ireland figures shown in tables 5 and 6.

The sources of the statistics are given in the notes to the tables, and there is, of course, a much greater wealth of detail available there, increasingly so from the beginning of the nineteenth century. The principle followed in the selection of items to be shown here has been to include those which were of relative importance at any time during the period, and to show them throughout when available. Items which were of importance for only a short time are, however, usually given in the notes; and the separate listing of the Civil List expenditure has been dropped after the 1801–2 break, since by that time it was relatively small, and on the succession of King William IV it became almost negligible. Perhaps this is the place to draw attention to one especially useful source of more detailed statistics on public finance for the first seventy years of the period here covered, namely P. G. M. Dickson, *The Financial Revolution in England*.[5]

[1] Sir John Sinclair, *The History of the Public Revenue of the British Empire, containing an account of the public income and expenditure from the remotest periods recorded in history to Michaelmas 1802* (London, 1804).

[2] Sir Charles Whitworth, *A Collection of the Supplies and Ways and Means from the Revolution to the Present Times* (London, 1763).

[3] *S.P.* 1868–9 XXXV. See Appendix 13 for a full annotation of the accounts written by the compiler, H. S. Chisholm, with the advice of the 'most experienced financial officers of the Government'.

[4] J. E. D. Binney, *British Public Finance and Administration 1774–92* (Oxford, 1958), 'Note on the Public Accounts'.

[5] (London, 1969).

Three further general points may be made about these first tables. First, it should be realised that from 1869 onwards, each figure comprises all items under the appropriate heading at the date in question. Thus no account is taken of transfers from, for example, customs to excise or funded to unfunded debt charges, except in so far as the compilers of the historical volume made such transfers effective throughout the period which they covered. In making comparisons over long periods especially, therefore, the possibility of such transfers having taken place should be borne in mind. The principal transfers are, of course, well known, and some of the more misleading ones, such as the separation of death duties from stamp duties, have been indicated in the tables.

A second point to note about the income and expenditure tables is that they are concerned with current account transactions – that is, they correspond to 'above the line' items in the present-day Finance Statement. This distinction was not made explicitly, however, until the 1890s, and it is likely that a few small items of capital expenditure, and of borrowing for such expenditure, are included in the accounts before then. But at that period and earlier they can hardly have been significant.

The third point concerns the exact nature of the income and expenditure which the tables show, namely the receipts and issues of the Exchequer. These are not quite the same as the actual receipts and expenditures of the various departments, which it would no doubt be preferable to show were they available for as long a period as the Exchequer statistics. Whatever the situation in the eighteenth century, however, it is doubtful if the differences between the two methods of accounting were ever very great in the nineteenth century; and for the period when easy comparison is possible, the differences are only significant in one or two periods during and immediately after the upheaval of war. In most years the differences were very much less than 1 per cent of the totals. Possibly more interesting than these minor variations between methods of recording the accounts are those between anticipated and realised results – between budgets and financial statements. Whilst there is not sufficient space here to show these, they can be found for an extensive period in Buxton and Iddesleigh in the last century, and Mallet and George in this.[6] These are also informative about the political and Parliamentary background to public finance in general in the periods with which they are concerned.

Tables 7 and 8, on the public debt of the United Kingdom and of the Republic of Ireland respectively, are fairly straightforward and do not appear to call for any special comment.

Until towards the end of the nineteenth century much less information is available on local than on central government finance, and what there is for the eighteenth and early nineteenth centuries is mainly scattered, discontinuous, and collected with little regard for uniformity among the various local authorities. Tables 9 and 10 have been included here as the best representatives of local finances in this period. These two series are by far the longest

[6] S. Buxton, *Finance and Politics, an Historical Study, 1783–1885* (2 vols., London, 1888); Lord Iddesleigh, *Twenty Years of Financial Policy* (London, 1862); B. Mallet, *British Budgets, 1887–1913* (London, 1913); B. Mallet and C. O. George, *British Budgets, 1913–1921* (London, 1929); and B. Mallet and C. O. George, *British Budgets, 1921–1933* (London, 1933).

available, and they cover much the largest fields of local taxation, at least until around the middle of the nineteenth century. There was, moreover, a greater degree of uniformity in their collection, and they were published in a more readily available form, than any other series. Nevertheless, it is sufficient to draw attention to the remarks of Goschen and of the author of the *Return* of 1839, quoted in the notes to the tables, to show that even these statistics are far from satisfactory. Additional statistics, not generally going back before the 1830s except for isolated dates, can be found scattered through the early and mid-nineteenth-century Blue Books. The 1843 *Report of Local Taxation* by the Poor Law Commissioners, which contained a full survey of the existing system of local taxation, summarised as follows the data available for previous years: 'The only distinct rates in respect of which comprehensive information has been obtained are the Church Rates for the years 1827, 1832 and 1838; the Highway Rate for the years 1812, 1813, 1814, 1827, and 1839; the County Rate for the years 1792 to 1841 complete; and the Poor's Rate for the several years 1748, 1749, 1750, 1776, 1783, 1784, 1785, 1803 and continuously from 1813 to 1841.'[7] From the middle of the century there exist municipal borough finance accounts for each town, audited and set out in individual fashion. But the many differences in definition, methods of collection, annual period covered, and accounting procedures have, in fact, discouraged anyone from attempting to aggregate the latter.

From 1860, official annual *Local Taxation Returns* were published in *Sessional Papers*, but their deficiencies at that time were so great, as Goschen pointed out, that nothing from them is included here. The latter's report in 1869[8] has been taken as the starting-point for modern statistics, though it was not until the Local Government Board took over the publication of the *Returns* in the early 1870s that the continuous series began; and it was not until twenty years later that Scotland followed suit. For the earliest attempt to bring together statistics of Scottish local authorities see the 1835 *Report* of the Royal Commisson on Scottish Municipal Corporations.[9] Skelton's *Report on Local Taxation in Scotland*[10] is also useful. The first regular Scottish *Local Taxation Returns* were published in 1882, and since statistics for Scotland, as for Ireland, were collected on different bases from England and Wales, they have been treated separately in tables 10 to 18. These are, with their notes, largely self-explanatory. The sources will yield very much more detail to those who require it.[11]

No tax for which much detailed statistical information exists compares for historical interest with the income tax, despite its youth relative to most other great sources of revenue, such as customs and excise. A straightforward summary is therefore included here as table 19

[7] *S.P.* 1843 XX. The passage given here is quoted in the I.D.S.E.R. *Guides to Official Sources No. 3, Local Government Statistics* (H.M.S.O., 1953), p. 4. This is a particularly useful example of that series.

[8] *S.P.* 1870 IV.

[9] *S.P.* 1835 XXVII and XXIX.

[10] *S.P.* 1894 LXXIV, Pt. II.

[11] There are useful data and discussion in some of the mid-century volumes of the *Journal of the Statistical Society*, especially in 1858, 1860, 1871, and 1877.

of the rates at which the tax has been levied. Many more data are available on the tax, of course, as, indeed, on most other taxes. The *Reports* of the Commissioners of Inland Revenue and of Customs and Excise are the first places to go for this, but two books may be mentioned as especially useful. The first is A. Hope-Jones, *Income Tax in the Napoleonic Wars*.[12] The other, which contains much valuable information on the political and legislative background of the tax, is F. Shehab, *Progressive Taxation*.[13]

[12] (Cambridge, 1939).
[13] (Oxford, 1953).

Public Finance 1. Net Receipts of the Public Income – Great Britain 1688–1801

NOTES

[1] SOURCE: *S.P.* 1868–9, xxxv.

[2] There are no transfers of component items from heading to heading in this table. Items appropriate to a particular heading at the end of the period were included in that heading throughout.

[3] Gross accounts are available for lotteries, as follows (in £ thousand):

	Receipts	Expenditure		Receipts	Expenditure
1769	770	—	1785	399	361
1770	600	602	1786	577	501
1771	610	502	1787	731	501
1772	760	452	1788	774	501
1773	40	601	1789	749	482
1774	740	—	1790	866	501
1775	740	601	1791	781	501
1776	20	601	1792	813	501
1777	495	—	1793	751	502
1778	405	501	1794	670	501
1779	541	482	1795	814	502
1780	446	491	1796	915	502
1781	480	481	1797	499	501
1782	427	482	1798	645	501
1783	529	406	1799	690	501
1784	286	481	1800 (*e*)	(275)	(—)
			1801	790	502

(in £ thousand sterling)

	Total Net Income	Principal Constituent Items (*a*)				
		Customs	Excise	Stamps	Post Office	Land and Assessed Taxes
1688–91 (*b*)	8,613	1,920	2,430	—	163	3,172
1692 (*c*)	4,111	898	1,214	—	57	1,611
1693	3,783	689	905	—	64	1,738
1694	4,004	892	879	45	60	1,914
1695	4,134	899	935	46	64	1,839
1696	4,823	1,028	919	65	76	2,528
1697	3,298	719	1,078	47	59	972
1698	4,578	1,133	1,365	65	63	1,508
1699	5,164	1,472	1,413	95	75	1,578
1700	4,344	1,523	1,030	89	77	1,483
1701	3,769	1,583	986	94	75	991
1702	4,869	1,469	1,396	94	79	1,772
1703	5,561	1,576	1,750	89	66	1,954
1704	5,394	1,554	1,657	94	66	1,914
1705	5,292	1,110	1,807	84	60	2,065
1706	5,284	1,271	1,682	86	61	2,061
1707	5,471	1,366	1,745	87	57	2,034
1708	5,208	1,213	1,682	93	57	1,983
1709	5,206	1,305	1,571	94	56	2,056
1710	5,248	1,338	1,548	98	62	2,074
1711	5,179	1,109	1,673	97	66	2,130
1712	5,748	1,481	1,805	195	92	2,152
1713	5,780	1,428	2,089	107	92	1,884
1714	5,361	1,599	2,056	117	87	1,289
1715	5,547	1,685	2,303	142	95	1,129
1716	5,582	1,504	2,372	130	88	1,368
1717	6,514	1,822	2,355	143	91	1,984
1718	6,090	1,687	2,413	139	95	1,619
1719	6,026	1,644	1,454	136	98	1,589
1720	6,323	1,673	2,478	176	95	1,537
1721	5,954	1,446	2,486	140	95	1,573
1722	6,150	1,493	2,676	142	90	1,575
1723	5,993	1,604	2,780	144	93	1,224
1724	5,773	1,624	2,633	151	90	1,207
1725	5,960	1,711	2,741	155	99	1,148

See p. 577 for footnotes.

Public Finance 1. *continued*

(in £ thousand sterling)

	Total Net Income	Principal Constituent Items (*a*) Customs	Excise	Stamps	Post Office	Land and Assessed Taxes
1726	5,518	1,427	2,659	151	95	1,140
1727	6,103	1,648	2,879	157	100	1,287
1728	6,741	1,833	2,626	162	91	1,977
1729	6,294	1,669	2,649	159	100	1,644
1730	6,265	1,601	2,810	154	92	1,558
1731	6,080	1,525	2,786	163	95	1,217
1732	5,803	1,689	2,712	143	90	1,129
1733	5,522	1,521	3,028	127	96	721
1734	5,448	1,560	2,918	138	93	710
1735	5,652	1,479	2,843	137	98	1,070
1736	5,762	1,540	2,837	137	91	1,127
1737	6,077	1,722	2,954	142	97	1,108
1738	5,716	1,370	2,921	138	95	1,145
1739	5,820	1,398	3,025	135	96	1,134
1740	5,745	1,420	2,817	133	89	1,252
1741	6,244	1,435	2,587	131	87	1,983
1742	6,416	1,280	2,815	132	78	2,083
1743	6,567	1,278	2,903	130	97	2,130
1744	6,576	1,141	3,111	135	86	2,079
1745	6,451	1,156	2,921	134	85	2,117
1746	6,249	1,017	2,951	129	64	2,061
1747	6,961	1,328	3,218	132	82	2,174
1748	7,199	1,395	3,410	136	78	2,152
1749	7,494	1,618	3,394	132	96	2,229
1750	7,467	1,537	3,454	136	93	2,212
1751	7,097	1,588	3,468	134	106	1,769
1752 (*d*)	6,992	1,635	3,402	135	98	1,685
1753	7,338	1,770	3,582	132	100	1,728
1754	6,827	1,587	3,692	135	100	1,288
1755	6,938	1,782	3,660	137	100	1,236
1756	7,006	1,699	3,649	165	86	1,375
1757	7,969	1,872	3,303	239	74	2,043
1758	7,946	1,918	3,477	277	81	2,139
1759	8,155	1,830	3,615	282	84	2,216
1760	9,207	2,113	4,218	289	87	2,407
1761	9,594	2,191	4,671	307	67	2,253
1762	9,459	1,824	4,816	289	99	2,386
1763	9,793	2,283	4,793	299	103	2,288
1764	10,221	2,282	5,027	302	122	2,316
1765	10,928	2,324	4,935	302	165	2,243
1766	10,276	2,514	4,879	308	157	2,225
1767	9,868	2,460	4,521	310	160	2,174
1768	10,131	2,453	4,746	322	165	1,895
1769	11,130	2,675	4,961	320	162	1,814
1770	11,373	2,841	5,139	336	162	1,796
1771	10,987	2,739	4,842	339	154	1,834
1772	11,033	2,457	4,995	336	152	2,092
1773	10,487	2,702	5,141	342	167	1,843
1774	10,613	2,557	4,922	345	161	1,821
1775	11,112	2,756	5,106	350	177	1,756

Public Finance 1. *continued*

(in £ thousand sterling)

	Total Net Income	Principal Constituent Items (*a*)				
		Customs	Excise	Stamps	Post Office	Land and Assessed Taxes
1776	10,576	2,684	5,383	383	172	1,875
1777	11,105	2,411	5,252	436	152	2,299
1778	11,436	2,348	5,369	442	139	2,497
1779	11,853	2,523	5,625	475	133	2,450
1780	12,524	2,774	6,081	542	136	2,523
1781	13,280	3,019	6,111	626	142	2,635
1782	13,765	2,898	6,420	656	144	2,724
1783	12,677	2,949	5,480	855	166	2,596
1784	13,214	3,026	6,139	991	201	2,460
1785	15,527	4,537	6,142	1,217	304	2,666
1786	15,246	3,783	6,413	1,300	262	2,774
1787	16,453	4,094	7,043	1,196	262	2,909
1788	16,779	3,996	7,257	1,322	330	3,013
1789	16,669	3,647	7,301	1,250	321	3,006
1790	17,014	3,462	7,698	1,324	366	2,993
1791	18,506	4,018	8,433	1,384	338	2,914
1792	18,607	4,100	8,741	1,463	378	3,020
1793	18,131	3,557	8,559	1,452	409	2,952
1794	18,732	4,348	8,387	1,462	471	3,034
1795	19,053	3,419	9,915	1,456	441	2,946
1796	19,391	3,645	9,096	1,785	483	3,021
1797	21,380	3,940	10,303	1,978	558	3,365
1798	26,946	4,741	11,571	2,273	677	4,591
1799	31,783	7,056	11,862	2,447	704	6,446
1800 (*e*)	(9,674)	(2,395)	(3,241)	(763)	...(*f*)	(1,600)
1801 (*g*)	31,585	6,785	10,594	2,621	...(*f*)	5,093

(*a*) The property and income tax, introduced in 1799, was a major constituent of public income at the end of the period, as follows: 1799, 16,71; 1800, (1,020); 1801, 4,513.

(*b*) 5th November 1688 to 29th September 1691

(*c*) Years ended 29th September henceforth to 1751.

(*d*) Years ended 10th October henceforth to 1799.

(*e*) Quarter ended 5th January.

(*f*) The heading *Post Office* does not appear in the accounts for these periods.

(*g*) Year ended 5th January.

Public Finance 2. Net Public Expenditure – Great Britain 1688–1801

NOTES

[1] Source: *S.P.* 1868–9, xxxv.

[2] There are no transfers of component items from heading to heading in this table. Items appropriate to a particular heading at the end of the period were included in that heading throughout.

(in £ thousand sterling)

	Total Net Expenditure	Principal Constituent Items: Debt Charges: Total	Funded	Terminable Annuities	Unfunded	Civil Government: Total	Civil List	Army	Navy	Ordnance
1688–91 (*a*)	11,543	189	—	—	189	1,792	1,730	5,200	3,098	659
1692 (*b*)	4,255	199	—	—	199	662	632	1,900	1,239	254
1693	5,576	222	—	—	222	702	697	2,346	1,925	380
1694	5,602	442	12	111	319	669	662	2,119	2,132	239
1695	6,220	581	107	190	284	774	774	2,559	1,890	417
1696	7,998	651	66	262	323	713	700	1,749	1,922	253
1697	7,915	1,044	127	283	634	871	746	2,646	2,822	521
1698	4,127	1,467	186	469	812	391	375	1,343	877	49
1699	4,691	1,484	243	305	898	913	856	1,018	1,232	44
1700	3,201	1,251	218	331	701	699	683	359	819	73
1701	3,442	1,200	222	304	675	704	688	442	1,046	50
1702	5,010	1,174	256	315	603	523	508	1,102	2,094	117
1703	5,313	1,042	285	307	450	605	590	1,770	1,724	173
1704	5,527	977	260	338	374	656	638	2,107	1,630	157
1705	5,873	1,036	260	435	367	737	725	2,146	1,772	183
1706	6,692	1,078	268	449	350	652	630	2,741	1,949	271
1707	8,747	1,846	322	680	842	1,129	706	3,188	2,297	287
1708	7,742	1,637	315	735	585	784	761	3,183	1,909	229
1709	9,160	2,014	311	1,070	602	777	701	3,969	2,117	282
1710	9,772	1,754	317	733	584	857	840	4,463	2,422	276
1711	15,145(*c*)	1,813	347	763	612	668	645	4,853(*c*)	7,476(*c*)	334(*c*)
1712	7,864	2,360	709	1,080	485	726	697	2,837	1,776	165
1713	6,362	2,888	943	1,414	531	656	604	1,267	1,457	95
1714	6,185	3,021	834	1,604	583	1,161	1,108	884	1,043	76
1715	6,228	3,276	1,237	1,540	492	734	693	924	1,205	90
1716	7,076	3,027	856	1,689	461	926	874	2,151	792	180
1717	5,885	3,440	1,112	1,870	458	983	901	980	443	39
1718	6,354	2,839	1,383	1,073	375	840	784	1,204	1,350	120
1719	6,152	2,706	1,465	1,003	208	808	698	1,186	1,293	159
1720	6,002	2,769	1,716	943	96	980	880	965	1,181	108
1721	5,873	3,314	2,857	362	88	1,002	890	754	705	99
1722	6,978	3,012	2,544	212	232	1,181	1,101	1,011	1,666	108
1723	5,671	2,919	2,523	267	105	942	847	895	827	89
1724	5,438	2,864	2,461	281	115	968	886	856	630	120
1725	5,516	2,796	2,432	268	86	1,251	1,157	773	601	95
1726	5,543	2,667	2,353	224	88	1,089	825	992	695	100
1727	5,860	2,783	2,448	203	122	939	625	1,191	833	115
1728	6,504	2,335	2,006	208	121	1,051	916	1,378	1,539	201
1729	5,711	2,284	1,998	184	97	1,044	932	1,293	925	164
1730	5,574	2,280	2,001	187	85	935	853	1,203	1,033	123
1731	5,347	2,120	1,850	186	83	918	862	1,353	815	140
1732	4,974	2,217	1,959	182	66	933	867	1,012	700	113
1733	4,595	2,143	1,888	182	73	957	893	791	555	148
1734	6,360	2,052	1,792	182	76	1,060	945	707	2,079	462
1735	5,852	2,174	1,863	186	125	941	856	1,037	1,545	155

See p. 580 for footnotes.

Public Finance 2. *continued*

(in £ thousand sterling)

Principal Constituent Items

	Total Net Expenditure	Debt Charges				Civil Government				
		Total	Funded	Terminable Annuities	Unfunded	Total	Civil List	Army	Navy	Ordnance
1736	5,793	2,127	1,829	179	119	949	853	1,185	1,390	142
1737	5,129	2,105	1,808	181	114	930	855	835	933	327
1738	4,725	2,059	1,753	184	122	886	828	846	819	115
1739	5,210	2,047	1,762	181	103	953	876	1,066	988	156
1740	6,161	2,102	1,790	185	128	846	792	1,418	1,607	187
1741	7,388	2,032	1,727	177	128	842	738	1,776	2,419	320
1742	8,533	2,041	1,690	182	170	834	783	2,523	2,795	340
1743	8,979	2,117	1,725	170	181	884	750	2,878	2,736	363
1744	9,398	2,178	1,824	154	191	921	797	3,227	2,709	364
1745	8,920	2,259	1,855	153	169	837	762	2,790	2,688	345
1746	9,804	2,316	1,945	172	189	784	685	3,729	2,396	579
1747	11,453	2,716	2,208	210	282	1,366	1,213	3,679	3,176	516
1748	11,943	2,842	2,306	219	194	997	770	4,172	3,361	571
1749	12,544(*c*)	2,981	2,449	217	162	1,082	793	2,339	5,606(*c*)	536(*c*)
1750	7,185	3,218	2,817	214	186	1,016	813	1,338	1,385	228
1751	6,425	2,978	2,588	212	176	1,068	829	1,383	895	102
1752 (*d*)	7,037	2,944	2,580	215	139	1,108	803	976	1,854	154
1753	5,952	2,762	2,394	212	150	1,068	853	1,140	849	133
1754	6,030	2,823	2,494	211	118	1,043	801	1,071	944	150
1755	7,119	2,731	2,419	211	99	997	785	1,399	1,814	177
1756	9,589	2,761	2,463	207	82	1,292	849	2,396	2,714	426
1757	11,214	2,805	2,525	205	53	1,083	841(*e*)	3,210	3,595	520
1758	13,200	2,895	2,492	239	151	1,279	840	4,586	3,893	547
1759	15,382	2,947	2,623	240	72	991	809	5,744	4,971	729
1760	17,993	3,372	2,915	237	193	1,152	852	8,249	4,539	682
1761	21,112	3,823	3,247	298	182	1,256	997	9,923	5,256	853
1762	20,040	4,404	3,681	418	225	1,218	942(*e*)	8,781	4,892	746
1763	17,723(*c*)	4,666	3,989	474	139	1,056	867(*e*)	4,067	7,464(*c*)	470
1764	10,686	4,887	4,230	474	171	1,137	865(*e*)	2,234	2,150	279
1765	12,017(*c*)	4,828	4,224	469	134	1,050	806	2,702	3,154(*c*)	282
1766	10,314	4,686	4,046	472	157	1,069	815(*e*)	1,815	2,467	276
1767	9,638	5,020	4,274	563	164	1,022	813(*e*)	1,696	1,657	243
1768	9,146	4,911	4,299	463	130	1,036	807(*e*)	1,472	1,431	296
1769	9,569	4,803	4,191	466	132	1,498	1,268(*f*)	1,438	1,527	303
1770	10,524	4,836	4,236	463	136	1,223	898(*f*)	1,545	2,082	236
1771	10,106	4,611	4,054	458	98	1,057	796	1,514	2,061	361
1772	10,725	4,686	4,466	459	142	1,017	797(*e*)	1,497	2,738	334
1773	9,977	4,649	4,041	456	150	1,032	803(*e*)	1,581	1,787	327
1774	9,566	4,612	4,040	450	122	1,095	809(*e*)	1,532	2,030	298
1775	10,365	4,674	4,010	452	210	1,211	905(*e*)	1,765	1,765	349
1776	14,045	4,632	3,991	446	192	1,271	811(*e*)	4,248	2,745	549
1777	15,259	4,709	4,036	455	212	1,769	1,386(*e*)	4,677	3,531	573
1778	17,940	5,030	4,414	506	181	1,425	1,112(*e*)	5,464	4,563	957
1779	19,714	5,618	4,543	750	252	1,158	970(*e*)	7,112	4,271	1,074
1780	22,605	5,995	4,675	964	266	1,251	1,039(*e*)	7,210	6,329	1,330

See p. 580 for footnotes.

Public Finance 2. *continued*

(in £ thousand sterling)

Principal Constituent Items

	Total Net Expenditure	Debt Charges				Civil Government				
		Total	Funded	Terminable Annuities	Unfunded	Total	Civil List	Army	Navy	Ordnance
1781	25,810	6,917	5,348	1,149	310	1,350	983(*e*)	8,928	6,589	1,546
1782	29,234	7,364	5,898	1,113	312	1,263	1,005(*e*)	7,755	10,807	1,564
1783	23,510	8,054	6,447	1,245	275	1,383	1,131(*e*)	5,332	6,994	1,341
1784	24,245(*c*)	8,678	6,959	1,323	372	1,324	1,055(*e*)	3,301	9,447(*c*)	1,014
1785	25,832(*c*)	9,229	7,431	1,299	467	1,451	989(*e*)	2,390	11,851(*c*)	551
1786	16,978	9,481	7,980	1,295	206	1,513	1,015(*e*)	1,984	3,127	372
1787	15,484	9,292	7,916	1,021	355	1,513	1,054(*e*)	1,803	1,991	384
1788	16,338	9,407	7,894	1,267	247	1,522	1,164(*e*)	2,099	2,262	547
1789	16,018	9,425	7,850	1,265	310	1,664	1,251(*e*)	1,899	2,073	475
1790	16,798	9,370	7,904	1,277	285	1,703	1,150(*e*)	2,197	2,482	545
1791	17,996	9,430	7,758	1,344	321	1,886	1,177(*e*)	2,009	3,400	769
1792	16,953	9,310	7,712	1,294	304	1,565	968(*e*)	1,829	3,331	417
1793	19,623	9,149	7,661	1,269	219	1,835	1,160(*e*)	4,829	2,464	844
1794	28,706(*c*)	9,797	8,016	1,272	452	1,572	1,118(*e*)	9,209	6,127(*c*)	1,501
1795	38,996(*c*)	10,470	8,595	1,351	331	1,751	1,235(*e*)	14,651	9,626(*c*)	1,996
1796	42,372(*c*)	11,602	9,582	1,453	237	2,014	1,272(*e*)	14,236	11,518(*c*)	2,500
1797	57,649(*c*)	13,594	11,609	1,499	246	2,527	1,311(*e*)	15,327	23,580(*c*)	2,122
1798	47,422	16,029	13,750	1,517	505	2,178	1,187(*e*)	14,142	12,793	1,780
1799	47,419	16,856	13,916	1,555	1,158	2,180	1,045(*e*)	14,289	11,614	1,980
1800 (*g*)	(12,383)	(3,387)	(2,382)	(742)	(44)	(537)	(225)	(4,151)	(3,843)	(465)
1801 (*h*)	50,991	16,749	13,872	1,780	922	2,072	1,039(*e*)	15,297	14,707	1,663

(*a*) 5th November 1688 to 29th September 1691.

(*b*) Years ended 29th September henceforth to 1751.

(*c*) These figures contain an element of debt funded in these years but contracted previously. The amounts are as follows:

1711 1,133 Army, 6,239 Navy, and 189 Ordnance,
1749 2,842 Navy, and 230 Ordnance,
1763 3,484 Navy,
1765 1,368 Navy,
1784 6,397 Navy and Ordnance combined – here attributed entirely to Navy,
1785 9,866 Navy and Ordnance combined – here attributed entirely to Navy,
1794 1,907 Navy,
1795 1,491 Navy,
1796 4,227 Navy,
1797 11,596 Navy.

(*d*) Years ended 10th October henceforth to 1799.

(*e*) The Civil List was swollen in these years by the addition of certain sums advanced from it for miscellaneous supply services on the understanding that they would be repaid in the following session. The amounts repaid were as follows:

1758	31	1776	7	1789	395
1763	6	1777	48	1790	219
1764	7	1778	85	1791	255
1765	2	1779	71	1792	118
1767	13	1780	124	1793	190
1768	11	1781	96	1794	202
1769	17	1782	97	1795	281
1770	14	1783	103	1796	474
1771	15	1784	145	1797	276
1772	7	1785	69	1798	207
1773	6	1786	123	1799	55
1774	10	1787	30	1800(¼)	—
1775	14	1788	293	1801	77

(*f*) These figures include grants for Civil List debts – 463 in 1769 and 50 in 1770.

(*g*) Quarter ended 5th January.

(*h*) Year ended 5th January.

Public Finance 3. Gross Public Income – United Kingdom 1801–1980

NOTES

[1] Sources: 1802–69 – *S.P.* 1868–9, xxxv; 1870–1980 – *Finance Accounts*, and its successor, *Consolidated Fund and Loan Fund Accounts*, and *Abstract*.

[2] The figures for Great Britain for the years ended 5th January 1802–17 are as follows:

	Total Gross Income	Customs	Excise	Stamps	Land and Assessed Taxes	Property and Income Tax	Post Office
1802	35·9	8·8	11·6	3·0	4·6	5·8	1·2
1803	37·4	7·7	15·5	3·2	5·3	3·3	1·3
1804	39·1	8·2	18·8	3·4	5·8	0·4	1·2
1805	46·5	9·4	21·5	3·5	6·0	3·7	1·3
1806	51·2	10·1	23·2	4·1	6·3	4·6	1·4
1807	55·7	10·8	24·1	4·3	6·4	6·2	1·5
1808	59·8	10·6	24·7	4·4	7·0	10·2	1·5
1809	62·9	10·3	25·6	4·7	7·6	11·4	1·5
1810	64·1	11·9	23·4	5·3	8·4	12·4	1·6
1811	69·6	12·4	25·8	5·5	7·7	13·5	1·7
1812	67·5	10·9	25·9	5·3	7·4	13·2	1·7
1813	64·7	11·6	23·6	5·3	7·5	13·1	1·8
1814	72·8	11·9	25·3	5·6	7·9	14·3	1·9
1815	74·3	12·6	26·4	5·8	8·0	14·5	2·0
1816	78·6	12·0	26·2	6·1	9·5	14·6	2·1
1817	65·2	10·1	24·2	6·2	7·3	11·8	2·0

[3] Statistics to 1854 are for years ended 5 January, and subsequently they are for years ended 31 March.

[4] The Indian Military Contribution and the Army and Navy Extra Receipts have been excluded throughout this table.

[5] Receipts from taxes assigned to local authorities in lieu of exchequer payments for the period 1890–1907 have been included in this table.

(in £ million sterling)

		Principal Constituent Items (*a*)					
	Total Gross Income	Customs	Excise	Stamps	Land and Assessed Taxes	Property and Income Tax	Post Office
1802	39·1	8·8	11·6	3·2	4·6	5·8	1·3
1803	41·2	7·7	15·5	3·4	5·3	3·3	1·4
1804	42·4	8·2	18·8	3·6	5·8	0·4	1·3
1805	50·2	9·4	21·5	3·9	6·0	3·7	1·4
1806	55·0	10·1	23·2	4·6	6·3	4·6	1·6
1807	60·1	10·8	24·1	4·9	6·4	6·2	1·6
		- - -	- - -				
1808	64·8	12·6(*b*)	26·7(*b*)	5·0	7·0	10·2	1·6
1809	68·2	12·6	27·6	5·4	7·6	11·4	1·6
1810	69·2	14·6	24·8	6·0	8·4	12·4	1·7
1811	73·0	14·4	27·4	6·2	7·7	13·5	1·9
1812	71·0	13·0	27·9	6·0	7·4	13·2	1·9
1813	70·3	14·0	25·9	6·0	7·5	13·1	2·0
1814	74·7	14·4	27·5	6·3	7·9	14·3	2·1
1815	77·9	14·8	29·5	6·5	8·0	14·5	2·2
1816	79·1	14·3	29·5	6·7	9·5	14·6	2·3
1817	69·2	11·9	26·9	6·8	7·3	11·8	2·2
1818	57·6	13·4	23·2	7·2	8·2	2·3	2·1
1819	59·5	13·9	26·4	7·2	8·2	0·6	2·1
1820	58·1	13·0	26·5	7·0	8·2	0·2	2·1
1821	59·9	11·9	29·6	6·9	8·2	..	2·1
1822	61·6	12·7	29·9	6·8	8·3	..	2·0
1823	59·9	13·0	29·1	6·9	7·7	—	2·1
1824	58·5	13·9	27·2	7·1	6·7	—	2·1
1825	59·7	13·5	28·5	7·6	5·3	—	2·2
1826	57·7	18·7	22·6	7·7	5·4	—	2·2
1827	55·2	19·5	20·8	7·0	5·1	—	2·3
1828	54·7	20·1	20·0	7·1	5·1	—	2·2
1829	56·5	19·3	22·2	7·4	5·2	—	2·2
1830	55·3	19·2	21·0	7·4	5·3	—	2·2
1831	54·5	19·4	20·0	7·3	5·4	—	2·2

See p. 586 for footnotes.

Public Finance 3. *continued*

(in £ million sterling)

	Total Gross Income	Principal Constituent Items (*a*)								
		Customs	Excise	Stamps (*d*)	Land and Assessed Taxes	Property and Income Tax	Post Office	Telegraph Service	Telephone Service	Death Duties (*d*)
1832	50·6	18·2	17·5	7·2	5·2	—	2·2	—	—	—
1833	51·1	18·5	17·9	7·2	5·2	—	2·2	—	—	—
1834	50·2	17·8	17·7	7·1	5·2	—	2·2	—	—	—
1835	50·4	20·0	16·1	7·2	4·8	—	2·2	—	—	—
1836	50·0	22·0	14·4	7·2	3·9	—	2·2	—	—	—
1837	52·6	23·1	15·7	7·4	3·9	—	2·3	—	—	—
1838	50·4	22·1	14·6	7·1	3·9	—	2·3	—	—	—
1839	51·3	22·4	14·8	7·2	3·9	—	2·3	—	—	—
1840	51·8	23·2	14·6	7·2	3·9	—	2·4	—	—	—
1841	51·6	23·4	14·9	7·4	4·2	—	1·3	—	—	—
1842	52·2	23·5	14·8	7·3	4·7	—	1·4	—	—	—
1843	51·1	22·6	13·6	7·2	4·5	0·6	1·6	—	—	—
1844	56·7	22·6	14·0	7·1	4·4	5·3	1·6	—	—	—
1845	58·2	24·1	14·4	7·3	4·4	5·3	1·7	—	—	—
1846	57·5	21·8	14·6	7·9	4·4	5·2	1·9	—	—	—
1847	58·2	22·2	15·0	7·7	4·5	5·5	2·0	—	—	—
1848	56·1	21·7	13·9	7·7	4·6	5·6	2·1	—	—	—
1849	57·8	22·6	15·2	6·8	4·5	5·5	2·2	—	—	—
1850	57·1	22·3	15·0	7·0	4·5	5·6	2·2	—	—	—
1851	57·1	22·0	15·3	6·7	4·6	5·5	2·3	—	—	—
1852	56·3	22·2	15·4	6·5	3·8	5·4	2·4	—	—	—
1853	57·3	22·1	15·7	6·9	3·6	5·7	2·4	—	—	—
1854	58·5	22·5	16·3	7·1	3·3	5·7	2·5	—	—	—
[1854](*c*)	[13·5]	[5·1]	[2·6]	[1·8]	[0·2]	[2·7]	[0·7]	—	—	—
1855	62·4	21·6	16·9	7·1	3·2	10·6	2·4	—	—	—
1856	69·7	23·2	17·5	7·1	3·1	15·1	2·8	—	—	—
1857	72·2	23·5	18·3	7·4	3·1	16·1	2·9	—	—	—
1858	66·9	23·1	17·8	7·4	3·2	11·6	2·9	—	—	—
1859	64·3	24·1	17·9	8·0	3·2	6·7	3·2	—	—	—
1860	70·1	24·5	20·4	8·0	3·2	9·6	3·3	—	—	—
1861	69·7	23·3	19·4	8·3	3·1	10·9	3·4	—	—	—
1862	69·0	23·7	18·3	8·6	3·2	10·4	3·5	—	—	—
1863	68·8	24·0	17·2	9·0	3·2	10·6	3·7	—	—	—
1864	68·4	23·2	18·2	9·3	3·2	9·1	3·8	—	—	—
1865	68·7	22·6	19·6	9·5	3·3	8·0	4·1	—	—	—
1866	66·1	21·3	19·8	9·6	3·4	6·4	4·3	—	—	—
1867	67·8	22·3	20·7	9·4	3·5	5·7	4·5	—	—	—
1868	67·8	22·7	20·2	9·5	3·5	6·2	4·6	—	—	—
1869	70·8	22·4	20·5	9·2	3·5	8·6	4·7	—	—	—
				---(*d*)						
1870	73·7	21·5	21·8	4·0	4·5	10·0	4·7	0·1	—	4·7
			---(*e*)		---(*e*)					
1871	68·2	20·2	22·8	3·6	2·7	6·4	4·8	0·5	—	4·8
1872	73·1	20·3	23·3	3·9	2·3	9·1	4·7	0·8	—	5·2
1873	74·7	21·0	25·8	4·1	2·3	7·5	4·8	1·0	—	5·1
1874	75·5	20·3	27·2	4·3	2·3	5·7	5·8	1·2	—	5·5
1875	73·6	19·3	27·4	4·2	2·4	4·3	5·7	1·1	—	5·6
1876	75·5	20·0	27·6	4·4	2·5	4·1	6·0	1·2	—	5·8
1877	76·8	19·9	27·7	4·3	2·5	5·3	6·0	1·3	—	5·9
1878	77·7	20·0	27·5	4·2	2·7	5·8	6·2	1·3	—	6·0
1879	81·2	20·3	27·4	4·3	2·7	8·7	6·2	1·3	—	5·6
1880	73·3	19·3	25·3	4·2	2·7	9·2	6·4	1·4	—	6·2

See p. 586 for footnotes.

Public Finance 3. *continued*

(in £ million sterling)

Principal Constituent Items (*a*)

	Total Gross Income	Customs	Excise	Stamps	Land and Assessed Taxes	Property and Income Tax (*f*)	Post Office	Telegraph Service (*g*)	Telephone Service (*g*)	Death Duties
1881	81·9	19·2	25·3	4·4	2·7	10·7	6·7	1·6	—	6·7
1882	84·0	19·3	27·2	4·3	2·7	9·9	7·0	1·6	—	7·1
1883	87·4	19·7	26·9	4·5	2·8	11·9	7·3	1·7	—	7·3
1884	86·2	19·7	27·0	4·2	2·9	10·7	7·7	1·7	—	7·4
1885	88·0	20·3	26·6	4·2	3·0	12·0	7·9	1·8	—	7·7
1886	89·6	19·8	25·5	4·2	2·9	15·2	8·2	1·7	—	7·4
1887	90·8	20·2	25·3	4·4	3·0	15·9	8·5	1·8	—	7·4
1888	89·8	19·6	25·6	4·8	3·0	14·4	8·7	2·0	—	8·2
1889	89·9	20·1	25·6	4·3	3·0	12·7	9·1	2·1	—	8·0
1890	94·6	20·4	27·2	5·0	3·0	12·8	9·5	2·3	—	9·1
1891	96·5	19·7	29·2	6·0	2·6	13·3	9·9	2·4	—	9·9
1892	98·6	19·9	30·2	5·4	2·5	13·8	10·2	2·5	—	11·1
1893	97·7	20·0	30·0	5·5	2·5	13·5	10·4	2·5	—	10·7
1894	98·4	20·0	29·8	5·3	2·5	15·2	10·5	2·5	—	9·9
1895	101·8	20·4	30·7	5·7	2·5	15·6	10·8	2·6	—	10·9
1896	109·4	21·1	31·5	7·4	2·5	16·1	11·4	2·8	—	14·1
1897	112·3	21·5	32·4	7·4	2·4	16·7	11·9	2·9	—	14·0
1898	116·1	22·1	33·3	7·7	2·4	17·3	12·2	3·0	—	15·3
1899	117·9	21·1	34·3	7·6	2·4	18·0	12·7	3·2	—	15·6
1900	129·9	24·1	37·3	8·5	2·5	18·8	13·3	3·4	—	18·5
1901	140·2	26·6	38·4	7·8	2·5	26·9	13·8	3·5	—	17·2
1902	152·7	31·2	36·8	7·8	2·5	34·8	14·3	3·5	—	18·5
1903	161·3	34·7	37·4	8·2	2·6	38·8	14·8	3·6	—	18·1
1904	151·3	34·1	36·9	7·5	2·7	30·8	15·5	3·7	—	17·2
1905	153·2	35·9	36·1	7·7	2·8	31·3	16·1	3·8	—	16·7
1906	153·9	34·6	35·6	8·2	2·7	31·4	16·9	4·1	—	17·3
1907	155·0	33·1	35·7	8·0	2·6	31·6	17·2	4·3	—	19·1
1908	156·5	32·5	35·7	8·0	2·7	32·4	17·9	4·4	—	19·1
								---(*g*)		
1909	151·6	29·2	33·7	7·8	2·6	33·9	17·8	3·0	1·5	18·4
1910	131·7	30·3	31·0	8·1	0·7	13·3	18·2	3·1	1·7	21·8
1911	203·9	33·1	40·0	9·8	4·3	61·9	19·2	3·2	2·0	25·5
1912	185·1	33·6	38·4	9·5	2·9	44·8	19·7	3·1	2·9	25·4
1913	188·8	33·5	38·0	10·1	2·7	44·8	20·3	3·1	5·8	25·2
1914	198·2	33·5	39·6	10·0	2·7	47·2	21·2	3·1	6·5	27·4
1915	226·7	38·7	42·3	7·6	2·6	69·4	20·4	3·0	6·3	28·4
1916	336·8	59·6	61·2	6·8	2·7	128·3	24·1	3·4	6·5	31·0
1917	573·4	70·6	56·4	7·9	2·6	205·0	24·4	3·4	6·4	31·2
1918	707·2	71·3	38·8	8·3	2·6	239·5	25·2	3·5	6·6	31·7
1919	889·0	102·8	59·4	12·4	2·5	291·2	29·4	3·8	6·8	30·3
1920	1,339·6	149·4	133·7	22·6	2·6	359·1	31·0	4·9	8·3	40·9
			---(*h*)							

See p. 586 for footnotes.

Public Finance 3. *continued*

(in £ million sterling)

Principal Constituent Items (*a*)

	Total Gross Income	Customs	Excise	Stamps	Land and Assessed Taxes	Property and Income Tax (*f*)	Profits Tax (*i*)	Post Office (*j*)	Telegraph Service (*j*)	Telephone Service (*j*)	Death Duties	Motor Vehicle Duties (*h*)	Broadcast Receiving Licences (*k*)
1921	1,426·0	134·0	199·8	26·6	2·6	394·1	—	36·1	5·2	8·2	47·7	7·1	...
1922	1,124·9	130·1	194·3	19·6	2·6	398·8	—	40·0	5·9	10·5	52·2	11·1	...
1923	914·0	123·0	157·3	22·2	2·8	379·0	—	34·2	5·5	13·6	56·9	12·3	...
1924	837·2	120·0	148·0	21·6	2·5	330·0	—	32·8	5·6	14·4	57·8	14·7	...
1925	799·4	99·3	135·1	22·9	1·2	336·5	—	34·9	5·6	15·0	59·5	16·2	...
1926	812·1	103·5	134·6	24·7	0·7	327·9	—	35·8	5·7	16·0	61·2	18·1	...
1927	805·7	107·5	133·0	24·8	0·7	300·6	—	35·6	5·9	17·4	67·3	21·4	...
1928	842·8	111·6	139·2	27·0	0·6	311·2	—	38·3	6·1	18·7	77·3	24·5	...
1929	836·4	119·0	134·0	30·1	0·6	293·8	—	39·0	6·2	20·1	80·6	25·4	...
1930	815·0	119·9	127·5	25·7	0·7	293·8	—	40·2	6·3	21·6	79·8	26·8	...
1931	857·8	121·4	124·0	20·7	0·6	323·9	—	40·3	6·3	22·6	82·6	27·8	...
1932	851·5	136·2	119·9	17·1	0·7	364·1	—	40·1	6·2	23·3	65·0	27·5	...
1933	827·0	162·2	120·9	19·2	0·6	312·2	—	39·9	6·3	24·0	77·1	27·9	...
1934	809·4	179·2	107·0	22·7	0·6	281·5	—	40·6	6·6	25·3	85·3	30·7	...
1935	804·6	185·1	104·6	24·1	0·6	280·0	—	41·5	7·0	25·6	81·4	31·5	...
1936	844·8	196·6	106·7	25·8	0·6	289·1	—	42·8	7·1	27·9	87·9	30·8	...
1937	896·6	211·3	109·5	29·1	0·5	310·8	—	45·4	7·6	30·0	88·0	32·7	...
1938	948·7	221·6	113·7	24·2	...	354·0	1·4	47·0	7·8	31·8	89·0	34·6	...
1939	1,006·2	226·3	114·2	21·0	...	398·4	21·9	47·3	7·8	33·4	77·4	35·6	...
1940	1,132·2	262·1	137·9	17·1	...	459·9	26·9	43·9	8·0	35·1	77·7	34·1	...
1941	1,495·3	304·9	224·1	13·7	...	600·0	96·2	54·5	8·7	38·5	80·8	38·0	...
1942	2,174·6	378·4	325·7	14·1	...	844·6	269·1	56·7	8·6	49·0	90·9	38·4	...
									---(*k*)				
1943	2,922·4	549·5	425·3	15·3	...	1,082·2	377·5	58·6	5·7	50·6	93·3	28·5	4·6
1944	3,149·2	560·8	482·2	17·7	...	1,259·6	500·1	65·6	4·9	40·5	99·5	27·3	4·8
1945	3,354·7	579·4	496·9	17·0	...	1,390·4	510·4	68·0	5·3	43·3	110·9	29·0	4·8
1946	3,401·2	569·8	540·8	25·1	...	1,430·4	466·4	63·8	5·7	46·0	120·3	43·2	5·2
1947	3,622·7	620·7	563·5	38·3	...	1,232·0	357·5	71·0	5·5	54·5	148·0	49·5	9·9
1948	4,011·3	791·1	629·7	56·3	...	1,280·9	288·7	76·3	5·5	61·5	172·0	49·1	11·2
1949	4,168·0	823·3	733·5	56·4	...	1,465·5	278·9	81·0	5·4	66·3	177·1	52·7	11·7
1950	4,098·0	813·3	706·4	51·5	...	1,553·1	297·0	85·3	5·1	71·8	189·6	55·8	12·6

1951	4,157·2	905·2	724·8	54·5	...	1,525·5	267·7	86·3	7·8	78·0	185·2	61·4	13·0
1952	4,629·0	998·5	753·3	61·9	...	1,798·3	315·4	97·3	10·0	82·8	183·0	65·2	14·2
1953	4,653·8	1,024·5	739·1	50·2	...	1,867·4	379·1	108·4	10·5	91·0	151·8	67·7	14·8
1954	4,606·0	1,042·4	722·0	56·6	...	1,863·4	254·3	112·5	13·3	106·2	164·5	73·1	16·4
1955	4,986·7	1,100·0	771·6	75·1	...	2,027·7	249·3	119·7	14·0	115·0	187·9	79·0	22·3
1956	5,160·4	1,148·6	864·5	70·6	...	2,081·5	211·0	122·6	15·4	126·9	175·7	87·0	25·8
1957	5,462·4	1,198·9	901·7	63·0	...	2,272·2	200·0	140·7	15·4	152·4	169·0	90·6	28·4
1958	5,678·7	1,207·5	942·4	63·7	...	2,365·7	255·2	154·8	16·1	172·4	170·6	100·7	30·7
1959	5,850·1	1,261·5	929·8	65·4	...	2,488·4	274·8	164·7	17·8	187·7	186·9	106·8	33·7
1960	6,015·6	1,373·3	908·6	97·3	...	2,423·9	261·8	173·3	18·5	201·1	226·5	108·4	36·1
1961	6,343·6	1,456·3	933·3	90·2	...	2,622·5	263·1	182·0	18·9	209·0	235·6	126·0	37·9
1962	6,644·9	1,616·3	978·4	96·6	...	2,950·8	335·1	...	...	...	262·2	141·0	39·5
1963	6,794·1	1,639·4	1,028·4	95·7	...	3,002·2	383·1	...	...	...	270·2	152·5	40·7
1964	6,890·2	1,723·0	1,042·9	88·2	...	2,922·5	390·4	...	...	...	310·2	171·1	50·4
1965	7,727·0	2,007·7	1,165·7	78·9	...	3,272·0	422·6	...	...	...	297·5	186·8	55·4

See p. 586 for footnotes.

Public Finance 3. *continued*

(in £ million sterling)

		Principal Constituent Items (*a*)								
	Total Gross Income	Customs & Excise (*l*)	Stamps	Income Tax (*f*)	Profits Tax & Corporation Tax (*i*)	Death Duties & Capital Transfer Tax (*m*)	Motor Vehicle Duties	Broadcast Receiving Licences	Capital Gains Tax	Value Added Tax
1966	8,673·9 ----(*n*) 9,144·4	3,401·2	75·9	3,881·1	437·7	292·9	234·9	68·6	—	—
1967	10,278·9	3,535·9	76·4	3,487·6	1,118·0	301·3	243·9	73·6	7·2	—
1968	11,855·1 ----(*n*) 11,227·3	3,721·3	97·1	4,068·3	1,252·8	331·3	269·0	81·2	15·5	—
1969	13,363·4	4,600·5	124·1	4,561·4	1,354·0	379·2	393·1	84·7	46·8	—
1970	15,266·6	4,952·5	120·2	5,155·3	1,688·6	365·5	416·7	101·2	126·8	—
1971	15,842·8	4,709·1	116·2	5,968·6	1,591·3	356·3	421·2	100·7	138·8	—
1972	16,931·8	5,325·3	166·3	6,798·1	1,559·6	452·4	473·3	122·0	155·5	—
1973	17,178·1	5,743·5	227·6	6,816·2	1,533·5	458·5	485·0	136·4	208·4	—
1974	18,226·4	3,772·2	190·3	7,443·1	2,263·2	412·2	533·5	152·9	323·6	1,447·4
1975	23,570·1	4,910·0	197·4	10,424·5	2,850·7	337·8	532·1	164·3	380·4	2,496·5
1976	29,417·1	5,781·4	281·1	15,162·7	1,998·0	330·2	780·7	229·6	387·1	3,395·0
1977	33,778·1	7,121·6	271·6	17,075·0	2,655·1	383·2	845·9	246·7	323·4	3,778·4
1978	38,773·2	8,053·7	376·4	17,452·3	3,343·2	397·9	1,071·7	294·3	340·0	4,230·4
1979	43,087·9	8,957·2	433·9	18,783·0	3,944·3	419·4	1,113·0	336·5	353·3	4,877·8
1980	54,331·5	10,027·8	619·1	20,574·5	4,638·1	432·1	1,148·9	272·8	430·3	8,004·1

(*a*) For short periods other items are of interest or importance, as follows:

Gross Income from Lotteries

1802	1·1	1809	1·1	1816	1·1	1823	0·8
1803	1·1	1810	0·8	1817	1·0	1824	0·6
1804	1·3	1811	1·1	1818	0·8	1825	0·6
1805	1·1	1812	0·9	1819	0·8	1826	1·0
1806	1·3	1813	1·0	1820	0·8	1827	0·3
1807	1·2	1814	0·9	1821	0·8		
1808	1·3	1815	1·1	1822	0·9		

Gross Income from Excess Profits Tax

1917	139·9	1919	285·0	1921	219·2
1918	220·2	1920	290·0	1922	30·5

Gross Income from Corporation Profits Tax

1922	17·6	1924	23·3	1926	11·7
1923	19·0	1925	18·1	1927	4·0

Gross Income from Selective Employment Tax

1967	600·1	1970	1,888·1	1973	993·5
1968	1,063·8	1971	1,989·6	1974	45·0
1969	1,362·7	1972	1,323·7	1975	2·0

Gross Income from Petroleum Revenue Tax

1979	183·0	1980	1,433·0

(*b*) Prior to 1808 the customs and excise revenues of Ireland cannot be separated. The combined figure has been included in Total Gross Income but not under the individual headings.

(*c*) Figures in this row are for the quarter ended 5 April. See note 3 above.

(*d*) Death duties are included with stamps to 1869. Fee and patent stamps were excluded from that heading at the same time as death duties were separated.

(*e*) From 1871 all assessed taxes except land tax and house duty were replaced by excise licences, and their revenue consequently transferred.

(*f*) Including supertax and surtax, the former introduced in 1911.

(*g*) Telephones are included with telegraph service to 1908.

(*h*) Motor licences are included with excises to 1920.

(*i*) Including National Defence Contribution, Excess Profits Duty, and Excess Profits Levy. Corporation tax was introduced in 1967. For the First World War profits taxes see footnote (*a*) above.

(*j*) The Post Office Act (1961) separated the finances of the Post Office from the Exchequer from 1 April 1961.

(*k*) Broadcast receiving licences are included with telegraph service to 1942.

(*l*) Customs and excise receipts cannot be shown separately on the same basis as before after 1965. The figures here are exclusive of V.A.T., which is shown separately.

(*m*) Capital transfer tax was introduced in 1976.

(*n*) Certain items, mainly interest and dividends, are included in 1966 (2nd line), 1967, and 1968 (1st line), but most of them are excluded subsequently.

Public Finance 4. Gross Public Expenditure – United Kingdom 1801–1980

NOTES

[1] SOURCES: 1802–69 – *S.P.* 1868–9, xxxv; 1870–1980 – *Finance Accounts* and its successor, *Consolidated Fund and Loan Fund Accounts*, and *Abstract*. The cost of the postal packet service in the period 1839–42 is taken from the *Navy Estimates* (see footnote (*f*) p. 595).

[2] All payments for capital investment, with certain minor exceptions before 1889, have been excluded from this table, as has all expenditure on debt redemption, other than through the payment of terminable annuities. All costs of collection are included.

[3] Statistics to 1854 are for years ended 5 January, and subsequently they are for years ended 31 March.

(in £ million sterling)

Principal Constituent Items (*a*)

		Debt Charges				Civil Government – Total and Main Constituents								Costs of Collection	
	Total Gross Expenditure	Total (*b*)	Funded	Terminable Annuities	Unfunded	Total (*c*)	Works and Buildings	Salaries, etc. of Public Departments	Law and Justice (*d*)	Education, Art and Science	Colonial, Consular, and Foreign	Army and Ordnance	Navy	Total	Post Office, Telegraphs, and Telephones
1802	65·5	19·9	16·1	1·9	1·1	5·6	0·09	0·07	0·10	0·06	0·17	20·1	17·3	2·4	0·4
1803	54·8	20·4	17·2	1·9	1·3	6·7	0·10	0·09	0·12	0·08	0·12	13·3	12·0	2·4	0·4
1804	53·0	20·7	17·9	1·9	0·9	5·1	0·13	0·08	0·11	0·08	0·26	15·5	8·1	2·4	0·4
1805	62·8	20·7	18·0	1·9	0·7	5·2	0·13	0·10	0·14	0·07	0·25	22·2	11·9	2·6	0·4
1806	71·4	22·3	18·6	1·9	1·4	5·2	0·22	0·13	0·17	0·10	0·28	25·8	14·3	2·7	0·4
1807	72·9	23·2	19·6	2·0	1·2	4·7	0·24	0·14	0·17	0·10	0·20	24·8	16·3	2·8	0·4
1808	73·3	23·8	19·9	2·0	1·6	5·3	0·39	0·21	0·16	0·12	0·19	24·0	16·9	3·2	0·4
1809	78·0	23·1	20·0	1·6	1·2	4·7	0·31	0·19	0·18	0·12	0·24	27·2	17·6	3·5	0·5
1810	81·5	24·2	20·4	1·6	2·1	5·2	0·21	0·20	0·17	0·11	0·29	28·9	19·4	3·6	0·5
1811	81·6	24·4	20·9	1·7	1·8	5·1	0·26	0·18	0·18	0·14	0·25	28·0	20·0	3·9	0·5
1812	87·3	24·6	21·5	1·6	1·4	5·2	0·24	0·22	0·24	0·20	0·23	33·8	19·6	3·9	0·5
1813	94·8	26·4	22·2	1·7	2·3	5·4	0·29	0·18	0·20	0·26	0·25	36·5	20·8	4·1	0·6
1814	111·1	27·3	23·5	1·8	1·7	5·3	0·36	0·23	0·23	0·13	0·29	49·6	22·5	4·4	0·6
1815	112·9	30·0	25·6	1·9	2·0	5·8	0·45	0·23	0·24	0·15	0·34	49·6	22·8	4·6	0·7
1816	99·5	32·2	26·3	1·9	3·9	6·1	0·41	0·26	0·23	0·15	0·28	39·6	16·8	4·7	0·7
1817	71·3	32·9	28·5	1·9	2·2	5·5	0·38	0·33	0·23	0·19	0·30	18·0	10·2	4·8	0·6
1818	58·7	31·5	27·8	1·9	1·8	5·0	0·30	0·40	0·27	0·08	0·28	11·1	6·6	4·5	0·6
1819	57·6	31·3	27·1	2·0	2·2	6·0	0·32	0·47	0·28	0·12	0·31	9·1	6·6	4·5	0·7
1820	57·5	31·1	28·2	2·0	0·8	5·4	0·16	0·46	0·34	0·09	0·36	10·3	6·4	4·4	0·6
1821	58·4	32·0	28·0	1·8	2·0	5·4	0·26	0·52	0·44	0·08	0·30	10·1	6·6	4·3	0·6
1822	58·4	31·9	28·4	1·8	1·7	5·6	0·21	0·49	0·29	0·07	0·30	10·4	6·3	4·3	0·6
1823	56·5	31·4	28·1	1·8	1·4	5·4	0·17	0·43	0·30	0·08	0·28	8·7	5·2	4·5	0·6
1824	54·3	30·0	26·7	2·2	1·1	5·4	0·24	0·45	0·30	0·08	0·36	8·7	5·6	4·5	0·6
1825	55·5	30·2	26·6	2·5	1·1	6·0	0·28	0·61	0·29	0·17	0·36	9·0	6·2	4·1	0·6
1826	54·1	29·2	25·8	2·5	0·8	5·8	0·39	0·56	0·22	0·11	0·39	9·2	5·8	4·0	0·6
1827	56·1	29·2	25·8	2·6	0·8	6·0	0·52	0·63	0·39	0·14	0·45	10·2	6·5	4·1	0·7
1828	55·9	29·4	26·0	2·6	0·9	6·2	0·39	0·65	0·38	0·09	0·58	9·8	6·4	4·1	0·7
1829	53·5	29·3	25·7	2·6	0·9	5·0	0·42	0·52	0·35	0·12	0·20	9·5	5·7	4·0	0·7
1830	53·7	29·1	25·7	2·6	0·9	5·4	0·69	0·52	0·38	0·10	0·36	9·3	5·9	4·0	0·7
1831	51·9	29·2	25·5	2·9	0·8	4·9	0·40	0·50	0·55	0·08	0·31	8·6	5·3	3·9	0·7
1832	51·5	28·3	24·4	3·3	0·7	5·0	0·73	0·57	0·57	0·04	0·39	8·7	5·7	3·7	0·7
1833	50·6	28·3	24·3	3·3	0·7	4·7	0·27	0·54	0·65	0·05	0·46	8·9	4·9	3·8	0·6
1834	48·8	28·5	24·3	3·5	0·8	4·3	0·23	0·50	0·77	0·06	0·49	7·9	4·4	3·7	0·6
1835	48·9	28·5	24·2	3·7	0·7	4·6	0·22	0·51	0·72	0·11	0·48	7·6	4·5	3·7	0·7
1836	65·2(*e*)	28·6	23·8	4·0	0·7	4·5	0·24	0·53	0·77	0·08	0·48	7·6	4·1	3·7	0·7
1837	54·0(*e*)	29·4	24·4	4·2	0·7	4·7	0·25	0·60	0·93	0·19	0·20	7·9	4·2	3·6	0·7
1838	51·1	29·6	24·5	4·2	0·9	5·1	0·30	0·76	1·03	0·18	0·58	8·0	[4·8](*f*)	[3·6](*f*)	[0·7](*f*)
1839	51·7	29·4	24·5	4·2	0·7	5·5	0·24	0·72	1·42	0·20	0·48	8·2	4·4	3·7	0·8
1840	53·4	29·6	24·4	4·3	0·8	5·6	0·25	0·68	1·32	0·17	0·36	8·5	5·3	3·8	0·9
1841	53·2	29·5	24·6	4·2	0·6	5·3	0·25	0·75	1·29	0·27	0·30	8·5	5·4	3·9	1·1
1842	54·3	29·7	24·5	4·1	0·9	5·6	0·24	0·69	1·51	0·29	0·38	8·2	6·2	4·0	1·2
1843	55·1	29·6	24·8	4·1	0·7	5·6	0·28	0·78	1·54	0·27	0·35	8·2	6·2	4·1	1·4
1844	55·4	29·4	24·8	3·9	0·7	6·0	0·26	0·74	1·66	0·25	0·42	7·9	6·2	4·2	1·4
1845	54·8	30·6	26·1	4·0	0·5	5·9	0·36	0·32	0·72	1·73	0·25	8·1	5·4	4·3	1·4
1846	53·7	28·6	24·0	4·0	0·4	5·4	0·38	0·75	1·42	0·29	0·29	8·9	6·3	4·6	1·7

See p. 595 for footnotes.

Public Finance 4. *continued*

(in £ million sterling)

		Principal Constituent Items (a)													
		Debt Charges				Civil Government – Total and Main Constituents								Costs of Collection	
	Total Gross Expenditure	Total (b)	Funded	Terminable Annuities	Unfunded	Total (c)	Works and Buildings	Salaries, etc. of Public Departments	Law and Justice (d)	Education, Art and Science	Colonial, Consular, and Foreign	Army and Ordnance	Navy	Total	Post Office, Telegraphs, and Telephones
1847	55·4	28·3	23·9	3·9	0·4	6·3	0·39	0·80	1·57	0·33	0·49	9·1	7·3	4·6	1·7
1848	59·1	28·4	24·0	3·9	0·4	8·1	0·61	0·91	1·96	0·30	0·40	10·5	7·5	4·7	1·7
1849	59·0	28·7	24·2	3·8	0·8	7·2	0·51	0·99	2·22	0·36	0·50	9·7	7·3	4·9	2·0
1850	55·5	28·5	24·2	3·7	0·6	7·0	0·48	0·94	2·28	0·37	0·41	8·9	6·2	4·9	2·1
1851	54·7	28·3	24·1	3·7	0·4	6·8	0·50	1·01	2·26	0·45	0·40	9·0	5·7	5·0	2·2
1852	54·0	28·2	24·0	3·8	0·4	6·9	0·50	1·01	2·20	0·46	0·46	8·7	5·0	4·9	2·1
1853	55·3	28·1	23·9	3·8	0·4	6·6	0·68	1·04	1·97	0·48	0·36	9·5	5·8	4·9	2·2
1854	55·8	28·1	23·8	3·8	0·4	7·2	0·78	1·06	2·22	0·56	0·34	9·4 }	[7·8](h)	[6·2](h)	[2·7](h)
[1854](g)	[14·0]	[6·6]	[5·8]	[0·6]	[0·2]	[2·1]	[0·15]	[0·25]	[0·78]	[0·17]	[0·17]	[2·2]			
1855	69·1	28·0	23·3	3·8	0·6	7·7	0·74	1·42	2·39	0·66	0·34	13·8	13·7	4·1	1·9
1856	93·1	28·2	23·4	3·9	0·9	8·7	0·77	1·32	3·04	0·83	0·34	27·8	18·9	5·3	2·4
1857	76·1	28·8	23·8	4·0	1·0	8·4	1·06	1·21	2·71	0·91	0·33	20·8	12·7	5·4	2·4
1858	68·2	28·7	23·8	4·0	1·0	10·1	0·85	1·43	3·07	1·06	0·39	12·9	9·6	5·3	2·7
1859	64·8	28·7	23·7	4·0	1·0	9·1	0·77	1·42	3·29	1·15	0·35	12·5	8·2	5·5	2·9
1860	69·6	28·7	23·9	4·3	0·4	9·7	0·68	1·47	3·44	1·27	0·42	14·1	10·8	5·4	2·9
1861	72·9	26·3	23·9	1·9	0·4	10·7	0·64	1·43	3·19	1·23	0·45	15·0	13·3	5·6	2·9
1862	72·3	26·3	23·9	1·8	0·6	10·8	0·72	1·46	3·40	1·35	0·73	16·5	12·6	5·6	3·0
1863	70·3	26·2	23·8	1·9	0·5	10·9	0·87	1·48	3·53	1·40	0·90	17·3	11·4	5·5	2·9
1864	67·8	26·2	23·8	2·0	0·4	10·8	0·93	1·51	3·50	1·29	0·59	15·4	10·8	5·4	2·9
1865	67·1	26·4	23·6	2·3	0·4	10·2	0·63	1·56	3·39	1·22	0·55	15·0	10·9	5·5	3·0
1866	66·5	26·2	23·5	2·4	0·3	10·3	0·65	1·54	3·66	1·28	0·55	14·4	10·3	5·4	2·9
1867	67·2	26·1	23·4	2·4	0·3	10·5	0·82	1·54	3·55	1·42	0·54	15·1	10·7	5·6	3·1
1868	71·8	26·6	22·9	3·4	0·3	11·2	0·72	1·73	3·87	1·60	0·55	15·9	11·2	5·7	3·1
1869	75·5	26·6	22·5	4·0	0·2	12·0	0·95	1·59	4·65	1·38	0·54	15·5	11·4	6·1	3·5
	---(i)											---(i)	---(i)		
1870	67·1	27·1	22·4	4·4	0·3	11·0	0·94	1·64	4·25	1·62	0·55	12·1	9·4	6·2	3·6
1871	67·8	26·8	22·3	4·4	0·2	12·0	1·3	1·7	4·6	1·8	0·5	12·1	9·0	6·5	3·9
1872	69·9	26·8	22·2	4·5	0·2	12·2	1·3	1·8	4·7	1·9	0·6	14·7	9·5	6·6	4·0
1873	68·8	26·8	22·1	4·5	0·1	11·8	1·1	1·8	4·5	2·2	0·6	13·8	9·3	7·2	4·6
1874	74·6	26·7	22·0	4·6	0·1	12·7	1·2	1·9	5·0	2·4	0·6	13·5	10·1	7·6	4·9
1875	73·0	27·1	21·8	5·2	0·1	13·6	1·3	2·1	5·2	2·6	0·7	14·0	10·5	7·8	5·1
1876	74·7	27·2	21·6	5·4	0·1	14·8	1·4	2·5	5·5	2·9	0·6	14·2	10·8	7·6	4·9
1877	75·7	27·4	21·6	5·4	0·1	14·9	1·4	2·6	5·5	3·2	0·7	14·5	11·0	7·9	5·2
1878	79·6	27·6	21·6	5·5	0·1	15·6	1·4	2·6	5·7	3·6	0·7	14·3	10·8	7·8	5·1
1879	82·8	28·0	21·5	5·7	0·1	16·6	1·4	2·2	6·3	4·0	0·6	16·9	11·8	8·0	5·2
1880	81·5	28·1	21·5	5·7	0·1	16·9	1·4	2·2	6·5	4·0	0·6	15·0	10·2	8·0	5·2
1881	80·6	29·2	21·5	6·9	0·1	17·4	1·4	2·3	6·5	4·3	0·6	14·7	10·5	8·2	5·4
1882	83·3	29·4	21·4	7·2	0·1	18·0	1·5	2·4	6·7	4·4	0·7	15·7	10·6	8·5	5·7
1883	87·1	29·5	21·4	7·3	0·1	18·9	1·8	2·4	7·1	4·6	0·7	15·1	10·3	8·9	6·1
1884	85·4	29·1	21·3	7·9	0·1	18·7	1·8	2·4	6·8	4·8	0·7	16·1	10·7	9·7	6·9
1885	88·5	29·0	19·2	9·1	0·1	19·0	1·8	2·4	6·8	5·1	0·7	18·6	11·4	9·9	7·1
1886	92·2	23·5	19·0	3·6	0·2	19·2	1·8	2·4	6·7	5·3	0·7	17·0	12·7	10·0	7·3
1887	90·0	28·0	19·0	8·2	0·2	19·3	1·8	2·4	6·7	5·5	0·6	18·4	13·3	10·8	8·1
1888	86·7	25·5	18·4	6·6	0·3	19·7	2·0	2·4	6·8	5·6	0·6	18·2	12·3	10·7	8·0
1889	86·5	25·1	18·6	5·9	0·4	19·4	1·4	2·4	6·8	5·7	0·6	16·0	13·0	11·0	8·3
1890	90·6	24·5	17·0	6·6	0·7	17·1	1·5	2·1	5·2	5·8	0·7	17·4	15·3	11·0	8·3
1891	93·4	23·9	16·2	6·6	1·0	17·6	1·7	2·1	5·0	6·1	0·7	17·8	15·6	11·3	8·7
1892	96·0	23·7	16·1	6·6	0·8	19·0	2·0	2·3	4·9	7·0	0·7	17·6	15·6	12·0	9·3
1893	95·8	23·5	16·2	6·4	0·7	19·3	1·6	1·9	4·3	8·9	0·7	17·5	15·7	12·4	9·8
1894	98·5	23·4	16·3	6·4	0·5	19·7	1·6	2·0	4·2	9·4	0·8	17·9	15·5	12·8	10·1
1895	100·9	23·3	16·4	6·4	0·5	20·4	1·7	2·0	4·1	9·8	0·9	17·9	17·5	12·9	10·3

See p. 595 for footnotes.

Public Finance 4. *continued*

(in £ million sterling)

Principal Constituent Items (*a*)

		Debt Charges				Civil Government – Total and Main Constituents								Costs of Collection	
	Total Gross Expenditure	Total (*b*)	Funded	Terminable Annuities	Unfunded	Total (*c*)	Works and Buildings	Salaries, etc. of Public Departments	Law and Justice (*d*)	Education, Art and Science	Colonial, Consular, and Foreign	Army and Ordnance	Navy	Total	Post Office, Telegraphs, and Telephones
1896	105·1	22·8	16·3	6·4	0·1	21·2	1·9	2·1	4·2	10·3	1·0	18·5	19·7	13·2	10·5
1897	109·7	23·6	16·3	7·2	0·1	21·4	1·9	2·1	4·1	10·7	0·9	18·3	22·2	13·6	10·8
1898	112·3	23·6	16·2	7·3	0·1	22·9	1·9	2·1	4·2	11·5	1·2	19·3	20·9	14·3	11·6
1899	117·7	23·6	16·2	7·3	0·1	23·4	1·9	2·1	4·2	12·0	1·6	20·0	24·1	15·0	12·2
1900	143·7	23·2	15·4	7·3	0·3	23·9	2·0	2·1	4·2	12·2	1·7	43·6	26·0	15·6	12·8
1901	193·3	19·8	15·3	2·8	0·4	24·9	2·0	2·4	4·2	12·5	2·1	91·5	29·5	16·3	13·5
1902	205·2	21·7	15·3	2·8	0·3	31·9	2·1	2·6	4·3	12·8	8·4	92·3	31·0	17·0	14·0
1903	194·2	27·2	15·2	7·3	0·4	37·6	2·3	2·5	4·3	13·3	13·3(*j*)	69·4	31·2	17·6	14·6
1904	155·3	25·5	16·6	6·5	2·4	28·3	2·5	2·5	4·3	14·6	2·2	36·7	35·5	18·2	15·1
1905	149·5	24·8	16·1	6·5	2·1	28·8	2·5	2·6	4·3	15·6	2·1	29·2	36·8	18·7	15·6

See p. 595 for footnotes.

Public Finance 4. *continued*

(in £ million sterling)

	Total Gross Expenditure	Debt Charges: Total (*b*)	Debt Charges: Funded	Debt Charges: Terminable Annuities	Debt Charges: Unfunded	Civil Expenditures and Main Constituents: Total (*c*)	Works and Buildings	Salaries etc. of Public Departments	Law and Justice (*d*)	Education, Art and Science	Colonial, Consular, and Foreign	Government Pensions	Contributions to Local Government	Health, Labour & Insurance (*k*)	Trade, Industry and Roads	Payments to Northern Ireland
1906	147·0	24·6	16·1	6·5	1·9	29·8	2·5	2·6	4·3	16·4	2·0	0·8	1·2	—	—	—
1907	143·7	22·5	16·0	4·7	1·7	30·6	2·7	2·6	4·3	16·9	1·9	0·8	1·2	—	—	—
1908	143·4	21·1	16·0	3·6	1·6	31·9	2·7	2·9	4·4	17·4	2·1	0·8	11·2	—	—	—
1909	144·8	21·5	15·8	3·6	1·2	33·8	2·9	2·9	4·5	17·4	1·8	0·8	9·8	2·1	—	—
1910	156·9	20·8	15·7	3·5	1·6	41·4	3·1	3·0	4·6	17·9	1·9	0·9	9·4	8·5	—	—
1911	167·9	20·4	15·6	3·5	1·4	45·9	3·2	3·4	4·8	18·7	2·0	0·8	9·9	9·8	1·4	—
1912	174·1	20·1	15·4	3·5	1·2	49·2	3·2	4·1	4·9	19·0	2·1	0·8	9·6	11·8	1·7	—
1913	184·0	19·9	15·2	3·5	1·2	54·6	3·5	4·3	5·0	19·5	2·2	0·8	9·7	17·0	1·2	—
1914	192·3	19·3	15·0	3·2	1·1	56·8	3·3	4·3	5·0	19·5	1·5	0·8	9·7	19·5	1·4	—
1915	559·5	21·7	14·8	2·9	1·8	60·0	3·7	4·6	5·3	20·2	1·8	0·8	9·5	20·4	1·5	—
1916	1,559·2	60·2	13·1	2·9	4·3	57·0	3·4	4·6	5·2	20·7	1·5	0·8	9·8	18·4	0·7	—
1917	2,198·1	127·3	8·3	2·9	8·6	53·9	3·0	4·8	5·0	20·3	1·2	0·8	9·9	20·5	—	—
1918	2,696·2	189·9	8·5	2·8	8·5	62·7	2·9	5·4	5·3	25·8	1·3	0·8	9·7	19·4	—	—
1919	2,579·3	270·0	8·7	2·6	12·4	69·5	3·4	7·6	7·1	25·6	1·2	0·8	9·7	20·7	—	—
1920	1,665·8	332·0	8·8	2·6	12·4	574·5(*m*)	10.0	15·1	14·6	43·2	2·7	100·5	10·7	33·3	—	—
1921	1,188·1	342·3	8·6	2·6	5·9	477·9	12·4	18·4	20·0	59·3	5·0	110·3	10·8	72·5	8·9	—
1922	1,070·1	323·2	8·7	2·6	4·1	465·0	11·2	17·1	22·9	65·4	32·5(*n*)	95·8	11·2	72·9	10·8	1·1
1923	812·5	324·0	8·8	3·4	1·9	302·5	6·1	10·8	15·0	49·8	12·3(*n*)	82·6	10·5	61·0	11·8	3·3
1924	748·8	307·3	33·5	0·4	273·4	257·5	5·9	12·1	11·5	47·7	18·1(*n*)	71·5	13·7	59·4	14·1	4·0
1925	750·8	312·2	34·0	0·4	277·7	244·8	6·5	8·9	11·5	48·7	6·8	71·3	14·0	64·5	15·6	3·8
1926	776·1	308·2	34·4	0·4	273·4	263·9	6·9	10·9	12·3	48·6	7·6	70·4	14·5	65·2	17·5	4·9
1927	782·4	318·6	36·4	0·4	281·7	260·7	6·4	13·7	12·6	53·2	7·4	65·8	14·2	74·6	17·4	5·8
									---(*o*)	---(*o*)				---(*o*)		
1928	773·6	313·8	43·3	0·4	270·2	253·1	— (*o*)	— (*o*)	12·6	53·3	7·7	62·3	15·4	72·9	29·6	5·3
1929	760·5	311·5	49·4	0·4	261·7	246·4	—	—	12·1	49·5	5·6	58·7	15·2	75·9	30·2	5·1
1930	781·7	307·3	52·5	0·4	254·3	271·7	—	—	12·4	50·1	5·5	56·2	28·6	85·8	32·3	5·5
1931	814·2	293·2	50·6	0·4	242·2	333·2	—	—	15·8	55·1	6·0	54·6	44·5	107·7	35·5	6·4
1932	818·6	289·5	50·0	0·4	239·0	345·7	—	—	16·0	55·4	5·6	52·1	44·8	121·3	36·6	6·3
1933	833·0	282·2	52·0	0·4	229·8	369·2	—	—	15·3	51·6	7·9	49·5	44·9	154·7	32·1	7·0
1934	770·5	216·3	118·1	0·4	97·7	368·3	—	—	15·7	51·1	8·4	48·6	45·3	150·7	34·8	6·6
1935	784·7	211·7	118·0	0·4	93·2	378·0	—	—	16·2	52·8	8·0	46·8	45·4	150·8	41·9	6·8
1936	829·4	211·5	117·8	0·4	93·3	394·5	—	—	17·2	55·9	8·6	45·9	45·3	161·9	42·8	7·2
1937	889·1	210·9	117·8	0·4	92·7	398·6	—	—	18·7	58·5	9·2	45·0	45·2	161·5	45·2	8·0
1938	909·4	216·2	117·6	0·4	98·2	400·4	—	—	22·2	59·9	8·6	43·9	54·1	161·6	31·0	8·9

(in £ million sterling)

	Costs of Collection		Defence Expenditures		
	Post Office	Other	Army & Ordnance	Navy	Air Force
1906	16·0	3·1	28·9	33·3	—
1907	16·6	3·2	27·8	31·4	—
1908	17·5	3·2	27·1	31·1	—
1909	18·1	3·3	26·8	32·2	—
1910	18·7	3·3	27·2	35·8	—
1911	19·7	3·9	27·4	40·4	—
1912	20·5	4·0	27·6	42·9	—
1913	23·0	4·2	28·1	44·4	—
1914	24·6	4·5	28·3	48·8	—
1915	26·1	4·6	28·9	51·6	—
1916	26·7	4·6	-- (*l*)	-- (*l*)	—
1917	26·5	4·7	-- (*l*)	-- (*l*)	—
1918	25·7	5·2	-- (*l*)	-- (*l*)	—
1919	26·4	5·5	-- (*l*)	-- (*l*)	-- (*l*)
1920	48·1	9·4	395·0	156·5	52·5
1921	53·7	11·3	181·5	88·4	22·3
1922	66·0	14·2	95·1	80·8	13·6
1923	49·9	11·3	45·4	56·2	9·4
1924	49·8	10·8	43·6	52·6	9·6
1925	50·4	11·0	44·8	55·6	14·3
1926	54·0	11·4	44·3	59·7	15·5
1927	54·9	11·5	43·6	57·6	15·5
1928	56·8	11·7	44·2	58·1	15·2
1929	57·2	11·6	40·5	56·9	16·1
1930	58·9	12·0	40·5	55·8	16·8
1931	59·0	11·4	40·5	52·6	17·8
1932	58·0	11·8	38·5	51·1	17·7
1933	59·3	12·4	35·9	50·0	17·1
1934	59·3	12·1	37·6	53·5	16·8
1935	61·8	12·6	39·7	56·6	17·6
1936	66·1	13·1	44·6	64·8	27·5
1937	71·9	13·4	54·8	81·1	50·1
1938	72·9	13·7	63·0(*p*)	78·0(*p*)	56·3(*p*)

See p. 595 for footnotes.

Public Finance 4. *continued*

(in £ million sterling)

	Total Gross Expenditure	Debt Charges: Total(b)	Debt Charges: Interest on Funded Debt	Debt Charges: Interest on Unfunded Debt	Civil Expenditures and Main Constituents: Total(c)	Home Dept., Law, and Justice	Education and Broadcasting	Common-wealth and Foreign	Government Pensions	Contributions to Local Government	Health, Labour, and Insurance	Trade, Industry, and Roads	Supply, Food, and Miscellaneous	Payments to Northern Ireland
1939	1,005·7	218·7	116·6	100·5	435·6	27·7	61·6	11·8	42·8	54·2	165·7	48·2	—	9·5
1940	1,401·0	228·6	116·6	110·5	448·5	30·3	63·1	17·4	41·9	53·3	167·2	45·6	—	9·6
1941	3,953·7	233·6	116·6	115·0	414·5	19·9	63·3	12·9	41·2	52·8	164·7	29·3	—	9·7
1942	4,876·3	278·0	116·6	157·7	415·1	20·1	65·6	11·8	40·9	52·8	170·0	22·2	—	9·1
1943	5,725·7	331·6	116·6	211·9	445·1	20·1	77·5	23·1	40·1	52·8	185·6	19·4	—	9·2
1944	5,899·0	385·1	116·6	265·7	446·0	20·0	79·5	14·9	39·3	52·8	198·7	17·3	—	9·0
1945	6,174·4	434·9	116·6	315·5	481·7	19·6	85·3	28·3	39·7	52·8	208·4	21·2	—	10·0
1946	5,591·5	474·9	116·6	355·1	567·7	22·8	117·7	36·4	41·6	62·9	218·6	33·5	—	12·3
1947	4,191·9	501·9	118·4	380·7	1,660·3(*m*)	28·4	149·6	92·6	96·9	65·2	334·4	144·4	663·2	20·3
1948	3,353·6	511·4	127·7	381·6	1,776·4	30·8	182·1	59·1	91·2	66·4	379·6	170·0	702·4	24·3
1949	3,314·2	497·1	130·3	364·7	1,994·3	41·2	213·0	67·3	96·0	653·7		171·3	504·3	32·3
1950	3,530·6	499·7	130·3	367·4	2,069·6	51·6	241·7	63·9	96·5	805·7		150·6	558·0	37·0
1951	3,417·3	514·9	130·2	374·0	1,911·7	51·0	252·9	78·0	93·5	834·9		134·7	374·1	37·7
1952	4,221·8	561·3	130·1	429·1	1,316·1	56·7	273·7	74·4	90·9	809·9		122·1	793·9	39·4
1953	4,530·5	640·6	129·6	505·1	2,241·1	74·8	288·0	91·1	100·3	884·4		159·3	548·2	44·7
											Trade Supply, etc.(*t*)	Transport Power, etc.(*u*)	Agri-culture & Food	
1954	4,476·8	667·1	128·9	528·4	2,199·4	79·6	303·0	84·7	97·2	903·0	183·1	65·0	389·8	50·1
									National Insurance, etc.(*s*)	Health, Housing, Local Govt.				
1955	4,517·4	673·7	128·2	539·9	2,166·5	82·0	338·0	102·3	418·5	618·5	98·4	119·6	293·9	50·2
1956	4,726·8	757·1	127·6	625·2	2,296·1	81·1	377·5	115·0	432·5	651·6	78·5	138·0	327·0	59·2
1957	5,135·7	857·4	126·9	718·4	2,473·8	89·1	434·1	91·5	462·9	750·4	71·7	156·6	310·9	66·4
1958	5,218·2	832·4	126·2	699·8	2,659·6	99·3	480·7	90·7	489·5	781·5	73·7	197·4	343·6	71·6
1959	5,434·8	868·8	125·4	726·8	2,795·5	102·8	523·2	100·9	575·1	793·8	74·3	222·4	295·4	76·5
1960	5,590·3	858·3	124·7	712·8	2,967·0	93·9	215·3	104·7	609·5	1,209·2	74·5	228·4	321·0	80·2
1961	6,157·1	934·6	124·0	797·1	3,323·8	105·9	204·1	119·1	634·0	1,384·2	88·4	330·0	336·7	89·0
1962	6,194·7	1,035·8	123·2	878·8	3,616·7	119·5	246·9	144·6	658·4	1,416·7	110·4	376·0	415·8	97·4

							Education & Science		Housing, Local Govt. & Social Services		Industry, Trade & Transport			
1963	6,400·5	981·7	122·5	831·0	3,861·0	132·5	181·8	154·9	2,349·3	—	431·1	—	374·1	101·8
1964	6,775·7	1,045·1	121·8	893·7	4,131·7	148·4	182·8	170·6	2,582·6	—	424·7	—	356·0	118·6
1965	7,264·6	1,065·5	121·1	911·6	4,490·4	158·7	224·4	239·0	2,796·7	—	460·3	—	318·0	138·6
1966	7,974·2 ----(v) 8,455·7	1,136·3	120·5	979·6	4,995·0	178·3	413·4	225·9	3,013·7	—	548·5	—	279·3	148·5
1967	9,541·4	1,238·0	...	...	5,895·7	194·0	461·7	261·6	3,378·3	—	897·2	—	282·5	164·6
1968	11,525·1	1,371·1	...	...	7,567·4	220·1	408·2		3,953·3	—	1,874·1	—	388·4	194·3

New Presentation

	Consolidated Fund Expenditure	Debt Charge (w)	Total Civil Supply Expenditure (c)	Law, Order, etc.	Education, Science, etc.	Trade, Industry & Transport	Agriculture etc.	Housing, Local Government & Social Services				Payments to Northern Ireland	Payments to the E.E.C.	Defence
1968	10,871	669	7,722	220	408	1,874	388	3,953				194	—	2,254
1969	11,615	552	8,578	237	430	2,152	379	4,481				224	—	2,232
1970	12,822	513	9,812	265	451	2,816	386	5,043				252	—	2,204
						Trade, Industry, & Employment		Environmental Services		Social Services				
1971	14,086	325	10,970	306	523	2,971	426	3,374		3,187		277	—	2,479
1972	15,549	334	12,021	377	582	2,240	478	3,714		3,656		342	—	2,797
1973	17,689	544	13,731	496	687	2,226	459	4,653		4,188		358	38	2,886
1974	19,965	677	15,491	724	751	2,244	493	5,630		4,506		350	219	3,133
								Housing	Roads & Transport	Health & Personal Services	Social Security			
1975	26,803	576	21,361(x)	654	1,015	2,435	1,080	1,442	1,229	3,680	2,487	421	243	4,245
1976	36,047	964	28,802(x)	933	1,285	3,796	1,146	1,565	1,358	4,768	3,472	576	382	5,270
1977	39,372	1,133	30,904(x)	1,071	1,514	3,086	844	2,144	1,296	5,417	4,225	638	549	6,163
1978	43,989	2,220	33,289(x)	1,182	1,645	2,683	653	2,498	1,261	6,015	5,227	689	977	6,754
1979	51,469	3,222	38,343(x)	1,297	1,795	3,965	545	2,674	1,273	6,807	6,892	765	1,669	7,419
1980	61,007	4,143	46,456(x)(y)	1,637	2,187	3,674	808	3,194	1,571	8,215	6,383	987	2,007	9,139

See p. 595 for footnotes.

Public Finance 4. *continued*

(in £ million sterling)

	Costs of Collection		Defence Expenditures			
	Post Office(q)	Other	Army	Navy	Air Force	Central (r)
1939	75·3	14·1	85·7(p)	95·9(p)	72·8(p)	—
1940	79·3	14·3	81·9(p)	69·4(p)	66·6(p)	—
1941	81·7	14·8	-- (l)	-- (l)	-- (l)	—
1942	93·7	16·0	-- (l)	-- (l)	-- (l)	—
1943	102·5	18·1	-- (l)	-- (l)	-- (l)	—
1944	110·6	18·7	-- (l)	-- (l)	-- (l)	—
1945	123·4	19·5	-- (l)	-- (l)	-- (l)	—
1946	124·3	20·5	-- (l)	-- (l)	-- (l)	—
1947	133·8	24·7	717·0	266·9	255·5	414·0
1948	146·0	27·2	383·6	194·3	181·9	94·1
1949	159·4	29·1	346·7	162·7	186·9	56·9
1950	168·2	31·0	291·8	186·8	201·6	60·5
1951	171·1	33·3	309·0	190·0	225·1	53·3
1952	198·4	38·5	422·3	271·3	322·3	94·3
1953	217·6	41·8	525·0	333·4	421·3	124·0
1954	232·9	44·2	487·8	324·1	416·4	136·2
1955	243·6	46·3	477·0	345·8	463·6	149·5
1956	277·4	49·0	462·9	337·7	431·1	173·2
1957	304·0	55·2	498·9	342·6	471·5	212·1
1958	335·5	58·2	387·9	353·0	474·0	214·8
1959	370·0	62·0	433·0	373·7	465·7	195·3
1960	384·5	67·6	428·2	364·6	485·1	197·8
1961	409·9	72·7	482·8	389·2	532·0	191·8
1962	—	81·1	508·4	413·8	547·3	219·2
1963	—	82·0	528·5	438·1	569·7	230·3
1964	—	85·7	489·0	433·6	499·2	369·9
1965	—	91·2	506·6	473·9	491·8	436·7
1966	—	101·8	553·7	512·0	533·0	457·2
1967	—	109·0	573·3	586·4	514·1	441·1
1968	—	117·9	620·3	648·0	536·4	449·7

(*a*) Some items of expenditure which were of importance for relatively short periods only have not been included in the main body of this table, viz:-

Gross Expenditure on Lotteries

1802	0·8	1809	0·5	1816	0·8	1823	0·6
1803	1·0	1810	0·6	1817	0·6	1824	0·6
1804	0·9	1811	0·6	1818	0·5	1825	0·4
1805	0·8	1812	0·6	1819	0·6	1826	0·7
1806	0·8	1813	0·6	1820	0·6	1827	0·4
1807	0·5	1814	0·5	1821	0·6	1828	0·2
1808	1·1	1815	0·7	1822	0·7		

Gross Expenditure on Special Expeditions, Votes of Credit, etc.
(for dates not shown the amount was nil)

1802	0·3	1823	1·3	1869	5·0	1887	0·1
1803	1·3	1849	1·1	1870	1·3	1888	0·1
1804	0·2	1852	0·3	1871	1·4	1915	357·0
1805	1·2	1853	0·4	1872	0·1	1916	1,399·7
1806	1·0	1854	0·3	1874	0·8	1917	1,973·7
1807	0·1	[1854*	--]	1875	0·1	1918	2,402·8
1808	1·9	1855	1·8	1877	--	1919	2,198·0
1809	0·2	1856	4·2	1878	3·5	1920	87·0
1810	0·2	1858	1·5	1879	1·5	1940	408·5
1811	0·2	1859	0·8	1880	3·2	1941	3,220·0
1812	0·2	1860	0·9	1881	0·6	1942	4,085·0
1813	1·5	1861	3·0	1882	1·1	1943	4,840·0
1814	2·0	1862	1·3	1883	4·4	1944	4,950·0
1815	--	1864	0·1	1884	1·0	1945	5,125·0
1816	--	1866	0·8	1885	0·6	1946	4,410·0
1817	--	1868	2·0	1886	9·7		

*=quarter ended 5 April.

(*b*) Debt charges which were regarded as outside the permanent charge of the national debt have been included in this total, but are not shown under the separate items. The only period when they were of much significance was 1915–23, when they were as follows:

1915	2·2	1920	308·3
1916	39·9	1921	325·1
1917	107·5	1922	307·8
1918	170·0	1923	309·8
1919	246·3		

Differences between the total and the sum of the constituent items represents management expenses and, after 1938, the small amount of terminable annuities.

(*c*) Total civil votes plus some items of Consolidated Fund expenditure but excluding (from 1947) some expenditures by the Ministry of Supply (and its successors) which should properly be included here, see footnote (*r*).

(*d*) This includes expenditure on courts up to 1927. From 1928 Home Department expenditure is included.

(*e*) These figures include compensatory payments to colonial slave owners – 16·7 in 1836 and 4·1 in 1837.

(*f*) In the period 1838–60 the postal packet service was paid for out of the navy vote, but in this table its cost has been transferred to *Costs of Collection*. In the year 1838, however, it cannot be separated from expenditure on the navy.

(*g*) Figures in this row are for the quarter ended 5 April. See note 4 above.

(*h*) These figures are for the 15 months ended 5 April 1854.

(*i*) Prior to 1870 expenditure out of the Indian Military Contribution and the Army and Navy Extra Receipts is included under these headings. Its exclusion in 1870 made a difference of about ten per cent under the *Army* heading and five per cent under the *Navy* heading.

(*j*) Including 8·0 grant-in-aid to Transvaal and the Orange Free State.

(*k*) Including Old Age Pensions.

(*l*) During these years all military payments, except purely nominal amounts, were made from votes of credit – see footnote (*a*).

(*m*) Many items of expenditure, civilian as well as military, were transferred from votes of credit after 1919 and again after 1946.

(*n*) These figures include exceptionally large sums for 'Middle-Eastern services' – 29·0 in 1922, 11·2 in 1923, and 7·0 in 1924. The normal expenditure on this item was about 4·0.

(*o*) There was a reorganisation of the system of accounting for civil government expenditure in 1928. See also footnote (*d*).

(*p*) Excluding amounts issued under the Defence Loans Act.

(*q*) The Post Office Act (1961) separated the finances of the Post Office from the Exchequer from 1 April 1961.

(*r*) This column comprises expenditures by the Ministry of Supply (and its successors) and the Ministry of Defence. The Ministry of Supply component includes expenditures up to 1970, which should properly be regarded as civil. They are as follows:

1947	414·0	1953	111·8	1959	181·0	1965	254·5
1948	94·1	1954	119·1	1960	181·3	1966	269·8
1949	56·3	1955	133·0	1961	176·4	1967	239·6
1950	59·8	1956	157·9	1962	203·9	1968	235·8
1951	49·3	1957	195·3	1963	212·0	1969	200·4
1952	83·0	1958	200·6	1964	207·5	1970	199·7

(*s*) Including National Assistance and all pensions.

(*t*) Variously described, as 'Trade, Materials and Supply'; 'Trade Labour, Materials and Supply'; and 'Trade, Labour and Supply'.

(*u*) Including industrial research.

(*v*) All Consolidated Fund expenditures are included subsequently.

(*w*) These figures are of payments from the Consolidated Fund to the National Loan Fund. Total debt charges met by the latter were as follows:

1969	1,354	1973	1,879	1977	4,534
1970	1,458	1974	2,340	1978	5,192
1971	1,457	1975	2,858	1979	6,458
1972	1,643	1976	3,560	1980	8,400

(*x*) Including rate support grants, etc. as follows:

1975	4,742	1977	7,737	1979	8,593
1976	7,184	1978	7,887	1980	11,916

(*y*) Including government investment in nationalised industries (1,236) for the first time.

Public Finance 5. Gross Public Income – Republic of Ireland, 1923–80

NOTES
[1] SOURCE: *Statistical Abstract of Ireland*.
[2] Statistics to 1974 are for years ended 31st March.

(in £ million Irish)

	Total	Main Constituent Items								
		Customs	Excise	Motor Vehicle Duties	Estate Duties, etc.	Stamps	Income Tax & Surtax	Corporation Profits Tax (*a*)	Value Added Tax, etc. (*b*)	Post Office
1923	27.9	2.5	16.5	0.1	1.0	0.5	5.0	0.3	—	1.3
1924	31.4	8.2	9.3	0.4	1.0	0.5	5.4	0.5	—	2.0
1925	26.9	7.7	7.5	0.5	0.8	0.5	5.9	0.3	—	1.7
1926	25.4	7.0	6.3	0.5	1.0	0.5	5.7	0.6	—	1.7
1927	25.1	6.8	6.7	0.6	1.0	0.5	5.1	0.5	—	1.7
1928	24.1	6.7	6.6	0.7	1.3	0.5	4.3	0.3	—	1.8
1929	24.2	7.2	6.8	0.7	1.0	0.5	4.3	0.4	—	1.8
1930	24.2	7.3	6.4	0.9	1.2	0.4	4.0	0.4	—	1.8
1931	24.4	7.5	6.3	0.9	1.3	0.4	4.2	0.4	—	1.8
1932	25.5	8.3	5.5	0.9	1.3	0.4	4.6	0.4	—	1.9
1933	30.0	9.3	5.4	0.9	1.1	1.1	5.2	0.6	—	1.9
1934	30.2	9.7	5.3	0.9	1.1	1.1	5.3	0.7	—	1.8
1935	28.8	9.4	5.6	0.9	1.0	1.1	4.9	0.7	—	1.8
1936	30.6	10.2	6.0	1.0	1.1	1.0	5.2	0.7	—	1.9
1937	31.0	10.0	6.1	1.1	1.1	1.0	5.3	0.7	—	2.0
1938	31.2	9.7	5.9	1.1	1.3	1.0	5.6	0.7	—	2.0
1939	31.9	10.1	6.1	1.2	1.2	1.0	5.8	0.7	—	2.0
1940	32.4	10.6	6.3	1.1	1.0	0.8	5.9	0.6	—	2.1
1941	34.6	11.7	6.6	0.9	1.2	0.5	7.3	0.6	—	2.0
1942	37.0	10.9	7.1	1.0	1.2	0.5	9.4	0.9	—	2.2
1943	39.7	10.7	7.4	0.6	1.4	0.5	10.1	2.8	—	2.4
1944	43.8	11.4	8.0	0.5	1.5	0.5	11.5	3.8	—	2.6
1945	46.2	11.3	8.9	0.6	1.5	0.5	12.5	4.0	—	2.7
1946	50.8	13.0	9.8	0.9	1.8	0.6	13.1	4.5	—	3.0
1947	54.4	16.5	9.5	1.5	1.8	0.9	12.4	4.5	—	3.2
1948	65.2	22.0	11.2	2.0	2.3	1.3	13.1	4.7	—	3.8
1949	71.7	23.8	12.7	2.4	2.3	1.6	16.1	3.5	—	4.1
1950	74.0	25.4	12.6	2.6	3.7	1.6	17.1	2.3	—	4.3
1951	77.4	27.3	13.2	2.8	2.5	1.7	17.8	2.5	—	4.5
1952	83.9	28.9	13.6	3.3	2.4	1.8	20.7	2.7	—	5.0
1953	95.9	33.8	16.4	3.9	2.6	1.5	23.0	2.9	—	5.4
1954	102.8	36.9	17.2	4.4	2.8	1.7	22.2	2.6	—	6.2
1955	106.7	37.0	16.9	4.8	3.0	1.8	23.5	2.9	—	6.6
1956	111.7	38.8	17.2	5.1	3.3	1.9	24.8	3.2	—	6.9
1957	117.7	45.1	17.4	4.8	2.3	2.0	24.1	3.1	—	7.8
1958	122.9	46.9	17.4	5.7	2.7	2.0	25.1	2.9	—	8.2
1959	126.4	48.3	17.5	5.5	2.9	2.1	25.0	2.8	—	8.7
1960	129.9	45.0	24.2	5.9	3.0	2.6	23.6	3.0	—	9.2
1961	138.8	41.0	30.2	6.5	3.2	2.7	28.0	3.3	—	9.7
1962	151.7	44.9	33.5	6.9	2.9	3.0	31.3	3.7	—	10.5
1963	163.5	46.9	34.7	7.4	3.5	3.1	36.2	4.5	—	11.4
1964	184.4	50.3	37.7	8.2	3.6	3.5	40.2	7.7	3.7	12.1
1965	219.0	55.7	42.9	8.8	4.4	3.9	47.8	8.4	13.4	14.9
1966	240.8	58.4	49.1	9.6	4.7	3.6	54.9	9.3	14.2	16.4
1967	272.8	67.8	55.0	10.4	4.6	3.5	64.0	9.4	17.2	18.3

Public Finance 5. *continued*

(in £ million Irish)

		Main Constituent Items								
	Total	Customs	Excise	Motor Vehicle Duties	Estate Duties, etc.	Stamps	Income Tax & Surtax	Corporation Profits Tax (*a*)	Value Added Tax, etc. (*b*)	Post Office
1968	305·4	70·1	62·2	11·6	6·0	4·2	70·0	12·1	23·4	20·5
1969	345·5	76·0	72·6	12·7	7·6	5·1	80·7	12·8	27·4	21·7
1970	411·0	87·7	87·9	13·4	7·7	5·5	93·3	14·9	40·6	27·4
1971	481·5	91·9	91·0	16·1	6·3	5·6	116·6	20·3	66·2	29·9
1972	569·4	101·3	96·9	17·8	9·0	7·7	152·9	21·1	80·0	36·6
1973	659·1	116·4	103·6	20·0	13·2	10·9	173·7	21·2	100·9	40·8
1974	792·9	138·6	115·6	24·4	14·0	13·9	221·6	22·8	137·0	46·3
1974	[651·4](*c*)	[108·6](*c*)	[89·3](*c*)	[19·1](*c*)	[11·5](*c*)	[9·4](*c*)	[170·5](*c*)	[19·0](*c*)	[112·3](*c*)	[42·5](*c*)
1975	1,091·2	175·4	157·4	27·9	13·5	13·3	331·7	26·5	175·1	69·0
1976	1,470·2	27·3	416·9	38·2	8·8	17·3	461·8	13·7	253·6	90·0
1977	1,756·9	28·6	448·7	32·7	6·7	24·6	521·9	8·0	321·2	121·5
1978	2,023·4	34·3	493·5	18·5	5·8	34·7	605·0	4·3	415·2	113·3
1979	2,383·9	39·3	602·0	19·7	3·4	43·6	731·5	2·3	420·6	109·0
1980	3,155·3	46·3	850·9	25·5	3·0	48·0	1,014·3	1·4	471·6	202·6

(*a*) Including Excess Profits Tax and Corporation Tax.
(*b*) Including Turnover Tax and Wholesale Tax.
(*c*) These figures are for the period April–December.

Public Finance 6. Gross Public Expenditure – Republic of Ireland, 1923–80

NOTES

[1] SOURCE: *Statistical Abstract of Ireland.*
[2] Statistics to 1974 are for years ended 31 March.
[3] Figures are stated to be not directly comparable from year to year in many cases owing to transfers of services from one vote to another.

(in £ million Irish)

	Total	Main Constituent Items (*a*)								
		Debt Service	Defence (*b*)	Education	Law & Justice	Posts & Telegraphs	Industry, Commerce, & & Energy (*c*)	Tourism and Transport	Agriculture, Forests, & Fisheries	Health & Social Welfare (*c*)
1923	...	0·1	7·5	4·4	1·2	2·9	0·3	0·1	0·7	3·6
1924	...	0·1	10·6	4·3	1·8	2·6	0·3	0·1	0·8	3·4
1925	...	0·9	3·1	4·1	1·8	2·4	0·4	0·1	1·0	3·1
1926	...	0·9	2·7	4·3	1·8	2·3	0·3	0·1	1·6	2·8
1927	28·3	1·1	2·5	4·4	1·8	2·3	0·3	0·1	2·0	2·9
1928	31·4	1·5	2·3	4·4	1·9	2·3	0·3 ---(*c*) 0·1	0·1	1·7	2·9 ---(*c*) 3·1
1929	29·1	1·6	1·9	4·5	1·9	2·2	0·1	0·1	1·7	3·2
1930	30·1	1·7	1·5	4·5	1·9	2·2	0·1	0·1	1·6	3·3
1931	31·1	2·0	1·3	4·6	1·9	2·1	0·1	0·1	1·7	3·3
1932	27·9	2·1	1·4	4·6	1·9	2·0	0·1	--	2·6	3·2
1933	36·9	2·3	1·4	4·6	2·0	2·0	0·1	--	2·8	3·4
1934	33·0	2·0	1·5	4·5	2·0	2·0	0·1	0·1	4·5	3·8
1935	32·2	2·3	1·6	4·7	2·1	1·9	0·2	--	3·5	4·6
1936	33·1	2·5	1·7	4·7	2·1	1·9	0·2	--	3·7	5·5
1937	33·5	2·0	1·8	4·7	2·1	2·0	0·3	--	3·6	5·1
1938	35·6	1·7	2·0	4·7	2·1	2·2	0·4	0·1	3·7	5·1
1939	52·2	2·2	2·4	5·0	2·1	2·3	0·5	0·1	4·0	5·4
1940	45·7	2·4	3·5	5·0	2·1	2·4	0·3	0·1	4·2	5·6
1941	39·2	2·6	7·2	5·0	2·4	2·5	0·3	0·1	4·0	5·3
1942	48·6	2·7	8·7	5·1	2·3	2·5	0·2	0·1	4·1	5·1
1943	45·2	2·9	9·1	5·0	2·3	2·6	0·3	0·1	3·7	5·2
1944	47·5	3·0	8·8	5·4	2·5	2·7	0·3	0·2	3·7	5·5
1945	50·7	2·9	8·7	5·5	2·6	3·0	0·3	0·2	3·3	6·9
1946	56·2	3·2	9·4	5·7	2·8	3·3	0·3	0·4	3·5	7·6
1947	62·1	3·3	5·8	6·7	3·0	3·9	5·1	0·8	3·8	7·9
1948	73·5	3·3	4·5	7·3	3·3	4·4	11·3	1·3	5·8	11·7
1940	99·2	3·5	4·5	7·5	3·3	4·6	14·5	0·7	6·4	12·5
1950	103·0	4·0	4·5	7·8	3·4	5·2	3·4	4·3	15·0	15·1
1951	109·2	5·4	5·0	9·2	3·4	5·5	2·3	1·7	19·2	15·7
1952	129·1	6·1	6·0	9·4	3·6	6·6	6·5	3·1	20·2	17·8
1953	154·2	8·1	8·0	10·9	4·0	7·1	8·2	3·6	13·9	24·2
1954	178·2	10·1	9·3	11·4	3·9	6·9	8·2	2·6	12·0	29·7
1955	180·5	11·7	8·1	12·3	5·4	7·7	9·2	2·1	14·7	27·9
1956	192·8	13·6	8·0	12·3	4·9	7·6	8·0	2·3	15·7	29·0
1957	212·8	15·9	7·9	13·4	5·2	8·4	7·4	3·5	16·6	31·0
1958	237·2	18·0	7·7	14·0	5·3	8·6	3·6	6·1	18·5	33·6
1959	236·0	19·6	7·7	14·1	5·4	8·8	1·4	4·6	20·6	33·4
1960	244·2	21·1	8·3	15·9	5·7	9·4	2·8	2·7	22·6	33·9
1961	299·4	23·3	8·8	16·6	6·3	10·1	2·7	3·3	26·7	35·0
1962	344·6	25·8	9·3	17·7	6·7	11·2	3·1	3·5	35·9	35·1
1963	423·1	28·6	10·3	20·6	7·4	13·0	3·5	4·2	38·4	38·6
1964	450·4	31·8	10·7	23·1	8·4	13·8	5·0	4·8	39·3	42·7
1965	529·8	35·8	13·6	28·9	9·4	17·8	5·2	6·7	48·4	49·7
1966	731·1	41·2	14·1	32·3	9·9	18·6	8·6	7·6	52·4	55·5
1967	684·8	47·5	13·0	34·7	11·0	19·5	10·1	7·4	58·7	62·6

Public Finance 6. *continued*

(in £ million Irish)

Main Constituent Items (*a*)

	Total	Debt Service	Defence (*b*)	Education	Law & Justice	Posts & Telegraphs	Industry, Commerce, & Energy (*c*)	Tourism and Transport	Agriculture, Forests, & Fisheries	Health & Social Welfare (*c*)
1968	744·4	53·9	13·7	40·1	10·6	21·0	9·9	8·8	72·7	68·0
1969	875·3	64·6	15·1	49·0	11·4	22·7	12·9	9·9	81·8	74·8
1970	1,038·9	76·5	17·3	62·7	13·4	26·1	18·3	14·1	93·9	92·2
1971	1,036·0	87·7	22·5	72·3	16·7	34·8	23·0	19·2	100·4	117·0
1972	1,439·9	99·5	23·5	83·3	20·0	36·7	28·8	16·8	109·8	121·4
1973	1,598·5	109·3	35·2	105·7	25·9	47·4	32·8	23·2	123·8	158·0
1974	1,899·4	125·9	40·6	127·9	36·3	55·2	34·4	25·1	104·8	231·8
1974	[1,771·7](*d*)	[113·7](*d*)	[36·4](*d*)	[108·6](*d*)	[35·6](*d*)	[50·0](*d*)	[26·5](*d*)	[24·5](*d*)	[85·8](*d*)	[220·3](*d*)
1975	3,440·0	194·6	69·7	216·9	62·0	91·0	63·0	45·6	140·4	427·0
1976	3,597·6	278·3	84·0	261·2	67·3	111·1	85·1	49·7	173·2	507·3
1977	3,987·7	334·1	97·5	298·7	69·7	131·4	100·1	57·6	201·7	597·9
1978	4,874·2	418·2	104·1	351·2	84·2	149·6	125·9	58·9	222·3	713·2
1979	7,043·6	574·4	127·7	436·3	113·2	184·8	178·0	83·0	216·0	866·9
1980	8,413·5	660·5	164·1	527·5	150·8	258·7	238·8	90·3	267·6	1,145·1

(*a*) Food allowances took a significant amount from 1942–47, as follows:

1942	0·2	1944	0·5	1946	0·6
1943	0·4	1945	0·6	1947	0·6

(*b*) Including pensions.

(*c*) Unemployment insurance was transferred from Industry etc. to Social Welfare in 1928.

(*d*) The figures are for the period April–December.

Public Finance 7. Nominal Amount of the Unredeemed Capital of the Public Debt of the United Kingdom at the End of Each Financial Year – 1691–1980

NOTES

[1] SOURCES: Funded Debt – 1691–1785 – *S.P.* 1898, LII, 1786–1890 – *S.P.* 1890–1, XLVIII, 1891–1939 – *Return Relating to the National Debt* published in *Finance Accounts* annually. Unfunded Debt – 1691–1835 – *S.P.* 1868–9, XXXV, 1836–1980 – *Return Relating to the National Debt*, and *Abstract*. Remaining figures – *Return relating to the National Debt*.

[2] Material prepared by the National Debt Commissioners has been preferred to the alternative source (*S.P.* 1868–9, XXXV). Differences between the two are slight, and the break in the unfunded series between 1835 and 1836 is inconsiderable. The mistaken attribution of the figures of unfunded debt to the year previous to that to which they actually apply, in *S.P.* 1868–9, XXXV, Part II, Appendix 12, has been corrected.

[3] All figures of the total national debt result from the addition of the two separate figures of funded and unfunded debt regardless of whether the financial years are the same for both.

[4] All statistics since 1919 exclude the amounts of Funding Loan and Victory Bonds tendered for duties under section 3(3) of the War Loan Act (1919), and held by the National Debt Commissioners.

[5] From 1940 the amount of the funded debt has changed very little, and it has not seemed worthwhile to continue to show it and the unfunded debt separately.

(in £ million sterling)

	Funded	Unfunded	Total		Funded	Unfunded	Total
1691 (*b*)	—	3·1	3·1	1724	48·6	5·2	53·8
1692	—	3·3	3·3	1725	48·6	4·1	52·7
1693	—	5·9	5·9	1726	49·1	3·8	52·9
1694	0·6	5·5	6·1	1727 (*b*)	48·4	4·5	53·0
1695	1·2	7·2	8·4	1728	48·5	4·2	52·7
1696	1·2	10·4	10·6	1729	48·4	3·7	52·1
1697	3·4	13·3	16·7	1730	47·4	4·0	51·4
1698	5·1	12·2	17·3	1731	47·9	3·7	51·7
1699	4·8	10·6	15·4	1732	46·4	3·7	50·1
1700	4·7	9·4	14·2	1733	46·4	3·6	50·0
1701	4·7	9·4	14·1	1734	45·4	3·7	49·1
1702	4·6	9·6	14·1	1735	45·4	3·9	49·3
1703	4·4	9·1	13·6	1736	46·0	3·7	49·7
1704	4·3	9·2	13·4	1737	45·0	3·6	48·5
1705	4·1	8·9	13·0	1738	44·0	3·5	47·5
1706	4·5	8·5	13·0	1739	43·3	3·7	46·9
1707	4·3	10·2	14·5	1740	43·3	4·2	47·4
1708	4·8	10·5	15·2	1741	43·3	5·4	48·8
1709	7·4	11·7	19·1	1742	45·0	6·4	51·3
1710	7·3	14·1	21·4	1743	47·6	5·9	53·5
1711	11·8	10·6	22·4	1744	50·4	6·7	57·1
1712	25·6	9·4	34·9	1745	52·4	7·7	60·1
1713	26·1	8·6	34·7	1746	56·3	8·5	64·9
1714	27·8	8·4	36·2	1747	61·8	7·6	69·4
1715	29·6	7·8	37·4	1748	68·7	7·4	76·1
1716	29·5	8·4	37·9	1749	71·8	6·0	77·8
1717	31·7	7·6	39·3	1750	72·8	5·2	78·0
1718	34·1	5·6	39·7	1751	72·4	5·7	78·1
1719	37·2	4·4	41·6	1752 (*b*)	71·5	5·5	76·9
1720	49·8	4·1	54·0	1753	71·0	4·1	75·0
1721	50·3	4·6	54·9	1754	70·9	1·3	72·2
1722	48·4	4·3	52·7	1755	71·8	0·7	72·5
1723	49·1	4·4	53·6	1756	73·8	0·8	74·6

See p. 603 for footnotes.

Public Finance 7. *continued*

(in £ million sterling)

	Funded	Un-funded	Total
1757	76·8	1·1	77·8
1758	81·8	1·4	82·1
1759	89·3	1·9	91·3
1760	97·6	4·2	101·7
1761	109·9	4·4	114·2
1762	121·9	4·7	126·6
1763	129·1	3·6	132·6
1764	129·2	5·0	134·2
1765	130·6	3·0	133·6
1766	131·2	2·1	133·3
1767	131·9	1·9	133·9
1768	130·3	2·3	132·6
1769	128·6	1·7	130·3
1770	128·6	2·1	130·6
1771	127·1	1·8	128·9
1772	126·4	2·2	128·7
1773	125·8	3·1	128·9
1774	125·3	2·4	127·7
1775	124·3	3·1	127·3
1776	125·9	5·3	131·2
1777	130·9	5·7	136·6
1778	137·1	6·0	143·1
1779	144·1	9·4	153·4
1780	156·1	11·2	167·2
1781	177·4	11·9	190·4
1782	197·5	16·8	214·3
1783	212·8	19·0	231·8
1784	228·7	14·2	242·9
1785	239·6	5·8	245·5
1786	239·7	6·4	246·2
1787 (*b*)	239·2	6·6	245·8
1788	237·7	7·4	245·1
1789	236·2	8·1	244·3
1790	234·6	9·4	244·0
1791	233·0	10·1	243·2
1792	231·5	10·0	241·6
1793	229·6	13·3	242·9
1794	234·0	15·6	249·6
1795	247·9	19·6	267·4
1796	301·9	8·5	310·4
1797	351·5	7·7	359·2
1798	378·6	12·6	391·2
1799	408·1	18·5	426·6
1800	411·4	...(*b*)	...(*b*)
1801 (*b*)	432·3	23·7	456·1
1802	478·1	20·5	498·6
1803	501·0	15·4	516·4
1804	504·3	19·5	523·8

	Funded	Un-funded	Total	Aggregate Gross Liabilities of the State
1805	514·2	25·3	539·6	...
1806	538·0	26·3	564·4	...
1807	556·0	27·1	583·1	...
1808	559·2	32·1	591·3	...
1809	559·8	39·3	599·0	...
1810	567·7	39·7	607·4	...
1811	570·8	37·9	609·6	...
1812	583·4	42·6	626·0	...
1813	607·5	44·8	652·3	...
1814	677·5	48·1	725·5	...
1815	684·6	60·3	744·9	...
1816	733·6	44·7	778·3	...
1817	716·3	49·8	766·1	...
1818 (*b*)	780·6	62·6	843·3	...
1819	795·6	48·7	844·3	...
1820	798·5	41·6	840·1	...
1821	804·9	33·3	838·3	...
1822	798·5	32·7	831·1	...
1823	797·4	38·7	836·1	...
1824	792·9	35·8	828·6	...
1825	782·3	37·9	820·2	...
1826	779·3	31·7	811·0	...
1827	785·0	25·0	810·0	...
1828	778·7	27·6	806·4	...
1829	773·6	27·7	801·3	...
1830	772·6	25·5	798·2	...
1831	758·9	27·3	786·2	...
1832	757·0	27·2	784·2	...
1833	755·6	27·4	783·0	...
1834	753·2	28·1	781·3	...
1835	745·3	29·6	774·9	...
		- - -		
1836	760·3	30·1(*c*)	790·4	846·1
1837	763·2	27·7	790·9	845·5
1838	763·6	25·3	788·9	841·9
1839	762·8	25·5	788·2	840·4
1840	768·0	20·6	788·7	839·0
1841	767·9	22·2	790·2	838·8
1842	774·3	19·6	793·9	840·8
1843	774·9	18·7	793·5	838·7
1844	774·0	20·5	794·5	838·3
1845	771·1	18·8	789·9	833·8
1846	768·8	18·4	787·2	829·8
1847	766·8	18·4	785·2	826·1
1848	774·7	18·0	792·7	831·6
1849	776·5	17·8	794·3	831·4
1850	775·7	17·8	793·5	828·9
1851	772·0	17·8	789·7	823·7
1852	767·9	17·7	785·7	818·0

See p. 603 for footnotes.

Public Finance 7. *continued*

(in £ million)

	Funded	Un-funded	Total	Out-standing Invest-ment Borrow-ing (*a*)	Aggre-gate Gross Liabili-ties of the State		Funded	Un-funded (*d*)	Total (*d*)	Out-standing Invest-ment Borrow-ing (*a*)	Aggre-gate Gross Liabili-ties of the State (*d*)
1853	764·5	17·7	782·3	—	813·5	1897	587·7	8·1	595·8	4·0	645·2
1854	758·4	16·0	774·4	—	803·6	1898	585·8	8·1	593·9	3·7	638·8
1855(*b*)	755·6	24·2	779·7	—	806·7	1899	583·2	8·1	591·3	7·4	635·4
1856	779·4	27·1	806·5	—	833·7	1900	552·6	16·1	568·7	10·0	638·9
1857	784·0	28·0	812·0	—	836·8	1901	551·2	78·1	629·3	14·5	703·9
1858	782·9	25·9	808·9	—	831·2	1902	609·6	75·1	684·7	20·2	765·2
1859	790·5	18·3	808·8	—	828·7	1903	640·1	75·1	715·2	27·6	798·3
1860	789·7	16·3	806·0	—	822·8	1904	637·6	73·6	711·3	31·9	794·5
1861	789·0	16·7	805·7	—	822·0	1905	635·7	71·6	707·3	41·7	796·7
1862	788·2	16·5	804·7	—	821·3	1906	634·0	65·7	699·8	45·8	789·0
1863	787·4	16·5	803·9	—	821·5	1907	631·9	51·7	683·6	49·7	779·2
1864	781·7	13·1	794·8	—	817·2	1908	625·6	44·0	669·6	50·9	762·3
1865	780·2	10·7	790·9	—	812·7	1909	621·8	42·8	664·7	51·4	754·1
1866	773·9	8·2	782·1	—	803·4	1910	614·9	62·5	677·4	49·2	762·5
1867	770·2	8·0	778·1	—	800·9	1911	610·3	40·5	650·8	47·8	733·1
1868	741·8	7·9	749·8	—	797·8	1912	602·2	33·1	635·3	50·1	718·4
1869	741·1	9·9	751·0	—	797·8	1913	593·5	31·5	625·0	54·8	711·3
1870	741·5	6·8	748·3	1·0	793·1	1914	586·7	33·5	620·2	56·4	706·2
1871	732·0	6·1	738·1	0·9	787·3	1915	583·3	493·6	1,076·9	57·0	1,162·0
1872	731·8	5·2	736·9	0·9	784·2	1916	318·5	1,788·5	2,107·0	56·7	2,189·8
1873	727·4	4·8	732·2	0·9	777·5	1917	317·8	3,669·6	3,987·4	52·2	4,063·6
1874	723·5	4·5	728·0	0·9	771·2	1918	317·7	5,532·2	5,849·9	49·2	5,921·1
1875	714·8	5·2	720·0	0·9	767·3	1919	317·6	7,096·7	7,414·3	46·1	7,481·1
1876	713·7	11·4	725·1	0·8	769·4	1920	315·0	7,494·5	7,809·5	46·9	7,875·6
1877	712·6	13·9	726·6	0·8	768·7	1921	314·8	7,241·8	7,556·7	48·7	7,623·1
1878	710·8	20·6	731·4	0·8	770·9	1922	580·6	7,057·5	7,638·1	66·2	7,720·5
1879	709·4	25·9	735·3	0·8	771·8	1923	997·8	6,730·7	7,728·6	70·3	7,812·6
1880	710·5	27·3	737·8	0·7	770·6	1924	980·3	6,647·3	7,627·6	66·5	7,707·5
1881	709·1	22·1	731·2	0·7	765·2	1925	1,022·7	6,562·1	7,584·8	68·0	7,665·9
1882	709·5	18·0	727·5	0·7	759·9	1926	1,073·5	6,472·5	7,546·0	75·1	7,633·7
1883	712·7	14·2	726·9	0·7	753·9	1927	1,219·8	6,322·6	7,542·4	98·1	7,652·7
1884	640·6	14·1	654·7	0·7	745·6	1928	1,350·0	6,165·3	7,515·3	103·2	7,631·0
1885	640·2	14·0	654·2	0·6	739·9	1929	1,478·3	6,009·5	7,487·8	120·5	7,620·9
1886	638·9	17·6	656·5	0·6	742·0	1930	1,456·0	6,000·9	7,456·9	127·2	7,596·2
1887	637·6	17·5	655·2	0·6	736·2	1931	1,425·0	5,976·3	7,401·3	169·6	7,582·9
1888	609·7	17·4	627·1	0·6	704·6	1932	1,467·1	5,995·1	7,422·2	214·0	7,648·0
1889	607·1	16·1	623·2	0·6	697·6	1933	3,376·3	4,255·6	7,631·9	215·9	7,859·7
1890	586·0	32·3	618·2	0·5	689·1	1934	3,374·3	4,435·9	7,810·2	208·1	8,030·4
1891	579·5	36·1	615·6	1·3	683·5	1935	3,368·1	4,420·2	7,788·4	102·0	7,902·4
1892	577·9	35·3	613·3	1·3	677·1	1936	3,366·5	4,417·3	7,783·7	105·8	7,901·6
1893	589·5	20·7	610·3	1·8	671·1	1937	3,364·9	4,420·2	7,785·1	112·6	7,909·9
1894	587·6	21·4	609·1	2·5	667·3	1938	3,364·8	4,648·8	8,013·6	122·8	8,149·0
1895	586·0	17·4	603·4	3·1	659·0	1939	3,364·6	4,785·0	8,149·6	138·0	8,301·1
								- - -(*d*)	- - -(*d*)		- - -(*d*)
								3,752·6	7,130·8		7,268·7
1896	589·1	10·0	599·1	4·0	652·3	1940	3,364·4	4,520·2	7,899·2	151·6	8,050·8

Public Finance 7. *continued*

(in £ million)

	Total National Debt	of which External Debt	Outstanding Investment Borrowing	Aggregate Liabilities of the State		Total National Debt	of which External Debt	Outstanding Investment Borrowing	Aggregate Liabilities of the State
1941	10,366·4	2·3	153·9	10,520·3	1961	28,251·7	1,979·1	186·8	28,438·5
1942	13,041·1	109·9	152·9	13,193·9	1962	28,674·4	1,922·2	0·1	28,674·5
1943	15,822·6	263·1	151·1	15,973·7	1963	29,847·6	1,874·6	—	(*e*)
1944	18,562·2	255·1	148·3	18,710·5	1964	30,226·3	1,835·0	—	
1945	21,365·9	236·1	142·9	21,508·8	1965	30,440·6	1,806·4	—	
1946	23,636·5	369·1	137·4	23,773·9	1966	31,340·7	1,795·0	—	
1947	25,630·6	767·5	139·9	25,770·6	1967	31,985·6	1,821·7	—	
1948	25,620·8	1,554·8	151·9	25,772·7	1968	34,193·9	2,302·0	—	
1949	25,167·6	1,595·3	164·2	25,331·8	1969	33,984·2	2,252·7	—	
1950	25,802·3	2,189·9	184·0	25,986·3	1970	33,079·4	2,233·6	—	
1951	25,921·6	2,192·1	203·5	26,125·1	1971	33,441·9	2,148·7	—	
1952	25,890·5	2,167·9	227·0	26,117·5	1972	35,839·9	1,879·2	—	
1953	26,051·2	2,162·5	263·5	26,314·7	1973	36,884·6	1,615·8	—	
1954	26,583·0	2,114·5	304·9	26,887·9	1974	40,457·0	1,875·2	—	
1955	26,933·7	2,130·4	300·1	27,233·8	1975	46,403·7	2,816·5	—	
1956	27,038·9	2,074·7	281·1	27,320·0	1876	56,585·2	3,450·4	—	
1957	27,007·5	2,065·3	261·2	27,268·7	1977	67,165·8	4,369·8	—	
1958	27,232·0	2,163·1	241·5	27,473·5	1978	79,179·9	4,629·9	—	
1959	27,376·3	2,186·5	222·3	27,598·6	1979	86,884·9	4,287·8	—	
1960	27,732·6	2,043·0	204·1	27,936·7	1980	95,314·2	3,948·5	—	

(*a*) This relates to loans under Telegraph Acts, Naval Works Act, Barracks Act, Telephone Transfer Acts, etc.

(*b*) Financial years ended on the following dates: *Great Britain (funded debt)* 1691–1751 – 29 September, 1752–86 – 10 October, 1787–1817 – 1 February; *Great Britain (except for funded debt)* 1691–1751 – 29 September, 1752–99 – 10 October, 1801–17 – 5 January; *Ireland* 1691–1726 – 25 December, 1727–1800 – 25 March, 1801–17 – 5 January; *United Kingdom* 1818–54 – 5 January, 1855–1980 – 31 March.

(*c*) See note 2.

(*d*) From 1916 to 1939 these columns include outstanding external debt arising out of the First World War as follows:

1916	60·6	1924	1,125·8	1932	1,090·8
1917	400·3	1925	1,121·6	1933	1,060·4
1918	1,048·7	1926	1,110·8	1934	1,036·5
1919	1,364·9	1927	1,101·5	1935	1,036·5
1920	1,278·7	1928	1,095·2	1936	1,036·5
1921	1,161·6	1929	1,084·7	1937	1,032·6
1922	1,088·7	1930	1,074·2	1938	1,032·5
1923	1,155·7	1931	1,066·7	1939	1,032·4

From 1939 (2nd line) this debt is excluded.

(*e*) The figures under this heading are identical subsequently with those of the total national debt.

Public Finance 8. Nominal Capital Liabilities – Republic of Ireland 1926–80

NOTES

[1] SOURCE: *Statistical Abstract of Ireland*.

[2] Figures to 1974 (1st line) relate to 31 March. Subsequently they relate to 31 December.

(in £ million)

1926	14·1	1940	64·8 ---(a) 69·3	1954	278·9	1968	840·6
1927	17·4	1941	69·6	1955	305·0	1969	931·8
1928	22·6	1942	77·0	1956	325·7	1970	1,027·2
1929	23·8	1943	78·7	1957	351·7	1971	1,110·9
1930	25·9	1944	78·9	1958	377·6	1972	1,329·9
1931	29·3	1945	79·5	1959	390·9	1973	1,483·7
1932	31·8	1946	81·3	1960	426·0	1974	1,724·8
1933	31·4	1947	86·8	1961	460·5	1974 (b)	2,077·5
1934	49·6	1948	91·0	1962	499·0	1975	2,743·8
1935	48·6	1949	100·9	1963	544·9	1976	3,611·8
1936	48·4	1950	140·6	1964	592·3	1977	4,218·8
1937	48·7	1951	178·9	1965	653·6	1978	5,166·1
1938	49·4	1952	213·6	1966	735·1	1979	6,540·1
1939	61·4	1953	243·8	1967	791·5	1980	7,896·4

(a) Subsequently including the liability in respect of an annuity payable to the British Government under an Agreement of December 1925.

(b) See note 2 above.

Public Finance 9. Produce of the Poor Rates and Expenditure on the Relief of the Poor – England & Wales 1748–1885

NOTES

[1] Sources: 1748–50, 1776, 1783–5, and 1803 – *S.P.* 1818, v; 1813–69 – *S.P.* 1870, LV; 1870–85 – *Poor Rate Returns* in sessional papers annually.

[2] As Goschen pointed out in his Report of 1870, the usefulness of the Poor Rates Receipts series is considerably reduced by the variations in the number of rates levied under the general title 'poor rates' at different periods. Up to and including 1815, Church and By-Highway rates were probably wholly or partially included; and from 1841 onwards Borough and Police rates were definitely included.

[3] Money collected under the title 'poor rates' for Highway Boards is not included in this table.

(in £ thousand)

	Poor Rates Receipts	Expenditure on Relief
1748–50 (*a*)	730	690
1776 (*b*)	1,720	1,531
1783–5 (*c*)	2,168	2,004
1803	5,348	4,268
1813	8,647	6,656
1814	8,389	6,295
1815	7,458	5,419
1816	6,937	5,725
1817	8,128	6,911
1818	9,320	7,871
1819	8,932	7,517
1820	8,720	7,330
1821	8,412	6,959
1822	7,761	6,359
1823	6,898	5,773
1824	6,837	5,737
1825	6,972	5,787
1826	6,965	5,929
1827	7,784	6,441
1828	7,715	6,298
1829	7,642	6,332
1830	8,111	6,829
1831	8,279	6,799
1832	8,623	7,037
1833	8,607	6,791
1834	8,338	6,317
1835	7,374	5,526
1836	6,355	4,718
1837	5,295	4,045
1838	5,186	4,124
1839	5,614	4,407
1840	6,015	4,577
1841	6,352	4,761
1842	6,553	4,911
1843	7,086	5,208
1844	6,847	4,976
1845	6,791	5,040
1846	6,801	4,954
1847	6,965	5,299
1848	7,817	6,181
1849	7,674	5,793
1850	7,270	5,395
1851	6,779	4,963
1852	6,552	4,898
1853	6,522	4,939
1854	6,973	5,283
1855	7,864	5,890
1856	8,201	6,004
1857	8,139	5,899
1858	8,189	5,879
1859	8,108	5,559
1860	7,716	5,455
1861	7,922	5,779
1862	8,511	6,078
1863	9,175	6,527
1864	9,448	6,423
1965	8,841	6,265
1866	8,995	6,440
1867	9,708	6,960
1868	10,440	7,498
1869	10,705	7,673
1870	10,921	7,644
1871	10,962	7,887
1872	11,442	8,007
1873	11,487	7,692
1874	11,565	7,665
1875	11,682	7,488
1876	11,270	7,336
1877	11,161	7,400
1878	11,615	7,689
1879	11,916	7,830
1880	12,043	8,015
1881	12,410	8,102
1882	13,050	8,232
1883	13,225	8,353
1884	13,451	8,403
1885	13,659	8,492

(*a*) Average of the three years ended Easter. The returns were incomplete, and Rickman added estimates of the deficiencies in 1818.

(*b*) Years ended 25th March henceforth.

(*c*) Average of three years.

Public Finance 10. County Receipts and Expenditure – England & Wales 1792–1871

NOTES

[1] SOURCES: 1792–1838 – *S.P.* 1839, XLIV (*Local Taxation Return*); 1839–71 – *Abstract of County Treasurers' Returns*, published in sessional papers annually.

[2] In the *Local Taxation Return* of 1839 the defects of the earlier statistics are pointed out. The introduction says that more than one-third of the Treasurers of Counties had no means of affording information of the earliest years concerning which questions were put to them by the Committee of 1825; so that in such an abstract as is now attempted, a defect to that extent is inevitable, and has been supplied by presuming the population of each county in the several years (as nearly as it could be estimated) to represent an equal expenditure in the counties which made no return as was the actual expenditure of the counties which made return'. The percentage increase which had to be added to the returns until, in 1819, they were complete, was as follows:

	England	Wales		England	Wales		England	Wales
1792	44	33	1801	27	33	1810	25	20
1793	45	33	1802	27	43	1811	25	20
1794	45	33	1803	31	38	1812	20	20
1795	45	33	1804	27	25	1813	20	20
1796	43	33	1805	25	25	1814	20	20
1797	38	33	1806	25	25	1815	20	20
1798	33	33	1807	25	33	1816	12	11
1799	31	33	1808	25	25	1817	12	11
1800	31	33	1809	25	25	1818	12	—

[3] The financial years of the different counties did not all end at the same time. The aggregates in this table do not, therefore, represent a genuine figure for any exactly defined period.

(in £ thousand)

	Receipts			Expenditure				
		Principal Constituents			Principal Constituents			
	Total	County and Police Rates	Treasury Grants	Total	Bridges	Gaols and Prisoners (a)	Constables and Vagrants	Prosecutions
1792	...	218	...	223	33	105	16	8
1793	...	212	...	217	41	92	12	7
1794	...	198	...	210	31	82	11	5
1795	...	217	...	225	43	68	13	7
1796	...	229	...	237	50	71	11	7
1797	...	247	...	275	45	60	11	9
1798	...	269	...	245	41	65	11	10
1799	...	289	...	267	43	76	11	12
1800	...	292	...	288	46	100	17	20
1801	...	326	...	348	52	108	21	24
1802	...	318	...	299	46	93	18	16
1803	...	286	...	273	42	90	15	16
1804	...	299	...	278	42	101	13	16
1805	...	325	...	327	58	121	14	16
1806	...	339	...	332	49	117	14	18
1807	...	367	...	339	52	118	14	17
1808	...	350	...	363	61	126	15	18
1809	...	393	...	411	77	145	15	21
1810	...	436	...	436	89	169	14	22
1811	...	497	...	474	97	168	15	21
1812	...	502	...	500	112	174	18	28
1813	...	548	...	547	122	169	22	33
1814	...	574	...	525	130	194	23	29
1815	...	542	...	573	151	214	30	38
1816	...	558	...	559	114	216	32	44

See p. 608 for footnotes.

Public Finance 10. *continued*

(in £ thousand)

	Receipts			Expenditure					
		Principal Constituents			Principal Constituents				
	Total	County and Police Rates	Treasury Grants	Total	Bridges	Gaols and Prisoners (*a*)	Constables and Vagrants	Prosecutions	Lunacy (*b*)
1817	...	567	...	590	95	276	45	55	...
1818	...	646	...	658	92	296	53	75	...
1819	...	658	...	664	86	292	57	89	...
1820	...	699	...	679	85	265	61	94	...
1821	...	672	...	653	61	281	59	104	...
1822	...	615	...	595	69	265	27	82	...
1823	...	577	...	579	62	252	19	80	...
1824	...	569	...	599	77	294	16	91	...
1825	...	673	...	664	102	314	17	91	...
1826	...	736	...	743	97	353	22	106	...
1827	...	732	...	762	90	344	27	134	...
1828	...	723	...	721	88	314	27	121	...
1829	...	691	...	714	78	312	30	132	...
1830	...	708	...	727	76	315	33	135	...
1831	...	755	...	773	84	323	42	149	...
1832	...	762	...	799	75	321	43	148	...
1833	...	759	...	745	77	267	36	145	...
1834	...	724	...	692	72	223	28	148	...
1835	...	671	...	649	54	221	23	129	...
1836	...	705	...	639	55	190	22	133	...
1837	...	638	...	652	55	199	22	138	...
1838	...	684	...	700	46	211	25	150	...
1839 (*c*)	...	[623]	[90]	[737]	...	...	...	...	...
							Rural Police		
1840	961	716	101	881	62	290	76	169	9
1841	1,078	832	96	999	64	289	137	174	10
1842	1,078	829	115	1,051	64	317	147	204	11
1843	1,233	886	112	1,111	57	327	160	209	20
1844	1,209	868	102	1,080	59	343	169	187	22
1845	1,213	860	96	1,084	53	335	179	170	23
1846	1,240	835	87	1,093	56	338	188	166	11
1847	1,325	877	148	1,177	57	349	195	179	12
1848	1,585	893	291	1,407	67	430	229	211	15
1849	1,542	865	290	1,382	64	419	226	204	29

See p. 608 for footnotes.

Public Finance 10. *continued*

(in £ thousand)

	Receipts			Expenditure							
		Principal Constituents			Principal Constituents						
	Total	County and Police Rates	Treasury Grants	Total	Bridges	Gaols and Prisoners (*a*)	Rural Police	Prosecutions	Lunacy (*b*)	Interest on Debt	Repayment of Debt
1850	1,574	796	396	1,380	54	381	223	182	185	...	...
1851	1,489	800	275	1,356	59	337	208	190	165	67	...
1852	1,409	810	274	1,252	52	309	219	178	80	109	...
1853	1,479	886	295	1,288	50	333	230	175	94	119	...
1854	1,550	884	298	1,396	58	366	253	185	100	95	...
1855	1,673	992	315	1,483	60	386	258	179	103	104	...
1856	1,701	1,010	292	1,485	56	379	301	142	128	127	...
1857	1,935	1,157	302	1,716	48	378	424	145	191	86	209
1858	2,047	1,222	301	1,841	52	377	563	127	181	94	93
1859	2,038	1,163	291	1,829	48	339	564	105	190	111	93
1860	2,037	1,223	347	1,801	51	336	579	103	175	114	110
1861	2,049	1,234	295	1,860	53	348	590	113	165	109	115
1862	2,044	1,322	294	1,830	55	360	573	131	144	115	121
1863	2,212	1,324	394	1,906	53	372	618	132	160	96	144
1864	2,249	1,305	389	1,959	49	389	620	127	196	115	141
1865	2,251	1,291	418	2,010	52	412	649	126	192	96	157
1866	2,670	1,359	434	2,416	50	447	685	123	209	121	134
1867	2,534	1,449	417	2,279	52	487	709	128	216	97	163
1868	2,545	1,501	488	2,327	53	551	745	132	246	115	169
1869	2,715	1,576	492	2,417	51	515	754	134	310	119	176
1870	2,762	1,556	526	2,412	59	494	760	122	287	121	178
1871	2,537	1,626	400	2,545	53	462	784	114	385	128	238

(*a*) This covers costs of maintenance of gaols and houses of correction, and of their inmates (including from 1868–71 the costs of reformatories), and the costs of conveying prisoners.

(*b*) This comprises the costs of maintenance of pauper lunatics, and (from 1850) the costs of lunatic asylums.

(*c*) Returns for the *Abstract of County Treasurers' Returns* for 1839 were incomplete in that there were none for Buckinghamshire Lancashire, and Oxfordshire, and there was a lack of uniformity in the treatment of the various items of expenditure. The figures shown for 1839 have been computed by adding estimates for the three missing counties based on their returns for 1840, namely 61 for total expenditure, 55 for receipts from rates, and 11 for receipts from the Treasury.

Public Finance 11. Receipts of Local Authorities – England & Wales 1868–1980

NOTES

[1] SOURCES: 1868 (Total Receipts) – *Abstract (1889)* (revision of the Goschen Report); 1868 (Rates) – *S.P.* 1893–4, LXXVII; 1868 (Loans) – *S.P.* 1870, LV (the Goschen Report); 1868 (Government Grants) – P. G. Craigie in the *Journal of the Statistical Society* (1877) (revision of the Goschen Report); 1871–9 (Total Receipts) – *Local Taxation Returns* in sessional papers annually; 1871–9 (Rates) – *S.P.* 1893–4, LXXVII; 1880–1939 (except Water and Gas 1883–5) – *Abstract*; 1883–5 (Water and Gas) – *Local Taxation Returns*, annually.

[2] The financial years of the various authorities did not all end on the same date, though the majority ended on the 25th or the 31st March. The figures are aggregates for the financial years ended in the years shown.

(in £ million)
Principal Constitutent Items

					Receipts from Main Trading Services			
	Total Receipts	Loans	Rates	Government Grants, etc.	Water	Gas	Electricity	Transport
1868	30·4	5·5	16·5	0·8	...	...	...	...
1871	30·2	...	...	...	...	...	...	...
1872	31·7	...	17·6	...	...	...	...	...
1873	32·8	...	18·1	...	...	...	...	...
1874	37·4	...	18·9	...	...	...	...	...
1875	43·6	...	19·3	...	...	...	...	...
1876	43·4	...	19·5	...	...	...	...	...
1877	48·1	...	20·1	...	...	...	...	...
1878	51·8	...	21·1	...	...	...	...	...
1879	54·4	...	21·8	...	...	...	...	...
	---(*a*)		---(*a*)					
1880	53·0	13·7	22·5	2·7	3·2 (Water and Gas)		...	...
1881	53·9	12·9	22·8	2·7	3·5 (Water and Gas)		...	...
1882	57·5	15·0	23·9	2·9	3·6 (Water and Gas)		...	...
1883	53·8	10·7	24·5	3·3	1·9	3·2	...	...
1884	51·2	7·2	24·9	3·5	2·0	3·4	...	0·1
1885	55·5	10·9	25·7	3·6	2·1	3·3	...	0·1
1886	56·0	11·0	26·2	3·8	2·1	3·3	...	0·1
1887	54·7	8·7	26·6	4·0	2·2	3·4	...	0·1
	---(*b*)	---(*c*)						
1888	55·0	8·6	27·2	4·3	2·3	3·5	...	0·1
1889	55·0	7·0	27·4	4·8	2·4	3·7	...	0·1
1890	57·3	7·1	27·7	6·5	2·5	3·9	...	0·1
1891	57·6	6·2	27·8	7·1	2·6	4·2	...	0·1
1892	63·3	10·0	28·5	8·0	2·7	4·3	--	0·1
1893	67·6	12·1	30·2	8·9	2·7	4·3	--	0·1
1894	72·6	14·3	32·2	8·8	2·8	4·5	--	0·2
1895	75·9	15·5	33·9	9·0	2·9	4·8	0·1	0·2
1896	75·5	12·2	35·9	9·2	3·0	4·7	0·2	0·3
1897	79·9	13·3	37·5	9·6	3·2	4·9	0·3	0·3
1898	83·6	14·5	37·6	11·0	3·3	5·1	0·4	0·6
1899	91·9	19·7	38·6	11·8	3·5	5·4	0·6	0·9
1900	100·6	23·4	40·7	12·2	3·7	6·0	0·9	1·6
1901	111·9	29·9	43·0	12·7	3·9	6·9	1·3	1·9
1902	121·6	34·4	46·4	12·5	4·0	7·0	1·7	2·7
1903	129·2	35·3	50·3	12·8	4·2	7·2	1·9	3·8
1904	[133·6](*e*)	[31·3](*e*)	52·9	15·6	4·3	7·4	2·3	4·8
1905	180·6(*f*)	67·5(*f*)	56·0	19·5	7·5(*f*)	7·1	2·6	5·4
1906	141·2	24·5	58·3	19·9	7·5	7·1	2·9	5·9
1907	141·2	20·4	59·6	21·0	7·5	7·2	3·1	7·1
1908	143·7	21·4	59·6	20·6	7·6	7·6	3·4	7·9
1909	145·5	20·6	61·3	21·4	7·8	7·5	3·5	8·0

See p. 611 for footnotes.

Public Finance 11. *continued*

(in £ million)

		Principal Constituent Items								
						Receipts from Main Trading Services				
	Total Receipts	Loans	Rates	Government Grants, etc.	House Rents	Water	Gas	Electricity	Transport	Harbours, etc. (*d*)
1910	171·9(*g*)	42·0(*g*)	63·3	20·9	...	8·0	7·5	3·7	8·5	...
1911	152·2	18·2	65·2	21·2	0·5	8·0	7·8	4·0	8·9	7·1
1912	157·0	17·8	66·4	22·3	0·5	8·3	8·0	4·4	9·5	7·7
1913	160·8	17·5	68·2	21·9	0·5	8·4	8·6	4·8	9·8	8·1
									---(*h*)	
1914	169·3	20·0	71·3	22·6	0·6	8·7	8·7	5·4	10·3	8·4
1915	175·7	22·4	73·7	23·2	0·6	8·9	8·6	5·7	10·7	8·5
1916	168·5	9·0	75·9	23·4	0·7	9·1	10·1	6·6	11·2	9·3
1917	165·6	5·4	72·9	22·9	0·7	9·3	10·8	8·1	12·1	9·5
1918	176·6	4·1	75·4	26·3	0·8	9·5	12·4	9·5	14·1	9·7
1919	199·2	4·3	84·7	28·9	0·8	9·7	13·9	10·7	16·9	12·3
1920	282·2	24·3	105·6	48·3	0·9	10·7	17·4	13·7	20·4	16·2
1921	457·2	116·1	151·8	63·0	2·3	11·5	21·6	17·9	23·6	18·5
1922	501·8	127·4	170·9	76·7	4·4	12·6	20·3	17·7	23·6	16·2
1923	422·2	61·1	157·3	75·8	6·7	14·9	18·1	18·3	23·4	15·1
1924	396·0	46·5	143·3	78·3	8·0	15·0	17·6	19·0	22·0	13·8
1925	424·4	69·6	142·0	81·7	9·3	15·2	16·7	20·3	22·6	14·4
1926	471·4	99·2	148·6	84·6	11·7	15·8	16·7	21·5	23·5	14·2
1927	515·1	119·4	159·0	87·0	15·3	15·9	20·9	24·5	23·1	13·8
1928	544·0	128·0	166·7	90·1	20·0	16·8	18·7	26·5	25·0	14·2
1929	516·5	92·9	166·5	92·3	23·5	17·3	17·2	27·1	25·8	14·5
	---(*i*)			---(*i*)	---(*i*)	---(*i*)	---(*i*)	---(*i*)	---(*i*)	---(*i*)
	516·8			89·4	18·9	17·0	17·1	26·7	25·6	13·6
1930	530·2	87·4	156·3	107·8	21·2	17·4	17·0	28·7	26·7	13·9
1931	566·1	100·0	149·9	130·2	22·9	18·1	16·8	30·6	26·7	12·9
1932	556·5	92·6	148·3	126·6	24·7	18·1	16·3	32·6	26·4	12·7
1933	537·1	80·8	146·3	120·5	26·0	18·4	16·3	34·6	25·7	11·7
1934	533·3	62·8	148·6	121·6	26·8	19·0	16·1	37·5	22·3	12·2
1935	539·6	64·8	154·8	125·0	27·5	19·3	16·0	40·6	21·6	12·3
			---(*j*)		---(*j*)					
1936	577·2	82·3	164·9	132·9	22·1	20·0	16·7	44·0	22·3	12·6
1937	621·1	101·1	172·8	135·6	22·5	20·6	17·2	48·6	23·1	12·9
1938	659·2	122·7	177·3	136·1	23·4	21·4	18·0	52·5	24·5	13·7
1939	692·3	129·8	191·4	140·2	24·9	21·7	17·7	56·9	25·2	13·6
1940	711·8	89·4	201·3	181·9(*k*)	26·7	22·3	18·3	59·3	25·3	13·4
1941	734·9	51·6	203·9	226·0(*k*)	27·6	23·7	20·9	64·9	27·0	11·7
1942	787·8	25·4	198·9	278·3(*k*)	27·3	24·9	24·1	74·4	31·4	13·4
1943	769·0	21·8	200·4	248·1(*k*)	27·6	25·6	26·3	76·2	34·3	13·3
1944	766·8	17·8	204·1	228·4(*k*)	27·6	26·2	28·5	82·4	35·3	18·9
1945	786·3	14·8	206·7	230·3(*k*)	27·5	27·0	30·5	88·1	36·7	20·9
1946	835·7	31·0	222·6	235·8	27·8	26·9	33·0	93·9	37·8	18·0
1947	1,034·8	149·9	243·2	252·1	30·1	28·6	37·1	107·8	41·3	20·0
1948	1,253·7	266·9	283·3	269·7	34·0	30·2	40·6	115·6	44·9	23·3
1949	1,196·1	287·3	284·4	284·9	42·3	32·6	46·8	—	47·0	23·8
1950	1,204·5	307·5	294·3	294·4	50·1	34·3	3·8	—	49·2	25·4
1951	1,261·3	340·4	304·9	304·6	58·2	34·5	—	—	49·9	26·0
1952	1,421·8	397·9	331·9	349·9	67·7	36·0	—	—	55·4	29·8
1953	1,579·1	473·9	351·0	384·8	77·9	38·0	—	—	59·7	29·2

Public Finance 11. *continued*

(in £ million)

Principal Constituent Items

	Total Receipts	Loans	Rates (*l*)	Government Grants, etc.	House Rents, etc.	Receipts from Main Trading Services: Water	Gas	Electricity	Transport	Harbours, Docks, etc.
1954	1,709·2	494·8	392·5	414·2	91·9	40·5	—	—	61·8	32·9
1955	1,784·8	491·4	410·5	452·9	105·3	42·6	—	—	62·9	33·4
1956	1,901·3	511·9	421·1	500·4	125·6	45·1	—	—	66·2	37·0
1957	2,097·4	501·0	513·5	568·0	148·1	50·8	—	—	70·7	38·1
1958	2,205·1	470·7	552·1	615·9	165·2	53·4	—	—	73·4	40·3
1959	2,311·0	463·7	579·3	658·8	182·9	55·3	—	—	75·7	41·1
1960	2,530·9	513·5	649·9	705·6	200·8	58·7	—	—	76·5	44·0
1961	2,701·2	530·4	696·7	756·0	216·3	62·1	—	—	78·2	46·0
1962	3,000·2	648·1	747·4	830·6	240·2	65·2	—	—	81·4	46·7
1963	3,303·7	704·7	831·3	907·0	268·2	69·2	—	—	84·1	51·6
1964	3,730·7	829·2	923·1	1,022·4	297·7	75·8	—	—	88·9	54·5
1965	4,214·2	1,069·5	991·2	1,103·0	325·6	83·4	—	—	90·5	57·7
1966	4,690·4	1,151·6	1,131·5	1,260·0	370·4	87·2	—	—	94·4	61·3
1967	5,151·3	1,231·0	1,266·1	1,389·1	418·5	95·5	—	—	96·3	55·3
1968	5,637·9	1,306·7	1,323·4	1,591·0	472·1	101·1	—	—	96·8	54·8
1969	6,029·1	1,341·7	1,398·0	1,712·9	525·7	110·5	—	—	97·5	68·1
1970	7,345·4	1,343·8	1,515·2	1,954·9	551·8	140·2	—	—	101·5	65·7
									---(*m*)	
1971	8,337·0	1,597·4	1,640·5	2,284·2	605·8	156·0	—	—	61·4	74·0
										---(*n*)
1972	9,561·3	1,701·7	1,911·7	2,653·9	687·9	171·1	—	—	71·1	61·6
										---(*n*)
1973	11,058·9	2,150·9	2,179·6	3,135·0	766·5	179·0	—	—	74·5	11·9
1974	13,602·0	2,960·5	2,414·6	3,897·3	870·4	199·1	—	—	78·1	13·6
1975	15,920·7	3,407·6	2,927·3	5,651·8	1,010·3	—	—	—	59·1	21·4
1976	19,801·0	3,457·7	3,795·7	7,666·1	959·1	—	—	—	78·5	21·6
1977	21,804·1	3,254·0	4,151·0	8,639·8	1,085·1	—	—	—	81·3	23·8
1978	23,155·2	2,815·9	4,686·7	9,138·3	1,242·7	—	—	—	95·8	31·0
1979	25,734·8	2,751·1	5,166·6	10,103·8	1,359·4	—	—	—	103·0	27·9
1980	29,979·7	3,135·9	6,122·5	11,684·4	1,595·1	—	—	—	122·8	32·5

(*a*) This is a very slight break resulting from the change in source.
(*b*) The inclusion of receipts from Pilotage and Light Dues was discontinued, resulting in a fall of about 2 per cent.
(*c*) From this year loans advanced out of the London County Council Consolidated Loans Fund are included. The break is very small.
(*d*) This covers docks, piers, and similar services.
(*e*) These figures do not include loans raised by school boards outside London and the county boroughs, the amount of which was never ascertained, but was probably a little over 1·0.
(*f*) These unusually large figures result from the formation of the Metropolitan Water Board.
(*g*) These unusually large figures result from the formation of the Port of London Authority.
(*h*) Takings from motor bus and trolley undertakings are included subsequently.
(*i*) Subsequently all receipts which were intended for expenditure on capital works were excluded from the individual items. No explanation can be offered for the small change in total receipts.
(*j*) From 1936 rates on local authority houses were excluded both as income and expenditure.
(*k*) Including grants to certain local authorities which lost rate income owing to war conditions, and the following grants and reimbursements for services arising solely from the war:

1939	2·8	1941	84·5	1943	83·7	1945	65·5
1940	42·5	1942	101·5	1944	69·6		

(*l*) Including payments made by nationalised undertakings in lieu of rates.
(*m*) Subsequently excluding Passenger Transport Executives.
(*n*) Excluding the Mersey Dock and Harbour Board from 1972, and the Port of London Authority and similarly constituted bodies from 1973.

Public Finance 12. Expenditure of Local Authorities other than out of Loans 1868–1929 and Other than on Capital Works 1929–80 – England & Wales

NOTES

[1] Sources: 1868 (Total Expenditure) – *S.P.* 1870, LV (the Goschen Report); 1868 (all other items) – P. G. Craigie in the *Journal of the Statistical Society* (1877) (revision of the Goschen Report); 1875 (Education, Poor Relief, and Lunacy) – Craigie, *loc. cit.*; 1872–1902 (all figures) – *Local Taxation Returns*, published annually in sessional papers; 1903–14 (Public Baths, Refuse Disposal, and Fire Service) and 1903–7 (Housing) – *ibid.*; all other figures – *Abstract*.

[2] The financial years of the various authorities did not always end on the same date, though the majority ended on 25 or 31 March. The figures are aggregates for the financial years ended in the years shown.

(in £ million)

		Principal Constituent Items									
	Total Expenditure	Education	Libraries and Museums	Poor Relief (*a*)	Housing	Highways and Bridges	Public Lighting	Fire Service	Sewerage	Refuse Disposal	Police
1868	30·2	..	...	7·4	...	...	...	...	...	...	...
1870	27·3	...	...	...	...	...	...	...	...	...	...
1871	29·9	...	...	...	...	...	...	...	...	...	...
1872	31·2	...	...	...	...	...	...	...	...	...	...
1873	32·7	...	...	...	...	...	...	...	...	...	...
1874	36·4	...	...	...	...	...	...	...	...	...	...
1875	40·7	2·2	...	6·7	...	...	...	...	...	...	...
1876	43·3	...	...	...	...	...	...	...	...	...	...
1877	48·4	...	...	...	...	...	...	...	...	...	...
1878	49·3	...	...	...	...	...	...	...	...	...	...
1879	52·2	...	...	...	...	...	...	...	...	...	...
1880	50·3	3·3	...	7·0	...	...	...	...	...	...	3·1
1881	52·6	3·2	...	7·1	...	5·7	...	...	...	...	3·1
1882	55·5	3·4	...	7·2	...	6·1	...	...	...	...	3·2
	---(*d*)	---(*d*)		---(*d*)		---(*d*)					---(*d*)
1883	43·5	2·7	...	6·8	...	6·3	...	...	0·6	...	3·3
1884	43·4	2·8	0·13	6·8	0·10	5·7	0·9	0·2	0·8	...	3·4
1885	44·1	3·2	0·14	6·8	0·11	5·6	0·9	0·2	0·9	...	3·5
1886	44·5	3·5	0·14	6·6	0·11	5·8	0·9	0·2	0·8	...	3·5
1887	45·1	3·6	0·14	6·5	0·05	5·7	0·9	0·2	1·0	...	3·8
1888	45·8	3·8	0·17	6·7	0·02	5·8	0·9	0·2	1·0	...	3·8
1889	47·1	3·9	0·18	6·6	0·02	6·1	0·9	0·2	0·9	...	3·9
1890	48·2	4·1	0·19	6·6	0·02	6·3	0·9	0·2	1·0	...	3·9
1891	50·7	4·3	0·22	6·7	0·02	6·4	1·0	0·2	1·1	...	4·1
1892	53·1	4·8	0·27	6·9	0·02	6·9	1·0	0·2	1·1	...	4·5
1893	56·2	5·4	0·29	7·2	0·04	7·4	1·0	0·3	1·2	...	4·7
1894	57·8	5·7	0·31	7·5	0·03	7·7	1·1	0·3	1·4	...	4·8
1895	59·7	6·4	0·32	7·7	0·04	7·4	1·1	0·3	1·3	...	4·6
1896	62·2	6·9	0·34	7·9	0·04	7·7	1·2	0·3	1·4	...	4·7
1897	64·7	7·5	0·37	8·0	0·03	7·9	1·2	0·3	1·4	...	4·8
1898	67·8	7·8	0·38	8·3	0·04	8·2	1·3	0·3	1·6	1·1	4·9
1899	71·2	8·2	0·39	8·6	0·05	8·7	1·3	0·4	1·7	1·4	5·0
1900	76·0	8·8	0·40	8·4	0·05	9·1	1·5	0·4	1·8	1·7	5·1
1901	82·4	9·5	0·42	8·8	0·09	9·6	1·8	0·4	1·9	1·8	5·2
1902	87·4	10·1	0·46	9·3	0·09	12·4	1·9	0·5	1·9	1·9	5·5
		---(*e*)	---(*e*)	---(*e*)		---(*e*)	---(*e*)		---(*e*)		---(*e*)
1903	92·9	12·9	0·53	10·7	0·10	12·7	2·0	0·5	3·9	2·0	5·8
1904	[98·5](*f*)	[15·6](*f*)	0·52	11·1	0·12	13·1	2·0	0·5	4·1	2·1	6·0
1905	[107·7](*f*)	[21·9](*f*)	0·63	11·5	0·12	13·5	2·0	0·5	4·2	2·1	6·1
1906	111·3	23·5	0·72	11·7	0·18	13·6	2·1	0·5	4·4	2·0	6·2
1907	114·1	24·7	0·75	11·6	0·20	13·5	2·2	0·5	4·5	2·1	6·3
					---(*e*)						
1908	118·7	25·7	0·73	12·0	0·56	13·5	2·2	0·6	4·6	2·1	6·4

See p. 618 for footnotes.

Public Finance 12. *continued*

(in £ million)

Principal Constituent Items

	Total Expend-iture	Educa-tion	Libraries and Museums	Poor Relief (*a*)	Housing	High-ways and Bridges	Public Lighting	Fire Service	Sewer-age	Refuse Disposal	Police
1909	121·9	26·8	0·70	12·3	0·55	13·9	2·2	0·6	4·7	2·1	6·6
1910	125·8	27·5	0·71	12·4	0·58	14·1	2·2	0·6	4·7	2·2	6·7
1911	129·4	28·3	0·72	12·5	0·58	14·6	2·3	0·6	4·8	2·2	6·9
	---(*g*)	---(*h*)									
1912	134·1	29·7	0·68	11·9	0·61	15·0	2·3	0·7	4·9	2·3	7·2
1913	140·3	30·6	0·69	12·3	0·64	15·6	2·3	0·7	5·1	2·4	7·5
1914	148·3	31·8	0·70	12·3	0·62	16·5	2·3	0·7	5·2	2·5	7·7
					---(*h*)	---(*h*)			---(*h*)		
1915	153·3	32·8	0·68	12·9	0·9	17·6	2·3	0·9	5·8	2·6	8·2
								---(*e*)		---(*e*)	
1916	154·0	32·6	0·68	13·0	1·0	15·8	1·7	0·9	8·6		8·1
1917	156·1	32·4	0·64	13·0	1·1	14·7	1·1	0·9	8·9		8·0
1918	170·0	37·2	0·69	13·7	1·0	15·1	1·1	1·0	9·6		8·6
1919	193·5	42·6	0·76	14·9	1·1	15·8	1·3	1·1	6·2	4·6	10·3
1920	265·5	56·4	1·0	19·2	1·4	26·4	2·4	1·4	7·3	6·5	17·4
1921	343·2	73·9	1·4	25·3	4·3	39·1	3·5	1·9	8·7	8·3	20·8
1922	365·0	77·8	1·5	34·8	10·2	42·1	3·7	2·0	8·9	7·9	21·3
						---(*k*)					
1923	346·7	74·8	1·5	35·7	14·6	40·2	3·7	1·9	8·1	6·9	18·9
1924	343·3	72·3	1·5	32·5	16·3	41·4	3·6	1·9	8·3	6·5	18·8
1925	354·9	73·9	1·6	31·4	18·1	45·8	3·7	2·0	8·7	6·6	19·1
1926	373·1	75·5	1·7	34·6	21·3	48·8	3·9	2·1	9·0	6·8	20·0
1927	402·2	76·0	1·8	43·7	26·2	49·5	3·9	2·1	9·3	6·9	21·0
1928	402·6	77·0	1·8	34·7	32·2	52·1	4·1	2·2	9·6	6·9	21·1
1929	414·7	81·7	1·9	33·4	36·6	51·4	4·2	2·2	9·8	6·9	21·4
	---(*l*)	---(*l*)	---(*l*)	---(*l*)	---(*l*)	---(*l*)	---(*l*)	---(*l*)	---(*l*)	---(*l*)	---(*l*)
	405·9	81·1	1·9	33·4	32·6	47·6	4·2	2·2	9·7	6·9	21·3
1930	423·7	83·7	2·0	33·9	35·1	50·9	4·3	2·3	10·1	7·1	21·7
1931	432·7	86·6	2·2	32·0	38·0	52·4	4·5	2·4	10·5	7·2	22·3
1932	435·0	85·1	2·2	30·4	40·1	51·9	4·6	2·5	10·7	7·3	22·3
1933	430·3	82·6	2·2	32·7	41·8	46·8	4·6	2·4	11·1	7·1	21·5
1934	433·2	83·4	2·3	33·9	42·8	46·3	4·7	2·5	11·4	7·1	21·5
1935	454·8	86·9	2·5	36·2	44·4	47·5	4·9	2·6	11·6	7·2	22·3
1936	470·9	92·2	2·6	37·8	39·8	48·6	5·1	2·7	11·8	7·5	23·9
1937	484·6	95·0	2·8	37·2	40·6	50·1	5·4	2·9	12·0	7·8	24·7

See p. 618 for footnotes.

(in £ million)

Principal Constituent Items

	Public Baths, etc.	Commons, Parks, etc.	Lunacy (*a*)	Hospitals	Water Supply	Gas Supply	Electricity Supply	Transport Services	Harbours, etc. (*b*)	Loan Charges (*c*)
1868	...	...	0·9	...	...	...	...	...	...	4·6
1870	...	...	...	...	...	...	...	...	...	...
1871	...	...	...	...	...	...	...	...	...	...
1872	...	...	...	...	...	...	...	...	...	...
1873	...	...	...	...	...	...	...	...	...	...
1874	...	...	...	...	...	...	...	...	...	...
1875	...	...	1·4	...	...	...	...	...	...	8·5
1876	...	...	...	...	...	...	...	...	...	...
1877	...	...	...	...	...	...	...	...	...	...
1878	...	...	...	...	...	...	...	...	...	...
1879	...	...	...	...	...	...	...	...	...	...
1880	...	...	1·4	...	...	...	...	...	...	...
1881	...	...	1·4	...	...	...	...	...	0·9	...
1882	...	...	1·5	...	...	...	...	...	1·4	10·6
									3·8	14·4
			---(*d*)						---(*d*)	---(*d*)
1883	...	...	1·3	...	0·8	2·6	...	...	1·1	10·5
1884	0·11	0·14	1·4	0·1	0·9	2·4	...	...	1·2	9·8
1885	0·12	0·15	1·5	0·1	0·8	2·4	...	--	1·2	9·9
1886	0·12	0·22	1·5	0·1	0·8	2·4	...	--	1·2	10·0
1887	0·12	0·17	1·4	0·1	0·8	2·5	...	--	1·1	10·7
1888	0·12	0·19	1·5	0·1	0·9	2·5	...	--	1·1	10·7
1889	0·13	0·21	1·5	0·2	0·9	2·6	...	--	1·1	11·2
1890	0·14	0·23	1·5	0·2	0·9	2·8	...	--	1·2	11·1
1891	0·16	0·27	1·6	0·2	1·0	3·3	...	--	1·4	11·4
1892	0·17	0·33	1·7	0·2	1·0	3·5	...	--	1·3	11·4
1893	0·21	0·35	1·8	0·3	1·0	3·5	...	0·1	1·4	11·9
1894	0·21	0·37	1·8	0·5	1·1	3·7	...	0·1	1·4	12·4
1895	0·22	0·40	1·8	0·4	1·1	3·6	...	0·1	1·4	12·7
1896	0·24	0·41	1·9	0·4	1·2	3·6	...	0·1	1·5	13·2
1897	0·25	0·44	2·0	0·4	1·2	3·8	0·2	0·2	1·6	13·8
1898	0·30	0·52	2·1	0·4	1·3	4·0	0·2	0·3	1·6	14·2
1899	0·31	0·51	2·2	0·5	1·4	4·1	0·3	0·7	1·6	14·7
1900	0·33	0·57	2·3	1·0	1·5	4·6	0·6	1·1	1·7	15·7
1901	0·37	0·58	2·5	1·0	1·6	5·7	0·8	1·4	1·9	16·9
1902	0·38	0·63	2·6	1·3	1·7	5·7	1·0	1·8	1·8	18·3
		---(*e*)	---(*e*)	---(*e*)	---(*e*)	---(*e*)	---(*e*)	---(*e*)	---(*e*)	
1903	0·39	1·1	3·3	2·0	4·6	6·7	1·9	3·3	3·3	20·3
1904	0·41	1·1	3·4	1·8	4·7	6·7	2·2	4·2	3·5	21·7
1905	0·44	1·1	3·4	1·7	7·4	6·6	2·5	4·9	3·6	24·5
1906	0·48	1·2	3·5	1·7	8·5	6·5	2·7	5·4	3·7	26·7
1907	0·46	1·2	3·6	1·9	8·0	6·5	3·0	6·5	3·9	27·2
1908	0·50	1·2	3·6	2·0	8·1	7·1	3·3	7·0	4·2	28·6

See p. 618 for footnotes.

(in £ million)

Principal Constituent Items

	Public Baths, etc.	Commons, Parks, etc.	Lunacy (*a*)	Hospitals and Health Services	Water Supply	Gas Supply	Electricity Supply	Transport Services	Harbours, etc. (*b*)	Loan Charges (*c*)
1909	0·51	1·3	3·7	1·9	8·3	7·2	3·3	7·3	4·3	29·3
1910	0·50	1·4	3·8	1·9	8·4	6·9	3·5	7·4	6·8	30·8
1911	0·51	1·4	3·9	1·8	8·6	7·2	3·7	8·0	7·0	31·1 ---(*g*)
1912	0·54	1·5	4·0	1·9	8·7	7·3	4·2	8·6	7·3	33·0
1913	0·56	1·5	4·2	2·0	9·0	7·8	4·7	9·2 ---(*i*)	8·4	35·0
1914	0·61	1·6 ---(*h*)	4·3 ---(*h*)	2·4	9·1	8·5	5·2	10·0	7·8	34·4
1915	0·88 ---(*e*)	1·7	4·5	2·9 ---(*j*)	9·4	8·6	5·5	10·5	8·2	35·3
1916	0·92	1·6	4·8	3·8	9·8	9·8	6·6	10·7	8·8	35·9
1917	0·93	1·5	5·0	3·8	10·2	10·8	8·0	11·5	8·9	36·5
1918	1·0	1·5	5·3	4·4	10·4	12·2	9·3	12·9	9·6	36·6
1919	1·1	1·7	5·7	5·4	11·3	13·8	10·7	15·6	11·0	36·5
1920	1·5	2·5	7·3	8·8 ---(*j*)	13·1	17·2	13·4	20·5	15·3	37·8
1921	2·0	3·5	9·3	13·6	15·6	21·7	17·9	25·2	17·7	41·7
1922	1·8	3·9	9·5	13·6	16·4	20·8	17·4	24·4	16·4	51·5
1923	1·6	3·5	8·9	11·9	15·1	16·8	16·0	22·5	15·3	57·6
1924	1·7	3·8	9·0	11·3	15·4	16·8	17·6	21·7	14·3	59·8
1925	1·7	4·2	9·0	11·6	15·8	17·0	19·1	22·5	14·2	61·5
1926	1·7	4·4	9·4	12·2	17·0	16·7	20·4	23·7	14·2	68·8
1927	1·8	4·5	9·6	13·1	17·3	21·4	25·2	24·1	13·8	74·2
1928	1·8	4·7	9·7	13·2	17·6	17·4	24·1	25·1	15·0	83·4
1929	1·9 ---(*l*)	5·0 ---(*l*)	9·9 ---(*l*)	13·8 ---(*l*)	18·2 ---(*l*)	16·8 ---(*l*)	25·5 ---(*l*)	26·1 ---(*l*)	14·5 ---(*l*)	89·4
	1·9	4·8	9·9	12·7	18·1	16·9	26·0	25·8	13·9	
1930	2·0	5·2	10·6	11·5	19·0	16·9	28·6	26·7	13·9	93·2
1931	2·2	5·4	10·8	16·1	19·3	16·7	30·4	27·0	13·4	99·6
1932	2·2	5·5	10·8	19·3	19·3	16·3	32·2	26·9	13·2	102·1
1933	2·4	5·3	11·0	20·2	19·6	16·0	34·2	26·2	12·2	106·7
1934	2·6	5·5	11·4	21·3	20·2	16·1	36·6	22·3	12·5	117·9
1935	2·6	5·7	11·8	22·6	20·5	16·1	40·3	21·8	12·7	109·3
1936	2·7	6·0	12·5	24·4	20·9	16·4	43·3	22·2	13·0	108·6
1937	2·8	6·3	13·2	26·6	21·7	17·1	47·9	23·0	13·2	111·0

See p. 618 for footnotes.

Public Finance 12. *continued*

(in £ million)

Principal Constituent Items

	Total Expenditure	Education	Libraries and Museums	Poor Relief (*a*) (*m*)	Housing (*n*)	Highways and Bridges	Public Lighting	Fire Service	Sewerage	Refuse Disposal	Police	Public Baths etc.
1938	505·6	98·0	3·0	34·3	42·3	49·6	5·6	3·0	12·5	8·3	25·3	3·0
1939	532·8	100·4	3·2	35·3	44·9	50·4	5·8	3·1	12·7	8·5	26·1	3·1
1940	578·8	98·6	3·2	35·3	47·5	44·7	3·1	3·4	12·8	8·7	31·0	3·1
1941	631·1	99·5	3·2	31·2	48·0	39·3	1·6	3·7	13·0	10·0	34·0	3·1
1942	707·4	105·4	3·5	28·3	48·1	38·9	1·5	29·4	13·3	11·2	37·4	3·2
1943	694·3	113·4	3·6	27·6	47·7	39·8	1·5	14·0	13·4	12·5	37·4	3·3
1944	698·1	120·5	3·9	28·4	47·6	38·9	1·5	6·9	13·7	12·8	36·1	3·4
1945	729·1	128·1	4·1	30·0	48·5	39·8	2·4	5·0	13·8	13·1	34·9	3·5
1946	779·9	156·3	4·4	32·5	49·1	43·4	4·8	3·5	13·8	14·0	35·1	3·7
1947	873·7	183·2	5·5	37·3	53·7	56·6	5·5	3·4	14·9	16·1	36·1	4·4
1948	959·9	209·4	6·5	42·5	61·0	61·2	5·7	3·5	15·6	18·3	41·1	4·9
	---(*r*)				---(*s*)							
1949	866·2	236·4	7·6	11·7	70·1	58·6	7·2	12·2	16·6	19·8	44·1	5·2
	---(*r*)											
1950	849·1	257·1	8·3	—	80·8	62·8	8·5	13·8	17·7	20·6	48·6	5·5
1951	887·4	268·7	8·8	—	91·2	62·8	9·1	14·9	18·0	21·7	54·4	5·6
1952	987·7	318·2	10·0	—	104·2	70·0	10·0	16·5	19·2	24·3	61·5	6·0
1953	1,062·3	345·4	10·7	—	122·2	74·4	11·0	17·9	20·8	26·2	66·3	6·3
1954	1,127·5	364·5	11·2	—	143·4	77·8	11·7	18·6	22·2	26·9	69·1	6·6
1955	1,225·3	409·1	12·1	—	163·7	84·6	12·2	19·1	23·7	28·0	71·8	6·7
1956	1,330·8	451·3	13·2	—	198·0	90·3	13·4	20·4	25·8	30·8	78·8	7·4
					---(*t*)							
1957	1,497·1	527·1	15·1	—	221·9	96·4	14·7	22·2	29·8	33·6	91·6	8·3
1958	1,630·2	587·0	16·5	—	244·9	103·9	15·7	24·1	33·4	35·3	95·2	8·8
1959	1,731·3	633·9	17·7	—	262·7	105·7	16·8	25·5	36·7	36·9	102·6	9·1
1960	1,865·7	696·8	19·6	—	279·1	112·8	17·6	27·1	40·0	38·1	108·2	9·4
1961	2,018·5	752·4	21·8	—	301·2	119·9	18·6	29·2	43·9	41·0	122·2	9·8
1962	2,232·3	830·7	24·1	—	332·7	133·7	19·9	32·0	49·2	45·2	136·8	11·0
1963	2,446·9	929·7	26·3	—	355·8	149·3	21·2	36·2	53·8	47·9	146·5	12·1
1964	2,667·5	1,019·3	28·8	—	386·5	165·8	22·1	38·7	58·3	50·9	162·4	12·9
1965	2,902·8	1,101·1	32·0	—	435·4	178·0	23·7	42·7	66·0	54·8	176·1	14·2
1966	3,306·4	1,262·4	37·0	—	500·0	197·1	25·6	46·7	75·0	62·3	196·9	16·6
1967	3,621·4	1,386·2	41·1	—	558·0	210·6	27·2	51·1	85·0	68·6	220·0	18·7
1968	3,988·4	1,525·6	46·2	—	619·0	247·2		55·5	94·5	75·5	245·6	21·3
1969	4,322·3	1,644·2	50·0	—	699·8	278·6		59·5	106·7	82·1	263·9	23·7
1970	5,405·3	1,894·7	58·3	—	797·2	284·8		67·0	131·9	95·8	303·2	...(*u*)
1971	6,185·5	2,145·5	66·8	—	896·5	305·2		75·1	150·8	109·0	367·5	31·5
1972	7,080·7	2,492·1	78·2	—	981·0	344·0		90·4	169·9	124·7	425·6	35·8
1973	8,004·2	2,902·8	91·0	—	1,150·2	415·6		106·0	196·3	143·5	466·7	41·0
1974	9,732·6	3,356·7	105·8	—	1,491·2	475·7		122·8	242·1	166·9	534·8	49·3
	---(*r*)											
1975	1,1734·3	4,404·4	139·4	—	2,033·2	559·9		165·2	—	229·7	660·9	...(*v*)
1976	1,4961·5	5,640·0	178·0	—	2,539·8	761·6		216·2	—	290·5	869·0	...
1977	17,132·6	6,434·5	204·6	—	3,036·9	1,104·6		247·9	—	328·6	1,033·1	...
1978	18,768·1	7,031·7	225·3	—	3,289·1	1,216·9		252·3	—	373·3	1,129·4	...
1979	21,409·8	7,965·8	253·9	—	3,809·9	1,300·3		305·9	—	428·1	1,272·4	...
1980	25,264·9	9,117·7	292·2	—	4,624·1	1,472·1		378·5	—	532·3	1,639·6	...

See p. 618 for footnotes.

Public Finance 12. *continued*

(in £ million)
Principal Constituent Items

	Commons, Parks, etc.	Lunacy (a) (m)	Health Services (o)	Welfare Services (p)	Local Health Authority Services (q)	Water Supply	Gas Supply (m)	Electricity Supply (m)	Transport Services	Harbours, etc. (b)	Loan Charges (c)
1938	6·9	14·3	30·2	—	—	22·5	17·9	52·5	24·2	14·1	114·7
1939	7·1	15·0	33·3	—	—	23·4	18·1	56·9	25·0	13·9	118·1
1940	6·7	15·3	32·8	—	—	24·4	18·8	59·6	25·1	14·3	118·8
1941	6·2	15·8	31·7	—	—	25·4	20·8	64·7	26·9	13·1	120·9
1942	6·1	16·6	33·0	—	—	27·0	23·9	74·0	30·5	14·2	120·6
1943	6·3	17·1	35·4	—	—	27·4	26·1	76·3	33·1	15·0	120·8
1944	6·6	17·9	39·6	—	—	27·2	28·1	81·4	35·0	18·3	121·2
1945	7·0	19·0	42·9	—	—	28·6	30·6	87·6	36·4	21·2	120·4
1946	7·8	19·9	49·4	—	—	29·2	32·9	94·2	37·7	19·4	112·2
1947	9·6	23·1	60·4	—	—	30·4	37·2	108·3	40·7	20·5	111·4
1948	11·3	26·6	72·7	—	—	32·1	40·6	119·0	44·4	22·8	117·0
			---(o)								
1949	12·5	7·5	24·4	16·3	24·5	33·3	46·9	—	48·3	23·7	101·6
			---(o)								
1950	13·8	—	9·6	25·0	32·1	35·5	3·8	—	49·9	25·4	111·2
1951	14·6	—	9·6	27·1	36·0	36·6	—	—	51·9	26·1	122·5
1952	15·8	—	10·5	31·7	38·5	38·4	—	—	56·7	29·8	136·8
1953	16·9	—	11·0	35·5	42·9	41·0	—	—	60·3	29·5	157·4
1954	17·6	—	11·3	37·9	43·0	44·0	—	—	61·2	32·9	183·5
1955	18·5	—	11·5	39·9	45·1	45·8	—	—	62·9	33·5	209·1
1956	20·4	—	12·7	42·6	49·1	49·9	—	—	66·2	37·2	236·5
1957	22·3	—	14·3	46·6	54·1	53·7	—	—	70·5	38·3	270·7
1958	24·1	—	15·4	50·4	57·8	58·7	—	—	73·6	40·3	311·5
1959	26·3	—	16·6	53·9	61·7	60·4	—	—	75·0	41·2	342·8
1960	27·1	—	17·7	57·3	68·1	63·8	—	—	76·1	43·8	372·3
1961	28·9	—	18·5	62·1	72·5	67·7	—	—	78·7	45·8	415·0
1962	30·7	—	20·8	68·9	81·3	72·0	—	—	82·8	48·2	466·4
1963	32·5	—	22·7	75·9	87·3	77·3	—	—	83·9	51·4	508·4
1964	36·1	—	24·6	84·6	95·7	80·8	—	—	89·1	53·9	561·9
1965	38·7	—	27·1	91·8	104·5	87·8	—	—	90·9	57·7	645·6
1966	43·3	—	30·1	105·6	118·0	94·8	—	—	95·4	60·6	740·0
1967	46·9	—	33·3	119·0	128·8	103·8	—	—	98·3	56·0	832·2
					---(q)						
1968	50·8	—	36·8	133·5	141·2	110·4	—	—	99·1	58·4	934·7
1969	55·9	—	37·8	147·5	152·7	120·1	—	—	102·5	72·6	1,059·2
1970	66·5	—	[71·6](u)	168·3	167·6	115·4	—	—	111·0	70·5	1,210·8
1971	74·2	—	50·3	199·4	199·2	160·8	—	—	68·8	78·4	1,371·0
				---(p)	---(q)					---(w)	
				Personal Social Services							
1972	89·0	—	55·8	314·4	141·9	175·7	—	—	75·9	63·2	1,449·3
										---(w)	
1973	107·0	—	62·7	390·5	165·0	185·5	—	—	82·0	13·3	1,620·9
1974	134·0	—	71·1	522·4	193·6	208·2	—	—	90·3	14·3	2,083·4
	---(v)				---(q)						
1975	263·6	—	104·1	753·1	1·3	—	—	—	74·2	23·5	2,290·4
1976	360·9	—	143·2	963·4	1·9	—	—	—	90·6	24·0	2,617·3
1977	414·4	—	168·1	1,131·2	2·1	—	—	—	90·5	25·5	3,116·1
1978	458·4	—	185·2	1,267·1	2·3	—	—	—	99·9	29·8	3,209·3
1979	527·3	—	213·4	1,441·0	2·5	—	—	—	108·9	36·5	3,643·6
1980	648·1	—	270·5	1,755·4	3·0	—	—	—	135·4	43·4	4,428·8

See p. 618 for footnotes.

(*a*) Expenditure on the maintenance of pauper lunatics is included under *Lunacy*.
(*b*) This covers docks, piers, and similar services.
(*c*) Figures under this heading are only transferred to total expenditure in so far as they are not already included under some other heading.
(*d*) Prior to 1883 all figures include expenditure out of loans, which was not at that time separately distinguished.
(*e*) Loan charges attributable to these items are not included with them previously.
(*f*) These figures are incomplete, since the total amounts spent in 1904, and the amounts spent on maintenance in 1905, by school boards outside London and the country boroughs were never ascertained.
(*g*) There is a very slight break in these series (and a completely negligible one in most other series) as a result of the London County Council substituting actual repayments of debt for payments into their sinking fund in reckoning their loan charges.
(*h*) Some small, previously unascertainable portion of loan charges is included from these dates.
(*i*) Prior to 1914 this heading covered tramways and light railways only, but from that year expenditure on motor bus and trolley undertakings is included.
(*j*) Maternity and child welfare and other public health expenditure was included under this heading in two stages, in 1916 and 1921.
(*k*) From 1923 expenditure on ferries is no longer included, making a difference of a little over 1 per cent.
(*l*) The first figure for 1929 excludes all expenditure out of loans, and is comparable with earlier years. The second figure excludes all expenditure on capital works, but may include a small amount of current expenditure out of loans, and is comparable with later years.
(*m*) Owing to legislative changes in the postwar years, these items disappear or emerge under other headings between 1948 and 1950.
(*n*) Including amounts advanced under the Small Dwellings Acquisition Acts.
(*o*) Hospitals etc. are excluded from 5 July 1948. Subsequently this heading mainly covers Public (Environmental) Health.
(*p*) Care of the Aged, Handicapped and Homeless, Protection of Children etc. From 1972 the heading includes some other items previously included under *Local Health Authority Services*.
(*q*) From 1968 Port Health Authorities are included (an addition of 0·6). Some Local Health Authority Services were transferred to *Personal Social Services* in 1972, and the remainder went to Regional Health Authorities in 1975.
(*r*) These breaks result from the transfer of various local authority services to nationalised undertakings, the National Health Service, and regional authorities.
(*s*) Subsequently excluding expenditure on town planning.
(*t*) Subsequently including expenditure in respect of requisitioned houses.
(*u*) Public baths are included with *Health Services* in 1970.
(*v*) Public baths are included with *Commons, Parks, etc.* from 1975. There were other additions under the latter heading.
(*w*) The Mersey Dock and Harbour Board is excluded from 1972 and the Port of London Authority and similarly constituted bodies from 1973.

Public Finance 13. Expenditure of Local Authorities out of Loans 1883–1929, and on Capital Works 1929–80 – England & Wales

NOTES

[1] SOURCES: 1883–1903 – *Local Taxation Returns*, published annually in sessional papers; 1904–80 – *Abstract* and *Local Government Financial Statistics*.

[2] The financial years of the various authorities did not always end on the same date in the earlier years, though the majority ended on 25th or 31st March and all were standardised at the latter date from 1929 at the latest. The figures are aggregates of the financial years ended in the years shown.

(in £ million)

		Principal Constituent Items											
	Total Expenditure	Education	Workhouses, etc.	Housing, etc. (*a*)	Highways and Bridges	Lunatic Asylums	Hospitals, etc. (*b*)	Sewerage	Water Supply	Gas Supply	Electricity Supply	Transport Services	Harbours, etc. (*c*)	Commons, Parks, etc.
1883	9·4	...	0·4	...	...	...	...	1·1	1·2	0·4	...	...	1·1	...
1884	8·8	1·2	0·5	0·1	1·8	0·3	--	0·9	1·2	0·5	...	0·1	0·7	0·1
1885	9·9	1·4	0·6	--	2·6	0·3	--	1·0	1·2	0·6	...	0·1	0·8	0·1
1886	9·4	1·4	0·6	0·1	2·2	0·2	--	1·1	1·1	0·7	...	0·1	0·6	0·1
1887	8·6	1·0	0·4	0·1	1·9	0·3	0·1	1·0	1·1	0·3	...	--	0·7	0·2
1888	9·3	0·7	0·3	0·2	1·4	0·2	0·1	0·9	3·3	0·2	...	--	0·6	0·2
1889	7·0	0·7	0·3	0·1	0·9	0·2	0·1	0·9	1·5	0·2	...	--	0·5	0·3
1890	7·1	0·8	0·4	0·1	1·1	0·1	0·1	0·9	1·3	0·2	...	--	0·6	0·4
1891	7·2	0·8	0·3	--	1·2	0·3	0·1	1·1	1·3	0·3	--	--	0·4	0·3
1892	10·6	1·0	0·3	0·1	1·2	0·3	0·1	1·2	1·3	0·5	0·1	--	0·5	0·2
1893	10·6	1·2	0·4	0·3	1·3	0·2	0·1	1·2	1·4	0·5	0·2	0·1	0·5	0·5
1894	14·0	1·6	0·7	0·2	1·4	0·4	0·2	1·5	1·7	0·8	0·4	0·2	0·6	0·5
1895	13·4	2·0	0·8	0·2	1·4	0·3	0·2	1·8	1·8	0·6	0·7	0·1	0·6	0·3
1896	13·4	2·3	0·8	0·2	1·6	0·5	0·2	2·2	1·6	0·5	0·6	0·2	0·7	0·2
1897	13·8	2·4	0·8	0·3	1·4	0·7	0·2	1·9	1·4	0·6	1·1	0·1	0·6	0·2
1898	17·1	2·0	1·2	0·3	2·1	0·8	0·2	2·0	1·9	0·8	0·8	1·7	0·9	0·3
1899	21·5	2·0	1·4	0·5	2·3	1·0	0·3	2·1	2·6	1·3	2·1	1·6	1·5	0·3
1900	24·9	2·1	1·2	0·8	3·2	1·0	0·4	2·0	4·2	1·0	2·8	1·4	1·6	0·5
1901	27·9	2·2	1·4	0·5	4·8	1·0	0·5	2·4	2·8	1·3	3·3	2·9	1·1	0·6
1902	33·9	2·6	1·6	0·8	5·4	1·1	0·9	2·6	3·2	1·9	3·9	4·7	1·3	0·6
1903	36·1	2·5	1·8	...	6·4	1·1	0·9	2·5	4·3	1·0	4·2	4·8	1·5	0·8
1904	[30·7](*d*)	[2·1](*d*)	1·3	1·0	4·9	0·8	0·6	2·4	3·8	0·7	3·4	4·3	1·8	0·5
1905	[65·5](*d*)	[2·4](*d*)	1·1	0·7	4·4	1·0	0·7	2·9	37·6(*e*)	0·8	4·2	4·3	2·0	0·4
1906	25·4	2·4	1·0	0·6	3·1	0·9	0·5	2·8	3·2	0·5	2·4	3·1	1·8	0·3
1907	23·4	2·8	0·8	0·5	2·1	0·8	0·3	2·6	2·8	0·4	1·8	4·2	1·5	0·3
1908	19·4	2·6	0·5	0·3	1·9	0·6	0·1	2·0	2·7	0·5	1·5	2·8	1·5	0·3
1909	18·4	3·0	0·5	0·3	1·9	0·3	0·1	2·0	2·9	0·5	1·3	2·0	1·4	0·3
1910	40·6	2·9	0·4	0·4	1·9	0·3	0·1	2·1	2·6	0·4	1·1	2·3	23·1(*f*)	0·3
1911	18·2	3·2	0·4	0·2	1·8	0·3	0·1	1·9	2·7	0·4	1·2	1·4	1·9	0·3
1912	17·1	2·7	0·4	0·2	1·7	0·3	0·1	1·8	2·3	0·4	1·4	1·3	1·4	0·4

See p. 622 for footnotes.

Public Finance 13. *continued*

(in £ million)

	Total Expenditure	Principal Constituent Items: Education	Workhouses, etc.	Housing, etc. (a)	Highways and Bridges	Lunatic Asylums	Hospitals, etc. (b)	Sewerage	Water Supply	Gas Supply	Electricity Supply	Transport Services	Harbours, etc. (c)	Commons, Parks, etc.
1913	18·3	3·0	0·6	0·4	1·9	0·3	0·1	1·7	2·0	0·5	1·6	1·3	1·3	0·4
1914	21·1	2·9	0·6	0·7	3·2	0·5	0·2	1·9	2·0	0·9	1·9	1·3	1·6	0·5
1915	21·8	2·7	0·6	0·9	3·0	0·6	0·3	1·8	1·8	0·7	2·4	1·4	1·6	0·5
1916	11·6	1·3	0·3	0·6	1·2	0·4	0·3	...	1·2	0·4	1·6	0·7	1·5	0·2
1917	5·8	0·3	0·1	0·5	0·4	0·1	0·1	...	0·6	0·3	1·7	0·2	0·7	--
1918	3·6	0·1	--	0·1	0·2	--	0·1	...	0·4	0·1	1·7	0·1	0·4	--
1919	4·6	0·1	--	0·1	0·1	--	0·1	0·1	0·3	0·2	2·1	0·1	1·0	--
1920	23·9	0·7	0·1	4·8	1·2	0·1	0·3	0·7	1·9	0·9	3·6	1·4	2·1	0·2
1921	94·5	1·9	0·2	52·2	---(g) 3·7	0·2	0·9 ---(b) 1·2	2·3	4·0	1·9	8·4	2·8	3·6	0·5
1922	128·7	1·8	0·3	81·8	6·2	0·3	1·1	3·5	5·5	2·9	11·5	3·5	2·6	0·9
1923	71·6	0·9	0·4	29·6	9·0	0·2	0·7	4·6	5·4	2·0	9·3	2·5	1·9	1·1
1924	50·0	0·9	0·5	11·3	8·4	0·2	0·6	4·8	5·2	1·2	8·5	2·1	2·0	1·3
1925	70·3	1·4	0·7	24·0	9·9	0·4	0·9	5·0	6·7	1·4	9·7	2·6	2·4	1·4
1926	100·7	3·1	0·9	47·0	10·0	0·4	1·0	5·6	6·5	1·9	11·8	2·6	2·2	1·8
1927	117·4	4·4	1·1	65·3	9·5	0·5	1·2	4·5	5·3	2·8	12·1	2·7	2·0	1·3
1928	120·0	5·7	1·3	66·2	8·4	0·4	0·9	4·2	4·9	2·3	13·1	2·6	3·7	1·2
	90·5	6·0	1·2	38·1	8·0	0·3	0·9	3·9	4·6	1·5	14·4	2·4	2·4	1·2
1929	---(h)	---(h)	---(h)	---(h)	---(h)	---(h)	---(h)	---(h)	---(h)	---(h)	---(h)	---(h)	---(h)	---(h)
	102·8	6·7	1·2	42·9	11·9	0·4	1·0	4·1	4·9	1·6	14·6	2·8	3·0	1·4
1930	108·9	6·0	0·9	42·8	16·2	0·9	1·2	4·5	5·1	1·5	15·3	2·4	1·7	1·7
1931	110·9	7·8	0·8	37·4	18·9	1·1	1·7	6·5	4·9	1·7	14·3	2·6	1·5	2·2
1932	116·8	9·8	0·6	39·6	19·0	1·1	1·5	9·0	5·5	1·4	13·6	2·7	2·0	1·7
1933	84·8	5·7	1·1	28·2	10·2	1·5	1·0	8·3	4·2	1·2	10·9	1·6	1·4	0·8
1934	89·3	3·9	0·6	30·6	8·7	1·4	0·9	5·7	3·7	1·2	11·4	11·1	1·3	0·8
1935	80·7	4·3	0·8	29·3	7·2	1·2	1·2	5·5	4·0	1·2	12·7	1·8	1·0	1·4
1936	96·9	5·8	0·7	37·7	8·3	1·4	1·7	5·3	4·7	1·4	15·3	1·6	0·9	1·9
1937	116·8	7·9	1·0	44·5	9·7	1·8	2·4	5·5	5·8	1·8	17·4	2·3	1·2	2·5
1938	142·1	11·1	1·2	53·7	12·2	2·2	2·9	6·3	6·2	2·2	19·5	4·0	2·2	3·5
1939	150·8	14·8	1·5	55·1	13·5	2·3	3·6	7·5	7·2	1·8	18·3	2·9	1·4	3·0
1940	117·0	14·4	1·0	29·3	9·8	1·9	3·5	5·7	6·3	1·8	14·9	2·1	1·5	1·4
1941	62·0	6·8	0·3	9·1	3·1	0·8	1·5	2·4	3·8	1·0	11·1	0·3	0·8	0·4

	Total Expenditure	Education	Workhouses, etc.	Housing, etc. (a)	Highways and Bridges	Lunatic Asylums	Hospitals & Public Health (b)	Sewerage	Water Supply	Gas Supply	Electricity Supply	Transport Services	Harbours, etc. (c)	Commons, Parks, etc.	Welfare Services
1942	47·3	1·9	0·2	5·4	1·5	0·3	0·9	1·3	2·8	0·9	11·8	0·1	0·9	0·1	
1943	38·2	0·8	0·1	6·0	1·8	0·1	0·5	1·2	2·1	1·3	12·1	0·4	1·1	0·1	
1944	25·4	0·6	0·1	7·2	0·6	0·1	0·3	0·7	1·6	1·0	8·0	0·5	0·5	0·1	
1945	23·8	0·4	0·1	7·8	1·4	0·1	0·2	0·4	1·2	0·9	6·7	0·7	0·6	0·1	
1946	46·5	0·8	0·1	24·9	0·5	0·2	0·5	0·6	1·6	1·3	11·2	1·1	0·6	0·2	
	(in £ million)														
1947	162·4	2·0	0·4	114·2	1·7	0·2	0·9	1·9	5·0	3·0	22·8	1·9	1·8	0·8	—
1948	303·5	8·3	0·7	221·0	3·4	0·5	1·6	4·5	6·3	4·2	31·4	5·0	1·8	1·0	—
							- - -								
1949	329·5	18·4	0·3	252·3	3·3	0·3	1·0(b)	7·3	11·2	6·0	—	8·1	3·5	1·0	1·2
							- - -								
1950	331·1	28·0	—	233·8	5·1	—	1·9	9·5	15·3	0·7	—	8·9	3·3	1·3	2·9
1951	368·8	39·8	—	248·8	5·8	—	1·9	11·0	17·5	—	—	7·3	4·4	1·5	3·5
1952	426·5	53·5	—	281·7	5·8	—	2·4	15·3	20·8	—	—	4·8	4·6	2·1	4·3
1953	497·8	58·0	—	342·9	6·3	—	2·0	17·6	23·5	—	—	3·7	4·6	2·0	4·2
1954	543·6	58·7	—	373·8	6·5	—	2·0	18·9	24·8	—	—	4·8	5·2	1·4	3·7
1955	525·7	60·1	—	360·2	8·1	—	2·2	19·5	23·8	—	—	3·0	5·0	2·1	3·3
				- - -(a)											
1956	541·1	68·8	—	349·2	10·8	—	2·2	23·7	24·4	—	—	3·7	5·7	2·6	3·9
1957	555·0	86·0	—	338·3	13·5	—	2·0	26·5	28·3	—	—	4·4	6·7	2·2	3·3
1958	528·6	96·3	—	309·9	15·1	—	1·9	27·3	25·8	—	—	3·2	5·4	1·3	3·1
1959	511·9	92·0	—	286·0	21·0	—	2·5	28·3	26·1	—	—	3·0	7·5	1·6	3·4
1960	571·5	89·2	—	321·2	26·5	—	3·5	35·2	28·1	—	—	2·3	7·4	2·6	4·9
1961	620·8	88·2	—	345·6	31·7	—	5·1	37·0	31·7	—	—	1·7	6·2	3·8	5·6
1962	741·2	111·0	—	399·4	35·7	—	7·1	46·4	34·4	—	—	1·7	7·8	5·7	7·3
1963	793·7	122·3	—	414·0	43·9	—	8·6	53·2	36·9	—	—	3·0	6·8	5·6	9·4
1964	979·4	123·9	—	556·1	59·7	—	10·1	58·4	39·0	—	—	3·6	6·0	6·8	10·2
1965	1,225·8	134·6	—	723·4	72·6	—	11·8	62·8	42·1	—	—	2·9	10·1	9·2	15·7
1966	1,289·3	129·3	—	779·9	69·4	—	10·8	62·0	43·8	—	—	3·8	14·2	9·5	15·5
1967	1,411·9	143·6	—	848·9	77·2	—	10·3	73·6	48·9	—	—	4·1	21·4	7·0	15·6
					112·3										
1968	1,563·3	187·6	—	894·7	- - -(i)	—	9·5	91·8	51·1	—	—	4·9	18·6	6·4	17·0
					124·7										
1969	1,597·2	195·4	—	873·6	145·1	—	9·1	101·6	48·5	—	—	7·5	17·3	8·3	18·6
1970	1,707·9	222·1	—	831·3	181·9	—	11·6	115·0	63·5	—	—	10·6	29·6	11·5	20·9
1971	2,050·2	264·1	—	953·6	219·3	—	4·1	142·7	83·5	—	—	6·9	31·8	18·6	24·7

See p. 622 for footnotes.

Public Finance 13. *continued*

(in £ million)

	Total Expendi- ture	Educa- tion	Housing, etc. (*a*)	Highways and Bridges	Hospitals & Public Health (*b*)	Sewer- age	Water Supply	Trans- port Services	Har- bours, etc. (*c*)	Com- mons, Parks, etc.	Personal Social Services
1972	2,231·6	315·3	1,006·7	242·9	5·0	163·6	95·0	6·6	---(*j*) 25·7 ---(*j*)	22·6	37·7
1973	2,794·8	385·3	1,292·7	266·8	6·2	211·7	113·5	7·9	7·6	37·5	50·8
1974	3,739·3	457·4	1,880·5	296·3	6·8	283·8	153·1	18·5	10·3	52·6	74·3
1975	4,075·7	415·0	2,686·7	359·7	6·1	—	—	6·1	10·3	89·9	72·3
1976	4,351·3	450·6	2,756·3	423·0	7·3	—	—	9·6	12·3	95·2	79·7
1977	4,337·9	428·2	2,813·5	399·8	6·9	—	—	9·0	11·8	83·1	68·3
1978	4,039·3	364·7	2,689·7	353·0	6·6	—	—	12·2	6·2	70·3	51·2
1979	4,229·8	332·8	2,788·5	368·8	8·5	—	—	13·5	6·6	82·9	61·6
1980	4,837·6	367·5	3,055·6	459·4	13·3	—	—	13·3	9·7	116·4	77·8

(*a*) Including town and country planning to 1955 and expenditure in respect of requisitioned houses subsequently.

(*b*) Including clinics and maternity services and various public health expenditures. Hospitals etc. are excluded on transfer to the National Health Service on 5 July 1948. From 1921 (2nd line) and again from 1950 additional items are included.

(*c*) Including docks, piers, and similar services.

(*d*) These figures are incomplete, since the total spent in 1904, and the amounts spent on maintenance in 1905, by school boards outside London and the county boroughs was never ascertained.

(*e*) This exceptionally large sum results from the formation of the Metropolitan Water Board.

(*f*) This exceptionally large sum results from the formation of the Port of London Authority.

(*g*) Subsequently excluding ferries. The break is negligible.

(*h*) The first row for 1929 is of expenditure out of loans, the second is of capital expenditures.

(*i*) Subsequently including public lighting.

(*j*) The Mersey Dock and Harbour Board is excluded from 1972, and the Port of London and similarly constituted authorities from 1973.

Public Finance 14. Receipts of Local Authorities – Scotland 1880–1980

NOTES

[1] Sources: *Abstract* and *Scottish Local Government Financial Statistics*.

[2] In the earlier years the financial years of the various authorities did not always end on the same date though the majority ended on 15 May. As from 1976 this was changed to 31 March. The figures are aggregates of the financial years ended in th years shown.

(in £ million)

	Total Receipts	Loans	Rates	Government Grants etc.	Housing Rents etc. (*a*)	Principal Trading Services: Water	Gas	Electricity	Transport
1880	6·1	1·1	2·6	0·6	...	...	...	...	...
1881	6·1	1·0	2·9	0·5	...	...	...	...	...
1882	6·3	1·1	3·1	0·6	...	...	...	...	...
1883	6·2	0·9	3·1	0·6	...	...	...	...	...
1884	7·3	1·7	3·3	0·6	...	...	...	...	...
1885	7·7	2·1	3·3	0·7	...	...	...	...	...
1886	8·1	2·5	3·4	0·7	...	...	...	...	...
1887	7·5	1·8	3·4	0·7	...	...	...	...	...
	...								
1888	7·6(*b*)	1·8	3·5	0·8	...	...	...	...	...
1889	7·5	1·5	3·5	0·8	...	...	...	...	...
1890	7·5	1·4	3·6	1·0	...	...	...	...	...
1891	8·0	1·8	3·2	1·1	...	0·5(*c*)	-- (*c*)	...	...
			---(*c*)						
1892	8·5	2·0	3·3	1·3	...	0·5	--	...	...
1893	9·8	1·9	3·3	1·4	...	0·5	1·2	--	...
1894	10·4	2·1	3·4	1·7	...	0·5	1·2	--	--
1895	11·0	2·0	3·4	1·6	...	0·6	1·2	--	0·2
1896	11·1	1·9	3·7	1·6	...	0·6	1·2	--	0·4
1897	12·7	3·1	3·8	1·7	...	0·6	1·3	0·1	0·4
1898	12·5	2·3	3·8	1·8	...	0·7	1·4	0·1	0·4
1899	13·6	3·1	4·0	1·9	...	0·7	1·5	0·1	0·5
1900	15·2	4·1	4·2	2·0	...	0·7	1·6	0·2	0·5
1901	16·5	4·7	4·5	2·0	...	0·7	1·8	0·2	0·6
1902	16·8	4·1	4·9	2·1	...	0·8	1·8	0·3	0·8
1903	16·7	3·5	5·0	2·1	...	0·8	1·8	0·3	0·8
1904	18·2	4·4	5·3	2·3	...	0·9	1·7	0·4	0·9
1905	17·9	3·6	5·5	2·4	...	0·9	1·7	0·4	1·0
1906	18·0	3·3	5·7	2·4	...	1·0	1·8	0·5	1·1
1907	18·4	3·1	5·9	2·6	0·1	1·0	1·8	0·5	1·2
1908	19·5	3·7	6·1	2·6	0·1	1·0	2·1	0·6	1·2
1909	18·5	2·5	6·4	2·6	0·1	1·0	1·9	0·6	1·2
1910	18·8	2·2	6·6	2·8	0·1	1·0	2·0	0·6	1·3
1911	19·5	2·2	6·8	2·9	0·1	1·1	2·0	0·6	1·3
1912	20·0	2·4	7·0	3·0	0·1	1·1	2·1	0·7	1·4
1913	20·7	2·2	7·4	2·9	0·1	1·1	2·3	0·7	1·4
1914	22·3	3·0	7·7	3·0	0·1	1·2	2·4	0·8	1·5
1915	23·1	3·3	8·2	3·1	0·1	1·2	2·4	0·8	1·5
1916	22·2	1·5	8·2	3·0	0·1	1·3	3·0	1·0	1·6
1917	22·4	1·2	8·1	3·2	0·1	1·3	3·1	1·1	1·7
1918	24·3	1·1	8·5	3·5	0·1	1·3	3·5	1·4	1·9
1919	27·1	1·3	9·3	3·9	0·2	1·4	4·1	1·6	2·1
1920	40·6	4·0	13·0	8·0	0·2	1·6	4·8	1·9	2·8
1921	55·0	9·8	18·1	8·3	0·2	1·9	6·0	2·6	3·7
1922	67·0	19·2	18·4	11·0	0·3	2·0	5·5	2·4	3·7
1923	55·6	10·2	17·3	10·3	0·6	2·0	5·1	2·2	3·6
1924	54·5	7·7	17·7	10·9	0·8	2·0	5·1	2·3	3·6

See p. 625 for footnotes.

Public Finance 14. *continued*

(in £ million)

	Total Receipts	Loans	Rates	Government Grants etc.	Housing Rents etc. (a)	Principal Trading Services			
						Water	Gas	Electricity	Transport
1925	57·5	9·4	18·1	11·4	0·9	2·0	4·7	2·5	3·8
1926	60·9	11·6	18·6	12·1	1·0	2·0	4·6	2·5	3·8
1927	66·4	12·3	20·5	12·8	1·3	2·1	5·6	3·0	3·9
1928	71·0	14·3	21·7	13·4	1·7	2·2	5·4	3·0	4·0
1929	68·1	11·5	21·9	13·3	2·0	2·2	4·7	3·2	4·1
1930	67·8	10·5	19·4	16·1	2·4	2·1	4·6	3·3	4·4
			---(*d*)			---(*d*)			
1931	70·3	10·9	19·6	19·7	2·6	0·8	4·4	3·1	4·5
1932	69·3	11·8	18·1	19·7	2·8	0·7	4·2	3·0	4·5
1933	68·4	10·8	18·6	18·8	3·0	0·7	4·2	3·1	4·4
1934	69·8	10·3	19·6	18·3	3·2	0·8	4·2	3·2	4·4
1935	70·1	9·3	20·1	18·9	3·6	0·8	4·2	3·6	4·7
1936	75·0	11·3	20·5	21·0	3·6	0·8	4·2	3·6	4·7
1937	81·2	15·4	21·6	21·3	3·8	0·9	4·5	4·1	4·9
1938	84·4	17·0	21·8	21·4	4·1	0·9	4·7	4·3	5·1
1939	89·0	19·2	22·4	22·0	4·4	0·9	4·6	4·6	5·4
1940	87·4	13·1	23·5	25·1	4·7	0·9	4·9	4·8	5·2
1941	88·4	8·3	23·7	27·3	5·0	1·1	5·9	5·4	5·9
			---(*e*)	---(*e*)					
1942	90·9	4·7	23·9	30·6	5·1	1·1	6·4	5·9	6·4
1943	89·5	2·9	24·0	28·5	5·3	1·2	7·0	6·0	6·8
1944	90·4	3·1	24·2	27·0	5·4	1·3	7·5	6·5	7·0
1945	91·4	3·6	25·8	25·3	5·5	1·2	8·3	6·7	7·2
1946	102·8	6·7	27·8	29·5	5·4	1·2	9·0	6·7	7·4
1947	127·1	22·7	29·7	32·6	5·8	1·3	9·9	7·6	7·9
1948	148·5	32·7	32·8	38·3	6·6	1·5	10·9	6·8(*f*)	8·2
1949	146·9	37·0	31·2(*g*)	36·6	7·3	1·5	11·3(*f*)	—	8·7
1950	143·3	39·3	31·7	38·2	8·0	1·5	—	—	8·9
1951	152·2	42·5	33·3	39·9	8·7	1·5	—	—	9·5
1952	177·9	54·0	38·2	44·9	9·5	1·6	—	—	10·8
1953	210·2	70·1	46·0	48·8	10·4	1·9	—	—	12·1
1954	225·1	71·7	50·7	54·6	11·6	2·2	—	—	13·0
1955	226·6	63·9	51·2	60·6	12·8	2·3	—	—	13·1
1956	247·1	70·2	55·6	66·8	13·5	2·8	—	—	15·2
1957	261·8	63·1	64·9	74·3	14·8	2·8	—	—	15·5
1958	270·1	60·7	68·8	84·1	10·9	2·9	—	—	15·6
1959	293·2	69·5	73·1	91·8	11·8	3·1	—	—	15·6
1960	304·4	67·0	76·9	96·5	13·7	2·9	—	—	16·1
1961	320·5	66·0	79·7	103·6	14·8	3·2	—	—	17·9
1962	360·2	81·6	94·6	112·6	16·4	3·2	—	—	16·9
1963	387·3	91·7	99·4	119·0	21·3	3·4	—	—	17·9
1964	444·4	119·2	107·9	135·2	23·4	3·5	—	—	17·2
1965	483·2	133·4	116·1	142·9	25·9	3·7	—	—	18·0
1966	530·8	145·1	126·5	157·4	29·7	3·9	—	—	19·4
1967	602·4	163·8	148·6	175·0	33·3	4·1	—	—	18·8
1968	668·9	191·2	150·9	197·3	37·2	4·5	—	—	18·9
1969	746·9	223·8	163·0	211·1	43·3	6·0	—	—	19·9
1970	809·9	228·1	177·1	244·4	52·1	7·3	—	—	21·1
1971	899·1	215·9	198·3	293·9	61·6	8·1	—	—	22·6
1972	1,013·2	222·2	227·4	339·9	68·8	8·9	—	—	24·3
1973	1,163·5	250·6	240·0	406·8	84·4	10·3	—	—	27·0
1974	1,429·0	341·8	267·4	524·6	114·5	11·1	—	—	10·8

Public Finance 14. *continued*

(in £ million)

	Total Receipts	Loans	Rates	Government Grants etc.	Housing Rents etc. (*a*)	Principal Trading Services: Water	Gas	Electricity	Transport
1975	1,802·3	418·6	304·5	727·5	129·2	13·7	—	—	12·8
	---(*h*)	---(*h*)	---(*h*)	---(*h*)	---(*h*)	---(*h*)			---(*h*)
1976	1,986·5	445·0	408·4	874·9	128·6	32·9	—	—	15·1
1977	2,455·1	489·5	470·9	1,048·4	178·8	43·7	—	—	19·9
1978	2,617·0	453·7	544·7	1,196·5	207·4	45·3	—	—	22·7
1979	2,934·5	481·9	616·6	1,308·2	231·5	50·0	—	—	27·7
1980	3,449·8	583·4	717·0	1,564·4	259·3	59·2	—	—	25·7

(*a*) Gross income from council houses, apart from rates and grants.
(*b*) Prior to 1888 receipts from Pilotage and Light Dues are included under this heading. Since these were not recorded separately for the different parts of the United Kingdom it is impossible to indicate the extent of the difference made by their exclusion, but it cannot have been large.
(*c*) Prior to 1891 receipts from water and gas services were included under the heading *Rates*.
(*d*) From 1931 water rates, which formed the bulk of the receipts of water services, were included with *Rates* generally.
(*e*) Up to 1941 *Government Grants etc.* includes Exchequer grants under Local Government (Scotland) Acts and compensation for loss of rates due to the derating provisions of the Acts of 1929. After 1941 these amounts are included under *Rates*.
(*f*) Owing to legislative changes these services disappear or emerge under other headings in the years 1949–50.
(*g*) From 1949 this heading includes payments in lieu of rates made by the British Transport Commission, British Electricity Authority (later South of Scotland Electricity Board), and the North of Scotland Hydro-Electric Board.
(*h*) Local government reorganisation was accompanied by changes in some of the categories of receipts. See also note 2 above.

Public Finance 15. Expenditure of Local Authorities other than out of Loans 1893–1948 and other than on Capital Works 1949–80 – Scotland

NOTES

[1] SOURCES: *Abstract*, and *Scottish Local Government Financial Statistics*.

[2] In the earlier years, the financial years of the various authorities did not always end on the same date, though the majority ended on 15 May. As from 1976 this was changed to 31 March. The figures are aggregates of the financial years ended in the years shown.

(in £ thousand)

	Total Expenditure	Principal Constituent Items								
		Education	Libraries and Museums	Highways and Bridges	Public Lighting	Police	Sewerage	Refuse Disposal	Commons, Parks, etc.	Lunacy (*a*)
1893 (*c*)	[8,976]	[1,575]	[16]	[674]	...	[438]	...	...	[45]	[101]
1894	8,070	1,373	4	663	140	455	...	...	45	11
1895	9,175	1,459	15	669	152	469	...	...	50	18
		---(*d*)	---(*d*)	---(*d*)	---(*d*)	---(*d*)			---(*d*)	---(*d*)
1896	9,315	1,821	18	760	166	504	158	...	82	87
1897	9,495	1,912	21	784	173	493	152	...	96	77
1898	10,188	1,965	26	855	180	513	158	...	116	77
1899	10,521	2,033	21	821	195	513	166	...	116	87
1900	11,103	2,140	28	865	215	532	182	...	131	104
1901	12,072	2,290	38	894	248	547	188	...	143	113
1902	12,472	2,371	42	959	265	568	199	...	135	113
1903	13,029	2,562	38	991	275	604	223	...	141	125
1904	13,579	2,686	42	1,030	278	620	259	...	145	152
1905	13,972	2,825	47	1,055	299	634	288	...	159	155
1906	14,491	2,921	53	1,069	315	636	298	...	160	162
1907	15,062	3,026	64	1,097	323	652	322	444	168	173
1908	15,758	3,186	70	1,121	342	663	335	455	175	190
1909	16,093	3,351	67	1,179	336	670	355	464	243	168
1910	16,457	3,653	66	1,194	332	677	371	462	183	162
1911	16,872	3,773	70	1,243	325	681	402	458	189	169
1912	17,413	3,910	74	1,305	320	707	405	483	204	163
1913	18,310	4,042	77	1,347	316	717	435	509	238	160
1914	19,054	4,156	82	1,413	311	755	469	535	222	157
										---(*a*)
1915	19,536	4,244	85	1,484	293	790	481	571	232	448
1916	20,333	4,270	86	1,368	230	773	499	584	217	512
1917	21,042	4,360	86	1,289	162	787	517	614	216	546
1918	22,958	4,879	94	1,362	195	848	518	696	216	543
1919	26,561	5,736	101	1,542	284	1,125	558	821	230	602
1920	36,666	9,483	119	2,600	517	1,920	626	1,062	333	772
1921	45,226	11,272	150	3,468	630	2,104	690	1,331	436	899
1922	47,274	11,488	169	3,942	634	2,329	666	1,266	540	787
1923	45,356	10,577	177	4,214	658	2,091	651	1,123	511	739
1924	46,698	10,550	187	4,691	652	2,131	680	1,124	587	763
1925	48,481	10,954	188	5,342	652	2,195	694	1,115	642	783
1926	50,219	11,356	200	5,711	671	2,299	709	1,158	676	781
1927	56,199	11,921	209	5,943	727	2,416	761	1,152	706	821
1928	53,994	11,932	208	6,072	770	2,351	758	1,176	690	825
1929	54,682	12,135	214	5,907	757	2,379	787	1,190	706	798
1930	56,811	12,566	225	6,282	774	2,403	791	1,214	716	938
										---(*a*)
1931	57,278	12,947	226	6,619	821	2,449	823	1,242	756	1,309
1932	57,963	12,435	234	7,169	832	2,420	864	1,226	757	1,255
1933	56,505	12,065	225	5,966	797	2,340	863	1,184	708	1,238
1934	57,661	12,024	231	5,494	787	2,349	909	1,201	742	1,208
1935	59,956	12,625	237	5,302	818	2,458	918	1,216	747	1,232
1936	62,610	13,188	245	5,285	853	2,582	957	1,261	783	1,267
1937	64,829	13,566	254	5,559	892	2,625	1,088	1,334	833	1,362

See p. 629 for footnotes.

Public Finance 15. *continued*

(in £ thousand)
Principal Constituent Items

	Hospitals, Clinics, etc.	Housing	Poor Relief (*a*)	Water Supply	Gas Supply	Electricity Supply	Transport Services	Harbours, etc.	Loan Charges (*b*)
1893 (*c*)	[113]	...	[938]	...	...	...	...	[721]	1,631
1894	...	...	936	...	934	15	...	400	1,790
1895	...	...	970	...	1,057	23	193	430	2,269
			---(*d*)		---(*d*)	---(*d*)	---(*d*)	---(*d*)	
1896	132	...	1,027	659	1,254	40	300	894	2,123
1997	148	...	1,069	629	1,253	58	352	883	2,129
1898	163	...	1,100	664	1,302	85	397	939	2,184
1899	185	...	1,105	685	1,423	108	479	950	2,211
			---(*e*)						
1900	205	...	1,109	726	1,619	165	534	925	2,338
1901	241	...	1,155	763	1,897	220	603	963	2,552
1902	264	...	1,184	823	1,759	288	748	961	2,801
1903	244	...	1,234	834	1,751	333	806	1,067	3,046
1904	277	...	1,301	883	1,769	364	864	1,057	3,324
1905	293	...	1,392	928	1,718	410	874	1,031	3,403
1906	278	...	1,406	969	1,750	460	1,070	1,069	3,626
1907	291	138	1,422	987	1,830	516	1,151	1,161	3,852
1908	318	137	1,471	1,036	2,055	562	1,183	1,129	3,898
1909	336	138	1,512	1,047	1,920	564	1,169	1,176	4,046
1910	367	140	1,552	1,047	1,940	570	1,198	1,173	4,178
1911	381	141	1,555	1,073	1,983	617	1,244	1,179	4,160
1912	383	136	1,546	1,108	2,025	658	1,316	1,230	4,251
1913	400	144	1,576	1,148	2,265	716	1,375	1,335	4,367
1914	432	148	1,598	1,191	2,467	775	1,456	1,308	4,506
	---(*f*)		---(*a*)						
1915	550	153	1,388	1,243	2,409	781	1,502	1,327	4,421
1916	598	168	1,412	1,245	2,883	1,003	1,577	1,327	4,592
1917	634	192	1,497	1,283	3,141	1,102	1,573	1,323	4,839
1918	687	193	1,538	1,366	3,564	1,446	1,687	1,357	4,636
1919	778	210	1,668	1,472	4,112	1,619	2,054	1,576	4,686
1920	961	269	2,075	1,671	4,672	1,922	2,931	1,961	4,983
1921	1,251	487	2,797	1,906	6,207	2,573	3,572	2,086	5,446
1922	1,259	979	3,775	1,967	5,972	2,367	3,524	1,989	6,289
1923	1,158	1,610	4,516	1,949	4,463	2,172	3,584	2,034	7,404
1924	1,165	1,919	4,370	2,030	4,839	2,362	3,542	1,915	7,698
1925	1,149	2,120	3,965	2,063	4,910	2,518	3,924	2,065	8,097
1926	1,148	2,436	4,352	2,120	4,750	2,526	3,964	1,902	8,588
1927	1,226	2,871	5,621	2,250	6,793	3,108	3,994	1,913	9,295
1928	1,211	3,536	4,888	2,240	4,559	2,847	4,035	2,043	10,012
1929	1,230	4,133	4,565	2,254	4,386	3,146	4,221	2,056	10,853
1930	1,252	4,669	4,672	2,241	4,468	3,299	4,442	1,967	11,404
			---(*a*)						
1931	1,286	5,047	3,868	2,253	4,422	3,119	4,468	1,794	11,848
1932	1,301	5,258	4,317	2,243	4,352	3,040	4,452	1,837	12,242
1933	1,341	5,475	5,080	2,270	4,072	3,106	4,357	1,699	12,599
1934	1,352	6,014	5,919	2,273	4,093	3,179	4,375	1,717	12,907
1935	1,382	6,142	6,896	2,298	4,119	3,466	4,428	1,747	[11,875](*b*)
1936	1,408	6,409	7,378	2,322	4,471	3,615	4,632	1,807	12,223
1937	1,440	6,841	7,128	2,416	4,436	4,055	4,829	1,834	12,422

See p. 629 for footnotes.

Public Finance 15. *continued*

(in £ million)

		Principal Constituent Items										
	Total Expenditure	Education	Libraries and Museums	Highways and Bridges	Public Lighting	Police	Sewerage	Refuse Disposal	Commons, Parks, etc.	Lunacy (*a*)	Hospitals, Clinics, etc. (*g*)	Individual Health (*h*)
1938	66·3	13·9	0·3	6·1	1·0	2·7	1·1	1·4	0·9	1·5	1·6	—
1939	69·0	14·1	0·3	6·3	1·0	2·8	1·2	1·4	0·9	1·6	2·0	—
1940	74·5	13·9	0·3	5·2	0·6	3·0	1·4	1·6	0·9	1·6	2·0	—
1941	78·6	14·0	0·3	4·6	0·6	3·4	1·3	1·8	0·9	2·0	2·4	—
1942	85·3	14·9	0·3	4·7	0·6	3·8	1·2	2·0	0·6	2·1	2·6	—
1943	84·4	15·7	0·3	4·6	0·6	3·9	1·3	2·0	0·8	2·1	2·7	—
1944	87·0	16·9	0·3	4·5	0·6	3·8	1·3	2·2	0·9	2·2	3·0	—
1945	89·0	18·1	0·3	4·4	0·7	3·8	1·3	2·2	0·9	2·3	3·5	—
1946	95·9	23·1	0·4	5·0	1·0	3·9	1·3	2·3	1·1	2·4	3·6	—
1947	105·2	25·0	0·4	6·6	1·1	4·2	1·4	2·7	1·2	2·7	4·1	—
1948	115·7	28·5	0·5	6·9	1·2	4·6	1·7	2·9	1·5	3·3	4·7	—
	---(*j*)	---(*j*)	---(*j*)	---(*j*)	---(*j*)	---(*j*)	---(*j*)	---(*j*)	---(*j*)	---(*j*)	---(*j*)	
1949	105·8	30·9	0·6	6·5	1·5	4·9	1·7	3·2	1·5	0·4	0·7	2·0
1950	100·3	32·8	0·6	7·0	1·8	5·4	1·7	3·3	1·7	—	—	2·6
1951	108·4	34·6	0·6	7·2	1·9	5·8	2·2	3·6	1·8	—	—	3·3
1952	122·8	40·4	0·7	8·1	2·0	6·5	2·1	4·1	2·0	—	—	3·5
1953	133·5	43·7	0·8	8·6	2·4	6·8	2·4	4·3	2·2	—	—	4·0
1954	142·0	45·5	0·8	8·7	2·5	7·1	2·6	4·5	2·2	—	—	4·1
1955	156·5	51·2	0·9	9·3	2·7	7·9	2·8	4·8	2·4	—	—	4·4
1956	170·8	55·9	1·0	10·2	2·9	8·5	3·2	5·3	2·8	—	—	4·7
1957	195·0	67·8	1·1	11·2	3·3	9·9	3·7	5·7	2·9	—	—	5·3
1958	202·3	71·7	1·2	12·2	3·4	10·6	3·4	6·2	3·1	—	—	6·0
1959	213·1	75·2	1·2	12·3	3·6	11·4	3·6	6·5	3·4	—	—	6·1
1960	221·2	79·7	1·3	12·9	3·7	12·0	3·7	6·8	3·7	—	—	6·5
1961	241·6	86·5	1·3	14·7	3·8	13·8	4·0	7·0	3·8	—	—	6·7
1962	264·4	96·7	1·5	15·9	4·0	15·2	4·6	7·8	4·3	—	—	7·0
1963	281·9	103·2	1·6	17·0	4·3	16·2	4·7	8·2	4·4	—	—	7·8
1964	307·7	113·8	1·6	20·1	4·6	17·9	5·2	9·4	4·6	—	—	8·2
1965	333·3	122·6	1·8	19·6	4·9	19·6	5·7	9·6	5·0	—	—	9·0
1966	365·8	134·0	2·0	21·6	5·2	21·6	6·5	10·7	5·5	—	—	10·1
1967	407·3	152·0	2·2	23·4	5·6	23·6	7·5	11·5	6·0	—	—	10·8
1968	445·0	158·9	2·4	27·4	5·4	25·8	8·2	12·8	6·7	—	—	11·6
1969	490·9	173·7	2·6	26·3	5·7	27·8	9·5	14·1	7·7	—	—	12·6
1970	554·4	191·6	2·9	28·6	6·9	30·2	10·5	16·0	8·3	—	—	7·3
1971	640·7	227·1	3·5	33·7	7·7	36·4	12·9	18·4	10·0	—	—	9·2
1972	721·6	254·9	6·8	39·1	9·0	41·5	14·3	20·7	11·6	—	—	11·2
1973	841·6	299·6	8·0	45·2	10·0	48·2	17·3	23·4	14·6	—	—	12·0
1974	1,001·4	353·0	9·6	53·6	10·9	55·7	22·5	28·1	18·2	—	—	12·7
1975	1,344·1	488·7	12·8	70·2	13·2	70·7	30·0	36·6	26·3	—	—	—
	---(*k*)	---(*k*)	---(*k*)	---(*k*)	---(*k*)	---(*k*)	---(*k*)	---(*k*)	---(*k*)			
									Leisure & Recreation			
1976	1,566·1	546·0	15·6	103·4		105·5	93·3	—	51·7	—	—	—
1977	1,963·6	674·6	19·4	124·4		134·4	[113·0](*l*)	—	67·4	—	—	—
1978	2,123·2	721·6	21·6	153·2		141·1	[125·3](*l*)	—	74·2	—	—	—
1979	2,442·3	830·2	26·6	180·2		166·2	153·6	—	91·4	—	—	—
1980	2,985·9	975·6	32·3	229·1		213·4	189·6	—	114·4	—	—	—

Public Finance 15. *continued*

(in £ million)
Principal Constituent Items

	Housing	Poor Relief (*g*)	L.A. Welfare Services (*i*)	Water Supply	Gas Supply (*g*)	Electricity Supply (*g*)	Transport Services	Harbours, etc.	Loan Charges (*b*)
1938	7·2	5·7	—	2·4	4·7	4·4	5·1	2·0	12·6
1939	7·9	5·4	—	2·5	4·8	4·6	5·4	1·9	13·3
1940	8·7	5·4	—	2·6	4·9	4·8	5·4	1·9	14·2
1941	9·1	4·4	—	2·7	5·8	5·4	5·9	2·2	14·6
1942	9·5	4·0	—	2·8	6·4	5·9	6·1	2·5	15·7
1943	9·4	3·9	—	2·8	7·0	6·0	6·4	2·5	14·6
1944	9·5	4·0	—	2·9	7·6	6·5	7·1	2·9	14·9
1945	9·8	4·4	—	2·8	8·4	6·6	7·5	2·7	14·5
1946	9·9	4·7	—	2·9	9·1	7·0	7·6	2·6	14·8
1947	10·9	4·9	—	3·0	10·0	7·6	7·9	2·4	14·5
1948	12·5	5·3	—	3·3	10·9	7·0	8·5	2·8	14·6
	---(*j*)	---(*j*)		---(*j*)	---(*j*)	---(*j*)	---(*j*)	---(*j*)	
1949	13·8	0·7	2·2	3·7	11·4	—	9·1	2·9	14·4
1950	15·2	—	2·7	3·6	—	—	9·5	3·1	14·1
1951	16·7	—	2·9	3·7	—	—	10·2	3·2	16·4
1952	19·1	—	3·2	4·1	—	—	11·3	3·3	19·2
1953	23·1	—	3·5	4·7	—	—	12·1	3·5	20·7
1954	26·9	—	4·0	5·2	—	—	12·9	3·7	24·7
1955	30·0	—	4·2	5·4	—	—	13·1	3·9	28·1
1956	33·7	—	4·5	6·4	—	—	14·1	4·3	31·7
1957	39·1	—	4·9	7·1	—	—	15·3	4·7	36·8
1958	36·9	—	5·3	7·5	—	—	15·9	5·0	42·2
1959	38·9	—	5·7	8·2	—	—	15·8	5·0	45·9
1960	41·0	—	5·9	8·4	—	—	15·8	5·0	49·4
1961	44·4	—	6·2	8·9	—	—	16·9	5·7	55·4
1962	48·9	—	7·0	9·6	—	—	16·8	6·1	63·0
1963	52·5	—	7·3	10·5	—	—	17·1	6·2	67·0
1964	56·0	—	8·3	11·2	—	—	17·9	6·1	72·9
1965	64·0	—	9·1	11·8	—	—	18·5	6·4	85·9
1966	71·7	—	10·2	12·9	—	—	19·3	6·7	95·1
1967	81·1	—	11·1	14·3	—	—	19·4	6·9	107·8
1968	91·0	—	12·5	14·8	—	—	19·9	6·7	120·6
1969	105·6	—	14·0	17·3	—	—	20·5	9·3	139·2
1970	124·5	—	23·0	21·2	—	—	21·5	8·9	170·3
1971	139·2	—	26·1	23·0	—	—	23·9	9·7	188·1
1972	146·8	—	33·3	27·2	—	—	26·2	10·7	199·3
1973	170·6	—	43·1	29·6	—	—	28·3	11·9	222·0
1974	227·0	—	56·3	33·5	—	—	12·2	12·8	283·2
1975	296·2	—	77·3	41·5	—	—	14·8	15·8	356·0
	---(*k*)		---(*k*)	---(*k*)			---(*k*)	---(*k*)	---(*k*)
			Social Work						
1976	309·2	—	93·3	45·9	—	—	16·5	0·6	371·8
1977	404·3	—	119·8	57·6	—	—	20·9	1·1	496·8
1978	431·5	—	129·8	59·1	—	—	23·0	1·4	514·8
1979	469·9	—	156·5	65·8	—	—	28·9	8·6	577·2
1980	578·3	—	196·2	79·2	—	—	30·2	11·5	713·9

(*a*) Until 1914 the whole cost of pauper lunatics was met out of poor relief. From 1914–30 the cost was halved between *Poor Relief* and *Lunacy*, whilst from 1931 the whole cost came under the latter heading.
(*b*) Figures under this heading are only included in total expenditure in so far as they are not already included under some other heading. They include small amounts which were paid out of the receipts from new loans, and are therefore also included under the appropriate item in table 15, except in the year 1935.
(*c*) The figures for 1893 include expenditure out of loans, which cannot be separately distinguished.
(*d*) Loan charges attributable to the various items are not included with those items until 1896.
(*e*) The cost of collection of school rates by the parish authorities is included previously.

(*f*) From 1915 the cost of tuberculosis treatment was included under this heading. In 1915 it amounted to 180.
(*g*) Owing to legislative changes these items disappear or emerge under other headings between 1948 and 1950.
(*h*) i.e. Local Authority Health Services from 5 July 1948.
(*i*) National Assistance, Child Welfare, etc.
(*j*) Subsequent statistics relate to expenditure other than on capital works than expenditure other than out of loans.
(*k*) Local government reorganisation was accompanied by a major functional reorganisation, which effected great changes in categories of expenditure. It is impossible to reconcile the previous format with that employed subsequently. See also note 2 above.
(*l*) Excluding crematoria and burial grounds.

Public Finance 16. Expenditure of Local Authorities out of Loans 1894–1948 and on Capital Works 1949–80 – Scotland

NOTES

[1] SOURCE: *Abstract* and *Scottish Local Government Financial Statistics*.

[2] In the earlier years, the financial years of the various authorities did not always end on the same date, though the majority ended on 15 May. As and from 1976 this was changed to 31 March. The figures are aggregates of the financial years ended in the year shown.

(in £ thousand)

	Total Expenditure	Principal Constituent Items												
		Education	Highways and Bridges	Sewerage	Commons, Parks, etc.	Lunatic Asylums (a)	Hospitals, Clinics, etc.	Housing	Work-houses, etc. (a)	Water Supply	Gas Supply	Electricity Supply	Transport Services	Harbours, Docks, etc.
1894	2,141	294	102	...	100	123	...	...	14	...	98	66	233	254
1895	2,318	323	129	...	73	118	...	...	21	...	95	125	389	194
1896	2,055	355	145	98	87	113	129	...	16	385	57	68	14	301
1997	2,780	356	182	126	114	127	118	...	24	368	273	125	178	291
1898	2,568	283	119	127	81	110	77	...	19	394	124	132	348	375
1899	3,069	275	119	132	58	102	124	...	14	454	270	341	329	366
1900	3,740	347	131	170	25	102	137	...	33	479	276	594	528	394
1901	4,491	376	98	183	155	86	169	...	41	469	383	510	1,100	302
1902	4,187	436	138	282	32	91	138	...	86	505	540	492	469	314
1903	4,092	394	163	501	25	153	149	...	250	563	508	409	222	190
1904	4,467	456	191	403	69	338	117	...	294	1,072	409	309	142	161
1905	3,729	432	166	272	57	132	124	...	184	588	363	381	189	311
1906	3,504	390	180	282	47	166	95	...	162	488	271	288	142	567
1907	3,308	409	126	321	49	138	95	38	114	367	225	338	170	430
1908	3,498	424	130	361	27	110	61	27	61	410	148	274	875(b)	304
1909	2,821	484	143	324	56	67	56	18	47	403	91	314	236	325
1910	2,426	445	156	349	47	46	55	9	25	375	80	184	143	262
1911	2,248	491	120	188	30	47	52	36	13	356	96	129	107	194
1912	2,352	477	131	116	50	43	42	7	19	456	250	142	40	328
1913	2,250	424	123	106	50	44	42	17	47	432	117	236	109	199
1914	2,997	472	212	139	49	65	90	67	40	294	295	347	102	338
1915	3,326	397	171	117	58	107	167	83	16	358	534	341	121	299
1916	1,855	223	105	58	15	53	142	114	2	242	170	243	107	128
1917	1,297	89	26	19	10	19	109	85	1	189	104	364	16	145
1918	1,064	50	31	14	4	2	96	32	—	157	65	404	4	50

1919	1,506	54	66	19	38	3	64	27	3	213	59	722	8	56
1920	4,425	118	178	43	75	44	127	795	1	396	402	1,406	307	212
1921	10,762	390	397	196	106	26	140	3,929	14	688	1,530	2,207	348	300
1922	16,656	421	811	300	187	24	299	8,928	6	918	1,392	1,735	764	288
1923	13,034	269	787	271	256	33	114	6,001	5	972	653	1,740	1,178	204
1924	8,897	267	979	211	250	25	78	2,785	12	833	412	1,001	1,149	297
1925	10,021	345	959	284	256	44	79	3,785	15	943	455	1,106	727	416
1926	11,791	498	1,116	341	158	112	172	5,227	15	869	484	1,183	365	577
1927	13,296	459	995	351	205	44	193	7,537	24	611	291	1,183	194	455
1928	13,530	546	746	304	126	108	223	8,058	27	560	327	943	250	554
1929	13,145	764	796	322	76	138	231	7,545	21	488	312	974	541	366
1930	11,081	998	1,301	292	131	153	178	5,195	29	498	253	714	412	280
						---(a)			---(a)					
1931	11,292	1,659	1,028	589	161	149	132	4,288	2	739	273	642	651	482
1932	11,797	1,139	1,179	822	104	157	76	5,325	19	928	235	539	249	396
1933	11,455	737	738	593	34	174	79	6,311	50	716	226	511	98	234
1934	11,836	574	545	441	69	218	57	7,696	30	493	193	589	83	214
1935	11,524	661	501	312	91	324	72	7,397	63	396	223	688	222	76
1936	12,193	831	449	540	190	339	132	7,068	52	526	254	796	373	90
1937	14,958	1,057	643	793	150	334	208	7,911	66	832	418	1,474	277	66
1938	18,650	1,231	798	1,051	158	161	188	10,297	118	810	383	1,658	686	68

See p. 633 for footnotes.

Public Finance 16. *continued*

(in £ million)

	Total Expenditure	Principal Constituent Items: Education	Highways and Bridges	Sewerage	Commons, Parks, etc.	Lunatic Asylums (*c*)	Health Services (*d*)	Housing	Work-houses, (*c*)	Water Supply	Gas Supply (*c*)	Electricity Supply (*c*)	Transport Services	Harbours, Docks, etc.	Welfare Services (*e*)
1939	20·4	1·2	0·8	1·2	0·1	0·2	0·3	12·0	0·1	0·8	0·6	1·5	0·4	0·3	—
1940	15·9	1·3	0·6	0·9	0·1	0·2	0·3	8·1	0·1	0·9	0·7	1·3	0·3	0·3	—
1941	7·2	0·7	0·2	0·3	--	0·1	0·2	3·3	--	0·5	0·4	0·6	0·1	0·1	—
1942	4·5	0·3	0·1	0·1	--	--	0·1	1·9	--	0·4	0·3	0·4	0·1	0·4	—
1943	4·0	0·1	--	0·2	--	--	0·1	1·7	--	0·5	0·3	0·6	0·1	0·2	—
1944	3·0	0·1	--	--	--	--	0·1	1·6	--	0·2	0·3	0·4	0·1	--	—
1945	3·7	0·2	--	0·1	--	--	--	2·3	--	0·1	0·4	0·3	0·1	--	—
1946	8·3	0·1	--	0·3	--	--	--	5·7	--	0·4	0·6	0·7	0·1	--	—
1947	21·7	0·2	0·4	1·0	--	0·1	0·1	16·4	--	0·8	1·0	1·2	0·2	--	—
1948	34·5	0·9	0·3	1·5	0·1	0·1	0·1	26·7	0·1	1·4	1·0	1·6	0·1	0·1	—
	---(*f*)(*g*)	---(*f*)	---(*f*)	---(*f*)	---(*f*)	---(*f*)	---(*f*)	---(*f*)	---(*f*)	---(*f*)	---(*f*)		---(*f*)	---(*f*)	
1949	42·4	1·7	0·7	1·6	0·1	--	0·1	32·5	--	2·0	0·9	—	1·3	0·5	0·1
	---(*g*)						---(*d*)								
1950	44·9	2·5	0·7	2·3	0·2	—	0·2	32·4	—	3·1	—	—	1·6	0·6	0·2
1951	47·4	3·4	0·8	1·9	0·2	—	0·3	33·7	—	3·8	—	—	0·9	0·8	0·3
1952	58·3	4·3	0·6	2·1	0·1	—	0·2	41·1	—	6·7	—	—	0·2	0·9	0·4
1953	69·2	5·5	0·8	3·1	0·2	—	0·2	49·4	—	6·1	—	—	0·3	1·0	0·3
1954	74·2	5·3	1·0	3·0	0·2	—	0·3	53·4	—	6·1	—	—	0·4	1·2	0·4
1955	73·2	6·7	1·2	3·5	0·2	—	0·3	49·0	—	5·2	—	—	3·1	1·0	0·3
1956	72·3	8·8	1·9	3·1	0·3	—	0·4	45·6	—	6·1	—	—	2·1	0·6	0·3
1957	70·7	10·4	2·1	2·4	0·3	—	0·2	44·0	—	4·7	—	—	1·8	1·2	0·4
1958	71·3	12·1	2·6	2·3	0·2	—	0·2	42·3	—	3·8	—	—	1·7	1·7	0·4
1959	71·3	12·8	4·3	2·1	0·2	—	0·3	40·0	—	3·7	—	—	1·8	2·1	0·2
1960	72·2	13·8	6·7	2·5	0·4	—	0·4	35·9	—	5·0	—	—	1·6	1·2	0·2
1961	78·4	14·1	9·0	2·7	0·5	—	0·5	38·4	—	6·0	—	—	1·0	0·7	0·3
1962	91·0	15·7	11·5	4·0	0·4	—	0·5	42·5	—	5·4	—	—	1·3	2·1	0·4
1963	99·6	18·7	9·8	4·3	0·5	—	0·4	47·7	—	5·2	—	—	1·5	2·3	0·4
1964	130·1	21·0	10·4	4·1	0·5	—	1·2	72·1	—	6·2	—	—	1·0	2·3	0·5
1965	146·9	22·3	11·8	5·8	0·8	—	1·0	78·3	—	9·7	—	—	0·9	2·0	0·6
1966	154·8	20·5	11·4	5·8	0·7	—	1·2	82·3	—	9·5	—	—	0·5	3·6	0·8
1967	187·5	21·1	15·7	7·0	0·9	—	1·1	103·7	—	10·6	—	—	0·9	4·6	1·2
1968	228·0	29·7	21·2	7·8	1·0	—	1·4	119·3	—	11·0	—	—	1·2	7·2	1·9

1969	257·8	38·1	20·2	10·5	2·0	—	1·4	131·2	—	13·1	—	—	0·7	8·3	1·9
1970	253·3	41·1	16·7	9·7	2·3	—	1·3	125·8	—	14·5	—	—	0·7	8·8	1·8
1971	251·3	40·1	22·4	11·6	1·9	—	2·2	122·0	—	14·0	—	—	1·5	4·0	2·2
1972	260·8	40·3	25·8	14·9	2·7	—	2·4	122·2	—	11·7	—	—	1·4	4·7	2·4
1973	303·7	51·2	32·9	22·1	4·2	—	2·1	127·4	—	13·1	—	—	2·6	5·5	4·5
1974	397·2	55·9	41·1	28·4	5·2	—	2·4	185·0	—	13·6	—	—	0·7	6·2	6·2
1975	493·4	62·7	49·0	29·8	6·0	—	1·9	244·0	—	13·6	—	—	1·5	12·4	7·4
	---(*h*)	---(*h*)	---(*h*)	---(*h*)	---(*h*)			---(*h*)		---(*h*)			---(*h*)	---(*h*)	---(*h*)
				Environ-mental Services	Leisure and Recreation										Social Work
1976	477·8	66·8	45·5	49·2	17·6	—	—(*d*)	218·7	—	16·9	—	—	2·6	6·6	7·4
1977	532·0	88·3	52·1	43·1	15·9	—	—	234·7	—	20·5	—	—	3·5	5·8	11·0
1978	499·3	75·8	46·5	40·3	12·2	—	—	229·4	—	21·3	—	—	2·0	14·8	8·1
1979	542·1	58·2	58·1	48·4	13·8	—	—	244·0	—	27·8	—	—	3·7	21·1	8·7
1980	658·5	56·8	77·7	64·3	20·7	—	—	293·8	—	38·0	—	—	3·2	20·4	11·7

(*a*) Up to 1930 expenditure on lunatic wards of poorhouses and on parochial asylums is included under *Workhouses etc.*, but from 1931 onwards it comes under the heading *Lunatic Asylums*.
(*b*) Of this figure, 734 was expenditure incurred in previous years and met out of contingent funds, etc.
(*c*) Owing to legislative changes these services disappear or emerge under other headings between 1948 and 1950.
(*d*) Including clinics and maternity services and various public health expenditures. Hospitals etc. were excluded on transfer to the National Health Service on 5 July 1948. From 1976, expenditures are included under other headings.
(*e*) Care of the aged, handicapped, and homeless; child welfare; etc.
(*f*) Subsequent statistics relate to expenditure on capital works, rather than expenditure out of loans.
(*g*) Nationalisation of municipal services affects comparability, both before and after 1949.
(*h*) Local government reorganisation was accompanied by a major functional reorganisation, which effected great changes in categories of expenditure. It is impossible to reconcile the previous format with that employed subsequently. See also note 2 above.

Public Finance 17. Receipts of Local Authorities, Ireland 1868–1980

NOTES

[1] SOURCES: *Abstract*, *Statistical Abstract of Ireland*, and *Local Taxation Returns*.

[2] In the earlier years the financial returns of the various authorities did not always end on the same date, though the majority ended on 31 March, which became standard. The figures are aggregates of the financial years ended in the years shown. Republic of Ireland figures from 1975 are for calendar years.

A. Ireland, 1868–1919

(in £ thousand)

		Principal Constituent Items						
					Receipts from Main Trading Services			
	Total Receipts	Loans	Rates (*a*)	Government Grants	Water Supply	Gas Supply	Electricity Supply	Transport Services
1868	3,055	237	2,284	78	...	...	...	—
1880	3,869	264	2,655	107	...	...	...	—
1881	3,872	402	2,657	115	...	...	...	—
1882	3,915	396	2,704	116	...	...	...	—
1883	4,089	403	2,853	115	...	...	...	—
1884	4,290	350	2,937	115	...	...	...	—
1885	4,250	295	2,990	118	...	...	...	—
1886	4,163	385	2,897	116	...	...	...	—
1887	4,215	475	2,842	114	...	...	...	—
1888	4,231 ---(*b*) 4,199	542	2,864	109	...	...	...	—
1889	4,438	705	2,912	120	...	...	...	—
1890	4,343	496	2,991	161	...	...	...	—
1891	4,456	547	2,826	348	...	...	...	—
1892	4,357 ---(*c*) 4,351	470	2,810	369 ---(*c*) 366	...	...	...	—
1893	4,740	775	2,869	361	...	...	...	—
1894	4,695	589	2,990	397	...	...	...	—
1895	4,765	682	2,974	326	...	...	...	—
1896	4,964	709	3,041	405	...	...	...	—
1897	5,245	881	3,136	368	...	...	...	—
1898	5,006	653	3,098	352	...	...	...	—
1899	5,195	592	3,234	473	...	...	...	—
1900	5,521	473	2,454	1,560	...	...	...	—
1901	6,478	944	3,174	1,296	...	...	...	—
1902	6,782	1,432	2,915	1,390	...	...	...	—
1903	6,434	1,029	3,007	1,325	...	...	...	—
1904	6,365	876	3,031	1,331	...	...	...	—
1905	6,839	1,288	3,008	1,360	...	...	...	—
1906	7,751	2,020	3,052	1,346	...	...	...	137
1907	6,980	942	3,159 ---(*a*)	1,441	...	...	...	183
1908	7,564	1,030	3,011	1,344	324	356	136	194
1909	8,106	1,464	3,123	1,359	331	361	136	195
1910	8,752	1,791	3,301	1,456	334	379	143	204
1911	8,776	1,788	3,317	1,364	341	393	166	218
1912	8,287	1,166	3,298	1,415	339	412	185	244
1913	8,804	1,602	3,301	1,410	345	429	210	256
1914	8,406	1,044	3,358	1,450	355	430	236	273
1915	8,832	1,265	3,490	1,439	374	418	259	270
1916	8,971	1,028	3,678	1,515	382	482	297	283
1917	8,788	634	3,747	1,442	392	556	317	302
1918	9,327	374	4,146	1,548	395	671	360	358
1919	10,354	271	5,017	1,476	432	756	398	409

See p. 637 for footnotes.

B. Northern Ireland, 1922–80

(in £ thousand)

		Principal Constituent Items							
						Receipts from Main Trading Services			
	Total Receipts	Loans	Rates	Government Grants	Housing Rents	Water Supply	Gas Supply	Electricity Supply	Transport Services
1922	7,392	1,392	2,953	514	...	125	950	410	668
1923	7,873	1,773	2,377	1,451	...	141	776	357	653
1924	7,041	1,059	2,147	1,520	...	136	778	386	602
1925	8,372	2,748	2,056	1,114	...	142	858	386	609
1926	7,254	1,547	2,233	821	...	140	861	399	624
1927	9,177	3,181	2,197	946	...	140	968	429	606
1928	7,278	1,135	2,287	954	...	144	968	429	605
1929	7,682	1,741	2,220	951	...	142	878	426	544
1930	8,630	2,475	1,657	1,574	...	154	868	441	655
1931	8,087	1,719	1,614	1,810	...	152	890	461	705
1932	7,725	1,339	1,633	1,798	...	152	865	487	698
1933	8,146	1,675	1,637	1,974	...	154	859	422	644
1934	9,400	2,763	1,778	1,948	...	149	889	457	653
1935	8,141	1,241	1,952	1,904	...	152	876	507	680
1936	8,812	1,357	2,062	2,191	59	152	897	585	714
1937	9,305	1,514	2,420	2,075	108	159	904	651	736
1938	9,678	1,948	2,415	1,969	110	160	949	721	746
1939	9,943	1,904	2,485	2,115	109	156	910	813	757
1940	9,767	1,458	2,608	2,170	...	...	...	...	...
1941	9,615	747	2,637	2,293	...	...	...	...	...
1942	11,589	597	2,713	3,522	...	...	...	...	...
1943	12,736	480	2,901	4,053	...	...	...	...	...
1944	12,611	359	2,879	3,486	...	...	...	...	...
1945	12,603	281	2,906	3,066	...	...	...	...	...
1946	13,205	632	2,966	3,162	116	234	1,738	1,717	1,500
1947	14,573	1,234	3,429	3,215	130	221	1,875	1,744	1,531
1948	18,470	3,348	3,913	4,057	179	223	2,033	1,880	1,679
1949	21,438	5,559	3,279	4,551	355	241	2,197	2,247	1,986
1950	26,924	8,418	3,583	5,451	418	258	2,245	1,650	1,989
1951	27,342	7,751	4,101	6,127	589	276	2,398	1,927	2,049
1952	31,962	10,111	4,389	7,234	680	307	2,598	2,095	2,212
1953	37,189	12,873	4,939	8,297	831	303	2,764	2,252	2,326
1954	45,991	14,144	5,724	8,983	1,003	438	3,047	4,244	2,625
1955	46,319	11,474	6,211	9,253	1,118	467	3,166	4,923	2,665
1956	50,228	13,058	6,836	10,489	1,227	537	3,342	5,595	2,660
1957	56,996	16,510	7,562	11,429	1,396	617	3,586	6,561	2,836
1958	63,447	16,267	9,386	13,735	1,579	651	3,935	7,675	2,844
1959	62,328	10,384	10,890	15,577	1,719	740	3,945	8,574	2,919
1960	71,346	14,831	10,860	19,368	1,924	790	3,984	9,131	2,939
1961	71,425	11,519	11,941	20,520	2,044	922	3,942	9,768	3,019
1962	77,551	12,603	12,660	23,632	2,332	979	4,106	10,478	3,056
1963	87,508	15,422	14,373	27,087	2,649	1,063	4,281	10,858	3,036
1964	98,298	19,032	15,907	30,319	3,051	1,173	4,332	10,875	3,179
1965	104,718	17,151	17,372	35,171	3,401	1,243	4,343	11,645	3,306
1966	116,651	21,180	18,537	39,840	4,017	1,332	4,520	13,164	3,584

See p. 637 for footnotes.

B. Northern Ireland, 1922–80 (*cont.*)

(in £ thousand)

		Principal Constituent Items				Receipts from Main Trading Services			
	Total Receipts	Loans	Rates	Government Grants	Housing Rents	Water Supply	Gas Supply	Electricity Supply	Transport Services
1967	132,368	26,064	20,816	45,743	4,279	1,683	4,656	13,755	3,591
1968	153,122	33,912	22,372	52,344	5,005	1,830	4,724	15,478	3,667
1969	159,693	32,297	24,417	52,457	5,867	2,039	4,403	16,481	3,686
1970	173,565	32,508	26,856	57,406	6,640	2,369	4,443	16,788	3,748
1971	180,425	39,621	29,285	56,150	7,807	2,668	4,639	12,240	3,992
1972	172,133	38,734	33,472	66,100	7,509	3,188	5,411	20,982	3,718
1973	222,268	19,706	38,212	84,759	3,593	3,334	5,740	23,074	3,389
1974	115,212	14,724	27,479	40,471	—(*d*)	2,088	5,707	—(*d*)	—(*d*)
1975	38,682	3,259	12,971	6,005	—	—(*d*)	7,583	—	—
1976	60,671	5,117	20,388	8,009	—	—	14,210	—	—
1977	68,907	3,970	25,397	9,292	—	—	15,423	—	—
1978	69,565	3,279	27,130	10,267	—	—	12,601	—	—
1979	78,285	3,871	30,376	10,754	—	—	15,118	—	—
1980	94,584	5,831	35,532	12,695	—	—	18,275	—	—

C. Republic of Ireland, 1923–80

(in £ thousand)

	Total Receipts	Loans	Rates	Government Grants
1923	7,655	341	4,153	1,402
1924	12,595	504	5,333	1,813
1925	11,200	1,361	5,311	2,403
1926	11,965	867	5,297	2,998
1927	10,730	853	5,224	2,888
1928	11,009	1,070	4,909	3,265
1929	9,430	1,072	4,906	3,303
1930	9,870	796	5,102	2,781
1931	10,412	974	5,208	3,066
1932	10,830	1,106	4,678	3,745
1933	11,319	1,036	4,279	4,792
1934	12,798	3,153	4,710	3,779
1935	13,257	2,793	5,151	3,746
1936	13,934	3,324	5,295	3,844
1937	14,309	3,026	5,515	4,264
1938	15,092	2,823	5,850	4,885
1939	17,412	3,950	6,271	5,145
1940	16,513	3,055	6,510	5,216
1941	16,742	3,031	6,631	5,236
1942	15,918	1,592	7,530	4,807
1943	16,894	1,517	7,814	5,335
1944	16,585	1,380	7,434	5,226
1945	16,825	1,121	7,804	5,247
1946	17,329	950	8,313	5,426
1947	18,756	921	7,999	7,269

Public Finance 17. *continued*

C. Republic of Ireland, 1923–80 (*cont.*)

(in £ million)

	Total Receipts	Loans	Rates	Government Grants
1948	22·3	0·7	9·1	9·6
1949	31·0	5·9	10·4	11·1
1950	45·0	14·2	11·6	14·0
1951	46·6	15·7	11·6	13·8
1952	56·5	20·9	12·7	16·3
1953	57·5	18·8	14·2	17·4
1954	58·9	15·7	16·0	19·6
1955	63·3	17·1	17·0	21·2
1956	68·3	20·0	17·7	21·9
1957	66·9	15·3	19·7	22·4
1958	69·2	14·2	20·1	24·7
1959	63·5	8·6	20·6	23·7
1960	66·4	9·0	21·4	24·5
1961	71·8	9·7	22·1	26·4
1962	75·8	10·9	23·2	28·8
1963	81·2	12·2	22·8	32·7
1964	90·0	14·8	24·5	34·9
1965	103·0	18·4	26·1	41·2
1966	117·0	24·2	29·8	46·5
1967	126·4	25·7	31·5	50·7
1968	145·9	31·3	34·7	57·5
1969	162·0	35·2	38·3	65·8
1970	187·0	40·9	43·0	76·9
1971	220·0	44·8	50·1	94·6
1972	259·1	52·5	59·8	116·4
1973	309·0	62·9	70·1	139·4
1974	392·9	92·4	71·2	187·5
1974	[382·7](*e*)	[92·5](*e*)	[61·3](*e*)	[187·6](*e*)
1975	640·1	150·0	84·0	337·1
1976	767·1	164·4	109·0	409·9
1977	891·6	170·3	110·4	511·2
1978	1,071·4	196·9	81·9	677·3
1979	1,303·7	235·3	90·4	835·0
1980	1,677·5	294·2	102·8	1,079·4

(*a*) Including water rates to 1907.
(*b*) Subsequently excluding pilotage and light dues.
(*c*) Subsequently the receipts of Clerks of the Peace and of the Crown were eliminated.
(*d*) Transferred to regional authorities.
(*e*) Figures are for the period April–December. See also note a above.

Public Finance 18. Local Authority Expenditure, Ireland 1868–1980

NOTES

[1] SOURCES: *Abstract*, *Statistical Abstract of Ireland*, *Local Taxation Returns*.

[2] In the earlier years the financial returns of the various authorities did not always end on the same date, though the majority ended on 31 March, which became standard. The figures are aggregates of the financial years ended in the years shown. Republic of Ireland figures from 1975 are for calendar years.

(in £ thousand)

A. Ireland – All Expenditures, 1868–1907

	Total Expenditure		Total Expenditure		Total Expenditure		Total Expenditure
1868	3,098	1885	4,327	1890	4,296	1895	4,830
		1886	4,219	1891	4,296	1896	4,994
1880	3,761	1887	4,288	1892	4,409 ---(*b*) 4,428	1897	5,031
1881	3,938	1888	4,288 ---(*a*) 4,168	1893	4,654	1898	5,160
1882	4,069	1889	4,365	1894	4,756	1899	5,244
1883	4,156						
1884	4,303						

		Principal Constituent Items									
	Total Expenditure	Education	Highways & Bridges	Hospitals, etc.	Lunacy	Poor Relief	Refuse Disposal	Sewerage (*c*)	Water Supply (*c*)	Transport Services	Loan Charges (*d*)
1900	5,661	39	935	197	368	945	91	160	235	120	648
1901	6,294	60	965	206	436	978	123	211	331	109	886
1902	6,489	107	968	211	428	1,027	122	278	273	88	1,035
1903	6,055	134	771	190	396	994	114	302	212	86	795
1904	6,447	129	976	214	451	1,024	119	265	184	85	884
1905	6,849	149	1,002	223	461	1,044	117	211	176	84	1,047
1906	8,036	161	1,053	221	448	1,074	122	247	215	212	1,027
1907	6,698	174	1,011	233	446	1,072	129	245	165	210	1,095

B. Ireland – Expenditure other than out of Loans, 1908–19

	Total Expendi-ture	Education	Highways & Bridges	Hospi-tals, etc.	Lunacy	Poor Relief	Refuse Disposal	Sewerage	Water Supply	Gas Supply	Electricity Supply	Transport Services	Loan Charges (*d*)
1908	6,673	140	944	236	460	1,080	122	167	117	340	94	210	1,171
1909	6,844	155	962	254	472	1,122	117	169	99	328	82	219	1,209
1910	6,845	174	950	269	478	1,098	118	193	100	341	87	223	1,199
1911	6,952	168	960	267	496	1,074	121	205	97	340	89	236	1,248
1912	7,134	174	1,016	273	507	1,002	128	203	116	352	103	234	1,271
1913	7,374	176	1,030	273	519	1,028	134	207	122	367	123	254	1,434
1914	7,438	188	1,054	291	528	1,030	124	205	100	367	139	267	1,417
1915	7,723	200	1,074	345	543	1,042	135	212	102	360	140	263	1,502
1916	7,875	199	1,058	366	622	1,092	142	209	109	395	175	264	1,532
1917	8,332	212	1,036	383	698	1,171	146	218	112	512	227	305	1,573
1918	8,931	223	1,133	405	797	1,296	146	274	121	604	221	324	1,562
1919	10,039	234	1,265	455	941	1,475	164	328	146	708	303	379	1,520

C. Ireland – Expenditure out of Loans, 1908–19

	Total Expenditure	Highways & Bridges	Sewerage	Water Supply	Gas Supply	Electricity Supply	Transport Services
1908	1,093	61	124	133	31	98	44
1909	1,290	90	88	84	21	74	14
1910	1,754	62	80	73	18	51	11
1911	1,696	92	95	73	52	57	9
1912	1,391	118	59	62	32	95	68
1913	1,494	162	70	66	32	120	196
1914	1,127	184	69	57	31	91	51
1915	1,232	204	67	69	87	86	15
1916	960	178	41	69	79	49	—
1917	547	70	16	22	45	66	..
1918	238	33	11	11	23	21	—
1919	348	23	6	9	5	143	—

See p. 644 for footnotes.

Public Finance 18. *continued*

D. Northern Ireland – Expenditure other than out of Loans 1922–30 and other than on Capital Works, 1931–80

(in £ thousand)

		Principal Constituent Items												
	Total Expenditure	Education	Highways & Bridges	Hospitals, etc.	Housing	Lunacy	Poor Relief	Refuse Disposal	Sewerage	Water Supply	Gas Supply	Electricity Supply	Transport Services	Loan Charges (*d*)
1922	5,601	118	853	111	15	218	355	111	148	86	872	287	519	749
1923	6,109	117	779	118	17	200	266	97	136	62	636	189	446	1,016
1924	5,870	111	767	122	24	199	257	101	137	93	679	185	441	1,074
1925	5,786	135	872	132	74	209	268	105	142	86	733	164	416	1,266
1926	5,510	152	964	131	62	208	286	102	130	107	726	163	422	1,088
1927	5,968	175	976	131	96	204	300	99	136	100	884	214	428	1,187
1928	5,746	190	929	136	139	195	294	94	130	95 ---(*e*) 96	748 ---(*e*) 873	117 ---(*e*) 294	419 ---(*e*) 570	1,213
1929	5,879	187	916	142	115	199	277	89	124	93	795	361	606	1,295
1930	6,034	207	928	139	137	204	284	92	121	86	802	406	599	1,384
1931	6,254	237	955	141	135	204	282	86	117	91	808	423	637	1,527
1932	6,315	257	968	144	126	202	309 ---(*e*) 340	76	125	99	819	433	633	1,541
1933	6,580	315	886	141 ---(*e*) 175	134	202	485	73	127	85	805	461	567	1,666
1934	6,829	430	890	223	48	194	643	74	132	95	834	462	557	1,692
1935	6,942	440	873	233	44	203	560	73	137	90	840	535	605	1,774
1936	7,278	538	898	239	45	212	518	78	143	88	837	612	624	1,877
1937	7,595	480	929	253	55	227	484	88	157	98	886	710	656	1,864
1938	7,803	559	1,259	266	52	150	403	81	156	103	969	694	673	1,842
1939	7,918	578	1,337	287	51	258	434	78	152	111	891	775	742	1,798
1940	8,027	578	...	[553](*f*)	...	...(*f*)	...	...	...	...	...	...	...	1,844
1941	8,721	602	...	[614](*f*)	...	...(*f*)	...	...	...	...	...	...	...	1,845
1942	10,580	638	...	[453](*f*)	...	...(*f*)	...	...	...	...	...	...	...	1,823
1943	11,413	774	...	[704](*f*)	...	...(*f*)	...	...	...	...	...	...	...	1,889
1944	11,654	841	...	[761](*f*)	...	...(*f*)	...	...	...	...	...	...	...	1,823
1945	11,762	814	...	[810](*f*)	...	...(*f*)	...	...	...	...	...	...	...	1,790
1946	12,118	890	1,455	278	60	403	634	103	280	170	1,695	1,693	1,412	1,701
1947	13,199	1,056	1,702	578	104	465	720	129	317	187	1,820	1,675	1,457	1,574
1948	15,626	1,253	1,999	655	151	644	815	125	348	202 ---(*e*)	1,973	1,854	1,674	2,395

See p. 644 for footnotes.

Public Finance 18. *continued*

D. Northern Ireland – Expenditure other than out of Loans 1922–30 and other than on Capital Works, 1931–80

(in £ thousand)

Principal Constituent Items

	Total Expenditure	Education	Highways & Bridges	Local Authority Health Services	Housing	Welfare Services	Refuse Disposal	Sewerage	Water Supply	Gas Supply	Electricity Supply	Transport Services	Loan Charges (d)
1949	15,604	1,819	2,258	278	540	108	131	401	454	2,057	2,193	1,951	1,723
1950	16,051	2,355	2,450	522	602	216	135	428	492	2,126	1,624	2,101	1,877
1951	18,730	3,150	2,692	592	799	269	172	452	1,049	2,312	1,889	2,102	2,778
1952	20,748	3,797	2,842	770	1,000	301	366	267	627	2,491	2,056	2,277	2,334
1953	23,262	4,338	3,348	780	1,715	404	360	349	842	2,713	2,321	2,381	2,990
1954	27,277	5,249	3,805	1,205	1,477	578	318	322	968	2,968	4,124	2,452	5,654
1955	28,958	5,652	3,531	1,259	1,660	666	343	365	1,096	3,150	4,802	2,544	6,770
1956	33,207	6,960	3,798	1,335	1,786	750	386	432	1,228	3,374	5,565	2,721	6,198
1957	36,762	7,763	4,394	1,429	2,074	812	446	452	1,361	3,613	6,461	2,742	6,958
1958	42,643	9,931	4,772	1,537	2,279	873	453	522	1,564	3,858	7,782	2,862	7,702
1959	47,378	11,396	6,066	1,635	2,481	938	466	609	1,818	3,865	8,345	2,842	7,723
1960	51,994	13,258	7,319	1,872	2,702	1,069	526	676	2,074	3,900	8,926	2,848	8,215
1961	55,210	14,727	7,245	2,045	2,979	1,263	573	741	2,252	3,981	9,433	3,000	8,905
1962	60,795	16,532	8,237	2,252	3,511	1,427	630	857	2,453	4,122	10,099	3,155	9,601
1963	67,465	19,335	9,672	2,416	3,989	1,625	693	937	2,738	4,317	10,419	3,079	10,404
1964	73,592	21,479	10,870	2,662	4,700	1,911	764	1,012	2,942	4,415	10,438	3,236	11,695
1965	81,282	24,047	12,552	2,827	5,590	2,111	845	1,232	3,118	4,455	11,579	3,246	12,883
1966	89,197	27,125	13,279	3,074	6,352	2,470	971	1,294	3,350	4,412	13,065	3,518	14,394
1967	100,696	31,716	15,955	3,226	6,966	2,798	1,136	1,448	3,702	4,609	14,033	3,770	15,834
1968	111,226	35,696	17,185	3,567	8,120	3,166	1,285	1,573	4,075	4,671	15,160	3,722	17,485
1969	117,850	39,744	13,700	3,805	9,740	3,478	1,420	1,771	4,593	4,166	16,402	3,899	21,256
1970	129,913	42,869	13,936	4,093	11,965	3,974	1,636	1,992	5,305	4,470	17,141	4,028	23,708
1971	139,151	39,388	14,380	5,019	13,962	5,130	1,909	2,422	6,123	4,935	18,663	4,839	27,089
1972	159,635	45,717	15,689	5,926	14,804	6,409	2,267	2,809	6,925	5,241	21,197	4,297	29,660
1973	183,306	52,198	17,101	6,608	3,319(g)	7,638	2,670	3,161	7,862	5,675	23,679	4,356	22,226
1974	96,427(g)	26,139(g)	9,569(g)	8,583	1,921(g)	4,532(g)	3,547	1,934(g)	5,359(g)	7,026	— (g)	— (g)	10,131
1975	33,880(g)	— (g)	— (g)	— (g)	1,143(g)	— (g)	4,810	— (g)	— (g)	10,540	—	—	4,072
1976	43,094	—	—	—	1,147	—	6,473	—	—	12,486	—	—	4,564
1977	50,593	—	—	—	1,111	—	7,618	—	—	13,313	—	—	5,292
1978	57,366	—	—	—	1,122	—	9,086	—	—	13,835	—	—	5,526
1979	65,267	—	—	—	1,094	—	10,295	—	—	16,363	—	—	5,757
1980	81,599	—	—	—	1,241	—	12,337	—	—	21,789	—	—	7,018

See p. 644 for footnotes.

Public Finance 18. *continued*

E. Northern Ireland – Expenditure out of Loans 1922–30 and on Capital Works 1931–80

(in £ thousand)

	Total Expenditure	Principal Constituent Items: Education	Highways & Bridges	Housing	Sewerage	Water Supply	Gas Supply	Electricity Supply	Transport Services
1922	1,284	...	9	260	15	36	112	302	244
1923	1,436	...	29	188	1	68	104	418	14
1924	1,923	...	96	23	11	113	268	343	11
1925	2,136	...	338	368	35	169	42	145	2
1926	2,053	...	378	434	24	215	71	154	182
1927	1,880	...	311	321	17	298	37	124	44
1928	1,527	...	157	512	8	194	51	167	4
1929	1,795	...	211	547	9	295	42	179	—
1930	1,966	...	382	416	16	311	56	209	3
1931	1,809	...	163	355	68	285	109	176	52
1932	1,773	...	221	224	89	263	59	192	54
1933	1,532	...	248	55	54	269	55	169	77
1934	2,172	...	194	37	80	773	69	175	41
1935	1,546	...	187	69	111	184	78	234	53
1936	1,783	...	133	190	62	274	89	427	145
1937	1,665	...	119	321	91	205	123	419	44
1938	1,689	...	172	77	83	277	197	427	29
1939	1,813	...	123	368	69	145	107	351	70
1940	1,587	...	...	...	...		546		...
1941	914	...	...	...	...		458		...
1942	607	...	...	...	...		339		...
1943	530	...	...	...	...		289		...
1944	523	...	...	...	...		297		...
1945	357	...	...	...	...		175		...
1946	615	...	2	125	18	56	124	62	100
1947	1,766	...	57	790	40	221	226	191	132
1948	3,066	...	53	1,543	114	280	172	354	315
1949	6,399	...	121	3,206	296	509	239	1,335	391
1950	9,715	406	141	6,225	336	738	295	976	403
1951	8,619	440	271	4,694	528	840	270	1,063	245
1952	11,712	981	428	5,896	689	1,005	322	1,662	204
1953	14,494	1,448	531	7,339	759	1,568	251	1,579	380
1954	17,893	1,954	712	8,198	661	2,389	291	2,654	374
1955	17,215	2,041	572	7,526	605	1,993	351	3,174	224
1956	17,214	2,000	654	6,659	771	3,241	411	2,531	413
1957	20,299	3,225	583	6,649	833	3,428	407	4,354	104
1958	20,048	3,720	732	4,889	928	4,627	298	4,012	73
1959	16,699	3,026	1,140	3,834	980	3,897	315	2,516	244
1960	17,589	2,673	899	5,786	1,193	4,242	419	1,382	44
1961	16,034	2,479	800	6,652	1,173	2,463	351	960	47
1962	16,009	2,627	777	6,674	1,078	2,316	377	773	62
1963	19,431	2,688	576	8,760	1,012	2,993	411	960	433
1964	23,354	2,911	1,234	10,283	1,703	2,702	899	1,568	468
1965	23,335	3,314	2,015	10,103	1,439	2,297	601	1,525	361
1966	27,047	4,112	2,323	10,957	1,222	2,406	684	2,528	36

Public Finance 18. *continued*

E. Northern Ireland – Expenditure out of Loans 1922–30 and on Capital Works 1931–80 (*cont.*)

(in £ thousand)

	Total Expenditure	Principal Constituent Items							
		Education	Highways & Bridges	Housing	Sewerage	Water Supply	Gas Supply	Electricity Supply	Transport Services
1967	31,036	4,826	2,022	12,991	1,960	3,570	889	2,147	58
1968	39,867	6,143	2,047	17,818	1,929	4,101	2,519	1,942	436
1969	44,311	6,600	2,442	20,198	2,056	5,207	1,203	1,713	250
1970	45,089	5,462	2,926	19,334	2,053	7,155	1,339	2,011	588
1971	51,322	5,900	3,563	22,148	3,210	6,412	1,846	2,968	850
1972	17,164(*g*)	5,454	4,681	−13,674(*g*)	3,469	7,371	1,404	2,236	64
1973	41,767(*g*)	7,870	6,386	6,387(*g*)	5,301	5,105	1,303	2,040	287
1974	29,483(*g*)	3,838(*g*)	4,025(*g*)	2,030(*g*)	3,262(*g*)	6,457(*g*)	1,019	—(*g*)	—(*g*)
1975	9,069(*g*)	—(*g*)	—(*g*)	1,477(*g*)	—(*g*)	—(*g*)	846	—	—
1976	13,371	—	—	1,301	—	—	1,250	—	—
1977	11,879	—	—	1,004	—	—	782	—	—
1978	13,377	—	—	850	—	—	528	—	—
1979	15,163	—	—	1,100	—	—	757	—	—
1980	21,318	—	—	1,815	—	—	419	—	—

F. Republic of Ireland – Expenditure on Revenue Account 1923–80

(in £ thousand)

	Total Expenditure	Principal Constituent Items							
		Education	Housing	Roads & Bridges (*h*)	Water Supply & Sanitary Services	Public Assistance	Health	Mental Hospitals	Loan Charges (*d*)
1923	8,354	209	—	1,593	486	1,558	339	...	685
1924	8,570	218	—	1,492	513	1,613	305	...	664
1925	9,465	240	—	1,886	511	1,521	288	...	686
1926	9,267	249	—	1,820	498	1,557	281	...	745
1927	9,193	260	48	1,767	358	1,612	334	...	984
1928	9,935	258	98	2,587	377	1,621	363	...	990
				---(*h*)					
1929	9,387	271	87	2,706	424	1,359	480	704	1,032
1930	8,672	263	91	2,311	440	1,426	497	691	1,058
1931	8,932	260	100	2,380	465	1,509	536	724	1,087
1932	9,230	303	97	2,612	489	1,564	538	770	1,096
1933	10,072	314	127	3,298	562	1,753	548	729	1,023
1934	9,948	325	159	2,820	561	1,909	559	730	1,088
1935	9,768	332	164	2,432	507	1,651	579	764	1,314
1936	10,005	353	99	2,466	498	1,626	573	807	1,440
1937	10,610	369	114	2,667	565	1,663	595	833	1,634
1938	11,688	387	135	3,130	572	1,735	642	900	1,845
1939	12,157	419	133	3,246	577	1,781	673	947	2,014
1940	12,921	437	146	3,466	592	1,871	682	998	2,184
1941	13,580	454	185	3,292	502	2,004	705	1,107	2,310
1942	13,254	456	185	2,751	478	2,116	703	1,122	2,416
1943	14,279	490	190	2,602	540	2,499	825	1,263	2,446
1944	14,212	507	216	2,341	653	2,022	585	1,343	2,406
1945	14,879	532	244	2,538	591	2,278	662	1,399	2,304
1946	15,690	566	273	2,694	601	2,334	824	871	2,427
1947	17,471	607	298	4,204	666	2,269	783	928	2,606

See p. 644 for footnotes.

Public Finance 18. *continued*

F. Republic of Ireland – Expenditure on Revenue Account 1923–80 (*cont.*)

(in £ million)

	Total Expenditure	Principal Constituent Items							
		Education	Housing	Roads & Bridges (*h*)	Water Supply & Sanitary Services	Public Assistance	Health	Mental Hospitals	Loan Charges (*d*)
1948	21·6	0·7	0·4	5·6	0·8	2·8	1·1	1·2	2·6
		---(*i*)							
1949	26·0	0·5	3·0	7·8	2·0	4·7	4·6		...
1950	28·5	0·6	3·1	6·0	2·1	4·6	5·3		...
1951	31·1	0·6	3·6	6·2	2·2	5·0	5·9		...
1952	35·5	0·7	4·3	7·1	2·5	6·3	7·1		...
1953	37·9	0·8	5·0	8·4	2·8	6·3	7·2		...
1954	42·8	0·8	5·9	10·8	2·9	6·7	7·8		...
1955	45·6	0·8	6·6	11·2	3·1	7·2	8·4		...
1956	49·1	0·9	7·1	11·6	3·4	1·1	16·2		...
1957	52·5	0·9	8·0	11·6	3·7	1·2	18·0		...
1958	52·3	0·9	8·7	10·7	3·9	1·2	18·5		...
1959	54·4	1·0	9·1	11·0	4·1	1·2	19·3		...
1960	56·4	1·1	9·6	11·6	4·4	1·1	19·6		...
1961	59·5	1·1	10·1	12·1	4·7	1·1	20·6		...
1962	64·5	1·2	10·7	13·9	5·0	1·1	22·3		...
1963	68·9	1·2	11·2	14·5	5·4	1·1	24·4		...
1964	73·0	1·5	11·8	15·1	5·8	1·2	26·0		...
1965	86·3	1·7	12·7	16·5	6·6	1·3	31·5		...
1966	92·4	2·0	13·9	17·4	7·1	1·4	35·2		...
1967	100·4	2·2	15·1	18·3	7·7	1·6	38·9		...
1968	111·5	2·3	17·1	18·3	8·4	1·7	42·2		...
1969	122·8	2·5	19·2	19·3	9·7	1·9	48·5		...
1970	146·4	2·7	22·9	21·7	11·2	2·1	60·5		...
1971	173·6	3·0	24·7	26·2	13·5	2·4	74·9		...
1972	205·4	3·2	27·2	29·1	16·0	2·2	85·5		...
1973	254·7	3·4	32·2	31·6	19·7	2·3	116·9		...
1974	320·0	3·4	37·3	38·8	23·7	2·4	154·6		...
1974	[303·7](*j*)	[2·8](*j*)	[43·3](*j*)	[38·8](*j*)	[25·5](*j*)	[2·3](*j*)	[134·3](*j*)		...
1975	503·0	4·4	62·5	54·7	39·8	3·9	240·4		...
		---(*k*)	---(*k*)	---(*k*)	---(*k*)	---(*k*)	...		
1976	596·9	7·1	76·0	69·1	32·1	—	344·6		...
1977	719·5	8·4	93·6	86·9	40·3	—	409·9		...
1978	868·1	9·9	103·9	107·3	47·9	—	500·2		...
1979	1,071·5	10·4	123·7	132·6	58·0	—	630·3		...
1980	1,396·2	11·6	151·0	156·3	72·9	—	849·4		...

From 1949, Health and Mental Hospitals are shown as a single combined figure.

See p. 644 for footnotes.

Public Finance 18. *continued*

G. Republic of Ireland – Expenditure on Loan Account 1923–80

		(in £ thousand) Principal Constituent Items		
	Total Expenditure	Housing	Roads & Bridges	Water Supply & Sanitary Services
1923	363	...	...	...
1924	497	...	...	...
1925	1,213	...	...	...
1926	944	...	...	...
1927	951	...	...	...
1928	931	...	...	...
1929	1,221	525	...	...
1930	1,032	663	...	...
1931	1,025	565	37	186
1932	1,440	572	55	321
1933	1,346	641	24	241
1934	3,134	1,894	50	270
1935	3,873	2,173	38	258
1936	3,528	1,658	34	308
1937	3,978	1,615	193	364
1938	3,659	1,280	102	454
1939	4,806	2,511	65	510
1940	3,646	1,421	69	510
1941	3,192	1,374	44	418
1942	2,637	1,215	11	217
1943	2,613	1,076	7	104
1944	2,032	1,152	44	245
1945	1,005	703	--	149
1946	1,458	701	31	106
1947	1,372	742	124	156
		(in £ million)		
1948	2·3	1·4	0·1	0·2
1949	5·6	4·3	0·3	0·5
1950	14·2	11·6	0·3	0·7
1951	16·4	12·9	0·2	1·0
1952	19·3	15·0	0·4	1·1

		(in £ million) Principal Constituent Items		
	Total Expenditure	Housing	Roads & Bridges	Water Supply & Sanitary Services
1953	19·8	14·3	0·6	1·4
1954	18·4	13·3	0·5	1·5
1955	18·0	12·6	0·6	1·5
1956	18·0	12·3	0·7	1·8
1957	17·0	10·8	0·6	2·0
1958	11·4	7·1	0·3	1·6
1959	9·6	6·0	0·3	1·6
1960	9·6	6·1	0·4	1·4
1961	9·8	6·5	0·3	1·4
1962	11·5	7·2	0·7	1·9
1963	13·3	8·5	0·5	2·2
1964	15·9	9·4	0·6	3·0
1965	20·3	11·9	0·5	3·7
1966	25·8	16·9	0·5	3·6
1967	25·8	18·4	0·4	2·8
1968	32·0	22·6	0·5	2·8
1969	38·1	26·4	1·0	4·0
1970	46·7	31·3	1·3	5·7
1971	42·4	25·2	1·1	6·6
1972	54·5	36·0	1·2	9·2
1973	63·7	43·2	0·8	10·2
1974	90·2	61·1	1·2	14·4
1974	[107·8](*j*)	[74·2](*j*)	[0·9](*j*)	[16·4](*j*)
1975	162·5	113·2	2·3	30·5
		---(*k*)	---(*k*)	---(*k*)
1976	153·7	101·1	2·1	...
1977	160·6	103·4	2·4	26·5
1978	184·7	116·6	2·4	28·4
1979	253·7	151·9	2·1	44·3
1980	324·5	200·0	3·2	65·7

(*a*) Subsequently excluding the pilot and light services.
(*b*) Revised figures were not carried back beyond 1892.
(*c*) Water supply in Rural Districts is included with sewerage to 1907.
(*d*) Figures under this heading are only included in total expenditure in so far as they are not already included under some other heading.
(*e*) Subsequently including the loan charges appropriate to the heading, though in the case of water supply, repayments are only included from 1949.
(*f*) Mental hospitals are included with other hospitals in these years.
(*g*) Many services were transferred to regional authorities in 1972–5.
(*h*) County Council expenditure only to 1928. The break is virtually negligible.
(*i*) County Council and County Borough Council expenditure only from 1949. The break is virtually negligible.
(*j*) Figures are for the period April–December. See also note a above.
(*k*) Reorganisation of the classification in 1976 results in breaks in the continuity of the series.

Public Finance 19. Standard Rate of Income Tax – United Kingdom 1799–1980

NOTES

[1] SOURCES: 1798–1918 – *S.P.* 1919 XXIII, Part I (*Report* of the Royal Commission on Income Tax), p. 131; 1919–80 – *Report of the Commissioners of Inland Revenue* and *Inland Revenue Statistics*.

[2] There was no income tax in force in 1803 and from 1817 to 1842.

[3] Standard rate was expressed as shillings and pence in the pound until 1969, whereafter it has been expressed as a percentage.

[4] The rates apply to years ended 5 April.

[5] Income tax was not levied in Ireland until 1854.

1799–1802	2/-	1877–1878	3d	1931	4/6
1804–1805	1/-	1879–1880	5d	1932–1933	5/-
1806	1/3	1881	6d	1934–1935	4/6
1807–1816	2/-	1882	5d	1936–1937	4/9
		1883	6½d	1938	5/-
1843–1853	7d				
1854	5d or 7d(*a*)	1884	5d	1939	5/6
1855	10d or 1/2(*a*)	1885	6d	1940	7/-
1856–1857	11½d or 1/4(*a*)	1886–1887	8d	1941	8/6
1858	5d or 7d(*a*)	1888	7d	1942–1946	10/-
		1889–1893	6d	1947–1951	9/-
1859	5d				
1860	6½d or 9d(*a*)	1894	7d	1952–1953	9/6
1861	7d or 10d(*a*)	1895–1900	8d	1954–1955	9/-
1862–1863	6d or 9d(*a*)	1901	1/-	1956–1959	8/6
1864	7d	1902	1/2	1960–1965	7/9
		1903	1/3	1966–1969	8/3
1865	6d				
1866–1867	4d	1904	11d	1970–1971	41·25%
1868	5d	1905–1909	1/-	1972–1973	38·75%
1869	6d	1910–1914	1/2		---(*b*)
1870	5d	1915	1/8	1974	30%
		1916	3/-	1975	33%
1871	4d			1976–1977	35%
1872	6d	1917–1918	5/-		
1873	4d	1919–1922	6/-	1978	34%
1874	3d	1923	5/-	1979	33%
1875–1876	2d	1924–1925	4/6	1980	30%
		1926–1930	4/-		

(*a*) The lower rate applied on income from £100 to £150 and the higher rate on income above £150.

(*b*) Subsequently basic rate. Higher rates are applied to higher income bands.

CHAPTER XII

FINANCIAL INSTITUTIONS

TABLES

In banking, as in so many other aspects of economic life, regular statistical information begins to be available for the period immediately following the revolution of 1688, despite the fact that in this case the majority of the statistics are not of government origin. Indeed, the only official series is that of coinage at the Mint, which can be carried back in Craig's book to 1273, but with gaps prior to 1662 which damage the usefulness of the statistics.[1] It is only from this last date that the figures have been included here, in table 1, and it is not continued beyond 1821. The excerpt thus covers the period of change from a silver standard to the firm nineteenth-century attachment to gold.

The Bank of England, founded in 1694, was treated exclusively as a private body, so far as the details of its operations were concerned, for well over a century afterwards. Nevertheless,

[1] Sir John Craig, *The Mint* (Cambridge, 1953).

a certain amount of statistical material about its operations for all except its earliest days has emerged over the centuries. This forms the basis of table 2. At the time of the suspension of cash payments in 1797, in 1810 during the Bullion Committee's proceedings, and again at each of the banking enquiries of the following forty years, a good deal of information about the Bank's position was obtained retrospectively and was published. But such information about the Bank's current position was not required by law until 1833, and not in detail until 1844. As a result, the latter year marks a clear division in any table of the Bank's operations.

The longest series before 1844 is that provided by the Bank's half-yearly statements in February and August, which were published for years back to 1778 by the Select Committee on Commercial Distress in 1847.[2] Clapham carried this series back to 1775 from the Bank's own records, and on the basis of a single annual statement he could push it back to 1720.[3] These sources together provide Part A of table 2, which could be filled out in more detail for various short periods from the 1790s onwards from the appendices to the *Reports* of the Bullion Committee,[4] the Committee on the Bank of England Charter,[5] the Committee on Banks of Issue,[6] and the aforementioned Committee on Commercial Distress. Part B of the table shows the Bank's operations after 1844 according to the returns required by the Bank Charter Act of that year. Apart from the column for Bankers' Deposits it is comparable (except for changes in the value of money) throughout. Gold continued to be valued at the old statutory price from 1931 to 1939 despite the depreciation of sterling, but shortly after the outbreak of war practically the whole of the Bank's holdings of gold coin and bullion was transferred to the Treasury.

For the commercial banks and other financial institutions, and for the money supply as a whole, the information is less complete. Even as recently as 1946, Balogh could write that 'information currently available about the assets and liabilities of the different banks is, even at the present, neither uniform nor comprehensive'.[7] More than a decade later, Johnson was claiming that only three important improvements in British monetary statistics had taken place in the meantime, all concerned with assets rather than with the liabilities which constitute deposit money.[8] Further progress has been made since then, partly in response to the Radcliffe *Report*,[9] but it was not until the 1970s that some currently published data first became available. Since the financial world is a constantly changing one, there will doubtless be more and different series published in the future.

For all the deficiencies of the available data, however, it has been possible to reconstruct reasonably firm and reliable estimates of the United Kingdom money supply back to 1870, and a summary of Capie and Webber's figures is given as table 10. Other estimates have been

[2] *S.P.* 1847–8 VIII.
[3] Sir John Clapham, *The Bank of England* (2 vols., Cambridge, 1944).
[4] *S.P.* 1810, III.
[5] *S.P.* 1831–2 VI.
[6] *S.P.* 1840 XV and *S.P.* 1841 (Sess. 1) V.
[7] T. Balogh, *Studies in Financial Organisation* (Oxford, 1949), p. 28.
[8] Harry G. Johnson, 'British Monetary Statistics', *Economica* XXVI (1959), p. 2.
[9] *Report* of the Committee on the Working of the Monetary System, *S.P.* 1958–9 XVII.

pushed as far back as 1833, which though not so reliable, and definitely in need of revision in one important respect, are still a basis for further refinement. The references here are to Collins's estimates of the money stock,[10] and to Huffman and Lothian's figures for high-powered money, which are also given in table 10. Both include as part of their aggregates the coin circulation figures estimated by Sheppard,[11] which have been shown to be substantially too high in the 1870s.[12] Presumably a revision needs to be applied to the years before 1870 also, so that, for the present, these figures can only be regarded as provisional.

Tables 3 to 9 give, amongst other things, details of some of the components of total money supply – bank deposits and monetary circulation – though these are incomplete, in their earlier years at least. No one ever seriously suggested that the private banks should publish details of their operations, except as regards note issues. As a result there is only a slender basis for estimation of their liabilities. But from quite early in the days of joint stock banking, there was pressure to get information from these banks. The number publishing balance sheets gradually increased, and these have been the essential foundation for all subsequent estimates of their deposits – including the earliest, those begun in the 1870s by *The Economist*,[13] as well as those by Collins reproduced here in table 3, and those by Capie and Webber in table 4.

Beginning in 1921, the London Clearing Banks issued joint monthly statements of their position on a selected day in each week. The annual averages of these statements are shown in tables 5 and 5A.[14] The user of these figures for years prior to 1947 should be aware of the fact that the selected day of the week for showing their position differed for all but two of the Big Five banks, and the opportunity for 'window-dressing' consequently remained considerable.

Attention was first focussed on the bank note circulation during the period of restriction of cash payments (i.e. suspension of the gold standard) after 1797, and it returned with each boom and crisis of the first half of the nineteenth century. Until 1833, however, the Bank of England was the only note-issuing bank about which exact information was available, even to the Parliamentary committees of secrecy. Argument about the country bank issues was conducted, perforce, on the basis of the stamping statistics. These are so seriously defective that it is not surprising that much of the argument seems irrelevant or misdirected. As Pressnell says: 'It is certainly unfortunate that statistics relating to private note issues are so defective, and that no alternative figures exist at present, but the hard facts have to be faced.

[10] Michael Collins, 'Long-Term Growth of the English Banking Sector and Money Stock 1844–80', *Economic History Review*, second series XXXVI, 3 (1983).

[11] David K. Sheppard, *The Growth and Role of U.K. Financial Institutions 1880–1962* (London, 1971).

[12] By Capie and Webber, whose own series from 1870 onwards is shown as part of table 7. See note 1 to that table for the reference.

[13] Discussed in René P. Higonnet, 'Bank Deposits in the United Kingdom, 1870–1914', *Quarterly Journal of Economics* (1957), and reproduced in the first version of this book.

[14] A useful discussion of this and other data, including summaries for the period 1900–54, can be found in W. Manning Dacey, 'Banking Statistics', *Journal of the Royal Statistical Society*, XCXXIX (1956). Johnson's article, cited in footnote 8 above, is also useful in this respect. For the 1930s to the 1950s it is worth consulting the *Memoranda of Evidence to the Committee on the Working of the Monetary System*. (See footnote 9 above.)

To yield to the temptation to use faulty statistics because no others are available may lead only to faulty conclusions.'[15] Statistics of note circulation, therefore, cannot be relied on until 1833, and consequently that is when the series in table 7 begin.

More detailed statistics on the circulation and on other aspects of banking in the nineteenth century can be found in Capie and Webber's book, in the reports of the various committees already mentioned, and in various contemporary books. Among these, three deserve mention: J. Dun's *British Banking Statistics*,[16] and two by R. H. I. Palgrave – *Bank Rate and the Money Market* and *Abstract of Evidence to the House of Commons Committee of 1875 on Banks of Issue*.[17]

Savings Bank deposits are, of course, part of the wider definitions of the money supply. But they have also attracted attention as evidence of the activities of small savers, and from some as having a bearing on debates about standards of living.[18] Tables 8 and 9 showing the totals remaining deposited in savings banks each year in the United Kingdom and the Republic of Ireland respectively are not, of course, a complete record of such small savings. But taken in conjunction with National Savings and related statistics available annually in *Finance Accounts*, they are a fair guide, until recently at least.

Whilst the commercial banks have until fairly recently shown great reluctance to publish details of their operations, the aggregate sum of their clearings has been available for over a century. The total of London clearings is broadly comparable throughout the period, though the merging of banks has taken many transactions out of the purview of the system. The continuity of the provincial series, on the other hand, was more seriously broken by the inclusion of new centres and the exclusion of old, and by many changes of area, of which only the most important are indicated in table 12.

The yield on Consols from their inception to the present day, shown in table 13, constitutes one of the longest unbroken and consistent series that we have, particularly since, as a ratio, it is not affected by changes in the value of money – or, at any rate, their effects are indirect. As a measure of the long-term rate of interest it perhaps comes as close as we can get to that theoretical abstraction, which requires a loan of infinite duration without any risk of default. However, this must be qualified. As Hicks said: 'It can hardly be maintained that at all points of this majestic sequence the Yield on Consols does satisfy these exacting conditions.'[19] The risk of default must have been felt at various times – for example, in 1781, 1798, 1917, or 1940; and the virtually constant fall in the value of money since 1940, with the general expectation, felt at least by the mid 1950s, that it would continue, may well be held to constitute a species of creeping default. A more specific – and, fortunately, avoidable – difficulty is provided by the risk of termination by conversion which existed in the 1880s and

[15] L. S. Pressnell, *Country Banking in the Industrial Revolution* (Oxford, 1956).
[16] (London, 1876).
[17] (London, 1903) and (printed for private circulation, 1876) respectively.
[18] E.g. R. M. Hartwell, 'The Rising Standard of Living in England, 1800–1850', *Economic History Review*, second series XIII, 3 (1961), p. 404.
[19] J. R. Hicks, 'The Future of the Rate of Interest', *Transactions of the Manchester Statistical Society* (1957–8).

1890s, when the price of first the Three per cent and then the Two-and-three-quarters per cent Consols rose above par. This problem, and a way round it suggested by Harley, is discussed in note 3 to table 13.[20]

Short-term rates of interest are represented here by two tables. Table 14, largely reproduced from Clapham, shows the date of every change in Bank Rate (and its successor, Minimum Lending Rate) from the beginning of the restriction period in 1797 to 1980, by which time the series was about to come to an end. Table 15 gives the average market rate of discount for first-class three months' bills, starting in 1824. It is believed to be reasonably comparable throughout.

Statistics of capital markets are represented by two tables in this chapter, though additional material on capital formation, including capital exports, can be found in chapter XVI. Table 16 part A shows the figures of new capital issues taken from *The Economist*'s annual 'Commercial History and Review' supplements, since this provides a long comparable series. These statistics reflect the nominal amounts of capital instruments offered for sale, not the actual amount of capital forthcoming. There is a breakdown by type of issue in the source, which is not shown here. It becomes progressively more detailed up to the end of the nineteenth century, when statistics at more frequent intervals also become available. Going backwards from the starting-point of the table in 1870, there are figures for a few earlier years in the same source, but they are not exactly comparable with the ones shown here. Parts B and C of the table show the fuller and more refined statistics that the Bank of England began to publish in the 1920s, when concern first arose at official level about the effects of the export of capital on economic activity at home.

Table 17 gives a selection of the indices of share prices on the London market going back to the beginning of the eighteenth century. These indices are entirely separate, of course, and even if internally consistent, can hope to do no more than be representative of market movements in the most general terms. However, the author of Part A specifically provided a link to Part B; and the authors of the latter included the previously unpublished index in Part C as a link with the later series, albeit they did so with some misgivings.[21]

The selection of life assurance statistics shown in table 19 is reasonably straightforward, but some warning is required for table 18, which gives statistics of the value of property insured against fire derived from the tax records up to the abolition of the fire insurance duty in 1869. These were much used in the nineteenth century in estimating national wealth. But, as Maywald pointed out, their usefulness for this purpose 'depends mainly on the following circumstances: (a) the specific conditions of valuation for insurance purposes, (b) the

[20] See also C. K. Harley, 'Goschen's Conversion of the National Debt and the Yield on Consols', *Economic History Review*, second series XXIX, 1 (1976).

[21] A. D. Gayer, W. W. Rostow, and A. J. Schwartz, *The Growth and Fluctuations of the British Economy, 1790–1860* (2 vols., Oxford, 1953), I, p. 457. In particular, they questioned whether Hayek's index could be legitimately linked to the subsequent L.C.E.S. index, in view of the former's heavy weighting with railway shares and the latter's exclusion of them. The latter did produce a version which includes them, however, and both versions are shown here.

insurance-mindedness of the owners of assets, and (c) the weight of the uninsurable assets in the total of national wealth'.[22] Comparability over a period depends on these circumstances remaining reasonably stable, and also on stable rates of duty or the possibility of making exact allowance for changes in those rates. It seems probable that none of these conditions was fulfilled until after the Napoleonic Wars. During the long period of three shillings per cent duty, from 1815 to 1865, it is not clear to what degree the other circumstances were stable, though they must have been more so than before. The proportion of uninsurable assets (mainly land) certainly fell steadily, and quite possibly there may have been an increase in insurance-mindedness. But changes were fairly slow, and any attempt at exact measurement and allowance for them must await a systematic investigation of the subject. Until then these statistics must be used with caution. This is particularly so because, until 1850, the annual data are unreliable because of the erratic timing of payment of duty by the fire insurance companies.[23]

The bankruptcy statistics, which appear in table 20 and for the Republic of Ireland in table 21, are certainly reliable and fairly straightforward from 1870 onwards, following the Act of 1869. Earlier figures, however, present many difficulties, though a selection is given here in response to users' demands.[24] The differences between different sources in the period up to 1847, when more than one source is available, may partly arise from differences in dates taken for the end of the year. Another cause is certainly the inclusion by some and the exclusion by others of Scotland and Ireland. In other cases it is clear that misprints have occurred, though the culprit cannot usually be identified. Finally, the statistics may quite legitimately differ if they apply to different stages of the bankruptcy procedures. At the risk of oversimplification, these may be described, prior to 1861, as (1) the striking of a docket with a view to securing the issue of a commission of bankruptcy (or a fiat from 1832); (2) the granting of such a commission (or fiat); (3) the subsequent announcement in the *London Gazette*; and (4) the putting into effect of the commission (or fiat). After 1849, stages 1 and 2 were, in effect, combined, for creditors could petition directly for an 'adjudication' of bankruptcy. At all times, the proceedings could be rescinded. Obviously, statistics could apply to each of these stages, and they might or might not take account of subsequent annulments. The scope for discrepancies was very great. As a result we have several different series, and it has seemed best to show several of these, both to bring out the nature of the problem and to provide long overlaps.

The last two tables in the chapter present information on the exchange rate of sterling, going back almost to the beginning of the seventeenth century. These, too, are included in

[22] K. Maywald, 'Fire Insurance in the Capital Coefficient in Great Britain, 1866–1952', *Economic History Review*, second series IX, 1 (1956).

[23] *S.P.* 1863 XXVI, p. 2.

[24] Some of the discrepancies which persuaded us not to put the bankruptcy statistics into the first version of this book were discussed there on pp. 245–6. There were others, and yet more have been discussed in Sheila Marriner, 'English Bankruptcy Records and Statistics before 1850', *Economic History Review*, second series XXXIII, 3 (1980). Nevertheless, probably more people have commented on the absence of these statistics than any others, and they have certainly been much cited in the past.

response to users' requests, though they may seem to be of limited interest except in periods when the exchange rate has been floating. There are many gaps, however, in the earlier years, and the figures are often based on very few quotations, so that they may not give a wholly reliable picture of the fluctuations of the pound. However, by the eighteenth century they are much more continuous, and based on an increasing number of transactions. Apart from the greater detail available in some of the sources cited, and from frequent press quotations since the middle of the nineteenth century, weekly rates can be found for the period 1718–1847 in various *Sessional Papers* of the first half of the nineteenth century.[25]

[25] *S.P.* 1810–1 X; *S.P.* 1819 III; *S.P.* 1840 IV; *S.P.* 1841 (Sess. 1) V; and *S.P.* 1847–8 VIII.

Financial Institutions 1. Gold and Silver Coinage – 1662–1821

NOTE
SOURCE: Sir John Craig, *The Mint* (Cambridge University Press, 1953), appendix 1.

(in £ thousand sterling)

	Gold	Silver		Gold	Silver
1662 (*a*)	4·4	243·6	1711	435·7	76·8
1663	31·3	364·4	1712	133·4	5·5
1664	9·6	216·5	1713	613·8	7·2
1665	69·3	75·4	1714	1,379·6	4·9
1666	92·5	32·8	1715	1,826·5	5·1
1666 (*b*)	42·3	34·8	1716	1,110·4	5·1
1667 (*c*)	117·3	53·4	1717	709·6	2·9
1668 (*d*)	222·4	122·7	1718	140·6	7·1
1669	120·7	46·4	1719	689·0	3·4
1670	117·6	132·6	1720	885·9	24·3
1671	194·1	124·2	1721	272·5	7·2
1672	86·9	274·0	1722	594·7	6·1
1673	127·2	304·9	1723	388·1	149·1
1674	87·5	41·2	1724	273·8	3·1
1675	53·9	5·8	1725	58·4	7·7
1676	242·4	314·8	1726	873·0	2·6
1677	243·0	451·7	1727	292·8	2·0
1678	130·2	24·7	1728	539·9	2·6
1679	560·1	253·0	1729	—	6·4
1680	603·8	198·1	1730	91·6	3·5
1681	312·4	92·2	1731	305·8	2·2
1682	186·5	29·6	1732	373·5	2·6
1683	376·7	229·7	1733	833·9	3·6
1684	319·2	53·7	1734	487·1	4·9
1685	564·2	94·8	1735	107·2	3·5
1686	648·3	59·8	1736	330·6	5·3
1687	421·4	250·6	1737	67·3	3·7
1688	589·4	76·2	1738	269·8	—
1689	134·9	96·6	1739	283·9	10·5
1690	51·2	2·0	1740	196·2	—
1691	57·2	3·7	1741	25·2	9·5
1692	120·2	4·2	1742	—	—
1693	54·1	2·0	1743	—	7·4
1694	64·8	9·3	1744	9·8	7·8
1695	753·1	0·2	1745	293·0	1·9
1696	145·5	2,511·9 (*e*)	1746	474·5	136·4
1697	126·5	2,192·2 (*e*)	1747	37·1	4·7
1698	495·1	326·6 (*e*)	1748	338·5	—
1699	148·4	60·4	1749	710·7	—
1700	126·2	14·9	1750	558·6	—
1701	1,249·5	116·2	1751	450·7	8·1
1702	170·2	0·4	1752	572·7	0·1
1703	1·6	2·2	1753	364·9	0·1
1704	—	12·4	1754	—	0·1
1705	4·9	1·3	1755	224·7	0·1
1706	25·1	2·9	1756	493·0	0·1
1707	28·4	3·6 (*f*)	1757	—	16·6
1708	47·2	11·6 (*f*)	1758	651·8	62·6
1709	115·3	78·8 (*f*)	1759	2,429·0	0·1
1710	173·6	2·5	1760	676.2	0·1

See p. 654 for footnotes.

Financial Institutions 1. *continued*

(in £ thousand sterling)

	Gold	Silver		Gold	Silver
1761	550·9	..	1791	2,456·6	—
1762	553·7	3·2	1792	1,171·9	0·3
1763	513·0	2·6	1793	2,747·4	—
1764	883·1	..	1794	2,558·9	—
1765	538·3	..	1795	493·4	0·3
1766	820·7	0·3	1796	464·7	—
1767	1,271·8	—	1797	2,000·3	—
1768	844·6	—	1798	2,967·5	—
1769	626·6	—	1799	450·0	—
1770	623·8	0·1	1800	189·9	0·1
1771	637·8	—	1801	450·2	..
1772	843·9	0·3	1802	437·0	0·1
1773	1,317·6	—	1803	596·4	0·1
1774	4,685·6	—	1804	718·4	0·1
1775	4,901·2	—	1805	54·7	0·2
1776	5,006·4	0·3	1806	405·1	—
1777	3,681·0	—	1807	—	0·1
1778	350·4	—	1808	371·7	—
1779	1,696·1	0·3	1809	298·9	0·1
1780	—	—	1810	316·9	0·1
1781	876·8	0·1	1811	312·3	—
1782	698·1	—	1812	—	0·1
1783	227·1	—	1813	519·7	0·1
1784	822·1	0·2	1814	—	0·2
1785	2,488·1	—	1815	—	—
1786	1,107·4	—	1816	—	1,805·3
1787	2,849·1	55·5	1817	4,275·3	2,436·3
1788	3,664·2	—	1818	2,862·4	576·3
1789	1,530·7	—	1819	3·6	1,267·3
1790	2,660·5	—	1820	949·5	847·7
			1821	9,520·8	433·7

(*a*) Year ended 29th September henceforth to 1666.
(*b*) 29th September to 21st December.
(*c*) Year ended 21st December.
(*d*) Calendar year henceforth.
(*e*) Plus Country Mints, 1696–8; 1,800·8.
(*f*) Plus Edinburgh, 1707–9; 320·4.

Financial Institutions 2. The Bank of England – 1720–1980

NOTES TO PART A

[1] SOURCES: 1720–77 and 1778–97 (Drawing Accounts only) – J. H. Clapham, *The Bank of England* (2 vols, Cambridge University Press, 1944), vol. I, appendix c; 1778–1844 – *S.P.* 1847–8, VIII (appendix to the Report of the Select Committee on the Commercial Distress, part II). The figures from Clapham's book are reproduced by permission of the Governor and Company of the Bank of England.

[2] There is an element of conjecture in the figures of circulation and of bullion for the years 1720–8 – *vide* Clapham, *loc. cit.*

[3] The years 1720–64 are represented by accounts drawn up on 31st August, 1766–73 by accounts drawn up on the last day of February, and later years by the means of accounts drawn up on the last days of February and August.

A. 1720–1844

(in £ thousand sterling)

	Circulation	Drawing Accounts	Rest	Bullion
1720	2,480	1,568	145	1,001
1721	1,925	1,108	133	1,048
1722	2,762	1,198	166	1,246
1723	3,323	791	410	1,658
1724	3,758	1,479	537	1,918
1725	4,470	1,233	283	1,178
1726	2,966	1,703	311	1,763
1727	4,465	2,129	303	2,961
1728	4,281	2,256	281	2,444
1729	4,200	1,919	290	2,324
1730	4,416	1,888	298	2,201
1731	5,250	1,805	295	2,691
1732	4,592	2,459	280	2,537
1733	4,543	2,038	275	3,356
1734	4,573	2,825	278	3,714
1735	4,739	2,917	284	3,736
1736	5,078	2,599	291	3,968
1737	4,415	2,607	309	3,317
1738	4,609	2,549	308	2,980
1739	4,062	2,671	307	4,087
1740	4,444	2,845	308	4,801
1741	4,084	3,203	300	4,075
1742	5,011	2,732	325	3,424
1743	4,250	2,745	352	2,613
1744	4,270	2,868	370	1,732
1745	3,465	2,172	346	808
1746	3,845	1,978	308	2,335
1747	3,652	2,441	279	1,938
1748	3,790	1,683	280	2,179
1749	4,183	1,880	338	2,062
1750	4,318	1,914	358	1,959
1751	5,195	1,933	330	2,970
1752	4,750	2,135	290	2,730
1753	4,420	1,723	262	2,289
1754	4,081	1,675	310	2,829
1755	4,115	2,259	285	3,789
1756	4,516	2,815	259	4,034
1757	5,150	3,052	265	3,727
1758	4,864	2,328	295	2,241
1759	4,800	1,620	363	2,208
1760	4,936	1,913	297	2,628
1761	5,247	1,814	347	2,020
1762	5,887	2,121	484	3,053
1763	5,315	1,550	515	367
1764	6,211	1,504	512	1,873
	-------(*a*)	-------(*a*)	----(*a*)	-------(*a*)

See p. 657 for footnotes.

Financial Institutions 2. *continued*

A. 1720–1844 (*cont.*)

(in £ thousand sterling)

	Circulation	Drawing Accounts	Deposits	Rest	Bullion	Securities	
						Total	Government
1765	...	...	...	...	...	...	...
1766	5,846	1,497	...	484	1,871	...	...
1767	5,511	1,568	...	384	818	...	...
1768	5,779	1,797	...	499	1,564	...	...
1769	5,707	1,810	...	437	1,379	...	...
1770	5,237	1,820	...	614	2,873	...	...
1771	6,823	1,716	...	593	2,278	...	...
1772	5,962	1,553	...	666	1,504	...	...
1773	6,037	1,784	...	648	1,192	...	...
	-------(*a*)	-------(*a*)		----(*a*)	-------(*a*)		
1774	...	...	...	...	...	...	...
1775	8,762	2,136	...	872	6,829	...	...
1776	8,626	2,108	...	859	5,141	...	...
1777	8,033	1,858	...	1,001	3,279	...	...
1778	7,099	2,182	4,689	1,206	2,570	10,424	7,219
1779	8,145	2,241	4,780	1,316	3,847	10,393	8,178
1780	7,376	2,306	5,690	1,437	3,880	10,623	7,943
1781	6,701	2,564	5,859	1,659	3,071	11,148	7,625
1782	7,394	2,520	6,445	1,857	2,057	13,639	9,667
1783	6,991	1,911	5,285	1,998	956	13,319	9,791
1784	5,898	1,970	5,086	2,186	1,098	12,072	8,113
1785	6,247	2,250	6,461	2,465	4,114	11,059	6,962
1786	7,883	2,506	6,009	2,618	6,145	10,366	7,412
1787	9,008	2,269	5,767	2,792	5,960	11,606	7,854
1788	9,782	2,399	5,353	2,904	6,321	11,717	8,337
1789	10,465	2,815	5,970	2,832	7,937	11,329	8,956
1790	10,737	2,957	6,211	2,729	8,510	11,168	9,197
1791	11,556	3,264	6,401	2,717	7,962	12,711	10,651
1792	11,157	2,564	5,525	2,718	5,913	13,487	10,327
1793	11,377	3,010	5,895	2,802	4,666	15,407	9,966
1794	10,515	2,776	6,914	2,935	6,879	13,486	9,407
1795	12,440	3,716	7,064	3,029	5,632	16,901	13,208
1796	9,988	2,522	6,179	3,246	2,331	17,083	11,914
1797	10,394	2,644	6,328	3,414	2,588	17,549	10,240
1798	12,638	...	7,225	3,399	6,188	17,075	11,086
1799	13,175	...	7,887	3,205	7,282	16,985	10,482
1800	15,946	...	7,699	3,784	5,647	27,781	13,781
1801	15,385	...	9,440	3,980	4,488	24,317	13,942
1802	16,142	...	8,299	4,118	4,022	24,537	13,864
1803	15,652	...	8,934	4,516	3,685	25,417	11,377
1804	17,116	...	9,196	4,726	4,626	26,413	14,839
1805	17,130	...	13,066	4,776	6,754	28,217	14,151
1806	19,379	...	9,809	4,946	6,101	28,032	14,491
1807	18,315	...	11,809	4,863	6,314	28,673	13,431
1808	17,650	...	12,487	5,112	6,936	28,314	14,553
1809	19,059	...	11,120	5,169	4,071	31,277	15,026
1810	22,907	...	13,037	5,579	3,347	38,176	15,761
1811	23,324	...	11,261	5,816	3,297	37,103	19,543
1812	23,218	...	11,722	6,203	3,041	38,101	21,646
1813	24,020	...	11,214	6,583	2,798	39,019	25,314
1814	26,585	...	13,653	7,082	2,151	45,168	29,306

A. 1720–1844 (*cont.*)

(in £ thousand sterling)

	Circulation	Deposits	Rest	Bullion	Securities	
					Total	Government
1815	27,255	12,199	7,975	2,723	44,706	25,853
1816	26,886	12,123	7,433	6,102	40,340	22,762
1817	28,471	9,955	5,691	10,675	33,442	26,319
1818	26,987	7,963	4,898	8,209	31,638	27,085
1819	25,190	6,359	3,939	3,890	31,598	23,887
1820	23,892	4,257	3,429	6,561	25,017	20,445
1821	22,090	5,721	3,377	11,552	19,636	15,882
1822	18,065	5,545	3,600	10,578	16,632	13,073
1823	18,812	7,504	3,099	11,521	17,894	12,751
1824	19,935	9,889	2,864	12,799	19,888	14,495
1825	20,076	8,290	2,869	6,207	25,029	18,431
1826	23,516	7,068	3,024	4,607	29,001	19,144
1827	22,319	8,427	2,930	10,311	23,364	19,247
1828	21,669	9,700	2,798	10,423	23,743	20,251
1829	19,709	9,295	2,835	6,815	25,023	19,905
1830	20,758	11,192	2,596	10,161	24,385	20,475
1831	19,069	10,141	2,675	7,328	24,557	18,992
1832	18,016	9,906	2,653	6,445	24,130	18,822
1833	19,500	12,492	2,580	9,697	24,875	19,149
1834	19,046	13,575	2,639	7,529	27,730	18,624
1835	18,110	12,282	2,755	6,231	26,917	17,447
1836	18,130	13,299	2,806	6,581	27,654	15,443
1837	18,487	10,485	2,965	5,381	26,556	13,202
1838	19,266	9,825	2,833	10,036	21,888	13,576
1839	17,958	7,979	2,792	4,618	24,110	13,534
1840	16,773	7,058	2,862	4,342	22,350	14,064
1841	16,971	7,215	2,830	4,630	22,386	14,289
1842	18,543	8,661	2,844	8,103	21,944	14,220
1843	19,812	11,285	3,009	11,722	22,383	16,446
1844	21,317	12,333	3,374	15,764	21,260	14,406

(*a* See note 3 above.

NOTES TO PART B

[1] SOURCES: The weekly returns of the Bank of England published in the *London Gazette* are the original source. The yearly averages shown here are taken from the United States National Monetary Commission's *Statistics for Great Britain, Germany and France* (Washington, 1910), and from the original source from 1910 onwards. *Bankers' Deposits* for 1844–77 are taken from R. H. I. Palgrave, *Bank Rate in England, France and Germany, 1844–78* (London, 1880), and from 1920 onwards from the Bank of England's *Statistical Summary* and *Abstract*. *Bankers' Deposits* for 1878–1919 (and the figure mentioned in footnote (*c*)) have not been previously published, and were kindly made available to us by the Bank of England.

[2] Statistics are averages of Wednesdays to 1971 (1st line), and are on the second Wednesday in December subsequently.

[3] Gold Coin and Bullion held by the Issue Department are not given here after 1939 because the amounts held since September 1939 have been negligible. The holding on 30 August 1939 was £263·0 million, which was practically all transferred to the Treasury. Issue Department holdings of other securities and of coin other than gold coin have also been negligible. Since 1938 the highest yearly averages have been: Other securities – £3·4 million (in 1940), and coin other than gold coin – £3·3 million (in 1951).

B. 1844–1980

(in £ million)

	Issue Department		Banking Department					
			Deposits			Securities		
	Circulation (*a*)	Bullion (*b*)	Total	Public	Bankers	Govern-ment	Other	Reserves of Notes
1844	20·3	13·9	13·6	5·2	1·0	14·4	9·5	7·9
1845	20·7	14·6	15·3	5·7	1·3	13·4	12·2	7·9
1846	20·3	14·2	19·2	6·3	1·6	13·1	16·7	7·9
1847	19·1	9·8	15·1	6·4	1·5	11·6	17·2	4·6
1848	18·1	13·2	15·0	5·2	2·4	12·4	12·0	9·1
1849	18·4	14·3	16·2	6·1	2·1	14·2	10·2	9·9
1850	19·4	15·9	17·6	7·8	1·7	14·3	11·0	10·5
1851	19·5	13·9	16·4	7·1	1·7	13·7	12·6	8·5
1852	21·9	20·1	18·8	6·0	3·2	13·8	11·4	12·2
1853	22·6	17·0	18·2	5·7	2·3	13·3	15·1	8·4
1854	20·7	13·3	14·7	3·6	2·7	11·6	14·7	6·6
1855	19·8	13·5	16·7	5·0	3·1	11·9	15·3	7·8
1856	19·7	10·3	16·0	4·8	3·0	11·7	17·1	5·1
1857	19·5	9·7	17·1	6·4	3·3	10·6	20·4	4·7
1858	20·2	17·1	20·0	5·9	4·6	10·4	16·3	11·2
1859	21·3	17·3	21·7	7·3	4·3	11·1	18·2	10·4
1860	21·3	14·5	20·2	6·6	4·3	9·8	20·5	7·7
1861	20·0	12·2	17·8	5·3	4·2	10·1	18·7	6·7
1862	20·8	15·5	21·7	7·1	5·0	11·2	19·0	9·3
1863	20·7	13·8	21·3	7·3	4·7	11·1	20·2	7·7
1864	20·6	12·8	20·1	6·9	4·9	11·0	20·3	6·8
1865	21·1	13·7	20·7	6·7	5·0	10·5	20·6	7·3
1866	23·2	14·0	22·1	5·3	6·3	11·0	23·0	5·8
1867	23·4	20·2	25·6	6·8	6·7	12·9	18·2	11·6
1868	23·9	19·7	25·1	4·9	6·8	14·1	17·6	10·7
1869	23·5	17·8	23·2	5·1	6·5	14·1	16·8	9·3
1870	23·3	19·9	25·7	7·6	6·6	13·2	18·6	11·6
1871	24·4	22·9	28·4	7·1	8·4	13·7	18·8	13·5
1872	25·5	21·9	28·9	8·9	7·6	13·8	21·5	11·4
1873	25·6	21·9	28·5	9·4	8·6	13·1	21·6	11·2
1874	26·3	21·6	25·1	6·3	8·3	14·2	18·5	10·3
1875	27·3	23·2	26·4	5·2	10·3	13·9	19·2	10·8
1876	27·7	27·9	30·3	6·8	11·9	15·2	17·5	15·1
1877	27·9	24·5	28·4	5·8	9·5	15·4	18·9	11·6
1878	28·1	22·9	28·8	5·6	10·8	15·6	20·4	9·9
1879	29·2	31·3	36·6	6·0	13·8	16·4	20·8	17·1
1880	26·9	26·7	33·0	6·9	11·0	16·1	19·2	14·7
1881	26·3	23·5	31·7	6·5	10·8	15·0	21·1	12·7
1882	26·0	21·0	29·5	5·7	10·7	12·9	23·0	10·8
1883	25·6	21·3	29·8	6·6	10·3	13·4	22·1	11·5

See p. 661 for footnotes.

B. 1844–1980 (*cont.*)

(in £ million)

	Issue Department		Banking Department					
			Deposits			Securities		
	Circulation (*a*)	Bullion (*b*)	Total	Public	Bankers	Government	Other	Reserves of Notes
1884	25·4	22·0	31·3	7·3	10·5	13·5	22·6	12·4
1885	24·7	23·0	33·5	6·2	12·8	14·7	21·2	14·1
1886	24·7	19·8	29·2	5·2	11·1	14·4	20·7	10·9
1887	24·4	20·5	29·4	5·4	11·4	14·4	19·6	12·0
1888	24·3	19·4	31·0	6·4	11·1	16·4	19·9	11·4
1889	24·4	20·5	32·5	7·2	11·7	15·8	21·6	12·3
1890	24·6	20·8	33·4	5·8	12·2	14·4	23·4	12·7
1891	25·1	23·4	38·0	6·6	15·3	10·9	29·7	14·6
1892	25·9	24·3	36·2	5·9	15·6	11·9	26·2	14·9
1893	25·9	24·6	36·0	5·7	15·2	11·5	25·6	15·2
1894	25·3	31·9	40·6	7·0	16·9	11·4	21·3	23·4
1895	25·8	36·4	48·2	7·6	17·9	14·1	22·1	27·3
1896	26·5	42·0	59·8	10·4	17·7	14·8	28·3	32·3
1897	27·2	33·2	49·8	10·0	18·1	13·9	28·9	22·8
1898	27·4	31·2	49·7	10·5	19·3	13·0	31·9	20·6
1899	27·9	30·3	49·6	10·0	21·4	13·6	32·8	19·3
1900	29·4	31·7	49·8	9·3	22·7	17·1	29·5	19·8
1901	29·6	33·8	50·4	9·7	23·3	15·7	28·8	22·0
1902	29·4	33·4	52·0	11·0	23·9	16·2	29·7	21·9
1903	28·9	32·3	50·1	8·8	24·4	16·4	28·0	21·7
1904	28·3	32·5	49·8	8·5	23·9	17·0	26·3	22·6
1905	28·8	33·9	54·1	11·8	23·4	16·7	30·1	23·5
1906	28·9	32·5	53·9	10·4	23·7	15·7	32·8	22·1
1907	28·9	33·6	53·7	9·2	25·7	15·2	32·1	23·1
1908	28·9	35·7	53·3	9·2	26·2	14·9	29·6	25·3
1909	29·2	35·9	54·3	10·5	25·7	15·5	30·1	25·2
1910	28·3	35·7	54·8	13·1	24·2	15·5	30·2	25·9
1911	28·6	37·1	55·5	13·1	24·3	14·9	30·5	26·9
1912	28·8	37·4	59·6	17·5	24·2	14·0	35·2	27·1
1913	28·7	36·2	54·9	13·4	24·6	12·7	32·3	25·9
1914	31·6	45·9	99·3	19·6	47·0	15·7	67·6	32·7
1915	33·8	58·7	189·1	85·9	48·0	36·3	126·6	43·4
1916	35·5	55·0	153·4	55·3	33·6	38·8	93·1	38·0
1917	40·2	53·2	178·7	48·7	39·1	62·5	100·5	31·5
1918	54·8	65·6	171·1	35·9	41·4	58·9	100·1	29·2
1919	78·0	84·8	144·7	24·0	52·2	56·0	81·8	24·5
					----- (*c*)			
1920	102·8	115·9	145·1	19·1	83·3	59·8	83·0	19·1
1921	107·9	126·6	139·7	16·7	85·9	53·3	84·8	17·7
1922	102·6	126·3	134·4	16·7	80·1	51·9	76·6	21·9
1923	101·9	125·8	125·0	15·4	70·0	47·8	72·2	21·2
1924	102·7	126·4	127·1	14·2	69·9	46·3	76·1	20·8
1925	91·8	145·6	126·9	14·1	71·7	41·1	75·0	26·9
1926	84·5	148·6	123·7	16·0	68·6	39·1	73·6	27·6
1927	80·7	150·1	119·4	16·4	66·4	43·6	59·5	32·9
1928	78·8 (*d*)	162·6	117·4	15·0	65·5	36·0	50·6	47·0

See p. 661 for footnotes.

Financial Institutions 2. *continued*

B. 1844–1980 (*cont.*)

(in £ million)

	Issue Department		Banking Department					
			Deposits			Securities		
	Circulation (*a*)	Bullion (*b*)	Total	Public (*f*)	Bankers (*g*)	Govern-ment	Other	Reserves of Notes
1929	362·3	146·9	114·4	14·5	62·9	55·9	31·1	44·6
1930	358·6	155·1	115·9	14·8	65·5	49·8	26·7	56·5
1931	354·8	139·7	118·3	15·4	64·7	45·5	38·6	51·3
1932	359·5	130·4	131·8	16·3	81·3	64·0	39·0	45·9
1933	371·2	176·6	157·8	17·7	99·9	79·6	25·9	69·1
1934	378·5	191·5	155·6	18·6	100·3	80·9	19·0	73·0
1935	394·7	193·7	150·1	15·3	96·7	87·0	21·5	59·0
1936	431·2	227·5	151·3	16·6	96·2	88·8	26·9	52·8
1937	479·6	321·4	153·9	19·5	97·2	98·4	28·0	44·5
1938	485·6	326·4	160·7	18·2	106·2	103·2	30·6	43·9
1939	507·3	211·5 (*e*)	161·9	21·3	102·5	107·0	31·4	40·6
1940	574·7	...	185·0	27·3	110·3	141·4	27·1	33·4
1941	651·1	...	192·1	16·8	122·4	144·3	30·8	33·6
1942	808·3	...	197·5	10·8	136·9	150·3	27·8	36·4
1943	966·3	...	223·4	8·7	158·9	179·8	23·5	36·8
1944	1,135·7	...	250·5	9·9	184·4	214·0	22·3	30·9
1945	1,284·2	...	285·7	12·8	217·9	251·8	24·2	26·6
1946	1,357·8	...	322·5	12·6	254·7	260·2	33·9	45·4
1947	1,383·3	...	397·8	12·8	295·9	313·1	35·0	66·4
1948	1,253·7	...	422·1	24·8	304·6	340·8	39·2	59·0
1949	1,269·0	...	432·0	41·0	296·4	354·3	45·5	45·7
1950	1,287·4	...	596·8	210·2	292·2	519·8	49·0	41·3
1951	1,342·4	...	406·2	20·2	297·6	341·4	41·6	40·6
1952	1,435·2	...	376·7	25·6	277·2	314·8	37·8	40·7
1953	1,531·9	...	390·4	43·2	277·6	341·4	26·3	38·7
1954	1,630·3	...	368·8	20·6	281·1	327·4	25·1	32·1
1955	1,760·0	...	340·6	19·2	254·0	283·4	37·9	35·1
1956	1,875·1	...	317·5	16·1	228·0	257·8	39·5	36·4
1957	1,966·3	...	303·6	13·3	216·2	239·4	47·9	32·2
1958	2,034·6	...	303·0	12·6	217·9	245·4	40·1	33·7
1959	2,104·5	...	313·9	13·0	236·0	258·0	37·0	36·2
1960	2,210·7	...	403·0	12·0	248·3	331·9	48·2	40·2
1961	2,306·2	...	516·2	13·0	250·0	423·8	74·7	35·0
1962	2,327·3	...	502·3	13·1	246·2	403·7	69·3	46·7
1963	2,398·2	...	334·3	12·5	249·3	227·7	81·3	42·5
1964	2,561·7	...	342·2	12·4	250·6	251·2	67·8	40·6
1965	2,727·4	...	424·9	12·3	323·0	311·1	82·7	48·5
	-------		-----		-----	-----	----	
1966	2,892·5 (*h*)	...	526·3 (*h*)	13·3	406·1 (*h*)	410·6 (*h*)	88·6 (*h*)	44·4
	-------		-----		-----	-----	----	
1967	2,971·5	...	605·0	12·5	479·4	451·3	130·7	40·4
1968	3,119·2	...	663·8	12·7	518·1	499·3	140·6	41·5
1969	3,243·5	...	652·8	14·2	494·8	465·6	162·3	41·8
1970	3,416·7	...	606·7	12·9	446·1	474·8	109·3	38·9
	------- (i)		----- (i)	---- (i)	----- (i)	----- (i)	----- (i)	----- (i)
	3,682·1		757·8	13·5	478·6	588·5	151·9	34·3
1971	------- (i)	...	----- (i)	---- (i)	----- (i)	----- (i)	----- (i)	----- (i)
	3,785		525	11	182	369	131	40
1972	4,379	...	615	21	343	488	120	21
1973	4,788	...	1,967	23	1,634	1,674	295	12

Financial Institutions 2. *continued*

B. 1844–1980 (*cont.*)

(in £ million)

	Issue Department		Banking Department					
			Deposits			Securities		
	Circulation (*a*)	Bullion (*b*)	Total	Public (*f*)	Bankers (*g*)	Govern-ment	Other	Reserves of Notes
1974	5,520	...	1,580	18	1,228	1,248	342	5
1975	6,138	...	1,751	21	1,311	1,405	348	12
1976	6,858	...	2,632	17	2,131	1,905	724	17
1977	8,019	...	2,222	23	1,613	1,591	640	6
1978	9,122	...	2,236	25	1,522	1,848	375	28
1979	10,089	...	1,984	20	1,267	1,462	526	11
1980	10,611	...	1,147	33	487	447	701	14

(*a*) This does not cover notes held in the Banking Department. Notes set aside against currency notes are excluded from 1919–28.
(*b*) This includes gold and silver coin as well as bullion.
(*c*) Prior to 1920 this series covers deposits of London bankers only at the Head Office (but not the branches) of the Bank; thereafter it includes total bankers' deposits. The size of the break is indicated by the Head Office only figure for 1920, which was 73·8.
(*d*) In determining this figure the last eight weeks of the year have been excluded from consideration, since the Treasury's currency notes were amalgamated with the Bank of England issue in that period.
(*e*) This figure is for the first eight months of the year only. See also note 3 above.

(*f*) From 1948 to 1955 this includes a Special Account of H.M. Treasury established in August 1948 under the Economic Co-operation Agreement between the United States and the United Kingdom. The amounts in this account were as follows:

1948	10·8	1951	4·2	1954	5·8
1949	28·6	1952	12·5	1955	3·9
1950	195·6	1953	29·7		

(*g*) Including 'Special Deposits', for which see table 5.
(*h*) After 31 March, Irish business of the National Bank is excluded. Deposits fell by about £80 milion and advances and investments by about £40 million and £20 million respectively.
(*i*) There was a change in methods of accounting in 1971. See also note 2.

Financial Institutions 3. Net Public Liabilities of Joint Stock Banks – England and Wales 1844–80

NOTES

[1] SOURCE: Michael Collins, "Long-Term Growth of the English Banking Sector and Money Stock, 1844–80", *E.H.R.*, second series XXXVI, 3 (1983).

[2] Estimates of the liabilities of private banks for quinquennia are as follows (in £ million):

1844–8	56·0	1859–63	96·9	1874–8	119·7
1849–53	68·8	1864–8	97·0	1876–80	110·7
1854–8	86·6	1869–73	104·9		

The estimates were not regarded as sufficiently reliable for publication on an annual basis. Estimates for all other quinquennia centred on years between 1847 and 1877 are available in the source.

[3] The figures are for the end of each year.

(in £ million)

	London Banks	Provincial Banks		London Banks	Provincial Banks		London Banks	Provincial Banks
1844	11·0	...	1857	47·8	39·7	1869	85·1	85·9
1845	14·1	29·8	1858	34·5	42·7	1870	80·6	79·4
1846	12·1	32·8	1859	34·4	48·4	1871	104·4	76·8
1847	10·8	26·0	1860	38·5	46·6	1872	110·0	100·1
1848	12·0	24·9	1861	45·5	49·4	1873	114·9	108·2
1849	16·3	29·3	1862	44·6	55·2	1874	120·5	115·1
1850	19·4	30·1	1863	69·6	66·0	1875	117·6	131·1
1851	19·0	31·7	1864	93·1	70·1	1876	137·4	138·1
1852	23·1	36·3	1865	77·7	72·8	1877	137·4	126·2
1853	22·3	36·7	1866	84·6	85·4	1878	124·4	157·4
1854	25·8	36·2	1867	71·3	84·5	1879	130·6	101·4
1855	32·4	38·9	1868	70·5	78·1	1880	128·3	120·4
1856	35·7	43·2						

Financial Institutions 4. Bank Deposits – United Kingdom, 1870–1982

NOTES

[1] SOURCE: Forrest Capie and Alan Webber, *A Monetary History of the United Kingdom, 1870–1982* (London, 1985), table II (1).

[2] The statistics are of gross bank deposits – i.e. including interbank deposits and items in transit.

[3] The figures are taken at end December.

[4] The first two columns are aggregates of London joint stock, private, and 'ephemeral' banks, provincial joint stock and private banks, Scottish banks, and Irish banks. The remaining figures are aggregates of the London clearing banks, non-clearing and other banks, Scottish banks and Irish banks.

(in £ million)

	Total Deposits		Total Deposits		Demand Deposits	Total Deposits		Demand Deposits	Total Deposits
1870	427·5	1899	812·8	1921	2,562	1,330	1952	7,636	4,804
					------- (*a*)	------- (*a*)			
1871	475·3	1900	839·1	1922	2,276	1,245	1953	7,901	4,890
1872	503·8	1901	833·7	1923	2,211	1,208	1954	8,228	5,082
1873	499·3	1902	840·6	1924	2,183	1,199	1955	7,833	4,894
1874	518·8	1903	815·0	1925	2,162	1,170	1956	7,861	4,808
1875	539·3	1904	825·9	1926	2,198	1,173	1957	8,152	4,707
1876	538·5	1905	845·9	1927	2,242	1,193	1958	8,419	4,802
1877	515·3	1906	867·1	1928	2,308	1,230	1959	8,709	5,052
1878	474·9	1907	886·8	1929	2,282	1,152	1960	8,806	4,928
1879	485·4	1908	908·6	1930	2,361	1,201	1961	8,840	4,760
1880	495·0	1909	919·2	1931	2,213	1,064	1962	9,219	4,996
1881	509·1	1910	955·9	1932	2,515	1,210	1963	9,706	5,447
1882	521·7	1911	976·2	1933	2,481	1,248	1964	10,414	5,646
1883	525·4	1912	1,016·6	1934	2,525	1,287	1965	10,943	5,708
1884	525·6	1913	1,064·1	1935	2,680	1,406	1966	11,033	5,592
1885	539·2	1914	1,168·4	1936	2,854	1,529	1967	11,941	6,064
1886	539·0	1915	1,286·6	1937	2,883	1,530	1968	12,457	6,264
1887	555·1	1916	1,499·0	1938	2,810	1,506	1969	12,436	6,128
1888	579·4	1917	1,762·9	1939	3,006	1,659	1970	12,374	6,502
1889	598·8	1918	2,075·3	1940	3,390	2,067	1971	14,510	7,560
1890	613·8	1919	2,423·6	1941	3,990	2,511	1972	19,363	8,755
1891	639·9	1920	2,572·9	1942	4,369	2,826	1973	26,098	9,212
1892	644·6			1943	4,862	3,163	1974	30,456	9,868
1893	635·0			1944	5,472	3,549	1975	48,143	12,550
1894	668·0			1945	5,872	3,820	1976	54,380	13,972
1895	695·5			1946	6,808	4,436	1977	61,092	17,005
1896	733·4			1947	7,120	4,603	1978	70,274	19,698
1897	762·5			1948	7,408	4,812	1979	87,169	23,112
1898	787·7			1949	7,399	4,808	1980	100,078	22,634
				1950	7,572	4,909	1981	132,875	25,811
				1951	7,505	4,920	1982	166,913	31,804

(*a*) Estimated Northern Irish deposits only subsequently.

Financial Institutions 5. Liabilities and Assets of London Clearing Banks – 1921–74

NOTES

[1] SOURCE: *Abstract*.

[2] Until September 1939 the figures were annual averages of weekly returns drawn up on varying days by the different banks. From then until the end of 1946 they were annual average figures for a single day in the second half of each month, each bank choosing a day convenient to itself. Since the beginning of 1947 the monthly figures have been drawn up on a single day for all banks.

(in £ million)

	Total Assets or Liabilities	Deposits	Cash and Balances at Bank of England	Balances at other Banks	Money at Call and Short Notice	Bills Discounted	Treasury Deposit Receipts	Investments	Advances to Customers and other Accounts	Acceptances, Endorsements, etc.
1921	1,997	1,812	211	48	105	363	—	331	833	63
1922	1,953	1,774	206	44	113	340	—	391	750	59
1923	1,874	1,674	197	45	110	275	—	356	761	79
1924	1,887	1,671	195	48	105	244	—	341	808	91
1925	1,888	1,662	196	52	117	226	—	286	856	100
1926	1,888	1,665	195	50	120	216	—	265	892	93
1927	1,942	1,713	198	52	137	218	—	254	928	98
1928	2,069	1,766	196	55	150	237	—	254	948	166
1929	2,139	1,800	194	55	145	229	—	257	991	203
1930	2,073	1,801	192	50	140	264	—	258	963	136
1931	2,010	1,760	182	46	121	256	—	301	919	114
1932	2,006	1,791	187	42	116	308	—	348	844	89
1933	2,182	1,953	212	43	102	354	—	537	758	102
1934	2,121	1,880	212	46	134	230	—	560	753	114
1935	2,235	1,999	215	48	142	266	—	615	769	106
1936	2,370 ------- (a) 2,456	2,142 ------- (a) 2,216	221 ---- (a) 228	54 --- (a) 56	158 ---- (a) 165	313 ---- (a) 320	—	614 ---- (a) 643	839 ---- (a) 865	99 --- (a) 105
1937	2,542	2,287	235	62	167	281	—	652	954	119
1938	2,536	2,277	241	60	151	280	—	637	976	118
1939	2,513	2,248	244	67	149	255	—	608	991	125
1940	2,765	2,506	268	87	148	370	73	666	955	118
1941	3,216	2,970	311	107	134	231	495	894	858	104
1942	3,512	3,275	345	116	133	234	642	1,069	797	95
1943	3,918	3,677	386	123	152	185	1,002	1,147	747	98
1944	4,396	4,153	437	131	180	171	1,387	1,165	750	99
1945	4,942	4,692	492	141	206	188	1,811	1,156	768	104
1946	5,397	5,097	523	165	300	457	1,492	1,345	888	153
1947	6,032	5,650	473	186	450	723	1,308	1,474	1,107	233
1948	6,311	5,913	486	199	473	744	1,284	1,479	1,319	248
1949	6,387	5,974	496	202	510	914	983	1,505	1,440	259
1950	6,476	6,014	497	203	550	1,298	430	1,505	1,603	307
1951	6,787	6,162	511	232	569	1,228	247	1,624	1,892	468
1952	6,667	6,083	505	226 ----(b) 301	529	1,062	7	1,983	1,922 -------(c) 1,860	427
1953	6,754	6,256	509	310	472	1,219	—	2,163	1,736	336
1954	7,014	6,495	528	343	457	1,206	—	2,321	1,833	349
1955	7,095	6,454	529	361	439	1,130	—	2,149	2,061	462
1956	6,902	6,288	516	367	431	1,270	—	1,978	1,907	432
1957	7,122	6,432	526	394	439	1,291	—	2,008	1,926	503
1958	7,339	6,636	543	406	434	1,277	—	2,149	1,991	506
1959	7,783	6,935	565	436	489	1,223	—	1,836	2,595	2601

Financial Institutions 5. *continued*

(in £ million)

	Total Assets or Liabilities	Deposits	Cash and Balances at Bank of England	Balances at other Banks	Money at Call and Short Notice	Bills Discounted	Investments	Advances to Customers and other Accounts	Acceptances, Endorsements, etc.	Special Deposits (*d*)
1960	8,259	7,236	588	493	562	1,149	1,407	3,195	745	74
	------- (*e*)	------- (*e*)	---- (*e*)	---- (*e*)	---- (*e*)	------- (*e*)	------- (*e*)	------- (*e*)	---- (*e*)	
1961	8,471	7,395	607	486	606 (*f*)	1,225 (*f*)	1,122	3,423 (*f*)	767	174
					----	-------		-------		
1962	8,443	7,611	623	527	718	1,205	1,194	3,467	461	159
1963	8,856	7,971	647	563	748	1,140	1,244	3,947	455	—
1964	9,479	8,550	696	658	738	1,155	1,220	4,395	490	—
1965	10,044	8,989	739	673	910	1,114	1,087	4,711	541	56
1966	10,488	9,376	767	704	1,006	1,135	1,137	4,794	567	137
1967	11,011	9,772	798	748	1,136	1,056	1,341	4,811	670	194
1968	11,817	10,431	851	787	1,335	995	1,375	5,160	768	208
1969	12,258	10,610	879	850	1,451	862	1,201	5,431	942	213
1970	11,410	10,151	826	584	1,467	921	1,115	5,739	1,212	256
1971	17,727	11,328	894	638	1,536	1,185	1,443	6,140	1,482	225
1972	16,166	14,580	823	732	1,434	856	1,650	9,451	1,760	5
1973	21,688	19,708	907	851	1,976	722	1,487	13,604	2,312	539
1974	27,371	24,715	974	935	2,840	864	1,689	17,433	3,212	615

(*a*) The District Bank was included from January 1936. The first line excludes it.
(*b*) The definition of this column up to 1951 (1st line) is 'Balances with, and cheques in course of collection on, other banks in the United Kingdom and the Irish Republic'. Subsequently there was added 'items in transit between offices of the same bank'.
(*c*) Figures from 1952 (2nd line) exclude items in transit between eight banks.
(*d*) Deposits called from banks not at their free disposal.
(*e*) Subsequently excluding the business of Lloyds Bank Eastern Branches.
(*f*) From February 1961, 'Bills discounted include' and 'Advances' exclude refinanceable export credits, and from October 1961 about £40 million was transferred from 'Advances' to 'Money at Call'.

Financial Institutions 5A. Liabilities and Assets of Banks in the United Kingdom – 1975–80

NOTES
[1] Source: *Abstract*.
[2] This table relates to all banks observing the common reserve ratio requirement introduced on 16 September 1971, including the National Girobank from October 1978.
[3] The figures are for the second Wednesday in December.

(in £ thousand million)

	Total Assets or Liabilities	Deposits	Cash and Balances at Bank of England	Money at Call	Bills Discounted (*a*)	Investments	Loans & Advances	Acceptances	Special Deposits
1975	140·1	129·4	1·5	1·8	3·8	4·3	122·3	2·1	1·0
1976	175·1	163·5	1·5	1·9	3·9	4·4	155·6	2·5	1·8
1977	191·6	178·2	1·8	2·8	4·0	5·5	169·3	2·6	1·2
1978	218·9	203·9	1·9	3·2	3·3	6·2	195·5	3·8	1·1
1979	263·8	246·4	1·9	3·6	3·7	6·9	237·9	6·3	0·8
1980	303·2	283·7	2·1	4·9	4·7	9·2	271·7	5·6	—

(*a*) Including British Government Stocks up to 1 year.

Financial Institutions 6. Liabilities and Assets of Associated Banks – Republic of Ireland, 1929–80

NOTES

[1] SOURCES: *Statistical Abstract of Ireland*, supplemented since 1970 by the *Statistical Supplement* to the *Central Bank of Ireland Bulletin*.

[2] Except as indicated in footnotes the figures relate to the end of December.

(in £ million)

	Total Assets or Liabilities	Assets or Liabilities within the State	Deposits		Cash and Balances with Banks	Money at Call and Short Notice	Bills Dis-counted	Invest-ments	Loans and Advances
			within the State	Elsewhere					
1929 (*a*)	...	...	124	41	...	...	...(*c*)	...	84 (*c*)
1930	...	...	123	41	...	...	...(*c*)	...	84 (*c*)
1931	193 (*b*)	145 (*b*)	122	41	...	...	...(*c*)	...	84 (*c*)
1932	207	153	132	45	15	13	12	89	70
1933	200	146	124	46	15	11	8	91	68
1934	196	139	120	45	14	11	7	87	69
1935	195	136	118	46	15	10	6	88	68
1936	196	137	119	46	15	11	7	88	68
1937	193	135	117	44	14	10	7	84	71
1938	189	133	114	43	15	9	8	77	72
1939	195	139	119	43	19	9	8	78	72
1940	210	148	128	46	28	11	5	85	72
1941	236	161	139	56	32	14	5	108	68
1942	259	176	154	61	36	18	4	123	67
1943	284	193	171	68	41	20	4	144	64
1944	306	209	189	74	47	21	4	158	67
1945	331	227	207	81	50	25	4	177	67
1946	361	246	225	92	52	24	4	195	76
1947	383	261	238	100	48	25	5	181	111
1948	390	263	238	106	49	24	6	175	121
1949	400	273	249	107	49	28	4	178	126
1950	418	285	260	110	49	22	4	186	139
1951	422	291	268	109	47	22	5	158	165
1952	420	293	283	107	55	32	10	150	155
1953	438	307	298	110	51	28	11	173	157
1954	460	323	291	116	54	29	14	179	167
1955	450	316	291	112	47	25	21	147	192
1956	461	320	307	117	52	37	24	137	190
1957	478	331	322	122	56	36	29	143	195
1958	495	344	328	126	56	40	20	158	203
1959	516	355	328	135	56	39	16	150	233
1960	535	371	345	138	59	42	19	137	256
1961	577	399	372	149	64	43	36	141	269
1962	618	429	402	156	66	41	28	161	296
1963	650	447	418	168	74	33	27	165	324
1964	700	485	454	177	88	33	31	154	364
1965	742	511	478	192	96	39	52	153	372
1966	776	582	531	159	113	21	53	169	371
1967	854	641	587	177	119	47	61	196	382
1968	980	746	684	193	128	51	54	239	453
1969	1,070	821	748	207	154	49	70	225	511
1970	...	...	...	...	...	...	...	...	...
1971	1,493	1,083	993	...	216		108	176	514
1972	1,608	1,085	965	321	330		1,192		
1973	2,107	1,301	1,143	401	572		1,452		

Financial Institutions 6. *continued*

(in £ million)

	Total Assets or Liabilities	Assets or Liabilities within the State	Deposits within the State	Deposits Elsewhere	Cash and Balances with Banks	Money at Call and Short Notice	Bills Discounted	Investments	Loans and Advances
1974	2,577	1,618	1,365	499	680			1,722	
1975	3,137	1,991	1,674	611	848			2,093	
1976	3,589	2,226	1,876	679	874			2,572	
1977	4,464	2,761	2,296	780	1,080			3,099	
1978	5,340	3,379	2,817	908	1,243			3,827	
1979	6,630	4,072	3,178	1,061	1,478			4,807	
1980	8,398	4,617	3,832	1,437	2,303			5,609	

(*a*) Mostly December.
(*b*) 31 March 1932.
(*c*) Bills discounted are included with 'Loans'.

Financial Institutions 7. Monetary Circulation – United Kingdom, 1833–1980; Republic of Ireland, 1929–80

NOTES

[1] SOURCES: 1833–44 – *S.P.* 1857–8 VIII (*Report* of the Select Committee on Commercial Distress); 1845–1909 – United States National Monetary Commission, *Statistics for Great Britain, Germany and France* (Washington, 1910); 1910 – the *Bankers' Magazine*; 1911–78 (1st line) – *Abstract*, *Statistical Abstract of Ireland*, and (for 'Irish notes' 1928–38), Bank of England *Statistical Summary*; 1978–80 (U.K.) – *Financial Statistics*. Coin – Forrest Capie and Alan Webber, *A Monetary History of the United Kingdom, 1870–1982* (London, 1985), Table III (1).

[2] Figures to 1841 are annual averages of the mean circulation in the twelve calendar months. For 1842–44 (Bank of England) and 1842–1978 (1st line) (Scottish and [Northern] Irish notes), the figures are annual averages of the mean circulation in thirteen four-week periods, as closely corresponding to the calendar year as possible. The 1845–1978 (1st line) Bank of England figures are averages of all the Wednesdays in the year. The Republic of Ireland figures are taken at the end of the calendar year. The 1978 (2nd line) – 1980 figures for the U.K. are averages of twelve figures on a day in the middle of each month.

[3] Figures relate to notes in the hands of the public.

(in £ thousand)

	Bank of England	Country Banks	Scottish Banks	Irish Banks	Coin
1833	[18,456] (*b*)	[9,991] (*b*)	[3,056] (*b*)	[5,334] (*b*)	...
1834	18,820	10,287	3,117	5,216	...
1835	18,107	10,700	3,098	5,186	...
1836	17,827	11,770	3,218	5,500	...
1837	18,288	10,609	3,074	5,119	...
1838	18,950	11,425	3,113	5,636	...
1839	17,677	11,716	3,247	5,848	...
1840	16,839	10,457	3,251	5,391	...
1841	16,948	9,728	3,195	5,356	...
	------- (*a*)	------- (*a*)	------- (*a*)	------- (*a*)	
1842	18,440	8,306	2,821	5,114	...
1843	19,523	7,647	2,732	5,168	...
1844	[21,216] (*b*)	8,175	2,951	5,937	...
	------- (*a*)				
1845	20,674	7,710	3,294	6,949	...
1846	20,252	7,730	3,405	7,260	...
1847	19,123	7,360	3,551	6,009	...
1848	18,086	6,280	3,176	4,829	...
1849	18,438	6,210	3,134	4,310	...
1850	19,448	6,330	3,225	4,512	...
1851	19,468	6,210	3,243	4,463	...
1852	21,910	6,410	3,404	4,818	...
1853	22,602	6,840	3,789	5,650	...
1854	20,688	6,830	4,055	6,296	...
1855	19,830	6,900	4,105	6,362	...
1856	19,667	6,790	4,093	6,652	...
1857	19,467	6,640	4,080	6,822	...
1858	20,248	5,990	3,926	6,183	...
1859	21,326	6,430	4,111	6,870	...
1860	21,252	6,450	4,228	6,840	...
1861	19,992	6,130	4,197	6,266	...
1862	20,835	6,120	4,153	5,658	...
1863	20,664	6,040	4,204	5,405	...
1864	20,605	5,980	4,262	5,594	...
1865	21,117	5,790	4,383	5,987	...
1866	23,159	5,150	4,440	5,884	...
1867	23,438	5,100	4,566	5,811	...
1868	23,932	5,050	4,608	6,181	...
1869	23,483	5,050	4,730	6,608	...
1870	23,327	4,910	4,933	6,880	85,449
1871	24,416	5,050	5,178	7,544	90,539
1872	25,492	5,100	5,332	7,674	97,776
1873	25,645	5,070	5,636	7,077	95,353
1874	26,264	4,980	5,900	6,768	96,392
1875	27,346	4,812	6,053	7,064	96,837
1876	27,734	4,714	6,099	7,500	93,154
1877	27,895	4,565	6,116	7,399	93,734

See p. 670 for footnotes.

Financial Institutions 7. *continued*

(in £ thousand)

	Bank of England	Country Banks	Scottish Banks	Irish Banks	Currency Notes	Coin
1878	28,058	4,362	5,841	6,968	—	91,094
1879	29,212	3,593	5,523	6,066	—	89,395
1880	26,915	3,440	5,538	5,727	—	86,888
1881	26,321	3,347	5,545	6,587	—	87,563
1882	25,985	3,408	5,682	7,297	—	90,197
1883	25,568	3,324	5,872	7,124	—	89,371
1884	25,358	3,150	5,860	6,514	—	88,496
1885	24,667	2,981	5,711	6,063	—	87,680
1886	24,659	2,748	5,687	6,019	—	87,511
1887	24,350	2,496	5,644	5,885	—	85,424
1888	24,283	2,452	5,744	6,114	—	85,014
1889	24,389	2,393	5,944	6,663	—	84,589
1890	24,561	2,350	6,296	6,800	—	90,626
1891	25,145	2,243	6,440	6,500	—	91,591
1892	25,863	2,122	6,471	6,189	—	96,267
1893	25,858	2,002	6,486	6,317	—	96,019
1894	25,300	1,820	6,566	6,327	—	92,157
1895	25,753	1,750	6,962	6,380	—	95,773
1896	26,470	1,619	7,174	6,287	—	98,917
1897	27,198	1,422	7,323	6,226	—	101,718
1898	27,448	1,378	7,497	6,144	—	102,211
1899	27,820	1,304	7,850	6,363	—	110,595
1900	29,366	1,243	7,946	6,830	—	114,688
1901	29,552	1,118	7,889	6,763	—	115,694
1902	29,407	877	7,865	6,810	—	115,124
1903	28,944	735	7,762	7,272	—	115,745
1904	28,313	650	7,497	6,713	—	112,188
1905	28,968	595	7,441	6,401	—	110,471
1906	28,926	546	7,469	6,470	—	116,601
1907	28,911	510	7,370	6,784	—	122,437
1908	28,840	435	7,101	6,681	—	118,652
1909	29,257	304	7,069	6,882	—	122,987
1910	28,300	197	7,074	7,439	—	129,354
1911	28,610	171	7,151	7,611	—	133,017
1912	28,788	159	7,317	7,410	—	137,467
1913	28,723	138	7,565	8,293	—	146,753
1914	31,605	440	8,189	9,095	[29,291] (*c*)	152,533
1915	33,761	110	10,808	13,585	56,189	152,002
1916	35,456	127	14,117	17,571	121,276	150,029
1917	40,195	145	17,049	20,880	166,233	136,814
1918	54,921	172	22,599	27,496	255,877	139,397
1919	78,114	174	27,023	30,580	335,138	133,041
1920	102,770	170	28,953	26,863	346,350	107,891
1921	107,869	[24] (*d*)	27,148	20,602	328,784	95,833
1922	102,541	—	23,986	18,067	297,862	92,333
1923	101,877	—	22,896	17,081	285,766	89,417
1924	102,727	—	22,224	16,559	288,068	88,500
1925	91,751	—	21,670	15,876	292,065	87,417
1926	84,465	—	20,833	15,013	291,866	87,917
1927	80,732	—	20,831	14,666	293,925	87,250

See p. 670 for footnotes.

Financial Institutions 7. *continued*

(in £ million)

	Bank of England	Scottish Banks	Irish Banks (*e*)	Currency Notes	U.K. Coin	Republic of Ireland (*f*)
1928	78·8 (*g*)	21·2	14·8	293·5 (*g*)	83·3	. . .
1929	362·3	21·2	16·9	—	83·5	14·2
1930	358·7	21·4	17·4	—	81·9	14·3
1931	354·8	21·0	16·6	—	79·5	13·4
1932	359·5	21·1	16·2	—	71·7	13·4
1933	371·2	21·1	16·8	—	69·3	13·7
1934	378·7	21·2	16·8	—	71·8	13·9
1935	394·7	21·7	17·5	—	72·5	14·3
1936	431·2	22·4	18·5	—	74·5	15·1
1937	479·6	23·1	19·5	—	75·9	15·7
1938	484·6	23·5	20·3 ------ (*e*) 5·3	—	78·5	15·9
1939	506·4	24·7	5·6	—	80·4	18·0
1940	573·7	28·7	7·6	—	86·9	21·2
1941	649·8	33·9	10·8	—	93·2	24·5
1942	807·4	43·9	14·2	—	100·7	30·3
1943	965·1	53·5	16·0	—	110·8	33·1
1944	1,134·5	61·1	16·3	—	119·7	37·8
1945	1,283·2	64·9	15·7	—	127·3	42·8
1946	1,356·6	68·1	16·0	—	138·2	45·0
1947	1,382·3	71·8	14·7	—	144·6	48·7
1948	1,252·5	66·0	12·2	—	158·0	50·4
1949	1,264·4	68·5	11·2	—	170·0	54·5
1950	1,282·6	70·1	10·0	—	167·3	57·3
1951	1,341·5	74·1	9·2	—	162·2	62·4
1952	1,433·6	81·2	8·9	—	163·0	67·4
1953	1,529·7	90·0	8·2	—	154·8	71·7
1954	1,627·9	95·5	8·3	—	159·3	75·3

	Bank of England	Scottish Banks	Northern Irish Banks	U.K. Coin	Republic of Ireland (*f*)
1955	1,757·6	101·8	8·4	162·9	77·2
1956	1,873·0	109·0	9·5	169·3	76·4
1957	1,963·9	116·8	9·9	176·0	80·7
1958	2,032·7	119·4	9·4	181·5	79·4
1959	2,103·6	120·5	8·9	184·4	77·8
1960	2,209·8	124·9	8·7	187·3	81·5
1961	2,305·4	128·0	8·5	197·6	86·8
1962	2,326·4	125·8	7·9	208·8	91·3
1963	2,397·3	126·1	7·4	206·8	99
1964	2,560·8	128·8	7·2	207·2	114
1965	2,726·5	130·3	7·4	210·2	112
1966	2,891·6	133·8	7·8	217·7	119
1967	2,970·9	136·1	8·9	223·1	125
1968	3,118·6	142·0	10·9	230·7	138
1969	3,239·5	147·6	12·9	270·5	144
1970	3,409·1	155·4	15·3	341·1	159
1971	3,678·1	163·7	22·0	358·1	169
1972	3,949·2	176·9	27·1	347·3	188
1973	4,425·4	195·9	28·4	366·9	231
1974	4,964·1	226·5	29·6	393·5	248
1975	5,717·5	266·0	33·8	429·5	295
1976	6,452·7	299·3	36·3	460·5	339
1977	7,183·4	332·9	40·5	491·1	389
1978	8,290 ------- (*a*) 8,234	390 ------ (*a*) 382	45 ----- (*a*) 45	535·6	469
1979	9,334	422	48	595·5	600
1980	10,035	468	51	654·8	680

(*a*) See note 2 above.
(*b*) Average of last four months of the year only.
(*c*) Average of third and fourth quarters, in the former of which there were issues for seven weeks only.
(*d*) Average of first two quarters only.

(*e*) The note issues of southern Irish banks continued to be included from 1922 to 1938 (1st line), with Irish legal tender notes also included from their inception in 1928.
(*f*) Circulation of legal tender notes and of bank notes of banks based in the Republic of Ireland.
(*g*) The first five weeks only of the last quarter are counted here, the period after the amalgamation of Treasury and Bank of England issues being ignored.

Financial Institutions 8. Savings Bank Deposits – United Kingdom 1817–1980

NOTES

[1] SOURCES: to 1939 – H. Oliver Horne, *A History of Savings Bank* (Oxford University Press, 1947), appendix II. These figures are reproduced by permission of the Trustee Savings Banks Association. Post Office 1940–67 – *Post Office Savings Bank* (H.M.S.O. annually to 1969); Post Office 1968–80 – *Abstract*; Trustee Savings Banks 1940–80 – *Trustee Savings Bank Year Book*.

[2] The Post Office/National Savings Bank figures are taken at 31 December to 1967 and 31 March subsequently. The Trustee Savings Bank figures are taken at 20 November.

[3] The Trustee Savings Bank figures are for cash only, and do not include stock owing to depositors.

(Amount due to depositors in £ million)

		Trustee Savings Banks	
	Post Office	Ordinary Departments	Special Investment Departments
1817	—	0·2 (*a*)	—
1818	—	1·7 (*a*)	—
1819	—	2·8 (*a*)	—
1820	—	3·5 (*a*)	—
1821	—	4·7 (*a*)	—
1822	—	6·5 (*a*)	—
1823	—	8·7 (*a*)	—
1824	—	11·7 (*a*)	—
1825	—	13·3 (*a*)	—
1826	—	13·1 (*a*)	—
1827	—	14·2 (*a*)	—
1828	—	15·4 (*a*)	—

1829	—	14·3	—
1830	—	14·6	—
1831	—	14·6	—
1832	—	14·4	—
1833	—	15·3	—
1834	—	16·3	—
1835	—	17·4	—
1836	—	18·8	—
1837	—	19·6	—
1838	—	21·4	—
1839	—	22·4	—
1840	—	23·5	—
1841	—	24·5	—
1842	—	25·3	—
1843	—	27·2	—
1844	—	29·5	—
1845	—	30·7	—
1846	—	31·7	—
1847	—	30·2	0·1
1848	—	28·1	0·1
1849	—	28·5	0·1
1850	—	28·9	. .
1851	—	30·3	. .
1852	—	31·8	. .
1853	—	33·4	. .
1854	—	33·7	. .
1855	—	34·3	. .
1856	—	34·9	0·1
1857	—	35·1	0·1
1858	—	36·2	0·2
1859	—	39·0	0·2
1860	—	41·3	0·2
1861	—	41·5	0·2
1862	1·7	40·6	0·2
1863	3·4	41·0	0·2
1864	5·0	39·3	0·2
1865	6·5	38·7	0·3
1866	8·1	36·4	0·3
1867	9·7	36·5	0·3
1868	11·7	36·9	0·3
1869	13·5	37·6	0·3
1870	15·1	38·0	0·3
1871	17·0	38·8	0·4
1872	19·3	39·7	0·6
1873	21·2	40·5	0·7
1874	23·2	41·5	0·8
1875	25·2	42·4	1·1
1876	27·0	43·3	1·3
1877	28·7	44·2	1·4
1878	30·4	44·3	1·6
1879	32·0	43·8	1·8
1880	33·7	44·0	2·0
1881	36·2	44·1	2·3
1882	39·0	44·6	2·6
1883	41·8	45·0	2·8
1884	44·8	45·8	3·1
1885	47·7	46·4	3·3
1886	50·9	46·8	3·6
1887	54·0	47·3	3·8
1888	58·6	46·4	4·0
1889	63·0	44·9	4·2
1890	67·6	43·6	4·4
1891	71·6	42·9	4·1
1892	75·9	42·4	4·3
1893	80·6	42·2	4·5
1894	89·3	43·5	4·6
1895	97·9	45·3	4·7
1896	108·1	46·7	4·7
1897	115·9	48·5	4·6
1898	123·1	50·0	4·6
1899	130·1	51·4	4·6
1900	135·5	51·5	4·5
1901	140·4	52·0	4·5
1902	144·6	52·5	4·6
1903	146·1	52·5	4·7
1904	148·3	52·3	4·9
1905	152·1	52·7	5·6
1906	156·0	53·0	6·4

See p. 672 for footnotes.

Financial Institutions 8. *continued*

(Amount due to depositors in £ million)

	Post Office	Trustee Savings Banks: Ordinary Departments	Trustee Savings Banks: Special Investment Departments
1907	157·5	52·2	7·1
1908	160·6	51·7	8·2
1909	164·6	52·2	9·8
1910	168·9	52·3	11·0
1911	176·5	53·0	12·2
1912	182·1	53·8	13·4
1913	187·2	54·3	14·4
1914	190·5	53·9	15·6
1915	186·3	51·4	15·4
1916	196·7	53·8	14·7
1917	203·3	52·4	14·1
1918	234·6	61·0	14·1
1919	266·3	71·9	14·9
1920	266·5	75·1	16·2
1921	264·2	73·1	19·3
1922	268·1	75·8	22·5
1923	273·1	79·6	23·6
1924	280·4	82·3	24·7
1925	285·5	83·4	27·0
1926	283·7	82·0	28·8
1927	284·6	81·4	32·5
1928	288·6	81·7	38·9
1929	285·0	79·3	45·1
1930	290·2	79·1	54·1
1931	289·4	77·9	65·1
1932	305·7	80·0	74·8
1933	326·7	88·8	82·6
1934	354·8	94·8	87·1
1935	390·3	107·6	89·8
1936	432·4	120·3	91·8
1937	470·5	131·3	93·3
1938	509·3	142·4	96·5
1939	551·4	152·3	99·4
1940	654·4	173·6	101·9
1941	822·9	214·8	108·6

	Post Office	Trustee Savings Banks: Ordinary Departments	Trustee Savings Banks: Special Investment Departments
1942	1,005·4	264·6	113·9
1943	1,240·6	333·0	115·2
1944	1,493·9	411·0	115·8
1945	1,776·6	488·5	114·6
1946	1,981·9	557·7	112·6
1947	1,943·2	621·9	109·6
1948	1,948·1	688·7	110·5
1949	1,947·6	744·4	112·5
1950	1,934·3	793·7	115·2
1951	1,875·9	816·6	115·7
1952	1,812·3	831·3	122·4
1953	1,746·8	824·9	143·7
1954	1,727·4	827·1	192·6
1955	1,700·0	827·3	226·2
1956	1,687·9	811·6	282·8
1957	1,676·6	823·3	316·8
1958	1,645·6	822·8	342·6
1959	1,679·0	858·6	380·5
1960	1,710·2	880·6	434·0
1961	1,736·6	902·4	499·0
1962	1,760·1	913·6	603·5
1963	1,791·6	951·6	733·4
1964	1,814·4	995·6	885·1
1965	1,822·5	1,028·0	994·0
1966	1,739·8	1,041·9	1,107·0
1967	1,672·7	1,050·3	1,215·4

---------- (*b*)

	Post Office: Ordinary Accounts	Post Office: Investment Accounts	Trustee Savings Banks: Ordinary Departments	Trustee Savings Banks: Special Investment Departments
1968	1,664·2	140·2	1,052·1	1,312·6
1969	1,589·9	208·3	1,041·0	1,375·6
1970	1,497·6	259·7	1,064·2	1,474·4
1971	1,474·7	322·5	1,143·3	1,636·1
1972	1,475·8	405·7	1,255·0	1,877·2
1973	1,517·7	528·8	1,379·8	2,025·6
1974	1,534·2	551·5	1,472·6	2,045·2
1975	1,539·9	581·2	1,635·6	2,216·5
1976	1,551·1	633·7	1,794·7	2,477·6
1977	1,549·5	670·3	1,894·2	2,622·9
1978	1,722·0	1,533·9	2,113·5	2,893·3
1979	1,848·8	1,303·2	2,025·2	3,404·2
1980	1,821·0	1,605·4	2,012·2	3,744·7

(*a*) The balance due by the National Debt Commissioners to trustees. In 1829 this was £500,000 greater than the amount owing to depositors – *vide S.P.*, 1860, XL.

(*b*) See note 1 above.

Financial Institutions 9. Savings Bank Deposits – Republic of Ireland 1923–80

NOTES
[1] SOURCE: *Statistical Abstract of Ireland*.

[2] The Post Office Savings Bank figures are taken at 31 December, and those for the Trustee Savings Bank at 20 November.

(amount due to depositors in £ million)

	British Post Office (a)	Post Office	Trustee Savings Banks		British Post Office (a)	Post Office	Trustee Savings Banks
1923	7·2	1·6	1·1	1952	0·9	57·1	8·8
1924	6·2	2·1	1·1	1953	0·9	61·8	9·5
1925	5·6	2·4	1·2	1954	0·8	66·7	10·6
1926	5·0	2·6	1·2	1955	0·8	71·2	11·2
1927	4·5	2·8	1·2	1956	0·8	73·5	11·8
1928	4·1	3·1	1·2	1957	—	76·0	12·1
1929	3·6	3·2	1·2	1958	—	78·7	12·7
1930	3·3	3·4	1·2	1959	—	82·5	13·9
1931	3·0	3·7	1·3	1960	—	86·7	15·1
1932	3·0	4·2	1·3	1961	—	91·5	16·5
1933	2·7	4·8	1·5	1962	—	97·2	17·7
1934	2·5	5·6	1·6	1963	—	101·9	18·4
1935	2·4	6·5	1·8	1964	—	107·5	19·6
1936	2·2	7·5	1·9	1965	—	109·9	19·8
1937	2·0	8·5	2·0	1966	—	110·5	20·6
1938	1·8	9·6	2·1	1967	—	116·3	21·8
1939	1·7	10·7	2·3	1968	—	118·3	22·8
							----- (b)
1940	1·5	11·8	2·4	1969	—	120·8	27·5
1941	1·4	13·6	2·6	1970	—	139·4	45·5
1942	1·3	16·7	2·9	1971	—	139·9	45·2
1943	1·3	20·9	3·4	1972	—	146·9	55·5
1944	1·3	26·4	4·0	1973	—	154·1	63·6
1945	1·2	32·7	4·7	1974	—	165·3	76·9
1946	1·2	36·4	5·3	1975	—	180·5	95·1
1947	1·2	36·9	5·4	1976	—	205·4	129·2
1948	1·1	39·0	5·7	1977	—	223·4	176·3
1949	1·1	43·9	6·6	1978	—	238·8	195·3
1950	1·0	48·1	7·3	1979	—	248·9	214·6
1951	1·0	53·4	8·2	1980	—	259·0	253·2

(a) Balances at offices in southern Ireland.

(b) Subsequently including special investment accounts.

Financial Institutions 10. Money Supply Estimates – United Kingdom 1870–1982

NOTES

[1] SOURCE: Forrest Capie and Alan Webber, *A Monetary History of the United Kingdom, 1870–1982* (London, 1985), tables I(1), I(4) and I(9).

[2] The money base is defined as cash in the hands of the public and the till money of banks (including the reserves of notes and coin held in the Banking Department of the Bank of England), and bankers' balances at the Bank of England. M1 is defined as notes and coin in the hands of the non-bank public plus sterling current accounts held by the private sector. M3 includes additionally all deposits of all residents with the U.K. banking sector.

[3] The statistics are annual averages.

(in £ million)

	Money Base	M3		Money Base	M1	M3		Money Base	M1	M3
1870	134	...	1908	208	...	967	1946	1,819	5,098	7,264
1871	144	540	1909	213	...	993	1947	1,894	5,528	8,044
1872	150	587	1910	217	...	1,021	1948	1,775	5,569	8,170
1873	148	587	1911	223	...	1,038	1949	1,786	5,679	8,240
1874	148	602	1912	227	...	1,067	1950	1,794	5,710	8,293
1875	153	623	1913	237	...	1,108	1951	1,847	5,835	8,454
1876	156	626	1914	288	...	1,198	1952	1,920	5,724	8,412
1877	150	608	1915	336	...	1,390	1953	2,006	5,824	8,652
1878	149	587	1916	385	...	1,531	1954	2,111	6,070	9,040
1879	156	564	1917	421	...	1,733	1955	2,223	6,150	9,076
1880	146	565	1918	531	...	2,103	1956	2,316	6,069	8,983
1881	145	580	1919	631	...	2,572	1957	2,396	6,119	9,184
1882	146	597	1920	659	...	2,889	1958	2,479	6,006	9,447
1883	144	601	1921	620	...	2,879	1959	2,560	6,354	9,838
				---- (*a*)		------- (*a*)				
1884	144	607	1922	585	1,536	2,662	1960	2,684	6,590	10,194
1885	146	612	1923	556	1,467	2,471	1961	2,794	6,613	10,520
1886	140	615	1924	558	1,447	2,448	1962	2,834	6,618	10,747
1887	139	624	1925	564	1,413	2,431	1963	2,901	6,983	11,184
1888	139	639	1926	557	1,403	2,420	1964	3,061	7,439	11,189
1889	139	663	1927	558	1,407	2,457	1965	3,263	7,613	12,524
1890	148	688	1928	568	1,418	2,498	1966	3,416	7,833	13,123
1891	154	710	1929	558	1,397	2,542	1967	3,514	8,039	13,646
1892	160	727	1930	565	1,377	2,549	1968	3,705	8,417	14,498
1893	160	722	1931	555	1,370	2,523	1969	3,839	8,412 ------- (*b*) 8,413	14,795 ------- (*b*) 16,014
1894	165	729	1932	560	1,337	2,571	1970	3,977	9,007	17,128
1895	174	769	1933	613	1,479	2,782	1971	4,296	10,205	19,127
1896	182	811	1934	627	1,471	2,721	1972	4,526	11,885 (*c*)	23,705 (*c*)
1897	178	843	1935	626	1,598	2,874	1973	5,063	12,923 (*c*)	30,077 (*c*)
1898	178	858	1936	658	1,748	3,080	1974	5,639	13,550	35,569
1899	188	894	1937	699	1,828	3,205	1975	6,436	16,223 (*c*)	38,951 (*c*)
1900	195	913	1938	717	1,862	3,218	1976	7,213	18,696	43,035
1901	199	913	1939	735	1,887	3,196	1977	7,995	21,421	47,063
1902	201	921	1940	805	2,175	3,514	1978	9,194	25,653	53,883
1903	201	913	1941	914	2,680	4,050	1979	10,423	28,598	60,106
1904	197	898	1942	1,105	3,128	4,568	1980	11,245	29,981	69,672
1905	195	911	1943	1,305	3,643	5,226	1981	11,807	33,003	83,923
1906	201	935	1944	1,495	4,158	5,934	1982	12,159	38,038	102,379
1907	209	963	1945	1,679	4,697	6,708				

(*a*) Subsequently excluding southern Ireland.

(*b*) Means of end-quarter data subsequently. Sterling deposits of U.K. residents with overseas banks are included in M1 and M3 subsequently.

(*c*) Minor changes in composition occurred in 1972, 1973, and June 1975.

Financial Institutions 11. Estimates of Velocity of Circulation – United Kingdom 1870–1982

SOURCE: Forrest Capie and Alan Webber, *A Monetary History of the United Kingdom, 1870–1982* (London, 1985) table I(a).

Year	M1 Velocity	M3 Velocity
1871		1·904
1872		1·871
1873		2·005
1874		1·912
1875		1·823
1876		1·789
1877		1·827
1878		1·836
1879		1·871
1880		1·949
1881		1·966
1882		1·978
1883		1·942
1884		1·871
1885		1·830
1886		1·857
1887		1·902
1888		1·978
1889		2·050
1890		2·025
1891		1·934
1892		1·834
1893		1·853
1894		1·956
1895		1·897
1896		1·846
1897		1·839
1898		1·907
1899		1·934
1900		1·953
1901		1·922
1902		1·924
1903		1·913
1904		1·931
1905		1·991
1906		2·053
1907		2·097
1908		1·994
1909		1·972
1910		2·001
1911		2·038
1912		2·101
1913		2·096
1914		1·959
1915		1·925
1916		2·074
1917	...	2·280
1918	...	2·268
1919	...	1·941
1920	...	1·969
1921	...	1·649
1922	2·622	1·513
1923	2·610	1·550
1924	2·737	1·618
1925	3·001	1·745
1926	2·873	1·665
1927	3·029	1·735
1928	3·018	1·713
1929	3·163	1·739
1930	3·163	1·709
1931	2·882	1·565
1932	2·866	1·491
1933	2·660	1·414
1934	2·850	1·541
1935	2·739	1·523
1936	2·646	1·502
1937	2·687	1·533
1938	2·752	1·592
1939	2·807	1·657
1940	2·745	1·699
1941	2·694	1·783
1942	2·551	1·747
1943	2·344	1·634
1944	2·108	1·477
1945	1·888	1·322
1946	1·737	1·219
1947	1·711	1·176
1948	1·878	1·280
1949	1·973	1·360
1950	2·060	1·418
1951	2·218	1·531
1952	2·445	1·664
1953	2·549	1·716
1954	2·605	1·749
1955	2·760	1·870
1956	3·036	2·051
1957	3·192	2·127
1958	3·398	2·160
1959	3·372	2·177
1960	3·462	2·238
1961	3·700	2·326
1962	3·870	2·383
1963	3·907	2·440
1964	3·933	2·461
1965	4·101	2·493
1966	4·224	2·521
1967	4·391	2·587
1968	4·502	2·613
1969	4·771 ------- (a) 4·643	2·712 ------ (a) 2·438
1970	4·803	2·525
1971	4·644	2·476
1972	4·621	2·321
1973	4·978	2·145
1974	6·137	2·338
1975	6·217	2·586
1976	6·682	2·904
1977	6·718	3·053
1978	6·469	3·079
1979	6·783	3·228
1980	7·528	3·242
1981	7·444	2·911
1982	7·149(b)	2·644 (b)

(*a*) See footnote (b) to table 10 above.

(*b*) Average of first three quarters only.

Financial Institutions 12. Bank Clearings 1868–1980

NOTES

[1] SOURCE: *Abstract*.

[2] Changes in the composition of the clearing whilst the Clearing Banks Emergency Operations were in force (September 1939 to August 1946) precludes strict comparability across that period.

(in £ million)

	London	Provinces	Total
1868	3,425	...	...
1869	3,626	...	...
1870	3,914	...	...
1871	4,826	...	...
1872	5,916	...	...
1873	6,071	...	...
1874	5,937	...	...
1875	5,686	...	...
1876	4,963	...	...
1877	5,042	...	...
1878	4,992	...	...
1879	4,886	...	...
1880	5,794	...	...
1881	6,357	...	...
1882	6,221	...	...
1883	5,929	...	...
1884	5,799	...	...
1885	5,511	...	...
1886	5,902	...	...
1887	6,077	...	...
1888	6,942	...	...
1889	7,619	...	...
1890	7,801	...	...
1891	6,848	...	...
1892	6,482	...	...
1893	6,478	...	...
1894	6,337	...	...
1895	7,593	386	7,979
1896	7,575	464	8,039
1897	7,491	483	7,974
1898	8,097	508	8,605
1899	9,150	571	9,721
1900	8,960	633	9,593
1901	9,561	606	10,167
1902	10,029	615	10,644
1903	10,120	625	10,745
1904	10,564	655	11,219
1905	12,288	665	12,953
1906	12,711	679	13,390
1907	12,730	723	13,453
1908	12,120	652	12,772
1909	13,525	690 (*a*)	14,215 (*a*)
1910	14,659	743	15,402
1911	14,614	774	15,388
1912	15,962	852 (*b*)	16,814 (*b*)
1913	16,436	900	17,336
1914	14,665	831	15,496
1915	13,408	990	14,398

	London	Provinces	Total
1916	15,275	1,212	16,487
1917	19,121	1,438	20,559
1918	21,198	1,777	22,975
1919	28,415	2,284	30,699
1920	39,019	3,134	42,153
1921	34,930	1,786	36,716
1922	37,161	1,797	38,958
1923	36,628	1,801	38,429
1924	39,533	1,881	41,414
1925	40,347	1,866	42,303
1926	39,825	1,628	41,453
1927	41,551	1,710	43,261
1928	44,204	1,673	45,877
1929	44,897	1,599	46,496
1930	43,558	1,348	44,906
1931	36,236	1,200	37,436
1932	32,112	1,238	33,350
1933	32,138	1,243	33,381
1934	35,484	1,295	36,779
1935	37,560	1,283	38,843
1936	40,617 (*c*)	1,394	42,011
1937	42,686	1,472	44,158
1938	39,611	1,258	40,869
1939	36,642	1,269	37,911
1940	40,019	1,408	41,427
1941	43,011	1,471	44,482
1942	48,657	1,480	50,137
1943	57,107	1,168	58,275
	(in £ thousand million)		
1944	62·6	0·9	63·6
1945	66·9	1·0	68·8
1946	69·0	1·3	70·3
1947	73·3	1·4	74·7
1948	80·2	1·7	81·9
1949	86·1	1·9	87·9
1950	94·2	2·1	96·3
1951	108·8	2·3	111·1
1952	110·6	2·1	112·6
1953	123·4	2·1	125·5
1954	144·3	2·3	146·6
1955	152·6	2·5	155·1
1956	160·9	2·4	163·3
1957	172·7	2·5	175·2
1958	180·9	2·4	183·4

Financial Institutions 12. *continued*

(in £ thousand million)

	London	Provinces	Total
1959	199·2	2·6	201·8
1960	225·4	2·8	228·2
1961	242·4	2·8	245·2
1962	272·9	2·8	275·6
1963	302·3	2·8	305·2
1964	355·7	2·9	358·7
1965	408·6	3·0	411·6
1966	452·3	3·2	455·5
1967	558·7	3·2	561·9
	------- (*d*)	---- (*d*)	
1968	599·5	0·6	600·2
1969	699·2	0·6	699·8
1970	772·5	0·6	773·1
1971	843·6	0·7	844·4
1972	1,071	0·7	1,072
1973	1,456	0·8	1,457
1974	1,640	0·9	1,641
1975	1,795	1·1	1,796
1976	2,204	1·2	2,205
1977	2,598	1·2	2,599
1978	2,846	1·1	2,847
1979	3,615	1·2	3,617
1980	4,457	1·4	4,458

(*a*) The first year in which records were kept at Nottingham.
(*b*) The first year in which records were kept at Bradford.
(*c*) The District Bank became a member of the London Clearing House in January 1936.
(*d*) All provincial clearings were ended in 1968 except one at Liverpool.

Financial Institutions 13. Yield on Consols – 1756–1980

NOTES

[1] Sources: 1756–1830 – T. S. Ashton, 'Some Statistics of the Industrial Revolution' in *Transactions of the Manchester Statistical Society* (1947–8); 1831–51 – G. F. Warren and F. A. Pearson, *Gold and Prices* (New York 1935), p. 403 (which also contains the figures up to 1934); 1852–1980 – *Abstract*.

[2] The nominal rate of interest on Consols was 3 per cent from their first issue until 1888. From 1889–1902 it was 2¾ per cent, and from 1903 onwards it has been 2½ per cent.

[3] When the price of 3% Consols rose above par (at which they were redeemable) and when the 2¾% did so in the 1890s, they ceased to be loans of infinite duration, and so, as C. Knick Harley pointed out in 'Goschen's Conversion of the National Debt and the Yield on Consols', *E.H.R.*, second series XXIX, 1 (1976), their yield did not fit precisely the concept of the long-term rate of interest. He offered the following substitute figures for the period 1879–1902, using the yield on 2½% Consols for 1879–88 and the yield on Goschen's Consols, less its annuity element subsequently. These are to be preferred to the conventional yield on Consols for most purposes.

1879	3·17	1885	2·85	1891	2·68	1897	1·96
1880	3·10	1886	2·81	1892	2·65	1898	2·00
1881	2·90	1887	2·72	1893	2·60	1899	2·18
1882	2·94	1888	2·62	1894	2·55	1900	2·53
1883	2·83	1889	2·63	1895	2·29	1901	2·67
1884	2·72	1890	2·67	1896	2·06	1902	2·66

(per cent)

1756	3·4	1801	4·9	1846	3·1	1891	2·9	1936	2·9
1757	3·4	1802	4·2	1847	3·4	1892	2·8	1937	3·3
1758	3·2	1803	5·0	1848	3·5	1893	2·8	1938	3·4
1759	3·6	1804	5·3	1849	3·2	1894	2·7	1939	3·7
1760	3·8	1805	5·0	1850	3·1	1895	2·6	1940	3·4
1761	3·9	1806	4·9	1851	3·1	1896	2·5	1941	3·1
1762	4·3	1807	4·9	1852	3·0	1897	2·5	1942	3·0
1763	3·4	1808	4·6	1853	3·1	1898	2·5	1943	3·1
1764	3·6	1809	4·6	1854	3·3	1899	2·6	1944	3·1
1765	3·4	1810	4·5	1855	3·3	1900	2·8	1945	2·9
1766	3·4	1811	4·7	1856	3·2	1901	2·9	1946	2·6
1767	3·4	1812	5·1	1857	3·3	1902	2·9	1947	2·8
1768	3·3	1813	4·9	1858	3·1	1903	2·8	1948	3·2
1769	3·5	1814	4·9	1859	3·2	1904	2·8	1949	3·3
1770	3·6	1815	4·5	1860	3·2	1905	2·8	1950	3·5
1771	3·5	1816	5·0	1861	3·3	1906	2·8	1951	3·8
1772	3·3	1817	4·1	1862	3·2	1907	3·0	1952	4·2
1773	3·5	1818	3·9	1863	3·2	1908	2·9	1953	4·1
1774	3·4	1819	4·2	1864	3·3	1909	3·0	1954	3·8
1775	3·4	1820	4·4	1865	3·4	1910	3·1	1955	4·2
1776	3·5	1821	4·1	1866	3·4	1911	3·2	1956	4·7
1777	3·8	1822	3·8	1867	3·2	1912	3·3	1957	5·0
1778	4·5	1823	3·8	1868	3·2	1913	3·4	1958	5·0
1779	4·9	1824	3·3	1869	3·2	1914	3·3	1959	4·8
1780	4·9	1825	3·5	1870	3·2	1915	3·8	1960	5·4
1781	5·2	1826	3·8	1871	3·2	1916	4·3	1961	6·2
1782	5·3	1827	3·6	1872	3·2	1917	4·6	1962	6·0
1783	4·8	1828	3·5	1873	3·2	1918	4·4	1963	5·6
1784	5·4	1829	3·3	1874	3·2	1919	4·6	1964	6·0
1785	4·8	1830	3·5	1875	3·2	1920	5·3	1965	6·4
1786	4·1	1831	3·8	1876	3·2	1921	5·2	1966	6·8
1787	4·1	1832	3·6	1877	3·1	1922	4·4	1967	6·7
1788	4·0	1833	3·4	1878	3·2	1923	4·3	1968	7·4
1789	3·9	1834	3·3	1879	3·1	1924	4·4	1969	8·9
1790	3·9	1835	3·3	1880	3·1	1925	4·4	1970	9·2
1791	3·6	1836	3·4	1881	3·0	1926	4·6	1971	9·1
1792	3·3	1837	3·3	1882	3·0	1927	4·6	1972	9·1
1793	4·0	1838	3·2	1883	3·0	1928	4·5	1973	10·8
1794	4·4	1839	3·3	1884	3·0	1929	4·6	1974	14·9
1795	4·5	1840	3·4	1885	3·0	1930	4·5	1975	14·7
1796	4·8	1841	3·4	1886	3·0	1931	4·4	1976	14·3
1797	5·9	1842	3·3	1887	3·0	1932	3·7	1977	12·3
1798	5·9	1843	3·2	1888	3·0	1933	3·4	1978	11·9
1799	5·1	1844	3·0	1889	2·8	1934	3·1	1979	11·4
1800	4·7	1845	3·1	1890	2·9	1935	2·9	1980	11·9

Financial Institutions 14. Changes in Bank Rate/Minimum Lending Rate – 1797–1980

NOTE

SOURCES: 1797–1914 – J. H. Clapham, *The Bank of England* (2 vols, Cambridge University Press, 1944), vol. II, pp. 429–32; 1915–80 – *Abstract*. The figures from Clapham's book are reproduced by permission of the Governor and Company of the Bank of England.

Year	Date	Rate
1797		5
1822	20 June	4
1825	13 December	5
1827	5 July	4
1836	21 July	4½
1836	1 September	5
1838	15 February	4
1839	16 May	5
1839	20 June	5½
1839	1 August	6
1840	23 January	5
1842	7 April	4
1844	5 September	2½ & 3 (*a*)
1845	13 March	2½
1845	16 October	3
1845	6 November	3½
1846	27 August	3
1847	14 January	3½
1847	21 January	4
1847	8 April	5
1847	5 August	5½
1847	30 September	6 (*b*)
1847	25 October	8
1847	22 November	7
1847	2 December	6
1847	23 December	5
1848	27 January	4
1848	15 June	3½
1848	2 November	3
1849	22 November	2½
1850	26 December	3
1852	1 January	2½
1852	22 April	2
1853	6 January	2½
1853	20 January	3
1853	2 June	3½
1853	1 September	4
1853	15 September	4½
1853	29 September	5
1854	11 May	5½
1854	3 August	5
1855	5 April	4½
1855	3 May	4
1855	14 June	3½
1855	6 September	4
1855	13 September	4½
1855	27 September	5
1855	4 October	5½
1855	18 October	6 or 7 (*c*)
1856	22 May	6
1856	29 May	5
1856	26 June	4½
1856	1 October	5
1856	6 October	6 or 7 (*c*)
1856	13 November	7
1856	4 December	6½
1856	18 December	6
1857	2 April	6½
1857	18 June	6
1857	16 July	5½
1857	8 October	6
1857	12 October	7
1857	19 October	8
1857	5 November	9
1857	9 November	10
1857	24 December	8
1858	7 January	6
1858	14 January	5
1858	28 January	4
1858	4 February	3½
1858	11 February	3
1858	9 December	2½
1859	28 April	3½
1859	5 May	4½
1859	2 June	3½
1859	9 June	3
1859	14 July	2½
1860	19 January	3
1860	31 January	4
1860	29 March	4½
1860	12 April	5
1860	10 May	4½
1860	24 May	4
1860	8 November	4½
1860	13 November	5
1860	15 November	6
1860	29 November	5
1860	31 December	6
1861	7 January	7
1861	14 February	8
1861	21 March	7
1861	4 April	6
1861	11 April	5
1861	16 May	6
1861	1 August	5
1861	15 August	4½
1861	29 August	4
1861	19 September	3½
1861	7 November	3
1862	9 January	2½
1862	22 May	3
1862	10 July	2½
1862	24 July	2
1862	30 October	3
1863	15 January	4
1863	28 January	5
1863	19 February	4
1863	23 April	3½
1863	30 April	3
1863	16 May	3½
1863	21 May	4
1863	2 November	5
1863	5 November	6
1863	2 December	7
1863	3 December	8
1863	24 December	7
1864	20 January	8
1864	11 February	7
1864	25 February	6
1864	16 April	7
1864	2 May	8
1864	5 May	9
1864	19 May	8
1864	26 May	7
1864	16 June	6
1864	25 July	7
1864	4 August	8
1864	8 September	9
1864	10 November	8
1864	24 November	7
1864	15 December	6
1865	12 January	5½
1865	26 January	5
1865	2 March	4½
1865	30 March	4
1865	4 May	4½
1865	25 May	4
1865	1 June	3½
1865	15 June	3
1865	27 July	3½
1865	3 August	4
1865	28 September	4½
1865	2 October	5
1865	5 October	6
1865	7 October	7
1865	23 November	6
1865	28 December	7
1866	4 January	8
1866	22 February	7
1866	15 March	6

See p. 682 for footnotes.

1866	3 May	7
1866	8 May	8
1866	11 May	9
1866	12 May	10
1866	16 August	8
1866	23 August	7
1866	30 August	6
1866	6 September	5
1866	27 September	4½
1866	8 November	4
1866	20 December	3½
1867	7 February	3
1867	30 May	2½
1867	25 July	2
1868	19 November	2½
1868	3 December	3
1869	1 April	4
1869	6 May	4½
1869	10 June	4
1869	24 June	3½
1869	15 July	3
1869	19 August	2½
1869	4 November	3
1870	21 July	3½
1870	23 July	4
1870	28 July	5
1870	4 August	6
1870	11 August	5½
1870	18 August	4½
1870	25 August	4
1870	1 September	3½
1870	15 September	3
1870	29 September	2½
1871	2 March	3
1871	13 April	2½
1871	13 July	2
1871	21 September	3
1871	28 September	4
1871	7 October	5
1871	16 November	4
1871	30 November	3½
1871	14 December	3
1872	4 April	3½
1872	11 April	4
1872	9 May	5
1872	30 May	4
1872	13 June	3½
1872	20 June	3
1872	18 July	3½
1872	18 September	4
1872	26 September	4½
1872	3 October	5
1872	10 October	6
1872	9 November	7
1872	28 November	6
1872	12 December	5
1873	9 January	4½
1873	23 January	4
1873	30 January	3½
1873	26 March	4
1873	7 May	4½
1873	10 May	5
1873	17 May	6
1873	4 June	7
1873	12 June	6
1873	10 July	5
1873	17 July	4½
1873	24 July	4
1873	31 July	3½
1873	21 August	3
1873	25 September	4
1873	29 September	5
1873	14 October	6
1873	18 October	7
1873	1 November	8
1873	7 November	9
1873	20 November	8
1873	27 November	6
1873	4 December	5
1873	11 December	5½
1874	8 January	4
1874	15 January	3½
1874	30 April	4
1874	28 May	3½
1874	4 June	3
1874	18 June	2½
1874	30 July	3
1874	6 August	4
1874	20 August	3½
1874	27 August	3
1874	15 October	4
1874	16 November	5
1874	30 November	6
1875	7 January	5
1875	14 January	4
1875	28 January	3
1875	18 February	3½
1875	8 July	3
1875	29 July	2½
1875	12 August	2
1875	7 October	2½
1875	14 October	3½
1875	21 October	4
1875	18 November	3
1875	30 December	4
1876	6 January	5
1876	28 January	4
1876	23 March	3½
1876	6 April	3
1876	20 April	2
1877	3 May	3
1877	5 July	2½
1877	12 July	2
1877	28 August	3
1877	4 October	4
1877	11 October	5
1877	29 November	4
1878	10 January	3
1878	31 January	2
1878	28 March	3
1878	30 May	2½
1878	27 June	3
1878	4 July	3½
1878	1 August	4
1878	12 August	5
1878	14 October	6
1878	21 November	5
1879	16 January	4
1879	30 January	3
1879	13 March	2½
1879	10 April	2
1879	6 November	3
1880	17 June	2½
1880	9 December	3
1881	13 January	3½
1881	17 February	3
1881	28 April	2½
1881	18 August	3
1881	25 August	4
1881	6 October	5
1882	30 January	6
1882	23 February	5
1882	9 March	4
1882	23 March	3
1882	17 August	4
1882	14 September	5
1883	25 January	4
1883	15 February	3½
1883	1 March	3
1883	10 May	4
1883	13 September	3½
1883	27 September	3
1884	7 February	3½
1884	13 March	3
1884	3 April	2½
1884	19 June	2
1884	9 October	3
1884	30 October	4
1884	6 November	5
1885	29 January	4
1885	19 March	3½
1885	7 May	3
1885	14 May	2½
1885	28 May	2
1885	12 November	3

Financial Institutions 14. *continued*

Year	Date	Rate
1885	17 December	4
1886	21 January	3
1886	18 February	2
1886	6 May	3
1886	10 June	2½
1886	26 August	3½
1886	21 October	4
1886	16 December	5
1887	3 February	4
1887	10 March	3½
1887	24 March	3
1887	14 April	2½
1887	28 April	2
1887	4 August	3
1887	1 September	4
1888	12 January	3½
1888	19 January	3
1888	16 February	2½
1888	15 March	2
1888	10 May	3
1888	7 June	2½
1888	9 August	3
1888	13 September	4
1888	4 October	5
1889	10 January	4
1889	24 January	3½
1889	31 January	3
1889	18 April	2½
1889	8 August	3
1889	29 August	4
1889	26 September	5
1889	30 December	6
1890	20 February	5
1890	6 March	4½
1890	13 March	4
1890	10 April	3½
1890	17 April	3
1890	26 June	4
1890	31 July	5
1890	21 August	4
1890	25 September	5
1890	7 November	6
1890	4 December	5
1891	8 January	4
1891	22 January	3½
1891	29 January	3
1891	16 April	3½
1891	7 May	4
1891	14 May	5
1891	4 June	4
1891	18 June	3
1891	2 July	2½
1891	24 September	3
1891	29 October	4
1891	10 December	3½
1892	21 January	3
1892	7 April	2½
1892	28 April	2
1892	20 October	3
1893	26 January	2½
1893	4 May	3
1893	11 May	3½
1893	18 May	4
1893	8 June	3
1893	15 June	2½
1893	3 August	3
1893	10 August	4
1893	24 August	5
1893	14 September	4
1893	21 September	3½
1893	5 October	3
1894	1 February	2½
1894	22 February	2
1896	10 September	2½
1896	24 September	3
1896	22 October	4
1897	21 January	3½
1897	4 February	3
1897	8 April	2½
1897	15 May	2
1897	23 September	2½
1897	14 October	3
1898	7 April	4
1898	26 May	3½
1898	2 June	3
1898	30 June	2½
1898	22 September	3
1898	13 October	4
1899	19 January	3½
1899	2 February	3
1899	13 July	3½
1899	3 October	4½
1899	5 October	5
1899	30 November	6
1900	11 January	5
1900	18 January	4½
1900	25 January	4
1900	24 May	3½
1900	16 June	3
1900	19 July	4
1901	3 January	5
1901	7 February	4½
1901	21 February	4
1901	6 June	3½
1901	13 June	3
1901	31 October	4
1902	23 January	3½
1902	6 February	3
1902	2 October	4
1903	21 May	3½
1903	18 June	3
1903	3 September	4
1904	14 April	3½
1904	21 April	3
1905	9 March	2½
1905	7 September	3
1905	28 September	4
1906	5 April	3½
1906	3 May	4
1906	21 June	3½
1906	13 September	4
1906	11 October	5
1906	19 October	6
1907	17 January	5
1907	11 April	4½
1907	25 April	4
1907	15 August	4½
1907	31 October	5½
1907	4 November	6
1907	7 November	7
1908	2 January	6
1908	16 January	5
1908	23 January	4
1908	5 March	3½
1908	19 March	3
1908	28 May	2½
1909	14 January	3
1909	1 April	2½
1909	7 October	3
1909	14 October	4
1909	21 October	5
1909	9 December	4½
1910	6 January	4
1910	20 January	3½
1910	10 February	3
1910	17 March	4
1910	2 June	3½
1910	9 June	3
1910	29 September	4
1910	20 October	5
1910	1 December	4½
1911	26 January	4
1911	16 February	3½
1911	9 March	3
1911	21 September	4
1912	8 February	3½
1912	9 May	3
1912	29 August	4
1912	17 October	5
1913	17 April	4½
1913	2 October	5
1914	8 January	4½
1914	22 January	4
1914	29 January	3
1914	30 July	4

Financial Institutions 14. *continued*

Year	Date	Rate
1914	31 July	8
1914	1 August	10
1914	6 August	6 (*d*)
1914	8 August	5
1916	19 July	6
1917	15 January	5½
1917	29 April	5
1919	6 November	6
1920	15 April	7
1921	28 April	6½
1921	23 June	6
1921	21 July	5½
1921	4 November	5
1922	18 February	4½
1922	22 April	4
1922	17 June	3½
1922	15 July	3
1923	7 July	4
1925	5 March	5
1925	6 August	4½
1925	1 October	4
1925	3 December	5
1927	21 April	4½
1929	7 February	5½
1929	26 September	6½
1929	31 October	6
1929	21 November	5½
1929	12 December	5
1930	6 February	4½
1930	6 March	4
1930	20 March	3½
1930	1 May	3
1931	14 May	2½
1931	23 July	3½
1931	30 July	4½
1931	21 September	6
1932	18 February	5
1932	10 March	4
1932	17 March	3½
1932	21 April	3
1932	12 May	2½
1932	30 June	2
1939	24 August	4
1939	28 September	3
1939	26 October	2
1951	8 November	2½
1952	12 March	4
1953	17 September	3½
1954	13 May	3
1955	27 January	3½
1955	24 February	4½
1956	16 February	5½
1957	7 February	5
1957	19 September	7
1958	20 March	6
1958	22 May	5½
1958	19 June	5
1958	14 August	4½
1958	20 November	4
1960	21 January	5
1960	23 June	6
1960	27 October	5½
1960	8 December	5
1961	26 July	7
1961	5 October	6½
1961	2 November	6
1962	8 March	5½
1962	22 March	5
1962	26 April	4½
1963	3 January	4
1964	27 February	5
1964	23 November	7
1965	3 June	6
1966	14 July	7
1967	26 January	6½
1967	16 March	6
1967	4 May	5½
1967	19 October	6
1967	9 November	6½
1967	19 November	8
1968	21 March	7½
1968	19 September	7
1969	27 February	8
1970	5 March	7½
1970	15 April	7
1971	1 April	6
1971	2 September	5
1972	22 June	6
	------------------------------	(*e*)
1972	13 October	7¼
1972	27 October	7½
1972	1 December	7¾
1972	8 December	8
1972	22 December	9
1973	19 January	8¾
1973	23 March	8½
1973	13 April	8
1973	19 April	8¼
1973	11 May	8
1973	18 May	7¾
1973	22 June	7½
1973	20 July	9
1973	27 July	11½
1973	19 October	11¼
1973	13 November	13
1974	4 January	12¾
1974	1 February	12½
1974	5 April	12¼
1974	11 April	12
1974	24 May	11¾
1974	20 September	11½
1975	17 January	11¼
1975	25 July	11
1975	3 October	12
1975	14 November	11¾
1975	28 November	11½
1975	24 December	11¼
1976	2 January	11
1976	16 January	10¾
1976	23 January	10½
1976	30 January	10
1976	6 February	9½
1976	5 March	9¼
1976	23 April	10½
1976	21 May	11½
1976	10 September	13
1976	7 October	15
1976	19 November	14¾
1976	17 December	14½
1976	24 December	14¼
1977	7 January	14
1977	21 January	13¼
1977	28 January	12¼
1977	3 February	12
1977	10 March	11
1977	18 March	10½
1977	31 March	9½
1977	7 April	9¼
1977	15 April	9
1977	22 April	8¾
1977	29 April	8¼
1977	13 May	8
1977	5 August	7½
1977	12 August	7
1977	9 September	6½
1977	16 September	6
1977	7 October	5½
1977	14 October	5
1977	25 November	7
1978	6 January	6½
1978	11 April	7½
1978	5 May	8¾
1978	12 May	9
1978	8 June	10
1978	9 November	12½
1979	8 February	14
1979	1 March	13
1979	5 April	12
1979	12 June	14
1979	15 November	17
1980	3 July	16
1980	24 November	14

(*a*) Bills 2½, Notes 3.
(*b*) One-month bills 5½.
(*c*) 60-day at 6.

(*d*) The Secretary of the Bank of England kindly informed us of a misprint in this place in the source.
(*e*) Minimum Lending Rate subsequently.

NOTES TO PART A

[1] SOURCE: *S.P.* 1857 (Sess. 2), x, p. 463–4.

[2] These figures are stated to be annual averages.

A. Overend, Gurney's Rates for First-class Three Months' Bills, 1824–56

1824	3·50	1835	3·71	1846	3·79
1825	3·88	1836	4·25	1847	5·85
1826	4·50	1837	4·44	1848	3·21
1827	3·25	1838	3·00	1849	2·31
1828	3·04	1839	5·13	1850	2·25
1829	3·38	1840	4·98	1851	3·06
1830	2·81	1841	4·90	1852	1·91
1831	3·69	1842	3·33	1853	3·67
1832	3·15	1843	2·17	1854	4·94
1833	2·73	1844	2·13	1855	4·67
1834	3·38	1845	2·96	1856	5·86

NOTES TO PART B

[1] SOURCES: 1845–1910 – T. T. Williams, 'The Rate of Discount and the Price of Consols', *J.R.S.S.* (1912). (Williams gives as his sources: R. H. I. Palgrave, *Bank Rate and the Money Market, 1844–1900* (London, 1903) and *The Economist*); 1911–38 – *The Bankers' Magazine* (also available from 1919 in the *Abstract*.)

[2] The figures for 1845–1910 are means of twelve monthly quotations, on or near the first of each month. Williams (*loc. cit.* p. 380) notes: 'It follows that the averages so obtained are uncertain to a degree not less than about 1 in 10, for frequently there is a considerable fluctuation in the rate of discount during a month, and this fluctuation bears little correspondence to the day of the month'.

[3] The figures from 1911–38 are means of the monthly means of, respectively, the highest and the lowest quotations on each day.

B. Rates for Three Months' Bank Bills, 1845–1938

					Max.	Min.
1845	3·00	1877	2·62	1909	2·28	
1846	3·75	1878	3·59	1910	3·16	
1847	5·87	1879	2·14			
1848	3·25	1880	2·53	1911	2·92	2·89
1849	2·25	1881	3·05	1912	3·64	3·59
1850	2·25	1882	3·55	1913	4·38	4·35
1851	3·00	1883	3·22	1914	2·94	2·87
1852	1·87	1884	2·57	1915	3·70	3·61
1853	3·50	1885	2·40	1916	5·24	5·15
1854	4·87	1886	2·33	1917	4·83	4·74
1855	4·55	1887	2·65	1918	3·58	3·55
1856	5·50	1888	2·53	1919	3·96	3·89
1857	6·65	1889	2·85	1920	6·45	6·36
1858	2·75	1890	3·88	1921	5·24	5·09
1859	2·50	1891	2·77	1922	2·68	2·59
1860	4·00	1892	1·76	1923	2·76	2·67
1861	5·00	1893	2·32	1924	3·50	3·41
1862	2·25	1894	1·18	1925	4·18	4·09
1863	4·25	1895	0·96	1926	4·51	4·44
1864	7·00	1896	1·56	1927	4·29	4·22
1865	5·32	1897	1·92	1928	4·18	4·13
1866	6·41	1898	2·62	1929	5·29	5·24
1867	2·66	1899	3·35	1930	2·59	2·55
1868	2·46	1900	3·70	1931	3·65	3·57
1869	3·37	1901	3·17	1932	1·91	1·80
1870	3·28	1902	2·97	1933	0·72	0·66
1871	2·89	1903	3·38	1934	0·84	0·81
1872	4·08	1904	2·68	1935	0·61	0·56
1873	4·70	1905	2·62	1936	0·62	0·60
1874	3·56	1906	3·97	1937	0·60	0·57
1875	3·14	1907	4·49	1938	0·65	0·62
1876	2·26	1908	2·29			

NOTES TO PART C

[1] Source: *Abstract*.

[2] The figures are the means of the market buying rate on working days as quoted in *The Times*.

C. Rates for Three Months' Bank Bills, 1938–80

(discounts in per cent per year)

	Jan.	Feb.	Mar.	Apr.	May	June	July	Aug.	Sept.	Oct.	Nov.	Dec.
1938	0·53	0·53	0·53	0·53	0·53	0·59	0·53	0·53	0·91	0·69	0·66	0·94
1939	0·56	0·53	0·63	1·41	0·72	0·75	0·78	1·59	3·53	1·88	1·19	1·22
1940	1·09	1·03	1·03	1·03	1·03	1·03	1·03	1·03	1·03	1·03	1·03	1·03
1941	1·03	1·03	1·03	1·03	1·03	1·03	1·03	1·03	1·03	1·03	1·03	1·03
1942	1·03	1·03	1·03	1·03	1·03	1·03	1·03	1·03	1·03	1·03	1·03	1·03
1943	1·03	1·03	1·03	1·03	1·03	1·03	1·03	1·03	1·03	1·03	1·03	1·03
1944	1·03	1·03	1·03	1·03	1·03	1·03	1·03	1·03	1·03	1·03	1·03	1·03
1945	1·03	1·03	1·03	1·03	1·03	1·03	1·03	1·03	1·03	1·03	0·53	0·53
1946	0·53	0·53	0·53	0·53	0·53	0·53	0·53	0·53	0·53	0·53	0·53	0·53
1947	0·53	0·53	0·53	0·53	0·53	0·53	0·53	0·53	0·53	0·53	0·53	0·53
1948	0·54	0·56	0·56	0·56	0·56	0·56	0·56	0·56	0·56	0·56	0·56	0·56
1949	0·56	0·56	0·56	0·58	0·63	0·63	0·63	0·67	0·69	0·69	0·69	0·69
1950	0·69	0·69	0·69	0·69	0·69	0·69	0·69	0·69	0·69	0·69	0·69	0·69
1951	0·69	0·69	0·69	0·69	0·69	0·69	0·93	1·00	1·00	1·00	1·38	1·50
1952	1·50	1·50	2·48	3·00	3·00	3·00	3·00	3·00	3·00	3·00	3·00	3·00
1953	3·00	3·00	3·00	3·00	3·00	3·00	3·00	3·00	2·67	2·19	2·19	2·19
1954	2·19	2·15	2·16	2·17	1·89	1·66	1·60	1·61	1·64	1·62	1·62	1·78
1955	2·02	2·58	3·81	3·83	3·94	3·99	4·00	4·06	4·15	4·16	4·21	4·22
1956	4·22	4·77	5·34	5·27	5·14	5·20	5·10	5·08	5·17	5·15	5·08	5·07
1957	4·84	4·44	4·25	4·18	4·04	4·08	4·06	4·17	5·40	6·81	6·77	6·67
1958	6·51	6·17	5·96	5·47	5·24	4·64	4·31	3·98	3·82	3·79	3·67	3·34
1959	3·28	3·23	3·41	3·40	3·44	3·54	3·57	3·60	3·59	3·58	3·55	3·72
1960	4·14	4·69	4·74	4·80	4·76	5·03	5·76	5·75	5·71	5·62	4·98	4·63
1961	4·44	4·48	4·61	4·63	4·55	4·64	5·10	6·91	6·84	6·32	5·67	5·61
1962	5·65	5·65	5·13	4·50	4·14	3·99	4·09	4·02	3·93	3·92	4·03	3·86
1963	3·69	3·63	3·70	3·88	3·88	3·84	3·87	3·85	3·88	3·86	3·91	3·91
1964	3·91	4·00	4·53	4·53	4·56	4·65	4·73	4·84	4·84	4·88	5·42	6·84
1965	6·84	6·75	6·74	6·78	6·73	6·04	5·97	5·97	5·97	5·92	5·91	5·91
1966	5·91	5·95	5·97	5·97	5·97	5·97	6·56	6·97	7·01	6·97	6·93	6·94
1967	6·77	6·40	6·18	5·69	5·51	5·44	5·47	5·53	5·54	5·79	6·88	7·78
1968	7·78	7·75	7·65	7·41	7·42	7·53	7·58	7·44	7·30	6·97	7·02	7·25
1969	7·28	7·33	8·35	8·41	8·45	8·68	8·88	8·88	8·88	8·88	8·88	8·88
1970	8·88	8·88	8·61	8·29	8·06	8·06	8·06	8·06	8·06	8·06	8·06	8·06
1971	8·06	8·06	8·06	7·06	7·05	6·74	6·43	6·02	5·30	4·91	4·77	4·51
1972	4·43	4·85	4·79	4·62	4·62	5·72	6·80	7·08	7·13	7·34	7·84	8·09
1973	8·75	9·35	9·77	8·72	8·46	8·07	8·74	12·55	12·59	11·98	12·40	13·76
1974	13·72	13·63	14·40	13·93	13·34	12·60	13·22	12·81	12·09	11·95	12·09	12·93
1975	11·91	11·42	10·37	9·53	10·10	9·68	9·92	10·52	10·46	11·40	11·19	10·92
1976	10·04	8·94	8·56	9·04	10·28	11·09	10·98	10·97	11·98	14·25	14·30	13·90
1977	13·02	11·33	10·00	8·34	7·58	7·71	7·61	6·74	5·87	4·83	5·14	6·58
1978	6·01	6·42	6·45	7·30	8·86	9·63	9·83	9·39	9·23	10·29	11·86	12·06
1979	12·37	12·89	11·68	11·50	11·55	12·94	13·74	13·87	14·10	14·10	16·04	16·65
1980	16·63	17·39	17·57	17·07	15·74	16·24	15·14	15·61	15·10	15·09	14·94	13·92

Financial Institutions 16. New Capital Issues on the London Money Market 1870–1980

NOTES TO PART A

[1] SOURCE: *The Economist*'s 'Commercial History and Review' supplements from 1883 annually to 1940.

[2] These figures were at first described as 'capital created and issued' and later as 'new capital applications'. A series of new capital issues excluding borrowing by the British government for purely financial purposes, shares issued to vendors, allotments arising from capitalisation of reserves etc., issues for conversion or redemption of securities previously held in the U.K., sales of already-issued securities, short-dated bills in anticipation of long-term borrowings, and the loans of local authorities which were not specifically limited, was published in the *Board of Trade Journal* annually in the inter-war years. It is as follows:

1919	237·5	1926	253·3	1933	132·9
1920	384·2	1927	314·7	1934	150·2
1921	215·8	1928	362·5	1935	182·8
1922	235·7	1929	253·7	1936	217·2
1923	203·8	1930	236·2	1937	170·9
1924	223·5	1931	88·7	1938	118·1
1925	219·9	1932	113·0	1939	66·3

A. *The Economist's* series, 1870–1939

1870	92·3	1888	160·3	1906	120·2	1923	271·4
1871	149·6 (*a*)	1889	207·0	1907	123·6	1924	209·3
1872	151·6	1890	142·6	1908	192·2	1925	232·2
1873	154·7	1891	104·6	1909	182·4	1926	230·8
1874	114·2	1892	81·1	1910	267·4	1927	355·2
1875	62·7	1893	49·1	1911	191·8	1928	369·1
1876	43·2	1894	91·8	1912	210·9	1929	285·2
1877	51·5	1895	104·7	1913	196·5	1930	267·8
1878	59·2	1896	152·7	1914	512·5	1931	102·1
1879	56·5	1897	157·3	1915	685·2	1932	188·9
1880	122·2	1898	150·2	1916	585·4	1933	244·8
1881	189·4	1899	133·2	1917	1,318·6	1934	169·1
1882	145·6	1900	165·5	1918	1,393·4	1935	236·1
1883	81·2	1901	159·3	1919	1,036·1	1936	255·7
1884	109·0	1902	153·8	1920	367·6	1937	251·6
1885	78·0	1903	108·5	1921	389·0	1938	180·1
1886	101·9	1904	123·0	1922	573·7	1939	91·7
1887	111·2	1905	167·2				

NOTES TO PARTS B AND C

[1] SOURCES: 1927–39 – Bank of England, *Statistical Summary*; 1946–80 – *Abstract*.

[2] The main difference between the 1927–60 series and the later one is that the latter does not include nationalised industries' stock issues. For a fuller account of the differences between the two series see Bank of England *Quarterly Bulletin*, vol. 1,no. 5 (Dec. 1961).

[3] Government stock is not included.

Part B. 1927–60

(in £ million)

	Total New Issues (*b*)	'Industrial' Issues (*c*)	Other U.K. Issues	Overseas Issues	Investment Trust Issues
1927	316·7	121·4	...	150·8	19·5
1928	360·6	159·4	...	150·1	33·9
1929	269·2	134·7	...	107·3	26·0
1930	244·8	92·9	...	112·8	9·5
1931	94·5	32·9	7·2	49·6	4·9
1932	117·8	77·5	10·2	29·4	0·7
1933	136·9	70·2	24·9	40·6	1·2
1934	164·6	91·0	28·2	42·0	3·4
1935	199·2	141·1	22·6	21·3	14·2
1936	244·6	165·6	41·5	32·4	5·2
1937	187·2	113·8	33·2	32·9	7·0
1938	131·8	76·7	26·0	28·1	1·1
1939	[72·3] (*d*)	38·9	14·5	18·9	...
1946	153·6	136·0	—	16·8	0·7
1947	187·3	154·2	—	32·5	0·6
1948	277·8	238·8	—	38·1	0·9
1949	157·1	113·1	—	41·9	2·1
1950	360·2	307·2	—	52·2	0·8

See p. 686 for footnotes.

Part B. 1927–60 *(cont.)*

(in £ million)

	Total New Issues (*b*)	'Industrial' Issues (*c*)	Other U.K. Issues	Overseas Issues	Investment Trust Issues
1951	292·2	239·7	—	50·2	2·3
1952	387·2	332·5	—	52·4	2·2
1953	435·1	350·4	19·4	57·4	7·8
1954	530·6	406·9	18·2	79·2	26·3
1955	634·5	539·0	8·8	63·6	23·1
1956	365·5	234·8	53·9	52·6	24·3
1957	367·3	261·6	25·7	65·1	14·9
1958	359·5	209·8	60·9	74·0	14·8
1959	541·4	413·9	45·2	48·8	33·6
1960	607·5	459·3	52·5	48·1	47·6

Part C. 1954–80

	Gross Issues	Gross Redemptions	Net Issues: Loan Capital	Net Issues: Pref. Shares	Net Issues: Ordinary Shares
1954	335·4	70·3	154·5	17·3	93·3
1955	355·1	80·3	113·0	16·7	145·1
1956	305·0	36·2	108·6	7·8	152·4
1957	391·5	50·8	185·3	−1·1	156·5
1958	387·4	92·5	194·1	0·1	100·7
1959	511·6	86·4	163·6	7·6	254·0
1960	573·5	91·0	144·5	4·1	333·9
1961	699·4	69·6	184·7	−1·1	446·2
1962	638·7	65·7	308·7	2·7	261·6
1963	649·3	108·5	337·3	10·0	193·3
1964	695·3	82·0	382·4	7·5	223·4
1965	779·2	150·1	556·5	−14·9	87·5
1966	1,050·9	205·0	657·9	28·4	159·6
1967	908·6	204·1	629·5	−2·4	77·4
1968	1,050·5	334·2	351·9	−10·0	374·4
1969	1,039·6	355·3	474·4	−0·6	210·5
1970	810·7	447·2	268·0	12·4	83·2
1971	1,263·3	490·3	508·0	11·4	253·6
1972	1,674·9	574·7	381·8	32·6	685·8
1973	754·9	586·2	6·9	21·7	140·1
1974	849·2	778·1	−64·9	15·6	120·4
1975	2,537·3	986·3	226·6	40·1	1,284·3
1976	2,296·8	1,182·5	27·9	31·0	1,055·4
1977	2,226·0	1,299·8	121·3	15·7	789·2
1978	1,983·2	1,163·5	−127·1	22·3	924·5
1979	1,743·1	1,005·0	−276·0	53·5	960·6
1980	2,083·3	1,310·1	−210·2	30·2	953·2

(*a*) The provenance of this figure is different from the remainder of the series, as it is compiled from totals of home new issues and foreign loans shown in a detailed breakdown in *The Economist*'s 'Commercial History and Review of 1871'.

(*b*) Investment trust issues were not included in the heading 'total new issues' in the source until 1946. They have been included here, but since the addition was of rounded figures there may be an error in the last digit.

(*c*) The heading was later changed to 'Public Corporation' and 'Public Companies' issues.

(*d*) Excludes investment trust issues.

Financial Institutions 17. Share Price Indices, 1700–1980

NOTES

[1] SOURCES: Part A – Philip Mirowski, "The Rise (and Retreat) of a Market: English Joint Stock Shares in the Eighteenth Century", *J.E.H.*, XLI, 3 (1981). Part B – based on monthly indices in A. D. Gayer, W. W. Rostow, and Anna J. Schwartz, *The Growth and Fluctuation of the British Economy 1790–1850* (2 vols, Oxford, 1953), I, p. 368. Part C – based on Hayek's monthly indices in *ibid.*, p. 456. Part D and Part E (1913–19) – K. C. Smith and G. F. Horne, *An Index Number of Securities 1867–1914* (L.C.E.S. Special Memorandum No. 37). Part E – A. L. Bowley, G. L. Schwartz, and K. C. Smith, *A New Index of Prices of Securities* (L.C.E.S. Special Memorandum No. 33) and L.C.E.S. *Bulletin*, 29. Part F – *Key Statistics, 1900–1970* (L.C.E.S., 1972) and *Financial Times* (Actuaries index).

[2] In linking indexes in the different parts, the following points should be kept in mind; (i) Mirowski specifically links Part A to Part B (excluding mines), (ii) Part B (including mines) is the more appropriate index to link to Part C, (iii) Part C does not include financial companies, but does include transport, and so should be linked to Part D (including transport), (iv) The link to 1913 provided in Part E is to the old L.C.E.S. index of 20 industrial shares.

A. 1700–1810 (1750=100)

1700	74·2	1728	98·7	1756	89·5	1784	70·1
1701	67·3	1729	96·8	1757	90·9	1785	78·3
1702	71·6	1730	101·0	1758	91·9	1786	90·7
1703	83·2	1731	104·0	1759	83·9	1787	93·8
1704	83·2	1732	104·6	1760	83·0	1788	98·2
1705	71·7	1733	101·6	1761	79·9	1789	100·5
1706	65·2	1734	92·8	1762	75·8	1790	100·9
1707	71·2	1735	96·6	1763	94·0	1791	107·8
1708	78·4	1736	107·8	1764	87·1	1792	119·2
1709	77·8	1737	109·9	1765	96·8	1793	103·8
1710	71·6	1738	108·6	1766	101·5	1794	95·3
1711	64·8	1739	99·9	1767	109·9	1795	93·5
1712	67·4	1740	96·9	1768	115·4	1796	94·9
1713	75·8	1741	97·6	1769	111·4	1797	76·3
1714	78·3	1742	98·5	1770	103·2	1798	74·4
1715	83·6	1743	101·8	1771	105·1	1799	87·0
1716	88·4	1744	99·2	1772	107·3	1800	97·8
1717	99·5	1745	98·3	1773	99·3	1801	97·9
1718	106·2	1746	91·1	1774	101·4	1802	107·5
1719	105·3	1747	89·8	1775	104·5	1803	91·3
1720	213·9	1748	89·8	1776	104·3	1804	89·0
1721	90·8	1749	96·0	1777	100·7	1805	97·2
1722	73·3	1750	100	1778	87·3	1806	104·8
1723	76·1	1751	102·2	1779	84·5	1807	108·9
1724	82·7	1752	106·4	1780	77·5	1808	111·7
1725	97·6	1753	107·6	1781	75·1	1809	119·5
1726	90·7	1754	104·5	1782	73·4	1810	120·3
1727	94·5	1755	97·2	1783	79·9	[1811	113·1] (*a*)

B. 1811–50 (June 1840=100)

	incl. mines	excl. mines		incl. mines	excl. mines		incl. mines	excl. mines
1811	103·1 (*b*)	77·9 (*b*)	1825	293·3	98·5	1838	104·9	95·8
1812	94·4	71·3	1826	142·9	84·7	1839	96·5	91·8
1813	89·2	67·4	1827	134·0	86·5	1840	94·3	92·9
1814	93·6	70·8	1828	138·8	89·7	1841	84·3	89·0
1815	87·0	65·7	1829	122·7	88·9	1842	88·3	91·3
1816	78·2	59·1	1830	128·2	87·2	1843	95·0	98·6
1817	84·1	63·5	1831	102·1	78·4	1844	111·2	113·9
1818	102·1	77·2	1832	95·9	78·7	1845	123·3	126·4
1819	101·6	76·8	1833	110·1	79·9	1846	117·7	119·5
1820	97·1	73·3	1834	107·4	81·3	1847	104·3	105·5
1821	101·3	76·5	1835	104·4	83·6	1848	89·4	90·6
1822	109·4	82·7	1836	123·8	104·6	1849	82·9	83·5
1823	115·7	87·4	1837	105·6	88·6	1850	82·6	82·4
1824	150·6	104·7						

See p. 689 for footnotes.

C. 1820–68 (1841 average=100)

1820	119·3	1833	102·4	1845	142·5	1857	114·1
1821	128·8	1834	109·3	1846	131·1	1858	113·8
1822	119·8	1835	110·3	1847	115·6	1859	113·3
1823	123·9	1836	129·0	1848	98·8	1860	115·6
1824	139·9	1837	115·9	1849	108·4	1861	124·8
1825	174·8	1838	119·9	1850	111·2	1862	142·4
1826	100·5	1839	123·0	1851	114·1	1863	168·6
1827	94·7	1840	117·0	1852	119·9	1864	170·2
1828	90·5	1841	100	1853	123·5	1865	180·0
1829	87·9	1842	102·6	1854	111·2	1866	153·8
1830	91·6	1843	112·5	1855	112·0	1867	145·3
1831	82·5	1844	124·3	1856	113·9	1868	140·4
1832	88·4						

D. 1867–1914 (June 1890=100)

	incl. transport	excl. transport		incl. transport	excl. transport		incl. transport	excl. transport
1867	[82·8] (*c*)	[81·7] (*c*)	1883	92·8	89·2	1899	152·0	164·9
1868	83·2	82·9	1884	88·4	85·5	1900	150·1	162·9
1869	86·9	88·7	1885	87·0	86·5	1901	142·3	154·9
1870	96·7	102·1	1886	88·1	88·7	1902	139·7	152·4
1871	109·0	116·4	1887	85·2	86·9	1903	136·4	148·8
1872	123·2	130·3	1888	87·9	87·9	1904	128·6	139·7
1873	126·6	132·6	1889	99·6	99·1	1905	136·4	148·3
1874	122·9	128·4	1890	99·7	100·4	1906	138·4	150·6
1875	115·8	120·7	1891	97·9	100·6	1907	135·9	148·2
1876	108·2	111·1	1892	96·7	99·2	1908	127·7	139·0
1877	102·5	102·5	1893	97·7	100·8	1909	127·2	138·8
1878	94·4	91·0	1894	101·0	105·2	1910	138·1	150·7
1879	87·1	80·3	1895	111·5	117·4	1911	144·6	157·6
1880	102·7	96·4	1896	134·9	144·2	1912	144·4	156·4
1881	101·6	92·9	1897	148·9	160·4	1913	142·5	154·0
1882	97·9	92·4	1898	148·1	159·3	1914	[140·4] (*d*)	[151·4] (*d*

E. 1913–50 (1938 average=100)

1913	51	1923	82	1933	84	1942	92
1914	50	1924	80 --- (*e*) 81	1934	102	1943	110
1915	48	1925	89	1935	113	1944	120
1916	54	1926	94	1936	131	1945	127
1917	61	1927	101	1937	122	1946	138
1918	73	1928	115	1938	100	1947	145
1919	86	1929	113	1939	93	1948	139
1920	86	1930	91	1940	77	1949	132
1921	59	1931	71	1941	82	1950	134
1922	67	1932	68				

F. 1950–80 (1963=100)

1950	31	1958	50	1966	101	1974	102
1951	36	1959	72	1967	108	1975	128
1952	30	1960	91	1968	153	1976	153
1953	32	1961	94	1969	151	1977	197
1954	42	1962	88	1970	134	1978	221
1955	49	1963	100	1971	158	1979	251
1956	46	1964	107	1972	201	1980	269
1957	49	1965	100	1973	174		

(*a*) Mirowski provides this figure as a link to the index (excluding mines) in Part B.
(*b*) Excluding January.
(*c*) Second half-year only.
(*d*) First half-year only.
(*e*) Subsequently the new index of industrial ordinary shares.

Financial Institutions 18. Fire Insurance – United Kingdom 1783–1869

NOTES

[1] SOURCE: *S.P.* 1870, XX (except for years marked *, which are taken from the Revised Report on Fire Insurance Duties, *S.P.* 1863, XXVI).

[2] The following rates of duty were charged: Great Britain – 1/6 from 1782 to the middle of 1797; 2/- from then to mid-1804; 2/6 from mid-1804 to mid-1815; 3/- from then to mid-1865, when for one year there was a reduction to 1/6 for stock-in-trade; from mid-1866 to abolition in 1869, 1/6. Ireland – 1/- from 1786 to mid-1812; 2/6 from mid-1812 to mid-1842; thereafter the same rates as in Great Britain.

(Value of Property Insured in £ million)

	England & Wales	Scotland	Ireland		England & Wales	Scotland	Ireland
1783 (*a*)	170·5*	...	...	1827	461·2	30·7	20·2

1784	153·2	2·0	...	1828	446·7	31·4	21·2
1785	136·4	1·8	...	1829	470·8	31·7	22·6
1786	132·6	1·7	...	1830	482·2	33·6	22·8
1787	134·3	1·8	...	1831	478·2	34·4	23·4
1788	135·1	1·9	...	1832	499·1	33·8	23·4
1789	139·9	2·1	...	1833	503·7	34·1	23·5
1790	144·9	2·2	...	1834	503·1	34·1	25·2
1791	150·9	2·5	...	1835	521·2	(33·7) (*c*)	(26·2) (*c*)
1792	162·1	2·7	...	1836	545·6	38·1	28·0
1793	177·3	2·9	...	1837	563·4	39·2	(29·6) (*c*)
1794	176·5	2·7	...	1838	582·2	41·5	32·4
1795	176·7	2·9	...	1839	604·6	43·0	33·5
1796	188·3	3·2	...	1840	625·1	43·6	35·2
1797	181·5	3·2	...	1841	641·4	43·2	36·7
1798	183·8*	...	...	1842	652·7	47·3	37·0
1799	198·6	3·5	...	1843	666·8	48·0	...
1800	211·4*	...	...	1844	670·2	47·8	33·0
1801 (*b*)	204·9	3·6	...	1845	678·6	49·8	33·6
1802	219·6	3·8	...	1846	696·5	51·6	34·8
1803	223·5	3·9	...	1847	709·9	54·8	35·9
1804	238·1	5·4	...	1848	727·0	53·4	36·7
1805	248·2*	...	14·5	1849	726·5	47·1	34·5
1806	256·9	5·8	14·2	1850	738·1	46·8	34·2
1807	273·0	7·8	8·2	1851	752·1	48·1	34·6
1808	281·6	9·1	30·3	1852	768·8	48·9	35·5
1809	303·1	9·6	34·9	1853	787·1	49·7	36·4
1810	324·8	10·7	39·5	1854	816·9	52·1	38·2
1811	347·3	13·1	44·8	1855 (*d*)	851·9	44·7	39·7
1812	358·2	13·8	42·7	1856	866·5	58·5	40·2
1813	362·6	12·5	...	1857	893·9	61·1	42·5
1814	349·9	12·7	21·3	1858	911·4	65·5	44·3
1815	389·2*	13·1	22·3	1859	940·9	68·1	46·1
1816	384·8	...	19·6	1860	956·5	71·6	48·6
1817	382·1	12·8	20·5	1861	983·2	77·9	52·2
1818	385·0	13·4	17·8	1862	1,006·6	86·4	54·8
1819	389·5	13·5	17·5	1863	1,035·4	89·5	55·1
1820	396·8	14·6	18·2	1864	1,068·6	92·7	57·0
1821	391·3	14·8	17·4	1865	1,132·1	98·2	59·4
1822	399·7	14·6	17·6	1866	1,172·9	103·4	64·8
1823	405·2	15·6	17·3	1867	1,228·1	114·1	69·2
					----(*e*)	----(*e*)	----(*e*)
1824	401·7	16·6	17·5	1868	1,263·5	124·6	57·3
1825	427·7	18·7	21·2	1869	1,358·0	140·9	12·2
1826	442·2	25·4	19·2				

(*a*) Year ended 1st August. The figure for 1783 is an estimate based on the revenue paid during the 401 days ended 1st August.

(*b*) Year ended 5th January.

(*c*) As from 24th June 1833 insurance of agricultural stock was exempt from duty, but returns of the value of such property continued to be made and are included here. These three bracketed figures are exceptions for which no record of exempt property is available.

(*d*) Year ended 31st March.

(*e*) From 25th December 1867 British insurance companies were required to account in Great Britain for insurances effected in Ireland.

Financial Institutions 19. Life Assurance Premiums and Funds – Great Britain 1881–1980

NOTES

[1] SOURCES: Board of Trade, *Summary of Statements of Insurance Business* and *Report of the Industrial Assurance Commissioner* annually. (The latter is included with the *Report of the Chief Registrar of Friendly Societies* from 1969).

[2] The statistics relate only to companies established within Great Britain.

[3] Prior to 1975, the accounting periods covered are those ending in the twelve months beginning 1 September of the year shown. Subsequently the figures cover accounting periods ending in the calendar year.

(in £ million)

	Ordinary Business		Industrial Business by Companies		Industrial Business by Collecting Societies	
	Premiums Income (*a*)	Life Fund at 31 Dec. (*b*)	Premiums Income	Life Fund at 31 Dec.	Premiums Income	Life Fund at 31 Dec.
1881	12·5	127·7	...	...	...	...
1882	12·8	131·9	...	...	...	...
1883	12·9	135·6	...	...	...	...
1884	13·2	139·5	...	...	...	...
1885	13·4	142·8	...	...	...	...
1886	13·7	146·1	...	...	...	...
1887	14·4	149·9	...	...	...	...
1888	15·0	154·9	...	...	...	...
1889	15·5	160·5	...	...	...	...
1890	16·0	165·9	...	...	...	...
1891	15·7	170·5	...	...	...	...
1892	17·9	176·4	...	...	...	...
1893	18·3	183·0	...	...	...	...
1894	19·4	190·2	...	...	...	...
1895	21·0	199·3	...	...	...	...
1896	21·9	209·2	...	...	...	...
1897	22·2	219·8	...	...	...	...
1898	23·2	228·9	...	...	...	...
1899	23·4	238·2	...	...	...	...
1900	23·5	246·1	...	...	...	...
1901	24·4	255·3	...	...	...	...
1902	25·0	265·0	...	...	...	...
1903	25·8	274·2	...	...	...	...
1904	27·3	284·5	...	...	...	...
1905	27·5	296·0	...	...	...	...
1906	28·1	306·4	...	...	...	...
1907	28·9	315·4	...	...	...	...
1908	30·0	325·9	...	...	...	...
1909	31·9	336·4	...	...	...	...
1910	31·3	348·6	...	...	...	...
1911	31·9	359·8	...	...	...	...
1912	32·8	370·5	...	...	...	...
1913	33·9	381·5	...	...	...	...
1914	34·3	390·1	18·0	58·7	...	...
1915	33·8	390·5	18·6	61·4	...	...
1916	34·0	395·2	19·6	65·0	...	...
1917	34·5	396·4	21·0	69·4	...	...
1918	38·6	411·0	22·4	74·0	...	...
1919	43·5	425·9	25·4	80·5	...	...
1920	47·5	437·5	29·3	89·7	...	...
1921	49·0	456·6	31·1	100·3	...	...
1922	51·5	479·5	31·6	111·5	...	...
1923	54·3	506·3	33·2	123·2	...	...
1924	58·8	532·7	34·1	136·4	8·1	29·3
1925	65·8	570·1	36·6	151·8	8·6	31·8

See p. 693 for footnotes.

Financial Institutions 19. *continued*

(in £ million)

	Ordinary Business		Industrial Business by Companies		Industrial Business by Collecting Societies	
	Premiums Income (*a*)	Life Fund at 31 Dec. (*b*)	Premiums Income	Life Fund at 31 Dec.	Premiums Income	Life Fund at 31 Dec.
1926	65·4	605·6	36·8	165·8	8·6	34·7
1927	71·4	640·4	38·8	179·1	9·2	37·7
1928	76·0	674·3	40·9	192·0	9·6	40·9
1929	78·0	710·1	42·0	203·1	10·0	43·6
1930	75·5	734·5	43·8	217·3	10·4	46·8
1931	75·4	754·3	45·4	226·3	10·7	50·4
1932	86·4	793	46·4	243·0	11·0	53·4
1933	90·1	833	47·7	259·3	11·3	56·9
1934	91·9	868	50·1	277·5	11·8	60·6
1935	95·6	903	51·5	296·7	12·2	63·9
1936	98·1	943	53·6	317·1	12·8	68·0
1937	99·7	984	55·8	337·3	13·4	72·4
1938	102·1	1,023	58·0	359·2	13·8	76·2
1939	99·5	1,042	59·8	374·4	14·3	80·7
1940	96·4	1,054	62·2	388·6	14·6	84·9
1941	95·5	1,081	63·6	407·0	15·0	90·0
1942	99·8	1,115	68·0	430·4	15·9	95·5
1943	103·6	1,153	72·2	456·0	17·0	102·4
1944	109·5	1,193	75·7	484·9	17·8	109·3
1945	117·5	1,244	79·4	526·9	18·4	116·6
1946	134·5	1,313	83·6	568·6	19·6	123·8
1947	158·9	1,391	91·2	604·1	21·2	132·5
1948	173·0	1,478	97·1	640·0	22·8	141·7
1949	185·8	1,573	100·3	671·1	23·8	150·4
1950	203·9	1,675	103·5	703·0	24·1	159·3
1951	232·4	1,786	108·2	724·9	24·9	167·2
1952	253·6	1,914	112·0	746·5	25·6	172·5
1953	274·7	2,078	116·6	786·5	26·4	182·6
1954	290·8	2,273	120·9	840·1	27·5	194·2
1955	331·0	2,484	127·4	889·9	28·6	203·4
1956	357·4	2,681	134·5	936·5	29·3	213·7
1957	396·9	2,907	140·1	972·1	30·3	225·3
1958	438·3	3,211	146·6	1,026·9	31·3	235·8
1959	478·5	3,557	153·5	1,090·6	32·6	249·0
1960	532·3	3,951	161·0	1,162·5	34·5	263·0
1961	589·4	4,385	168·6	1,227·5	35·0	274·5
1962	651·0	4,840	181·2	1,296·6	34·9	280·5
1963	759·1	5,408	185·1	1,368·7	36·1	296·1
1964	836·1	6,046	194·2	1,458·5	37·4	312·4
1965	849·3	6,680	204·0	1,561·2	38·8	329·4
1966	928·1	7,315	214·0	1,639·9	40·2	343·8
1967	1,080·7	8,156	223·5	1,719·6	41·1	359·6
	------- (*c*)	------- (*c*)				
1968	1,217·1	9,118	234·8	1,812·8	42·0	372·3
	------- (*d*)	------- (*d*)				
1969	1,221	9,831	244·0	1,896·9	43·5	388·6
1970	1,397	10,784	255·1	1,975·5	44·8	404·4

Financial Institutions 19. *continued*

(in £ million)

	Ordinary Business		Industrial Business by Companies		Industrial Business by Collecting Societies	
	Premiums Income (*a*)	Life Fund at 31 Dec. (*b*)	Premiums Income	Life Fund at 31 Dec.	Premiums Income	Life Fund at 31 Dec.
1971	1,705	12,046	267·3	2,082·6	46·5	422·3
1972	2,486	14,099	283·7	2,179·1	48·8	439·2
1973	2,696	15,876	307·0	2,299·5	51·1	458·7
1974	2,622	14,880	329·6	2,187·3	54·5	477·0
	------- (*e*)					
1975	2,703	18,047	361·5	2,430·9	58·5	493·2
1976	3,344	20,261	401·3	2,581·9	63·1	509·4
1977	3,770	24,181	447·3	2,814·9	68·3	540·9
1978	...	...	501·7	3,082·0	74·1	576·8
1979	...	...	657·2	3,463·3	92·0	631·9
1980	...	...	781·2	3,930·8	105·3	695·7

(*a*) Including considerations for annuities.
(*b*) Including Annuity Fund.
(*c*) Subsequently excluding those exempt from submitting fully detailed accounts under Section 92 of the Companies Act (1967).
(*d*) Reporting requirements were altered substantially from 1969, and much overseas business was excluded subsequently.

Financial Institutions 20. Bankruptcies – England & Wales/United Kingdom 1700–1869 and Great Britain 1870–1980

NOTES TO PART A

[1] SOURCES: G. Chalmers, *Estimate of the Comparative Strength of Great Britain* (London, editions of 1794, 1804, and 1812); T. S. Ashton, *An Economic History of England: The Eighteenth Century* (London, 1955) citing the *London Gazette* for 1738–41 and 1786–1800 and *The Gentleman's Magazine* for the remainder; *The Annual Register* (with a few gaps in the early years filled from J. R. McCulloch, *Statistical Account of the British Empire* (London, 1854), whose series is the same at that period); N. J. Silberling, "British Prices and Business Cycles 1779–1850", *Review of Economic Statistics*, v (1923), citing the *London Gazette*; *Report* of the Select Committee of the House of Lords on the Resumption of Cash Payments (*S.P.* 1819 III); *Report* of the Select Committee on Commercial Distress (*S.P.* 1847–8 VIII); *Return of Bankrupts* (*S.P.* 1847–8 LI); and *Bankruptcy Returns* (1863–70).

[2] Ashton's figures are said to be for years ended 30 September, the *Annual Register* figures to 1819 for years ended 20 December and subsequently for calendar years; and the 1862–9 figures are for years ended 11 October. Other series are for undefined dates.

[3] The official figures are apparently for the United Kingdom, as are those in the *Annual Register* from 1837. Others are not stated, except that the *Annual Register* series is for England only to 1819. The numbers of Scottish and Irish bankruptcies in 1837 were 98 and 81 respectively.

[4] The figures from official sources are of commissions sealed (or fiats issued). Other series are undefined but presumably are of commissions (or fiats) gazetted.

A. 1700–1869

	Chalmers	Ashton
1700	38	...
1701	38	...
1702	30	...
1703	...	...
1704	...	...
1705	...	...
1706	...	...
1707	...	...
1708	...	...
1709	...	...
1710	200	...
1711	...	...
1712	...	...
1713	...	...
1714	173	...
1715	169	...
1716	...	...
1717	...	...
1718	...	...
1719	...	...
1720	235	...
1721	...	...
1722	...	...
1723	...	...
1724	...	...
1725	...	...
1726	415	...
1727	446	...
1728	388	...
1729	...	...
1730	...	...
1731	...	...
1732	...	164
1733	...	170
1734	...	207
1735	...	218
1736	240	212
1737	220	222
1738	232	210
1739	263	265

	Chalmers	Ashton	*Annual Register*	Silberling
1740	288	291	...	...
1741	255	255	...	...
1742	...	...	...	...
1743	...	185	...	...
1744	197	162	...	...
1745	200	175	...	...
1746	159	167	...	...
1747	...	179		
1748	226	201	...	...
			...	...
1749	200	207	...	...
1750	...	211	...	...
1751	...	172	...	...
1752	158	170	...	...
1753	214	197	...	...
1754	244	243	...	...
1755	270	231	...	...
1756	...	236	...	...
1757	274	250	...	...
1758	...	278	...	...
1759	...	280	...	...
1760	...	216	...	...
1761	...	178	...	...
1762	205	188	...	...
1763	233	214	...	...
1764	301	284	...	...
1765	...	223	...	...
1766	...	288	...	...
1767	...	334	...	...
1768	...	303	...	...
1769	...	309	...	...
1770	...	393	...	...
1771	...	345	...	...
1772	525	484	...	...
1773	562	556	...	...
1774	360	338	...	...
1775	...	332	...	...
1776	...	388	...	...
1777	...	489	...	...
1778	675	662	...	...
1779	544	575	...	538
1780	449	454	458	445

	Chalmers	Ashton	*Annual Register*	Silberling	Official Sources
1781	438	381	458	444	...
1782	537	411	558	557	...
1783	528	540	532	535	...
1784	517	534	521	544	...
1785	...	383	502	485	...
1786	...	509	510	512	...
1787	...	487	509	506	...
1788	...	697	707	754	...
1789	...	560	562	586	...
1790	...	574	585	596	747
1791	604	603	583	615	769
1792	628	609	636	638	934
1793	1,304	1,256	1,302	1,377	1,956
1794	...	857	816	844	1,041
1795	...	731	708	690	879
1796	...	720	760	749	954
1797	...	905	869	871	1,115
1798	...	767	...	714	911
1799	...	512	...	546	717
1800	...	727	...	738	951
1801	...	...	...	881	1,198
1802	...	...	852	833	1,092
1803	...	...	901	899	1,184
1804	...	...	910	896	1,123
1805	...	...	866	867	1,128
1806	...	...	865	992	1,306
1807	...	...	1,028	1,076	1,358
1808	...	...	1,058	1,098	1,424
1809	...	...	1,089	1,098	1,386
1810	...	...	1,690	1,799	2,282
1811	...	...	2,000	2,112	2,483
1812	...	...	1,616	1,813	2,309
1813	...	...	1,599	1,583	1,945
1814	...	...	1,066	1,258	1,598
1815			1,285	1,759	2,271
1816	...	...	2,029	2,145	2,701
1817	...	...	1,575	1,578	1,917
1818	...	...	1,056	1,012	1,241
1819	...	...	1,499	1,582	2,043
	...	...	------- (*a*)		
1820	...	...	1,381	1,385	1,685
1821	...	...	1,238	1,268	1,572

A. 1700–1869 (*cont.*)

	Annual Register	Silberling	Official Sources
1822	1,113	822	1,412
1823	953	988	1,238
1824	923	999	1,231
1825	1,107	1,141	1,469
1826	2,583	2,590	3,301
1827	1,040	1,372	1,680
1828	1,223	1,214	1,512
1829	1,590	1,656	2,161
1830	1,308	1,380	1,716
1831	1,433	...	1,918
1832	1,365	...	1,734
1833	1,020	...	1,294
1834	1,101	...	1,370
1835	1,032	...	1,309
1836	929	...	1,189
	------- (*b*)		
1837	1,668	...	1,954

	Annual Register	Official Sources
1838	978	1,086
1839	1,293	1,468
1840	1,870	1,887
1841	1,789	1,837
1842	1,923	1,655
1843	1,575	1,259
1844	1,313	1,099
1845	1,263	1,160
1846	1,730	1,532
1847	2,136	1,910
1848	2,370	...
1849	1,693	...
1850	1,253	...
1851	1,381	...
1852	1,222	...

	Annual Register	Official Sources
1853	1,009	...
1854	1,608	...
1855	1,800	...
1856	1,589	...
1857	2,014	...
1858	2,116	...
1859	1,505	...
1860	1,826	...
1861	...	...
		------- (*c*)
1862	...	9,663
1863	...	8,470
1864	...	7,224
1865	...	8,305
1866	...	8,126
1867	...	8,994
1868	...	9,195
1869	...	10,396

(*a*) See notes 2 and 3 above.

(*b*) See note 3 above.

(*c*) Subsequent figures are of adjudications of bankruptcy.

NOTES TO PART B

[1] SOURCE: *Abstract*.

[2] Scottish figures up to 1896 are for years ended 31 October. Subsequent Scottish figures and all English ones are for calendar years.

B. 1870–1980

	England & Wales						Scotland		
	Numbers Adjudicated Bankrupt	Bankrupts' Liabilities (£ thousand)	Bankrupts' Assets (£ thousand)	Number of Deeds of Arrangement	Liabilities Involved in Deeds (£ thousand)	Assets Involved in Deeds (£ thousand)	Sequestrations Awarded (*a*)	Bankrupts' Liabilities (£ thousand)	Bankrupts' Assets (£ thousand)
1870	1,351	7,933	1,966				555	1,004	434
1871	1,238	3,975	555				490	1,429	422
1872	933	2,650	622				368	1,002	492
1873	915	4,045	675				391	786	498
1874	930	3,789	485				382	798	353
1875	965	6,981	961				441	743	348
1876	976	3,834	518				482	2,269	1,113
1877	967	2,924	487				543	1,666	725
1878	1,084	9,287	1,951				717	1,614	748
1879	1,156	4,299	571				1,077	1,164	591
1880	995	2,733	337				582	1,243	602
1881	1,005	2,728	320				450	1,610	696
1882	995	3,367	401				452	14,296 (*b*)	871
1883	1,046	4,321	462				342	1,625	740
1884	2,998	8,590	2,192				406	7,596 (*b*)	521
1885	3,965	7,497	2,416				362	1,137	934
1886	4,566	6,673	2,101				450	1,337	294
1887	4,681	8,129	2,368				444	1,530	790
1888	4,695	6,584	2,013	3,495	4,803	2,417	442	1,804	721
1889	4,415	5,481	1,627	3,337	4,774	2,719	388	8,956 (*b*)	1,244
1890	3,924	5,526	1,787	3,097	4,360	2,353	339	7,994 (*b*)	454
1891	4,150	7,370	2,520	3,008	5,092	3,107	348	8,048 (*b*)	1,278
1892	4,575	8,531	2,996	3,333	5,957	2,937	346	1,548	543
1893	4,805	7,216	2,707	3,938	7,574	3,441	356	918	544
1894	4,702	6,791	2,296	3,894	6,419	3,162	341	7,504 (*b*)	560

See p. 697 for footnotes.

B. 1870–1980 (*cont.*)

	England & Wales						Scotland		
	Numbers Adjudicated Bankrupt	Bankrupts' Liabilities (£ thousand)	Bankrupts' Assets (£ thousand)	Number of Deeds of Arrangement	Liabilities Involved in Deeds (£ thousand)	Assets Involved in Deeds (£ thousand)	Sequestrations Awarded (*a*)	Bankrupts' Liabilities (£ thousand)	Bankrupts' Assets (£ thousand)
1895	4,349	6,247	1,937	3,462	4,879	2,542	356	909	398
1896	4,109	5,796	2,275	3,271	4,480	2,339	317	1,475	626
1897	4,032	5,546	2,520	3,208	3,981	1,910	278	1,019	484
1898	4,247	6,686	2,451	3,246	3,847	1,979	282	873	788
1899	4,045	5,784	1,895	2,974	3,372	1,774	297	1,572	391
1900	4,343	6,325	2,555	3,354	4,264	2,487	341	662	322
1901	4,176	6,513	3,111	3,369	4,000	2,255	312	1,008	326
1902	4,145	5,435	2,729	3,305	4,483	2,757	294	1,918	470
1903	4,243	5,255	2,506	3,622	4,354	2,506	302	1,473	611
1904	4,481	6,801	2,757	4,085	5,125	2,967	317	693	310
							- - - (*a*)	- - - - (*c*)	- - - (*c*)
1905	4,700	5,785	2,287	3,839	3,759	2,047	259	538	178
1906	4,366	5,542	1,771	3,641	4,364	2,619	259	809	287
1907	4,051	5,440	1,828	3,488	5,215	3,101	257	805	227
1908	4,241	5,275	2,033	3,822	5,858	3,545	284	857	182
1909	3,998	5,600	2,035	3,491	3,911	2,033	278	880	287
1910	3,790	7,642	2,742	3,364	3,451	1,937	228	845	202
1911	3,670	6,526	1,923	2,950	4,006	2,084	230	1,010	311
1912	3,497	4,661	1,716	2,770	3,140	1,655	204	584	145
1913	3,275	4,900	1,659	2,411	2,766	1,513	169	410	87
1914	2,791	5,905	2,036	1,776	3,826	1,719	195	397	121
1915	2,285	3,465	1,088	1,652	2,064	996	199	424	102
1916	1,503	2,634	933	1,050	1,465	751	126	255	69
1917	1,045	1,637	1,119	612	1,026	529	109	326	52
1918	592	851	869	198	414	176	65	167	43
1919	709	1,740	615	165	551	320	65	73	18
1920	1,521	4,638	1,920	451	2,150	1,085	77	91	30
1921	3,397	13,359	3,856	1,368	8,067	4,908	209	583	173
1922	4,635	15,967	3,859	1,847	8,604	3,534	259	763	158
1923	4,965	10,515	2,269	1,808	5,249	2,472	291	707	148
1924	4,706	12,224	2,284	1,901	4,329	1,967	247	1,993	199
1925	4,627	9,946	1,907	1,877	4,455	1,974	248	690	148
1926	4,149	9,357	2,724	1,763	4,232	1,959	199	686	88
1927	4,234	8,015	1,737	1,856	4,392	1,967	252	463	151
1928	4,081	7,668	1,638	2,054	4,375	2,132	208	485	135
1929	3,856	8,890	2,637	1,971	5,263	2,496	216	791	99
1930	4,063	9,064	1,721	2,154	5,574	2,555	209	501	137
1931	4,317	10,787	2,154	2,415	5,412	2,685	203	1,213	128
1932	4,547	9,864	1,996	2,676	6,291	3,167	230	660	142
1933	4,030	6,366	1,250	2,102	3,818	1,771	202	417	89
1934	3,544	5,977	1,223	1,861	3,447	1,399	185	389	121
1935	3,449	5,565	1,034	1,635	5,166	1,592	156	233	49
1936	3,170	4,602	1,286	1,598	2,701	1,186	153	352	67
1937	3,034	5,144	1,002	1,630	3,500	1,825	140	261	60
1938	3,024	6,711	1,787	1,663	3,380	1,579	112	517	41
1939	2,590	6,278	1,195	1,417	2,568	1,318	112	179	41
1940	1,552	3,748	1,271	934	1,619	968	71	127	51
1941	575	1,391	489	184	335	233	38	89	13
1942	332	839	200	64	105	56	28	38	24
1943	229	694	177	44	164	83	21	49	57
1944	210	458	198	21	43	23	7	8	2

B. 1870–1980 (*cont.*)

	England & Wales						Scotland		
	Numbers Adjudi-cated Bankrupt	Bankrupts' Liabilities (£ thousand)	Bankrupts' Assets (£ thousand)	Number of Deeds of Arrange-ment	Liabilities Involved in Deeds (£ thousand)	Assets Involved in Deeds (£ thousand)	Sequestra-tions Awarded (*a*)	Bankrupts' Liabilities (£ thousand)	Bankrupts' Assets (£ thousand)
1945	194	542	203	26	50	29	17	50	25
1946	311	997	403	31	136	98	6	15	6
1947	607	1,618	498	90	198	141	23	70	12
1948	1,114	2,741	917	152	549	388	37	113	42
1949	1,463	4,639	1,168	202	1,123	609	59	176	62
1950	1,797	5,414	1,702	232	866	463	71	362	113
1951	1,789	4,817	1,468	261	1,120	740	80	265	80
1952	1,987	6,374	1,681	301	1,253	700	125	713	158
1953	2,179	6,493	2,433	302	1,099	553	92	594	116
1954	2,142	6,533	2,172	315	1,376	670	90	601	198
1955	2,119	6,893	1,852	301	1,843	792	100	641	177
1956	2,081	6,444	1,994	325	1,399	889	77	543	133
1957	2,030	6,164	2,224	313	1,445	788	99	530	127
1958	2,215	7,656	1,959	276	1,538	910	85	486	160
1959	2,277	7,250	2,182	255	1,418	698	89	565	195
1960	2,767	10,415	2,087	276	1,677	810	82	816	173
1961	3,482	14,503	2,576	299	1,930	903	106	1,440	295
1962	4,112	14,237	3,089	315	3,779	2,349	85	917	184
1963	3,929	12,779	2,605	235	1,353	654	89	888	138
1964	3,333	13,173	3,641	205	1,774	614	78	705	175
1965	3,375	17,097	3,932	198	1,463	669	83	630	184
1966	3,672	16,298	3,390	194	2,280	1,146	69	987	161
1967	3,995	19,253	4,581	160	1,947	1,013	89	1,099	416
1968	3,896	17,384	4,558	138	1,380	775	59	774	232
1969	4,347	19,173	6,630	212	2,875	1,522	82	830	327
1970	4,622	21,775	6,526	174	2,540	1,141	84	1,545	373
1971	4,353	29,284	6,595	145	2,391	939	64	843	196
1972	3,860	20,237	8,231	92	1,187	673	75	1,206	404
1973	3,363	19,102	8,640	95	1,338	688	47	968	535
1974	5,191	41,681	14,562	106	7,834	3,565	63	1,619	559
1975	6,676	81,553	21,215	123	62,902	1,876	89	3,461	1,513
1976	6,681	76,692	22,300	96	36,533	1,769	80	3,171	1,305
1977	4,078	104,674	15,834	82	9,290	2,611	76	3,213	1,025
1978	3,526	205,809	20,093	70	10,829	1,495	80	4,338	648
1979	3,158	65,805	21,678	44	7,582	858	66	2,470	994
1980	3,634	68,580	39,327	52	3,156	1,704	111	4,843	2,060

(*a*) After 1904 the figures are of the net number of sequestrations *concluded* during the year. The number awarded during 1905 was 278.

(*b*) These figures are affected by bankruptcies arising out of the failure of the City of Glasgow Bank.

(*c*) Up to 1904 the figures are of gross liabilities and assets, subsequently they are of net liabilities and assets. Gross figures for 1905 (in £000) were 821 and 407 respectively.

Financial Institutions 21. Bankruptcies – Ireland 1901–80

NOTE
SOURCES: *Abstract* and *Statistical Abstract of Ireland*.

	All Ireland						
	Numbers Adjudicated Bankrupt	Bankrupts' Liabilities (£ thousand)	Bankrupts' Assets (£ thousand)	Number of Deeds of Arrangement (*a*)	Liabilities Involved in Deeds (£ thousand)	Assets Involved in Deeds (£ thousand)	Republic of Ireland Number of Bankruptcies (*b*)
1901	195	211	61	175	328	236	...
1902	199	200	61	129	166	106	...
1903	182	170	50	184	246	169	...
1904	186	165	56	137	136	103	...
1905	208	139	47	151	194	132	...
1906	176	207	43	111	100	52	...
1907	173	150	54	125	138	70	...
1908	188	170	71	131 ----(*a*) 232	169 ----(*a*) 290	121 ----(*a*) 183	... ...
1909	154	128	20	239	327	181	...
1910	157	170	44	247	195	155	
1911	126	132	48	190	197	75	...
1912	128	223	41	244	176	112	...
1913	142	144	35	161	187	110	...
1914	96	115	25	140	192	81	...
1915	106	84	29	112	86	51	...
1916	70	68	24	106	90	40	...
1917	77	70	32	124	130	86	...
1918	21	9	3	43	68	24	...
1919	24	13	7	16	12	2	...
1920	50	49	15	33	74	276	...
	Northern Ireland						
1921	40	218	23	60	178	69	...
1922	60	126	27	86	853	173	...
1923	66	108	28	106	352	168	...
1924	51	79	20	93	192	79	...
1925	52	84	27	97	378	200	...
1926	56	86	23	94	503	208	...
1927	54	85	15	82	200	87	61
1928	38	55	14	99	235	98	47
1929	37	39	9	98	129	71	56
1930	53	69	11	93	123	40	52
1931	39	91	18	90	262	130	48
1932	61	104	14	94	179	95	51
1933	32	17	7	73	172	85	68
1934	26	28	9	35	78	27	52 ---- (*b*) 49
1935	29	52	12	67	130	54	35
1936	47	58	21	31	44	20	42
1937	31	145	29	57	174	59	41
1938	33	27	8	38	104	56	40
1939	28	37	11	34	67	27	34
1940	13	16	11	32	92	39	37

Financial Institutions 21. *continued*

	Northern Ireland						Republic of Ireland
	Numbers Adjudicated Bankrupt	Bankrupts' Liabilities (£ thousand)	Bankrupts' Assets (£ thousand)	Number of Deeds of Arrangement (a)	Liabilities Involved in Deeds (£ thousand) (a)	Assets Involved in Deeds (£ thousand) (a)	Number of Bankruptcies
1941	9	9	5	7	8	4	25
1942	7	8	2	—	—	—	21
1943	9	6	3	2	2	1	10
1944	5	2	2	2	5	2	11
1945	3	1	—	1	3	—	18
1946	5	3	2	—	—	—	4
1947	5	7	6	2	9	5	16
1948	13	61	29	4	9	6	18
1949	11	20	15	6	7	3	19
1950	24	109	46	11	59	23	25
1951	23	56	18	7	51	32	31
1952	24	52	24	17	100	38	24
1953	21	84	30	10	26	8	23
1954	16	36	13	16	55	20	20
1955	21	51	27	11	83	44	19
1956	27	72	37	18	97	55	19
1957	22	69	18	15	61	27	32
1958	22	205	109	17	82	82	31
1959	21	91	57	11	39	13	13
1960	21	88	15	22	105	29	12
1961	46	205	45	24	138	48	13
1962	37	186	53	19	160	42	13
1963	28	124	67	18	137	70	14
1964	22	98	21	18	112	37	21
1965	30	113	31	20	157	72	11
1966	19	94	39	25	130	56	10
1967	12	48	21	20	268	168	3
1968	30	383	101	18	120	49	8
1969	15	219	92	25	203	63	10
1970	23	189	67	36	395	152	16
1971	27	320	30	35	698	421	28
1972	20	646	97	14	150	38	20
1973	19	196	19	4	90	49	22
1974	25	466	98	5	159	55	25
1975	37	1,008	175	5	424	105	21
1976	49	970	554	1	10	5	40
1977	39	588	299	10	153	74	31
1978	36	1,147	267	8	323	258	15
1979	23	551	154	8	513	235	24
1980	28	1,276	252	9	576	184	27

(*a*) Including arrangements under the control of the Court from 1907 (2nd line). (*b*) Figures to 1934 (1st line) are of petitions filed in the year ending 31 March.

Financial Institutions 22. Foreign Exchange Rates – 1609–1980

NOTES

[1] Sources: To 1775 – John J. McCusker, *Money and Exchange in Europe and America, 1600–1775: A Handbook* (Chapel Hill, N.C., 1978). 1776–89 – *S.P.* 1810–11 x, p. 197. 1790–1818 – *S.P.* 1819 III, Appendix to the second *Report* from the Select Committee on the Expediency of the Bank Resuming Cash Payments. 1819–47 – *S.P.* 1840 IV, *S.P.* 1841 (1) V, and *S.P.* 1847–8 VIII. 1848–99 and 1914–18 *J.R.S.S.*, "Periodical Returns" and *The Bankers' Magazine*. 1900–13 and 1919–38 – L.C.E.S., *The British Economy: Key Statistics 1900–64*. 1939–80 – *Abstract*.

[2] McCusker's figures are averages of monthly data; figures for 1776–1899 and 1914–18 are averages of the last available quotations in February, May, August, and November; all other figures are averages of daily quotations.

[3] The Hamburg exchange rate is expressed in schillings vlamische Banco to 1827 and in marks, subsequently. (One schilling vls. equalled 2·66 marks.) The Paris exchange rate is expressed in pence sterling per écu (of 3 livres tournois) to 1793 and in francs per pound sterling subsequently. The colonial exchange rates are expressed in local pounds per £100 sterling, and U.S. rates in dollars and cents per pound sterling.

[4] The longer continuous series of the two given by McCusker for the Paris rate has been preferred here. Some of the missing years may be filled from the other series, and these are shown here in square brackets.

[5] The figures in round brackets following the Hamburg and Paris rates prior to 1698 indicate the number of months for which there are quotations.

	Hamburg sch. vls. per £1	Paris pence per écu
1609	26·73(1)	...
1619	30·27(1)	71·43(1)
1624	35·36(7)	69·39(7)
1625	35·45(8)	68·76(8)
1626	34·67(8)	67·77(9)
1628	34·56(1)	69·51(1)
1630	35·58(3)	67·10(3)
1631	34·88(7)	64·03(6)
1632	35·43(4)	63·26(3)
1633	35·72(4)	63·50(4)
1634	36·08(1)	63·77(1)
1635	35·11(3)	62·84(3)
1636	34·31(4)	59·60(3)
1637	35·43(2)	56·44(2)
1638	34·44(2)	54·23(2)
1640	35·98(1)	51·82(1)
1641	37·22(2)	51·99(2)
1642	36·89(4)	52·68(4)
1643	37·29(3)	51·71(3)
1645	37·35(5)	51·58(5)
1646	36·53(12)	53·09(12)
1648	32·13(4)	61·26(3)

	Hamburg sch. vls. per £1	Paris pence per écu	Massachusets local pounds per £100 stg.
1649	31·21(8)	...	112·00
1650	31·79(5)	63·29(4)	...
1651	35·87(1)	53·09(1)	...
1652	33·84(2)	56·15(2)	...
1653	35·00(2)	51·16(2)	...
1654	34·98(5)	51·64(5)	...
1660	...	...	112·00
1663	...	[55·38(1)]	112·00
1664	34·01(1)	56·22(1)	113·33
1665	32·62(1)	55·45(1)	115·33
1667	...	[57·25(1)]	116·00
1668	...	[57·07(4)]	115·75
1669	35·02(6)	55·92(6)	116·00
1670	...	...	125·00
1671	34·93(2)	54·87(2)	125·00
1672	34·09(3)	55·60(3)	125·00
1673	...	[55·24(12)]	125·00
1674	31·68(6)	56·96(6)	125·00
1675	32·76(1)	57·02(1)	123·89
1676	34·16(2)	54·92(2)	129·17
1677	34·85(5)	54·88(5)	128·00
1678	34·29(1)	53·60(1)	128·00
1679	34·40(2)	54·24(2)	122·00

	Hamburg sch. vls per £1	Paris pence per écu	Massa-chusetts local pounds per £100 stg.	Penn-sylvania local pounds per £100 stg.
1680	34·70(2)	55·25(2)	120·25	...
1681	34·61(1)	55·20(1)	124·88	...
1682	34·62(2)	55·36(2)	128·00	125·00
1683	33·70(1)	54·33(1)	128·00	125·00
1684	...	[54·86(12)]	130·00	...
1685	34·34(1)	55·65(1)	127·50	...
1686	34·53(2)	54·02(2)	125·00	...
1687	34·67(1)	53·70(1)	120·94	...
1688	34·15(1)	52·98(1)	140·00	...
1689	...	[55·94(1)]	...	130·00
1690	...	...	128·33	...
1891	32·63(1)	52·64(1)	131·25	...
1692	32·51(1)	52·37(1)	130·50	...
1693	31·67(6)	53·27(6)	130·00	...
1694	30·62(7)	56·70(7)	133·66	135·86
1695	...	60·39(10)	139·86	...
1696	...	56·76(5)	129·17	115·00
1697	...	48·38(4)	136·00	...
1698	34·41	45·71	...	155·00
1699	33·98	46·46	40·48	...
1700	34·38	46·09	139·43	155·00
1701	35·30	44·45	136·50	147·92
1702	34·08	44·04 (*a*)	130·00	150·72
1703	32·55	...	140·00	150·84
1704	32·62	...	140·00	150·00
1705	32·76	...	135·00	150·14
1706	33·50	...	150·00	150·58
1707	33·67	...	...	152·58
1708	33·48	...	...	153·96
1709	32·76	...	151·06	120·05
1710	32·70	...	155·00	128·16
1711	33·31	...	146·67	...
1712	33·23	...	150·00	128·93
1713	34·41	37·12 (*b*)	150·00	130·36
1714	34·83	39·58	153·33	132·50
1715	35·11	47·55	160·33	130·36
1716	34·46	45·36	162·50	133·52
1717	33·81	47·34	170·00	134·72
1718	33·82	36·68	200·00	132·32
1719	34·53	28·38	216·68	135·42
1720	34·16	16·47	219·43	138·75
1721	34·18	24·31	225·98	137·50
1722	35·04	23·06	229·79	135·01
1723	34·54	22·54	241·81	140·37
1724	34·02	30·38	267·92	143·11
1725	33·94	38·02	289·11	139·34
1726	34·71	36·12	290·98	...
1727	34·82	32·97	291·98	149·58
1728	33·85	32·86	298·82	150·62
1729	33·43	32·68	313·33	148·61
1730	33·20	32·48	337·71	152·03
1731	33·97	31·67	334·31	153·28
1732	34·18	32·20	339·51	160·90
1733	34·36	31·67	350·00	166·94
1734	35·61	31·33	355·00	170·00
1735	35·33	31·21	360·00	166·11
1736	34·65	31·36	430·00	167·00
1737	33·94	32·34	516·67	170·25
1738	33·96	31·98	500·00	160·42
1739	34·32	31·22	500·00	169·69
1740	34·12	32·31	525·00	165·45
1741	33·55	32·54	548·44	146·14
1742	33·63	31·52	550·28	159·38
1743	33·64	32·37	550·70	159·79
1744	33·56	32·60	588·61	166·67
1745	34·20	31·81	644·79	174·77
1746	35·62	30·68	642·50	179·86
1747	35·04	31·60	925·00	183·78
1748	34·78	30·75	912·50	174·12
1749	34·36	31·30	1,033·33	171·39
1750	33·56	31·52	137·33	170·60
1751	33·58	31·12	133·33	169·86
1752	33·40	31·68	...	166·85
1753	33·30	32·10	130·00	167·49
1754	33·53	31·43	133·33	168·35
1755	34·48	30·96	133·33	168·79
1756	35·76	30·30	133·33	172·57
1757	36·18	30·30	133·33	166·07
1758	35·69	31·20	128·34	159·00
1759	37·05	30·59	...	153·52
1760	33·98	30·62	129·54	158·61
1761	32·34	31·29	140·10	172·71
1762	34·34	30·60	142·33	176·26
1763	34·31	31·65	136·00	173·00
1764	35·04	30·52	133·75	172·86
1765	34·66	31·19	133·54	169·90
1766	35·04	31·81	133·03	162·96
1767	35·55	31·57	133·33	166·02
1768	34·18	31·38	133·33	166·62
1769	33·41	31·70	129·86	157·56
1770	33·26	31·60	126·31	153·92
1771	33·20	31·64	133·33	165·69
1772	33·24	31·53	131·00	160·83
1773	34·72	29·88	132·19	166·27
1774	34·56	30·21	135·30	169·46
1775	34·28	30·70	117·45	161·12

See p. 703 for footnotes.

	Hamburg sch. vls per £1	Paris pence per écu		Hamburg sch. vls per £1	Paris francs per £1	New York dollars per £1 (*g*)		Hamburg marks per £1 (*f*)	Paris francs per £1	New York dollars per £ (*g*)
1776	33·50	30·56	1821	318·0	25·73	...	1866	13·63	25·53	7·18
1777	32·56	31·31	1822	37·58	25·44	...	1867	13·62	25·38	5·32
1778	34·08	29·91	1823	38·04	25·80	...	1868	13·65	25·38	5·32
1779	35·25	29·22	1824	37·17	25·35	...	1869	13·80	25·41	5·31
1780	34·54	29·38	1825	36·92	25·21	...	1870	13·70	25·62	5·32
1781	32·98	30·75	1826	37·60	25·68	...	1871	13·66	25·94	5·34
1782	32·29	31·59	1827	37·02	25·45	...	1872	13·69	25·94	5·31
				marks per £1				Reichsmarks per £1		
1783	32·25	31·55	1828	13·80	25·35	...	1873	20·56	25·88	5·28
										----- (*g*
1784	34·15	29·73	1829	13·93	25·66	...	1874	20·41	25·41	4·864
1785	35·17	28·55	1830	13·98	25·56	...	1875	20·71	25·49	4·856
1786	34·60	29·00	1831	13·73	25·24	...	1876	20·58	25·45	4·860
1787	34·75	29·19	1832	13·98	25·79	...	1877	20·67	25·36	4·841
1788	35·08	28·70	1833	13·84	25·74	...	1878	20·65	25·42	4·823
1789	35·21	27·97	1834	13·75	25·46	...	1879	20·61	25·48	4·839
1790	35·37	26·45	1835	13·88	25·60	...	1880	20·65	25·51	4·826
1791	35·58	23·16	1836	13·84	25·59	...	1881	20·71	25·58	4·823
1792	34·37	17·88	1837	13·84	25·59	...	1882	20·70	25·53	4·839
1793	36·35	[10·54] (*c*)	1838	13·78	25·63	...	1883	20·68	25·53	4·825
1794	35·27	...	1839	13·77	25·41	...	1884	20·61	25·41	4·838
1795	33·75	...	1840	13·70	25·39	...	1885	20·60	25·44	4·842
1796	33·73	...	1841	13·61	25·63	...	1886	20·55	25·42	4·843
1797	37·00	...	1842	13·70	25·79	...	1887	20·54	25·48	4·837
1798	37·52	...	1843	13·78	25·84	...	1888	20·59	25·54	4·848
1799	34·54	...	1844	13·72	25·73	...	1889	20·60	25·42	4·847
1800	32·56	...	1845	13·86	25·92	...	1890	20·66	25·46	4·819
1801	31·52	...	1846	13·81	25·93	...	1891	20·58	25·47	4·833
		francs per £1								
1802	33·06	[23·77] (*d*)	1847	13·73	25·76	...	1892	20·52	25·32	4·858
1803	34·02	24·39	1848	14·05	25·80	...	1893	20·62	25·40	4·844
1804	35·56	25·18	1849	13·82	25·67	...	1894	20·54	25·32	4·862
1805	34·85	25·55	1850	13·70	25·54	...	1895	20·59	25·34	4·876
1806	34·08	24·29	1851	13·52	25·29	...	1896	20·60	25·33	4·850
1807	34·54	24·35	1852	[13·44] (*e*)	[25·45] (*e*)	...	1897	20·56	25·31	4·839
1808	34·10	23·28	1853	13·44	25·28	...	1898	20·64	25·43	4·831
1809	29·75	20·21	1854	13·37	25·31	...	1899	20·68	25·42	4·834
1810	29·81	20·75	1855	13·52	25·47	...	1900	20·72 (*f*)	25·38	4·834 ----- (*h* 4·872
1811	24·75	17·93	1856	13·61	25·73	...	1901	20·62	25·35	4·879
1812	28·06	19·25	1857	13·61	25·53	...	1902	20·61	25·33	4·876
1813	28·00	19·93	1858	13·46	25·39	...	1903	20·63	25·36	4·868
1814	29·96	21·05	1859	13·34	25·38	5·38	1904	20·61	25·33	4·872
1815	31·68	21·53	1860	13·39	25·45	5·31	1905	20·62	25·31	4·866
1816	36·06	25·36	1861	13·63	25·74	5·19	1906	20·71	25·37	4·857
1817	35·29	24·68	1862	13·69	25·45	6·05	1907	20·78	25·43	4·867
1818	34·02	24·00	1863	13·52	25·56	7·67	1908	20·66	25·32	4·868
1819	35·31	24·59	1864	13·58	25·73	11·11	1909	20·66	25·36	4·876
1820	36·83	25·55	1865	13·63	25·48	8·54	1910	20·71	25·45	4·868

Financial Institutions 22. *continued*

	Berlin Reichs-marks per £1	Paris francs per £1	New York dollars per £1		Berlin (*j*) Reichs-marks per £1	Paris francs per £1	New York dollars per £1		Frankfurt Deutsch-marks per £1	Paris francs per £1	New York dollars per £1
1911	20·71	25·49	4·866	1935	12·18	74·27	4·903	1958	11·72	1,177·56 new francs per £1	2·81
1912	20·75	25·50	4·870	1936	12·33	82·97	4·971	1959	11·74	13·77	2·81
1913	20·78	25·56 ----- (*h*)	4·868	1937	12·29	124·61	4·944	1960	11·71	13·77	2·81
1914	...	25·16	4·884 ----- (*h*) 4·876	1938	12·17	170·65	4·890	1961	11·256	13·745	2·8023
1915	...	26·51	4·748	1939	...	176·65	4·460	1962	11·224	13·758	2·8078
1916	...	28·04	4·766	1940	...	176·62	4·03	1963	11·161	13·721	2·8003
1917	...	27·47	4·764	1941	...	...	4·03	1964	11·099	13·684	2·7927
1918	...	26·72 ----- (*h*)	4·765	1942	...	...	4·03	1965	11·165	13·702	2·7962
1919	226·98	31·75	4·402 ----- (*h*) 4·429	1943	...	...	4·03	1966	11·168	13·723	2·7932
1920	404·59	52·47	3·661	1944	...	...	4·03	1967	10·971	13·539	2·7563
1921	8,155·85	51·89	3·846	1945	...	203·89	4·03	1968	9·555	11·855	2·3937
1922	...	54·60	4·427	1946	...	480·00	4·03	1969	9·379	12·424	2·3903
1923	18·90	75·64	4·574	1947	...	480·00	4·03	1970	8·736	13·244	2·3960
1924	20·28	85·24	4·417	1948	...	879·73	3·68	1971	8·496	13·471	2·4460
1925	20·41	102·54	4·829	1949	...	1,053·06	2·80	1972	7·979	12·621	2·5029
1926	20·46	152·38	4·858	1950	...	980·00	2·80	1973	6·540	10·899	2·4526
1927	20·39	123·85	4·861	1951	...	979·74	2·79	1974	6·049	11·246	2·3402
1928	20·39	124·10	4·866	1952	...	981·48	2·81	1975	5·4470	9·5003	2·2200
					Deutsch-marks per £1						
1929	20·40	124·02	4·857	1953	11·70	982·76	2·81	1976	4·5520	8·6081	1·8049
1930	20·38	123·88	4·862	1954	11·73	981·64	2·79	1977	4·0504	8·5733	1·7455
1931	20·52 ----- (i) 15·73	124·06 ----- (i) 94·02	4·859 ----- (i) 3·694	1955	11·74	978·10	2·80	1978	3·8500	8·6446	1·9197
1932	14·74	89·19	3·504	1956	11·71	982·74	2·79	1979	3·8875	9·0253	2·1225
1933	13·98	84·59	4·218	1957	11·73	1,060·24	2·81	1980	4·2269	9·8250	2·3281
1934	12·80	76·94	5·041								

(*a*) First 4 months.
(*b*) Last 8 months.
(*c*) Average of February, May, and August.
(*d*) Average of May, August, and November.
(*e*) November only.
(*f*) Berlin from 1909.
(*g*) 60 day money to 1873.
(*h*) This break occurs on a change of source. See note 1 above. The Paris rate for 1913 in the old source is 25.24, and that for 1919 is 32.16.
(*i*) The first figure is for the period prior to leaving the gold standard in September, the second figure relates to the remainder of the year.
(*j*) Frankfurt from 1953.

Financial Institutions 23. Variations from Mint Parity in Sterling Dollar Exchange Rates – 1791–1900

NOTES

[1] SOURCES: To 1834 – based on Lawrence Officer, "Dollar–Sterling Mint Parity and Exchange Rates, 1791–1834", *J.E.H.* XLIII, 3 (1983); 1835 onwards – based on Edwin J. Perkins, "Foreign Interest Rates in American Financial Markets: A Revised Series of Dollar–Sterling Exchange Rates, 1835–1900", *J.E.H.* XXXVIII, 2 (1978).

[2] The rates are expressed as deviations from the "true mint parity", as defined and described by Officer in the source for the period before the United States went effectively on to the gold standard in 1834, and as deviations from the parity then established subsequently. A negative sign means that sterling was at a discount to parity.

[3] The original data for all series were actual transactions in bills of exchange. The interest element in such transactions has been removed in arriving at the figures shown here.

[4] Since the series represent deviations from mint parity, depreciation of paper currency in terms of specie has been allowed for, except in 1837–42.

[5] Of the two series shown by Officer, the one based on information compiled by John White, Cashier of the Bank of the United States in 1829, has been preferred where available. There is consequently, a slight break in continuity between 1829 and 1830.

[6] The quarterly figures given in the sources have been converted to annual averages here.

Year		Year		Year		Year	
1791	−0·08	1819	2·14	1847	−1·31	1874	0·55
1792	−2·77	1820	−5·05	1848	0·40	1875	0·34
1793	−0·73	1821	−0·44	1849	−0·73	1876	0·35
1794	2·27	1822	4·12	1850	0·37	1877	0·03
1795	−3·14	1823	0·14	1851	1·23	1878	0·10
1796	−9·49	1824	1·30	1852	1·02	1879	0·06
1797	−1·19	1825	1·28	1853	0·69	1880	−0·13
1798	−5·86	1826	2·79	1854	0·64	1881	−0·44
1799	−6·96	1827	3·25	1855	0·64	1882	0·39
1800	7·49	1828	2·84	1856	1·04	1883	−0·04
1801	8·51	1829	1·54	1857	0·70	1884	0·06
			---- (*a*)				
1802	6·98	1830	−0·87	1858	0·07	1885	0·11
1803	5·72	1831	1·83	1859	0·98	1886	0·22
1804	4·76	1832	1·71	1860	−0·08	1887	0·02
1805	−1·96	1833	−0·63	1861	−1·71	1888	0·40
1806	3·95	1834	−13·08 (*b*)	1862	1·20	1889	0·37
			---- (*c*)				
1807	3·85	1835	−0·05	1863	0·45	1890	0·10
1808	1·84	1836	−0·75	1864	1·95	1891	0·11
1809	4·03	1837	5·12	1865	0·91	1892	0·36
1810	2·41	1838	0·84	1866	0·70	1893	0·17
1811	−1·79	1839	2·68	1867	0·78	1894	0·43
1812	−4·54	1840	3·05	1868	0·84	1895	0·67
1813	3·18	1841	2·81	1869	0·42	1896	0·34
1814	8·16	1842	−1·03	1870	0·37	1897	0·14
1815	4·91	1843	−1·07	1871	0·65	1898	−0·16
1816	−0·31	1844	0·49 (*b*)	1872	−0·11	1899	0·14
1817	3·64	1845	0·30	1873	0·60	1900	0·17
1818	5·76	1846	−0·85				

(*a*) See note 5 above.
(*b*) Based on three quarters.
(*c*) There may be a slight break on the change of source.

CHAPTER XIII

CONSUMPTION

TABLES

Statistics of personal consumption were not collected specifically in Britain until the Second World War, and the first easily obtained publication in which they appeared was the initial postwar *Annual Abstract of Statistics*. But for certain wholly imported commodities they can be constructed from the external trade and population statistics of the country for much earlier periods. There are also other indicators which have been used.

Table 1 consists of such series, namely the numbers of cattle and sheep brought for sale to Smithfield Market in London in the period 1732–1854. Hobsbawm thought in the 1950s that these could be used 'without too much hesitation'[1] as indicators of working-class living standards. Others would be less confident, for a variety of reasons. The statistics relate to animals brought for slaughter, and contain no information on changes which may have taken place in the weight of and the proportion of meat on such animals. Fussell discussed this problem so far as the eighteenth century was concerned many years ago,[2] but was unable to come to any conclusion about sheep. For cattle, he found that the usual view held up to then, that there was a substantial increase in weight, was exaggerated, for 'the effect of Bakewell's improvements, although remarkable, cannot have been approximately universal'. However, the effect of the changes in breed had been mainly 'towards producing more meat and less bone.'

Great doubt is thrown on the use of the Smithfield statistics to suggest changes in living standards not so much by these speculations about the meat per beast as by two other things.

[1] E. J. Hobsbawm, 'The British Standard of Living 1790–1850', *Economic History Review*, second series X, 1 (1957), p. 65. This was reprinted in his *Labouring Men* (London, 1964) with the additional remark that 'since the original publication of this paper it has increasingly been so used' and a reference in support to the first version of this book (p. 100). In view of that I should like to call particular attention to the drawbacks of the Smithfield series mentioned in the rest of this paragraph and in the next one.

[2] G. E. Fussell, 'The Size of English Cattle in the Eighteenth Century', *Agricultural History* (1929); and G. E. Fussell and Constance Goodman, 'Eighteenth Century Estimates of British Sheep and Wool Production', *Agricultural History* (1930).

First, they do not include pigs, and pigmeat was traditionally the most important sort of flesh consumed by the poorer classes.[3] And second, the statistics could, at most, only be taken as applying to London; and then only if the proportion of the London population fed from Smithfield remained constant. It is impossible to believe that this was the case, for other markets were established at Newgate, Leadenhall, Faringdon, and Whitechapel, and they grew faster; and, moreover, country-killed meat began to come in by cart as the roads were improved, even before the railways magnified its volume greatly. The figures in table 1, therefore, are retained for their historiographical interest. But until and unless more can be said about other sources of supply, they cannot be safely used to indicate London's meat – or even beef and lamb – consumption.

Table 2 gives statistics of *per caput* consumption up to 1938 of four commodities which, with the partial exception of sugar in the 1920s and 1930s, were wholly imported. They are based where possible on the Customs figures of imports entered for home consumption (less quantities over-entered). For the periods when these are not available (for example, when the goods have been duty-free), imports less re-exports have been used. These figures will be found to differ from some previously published.[4] The differences result from minor variations in definition, from small revisions in the Registrar General's estimates of population, and from differences in the trade statistics published in early-nineteenth-century Blue Books. In general, the policy preferred here has been to prefer those statistics which were published latest; and, in particular, to use those in the Customs historical volume of 1898.[5]

The use of these *per caput* consumption statistics as indicators of the standard of living is, of course, fraught with dangers in interpretation. All the commodities for which the series exist were imported and were therefore subject in the early and more controversial period to annual variations arising from wars and the slow, irregular pace of ocean shipping.[6] There were secular trends in the consumption of at least three of these commodities at different times – a trend towards tea-drinking away from beer in the eighteenth and early nineteenth centuries; a swing of fashion against tobacco in early Victorian times; and the well-known decline in the popularity of coffee in the second half of the nineteenth century. One must agree with Hobsbawm that 'sugar is the most sensitive indicator',[7] though that, too, was

[3] A general account of the diet of different classes in England from the Middle Ages to fairly modern times can be found in J. C. Drummond and Anne Wilbraham, *The Englishman's Food* (London, 1939), though it contains no serious attempt to estimate exactly how much of his chosen foods the poorer Englishman was able to buy. The same is, in the main, true of John Burnett, *Plenty and Want* (London, 1966). Contemporary sources of labourers' diet in the late eighteenth century are David Davies, *The Case of the Labourers in Husbandry* (Lonodn, 1795), and Sir Frederick M. Eden, *The State of the Poor* (3 vols., London, 1797).

[4] Those in the *Statistical Abstract* for some years, and those given in A. Rive, 'The Consumption of Tobacco since 1600', *Economic History*, I (1926).

[5] *S.P.* 1898 LXXXV.

[6] This does not seriously affect the *per caput* figures shown here, only the absolute figures in the notes. An exception may be tobacco in the early nineteenth century according to Rive, 'A Short History of Tobacco Smuggling', *Economic History*, I.

[7] E. J. Hobsbawm, *loc. cit.*, p. 57.

subject to outside factors, such as the growth of a factory confectionery industry in the late nineteenth century, and the imposition and removal of duties. In general, it would not be unfair to say that the consumption statistics that we have are a poor measure of the standard of living, particularly for the period before 1850 for which good indicators are most needed. Only pronounced trends can be interpreted clearly, and there are none of those before the 1840s.[8] Some, indeed, would echo Burnett, that 'this line of inquiry seems to be unrewarding since it can only inform us about average consumption per head and not about the actual diet of real people'.[9] This is going too far. Averages may conceal some things, but they do reveal others.

In his very detailed *History . . . of the Potato*, Salaman makes some estimates of wheat and potato consumption from the late eighteenth to the early twentieth centuries which, though only rough approximations based on a number of debatable assumptions, are not without interest. These are shown in table 3. Finally, the modern statistics, begun with the difficulty of feeding the population in the Second World War, are given in table 4.

[8] A. J. Taylor, 'Progress and Poverty in Britain, 1780–1959: A Reappraisal', *History*, XLV (1960), pp. 22–3, in effect questioned the use of a limited range of consumption statistics when he wrote that 'it was outside the field of necessities, in the narrow sense, that increasing consumption was most evident . . . If these improvements were purchased in part at the expense of so-called necessities, and specifically of food, this was a matter of the consumer's choice.'

[9] John Burnett, *op. cit.*, p. 31.

Consumption 1. Cattle and Sheep Brought for Sale at Smithfield Market 1732–1854

NOTES

[1] SOURCES: 1732–89 – *Report on Waste Lands* (1795), pp. 202–3; 1790–1819 – *S.P.* 1822, XXI; 1820–47 – Porter's Tables; 1848–54 – G. Dodd, *The Food of London* (London, 1856), pp. 240–1.

[2] The *Report on the Waste Lands* gives slightly different figures for the years 1790–4. The only material differences are in the numbers of sheep in 1790–2, which are given (in thousands) as:

1790	730	1791	730	1792	753

[3] *S.P.* 1822, XXI, gives the number of cattle in 1821 as 142 thousand.

[4] For the period 1842–7 Dodd, *op. cit.*, gives slightly different figures from the ones used here.

[5] Earlier estimates of sales at Smithfield were made for 1698 and 1725, as follows (in thousands):

	Cattle	Sheep		Cattle	Sheep
1698	70	540	1725	74	556

The sources are, respectively, Stowe, *Survey* (1754 edition), p. 719, and Maitland, *History of London* (1772 edition), pp. 756–7.

(in thousands)

	Cattle	Sheep		Cattle	Sheep		Cattle	Sheep
1732	76	515	1773	90	610	1814	135	871
1733	80	555	1774	90	585	1815	125	963
1734	79	567	1775	94	624	1816	120	969
1735	84	591	1776	98	672	1817	130	1,045
1736	88	587	1777	94	715	1818	138	963
1737	90	607	1778	97	659	1819	135	950
1738	87	589	1779	97	677	1820	133	948
1739	87	569	1780	102	707	1821	129	1,107
1740	85	501	1781	103	743	1822	142	1,340
1741	78	536	1782	101	729	1823	150	1,265
1742	80	503	1783	102	702	1824	164	1,240
1743	76	468	1784	98	616	1825	157	1,130
1744	77	491	1785	99	641	1826	143	1,271
1745	74	564	1786	92	666	1827	138	1,335
1746	72	621	1787	95	669	1828	148	1,288
1747	71	622	1788	93	679	1829	158	1,240
1748	68	610	1789	93	694	1830	160	1,287
1749	73	624	1790	104	750	1831	148	1,189
1750	71	656	1791	101	740	1832	159	1,257
1751	70	632	1792	107	761	1833	152	1,168
1752	74	642	1793	117	728	1834	162	1,237
1753	75	648	1794	109	719	1835	170	1,382
1754	70	631	1795	131	746	1836	164	1,220
1755	74	647	1796	117	759	1837	172	1,329
1756	77	625	1797	108	694	1838	183	1,403
1757	83	575	1798	107	753	1839	181	1,360
1758	84	551	1799	123	834	1840	177	1,372
1759	86	582	1800	125	842	1841	...	...
1760	89	622	1801	135	761	1842	175	1,469
1761	83	666	1802	126	743	1843	175	1,572
1762	103	722	1803	118	787	1844	186	1,609
1763	81	653	1804	113	904	1845	192	1,442
1764	75	556	1805	125	912	1846	200	1,459
1765	82	537	1806	120	859	1847	221	1,438
1766	76	515	1807	134	924	1848	220	1,344
1767	77	574	1808	144	1,015	1849	224	1,514
1768	80	626	1809	138	989	1850	227	1,540
1769	82	643	1810	132	963	1851	241	1,564
1770	87	649	1811	125	966	1852	259	1,565
1771	94	632	1812	134	954	1853	277	1,461
1772	90	610	1813	138	891	1854	263	1,539

Consumption 2. *Per Caput* Consumption of Coffee, Tea, Sugar and Tobacco – United Kingdom 1789–1938

NOTES

[1] Sources: Coffee 1789–1839 – *S.P.* 1829, xv and *S.P.* 1843, LII; tea 1789–1896 – *S.P.* 1898, LXXXV; sugar 1793–1814 – *S.P.* 1847–8, LVIII; sugar 1815–96 – *S.P.* 1898, LXXXV; sugar 1897–1901 – *Annual Statement of Trade*; tobacco 1790–1870 – *S.P.* 1898, LXXXV; all other figures – *Abstract*. The population figures used were the latest estimates in the *Reports of the Registrar General* for the various kingdoms, after 1801, and our own estimates based on extrapolation of later trends, for 1789–1800.

[2] For the years before 1789, for which population estimates are not sufficiently sure to be used to extend this table, the following statistics of quantities entered for home consumption are available:

Tea, in thousands of pounds: (source: *S.P.* 1898, LXXXV)

1740	1,494	1748	3,151	1756	3,813	1764	5,223
1741	1,192	1749	3,335	1757	3,723	1765	5,204
1742	474	1750	2,296	1758	3,521	1766	5,186
1743	711	1751	3,656	1759	3,246	1767	4,921
1744	1,723	1752	2,273	1760	3,861	1768	7,676
1745	2,423	1753	3,253	1761	4,308	1769	9,115
1746	2,496	1754	3,049	1762	4,218	1770	8,634
1747	215	1755	3,437	1763	5,307	1771	6,307
1772	6,722	1777	5,120	1782	6,202	1787	15,726
1773	3,776	1778	4,180	1783	4,742	1788	14,765
1774	6,729	1779	6,342	1784	10,160		
1775	6,156	1780	7,328	1785	14,801		
1776	4,468	1781	4,884	1786	15,852		

Tobacco, in thousands of pounds: (source: A. Rive, 'The Consumption of Tobacco since 1600', in *Economic History*, vol. 1 (1926)).

1614–21 (annual average)	140	
1628	400	
1632–4 (annual average)	600	
1699–1709 (annual average)	11,300	
1732	5,200	—much smuggling
1744–6 (annual average)	7,000	—much smuggling
1770	10,000	
1775	27,000	—fear of shortage due to political situation.
1775–82 (annual average)	5,000	
1786	6,800	
1787	6,700	
1788	6,900	

(in lb.)

	Coffee		Tea	Sugar	Tobacco
	G.B.	U.K.	U.K.	U.K.	U.K. (*a*)
1789	0·10	...	1·16	...	...
1790	0·10	...	1·14	...	0·75
1791	0·11	...	1·18	...	0·94
1792	0·10	...	1·21	...	0·92
1793	0·11	...	1·18	14·70	0·81
1794	0·10	...	1·25	13·95	1·05
1795	0·10	...	1·42	12·72	1·16
1796	0·04	...	1·34	13·56	1·18
1797	0·06	...	1·23	11·74	1·12
1798	0·07	...	1·45	13·21	1·32
1799	0·07	...	1·46	22·22	1·03
1800	0·08	...	1·48	15·32	1·24
1801	0·07	...	1·49	22·53	1·23
1802	0·08	...	1·58	20·39	1·06
1803	0·08	...	1·53	14·39	1·23
1804	0·10	...	1·34	18·15	1·14
1805	0·11	...	1·45	17·12	1·08
1806	0·10	...	1·31	21·74	1·09
1807	0·10	...	1·39	18·85	1·01
1808	0·09	...	1·45	22·34	1·01
1809	0·78	...	1·19	20·39	0·96
1810	0·44	...	1·37	24·64	1·18
1811	0·53	...	1·24	23·15	1·23
1812	0·66	...	1·34	19·66	1·21
1813	0·70	...	1·36	16·97	1·05
1814	0·50	...	1·29	15·48	0·94
				- - -	
1815	0·47	0·34	1·35	14·71(*b*)	0·86
1816	0·57	0·40	1·16	16·27	0·95
					- - -
1817	0·65	0·47	1·24	20·79	0·93(*a*)
1818	0·59	0·42	1·32	11·83	0·90
1819	0·54	0·38	1·24	17·09	0·81

See p. 711 for footnotes.

Consumption 2. *continued*

(in lb.)

	Coffee U.K.	Tea U.K.	Sugar U.K.	Tobacco U.K. (*a*)
1820	0·34	1·22	17·74	0·76
1821	0·36	1·27	18·19	0·75
1822	0·36	1·29	16·71	0·77
1823	0·39	1·25	17·92	0·79
1824	0·38	1·26	18·30	0·77
1825	0·50	1·31	16·44	0·85
1826	0·58	1·29	18·80	0·79
1827	0·68	1·31	17·33	0·82
1828	0·74	1·26	18·73	0·80
1829	0·83	1·25	18·15	0·81
1830	0·95	1·26	19·08	0·81
1831	0·94	1·24	18·92	0·81
1832	0·94	1·29	17·83	0·83
1833	0·92	1·29	17·15	0·84
1834	0·96	1·41	17·70	0·86
1835	0·93	1·46	17·93	0·88
1836	0·98	1·93	15·84	0·88
1837	1·03	1·19	17·68	0·88
1838	0·99	1·25	17·39	0·91
1839	1·02	1·34	16·37	0·88
1840	1·08	1·22	15·20	0·87
1841	1·06	1·37	16·99	0·83
1842	1·06	1·38	16·04	0·83
1843	1·10	1·48	16·55	0·85
1844	1·14	1·50	16·80	0·89
1845	1·23	1·59	19·58	0·94
1846	1·31	1·67	20·95	0·96
1847	1·34	1·66	23·24	0·95
1848	1·33	1·75	24·91	0·98
1849	1·24	1·81	24·20	1·00
1850	1·13	1·86	25·26	1·00
1851	1·19	1·97	26·87	1·02
1852	1·27	1·99	29·27	1·04
1853	1·34	2·14	30·45	1·07
1854	1·35	2·24	33·74	1·10
1855	1·29	2·28	30·38	1·09
1856	1·25	2·26	28·27	1·16
1857	1·22	2·45	29·48	1·16
1858	1·24	2·58	34·51	1·20
1859	1·20	2·67	34·80	1·21
1860	1·23	2·67	34·14	1·22
1861	1·21	2·69	35·49	1·20
1862	1·18	2·69	35·92	1·21
1863	1·11	2·89	35·92	1·13
1864	1·06	2·99	36·74	1·28
1865	1·02	3·27	39·69	1·30
1866	1·02	3·39	41·11	1·34
1867	1·03	3·65	43·06	1·34
1868	0·99	3·48	41·89	1·34
1869	0·93	3·61	42·44	1·34
1870	0·97	3·76	47·11	1·32
1871	0·97	3·91	46·73	1·35
1872	0·98	4·01	47·32	1·37
1873	0·99	4·10	51·50	1·41
1874	0·96	4·22	53·07	1·43
1875	0·98	4·43	59·35	1·46
1876	0·99	4·49	54·74	1·46
1877	0·96	4·50	60·98	1·49
1878	0·97	4·64	55·14	1·44
1879	0·99	4·68	63·03	1·40
1880	0·92	4·57	60·28	1·42
1881	0·89	4·58	64·44	1·41
1882	0·89	4·69	67·31	1·42
1883	0·89	4·82	68·41	1·43
1884	0·90	4·90	68·60	1·45
1885	0·91	5·06	71·84	1·46
1886	0·87	4·92	64·05	1·44
1887	0·80	5·02	72·00	1·45
1888	0·83	5·03	69·02	1·48
1889	0·76	4·99	74·92	1·51
1890	0·75	5·17	71·09	1·55
1891	0·76	5·35	78·01	1·61
1892	0·74	5·43	75·15	1·64
1893	0·69	5·40	75·49	1·62
1894	0·68	5·51	76·92	1·66
1895	0·70	5·65	85·15	1·66
1896	0·69	5·75	82·19	1·72
1897	0·68	5·79	78·12	1·75
1898	0·68	5·83	82·73	1·82
1899	0·71	5·95	82·07	1·88
1900	0·71	6·07	85·53	1·95
1901	0·76	6·16	91·39	1·89

1902	0·68	6·07	73·86(*c*)	1·93
1903	0·71	6·04	66·99	1·94
1904	0·68	6·02	78·16	1·96
1905	0·67	6·02	70·41	1·97
1906	0·66	6·22	77·08	1·99
1907	0·67	6·26	78·83	2·04
1908	0·66	6·24	77·19	2·04
1909	0·67	6·36	80·42	1·97
1910	0·65	6·39	78·00	2·00
1911	0·62	6·48	80·27	2·06
1912	0·62	6·50	79·53	2·06
1913	0·62	6·69	83·22	2·10
1914	0·63	6·89	79·87	2·19
1915	0·74	7·15	81·14	2·44
1916	0·66	6·91	68·99	2·35
1917	1·05	6·41	54·73	2·44
1918	1·11	7·21	47·78	2·51
1919	0·76	8·70	75·64	3·26
1920	0·72	8·44	52·15	2·99
1921	0·71	8·69	64·92	2·96
1922	0·74	8·67	74·98	2·82
	---	---	---	---
1923 (*d*)	(0·79)	(8·68)	(72·77)(*e*)	(2·90)
1924	0·78	8·81	78·49	2·87
1925	0·79	8·85	84·50	2·96
1926	0·77	8·91	87·08	3·00
1927	0·80	9·03	84·74	3·04

Consumption 2. *continued*

(in lb.)

	Coffee U.K.	Tea U.K.	Sugar U.K.	Tobacco U.K. (*a*)
1928	0·78	9·16	91·39	3·11
1929	0·76	10·16	91·97	3·24
1930	0·77	9·87	92·68	3·31
1931	0·81	9·67	99·02	3·27
1932	0·76	10·53	94·86	3·23
1933	0·70	9·36	92·32	3·22
1934	0·72	9·22	97·42	3·41
1935	0·70	9·42	98·15	3·51
1936	0·72	9·31	101·08	3·72
1937	0·72	9·19	102·11	3·87
1938	0·72	9·09	100·51	4·00

(*a*) For the period up to 1816 inclusive these statistics are for years ended 5th July. The half-year ended 5th January 1817 is not represented in the table. In that period 8,959,000 pounds were entered for home consumption.
(*b*) In the Customs historical volume (*S.P.* 1898, LXXXV) it is said of sugar that 'it is impracticable to obtain an accurate view of the consumption of any single year' before 1815. The annual average *per caput* consumption for 1800–14 is put at 16·54 lb. The pre-1815 figures given here, which show an annual average of 18·83 lb. should not, therefore, be used for comparisons with later figures without bearing this difference in mind.
(*c*) Before 1902 the statistics relate to the combined unweighted quantities of refined and unrefined sugar, whereas later they represent the equivalent in refined sugar of total consumption. The effect of this change is to lower the *per caput* figure by about 10 per cent.
(*d*) Southern Ireland was treated as foreign from 1st April 1923. The 1923 figures are not exactly comparable with those for any other years, since they include southern Irish consumption before 1st April but are divided by the population of Great Britain and Northern Ireland only.
(*e*) Prior to 1923 sugar exported in composite articles was not deducted from imports, and is consequently reckoned as part of home consumption. From 1923 the consumption figures express the estimated equivalent in sugar exceeding 98° polarisation of all sugar refined and unrefined (including sugar in composite articles) entered for home consumption, less sugar re-exported on drawback (including sugar in composite articles). From 25th April 1928 the degree of polarisation was changed to over 99° for Empire sugar – a change which does not affect the *per caput* statistics.

Consumption 3. Wheat and Potatoes Available *Per Caput*, 1760–1914

NOTES

[1] SOURCE: R. N. Salaman, *The History and Social Influence of the Potato* (Cambridge University Press, 1949), pp. 613–7.

[2] This table relates to availability for either direct consumption by humans, or as animal feeding-stuffs, or for industrial use.

(in lb. per day)

	U.K. Wheat		England & Wales Potatoes
1760's	1·5		
1770's	1·3	1775	0·25
1780's	1·4		
1790's	1·36	1795	0·40
1800's	1·3		
1810's	1·05	1814	0·47
1820's	0·95		
1830's	0·9	1838	0·62
1840's	0·85		
1850's	0·85	1851	0·70
1860's	1·03	1866	0·80
1870's	1·05	1871	0·90
1880's	1·05	1881	0·64
1890's	1·04	1891	0·65
1900's	1·03	1901	0·58
1910–14	1·05	1911	0·60
		1914	0·53

Consumption 4. Supplies Available *Per Caput* – United Kingdom, 1834–8 to 1980

NOTES

[1] Source: *Abstract*, except for tobacco, which is derived from the *Reports of the Commissioners of Customs and Excise* and the Registrar General's mid-year estimates of population.

[2] The series for tobacco is derived by the same method as in table 3, i.e. net duty-paid clearances divided by population. However, total population estimates are used up to 1951 (1st line) since *de facto* population estimates are not available for the war and immediate postwar period.

(in lb. or pints to 1972, kg. or litres subsequently (*a*)

	Butter	Coffee	Fish	Flour	Fresh Fruit	Liquid Milk (pints)	Margarine	Meat (*b*)	Potatoes	Sugar	Tea	Tobacco
1934–8 (average)	24·7	0·7	25·3	194·5	78·5	...	8·7	129·3	181·9	102·9	9·3	(*c*)
1940	14·0	1·2	16·3	208·6	...	...	15·4	116·3	166·4	71·8	8·6	3·96
1941	10·2	1·2	14·7	237·1	...	...	17·5	99·3	188·2	67·4	8·1	4·60
1942	7·7	1·2	15·9	226·6	...	...	17·4	101·5	224·9	69·2	8·2	4·83
1943	7·6	1·0	17·3	230·2	28·7	231·8	17·0	98·5	248·8	69·3	7·0	4·55
1944	7·7	1·2	19·3	233·5	32·3	239·1	17·8	110·0	274·6	74·0	7·4	4·51
1945	8·5	1·2	23·6	240·7	35·9	243·8	17·1	100·4	260·2	70·8	8·2	4·76
1946	11·0	1·4	29·8	221·2	51·7	242·8	15·1	105·6	281·2	79·5	8·8	5·08
1947	11·2	1·6	31·3	224·9	68·0	237·6	15·0	95·6	285·9	83·8	8·5	4·54
1948	12·6	1·7	30·5	232·9	71·0	250·1	17·9	87·0	238·9	85·1	8·0	4·28
1949	13·9	1·8	26·7	222·2	64·0	263·9	18·4	88·0	258·3	93·1	8·3	4·19
1950	16·9	1·5	21·1	205·8	60·3	269·7	17·0	112·5	246·4	85·5	8·5	4·23
1951	14·6	1·7	23·3	203·6	68·3	268·0	18·7	89·8 / 95·3 (*b*)	234·7	95·0	8·1	4·37 / 4·39 (*d*)
1952	10·9	1·5	21·9	201·7	65·6	263·0	19·3	105·7	251·8	90·4	8·5	4·32
1953	13·2	1·3	19·7	192·7	68·5	255·8	17·8	116·1	245·3	98·7	9·5	4·43
1954	14·1	1·3	20·1	187·2	66·0	254·8	18·3	129·8	242·3	106·1	9·7	4·59
1955	14·7	1·3	20·6	182·5	66·5	251·8	17·9	136·7	234·2	108·8	9·3	4·63
1956	15·5	1·5	21·7	178·7	65·7	251·1	17·1	139·1	224·5	109·8	10·1	4·61
1957	17·3	1·6	21·1	172·5	67·8	246·8	15·5	142·9	223·8	111·7	9·8	4·72
1958	20·0	1·7	22·0	171·5	64·0	247·6	13·7	143·3	212·0	115·5	9·9	4·75
1959	18·5	1·9	21·0	168·3	74·2	247·4	14·8	131·2	214·8	111·3	9·7	4·91
1960	18·3	2·1	18·7	165·9	73·8	249·1	14·7	144·7	223·7	112·0	9·3	4·98
1961	19·6	2·1	18·2	164·0	69·6	248·8	13·3	150·5	226·7	113·6	9·8	4·91
1962	20·2	2·9	20·0	160·7	72·2	249·8	13·2	155·8	213·9	111·3	9·5	4·72
1963	19·1	3·1	18·2	161·3	71·8	250·2	13·4	155·4	227·5	111·7	9·5	4·77
1964	19·8	2·7	20·2	156·1	74·0	251·0	13·4	152·6	226·9	108·0	9·4	4·68
1965	19·5	2·9	20·0	154·9	73·5	249·4	12·0	152·3	222·5	108·4	9·0	4·41
1966	20·1	3·1	18·6	153·9	74·6	248·8	12·1	153·2	224·7	109·4	8·8	4·35
1967	20·6	3·3	19·0	147·6	68·0	248·4	11·7	155·9	224·1	107·3	9·1	4·38
1968	19·8	3·5	20·0	145·4	72·1	245·7	11·4	156·6	227·1	106·0	8·8	4·32
1969	19·6	4·0	18·8	146·5	73·5	243·5	11·9	156·0	221·3	107·1	8·5	4·20
1970	19·4	4·4	18·4	146·0	76·4	241·5	11·9	156·7	228·2	106·0	8·6	4·12
1971	18·0	4·7	17·3	143·5	77·3	237·9	12·7	159·3	221·4	104·1	8·2	3·94
1972	15·9	4·4	17·1	141·8	70·5	238·0	14·0	159·3	215·4	105·6	8·0	4·17
	---	---	---	---	---	---	---	---	---	---	---	
						litres						
1973	7·6	2·7	7·5	63·6	32·7	136·5	5·8	68·4	99·0	47·0	3·4	4·40
1974	8·3	2·1	7·4	61·6	32·7	139·5	4·9	69·7	99·5	47·9	3·5	4·20
1975	8·4	2·2	7·3	64·5	31·6	142·3	5·0	69·5	101·9	42·8	3·5	3·98
1976	8·3	2·1	7·7	66·2	33·5	140·4	5·8	67·1	85·0	42·9	3·6	4·08
1977	7·8	1·7	6·9	65·3	31·1	135·3	6·5	68·5	95·8	42·6	3·2	3·87
1978	7·5	1·9	6·1	63·7	32·3	133·4	6·3	70·6	101·6	42·9	2·9	...(*e*)
1979	6·8	2·5	6·2	63·1	35·5	131·9	6·5	72·9	105·8	42·3	3·1	...
1980	6·3	2·1	6·8	61·4	37·9	128·9	6·9	68·9	[105·0](*f*)	39·9	3·2	...

(*a*) Except for tobacco, which continues to be given in pounds.

(*b*) Poultry meat is not included until 1951 (2nd line).

(*c*) Figures for 1938 and 1939 on the same basis as 1940 to 1951 (1st line) are:
1938 3·98 1939 4·17

(*d*) See note 2 above.

(*e*) The series for net duty-paid clearances ceases with 1977.

(*f*) The 1980 figure is on a slightly different basis to previously.

CHAPTER XIV

PRICES

TABLES

Beveridge began the first, and as yet only, volume to come from the Price and Wage History Research group, nearly fifty years ago, by saying this: 'The importance to economic and social science of having a comprehensive history of prices and wages hardly needs to be emphasised. Prices and wages are the social phenomena most susceptible of objective statistical record over long periods of time.'[1] Not everyone, perhaps, would agree with the last statement, but the first would be widely accepted. Yet prior to the efforts of Lord Beveridge and his colleagues, there were only a few long series of prices published, and, as

[1] Sir William Beveridge and others, *Prices and Wages in England*, vol. I (London, 1939), p. 1.

we saw in chapter II, still fewer of wages. However, thanks to the Beveridge group 'the material now available on wages and prices is incomparably richer than anything hitherto known or imagined'.[2] Nevertheless, it remains true thirty years after that remark that relatively little further has been added to the corpus of data left when Beveridge was called away to other duties in 1939, certainly for the eighteenth century and earlier; and perhaps even those data have not been mined as thoroughly as they could have been.

Most of the lengthy price series which have survived from before the nineteenth century are those which were paid by institutions, often on contracts rather than in the market place, and these are closer to wholesale than to retail prices, which are the chief desiderata for most students. Their rigidity suggests that, for some goods at least, they were partially insulated from ordinary, week-to-week fluctuations, though this view is not universally accepted, and it scarcely seems to have applied to some of the more important consumers' goods, such as coal and corn. Institutional prices can safely be used as a measure of *general* price trends for periods before the nineteenth century; and after that more varied quotations become available. But the information which they give on short-period movements of prices is unreliable, or perhaps it would be more accurate to say imprecise as to timing, and probably also as to amplitude. There is also some question as to how well institutional prices represent retail prices. It is likely, of course, that bulk purchase by institutions kept the prices they paid below the averages in the market – although they may not always have bargained as efficiently as individual customers. But it is almost inconceivable that institutional price trends varied significantly in the long term from ordinary retail prices unless (and except as) costs of distribution to retail markets rose or fell disproportionately, or there was a trend in retailers' profit margins. Perhaps transport improvements from the end of the seventeenth century onwards did reduce costs of distribution disproportionately; and perhaps increasing competition amongst the growing numbers of retail outlets over the same period did reduce sellers' margins – but neither effect is likely to have been very pronounced, and both must have been very gradual.

It would seem, then, that attempts to construct cost-of-living indices out of the sort of price data which constitute the great majority of what we have until the nineteenth century are not inherently unacceptable. However, there have been few attempts to do so, and most who have endeavoured to distil the material into index numbers have produced something closer to wholesale prices. One of the first of these, constructed by Elizabeth Schumpeter and Elizabeth Gilboy, is shown as table 1. The two indices are rather crude, unweighted ones, and Part A is particularly short on foodstuffs. They could certainly be improved upon by competent statistical work, as well as by additional material. Nevertheless, no one has yet attempted this systematically, and they have been much used as a broad guide to secular price trends, safely enough in all probability. In view of their lack of weighting, however, it is probably unwise to use any of them as a cost-of-living index.

[2] Lord Beveridge, 'Wages and Inflation in the Past', *The Incorporated Statistician* (Oct. 1957). The material is deposited in the library of the Institute of Historical Research at London University.

The next five tables are also indices of general prices, mainly wholesale and import prices. In selecting tables 2 to 5, an attempt has been made to cover fully the period since 1790 with the best available indices and to include those which have been most used. For the years to 1850, the Gayer-Rostow-Schwartz series, despite some mostly minor criticisms,[3] have replaced their predecessors – Silberling,[4] Jevons,[5] and Sauerbeck[6] – and they form table 2 here. The Rousseaux indices also cover the greater part of this period, as well as continuing up to 1913. They are not based on such comprehensive material as the Gayer-Rostow-Schwartz series, but they have been included here, as table 3, for two reasons. First, Rousseaux presents a breakdown into a number of commodity sub-groups, instead of the domestic/imported breakdown of Gayer-Rostow-Schwartz; and second, the long period of coverage on the same basis has led many people to use the Rousseaux indices, for convenience if nothing else. However, this is not a very strong argument for employing them since changes in weightings are a desirable part of keeping up with changes in patterns of commodity use.[7]

With the Sauerbeck-*Statist* index, shown in table 4, more detailed commodity breakdowns were available than could be made for earlier periods,[8] though only the main sub-groups are shown here. The principal criticism of this index is that these sub-groups do not contain enough commodities. But it covers a period for which no other detailed series are yet available, namely 1851–70; and its continuation to 1966 gives a long period for comparison, even though the commodities tended to become less and less representative as time went on. Finally, with 1871 there began the modern type of official wholesale price indices, produced by the Board of Trade and its successors. These are given in table 5, with the Irish equivalent (begun only in 1938) in table 6. A similar index for agricultural prices only is shown in table 8.

When compared with the information available on institutional or wholesale prices, what we know about retail prices or the cost-of-living in history is almost negligible – though, as was argued above, the long-run link between institutional and retail prices was probably stable or very slow to change. Apart from the London and Dublin bread prices, shown in tables 21 and 22, there is scarcely a series of any length until the nineteenth century, though many scattered retail price quotations can be found in innumerable sources. Some of these,

[3] For example, the 'overweighting of mutton as compared with beef, and of soap and tallow as compared with leather and hides, and of wheat in relation to all other commodities', mentioned in T. S. Ashton, 'Economic Fluctuation 1790–1850', *Economic History Review*, second series VII, 3 (1955), p. 381.

[4] N. J. Silberling, 'British Prices and Business Cycles, 1779–1850', *Review of Economic Statistics*, V (1923), pp. 232–3.

[5] W. S. Jevons, *Investigations in Currency and Finance* (London, 1884), pp. 144–5.

[6] A. Sauerbeck, 'Prices of Commodities and the Precious Metals', *Journal of the Statistical Society*, XLIX (1886). This refers to his index for 1818–50, not to the one reproduced here as table 4.

[7] A similar long-period index was constructed for 1786–1924 by Kondratieff, but the method, which employed no weights, was excessively crude.

[8] This may not be true now if someone were to use the material listed as available in A. D. Gayer, W. W. Rostow, and A. J. Schwartz, *The Growth and Fluctuation of the British Economy 1790–1850* (2 vols., Oxford, 1953), pp. 975–7 and 981.

together with many of such longer runs as there are, can be found in the record of the Board of Trade's enquiry into prices of 1903.[9]

The first official cost-of-living index was established at the outset of the First World War, and was based on a family budget enquiry made in 1904. This index was pushed back by the Labour Department statisticians to 1892, though it can hardly be described as very satisfactory for that period, since it related only to London, was limited as to its constituents, and relied for its data on large stores, where movements may not always have been the same as in working-class districts. This index is shown in table 10, along with the fresh, better-based index constructed after the First World War. All cost-of-living indices using fixed weights are liable to become out-of-date as expenditure patterns change, but the interwar index suffered particularly in this respect since its weighting was based on 1904 patterns. It was especially affected by the fall in food prices in the 1930s, and the fall in the cost of living which it indicates is almost certainly somewhat excessive. Since 1947, however, the retail price indices have been regularly rebased and reweighted, though until the mid 1950s the family budget enquiry of 1937–8 (not used until 1947) was still the basis for its weighting.

The Irish consumer price indices, shown in table 11, though not rebased so frequently as the British ones, have, generally speaking, been kept up to date by fairly frequent revision in the period since the Second World War.

For periods before the official cost-of-living index – and, indeed, carrying on later and overlapping it – there have been various unofficial indices constructed. Some of these were shown in tables in chapter II to indicate the derivation of real wage indices. Two are shown here. Table 8 gives Lindert and Williamson's 'best guess' index using southern urban weights. They produced others with both northern and rural weights. This index was the subject of comment in the introduction to chapter II.[10] Table 9 shows Bowley's pre-1914 indices, which, in effect, pushed back the official cost-of-living index to 1880 on the basis of virtually similar material, and then went back more tentatively to 1846, using mostly the material collected by Sauerbeck for his wholesale price indices. G. H. Wood's index, shown in table 21, was similarly derived. As careful estimates by experienced investigators these must be seen as valuable guides; but their limitations must be recognised. Bowley himself assessed the margin of error in his index at plus or minus 5.[11]

The remainder of the tables in this chapter consist of figures of actual prices for a number of the most important commodities. None of these tables pretends to be an exhaustive survey of all the data available on a particular commodity. Far from it: most of the sources cited give a much greater amount of detail than is reproduced here, as well as covering other commodities. The aim here has been to present series which cover a lengthy period for representative varieties of the commodities concerned. For this reason many sources of

[9] *S.P.* 1903 LXVIII.

[10] See above, p. 98.

[11] A. L. Bowley, *Wages and Income since 1860* (Cambridge, 1937), p. 31, and the discussion in appendix D, pp. 114–26.

scattered price quotations, or of prices of other commodities, have not been used. One could multiply examples of these, since scarcely a monograph on industrial or commercial history fails to provide some additional price data. However, two major studies of prices additional to those already mentioned or referred to in table source notes, and two collections of material, do deserve to be singled out for mention. The two works are Thomas Tooke's[12] and Thorold Rogers'.[13] The latter, like Beveridge's group, worked mainly in the field of institutional prices, covering a long span up to the eighteenth century. He was the main source for Phelps Brown and Hopkins' index, shown in table 31 of chapter II. Tooke, in contrast, tackled a shorter period, during his own lifetime, and based his work mainly on market prices derived from *Prince's Price Current*. A collection of series from this and similar price currents, going back to 1779, was transcribed by Silberling when he was constructing his index, and is in the care of the Harvard Committee on Economic Research.[14] After the Second World War, other price currents came to light, going back into the late seventeenth century, and photostat copies of these are available in the Goldsmith Library at London University and the Kress Library of the Harvard Business School.[15]

[12] T. Tooke, *A History of Prices, 1793–1847* (4 vols., London, 1838–48), continued for a further decade by William Newmarch in two more volumes.

[13] J. E. T. Rogers, *A History of Agriculture and Prices in England* (7 vols., Oxford, 1866–1902).

[14] A list of the available material is in Gayer, Rostow, and Schwartz, *op. cit.*, pp. 475–8. The originals came from the London Guildhall Library, the library of the Board of Trade, and the British Library.

[15] This information comes from J. M. Price, 'Notes on Some London Price Currents, 1667–1715', *Economic History Review*, second series VII, 2 (1954). The author discusses the advantages and disadvantages of this type of source.

Prices 1. The Schumpeter-Gilboy Price Indices – 1661–1823

NOTES TO PART A

[1] SOURCE: Elizabeth B. Schumpeter, 'English Prices and Public Finance, 1660–1822', *Review of Economic Statistics* (1938).

[2] The indices are based very largely on contract prices paid by institutions.

[3] All figures are for years ended Michaelmas.

Part A. 1697=100

	Consumers' Goods (*a*)	Producers' Goods (*b*)
1661	109	96
1662	113	105
1663	111	97
1664	105	95
1665	105	101
1666	101	108
1667	96	112
1668	96	102
1669	92	92
1670	93	92
1671	92	97
1672	89	91
1673	88	96
1674	94	92
1675	101	89
1676	96	91
1677	89	87
1678	90	85
1679	95	86

	Consumers' Goods (*a*)	Producers' Goods (*b*)
1680	93	82
1681	90	79
1682	90	80
1683	88	84
1684	89	83
1685	91	75
1686	92	69
1687	81	71
1688	81	70
1689	80	77
1690	82	89
1691	83	97
1692	82	87
1693	86	89
1694	95	88
1695	95	92
1696	96	101
1697	100	100

(*a*) *Viz*. broadcloth, kersey, leather backs, tallow candles, and wheat.

(*b*) *Viz*. deals ordinary, deals sprutia, duck, timber firr, tarr Stockholm, bricks, copper wrought, hemp, lead, and train oil.

B. 1701=100

	Consumers' Goods (*a*)	Consumers' Goods other than Cereals (*b*)	Producers' Goods (*c*)
1696	121	112	112
1697	122	115	109
1698	128	119	101
1699	132	124	102
1700	115	107	99
1701	100	100	100
1702	99	99	104
1703	94	102	104
1704	98	95	102
1705	89	88	102
1706	101	100	98
1707	88	90	95
1708	92	89	97
1709	107	94	100
1710	122	104	106
1711	135	131	109
1712	101	98	98
1713	97	95	96
1714	103	95	91
1715	104	99	86
1716	99	96	89
1717	95	97	90

	Consumers' Goods (*a*)	Consumers' Goods other than Cereals (*b*)	Producers' Goods (*c*)
1718	93	94	91
1719	97	99	92
1720	102	96	91
1721	100	100	89
1722	92	96	91
1723	89	91	86
1724	94	89	87
1725	97	93	87
1726	102	97	92
1727	96	92	97
1728	99	92	95
1729	104	94	95
1730	95	91	98
1731	88	86	95
1732	89	90	90
1733	85	87	86
1734	88	87	86
1735	89	84	83
1736	87	81	82
1737	93	89	81
1738	91	85	81
1739	89	85	87

See p. 720 for footnotes.

B. 1701=100 (*cont.*)

	Consumers' Goods (*a*)	Consumers' Goods other than Cereals (*b*)	Producers' Goods (*c*)
1740	100	85	89
1741	108	95	97
1742	99	97	97
1743	94	91	91
1744	84	86	98
1745	85	87	81
1746	93	94	91
1747	90	89	86
1748	94	95	89
1749	96	93	91
1750	95	91	88
1751	90	85	85
1752	93	87	81
1753	90	85	81
1754	90	85	89
1755	92	88	91
1756	92	89	93
1757	109	92	94
1758	106	94	101
1759	100	96	101
1760	98	97	102
1761	94	91	101
1762	94	90	102
1763	100	92	102
1764	102	94	101
1765	106	97	99
1766	107	96	99
1767	109	93	99
1768	108	92	98
1769	99	92	92
1770	100	92	94
1771	107	96	94
1772	117	103	98
1773	119	102	99
1774	116	101	98
1775	113	96	98
1776	114	102	101
1777	108	99	102
1778	117	106	104
1779	111	102	110
1780	110	106	113
1781	115	105	110

	Consumers' Goods (*a*)	Consumers' Goods other than Cereals (*b*)	Producers' Goods (*c*)
1782	116	106	120
1783	129	113	117
1784	126	111	108
1785	120	109	107
1786	119	106	113
1787	117	106	111
1788	121	111	113
1789	117	108	107
1790	124	112	107
1791	121	109	107
1792	122	113	111
1793	129	117	124
1794	136	121	119
1795	147	119	122
1796	154	122	138
1797	148	142	141
1798	148	142	129
1799	160	146	128
1800	212	168	144
1801	228	166	162
1802	174	149	...
1803	156	148	...
1804	161	151	...
1805	187	158	...
1806	184	159	...
1807	186	159	...
1808	204	167	...
1809	212	169	...
1810	207	169	...
1811	206	183	...
1812	237	181	...
1813	243	190	...
1814	209	189	...
1815	191	190	...
1816	172	160	...
1817	189	155	...
1818	194	170	...
1819	192	174	...
1820	162	148	...
1821	139	135	...
1822	125	129	...
1823	128	121	...

(*a*) *Viz*. barley, beans, biscuits, break, flour, oats, peas, rye, wheat, beef for salting, butter, cheese, pork, ale, beer, cider, hops, malt, pepper, raisins, sugar, tea, tallow candles, coal, broadcloth, hair, felt hats, kersey, leather backs, Brussels linen, Irish linen, blue yarn stockings.

(*b*) *Viz*. all items after wheat in footnote (*a*).

(*c*) *Viz*. bricks, coal, lead, pantiles, plain tiles, hemp (to 1794), leather backs (to 1793), train oil (to 1783), tallow (to 1780), lime (to 1779), glue (to 1778), and copper (to 1776).

Prices 2. Indices of British Commodity Prices 1790–1850, Based on the Gayer, Rostow and Schwartz Monthly Indices

NOTES

[1] SOURCE: Annual average of the monthly figures in A. D. Gayer, W. W. Rostow and A. J. Schwartz, *The Growth and Fluctuation of the British Economy 1790–1850* (2 vols, Oxford, 1953), vol. 1, pp. 468–70.

[2] The composition and weighting of the indices is as follows:

Domestic		Imported			
Wheat	745	Sugar	166	Pepper	3
Oats	497	Cotton	163	Beeswax	2
Mutton	461	Wool	119	Brimstone	2
Beef	239	Tea	111	Cochineal	2
Coal	216	Raw Silk	61	Isinglass	2
Tallow	132	Tobacco	58	Liquorice	2
Butter	116	Timber	38	Logwood	2
Pork	116	Rum	28	Madder	2
Iron Bars	83	Flax	27	Mahogany	2
Iron Pigs	66	Brandy	22	Shumac	2
Leather Butts	41	Port wine	22	Annatto	1
Hard Soap	41	Staves	20	Balsam	1
Hides	38	Indigo	19	Barwood	1
Tinplates	21	Hemp	18	Brazilwood	1
Tin	6	Hides	18	Cinnamon	1
Mottled Soap	4	Coffee	18	Cocoa	1
Starch	3	Thrown Silk	13	Fustic	1
Alum	1	Linseed	11	Geneva Spirits	1
Camphor	1	Olive Oil	5	Ginger	1
Linseed Oil	1	Pearl Ashes	4	Jalap	1
Rape Oil	1	Bristles	4	Castor Oil	1
Vitriol	1	Tar	4	Opium	1
Sal-ammoniac	1	Turpentine	4	Whale Oil	1
Clover Seeds	1	Saltpetre	4	Whale Fins	1
		Barilla	3	Quicksilver	1
		Iron	3	Quinine	1

[3] It may seem surprising that in some years the value of the joint index of domestic and imported commodities lies above the values of both its components. This arises apparently from a method of calculation based upon the use of geometric means, together with the decision to make the arithmetic mean of the monthly values of the years 1821–5 equal 100. If the joint index had been calculated simply on the weighted geometric mean of its components the arithmetic average value for this period would not have been 100. To obtain this result each value of the joint series would have to be multiplied by a constant factor, with the effect that some values of this series would lie outside the average of its components.

Suppose we have two indices, A_t, B_t with an arithmetic mean over n value of 100. Then

$$\frac{1}{n}\sum_1^n A_t = \frac{1}{n}\sum_1^n B_t = 100.$$

Now if we calculate a joint index $A_t^{\kappa} B_t^{1-\kappa}$ and take the average over the same years we find that

$$\frac{1}{n}\sum_1^n A_t^{\kappa} B_t^{1-\kappa} = c,$$

where c is not in general equal to 100. Then in order to obtain a base of 100 for this series we must multiply each individual value by $\frac{1}{c}$ giving as the joint index $\frac{1}{c}A_t^{\kappa} B_t^{1-\kappa}$.

(We are indebted to Mr A. D. Bain for this note.)

(Monthly average of 1821–5=100)

	Domestic and Imported Commodities	Domestic Commodities	Imported Commodities		Domestic and Imported Commodities	Domestic Commodities	Imported Commodities
1790	89·3	87·1	87·5	1821	99·7	98·4	101·8
1791	89·7	84·5	94·6	1822	87·9	83·9	100·2
1792	88·1	80·6	99·0	1823	97·6	97·0	99·3
1793	96·6	91·6	100·6	1824	101·9	104·2	95·3
1794	98·5	96·3	95·9	1825	113·0	116·5	103·4
1795	114·9	113·6	109·5	1826	100·0	106·7	83·1
1796	116·1	115·8	108·6	1827	99·3	106·2	82·1
1797	106·2	100·8	114·2	1828	96·4	102·9	80·0
1798	107·9	100·2	123·4	1829	95·8	102·8	78·2
1799	124·6	119·9	129·8	1830	94·5	101·7	76·5
1800	151·0	156·6	122·5	1831	95·3	103·0	76·3
1801	155·7	161·7	127·3	1832	91·5	97·9	75·2
1802	122·2	122·3	113·2	1833	88·6	92·2	79·1
1803	123·6	120·4	125·9	1834	86·5	88·4	85·2
1804	124·3	119·7	132·8	1835	84·5	84·3	85·2
1805	136·2	133·5	138·6	1836	95·2	98·4	87·1
1806	134·5	131·9	137·5	1837	94·3	101·6	76·1
1807	131·2	128·3	137·0	1838	97·8	106·0	78·0
1808	144·5	141·3	152·1	1839	104·3	113·4	82·2
1809	155·0	153·8	157·1	1840	102·5	110·4	83·1
1810	153·4	153·5	151·4	1841	97·7	105·9	77·9
1811	145·4	149·2	133·4	1842	88·8	95·3	72·5
1812	163·7	172·2	141·1	1843	79·7	84·5	67·6
1813	168·9	173·1	155·8	1844	81·1	86·7	67·2
1814	153·7	148·5	167·0	1845	83·3	92·0	62·9
1815	129·9	124·6	144·3	1846	86·0	97·2	60·8
1816	118·6	115·0	128·3	1847	96·8	114·0	61·3
1817	131·9	131·8	130·7	1848	81·8	94·8	54·1
1818	138·7	139·8	133·9	1849	73·9	81·4	56·1
1819	128·1	130·4	120·3	1850	73·5	77·4	63·3
1820	115·4	117·4	108·7				

Prices 3. The Rousseaux Price Indices – 1800–1913

NOTES

[1] Source: P. Rousseaux, *Les Mouvements de Fond de l'Economie Anglaise, 1800–1913* (Brussels, 1938).

[2] The overall index is an unweighted average of the indices of total agricultural products and of principal industrial products.

[3] The prices used in constructing these indices are mainly wholesale prices and unit-values of imports.

(Average of 1865 and 1885=100)

	Vegetable Products (a)	Animal Products (b)	Total Agricultural Products	Principal Industrial Products (c)	Overall Index
1800	232	111	188	163	175
1801	247	143	210	166	188
1802	184	112	158	146	152
1803	183	116	160	162	161
1804	185	127	157	160	159
1805	211	111	175	166	170
1806	193	107	162	170	166
1807	183	105	155	167	161
1808	207	120	176	202	189
1809	214	129	184	229	206
1810	222	133	190	196	193
1811	190	135	170	186	178
1812	242	140	207	186	196
1813	250	157	216	189	203
1814	243	150	210	195	202
1815	190	117	164	164	164
1816	185	96	152	136	144
1817	229	111	184	137	161
1818	217	121	182	138	160
1819	187	111	160	134	147
1820	169	100	143	121	132
1821	149	88	127	115	121
1822	138	78	116	116	116
1823	151	80	125	116	120
1824	143	84	122	122	122
1825	171	96	144	121	133
1826	144	93	126	107	117
1827	149	90	128	106	117
1828	137	91	122	102	112
1829	141	87	122	98	110
1830	145	86	124	94	109
1831	146	91	126	97	112
1832	145	89	125	93	109
1833	145	80	121	92	107
1834	141	80	119	104	112
1835	140	79	118	106	112
1836	149	94	129	116	123
1837	147	94	129	107	118
1838	156	93	133	105	119
1839	173	93	143	116	130
1840	170	90	141	115	128
1841	149	97	131	110	121
1842	136	94	122	100	111
1843	127	86	113	96	105
1844	137	87	119	96	108
1845	141	83	120	99	110
1846	136	84	118	99	109
1847	142	92	125	104	115
1848	113	91	107	92	100
1849	109	86	102	87	95

See p. 724 for footnotes.

Prices 3. *continued*

(Average of 1865 and 1885=100)

	Vegetable Products (*a*)	Animal Products (*b*)	Total Agricultural Products	Principal Industrial Products (*c*)	Overall Index
1850	104	81	98	93	95
1851	99	82	94	89	91
1852	100	80	94	93	94
1853	119	96	113	112	112
1854	131	109	125	126	125
1855	134	111	128	122	125
1856	134	109	128	120	124
1857	138	109	130	124	127
1858	114	99	110	112	111
1859	117	103	113	116	115
1860	129	108	122	117	120
1861	121	107	117	114	115
1862	121	102	116	124	120
1863	120	99	114	128	121
1864	117	99	113	125	119
1865	119	109	116	118	117
1866	126	114	123	118	120
1867	137	106	122	114	118
1868	124	104	118	112	115
1869	116	108	114	100	107
1870	113	107	112	109	110
1871	123	105	119	112	115
1872	124	107	129	127	128
1873	130	110	124	129	127
1874	133	111	127	115	121
1875	126	117	124	110	117
1876	126	115	123	107	115
1877	120	109	117	103	110
1878	113	102	110	92	101
1879	111	97	107	88	98
1880	112	100	109	95	102
1881	108	100	105	92	99
1882	107	106	107	95	101
1883	110	106	109	94	101
1884	102	98	101	89	95
1885	91	91	91	85	88
1886	86	84	86	79	83
1887	83	79	82	79	81
1888	88	81	86	82	84
1889	86	83	85	84	84
1890	91	81	91	83	87
1891	96	82	92	79	86
1892	87	85	87	77	82
1893	85	87	86	78	82
1894	77	80	78	71	74
1895	73	75	74	71	72
1896	74	71	72	73	73
1897	79	74	78	71	74
1898	85	74	82	75	78
1899	84	73	81	87	84

See p. 724 for footnotes.

Prices 3. *continued*

(Average of 1865 and 1885=100)

	Vegetable Products (*a*)	Animal Products (*b*)	Total Agricultural Products	Principal Industrial Products (*c*)	Overall Index
1900	90	77	87	95	91
1901	86	78	84	87	86
1902	88	82	87	85	86
1903	87	80	85	86	86
1904	82	75	81	86	83
1905	83	78	82	91	86
1906	84	81	83	103	93
1907	90	87	89	104	97
1908	87	86	87	87	87
1909	89	87	89	93	91
1910	93	94	94	100	97
1911	104	87	101	103	102
1912	103	92	100	108	104
1913	100	95	99	114	106

(*a*) *Viz*. up to 1850 – wheat, rye, oats, bread, peas, flour, hops, beans, oatmeal, tea, coffee, rice, logwood, olive oil, tobacco, pepper, cinnamon, sugar, and rum; after 1850 – wheat, flour, barley, oats, hops, bread, potatoes, linseed oil, oatmeal, cocoa, coffee, tea, rice, lemons, oranges, figs, sago, tobacco, cinnamon, pepper, ginger, rum, linseed, currants, palm oil, olive oil, logwood, raisins, raw sugar, linseed oil cake.

(*b*) *Viz*. up to 1850 – beef, mutton, pig-meat, butter, tallow, cheese, whale oil, and milk; after 1850 – beef, mutton, pigmeat, bacon, butter, native tallow, foreign tallow, cheese, whale oil, cod-liver oil.

(*c*) *Viz*. up to 1850 – coal, pig iron, mercury, tin, lead, copper, hemp, cotton, wool, flax, tar, tobacco, hides, skins, tallow, hair, silk, and building wood; after 1850 – coal, pig iron, tin, lead, copper, wool (two quotations), hemp, cotton, linseed oil, palm oil, flax, tar, jute, hides, skins, tobacco, silk, foreign tallow, native tallow, and building wood.

Prices 4. The Sauerbeck-*Statist* Price Indices – 1846–1966

NOTES

[1] SOURCE: A. Sauerbeck, 'Prices of Commodities and the Precious Metals', *J.S.S.* (1886), continued annually thereafter in the same source by Sauerbeck and subsequently by the editor of *The Statist*.

[2] These indices are based on wholesale prices and unit values of imports.

(Average of 1867–77=100)

	Food				Raw Materials				
	Vegetable (*a*)	Animal (*b*)	Sugar, Tea and Coffee (*c*)	Total	Minerals (*d*)	Textile Fibres (*e*)	Sundry (*f*)	Total	Overall Index
1846	106	81	98	95	92	77	86	85	89
1847	129	88	87	105	94	78	86	86	95
1848	92	83	69	84	78	64	77	73	78
1849	79	71	77	76	77	67	75	73	74
1850	74	67	87	75	77	78	80	78	77
1851	73	68	84	74	75	75	79	76	75
1852	80	69	75	75	80	78	84	81	78
1853	100	82	87	91	105	87	101	97	95
1854	120	87	85	101	115	88	109	104	102
1855	120	87	89	101	109	84	109	101	101
1856	109	88	97	99	110	89	109	102	101
1857	105	89	119	102	108	92	119	107	105
1858	87	83	97	88	96	84	102	94	91
1859	85	85	102	89	98	88	107	98	94
1860	99	91	107	98	97	90	111	100	99
1861	102	91	96	97	91	92	109	99	98
1862	98	86	98	94	91	123	106	107	101
1863	87	85	99	89	93	149	101	115	103
1864	79	89	106	88	96	162	98	119	105
1865	84	97	97	91	91	134	97	108	101
1866	95	96	94	95	91	130	99	107	102
1867	115	89	94	101	87	110	100	100	100
1868	113	88	96	100	85	106	102	99	99
1869	91	96	98	94	89	109	100	100	98
1870	88	98	95	93	89	106	99	99	96
1871	94	100	100	98	93	103	105	101	100
1872	101	101	104	102	127	114	108	115	109
1873	106	109	106	107	141	103	106	114	111
1874	105	103	105	104	116	92	96	100	102
1875	93	108	100	100	101	88	92	93	96
1876	92	108	98	99	90	85	95	91	95
1877	100	101	103	101	84	85	94	89	94
1878	95	101	90	96	74	78	88	81	87
1879	87	94	87	90	73	74	85	78	83
1880	89	101	88	94	79	81	89	84	88
1881	84	101	84	91	77	77	86	80	85
1882	84	104	76	89	79	73	85	80	84
1883	82	103	77	89	76	70	84	77	82
1884	71	97	63	79	68	68	81	73	76
1885	68	88	63	74	66	65	76	70	72
1886	65	87	60	72	67	63	69	67	69
1887	64	79	67	70	69	65	67	67	68
1888	67	82	65	72	78	64	67	69	70
1889	65	86	75	75	75	70	68	70	72
1890	65	82	70	73	80	66	69	71	72

See p. 727 for footnotes.

Prices 4. *continued*

(Average of 1867–77=100)

	Food				Raw Materials				
	Vegetable (*a*)	Animal (*b*)	Sugar, Tea and Coffee (*c*)	Total	Minerals (*d*)	Textile Fibres (*e*)	Sundry (*f*)	Total	Overall Index
1891	75	81	71	77	76	59	69	68	72
1892	65	84	69	73	71	57	67	65	68
1893	59	85	75	72	68	59	68	65	68
1894	55	80	65	66	64	53	64	60	63
1895	54	78	62	64	62	52	65	60	62
1896	53	73	59	62	63	54	63	60	61
1897	60	79	52	65	66	51	62	59	62
1898	67	77	51	68	70	51	63	61	64
1899	60	79	53	65	92	58	65	70	68
1900	62	85	54	69	108	66	71	80	75
1901	62	85	46	67	89	60	71	72	70
1902	63	87	41	67	82	61	71	71	69
1903	62	84	44	66	82	66	69	72	69
1904	63	83	50	68	81	71	67	72	70
1905	63	87	52	69	87	72	68	75	72
1906	62	89	46	69	101	80	74	83	77
1907	69	88	48	72	107	77	78	86	80
1908	70	89	48	72	89	62	73	74	73
1909	71	89	50	73	86	64	76	75	74
1910	65	96	54	74	89	73	81	81	78
1911	70	90	61	75	93	76	81	83	80
1912	78	96	62	81	110	76	82	88	85
1913	69	99	54	77	111	84	83	91	85
1914	75	100	58	81	99	81	87	88	85
1915	108	126	70	107	126	92	109	108	108
1916	133	152	86	130	158	129	136	140	136
1917	177	192	113	169	172	192	174	179	179
1918	168	207	130	174	192	222	202	206	192
1919	179	213	147	185	220	228	219	222	206
1920	227	263	198	234	295	262	244	264	251
1921	143	218	83	158	181	140	145	153	155
1922	107	184	82	130	142	134	124	132	131
1923	98	162	101	122	155	140	117	134	129
1924	119	158	105	130	158	170	120	146	139
1925	118	162	89	128	154	165	119	143	136
1926	108	150	88	119	154	133	114	131	126
1927	108	138	83	114	141	131	118	129	122
1928	107	142	78	114	123	136	117	124	120
1929	99	146	72	110	126	122	111	119	115
1930	77	142	54	96	112	84	97	97	97
1931	68	119	50	83	100	63	85	82	83
1932	72	105	50	79	99	64	81	81	80
1933	60	106	47	74	107	67	80	83	79
1934	63	108	50	77	109	72	80	85	82
1935	66	107	42	76	112	80	83	90	84
1936	76	109	41	81	118	83	88	94	89
1937	93	117	49	93	142	93	101	110	102
1938	81	111	43	84	136	75	87	96	91
1939	74	115	47	83	137	93	88	102	94
1940	112	141	58	111	167	149	117	140	128

Prices 4. *continued*

(Average of 1867–77=100)

	Food				Raw Materials				
	Vegetable (*a*)	Animal (*b*)	Sugar, Tea and Coffee (*c*)	Total	Minerals (*d*)	Textile Fibres (*e*)	Sundry (*f*)	Total	Overall Index
1941	140	142	65	125	181	162	131	154	142
1942	170	148	66	140	184	163	142	160	151
1943	156	156	72	138	187	166	156	167	155
1944	152	156	73	137	197	182	161	178	160
1945	155	156	78	139	209	189	159	182	164
1946	155	154	88	140	239	231	198	219	186
1947	191	149	100	156	304	295	263	284	230
1948	217	155	107	171	368	348	279	324	260
1949	240	185	151	201	382	356	273	328	274
1950	268	204	224	235	416	491	299	390	324
1951	305	227	249	265	516	639	394	501	401
1952	336	285	227	294	532	475	363	443	380
1953	365	317	261	325	473	430	329	399	366
1954	330	325	320	326	476	429	298	386	361
1955	313	367	281	329	529	410	310	400	370
1956	319	351	282	326	581	400	352	428	384
1957	295	343	298	313	570	408	338	422	376
1958	314	347	251	313	539	346	319	386	355
1959	303	350	230	305	528	369	324	393	356
1960	277	356	230	296	518	416	325	405	359
1961	274	322	207	277	524	433	322	411	354
1962	311	343	213	301	541	404	314	416	360
1963	308	343	285	328	552	417	324	413	374
1964	316	397	280	339	649	441	318	445	401
1965	309	403	221	325	705	428	330	461	404
1966	333	417	205	337	698	438	310	453	404

(*a*) *Viz.* English wheat, American (later Canadian) wheat, flour, barley, oats, maize, potatoes, and rice.

(*b*) *Viz.* prime beef, middling beef, prime mutton, middling mutton, pork, bacon, and butter.

(*c*) *Viz.* West Indian sugar, beet sugar, Java sugar, and averages of various types of coffee and tea.

(*d*) *Viz.* iron, copper, tin, lead, coal in London, and coal for export.

(*e*) *Viz.* uplands cotton, Dhollerah (later Sudan) cotton, flax, hemp, jute, English wool, merino wool, and silk.

(*f*) *Viz.* hides, leather, tallow, palm oil, olive oil, linseed oil, and seeds, petroleum (later motor spirit, kerosene, and gas oil), soda crystals, nitrate of soda, indigo, and timber.

Prices 5. Board of Trade Wholesale Price Indices – 1871–1980

NOTES TO PART A

[1] SOURCE: 18th *Abstract of Labour Statistics* (collected from the *Board of Trade Journal* and revised).

[2] These indices are based on market prices and on unit values of imports and exports.

A. 1871–1920. 1900=100

			Food and Drink						
	Coal and Metals (*a*)	Textile Fibres (*b*)	Corn, etc. (*c*)	Animal Products (*d*)	Sugar, Tea, Tobacco, etc. (*e*)	Wine and Foreign Spirits (*f*)	Total	Miscellaneous Materials (*g*)	Total Index
1871	68·3	146·4	163·5	110·6	239·2	122·7	144·1	145·1	135·6
1872	102·9	166·5	169·2	111·9	242·1	122·8	147·3	151·5	145·2
1873	128·3	161·9	178·3	119·3	229·7	124·4	153·4	156·8	151·9
1874	104·8	151·1	178·5	120·1	216·2	119·2	152·5	154·5	146·9
1875	84·6	147·3	161·6	127·3	213·4	116·1	148·9	140·3	140·4
1876	72·4	137·9	160·2	127·7	207·9	112·4	148·0	141·1	137·1
1877	67·5	135·2	175·5	125·3	228·2	113·2	154·8	139·3	140·4
1878	62·8	131·4	159·7	121·1	202·6	114·8	144·1	125·1	131·1
1879	58·7	123·0	157·4	114·4	192·0	116·9	138·9	113·8	125·0
1880	64·8	130·0	159·0	116·1	197·1	119·1	140·9	124·4	129·0
1881	61·9	127·6	154·1	116·3	192·9	112·9	138·6	123·0	126·6
1882	62·2	123·4	153·7	122·1	191·3	109·4	141·0	123·7	127·7
1883	60·7	119·1	150·5	123·4	183·6	111·3	139·7	121·6	125·9
1884	57·5	115·2	130·1	114·4	150·4	109·5	123·9	114·5	114·1
1885	54·6	108·9	123·6	104·7	137·6	109·8	115·4	111·4	107·0
1886	52·6	99·9	116·4	100·7	112·8	112·8	109·9	101·7	101·0
1887	53·9	102·7	115·4	96·2	120·8	111·3	106·5	95·3	98·8
1888	56·6	101·2	115·3	102·4	131·4	114·4	110·5	98·0	101·8
1889	62·7	105·1	114·0	101·2	141·2	116·3	110·4	103·1	103·4
1890	74·9	105·4	115·3	99·5	125·3	113·2	108·5	99·4	103·3
1891	70·1	101·4	134·3	99·7	127·2	113·4	116·3	95·0	106·9
1892	65·2	95·6	117·9	99·9	127·8	110·3	109·9	92·5	101·1
1893	59·0	96·4	108·9	103·6	132·8	112·4	108·6	89·3	99·4
1894	60·0	88·6	100·7	99·4	117·8	109·6	101·9	84·5	93·5
1895	56·8	84·3	100·1	96·0	106·7	108·0	98·9	84·9	90·7
1896	55·5	92·9	92·7	90·1	107·8	112·3	93·3	86·5	88·2
1897	56·3	86·8	101·7	92·5	100·8	116·4	97·4	86·9	90·1
1898	61·7	80·0	117·5	89·8	99·9	113·4	102·2	89·7	93·2
1899	72·4	82·9	101·6	94·5	99·6	103·5	98·0	91·3	92·2
1900	100	100	100	100	100	100	100	100	100
1901	82·2	93·3	102·6	99·3	94·7	96·7	100·1	96·3	96·7
1902	76·1	92·3	102·3	104·4	84·4	91·8	101·4	92·5	96·4
1903	74·1	101·7	102·2	102·1	86·4	99·5	100·6	91·7	96·9
1904	70·9	112·9	106·9	98·3	92·5	100·8	101·2	88·3	98·2
1905	71·3	106·7	104·2	97·7	104·8	107·9	101·2	91·1	97·6
1906	78·3	121·1	102·3	102·2	88·7	103·2	101·0	95·6	100·8
1907	86·9	127·4	109·3	104·8	94·2	100·0	105·5	99·7	106·0
1908	78·5	109·8	113·8	103·3	99·0	97·8	107·0	94·8	103·0
1909	73·6	112·4	114·7	105·8	100·4	99·0	108·7	96·5	104·1
1910	76·6	136·2	105·9	111·7	111·7	100·2	109·2	104·3	108·8
1911	74·7	128·9	114·3	109·2	114·1	104·1	111·6	105·5	109·4
1912	84·9	119·6	124·0	116·8	120·4	111·9	119·9	110·1	114·9
1913	92·5	135·0	118·6	119·6	106·8	106·4	117·7	109·4	116·5
1914	86·7	128·8	118·2	122·7	127·0	102·1	120·9	111·3	117·2
1915	116·7	119·8	163·8	145·9	169·8	87·8	154·1	143·8	143·9

A. 1871–1920. 1900=100 (*cont.*)

	Coal and Metals (*a*)	Textile Fibres (*b*)	Food and Drink: Corn, etc. (*c*)	Animal Products (*d*)	Sugar, Tea, Tobacco, etc. (*e*)	Wine and Foreign Spirits (*f*)	Total	Miscel-laneous Materials (*g*)	Total Index
1916	165·8	180·1	209·5	175·1	196·7	103·6	189·4	204·0	186·5
1917	182·0	270·4	272·5	228·8	248·6	136·7	246·2	256·3	243·0
1918	204·9	354·4	259·3	263·8	256·9	210·6	260·3	268·6	268·1
1919	280·2	373·3	287·5	273·7	284·4	244·3	279·7	317·8	296·5
1920	419·2	503·7	354·8	306·8	401·6	265·8	334·1	336·6	368·8

(*a*) *Viz.* coal (34), pig iron (16), copper (5), lead (1½), tin (1½), and zinc (1½).
(*b*) *Viz.* cotton (38), British wool (6), foreign wool (13), silk (9), flax (4), and jute (3).
(*c*) *Viz.* British wheat (14), imported wheat (33), British barley (12), imported barley (5), British oats (17), imported oats (4), maize (8), hops (4), rice (1), and potatoes (33).
(*d*) *Viz.* English beef (52), English mutton (31), imported bacon and ham (21), milk (29), butter and margarine (12), imported cheese (4), imported eggs (5), and fish (7).
(*e*) *Viz.* sugar (2), tobacco (2), tea (8), coffee (1), and cocoa (½).
(*f*) *Viz.* wine (5), and foreign spirits (1½).
(*g*) *Viz.* cotton seed (2), linseed (5), olive oil (1), palm oil (½), paraffin and paraffin wax (½), petroleum (2), rubber (1½), bricks (3), wood and timber (20), and hides (8).

NOTES TO PART B
[1] Source: *Board of Trade Journal.*
[2] Statistics separating coal from other minerals, and wool from other textiles, were not published for the year 1920. Combined indices for 1920 and 1921 were as follows:

	Coal and Other Minerals	Wool and Other Textiles
1920	251·5	358·9
1921	178·9	171·6

[3] These indices are based on market prices.

B. 1920–34. 1913=100

	Food: Cereals (*a*)	Meat and Fish (*b*)	Other Foods (*c*)	Total	Metals and Minerals: Coal	Iron and Steel	Other (*d*)	Textile Materials: Cotton	Wool	Other (*e*)	Other Articles (*f*)	Total Index (*g*)
1920	273·4	262·5	278·9	271·8	...	357·8	...	480·2	...	...	272·9	307·3
1921	194·3	218·5	214·1	209·0	242·9	209·9	131·9	192·3	158·3	193·7	195·6	197·2
1922	151·1	172·1	172·3	165·2	171·7	136·8	116·2	182·2	160·6	173·3	166·0	158·8
1923	139·2	155·7	168·4	154·5	179·3	147·2	114·1	201·9	179·2	159·7	161·9	158·9
1924	160·1	153·6	184·4	166·3	172·4	142·9	120·3	227·8	219·0	165·6	157·6	166·2
1925	163·5	161·7	173·2	166·5	146·0	126·0	121·6	209·8	196·9	171·9	157·4	159·1
1926	150·2	153·8	159·7	154·8	184·6	123·5	120·1	158·3	169·5	147·5	145·0	148·1
1927	152·7	137·5	165·4	152·0	133·6	119·9	111·9	154·7	170·2	138·5	142·5	141·6
1928	149·1	140·9	166·7	152·3	117·9	112·3	107·1	164·2	185·9	137·8	142·3	140·3
1929	137·8	146·2	151·9	145·3	124·5	114·2	116·0	154·4	165·6	131·6	135·5	136·5
1930	109·1	140·2	132·4	126·6	121·4	112·7	95·0	121·2	122·4	101·7	123·8	119·5
1931	89·8	116·0	131·0	111·5	123·1	104·9	78·2	96·8	99·9	80·5	105·6	104·2
1932	96·7	105·7	130·4	110·6	123·3	103·7	80·5	95·8	90·2	79·2	96·2	101·6
1933	90·4	107·1	113·3	103·4	122·3	105·8	84·0	96·2	99·9	74·0	101·4	100·9
1934	93·8	110·1	111·2	104·8	126·0	109·6	81·2	106·9	114·2	69·2	105·2	104·1

(*a*) *Viz.* wheat (7), barley (5), oats (2), maize (1), and rice (2).
(*b*) *Viz.* beef and veal (6), mutton and lamb (3), pig-meat (5), poultry and eggs (1), and fish (1).
(*c*) *Viz.* dairy products (7), fruit and vegetables (5), sugar (2), tea, coffee and cocoa (3), and tobacco (2).
(*d*) *Viz.* copper (4), tin (1), lead (1), zinc (1), nickel (1), and petroleum (2).
(*e*) *Viz.* silk and artificial silk (2), linen (2), jute (1), and hemp (1).
(*f*) *Viz.* paper (2), leather (4), rubber (1), timber (4), bricks (1), stone and slate (2), and glass, china, etc. (1).
(*g*) The weights are as follows: Total Food – 52; Coal – 10; Iron and Steel – 24; Other Metals and Minerals – 10; Cotton – 16; Wool – 9; Other Textile Materials – 6; Other Articles – 15.

Prices 5. *continued*

NOTES TO PARTS C to G

[1] SOURCE: *Board of Trade Journal* and *Abstract*. The full revised series for 1938–50 was kindly supplied by the Statistics Division of the Board of Trade.

[2] In part G, the indices based on 1970 have been spliced on to those based on 1975 at 1974.

C. 1930–50: 1930=100

	Food, Drink, and Tobacco				Industrial Materials and Manufactures									
	Cereals (*a*)	Meat and Fish (*b*)	Other Foods and Tobacco (*c*)	Total	Coal	Iron and Steel	Non-ferrous Metals (*d*)	Cotton	Wool	Other Textiles (*e*)	Chemicals and Oils (*f*)	Miscel-laneous (*g*)	Total	Total Index (All Articles)
1930	100	100	100	100	100	100	100	100	100	100	100	100	100	100
1931	82·0	82·9	97·9	88·5	102·6	92·8	80·9	79·0	81·4	78·6	89·8	86·6	87·4	87·8
1932	88·2	75·4	97·3	87·7	103·0	91·5	82·9	78·3	74·6	77·1	90·7	80·3	84·6	85·6
1933	83·3	76·9	87·2	82·9	101·5	94·3	87·2	78·7	84·9	73·1	90·3	84·4	87·2	85·7
1934	86·4	81·2	86·9	85·0	102·5	98·7	83·9	87·5	95·0	66·4	87·4	88·0	89·7	88·1
1935	89·6	80·1	89·9	86·8	102·5	100·5	86·9	86·7	90·0	69·2	91·0	86·3	90·1	89·0
1936	99·1	81·1	94·8	91·7	107·6	106·6	93·0	88·8	105·0	72·5	93·5	92·3	95·7	94·4
1937	127·0	86·4	98·7	102·2	124·9	129·6	117·4	97·7	127·5	76·3	99·4	110·2	112·0	108·7
1938	109·9	85·9	97·5	97·3	123·2	139·1	94·4	83·6	101·4	68·7	94·7	93·2	103·5	101·4
1939	96·5	88·7	104·6	97·3	121·1	131·5	100·4	88·5	105·8	79·7	95·3	98·7	105·5	102·8
1940	138·0	114·6	143·3	132·7	140·1	159·2	123·2	125·3	157·3	108·5	117·1	142·6	138·4	136·6
1941	150·4	118·1	166·5	146·1	159·5	181·1	123·9	138·2	170·1	120·2	126·9	169·1	155·8	152·6
1942	188·8	116·7	171·3	157·5	171·1	182·5	125·8	140·9	172·9	128·4	136·0	172·0	160·1	159·4
1943	179·3	121·7	179·0	159·8	185·8	182·8	126·0	136·7	177·3	132·8	146·3	177·1	164·0	162·8
1944	167·3	121·8	182·4	157·8	209·1	184·1	127·8	153·6	183·7	134·3	151·4	184·2	170·2	166·2
1945	164·7	121·8	184·7	157·9	237·0	188·8	127·1	161·9	185·2	139·1	149·3	188·6	174·7	169·0
1946	166·9	123·5	181·6	158·1	244·0	209·2	150·9	173·3	186·5	151·1	148·3	188·7	184·2	175·2
1947	172·2	121·6	197·9	164·6	251·7	221·5	222·5	199·9	212·1	165·8	175·6	210·9	207·0	191·7
1948	176·7	136·0	225·1	180·8	297·4	235·6	241·7	300·4	276·3	167·8	190·7	266·6	241·8	219·3
1949	196·7	156·1	230·6	196·3	303·8	252·9	255·3	322·1	304·9	169·8	191·1	256·6	249·1	230·0
1950	235·3	173·6	251·3	221·1	304·5	260·8	337·1	397·5	505·6	197·2	208·4	293·6	285·8	262·4

(*a*) *Viz.* wheat (8), barley (8), oats (1), maize (2), and rice (1).
(*b*) *Viz.* beef and veal (6), mutton and lamb (3), pig-meat (6), poultry and eggs (3), and fish (2).
(*c*) *Viz.* dairy products (9), fruit and vegetables (7), sugar (4), tea, coffee and cocoa (3), and tobacco (5).
(*d*) *Viz.* copper (4), lead (1), tin (1), zinc (1), and nickel and aluminium (1).
(*e*) *Viz.* silk and artificial silk (5), linen (2), jute (1), and hemp (1).
(*f*) *Viz.* chemicals, drugs, dyes, etc. (6), oils and fats (3), paints (2), and petroleum (4).
(*g*) *Viz.* paper (9), leather (5), rubber (2), timber (8), bricks (2), tiles (1), stone and slate (2), cement (1), sand, lime, etc. (1), glass (1), and china, etc. (1).

D. 1946–57: 30 June 1949=100

	Materials Used in Broad Sectors of Industry						Fuel Used in all Manu-facturing Industry	Output of Broad Sectors of Industry							
	All Non-Food Manu-facturing	Mechanical Engin-eering	Electrical Machinery	Textiles	Building and Civil Engin-eering	House Building		All Non-Food Manu-factured Products	Chemicals	Iron and Steel	Textiles	Clothing and Footwear	Food	Paper
1946	...	83·2	82·5	...	83·2	83·6	...	...	...	...	...	...	...	...
1947	...	93·6	98·9	...	94·3	93·7	...	...	...	...	...	...	...	...
1948	...	97·4	101·9	...	100·6	100·8	...	...	...	90·4	...	...	...	...
1949	...	101·5	104·2	...	102·0	101·8	...	...	...	97·7	...	...	...	...
1950	138·6	113·2	122·0	155·0	106·1	105·2	103·0	106·8	103·7	101·0	131·1	103·7	...	101·4
1951	193·3	134·3	151·9	211·0	125·6	123·0	112·2	124·8	120·9	113·2	178·5	124·7	118·0	168·4
1952	162·1	149·9	165·4	154·7	133·6	130·6	124·1	127·8	131·0	136·5	136·4	114·9	132·5	160·9
1953	145·8	145·7	155·2	145·7	130·4	128·7	130·8	125·2	130·4	139·8	129·4	113·7	138·6	131·0
1954	143·5	150·4	160·5	147·4	131·4	130·7	136·2	125·5	130·8	141·3	130·3	114·2	139·1	133·3
1955	152·4	168·1	185·7	140·7	137·3	137·1	147·2	129·6	133·1	148·1	126·1	113·6	143·9	140·3
1956	156·2	177·3	190·0	144·1	142·4	142·3	163·2	135·6	138·8	158·9	126·7	115·3	148·1	146·0
1957	154·7	183·9	181·7	148·1	146·9	146·4	175·4	139·9	143·2	176·5	131·8	118·3	156·3	147·7

E. 1955–65: 1954=100

	Materials Purchased by Broad Sectors of Industry								
	All Basic Materials and Fuel Used in Manufacturing Industry	Basic Materials Used in Manufacturing Industry	Fuel Used in (*a*) Manufacturing Industry	Materials and Fuel Used in				Construction Materials	House Building Materials
				Food Manufacturing	Mechanical Engineering	Electrical Machinery	Textiles		
1955	103·0	102·7	106·1	97·8	110·2	110·2	96·0	104·7	105·2
1956	106·7	105·3	116·9	100·1	116·5	114·3	98·0	109·5	109·4
1957	107·4	105·3	123·4	97·3	121·9	114·9	103·1	113·7	112·3
1958	100·8	97·1	129·0	96·7	123·5	114·5	88·7	114·2	111·9
1959	101·7	98·4	127·5	98·6	124·5	115·6	88·1	113·4	111·0
1960	101·8	98·5	127·6	96·1	126·2	116·9	91·6	115·1	114·0
1961	100·6	96·4	133·0	93·0	128·1	118·3	92·9	118·2	118·0
1962	100·6	95·9	136·5	95·3	130·1	120·0	91·3	120·4	120·2
1963	103·0	98·5	137·8	99·6	130·8	120·9	96·6	121·9	121·7
1964	107·0	103·0	138·3	103·8	135·3	125·0	98·7	125·8	126·2
1965	107·5	103·1	141·6	102·3	140·5	131·2	94·5	130·4	131·5

See p. 734 for footnote.

Prices 5. *continued*

E. 1955–65: 1954=100 (*cont.*)

Output of Broad Sectors of Industry

	All Manufactured Products		Food Manufactures	Chemicals		Iron and Steel		Textiles		Clothing and Footwear	Paper
	Total Sales	Home Sales	Home Sales	Total Sales	Home Sales	Total Sales	Home Sales	Total Sales	Home Sales	Home Sales	Home Sales
1955	103·4	102·6	102·1	99·9	99·5	104·0	104·7	98·3	97·7	100·1	104·9
1956	106·7	107·0	105·8	102·9	103·1	112·1	112·8	98·1	97·5	101·7	109·2
1957	110·2	110·4	107·1	105·9	106·5	123·9	125·2	101·1	100·9	104·4	110·3
1958	111·0	111·1	104·9	104·6	105·6	127·7	129·9	98·9	97·9	105·5	109·7
1959	111·4	111·5	106·9	105·3	106·6	125·4	129·0	96·5	96·0	105·2	107·6
1960	113·1	113·0	106·9	104·4	106·0	125·6	128·5	101·4	100·8	107·1	107·6
1961	115·7	116·0	107·2	103·1	105·1	126·1	129·7	104·3	103·3	108·9	109·8
1962	118·0	118·6	111·1	102·6	104·5	128·7	133·3	103·8	102·5	110·4	111·0
1963	119·5	119·9	114·2	103·3	104·6	128·8	133·7	105·7	103·9	110·7	111·6
1964	123·2	123·9	118·1	105·4	106·8	129·3	134·3	110·1	107·9	112·6	114·3
1965	128·4	129·7	120·6	108·1	109·4	131·6	136·6	111·6	110·1	115·3	118·7

F. 1963–1971: 1963=100

Materials Purchased by Broad Sectors of Industry

	All Basic Material and Fuel used in Manufacturing Industry	Basic Materials used in Manufacturing Industry	Fuel used in Manufacturing Industry (*a*)	Materials and Fuel Used in: Food Manufacturing	Mechanical Engineering	Electrical Machinery	Textiles	Construction Materials	House Building Materials
1963	100	100	100	100	100	100	100	100	100
1964	104·1	104·4	101·8	104·3	103·1	103·5	102·0	102·9	103·3
1965	105·4	104·9	108·6	103·0	106·8	108·5	97·8	106·1	107·2
1966	108·7	107·3	112·9	104·2	112·3	118·0	99·8	108·6	109·7
1967	107·5	106·3	115·4	106·0	112·0	115·8	95·9	109·1	110·1
1968	117·3	117·0	119·7	110·6	117·1	124·9	102·6	114·8	116·8
1969	121·4	121·6	120·1	114·2	125·0	134·9	103·6	119·1	121·5
1970	126·2	126·2	125·7	122·0	137·9	147·8	104·0	129·2	131·4
1971	132·6	131·2	140·9	128·2	145·8	152·0	108·6	141·7	143·5

Output of Broad Sectors of Industry

	All Manufactured Products		Food Manufactures	Chemicals		Iron and Steel		Textiles		Clothing and Footwear	Paper
	Total Sales	Home Sales	Home Sales	Total Sales	Home Sales	Total Sales	Home Sales	Total Sales	Home Sales	Home Sales	Home Sales
1963	100	100	100	100	100	100	100	100	100	100	100
1964	102·7	102·9	103·9	100·6	100·1	100·4	100·5	102·8	102·5	101·3	102·0
1965	106·1	106·8	106·2	102·2	101·0	101·6	101·9	104·1	103·7	103·4	105·6
1966	109·5	109·6	107·9	103·2	101·7	104·3	104·9	105·6	105·2	106·4	107·4
1967	111·1	110·9	109·9	103·7	102·1	105·4	106·1	104·9	104·1	107·2	107·6
1968	116·7	115·3	114·5	108·1	105·4	107·5	107·1	108·7	107·8	108·9	113·1
1969	120·9	119·8	118·6	109·6	106·4	113·2	112·4	112·8	111·5	111·5	118·2
1970	128·8	127·7	128·2	115·3	111·2	130·4	130·1	116·9	115·8	115·6	130·5
1971	139·4	137·7	140·1	123·3	120·2	140·5	141·2	122·5	121·3	122·5	139·8

G. 1968–1980: 1975=100

Materials Purchased by Broad Sectors of Industry

	All Basic Material and Fuel used in Manufacturing Industry	Basic Materials used in Manufacturing Industry	Fuel used in Manufacturing Industry (*a*)	Materials and Fuel Used in				Construction Materials	House Building Materials
				Food Manufacturing	Mechanical Engineering	Electrical Machinery	Textiles		
1968	36·9	36·1	48·9	42·8	38·8	42·2	45·7	42·3	42·2
1969	38·3	37·7	49·4	44·2	40·9	45·0	46·4	43·9	43·9
1970	40·3	39·6	52·3	47·7	45·3	49·4	47·0	47·7	47·6
1971	42·2	41·3	56·4	51·1	48·8	51·7	49·3	52·0	52·3
1972	44·0	43·0	58·5	53·9	51·1	53·8	56·0	55·5	56·3
1973	58·3	58·5	59·3	70·4	57·8	62·4	78·4	65·1	67·2
1974	86·8	88·3	75·4	85·1	79·2	84·3	89·3	83·6	84·7
1975	100	100	100	100	100	100	100	100	100
1976	127·0	128·2	117·5	125·7	121·0	119·8	124·2	122·4	122·7
1977	145·6	146·6	138·1	152·3	140·2	138·6	142·1	145·9	146·4
1978	144·6	143·8	151·1	157·2	153·9	150·8	145·5	158·0	157·9
1979	167·6	167·1	169·8	169·1	171·3	170·8	164·0	182·2	182·4
1980	200·9	198·8	215·7	181·6	189·1	192·7	179·8	216·5	218·1

See p. 734 for footnote.

G. 1968–80: 1975=100 *(cont.)*

Output of Broad Sectors of Industry (Home Sales)

	All Manufactured Products	Food Manufactures	Chemicals	Steel	Textiles	Clothing and Footwear	Paper
1968	48·4	45·0	50·9	36·8	52·5	57·7	39·3
1969	50·3	46·6	51·3	38·5	54·1	59·1	41·0
1970	53·9	50·1	53·7	44·6	55·8	61·5	45·4
1971	58·7	54·7	58·1	48·6	58·5	65·5	48·8
1972	61·9	57·1	61·1	51·2	62·6	69·7	51·5
1973	66·4	66·4	63·9	56·1	73·5	75·0	56·0
1974	81·9	82·8	82·1	78·1	90·5	87·1	77·6
1975	100	100	100	100	100	100	100
1976	117·3	118·6	114·8	120·0	115·3	113·0	111·9
1977	140·5	148·2	133·1	141·4	135·6	128·7	129·1
1978	153·3	161·7	143·7	154·7	147·2	142·9	134·6
1979	172·0	177·9	165·1	168·4	163·0	159·7	152·0
1980	200·0	199·3	191·1	179·1	180·4	181·6	176·7

(*a*) i.e. coal (other than for carbonising), electricity and gas.

Prices 6. General Wholesale Price Index – Republic of Ireland 1938–80

NOTE
Source: *Statistical Abstract of Ireland.*

Oct 1938	100	1953	100	1968	145·9
1939	105·4	1954	98·6	1969	156·4
1940	131·8	1955	101·6	1970	164·7
1941	148·0	1956	103·1	1971	173·6
1942	170·2	1957	109·9	1972	191·7
1943	189·4	1958	113·5	1973	225·4
1944	198·2	1959	113·5	1974	255·9
1945	197·5	1960	112·9	1975	318·6
1946	197·5	1961	114·7		
1947	219·4	1962	118·3	1975	100
				1976	119·6
1948	232·1	1963	119·8	1977	140·1
1949	231·1	1964	126·8	1978	152·6
1950	244·2	1965	131·6	1979	171·2
1951	282·7	1966	134·2	1980	189·2
1952	298·6	1967	137·7		
1953	299·1				

Prices 7. Indices of Agricultural Prices – England and Wales 1909–80

NOTES
[1] Sources: Part A – *A Century of Agricultural Statistics* (H.M.S.O., 1968). Parts B, C, and D – *Abstract*.
[2] From 1932, index numbers are based on prices inclusive of subsidies.
[3] In Part D, indices based on the averages of 1964/5 to 1966/7 have been spliced on to those based on 1968/9 to 1971/2 at 1969/70.
[4] The index in Part A is continued in the source to 1966.
[5] In Parts C and D the numbers relate to harvest years.

A. 1906–8=100, All Products

1909	99	1919	284	1929	158
1910	104	1920	321	1930	145
1911	106	1921	241	1931	134
1912	112	1922	186	1932	129
1913	112	1923	173	1933	123
1914	111	1924	177	1934	124
1915	140	1925	175	1935	131
1916	176	1926	166	1936	132
1917	221	1927	158	1937	145
1918	255	1928	163	1938	144

B. 1936–8=100

	All Products	Cereals and Farm Crops	Livestock and Livestock Products (*a*)	Fruit, Vegetables, and Glasshouse Produce
1935	93	89	91	109
1936	94	101	93	91
1937	103	106	104	98
1938	102	93	104	111
1939	103	99	106	94
1940	143	138	143	153
1941	173	169	162	237
1942	184	201	178	197
1943	187	194	180	216
1944	191	192	185	216
1945	197	198	192	204
1946	207	198	208	211
1947	241	214	233	302
1948	249	238	252	244
1949	260	239	267	259
1950	270	250	281	249
1951	296	283	310	254
1952	306	279	323	273
1953	312	283	331	275
1954	310	282	325	281
1955	327	299	340	310
1956	328	319	331	335
1957	319	290	325	334
1958	327	353	322	317
1959	317	321	319	295
1960	302	276	313	287

See p. 736 for footnotes.

Prices 7. *continued*

C. 1954/5 to 1956/7=100

	All Products	Farm Crops	Fatstock	Livestock Products and Poultry	Fruit and Vegetables
1954/5	99·7	98·6	99·7	100·7	97·8
1955/6	102·2	106·6	98·7	101·8	107·4
1956/7	98·1	94·9	101·6	97·5	94·7
1957/8	101·6	112·6	98·0	96·7	113·7
1958/9	101·2	117·0	100·0	95·4	98·1
1959/60	96·4	96·9	99·3	92·1	104·8
1960/1	93·5	93·6	98·1	90·2	91·8
1961/2	97·4	105·7	99·1	86·1	127·3
1962/3	97·2	108·8	98·0	87·7	113·8
1963/4	95·9	98·9	100·5	88·7	106·2
1964/5	98·3	96·8	104·2	90·8	115·2
1965/6	99·6	95·1	104·9	93·3	119·4
1966/7	102·5	105·2	107·0	91·9	130·2
1967/8	103·5	98·3	111·3	92·2	139·0
1968/9	106·1	99·9	116·1	93·9	140·9

D. 1968/9 to 1971/2=100

	All Products	Farm Crops	Fatstock	Livestock Products and Poultry	Fruit and Vegetables
1964/5	86·9	88·8	80·7	93·0	83·7
1965/6	87·6	85·2	81·4	95·6	86·1
1966/7	89·4	93·1	81·9	93·9	94·3
1967/8	90·1	88·8	85·8	93·4	99·9
1968/9	92·7	89·9	90·0	95·4	100·6
1969/70	96·8	103·9	95·0	95·1	95·8
1970/1	102·9	101·7	104·7	103·1	97·6
1971/2	107·2	103·5	110·4	107·0	104·1
1972/3	124·1	116·2	142·2	111·5	130·9
1973/4	157·1	169·7	161·3	149·7	147·1
1974/5	177·1	190·8	175·1	172·8	174·1
1975/6	230·7	311·4	223·0	200·5	217·9
1976/7	276·4	386·7	257·0	235·5	290·2

E. 1975=100

	All Products	Farm Crops & Horticultural Products	Fatstock & Livestock Products	Main Constituents						
				Cereals	Root Crops	Fresh Vegetables	Fresh Fruit	Animals for Slaughter	Milk	Eggs
1973	72·4	65·3	76·3	82·4	32·6	63·0	77·9	80·5	63·7	96·0
1974	82·1	80·6	82·9	102·1	43·5	76·3	86·4	81.4	79·0	106·1
1975	100	100	100	100	100	100	100	100	100	100
1976	128·6	143·7	120·4	131·5	186·4	118·9	112·3	122·4	117·9	117·9
1977	133·7	130·9	135·2	136·3	95·0	125·8	181·0	139·1	128·8	133·2
1978	137·8	121·8	146·5	145·2	66·6	112·4	153·9	157·6	133·1	126·3
1979	152·1	141·4	157·9	161·9	97·5	141·8	135·3	169·2	142·5	145·1
1980	160·7	141·2	171·1	166·0	82·1	140·8	139·6	178·2	161·6	164·0

(*a*) Excluding store stock.

Prices 8. Lindert & Williamson's "Best Guess" Cost of Living Index using Southern Urban England Weights – 1781–1850

NOTE
SOURCE: Peter H. Lindert and Jeffrey G. Williamson, "English Workers' Living Standards during the Industrial Revolution: A New Look", *E.H.R.*, second series XXXVI, 1 (1983), as revised in *J.E.H.*, XLV, 1 (1985). The revised figures for years prior to 1805 (except 1781, 1785, 1790, 1795, and 1800) are interpolations kindly supplied by Professor Williamson.

	1850=100	Revised 1851=100		1850=100	Revised 1851=100		1850=100	Revised 1851=100		1850=100	Revised 1851=100		1850=100	Revised 1851=100
1781	118·8	111·1	1795	153·8	146·3	1809	204·9	196·6	1823	146·0	134·0	1837	129·2	129·2
1782	119·3	111·0	1796	159·5	153·0	1810	215·4	207·1	1824	154·6	143·7	1838	138·3	139·2
1783	121·9	113·5	1797	138·8	133·2	1811	204·5	196·0	1825	162·3	151·1	1839	142·3	143·6
1784	118·4	110·2	1798	136·9	131·4	1812	235·7	227·5	1826	144·4	135·9	1840	138·4	139·8
1785	112·3	104·1	1799	155·7	149·4	1813	230·0	221·9	1827	140·9	131·9	1841	133·3	134·9
1786	109·6	102·1	1800	207·1	200·1	1814	203·3	192·7	1828	143·2	135·4	1842	123·4	126·0
1787	112·5	104·8	1801	218·2	209·2	1815	182·6	164·3	1829	143·9	138·8	1843	109·6	113·0
1788	115·9	107·9	1802	160·9	154·3	1816	192·1	180·8	1830	141·3	135·4	1844	114·5	117·9
1789	122·3	113·9	1803	156·8	150·3	1817	197·5	186·7	1831	141·3	136·6	1845	112·0	115·2
1790	125·9	117·6	1804	160·2	153·6	1818	192·4	179·1	1832	133·9	130·4	1846	116·4	120·7
1791	121·2	114·4	1805	186·7	177·5	1819	182·9	166·6	1833	124·7	122·5	1847	138·0	141·4
1792	118·3	111·6	1806	178·5	169·1	1820	170·1	151·0	1834	117·6	116·4	1848	110·9	115·5
1793	127·3	120·1	1807	169·1	161·2	1821	155·5	138·2	1835	112·8	109·4	1849	101·2	105·0
1794	130·7	123·3	1808	180·5	172·8	1822	139·8	126·3	1836	126·4	125·6	1850	100	102·4

Prices 9. Bowley's Cost of Living Index – United Kingdom 1846–1914

[1] SOURCE: A. L. Bowley, *Wages and Income in the United Kingdom since 1860* (Cambridge, 1937), pp. 121–2.
[2] The figures to 1879 are described by Bowley as an "empirical estimate" and are based on the assumption that retail prices (and rent) bore the same relationship to wholesale prices before 1880 as they did after.
[3] The component indices, on a 1900=100 in the source, have been converted to January–June 1914=100.

(January to June 1914=100)

1846	106	1853	108	1860	113	1867	114	1874	115
1847	110	1854	115	1861	112	1868	113	1875	111
1848	96	1855	114	1862	113	1869	111	1876	110
1849	93	1856	114	1863	115	1870	110	1877	110
1850	94	1857	117	1864	115	1871	113	1878	104
1851	94	1858	106	1865	113	1872	120	1879	101
1852	96	1859	108	1866	114	1873	122		

	Food	Rent	Clothing	Fuel	Sundries	Overall Index
1880	115	91	86	86	95	105
1881	112	91	86	90	91	103
1882	111	92	85	85	91	102
1883	112	92	83	88	87	102
1884	104	93	82	87	83	97
1885	94	93	81	87	80	91
1886	91	93	81	85	76	89
1887	88	93	81	84	76	88
1888	89	93	80	85	78	88
1889	91	93	79	86	80	89
1890	90	93	81	93	81	89
1891	92	94	81	91	77	89
1892	93	95	80	91	74	90
1893	88	96	79	99	74	89
1894	85	96	79	85	68	85
1895	82	97	78	83	68	83
1896	82	98	79	84	68	83
1897	85	98	78	85	68	85

	Food	Rent	Clothing	Fuel	Sundries	Overall Index
1898	88	99	77	85	67	88
1899	85	99	76	92	69	86
1900	89	100	79	116	91	91
1901	89	100	72	103	82	90
1902	90	100	73	99	81	90
1903	92	100	79	94	82	91
1904	91	100	86	92	82	92
1905	92	100	87	91	85	92
1906	91	100	96	92	95	93
1907	94	100	93	103	97	95
1908	96	100	75	100	82	93
1909	96	100	77	98	85	94
1910	97	100	88	98	92	96
1911	97	100	94	99	95	97
1912	102	100	94	101	100	100
1913	103	100	101	100	104	102
1914(*a*)	100	100	100	100	100	100

(*a*) January to June.

Prices 10. Ministry of Labour/Department of Employment Indices of Retail Prices – United Kingdom, 1892–1980

NOTE
SOURCES: Part A – *18th Abstract of Labour Statistics* (1926); Other Parts – *Abstract*.

A. Partial Indices 1892–1914, 1900=100

	Food	Coal	Clothing		Food	Coal	Clothing
1892	103·9	74·4	101·0	1904	102·4	79·4	102·3
1893	99·3	83·4	100·3	1905	102·8	78·4	103·0
1894	94·9	70·5	99·1	1906	102·0	79·5	104·5
1895	92·1	68·8	97·8	1907	105·0	88·9	106·2
1896	91·7	68·2	98·6	1908	107·5	85·6	107·1
1897	95·5	70·2	98·2	1909	107·6	84·1	108·4
1898	99·5	72·1	97·0	1910	109·4	83·8	110·7
1899	95·4	79·3	96·2	1911	109·4	85·1	112·4
1900	100·0	100·0	100·0	1912	114·5	87·0	115·5
1901	100·4	89·0	100·6	1913	114·8	90·7	115·9
1902	101·0	84·6	99·9	Jan –July 1914	111·6	92·5	117·4
1903	102·8	80·9	99·7				

B. Working Class Cost of Living Indices for Food and All Items, 1915–38, 1914 (July)=100

	Food	All Items		Food	All Items
1915	131	123	1927	160	167½
1916	160	146	1928	157	166
1917	198½	176	1929	154	164
1918	215	203	1930	145	158
1919	219	215	1931	131	147½
1920	256	249	1932	126	144
1921	229½	226	1933	120	140
1922	176	183	1934	122	141
1923	169	174	1935	125	143
1924	170	175	1936	130	147
1925	171	176	1937	139	154
1926	164	172	1938	141	156

C. Working Class Cost of Living Indices

	All Items		Food	Clothing	Fuel and Light	Rent and Rates
	July 1914=100	1 September 1939=100				
1938	156	101	102	100	99	99
1939	158	102	102	103	101	100
1940	184	119	119	137	115	101
1941	199	128	122	177	125	101
1942	200	129	117	192	129	101
1943	199	128	120	169	134	101
1944	201	130	122	166	141	101
1945	293	131	123	167	149	102
1946	203·5	131	122	166	152	103
1947 (June)	203	131	117	166	155	108

D. Interim Index of Retail Prices

17 June 1947=100

	All Items	Food	Clothing	Fuel and Light	Rent and Rates	Household Durable Goods	Miscel-laneous Goods	Services	Alcoholic Drink and Tobacco
Weights 1947	*1,000*	*348*	*97*	*65*	*88*	*71*	*35*	*79*	*217*
1948	108	108·2	109·3	110·9	99·5	107·9	109·7	104·7	109·1
1949	111	114·1	117·7	113·0	100·0	108·5	112·1	105·4	108·3
1950	114	122·7	119·8	116·5	101·1	112·3	113·1	108·4	105·1
1951	125	136·3	138·3	128·0	103·3	132·1	128·2	117·9	106·3
1952 (15 Jan.)	132	149·7	147·1	140·1	104·2	136·6	137·3	123·9	108·5

	17 June 1947=100	15 January 1952=100									
	All Items	All Items	Food	Clothing	Fuel and Light	Rent and Rates	Household Durable Goods	Miscel-laneous Goods	Services	Alcoholic Drink	Tobacco
Weights 1952		*1,000*	*399*	*98*	*66*	*72*	*62*	*44*	*91*	*78*	*90*
1952	136	102·6	105·4	97·7	101·3	102·2	98·6	102·5	103·8	100·7	100·0
1953	140	105·8	111·3	95·6	106·5	107·7	96·1	100·9	108·2	101·2	100·3
1954	143	107·7	114·2	96·2	111·3	111·7	95·3	100·0	110·6	101·6	100·3
1955	149	112·6	122·8	96·5	117·6	115·0	96·8	101·9	115·1	102·8	100·9
1956	153·4	115·8	125·4	98·7	127·6	117·9	102·5	106·6	119·1	103·1	102·9

E. Index of Retail Prices

	All Items	Food	Alcoholic Drink	Tobacco	Housing	Fuel and Light	Household Durable Goods	Clothing and Footwear	Transport and Vehicles	Miscel-laneous Goods	Services	Meals Bought and Consumed out of the Home
	17 January 1956=100											
Weights 1956	*1,000*	*350*	*71*	*80*	*87*	*55*	*66*	*106*	*68*	*59*	*58*	—
1956	102·0	102·2	101·3	103·5	102·8	101·3	101·0	100·6	102·1	102·4	103·5	—
1957	105·8	104·9	104·3	106·1	110·1	107·9	101·1	102·2	110·2	107·7	109·4	—
1958	109·0	107·1	105·8	107·8	121·7	113·3	100·5	103·0	112·9	113·0	114·5	—
1959	109·6	108·2	100·0	107·9	127·8	114·5	98·5	102·6	114·7	113·5	116·1	—
1960	110·7	107·4	98·2	111·9	131·7	117·3	98·3	103·9	118·1	115·0	120·1	—
1961	114·5	109·1	102·5	117·7	137·6	124·7	100·3	105·6	123·0	124·3	126·2	—
1962 (16 Jan.)	117·5	110·7	108·2	123·6	140·6	130·6	102·1	106·6	126·7	128·2	130·1	—
	16 January 1962 = 100											
Weights 1962	*1,000*	*319*	*64*	*79*	*102*	*62*	*64*	*98*	*92*	*65*	*56*	—
1962	101·6	102·3	100·3	100·0	103·3	101·3	100·4	102·0	100·5	100·6	101·9	—
Weights 1963	*1,000*	*319*	*63*	*77*	*104*	*63*	*64*	*98*	*93*	*63*	*56*	—
1963	103·6	104·8	102·3	100·0	108·4	106·0	100·1	103·5	100·5	101·9	104·0	—
Weights 1964	*1,000*	*314*	*63*	*74*	*107*	*66*	*62*	*95*	*100*	*63*	*56*	—
1964	107·0	107·8	107·9	105·8	114·0	109·3	102·3	104·9	102·1	105·0	106·9	—
Weights 1965	*1,000*	*311*	*65*	*76*	*109*	*65*	*59*	*92*	*105*	*63*	*55*	—
1965	112·1	111·6	117·1	118·0	120·5	114·5	104·8	107·0	106·7	109·0	112·7	—
Weights 1966	*1,000*	*298*	*67*	*77*	*113*	*64*	*57*	*91*	*116*	*61*	*56*	—
1966	116·5	115·6	121·7	120·8	128·5	120·9	107·2	109·9	109·9	112·5	120·5	
Weights 1967	*1,000*	*293*	*67*	*72*	*118*	*62*	*59*	*92*	*118*	*61*	*58*	—
1967	119·4	118·5	125·3	120·8	134·5	124·3	109·0	111·7	112·2	113·7	126·4	—
Weights 1968	*1,000*	*263*	*63*	*66*	*121*	*62*	*59*	*89*	*120*	*60*	*56*	*41*
1968	125·0	123·2	127·1	125·5	141·3	133·8	113·2	113·4	119·1	124·5	132·4	126·9
Weights 1969	*1,000*	*254*	*64*	*68*	*118*	*61*	*60*	*86*	*124*	*66*	*57*	*42*
1969	131·8	131·0	136·2	135·5	147·0	137·8	118·3	117·7	123·9	132·3	142·5	135·0
Weights 1970	*1,000*	*255*	*66*	*64*	*119*	*61*	*60*	*86*	*126*	*65*	*55*	*43*
1970	140·2	140·1	143·9	136·3	158·1	145·7	126·0	123·8	132·1	142·8	153·8	145·5
Weights 1971	*1,000*	*250*	*65*	*59*	*119*	*60*	*61*	*87*	*136*	*65*	*54*	*44*
1971	153·4	155·6	152·7	138·5	172·6	160·9	135·4	132·2	147·2	159·1	169·6	165·0

E. Index of Retail Prices (*cont.*)

	All Items	Food	Alcoholic Drink	Tobacco	Housing	Fuel and Light	Household Durable Goods	Clothing and Footwear	Transport and Vehicles	Miscel-laneous Goods	Services	Meals Bought and Consumed out of the Home
					16 January 1962=100							
Weights 1972	*1,000*	*251*	*66*	*53*	*121*	*60*	*58*	*89*	*139*	*65*	*52*	*46*
1972	164·3	169·4	159·0	139·5	190·7	173·4	140·5	141·8	155·9	168·0	180·5	180·3
Weights 1973	*1,000*	*248*	*73*	*49*	*126*	*58*	*58*	*89*	*135*	*65*	*53*	*46*
1973	179·4	194·9	164·2	141·2	213·1	178·3	148·7	155·1	165·0	172·6	202·4	211·0
Weights 1974	*1,000*	*253*	*70*	*43*	*124*	*52*	*64*	*91*	*135*	*63*	*54*	*51*
1974	208·2	230·0	182·1	164·8	238·2	208·8	170·8	182·3	194·3	202·7	227·2	248·3
14 January 1974	191·8	216·7	166·0	142·2	225·1	188·6	158·3	166·6	175·0	182·2	212·8	229·5
					15 January 1974=100							
Weights 1974	*1,000*	*253*	*70*	*43*	*124*	*52*	*64*	*91*	*135*	*63*	*54*	*51*
1974	108·5	106·1	109·7	115·9	105·8	110·7	107·9	109·4	111·0	111·2	106·8	108·2
Weights 1975	*1,000*	*232*	*82*	*46*	*108*	*53*	*70*	*89*	*149*	*71*	*52*	*48*
1975	134·8	133·3	135·2	147·7	125·5	147·4	131·2	125·7	143·9	138·6	135·5	132·4
Weights 1976	*1,000*	*228*	*81*	*46*	*112*	*56*	*75*	*84*	*140*	*74*	*57*	*47*
1976	157·1	159·9	159·3	171·3	143·2	182·4	144·2	139·4	166·0	161·3	159·5	157·3
Weights 1977	*1,000*	*247*	*83*	*46*	*112*	*58*	*63*	*82*	*139*	*71*	*54*	*45*
1977	182·0	190·3	183·4	209·7	161·8	211·3	166·8	157·4	190·3	188·3	173·3	185·7
Weights 1978	*1,000*	*233*	*85*	*48*	*113*	*60*	*64*	*80*	*140*	*70*	*56*	*51*
1978	197·1	203·8	196·0	226·2	173·4	227·5	182·1	171·0	207·2	206·7	192·0	207·8
Weights 1979	*1,000*	*232*	*77*	*44*	*120*	*59*	*64*	*82*	*143*	*69*	*59*	*51*
1979	223·5	228·3	217·1	247·6	208·9	250·5	201·9	187·2	243·1	236·4	213·9	239·9
Weights 1980	*1,000*	*214*	*82*	*40*	*124*	*59*	*69*	*84*	*151*	*74*	*62*	*41*
1980	263·7	255·9	261·8	290·1	269·5	313·2	226·3	205·4	288·7	276·9	262·7	290·0

Prices 11. Consumer Price Indices – Republic of Ireland 1922–80

NOTE
SOURCE: *Statistical Abstract of Ireland.*

A. 1922–47: July 1914=100

	All Items	Food	Clothing	Fuel and Light
1922	188·3	190·7	...	...
1923	184·3	188·3	...	...
1924	185·5	190·3	...	...
1925	189·8	192·5	...	...
1926	184·8	178·5	...	...
1927	174·8	170·3	...	...
1928	174·0	168·5	...	...
1929	175·8	169·0	...	...
1930	170·8	160·0	...	...
1931	160·5	147·0	...	...
1932	157·3	141·0	202·3	172·8
1933	151·0	131·3	201·5	172·8
1934	152·5	134·8	200·8	166·5
1935	155·5	139·5	199·3	171·3
1936	160·3	146·5	202·5	171·0
1937	170·5	156·0	219·8	176·8
1938	173·3	159·3	225·8	181·3
1939	177·8	163·3	230·3	187·8
1940	205·3	183·3	288·3	235·0
1941	225·8	201·5	310·3	289·0
1942	250·0	222·5	346·5	321·0
1943	281·5	247·5	420·0	334·0
1944	295·0	261·5	442·5	336·5
1945	294·5	263·5	436·0	330·5
1946	290·5	263·0	425·5	308·3
1947	306·3	284·0	434·3	304·7

B. 1948–53: August 1947=100

	All Items	Food	Clothing	Fuel and Light	Rent
1948	101·3	99·3	98·0	102·0	101·5
1949	99·5	97·8	102·3	99·5	106·0
1950	101·0	98·0	111·0	102·9	109·0
1951	109·0	104·5	130·0	114·5	110·3
1952	118·5	116·3	132·3	121·0	114·3
1953	124·7	125·0	131·0	123·0	115·0

C. 1954–1968: August 1953=100

	All Items	Food	Alcoholic Drink and Tobacco	Clothing	Fuel and Light	Housing	Household Durable Goods	Other Goods and Services
1954	100·1	99·6	...	100·0	99·9	103·0	100·3	
1955	102·7	103·6	...	100·3	103·2	106·2	101·9	
1956	107·1	104·8	...	101·8	113·8	110·9	109·9	
1957	111·5	109·2	...	102·8	121·0	115·6	115·0	
1958	116·5	118·6	...	103·3	119·4	117·8	118·0	
1959	116·5	118·1		104·0	111·3	120·3	119·4	
1960	117·0	116·5	...	105·7	109·4	124·0	122·2	
1961	120·2	120·6	129·5	106·7	113·3	128·2	112·2	124·1
1962	125·3	123·2	142·0	109·5	120·3	133·7	114·1	130·8
1963	128·4	125·0	146·9	112·1	125·1	139·8	115·7	134·6
1964	137·0	132·8	159·3	118·4	132·3	147·3	121·1	145·9
1965	143·9	140·1	168·8	121·5	132·4	156·4	124·1	153·8
1966	149·6	141·7	181·7	123·2	134·4	166·3	126·9	160·9
1967	152·9	144·4	191·3	125·0	139·1	176·4	132·4	166·4
1968	160·1	152·7	199·3	127·1	144·0	188·6	135·0	174·4
Nov. 1968	162·7	152·6	208·3	128·0	147·2	198·9	136·6	176·6

Prices 11. *continued*

D. 1969–80: November 1968=100

	All Items	Food	Alcoholic Drink	Tobacco	Clothing	Fuel and Light	Housing	Household Durable Goods	Other Goods	Transport	Services
1969	105·7	106·1	109·5	102·8	102·7	102·9	105·1	106·0	109·3	107·5	104·3
1970	114·4	114·2	118·0	108·0	111·4	112·2	114·9	114·5	123·1	116·1	113·7
1971	124·6	122·6	127·5	109·5	122·0	123·3	126·8	123·6	137·3	131·7	126·5
1972	135·4	137·1	131·7	109·6	134·0	137·8	141·5	134·0	150·4	138·6	136·4
1973	150·8	159·7	141·6	115·2	155·3	147·7	151·2	150·2	157·6	149·1	151·3
1974	176·4	183·1	155·5	124·2	187·0	222·9	164·6	180·1	190·5	178·6	172·8
1975	213·2	222·4	197·2	155·2	215·8	259·4	183·0	209·4	244·2	224·4	207·8
1976	251·6	259·2	253·4	179·1	238·8	293·9	208·9	236·1	277·7	278·3	250·3
1977	285·9	301·6	269·4	188·4	273·6	352·1	226·9	269·6	320·6	314·0	293·9
1978	307·7	331·6	286·3	196·2	305·5	364·8	201·5	296·1	348·7	333·6	332·9
1979	348·4	380·8	325·6	226·2	336·4	414·4	220·5	323·7	379·9	383·4	377·9
1980	411·9	421·5	401·1	282·7	385·3	590·9	264·0	373·1	444·6	469·0	450·9

Prices 12. Prices of Coal Delivered at Westminster School 1585–1830, and at Greenwich Hospital 1716–1828

NOTES

[1] SOURCE: Sir William Beveridge and others, *Prices and Wages in England*, vol. I (London, Longmans Green & Co., 1939), pp. 193–6 and 294–5.

[2] The London chaldron weighed between 26 and 27 cwt.

[3] Both institutions ordered coal in summer.

[4] Both series include all duties. Except during the Interregnum, these were small prior to the Great Fire of London. According to Professor Nef (*The Rise of the British Coal Industry* (London, 1932), vol. II, p. 83 note) they came to 8d–10d per (London) chaldron, and according to the Beveridge group (*op. cit.* p. 177) they were about 1/- up to 1645 and 2/- when the records restart. A tax of 3/- per chaldron was in force in the 1670's, imposed for rebuilding the London churches, and this continued for over a century afterwards. In 1694 a national tax of 5/- per chaldron was imposed, and 8/- continued to be the rate of the main duties at London up to 1778. The following changes of rate are recorded in the Greenwich accounts thereafter: (Beveridge group: *op. cit.* p. 269)

1778	8/- + 5 per cent	1804	11·67/-
1781	8/- + 10 per cent	1806	12·47/-
1786	8·83/-	1809	12·50/-
1797	8·83/- + 5 per cent	1814	9·33/-
1802	9·33/-	1823	6·00/-
1802	9·33/- + 12½ per cent		

Other minor dues included the Richmond shilling (i.e. 6d per London chaldron), metage dues of 4d per chaldron, and various others amounting together at their maximum during the Napoleonic Wars to about 8d per chaldron.

[5] Costs of carriage for the coal delivered at Westminster were around 9d–11d per chaldron in the 1590's. From 1610–42 they rose from about 2/–2/6 per chaldron, and during the eighteenth century they were about 4/–5/-. (Beveridge group: *op. cit.* p. 174.) Costs of unloading and porterage for the Greenwich coal were as follows for selected years from 1741 onwards: (Beveridge group: *op. cit.* p. 271.)

1741	4·75/- per chaldron
1749	5·02/- ,, ,,
1759	5·48/- ,, ,,
1768	5·37/- ,, ,,
1779	6·50/- ,, ,,
1791	5·89/- ,, ,,
1799	7·18/- ,, ,,
1809	8·29/- ,, ,,
1819	8·38/- ,, ,,
1827	8·54/- ,, ,,

[6] There is no indication of the quality of coal delivered at Westminster, but at Greenwich Bucksnook followed by Main Team coal was used up to 1797 (and by the brewery until 1811). From 1798 Wallsend or Hebburn (i.e. what was described in the nineteenth century as 'best') was used mainly.

(in shillings per London chaldron)

	Westminster		Westminster		Westminster		Westminster
1585	15·75	1606	17·19	1627	21·55	1672	61·13
1586	15·69	1607	18·66	1628	18·07	1673	...
1587	15·46	1608	18·64	1629	21·42	1674	27·47
1588	19·45	1609	15·91	1630	22·25	1675	...
1589	17·76	1610	15·83	1631	21·25	1676	26·00
1590	14·75	1611	15·67	1632	20·80	1677	24·36
1591	13·07	1612	16·20	1633	20·78	1678	26·40
1592	12·75	1613	18·50	1634	20·32	1679	22·81
1593	15·25	1614	18·53	1635	21·96	1680	...
1594	13·59	1615	19·25	1636	22·17	1681	...
1595	16·92	1616	19·11	1637	20·34	1682	21·00
1596	15·92	1617	15·61	1638	...	1683	...
1597	14·26	1618	15·50	1639	22·13	1684	...
1598	13·97	1619	16·86	1664	29·32	1685	20·53
1599	...	1620	16·42	1665	...	1686	...
1600	13·83	1621	15·50	1666	47·19	1687	...
1601	14·00	1622	15·50	1667	32·54	1688	...
1602	13·85	1623	...	1668	23·32	1689	...
1603	13·42	1624	...	1669	...		
1604	12·50	1625	...	1670	...		
1605	15·50	1626	19·80	1671	...		

Prices 12. *continued*

(in shillings per London chaldron)

	Westminster	Greenwich		Westminster	Greenwich
1690	...	...	1744	35·00	30·04
1691	36·27	...	1745	34·13	29·45
1692	31·92	...	1746	32·82	28·05
1693	33·08	...	1747	31·06	27·63
1694	28·58	...	1748	32·12	28·61
1695	34·40	...	1749	31·77	27·30
1696	27·35	...	1750	29·90	26·14
1697	27·70	...	1751	31·13	28·18
1698	22·04	...	1752	32·04	27·62
1699	25·00	...	1753	32·10	27·57
1700	24·30	...	1754	34·58	31·38
1701	27·77	...	1755	40·59	34·90
1702	33·21	...	1756	38·24	35·70
1703	34·83	...	1757	38·39	36·10
1704	39·03	...	1758	36·78	35·01
1705	30·38	...	1759	34·37	32·13
1706	...	...	1760	36·39	34·44
1707	27·70	...	1761	37·30	37·00
1708	33·72	...	1762	33·97	31·47
1709	32·58	...	1763	35·93	33·42
1710	30·68	...	1764	36·02	33·36
1711	32·03	...	1765	34·56	31·17
1712	30·53	...	1766	33·05	30·01
1713	31·57	...	1767	33·05	30·79
1714	30·38	...	1768	32·07	30·19
1715	28·95	...	1769	32·54	30·19
1716	29·53	30·63	1770	33·88	32·90
1717	32·03	23·81	1771	36·56	32·89
1718	32·53	29·83	1772	34·55	31·08
1719	32·08	28·54	1773	34·39	31·43
1720	28·03	26·85	1774	36·93	32·53
1721	29·33	26·58	1775	38·93	35·58
1722	28·58	25·71	1776	38·44	36·63
1723	28·08	26·10	1777	38·44	38·32
1724	28·40	26·10	1778	38·93	39·96
1725	31·03	27·19	1779	39·90	40·08
1726	28·63	25·71	1780	39·90	41·58
1727	28·45	26·54	1781	42·83	42·68
1728	30·60	28·74	1782	35·03	35·75
1729	28·47	25·00	1783	34·92	34·21
1730	36·33	28·78	1784	36·98	35·76
1731	29·19	25·86	1785	36·39	34·94
1732	27·98	26·41	1786	36·88	34·80
1733	28·84	26·78	1787	38·52	34·54
1734	29·00	27·30	1788	37·53	35·43
1735	...	27·18	1789	39·00	...
1736	29·50	27·25	1790	38·53	37·23
1737	30·12	28·37	1791	38·52	35·87
1738	30·69	...	1792	41·47	41·20
1739	33·67	31·62	1793	46·47	42·03
1740	30·76	26·49	1794	48·35	41·70
1741	30·98	27·89	1795	35·06	39·83
1742	31·63	26·74	1796	...	39·62
1743	33·88	32·65	1797	48·31	40·37

Prices 12. *continued*

(in shillings per London chaldron)

	Westminster	Greenwich			Westminster	Greenwich	
1798	58·77	...(*a*)	50·81(*b*)	1815	63·94	...(*a*)	52·32(*b*)
1799	56·70	...	54·33	1816	59·55	...	49·79
1800	50·42	...	47·76	1817	59·55	...	52·50
1801	51·34	42·70	46·78	1818	59·55	...	50·72
1802	58·67	49·30	52·87	1819	57·46	...	50·14
1803	63·10	...	54·25	1820	60·44	...	49·19
1804	65·20	51·56	54·65	1821	56·26	...	47·84
1805	...	52·90	56·14	1822	58·35	...	49·83
1806	65·20	53·25	57·49	1823	49·60	...	47·25
1807	65·20	...	58·77	1824	49·60	...	46·20
1808	70·41	58·77	65·25	1825	49·60	...	43·36
1809	72·53	58·43	64·60	1826	49·08	...	44·40
1810	...	...	64·11	1827	49·08	...	44·03
1811	68·34	54·37	59·90	1928	48·77	...	38·88
1812	71·12	...	60·54	1829	49·29	...	...
1813	71·26	...	66·32	1830	46·29	...	...
1814	69·17	...	58·73				

(*a*) This column relates to 'ordinary' coal, and continues the previous Greenwich series.

(*b*) This column relates to best coal.

Prices 13. Average Prices of Coal in London and for Export – 1788–1980

NOTES TO PART A

[1] SOURCES: 1788–1800 – *S.P.* 1830, VII (*Report of the Select Committee on the Coal Trade*, p. 7); 1805–19 – *S.P.* 1871, XVIII (*Report of the Royal Commission on Coal Supply*, committee E, appendix, p. 208); 1820–80 – *S.P.* 1881, LXXXIII; 1881–9 – *S.P.* 1890, LXVII.

[2] The London chaldron weighed between 26 and 27 cwt.

[3] The main government duty is included in the figures for 1805–19 in the source. It has been added to other figures at the following rates: (See table 7, note 4.)

1788–96	8/10	per chaldron
1797–1800	9/3	,, ,,
1820–3	9/4	,, ,,
1824–31	6/-	,, ,,

The duty was abolished after 1831.

A. Annual Average Price of Best Coals at the Ships' Side in London, 1788–1889

	per chaldron	
	s.	d.
1788	39	2¾
1790	41	7¼
1792	39	7
1793	43	10¾
1795	50	8½
1797	44	5½
1799	51	3¾
1800	61	6½
	...	...
1805	44	9(*a*)
1806	44	5
1807	45	10
1808	49	3
1809	54	6
1810	51	8
1811	47	8
1812	44	10
1813	52	5
1814	59	1
1815	46	9
1816	41	8
1817	40	4
1818	39	10
1819	41	10(*a*)
	...	...
1820	41	9
1821	42	6
1822	41	10
1823	45	1
1824	40	6
1825	39	10
1826	36	2
1827	37	4
1828	37	0
1829	33	11
1830	35	2
1831	32	4

	per ton	
	s.	d.
1832	20	10
1833	17	2
1834	19	5
1835	20	10
1836	21	10
1837	22	11
1838	23	5
1839	22	7
1840	22	6
1841	21	3
1842	20	1
1843	19	1
1844	21	9
1845	18	1
1846	16	10
1847	19	9
1848	17	1
1849	16	7
1850	16	0
1851	15	0
1852	15	5
1853	20	1
1854	22	8
1855	20	10
1856	17	10
1857	17	7
1858	17	4
1859	17	3
1860	19	0

	per ton	
	s.	d.
1861	18	5
1862	16	6
1863	17	1
1864	19	0
1865	19	1
1866	19	0
1867	19	8
1868	17	7
1869	17	8
1870	17	5
1871	18	2
1872	23	10
1873	31	3
1874	24	8
1875	22	9
1876	20	2
1877	18	5
1878	16	10
1879	16	11
1880	14	11
1881	16	5
1882	16	2
1883	17	5
1884	15	9
1885	15	9
1886	15	1
1887	15	2
1888	15	3
1889	16	8

(*a*) The figures for 1805–19 are inclusive of all duties, not merely the government duty. The minor duties came to 1/2 per chaldron in 1819.

NOTE TO PART B

SOURCES: 1831–45 – *Porter's Tables*; 1846–1980 – A. Sauerbeck, 'Prices of Commodities and the Precious Metals', *J.S.S.* (1886), continued annually thereafter in that journal by Sauerbeck and subsequently by the editor of *The Statist* until the latter ceased publication in 1967. Subsequent figures of average export values are from the *Annual Statement of Trade* and *Overseas Trade Statistics of the United Kingdom*.

B. Annual Average Price of Best Coal in London and of All Exports, 1831–1980

(per ton)

	Wallsend, Hetton in London s.	d.	All Exports f.o.b. shillings		Wallsend, Hetton in London s.	d.	All Exports f.o.b. shillings
1831	...		7·82	1874	25	0	17·21
1832	...		7·77	1875	24	0	13·28
1833	...		7·29	1876	21	0	10·93
1834	...		7·18	1877	20	0	10·17
1835	...		6·65	1878	18	0	9·46
1836	...		7·26	1879	18	0	8·77
1837	...		7·75	1880	15	6	8·95
1838	...		7·38	1881	17	0	8·97
1839	...		7·49	1882	17	0	9·14
1840	...		7·18	1883	18	0	9·35
1841	...		7·31	1884	16	6	9·29
1842	...		7·34	1885	16	6	8·95
1843	...		7·40	1886	16	0	8·45
1844	...		7·66	1887	16	0	8·32
1845	...		7·69	1888	16	6	8·41
1846	18	0	7·67	1889	17	6	10·21
1847	20	6	7·80	1890	19	0	12·62
1848	18	0	7·81	1891	19	0	12·16
1849	17	6	7·69	1892	18	6	11·04
1850	17	0	7·66	1893	19	6	9·90
1851	16	0	7·51	1894	16	6	10·50
1852	16	6	7·54	1895	15	0	9·33
1853	22	0	8·16	1896	15	0	8·85
1854	23	6	9·87	1897	15	9	8·98
1855	22	0	9·83	1898	16	9	9·92
1856	18	6	9·61	1899	18	6	10·72
1857	18	6	9·52	1900	23	6	16·75
1858	18	0	9·33	1901	20	0	13·86
1859	18	6	9·33	1902	18	6	12·29
1860	20	6	9·06	1903	16	6	11·70
1861	20	0	9·19	1904	16	3	11·13
1862	18	0	9·05	1905	15	6	10·56
1863	18	0	9·00	1906	16	6	10·90
1864	20	0	9·48	1907	19	9	12·75
1865	20	0	9·69	1908	18	0	12·77
1866	19	6	10·29	1909	17	6	11·30
1867	20	0	10·39	1910	17	3	11·72
1868	18	6	9·92	1911	17	9	11·43
1869	18	6	9·62	1912	21	9	12·70
1870	18	6	9·64	1913	21	6	13·94
1871	19	0	9·80	1914	21	3	13·65
1872	25	6	15·83	1915	30	9(*a*)	16·96
1873	32	0	20·90				

B. Annual Average Price of Best Coal in London and of All Exports, 1831–1980 (*cont.*)

(per ton)

	Best Yorks. House s.	d.	All Exports f.o.b. shillings
1916	27	6(*a*)	24·64
1917	27	6(*a*)	27·16
1918	33	7	30·6
1919	45	4	46·2
1920	32	0	79·8
1921	32	3	34·83
1922	34	5	24·16
1923	32	5	25·13
1924	27	6	23·38
1925	29	8	20·08
1926 (*b*)	(30	4)	(18·59)
1927	23	1	17·80
1928	21	5	15·67
1929	23	5	16·13
1930	24	9	16·64
1931	24	8	15·98
1932	23	5	16·27
1933	22	8	16·08
1934	20	3	16·08
1935	20	3	16·30
1936	23	1	16·98
1937	24	6	19·05
1938	25	8	21·32
1939	25	4	21·12
1940	28	1	27·23
1941	30	10	32·22
1942	32	6	34·87
1943	34	11	36·91
1944	38	10	39·19
1945	42	8	40·27
1946	45	2	40·94
1947	48	2	47·61
1948	54	9	74·07
1949	54	9	72·97
1950	53	0	73·65
1951	58	6	74·88
1952	64	11	94·38
1953	69	6	89·03
9154	62	6	86·75
1955	66	4	86·96
1956	74	3	105·41
1957	79	9	116·23
1958	82	10	105·31
1959	81	7	87·06
1960	84	5	73·40
1961	89	9	72·04
1962	88	9	85·58
1963	89	11	87·4
1964	88	8	92·3
1965	88	1	96·3
1966	88	1	92·8 ---(*c*) 94·3
1967	...(*d*)		93·1
1968	...		91·1
			£
1969	...		4·76
1970	...		5·30
1971	...		4·99
1972	...		5·55
1973	...		5·64
1974	...		11·13
1975	...		16·53
1976	...		21·33
1977	...		22·53
1978	...		22·73
1979	...		26·66
1980	...		28·76

(*a*) Approximate figures only.

(*b*) Figures for January to April only.

(*c*) This break occurs on a change of source (see note above), and is probably the result of excluding various sorts of manufactured fuel.

(*d*) A series of typical December retail prices in London is given in the *Digest of Energy Statistics* as follows, in new pence per hundredweight:

1965	59	1969	75	1973	108	1977	242
1966	66	1970	85	1974	133	1978	264
1967	66	1971	98	1975	175	1979	323
1968	70	1972	107	1976	202	1980	404

Prices 14. Index of Coal Prices – England, 1700–1830

NOTES

[1] Source: M. W. Flinn, *The History of the British Coal Industry*, vol. 2 (Oxford, 1984), table 9.4.

[2] The index is based on contract prices for various institutions, on London prices, and on some North-Eastern colliery records.

(average of 1770–9=100)

Year	Index	Year	Index	Year	Index	Year	Index	Year	Index
1700	74·8	1727	77·4	1753	85·0	1779	109·4	1805	146·2
1701	85·8	1728	81·5	1754	92·3	1780	108·5	1806	145·4
1702	98·2	1729	78·5	1755	102·5	1781	111·5	1807	148·1
1703	94·9	1730	84·7	1756	104·3	1782	101·7	1808	151·3
1704	92·1	1731	79·0	1757	101·0	1783	94·3	1809	167·7
1705	83·7	1732	79·3	1758	100·6	1784	100·7	1810	152·9
1706	78·7	1733	80·2	1759	97·8	1785	100·9	1811	162·6
1707	88·1	1734	78·6	1760	99·4	1786	99·0	1812	159·3
1708	91·1	1735	79·5	1761	100·7	1787	99·7	1813	171·9
1709	91·7	1736	78·2	1762	96·9	1788	98·2	1814	172·6
1710	91·8	1737	80·1	1763	99·6	1789	104·7	1815	158·0
1711	77·1	1738	80·4	1764	99·1	1790	105·5	1816	146·1
1712	77·9	1739	93·1	1765	92·3	1791	106·5	1817	143·6
1713	78·7	1740	87·4	1766	91·0	1792	110·6	1818	141·0
1714	77·3	1741	85·7	1767	90·3	1793	115·2	1819	138·7
1715	74·4	1742	85·0	1768	89·5	1794	123·7	1820	140·3
1716	79·1	1743	89·6	1769	91·3	1795	108·8	1821	141·7
1717	82·2	1744	89·2	1770	98·5	1796	107·3	1822	139·1
1718	83·3	1745	90·1	1771	98·8	1797	108·9	1823	141·6
1719	81·1	1746	88·2	1772	93·0	1798	128·1	1824	136·9
1720	80·2	1747	86·0	1773	91·5	1799	136·5	1825	131·7
1721	78·1	1748	84·6	1774	93·8	1800	122·6	1826	125·6
1722	77·1	1749	82·9	1775	100·9	1801	121·1	1827	129·3
1723	76·9	1750	80·9	1776	103·5	1802	128·6	1828	131·6
1724	78·1	1751	83·2	1777	107·1	1803	138·6	1829	127·0
1725	80·6	1752	84·9	1778	106·4	1804	142·4	1830	127·5
1726	79·0								

Prices 15. Indices of Average Pitmouth Value of Coal in Four Main Coalfields – Great Britain, 1805–1914

NOTES

[1] SOURCE: B. R. Mitchell, *The Economic Development of the British Coal Industry, 1800–1914* (Cambridge, 1984), table 9.3.

[2] These indices are based on average export values and on average receipts of certain collieries to 1881, and on official statistics thereafter.

(1886=100)

	North-East	Yorkshire	South Wales	Scotland
1805	51	...	...	...
1810	84	...	...	...
1815	103	...	...	...
1818	92	...	...	...
1819	123	...	...	...
1820	130	...	...	...
1821	135	...	...	...
1822	131	...	...	...
1823	127	...	...	...
1824	134	...	...	...
1825	131	...	...	...
1826	122	...	...	...
1827	123	...	...	...
1828	129	...	...	...
1829	113	...	...	...
1830	122	...	...	...
1831	98	...	...	...
1832	123	...	...	107
1833	97	120	96	107
1834	106	100	86	89
1835	111	100	84	99
1836	119	112	95	113
1837	119	131	107	131
1838	113	122	105	113
1839	120	122	107	101
1840	114	120	113	90
1841	123	113	113	107
1842	117	113	107	99
1843	119	114	108	91
1844	105	124	100	96
1845	102	116	105	133
1846	94	110	110	136
1847	109	115	112	127
1848	97	115	113	104
1849	93	113	109	102
1850	92	105	108	103
1851	85	100	106	99
1852	88	100	105	99
1853	111	111	118	134
1854	135	129	125	143
1855	130	126	123	146
1856	113	124	121	143
1857	112	113	121	125
1858	109	114	118	116
1859	107	114	115	117
1860	115	116	114	111
1861	113	120	116	106
1862	102	117	113	95
1863	104	121	111	102

	North-East	Yorkshire	South Wales	Scotland
1864	116	119	126	128
1865	119	120	128	131
1866	127	121	130	151
1867	132	125	131	129
1868	119	123	127	117
1869	117	120	124	112
1870	117	117	126	116
1871	123	117	129	135
1872	185(*a*)	188(*a*)	201(*a*)	225(*a*)
1873	245(*a*)	249(*a*)	249(*a*)	264(*a*)
1874	197	215	214	198
1875	162	176	163	155
1876	141	159	124	136
1877	129	146	114	136
1878	117	134	111	125
1879	108	125	108	116
1880	103	114	109	119
1881	106	112	113	111
1882	107	130	114	110
1883	113	115	122	129
1884	106	109	122	114
1885	103	105	114	110
1886	100	100	100	100
1887	100	98	104	99
1888	99	107	114	98
1889	117	139	155	129
1890	158	180	201	171
1891	158	171	201	159
1892	141	160	171	143
1893	126	155	146	143
1894	128	142	129	150
1895	117	126	120	132
1896	114	125	128	127
1897	120	127	132	130
1898	133	134	119	151
1899	156	152	173	186
1900	231	214	236	271
1901	193	187	228	196
1902	165	169	205	165
1903	158	157	184	155
1904	145	146	177	146
1905	143	135	171	144
1906	155	136	182	160
1907	195	166	226	219
1908	195	171	216	191
1909	167	150	210	165
1910	177	153	216	169
1911	166	154	219	169
1912	203	166	217	209
1913	235	189	232	240
1914	224	186	233	223

(*a*) The estimates for these years may be up to 10% too low.

Prices 16. Wheat Prices at Exeter 1316–1820, at Eton 1594–1820, and at Winchester, 1630–1817

NOTES

[1] SOURCES: Exeter series – Sir William Beveridge, 'A Statistical Crime of the Seventeenth Century', *Journal of Economic and Business History* (1929); Winchester series – Sir William Beveridge and others, *Prices and Wages in England*, vol. 1 (London, Longmans Green & Co., 1939), pp. 81–4; Eton series – not previously published, this series was very kindly made available to us by Lord Beveridge.

[2] All figures in the original sources were adjusted by the Beveridge group to the Winchester quarter (97 per cent of the Imperial quarter).

(in shillings per Winchester quarter)

	Exeter		Exeter		Exeter		Exeter
1316 (*a*)	15·42	1340	3·81	1364	12·09	1388	3·42
1317	8·11	1341	4·17	1365	7·48	1389	5·50
1318	4·17	1342	3·67	1366	5·80	1390	8·25
1319	5·98	1343	5·42	1367	8·02	1391	6·50
1320	6·00	1344	3·70	1368	8·42	1392	3·50
1321	9·90	1345	4·82	1369	10·12	1393	3·25
1322	8·75	1346	6·96	1370	8·92	1394	3·50
1323	7·35	1347	5·82	1371	8·52	1395	3·80
1324	6·36	1348	4·72	1372	7·42	1396	5·25
1325	4·56	1349	6·92	1373	6·25	1397	4·30
1326	3·87	1350	8·78	1374	10·02	1398	5·03
1327	4·75	1351	9·25	1375	7·75	1399	8·00
1328	6·13	1352	5·59	1376	5·32	1400	6·00
1329	6·42	1353	4·55	1377	3·92	1401	9·07
1330	7·30	1354	6·42	1378	3·75	1402	9·33
1331	8·25	1355	7·92	1379	6·42	1403	6·33
1332	6·39	1356	7·52	1380	6·42	1404	5·86
1333	5·11	1357	7·52	1381	6·42	1405	4·21
1334	4·78	1358	7·47	1382	5·50	1406	5·00
1335	4·60	1359	6·37	1383	6·40	1407	5·20
1336	3·64	1360	6·00	1384	5·00	1408	5·69
1337	2·92	1361	4·92	1385	6·40	1409	7·51
1338	...	1362	8·28	1386	6·00	1410	6·00
1339	...	1363	11·62	1387	3·50	1411	5·20

See p. 755 for footnote.

Prices 16. *continued*

(in shillings per Winchester quarter)

	Exeter		Exeter		Exeter		Exeter
1412	6·00	1455	5·55	1498	6·10	1541	8·27
1413	4·88	1456	6·55	1499	6·10	1542	7·66
1414	4·66	1457	7·14	1500	9·38	1543	9·65
1415	7·34	1458	7·86	1501	7·39	1544	12·70
1416	8·68	1459	4·70	1502	...	1545	19·10
1417	6·40	1460	7·41	1503	7·98	1546	6·46
1418	8·00	1461	8·14	1504	7·98	1547	6·67
1419	6·00	1462	4·05	1505	5·87	1548	9·33
1420	5·40	1463	4·19	1506	...	1549	15·06
1421	5·40	1464	4·80	1507	7·14	1550	15·79
1422	4·70	1465	...	1508	...	1551	20·20
1423	5·20	1466	6·46	1509	5·02	1552	12·66
1424	6·54	1467	6·96	1510	...	1553	10·03
1425	5·60	1468	6·94	1511	6·70	1554	14·51
1426	4·40	1469	7·96	1512	6·83	1555	24·77
1427	5·16	1470	6·64	1513	6·68	1556	32·41
1428	9·27	1471	7·44	1514	5·57	1557	11·47
1429	5·60	1472	5·20	1515	9·14	1558	...
1430	7·04	1473	5·82	1516	6·06	1559	20·64
1431	5·60	1474	5·12	1517	5·51	1560	22·62
1432	7·14	1475	6·15	1518	5·68	1561	15·50
1433	5·28	1476	5·26	1519	8·54	1562	26·96
1434	5·70	1477	6·78	1520	12·94	1563	20·32
1435	7·20	1478	7·54	1521	10·14	1564	21·84
1436	5·34	1479	5·58	1522	6·40	1565	27·03
1437	9·93	1480	5·46	1523	6·94	1566	12·84
1438	11·77	1481	6·15	1524	5·52	1567	14·06
1439	8·25	1482	8·55	1525	6·46	1568	17·06
1440	4·16	1483	9·00	1526	7·04	1569	18·88
1441	4·80	1484	7·28	1527	10·56	1570	...
1442	4·70	1485	5·84	1528	11·21	1571	17·38
1443	5·02	1486	6·22	1529	...	1572	18·21
1444	4·36	1487	7·67	1530	...	1573	20·47
1445	4·76	1488	6·40	1531	...	1574	21·21
1446	7·70	1489	6·31	1532	10·30	1575	29·16
1447	5·66	1490	8·83	1533	8·43	1576	...
1448	5·94	1491	5·44	1534	6·58	1577	22·40
1449	6·68	1492	4·34	1535	10·87	1578	...
1450	7·80	1493	4·97	1536	8·43	1579	...
1451	8·13	1494	5·42	1537	6·64	1580	...
1452	6·64	1495	4·86	1538	7·56	1581	24·38
1453	4·90	1496	6·07	1539	8·70	1582	21·25
1454	5·12	1497	7·51	1540	7·78	1583	...

Prices 16. *continued*

(in shillings per Winchester quarter)

	Exeter	Eton (*b*) College	Winchester (*c*) College		Exeter	Eton (*b*) College	Winchester (*c*) College		Exeter	Eton (*b*) College	Winchester (*c*) College
1584	21·21	...	...	1635	33·84	45·62	37·51	1686	30·83	30·06	31·03
1585	32·02	...	...	1636	39·08	44·34	30·94	1687	28·00	24·45	22·74
1586	40·57	...	...	1637	46·52	49·40	44·02	1688	20·50	20·17	18·95
1587	22·32	...	...	1638	40·66	37·76	30·50	1689	24·36	28·47	29·30
1588	19·60	...	...	1639	35·40	33·15	27·37	1690	28·01	26·58	23·40
1589	26·66	...	...	1640	38·32	42·68	32·00	1691	39·65	33·47	37·18
1590	20·88	...	...	1641	40·54	35·42	29·35	1692	43·29	42·67	45·92
1591	17·76	...	...	1642	44·38	...	34·17	1693	43·46	62·51	57·67
1592	22·41	...	...	1643	40·92	...	29·36	1694	24·56	34·36	34·59
1593	28·63	...	...	1644	39·53	33·83	25·02	1695	38·69	56·78	53·98
1594	38·88	32·25	...	1645	45·05	35·42	29·59	1696	57·68	44·33	49·24
1595	32·00	32·25	...	1646	50·65	54·22	48·88	1697	55·29	54·00	56·74
1596	62·94	51·59	...	1647	62·72	64·73	54·82	1698	41·25	55·04	55·55
1597	39·92	48·33	...	1648	44·01	69·25	51·94	1699	36·67	39·49	37·53
1598	19·76	30·06	...	1649	43·36	60·58	52·33	1700	33·40	30·59	32·59
1599	20·55	24·33	...	1650	53·88	60·13	48·26	1701	27·20	25·52	24·87
1600	23·83	32·76	...	1651	52·13	47·29	35·89	1702	24·90	23·76	26·52
1601	24·54	23·33	...	1652	40·89	33·01	28·97	1703	27·97	40·25	38·49
1602	...	27·94	...	1653	30·34	25·00	22·18	1704	...	26·89	26·52
1603	...	25·52	...	1654	26·47	19·64	15·80	1705	25·79	21·75	22·29
1604	...	27·64	...	1655	44·56	34·67	28·56	1706	28·01	20·92	23·03
1605	27·98	26·06	...	1656	44·84	33·54	28·98	1707	32·93	24·70	26·91
1606	25·46	30·59	...	1657	47·78	41·08	41·84	1708	55·27	47·00	48·36
1607	42·61	31·73	...	1658	43·66	59·09	46·80	1709	59·47	74·10	69·52
1608	45·58	49·91	...	1659	45·50	49·40	46·21	1710	38·63	45·92	44·98
1609	28·59	32·48	...	1660	50·78	47·52	43·25	1711	34·12	45·39	40·81
1610	28·80	27·42	...	1661	58·37	67·68	53·33	1712	37·02	30·60	35·26
1611	30·13	33·02	...	1662	42·16	46·73	33·53	1713	45·40	50·76	48·89
1612	...	37·31	...	1663	39·50	45·92	34·52	1714	30·29	30·07	31·11
1613	...	38·37	...	1664	36·76	41·39	31·78	1715	34·35	39·50	43·56
1614	31·46	30·06	...	1665	34·94	35·41	30·73	1716	32·08	37·46	38·07
1615	33·08	32·77	...	1666	30·16	25·76	22·36	1717	29·60	35·41	34·96
1616	...	35·41	...	1667	29·32	30·06	24·00	1718	27·80	27·57	25·04
1617	...	39·49	...	1668	45·07	37·61	33·99	1719	39·12	29·53	31·55
1618	37·31	32·25	...	1669	41·16	33·83	27·25	1720	36·39	31·42	31·55
1619	...	35·92	...	1670	35·17	32·78	32·00	1721	29·36	28·56	25·81
1620	22·57	23·33	...	1671	31·91	33·82	27·45	1722	30·69	27·94	28·77
1621	30·73	33·31	...	1672	34·19	33·03	27·65	1723	29·05	29·00	27·99
1622	43·10	52·11	...	1673	54·79	50·46	49·52	1724	34·57	32·25	36·15
1623	37·13	35·94	...	1674	52·11	52·10	46·36	1725	41·04	43·13	38·07
1624	36·30	41·92	...	1675	30·89	35·95	28·89	1726	30·72	31·03	29·55
1625	27·74	41·92	...	1676	30·77	28·16	28·29	1727	46·78	41·18	44·37
1626	33·44	33·53	...	1677	43·20	41·91	46·39	1728	...	42·08	44·22
1627	33·69	24·48	...	1678	39·44	49·92	45·33	1729	...	32·64	30·22
1628	32·88	27·42	...	1679	31·55	36·25	34·81	1730	...	28·16	26·96
1629	36·53	36·49	...	1680	32·00	36·54	37·50	1731	20·00	23·87	22·74
1630	54·68	58·74	48·15	1681	40·69	36·54	33·03	1732	24·46	22·06	22·94
1631	39·33	41·92	35·42	1682	37·90	37·08	34·19	1733	29·22	24·70	24·68
1632	35·02	46·23	34·91	1683	36·21	30·59	32·37	1734	36·53	33·01	31·10
1633	41·53	46·75	39·75	1684	36·00	40·78	43·21	1735	34·67	34·14	33·19
1634	38·00	43·50	38·62	1685	25·12	29·01	26·21	1736	28·50	32·42	26·91

Prices 16. *continued*

(in shillings per Winchester quarter)

	Exeter	Eton (*b*) College	Win- chester (*c*) College		Exeter	Eton (*b*) College	Win- chester (*c*) College		Exeter	Eton (*b*) College	Win- chester (*c*) College
1737	27·68	29·83	25·94	1765	40·17	39·04	38·35	1793	51·46	45·98	51·17
1738	28·50	27·94	26·50	1766	50·23	46·29	51·60	1794	60·97	57·98	63·08
1739	40·84	34·73	36·39	1767	46·73	52·96	51·46	1795	80·67	85·16	99·83
1740	50·74	48·73	50·20	1768	40·50	41·30	40·72	1796	56·42	54·96	57·25
1741	29·34	28·16	26·64	1769	38·85	35·30	35·00	1797	58·36	56·78	64·75
1742	24·11	22·74	20·92	1770	44·85	44·71	43·37	1798	60·47	51·34	56·83
1743	22·00	19·49	18·13	1771	45·83	49·17	49·79	1799	99·51	98·45	112·00
1744	22·50	20·16	18·55	1772	49·81	54·37	54·94	1800	119·15	138·32	148·50
1745	28·97	28·77	26·22	1773	46·42	50·76	49·37	1801	64·80	67·04	83·75
1746	33·16	29·38	28·03	1774	50·89	52·56	56·34	1802	59·32	57·38	61·75
1747	29·45	27·64	26·98	1775	41·69	39·04	37·37	1803	55·65	53·76	57·04
1748	29·08	29·83	28·58	1776	44·64	40·26	40·79	1804	82·60	76·10	100·50
1749	29·80	27·80	26·78	1777	49·65	45·92	46·54	1805	82·91	76·10	82·50
1750	31·92	26·96	27·61	1778	36·59	34·06	34·62	1806	82·47	78·52	86·21
1751	37·84	37·76	34·93	1779	35·23	33·46	34·34	1807	71·52	66·22	76·50
1752	36·75	35·20	34·59	1780	48·11	47·52	49·78	1808	86·30	88·79	96·00
1753	31·15	32·70	33·19	1781	49·98	44·33	48·07	1809	106·92	105·10	119·00
1754	28·69	25·52	25·94	1782	52·90	52·80	51·73	1810	110·50	94·22	104·50
1755	36·39	29·23	30·40	1783	46·50	47·89	48·59	1811	119·73	112·34	134·50
1756	51·91	49·17	49·92	1784	44·04	45·54	44·45	1812	119·90	115·97	128·25
1757	36·77	43·52	42·12	1785	45·78	39·87	39·56	1813	81·30	85·77	84·08
1758	30·39	34·67	31·24	1786	42·50	38·30	39·42	1814	71·20	74·29	75·00
1759	29·40	29·17	29·00	1787	45·84	45·54	46·76	1815	73·87	65·23	69·00
1760	34·12	27·41	28·59	1788	50·10	46·90	48·13	1816	111·79	101·47	122·00
1761	27·96	28·39	28·59	1789	54·11	50·98	56·48	1817	95·78	92·41	96·00
1762	29·92	30·36	30·54	1790	48·05	48·95	52·33	1818	78·54	77·92	...
1763	36·79	35·28	37·93	1791	40·35	38·67	42·22	1819	73·69	70·67	...
1764	37·92	42·67	39·12	1792	49·10	48·72	51·85	1820	61·09	62·82	...

(*a*) Years beginning at Michaelmas.
(*b*) Means of twice-yearly quotations, adjusted to middling quality wheat by the Beveridge group by reducing the original figures by 9.4 per cent.

(*c*) Means of four quotations each year, adjusted to middling quality wheat by the Beveridge group by reducing the original figures by 9·0 per cent.

Prices 17. Average Prices of British Corn – England & Wales 1771–1980

NOTES

[1] SOURCES: 1771–1839 – *S.P.* 1843, LIII; 1840–1979 – *Abstract*. The original source, from which the 1980 figures are derived, is the *London Gazette* (though the quotations there up to 1824 were converted into Imperial quarters).

[2] The prices are based on statutory returns from a large number of towns in the British Isles. Before 1801 Ireland, and after 1922 Southern Ireland, are excluded.

[3] Subsidies, payments under the Cereal Deficiency Payments Scheme, etc. are excluded.

(per Imperial quarter)

Calendar Year	Wheat s.	Wheat d.	Barley s.	Barley d.	Oats s.	Oats d.
1771	48	7	26	5	17	2
1772	52	3	26	1	16	8
1773	52	7	29	2	17	8
1774	54	3	29	4	18	4
1775	49	10	26	9	17	0
1776	39	4	20	9	15	5
1777	46	11	21	1	16	1
1778	43	3	23	4	15	7
1779	34	8	20	1	14	5
1780	36	9	17	6	13	2
1781	46	0	17	8	14	1
1782	49	3	23	2	15	7
1783	54	3	31	3	20	5
1784	50	4	28	8	18	10
1785	43	1	24	9	17	8
1786	40	0	25	1	18	6
1787	42	5	23	4	17	2
1788	46	4	22	8	16	1
1789	52	9	23	6	16	6
1790	54	9	26	3	19	5
1791	48	7	26	10	18	1
1792	43	0	...		16	9
1793	49	3	31	1	20	6
1794	52	3	31	9	21	3
1795	75	2	37	5	24	5
1796	78	7	35	4	21	10
1797	53	9	27	2	16	3
1798	51	10	29	0	19	5
1799	69	0	36	2	27	6
1800	113	10	59	10	39	4
1801	119	6	68	6	37	0
1802	69	10	33	4	20	4
1803	58	10	25	4	21	6
1804	62	3	31	0	24	3
1805	89	9	44	6	28	4
1806	79	1	38	8	27	7
1807	75	4	39	4	28	4
1808	81	4	43	5	33	4
1809	97	4	47	0	31	5
1810	106	5	48	1	28	7
1811	95	3	42	3	27	7
1812	126	6	66	9	44	6
1813	109	9	58	6	38	6
1814	74	4	37	4	25	8
1815	65	7	30	3	23	7
1816	78	6	33	11	27	2
1817	96	11	49	4	32	5
1818	86	3	53	10	32	5
1819	74	6	45	9	28	2
1820	67	10	33	10	24	2
1821	56	1	26	0	19	6
1822	44	7	21	10	18	1
1823	53	4	31	6	22	11
1824	63	11	36	4	24	10
1825	68	6	40	0	25	8
1826	58	8	34	4	26	8
1827	58	6	37	7	28	2
1828	60	5	32	10	22	6
1829	66	3	32	6	22	9
1830	64	3	32	7	24	5
1831	66	4	38	0	25	4
1832	58	8	33	1	20	5
1833	52	11	27	6	18	5
1834	46	2	29	0	20	11
1835	39	4	29	11	22	0
1836	48	6	32	10	23	1
1837	55	10	30	4	23	1
1838	64	7	31	5	22	5
1839	70	8	39	6	25	11
1840	66	4	36	5	25	8
1841	64	4	32	10	22	5
1842	57	3	27	6	19	3
1843	50	1	29	6	18	4
1844	51	3	33	8	20	7
1845	50	10	31	8	22	6
1846	54	8	32	8	23	8
1847	69	9	44	2	28	8
1848	50	6	31	6	20	6
1849	44	3	27	9	17	6
1850	40	3	23	5	16	5
1851	38	6	24	9	18	7
1852	40	9	28	6	19	1
1853	53	3	33	2	21	0
1854	72	5	36	0	27	11
1855	74	8	34	9	27	5
1856	69	2	41	1	25	2
1857	56	4	42	1	25	0
1858	44	2	34	8	24	6
1859	43	9	33	6	23	2
1860	53	3	36	7	24	5
1861	55	4	36	1	23	9
1862	55	5	35	1	22	7
1863	44	9	33	11	21	2
1864	40	2	29	11	20	1
1865	41	10	29	9	21	10
1866	49	11	37	5	24	7
1867	64	5	40	0	26	0
1868	63	9	43	0	28	1
1869	48	2	39	5	26	0
1870	46	11	34	7	22	10

Prices 17. *continued*

Calendar Year	Wheat (per Imperial quarter) s.	d.	Barley s.	d.	Oats s.	d.
1871	56	8	36	2	25	2
1872	57	0	37	4	23	2
1873	58	8	40	5	25	5
1874	55	9	44	11	28	10
1875	45	2	38	5	28	8
1876	46	2	35	2	26	3
1877	56	9	39	8	25	11
1878	46	5	40	2	24	4
1879	43	10	34	0	21	9
1880	44	4	33	1	23	1
1881	45	4	31	11	21	9
1882	45	1	31	2	21	10
1883	41	7	31	10	21	5
1884	35	8	30	8	20	3
1885	32	10	30	1	20	7
1886	31	0	26	7	19	0
1887	32	6	25	4	16	3
1888	31	10	27	10	16	9
1889	29	9	25	10	17	9
1890	31	11	28	8	18	7
1891	37	0	28	2	20	0
1892	30	3	26	2	19	10
1893	26	4	25	7	18	9
1894	22	10	24	6	17	1
1895	23	1	21	11	14	6
1896	26	2	22	11	14	9
1897	30	2	23	6	16	11
1898	34	0	27	2	18	5
1899	25	8	25	7	17	0
1900	26	11	24	11	17	7
1901	26	9	25	2	18	5
1902	28	1	25	8	20	2
1903	26	9	22	8	17	2
1904	28	4	22	4	16	4
1905	29	8	24	4	17	4
1906	28	3	24	2	18	4
1907	30	7	25	1	18	10
1908	32	0	25	10	17	10
1909	36	11	26	10	18	11
1910	31	8	23	1	17	4
1911	31	8	27	3	18	10
1912	34	9	30	8	21	6
1913	31	8	27	3	19	1
1914	34	11	27	2	20	11
1915	52	10	37	4	30	2
1916	58	5	53	6	33	5
1917	75	9	64	9	49	10
1918	72	10	59	0	49	4
1919	72	11	75	9	52	5
1920	80	10	89	5	56	10

Calendar Year	Wheat (per Imperial quarter) s.	d.	Barley s.	d.	Oats s.	d.
1921	71	6	52	2	34	2
1922	47	10	40	1	29	1
			(per cwt)			
1923	9	10	9	5	9	7
1924	11	6	13	1	9	9
1925	12	2	11	9	9	9
1926	12	5	10	4	9	0
1927	11	6	11	9	9	0
1928	10	0	11	0	10	5
1929	9	10	9	11	8	10
1930	8	0	7	11	6	2
1931	5	9	7	11	6	3
1932	5	11	7	7	7	0
1933	5	4	7	11	5	7
1934	4	10	8	8	6	3
1935	5	2	7	11	6	8
1936	7	2	8	3	6	4
1937	9	4	10	11	8	7
1938	6	9	10	2	7	7
1939	5	0	8	10	6	11
1940	10	0	18	2	13	4
1941	14	8	24	0	14	8
1942	15	11	45	8	14	11
1943	16	3	31	5	15	8
1944	14	11	26	5	16	3
1945	14	5	24	5	16	5
1946	14	10	24	3	16	3
1947	16	9	24	0	18	3
1948	21	0	26	10	20	10
1949	23	3	25	10	21	0
1950	25	10	27	11	21	7
1951	28	8	38	10	26	2
1952	29	7	32	7	26	9
1953	31	2	30	1	24	7
1954	28	3	25	9	22	7
1955	22	11	26	0	26	3
1956	25	6	25	8	24	8
1957	21	7	23	2	22	10
1958	21	9	22	11	23	10
1959	21	0	22	7	22	7
1960	21	4	21	3	22	6
1961	20	7	19	10	19	5
1962	21	10	23	0	23	0

Prices 17. *continued*

	Wheat	Barley	Oats
	(in £ per cwt)		
1963	1·05	1·03	1·05
1964	1·10	1·06	1·07
1965	1·08	1·09	1·06
1966	1·09	1·055	1·065
1967	1·10	1·05	1·01
1968	1·12	1·065	0·99
1969	1·16	1·095	1·005
1970	1·34	1·36	1·15
1971	1·245	1·275	1·13
1972	1·48	1·37	1·12

	Wheat	Barley	Oats
1973	2·56	2·34	2·03
1974	3·12	3·04	2·80
1975	2·96	3·02	2·86
1976	3·83	3·88	3·55
1977	4·13	3·85	3·66
1978	4·43	4·05	3·65
1979	4·94	4·67	4·51
1980	4·93	4·61	4·77

Prices 18. Raw Cotton Prices – Great Britain 1706–1966

NOTES TO PART A

[1] SOURCE: Thomas Tooke, *A History of Prices* (London, 1838–58), vol. II, pp. 401–2. These prices are stated to be drawn from *Prince's Price Current*.

[2] According to T. Ellison, *The Cotton Trade of Great Britain* (London, 1886), the price range of West Indian cotton in the following periods was:

1771–5	9½d to 14d
1776–80	16d to 25d
1781	19d to 48d

[3] E. Baines, *A History of the Cotton Manufacture* (London, 1835) gives a different series of prices, taken from circulars of Messrs George Holt & Co. of Liverpool, from 1806 for Bowed Georgia and Pernambuco:

	Upland (i.e. Bowed Georgia)	Pernambuco
1806	15 to 21½	23½ to 29
1807	15½ to 19	24½ to 26½
1808	15½ to 36	25½ to 42
1809	14 to 34	22½ to 38
1810	14½ to 22½	23 to 29
1811	12½ to 16	18 to 23½
1812	13 to 23½	19 to 27½
1813	21 to 30	24 to 34
1814	23 to 37	28½ to 41
1815	18 to 25½	25½ to 37
1816	15 to 21	23 to 30
1817	16½ to 23½	22 to 27¾
1818	16½ to 22	22 to 27
1819	10 to 19¾	16 to 23½
1820	8 to 13¾	11½ to 18½

A. Highest and Lowest Prices in Each Year, West Indies, American and Brazilian, 1782–1820

(old) pence per lb.

	West Indies, Surinam and Berbice	Bowed Georgia	Pernambuco
1782	20 to 42	—	—
1783	13 to 36	—	—
1784	12 to 25	—	—
1785	14 to 28	—	—
1786	22 to 42	—	—
1787	19 to 34	—	—
1788	14 to 33	—	18 to 31
1789	12 to 22	—	16 to 22
1790	12 to 21	—	19 to 22
1791	13 to 30	—	18 to 31
1792	20 to 30	—	22 to 30
1793	12 to 27	13 to 22	21 to 27
1794	13 to 26	12 to 18	18 to 25
1795	15 to 30	15 to 27	21 to 30
1796	19 to 30	12 to 29	22 to 30
1797	17 to 40	12 to 37	23 to 41
1798	25 to 40	22 to 45	37 to 41
1799	18 to 55	17 to 60	29 to 52
1800	20 to 38	16 to 36	33 to 37
1801	21 to 30	17 to 38	32 to 36
1802	15 to 33	12 to 38	24 to 35
1803	14 to 27	8 to 15	24 to 29
1804	12 to 28	10 to 18	21 to 30
1805	17 to 28	14 to 19	23 to 30
1806	14 to 26	12 to 15	20 to 24
1807	14 to 22	10 to 14	21 to 23
1808	14 to 33	9 to 30	21 to 33
1809	14 to 36	10 to 18	20 to 34
1810	17 to 27	10 to 19	21 to 27
1811	9 to 21	7 to 14	14 to 22
1812	11 to 18	11 to 14	17 to 20
1813	12 to 30	16 to 26	23 to 34
1814	22 to 34	22 to 30	26 to 36
1815	18 to 32	14 to 23	22 to 33
1816	16 to 24	15 to 20	22 to 29
1817	18 to 25	17 to 22	21 to 25
1818	15 to 26	16 to 22	21½ to 26
1819	11 to 23	11 to 19	16½ to 23
1820	8 to 17	8 to 14	12 to 18

NOTES TO PART B

[1] Sources: 1801–1902 – *S.P.* 1903, LXVIII; 1903–66 – A. Sauerbeck, 'Prices of Commodities and the Precious Metals', *J.R.S.S.* (1904) and subsequent issues, being continued by the editor of *The Statist* until that journal ceased publication in 1967.

[2] The term 'middling American' is used in *S.P.* 1903, LXVIII though this is an anachromism for the first half of the nineteenth century, until the establishment of the Liverpool Universal Standards. The contemporary designation 'upland' or 'bowed Georgia' does, however, correspond to the later 'middling American' reasonably closely.

B. Average Prices of Upland or Middling American, 1801–1966

(old) pence per lb.

Year	Price	Year	Price	Year	Price	Year	Price
1801	18·00	1846	4·88	1891	4·69	1936	6·70
1802	16·00	1847	6·13	1892	4·19	1937	6·43
1803	12·50	1848	4·13	1893	4·63	1938	4·93
1804	14·00	1849	5·13	1894	3·81	1939	5·95
1805	16·50	1850	7·00	1895	3·81	1940	8·10
1806	18·25	1851	5·50	1896	4·32	1941	9·14
1807	14·50	1852	5·31	1897	3·94	1942	8·83
1808	22·00	1853	5·75	1898	3·31	1943	7·83
1809	20·00	1854	5·38	1899	3·56	1944	11·32
1810	15·25	1855	5·63	1900	5·50	1945	12·75
1811	12·50	1856	6·31	1901	4·75	1946	14·87
1812	16·75	1857	7·75	1902	4·88	1947	21·21
1813	23·00	1858	6·88	1903	6·03	1948	23·23
1814	29·50	1859	6·75	1904	6·60	1949	24·85
1815	20·75	1860	6·25	1905	5·09	1950	36·15
1816	18·25	1861	8·56	1906	5·95	1951	46·01
1817	20·13	1862	17·25	1907	6·55	1952	38·92
1818	20·00	1863	23·25	1908	5·72	1953	31·83
1819	13·50	1864	27·50	1909	6·33	1954	32·72
1820	11·50	1865	19·00	1910	8·00	1955	31·70
1821	9·50	1866	15·50	1911	7·04	1956	26·95
1822	8·25	1867	10·88	1912	6·45	1957	25·35
1823	8·25	1868	10·50	1913	7·01	1958	24·21
1824	8·50	1869	12·13	1914	6·41	1959	21·49
1825	11·63	1870	9·94	1915	5·87	1960	21·66
1826	6·75	1871	8·56	1916	9·00	1961	23·27
1827	6·50	1872	10·56	1917	16·55	1962	23·66
1828	6·38	1873	9·00	1918	22·30	1963	22·80
1829	5·75	1874	8·00	1919	19·65	1964	22·48
1830	6·88	1875	7·38	1920	23·14	1965	22·49
1831	6·00	1876	6·25	1921	9·40	1966	21·70
1832	6·63	1877	6·31	1922	12·10		
1833	8·50	1878	6·13	1923	15·25		
1834	8·63	1879	6·31	1924	16·26		
1835	10·25	1880	6·94	1925	12·64		
1836	9·88	1881	6·44	1926	9·40		
1837	7·00	1882	6·63	1927	9·54		
1838	7·00	1883	5·75	1928	10·92		
1839	7·88	1884	6·00	1929	10·26		
1840	6·00	1885	5·63	1930	7·49		
1841	6·25	1886	5·13	1931	5·90		
1842	5·38	1887	5·50	1932	5·24		
1843	4·63	1888	5·56	1933	5·54		
1844	4·88	1889	5·94	1934	6·68		
1845	4·13	1890	6·00	1935	6·71		

Prices 19. Average Value of Cotton Piece Goods Exported – United Kingdom 1821–1961

NOTES

[1] Sources: 1821–84 – T. Ellison, *The Cotton Trade of Great Britain* (London, 1886), pullout table 2; 1885–1961 – *Annual Statement of Trade*.

[2] Quantities exported have been recorded in various units, and it is difficult, if not impossible, to achieve a uniform series.

(pence per linear yard)

Year	Value	Year	Value	Year	Value	Year	Value
1821	11·73	1860	3·49	1898	2·20	1935	4·71
1822	10·96	1861	3·38	1899	2·24	1936	4·86
1823	10·32	1862	4·07	1900	2·50	1937	5·31
1824	10·06	1863	5·28	1901	2·53	1938	5·30
1825	10·15	1864	6·01	1902	2·49	1939	5·25
1826	8·87	1865	5·34	1903	2·57	1940	7·38
1827	8·50	1866	5·39	1904	2·75	1941	8·48
1828	8·24	1867	4·50	1905	2·74	1942	11·03
1829	7·46	1868	4·05	1906	2·89	1943	12·21
1830	7·62	1869	4·18	1907	3·09	1944	12·45
1831	6·92	1870	3·90	1908	3·05	1945	14·71
1832	5·99	1871	3·73	1909	2·86	1946	17·57
1833	6·02	1872	3·97	1910	3·14	1947	21·12
1834	6·10	1873	3·86	1911	3·26	1948	25·69
1835	6·53	1874	3·63	1912	3·18	1949	26·89
1836	6·47	1875	3·61	1913	3·32	1950	28·28
1837	5·75	1876	3·28	1914	3·31	1951	35·85
1838	5·41	1877	3·26	1915	3·27	1952	32·91
1839	5·37	1878	3·17	1916	4·06	1953	28·83
1840	4·95	1879	3·01	1917	5·44	1954	30·05
1841	4·79	1880	3·06	1918	8·99	1955	29·79
1842	4·21	1881	2·95	1919	12·20	1956	26·42
1843	3·96	1882	3·03	1920	(16·32)(*a*)	1957	27·49
1844	4·04	1883	2·92	1921	10·83	1958	31·15
1845	3·96	1884	2·81	1922	7·93	1959	30·35
1846	3·76	1885	2·65	1923	7·67	1960	31·66
1847	4·13	1886	2·48	1924	8·03	1961	33·57
1848	3·44	1887	2·53	1925	7·80		
1849	3·37	1888	2·50	1926	7·10		
1850	3·63	1889	2·47	1927	6·30		
1851	3·43	1890	2·54	1928	6·49		
1852	3·41	1891	2·56	1929	6·33		
1853	3·60	1892	2·40	1930	5·91		
1854	3·33	1893	2·44	1931	5·00		
1855	3·24	1894	2·27	1932	4·55		
1856	3·36	1895	2·23	1933	4·56		
1857	3·49	1896	2·49	1934	4·64		
1858	3·31	1897	2·29				
1859	3·46						

(*a*) Exports were measured in square yards only in 1920. The 1921 ratio between square and linear yards has been used to convert the 1920 figure to linear yards in order to calculate this figure. The 1920 average value in pence per square yard was 17·08.

Prices 20. Prices of Iron – Great Britain 1801–1968

NOTES TO PART A

[1] SOURCES: Midland Forge Pig Iron – *S.P.* 1833 (evidence of Barclay to the Select Committee on Manufactures); Bar Iron – G. R. Porter, *The Progress of the Nation* (London, 2nd edition, 1847), p. 586.

[2] T. S. Ashton, quoting these pig iron figures, wrote: 'though ... there was a tendency in times of bad trade for individuals to break away from the associations and to sell at something below official values ... the figures ... may be taken as a rough indication of industrial vicissitudes'. (*Iron and Steel in the Industrial Revolution* (Manchester, 1924), pp. 155–6.)

[3] *The Progress of the Nation* (London, edition of F. W. Hirst, 1912) gives the following prices of merchant bars at Liverpool:

	£	s.	d.
1880	5	15	0
1890	6	0	0
1900	9	10	0

A. Midland Forge Pig Iron and English Merchant Bar Iron, 1801–45

(per ton)

	Midland Forge Pig Iron £ s. d.	English Merchant Bar Iron at Liverpool £ s. d.		Midland Forge Pig Iron £ s. d.	English Merchant Bar Iron at Liverpool £ s. d.
1801	6 15 0	...	1824	5 0 0	8 15 0
1802	6 0 0	...	1825	7 10 0	14 0 0
1803	6 0 0	...	1826	5 0 0	11 0 0
1804	5 16 6	...	1827	4 10 0	10 0 0
1805	6 8 0	...	1828	4 0 0	9 0 0
1806	6 15 0	17 10 0	1829	3 12 6	7 15 0
1807	6 1 3	16 0 0	1830	3 8 9	6 12 6
1808	6 5 0	15 0 0	1831	...	6 5 0
1809	6 5 0	15 10 0	1832	...	6 5 0
1810	6 6 0	14 10 0	1833	...	6 5 0
1811	6 5 0	15 0 0	1834	...	7 15 0
1812	5 10 0	14 0 0	1835	...	6 10 0
1813	5 2 6	13 0 0	1836	...	10 10 0
1814	6 0 0	13 0 0	1837	...	10 10 0
1815	5 0 0	13 5 0	1838	...	9 15 0
1816	3 15 0	11 10 0	1839	...	10 5 0
1817	4 5 0	8 15 0	1840	...	9 0 0
1818	5 10 0	13 0 0	1841	...	8 0 0
1819	6 2 6	12 10 0	1842	...	6 10 0
1820	4 10 0	11 0 0	1843	...	5 5 0
1821	4 0 0	9 0 0	1844	...	4 15 0
1822	3 15 0	8 0 0	1845	...	6 10 0
1823	4 0 0	8 10 0			

NOTES TO PART B

[1] Sources: Scottish Pig Iron and Common Bars – A. Sauerbeck, 'Prices of Commodities and the Precious Metals', in the *J.S.S.* (1886) continued annually thereafter in the same source by Sauerbeck and subsequently by the editor of *The Statist*; Cleveland Pig Iron and steel billets – *S.P.* 1903, LXVIII up to 1902, and British Iron and Steel Federation/Iron and Steel Board, *Statistical Year Book* (later *Annual Statistics*) thereafter.

[2] R. Meade, *The Coal and Iron Industries of the United Kingdom* (London, 1882), p. 741, gives prices of Scottish pig iron back to 1830 differing from Sauerbeck's for the overlap period. They are as follows:

	s.	d.		s.	d.		s.	d.
1830	100	0	1841	60	0	1852	45	4
1831	90	0	1842	50	0	1853	61	6
1832	90	0	1843	56	0	1854	79	9
1833	80	0	1844	54	9	1855	79	9
1834	85	0	1845	...		1856	70	9
1835	90	0	1846	...		1857	69	2
1836	135	0	1847	...		1858	54	5
1837	90	0	1848	44	5	1859	51	11
1838	80	0	1849	46	1	1860	53	9
1839	90	0	1850	44	5	1861	49	3
1840	75	0	1851	40	3	1862	53	0

[3] G. R. Porter, *The Progress of the Nation* (London, 2nd edition, 1847), p. 586, also gives a different series of Scottish pig iron prices for part of this period, as follows:

	s.	d.		s.	d.		s.	d.
1835	82	6	1838	90	0	1841	67	6
1836	133	0	1839	85	0	1842	50	0
1837	92	0	1840	78	0	1843 (Jan.)	55	0

(The figure for 1843 is given as 45/- in the 1847 edition, but was subsequently corrected.)

[4] Indices for steel, then iron and steel, prices are given after the 1969 issue of *Annual Statistics* as follows (1975=100):

1966	35·6	1971	48·1	1976	119·6
1967	36·0	1972	50·7	1977	141·9
1968	36·3	1973	55·5	1978	154·2
1969	38·1	1974	77·3	1979	167·6
1970	44·1	1975	100	1980	180·5

B. Scottish and Cleveland Pig Iron and Common Bar Iron, 1846–1968 and Steel Billets, 1923–68

(per ton)

	Scottish Pig Iron		Cleveland No. 3 Pig Iron		Common Bars		
	s.	d.	s.	d.	£	s.	d.
1846	67	3	...		9	10	0
1847	65	4	...		9	15	0
1848	40	4	...		7	0	0
1849	45	6	...		6	5	0
1850	44	2	...		5	17	6
1851	39	9	...		5	10	0
1852	45	1	...		6	5	0
1853	62	3	...		9	5	0
1854	79	8	...		10	0	0
1855	70	9	...		8	10	0
1856	72	6	...		8	17	6
1857	69	2	...		8	5	0
1858	54	4	...		7	0	0
1859	51	9	...		6	15	0
1860	53	6	...		6	10	0
1861	49	3	...		6	0	0
1862	53	0	...		6	5	0
1863	55	9	...		7	0	0
1864	57	3	...		8	5	0
1865	54	9	48	1	7	15	0
1866	60	6	49	8	7	5	0
1867	53	6	44	11	6	15	0
1868	52	9	42	11	6	7	6
1869	53	3	43	10	6	15	0
1870	54	4	46	11	7	7	6
1871	58	11	47	2	7	12	6
1872	101	10	65	4	11	0	0
1873	117	3	98	5	12	10	0
1874	87	6	70	1	10	5	0
1875	65	9	53	4	8	7	6
1876	58	6	46	7	7	5	0
1877	54	4	42	0	6	15	0
1878	48	5	38	10	5	12	6
1879	47	0	34	11	5	15	0
1880	54	6	41	7	6	15	0
1881	49	1	38	4	5	15	0
1882	49	4	42	8	6	5	0
1883	46	9	39	11	5	15	0
1884	42	1	36	5	5	2	6
1885	41	10	33	7	4	17	6
1886	39	11	30	9	4	12	6
1887	42	3	33	0	4	12	6
1888	39	11	32	6	4	17	6
1889	47	9	38	3	6	5	0
1890	49	7	47	8	6	7	6
1891	47	2	40	5	5	12	6
1892	41	10	38	5	5	10	0
1893	42	4	34	6	5	0	0
1894	42	8	35	3	4	17	6
1895	44	5	35	3	4	17	6
1896	46	10	37	6	5	0	0
1897	45	4	40	0	5	5	0
1898	47	2	40	11	5	10	0
1899	63	9	53	0	7	5	0
1900	69	4	68	1	9	0	0
1901	53	9	47	2	6	10	0
1902	54	6	46	10	6	2	6
1903	52	3	46	7	6	5	0
1904	51	5	42	10	6	2	6
1905	53	6	46	6	6	10	0
1906	58	9	51	4	7	5	0
1907	63	6	55	10	7	10	0
1908	56	1	50	2	6	15	0
1909	55	1	48	7	6	10	0
1910	56	1	50	6	6	10	0
1911	53	5	48	4	6	7	6
1912	64	2	53	3	7	7	6
1913	65	6	60	0	7	15	0

Prices 20. *continued*

B. Scottish and Cleveland Pig Iron and Common Bar Iron, 1846–1968 and Steel Billets, 1923–68 (*cont.*)

(per ton)

	Scottish Pig Iron		Cleveland No. 3 Pig Iron		Common Bars			Steel Billets (soft, basic)		
	s.	d.	s.	d.	£	s.	d.	£	s.	d.
1914	57	1	51	2	7	0	0		...	
1915	71	2	60	8	10	10	0		...	
1916	90	0	82	10	13	15	0		...	
1917	95	7	97	3	13	15	0		...	
1918	101	0	113	8	14	0	0		...	
1919	143	1	145	0	19	6	8		...	
1920	214	11	206	0	28	6	8		...	
1921	168	6	141	11	19	2	6		...	
1922	99	10	86	4	11	4	0		...	
1923	108	0	99	11	11	17	6	8	8	8
1924	96	8	90	1	12	10	0	7	19	5
1925	83	4	73	0	11	17	6	7	5	1
1926	87	2	80	7	11	10	0	6	14	11
1927	80	5	71	2	11	5	0	6	12	1
1928	69	9	63	1	9	18	9	6	5	0
1929	74	0	65	5	9	15	0	6	10	3
1930	76	0	63	11	9	19	4½	6	2	9
1931	71	0	54	5	10	1	10½	5	6	4
1932	68	2	52	2	10	0	0	5	5	5
1933	66	0	51	2	9	13	9	5	6	11
1934	69	6	55	10	9	10	7½	5	10	2½
1935	70	6	58	10	9	12	6	5	10	0
1936	78	6	61	9	10	3	9	6	0	2½
1937	104	6	72	9 (*a*)	12	6	9	7	6	8
1938	118	0	109	0	13	5	0	8	7	6
1939	104	3	100	7	12	7	6	7	15	10
1940	104	10	116	4	14	6	3	10	7	11
1941	123	0	128	0	15	12	6	12	10	0
1942	123	0	128	0	15	12	6	12	10	0
1943	123	0	128	0	15	12	6	12	10	0
1944	123	0	128	0	16	10	0	12	10	0
1945	139	11	140	6	18	0	0	12	10	0
1946	167	0	165	6	19	12	6	12	19	5
1947	176	9	175	5	20	8	9	13	6	3
1948	194	6	193	6	21	5	0	14	4	7
1949	228	11	204	7	20	0	0	16	8	2
1950	239	6	209	1	20	0	0	17	1	6
1951	252	1	221	10	21	17	6	19	3	6
1952	291	10	255	8	26	16	0	25	3	2
1953	328	9	274	10	28	7	6	26	0	11
1954	344	8	296	3	31	5	0	26	2	0
1955	372	4	324	7	38	17	6	26	9	1
1956	428	2	350	5	43	7	6	28	16	4
1957	464	6	401	0	45	0	0	32	1	5
1958	464	6	401	0	45	0	0	33	7	0
1959	464	6	401	0	45	0	0	32	13	9
1960	469	4	423	0	43	5	0	32	5	6
1961	470	0	426	0	43	0	0	32	8	11
1962	488	4	447	0	44	2	6	32	19	2
1963	488	3	445	2	44	0	0	33	0	6
1964	492	0	449	0	44	3	0	32	12	9
1965	492	0	449	0	44	3	0	32	14	10
1966	507	0	464	0	46	14	0	33	15	4
1967	...					...		34	1	6
1968	...		435	0		...		34	1	6

(*a*) Average of first three quarters only.

Prices 21. Raw Wool Prices – Great Britain 1706–1980

NOTE TO PART A

SOURCES: Anon. (Sir Joseph Banks), *The Propriety of Allowing a Qualified Exportation of Wool* (London, 1782), pp. 83–4.

A. Lincoln Long, per tod of 28 lb., 1706–81

	s.	d.		s.	d.		s.	d.		s.	d.
1706	17	6	1728	18	0	1746	17	0	1764	20	0
1707	16	6	1729	18	0	1747	17	3	1765	21	0
			1730	19	0	1748	18	6	1766	21	6
1712	15	0	1731	19	0	1749	19	0	1767	20	0
1713	...		1732	19	0	1750	18	6	1768	16	0
1714	18	0	1733	18	6	1751	18	6	1769	15	3
1715	...		1734	16	0	1752	20	0	1770	14	0
1716	...		1735	14	0	1753	15	0	1771	15	0
1717	23	0	1736	14	0	1754	14	6	1772	15	6
1718	27	0	1737	14	0	1755	14	0	1773	15	6
1719	21	0	1738	13	6	1756	15	6	1774	17	6
1720	21	6	1739	13	0	1757	18	0	1775	18	6
1721	20	0	1740	14	0	1758	20	0	1776	18	6
1722	20	0	1741	14	0	1759	20	0	1777	18	3
1723	17	6	1742	15	0	1760	18	6	1778	17	0
1724	16	0	1743	19	6	1761	18	0	1779	18	6
1725	16	0	1744	21	0	1762	17	0	1780	19	6
1726	15	9	1745	16	6	1763	20	0	1781	20	0
1727	16	0									

NOTES TO PART B

[1] SOURCES: Southdown and Kent Long – *S.P.* 1828, VIII (*Committee of the House of Lords on the State of the Wool Trade*, evidence of T. Legg) for 1759–91; *ibid.* (evidence of W. Nottidge) for 1792–1827; and J. R. McCulloch, *Dictionary of Commerce* (1882 edition), p. 1,541 for 1828–45. Lincoln Half-Hogg – *S.P.* 1903, LXVIII (quoting tables printed by the *Bradford Daily Observer*).

[2] For the period 1759–91 a single price is quoted for each year. This series continues to 1827, but for the period 1792–1827 a series giving two quotations for each year for Southdown wool has been preferred.

[3] After 1845 prices of Southdown wool are quoted in Mc Culloch, *op. cit.* and in *The Economist* price current, but in a slightly different form.

[4] The Lincoln Half-Hogg series links directly on to that given in Part C.

B. Southdown, Kent Long and Lincoln Half-Hogg, pence per lb., 1759–1845

	Southdown	Kent Long
1759	8½	7½
1760	8½	7½
1761	6½	6
1762	6½	6
1763	8	7
1764	8	8
1765	7½	7½
1766	8	8
1767	9	7½
1768	7	6½
1769	7	6½
1770	7½	7
1771	8	7½
1772	7	6½
1773	7	7
1774	8	7
1775	9	8
1776	8½	8
1777	8	7½
1778	6½	5½
1779	6	6
1780	7½	6½
1781	7½	5
1782	8	5½
1783	8	6½
1784	8½	7
1785	9	7
1786	9	7½
1787	11	9½
1788	12	9
1789	12	8½
1790	12½	9½
1791	11½	9
1792	15	11½
1793	11½	9½
1794	12½	9½
1795	15	10
1796	16	9½
1797	15¼	9½
1798	14½	9½
1799	19	12
1800	17	12½
1801	18	12½
1802	18½	14

	Southdown	Kent Long	Lincoln Half-Hogg
1803	18¾	13½	...
1804	21	15	...
1805	23½	16	...
1806	21½	14½	...
1807	21½	14	...
1808	20	12	...
1809	27½	15	...
1810	30	16	...
1811	19	13	...
1812	18¾	13½	...
1813	21	15	...
1814	25¼	21	19
1815	23½	22	22
1816	16½	15	16
1817	19½	15	15
1818	26	24	22
1819	20½	15	16½
1820	16½	16	16½
1821	14¼	13	14
1822	14	11	12
1823	14¾	12	11¼
1824	12½	13	12
1825	16	16	17½
1826	10	11	13
1827	9	10½	11½
1828	8	12	11
1829	6	9	10
1830	10	10½	9
1831	13	10½	12
1832	12	12½	13
1833	17	10½	14
1834	19	19½	15½
1835	18	18	15½
1836	20	20½	16
1837	15	15	13½
1838	16	17	14
1839	16	17	17
1840	15	14½	14
1841	12	11	12½
1842	11½	10	11
1843	11¼	11	10
1844	14	14	11
1845	16	15	13

NOTES TO PART C

[1] Sources: Lincoln and Port Philip – A. Sauerbeck, 'Prices of Commodities and the Precious Metals', in the *J.S.S.* (1886), continued annually thereafter in the same source by Sauerbeck and subsequently by the editor of *The Statist*; Import Value – *Annual Statement of Trade* and its successor.

[2] An index of wool prices based on those appearing in *Agricultural Statistics of the United Kingdom* for the period after 1966 is as follows (1975 = 100):

1966	79·7	1969	80·6	1972	81·2	1975	100	1978	164·3
1967	78·4	1970	78·1	1973	81·8	1976	121·7	1979	171·1
1968	78·0	1971	79·5	1974	84·4	1977	163·2	1980	158·1

C. Lincoln Half-Hogg, Port Philip Merino and Average Import Values, pence per lb. 1846–1980

	Lincoln Half-Hogg	Port Philip Merino Average Fleece	Average Import Value
1846	13	18	...
1847	12	16	...
1848	11	13	...
1849	10	16	...
1850	11	17	...
1851	12½	17	...
1852	13⅝	19½	...
1853	16	20	...
1854	15½	18	...
1855	13	19½	15·8
1856	16	23	17·9
1857	20½	23	17·9
1858	15⅝	22½	17·0
1859	18⅝	23½	17·7
1860	20⅛	24	17·8
1861	19½	22	15·8
1862	20½	22	16·4
1863	22⅝	22	16·1
1864	27⅜	23	18·0
1865	25¾	22½	16·9
1866	23½	23½	17·6
1867	18⅞	21½	16·6
1868	17½	20	14·4
1869	18⅛	17	13·6
1870	16¾	17	14·4
1871	21⅜	21	13·3
1872	25⅝	26	14·5
1873	24½	25	14·7
1874	20¾	23½	14·7
1875	19¾	22	15·4
1876	17¾	20¼	14·5
1877	16¼	20¼	14·4
.878	15	20	13·9
1879	12½	18¾	13·6
1880	15⅛	21½	13·7
1881	12⅜	19½	13·9
1882	11¼	19¾	12·3
1883	10	19	12·1
1884	10	18¼	12·1
1885	9⅞	16½	10·0
1886	10	15½	9·1
1887	10½	15¾	10·1
1888	10⅜	15¾	9·8
1889	11	17½	9·8
1890	11	16	10·3
1891	9¾	14¾	9·3
1892	8¾	13	8·7
1893	10¼	12¾	8·7
1894	10⅛	11¾	8·5
1895	12	12	8·1
1896	11½	13	8·4
1897	9⅝	12¼	8·0
1898	8¾	13¼	8·1
1899	8¼	17¼	8·6
1900	7⅞	15¾	9·5
1901	6⅞	13	7·5
1902	6¼	15	7·5
1903	7¼	16	8·3
1904	10⅛	16	8·7
1905	12⅜	17¼	9·3
1906	13⅜	18	10·2
1907	12¼	18	10·3
1908	8½	15¾	9·3
1909	9	17¾	9·5
1910	9⅞	18¼	10·2
1911	10	17¼	10·0
1912	10½	17½	9·9
1913	12⅜	18	10·3
1914	12⅝	18½	10·5
1915	17⅜	21⅜	10·9
1916	20	32¾	14·6
1917	20⅞	46½	19·1
1918	18¾	47¼	21·1
1919	22⅝	67	22·3
1920	22	79⅞	24·1 (a)
1921	8⅜	31⅞	13·1
1922	9¾	39	12·8
1923	12·0	43·7	15·2
1924	18·9	53·4	22·1
1925	17·2	41·1	23·7
1926	15·0	36·5	18·5
1927	15·3	38·1	17·5
1928	17·9	37·0	18·6
1929	16·1	35·4	17·6
1930	10·75	18·3	13·0
1931	8·5	14·7	9·3
1932	5·8	15.0	8·5
1933	5·9	19·9	9·0
1934	7·0	21·25	11·3
1935	7·3	20·1	9·9

See p. 768 for footnote.

C. Lincoln Half-Hogg, Port Philip Merino and Average Import Values, pence per lb. 1846–1980 (*cont.*)

(Old pence per lb. to 1971, new pence subsequently)

	Lincoln Half-Hogg	Port Philip Merino Average Fleece	Average Import Value
1936	10·4	24·7	11·5
1937	16·9	26·9	15·2
1938	11·9	18·6	11·2
1939	12·2	17·9	10·3
1940	19·4	29·6	14·5
1941	21·0	32·0	15·3
1942	21·0	32·0	15·7
1943	21·0	32·0	16·6
1944	21·1	32·0	16·7
1945	21·1	31·6	16·8
1946	20·7	35·2	19·0
1947	22·7	58·2	23·2
1948	33·0	91·2	30·7
1949	38·4	92·4	37·4
1950	65·75	157·45	63·2
1951	99·0	177·25	113·1
1952	49·5	120·0	59·0
1953	60·0	126·25	66·6
1954	63·25	111·25	64·8
1955	61·75	99·4	58·9
1956	61·9	102·6	57·6
1957	68·5	100·75	67·1
1958	53·5	70·75	48·8
1959	55·2	75·75	46·9
1960	57·8	71·25	50·0
1961	58·5	79·5	48·2
1962	58·25	85·5	47·5
1963	59·75	64·3	53·4
1964	66·83	63·6	61·2
1965	53·7	87·3	49·6
1966	52·5	60·4	50·6
1967	...	...	46·2
1968	...	...	43·5
1969	...	...	46·0
1970	...	...	42·0
1971	...	...	37·6
			new pence per lb.
1972	...	...	22·1
1973	...	...	44·3
1974	...	...	43·0
1975	...	...	32·7
1976	...	...	49·2
1977	...	...	58·3
1978	...	...	59·0
1979	...	...	61·6
1980	...	...	63·2

(*a*) Prior to 1920 the value of wool imports includes noils.

Prices 22. Average Price of Bread in London – 1545–1925

NOTES

[1] Sources: 1545–1757 – material collected by Lord Beveridge's Price and Wage History Research Group, not previously published. This was kindly made available to us by Lord Beveridge. 1758–1800 – *S.P.* 1903, LXVIII (based on assize price of a quartern loaf of 4 lb. 5½ oz.); 1801–1903 – *S.P.* 1904, LXXIX (based on various sources detailed in this volume); 1904–25 – 18th *Abstract of Labour Statistics*.

[2] The table relates to wheaten or household bread.

(in pence per 4 lb.)

1545 (*a*)	1·8	1595	...	1645	5·3	1695	7·1
1546	1·0	1596	6·5	1646	6·8	1696	7·1
1547	1·0	1597	5·6	1647	9·0	1697	8·0
1548	1·3	1598	3·7	1648	8·6	1698	7·3
1549	2·2	1599	4·3	1649	9·0	1699	5·7
1550	...	1600	4·0	1650	7·4	1700	4·8
1551	2·4	1601	3·3	1651	6·4	1701	4·3
1552	1·8	1602	3·4	1652	4·8	1702	4·4
1553	2·0	1603	3·6	1653	3·9	1703	5·7
1554	2·3	1604	3·9	1654	3·9	1704	4·7
1555	3·2	1605	3·4	1655	5·6	1705	4·1
1556	2·7	1606	3·9	1656	5·7	1706	4·1
1557	1·3	1607	5·4	1657	7·5	1707	4·7
1558	1·6	1608	5·1	1658	7·3	1708	7·0
1559	2·4	1609	4·0	1659	7·4	1709	8·7
1560	2·7	1610	4·2	1660	7·5	1710	6·2
1561	2·2	1611	5·3	1661	9·7	1711	5·9
1562	3·8	1612	4·8	1662	6·1	1712	5·4
1563	2·0	1613	5·3	1663	6·0	1713	6·3
1564	2·1	1614	4·5	1664	5·7	1714	4·9
1565	2·6	1615	4·8	1665	5·0	1715	5·5
1566	2·0	1616	...	1666	4·2	1716	5·4
1567	1·9	1617	5·3	1667	4·6	1717	4·7
1568	2·2	1618	4·0	1668	5·9	1718	4·1
1569	1·9	1619	3·5	1669	5·4	1719	4·6
1570	2·0	1620	3·9	1670	5·4	1720	4·8
1571	2·4	1621	5·3	1671	5·4	1721	4·5
1572	2·8	1622	5·8	1672	5·6	1722	4·7
1573	3·8	1623	5·4	1673	7·6	1723	4·8
1574	2·6	1624	6·0	1674	7·4	1724	5·4
1575	2·4	1625	5·3	1675	5·4	1725	6·0
1576	2·9	1626	4·2	1676	5·1	1726	5·1
1577	2·6	1627	3·6	1677	6·9	1727	6·5
1578	2·2	1628	4·5	1678	7·5	1728	6·2
1579	2·2	1629	6·0	1679	5·9	1729	4·6
1580	2·4	1630	7·0	1680	6·2	1730	4·5
1581	...	1631	5·5	1681	5·6	1731	4·0
1582	2·4	1632	6·1	1682	5·8	1732	4·1
1583	2·3	1633	...	1683	5·6	1733	4·7
1584	2·3	1634	5·8	1684	6·6	1734	5·1
1585	...	1635	6·1	1685	4·8	1735	5·2
1586	4·8	1636	5·4	1686	5·2	1736	5·3
1587	2·2	1637	6·2	1687	4·5	1737	4·8
1588	...	1638	5·0	1688	4·4	1738	5·0
1589	2·9	1639	4·6	1689	5·3	1739	6·2
1590	...	1640	5·8	1690	5·0	1740	6·4
1591	2·2	1641	5·1	1691	6·4	1741	4·7
1592	2·6	1642	5·3	1692	7·8	1742	4·1
1593	2·9	1643	5·1	1693	8·5	1743	3·9
1594	4·7	1644	4·8	1694	5·6	1744	4·0

See p. 770 for footnote.

Prices 22. *continued*

(in pence per 4 lb.)

Year	Price
1745	4·9
1746	4·9
1747	4·8
1748	5·0
1749	4·9
1750	4·9
1751	5·4
1752	5·6
1753	5·0
1754	4·5
1755	5·0
1756	7·2
1757	6·1

1758 (*b*)	5·2
1759 (*c*)	4·7
1760	4·7
1761	4·1
1762	4·9
1763	5·1
1764	5·8
1765	6·7
1766	6·0
1767	7·3
1768	7·1
1769	5·7
1770	5·8
1771	6·5
1772	7·3
1773	7·3
1774	7·0
1775	6·9
1776	5·8
1777	6·6
1778	6·5
1779	5·5
1780	5·7
1781	7·0
1782	7·0
1783	7·0
1784	6·9
1785	6·1
1786	5·5
1787	5·7
1788	6·4
1789	6·0

Year	Price
1790	7·0
1791	6·3
1792	5·9
1793	6·8
1794	7·0
1795	9·6
1796	9·7
1797	7·6
1798	7·7
1799	9·6
1800	15·3
1801	15·5
1802	9·5
1803	8·7
1804	9·7
1805	13·1
1806	11·7
1807	10·8
1808	11·6
1809	13·7
1810	14·7
1811	14·0
1812	17·0
1813	15·7
1814	11·4
1815 (*d*)	10·4
	---- (*e*)
1816	. . . (*f*)
1817	. . . (*f*)
1818	. . . (*f*)
1819	. . . (*f*)
	---- (*e*)
1820	10·1
1821	9·5
1822	9·5
1823	10·3
1824	10·5
1825	10·5
1826	9·5
1827	9·5
1828	9·5
1829	10·5
1830	10·5
1831	10·0
1832	10·0
1833	8·5
1834	8·0

Year	Price
1835	7·0
1836	8·0
1837	8·5
1838	10·0
1839	10·0
1840	10·0
1841	9·0
1842	9·5
1843	7·5
1844	8·5
1845	7·5
1846	8·5
1847	11·5
1848	7·5
1849	7·0
	---- (*e*)
1850	6·75
1851	6·75
1852	6·75
1853	8·33
1854	10·50
1855	10·75
1856	10·75
1857	9·00
1858	7·50
1859	7·50
1860	8·75
1861	9·00
1862	8·50
1863	7·50
1864	7·00
1865	7·50
	---- (*e*)
1866	8·75
1867	10·25
1868	9·25
1869	7·75
1870	8·00
1871	9·00
1872	9·75
1873	8·00
1874	7·25
	---- (*e*)
1875	6·83
1876	7·15
1877	8·13
1878	7·50
1879	7·13

Year	Price
1880	6·98
1881	7·04
1882	7·38
1883	7·00
1884	6·78
1885	6·23
1886	6·25
1887	5·63
1888	5·69
1889	6·02
1890	6·00
1891	6·21
1892	6·23
1893	5·75
1894	5·48
1895	5·08
1896	5·09
1897	5·50
1898	6·02
1899	5·09
1900	5·23
1901	5·00
1902	5·28
1903	5·59
	----(*e*)
1904	5·5
1905	5·5
1906	5·5
1907	5·4
1908	5·8
1909	6·1
1910	5·9
1911	5·5
1912	5·8
1913	5·8
1914	5·8
1915	8·0
1916	9·0
1917	10·6
1918	8·9
1919	9·1
1920	11·6
1921	12·4
1922	9·2
1923	8·5
1924	8·7
1925	9·9

(*a*) Harvest years (September-August) **beginning** in the year shown.
(*b*) 10th October to 31st December.
(*c*) Calendar years.
(*d*) 1st January to 11th March henceforth.
(*e*) These minor breaks, resulting from changes in original source, are probably negligible.
(*f*) Prices paid by Charterhouse for the harvest years are given in Sir William Beveridge and others, *Prices and Wages in England*, vol. 1 (London, Longmans Green & Co., 1939), p. 207, and are as follows (translated into pence per 4 lb.):

1814	12·0	1816	16·8	1818	11·6	1820	10·2
1815	11·5	1817	13·3	1819	11·5		

Prices 23. Average Price of Bread in Dublin 1745–1945

NOTES

[1] Source: John Swift, *History of the Dublin Bakers and Others* (Dublin, n.d.), Appendix IX.

[2] The figures to 1848 have been converted to the unit used subsequently.

[3] The table relates to second quality bread from 1849 to 1877, and to ordinary batch bread subsequently. Prior to 1849 it is not defined.

(in pence per 4 lb.)

Year	Price	Year	Price	Year	Price	Year	Price
1745	3·34	1795	8·71	1845	6·45	1895	4·5
1746	3·38	1796	8·35	1846	6·91	1896	5
1747	3·37	1797	8·26	1847	8·75	1897	5·5
1748	3·67	1798	8·35	1848	7·37	1898	6·5
1749	3·76	1799	7·38	1849	5·5	1899	5·5
1750	3·76	1800	16·70	1850	5	1900	5·5
1751	3·92	1801	14·22	1851	5·5	1901	5
1752	4·02	1802	7·38	1852	5·5	1902	5·5
1753	4·28	1803	8·73	1853	7	1903	5·5
1754	4·15	1804	7·03	1854	9	1904	5·5
1755	3·73	1805	11·07	1855	9	1905	6
1756	4·41	1806	10·36	1856	8·5	1906	5·5
1757	5·12	1807	9·67	1857	8	1907	6
1758	4·27	1808	12·43	1858	6	1908	6·5
1759	3·47	1809	11·97	1859	6	1909	6
1760	3·93	1810	12·89	1860	7	1910	6·5
1761	3·83	1811	14·27	1861	7	1911	6
1762	4·35	1812	17·27	1862	8	1912	6·5
1763	4·53	1813	16·12	1863	7	1913	6
1764	4·43	1814	10·36	1864	6	1914	6·5
1765	5·05	1815	9·21	1865	6·5	1915	7·5
1766	5·53	1816	14·27	1866	6·5	1916	9·5
1767	6·18	1817	19·80	1867	8	1917	11
1768	5·05	1818	12·43	1868	7	1918	9
1769	5·53	1819	11·51	1869	7	1919	10
1770	5·15	1820	9·21	1870	7	1920	13·5
1771	5·64	1821	7·83	1871	7·5	1921	11·5
1772	5·60	1822	7·37	1872	7·5	1922	11
1773	5·64	1823	7·60	1873	8·5	1923	11·5
1774	6·00	1824	9·44	1874	9·5	1924	11·5
1775	5·41	1825	9·21	1875	7·5	1925	11
1776	4·36	1826	8·52	1876	7·5	1926	11
1777	4·92	1827	8·29	1877	7·5	1927	11
1778	5·22	1828	7·37	1878	7·5	1928	10·5
1779	4·36	1829	9·21	1879	7·5	1929	10
1780	4·29	1830	8·75	1880	7·5	1930	10·5
1781	5·18	1831	8·52	1881	7·5	1931	8·5
1782	5·68	1832	7·60	1882	7·5	1932	8·5
1783	6·50	1833	7·37	1883	7	1933	9
1784	6·17	1834	6·91	1884	6·5	1934	9
1785	5·47	1835	7·37	1885	6	1935	9
1786	5·40	1836	6·91	1886	6·5	1936	9·5
1787	5·15	1837	8·29	1887	6	1937	9·5
1788	5·09	1838	8·75	1888	6·5	1938	10
1789	5·73	1839	8·75	1889	7	1939	10·5
1790	6·23	1840	7·83	1890	6·5	1940	11·5
1791	6·14	1841	7·37	1891	6·5	1941	11·5
1792	5·15	1842	6·91	1892	6	1942	12
1793	6·40	1843	5·99	1893	5·5	1943	13
1794	6·86	1844	6·45	1894	5	1944	13·5
						1945	13·5

CHAPTER XV

MISCELLANEOUS STATISTICS

TABLES

The tables in this chapter cover three main topics, more of a social than an economic nature – crime, elections, and education. The first five are derived from the official *Judicial* (or *Criminal*) *Statistics*, first published regularly in Blue Books from 1834, with earlier, occasional returns taking some series back to 1805. These statistics, especially those for the nineteenth century, have been subjected to a good deal of criticism at various times, both by contemporaries, including official enquiries,[1] and by historians. Perhaps the most hostile of the latter has been Tobias, who went so far as to say that 'the criminal statistics have little to tell us about crime and criminals in the nineteenth century'.[2] He was especially critical of the overall statistics, such as are shown here, believing that their defects 'are enough to rule out any use of national totals'. But this conclusion seems to have been based on the idea that 'the national totals are as strong only as the weakest component', which for most purposes is surely not true. The weakness of the statistics in different areas at different times can be expected to have had some mutually offsetting effect, at any rate once the system of reporting

[1] E.g. The Departmental Committee on Criminal Statistics (*S.P.* 1895 CVIII). The *Journal of the Statistical Society* contained many articles about these statistics, especially up to the 1860s, but again in the 1890s. A more recent one is by Lodge in *Journal of the Royal Statistical Society*, XCXXVI (1953).

[2] J. Tobias, *Crime and Industrial Society in the 19th Century* (London, 1967), p. 21.

and recording had been established for a few years. Local data, on the other hand, are best treated with a good deal of distrust, and perhaps should be left to specialists, for Tobias may be right to say that 'changes of chief constable had more effect on the rate of indictable crime than had anything else' in individual cases.[3] When one sees the way that different chief constables change the emphasis of policing nowadays, such a belief probably still contains a substantial element of the truth. Nevertheless, though this may affect national *levels*, it is unlikely to have a significant effect on national *trends*.

It would appear, in fact, that there are actually worse drawbacks to the criminal statistics than those which Tobias found so objectionable. These are enumerated and discussed in a study by Gatrell and Haddon, which nevertheless concludes that 'if . . . we are not to abdicate entirely from a systematic examination of nineteenth-century criminal behaviour, it is only by returning to the official statistics that we can hope to attain a wider perspective than contemporary observers, to avoid repeating their prejudices, and to arrive at conclusions based on a greater awareness of the possible distortion in the criminal records than that which they usually exhibited.[4]

It is, of course, clear that, as Gatrell and Haddon put it, 'the real incidence of criminal activity ... must always remain a matter for informed judgement rather than precise quantification'.[5] An unknown, and at times changing, amount of crime goes unreported. But this does not mean that an analysis of *known* offences is uninteresting, or that it cannot be used as an indicator of crime *in toto*, though there are limitations and qualifications to this.

The best of the criminal statistics as an indicator of overall crime are generally accepted as being those closest to the offence,[6] in other words, the police statistics of the number of offences known, given here in table 1 and, for Ireland, table 4. However, the ratio between these and the committals, shown in tables 3 and 5, seems to have been relatively constant, so that the latter are not *necessarily* misleading for the period when they alone are available. However, even the best statistics in this field are subject to qualification, and it is likely that the qualifications will be strongest in the first half of the nineteenth century.

Changes in public attitudes both to crime and to policing must have affected the extent to which crime was reported and criminals were apprehended. There is good reason to believe that both changed in ways which increased the numbers both of crimes known and of criminals tried. However, it is very probable that the effects of these changes had largely run their course by about 1850,[7] though there must have been occasional effects from specific, limited changes subsequently, such as the recent increase in reported rapes.

A larger effect on the statistics was probably caused by the progressive extension of police control, in the period from the 1820s to the 1860s at any rate. However, this is likely to have

[3] *Ibid.*, p. 258.
[4] V. A. C. Gatrell and T. B. Haddon in E. A. Wrigley (ed.), *Nineteenth-century Society* (Cambridge, 1972), p. 339.
[5] *Ibid.*, p. 351.
[6] *Ibid.*, p. 351, and Tobias, *op. cit.*, p. 256.
[7] Gatrell and Haddon, *loc. cit.*, p. 353.

had contrary effects. The initial impact of improved policing should be to raise reported crime rates and secure more convictions. But, sooner or later, the resulting deterrent effects might be expected to reduce them. It is not really possible to generalise about the timing and significance of these effects.

Other changes in the levels of reported crime have resulted at various times from changes in the law itself and in administrative arrangements. The more significant of these are referred to in footnotes to the tables. The most important kind have involved extensions of summary jurisdiction, though the change in 1893 had the opposite effect, since it stopped the previous practice of deducting indictable offences tried summarily from the records of the total known to the police.

Perhaps one can best sum up by saying that the criminal statistics as shown here must be used with care. Over long periods, especially where they include the major legal or administrative changes indicated, it is impossible to assume that the ratio between recorded and actual crime was constant. But for other and shorter periods the discontinuities are probably tolerable, certainly after about 1860.

Only the broadest overall statistics of electorate, votes cast and members elected at general elections are included in the three electoral tables given here – 6 and 7 for the United Kingdom and 8 for the Irish Republic – though, obviously, much more statistical material is available on elections, going back at least as far as the sixteenth century. But most, if not all, of this requires careful interpretation, and is too much a matter for specialist analysis to be included in a volume such as this. Nevertheless, from at least the 1880s, if not 1832, there is a mass of data which is fairly readily comprehensible. The trouble is that there is so much of it that it would be difficult to establish a satisfactory principle of selection. It has, perhaps, been the coward's way out not to include any other than the national party totals in table 7. For those who require it, the best sources simply for data are Craig's various publications.[8]

Finally, there are six tables of statistics about education, selected from the much greater amount of badly organised material which is available in the sources, beginning in the middle of the nineteenth century. There are, of course, earlier statistics of various kinds, though, apart from the Census, they are local ones.[9] The nature of what is available may be judged from Sanderson's survey, which concludes that it is not yet possible to draw up a national balance sheet even as to literacy.[10]

It was with some hesitation that even the schools statistics for the nineteenth century were included here, because the material is far from easily tractable. The authorities changed the coverage of the statistics which they collected, and their methods of collection as well, on numerous occasions, often with little to indicate to the user what changes had taken place.

[8] F. W. S. Craig, *British Parliamentary Election Results* (5 vols., London and Chichester, 1974–84); and *British Electoral Facts 1832–1980* (Chichester, 1981) are the main ones for this purpose.

[9] B. I. Coleman in E. A. Wrigley (ed.), *op. cit.* deals with the Census material, but for all his ingenuity it is likely to remain the case that 'the standard histories of education are remarkably uninformative on the prevalence of education in nineteenth-century England' (p. 397).

[10] Michael Sanderson, *Education, Economic Change and Society in England 1780–1870* (London, 1983).

This applied equally to the Irish statistics, given in table 10, as to the English and Scottish ones in table 9. I have attempted to compile consistent series and to indicate the major breaks in continuity as far as possible; but it is certain that the attempt has not always been successful. Moreover, the figures for this period do not include privately financed schools, even though they were at that time a relatively important part of the educational system. The statistics up to about 1900, therefore, must be taken only as rough indicators of the growth of public education. Coverage after about 1900 was greatly improved, and changes have been much more clearly indicated, though private schools continued to be excluded from the statistics until after the Second World War. Data for these then became available for secondary education, in which private schools were a significant feature, and they are summarised in table 12.

It is perhaps worthwhile at this point to draw the user's attention to the difference between the statistics of pupils on the rolls of schools, pupils in attendance on a particular date during the year, and average daily attendance. The nature of each series shown is indicated, but it should be realised that the actual numbers can vary very considerably.

Whilst the schools statistics up to the twentieth century are incomplete but usable, those for universities have too many gaps before 1922 to be worth including here. A minor exception is provided by the figures of overall student numbers for the universities in the Republic of Ireland, which were carried back to 1909 in the early *Statistical Abstracts of Ireland*. It is likely that these could be continued further backwards without too much trouble. It is equally likely that the figures for Northern Ireland before 1948, which were not published, officially at least, at the time, could also be pushed back.

Miscellaneous Statistics 1. Crimes (Indictable Offences) Known to the Police – England & Wales 1857–1980 and Scotland 1868–1980

NOTES

[1] SOURCE: *Judicial Statistics* (later called *Criminal Statistics*) published for each year, separately for England & Wales and for Scotland, in *Sessional Papers*.

[2] The English figures for years up to and including 1892, and the Scottish figure for 1868, are for twelve months ended 29 September in the year indicated. All other figures are for calendar years.

[3] The Scottish figures up to 1896 are for crimes and offences, i.e. they include the equivalent of non-indictable offences in England.

[4] The English figures do not include certain offences which may be tried either on indictment or summarily.

(in thousands)

	Total		Against the Person		Against Property with Violence		Against Property without Violence	
	England and Wales	Scotland (*a*)	England and Wales	Scotland (*a*)	England and Wales	Scotland (*a*)	England and Wales	Scotland (*a*)
1857	92	...	2·8	...	6·5	...	78	...
1858	93	...	2·7	...	5·7	...	80	...
1859	85	...	2·6	...	4·4	...	75	...
1860	83	...	2·2	...	4·1	...	74	...
1861	88	...	2·5	...	5·1	...	78	...
1862	95	...	2·5	...	5·7	...	83	...
1863	93	...	3·0	...	5·4	...	80	...
1864	90	...	3·1	...	5·0	...	78	...
1865	93	...	3·1	...	5·2	...	81	...
1866	89	...	2·9	...	5·1	...	78	...
1867	96	...	2·8	...	5·9	...	84	...
1868	101	104	3·0	...	6·4	...	89	...
1869	100	108	3·0	7·1	6·0	25	88	...
1870	91	118	2·7	7·4	5·2	24	80	...
1871	82	122	2·6	7·6	4·2	22	72	...
1872	81	130	2·6	8·3	3·9	22	72	...
1873	83	133	2·5	8·7	4·0	23	74	...
1874	86	132	2·9	9·1	4·2	24	76	...
1875	82	123	3·2	9·1	4·1	23	72	...
1876	85	125	3·2	8·8	4·1	24	75	...
1877	89	128	3·0	8·9	4·5	26	79	...
1878	94	125	2·9	8·2	6·7	26	81	...
1879	91	112	2·6	7·4	5·9	26	80	...
1880	98	123	2·9	8·5	6·8	26	85	...
1881	97	124	2·9	8·5	6·7	25	84	...
1882	100	127	3·2	9·1	7·1	25	87	...
1883	96	130	2·8	...	6·1	...	84	...
1884	92	127	3·2	...	6·1	...	80	...
1885	87	115	3·1	...	6·0	...	74	...
1886	87	116	3·6	...	6·6	...	74	...
1887	85	120	3·5	...	6·6	...	72	...
1888	88	124	3·6	...	6·9	...	75	...
1889	87	128	3·4	...	6·5	...	74	...
1890	82	137	3·5	...	6·1	...	69	...
1891	80	134	3·4	...	5·9	...	68	...
1892	85	136	3·5	...	6·8	...	72	...
1893	86	134	3·9	...	8·0	...	71	...
1894	86	139	3·9	...	7·9	...	71	...
1895	81	134	3·9	...	7·9	...	66	...
1896	79	144	3·8	...	7·6	...	64	...

See p. 778 for footnote.

Miscellaneous Statistics 1. *continued*

(in thousands)

	Total		Against the Person		Against Property with Violence		Against Property without Violence	
	England and Wales	Scotland (*a*)	England and Wales	Scotland (*a*)	England and Wales	Scotland (*a*)	England and Wales	Scotland (*a*)
1897	79	143 ----- (*a*) 33	3·8	5·8	8·0	3·2	64	19
1898	82	33	3·9	5·7	8·8	3·2	66	20
1899	76	33	3·7	5·3	7·4	3·2	61	19
1900	78	33	3·5	5·1	7·8	3·5	64	20
1901	81	35	3·7	5·0	8·8	4·1	65	21
1902	83	35	3·6	5·1	9·1	4·0	67	20
1903	86	36	3·5	5·1	9·9	4·7	69	21
1904	93	39	3·4	4·6	11	4·8	74	25
1905	95	40	3·5	4·5	11	4·7	76	26
1906	92	40	3·8	4·8	11	4·5	73	27
1907	99	42	3·9	4·9	12	4·5	79	28
1908	105	42	3·8	4·7	13	5·2	84	28
1909	105	40	3·9	3·7	14	5·6	83	26
1910	103	38	3·9	3·8	14	4·4	81	26
1911	97	37	4·2	4·3	12	4·1	76	24
1912	102	39	4·6	4·6	12	4·8	81	24
1913	98	39	4·7	5·0	12	4·6	77	24
1914	89	38	4·2	4·7	11	4·9	70	24
1915	78	34	3·5	3·5	7·8	3·6	64	21
1916	81	32	3·2	2·5	8·6	4·1	67	22
1917	89	32	2·7	1·9	10	5·2	74	21
1918	88	29	3·0	1·7	11	5·1	72	19
1919	88	34	4·2	2·7	14	6·5	67	21
1920	101	39	4·6	4·2	16	6·9	77	25
1921	103	40	4·2	3·3	16	7·6	80	25
1922	107	37	4·3	2·8	18	6·8	82	24
1923	110	35	4·3	2·9	18	6·1	85	23
1924	113	33	4·4	3·0	18	5·9	87	20
1925	114	33	4·6	3·0	18	6·6	88	20
1926	133	38	5·1	3·0	20	7·8	105	23
1927	126	31	5·4	2·8	20	7·7	96	17
1928	130	34	5·3	3·0	22	8·8	99	18
1929	135	35	5·5	3·0	23	9·8	101	19
1930	147	37	5·7	3·1	26	10	110	19
1931	159	38	5·3	3·0	32	12	117	19
1932	208	49	5·2	2·9	41	16	157	26
1933	227	50	5·6	2·9	37	16	178	27
1934	233	52	6·2	3·0	37	16	184	29
1935	234	60	6·3	3·2	36	16	186	35
1936	249	59	6·9	3·4	39	15	197	35
1937	266	59	7·4	3·4	45	14	207	34
1938	283	59	7·7	3·6	50	15	219	34
1939	304	60	7·9	3·1	53	16	237	34
1940	305	62	7·1	2·6	50	16	243	36
1941	359	67	8·3	2·8	53	17	290	41
1942	365	69	9·8	2·8	57	18	289	41
1943	373	71	11	3·0	59	20	293	42
1944	415	72	12	3·1	75	21	320	40
1945	478	86	13	2·7	109	32	347	43
1946	472	77	13	2·5	116	27	333	40

See p. 778 for footnote.

Miscellaneous Statistics 1. *continued*

(in thousands)

	Total		Against the Person		Against Property with Violence		Against Property without Violence	
	England and Wales	Scotland (*a*)	England and Wales	Scotland (*a*)	England and Wales	Scotland (*a*)	England and Wales	Scotland (*a*)
1947	499	75	14	2·5	113	26	358	40
1948	523	82	16	2·4	114	30	378	42
1949	460	71	17	2·4	93	26	336	37
1950	461	75	19	2·4	94	27	334	39
1951	525	83	21	2·8	97	28	393	45
1952	513	82	22	2·7	99	28	378	44
1953	473	77	23	2·9	90	27	344	42
1954	434	75	24	3·0	77	27	318	37
1955	438	75	25	2·8	76	26	325	39
1956	480	80	26	2·8	87	29	354	45
		----- (*b*)						
1957	546	80	30	3·2	106	33	396	44
		----- (*c*)						
1958	627	92	30	3·5	133	43	449	40
1959	676	96	34	3·7	136	44	490	46
1960	743	103	36	4·3	154	46	537	50
1961	807	109	38	4·2	168	50	585	52
1962	896	118	38	4·5	195	55	648	55
1963	978	128	41	4·6	222	62	699	59
1964	1,068	134	43	5·5	237	61	770	64
1965	1,134	140	46	6·3	257	64	812	65
1966	1,200	148	48	6·5	281	67	849	69
1967	1,207	153	52	7·2	271	69	859	71
1968	1,289 ----- (*d*) 1,400	152	55	7·4	292 ----- (*e*)	66	913 ----- (*f*)	73
1969	1,499	156	61	7·0	427	68	1,005	74
1970	1,568	167 ----- (*g*) 191	65	6·8 ----- (*g*) 11	438	73	1,060	80
1971	1,666	211	71	12	459	80	1,130	83
1972	1,690	213	76	12	448	77	1,160	83
1973	1,658	208	87	12	401	66	1,162	81
1974	1,963	234	88	12	492	77	1,374	93
1975	2.106	282	95	13	533	87 ----- (*h*) 101	1,469	102 ----- (*h*) 107
1976	2,136	318	100	14	527	114	1,499	119
1977	2,463	363	104	14	618	130	1,732	134
1978	2,396	335	110	15	579	112 ----- (*e*) 108	1,704	125
1979	2,377	347	117	15	562	110	1,695	...
	----- (*i*)		----- (*i*)		----- (*i*)		------- (*i*)	
1980	2,521	365	118	16	638	115	1,761	...

(*a*) See note 3 above.
(*b*) Subsequently excluding petty cases of malicous damage and cases of false fire alarms.
(*c*) Subsequently excluding cases of taking a motor vehicle without consent.
(*d*) This increase resulted from changes produced by the Theft Act (1968).
(*e*) Subsequently 'burglary and robbery'.
(*f*) Subsequently 'other offences against property'.
(*g*) This break results from changes in categories and procedures made at later dates, when revised statistics were carried back to 1970. The main changes are referred to in the next footnote.
(*h*) This break results from better reporting procedures.
(*i*) The 1980 figures are not exactly comparable with earlier ones because of improvements in the recording of multiple, continuous, and repeated offences.

Miscellaneous Statistics 2. Proceedings and Convictions in Courts of Summary Jurisdiction – England & Wales 1857–1980, Scotland 1868–1980

NOTES

[1] SOURCE: *Judicial Statistics* (later called *Criminal Statistics*) published for each year, separately for England & Wales and for Scotland in *Sessional Papers*.

[2] The English figures for years up to and including 1892, and the Scottish figures for 1868, are for twelve months ended 29 September in the year indicated. All other figures are for calendar years.

(in thousands)

	England & Wales				Scotland			
	Persons Dealt with Summarily for Offences		Convictions		Persons Proceeded against Summarily for		Convictions	
	Indictable	Non-indictable	Indictable	Non-indictable	Crimes (i.e. indictable)	Offences (i.e. non-indictable)	Crimes	Offences
1857	34·4	329·0	233·8					
1858	34·6	355·5	260·3					
1859	33·4	343·9	257·8					
1860	32·5	338·7	255·8					
1861	37·7	343·2	263·5					
1862	41·3	352·9	273·0					
1863	40·6	365·0	283·6					
1864	38·9	386·5	300·7					
1865	40·3	402·6	312·9					
1866	38·8	427·1	339·1					
1867	40·5	417·1	335·4					
1868	42·3	430·0	347·5		87·2		81·9	
1869	42·0	457·5	372·7		90·8		84·8	
1870	38·6	467·4	389·7		101·5		95·2	
1871	36·8	482·2	407·9		95·0		87·9	
1872	37·1	499·7	423·6		101·1		94·6	
1873	38·6	530·6	456·7		103·8		97·4	
1874	38·3	559·4	486·8		109·9		103·1	
1875	35·3	589·6	512·4		124·2		117·2	
1876	35·9	599·9	526·9		120·8		114·0	
1877	38·0	590·1	519·8		120·8		113·1	
1878	39·7	606·4	538·2		119·6		112·3	
1879	38·7	573·9	506·3		104·5		96·9	
1880	46·0	589·1	517·4		117·0		108·7	
1881	45·9	595·3	531·0		117·2		108·7	
1882	48·1	637·6	575·6		120·5		111·9	
1883	46·2	651·7	588·7		104·3		96·3	
1884	45·3	648·9	583·3		105·1		97·0	
1885	42·9	613·2	548·4		95·4		88·0	
1886	42·3	572·0	509·1		97·7		90·1	
1887	43·0	594·9	529·4		101·4		93·9	
1888	44·8	598·4	538·9		106·1		98·9	
1889	45·6	616·2	559·0		108·4		101·0	
1890	43·1	667·8	605·9		113·0		105·3	
1891	42·5	663·2	602·6		112·3		104·8	
1892	46·2	640·6	579·9		113·8		105·2	
	- - - (*a*)	- - - - (*a*)	—— (*b*)					

See p. 782 for footnotes.

Miscellaneous Statistics 2. *continued*

(in thousands)

	England & Wales				Scotland			
	Persons Dealt with Summarily for Offences		Convictions		Persons Proceeded against Summarily for		Convictions	
	Indictable	Non-indictable	Indictable	Non-indictable	Crimes (i.e. indictable)	Offences (i.e. non-indictable)	Crimes	Offences
1893	45·1	600·2	34·1	471·1	113·7		105·9	
1894	44·2	630·3	34·0	494·7	119·1		112·1	
1895	39·3	624·6	30·6	490·2	114·1		107·2	
1896	39·6	666·0	31·0	525·7	122·3		115·3	
1897	39·5	694·6	31·4	553·3	21·6	130·5	16·8	94·0
1898	41·1	739·3	32·8	600·7	21·8	141·8	16·8	103·0
1899	39·6	755·5	31·9	616·5	22·0	152·4	17·0	110·3
1900	43·5	706·8	35·3	581·4	24·0	153·7	18·7	110·9
1901	44·7	727·9	36·4	602·1	24·1	160·2	19·1	118·2
1902	45·7	721·5	37·5	596·7	33·2	156·9	18·2	115·7
1903	46·6	737·6	38·6	612·1	23·1	140·4	18·4	103·8
1904	47·8	740·3	39·6	615·8	23·5	138·0	18·7	103·3
1905	49·1	724·0	40·8	599·6	23·7	138·3	18·4	103·5
1906	46·3	695·9	38·4	573·7	19·2	114·6	17·9	111·8
1907	48·8	680·6	39·9	557·1	23·5	155·2	18·4	115·7
1908	54·0	683·8	33·0	548·2	25·0	152·3	18·6	115·1
1909	53·4	654·5	31·8	519·9	23·3	130·1	17·4	99·1
1910	52·7	631·9	29·2	496·7	23·8	125·0	16·9	93·8
1911	49·4	635·1	27·2	500·9	23·4	130·8	16·8	96·9
1912	54·2	663·1	29·5	526·0	25·5	135·9	18·5	100·2
1913	50·8	680·3	27·1	542·8	24·7	147·3	17·6	106·9
1914	47·8	626·8	24·9	491·8	24·0	141·8	17·0	102·1
1915	49·5	532·4	24·9	423·4	22·9	119·3	16·2	76·3
1916	53·6	610·2	28·2	512·5	19·6	106·7	13·8	71·6
1917	57·4	445·8	31·0	362·8	21·1	82·7	14·8	51·4
1918	52·5	375·1	28·4	299·6	18·9	60·5	13·5	36·0
1919	45·7	493·0	25·3	397·1	19·2	81·1	14·0	54·4
1920	51·5	611·8	28·1	497·1	20·8	120·7	15·6	83·5
1921	52·4	523·7	28·5	419·3	24·1	89·7	18·7	65·9
1922	49·7	524·7	25·0	421·8	20·5	84·1	14·7	65·4
1923	48·6	546·6	22·6	441·9	19·5	86·4	14·6	67·2
1924	49·5	584·5	21·5	477·5	19·4	91·0	14·7	70·5
1925	49·4	610·8	21·2	499·2	19·8	94·2	14·8	73·6
1926	69·7	602·6	33·3	492·2	28·1	92·8	21·9	73·9
1927	56·3	617·8	25·2	513·2	19·5	99·5	14·6	78·5
1928	54·2	597·6	23·0	493·9	18·7	98·6	13·8	78·4
1929	52·8	585·4	21·9	480·1	18·3	97·2	13·0	77·4
1930	55·7	609·7	22·6	499·2	18·7	89·6	13·4	71·0
1931	58·3	572·0	24·2	462·1	19·1	83·4	13·8	67·0
1932	62·1	540·3	26·1	436·8	20·1	75·3	14·7	61·5
1933	61·3	578·4	24·9	473·3	20·2	74·9	14·7	61·6

Miscellaneous Statistics 2. *continued*

(in thousands)

	England & Wales				Scotland			
	Persons Proceeded against for Offences (*c*)		Persons Found Guilty at Summary Courts (*c*)		Persons Proceeded against Summarily for		Persons Found Guilty at Summary Courts (*c*)	
	Indictable	Non-indictable (*d*)	Indictable	Non-indictable (*d*)	Crimes	Offences (*d*)	Crimes	Offences (*d*)
1933	72·2	581·5	54·9	541·0	20·2	74·9	17·9	62·4
1934	75·8	634·2	58·4	592·0	21·0	81·6	18·8	70·9
1935	79·6	733·2	63·0	689·6	21·1	95·3	18·9	83·9
1936	82·5	795·7	65·7	752·2	21·6	106·1	19·5	94·3
1937	87·3	770·4	69·9	727·8	21·5	113·3	19·4	100·4
1938	88·3	751·2	69·9	709·0	21·1	115·4	19·2	102·0
1939	88·6	658·5 (*d*)	69·6	617·8 (*d*)	21·2	111·2	19·0	96·7
1940	99·0	764·7 (*d*)	83·1	713·8 (*d*)	24·2	123·6 (*d*)	21·8	101·4 (*d*)
1941	118·7	760·9 (*d*)	99·1	695·1 (*d*)	25·7	121·4 (*d*)	23·1	95·1 (*d*)
1942	118·3	641·5 (*d*)	97·3	581·8 (*d*)	26·1	101·4 (*d*)	23·4	79·6 (*d*)
1943	115·5	508·5 (*d*)	94·6	464·6 (*d*)	25·7	87·6 (*d*)	23·2	69·7 (*d*)
1944	118·8	435·2 (*d*)	96·0	393·6 (*d*)	24·5	80·3 (*d*)	22·3	66·2 (*d*)
1945	128·7	388·8 (*d*)	101·9	351·4 (*d*)	26·5	64·1 (*d*)	24·2	53·5 (*d*)
1946	119·8	467·8 (*d*)	92·0	434·4 (*d*)	22·4	75·5 (*d*)	20·3	64·3 (*d*)
1947	128·5	554·1 (*d*)	97·7	517·4 (*d*)	21·6	82·7 (*d*)	19·7	71·2 (*d*)
1948	141·6	589·5	108·7	547·5	24·1	82·3	22·1	71·4
1949	124·4	575·9	96·9	536·1	21·0	83·4	19·2	72·2
1950	125·6	612·6	99·0	572·5	22·0	85·4	20·2	74·7
1951	143·6	632·6	114·8	590·4	24·3	86·9	22·5	76·0
1952	141·3	663·0	111·1	621·9	25·2	91·0	23·3	79·6
1953	124·9	627·4	97·6	588·6	22·6	95·7	21·1	84·0
1954	114·4	657·2	89·7	619·2	21·4	100·0	19·9	88·2
1955	115·2	665·3	91·2	627·8	21·7	105·4	20·3	93·2
1956	124·0	704·7	98·2	668·3	22·9	114·7	21·5	101·3
1957	140·2	771·1	110·2	733·5	22·5	119·3	21·2	106·2
1958	157·1	886·5	121·5	846·7	23·9	129·0	22·5	116·8
1959	163·0	927·9	126·3	887·6	24·6	141·7	23·2	129·8
1960	174·7	912·5	135·7	871·7	25·1	150·0	23·7	138·0
1961	192·7	1,013·6	150·9	970·2	27·9	142·1	26·3	130·2
1962	212·5	1,107·1	174·2	1.062·8	30·4	145·0	28·7	133·4
1963	222·6	1,154·1	189·5	1,107·4	32·7	149·1	30·5	138·2
1964	220·8	1,177·2	184·9	1,122·4	30·8	156·0	28·9	145·5
1965	235·1	1,203·9	196·1	1,149·6	32·5	159·9	30·2	148·6
1966	250·2	1,269·3	208·5	1,213·1	34·8	168·0	32·0	156·0
1967	261·2	1,402·7	216·6	1,337·4	36·1	175·7	33·5	164·7
1968	277·7	1,387·7	229·9	1,319·5	36·4	166·1	33·8	155·7
	---- (*e*)	----- (*e*)	---- (*e*)	----- (*e*)				
1969	329·7	1,372·6	271·6	1,302·7	39·1	172·7	36·2	162·4
1970	350·7	1,426·1	285·4	1.351·1	42·7	176·8	39·4	167·1
1971	350·9 (*f*)	1,444·9 (*f*)	282·1 (*f*)	1,366·1 (*f*)	36·6 (*g*)	185·2 (*g*)	33·4 (*g*)	175·3 (*g*)
1972	373·3	1,569·2	296·9	1,486·2	31·0	181·5	28·6	172·5
1973	365·5	1,673·6	292·7	1,591·2	30·1	201·8	27·3	190·0
1974	406·3	1,645·4	328·1	1,558·7	33·0	205·0	29·9	192·2
1975	439·2	1,671·7	349·9	1,586·2	35·5	198·2	32·1	184·8

See p. 782 for footnote.

Miscellaneous Statistics 2. *continued*

(in thousands)

	England & Wales				Scotland			
	Persons Proceeded against for Offences (*c*)		Persons Found Guilty at Summary Courts (*c*)		Persons Proceeded against Summarily for		Persons Found Guilty at Summary Courts (*c*)	
	Indictable	Non-indictable (*d*)	Indictable	Non-indictable (*d*)	Crimes	Offences (*d*)	Crimes	Offences (*d*)
1976	456·7	1,753·2	359·3	1,657·1	37·4	183·2	33·8	170·5
1977	474·3	1,687·6	371·5	1,573·3	39·0	169·8	35·3	158·0
1978	470·2	1,623·3	367·1	1,509·5	41·1	183·4	36·9	171·0
				- - - - - (*h*)	- - - - - (*h*)		- - - - - (*h*)	
				1,462·5				
1979	460·3	1,588·5	361·7	1,485·8	220·0		205·3	
1980	506·7	1,871·3	396·4	1,756·3	260·7		242·9	

(*a*) This break results from a reorganisation of the statistics. In the 1893 and subsequent volumes of *Judicial Statistics*, however, comparative tables were published which adjusted the 1857–92 figures to the new basis so far as possible. Later still slightly revised figures were published for non-indictable offences back to 1893. The figure for the latter in 1893 shown in the 1893 volume, and supposedly quite closely comparable with earlier figures, was 604·3.
(*b*) No comparative table was published for convictions, and it is impossible to estimate the size of the break here.
(*c*) The figures of those proceeded against summarily can be pushed back much earlier than this, and the decision to make the break at this point has been made because it is no longer possible to give exactly comparable figures of convictions after 1933. The figures of persons found guilty at summary courts can also be pushed back much further in the original sources. The English figures for those proceeded against for offences include people tried in superior courts.
(*d*) Including offences against the Defence Regulations at all times. For the period when these were important, the numbers of such offences and findings of guilty are shown in the next column.

	Persons Proceeded against for Offences against the Defence Regulations		Persons Found Guilty of Offences against the Defence Regulations	
	E. & W.	Scot.	E. & W.	Scot.
1939	61·4	—	59·9	—
1940	340·3	35·6	332·4	34·7
1941	286·4	34·0	278·1	32·9
1942	234·5	27·0	227·4	26·0
1943	194·8	24·5	186·4	23·2
1944	144·1	22·6	137·7	21·5
1945	58·1	7·6	54·0	7·0
1946	22·4	3·2	20·2	3·1
1947	20·9	2·4	18·7	2·3

(*e*) This break results from changes under the Theft Act (1968).
(*f*) On 14 October 1971 most non-indictable offences of criminal damage became indictable.
(*g*) Changes in the treatment of juvenile offenders resulted in a fall in the number of prosecutions from April.
(*h*) The basis of recording was changed in 1978.

Miscellaneous Statistics 3. Trials and Convictions in Superior Courts – England & Wales 1805–19, Scotland 1830–19

NOTES

[1] Sources: 1805–57 – *Returns of Criminal Offenders* and/or *of Committals*, published from time to time in *Sessional Papers*; after 1857 – *Judicial Statistics* (later called *Criminal Statistics*), published for each year, separately for England & Wales and for Scotland, in *Sessional Papers*.

[2] In the earlier years a few people tried by lower courts on criminal charges are included in the statistics. This practice ceased after 1892 in England & Wales, but it is not clear when it ceased in Scotland.

[3] The figures of convictions in England & Wales include those of incorrigible rogues sent for sentence to Quarter Sessions.

[4] The figures of convictions in Scotland do not include those outlawed or cases where bail was forfeited for non-appearance.

	Numbers for Trial		Numbers Convicted	
	E. & W.	Scot.	E. & W.	Scot.
1805	4,605	...	2,783	...
1806	4,346	...	2,515	...
1807	4,446	...	2,567	...
1808	4,735	...	2,723	...
1809	5,330	...	3,238	...
1810	5,146	...	3,158	...
1811	5,337	...	3,163	...
1812	6,576	...	3,913	...
1813	7,164	...	4,422	...
1814	6,390	...	4,025	...
1815	7,818	...	4,883	...
1816	9,091	...	5,797	...
1817	13,932	...	9,056	...
1818	13,567	...	8,958	...
1819	14,254	...	...	...
1820	13,710	...	9,318	...
1821	13,115	...	8,788	...
1822	12,241	...	8,209	...
1823	12,263	...	8,204	...
1824	13,698	...	9,425	...
1825	14,437	...	9,964	...
1826	16,164	...	11,107	...
1827	17,924	...	12,567	...
1828	16,564	...	11,723	...
1829	18,675	...	13,261	...
1830	18,107	1,429	12,805	1,274
1831	19,647	...	13,830	...
1832	20,829	1,758	14,947	1,577
1833	20,072	2,038	14,446	1,796
1834	20,168	1,987	14,261	1,790
	---- (*a*)		---- (*a*)	
1834	22,451		15,995	
1835	20,731	2,156	14,729	1,902
1836	20,984	2,414	14,771	2,152
1837	23,612	2,594	17,090	2,332
1838	23,094	2,885	16,785	2,623
1839	24,443	2,837	17,832	2,585
1840	27,187	3,213	19,927	2,909
1841	27,760	2,907	20,280	2,667
1842	31,309	3,572	22,733	3,145
1843	29,591	2,937	21,092	2,584
1844	26,542	3,023	18,919	2,719
1845	24,303	2,973	17,402	2,679
1846	25,107	3,409	18,144	3,092
1847	28,833	3,881	21,542	3,558
1848	30,349	3,975	22,900	3,689
1849	27,816	3,543	21,001	3,274

	Numbers for Trial		Numbers Convicted	
	E. & W.	Scot.	E. & W.	Scot.
1850	26,813	3,638	20,537	3,363
1851	27,960	3,328	21,579	3,070
1852	27,510	3,288	21,304	3,018
1853	27,057	3,109	20,756	2,821
1854	29,359	3,994	23,047	2,989
1855	25,972	3,630	19,971	2,689
1856	19,437	3,713	14,734	2,723
1857	20,269	3,840	15,307	2,920
1858	17,855	3,782	13,246	2,850
1859	16,674	3,472	12,470	2,563
1860	15,999	3,287	12,068	2,414
1861	18,326	3,229	13,879	2,418
1862	20,001	3,630	15,312	2,693
1863	20,818	3,404	15,799	2,438
1864	19,506	3,212	14,726	2,359
1865	19,614	3,117	14,740	2,355
1866	18,849	3,003	14,254	2,292
1867	18,971	3,305	14,207	2,510
1868	20,091	3,384	15,033	2,490
1869	19,318	3,510	14,340	2,592
1870	17,578	3,046	12,953	2,400
1871	16,269	2,948	11,946	2,184
1872	14,801	3,044	10,862	2,259
1873	14,893	2,755	11,089	2,110
	----- (*b*)			
1874	15,111	2,880	11,509	2,231
1875	14,665	2,872	10,954	2,205
1876	16,012	2,716	12,195	2,051
1877	15,809	2,684	11,942	2,009
1878	16,305	2,922	12,473	2,273
1879	16,303	2,700	12,525	2,091
1880	14,711	2,583	11,214	2,046
1881	14,708	2,444	11,353	1,832
1882	15,190	2,469	11,699	1,943
1883	14,572	2,567	11,347	1,916
1884	14,336	2,610	11,134	2,085
1885	13,494	2,535	10,500	1,956
1886	13,923	2,437	10,686	1,838
1887	13,215	2,357	10,338	1,843
1888	13,684	2,352	10,561	1,853
1889	12,006	2,250	9,348	1,737
1890	11,897	2,312	9,242	1,825
1891	11,605	2,354	9,055	1,823
1892	12,130	2,252	9,607	1,778
			---- (*c*)	
1893	12,296	2,394	9,694	1,903
1894	12,033	2,371	9,518	1,937

See p. 784 for footnotes.

Miscellaneous Statistics 3. *continued*

	Numbers for Trial		Numbers Convicted	
	E. & W.	Scot.	E. & W.	Scot.
1895	11,516	2,027	6,155	1,652
1896	11,103	2,120	8,745	1,704
1897	11,215	2,203	8,867	1,796
1898	11,454	2,290	9,133	1,877
1899	10,902	2,153	8,608	1,785
1900	10,149	2,167	7,975	1,835
1901	10,797	2,291	8,631	1,872
1902	11,392	2,477	9,138	2,052
1903	11,882	2,590	9,642	2,114
1904	12,158	2,631	9,918	2,208
1905	12,325	2,832	10,118	2,314
1906	12,757	2,631	10,390	2,157
1907	12,599	2,456	10,382	2,102
1908	14,122	2,559	11,628	2,115
1909	13,749	1,977	11,328	1,618
1910	13,680	1,488	11,337	1,225
1911	12,951	1,401	10,646	1,121
1912	13,286	1,533	10,931	1,189
1913	12,511	1,358	10,165	1,056
1914	10,800	1,292	8,668	1,012
1915	6,010	1,095	4,677	822
1916	5,011	1,085	3,878	874
1917	5,586	997	4,384	826
1918	5,904	780	4,694	630
1919	7,883	1,294	6,192	1,018
1920	9,130	1,550	7,225	1,231
1921	8,934	1,825	7,152	1,386
1922	8,435	1,774	6,784	1,413
1923	8,126	1,415	6,541	1,170
1924	7,845	1,188	6,379	981
1925	8,139	1,196	6,639	953
1926	7,924	1,197	6,350	994
1927	7,136	1,214	5,773	963
1928	7,282	1,180	6,019	929
1929	7,072	1,049	5,879	872
1930	8,384	1,131	6,921	894
1931	8,667	1,174	7,389	932
1932	10,410	1,199	8,968	957
1933	9,201	1,307	7,759	1,083
1934	8,675	1,395	7,297	1,114
1935	8,270	1,303	6,828	1,014
1936	8,492	1,217	7,079	1,006
1937	9,083	1,142	7,649	928
1938	10,003	1,130	8,612	912
1939	9,751	1,072	8,428	858
1940 (*d*)	7,829	1,271	6,825	1,072
1941	10,079	1,931	8,832	1,646
1942	11,565	1,907	10,176	1,512
1943	11,944	2,480	10,653	2,007
1944	12,279	1,656	10,894	1,434
1945	15,903	1,886	14,397	1,612
1946	17,750	1,843	16,062	1,505
1947	20,216	1,831	18,138	1,485
1948	23,018	1,771	20,890	1,434
1949	19,544	1,638	17,552	1,400
1950	19,935	1,618	17,149	1,357
1951	19,989	1,823	18,092	1,420
1952	22,153	1,778	19,971	1,443
1953	20,263	1,791	18,259	1,471
1954	18,736	1,646	16,740	1,301
1955	18,091	1,656	16,249	1,384
1956	19,572	1,701	17,700	1,378
1957	22,935	1,859	20,728	1,517
1958	27,801	2,204	25,305	1,902
1959	29,601	2,289	26,931	1,975
1960	30,591	2,283	27,830	2,032
1961	34,324	2,526	31,283	2,200
1962	33,009	2,811	29,570	2,363
1963	25,594	2,832	22,267	2,376
1964	24,369	2,687	20,397	2,217
1965	26,864	2,591	22,355	2,079
1966	28,838	3,236	24,404	2,614
1967	30,265	3,425	25,585	2,691
1968	32,347	2,979	27,395	2,579
1969	38,127	2,915	32,433	2,548
1970	44,134	3,300	37,519	2,883
1971	47,588	3,513	39,776	3,033
1972	51,921	3,271	43,131	2,772
1973	54,408	2,954	44,774	2,528
1974	56,403	2,979	46,790	2,728
1975	63,129	3,313	52,587	3,094
1976	67,975	3,461	56,236	3,167
1977	68,721	3,737	57,225	3,324
1978	69,143	3,399	56,966	3,200
1979	61,237	3,129	49,303	2,747
1980	73,892	4,097	59,008	3,387

(*a*) Seven categories of offences were included in the figures for the first time in 1834. Figures are given here for that year both including and excluding these categories.

(*b*) The figures do not subsequently include incorrigible rogues sent for sentence to Quarter Sessions.

(*c*) See note [2] above.

(*d*) Subsequently includes offences against the Defence Regulations. For the period when these were of some significance these were as follows:

	Numbers for Trial England & Wales	Numbers Convicted England & Wales
1940	107	84
1941	373	312
1942	387	327
1943	464	396
1944	407	348
1945	360	287
1946	253	214
1947	191	156
1948	269	221
1949	182	147
1950	56	140

Miscellaneous Statistics 4. Indictable Offences Known to the Police – Ireland 1864–1980

NOTES TO PART A

[1] SOURCES: *Judicial Statistics* (later *Criminal Statistics*) in *Sessional Papers*.

[2] Statistics to 1876 (1st line) are of offences about which proceedings were instituted.

A. Ireland, 1864–1919 (*a*)

	Total	Against the Person	Against Property with Violence	Against Property without Violence
1864	10,865	1,701	547	6,501
1865	9,766	1,585	483	5,592
1866	9,082	1,330	424	5,153
1867	9,260	1,306	532	5,624
1868	9,090	1,399	521	5,748
1869	9,178	1,406	623	5,459
1870	9,517	1,448	657	5,515
1871	8,155	1,469	497	4,801
1872	7,716	1,757	446	4,326
1873	6,942	1,370	432	4,143
1874	6,662	1,329	388	4,149
1875	6,598	1,635	354	3,935
1876	6,261 ----- (*b*) 9,175	1,627	376	3,549 ----- (*b*) 6,463
1877	9,674	1,625	361	6,804
1878	10,933	1,578	485	7,814
1879	12,432	1,457	592	8,454
1880	12,779	1,369	584	7,235
1881	15,550	1,475	754	7,683
1882	13,966	1,503	560	7,464
1883	10,585	1,197	416	7,348
1884	10,593	1,392	329	7,285
1885	10,435	1,294	359	6,944
1886	10,544	1,458	535	6,364
1887	9,876	1,274	355	6,372
1888	9,544	1,224	347	6,428
1889	9,221	1,089	308	6,364
1890	8,603	1,073	389	5,733
1891	8,689	1,013	294	6,030
1892	8,468	986	326	5,758
1893	8,935	1,066	386	5,933
1894	8,734	1,110	374	6,069
1895	7,471	776	382	5,087
1896	8,801	867	456	6,285
1897	9,464	803	544	6,911
1898	9,988	877	537	7,217
1899	9,144	803	480	6,485
1900	8,972	681	456	6,548
1901	9,003	651	630	6,518
1902	8,736	650	719	6,347
1903	9,137	614	693	6,900
1904	9,617	622	771	7,270
1905	9,728	583	756	7,310
1906	9,465	526	783	7,152
1907	9,418	526	769	6,949
1908	10,266	627	828	7,393
1909	9,873	523	913	7,134
1910	9,870	574	732	7,064
1911	9,831	580	867	6,878
1912	9,931	544	960	7,196
1913	9,241	672	831	6,525
1914	8,504	587	709	6,067
1915	7,873	457	646	5,841
1916	7,397	375	735	5,417
1917	7,401	329	800	5,281
1918	7,457	338	735	4,758
1919	8,130	507	1,115	4,166

See p. 787 for footnotes.

NOTES TO PART B

[1] Source: *Abstract.*

[2] The analysis of the total is not continued in the source after 1938, but a similar breakdown of those found guilty is substituted, and this is given in Part B of table 5.

[3] Hybrid offences, which become indictable only if tried on indictment, are included in this table. They seem to be the main reason for the increase since 1967.

B. Northern Ireland, 1928–80

	Total	Against the Person	Against Property with Violence	Against Property without Violence		Total		Total
1928	2,402	104	507	1,625	1946	6,112	1964	10,428
1929	2,324	126	559	1,462	1947	6,894	1965	12,846
1930	2,471	95	505	1,665	1948	7,581	1966	14,673
1931	2,753	97	491	1,794	1949	6,241	1967	15,404
1932	3,587	155	774	2,009	1950	7,475	1968	16,294
1933	3,105	118	733	1,963	1951	8,048	1969	20,303
1934	3,710	132	772	2,336	1952	7,498	1970	24,810
1935	4,350	219	762	2,190	1953	6,890	1971	30,828
1936	3,642	109	877	2,367	1954	6,428	1972	35,884
1937	3,016	133	764	1,794	1955	6,049	1973	32,057
1938	2,818	108	606	1,739	1956	6,427	1974	33,314
1939	2,579	...	...	...	1957	6,555	1975	37,239
1940	2,990	...	...	...	1958	7,594	1976	39,914
1941	3,586	...	...	...	1959	7,606	1977	45,571
1942	4,307	...	...	...	1960	8,460	1978	46,499
1943	4,566	...	...	...	1961	9,850	1979	49,975
1944	5,123	...	...	...	1962	10,286	1980	52,384
1945	5,709	...	...	...	1963	10,859		

NOTES TO PART C

[1] SOURCE: *Statistical Abstract of Ireland*.

[2] For the period 1958–74 the statistics relate to years ended 30 September.

C. Republic of Ireland, 1927–80

	Total	Against the Person	Against Property with Violence	Against Property without Violence
1927	7,091	504	908	4,574
1928	6,061	499	810	3,881
1929	5,877	426	759	3,956
1930	6,000	430	695	4,099
1931	6,341	490	884	4,188
1932	6,390	410	980	4,296
1933	6,954	548	968	4,478
1934	7,229	565	1,047	4,244
1935	6,538	507	1,032	4,144
1936	6,484	548	1,197	4,197
1937	6,232	518	1,000	4,292
1938	6,769	453	1,102	4,850
1939	8,202	387	1,186	6,186
1940	9,014	401 / 442 (c)	1,407 / 1,658 (c)	6,771 / 6,748 (c)
1941	13,180	459	2,179	10,391
1942	17,213	505	2,858	13,649
1943	17,305	545	2,879	13,714
1944	15,863	571	2,497	12,593
1945	16,786	639	2,732	13,227
1946	15,078	638	2,077	11,782
1947	15,329	436	2,727	12,004
1948	14,949	535	2,883	11,354
1949	12,171	496	2,407	9,130
1950	12,231	499	2,445	9,157
1951	14,127	446	2,996	10,513
1952	14,720	465	2,728	11,301
1953	15,602	531	3,032	11,813
1954	11,917	455	2,538	8,753
1955	11,531	525	2,325	8,555
1956	12,782	542	2,695	9,365
1957	14,037	473	3,061	10,339
1958	16,567 (d)	558 (d)	3,645 (d)	12,219 (d)
1959	17,865	587	3,824	13,270
1960	15,375	675	2,982	11,470
1961	14,818	701	3,186	10,623
1962	15,307	885	3,466	10,666
1963	16,203	1,047	4,006	10,823
1964	17,700	1,045	4,282	11,972
1965	16,736	1,113	4,213	11,014
1966	19,029	1,132	4,957	12,631
1967	20,558	1,149	5,575	13,452
1968	23,104	1,151	6,469	15,091
1969	25,972	1,170	7,563	16,764
1970	30,756	1,142	9,577	19,557
1971	37,781	1,256	10,654	24,929
1972	39,237	1,321	11,600	25,568
1973	38,022	1,655	11,800	23,567
1974	40,096 (d)	1,709 (d)	12,973 (d)	24,345 (d)
1975	48,387	1,456	16,432	30,335
1976	54,382	1,714	20,903	31,540
1977	62,946	2,063	23,154	37,465
1978	62,000	2,266	21,119	38,397
1979	64,057	2,326	21,535	39,980
1980	72,780	2,351	24,878	45,298

(*a*) Figures for 1863 exclusive of the Dublin Metropolitan Police District are 9,214, 2,166, 569, and 5,433 respectively.

(*b*) See note 2 above.

(*c*) There was a rearrangement of the classification in 1940.

(*d*) See note 2 above. Figures for the last quarter of 1974 are 10,511, 349, 3,590, and 6,338 respectively.

Miscellaneous Statistics 5. Judicial Proceedings and Convictions – Ireland 1851–1980

NOTES TO PART A

[1] Source: *Judicial Statistics* (later *Criminal Statistics*) in *Sessional Papers*.

[2] In this part cases where the charge was proved but the offender was not actually convicted are not included under 'Convictions'.

A. Ireland, 1851–1919

	Persons Proceeded Against			Convictions	
	Indictable Offences (in thousands) (*a*)	Non-Indictable Offences (in thousands) (*a*)	Persons Tried in Higher Courts	Higher Courts	Summary Courts (in thousands)
1851	...	...	24,684	14,377	...
1852	...	...	17,678	10,454	...
1853	...	...	15,144	8,714	...
1854	...	...	11,788	7,051	...
1855	...	...	9,012	5,220	...
1856	...	...	7,099	4,024	...
1857	...	...	7,210	3,925	...
1858	...	...	6,308	3,350	...
1859	...	...	5,865	3,109	...
1860	...	...	5,386	2,979	...
1861	...	...	5,586	3,271	...
1862	...	...	6,666	3,796	...
1863	9·2 (*a*)	227·5 (*a*)	6,078	3,285	187·0
1864	10·9	232·4	5,086	3,000	191·6
1865	9·8	233·9	4,657	2,661	194·2
1866	9·1	236·8	4,326	2,418	192·1
1867	9·3	259·7	4,561	2,732	215·7
1868	9·1	238·3	4,127	2,394	200·0
1869	9·2	239·4	4,151	2,452	196·4
1870	9·5	234·0	4,936	3,048	192·4
1871	8·2	220·2	4,485	2,557	183·4
1872	7·7	211·5	4,476	2,565	177·5
1873	6·9	223·8	4,544	2,541	191·2
1874	6·7	228·5	4,130	2,367	193·1
1875	6·6	243·1	4,248	2,484	209·2
1876	6·3 ---- (*a*) 7·1	256·3 ---- (*a*) 250·4	4,146	2,343	219·7
1877	7·2	259·9	3,870	2,300	229·7
1878	8·2	262·4	4,183	2,293	226·5
1879	8·7	249·3	4,363	2,217	212·3
1880	8·9	233·6	4,716	2,383	194·4
1881	8·9	199·0	5,310	2,698	166·3
1882	7·7	211·5	4,301	2,255	179·7
1883	6·4	219·2	3,025	1,740	190·2
1884	6·4	226·6	2,925	1,546	198·2
1885	6·3	218·7	2,850	1,573	188·1
1886	6·3	209·2	3,028	1,619	180·0
1887	6·2	212·9	2,694	1,411	182·8
1888	5·8	223·5	2,188	1,220	195·3
1889	5·6	227·3	2,181	1,225	199·5
1890	5·4	229·9	2,061	1,193	202·0
1891	5·5	226·6	2,112	1,255	198·0
1892	5·5	220·2	2,031	1,196	192·8
1893	5·9	211·6	2,339	1,378	183·5
1894	6·0	213·0	2,408	1,469	187·4
1895	5·1	180·5	1,775	1,096	153·0

See p. 792 for footnotes.

A. Ireland, 1851–1919 (*cont.*)

	Persons Proceeded Against			Convictions	
	Indictable Offences (in thousands) (*a*)	Non-Indictable Offences (in thousands) (*a*)	Persons Tried in Higher Courts	Higher Courts	Summary Courts (in thousands)
1896	5·4	192·8	2,055	1,310	164·0
1897	5·4	229·0	1,885	1,242	199·0
1898	5·6	228·8	2,111	1,367	201·8
1899	5·2	228·2	1,953	1,329	201·4
1900	5·1	202·3	1,682	1,087	175·7
1901	5·1	182·6	1,856	1,211	158·3
1902	5·0	188·5	1,717	1,086	163·7
1903	5·1	183·5	1,733	1,169	158·8
1904	5·6	178·9	1,837	1,296	156·5
1905	6·0	179·1	2,060	1,367	157·5
1906	5·9	169·7	2,072	1,303	148·2
1907	6·2	168·5	2,193	1,338	147·1
1908	6·7	200·2	2,242	1,375	177·2
1909	6·5	201·7	2,219	1,507	176·6
1910	6·3	193·6	2,036	1,373	167·9
1911	6·4	185·3	2,114	1,496	159·0
1912	6·9	195·2	2,109	1,443	168·7
1913	6·5	178·1	2,238	1,483	152·5
1914	5·8	163·0	1,970	1,410	138·8
1915	5·7	152·1	1,717	1,084	128·8
1916	5·3	132·8	1,426	920	112·2
1917	5·0	106·5	1,414	918	89·0
1918	3·9	95·7	1,181	737	78·9
1919	3·8	96·0	1,479	948	80·1

NOTES TO PART B

[1] SOURCE: *Abstract*.
[2] The analysis of those found guilty is not given in the source prior to 1938, but a similar breakdown of offences known to the police is given for earlier years in part B of table 4.
[3] In this part all cases where the charges were proved are included under 'Found Guilty', except as indicated in footnote (*d*).
[4] Hybrid offences, which become indictable only if tried on indictment, are included with indictable offences, except as indicated in footnote (*e*).

B. Northern Ireland, 1924–80

	Persons Proceeded Against		Persons Found Guilty (*d*)		Persons Found Guilty of	
	Indictable Offences (in thousands)	Non-Indictable Offences (in thousands)	Indictable Offences (in thousands)	Non-Indictable Offences (in thousands)	Offences against the Person	Breaking and Entering (*b*)
1924	1·9	37·0	0·5	31·4	...	...
1925	1·9	33·9	0·5	28·4	...	...
1926	2·3	31·3	0·5	26·3	...	...
1927	2·0	33·4	0·5	28·1	...	...
1928	1·9	31·3 ----- (*c*) 32·2	0·5 ---- (*d*) 1·3	25·3 ----- (*d*) 25·8	...	...
1929	1·8	31·9	1·2	26·7	...	...
1930	1·7	32·4	1·3	28·6	...	...
1931	1·7	32·6	1·3	29·0	...	...
1932	2·0	36·9	1·6	33·2	...	...
1933	1·7	41·6	1·3	37·2	...	...

See p. 792 for footnotes.

B. Northern Ireland, 1924–80 (*cont.*)

	Persons Proceeded Against		Persons Found Guilty		Persons Found Guilty of	
	Indictable Offences (in thousands)	Non-Indictable Offences (in thousands)	Indictable Offences (in thousands)	Non-Indictable Offences (in thousands)	Offences against the Person	Breaking and Entering (*b*)
1934	2·0	47·0	1·6	42·8	...	...
1935	2·2	43·1	1·7	38·6	99	331
1936	2·2	46·8	1·8	42·5	70	274
1937	2·4	45·5	2·0	41·1	95	352
1938	2·3	43·1	1·9	39·6	99	327
1939	2·2	41·9	2·0	38·5	89	382
1940	2·8	46·3	2·5	43·5	54	449
1941	2·9	52·9	2·5	50·1	76	443
1942	3·4	49·5	2·9	46·4	107	433
1943	3·5	50·5	3·0	47·2	109	499
1944	3·3	51·3	2·8	48·1	108	448
1945	3·2	41·7	2·7	39·2	105	505
1946	3·1	40·6	2·7	38·6	122	436
1947	3·0	38·1	2·6	35·4	114	508
1948	3·5	39·6	3·1	36·2	136	555
1949	2·9	41·4	2·7	38·1	117	542
1950	2·9	41·4	2·7	38·6	145	575
1951	3·4	41·7	3·1	38·9	144	626
1952	3·3	44·4	3·0	42·0	113	553
1953	3·0	42·7	2·7	40·3	160	548
1954	2·9	45·7	2·7	43·0	155	546
1955	2·7	46·3	2·5	43·4	183	488
1956	3·0	47·3	2·8	44·6	228	576
1957	2·9	38·9	2·7	36·7	196	623
1958	3·3	44·1	3·1	41·9	209	814
1959	3·4	47·6	3·2	45·4	315	855
1960	3·4	48·5	3·3	46·4	271	894
1961	3·6	49·9	3·4	47·9	278	933
1962	3·8	48·8	3·6	46·1	321	930
1963	4·1	46·7	3·9	43·7	361	1,081
1964	3·7	43·7	3·5	41·2	349	920
1965	3·9	43·4	3·7	40·7	330	959
1966	4·2	39·0	4·0	36·3	365	1,228
1967	4·5	39·6	4·2	36·8	378	1,243
1968	4·8	41·1	4·6	38·3	481	1,224
1969	4·6	34·9	4·4	32·0	382	1,250
1970	4·3	41·0	4·2	37·8	338	1,380
1971	4·6	39·3	4·3	35·4	349	1,271
1972	3·3	29·1	3·2	26·1	355	819
1973	3·8	33·7	3·5	31·0	439	791
1974	5·0	35·0	4·5	32·2	631	1,376
	---- (*e*)	----- (*e*)				
1975	5·4	38·1	5·0	35·5	746	1,511
1976	5·3	41·6	4·9	38·8	592	1,721
1977	5·6	44·2	5·2	41·1	656	1,831
1978	5·1	47·6	4·8	44·3	574	1,603
1979	7·1	46·2	6·6	42·0	825	2,020
1980	7·0	46·5	6·6	40·6	704	2,192

See p. 792 for footnotes.

NOTES TO PART C

[1] SOURCE: *Statistical Abstract of Ireland*.

[2] For the period 1958–74 the statistics relate to years ended 30 September.

[3] In this part all cases where the charges were proved are included under 'Found Guilty'.

C. Republic of Ireland, 1927–80

	Persons Proceeded Against		Persons Found Guilty		
	Indictable Offences (in thousands)	Non-Indictable Offences (in thousands)	Indictable Offences (in thousands) (*f*)	Non-Indictable Offences (in thousands)	Convictions in Higher Courts
1927	4·9	74	2·6	64	671
1928	5·0	90	2·8	79	670
1929	4·5	94	2·6	83	600
1930	4·8	99	2·9	88	588
1931	4·5	80	2·8	72	505
1932	4·8	83	3·1	72	494
1933	5·0	84	3·0	72	577
1934	6·1	90	3·7	79	600
1935	5·9	103	4·1	92	615
1936	5·8	102	3·6	93	591
1937	5·3	99	3·4	90	496
1938	5·0	104	3·5	96	429
1939	4·8	104	3·4	95	505
1940	5·4	85	4·0	78	540
1941	8·2	98	6·1	91	612
1942	10·8	105	8·2	96	644
1943	10·7	108	8·1	100	690
1944	9·5	128	7·2	119	611
1945	9·8	151	7·4	142	610
1946	8·5	151	6·2	143	550
1947	8·6	152	6·5	142	490
1948	7·9	167	5·9	157	497
1949	6·7	165	5·1	156	406
1950	6·9	148	5·3	140	394
1951	7·6	146	6·1	138	257
1952	6·8	140	5·4	132	241
1953	7·1	131	5·7	123	312
1954	6·1	110	4·9	104	207
1955	6·2	99	4·7	94	211
1956	6·8	94	5·3	88	243
1957	6·7	87	5·1	81	250
1958	7·7 (*g*)	83 (*g*)	6·4 (*g*)	77 (*g*)	297 (*g*)
1959	8·2	89	7·1	83	297
1960	8·5	103	7·1	95	363
1961	8·9	104	7·7	96	249
1962	9·4	105	7·6	96	702
1963	10·2	101	8·2	92	725
1964	10·2	121	8·2	109	679
1965	10·6	140	8·7	128	585
1966	11·2	150	9·2	139	678
1967	11·6	164	9·5	149	637
1968	12·7	174	10·5	154	680
1969	14·3	178	12·1	155	448
1970	13·7	170	11·6	146	697
1971	16·1	198	13·4	173	672

See p. 792 for footnotes.

C. Republic of Ireland, 1927–80 (*cont.*)

	Persons Proceeded Against		Persons Found Guilty		
	Indictable Offences (in thousands)	Non-Indictable Offences (in thousands)	Indictable Offences (in thousands) (*f*)	Non-Indictable Offences (in thousands)	Convictions in Higher Courts
1972	15·7	190	13·2	162	850
1973	16·8	240	13·5	199	948
1974	17·9	299	14·9	247	975
1975	19·5 (*g*)	308 (*g*)	16·2 (*g*)	243 (*g*)	769 (*g*)
1976	21·0	295	7·7	. . . (*h*)	762
1977	22·6	388	7·2	294	682
1978	23·2	346	10·0	271	773
1979	23·9	338	9·7	268	832
1980	26·8	403	9·4	321	552

(*a*) To 1876 (1st line) the figures are of offences dealt with on indictment and offences dealt with summarily.
(*b*) Later 'burglary and robbery'.
(*c*) Previously excluding proceedings in Juvenile Courts.
(*d*) Convictions in higher courts and in Summary Courts to 1928 (1st line).
(*e*) Hybrid offences are subsequently included with non-indictable offences.
(*f*) In Summary Courts only.
(*g*) See note 2 above. Figures for the last quarter of 1974 for the first two columns and the last are 4·4, 66, and 62 respectively.
(*h*) 196 thousand were actually convicted, compared with 212 thousand in the previous year.

Miscellaneous Statistics 6. Electorate and Votes Cast at General Elections – United Kingdom, 1832–1983

NOTE
SOURCE: F. W. S. Craig, *British Electoral Facts 1832–1980* (Chichester, 1981), and, for 1983, *Return of Election Expenses*.

(electorate and votes recorded in thousands)

	England					Wales				
	Total Electorate	Electorate in Contested Seats	Votes Recorded	Seats Contested	Unopposed Returns	Total Electorate	Electorate in Contested Seats	Votes Recorded	Seats Contested	Unopposed Returns
1832	610	477	668	351	113	42	11	14	10	22
1835	625	362	492	287	177	42	13	15	10	22
1837	741	507	669	324	140	50	22	22	15	17
1841	777	384	510	255	209	55	11	8	8	24
1847	828	339	404	221	241	55	10	13	5	27
1852	858	483	568	295	165	55	13	12	11	21
1857	879	446	525	246	214	56	11	11	5	27
1859	900	387	461	222	238	56	6	4	4	28
1865	970	557	698	282	182	62	8	6	5	27
1868	1,880	1,567	1,997	355	100	127	74	82	19	14
1874	2,097	1,602	1,941	325	126	137	95	89	21	12
1880	2,339	2,046	2,726	385	66	150	101	101	23	10
1885	4,095	4,052	3,530	451	5	282	249	205	30	4
1886	4,095	2,829	2,285	328	128	282	175	130	22	12
1892	4,479	4,177	3,506	424	32	315	275	220	30	4
1895	4,620	3,425	2,939	342	114	323	302	251	32	2
1900	4,929	3,282	2,708	305	151	340	226	179	23	11
1906	5,417	5,189	4,658	439	17	388	239	211	22	12
1910 Jan.	5,775	5,721	5,388	450	6	426	426	378	34	—
1910 Dec.	5,775	4,749	4,199	386	70	426	302	247	23	11
1918	16,022	13,998	8,051	422	63	1,171	803	529	24	11
1922	16,727	15,454	11,696	448	37	1,236	1,125	893	31	4
1923	17,080	16,129	11,927	456	29	1,259	1,093	845	30	5
1924	17,471	16,859	13,562	467	18	1,288	986	789	27	8
1929	23,425	23,295	18,502	482	3	1,599	1,599	1,317	35	—
1931	24,424	22,763	18,083	448	37	1,625	1,373	1,089	29	6
1935	25,619	24,807	18,273	466	19	1,670	1,140	871	24	11
1945	27,046	27,024	20,539	509	1	1,798	1,759	1,331	34	1
1950	28,374		23,954	506	—	1,802		1,529	36	—
1951	28,813		23,826	506	—	1,813		1,529	36	—
1955	28,790		22,136	511	—	1,801		1,434	36	—
1959	29,303		23,128	511	—	1,806		1,491	36	—
1964	29,805		22,937	511	—	1,805		1,447	36	—
1966	29,894		22,693	511	—	1,801		1,423	36	—
1970	32,737		23,361	511	—	1,959		1,517	36	—
1974 Feb.	33,078		26,142	516	—	1,994		1,594	36	—
1974 Oct.	33,341		24,191	516	—	2,008		1,538	36	—
1979	34,211		25,972	516	—	2,061		1,637	36	—
1983	35,143		25,473	523	—	2,114		1,609	38	—

Miscellaneous Statistics 6. *continued*

(electorate and votes recorded in thousands)

	Scotland					Ireland				
	Total Electorate	Electorate in Contested Seats	Votes Recorded	Seats Contested	Unopposed Returns	Total Electorate	Electorate in Contested Seats	Votes Recorded	Seats Contested	Unopposed Returns
1832	64	50	54	37	16	90	65	89	69	34
1835	73	49	44	30	23	98	56	60	56	47
1837	84	53	41	31	22	122	64	65	50	53
1841	84	36	27	24	29	94	44	49	34	69
1847	89	32	24	16	37	125	59	32	41	62
1852	99	45	28	20	33	164	109	132	71	32
1857	100	40	36	15	38	191	118	142	58	45
1859	106	12	8	8	45	200	66	93	41	62
1865	105	42	48	16	37	203	83	93	48	55
1868	231	144	149	32	26	223	74	93	36	67
1874	271	209	212	36	22	223	183	225	83	18
1880	294	240	270	46	12	229	194	251	86	15
1885	561	530	447	65	5	738	592	451	80	21
1886	561	480	358	61	9	738	245	195	32	69
1892	590	590	475	70	—	741	569	393	81	20
1895	616	580	456	65	5	732	289	221	42	59
1900	662	628	486	67	3	758	233	149	32	69
1906	729	721	597	69	1	687	164	135	21	80
1910 Jan.	762	762	660	70	—	684	263	221	40	63
1910 Dec.	779	689	578	58	12	684	264	208	41	62
1918	2,205	1,989	1,127	63	8	1,926	1,451	1,039	76	25
						Northern Ireland				
1922	2,232	2,149	1,569	68	3	609	161	208	3	9
1923	2,251	2,145	1,501	67	4	615	210	242	4	8
1924	2,280	2,208	1,717	68	3	610	522	519	10	2
1929	2,940	2,940	2,243	71	—	772	573	510	9	3
1931	2,992	2,701	2,174	63	8	773	252	282	4	8
1935	3,116	3,074	2,324	70	1	805	401	451	6	6
1945	3,343		2,390	71	—	836	767	720	11	1
1950	3,370		2,727	71	—	865	725	561	10	2
1951	3,421		2,778	71	—	872	580	463	8	4
1955	3,388		2,543	71	—	873		647	12	—
1959	3,414		2,668	71	—	875		576	12	—
1964	3,393		2,635	71	—	891		638	12	—
1966	3,360		2,552	71	—	902		596	12	—
1970	3,629		2,688	71	—	1,017		779	12	—
1974 Feb.	3,656		2,887	71	—	1,027		718	12	—
1974 Oct.	3,687		2,758	71	—	1,037		702	12	—
1979	3,796		2,917	71	—	1,027		696	12	—
1983	3,887		2,825	72	—	1,049		765	20	—

Miscellaneous Statistics 6. *continued*

(electorate and votes recorded in thousands)

	Universities					United Kingdom				
	Total Electorate	Electorate in Contested Seats	Votes Recorded	Seats Contested	Unopposed Returns	Total Electorate	Electorate in Contested Seats	Votes Recorded	Seats Contested	Unopposed Returns
1832	7	2	3	2	4	813	606	828	469	189
1835	7	—	—	—	6	846	480	611	383	275
1837	7	2	2	2	4	1,005	647	798	422	236
1841	7	—	—	—	6	1,017	475	593	319	337
1847	9	9	10	6	—	1,106	449	482	289	367
1852	9	3	3	2	4	1,184	653	744	399	255
1857	10	2	2	2	4	1,236	617	717	326	328
1859	10	—	—	—	6	1,272	471	566	275	379
1865	11	5	10	4	2	1,350	695	855	355	303
1868	22	11	12	4	5	2,485	1,871	2,333	446	212
1874	23	—	—	—	—	2,752	1,889	2,466	465	187
1880	29	14	11	3	6	3,040	2,597	3,359	543	109
1885	33	7	5	1	8	5,708	5,430	4,638	627	43
1886	33	7	6	3	6	5,708	3,735	2,974	546	224
1892	37	4	5	2	7	6,161	5,614	4,598	607	63
1895	39	—	—	—	—	6,331	4,598	3,866	481	189
1900	42	—	—	—	—	6,731	4,369	3,523	427	243
1906	45	34	26	5	4	7,265	6,348	5,626	556	114
1910 Jan.	48	29	21	3	6	7,695	7,201	6,667	595	75
1910 Dec.	47	6	4	1	8	7,710	6,011	5,235	507	163
1918	68	68	41	15	—	21,392	18,311	10,787	600	107
1922	72	39	26	8	4	20,874	18,928	14,392	558	57
1923	78	34	32	8	4	21,283	19,621	14,548	565	50
1924	82	51	53	11	1	21,731	20,655	16,640	583	32
1929	119	116	76	11	1	28,855	28,522	22,648	608	7
1931	138	40	28	4	8	29,952	27,130	21,656	548	67
1935	165	134	78	9	3	31,374	29,556	21,997	575	40
1945	217	217	116	12	—	33,240	33,111	25,095	637	3
1950	—	—	—	—	—	34,412	34,272	28,771	623	2
1951	—	—	—	—	—	34,919	34,627	28,597	621	4
1955	—	—	—	—	—	34,852		26,760	630	—
1959	—	—	—	—	—	35,397		27,863	630	—
1964	—	—	—	—	—	35,894		27,657	630	—
1966	—	—	—	—	—	35,957		27,265	630	—
1970	—	—	—	—	—	39,342		28,345	630	—
1974 Feb.	—	—	—	—	—	39,754		31,340	635	—
1974 Oct.	—	—	—	—	—	40,073		29,189	635	—
1979	—	—	—	—	—	41,096		31,221	635	—
1983	—	—	—	—	—	42,193		30,671	650	—

Miscellaneous Statistics 7. Party Votes and Members Elected at General Elections – United Kingdom 1832–1983

NOTES

[1] SOURCES: As for table 6.

[2] Communist Party, Plaid Cymru, and Scottish National Party votes from 1922 have been as follows:

	Comm.	P.C.	S.N.P.		Comm.	P.C.	S.N.P.
1922	34	—	—	1955	33	45	12
1923	39	—	—	1959	31	78	22
1924	55	—	—	1964	46	70	64
1929	51	1	3	1966	62	61	128
1931	75	2	21	1970	38	175	307
1935	27	3	30	1974 Feb.	33	171	633
1945	103	16	31	1974 Oct.	17	166	840
1950	92	18	10	1979	17	133	504
1951	22	11	7	1983	12	125	332

[3] One Communist M.P. was elected in each of the 1922, 1924, and 1935 elections and two in 1945. Plaid Cymru and Scottish National Party M.P.'s were elected as follows:

	P.C.	S.N.P.
1970	—	1
1974 Feb.	2	7
1974 Oct.	3	11
1979	2	2
1983	2	2

	Votes for Main Parties (thousands)			M.P.'s Elected			of which unopposed returns		
	Con (*a*)	Lib (*b*)	Lab	Con (*a*)	Lib (*b*)	Lab	Con (*a*)	Lib (*b*)	Lab
1832	241	555	—	175	441	—	66	109	—
1835	261	350	—	273	385	—	121	154	—
1837	380	418	—	314	344	—	121	115	—
1841	306	274	—	367	271	—	212	113	—
1847	205	259	—	324	293	—	212	137	—
1852	317	426	—	330	324	—	160	95	—
1857	240	464	—	264	377	—	148	176	—
1859	193	372	—	297	357	—	195	184	—
1865	346	508	—	288	370	—	143	160	—
1868	903	1,429	—	271	387	—	91	121	—
1874	1,092	1,281	—	350	242	—	125	52	—
1880	1,426	1,836	—	237	352	—	58	41	—
1885	2,021	2,200	—	249	319	—	10	14	—
1886	1,521	1,354	—	393	192	—	118	40	—
1892	2,159	2,088	—	313	272	—	40	13	—
1895	1,895	1,765	—	411	177	—	132	11	—
1900	1,768	1,572	63	402	183	2	163	22	—
1906	2,422	2,751	322	156	399	29	13	27	—
1910 Jan.	3,104	2,866	506	272	274	40	19	1	—
1910 Dec.	2,420	2,294	372	271	272	42	72	35	3
1918	4,144	2,785	2,246	382	163	57	41	27	11
1922	5,502	4,139	4,237	344	115	142	42	10	4
1923	5,515	4,301	4,440	258	158	191	35	11	3
1924	7,855	2,929	5,489	412	40	151	16	6	9
1929	8,656	5,309	8,370	260	59	287	4	—	—
1931	13,157	1,476	6,650	522	36	52	61	5	6
1935	11,756	1,443	8,325	429	21	154	26	—	13
1945	9,972	2,252	11,968	210	12	393	1	—	2
1950	12,492	2,621	13,266	298	9	315	2	—	—
1951	13,718	731	13,949	321	6	295	4	—	—
1955	13,311	722	12,405	345	6	277	—	—	—
1959	13,751	1,641	12,216	365	6	258	—	—	—
1964	12,003	3,099	12,206	304	9	317	—	—	—
1966	11,418	2,327	13,097	253	12	364	—	—	—
1970	13,145	2,117	12,209	330	6	288	—	—	—
1974 Feb.	11,872	6,060	11,646	297	14	301	—	—	—
1974 Oct.	10,463	5,347	11,457	277	13	319	—	—	—
1979	13,698	4,314	11,532	339	11	269	—	—	—
1983	13,012	4,210 (*c*)	8,457	397	17 (*c*)	209	—	—	—

(*a*) Including Liberal-Conservative 1847–59, Liberal-Unionist 1886–1910; National, National Liberal, and National Labour from 1931.

(*b*) Including Whig, National Liberal in 1922, and Independent Liberals in 1931.

(*c*) Votes for the Social Democratic Party were 3,571 thousands, making the total Alliance vote 7,781 thousand. Six S.D.P. members were elected.

Miscellaneous Statistics 8. General Elections – Republic of Ireland 1927–82

NOTE
SOURCE: *Statistical Abstract of Ireland*.

(in thousands)

	Electorate	Votes Recorded		Electorate	Votes Recorded
1927 June	1,725 (*a*)	1,175 (*a*)	1954	1,763	1,348
1927 Sept.	1,725 (*a*)	1,191 (*a*)	1957	1,738	1,239
1932	1,688 (*a*)	1,292 (*a*)	1961	1,671	1,180
1933	1,720 (*a*)	1,397 (*a*)	1965	1,683	1,264
1937	1,775	1,352	1969	1,735	1,335
1938	1,770	1,302	1973	1,784	1,366
1943	1,816	1,348	1977	2,119	1,617
1944	1,816	1,230	1981	2,275	1,734
1948	1,800	1,337	1982 Feb.	2,275	1,680
1951	1,785	1,344	1982 Nov.	2,335	1,701

(*a*) Excluding University electors and seats.

Miscellaneous Statistics 9. Primary Schools – England & Wales and Scotland 1850–1980

NOTES

[1] SOURCES: England & Wales: 1850–64 – M. E. Sadler and J. W. Edwards, 'Summary of Statistics, Regulations, etc., of Elementary Education in England and Wales', in *Special Reports on Educational Subjects*, vol. 2 (London, H.M.S.O., 1898); 1854–99 – *Report of the Committee of Council on Education (England and Wales)* (annually in *Sessional Papers*); 1900–54 – *Statistics of Public Education in England and Wales* (annually in *Sessional Papers*); 1955–77 – *Statistics of Education* (published annually from 1962 to 1978 by the Ministry of Education). Scotland: 1850–74 (except teachers) – *Abstract*; 1875–99 and teachers 1865–74 – *Report of the Committee of Council and Education (Scotland)* (annually in *Sessional Papers*); 1900–73 – *Statistics of Public Education in Scotland* (annually in *Sessional Papers*) followed by *Scottish Educational Statistics* from 1966 to 1974.

[2] The description primary schools is used in the title of this table though they were not known as such for the whole period, at any rate in England & Wales. The exact coverage is indicated in column headings and the footnotes.

[3] The figures apply to the following annual periods: England & Wales 1850–2 – year ended 31 October; 1854–1914 – year ended 31 August; 1920–38 – year ended 31 March; 1946 onwards – in January. Scotland: 1850–2 – year ended 31 October; 1854–79 – year ended 31 August; 1880–1901 – year ended 30 September; 1902–38 – year ended 31 August; 1946–7 – at 31 July; 1948–53 (except teachers) – at 31 March; 1954–74 – at 1 January; 1975–80 at 30 September; teachers 1951–64 at 1 October; 1965 in September; 1966–74 in December; 1975–80 at 30 September.

[4] Subsequent figures for both England & Wales and Scotland are calculated from *Educational Statistics of the U.K.* and from figures in the *Scottish Abstract of Statistics*, the *Digest of Welsh Statistics*, and the *Digest of Statistics, Northern Ireland*.

	England & Wales			Scotland		
	Number of Schools or Departments Inspected (*a*)	Average Number of Children Attending Inspected Day Schools (thousands)	Number of Full-time Teachers (*b*) (thousands)	Number of Schools Inspected	Average Number of Children Attending Inspected Day Schools (thousands)	Number of Full-time Teachers (*b*) (thousands)
1850	1,943 (*c*)	...	...	319	28	...
1851	2,093 (*c*)	250 (*c*)	...	315	32	...
1852	2,375 (*c*)	323 (*c*)	...	533	64	...
1853 (*d*)	2,384 (*c*)	285 (*c*)	2·0	577	60	...
1854	3,147 (*c*)	394 (*c*)	2·4	678	68	...
1855	3,853 (*c*)	447 (*c*)	3·0	974	91	...
1856	4,237 (*c*)	480 (*c*)	3·7	942	92	...
1857	4,438 (*c*)	531 (*c*)	4·4	960	95	...
1858	5,435 (*c*)	636 (*c*)	5·1	1,206	125	...
1859	5,531 (*c*)	675 (*c*)	6·0	1,055	127	...
1860	6,012 (*c*)	751 (*c*)	6·7	1,260	133	...
1861	6,259 (*c*)	774 (*c*)	7·6	1,446	146	...
1862	6,113 (*c*)	799 (*c*)	8·0	1,456	151	...
	----	----				
1863	6,188	826	8·8	1,512	162	...
1864	6,428	829	9·7	1,421	148	...
	---- (*e*)	---- (*e*)	---- (*f*)			
1864	8,675	797	9·1			
1865	9,347	848	10·3	1,573	156	1·9
1866	9,984	863	10·9	1,619	162	2·0
1867	10,364	912	11·7	1,739	169	2·2
1868	10,857	979	12·4	1,843	182	2·3
1869	11,404	1,063	13·0	1,745	179	2·2
1870	12,061	1,152	13·7	1,963	198	2·5
1871	12,788	1,231	14·4	1,944	201	2·4
1872	14,101	1,336	16·4	1,962	206	2·6
1873	15,929	1,482	18·8	2,043	213	2·7
1874	17,646	1,679	21·2	2,587	275	3·2
				---- (*g*)	---- (*g*)	---- (*g*)
1875	19,245	1,837	23·7	2,890	312	3·9
1876	20,782	1,985	26·8	2,912	333	4·3
1877	22,033	2,151	30·0	2,931	360	4·9
1878	23,618	2,405	34·5	2,998	377	5·2
1879	24,890	2,595	38·5	3,003	385	5·5
1880	25,601	2,751	41·4	3,056	405	5·8
1881	26,376	2,864	44·6	3,074	410	6·1
1882	26,779	3,015	48·1	3,073	421	6·4
1883	27,330	3,127	52·7	3,090	433	6·9
1884	27,958	3,273	57·8	3,131	448	7·2

See p. 801 for footnotes.

Miscellaneous Statistics 9. *continued*

	England & Wales			Scotland		
	Number of Schools or Departments Inspected (*a*)	Average Number of Children Attending Inspected Day Schools (thousands)	Number of Full-time Teachers (*b*) (thousands)	Number of Schools Inspected	Average Number of Children Attending Inspected Day Schools (thousands)	Number of Full-time Teachers (*b*) (thousands)
1885	28,356	3,371	61·6	3,081	456	7·4
1886	28,645	3,438	64·3	3,092	477	7·9
1887	28,935	3,537	66·5	3,111	492	8·2
1888	29,056	3,615	68·7	3,105	496	8·5
1889	29,119	3,683	70·8	3,116	503	8·8
1890	29,339	3,718	73·5	3,076	513	9·1
1891	29,533	3,750	77·0	3,105	538	9·6
1892	29,672	3,871	79·3	3.030	539	9·9
1893	29,804	4,100	83·0	3,004	543	10·2
1894	30,003	4,226	87·0	3,054	567	10·7
1895	30,237	4,325	92·6	3,034	575	10·9
1896	30,521	4,423	94·9	3,083	593	11·5
1897	30,847	4,489	100·7	3,086	605	11·9
1898	30,911	4,554	101·7	3,067	606	12·2
1899	31,173	4,637	109·0	3,062	612	12·7
1900	31,234	4,666	114·0	3,104	626	13·3
1901	31,288	4,754	118·9	3,107	633	13·9
1902	31,397	4,923	121·9	3,110	643	14·2
1903	31,626	5,057	127·4	3,113	665	14·8
1904	31,862	5,177	134·2	3,115	672	15·5
1905	31,960	5,258	140·6	3,123	682	16·3
1906	32,029	5,312	148·5	3,125	689	17·0
1907	32,029	5,302	152·6	3,138	693	17·6
	----- (*h*)					
1908	32,071	5,301	156·3	3,143	692	18·1
1909	32,112	5,355	160·0	3,149	705	19·0
1910	32,185	5,375	162·3	3,156	719	19·7
1911	32,255	5,382	163·7	3,173	732	20·0
1912	32,290	5,367	164·1	3,164	734	20·4
1913	32,380	5,376	164·7	3,177	729	20·6
1914	32,480	5,393	166·0	3,171	728	20·8
1915	...	...	...	3,168	725	21·3
1916	...	...	...	3,168	716	21·9
1917	...	...	...	3,167	715	22·0
1918	...	...	...	3,163	694	21·7
1919	...	...	...	---- (*i*)	----- (*i*)	---- (*i*)
1920	32,233	5,199	...	2,917	620	18·3
	----- (*j*)	---- (*j*)	---- (*j*)			
	32,145	5,187	165·5			
1921	32,106	5,206	167·2	2,907	627	17·9
1922	31,969	5,181	168·1	2,904	615	17·8
1923	31,538	5,136	163·6	2,901	608	17·8
1924	31,188	5,025	163·2	2,895	588	17·8
1925	31,001	4,934	164·5	2,894	584	18·1
1926	30,872	4,950	165·6	2,896	587	18·4

See p. 801 for footnotes.

Miscellaneous Statistics 9. *continued*

	England & Wales			Scotland		
	Number of Schools or Departments Inspected (*a*)	Average Number of Children Attending Inspected Day Schools (thousands)	Number of Full-time Teachers (*b*) (thousands)	Number of Schools Inspected	Average Number of Children Attending Inspected Day Schools (thousands)	Number of Full-time Teachers (*b*) (thousands)
1927	30,724	4,967	166·2	2,903	591	18·7
1928	30,591	4,981	(167·9) (*k*)	2,919	587	18·8
1929	30,522	4,909	167·3	2,915	585	19·1
1930	30,429	4,941	168·0	2,923	591	19·5
1931	30,363	4,930	168·9	2,924	595	19·5
1932	30,226	5,006	170·0	2,924	601	19·4
1933	29,959	5,049	170·6	2,920	606	19·4
1934	29,701	5,066	170·9	2,909	607	19·4
1935	29,589	4,907	170·6	2,898	592	19·4
1936	29,478	4,748	169·6	2,900	581	19·5
1937	29,359	4,588	168·0	2,898	567	19·7
1938	29,224	4,527	166·7	2,895	557	19·6
1939–45			not available			
	——(*l*)	——(*l*)	——(*l*)	——(*l*)	——(*l*)	——(*l*)
1946	23,991	3,736	116·8	2,144	383	...
1947	23,602	3,700	123·3	2,076	361	...
1948	21,396	3,812	126·3	2,042	364	...
1949	23,201	3,874	127·8	2,150	363	...
1950	23,133	3,955	130·0	2,151	367	...
				——(*m*)	——(*m*)	
1951	23,106	4,005	133·6	2,939	551	18·9
1952	23,188	4,214	137·3	2,947	566	19·4
1953	23,349	4,436	141·2	2,930	586	19·9
1954	23,501	4,554	144·8	2,937	595	20·0
1955	23,664	4,601	148·7	2,946	603	19·7
1956	23,731	4,592	150·5	2,955	607	19·8
1957	23,765	4,590	151·5	2,973	608	20·2
1958	23,725	4,508	149·8	2,980	610	20·1
1959	23,615	4,308	146·5	2,982	608	20·2
1960	23,488	4,201	144·7	2,976	598	19·7
1961	23,312	4,133	144·2	2,933	589	20·1
1962	23,191	4,130	145·0	2,902	587	19·9
1963	23,083	4,145	144·3	2,845	589	20·2
1964	22,941	4,204	146·5	2,800	595	20·8
1965	22,882	4,273	151·1	2,788	601	20·8
1966	22,822	4,366	155·9	2,773	608	21·4
1967	22,831	4,495	161·5	2,782	613	21·3
1968	22,932	4,647	166·9	2,771	622	21·8
1969	23,055	4,789	173·5	2,753	632	22·0
1970	23,075	4,914	180·0	2,738	642	23·2
1971	23,073	5,023	187·6	2,731	649	24·1
1972	23,160	5,115	196·9	2,755	658	25·5
1973	23,173	5,151	203·6	2,767	661	26·4
1974	23,240	5,149	208·8	2,825	663	28·0
1975	23,280	5,100	213·1	2,862	656	26·1

Miscellaneous Statistics 9. *continued*

	England & Wales			Scotland		
	Number of Schools or Departments Inspected (*a*)	Average Number of Children Attending Inspected Day Schools (thousands)	Number of Full-time Teachers (*b*) (thousands)	Number of Schools Inspected	Average Number of Children Attending Inspected Day Schools (thousands)	Number of Full-time Teachers (*b*) (thousands)
1976	23,353	5,048	213·7	2,909	651	27·1
1977	23,364	4,943	210·7	2,968	645	27·3
1978	23,312	4,800	207·0	3,015	631	26·7
1979	23,239	4,664	206·0	3,047	607	26·6
1980	23,167	4,305	...	3,059	584	26·8

(*a*) Up to 1864 evening schools are included, but thereafter the figures are of day schools only.
(*b*) Excluding pupil teachers and probationers. From 1946 part-time teachers are included on a full-time equivalent basis in England and Wales.
(*c*) Including Roman Catholic schools in Scotland.
(*d*) The figures are for schools inspected during a ten-month period only.
(*e*) Subsequent figures are of the number of departments with separate head teachers.
(*f*) Earlier figures relate to certificated and assistant teachers employed in *all* schools. Subsequently they relate to Annual Grant schools inspected.
(*g*) Previous figures of schools and attendance exclude Roman Catholic schools. The previous figures of teachers relate to a rather smaller number of schools than those shown here. In 1874 they relate to 2,366 schools with an attendance of 264 thousand.
h) The figures for 1908–14 are revised ones obtained from the 1924 *Annual Abstract*, and are 3 or 4 higher than those in the original source.
(*i*) There was a reorganisation of Scottish schools between 1919 and 1920. Figures for 1913 on a comparable basis to the later series are 2,948 schools, 641 thousand attendance, and 16·9 thousand teachers.
(*j*) Subsequent figures relate to Local Authority maintained schools only. Figures for 1913 on this basis are 32,300 departments, 5,356 thousand attendance, and 162·6 thousand teachers.
(*k*) Including some occasional emergency teachers.
(*l*) Comparability across the years of the Second World War is impossible owing to the reorganisation following the 1944 Education Act. In the second and fifth columns the number of registered pupils is substituted for attendance figures.
(*m*) Primary departments of secondary schools are subsequently included here.

Miscellaneous Statistics 10. Primary Schools – Ireland 1833–1980

NOTES TO PART A

[1] SOURCE: *Reports of the Commissioners of National Education in Ireland.*

[2] The description primary schools is used though they were not known as such during the period.

[3] Except as indicated in footnotes the statistics relate to 31 December or, in the case of the figures of average attendance, to periods ended 31 December.

A. Ireland, 1833–1920

	Number of Schools	Pupils on Rolls (thousands)	Average Number Attending (thousands)	Number of Teachers (b) (thousands)
1833	789	107	...	...
1835 (c)	1,106	146	...	...
1836 (c)	1,181	154	....	...
1837 (c)	1,300	167	...	...
1838 (c)	1,384	170	...	...
1839	1,581	193	...	...
1840	1,978	233	...	...
1841	2,337	282	...	...
1842	2,721	320	...	...
1843	2,912	355	...	...
1844	3,153	396	...	...
1845	3,426	433	...	...
1846	3,637	456	...	...
1847	3,825	403	...	...
1848	4,109	507	...	...
1849	4,321	481	...	...
1850	4,547	511	...	...
1851	4,704	520	...	4·6 (c)
1852	4,875	545	280	...
1853	5,023	551	271	4·9
1854	5,178	551	267	5·1
1855	5,124	536	252	5·0
		---- (a)		
1856	5,245	560	258	5·4
1857	5,337	776	268	5·5
1858	5,408	804	266	5·6
1859	5,496	807	269	5·6
1860	5,632	804	263	6·0
1861	5,830	803	285	6·4
1862	6,010	813	285	7·0
1863	6,163	841	297	7·2
1864	6,263	870	315	7·5
1865	6,372	922	321	7·8
1866	6,453	911	316	7·8
1867	6,520	913	322	8·0
1868	6,586	968	355	8·3
1869	6,707	991	359	8·6
1870	6,806	999	359	8·8
1871	6,914	1,022	364	9·0
1872	7,050	1,010	356	9·4
1873	7,160	1,020	373	9·5
1874	7,257	1,007	395	9·9
1875	7,267	1,012	390	10·1
1876	7,334	1,032	417	10·3(d)
1877	7,370	1,024	418	10·5
1878	7,443	1,037	437	10·7
1879	7,522	1,032	435	10·8
1880	7,590	1,083	469	10·7
1881	7,648	1,066	454	10·6
1882	7,705	1,083	469	10·5
1883	7,752	1,081	468	10·6
1884	7,832	1,089	493	10·7
1885	7,936	1,076	502	11·0
1886	8,024	1,072	490	11·0
1887	8,112	1,072	515	11·2
1888	8,196	1,061	494	11·1
1889	8,251	1,053	508	11·2
1890	8,298	1,037	489	11·1
1891	8,346	1,022	506	11·3
1892	8,403	1,020	495	11·4
1893	8,459	1,032	527	11·6
1894	8,505	1,028	526	11·8
1895	8,557	1,018	520	11·9
1896	8,606	809	535	12·0
1897	8,631	799	[521] (f)	12·0
1898 (e)	8,651	795	[519] (f)	12·0
1899 (e)	8,670	785	[514] (f)	12·1
1900	8,684	746	478	11·9
1901	8,692	741	482	11·9
1902	8,712	737	487	12·0
1903	8,720	727	482	12·0
1904	8,710	730	484	12·3
1905	8,659	738	500	12·5
1906	8,602	728	494	12·6
1907	8,538	675	486	12·7
1908	8,468	689	495	12·7
1909	8,401	679	501	12·8
1910	8,337	679	496	12·8
1911	8,289	685	513	13·0
1912	8,255	669	499	13·2
1913	8,229	682	503	13·3
1914	8,207	680	508	13·5
1915	8,163	679	500	13·5
1916	8,118	678	494	13·4
1917	8,060	684	489	13·4
1918	8,002	689	488	13·4
1919	7,947	683	488	13·3
1920	7,898	692	482	...

See p. 804 for footnotes.

NOTES TO PART B

[1] SOURCE: *Abstract* and *Digest of Statistics: Northern Ireland.*

[2] The description primary schools is used, though they were not known as such for all of this period.

[3] The statistics relate to 31 December or to the January immediately following.

B. Northern Ireland, 1922–80

	Number of Schools	Pupils on Rolls (thousands)	Average Numbers Attending (thousands)	Number of Teachers (*b*) (*g*) (thousands)
1922	2,066	198	153	4·2
1923	2,054	196	156	4·3
1924	2,041	199	157	4·3
1925	2,006	200	165	4·3
1926	1,970	201	170	4·4 ---- (*g*) 5·7
1927	1,948	200	169	5·3
1928	1,933	200	169	5·3
1929	1,920	200	168	5·4
1930	1,893	202	172	5·3
1931	1,868	204	174	5·4
1932	1,837	207	177	5·4
1933	1,814	207	177	5·5
1934	1,790	204	174	5·4
1935	1,775	201	172	5·4
1936	1,753	197	171	5·3
1937	1,727	194	167	5·3
1938	1,700	192	166	5·3
1939	...	...	...	...
1940	...	...	...	...
1941	...	...	...	...
1942	...	...	...	...
1943	...	...	...	...
1944	...	...	...	...
1945	...	185	...	4·9
1946	1,649	187	...	4·9
1947	1,642 ------- (*h*)	185	...	5·4
1948	1,651	183 ---- (*h*) 184	...	5·7
1949	1,650	187	...	5·7
1950	1,665	189	...	5·8
1951	1,665	194	...	5·9

	Number of Schools	Pupils on Rolls (thousands)	Number of Teachers (*b*) (thousands)
1952	1,662	200	6·1
1953	1,655	204	6·1
1954	1,641	205	6·3
1955	1,635	207	6·3
1956	1,635	208	6·5
1957	1,615	206	6·4
1958	1,597	203	6·4
1959	1,584	197	6·4
1960	1,568	196	6·4
1961	1,550	192	6·4
1962	1,526	192	6·4
1963	1,505	193	6·4
1964	1,484	192	6·5
1965	1,443	194	6·7
1966	1,411	197	6·9
1967	1,376	202	7·1
1968	1,335	207	7·2
1969	1,302	211	7·4
1970	1,266	215	7·6
1971	1,250	218	7·8
1972	1,209	217	7·9
1973	1,190	217	8·1
1974	1,176	216	8·2
1975	1,176	216	8·3
1976	1,164	213	8·6
1977	1,165	210	8·9
1978	1,163	207	8·8
1979	1,151	202	8·6
1980	1,161	199	8·5

See p. 804 for footnotes.

NOTES TO PART C

[1] SOURCE: *Statistical Abstract of Ireland*.

[2] The description primary schools is used, though they were not known as such for all of this period.

[3] Except as indicated in footnotes, the statistics relate to the school year ending in the year shown or to the last day of that school year (i.e. 30 June).

C. Republic of Ireland, 1921–80

	Number of Schools	Pupils on Rolls (thousands)	Average Number Attending (thousands)	Number of Teachers (b) (thousands)
1921 (i)	5,746	498	365	...
1922 (i)	5,696	496	356	...
1923 (i)	5,684	497	369	...
1924 (i)	5,636	493	363	...
1925	...	...	...	[11·4] (j)
1926	5,648	522	399	13·2
1927	5,641	524	413	13·3
1928	5,555	517	424	13·6
1929	5,447	515	420	13·7
1930	5,401	512	421	13·6
1931	5,378	509	417	13·7
1932	5,361	508	417	13·6
1933	5,334	513	422	13·6
1934	5,306	505	422	13·7
1935	5,280	496	413	13·6
1936	5,243	489	405	13·5
1937	5,212	482	393	13·4
1938	5,166	474	393	13·4
1939	5,127	470	385	13·3
1940	5,114	471	389	13·3
1941	5,076	472	381	13·1
1942	5,034	466	382	13·1
1943	5,064	465	381	13·1
1944	5,032	464	373	12·9
1945	5,009	463	375	12·8
1946	4,957	458	371	12·8
1947	4,946	453	355	12·8
1948	4,922	457	374	12·6
1949	4,896	459	377	12·7
1950	4,886	464	382	12·9
1951	4,878	468	377	12·8
1952	4,876	476	393	12·9
1953	4,880	484	401	13·0
1954	4,874	490	405	13·1
1955	4,872	495	405	13·2
1956	4,871	501	419	13·3
1957	4,869	503	424	13·4
1958	4,869	504	420	13·6
1959	4,878	505	425	13·8
1960	4,882	506	431	13·9
1961	4,880	503	428	14·0
1962	4,867	501	421	14·1
1963	4,864	502	428	14·2
		----- (k)		
1964	4,848	476	435	14·3
1965	4,847	473	449	14·5
1966	4,797	476	434	14·6
1967	4,685	481	447	14·7
1968	4,450	479 ----- (k) 494	444	14·8
1969	4,295	500	445	14·7
1970	4,117	506	453	14·9
1971	4,012	511	458	15·1
1972	3,879	517	463	15·4
1973	3,776	523	464	15·6
1974	3,688	522	465	16·1
1975	3,585	530	474	16·7
1976	3,508	538	481	17·1
1977	3,468	543	488	17·3
1978	3,449	546	496	17·6
1979	3,432	548	497	18·4
1980	3,415	552	503	18·8

(a) Statistics to 1855 are for the half-year to 30 September. Though the 1856 figure was said to be at 31 December, it was in the following year that the results of the changed system of reporting became apparent.

(b) Excluding unqualified assistants.

(c) At 31 March.

(d) At 31 March in the following year.

(e) The figures for this year are at 30 September, except as indicated in footnote (f).

(f) The figures are for the "results year" for each school examined.

(g) Statistics to 1926 (1st line) relate to teachers receiving personal salaries from the Ministry of Education.

(h) Subsequently including state-maintained nursery and special schools.

(i) The figures for this year are at 31 December.

(j) Excluding members of religious orders, who number 1·7 thousand in 1926.

(k) From 1964 to 1968 (1st line) at 1 February, and subsequently at 30 September.

Miscellaneous Statistics 11. Secondary Schools – England & Wales 1905–80, Scotland 1899–1980, and Ireland 1924–80

NOTES

[1] SOURCES: *Abstract*, *Statistical Abstract of Ireland* and *Statistics of Education* (published annually from 1961 to 1974 for Scotland and 1979 for England) and *Abstracts* of Scottish, Welsh and Northern Ireland statistics.

[2] The definition of a secondary school was changed in Scotland in 1920, and in both England & Wales and Scotland as a result of the 1944 Act.

[3] All figures relate to public and grant-aided schools only.

A. England and Wales, and Scotland

	England & Wales			Scotland		
	Number of Schools on 31 Jan.	Number of Pupils on 31 Jan.	Number of Full-time Teachers on 31 Jan.	Number of Schools, year ended 30 Sept.	Number of Pupils at end of school year	Number of Full-time Teachers at 11 March
1899				55	18,251	...
1900				55	18,215	...
1901				55	17,687	937
				year ended 31 Aug.		
1902				55	17,856	884
1903				55	17,921	997
1904				55	18,076	983
1905	575	94,698	...	55	18,210	996
1906	689	115,688	...	55	18,086	997
1907	769	125,802	...	55	18,316	983
1908	843	138,106	...	55	18,973	1,126
1909	912	150,794	9,328	57	20,904	1,117
1910	950	156,266	9,540	57	21,008	1,134
1911	971	160,477	9,832	56	20,532	1,147
1912	995	165,572	10,088	56	20,484	1,175
1913	1,010	174,423	10,398	56	19,557	1,197
1914	1,027	187,647	10,824	56	19,780	1,218
1915	1,047	198,884	...	56	19,866	1,196
1916	1,049	208,690	...	56	20,317	1,334
1917	1,049	218,900	12,045	56	21,012	1,481
1918	1,061	238,528	...	56	22,317	1,323
1919	1,081	269,887	14,499	56	23,978	1,398
				---- (*a*)	------- (*a*)	------ (*a*)
1920	1,141	308,266	16,037	252	155,141	5,053
1921	1,205	336,836	17,668	252	154,256	5,679
1922	1,249	354,956	18,964	249	155,024	5,694
1923	1,264	354,165	18,485	249	154,813	5,961
1924	1,270	349,141	18,658	249	153,044	6,103
1925	1,284	352,605	19,069	249	148,699	6,053
1926	1,301	360,503	19,640	249	150,490	6,209
1927	1,319	371,493	19,254	251	151,343	6,280
1928	1,329	377,540	20,102	252	152,804	6,424
1929	1,341	386,993	20,514	252	151,356	6,452
1930	1,354	394,105	21,165	250	151,031	6,573
1931	1,367	411,309	21,694	251	154,072	6,571
1932	1,379	432,061	22,293	251	159,732	6,717
1933	1,378	441,883	22,754	251	161,991	6,708
1934	1,381	448,421	23,024	251	159,218	6,714
1935	1,380	456,783	23,425	251	157,460	6,733
1936	1,389	463,906	24,003	251	154,376	6,764
1937	1,393	466,245	24,451	252	151,989	6,802
1938	1,398	470,003	25,039	252	152,781	6,908
1939–45			not available			

See p. 809 for footnotes.

Miscellaneous Statistics 11. *continued*

A. England and Wales, and Scotland (*cont.*)

Maintained Secondary Schools in England and Wales

	Modern			Grammar			Technical		
	Number of Schools in Jan.	Number of Pupils in Jan. (thousands)	Number of Full-time Teachers (*b*) at 31 March (thousands)	Number of Schools in Jan.	Number of Pupils in Jan. (thousands)	Number of Full-time Teachers (*b*) at 31 March (thousands)	Number of Schools in Jan.	Number of Pupils in Jan. (thousands)	Number of Full-time Teachers (*b*) at 31 March (thousands)
1946	...	720	...	...	489	...	...	60	...
1947	3,019	764	34·8	1,207	505	25·3	317	66	3·6
1948	3,063	961	39·7	1,212	512	25·9	319	72	3·8
1949	3,141	1,058	44·3	1,229	524	27·0	310	72	3·9
1950	3,227	1,095	47·1	1,192	503	26·5	301	72	3·9
1951	3,301	1,127	49·6	1,190	501	27·0	296	73	3·9
1952	3,365	1,138	51·1	1,189	506	27·4	291	74	4·0
1953	3,423	1,136	52·0	1,184	513	27·7	292	79	4·2
1954	3,480	1,167	53·4	1,181	518	28·0	300	85	4·5
1955	3,550	1,234	55·9 ---- (*b*) 56·8	1,180	528	28·5 ---- (*b*) 29·2	302	87	4·7 ---- (*b*) 5·1
1956	3,636	1,341	60·0	1,193	544	30·0	298	91	5·2
1957	3,719	1,424	63·8	1,206	559	30·9	290	95	5·4
1958	3,690	1,435	64·6	1,241	599	32·7	279	95	5·3
1959	3,808	1,596	70·8	1,252	641	34·5	264	99	5·4
1960	3,837	1,638	74·3	1,268	673	36·4	251	102	5·5
1961	3,872	1,698	78·2	1,284	697	38·1	228	97	5·4
1962	3,899	1,676	80·7	1,287	708	39·3	220	97	5·5
1963	3,906	1,609	80·0	1,295	722	40·4	204	93	5·2
1964	3,906	1,641	80·9	1,298	726	41·5	186	89	5·1
1965	3,727	1,555	78·6	1,285	719	41·9	172	85	5·0
1966	3,642	1,524	78·5	1,273	713	42·2	150	74	4·4
1967	3,494	1,459	76·4	1,236	695	41·4	141	70	4·2
1968	3,200	1,367	71·6	1,155	656	39·5	121	62	3·7
1969	2,954	1,304	68·9	1,098	632	38·3	109	57	3·4
1970	2,691	1,227	65·3	1,038	605	36·9	82	44	2·7
			---- (*c*)			----- (*c*)			----- (*c*)
1971	2,464	1,163	61·3	970	574	34·4	67	38	2·3
1972	2,218	1,086	58·7	893	540	32·8	58	33	2·0
1973	1,915	966	54·1	819	497	30·6	43	25	1·5
1974	1,509	857	46·1	675	411	25·5	35	21	1·3
1975	1,216	698	38·7	566	344	21·4	29	18	1·1
1976	1,002	589	33·2	477	295	18·2	23	15	0·9
1977	837	493	28·0	407	256	15·7	21	14	0·8
1978	660	397	22·5	320	203	12·4	19	12	0·7
1979	547	334	19·2	261	167	10·2	19	12	0·7
1980	...	235	...	...	135	...	...	10	...

See p. 809 for footnotes.

Miscellaneous Statistics 11. *continued*

A. England and Wales, and Scotland (*cont.*)

	Maintained Secondary Schools in England and Wales (continued)								
	Comprehensive (*d*)			Other Maintained Secondary			Scotand		
	Number of Schools in Jan.	Number of Pupils in Jan. (thousands)	Number of Teachers (*b*) (thousands)	Number of Schools in Jan.	Number of Pupils in Jan. (thousands)	Number of Teachers (*b*) (thousands)	Number of Schools (*e*)	Number of Pupils (*e*) (thousands)	Number of Full-time Teachers (*g*) (thousands)
1946	...	...	...	...	...	...	983	348	...
1947	...	...	...	...	...	...	1,037	367	...
							------- (*e*)	----- (*e*)	...
1948	...	...	...	...	...	...	1,050	403	...
1949	...	...	...	...	...	...	927	417	...
1950	...	...	...	45	25	1·2	913	419	...
							------- (*f*)	----- (*f*)	
1951	...	...	...	60	32	1·6	909	233	13·8
1952	...	...	...	69	38	1·9	869	236	14·0
1953	...	...	...	77	42	2·2	871	237	14·2
							------- (*e*)	----- (*e*)	
1954	13	12	0·6	80	40	2·0	817	225	14·5
1955	16	16	0·8	96	49	2·5 ----- (*b*) 2·5	809	227	15·1
1956	31	27	1·4	104	54	2·8	803	232	15·4
1957	43	42	2·2	122	67	3·5	787	240	15·5
1958	86	75	3·8	254	126	5·9	785	239	15·9
1959	111	107	5·3	280	150	6·9	776	249	16·8
1960	130	129	6·7	315	182	8·7	791	272	17·9
1961	138	142	7·5	325	195	9·6	771	288	18·2
1962	152	157	8·4	332	197	9·9	752	292	18·8
1963	175	179	9·6	311	177	9·2	744	286	19·2
1964	195	199	10·8	309	175	9·2	726	288	19·3
									----- (*g*)
1965	262	240	13·4	417	221	11·9	704	285	19·7
									----- (*g*)
1966	387	312	17·7	346	194	10·5	680	284	20·0
1967	508	408	23·0	350	201	11·1	665	288	20·0
1968	748	606	34·0	352	204	11·2	640	296	20·7
1969	962	773	43·5	331	195	10·8	616	307	20·4
1970	1,145	937	53·7	324	197	11·0	573	317	21·3
1971	1,373	1,128	64·3	274	186	10·5	541	328	22·3
1972	1,591	1,337	77·7	266	180	10·4	516	338	23·8
1973	1,835	1,580	94·6	245	171	10·1	492	352	25·4
1974	2,273	2,137	124·3	183	125	7·3	478 ----- (*e*) 472	385 ----- (*e*) 407	26·4 ----- (*g*) 25·3
1975	2,596	2,460	145·5	155	100	5·9	467	412	26·5
1976	2,878	2,753	164·4	93	60	3·6	464	416	27·9
1977	3,083	2,982	178·0	76	48	2·9	458	420	28·3
1978	3,290	3,179	190·6	72	45	2·8	466	422	28·8
1979	3,427	3,294	199·9	64	42	2·6	468	422	29·1
1980	...	3,398	...	...	35	...	467	419	29·1

See p. 809 for footnotes.

B. Ireland

	Northern Ireland			Republic of Ireland		
	Number of Schools	Number of Pupils (thousands)	Number of Full-time Teachers	Number of Schools	Number of Pupils (thousands)	Number of Teachers
1924	...	...	...	278	23	...
1925	69	8·5	...	283	25	2,133
1926	70	9·0	552	285	25	2,298
1927	71	9·9	566	287	26	2,256
1928	72	10·6	598	290	27	2,374
1929	74	11·6	650	294	28	2,391
1930	73	12·1	668	300	29	2,551
1931	73	12·3	706	306	30	2,643
1932	72	12·3	710	311	31	2,643
1933	73	12·7	740	315	32	2,675
1934	74	13·0	741	319	33	2,801
1935	73	13·2	739	327	35	2,861
1936	73	13·4	756	331	36	2,879
1937	76	13·7	777	336	36	2,948
1938	76	14·1	790	342	37	2,969
1939	...	...	...	345	38	3,019
1940	...	...	...	352	39	3,144
1941	...	...	...	362	40	3,173
1942	...	...	...	371	40	3,251
1943	...	...	...	377	40	3,357
1944	...	...	...	379	41	3,386
1945	...	19·9	1,080	385	42	3,497
1946	76	21·0	1,096	393	43	3,512
1947	77	22·0	1,124	404	44	3,584
	-----(*h*)	-----(*h*)				
1948	115	33·7	1,184	409	45	3,671
1949	117	37·2	1,455	416	47	3,863
1950	118	39·6	1,566	424	49	3,844
1951	120	41·2	1,700	434	50	3,929
1952	123	42·5	1,758	441	52	4,043
1953	128	44·2	1,816	447	54	4,170
1954	134	47·6	1,915	458	56	4,097
1955	140	50·1	2,023	474	59	4,417
1956	146	52·8	2,303	480	62	4,564
1957	168	63·5	2,726	489	66	4,739
1958	187	77·0	3,262	494	70	4,957
1959	205	86·5	3,320	512	73	5,032
1960	214	89·1	3,867	526	77	5,178
1961	228	97·1	4,258	542	80	5,282
1962	232	100·0	4,511	557	85	5,630
1963	238	103·2	4,718	569	89	5,908
1964	244	108·0	4,980	573	93	6,161
1965	250	111·8	5,408	585	99	6,477
1966	256	116·8	5,788	588	104	6,795
1967	260	124·5	6,061	595	119	7,248
1968	264	129·2	6,483	598	134	8,165

B. Ireland (*cont.*)

	Northern Ireland			Republic of Ireland		
	Number of Schools	Number of Pupils (thousands)	Number of Full-time Teachers	Number of Schools	Number of Pupils (thousands)	Number of Teachers
1969	266	132·6	6,800	600	144	9,130
1970	265	136·7	7,192	599	151	9,603
1971	261	139·4	7,487	593	157	10,254
1972	259	141·3	7,805	574	162	10,705
1973	259	152·0	8,492	554	167	11,250
1974	261	154·3	8,683	541	173	12,076
1975	262	157·5	8,999	539	183	11,798
1976	262	160·8	9,512	537	189	12,212
1977	261	162·1	9,978	532	193	12,740
1978	261	163·5	10,300	531	197	13,248
1979	262	164·2	10,429	527	199	13,407
1980	261	164·2	10,424	524	201	13,533

(*a*) See note 2 above. Figures for 1913 on the same basis as the 1920 and subsequent figures were as follows: 249 schools, 130,255 pupils, 4,479 teachers.
(*b*) Part-time teachers are included on a full-time equivalent basis from 1955 (2nd line) or from 1954 for comprehensive schools.
(*c*) Subsequently excluding untrained teachers.
(*d*) Comprehensive schools are included with 'other' schools prior to 1954.
(*e*) In July 1946 and 1947, March from 1948 to 1953, January from 1954 to 1974 (1st line) and in September subsequently. Statistics from 1974 (2nd line) are not strictly comparable with earlier ones.
(*f*) Primary departments of secondary schools are transferred subsequently to the 'primary' heading.
(*g*) In October to 1964, September to 1965, December from 1966 to 1974 (1st line), and in September subsequently.
(*h*) Including technical schools subsequently.

Miscellaneous Statistics 12. Direct Grant and Independent Schools – England & Wales 1946–79

NOTES

[1] SOURCES: 1947–54 – *Statistics of Public Education in England and Wales* (annually in *Sessional Papers*); 1955–79 and all figures of pupils – *Statistics of Education* (published annually from 1962 to 1979 by the Ministry of Education).

[2] All figures relate to a date in January.

	Direct Grant Grammar Schools (*a*)			Independent Schools (except Nursery Schools) Recognised as Efficient		
	Schools or Departments	Pupils	Full-time Teachers (*b*)	Schools or Departments	Pupils	Full-time Teachers (*b*)
1946	...	88	...	...	144	...
1947	194	81	4·2	945	165	12·8
1948	190	83	4·2	985	178	13·5
1949	186	84	4·3	1,035	189	14·2
1950	181	85	4·4	1,105	204	15·0
1951	181	86	4·5	1,191	219	16·0
1952	178	87	4·6	1,271	234	16·9
1953	176	89	4·7	1,313	244	17·3
1954	176	90	4·8	1,315	249	17·5
1955	173	91	4·8 ----(*b*) 5·0	1,348	259	17·9 ----(*b*) 19·7
1956	173	92	5·1	1,363	268	20·2
1957	172	94	5·2	1,408	279	20·9
1958	181	103	5·7	1,436	281	21·2
1959	182	106	5·8	1,467	288	21·8
1960	186	110	6·1	1,479	294	22·2
1961	186	112	6·3	1,498	300	22·8
1962	186	113	6·5	1,493	300	23·2
1963	186	114	6·6	1,509	305	23·4
1964	186	115	6·7	1,541	307	24·0
1965	185	116	6·9	1,530	306	24·0
1966	185	116	7·0	1,529	309	24·2
1967	185	118	7·1	1,497	305	24·0
1968	184	119	7·1	1,465	300	23·5
1969	182	119	7·1	1,437	301	23·9
1970	182	120	7·2	1,413	304	24·0
1971	179	119	7·3	1,393	305	24·0
1972	179	119	7·3	1,405	311	24·5
1973	179	121	7·5	1,382	315	24·8
1974	180	122	7·5	1,370	324	25·4
1975	178	122	7·6	1,358	329	25·6
1976	174	122	7·6	1,350	324	25·7
1977	169	119	7·5	1,341	323	26·0
1978	154	109	6·9	...	...	...
1979	142	101	6·4	...	...	...

(*a*) Including institutional and technical schools.

(*b*) Part-time teachers are included on a full-time equivalent basis from 1955 (2nd line).

Miscellaneous Statistics 13. University Education – Great Britain 1922–76, United Kingdom 1977–80

NOTES
[1] SOURCE: *Abstract*.
[2] All series cover full-time students and staff only, except the figures of total numbers taking courses, which include part-time students.
[3] Postgraduate and Diploma students are included.

	New Students Admitted		Numbers Taking Courses		Courses Taken at Universities										Teaching Staff
					Arts (*a*)		Pure Science		Medicine (*b*)		Technology (*c*)		Agriculture		
	Men	Women	Men	Women	Men	Women	Men	Women	Men	Women	Men	Women	Men	Women	
1922/3	8,424	3,878	42,512	16,440	10,232	7,999	5,634	2,129	9,498	2,368	5,849	78	1,091	101	...
1923/4	8,005	3,842	40,381	16,306	10,393	8,588	5,203	2,199	8,866	1,998	4,652	57	758	98	...
1924/5	8,194	3,910	39,671	16,251	10,950	8,941	5,165	2,164	7,896	1,631	4,156	54	746	96	...
1925/6	8,468	3,865	40,156	16,140	11,622	9,138	5,250	2,081	7,288	1,402	3,999	54	676	96	3,023
1926/7	8,826	3,902	40,859	16,282	12,486	9,426	5,180	2,043	7,179	1,236	3,925	45	723	111	3,085
1927/8	8,945	4,002	41,552	16,203	13,367	9,694	5,229	2,003	7,074	1,148	3,877	54	703	113	3,169
1928/9	9,296	3,704	42,596	15,952	14,005	9,620	5,405	1,972	7,279	1,108	1,108	66	705	133	3,259
1929/30	9,877	3,931	43,561	15,913	14,657	9,652	5,596	1,942	7,623	1,136	4,081	71	725	120	3,349
1930/1	10,078	3,967	46,057	16,255	15,091	9,582	5,866	2,002	8,702	1,187	4,197	77	773	110	3,501
1931/2	10,423	3,879	46,820	15,707	15,384	9,284	6,125	2,006	9,107	1,272	4,401	87	734	110	3,590
1932/3	10,977	4,073	48,200	15,915	15,952	9,223	6,328	2,066	9,835	1,412	4,443	91	700	105	3,629
1933/4	11,031	3,830	49,114	15,306	16,129	8,659	6,598	2,159	10,426	1,525	4,344	95	701	101	3,669
1934/5	10,808	3,679	49,061	14,989	15,898	8,245	6,658	2,126	10,854	1,646	4,274	95	722	120	3,735
1935/6	10,687	3,504	49,153	14,467	15,799	7,885	6,583	2,019	11,176	1,747	4,344	88	748	140	3,772
1936/7	10,424	3,344	48,490	14,002	15,461	7,431	6,231	1,871	11,430	1,833	4,410	82	803	137	3,845
1937/8	10,505	3,558	48,228	14,042	15,046	7,304	5,900	1,849	11,428	1,913	4,690	87	826	146	3,907
1938/9	11,220	3,933	49,202	14,218	14,841	7,533	5,815	1,846	11,623	2,013	5,199	89	890	153	3,994
1939/40	10,514	3,551	37,865	11,900	11,023	6,871	4,980	1,705	11,224	2,102	4,484	80	713	138	...
1940/1	8,784	3,500	32,083	11,951	7,205	6,830	3,947	1,685	10,691	2,261	3,894	75	563	133	...
1941/2	9,258	4,047	33,055	13,402	6,010	7,186	4,224	1,798	10,321	2,411	4,445	129	630	170	...
1942/3	9,543	4,544	33,541	14,488	4,761	7,691	4,158	1,923	9,793	2,529	4,879	145	664	221	...
1943/4	7,816	5,095	33,270	15,643	3,464	8,111	4,034	2,023	9,251	2,620	4,894	188	806	257	...
1944/5	8,573	5,484	32,873	16,936	3,904	8,770	4,472	2,311	9,219	2,772	5,036	181	904	270	...
1945/6	12,701	6,165	46,042	21,132	10,466	10,815	6,269	3,040	10,262	2,948	6,008	276	1,209	329	...
1946/7	16,791	5,754	63,785	22,551	18,944	11,829	9,263	3,253	11,400	3,004	8,474	293	1,683	309	...
1947/8	17,325	6,182	73,501	23,003	23,022	12,195	11,234	3,310	12,720	3,187	9,857	289	2,232	461	6,536
1948/9	18,857	5,969	79,141	22,729	25,028	12,119	12,843	3,256	13,635	3,382	10,620	264	2,516	403	7,390
1949/50	18,104	6,227	80,514	22,567	25,106	12,137	13,614	3,303	14,234	3,321	10,709	224	2,405	368	7,930
1950/1	16,537	5,686	79,422	22,590	24,509	12,279	13,862	3,306	14,836	3,325	10,384	207	2,240	366	8,603
1951/2	16,733	5,681	77,934	22,582	23,587	12,349	13,749	3,304	14,507	3,329	10,034	181	2,093	325	8,952

Miscellaneous Statistics 13. *continued*

	New Students Admitted		Numbers Taking Courses		Courses Taken at Universities										Teaching Staff
					Arts (*a*)		Pure Science		Medicine (*b*)		Technology (*c*)		Agriculture		
	Men	Women	Men	Women	Men	Women	Men	Women	Men	Women	Men	Women	Men	Women	
1952/3	15,605	5,750	74,861	22,468	22,432	12,484	13,559	3,442	14,020	3,265	9,822	171	1,953	326	9,134
1953/4	15,513	5,640	73,809	22,548	22,065	12,608	13,488	3,483	13,565	3,291	9,891	145	1,784	282	9,514
1954/5	16,487	5,976	74,687	23,164	22,109	12,996	13,656	3,671	13,406	3,354	10,438	148	1,686	241	9,810
1955/6	16,458	5,956	77,323	24,171	22,934	13,713	14,203	3,930	13,694	3,414	11,226	153	1,706	221	10,202
1956/7	18,796	6,769	80,854	25,220	24,293	14,354	15,549	4,350	13,362	3,448	12,329	167	1,677	237	10,485
1957/8	20,646	7,030	85,526	26,402	26,149	14,972	16,985	4,722	13,317	3,455	13,655	204	1,749	234	10,846
1958/9	21,236	7,041	89,080	27,003	27,909	15,223	18,373	5,029	12,995	3,571	14,788	255	1,814	247	11,125
1959/60	20,823	7,194	92,339	27,602	29,119	15,476	19,481	5,267	12,968	3,665	15,606	326	1,863	238	11,789
1960/1	21,464	8,046	96,423	29,107	30,008	16,378	20,735	5,718	12,901	3,712	15,880	345	1,806	216	12,417
1961/2	22,964	9,196	100,330	31,592	30,658	17,959	22,243	6,433	12,889	3,679	16,819	413	1,816	234	13,104
1962/3	23,956	9,721	101,410	34,018	31,580	19,626	24,460	7,347	13,118	3,749	16,663	348	1,833	280	14,132
1963/4	24,666	10,107	106,402	36,571	33,247	21,290	26,187	8,129	13,330	3,742	18,078	415	1,794	233	15,259
1964/5	27,609	11,959	115,460	41,328	36,991	24,905	27,990	8,796	13,738	3,883	19,781	481	1,881	265	17,117
1965/6	36,919 ------- (*d*) 37,166	14,872 ------- (*d*) 15,059	129,178 ------- (*d*) 133,963	46,426 ------- (*d*) 47,089	41,843	28,846	32,579 ------- (*e*) 35,492	9,534 ------- (*e*) 9,835	13,949 ------- (*b*) 14,089	3,832 ------- (*b*) 4,448	33,659 ------- (*e*) 29,503	1,985 ------- (*e*) 884	2,057 ------- (*e*) 3,160	323 ------- (*e*) 497	25,294
1966/7	37,890	15,685	147,797	52,927	46,585	32,512	37,675	10,884	14,769	4,920	32,174	899	3,240	545	27,471 ------- (*f*) 23,609
1967/8	40,539	16,588	159,354	58,275	51,084	35,873	40,782	11,857	15,244	5,251	34,540	1,103	3,306	632	25,353
1968/9	41,672	17,706	169,319	62,818	54,805	38,686	42,211	12,420	15,733	5,477	36,490	1,225	3,557	690	26,067
1969/70	43,063	19,156	176,169	66,842	58,093	40,628	42,085	12,416	15,901	5,838	37,923	1,486	3,649	749	26,904
1970/1	43,222	20,373	179,229	71,265	60,194	43,627	43,253	13,274	16,368	6,491	38,621	1,586	3,689	853	27,974
1971/2	43,889	21,074	182,887	74,683	61,138	45,469	44,696	14,277	16,405	7,206	39,564	1,843	3,475	912	28,908
1972/3	43,919	22,192	183,155	78,837	62,073	47,617	44,939	14,964	16,679	7,945	38,543	2,105	3,493	1,008	29,985
1973/4	43,621	23,580	184,000	83,384	63,519	50,216	44,326	15,353	17,318	8,711	37,779	2,293	3,497	1,082	30,680
1974/5	45,385	25,304	186,001	88,709	64,923	53,317	44,015	16,010	17,684	9,421	38,846	2,605	3,580	1,161	31,338
1975/6	48,110	26,592	191,819	94,448	68,509	56,849	44,433	16,517	17,930	10,001	38,830	2,936	3,785	1,361	31,381
1976/7	49,547	27,776	198,081	99,702	70,841	60,093	45,007	17,044	18,447	10,497	41,001	3,359	3,993	1,486	32,209
	------- (*g*)	------- (*g*)	------- (*g*)	------- (*g*)	------- (*g*)	------- (*g*)	------- (*g*)	------- (*g*)	------- (*g*)	------- (*g*)	------- (*g*)	------- (*g*)	------- (*g*)	------- (*g*)	------- (*g*)
1977/8	52,359	30,463	208,155	108,659	73,347	65,263	46,741	18,125	19,407	11,343	43,329	3,798	4,089	1,693	32,984
1978/9	52,870	32,014	211,364	114,112	74,844	68,246	47,650	18,973	19,633	11,954	44,360	4,234	4,271	1,858	33,695
1979/80	51,997	33,906	211,613	120,325	73,857	71,175	47,875	20,015	19,553	12,657	44,422	4,612	4,310	2,050	34,250
1980/1	52,214	34,613	213,487	126,438	73,922	73,974	48,694	21,229	19,368	13,280	44,754	5,095	4,185	2,113	34,297

(*a*) Including theology, fine art, law, music, commerce, economics, and education.
(*b*) Including dentistry, and, until 1965/6 (1st line), veterinary science.
(*c*) Including engineering, applied chemistry, mining, metallurgy, and architecture.
(*d*) Subsequently including students on courses 'not of university standard'.
(*e*) There was a rearrangement of categories.
(*f*) Subsequently full-time staff only.
(*g*) Northern Ireland is included subsequently and there may be other breaks in continuity.

Miscellaneous Statistics 14. University Education – Ireland 1909–80

NOTES

[1] SOURCES: *Abstract* and *Statistical Abstract of Ireland*.

[2] Except as indicated in headings or footnotes the statistics relate to all full-time students.

A. Northern Ireland 1948–76

	New Students Admitted (*d*)		Numbers Taking Courses		Courses Taken at Universities: Arts (*a*)		Science		Medicine (*b*)		Technology (*c*)		Agriculture		Full-time Teaching Staff
	Men	Women	Men	Women	Men	Women	Men	Women	Men	Women	Men	Women	Men	Women	
1948/9	472	173	2,251	607	521	307	243	84	583	160	502	9	79	—	167
1949/50	412	145	2,213	616	513	332	261	71	567	152	467	8	78	—	184
1950/1	397	159	2,057	618	505	360	261	71	557	127	413	4	64	1	204
1951/2	446	183	2,102	672	513	398	264	70	546	133	336	2	60	1	238
1952/3	411	149	2,107	648	520	371	276	68	540	128	332	2	51	—	260
1953/4	343	174	2,014	688	498	406	269	79	515	125	310	2	50	—	275
1954/5	383	154	2,017	692	511	385	269	75	468	127	311	2	50	—	296
1955/6	400	165	2,002	724	505	426	301	82	449	109	332	3	45	—	309
1956/7	456	174	2,080	691	557	413	330	74	430	113	368	2	45	—	303
1957/8	620	178	2,296	695	623	413	377	78	448	108	403	5	53	—	320
1958/9	618	216	2,583	775	718	448	485	99	436	102	450	8	61	—	284
1959/60	711	223	2,907	783	786	497	537	110	478	114	532	12	67	—	331
1960/1	714	283	3,076	921	844	562	605	138	476	140	587	14	79	—	348
1961/2	864	361	3,382	1,075	992	696	678	168	487	140	624	23	85	—	391
1962/3	756	314	3,451	1,113	1,017	697	713	179	487	152	676	24	86	—	405
1963/4	784	325	3,758	1,243	1,095	797	799	203	491	158	706	28	95	—	465
1964/5	947	360	3,923	1,307	1,264	872	758	187	506	164	733	31	98	—	508
1965/6	1,054	457	4,229	1,481	1,308	939	1,017	314	422	152	832	17	77	—	520
1966/7	1,109	420	4,771	1,632	1,482	1,028	1,037	318	426	145	928	22	77	1	578
1967/8	1,107	544	5,083	1,841	1,557	1,125	1,170	379	474	160	1,014	39	41	—	660
1968/9	1,323	785	5,361	2,138	1,643	1,331	1,310	427	489	177	1,029	44	41	3	744
1969/70	1,331	722	5,583	2,414	1,964	1,637	1,107	330	598	247	1,026	59	115	7	788
1970/1	1,310	770	5,700	2,715	2,104	1,887	1,222	367	549	254	957	65	117	11	838
1971/2	1,213	730	5,753	2,800	2,118	1,941	1,203	375	549	258	965	58	116	10	896
1972/3	1,194	680	5,542	2,808	2,095	1,938	1,165	377	575	288	841	52	114	10	925
1973/4	978	720	5,222	2,917	1,927	1,988	980	347	613	318	763	60	101	9	967
1974/5	1,148	806	5,220	2,979	1,973	2,007	923	349	648	339	676	87	93	6	971
1975/6	1,184	853	5,472	3,186	2,055	2,136	932	341	697	369	685	101	111	11	1,039
1976/7	1,085	794	5,445	3,312	2,060	2,187	888	372	725	411	680	91	88	9	988

Miscellaneous Studies 14. *continued*

B. Republic of Ireland, 1909–80

	Number of Students		Number of Students		Number of Students		Number of Students
1909/10	2,254	1914/15	2,362	1919/20	3,647	1924/25	3,249
1910/11	2,531	1915/16	2,321	1920/21	3,658	1925/26	3,159
1911/12	2,638	1916/17	2,431	1921/22	3,492	1926/27	3,037
1912/13	2,751	1917/18	2,725	1922/23	3,446	1927/28	3,171
1913/14	2,507	1918/19	3,383	1923/24	3,322	1928/29	3,532

	Number of Students		Courses Taken at Universities						
	Full-time	Part-time	Arts	Science	Technology	Medicine (*b*)	Law	Agriculture	Veterinary Medicine
1929/30	3,896		...	...	237	769	188	95	...
1930/1	4,311		...	...	259	860	184	109	...
1931/2	4,639		...	...	251	1,025	179	126	...
1932/3	4,954		...	...	252	1,121	182	138	...
1933/4	4,965		...	...	258	1,229	197	189	...
1934/5	5,054		...	...	272	1,400	207	226	...
1935/6	5,011		...	...	305	1,510	188	121	...
1936/7	5,163		...	...	372	1,613	214	154	...
1937/8	5,336		...	...	478	1,700	221	210	...
1938/9	5,370		...	...	554	1,797	202	235	...
1939/40	5,425		...	...	658	1,908	198	209	...
1940/1	5,430		...	...	662	2,001	159	258	...
1941/2	5,549		...	...	654	1,920	131	253	...
1942/3	5,758		...	...	694	1,950	115	234	...
1943/4	5,938		...	...	682	2,049	112	238	...
1944/5	6,341		...	...	720	2,109	111	243	...
1945/6	6,620		...	...	750	2,234	120	235	...
1946/7	7,022		...	...	771	2,178	148	241	...
1947/8	6,985		...	757	756	2,045	178	239	...
1948/9	7,319		...	778	734	2,001	165	206	...
1949/50	7,458		...	784	769	2,023	138	186	85
1950/1	7,231		3,083	625	776	2,071	57	188	111
1951/2	6,794	669	3,015	592	778	1,996	87	213	113
1952/3	6,917	684	3,093	601	829	1,919	83	279	111
1953/4	7,011	718	3,162	523	886	1,877	96	335	132
1954/5	7,284	693	3,278	606	874	1,830	108	418	170
1955/6	7,278	788	3,178	647	902	1,712	142	495	202
1956/7	7,669	724	3,386	762	879	1,659	153	558	227
1957/8	8,019	763	3,589	894	834	1,679	142	610	271
1958/9	8,676	724	4,073	1,143	786	1,699	128	534	313
1959/60	9,155	842	4,387	1,336	791	1,669	144	482	345
1960/1	10,021	830	4,947	1,420	827	1,831	136	492	288
1961/2	10,297	1,498	4,880	1,627	848	1,918	161	450	323
1962/3	11,119	1,592	5,479	1,720	918	1,993	198	484	327
1963/4	12,085	1,743	5,958	1,821	1,065	2,140	220	542	339
1964/5	13,006	1,655	6,591	1,837	1,181	2,184	277	586	350
1965/6	14,147	2,044	7,315	1,830	1,267	2,346	367	655	367
1966/7	15,278	1,937	8,100	1,973	1,208	2,612	409	715	362
1967/8	15,838	2,272	8,609	1,935	1,297	2,544	427	682	344
1968/9	16,908	2,968	9,433	1,995	1,419	2,604	394	700	363

B. Republic of Ireland, 1909–80

	Number of Students		Courses Taken at Universities						
	Full-time	Part-time	Arts	Science	Technology (*c*)	Medicine (*b*)	Law	Agriculture	Veterinary Medicine
1969/70	18,045	3,232	10,276	2,083	1,468	2,652	530	652	384
1970/1	18,793	2,871	10,792	2,206	1,696	2,591	592	598	418
1971/2	19,686	2,535	10,804	2,208	1,732	2,581	605	583	321
1972/3	20,178	2,203	10,781 -------(*e*) 11,657	2,259 ------(*e*) 2,327	1,743	2,740	757	631	323
1973/4	20,435	1,936	11,575	2,628	1,828	2,677	849	554	324
1974/5	20,771	2,686	11,577	2,824	1,867	2,678	963	538	324
1975/6	20,276	2,473	11,652	2,833	1,979	2,775	1,122	585	327
1976/7	21,001	2,465	9,284	2,997	2,146	2,555	1,147	610	350
1977/8	21,706	2,643	9,699	3,216	2,257	2,760	1,027	608	332
1978/9	21,739	2,583	9,482	3,348	2,290	2,802	957	653	327
1979/80	21,934	2,720	9,541	3,464	2,391	2,657	923	700	319
1980/1	22,266	3,619	9,408	3,693	2,552	2,650	907	698	334

(*a*) Including theology, law, fine art, music, economics, education, etc.
(*b*) Including dentistry.
(*c*) Including engineering and architecture.
(*d*) Undergraduates only.
(*e*) There was a change in categorisation.

CHAPTER XVI

NATIONAL ACCOUNTS

TABLES

The fact that not only is this chapter a great deal longer than its equivalent in the original version of this volume, but scarcely any of the numbers there survive into the present work, reflects the immense amount of work that has gone into making and refining estimates of the country's national accounts since the 1950s. Nevertheless, some of the preliminary remarks made in that earlier work are worth repeating now.

Attempts to calculate aggregate indicators of national wealth and income first seem to have been made towards the end of the seventeenth century. For earlier periods the data are scanty and incomplete, and no contemporary was concerned with the national picture until the second half of the sixteenth century. There are tax records and manorial surveys stretching back to medieval times; but even attempts to assess the incomes of particular social or economic groups at specific points of time yield uncertain and rather dubious results.[1]

With the reign of Queen Elizabeth I, some officials at last began to take an interest in statistics of national economic activity considered as a whole. According to Lawrence Stone, 'the first and most extensive compilation of quantitative material was made during a balance of trade scare of the early 1560s, when a serious attempt was made to discover the precise nature of English commerce'.[2] The Tudor interest in statistics 'ranged over the whole field of governmental activity. The confused system for public finance was made to yield essential tabular information, the best examples of which are the remarkable estimates of the costs of the two wars from 1539–51 and from 1585–1603. Detailed surveys of English resources in ships and seamen were carried out repeatedly between 1550 and 1583 and provide a wealth of information on these subjects to which there is no parallel until after the Restoration.'[3] For all its qualities, however, this sixteenth-century material was partial rather than aggregative in nature.

At the end of the seventeenth century, however, an unusual combination of circumstances produced a wealth of economic and statistical data which were more complete than any which had preceded it. It was also more systematically and informatively analysed by contemporaries than anything which was produced for the next hundred years. The most important factor in this combination was the 'spirit of the age'. It was characteristic of this period of eager enquiry into scientific questions that writers on political and economic matters should try to comprehend the economic system as a whole, and should try to describe it in quantitative terms.

The inventor of 'political arithmetic' was Sir William Petty, who produced the first known national income estimate for this country. For him, as for later exponents of this method, the key figure in the matrix which gave the final aggregates was the population figure, and he had very little material on which to formulate a sound estimate.[4] Gregory King, who seems to have become interested in political arithmetic in connection with a new tax on births, burials and marriages, imposed at graduated rates for different sections of the population, was more fortunate. He presumably had access to the records of the new tax, which came into operation in 1695 (and provided for the most complete 'census' of the population yet attempted), and also to various tax records (e.g. hearth tax, excise and house duties) which did not exist, or were not returned, by the collectors in Petty's time; and, of course, he had the advantage of being able to use the first systematically compiled returns of overseas trade

[1] See, for example, H. L. Gray, 'Incomes from Land in 1436', *English Historical Review*, XLIX (1934); M. M. Postan, 'Some Economic Evidence of Declining Population in the Later Middle Ages', *Economic History Review*, second series (1950); and C. D. Ross and T. B. Pugh, 'Materials for the Study of Baronial Incomes in Fifteenth-Century England', *Economic History Review*, second series (1953), p. 34.

[2] Lawrence Stone, 'Elizabethan Overseas Trade', *Economic History Review*, second series (1949).

[3] *Ibid.*, pp. 31–2.

[4] The first scientific study of the only available vital statistics was Graunt's analysis of the London Bills of Mortality for the period 1603–60. See J. Graunt, *Natural and Political Observations on the Bills of Mortality* (1662), included in C. H. Hull, *The Economic Writings of Sir William Petty*, vol. II (Cambridge, 1899).

for the country as a whole. Not until the assessments to Pitt's income tax and the 1801 census became available at the beginning of the nineteenth century were would-be national income investigators as well supplied with relevant statistics as King had been.[5]

The works of King, and his rather pale imitator in the middle of the eighteenth century, Joseph Massie, together with the efforts of Colquhoun and other early-nineteenth-century investigators, have been part of the basis of modern attempts to assess the growth of the national product and some of its main components for the period before the creation of detailed annual estimates becomes a feasible proposition. The pioneers in the field were Deane and Cole, though the only overall national series which they published, other than the figures reproduced here in part A of table 2, were index numbers of real output by broad sectors at decade intervals from 1700. These have not been shown here, mainly because of the cricitism to which they have been subjected, especially by Harley and by Crafts.[6] Instead, Crafts's suggested alternative estimates of growth rates are shown in note 4 to table 8, even though he himself describes the figures as 'essentially a set of hypotheses'[7] and appears to suggest that his growth rate for the industry component may even be too high.[8]

Lindert and Williamson have also attempted to derive estimates of the size (and distribution) of the national income with the work of contemporaries as their main base. The principal results are shown here in table 1, though it goes without saying that a very substantial margin of error must attach to these figures.

It is only since the First World War that there has been any attempt to make a continuous historical series of estimates of the national accounts, and only following the Second World War that there was much success. The first steps were taken by Bowley and Stamp, though neither produced a connected series for any lengthy period, any more than had their predecessor Giffen, or Clark, who worked in the field in the 1930s.[9] The first such series was

[5] For a critical evaluation of contemporary estimates made up to the end of the nineteenth century, see the following articles by Phyllis Deane: 'The Implications of Early National Income Estimates for the Measurement of Long-Term Growth in the United Kingdom', *Economic Development and Cultural Change* IV, 1 (1955); 'Contemporary Estimates of the National Income in the First Half of the Nineteenth Century', *Economic History Review*, second series VIII, 3 (1956); 'The Industrial Revolution and Economic Growth: The Evidence of Early British National Income Estimates', *Economic Development and Cultural Change*, V, 2 (1957); and 'Contemporary Estimates of the National Income in the Second Half of the Nineteenth Century', *Economic History Review*, second series IX, 3 (1957).

[6] C. Knick Harley, 'British Industrialization before 1841: Evidence of Slower Growth during the Industrial Revolution', *Journal of Economic History*, XLII, 2 (1982); N. F. R. Crafts, 'English Economic Growth in the Eighteenth Century: A Re-examination of Deane and Cole's Estimates', *Economic History Review*, second series XXIX, 2 (1976); and N. F. R. Crafts, *British Economic Growth during the Industrial Revolution* (Oxford, 1985), especially chapter 2.

[7] *Ibid.*, p. 46.

[8] *Ibid.*, p. 44. This index is shown separately in chapter VIII table 21, part B, along with Harley's, which has an even lower growth rate.

[9] Sir J. C. Stamp, *British Income and Property* (London, 1916); A. L. Bowley, *The Change in the Distribution of the National Income, 1880–1913* (London, 1920) – reprinted in Bowley and Stamp, *Three Studies in the National Income* (London, 1938); A. L. Bowley, *Wages and Income since 1860* (Cambridge, 1937); Sir Robert Giffen, *Economic Enquiries and Studies* (2 vols., London, 1904); Sir Robert Giffen, *The Growth of Capital* (London, 1889); and Colin Clark, *The National Income 1924–1931* (London, 1932), and its expanded and rewritten successor, *National Income and Outlay* (London, 1937).

Prest's, published in 1948, which went back continuously to 1870.[10] Various people have since worked at refining these estimates and pushing them further back in time, most notably Phyllis Deane and Charles Feinstein, whose work lies behind so many of the tables in this chapter.

It is impossible to summarise here the long and detailed calculations involved in these estimates, and anyone requiring information on their provenance must consult the sources, where there is frequent reference to the degrees of reliability of the figures as well as to how they were arrived at. Broadly speaking, the best estimates – which include most series since 1946,[11] and many in the interwar period – are reckoned to have a margin of error of less than 10 per cent, with many less than 5. In others, including some of those for the major war periods of the twentieth century, the margin may rise to as much as 25 per cent.

Only one further point will be made here about the national product tables in this chapter, and that concerns the provision of alternative estimates for the main aggregates. This arises because the estimates were made in two different ways – by assessing and aggregating expenditures of different kinds, and by doing the same for incomes from different sources. In principle, the two resulting aggregates should be the same; but in practice they are not. The differences between them may well be instructive, and, since it was felt that either or both of the alternatives might be required by some users, they are both given – in tables 4 and 5 (though only the expenditure side is given in constant price form). However, for the non-specialist who simply wants an expression of the overall size and growth of the country's product, probably the most useful table will be 5A, which presents Feinstein's own 'compromise' between the two alternative estimates of Gross Domestic Product.

The national accounting framework, which underlies almost all the tables in this chapter, was first employed officially during the Second World War, with the publication in 1941 of a White Paper giving official estimates of national income and expenditure. Others followed regularly, and in 1952 they were joined by the C.S.O.'s first *National Income Blue Book*. For those not familiar with the framework, there is a useful introduction by the Stones, and the more detailed official descriptive publication.[12]

The last two tables in the chapter show United Kingdom and Irish balance of payments estimates. These arrived rather late on the statistical scene in view of the seventeenth-century mercantilist concern about the balance of trade, for it was not until the interwar period that the wider concept was fully developed, largely as a result of the disruptions of international trading and financial relations arising out of the First World War. Even then, the contemporary estimates for that period were highly imperfect. It was with Imlah's estimates, published in the 1950s, that the first reasonably acceptable estimates of the major

10 A. R. Prest, 'National Income of the United Kingdom 1870–1946', *Economic Journal*, LVIII (1948).

11 A major exception is capital stock statistics, where the margins of error may be up to 25 per cent at all times, and perhaps more before 1913. Of course, it is almost inconceivable that the margins of error are not fairly consistent (i.e. close from year to year).

12 Richard and Giovanna Stone, *National Income and Expenditure* (London, 1961 – with later editions); and C.S.O., *United Kingdom National Accounts: Sources and Methods* (3rd edition, 1985).

historical balance of payments magnitudes became available, and these form part A of table 15. They have been widely and sometimes uncritically used since they appeared, though the fact that there has been no attempt to improve them suggests that such a task is difficult if not impossible. However, it is necessary to draw attention to the essential fragility of the estimates. A number of (necessarily) arbitrary assumptions had to be made about some of the invisible items, and only small changes in these would considerably affect the overall balances. This impressed Davis so much that he was convinced that it is impossible to determine the balance of payments, certainly prior to the 1850s, probably until the twentieth century. Differences of 5 per cent or so, he pointed out, 'are so large that possible error swamps the balancing figure that is aimed at'.[13] This is an extreme position, and others would not fully accept it, including Feinstein, whose own estimates, in part B of table 15, are essentially readjustments of Imlah's up to 1913.

Attention should be drawn to two of the main differences between Imlah's estimates and later ones. First, there is his inclusion of bullion and specie movements in the overall balance on current account. This was standard practice prior to 1932, but it had already become inappropriate in the 1920s, when most bullion movements had begun to be more of the nature of capital rather than current transactions. Second, he followed the normal practice in the trade statistics of valuing imports c.i.f., whereas modern balance of payments estimates value both imports and exports f.o.b. The older practice, of course, exaggerates the deficit of the visible balance and the surplus of the invisible balance.

[13] Ralph Davis, *The Industrial Revolution and British Overseas Trade* (Leicester, 1979), p. 85.

National Accounts 1. National Income and its Constituents – England and Wales, 1688–1801/3

NOTES

[1] SOURCE: P. H. Lindert and J. G. Williamson, "Revising England's Social Tables, 1688–1913", *Explorations in Economic History* 19 (1982), as corrected in *ibid.*, 20 (1983).

[2] For discussion of the problems of categorisation see the source.

(in £ million)

	1688	1759	1801/3
High Titles and Gentlemen	8·81	11·74	27·54
Professions	4·46	5·09	17·31
Military and Maritime	2·13	2·13	10·38
Commerce (*a*)	10·90	14·01	39·21
Industry and Building (*b*)	9·58	11·72	51·07
Agriculture (*c*)	12·21	16·66	38·00
Labourers (*b*)	4·27	4·20	10·54
Cottagers and Paupers (*d*)	2·04	1·25	2·60
Vagrants	0·04	0·04	1·92
Total	54·44	66·84	198·58

(*a*) Includes tradesmen, some of whom should properly be in 'industry and building'.

(*b*) In 1801/3, those described as 'labourers in industry' are included in 'industry and building'. In previous years there was no distinction made between labourers in different sectors.

(*c*) Freeholders and farmers only.

(*d*) Described as "paupers" in 1801/3.

National Accounts 2. Gross National or Domestic Product by Sector of Origin – Great Britain 1801–1924 and United Kingdom 1920–80

NOTES TO PART A

[1] SOURCE: Phyllis Deane and W. A. Cole, *British Economic Growth, 1688–1959* (Cambridge, 1962).

[2] The difference between the totals and the sums of the constituent items represents government, professional and other non-domestic services, income from abroad, and errors and omissions.

A. G.N.P. at Factor Cost – Great Britain 1801–1924

(in £ million)

	Agriculture, Forestry and Fishing	Mining, Manufacturing and Building (a)	Trade and Transport	Domestic and Personal Services	Housing	Total
1801	75·5	54·3	40·5	12·8	12·2	232·0
1811	107·5	62·5	50·1	15·7	17·2	301·1
1821	76·0	93·0	46·4	16·6	17·9	291·0
1831	79·5	117·1	59·0	19·2	22·0	340·0
1841	99·9	155·5	83·3	26·9	37·0	452·3
1851	106·5	179·5	97·8	27·4	42·6	523·3
1861	118·8	243·6	130·7	35·0	50·3	668·0
1871	130·4	348·9	201·6	45·5	69·4	916·6
1881	109·1	395·9	241·9	51·7	89·1	1,051·2
1891	110·9	495·2	289·6	70·6	104·0	1,288·2
1901	104·6	660·7	383·0	78·5	134·2	1,642·9
1907	120·1	737·7	547·3	75·8	148·4	1,995·5
1924	168·5	1,655·9	1,234·0	141·4	265·2	4,121·1

(*a*) Including Gas, Electricity, and Water.

NOTES TO PART B

[1] Source: C. H. Feinstein, *National Income, Expenditure and Output of the United Kingdom 1855–1965* (Cambridge, 1972), appendix table 9.

[2] The difference between the totals and the sums of the constituent items represents income not allocated and stock appreciation.

B. G.D.P. at Factor Cost (Income-based) – United Kingdom, 1920–1938

(in £ million)

	Agriculture, Forestry, and Fishing	Mining and Quarrying	Electricity, Gas and Water Supply	Manufacturing	Building and Contracting	Transport	Communications	Distributive Trades	Insurance, Banking, & Finance (*a*)	Ownership of Dwellings	Public Administration and Defence	Other Services	G.D.P.
1920	324	347	77	1,586	228	440	53	579	166	143	316	596	5,266
1921	279	216	74	1,132	204	411	58	486	149	163	255	573	4,424
1922	220	185	80	1,112	157	365	50	527	159	175	217	514	3,851
1923	187	216	82	1,073	146	327	46	517	157	177	194	505	3,653
1924	183	218	81	1,114	155	333	47	522	167	181	193	519	3,763
1925	179	183	85	1,130	174	337	49	545	184	183	195	537	4,010
1926	176	111	84	1,079	176	305	51	541	189	190	196	546	3,794
1927	157	154	93	1,166	192	350	54	575	202	197	197	560	4,014
1928	164	129	95	1,159	188	346	55	594	223	203	196	571	4,041
1929	164	151	98	1,177	189	350	56	595	223	211	200	582	4,178
1930	169	142	102	1,062	189	325	58	563	214	219	204	580	4,142
1931	153	130	103	949	178	306	57	542	214	226	204	565	3,786
1932	149	117	105	945	164	283	57	528	236	232	200	560	3,706
1933	170	115	108	1,005	171	291	57	564	243	238	198	569	3,779
1934	183	123	107	1,100	186	313	59	573	250	242	204	593	4,026
1935	176	126	113	1,171	201	324	61	604	263	249	213	619	4,194
1936	190	143	119	1,295	219	347	65	647	268	257	223	651	4,431
1937	166	163	124	1,426	229	375	69	667	272	265	237	674	4,709
1938	176	165	128	1,424	236	365	73	646	279	271	259	690	4,932

(*a*) Including income arising from land and buildings rented to trading concerns or public authorities (irrespective of the industry in which the owner of the building is engaged) plus the imputed rental of buildings owned and used by public authorities other than for their trading activities. The figures are measured after deducting net receipts of interest by financial concerns.

NOTES TO PARTS C and D

[1] SOURCE: C.S.O., *National Income and Expenditure* (renamed *United Kingdom National Accounts* from 1984).

[2] The difference between the totals and the sums of the constituent items to 1962 (2nd line) represents stock appreciation. The difference from 1962 (2nd line) onwards represents adjustment for financial services.

[3] The 1958 and 1968 Standard Industrial Classifications are used in Part C, the 1980 one in Part D.

C. G.D.P. at Factor Cost (Income-based) – United Kingdom, 1948–72

(in £ million)

	Agriculture, Forestry, and Fishing	Mining and Quarrying	Electricity, Gas, and Water Supply	Manufacturing	Building and Contracting	Transport	Communications	Distributive Trades	Insurance, Banking, and Finance	Ownership of Dwellings	Public Administration and Defence	Public Health & Education Services	Other Services	G.D.P.
1948	645	384	210	3,539	570	871		1,436	281	296	673	260	1,359	10,234
1949	693	398	223	3,733	617	916		1,521	300	297	686	326	1,430	10,985
1950	686	413	251	4,169	639	966		1,661	332	367	720	357	1,410	11,391
1951	726	449	274	4,725	699	1,140		1,810	380	323	828	403	1,508	12,617
1952	770	505	307	4,738	752	1,203		1,737	373	354	917	462	1,517	13,760
1953	786	544	335	5,116	830	1,195		1,839	391	409	950	488	1,583	14,633
1954	777	567	367	5,618	893	1,032	244	1,974	453	517	985	524	1,684	15,579
1955	801	589	401	6,168	977	1,144	274	2,150	500	557	1,011	566	1,876	16,847
1956	825	678	446	6,515	1,100	1,255	304	2,274	503	594	1,117	626	2,007	18,053
1957	863	710	474	6,888	1,127	1,305	340	2,375	522	638	1,158	700	2,069	19,019
1958	872	713	525	7,006	1,180	1,220	377	2,435	568	765	1,220	749	2,165	19,827
		---(a)		---(a)	---(a)			---(a)					---(a)	
1959	877	689	571	7,509	1,236	1,293	393	2,570	625	835	1,262	822	2,340	20,935
1960	913	680	617	8,244	1,363	1,532	421	2,756	681	901	1,323	906	2,545	22,759
1961	955	700	667	8,417	1,515	1,574	448	2,828	774	964	1,383	976	2,890	24,247
	992	744	734	8,545	1,650			2,968	855				3,012	
1962	---(b)	---(b)	---(b)	---(b)	---(b)	1,636	479	---(b)	---(b)(c)	1,052	1,458	1,082	---(b)	25,474
	978	744	740	8,538	1,666			2,969	1,539				2,994	
1963	964	744	839	8,974	1,768	1,766	522	3,145	1,771	1,149	1,551	1,183	3,172	27,188
1964	996	744	916	9,855	2,007	1,863	580	3,323	1,894	1,265	1,681	1,272	3,453	29,473
1965	1,027	708	1,006	10,624	2,153	1,984	646	3,605	2,092	1,395	1,805	1,430	3,651	31,750
1966	1,061	689	1,069	11,003	2,261	2,079	703	3,756	1,929	1,535	2,095	1,646	4,037	33,530
1967	1,105	675	1,145	11,194	2,373	2,087	753	3,910	2,137	1,672	2,247	1,779	4,416	35,124
1968	1,122	670	1,301	11,999	2,560	2,349	813	4,054	2,464	1,849	2,402	1,929	4,819	37,777
1969	1,198	614	1,387	13,094	2,704	2,493	925	4,213	2,710	2,080	2,635	2,093	5,082	40,487
1970	1,266	639	1,385	14,309	3,050	2,749	1,005	4,603	3,097	2,368	2,963	2,363	5,665	44,541
1971	1,435	686	1,575	15,712	3,431	2,932	1,166	5,321	3,631	2,627	3,501	2,762	5,902	49,676
1972	1,556	795	1,753	17,244	4,328	3,325	1,345	6,158	4,346	3,011	3,955	3,319	6,832	56,461

(a) There is a minor break in continuity caused by the charge from the 1958 to the 1968 S.I.C.

(b) See note 2 above.

(c) Subsequently measured before deducting financial companies' receipts of interest.

D. G.D.P. at Factor Cost (Income-based) – United Kingdom, 1972–80

(in £ million)

	Agriculture, Forestry, and Fishing	Energy and Water Supply	Manufac-turing	Construc-tion	Transport	Communica-tions	Distribution, Hotels and Catering, Repairs	Banking, Finance, etc. (a)	Ownership of Dwellings	Public Adminis-tration & Defence (b)	Education and Health Services	Other Services	G.D.P.
1972	1,577	2,771	17,876	4,017	2,896	1,357	7,742	5,807	3,011	3,743	4,460	2,964	56,461
1973	2,006	3,018	20,919	4,995	3,248	1,608	8,982	7,365	3,525	4,220	5,276	3,507	65,874
1974	2,097	3,337	22,772	5,266	3,707	2,118	9,883	8,273	4,556	5,113	6,636	4,321	74,575
1975	2,574	4,797	27,537	6,425	4,860	2,716	12,064	9,769	5,589	6,849	9,240	5,476	94,520
1976	3,126	6,453	31,617	7,311	5,724	3,363	13,853	11,703	6,735	7,988	10,696	6,294	110,406
1977	3,367	8,788	38,003	8,107	6,503	3,483	16,792	13,904	7,516	8,456	11,413	7,499	128,792
1978	3,586	10,427	43,580	9,457	7,544	3,933	19,747	15,979	8,571	9,636	12,636	8,812	148,005
1979	3,910	13,757	48,646	11,007	8,501	4,403	22,511	19,574	10,311	10,774	14,390	10,093	171,352
1980	4,293	19,246	53,072	12,485	8,940	5,199	25,162	23,126	12,139	13,577	18,344	11,808	199,383

(a) Including insurance, business services, and leasing.

(b) Including compulsory social security.

National Accounts 3. Gross Domestic Product by Sector of Origin – Republic of Ireland 1947–80

NOTES

[1] Sources: Part A – G. A. Duncan, "The Social Income of the Irish Free State", *Journal of the Statistical and Social Inquiry Society of Ireland*, XVI (1939–40), p. 9. Parts B, C and D – National Statistics Office, Dublin, *National Income and Expenditure*.

[2] The figures are measured before adjustment for stock changes and for financial services. Because of this, the figures of total GDP for 1971–80 differ from those given in table 7.

(in £ million)

A. Net National Product 1926–37 (at Current Prices)

	Agriculture and Fishing	Industry (*a*)	Distribution	Personal Services	Housing	Income from Abroad	Total
1926	50·2	26·5	25·2	29·4	10·5	12·3	154·1
1929	52·7	30·4	26·1	29·2	10·7	12·3	161·4
1931	42·5	29·6	24·4	29·3	10·8	10·3	146·9
1933	29·7	29·5	21·9	27·6	10·9	15·0	134·5
1936	38·8	35·9	24·9	29·3	11·5	13·5	154·0
1937	40·2	36·2	25·1	29·4	11·8	13·1	155·8

B. Net Domestic Product 1947–57 (at Current Prices)

	Agriculture, Forestry, and Fishing	Industry (*a*)	Distribution, Transport, and Communications	Public Administration and Defence	Other Services	Total
1947	81·5	64·0	52·0	16·1	57·5	271·1
1948	92·2	71·5	53·8	17·7	59·6	294·8
1949	99·5	81·6	57·0	17·3	61·1	316·5
1950	94·1	88·7	60·9	20·3	66·1	330·1
1951	100·6	97·2	64·2	21·6	71·4	355·0
1952	116·9	100·7	63·9	23·3	73·1	377·9
1953	126·7	113·4	67·4	25·3	76·9	409·7
1954	119·0	119·5	67·6	25·1	79·7	410·9
1955	130·8	123·3	70·3	25·9	85·1	435·4
1956	118·7	126·5	71·8	27·3	90·3	434·6
1957	130·7	123·1	71·5	27·3	93·2	445·8
C. Gross Domestic Product, 1958–80 (at Current Prices)						
1958	126·3	141·1	80·4	28·0	110·3	486·1
1959	136·8	150·5	88·1	29·0	116·5	520·9
1960	139·9	165·5	95·6	31·0	126·7	558·7
1961	146·8	185·5	105·5	33·0	135·4	606·2
1962	151·9	208·0	114·8	36·4	146·5	657·6
1963	150·1	227·7	126·8	39·3	158·4	702·3
1964	174·6	249·2	141·7	47·6	181·0	794·1
1965	176·7	272·1	151·5	50·6	193·5	844·4
1966	170·5	291·3	158·4	53·5	207·9	881·6
1967	183·4	329·0	169·1	56·2	229·8	967·5
1968	208·3	374·6	190·9	60·4	256·3	1,090·5
1969	216·4	442·1	221·8	68·7	301·4	1,250·4
1970	232·9	500·0	262·4	84·2	340·1	1,399·7
1971	258·0	570·2	293·8	96·2	399·0	1,617·2
1972	349·3	686·0	340·3	116·7	469·7	1,962·0
1973	438·9	805·2	421·7	142·6	570·1	2,378·5
1974	422·5	908·4	511·9	168·9	671·4	2,683·1
1975	589·2	1,214·3	599·8	235·7	866·1	3,505·1
1976	672·8	1,413·8	723·9	275·3	1,076·6	4,162·4
1977	913·6	1,812·2	923·3	307·0	1,345·7	5,301·8
1978	1,037·8	2,246·7	1,155·8	364·4	1,642·4	6,447·1
1979	971·6	2,706·1	1,385·3	457·7	2,021·0	7,541·7
1980	932·4	3,111·7	1,553·9	576·6	2,507·7	8,682·3

National Accounts 3. *continued*

(in £ million)

D. Gross Domestic Product, 1958–80 (at Constant Prices)

	Agriculture, Forestry, and Fishing	Industry (*a*)	Distribution, Transport, and Communications	Public Administration and Defence	Other Services	Total
1958 Prices						
1958	126·3	141·1	80·4	28·0	110·3	486·1
1959	137·8	152·1	82·8	28·1	112·6	513·4
1960	144·4	162·0	87·6	28·5	116·1	538·6
1961	145·7	175·4	92·4	28·9	118·7	561·1
1962	147·0	187·7	96·1	29·9	120·8	581·5
1963	144·5	199·1	100·9	30·4	123·7	598·6
1964	151·1	215·2	105·9	30·7	128·2	631·1
1965	145·5	223·8	108·0	31·2	129·6	638·1
1968 Prices						
1965	191·5	311·8	162·5	57·6	234·1	957·5
1966	191·2	318·5	165·7	58·5	237·7	799·6
1967	196·3	342·1	174·1	60·6	247·1	1,020·2
1968	208·3	374·6	190·9	60·4	256·3	1,090·5
1969	203·4	403·2	200·1	63·7	266·0	1,136·4
1970	207·0	410·3	208·7	66·6	269·6	1,162·2
1975 Prices						
1970	446·7	973·3	498·2	180·1	688·4	2,786·7
1971	473·2	1,049·2	509·4	187·6	736·5	2,955·9
1972	509·8	1,108·5	554·9	200·0	773·4	3,146·6
1973	494·9	1,168·9	603·9	211·6	810·2	3,289·5
1974	531·8	1,202·6	612·0	225·1	833·7	3,405·2
1975	589·2	1,214·3	599·8	235·7	866·1	3,505·1
1976	525·3	1,302·9	613·6	240·0	907·4	3,589·2
1977	576·2	1,402·5	658·7	242·3	942·9	3,822·6
1978	585·7	1,532·4	710·4	256·0	1,012·3	4,096·8
1979	513·9	1,700·0	741·8	280·6	1,076·2	4,312·5
1980	554·1	1,652·7	769·6	297·6	1,100·2	4,374·2

(*a*) Including construction and utilities.

National Accounts 4. Gross National Product at Factor Cost and Its Component Incomes at Current Prices – United Kingdom 1855–1980

NOTES

[1] SOURCES: 1855–1948 – C. H. Feinstein, *National Income, Expenditure and Output of the United Kingdom, 1855–1965* (Cambridge, 1972) and extensions and revisions thereto kindly provided by Professor Feinstein; 1948–80 C.S.O., *National Income and Expenditure* (later *National Accounts*) annually.

[2] Southern Ireland is included to 1920 (1st line) and excluded subsequently.

[3] Alternative estimates of G.N.P., G.D.P., and National Income from the expenditure side are given in table 5, and Feinstein's "compromise" estimate of G.D.P. is given in table 5A.

(in £ million)

	Income from Employment	Income from Self-Employment (*a*)	Gross Trading Profits of Companies(*a*)	Gross Trading Surplus of Public Enterprises (*a*)	Rent (*b*)	Stock Appreciation	Gross Domestic Product	Net Property Income from Abroad	Gross National Product	Capital Consumption	National Income
1855	328		199		93	...	620	13	633	32	601
1856	336		218		94	...	648	15	663	33	630
1857	321		216		97	...	634	16	650	33	617
1858	308		219		99	...	626	16	642	32	610
1859	337		212		102	...	651	17	668	32	636
1860	350		222		102	...	674	19	693	33	660
1861	350		252		106	...	708	20	728	34	694
1862	352		266		108	...	726	21	747	35	712
1863	364		284		109	...	757	21	778	36	742
1864	376		295		112	...	783	23	806	39	767
1865	398		300		115	...	813	24	837	40	797
1866	409		308		116	...	833	26	859	42	817
1867	409		293		117	...	819	28	847	43	804
1868	400		299		119	...	818	31	849	43	806
1869	414		310		121	...	845	33	878	44	834
1870	431		354		127	...	912	35	947	46	901
1871	457		395		130	...	982	39	1,021	49	972
1872	512		403		133	...	1,048	44	1,092	56	1,036
1873	559		425		137	...	1,121	52	1,173	64	1,109
1874	547		404		140	...	1,091	57	1,148	66	1,082
1875	544		387		143	...	1,074	58	1,132	63	1,069
1876	542		366		149	...	1,057	57	1,114	62	1,052
1877	545		354		152	...	1,051	55	1,106	61	1,045
1878	526		337		155	...	1,018	55	1,073	60	1,013
1879	518		319		156	...	993	56	1,049	59	990
1880	529		353		157	...	1,039	58	1,097	63	1,034
1881	547		370		159	...	1,076	59	1,135	62	1,073
1882	580		372		161	...	1,113	63	1,176	64	1,112
1883	587		352		161	...	1,100	64	1,164	65	1,099
1884	568		335		162	...	1,065	67	1,132	64	1,068
1885	555		327		165	...	1,047	70	1,117	63	1,054
1886	551		347		166	...	1,064	74	1,138	61	1,077
1887	579		360		166	...	1,105	79	1,184	61	1,123
1888	614		395		168	...	1,177	84	1,261	62	1,199
1889	674	295	125	4	170	...	1,268	89	1,357	66	1,291
1890	704	292	122	5	172	...	1,295	94	1,389	70	1,319
1891	705	280	114	5	172	...	1,276	94	1,370	69	1,301
1892	701	250	107	5	174	...	1,237	95	1,332	70	1,262
1893	704	241	115	6	177	...	1,243	95	1,338	70	1,268
1894	722	278	142	6	184	...	1,332	93	1,425	70	1,355
1895	737	281	151	6	189	...	1,364	94	1,458	70	1,388
1896	766	279	157	6	192	...	1,400	96	1,496	73	1,423
1897	785	290	174	6	196	...	1,451	97	1,548	76	1,472
1898	824	303	200	7	200	...	1,534	101	1,685	80	1,555
1899	857	331	226	7	204	...	1,625	103	1,728	87	1,641

See p. 830 for footnotes.

National Accounts 4. *continued*

(in £ million)

	Income from Employment	Income from Self-Employment (a)	Gross Trading Profits of Companies (a)	Gross Trading Surplus of Public Enterprises (a)	Rent (b)	Stock Appreciation	Gross Domestic Product	Net Property Income from Abroad	Gross National Product	Capital Consumption	National Income
1900	909	322	229	8	209	...	1,677	104	1,781	96	1,685
1901	908	304	216	8	213	...	1,649	106	1,755	96	1,659
1902	899	315	224	10	217	...	1,665	109	1,774	97	1,677
1903	908	287	209	11	221	...	1,636	112	1,748	98	1,650
1904	893	286	205	14	225	...	1,623	113	1,736	100	1,636
1905	913	311	230	13	227	...	1,694	123	1,817	103	1,714
1906	952	334	260	14	230	...	1,790	134	1,924	109	1,815
1907	1,008	350	274	15	233	...	1,880	144	2,024	115	1,909
1908	975	313	245	15	235	...	1,783	151	1,934	114	1,820
1909	987	317	249	17	237	...	1,807	158	1,965	116	1,849
1910	1,027	332	265	17	239	...	1,880	170	2,050	120	1,930
1911	1,065	358	278	18	243	...	1,962	177	2,139	125	2,014
1912	1,114	371	314	21	246	...	2,066	187	2,253	134	2,119
1913	1,160	372	332	20	249	...	2,133	200	2,333	141	2,192
1914	1,260	689		21	252	50	2,172	190	2,362	145	2,217
1915	1,556	876		26	259	200	2,517	165	2,682	165	2,517
1916	1,858	1,175		31	272	350	2,986	200	3,186	198	2,988
1917	2,340	1,348		49	278	250	3,765	195	3,960	235	3,725
1918	2,881	1,482		71	281	100	4,615	175	4,790	281	4,509
1919	3,076	1,662		36	284	200	4,858	165	5,023	347	4,676
1920	3,525	1,380		20	259	−200	5,384	254	5,638	414	5,224
	---(c)		---(c)	---(c)	---(c)	---(c)	---(c)	---(c)	---(c)	---(c)	---(c)
	3,449	752	621	20	224	−200	5,266	246	5,512	435	5,077
1921	2,835	618	343	25	252	−350	4,423	178	4,601	352	4,249
1922	2,411	626	437	44	270	− 62	3,850	177	4,027	314	3,713
1923	2,318	614	456	44	267	45	3,654	176	3,830	288	3,542
1924	2,376	633	477	40	278	40	3,764	196	3,960	283	3,677
1925	2,419	652	468	42	290	−139	4,010	232	4,242	283	3,959
1926	2,336	642	420	40	299	− 56	3,793	237	4,030	283	3,747
1927	2,505	653	478	48	311	− 28	4,023	239	4,262	279	3,983
1928	2,497	670	474	51	330	− 18	4,040	240	4,280	284	3,996
1929	2,545	668	485	52	347	− 80	4,177	243	4,420	293	4,127
1930	2,485	616	411	54	362	−213	4,141	215	4,356	291	4,065
1931	2,382	552	360	55	373	− 63	3,785	163	3,948	290	3,658
1932	2,357	548	321	59	387	− 34	3,706	127	3,833	283	3,550
1933	2,402	590	380	62	390	45	3,779	154	3,933	283	3,650
1934	2,507	596	464	67	396	5	4,025	167	4,192	282	3,910
1935	2,597	629	514	68	413	26	4,195	181	4,376	298	4,078
1936	2,744	663	627	69	425	98	4,430	195	4,625	317	4,308
1937	2,908	631	717	71	448	67	4,708	205	4,913	357	4,556
1938	2,989	615	687	72	460	109	4,932	192	5,124	370	4,754
1939	3,215	696	865	76	480	200	5,132	160	5,292	390	4,907
1940	3,843	791	1,109	77	485	500	5,805	160	5,965	440	5,530
1941	4,535	892	1,238	90	475	150	7,080	140	7,220	500	6,720
1942	5,042	949	1,377	136	475	100	7,879	100	7,979	530	7,449
1943	5,472	977	1,405	149	495	50	8,448	90	8,538	620	7,918
1944	5,751	991	1,388	134	470	50	8,684	80	8,764	650	8,114

See p. 830 for footnotes.

National Accounts 4. *continued*

(in £ million)

	Income from Employment	Income from Self-Employment (*a*)	Gross Trading Profits of Companies(*a*)	Gross Trading Surplus of Public Enterprises (*a*)	Rent (*b*)	Stock Appreciation	Gross Domestic Product	Net Property Income from Abroad	Gross National Product	Capital Consumption	National Income
1945	5,889	1,074	1,350	119	405	50	8,787	80	8,867	640	8,227
1946	5,758	1,126	1,476	106	429	125	8,770	85	8,855	690	8,165
1947	6,227	1,210	1,694	155	472	450	9,308	150	9,458	770	8,688
1948	6,785	1,305	1,793	220	456	325	10,234	235	10,469	848	9,621
1949	7,246	1,363	1,843	258	475	200	10,985	219	11,204	893	10,311
1950	7,627	1,402	2,126	335	551	650	11,391	396	11,787	964	10,823
1951	8,501	1,438	2,483	381	564	750	12,617	342	12,959	1,129	11,830
1952	9,107	1,490	2,180	322	611	− 50	13,760	252	14,012	1,283	13,729
1953	9,634	1,538	2,313	388	685	− 75	14,633	229	14,862	1,333	13,529
1954	10,284	1,577	2,576	466	751	75	15,579	250	15,829	1,392	14,437
1955	11,244	1,660	2,886	431	822	196	16,847	174	17,021	1,517	15,504
1956	12,267	1,713	2,928	472	881	208	18,053	229	18,282	1,657	16,625
1957	12,963	1,773	3,075	458	937	187	19,019	249	19,268	1,781	17,487
1958	13,470	1,783	2,983	501	1,085	− 5	19,827	293	20,120	1,888	18,232
1959	14,107	1,885	3,317	560	1,164	98	20,935	262	21,197	1,947	19,250
1960	15,174	2,008	3,730	723	1,246	122	22,759	233	22,992	2,047	20,945
1961	16,396	2,314	3,625	747	1,336	171	24,247	254	24,501	2,184	22,317
1962	17,298	2,469	3,581	829	1,449	152	25,474	334	25,808	2,380	23,428
1963	18,190	2,586	4,094	948	1,522	152	27,188	398	27,586	2,615	24,971
1964	19,730	2,729	4,546	1,043	1,668	243	29,473	406	29,879	2,793	27,086
1965	21,310	2,989	4,761	1,117	1,864	291	31,750	448	32,198	3,000	29,198
1966	22,842	3,183	4,618	1,166	2,026	305	33,530	403	33,933	3,247	30,686
1967	23,799	3,338	4,661	1,259	2,204	137	35,124	400	35,524	3,432	32,092
1968	25,455	3,646	5,302	1,514	2,443	583	37,777	359	38,136	3,732	34,404
1969	27,227	3,893	5,731	1,626	2,743	733	40,487	532	41,019	4,078	36,941
1970	30,553	4,191	6,105	1,627	3,126	1,061	44,541	595	45,136	4,613	40,523
1971	33,489	4,890	7,131	1,726	3,495	1,055	49,676	551	50,227	5,325	44,902
1972	37,870	5,866	8,161	1,845	4,009	1,290	56,461	593	57,054	6,138	50,916
1973	43,877	7,505	10,418	2,214	4,666	2,806	65,874	1,327	67,201	7,325	59,876
1974	52,379	8,118	11,457	2,693	6,037	6,109	74,575	1,507	76,082	9,081	67,001
1975	68,494	9,195	11,762	3,210	7,380	5,521	94,520	890	95,410	11,624	83,786
1976	78,005	10,918	14,714	4,636	8,814	6,681	110,406	1,557	111,963	13,990	97,973
1977	86,685	12,156	19,865	5,255	9,926	5,095	128,792	246	129,038	16,547	112,491
1978	98,995	13,813	22,567	5,576	11,282	4,228	148,005	827	148,832	19,260	129,572
1979	115,807	15,998	29,195	5,745	13,449	8,832	171,352	1,188	172,540	22,929	149,611
1980	137,353	17,557	29,024	6,293	15,888	6,732	199,383	−219	199,164	27,900	171,264

(*a*) Before providing for depreciation and stock appreciation.
(*b*) Including the imputed charge for consumption of non-trading capital, which was not identified separately prior to the 1977 Blue Book. The figures are before providing for depreciation.
(*c*) See note 2 above.

National Accounts 5. Gross National Product and National Income by Category of Expenditure at Current Prices – United Kingdom 1830–1980

NOTES

[1] SOURCES: As for table 4. Professor Feinstein's extensions back to 1830 are based in part on Phyllis Deane, "New Estimates of Gross National Product for the United Kingdom 1830–1914", *The Review of Income and Wealth*, series 14, 2 (1968).

[2] Southern Ireland is included to 1920 (1st line) and excluded subsequently.

[3] Alternative estimates of G.N.P., G.D.P., and National Income from the income side for the period since 1855 are given in table 4, and Feinstein's "compromise" estimate of G.D.P. is given in table 5A.

[4] The figures for Consumers' Expenditure given in this table differ slightly for 1961–80 from those given in table 9. This is because the figures in the latter table are taken from the 1983 Blue Book (rather than the latest available) in order to correspond to the constant price series in 1975 prices given there and to the component categories employed there.

(in £ million)

	Consumers' Expenditure	Public Authorities' Current Expenditure on Goods and Services	Gross Domestic Fixed Capital Formation	Value of Physical Increase in Stocks (a)	Exports less Imports (b)	Gross Domestic Product at Market Prices	Net Property Income from Abroad	Gross National Product at Market Prices	Factor Cost (c) Adjustment	Gross Domestic Product at Factor Cost	Gross National Product at Factor Cost	Capital Consumption	National Income at Factor Cost
1830	448	31	25	0	−3	501	4	505	61	440	444	16	428
1831	440	30	28	2	−2	498	4	502	56	442	446	17	429
1832	423	31	21	−1	2	476	4	480	57	419	423	17	406
1833	419	30	21	1	−1	470	5	475	58	412	417	18	399
1834	440	29	25	4	1	499	6	505	59	440	446	18	428
1835	449	29	39	5	5	527	8	535	56	471	479	19	460
1836	494	28	42	1	−3	562	9	571	54	508	517	19	498
1837	471	29	46	0	−6	540	8	548	56	484	492	20	472
1838	490	30	53	4	−4	573	8	581	54	519	527	20	507
1839	518	31	56	4	−5	604	8	612	55	549	557	21	536
1840	490	33	55	−3	−9	566	7	573	56	510	517	21	496
1841	483	33	35	−8	−4	539	6	545	58	481	487	22	465
1842	460	34	31	−4	−3	518	6	524	59	459	465	22	443
1843	441	35	27	6	7	516	7	523	57	459	466	22	444
1844	479	36	30	12	6	563	8	571	57	506	514	23	491
1845	502	34	46	13	1	596	10	606	59	537	547	23	524
1846	517	35	69	16	0	637	10	647	57	580	590	23	567
1847	555	36	88	−3	−14	662	11	673	58	604	615	23	592
1848	522	41	71	10	−7	637	9	646	57	580	589	24	565
1849	547	41	60	5	−5	648	8	656	60	588	596	24	572
1850	508	38	47	−2	2	593	9	602	59	534	543	24	519
1851	532	39	46	6	0	623	10	633	58	565	575	24	551
1852	532	39	53	4	1	629	11	640	57	572	583	25	558
1853	605	39	59	5	−5	703	12	715	57	646	658	29	629
1854	635	47	64	4	−5	745	13	758	59	686	699	32	667

See p. 835 for footnotes.

National Accounts 5. *continued*

(in £ million)

	Consumers' Expenditure	Public Authorities' Current Expenditure on Goods and Services	Gross Domestic Fixed Capital Formation	Value of Physical Increase in Stocks (a)	Exports less Imports (b)	Gross Domestic Product at Market Prices	Net Property Income from Abroad	Gross National Product at Market Prices	Factor Cost (c) Adjustment	Gross Domestic Product at Factor Cost	Gross National Product at Factor Cost	Capital Consumption	National Income at Factor Cost
1855	634	61	62	4	5	766	13	779	59	707	720	32	688
1856	672	52	56	9	8	797	15	812	63	734	749	33	716
1857	693	48	53	3	8	805	16	821	64	741	757	33	724
1858	659	46	51	1	12	769	16	785	64	705	721	32	689
1859	695	49	54	12	20	830	17	847	65	765	782	32	750
1860	715	51	59	−1	4	828	19	847	67	761	780	33	747
1861	763	52	63	13	−6	885	20	905	65	820	840	34	806
1862	775	51	68	8	−9	893	21	914	65	828	849	35	814
1863	792	51	78	22	6	949	21	970	67	882	903	36	867
1864	849	51	88	12	1	1,001	23	1,024	66	935	958	39	919
1865	865	49	91	23	12	1,040	24	1,064	65	975	999	40	959
1866	925	51	89	11	9	1,085	26	1,111	66	1,019	1,045	42	1,003
1867	926	54	80	3	15	1,078	28	1,106	69	1,009	1,037	43	994
1868	932	57	76	8	6	1,079	31	1,110	71	1,008	1,039	43	996
1869	933	53	77	11	14	1,088	33	1,121	73	1,015	1,048	44	1,004
1870	954	55	87	40	17	1,153	35	1,188	74	1,079	1,114	46	1,068
1871	1,004	56	99	6	43	1,208	39	1,247	75	1,133	1,172	49	1,123
1872	1,065	57	118	−22	54	1,272	44	1,316	78	1,194	1,238	56	1,182
1873	1,123	55	125	9	30	1,342	52	1,394	80	1,262	1,314	64	1,250
1874	1,123	58	141	56	14	1,392	57	1,449	80	1,312	1,369	66	1,303
1875	1,118	60	137	6	−4	1,317	58	1,375	81	1,236	1,294	63	1,231
1876	1,126	61	139	−10	−32	1,284	57	1,341	83	1,201	1,258	62	1,196
1877	1,133	62	135	−42	−47	1,241	55	1,296	84	1,157	1,212	61	1,151
1878	1,120	64	120	48	−41	1,311	55	1,366	85	1,226	1,281	60	1,221
1879	1,057	69	106	−57	−15	1,160	56	1,216	82	1,078	1,134	59	1,075
1880	1,146	70	107	85	−29	1,379	58	1,437	82	1,297	1,355	63	1,292
1881	1,125	71	109	−2	4	1,307	59	1,366	85	1,222	1,281	62	1,219
1882	1,157	74	110	−7	−3	1,331	63	1,394	87	1,244	1,307	64	1,243
1883	1,190	76	113	39	−16	1,402	64	1,466	87	1,315	1,379	65	1,314
1884	1,162	76	106	27	4	1,375	67	1,442	88	1,287	1,354	64	1,290

1885	1,138	83	96	6	−8	1,315	70	1,385	87	1,228	1,298	63	1,235
1886	1,126	80	85	20	4	1,315	74	1,389	87	1,228	1,302	61	1,241
1887	1,162	78	86	18	6	1,350	79	1,429	88	1,262	1,341	61	1,280
1888	1,186	78	90	−2	10	1,362	84	1,446	90	1,272	1,356	62	1,294
1889	1,227	80	100	22	−6	1,423	89	1,512	93	1,330	1,419	66	1,353
1890	1,253	85	106	15	9	1,468	94	1,562	95	1,373	1,467	70	1,397
1891	1,315	87	107	8	−22	1,495	94	1,589	96	1,399	1,493	69	1,424
1892	1,314	87	108	11	−31	1,489	95	1,584	97	1,392	1,487	70	1,417
1893	1,310	89	109	−12	−41	1,455	95	1,550	98	1,357	1,452	70	1,382
1894	1,336	91	111	46	−48	1,536	93	1,629	102	1,434	1,527	70	1,457
1895	1,355	97	115	19	−40	1,546	94	1,640	107	1,439	1,533	70	1,463
1896	1,406	102	127	41	−45	1,631	96	1,727	111	1,520	1,616	73	1,543
1897	1,435	106	144	−10	−56	1,619	97	1,716	113	1,506	1,603	76	1,527
1898	1,500	112	172	25	−78	1,731	101	1,832	115	1,616	1,717	80	1,637
1899	1,561	136	192	37	−55	1,871	103	1,974	121	1,750	1,853	87	1,766
1900	1,637	182	205	−24	−78	1,922	104	2,026	128	1,794	1,898	96	1,802
1901	1,677	202	210	47	−87	2,049	106	2,155	136	1,913	2,019	96	1,923
1902	1,686	190	213	4	−93	2,000	109	2,109	146	1,854	1,963	97	1,866
1903	1,699	169	208	−17	−71	1,988	112	2,100	146	1,842	1,954	98	1,856
1904	1,719	163	203	2	−60	2,027	113	2,140	151	1,876	1,989	100	1,889
1905	1,736	163	198	27	−36	2,088	123	2,211	152	1,936	2,059	103	1,956
1906	1,766	163	192	5	−16	2,110	134	2,244	153	1,957	2,091	109	1,982
1907	1,811	163	176	−16	18	2,152	144	2,296	155	1,997	2,141	115	2,026
1908	1,813	167	145	−7	9	2,127	151	2,278	150	1,977	2,128	114	2,014
1909	1,831	173	154	23	−19	2,162	158	2,320	151	2,011	2,169	116	2,053
1910	1,877	182	158	−2	1	2,216	170	2,386	164	2,052	2,222	120	2,102
1911	1,936	188	163	11	32	2,330	177	2,507	167	2,163	2,340	125	2,215
1912	2,006	196	171	−13	18	2,378	187	2,565	172	2,206	2,393	134	2,259
1913	2,070	203	192	31	33	2,529	200	2,729	175	2,354	2,554	141	2,413
1914	2,074	324	193	50	−87	2,554	190	2,744	171	2,383	2,573	145	2,428
1915	2,384	1,045	170	−200	−216	3,183	165	3,348	208	2,975	3,140	165	2,975
1916	2,581	1,332	159	−300	−101	3,671	200	3,871	222	3,449	3,649	198	3,451
1917	2,979	1,685	203	−100	−169	4,598	195	4,793	199	4,399	4,594	235	4,359
1918	3,600	1,842	286	100	−422	5,406	175	5,581	181	5,225	5,400	281	5,119
1919	4,535	935	434	100	−175	5,829	165	5,994	283	5,546	5,711	347	5,364
1920	5,246	520	578	−100	112	6,356	254	6,610	386	5,970	6,224	414	5,810
	---(*d*)	---(*d*)	---(*d*)	---(*d*)	---(*d*)	---(*d*)	---(*d*)	---(*d*)	---(*d*)	---(*d*)	---(*d*)	---(*d*)	---(*d*)
	5,020	488	482	−100	92	5,982	246	6,228	370	5,612	5,858	435	5,423
1921	4,315	489	458	−100	−28	5,134	178	5,312	402	4,732	4,910	352	4,558
1922	3,842	435	381	−91	12	4,579	177	4,756	439	4,140	4,317	314	4,003
1923	3,717	395	334	−65	4	4,385	176	4,561	454	3,931	4,107	288	3,819
1924	3,777	398	374	−6	−124	4,419	196	4,615	430	3,989	4,185	283	3,902

See p. 835 for footnotes.

National Accounts 5. *continued*

(in £ million)

	Consumers' Expenditure	Public Authorities' Current Expenditure on Goods and Services	Gross Domestic Fixed Capital Formation	Value of Physical Increase in Stocks (*a*)	Exports less Imports (*b*)	Gross Domestic Product at Market Prices	Net Property Income from Abroad	Gross National Product at Market Prices	Factor Cost (*c*) Adjustment	Gross Domestic Product at Factor Cost	Gross National Product at Factor Cost	Capital Consumption	National Income at Factor Cost
1925	3,878	412	420	133	−199	4,644	232	4,876	429	4,215	4,447	283	4,164
1926	3,833	420	401	17	−275	4,396	237	4,633	449	3,947	4,184	283	3,901
1927	3,887	423	426	44	−167	4,613	239	4,852	479	4,134	4,373	279	4,094
1928	3,939	425	420	18	−143	4,659	240	4,899	493	4,166	4,406	284	4,122
1929	3,983	435	442	40	−175	4,727	243	4,970	476	4,251	4,494	293	4,201
1930	3,932	443	435	91	−216	4,685	215	4,900	457	4,228	4,443	291	4,152
1931	3,805	431	408	−3	−294	4,359	163	4,522	459	3,900	4,063	290	3,773
1932	3,683	430	347	1	−186	4,276	127	4,403	490	3,786	3,913	283	3,630
1933	3,696	446	357	−58	−166	4,259	154	4,413	486	3,773	3,927	283	3,644
1934	3,802	483	427	29	−191	4,513	167	4,680	507	4,006	4,173	282	3,891
1935	3,935	483	456	5	−158	4,721	181	4,902	522	4,199	4,380	298	4,082
1936	4,080	536	517	−6	−222	4,905	195	5,100	557	4,348	4,543	317	4,226
1937	4,289	617	574	60	−251	5,289	205	5,494	582	4,707	4,912	357	4,555
1938	4,392	749	592	83	−244	5,572	192	5,764	587	4,985	5,177	370	4,807
1939	4,539	1,179	540	100	−400	5,958	160	6,118	640	5,318	5,478	390	5,088
1940	4,799	2,952	520	200	−950	7,521	160	7,681	803	6,718	6,878	440	6,438
1941	5,104	4,097	480	100	−950	8,831	140	8,971	1,050	7,781	7,921	500	7,421
1942	5,410	4,581	450	−100	−750	9,591	100	9,691	1,151	8,440	8,540	530	8,010
1943	5,525	4,983	360	100	−760	10,208	90	10,298	1,218	8,990	9,080	620	8,460
1944	5,846	5,056	300	−200	−730	10,272	80	10,352	1,212	9,060	9,140	650	8,490
1945	6,391	4,190	350	−200	−900	9,831	80	9,911	1,157	8,674	8,754	640	8,114
1946	7,273	2,282	925	−126	−395	9,959	85	10,044	1,189	8,770	8,855	690	8,165
1947	8,028	1,735	1,199	269	−576	10,656	150	10,805	1,347	9,308	9,458	770	8,688
1948	8,609	1,756	1,422	175	−238	11,724	235	11,959	1,442	10,282	10,517	848	9,669
1949	8,907	2,039	1,577	65	−202	12,386	219	12,605	1,470	10,916	11,135	893	10,242
1950	9,400	2,120	1,708	−210	−81	12,937	396	13,333	1,586	11,351	11,747	964	10,783
1951	10,150	2,486	1,905	575	−683	14,433	342	14,775	1,794	12,639	12,981	1,129	11,852
1952	10,691	2,957	2,134	50	−173	15,659	252	15,911	1,865	13,794	14,046	1,283	12,763
1953	11,402	3,099	2,395	125	−148	16,873	229	17,102	1,992	14,881	15,110	1,333	13,777
1954	12,091	3,182	2,595	56	−124	17,800	250	18,050	2,070	15,730	15,980	1,392	14,588

1955	13,045	3,262	2,882	300	−304	19,185	174	19,359	2,291	16,894	17,068	1,517	15,551
1956	13,756	3,519	3,164	259	44	20,742	229	20,971	2,453	18,289	18,518	1,657	16,861
1957	14,519	3,667	3,451	238	58	21,933	249	22,182	2,543	19,390	19,639	1,781	17,858
1958	15,306	3,751	3,569	111	127	22,864	293	23,157	2,637	20,227	20,520	1,888	18,632
1959	16,118	3,988	3,816	178	−29	24,071	262	24,333	2,813	21,258	21,520	1,947	19,573
1960	16,939	4,224	4,190	562	−393	25,522	233	25,755	2,885	22,637	22,870	2,047	20,823
1961	18,020	4,557	4,704	279	−119	27,441	254	27,695	3,034	24,407	24,661	2,184	22,477
1962	19,110	4,882	4,904	−8	−82	28,806	334	29,140	3,271	25,535	25,869	2,380	23,489
1963	20,322	5,155	5,144	161	−150	30,632	398	31,030	3,443	27,189	27,587	2,615	24,972
1964	21,697	5,481	6,123	700	−619	33,382	406	33,788	3,899	29,483	29,889	2,793	27,096
1965	23,112	6,011	6,630	461	−358	35,856	448	36,304	4,351	31,505	31,953	3,000	28,953
1966	24,461	6,539	7,063	288	−93	38,258	403	38,661	4,821	33,437	33,840	3,247	30,593
1967	25,703	7,230	7,708	286	−468	40,459	400	40,859	5,150	35,309	35,709	3,432	32,277
1968	27,679	7,681	8,506	452	−400	43,918	359	43,918	5,860	38,058	38,417	3,732	34,685
1969	29,374	8,018	8,832	537	159	46,920	532	46,920	6,879	40,041	40,573	4,078	36,495
1970	31,932	9,033	9,736	382	382	51,465	595	51,465	7,468	43,997	44,592	4,613	39,979
1971	35,753	10,298	10,894	114	734	57,793	551	57,793	7,714	50,079	50,630	5,325	45,305
1972	40,422	11,740	11,940	25	130	63,997	593	63,997	8,037	55,960	56,553	6,138	50,415
1973	46,012	13,396	14,726	1,529	−1,902	73,761	1,327	73,761	8,570	65,191	66,518	7,325	59,193
1974	53,069	16,714	17,497	1,045	−4,402	83,923	1,507	85,430	8,318	75,605	77,112	9,081	68,031
1975	65,211	23,119	21,035	−1,354	−1,997	106,014	890	106,904	10,361	95,653	96,543	11,624	84,919
1976	75,675	27,040	24,504	901	−1,684	126,436	1,557	127,993	12,863	113,573	115,130	13,990	101,140
1977	86,478	29,473	27,036	1,824	754	145,565	246	145,811	16,642	128,923	129,169	16,547	112,622
1978	99,648	33,396	31,060	1,804	1,936	167,844	827	168,671	19,137	148,707	149,534	19,260	130,274
1979	118,156	38,852	36,855	2,160	355	196,378	1,188	197,566	25,225	171,153	172,341	22,929	149,412
1980	136,995	48,906	41,588	−2,875	5,397	230,011	−219	229,792	30,765	199,246	199,027	27,900	171,127

(*a*) Including work in progress.
(*b*) Including services as well as goods.
(*c*) Taxes on expenditure *less* subsidies.
(*d*) See note 2 above.

National Accounts 5A. "Compromise" Estimate of Gross Domestic Product at Factor Cost – United Kingdom 1855–1948

NOTES

[1] SOURCE: As for table 4.

[2] The estimates in this table are arithmetic means of those in tables 4 and 5, after adjustment of the figures from the expenditure side for trend and for stock building.

[3] Southern Ireland is included to 1920 (1st line) and excluded subsequently.

(current prices in £ million; constant prices index 1913=100)

	Current Prices	Constant Prices
1855	646	31·7
1856	673	33·2
1857	669	33·2
1858	648	33·3
1859	689	34·7
1860	699	35·3
1861	744	36·1
1862	756	36·5
1863	798	37·4
1864	836	38·0
1865	870	39·7
1866	901	40·0
1867	889	39·5
1868	888	40·8
1869	905	41·6
1870	969	45·1
1871	1,031	46·8
1872	1,095	46·9
1873	1,186	48·4
1874	1,156	48·7
1875	1,133	50·0
1876	1,110	50·3
1877	1,106	51·0
1878	1,086	50·7
1879	1,048	51·1
1880	1,130	53·0
1881	1,138	55·2
1882	1,184	56·7
1883	1,184	57·3
1884	1,170	57·6
1885	1,134	57·2
1886	1,144	58·2
1887	1,184	60·3
1888	1,224	62·8
1889	1,324	66·5
1890	1,349	66·9
1891	1,328	66·5
1892	1,294	64·9
1893	1,290	64·8
1894	1,383	69·9
1895	1,402	72·0
1896	1,460	74·5
1897	1,478	75·0
1898	1,575	79·0
1899	1,688	82·6
1900	1,756	81·4
1901	1,761	82·3
1902	1,760	83·8
1903	1,739	82·5
1904	1,750	83·4
1905	1,815	86·6
1906	1,874	88·7
1907	1,938	90·6
1908	1,880	87·1
1909	1,909	89·5
1910	1,966	91·7
1911	2,062	94·9
1912	2,136	96·1
1913	2,244	100.0
1914	2,278	102·3
1915	2,746	108·8
1916	3,218	110·9
1917	4,082	111·7
1918	4,920	114·1
1919	5,202	102·8
1920	5,677 ---(a)	94·8 ---(a)
	5,439	91·3
1921	4,578	83·9
1922	3,995	88·2
1923	3,793	91·0
1924	3,877	94·8
1925	4,113	99·4
1926	3,870	95·7
1927	4,079	103·4
1928	4,103	104·7
1929	4,214	107·8
1930	4,185	107·0
1931	3,843	101·5
1932	3,746	102·3
1933	3,776	105·3
1934	4,016	112·2
1935	4,197	116·5
1936	4,389	121·8
1937	4,708	126·1
1938	4,959	127·6
1939	5,225	128·9
1940	6,262	141·8
1941	7,431	154·7
1942	8,160	158·5
1943	8,719	162·0
1944	8,872	155·6
1945	8,731	148·8
1946	8,770	142·3
1947	9,308	140·2
1948	10,258	144·7

(a) See note 3 above.

National Accounts 6. Gross National Product and National Income by Categories of Expenditure at Constant Prices – United Kingdom 1830–1980

NOTES

[1] SOURCES: As for table 4.

[2] Southern Ireland is included to 1920 (1st line) and excluded subsequently.

A. 1830–1913 at 1900 Prices

(in £ million)

	Consumers' Expenditure	Public Authorities' Current Expenditure on Goods and Services	Gross Domestic Fixed Capital Formation	Value of Physical Increase of Stocks (a)	Exports less Imports (b)	Gross Domestic Product at Market Prices	Net Property Income from Abroad	Gross National Product at Market Prices	Factor Cost (c) Adjustment	Gross Domestic Product at Factor Cost	Gross National Product at Factor Cost	Capital Consumption	National Income at Factor Cost
1830	424	28	26	0	−8	470	3	473	38	432	435	17	418
1831	433	28	31	2	−3	491	3	494	39	452	455	17	438
1832	434	29	23	−1	−1	484	3	487	39	445	448	17	431
1833	440	29	23	1	−2	491	3	494	39	452	455	18	437
1834	452	28	28	3	1	512	4	516	40	472	476	18	458
1835	462	28	41	4	3	538	5	543	41	497	502	19	483
1836	482	28	39	1	−2	548	5	553	43	505	510	19	491
1837	476	29	46	0	−7	544	6	550	42	502	508	20	488
1838	490	30	53	3	−2	574	5	579	44	530	535	20	515
1839	509	31	55	3	1	599	5	604	45	554	559	21	538
1840	498	34	55	−2	−3	582	4	586	44	538	542	21	521
1841	495	35	36	−6	1	561	4	565	44	517	521	21	500
1842	488	36	33	−3	3	557	4	561	43	514	518	22	496
1843	492	37	31	5	9	574	5	579	44	530	535	22	513
1844	518	37	33	10	7	605	6	611	46	559	565	23	542
1845	542	36	47	11	1	637	7	644	48	589	596	24	572
1846	559	39	66	14	2	680	8	688	50	630	638	25	613
1847	552	38	82	−2	−7	663	8	671	49	614	622	26	596
1848	567	42	73	9	−7	684	8	692	50	634	642	27	615
1849	580	42	69	5	−2	694	7	701	52	642	649	28	621
1850	578	42	57	−2	7	682	8	690	51	631	639	28	611
1851	601	42	58	6	5	712	9	721	53	659	668	29	639
1852	606	43	64	4	9	726	9	735	54	672	681	29	652
1853	629	42	63	4	9	747	8	755	56	691	699	31	668
1854	634	46	64	3	13	760	8	768	56	704	712	31	681

See p. 841 for footnotes.

National Accounts 6. *continued*

A. 1830–1913 at 1900 Prices (*cont.*)

(in £ million)

	Consumers' Expenditure	Public Authorities' Current Expenditure on Goods and Services	Gross Domestic Fixed Capital Formation	Value of Physical Increase of Stocks (*a*)	Exports *less* Imports (*b*)	Gross Domestic Product at Market Prices	Net Property Income from Abroad	Gross National Product at Market Prices	Factor Cost (*c*) Adjustment	Gross Domestic Product at Factor Cost	Gross National Product at Factor Cost	Capital Consumption	National Income at Factor Cost
1855	624	60	61	3	23	771	8	779	56	715	723	32	691
1856	653	59	56	7	28	803	10	813	58	745	755	33	722
1857	672	51	55	2	33	813	10	823	60	753	763	34	729
1858	669	52	55	1	24	801	11	812	60	741	752	34	718
1859	696	55	60	11	33	855	11	866	62	793	804	35	769
1860	703	58	64	−1	26	850	12	862	63	787	799	36	763
1861	734	56	70	10	15	885	13	898	65	820	833	36	797
1862	746	55	76	6	5	888	14	902	66	822	836	38	798
1863	758	55	86	15	14	928	14	942	67	861	875	40	835
1864	778	54	92	8	12	944	13	957	69	875	888	40	848
1865	808	53	96	17	17	991	15	1,006	72	919	934	42	892
1866	836	53	92	8	11	1,000	16	1,016	74	926	942	43	899
1867	841	54	85	2	19	1,001	17	1,018	75	926	943	45	898
1868	866	56	82	6	24	1,034	19	1,053	77	957	976	45	931
1869	883	54	82	9	28	1,056	21	1,077	79	977	998	46	952
1870	928	57	90	30	38	1,143	22	1,165	80	1,063	1,085	48	1,037
1871	963	57	100	5	43	1,168	26	1,194	84	1,084	1,110	49	1,061
1872	976	56	107	−13	35	1,161	27	1,188	87	1,074	1,101	51	1,050
1873	998	52	105	6	16	1,177	32	1,209	90	1,087	1,119	53	1,066
1874	1,032	56	119	26	15	1,248	36	1,284	93	1,155	1,191	54	1,137
1875	1,047	59	126	4	5	1,241	39	1,280	95	1,146	1,185	55	1,130
1876	1,058	61	132	−7	−3	1,241	39	1,280	96	1,145	1,184	58	1,126
1877	1,072	62	132	−28	−10	1,228	37	1,265	96	1,132	1,169	59	1,110
1878	1,084	65	124	33	−6	1,300	40	1,340	96	1,204	1,244	61	1,183
1879	1,070	72	114	−41	10	1,225	42	1,267	94	1,131	1,173	63	1,110
1880	1,126	71	110	61	4	1,372	42	1,414	96	1,276	1,318	64	1,254
1881	1,118	73	116	−2	37	1,342	43	1,385	96	1,246	1,289	65	1,224
1882	1,138	76	115	−5	30	1,354	46	1,400	96	1,258	1,304	67	1,237
1883	1,176	79	119	31	25	1,430	48	1,478	98	1,332	1,380	68	1,312
1884	1,180	81	117	24	34	1,436	53	1,489	98	1,338	1,391	69	1,322

1885	1,191	89	109	6	18	1,413	59	1,472	98	1,315	1,374	71	1,303
1886	1,198	88	100	20	24	1,430	66	1,496	98	1,332	1,398	72	1,326
1887	1,243	86	103	19	23	1,474	73	1,547	100	1,374	1,447	73	1,374
1888	1,260	86	107	−3	39	1,489	75	1,564	100	1,389	1,464	74	1,390
1889	1,286	87	114	21	27	1,535	78	1,613	103	1,432	1,510	75	1,435
1890	1,310	89	116	15	28	1,558	84	1,642	105	1,453	1,537	77	1,460
1891	1,365	92	122	8	−1	1,586	83	1,669	108	1,478	1,561	78	1,483
1892	1,359	92	125	11	−8	1,579	88	1,667	109	1,470	1,558	80	1,478
1893	1,365	95	127	−13	−25	1,549	90	1,639	108	1,441	1,531	81	1,450
1894	1,420	99	132	50	−33	1,668	94	1,762	111	1,557	1,651	83	1,568
1895	1,455	105	138	20	−18	1,700	98	1,798	114	1,586	1,684	84	1,600
1896	1,515	110	150	47	−46	1,776	100	1,876	117	1,659	1,759	86	1,673
1897	1,524	113	167	−11	−49	1,744	101	1,845	119	1,625	1,726	88	1,638
1898	1,588	116	193	26	−63	1,860	104	1,964	122	1,738	1,842	90	1,752
1899	1,641	140	204	41	−41	1,985	104	2,089	127	1,858	1,962	93	1,869
1900	1,637	182	205	−24	−85	1,915	98	2,013	128	1,787	1,885	96	1,789
1901	1,669	204	216	49	−89	2,049	103	2,152	130	1,919	2,022	99	1,923
1902	1,678	193	227	4	−82	2,020	108	2,128	130	1,890	1,998	103	1,895
1903	1,685	171	225	−17	−64	2,000	109	2,109	129	1,871	1,980	107	1,873
1904	1,709	165	223	2	−59	2,040	109	2,149	129	1,911	2,020	111	1,909
1905	1,719	164	220	27	−25	2,105	119	2,224	131	1,974	2,093	114	1,979
1906	1,749	162	207	5	−15	2,108	125	2,233	132	1,976	2,101	118	1,983
1907	1,772	159	185	−15	17	2,118	128	2,246	134	1,984	2,112	120	1,992
1908	1,766	163	156	−7	−2	2,076	139	2,215	132	1,944	2,083	123	1,960
1909	1,774	170	167	22	6	2,139	144	2,283	129	2,010	2,154	126	2,028
1910	1,803	176	169	−2	32	2,178	147	2,325	131	2,047	2,194	129	2,065
1911	1,857	181	172	10	39	2,259	157	2,416	135	2,124	2,281	132	2,149
1912	1,869	184	172	−11	25	2,239	163	2,402	136	2,103	2,266	135	2,131
1913	1,937	188	189	27	28	2,369	173	2,542	140	2,229	2,402	138	2,264

B. 1913–1948 at 1938 Prices

1913	3,544	370	325	50	342	4,632	204	4,836	511	4,121	4,325	241	4,084
1914	3,560	530	325	80	216	4,711	197	4,908	507	4,204	4,401	248	4,153
1915	3,637	1,590	256	−300	−29	5,154	146	5,300	517	4,637	4,783	251	4,532
1916	3,335	1,810	201	−350	157	5,153	135	5,288	480	4,673	4,808	253	4,555
1917	3,074	1,980	215	−100	−18	5,151	106	5,257	415	4,736	4,842	253	4,589
1918	3,045	1,890	261	80	−108	5,168	100	5,268	405	4,763	4,863	257	4,606
1919	3,485	830	342	80	45	4,782	72	4,854	474	4,308	4,380	267	4,113
1920	3,493 ---(d) 3,343	475 ---(d) 446	397 ---(d) 284	−60 ---(d) −60	68 ---(d) 83	4,373 ---(d) 4,096	73 ---(d) 70	4,446 ---(d) 4,166	513 ---(d) 489	3,860 ---(d) 3,607	3,933 ---(d) 3,677	276 ---(d) 251	3,657 ---(d) 3,426

See p. 841 for footnotes.

National Accounts 6. *continued*

B. 1913–1948 at 1938 Prices (*cont.*)

(in £ million)

	Consumers' Expenditure	Public Authorities' Current Expenditure on Goods and Services	Gross Domestic Fixed Capital Formation	Value of Physical Increase of Stocks (*a*)	Exports less Imports (*b*)	Gross Domestic Product at Market Prices	Net Property Income from Abroad	Gross National Product at Market Prices	Factor Cost (*c*) Adjustment	Gross Domestic Product at Factor Cost	Gross National Product at Factor Cost	Capital Consumption	National Income at Factor Cost
1921	3,143	452	326	−70	6	3,857	96	3,953	455	3,402	3,498	256	3,242
1922	3,254	424	300	−63	77	3,992	102	4,094	450	3,542	3,644	260	3,384
1923	3,349	400	308	−45	103	4,115	121	4,236	458	3,657	3,778	264	3,514
1924	3,428	403	359	−4	52	4,238	129	4,367	473	3,765	3,894	272	3,622
1925	3,508	417	410	88	26	4,449	153	4,602	483	3,966	4,119	279	3,840
1926	3,496	424	397	12	−86	4,243	170	4,413	474	3,769	3,939	283	3,656
1927	3,631	430	442	33	3	4,539	180	4,719	494	4,045	4,225	288	3,937
1928	3,690	435	438	14	40	4,617	178	4,795	500	4,117	4,295	292	4,003
1929	3,765	444	461	31	25	4,726	184	4,910	510	4,216	4,400	303	4,097
1930	3,822	455	463	79	−99	4,720	185	4,905	510	4,210	4,395	313	4,082
1931	3,863	466	454	−3	−300	4,480	173	4,653	500	3,980	4,153	321	3,832
1932	3,839	466	396	1	−209	4,493	146	4,639	485	4,008	4,154	326	3,828
1933	3,937	471	409	−72	−201	4,544	183	4,727	498	4,046	4,229	330	3,899
1934	4,051	482	498	34	−214	4,851	192	5,043	517	4,334	4,526	330	4,196
1935	4,163	515	518	6	−169	5,033	206	5,239	537	4,496	4,702	337	4,365
1936	4,285	562	565	−6	−216	5,190	210	5,400	557	4,633	4,843	345	4,498
1937	4,357	627	584	56	−213	5,411	192	5,603	577	4,834	5,026	361	4,665
1938	4,392	749	592	83	−244	5,572	192	5,764	587	4,985	5,177	370	4,807
1939	4,416	1,134	530	100	−390	5,790	158	5,948	600	5,190	5,348	380	4,968
1940	3,999	2,646	460	150	−630	6,625	114	6,739	589	6,036	6,150	390	5,760
1941	3,837	3,317	370	60	−560	7,024	88	7,112	610	6,414	6,502	390	6,112
1942	3,796	3,478	320	−50	−450	7,094	61	7,155	607	6,487	6,548	380	6,168
1943	3,751	3,594	220	60	−400	7,225	49	7,274	613	6,612	6,661	380	6,281
1944	3,864	3,364	170	−120	−380	6,898	42	6,940	614	6,284	6,326	370	5,956
1945	4,108	2,733	190	−120	−440	6,471	40	6,511	631	5,840	5,880	360	5,520
1946	4,533	1,500	480	70	−150	6,433	40	6,473	643	5,790	5,830	360	5,470
1947	4,675	1,058	560	140	−155	6,278	58	6,336	637	5,641	5,699	365	5,334
1948	4,719	1,017	603	80	20	6,439	82	6,521	633	5,806	5,888	368	5,520

C. 1948–65 at 1958 Prices

1948	12,531	3,072	2,135	250	−215	17,773	321	18,094	2,053	15,720	16,041	1,267	14,774
1949	12,670	3,359	2,333	40	−135	18,317	292	18,609	2,099	16,218	16,510	1,313	15,197
1950	13,037	3,349	2,472	−275	327	18,910	466	19,376	2,140	16,770	17,236	1,377	15,859
1951	12,864	3,592	2,490	615	34	19,595	306	19,901	2,218	17,377	17,683	1,440	16,243
1952	12,788	3,959	2,511	65	241	19,564	230	19,794	2,181	17,383	17,613	1,490	16,123
1953	13,367	4,056	2,791	135	118	20,467	231	20,698	2,269	18,198	18,429	1,545	16,884
1954	13,914	4,043	3,032	54	201	21,244	253	21,497	2,382	18,862	19,115	1,617	17,498
1955	14,494	3,944	3,209	313	57	22,017	171	22,188	2,477	19,540	19,711	1,686	18,025
1956	14,618	3,910	3,359	244	239	22,370	223	22,593	2,465	19,905	20,128	1,748	18,380
1957	14,922	3,840	3,539	250	247	22,798	236	23,034	2,523	20,275	20,511	1,823	18,688
1958	15,306	3,751	3,569	111	127	22,864	293	23,157	2,637	20,227	20,520	1,888	18,632
1959	16,022	3,809	3,847	173	−44	23,807	262	24,069	2,900	20,907	21,169	1,961	19,208
1960	16,689	3,879	4,203	562	−352	24,981	230	25,211	3,056	21,925	22,155	2,051	20,104
1961	17,244	4,019	4,607	281	−148	26,003	250	26,253	3,090	22,913	23,163	2,135	21,028
1962	17,629	4,442	4,666	−8	−171	26,558	330	26,888	3,098	23,460	23,790	2,267	21,523
1963	18,491	4,215	4,803	156	−183	27,482	384	27,866	3,279	24,203	24,587	2,458	22,129
1964	19,184	4,289	5,607	636	−496	29,220	379	29,599	3,488	25,732	26,111	2,574	23,537
1965	19,553	4,459	5,841	404	−297	29,960	414	30,374	3,448	26,512	26,926	2,671	24,255

D. 1965–80 at 1980 Prices

1965	100,348	35,444	23,398	2,193	−2,142	168,364	2,042	170,760	21,227	147,065	149,354	15,091	134,036
1966	102,121	36,386	23,749	1,332	−1,607	171,603	1,808	173,769	21,606	149,927	151,976	15,692	136,081
1967	104,589	38,445	25,083	1,070	−3,602	176,378	1,772	178,516	22,227	154,074	156,091	16,482	139,430
1968	107,498	38,594	24,815	1,701	−2,334	183,689	1,434	185,500	22,742	160,951	162,626	17,388	145,115
1969	108,092	37,887	24,004	1,885	−107	186,074	2,072	188,535	22,658	163,499	165,837	18,050	147,637
1970	110,995	38,513	24,026	1,412	2	190,298	2,173	192,870	23,543	166,763	169,211	19,071	150,039
1971	114,436	39,656	24,460	368	754	195,468	1,937	197,809	24,437	170,986	173,192	19,941	153,182
1972	121,464	41,332	24,912	−98	−3,007	200,031	2,024	202,471	26,324	173,397	175,697	20,846	154,829
1973	127,678	43,119	25,661	5,025	−3,395	215,402	3,665	219,537	28,013	187,122	191,144	21,626	169,411
1974	125,828	43,926	26,563	2,278	−468	213,351	2,928	216,625	27,080	185,834	189,024	22,215	166,730
1975	124,918	46,377	28,037	−2,644	1,846	211,906	1,518	213,528	26,999	184,499	186,096	23,269	162,792
1976	125,307	46,951	28,634	1,235	4,380	219,986	2,175	222,372	28,120	191,466	193,801	24,147	169,615
1977	124,631	46,175	28,323	2,602	7,434	222,266	301	222,456	28,242	193,576	193,791	25,117	168,667
1978	131,621	47,220	28,676	2,208	6,532	230,307	984	231,291	31,048	199,259	200,243	26,195	174,048
1979	137,552	48,257	29,170	2,534	3,238	235,436	1,302	236,738	31,890	203,546	204,848	27,046	177,802
1980	136,995	48,906	29,940	−2,875	5,397	230,011	−219	229,792	30,765	199,246	199,027	27,900	171,127

(*a*) Including work in progress.
(*b*) Including services as well as goods.
(*c*) Taxes on expenditure *less* subsidies.
(*d*) See note 2 above.

National Accounts 7. Gross National Product by Categories of Expenditure – Republic of Ireland 1938–80

NOTES

[1] SOURCES: To 1970 (1st line) – the Irish official publication, *National Income and Expenditure*, using the latest revisions published. From 1970 (2nd line) – United Nations Organisation, *Yearbook of National Accounts Statistics*, which has been preferred because it gives longer series on a revised basis.

[2] The break in continuity in 1970 results from changes in concept rather than from the change in source. Other changes in concept which affect substantially the comparability of the series are indicated by footnotes but minor changes are not indicated here.

[3] The constant price statistics for 1964–9 at 1975 prices are based on the current price statistics shown here, but deflated by the implicit price indices given in the U.N. *Yearbook*. (The figure for stocks is a residual.)

A. At Current Prices

(in £ million)

	Consumers' Expenditure	Public Authorities' Current Expenditure	Gross Domestic Fixed Capital Formation	Value of Increase of Stocks	Exports *less* (*a*) Imports	Gross Domestic Product at Market Prices	Net Factor Income from Abroad	Gross National Product at Market Prices	Factor Cost (*b*) Adjustment	Gross Domestic Product at Factor Cost	Gross National Product at Factor Cost	Capital Consumption	National Income
1938 (*d*)	141·5	22·9	17·1	[+0·2] (*c*)	+2·0	171·4	+12·3	183·7	22·1	149·3	161·6	4·2	157·4
1947	277·9	38·9	31·5	+13·4	−29·8	307·6	+24·3	331·9	31·4	276·2	300·5	12·2	288·3
1948	292·1	42·6	40·9	+9·1	−19·6	340·5	+24·6	365·1	32·5	308·0	332·6	13·5	319·1
1949	299·5	41·7	54·2	+5·6	−9·7	366·4	+24·9	391·3	36·1	330·3	355·2	14·6	340·6
1950	313·9	45·1	64·5	+5·0	−30·2	372·2	+26·1	398·3	38·6	333·6	359·7	16·5	343·2
1951	339·3	53·9	77·5	+10·6	−61·6	391·9	+27·8	419·7	37·7	354·2	382·0	18·0	364·0
1952	352·7	56·5	81·5	−4·2	−8·9	450·4	+27·2	477·6	54·4	395·9	423·1	19·3	403·8
1953	381·5	61·9	81·4	+6·7	−7·0	495·8	+28·7	524·5	63·4	432·4	461·1	21·8	439·8
1954	389·5	63·0	86·3	−5·4	−5·5	498·1	+29·7	527·9	62·5	435·6	465·2	23·7	441·5
1955	419·9	64·7	91·9	+9·7	−35·5	522·1	+28·6	550·7	64·8	457·3	485·9	25·2	460·7
1956	420·9	68·6	91·6	−7·9	−14·4	530·1	+28·7	558·8	72·7	457·4	486·1	29·7	456·4
1957	430·4	67·6	80·2	−6·6	+9·2	548·8	+31·9	580·8	78·5	470·4	502·3	31·9	470·4
1958	459·2	70·4	83·0	−7·7	−33·4	568·5	+32·4	600·9	82·4	486·1	518·5	33·8	484·7
1959	466·1	73·8	83·3	+24·3	−39·9	607·6	+31·2	638·8	86·7	520·9	552·1	37·3	514·8
1960	496·1	78·1	90·3	+12·4	−34·0	642·9	+33·2	676·1	84·2	558·7	591·9	40·1	551·8
1961	523·5	83·6	108·9	+10·0	−34·5	691·5	+35·7	727·2	85·3	606·2	641·9	45·2	596·7
1962	564·2	91·4	129·0	+12·6	−49·3	747·9	+35·9	783·8	90·3	657·6	693·5	52·2	641·3
1963	602·1	99·4	147·7	+12·6	−57·7	804·1	+35·6	839·7	101·8	702·3	737·9	59·1	678·8
1964	670·9	118·8	173·3	+20·0	−68·5	914·5	+37·1	951·6	120·4	794·1	831·2	65·4	765·8
1965	704·8	128·6	200·1	+27·3	−86·8	974·0	+25·5	999·5	129·6	844·4	869·9	72·7	797·2
1966	746·3	135·1	200·0	+7·8	−60·3	1,028·9	+23·2	1,052·1	147·3	881·6	904·8	78·2	826·8
1967	796·7	144·2	220·9	−4·5	−33·5	1,123·8	+24·6	1,148·4	156·3	967·5	992·1	87·2	904·9
1968	910·3	163·2	258·5	+16·1	−79·7	1,268·4	+31·7	1,300·1	177·9	1,090·5	1,122·2	100·7	1,021·5
1969	1,028·8	196·2	332·5	+37·1	−129·2	1,465·4	+28·3	1,493·7	215·0	1,250·4	1,278·7	121·3	1,157·4
	1,141·3	239·1	361·1	+34·9		1,646·8		1,675·1	247·1	1,399·7	1,428·0	133·0	1,295·0
1970	---(*e*)	---(*e*)	---(*e*)	---(*e*)	−129·6	---(*e*)	+28·3	---(*e*)	---(*e*)	---(*e*)	---(*e*)	---(*e*)	---(*e*)
	1,116·0	237·3	368·5	+20·8		1,620·2		1,648·5	235·6	1,384·6	1,412·9	134·9	1,278·0
1971	1,260·9	282·5	438·2	+6·3	−134·8	1,853·1	+26·6	1,879·7	271·9	1,581·2	1,607·8	155·4	1,452·4

	Consumers' Expenditure	Public Authorities' Current Expenditure	Gross Domestic Fixed Capital Formation	Value of Increase of Stocks	Exports *less* (a) (f) Imports	Gross Domestic Product at Market Prices	Net Factor Income from Abroad	Gross National Product at Market Prices	Factor Cost (g) Adjustment	Gross Domestic Product at Factor Cost	Gross National Product at Factor Cost	Capital Consumption (h)	National Income
1972	1,453·8	343·0	529·7	+30·9	−119·9	2,237·5	+29·6	2,267·1	319·7	1,917·8	1,947·4	184·6	1,762·8
1973	1,738·2	422·8	682·2	+42·4	−184·6	2,701·0	+12·5	2,713·5	375·3	2,325·7	2,338·2	215·1	2,123·1
1974	2,044·3	513·1	735·8	+131·0	−436·7	2,987·5	+19·2	3,006·7	376·2	2,611·2	2,630·4	258·6	2,371·8
1975	2,387·8	708·1	842·8	−15·7	−195·0	3,728·0	+7·3	3,735·3	389·2	3,338·8	3,346·1	297·7	3,048·4
1976	2,917·8	841·6	1,134·9	+2·3	−314·8	4,581·8	−24·3	4,557·5	593·0	3,988·8	3,964·5	365·4	3,599·1
1977	3,466·1	990·8	1,371·9	+113·7	−439·8	5,502·7	−70·9	5,431·8	533·3	4,969·4	4,898·5	458·3	4,440·2
1978	3,967·2	1,174·0	1,838·6	+12·1	−569·6	6,422·3	−125·1	6,297·2	482·0	5,940·3	5,815·2	585·3	5,229·9
1979	4,701·3	1,451·5	2,344·0	+160·2	−1,190·8	7,466·2	−175·8	7,290·4	526·3	6,939·9	6,764·1	708·0	6,056·1
1980	5,619·1	1,886·2	2,592·5	−64·5	−1,367·3	8,866	−233·0	8,633·0	832·4	8,033·6	7,800·6	852·1	6,948·5

B. At Constant Prices

1947–64 at 1958 Prices

(in £ million)

	Consumers' Expenditure	Public Authorities' Current Expenditure	Gross Domestic Fixed Capital Formation	Value of Increase of Stocks	Exports *less* (a) (f) Imports	Gross Domestic Product at Market Prices	Net Factor Income from Abroad	Gross National Product at Market Prices	Factor Cost (g) Adjustment	Gross Domestic Product at Factor Cost	Gross National Product at Factor Cost	Capital Consumption (h)	National Income
1947	406·8	60·0	43·2	+15·1	−19·7	...	...	505·4	47·8	...	457·6	16·7	440·9
1948	416·5	63·4	51·9	+12·9	−15·3	...	...	529·4	47·1	...	482·3	17·1	465·2
1949	430·4	60·2	69·4	+8·3	−13·2	...	...	551·0	50·8	...	500·2	18·7	481·5
1950	441·2	62·7	81·6	+7·2	−30·7	...	...	562·0	54·5	...	507·5	20·9	486·6
1951	441·4	67·5	93·6	+12·1	−41·9	...	...	572·7	51·4	...	521·3	21·7	499·6
1952	424·2	69·0	92·3	−4·6	+4·9	...	...	585·8	66·8	...	519·0	21·9	497·1
1953	438·0	71·9	92·5	+7·5	−9·2	...	...	600·7	72·6	...	528·1	24·8	503·3
1954	444·6	73·5	99·3	−5·8	−4·9	...	...	606·7	71·8	...	534·9	27·3	507·6
1955	467·4	72·7	103·0	+10·0	−34·2	...	...	618·9	72·8	...	546·1	28·2	517·9
1956	455·1	73·2	97·0	−8·9	−6·0	...	...	610·4	79·4	...	531·0	31·5	499·5
1957	446·6	70·9	81·4	−7·5	+23·0	...	...	614·4	83·0	...	531·4	32·4	499·0
					- - -(f)								
1958	459·2	70·4	80·0	−7·7	−33·4	568·5	+32·4	600·9	82·4	486·1	518·5	33·8	484·7
1959	464·2	71·7	83·2	+24·9	−49·2	594·8	+31·8	626·6	88·5	506·3	538·1	37·3	500·8
1960	489·8	73·3	88·5	+12·2	−38·2	625·6	+33·3	658·9	86·5	539·1	572·4	39·3	533·1
1961	505·2	75·0	103·3	+9·6	−36·8	656·3	+35·5	691·8	93·4	562·9	598·4	42·9	555·5
1962	524·1	77·4	118·5	+12·5	−53·7	678·8	+35·6	714·4	92·1	586·7	622·3	48·0	574·3
1963	545·5	80·6	132·9	+12·0	−61·9	709·1	+34·7	743·8	97·8	611·3	646·0	53·2	592·8
1964	570·0	82·8	146·9	+18·0	−82·0	735·7	+35·7	771·4	105·4	630·3	666·0	55·4	610·6

1964–80 at 1975 Prices

	Consumers' Expenditure	Public Authorities' Current Expenditure	Gross Domestic Fixed Capital Formation	Value of Increase of Stocks	Exports *less* (a) (f) Imports	Gross Domestic Product at Market Prices	Net Factor Income from Abroad	Gross National Product at Market Prices	Factor Cost (g) Adjustment	Gross Domestic Product at Factor Cost	Gross National Product at Factor Cost	Capital Consumption (h)	National Income
1964	1,715·9	366·7	458·5	+94·4	−203·3	2,432·2	+99·7	2,531·9	320·2	2,112·0	2,211·7	173·0	2,038·7
1965	1,723·2	378·2	522·5	+95·0	−240·5	2,478·4	+66·8	2,545·2	329·8	2,148·6	2,215·4	189·8	2,025·6
1966	1,768·5	382·7	520·8	+38·7	−188·9	2,521·8	+60·6	2,582·4	361·0	2,160·8	2,221·4	203·6	2,017·8
1967	1,831·5	400·6	553·6	+2·7	−137·9	2,650·5	+64·6	2,715·1	368·6	2,281·9	2,346·5	218·5	2,128·0
1968	1,987·6	419·5	622·9	+59·8	−226·6	2,863·2	+76·9	2,940·1	401·6	2,461·6	2,478·5	242·7	2,235·8

See p. 844 for footnotes.

National Accounts 7. *continued*

B. At Constant Prices (*cont.*)
1964–80 at 1975 Prices (*cont.*)

	Consumers' Expenditure	Public Authorities' Current Expenditure	Gross Domestic Fixed Capital Formation	Value of Increase of Stocks	Exports *less* (*a*) (*f*) Imports	Gross Domestic Product at Market Prices	Net Factor Income from Abroad	Gross National Product at Market Prices	Factor Cost (*g*) Adjustment	Gross Domestic Product at Factor Cost	Gross National Product at Factor Cost	Capital Consumption (*h*)	National Income
1969	2,091·1	461·6	737·3	+109·8	−359·6	3,040·2	+66·0	3,106·2	446·1	2,594·1	2,660·1	269·0	2,391·1
	2,163·0	497·2	719·8	+67·6	−356·2	3,091·4	+62·6	3,154·0	463·6	2,627·8	2,690·4	264·9	2,425·5
1970	- - -(*e*)	- - -(*e*)	- - -(*e*)	- - -(*e*)	- - -(*e*)	- - -(*e*)	- - -(*e*)	- - -(*e*)	- - -(*e*)	- - -(*e*)	- - -(*e*)	- - -(*e*)	- - -(*e*)
	2,115·1	493·5	734·5	+54·6	−356·2	3,041·5	+62·6	3,104·1	442·0	2,599·5	2,662·1	268·7	2,393·4
1971	2,183·6	536·2	799·1	+7·1	−379·8	3,146·2	+55·8	3,202·0	461·6	2,684·6	2,740·4	283·6	2,456·8
1972	2,295·9	576·5	858·0	+34·6	−418·0	3,347·0	+58·7	3,405·7	477·9	2,869·1	2,927·8	299·2	2,628·6
1973	2,460·7	615·4	996·7	+39·6	−607·4	3,505·0	+21·7	3,526·7	486·8	3,018·2	3,039·9	314·5	2,725·4
1974	2,501·1	662·0	880·9	+158·9	−548·6	3,654·3	+23·1	3,677·4	460·0	3,194·3	3,217·4	309·7	2,907·7
1975	2,387·8	708·1	842·8	−15·7	−195·0	3,728·0	+7·3	3,735·3	389·2	3,338·8	3,346·1	297·7	3,048·4
1976	2,454·2	725·6	951·4	+1·7	−324·1	3,808·8	−20·4	3,788·4	492·9	3,315·9	3,295·5	306·3	2,989·2
1977	2,585·3	751·7	986·7	+91·6	−348·0	4,067·3	−51·0	4,016·3	394·2	3,673·1	3,622·1	329·7	3,282·4
1978	2,764·5	804·2	1,187·9	+16·2	−468·2	4,304·6	−86·0	4,218·6	323·1	3,981·5	3,895·5	378·1	3,517·4
1979	2,888·4	859·7	1,328·4	+85·9	−711·8	4,450·6	−106·4	4,344·2	313·6	4,137·0	4,030·6	401·1	3,629·5
1980	2,911·2	917·2	1,244·8	−30·2	−426·2	4,616·8	−119·3	4,497·5	433·5	4,183·3	4,064·0	409·1	3,654·9

(*a*) Including services as well as goods.
(*b*) Taxes on expenditure minus subsidies.
(*c*) Farm livestock only.
(*d*) The following unrevised figures are available for 1944–6, with the equivalent figures for 1938 and 1947:

	Consumers' Expenditure	Public Authorities' Current Expenditure	Gross Domestic Fixed Capital Formation	Value of Increase in Stocks	Exports *less* Imports	G.D.P. at Market Prices	Net Factor Income from Abroad	G.N.P. at Market Prices	Factor Cost Adjustment	G.D.P. at Factor Cost	G.N.P. at Factor Cost	Capital Consumption	National Income
1938	146·2	22·1	14·2	[+0·2]	+2·0	...	+12·3	...	...	...	...	...	158·2
1944	212·0	30·5	8·9	−2·5	+11·3	260·2	+21·3	281·5	23·1	237·1	258·4	4·6	253·8
1945	226·3	33·3	11·8	+1·5	+13·4	286·3	+21·2	307·5	25·6	260·7	281·9	4·8	277·1
1946	241·5	33·4	19·0	+11·9	−1·9	303·9	+21·6	325·5	29·8	274·1	295·7	5·9	289·8
1947	289·3	35·5	32·8	+28·6	−54·2	332·0	+24·3	356·3	30·7	301·3	325·6	7·5·	318·1

(*e*) See note 2 above.
(*f*) Including net factor income from abroad to 1957.
(*g*) The 1947–57 figures are derived from Part A by deflating by the implicit G.N.P. price index.
(*h*) The figures are derived from Part A by deflating the implicit capital formation price index.

National Accounts 8. Index Numbers of Output at Constant Factor Cost – United Kingdom 1855–1980

NOTES

[1] SOURCES: Part A – C. H. Feinstein, *National Income, Expenditure and Output of the United Kingdom, 1855–1965* (Cambridge, 1972), appendix table 8. Part B – Kindly supplied by Mr M. Clary of the Central Statistical Office.

[2] The indices in part A are chained with the year 1913 shown as equal to 100. Different base years and weights for sub-periods are detailed on pp. 207–8 of C. H. Feinstein, *op. cit.* A similar chaining process is applied by the Central Statistical Office (see successive editions of the National Income Blue Book).

[3] The index of G.D.P. shown here is from the expenditure side. A "compromise" estimate between this and an index from the income side is shown in table 5A for the period to 1948.

[4] Conceptually similar to the index numbers in this table are Crafts's estimates of the rate of growth of national product (by sector) at constant prices (% per annum) for the period 1700 to 1831. These are as follows (the figures relating, in principle, to Great Britain to 1801 and to the United Kingdom subsequently):

	Agriculture	Industry	Government Services	Rent	Personal Services	G.N.P.†
1700–60	0·60	0·71	1·91	0·38		0·69
1760–80	0·13	1·51	1·29	0·69		0·70
1780–1801	0·75	2·11	2·11	0·97		1·32
1801–31	1·18	3·00	1·37*	1·53	1·37	2·13

*Government, professional and miscellaneous services.

†The commercial sector is not shown separately since it has been assumed to have grown at the same rate as overall G.N.P.

[Source: N. F. R. Crafts, *British Economic Growth during the Industrial Revolution* (Oxford, 1985), chapter 2.]

[5] Southern Ireland is excluded from 1920 (2nd line).

A. 1913=100

	Agriculture, Forestry, and Fishing	Industry (*a*)	Transport and Communication	Distribution and Other Services	G.D.P.
1855	99·3	26·3	19·7	33·1	33·5
1856	99·3	28·1	21·4	34·3	35·0
1857	100·0	29·1	21·8	35·0	35·6
1858	100·0	28·5	21·4	35·0	35·5
1859	100·7	30·0	23·1	35·9	36·6
1860	100·7	31·7	24·0	36·9	37·8
1861	101·5	31·7	24·5	37·3	38·1
1862	101·5	32·4	24·5	37·8	38·7
1863	102·1	32·5	25·3	38·3	38·9
1864	102·1	35·0	25·3	38·8	40·3
1865	102·9	37·3	27·1	39·9	41·7
1866	103·6	38·7	28·4	40·8	42·9
1867	100·7	36·4	27·9	40·9	41·8
1868	107·8	36·4	29·7	42·1	43·0
1869	103·6	35·8	29·7	42·5	42·7
1870	107·2	40·2	31·4	43·8	45·3
1871	104·3	43·5	34·1	45·5	47·4
1872	99·3	44·8	34·1	45·9	47·9
1873	102·1	45·3	34·9	47·0	48·9
1874	110·0	46·4	36·2	48·2	50·3
1875	110·7	46·7	37·1	49·2	51·0
1876	104·3	47·5	37·6	49·8	51·3
1877	95·0	47·4	38·4	50·4	51·0
1878	102·9	47·3	38·9	51·1	51·9
1879	82·8	45·6	38·9	51·2	50·0
1880	100·0	50·3	41·9	53·8	54·5
1881	100·0	53·5	43·2	55·0	56·2
1882	95·0	55·7	45·0	56·2	57·4
1883	101·5	56·5	46·7	57·6	59·0
1884	103·6	54·4	46·3	57·7	58·4
1885	100·7	52·1	46·3	58·1	57·5
1886	104·3	51·0	46·7	58·7	57·7
1887	97·9	55·1	49·3	60·4	59·6
1888	100·0	58·3	51·5	62·3	62·3
1889	102·1	62·4	54·6	64·3	65·3
1890	103·6	63·3	55·5	65·2	66·2
1891	106·4	64·1	57·2	66·4	67·3
1892	102·9	61·0	56·8	66·7	66·1
1893	98·7	60·0	56·3	66·6	65·4
1894	100·7	63·5	59·4	69·0	68·1

National Accounts 8. *continued*

A. 1913=100 *(cont.)*

	Agriculture, Forestry, and Fishing	Industry *(a)*	Transport and Communication	Distribution and Other Services	G.D.P.
1895	99·3	66·5	62·0	70·7	70·2
1896	99·3	71·4	65·1	72·4	73·3
1897	96·4	73·4	66·4	73·7	74·5
1898	100·7	77·0	68·6	75·7	77·2
1899	97·9	80·1	70·3	76·9	79·0
1900	95·8	80·1	71·2	78·2	79·6
1901	97·2	80·3	72·5	80·1	80·8
1902	100·7	81·7	74·2	81·5	82·4
1903	92·2	80·0	75·1	81·5	81·2
1904	97·2	81·0	77·3	82·4	82·5
1905	98·7	85·7	79·9	84·6	85·7
1906	92·2	89·3	82·5	86·4	87·8
1907	100·0	91·0	85·6	88·5	90·2
1908	102·9	83·7	83·8	88·4	87·3
1909	105·0	84·3	86·0	90·1	88·7
1910	103·6	85·5	88·6	91·9	90·2
1911	101·5	91·5	92·1	94·5	93·8
1912	100·0	93·9	96·1	97·4	96·4
1913	100·0	100·0	100·0	100·0	100·0
1920	93·0 ---*(b)* 71·5	99·3 ---*(b)* 97·9	98·0 ---*(b)* 95·1	97·3 ---*(b)* 93·8	97·5 ---*(b)* 93·7
1921	72·8	79·7	85·9	85·2	82·3
1922	73·7	92·2	99·9	86·6	88·5
1923	74·9	97·6	109·3	87·1	91·4
1924	72·6	108·4	113·0	88·8	96·0
1925	78·2	112·7	114·6	90·6	98·9
1926	80·5	106·6	109·6	90·8	96·6
1927	80·7	122·8	120·8	94·5	105·0
1928	85·4	119·5	122·4	95·9	105·0
1929	85·6	125·5	127·2	96·2	107·7
1930	87·7	120·1	126·5	96·6	106·0
1931	79·9	112·3	120·3	96·2	102·3
1932	83·7	111·9	116·0	96·9	102·5
1933	89·7	119·3	118·2	99·3	106·8
1934	90·8	131·2	122·1	101·9	112·6
1935	88·5	141·2	125·7	104·7	117·6
1936	87·1	153·9	132·0	107·9	124·0
1937	86·7	163·1	137·9	110·0	128·7
1938	85·7	158·7	137·6	110·1	127·1
1946	94·9	162·6	157·0	118·1	133·6
1947	91·0	171·3	164·0	113·4	135·0
1948	97·9	186·0	176·4	112·7	141·1

National Accounts 8. *continued*

B. 1980=100

	Agriculture, Forestry, and Fishing	Energy and Water	Manufacturing	Construction	Transport and Communications	Distribution, Hotels, Catering, and Repairs	Other Services	G.D.P.
1948	45·4	32·5	49·3	61·8	42·5	54·0	50·0	47·9
1949	48·6	34·1	52·9	64·7	44·7	56·1	50·5	49·7
1950	49·2	35·6	56·8	64·8	46·1	57·6	51·0	51·5
1951	50·5	37·6	58·5	62·3	48·2	56·8	51·8	52·4
1952	51·9	38·6	55·6	64·2	49·6	55·8	52·1	52·1
1953	52·8	39·7	59·6	68·8	51·2	59·3	52·7	54·2
1954	53·5	41·4	62·8	71·9	52·3	62·2	53·6	56·4
1955	53·0	41·9	66·8	72·1	53·6	65·2	54·5	58·3
1956	56·1	43·0	66·6	76·0	54·5	65·9	54·3	58·9
1957	57·2	43·5	68·2	75·8	54·4	67·4	55·5	60·0
1958	56·1	43·7	67·6	75·6	53·9	69·1	56·4	59·9
1959	58·2	43·5	71·5	79·8	56·3	73·0	58·3	62·6
1960	62·0	44·3	77·2	84·0	59·2	76·6	59·2	66·0
1961	62·4	44·8	77·4	90·5	60·5	78·1	60·9	67·2
1962	64·4	47·0	77·6	91·3	61·0	78·6	62·2	68·1
1963	66·9	48·1	80·3	91·1	63·0	81·8	63·9	70·4
1964	69·6	49·3	87·6	100·4	67·0	85·4	65·9	74·6
1965	71·4	50·5	90·1	105·1	68·5	87·1	67·9	76·7
1966	71·7	50·6	91·8	107·0	70·4	87·8	69·6	78·1
1967	74·0	51·3	92·3	111·3	71·2	88·6	71·9	79·5
1968	74·0	49·6	99·4	114·2	74·2	91·2	73·3	82·8
1969	73·8	50·2	103·1	113·3	77·1	91·7	74·3	84·5
1970	78·3	51·0	103·4	111·1	80·4	94·3	76·1	86·0
1971	82·4	52·6	102·3	113·1	82·5	96·4	78·3	87·2
1972	85·1	52·2	104·5	115·2	86·5	101·7	80·7	89·9
1973	87·8	55·8	114·2	117·9	93·0	106·5	83·3	95·1
1974	88·8	52·2	112·8	105·7	93·3	102·3	84·9	93·7
1975	81·9	54·5	105·0	100·1	92·2	98·6	88·1	92·0
1976	75·3	60·9	107·0	98·7	91·6	99·6	91·1	93·8
1977	85·1	74·8	109·0	98·4	94·2	99·0	92·8	96·5
1978	91·5	85·0	109·7	105·0	96·6	104·8	94·9	99·8
1979	90·1	100·5	109·5	105·8	101·3	107·9	97·6	103·0
1980	100.0	100.0	100.0	100.0	100.0	100.0	100.0	100.0

(*a*) Including extractive industries, building, and utilities.

(*b*) See note 3 above.

National Accounts 9. Consumers' Expenditure – United Kingdom 1900–1980

NOTES

[1] Sources: Parts A, C, and D – C. H. Feinstein, *National Income, Expenditure and Output of the United Kingdom, 1855–1965* (Cambridge, 1972). Parts B and E – C.S.O., *Economic Trends Annual Supplement* and C.S.O. *National Income and Expenditure*.

[2] Parts A, C, and D employ the definitions used in the 1967 National Income Blue Book, parts B and E use those used in the 1983 Blue Book.

[3] Southern Ireland is included to 1920 (1st line) and excluded subsequently.

(in £ million)

A. 1900–1957 at Current Prices

	Food (a)	Alcoholic Drink (b)	Tobacco	Housing (c)	Fuel and Light (d)	Clothing (e)	Durable Household Goods (f)	Motor Cars and Motor Cycles	Other Goods (g)	Other Services (h)	Adjust-ment (i)	Total Consumers' Expenditure
1900	464	187	27	167	75	153	61	2	97	390	14	1,637
1901	473	185	28	174	71	162	62	2	98	402	20	1,677
1902	481	183	29	180	70	153	62	2	101	405	20	1,686
1903	496	179	30	186	68	149	61	2	102	413	13	1,699
1904	499	173	30	191	67	154	63	4	105	420	13	1,719
1905	502	172	31	194	63	157	63	4	108	430	12	1,736
1906	507	171	32	198	64	161	63	5	113	440	12	1,766
1907	510	171	33	201	74	162	68	5	118	457	12	1,811
1908	515	163	33	203	70	168	67	4	113	462	15	1,813
1909	525	154	34	211	68	174	63	3	115	469	15	1,831
1910	534	163	37	211	67	178	63	8	119	479	16	1,877
1911	551	169	38	212	70	195	66	8	122	489	16	1,936
1912	576	168	39	215	74	202	70	10	128	508	16	2,006
1913	586	175	40	220	76	210	79	12	134	521	17	2,070
1914	557	188	42	224	74	173	77	9	131	526	73	2,074
1915	724	179	49	227	83	193	84	4	151	538	152	2,384
1916	846	207	57	227	100	169	81	1	177	531	185	2,581
1917	1,012	201	65	229	108	212	105	1	211	564	271	2,979
1918	1,132	232	80	237	122	364	141	3	273	683	333	3,600
1919	1,327	391	115	254	151	670	217	35	307	943	125	4,535
							---(f)		---(g)			
	1,624	474	127	285	183	827	149	41	556	953	27	5,246
1920	---(j)	---(j)	---(j)	---(j)	---(j)	---(j)	---(j)	---(j)	---(j)	---(j)	---(j)	---(j)
	1,547	450	120	272	174	795	143	40	536	917	26	5,020
1921	1,405	409	116	317	169	485	119	19	422	858	−4	4,315
1922	1,196	356	112	329	158	434	109	28	378	748	−6	3,842
1923	1,204	332	109	323	148	409	107	31	353	713	−12	3,717
1924	1,213	337	112	322	160	418	107	39	352	730	−13	3,777
1925	1,241	338	116	325	158	432	113	51	362	753	−11	3,878
1926	1,216	323	117	336	144	417	113	47	371	762	−13	3,833
1927	1,193	320	124	349	166	424	120	44	382	784	−19	3,887
1928	1,209	310	131	356	152	435	125	41	394	804	−18	3,939
1929	1,204	311	136	365	162	439	130	38	397	817	−16	3,983

1930	1,163	301	140	375	162	418	133	34	396	822	−12	3,932
1931	1,093	282	140	382	162	395	133	27	385	810	−4	3,805
1932	1,042	264	139	386	157	364	130	26	370	809	−4	3,683
1933	1,006	258	142	394	158	366	136	30	384	820	2	3,696
1934	1,027	262	146	402	161	371	151	38	407	839	−2	3,802
1935	1,054	273	153	416	164	388	160	44	424	861	−2	3,935
1936	1,082	283	161	431	176	402	169	47	440	893	−4	4,080
1937	1,136	297	169	443	185	426	178	49	483	930	−7	4,289
1938	1,157	294	176	455	188	438	174	43	498	965	4	4,392
					---(d)				---(g)			
1939	1,216	311	204	513	199	461	(f)	37	636	928	34	4,539
1940	1,244	378	260	528	222	501	(f)	5	735	961	103	4,799
1941	1,288	468	317	531	237	460	(f)	1	763	1,051	164	5,104
1942	1,334	550	414	536	238	498	(f)	1	772	1,106	192	5,410
1943	1,267	634	491	553	233	441	(f)	—	776	1,153	244	5,525
1944	1,348	678	507	575	240	511	(f)	—	796	1,210	258	5,846
1945	1,398	705	562	616	259	535	(f)	2	921	1,347	328	6,391
									---(g)			
1946	1,580	696	602	692	280	638	197	36	743	1,581	228	7,273
1947	1,826	726	689	757	300	736	269	49	841	1,667	168	8,028
1948	1,975	802	764	787	327	902	310	48	854	1,724	116	8,609
1949	2,148	755	753	801	335	1,013	360	61	927	1,716	100	8,969
1950	2,371	734	766	841	356	1,063	424	64	993	1,760	89	9,461
1951	2,599	774	800	886	392	1,116	480	74	1,095	1,880	119	10,215
1952	2,857	779	821	934	424	1,097	462	117	1,145	2,000	110	10,766
1953	3,156	795	837	1,001	451	1,115	528	186	1,204	2,101	101	11,475
1954	3,327	794	855	1,056	490	1,205	603	234	1,287	2,198	114	12,163
1955	3,615	832	880	1,122	528	1,297	624	310	1,443	2,350	109	13,110
1956	3,820	866	935	1,183	597	1,378	616	268	1,556	2,496	106	13,821
1957	3,962	906	981	1,276	618	1,439	685	320	1,650	2,648	97	14,582

See p. 853 for footnotes.

National Accounts 9. *continued*

(in £ million)

B. 1952–1980 at Current Prices (*l*)

	Food (*a*)	Alcoholic Drink (*b*)	Tobacco	Housing (*c*)	Fuel and Light (*d*)	Clothing (*e*)	Durable Household Goods (*f*)	Motor Cars and Motor Cycles	Other Goods (*g*)	Other Services (*h*)	Adjustment (*i*)	Total Consumers' Expenditure (*k*)
1952	2,824	779	821	921	424	1,097	462	117	1,145	1,991	110	10,691
1953	3,122	795	837	988	451	1,115	528	186	1,207	2,072	101	11,402
1954	3,295	794	855	1,043	490	1,205	603	234	1,292	2,166	114	12,091
1955	3,585	832	880	1,111	529	1,297	624	310	1,451	2,316	109	13,045
1956	3,787	866	935	1,172	596	1,378	616	268	1,569	2,463	106	13,756
1957	3,928	906	981	1,264	619	1,439	679	320	1,664	2,622	97	14,519
1958	4,028	909	1,031	1,434	690	1,458	741	425	1,786	2,716	92	15,306
1959	4,157	920	1,061	1,553	687	1,525	858	506	1,911	2,855	85	16,118
1960	4,225	963	1,140	1,643	752	1,664	832	568	2,061	3,011	80	16,939
1961	4,366	1,075	1,217	1,758	795	1,729	851	500	2,246	3,215	89	17,841
1962	4,560	1,162	1,242	1,935	910	1,771	881	538	2,396	3,436	100	18,930
1963	4,689	1,232	1,286	2,151	1,010	1,873	945	640	2,546	3,635	130	20,137
1964	4,889	1,390	1,343	2,338	1,001	1,971	1,008	733	2,811	3,857	161	21,501
1965	5,059	1,499	1,428	2,616	1,087	2,099	1,052	707	3,094	4,101	191	22,933
1966	5,297	1,626	1,504	2,860	1,160	2,154	1,046	703	3,360	4,382	194	24,330
1967	5,485	1,739	1,512	3,088	1,208	2,219	1,110	777	3,619	4,636	135	25,529
1968	5,696	1,870	1,578	3,397	1,341	2,375	1,242	875	4,092	4,997	65	27,528
1969	6,019	2,029	1,694	3,679	1,430	2,505	1,254	809	4,403	5,400	11	29,233
1970	6,349	2,300	1,720	4,048	1,495	2,753	1,397	997	4,832	5,921	−54	31,778
1971	6,974	2,593	1,691	4,619	1,619	2,990	1,636	1,438	5,408	6,663	−63	35,599
1972	7,412	2,910	1,808	5,279	1,797	3,365	2,069	1,793	6,184	7,599	−45	40,183
1973	8,471	3,423	1,945	6,254	1,897	3,847	2,429	1,799	7,033	8,725	−57	45,759
1974	9,759	3,915	2,238	7,410	2,270	4,474	2,678	1,586	8,600	9,923	−237	52,626
1975	11,961	4,856	2,748	9,221	2,914	5,166	3,232	2,135	10,534	12,252	−367	64,652
1976	13,941	5,759	3,107	10,635	3,590	5,749	3,742	2,654	12,019	14,470	−816	74,850
1977	16,047	6,645	3,632	12,422	4,258	6,527	4,066	3,017	13,960	16,698	−1,334	85,948
1978	17,927	7,462	3,910	14,020	4,656	7,704	4,849	4,350	15,873	19,252	−1,136	98,867
1979	20,364	8,847	4,270	16,756	5,340	8,947	6,035	5,686	18,921	22,893	−978	117,071
1980	22,873	10,153	4,867	20,443	6,413	9,750	6,469	5,211	22,788	27,421	−650	135,738

(in £ million)

C. 1900–1948 at 1938 Prices

	Food (*a*)	Alcoholic Drink (*b*)	Tobacco	Housing (*c*)	Fuel and Light (*d*)	Clothing (*e*)	Durable Household Goods (*f*)	Motor Cars and Motor Cycles	Other Goods (*g*)	Other Services (*h*)	Adjustment (*i*)	Total Consumers' Expenditure
1900	768	615	72	267	130	342	124	2	144	756	27	3,247
1901	777	610	70	273	130	357	127	2	146	768	39	3,299
1902	778	601	72	278	135	339	127	2	150	769	38	3,289
1903	794	581	74	283	133	326	123	2	152	770	27	3,265
1904	807	567	75	288	134	331	130	2	154	779	25	3,292
1905	807	558	76	292	127	325	127	2	159	790	23	3,286
1906	815	554	77	296	126	328	128	2	165	800	23	3,314
1907	810	556	79	301	136	326	135	2	169	809	22	3,345
1908	807	529	79	304	133	338	133	2	164	823	27	3,339
1909	815	486	77	308	133	350	126	2	161	829	27	3,317
1910	809	484	79	311	136	353	127	4	171	837	29	3,340
1911	839	502	83	315	140	378	130	4	177	846	28	3,442
1912	836	500	83	319	126	379	134	6	182	859	27	3,451
1913	841	519	86	322	138	391	148	8	192	870	29	3,544
1914	830	508	89	327	136	336	145	6	189	873	121	3,560
1915	841	490	96	329	144	363	137	2	196	829	210	3,637
1916	811	435	91	329	143	253	110	—	191	761	211	3,335
1917	756	301	92	330	139	236	104	—	184	790	242	3,074
1918	740	287	95	332	124	226	110	2	200	696	233	3,045
1919	840	428	127	336	134	369	142	12	200	813	84	3,485
							---(*f*)		---(*j*)			
	877	440	124	356	145	398	92	13	341	696	11	3,493
1920	---(*j*)	---(*j*)	---(*j*)	---(*j*)	---(*j*)	---(*j*)	---(*j*)	---(*j*)	---(*j*)	---(*j*)	---(*j*)	---(*j*)
	835	419	118	339	138	383	89	13	328	670	11	3,343
1921	867	363	115	340	119	316	82	7	291	648	−5	3,143
1922	925	319	111	343	135	357	95	11	311	653	−6	3,254
1923	988	321	109	346	139	361	102	15	321	658	−11	3,349
1924	999	336	112	349	148	366	103	21	329	678	−13	3,428
1925	1,006	338	117	352	150	373	109	27	346	700	−10	3,508
1926	1,011	323	118	359	130	374	114	26	342	711	−12	3,496
1927	1,027	321	123	367	162	395	124	28	364	738	−18	3,631
1928	1,047	310	128	375	157	397	130	28	378	767	−17	3,690
1929	1,054	310	133	380	164	405	137	28	393	777	−16	3,765
1930	1,082	300	136	388	163	400	141	27	400	798	−13	3,822
1931	1,118	273	137	394	162	408	147	23	399	806	−4	3,863
1932	1,119	238	134	399	158	391	159	25	397	822	−3	3,839
1933	1,119	250	139	405	161	406	164	29	414	848	2	3,937
1934	1,134	262	143	412	166	410	179	36	438	873	−2	4,051

See p. 853 for footnotes.

National Accounts 9. *continued*

(in £ million)

C. 1900–1948 at 1938 Prices (*cont.*)

	Food (*a*)	Alcoholic Drink (*b*)	Tobacco	Housing (*c*)	Fuel and Light (*d*)	Clothing (*e*)	Durable Household Goods (*f*)	Motor Cars and Motor Cycles	Other Goods (*g*)	Other Services (*h*)	Adjust-ment (*i*)	Total Consumers' Expenditure
1935	1,129	273	150	423	172	425	190	43	464	896	−2	4,163
1936	1,144	283	159	434	180	439	195	48	482	925	−4	4,285
1937	1,153	296	168	445	186	437	187	49	499	944	−7	4,357
1938	1,157	294	176	455	188	438	174	43	498	965	4	4,392
					---(*d*)				---(*g*)			
1939	1,177	297	182	506	198	447	(*f*)	39	623	915	32	4,416
1940	1,012	278	178	513	201	376	(*f*)	5	497	856	83	3,999
1941	951	291	196	510	203	280	(*f*)	1	408	880	117	3,837
1942	976	270	206	511	196	279	(*f*)	1	331	893	133	3,796
1943	983	273	204	517	183	254	(*f*)	—	322	898	167	3,751
1944	983	279	204	529	188	285	(*f*)	—	316	912	168	3,864
1945	998	304	224	542	191	290	(*f*)	1	373	982	203	4,108
									---(*g*)			
1946	1,214	283	236	592	210	345	97	16	432	988	120	4,533
1947	1,303	290	206	612	224	389	123	20	460	973	76	4,675
1948	1,331	278	198	629	226	431	132	18	445	982	49	4,719

D. 1946–57 at 1958 Prices

	Food (*a*)	Alcoholic Drink (*b*)	Tobacco	Housing (*c*)	Fuel and Light (*d*)	Clothing (*e*)	Durable Household Goods (*f*)	Motor Cars and Motor Cycles	Other Goods (*g*)	Other Services (*h*)	Adjust-ment (*i*)	Total Consumers' Expenditure
1946	3,098	869	1,051	1,205	537	926	282	71	1,080	2,617	416	12,152
1947	3,320	872	920	1,261	560	1,043	367	84	1,175	2,698	257	12,557
1948	3,365	832	890	1,261	563	1,156	398	71	1,122	2,684	189	12,531
1949	3,492	805	864	1,259	559	1,248	468	91	1,224	2,606	148	12,765
1950	3,648	816	870	1,282	583	1,293	530	94	1,278	2,604	118	13,116
1951	3,580	843	898	1,272	601	1,171	526	90	1,247	2,577	136	12,941
1952	3,545	835	915	1,281	595	1,153	476	124	1,251	2,582	119	12,876
1953	3,747	849	929	1,306	600	1,182	560	215	1,360	2,592	110	13,450
1954	3,811	845	949	1,340	625	1,267	653	271	1,469	2,645	120	13,995
1955	3,902	879	973	1,378	640	1,359	664	354	1,597	2,703	110	14,559
1956	3,963	899	986	1,404	661	1,413	615	282	1,637	2,716	106	14,682
1957	4,017	914	1,012	1,420	646	1,452	680	325	1,676	2,745	98	14,985

(in £ million)

E. 1952–80 at 1975 Prices (l)

	Food (a)	Alcoholic Drink and Tobacco (b)	Housing (c)	Fuel and Light	Clothing (e)	Durable Household Goods (f)	Motor Cars and Motor Cycles	Other Goods (g)	Other Services (h)	Total Consumers' Expenditure (k)
1952	8,988	4,337	5,315	1,725	2,483	990	210	3,665	8,064	35,238
1953	9,506	4,406	5,420	1,739	2,545	1,165	365	3,964	8,077	36,831
1954	9,704	4,446	5,565	1,812	2,728	1,358	460	4,248	8,279	38,347
1955	10,048	4,590	5,722	1,846	2,927	1,381	599	4,568	8,475	39,904
1956	10,210	4,672	5,832	1,916	3,043	1,279	478	4,670	8,552	40,289
1957	10,363	4,773	5,907	1,872	3,127	1,414	550	4,760	8,633	41,118
1958	10,488	4,808	6,019	2,000	3,140	1,541	721	5,036	8,540	42,095
1959	10,689	5,007	6,183	1,972	3,309	1,806	886	5,379	8,822	43,911
1960	10,919	5,230	6,350	2,145	3,563	1,751	1,017	5,749	9,016	45,623
1961	11,100	5,454	6,479	2,178	3,642	1,765	898	6,026	9,293	46,680
1962	11,211	5,370	6,698	2,392	3,626	1,790	1,003	6,200	9,608	47,653
1963	11,332	5,594	6,968	2,570	3,777	1,931	1,318	6,527	10,003	49,725
1964	11,495	5,736	7,081	2,460	3,933	2,006	1,528	6,993	10,311	51,274
1965	11,508	5,608	7,317	2,549	4,085	2,035	1,475	7,335	10,532	52,131
1966	11,727	5,809	7,521	2,577	4,083	1,982	1,470	7,711	10,629	53,184
1967	11,826	5,949	7,799	2,590	4,145	2,064	1,616	8,092	10,623	54,385
1968	11,920	6,107	8,191	2,664	4,371	2,207	1,720	8,475	10,676	56,026
1969	11,950	6,139	8,343	2,761	4,442	2,132	1,535	8,520	10,832	56,313
1970	12,041	6,374	8,443	2,782	4,635	2,228	1,759	8,772	11,076	57,814
1971	12,090	6,519	8,714	2,752	4,715	2,429	2,345	9,118	11,306	59,724
1972	11,988	6,960	8,917	2,854	4,964	2,986	2,811	9,956	11,964	63,270
1973	12,181	7,694	9,181	2,930	5,183	3,396	2,668	10,760	12,339	66,332
1974	12,027	7,777	9,081	2,984	5,109	3,269	2,033	10,840	11,929	65,049
1975	11,961	7,604	9,221	2,914	5,166	3,232	2,135	10,635	11,784	64,652
1976	12,047	7,591	9,238	2,887	5,194	3,419	2,222	10,734	11,375	64,707
1977	11,897	7,546	9,406	2,959	5,232	3,215	2,009	10,880	11,373	64,517
1978	12,233	8,053	9,596	3,013	5,716	3,531	2,474	11,414	12,197	68,227
1979	12,461	8,293	10,079	3,179	6,100	3,999	2,751	11,585	13,152	71,599
1980	12,474	8,034	10,293	3,073	6,142	3,904	2,200	11,633	13,797	71,550

(a) Food consumed in hotels, restaurants, etc., is included in "other services". Non-alcoholic drink is included.
(b) Including consumption in licensed premises.
(c) Rent, rates, water charges, and occupiers' costs of maintenance, repairs, and improvements.
(d) Including candles to 1938.
(e) Excluding repairs and alterations.
(f) Furniture, floor coverings, electrical appliances, bicycles, and, to 1919, bicycle repairs, household textiles, hardware, pottery, glassware, cutlery, and minor electrical goods. Prams and musical instruments are included from 1920.
(g) Matches, cleaning materials, books, recreational goods, travel goods, stationery, chemists' goods, etc., and, vehicle running costs and, to 1919, prams and musical instruments. From 1920 household textiles, hardware, etc., and pets and pet foods are included.
(h) Public travel and communication, catering, private education, entertainment, life assurance and insurance (other than motor vehicles), medical and funeral services, laundries, etc., hairdressing, other miscellaneous services, hire of domestic equipment, and repairs to clothing, furniture, watches, etc. Pets and pet foods are included to 1919 and bicycle repairs are included from 1920.
(i) Income in kind of the Armed Forces and consumers' expenditure abroad *less* expenditures of non-residents in the U.K.
(j) See note 3 above.
(k) Totals differ slightly from those given in earlier tables which are derived from later editions of the Blue Book.
(l) See note 2 above.

National Accounts 10. Consumers' Expenditure – Republic of Ireland 1938–80

NOTES

[1] Sources: Statistical Office, Dublin, *National Income and Expenditure*.

[2] The total of the columns in this table, minus the last column, is not always the same as the figure for consumers' expenditure given in table 6 owing to the unavailability of all revised figures in the source.

A. At Current Prices

(in £ million)

	Food (*a*)	Alcoholic Drink (*b*)	Tobacco	Clothing (*c*)	Fuel and Power (*d*)	Durable Household Goods	Transport Equipment	Other Goods	Rent (*e*)	Travel within the State (*f*)	Expenditure outside the State	Entertainment and Sport	Professional Services	Domestic Services	Other	Expenditure by Non-Residents (*g*)
1938	48·9	20·1		15·3	11·8					2·4	...	2·0	5·1	3·2	5·6	...
1947	106·2	33·6		39·7	19·2		36·6		13·4	7·2	...	3·2	7·2	5·8	9·9	...
1948	103·3	36·6		40·6	16·7		48·2		13·8	9·7	...	4·0	7·9	6·2	10·2	...
1949	103·5	39·2		45·5	20·1		46·3		14·3	10·2	...	4·2	8·4	6·2	11·1	...
1950	107·2	39·5		47·6	21·3		50·2		14·1	13·1	...	4·5	8·5	6·1	12·5	...
1951	112·3	43·1		51·9	27·0		57·8		15·0	13·5	...	4·7	9·1	6·7	13·6	...
	---(*a*)(*g*)	---(*b*)(*g*)		--- (*g*)	--- (*g*)		--- (*g*)		--- (*g*)	--- (*g*)		--- (*g*)	--- (*g*)	--- (*g*)	--- (*g*)	--- (*g*)
1952	128·1	33·4	30·9	46·7	25·8		53·0		15·1	19·9	...	6·6	9·2	6·3	15·4	29·5
					--- (*d*)				--- (*e*)	--- (*f*)						
1953	149·0	31·1	31·6	48·5	19·0	14·4	7·5	19·8	19·3	17·7	10·9	6·9	10·8	6·6	17·0	26·8
1954	151·7	32·2	29·8	47·0	19·2	15·3	9·5	20·6	20·5	18·4	11·6	7·3	11·1	6·5	17·7	27·7
1955	164·2	34·4	30·9	48·4	23·3	16·9	10·7	22·8	21·9	19·6	11·9	7·6	12·0	6·5	18·9	28·9
1956	161·8	34·8	31·8	49·8	23·9	16·6	7·0	23·0	23·6	21·2	12·7	8·5	12·7	6·6	19·7	31·3
1957	165·1	35·5	34·9	46·6	22·7	15·9	7·4	23·5	25·4	21·7	13·9	8·7	13·4	6·5	20·2	30·3
1958	173·4	36·8	37·1	47·5	23·4	18·4	9·9	25·2	27·6	23·7	13·8	11·1	14·1	6·5	23·0	32·3
1959	175·5	37·9	37·7	46·6	23·7	20·6	10·5	26·4	28·5	24·4	13·0	11·3	14·5	6·2	24·7	35·4
1960	181·0	40·7	39·6	51·5	24·1	22·6	13·7	29·2	29·8	27·0	14·9	11·8	16·1	6·1	27·7	39·7
1961	185·2	44·2	43·0	56·1	26·0	26·4	14·3	31·5	31·4	28·0	16·3	11·8	17·0	6·0	29·8	43·5
1962	194·6	51·1	45·6	57·5	28·3	29·8	15·9	34·4	33·3	30·5	19·2	12·4	18·8	6·0	32·4	45·6
1963	200·2	55·2	49·8	61·3	29·1	33·5	18·8	39·4	35·4	32·2	22·4	13·1	20·5	6·1	34·9	49·8
1964	222·6	62·6	52·6	68·0	31·1	38·7	22·9	43·6	38·4	37·5	25·9	14·3	24·2	6·5	40·8	58·8
1965	236·5	68·5	55·6	76·4	31·9	36·7	23·1	40·7	42·0	41·5	28·2	14·7	26·0	6·8	43·9	67·7
1966	243·8	73·2	59·0	75·1	33·3	37·8	23·3	46·9	46·0	44·8	31·6	15·1	28·0	6·8	46·7	65·1
1967	250·5	80·5	63·8	86·8	35·2	41·0	25·5	50·5	50·4	48·9	30·1	15·4	29·6	6·7	50·7	68·9
1968	287·7	91·8	66·4	94·7	38·9	45·2	32·8	66·1	56·1	56·5	36·3	16·2	32·2	6·6	58·5	75·7
1969	302·7	108·7	73·4	111·8	43·6	52·8	38·7	79·8	65·3	64·3	37·8	18·0	37·2	6·9	65·9	78·1
1970	331·2	128·3	78·0	119·1	48·3	56·4	41·4	87·8	75·4	59·7	40·1	20·3	45·7	6·7	69·8	74·3
1971	346·7	145·9	79·4	132·3	55·9	64·5	44·8	107·2	87·6	70·5	42·8	22·5	52·2	6·8	80·6	79·0

1972	390·9	165·8	83·9	146·9	66·1	79·0	58·8	125·9	101·0	81·2	46·9	24·4	57·3	7·1	90·0	70·4
1973	492·4	196·5	93·5	175·2	70·8	96·5	83·8	148·8	106·7	96·7	60·3	27·2	65·0	7·6	102·3	84·8
1974	582·2	233·0	105·1	202·3	102·1	110·7	84·0	172·6	122·8	120·6	72·8	30·5	78·4	8·2	122·0	102·3
1975	657·8	303·3	128·9	209·9	125·0	128·6	92·2	199·4	143·8	177·8	94·2	37·4	97·6	9·4	146·6	118·0
1976	757·0	382·2	150·0	231·9	153·0	165·3	162·3	249·6	179·5	214·0	109·4	60·8	114·9	10·2	170·0	137·2
1977	934·8	422·8	151·0	285·1	197·6	188·6	234·5	332·3	209·9	248·9	135·6	72·8	141·3	9·0	218·8	184·6
1978	1,066·8	486·2	170·1	359·6	212·7	224·7	305·8	394·4	213·0	300·2	183·8	91·2	158·0	9·1	269·4	215·9
1979	1,269·0	574·5	193·7	444·3	267·7	261·3	312·3	463·6	274·7	352·8	251·4	110·7	188·0	12·2	325·8	257·4
1980	1,472·5	695·9	239·1	518·7	351·4	297·4	314·6	547·2	327·8	465·9	283·4	128·0	236·0	17·8	377·9	281·9
B. At Constant Prices																
1938 and 1952–58 at 1953 Prices																
1938 (*g*)	[120·0](*a*)	[44·6](*b*)		43·3	[27·8](*d*)		36·7					[49·5](*e*)(*f*)				. . .
1952	137·7	66·5		46·0	[25·6](*d*)		53·0					76·0				31·1
1953	149·0	62·7		48·5	19·0	14·4	7·5	19·8				89·2				26·8
1954	150·9	61·9		47·0	19·2	15·5	9·7	20·4				92·2				27·7
1955	156·6	64·8		48·4	22·6	17·0	10·8	22·0				95·0				28·1
1956	155·5	62·3		48·9	21·5	15·9	6·7	20·8				96·7				29·2
1957	153·4	61·1		45·4	19·4	14·8	6·8	20·4				96·1				27·2
1958	152·0	61·7		45·9	20·4	16·8	8·9	21·5				101·5				27·7
1958–65 at 1958 Prices																
1958	173·4	73·9		47·5	23·4	18·4	9·9	25·2				119·8				32·3
1959	177·2	73·6		46·4	24·5	20·4	10·3	26·1				121·1				35·4
1960	183·5	77·2		50·3	25·6	22·2	13·5	28·3				128·7				39·5
1961	183·1	81·3		54·3	27·1	25·6	13·9	30·0				132·1				42·2
1962	188·4	82·6		54·2	28·8	28·4	15·3	31·1				137·7				42·4
1963	191·4	86·5		56·5	28·8	31·6	17·8	34·7				143·4				45·2
1964	198·7	86·7		59·4	30·1	34·9	21·4	35·6				153·2				50·0
1965	199·5	88·9		64·9	31·1	32·3	20·9	31·6				157·9				54·8
1965–70 at 1968 Prices																
1965	259·2	147·6		80·0	33·7	39·8	26·5	45·9				234·3				75·4
1966	264·9	145·8		76·4	34·8	40·2	25·7	48·8				239·9				70·3
1967	267·5	150·7		88·3	35·7	42·0	26·3	52·8				245·6				72·1
1968	287·7	158·2		94·7	38·9	45·2	32·8	66·1				262·4				75·7
1969	286·0	162·2		108·2	42·1	49·4	34·6	72·4				283·5				72·7
1970	291·1	172·5		106·1	41·4	49·0	33·3	71·0				271·0				63·9

See p. 856 for footnotes.

National Accounts 10. *continued*

B. At Constant Prices
1970–80 at 1975 Prices

(in £ million)

	Food (*a*)	Alcoholic Drink (*b*)	Tobacco	Clothing (*c*)	Fuel and Power (*d*)	Durable Household Goods	Transport Equipment	Other Goods	Rent (*e*)	Travel within the State (*f*)	Expenditure outside the State	Entertainment and Sport	Professional Services	Domestic Services	Other	Expenditure by Non-Residents (*g*)
1970	617·1	227·7	117·4	231·4	111·2	102·1	75·7	165·6	120·2	126·0	74·7	37·1	98·9	15·3	132·9	138·4
1971	632·9	240·5	115·5	234·7	116·2	103·4	72·9	181·3	121·0	130·1	73·3	37·6	100·1	13·8	140·2	135·3
1972	632·5	261·6	122·3	236·8	123·2	121·1	88·6	191·8	125·4	142·2	73·9	37·5	95·5	12·5	143·6	110·9
1973	682·1	280·6	126·4	240·7	126·1	132·9	115·3	217·3	130·3	155·9	85·3	37·4	93·8	11·5	145·4	119·9
1974	710·3	299·7	138·3	234·4	126·3	128·4	101·4	214·5	134·1	155·1	88·0	37·6	98·2	10·4	149·0	123·7
1975	657·8	303·3	128·9	209·9	125·0	128·6	92·2	199·4	143·8	177·8	94·2	37·4	97·6	9·4	146·6	118·0
1976	632·3	300·9	133·4	209·0	133·5	146·6	129·3	214·4	149·3	175·7	92·7	50·3	96·1	8·5	146·1	116·3
1977	680·9	313·0	127·4	224·2	145·0	147·9	159·8	246·7	155·2	183·7	101·1	51·9	102·7	6·2	163·6	137·7
1978	716·2	339·4	140·1	253·1	152·0	161·0	185·8	268·3	160·4	211·0	127·4	56·0	101·5	5·4	185·0	149·6
1979	718·2	352·6	138·3	284·8	168·7	170·3	168·7	288·5	168·2	214·3	153·9	59·3	101·4	6·0	201·9	157·5
1980	760·7	341·6	137·2	289·8	156·7	168·1	168·8	291·6	175·9	221·2	146·7	57·5	106·2	7·0	199·7	145·9

(*a*) Including non-alcoholic drink from 1952.
(*b*) Including non-alcoholic drink to 1951.
(*c*) Including 'personal equipment'.
(*d*) Excluding motor spirit from 1953.
(*e*) Personal rent only to 1952.
(*f*) 'Travel' to 1951. Including petrol from 1952.
(*g*) Expenditure by non-residents is excluded, in principle, prior to 1952.

National Accounts 11. Gross Domestic Fixed Capital Formation – Great Britain 1761–1860 and United Kingdom 1851–1920

NOTES
[1] SOURCE: Kindly supplied by C. H. Feinstein.
[2] These are new estimates, which replace those in earlier published works.
[3] Southern Ireland is included in part B of this table.

A. Great Britain – annual averages of decades, 1761–1860

(in £ million)

	at current prices		at 1851–60 prices	
	Total	Buildings and Works	Total	Buildings and Works
1761–70	4·25	2·94	7·38	5·39
1771–80	5·59	3·86	9·37	6·85
1781–90	6·95	4·75	11·16	7·96
1791–1800	11·26	7·84	13·72	10·08
1801–10	20·13	14·14	16·00	11·77
1811–20	25·13	18·48	19·23	14·37
1821–30	27·64	20·12	25·05	18·39
1831–40	36·93	26·47	35·09	25·47
1841–50	48·08	34·52	46·88	33·59
1851–60	53·29	33·81	53·29	33·81

B. United Kingdom 1851–1920

	at current prices		at 1900 prices	
	Total	Buildings and Works	Total	Buildings and Works
1851	46·3	31·8	58·2	41·6
1852	52·6	36·7	63·9	46·5
1853	59·3	39·7	63·3	44·4
1854	63·5	37·6	63·8	40·8
1855	62·2	35·0	61·4	38·4
1856	55·8	32·7	56·4	37·2
1857	53·0	33·4	54·8	38·0
1858	51·3	33·0	55·2	39·0
1859	54·2	36·1	60·0	43·2
1860	58·6	36·8	64·2	43·7
1861	63·2	40·9	70·6	48·8
1862	67·5	42·8	75·8	51·5
1863	77·9	48·1	85·5	56·8
1864	88·2	50·8	92·5	58·6
1865	91·1	53·6	96·0	62·4
1866	89·3	53·9	92·3	60·7
1867	79·9	50·1	84·7	57·2
1868	76·2	48·6	82·2	55·8
1869	77·0	49·6	82·4	56·5
1870	86·9	53·4	90·4	60·0
1871	98·9	59·1	100·1	65·2
1872	118·4	69·6	107·3	70·1
1873	125·2	76·4	104·5	70·4
1874	140·7	85·1	119·3	80·2
1875	136·9	86·9	126·0	87·5
1876	138·5	90·1	132·3	92·6
1877	134·7	87·4	132·4	91·1
1878	119·7	78·7	123·6	85·9
1879	106·8	68·0	114·0	77·4
1880	107·2	67·0	109·7	73·0

National Accounts 11. *continued*

B. United Kingdom 1851–1920 (*cont.*)

(in £ million)

	at current prices		at 1900 prices	
	Total	Buildings and Works	Total	Buildings and Works
1881	109·4	67·6	116·2	76·2
1882	110·5	65·7	114·5	73·0
1883	112·9	64·9	119·5	73·3
1884	105·8	67·6	117·4	78·5
1885	96·2	60·8	109·2	71·5
1886	85·1	55·8	99·7	67·2
1887	86·5	56·3	103·2	68·6
1888	90·0	54·8	106·9	66·8
1889	100·1	57·9	114·3	68·1
1890	105·9	61·0	116·3	68·4
1891	106·9	62·3	121·6	71·5
1892	108·3	63·2	124·7	73·2
1893	108·6	66·1	127·5	78·0
1894	110·7	66·7	131·8	79·4
1895	114·8	69·2	138·1	83·0
1896	126·8	76·1	150·2	90·0
1897	144·1	87·0	166·9	100·5
1898	172·1	102·9	193·2	114·0
1899	191·6	110·5	203·9	117·0
1900	204·9	115·1	204·9	115·1
1901	210·3	118·1	216·4	120·9
1902	213·0	119·9	226·6	128·6
1903	208·0	115·1	225·2	125·6
1904	203·2	109·0	223·3	120·4
1905	198·4	103·8	219·8	116·1
1906	191·9	100·7	207·4	110·4
1907	175·7	92·0	185·3	98·1
1908	144·7	77·2	156·2	84·6
1909	153·8	77·3	166·4	85·6
1910	158·4	78·0	169·4	84·7
1911	163·4	75·1	171·8	79·2
1912	171·3	75·9	172·3	76·2
1913	192·2	85·3	189·1	82·6
1914	192·8	80·6	188·9	77·3
1915	170·5	67·2	149·4	55·3
1916	158·7	57·7	117·4	40·9
1917	202·7	57·9	124·6	35·5
1918	285·7	78·7	152·5	39·1
1919	433·9	134·1	199·3	54·6
1920	577·6	252·4	231·0	86·7

National Accounts 12. Gross Domestic Fixed Capital Formation by Type of Asset – United Kingdom 1920–80

NOTES

[1] Sources: To 1947 – C. H. Feinstein, *National Income, Expenditure and Output of the United Kingdom, 1855–1965* (Cambridge, 1972), tables 39 and 40. From 1948 – C.S.O., *Economic Trends Annual Supplement* (1983 edition), using the price index implicit in Feinstein's work for constant price statistics.

[2] Southern Ireland is excluded in this table.

A. At current prices

(in £ million)

	Dwellings	Other New Buildings and Works (*a*)	Plant and Machinery	Vehicles (*b*)	Ships	Total
1920	62	180	131	53	56	482
1921	104	128	135	43	48	458
1922	75	94	80	39	93	381
1923	64	104	83	42	41	334
1924	94	111	89	50	30	374
1925	119	124	102	42	33	420
1926	144	106	93	45	13	401
1927	156	103	108	46	13	426
1928	117	102	122	42	37	420
1929	133	118	117	46	28	442
1930	122	138	110	45	20	435
1931	122	114	124	37	11	408
1932	118	89	108	30	2	347
1933	151	85	91	30	--	357
1934	170	97	119	37	4	427
1935	165	109	126	45	11	456
1936	170	128	143	53	23	517
1937	168	162	166	57	21	574
				---(*b*)		
1938	169	160	184	53	26	592
1939	280		190	60	10	540
1940	170		300	20	30	520
1941	140		270	30	40	480
1942	110		240	30	70	450
1943	80		180	40	60	360
1944	80		130	40	50	300
1945	140		120	50	40	350
1946	550		200	120	50	925
1947	330	280	360	160	70	1,199
1948	337	339	501	249		1,426
1949	332	415	562	272		1,581
1950	331	477	642	262		1,712
1951	376	527	750	256		1,909
1952	494	588	792	260		2,134
1953	630	629	828	308		2,395
1954	645	694	924	332		2,595
1955	639	824	1,050	369		2,882
1956	634	951	1,153	426		3,164
1957	615	1,042	1,296	498		3,451
1958	582	1,119	1,338	530		3,569
1959	646	1,179	1,420	571		3,816

See p. 861 for footnotes.

A. At current prices *(cont.)*

(in £ million)

	Dwellings	Other New Buildings and Works (*a*)	Plant and Machinery	Vehicles (*b*)	Ships	Total
1960	721	1,301	1,532	636		4,190
1961	791	1,507	1,808	598		4,704
1962	856	1,641	1,820	516		4,833
1963	956	1,669	1,926	515		5,066
1964	1,217	1,981	2,222	621		6,041
1965	1,286	2,120	2,474	624		6,504
1966	1,374	2,229	2,750	570		6,923
1967	1,525	2,467	2,886	646		7,524
1968	1,675	2,714	2,994	817		8,200
1969	1,667	2,867	3,198	859		8,591
1970	1,643	3,195	3,653	979		9,470
1971	1,898	3,576	3,936	1,107		10,517
1972	2,254	3,983	4,017	1,352		11,606
1973	2,686	5,031	4,865	1,656		14,238
1974	3,187	6,164	5,653	1,821		16,825
1975	4,149	7,560	6,658	2,041		20,408
1976	4,726	8,294	8,141	2,395		23,556
1977	4,695	8,349	9,537	3,146		25,727
1978	5,368	9,140	11,269	3,966		29,743
1979	5,673	10,806	13,335	4,655		34,469
1980	5,984	13,032	15,343	5,052		39,411
B. 1920–48 at 1938 prices						
1920	37	108	76	28	35	284
1921	76	91	111	23	25	326
1922	68	85	87	24	36	300
1923	61	99	95	32	21	308
1924	87	104	100	39	29	359
1925	109	119	115	33	34	410
1926	137	103	107	40	10	397
1927	150	104	122	42	24	442
1928	117	103	136	39	43	438
1929	133	122	127	45	34	461
1930	124	146	131	40	22	463
1931	130	122	158	33	11	454
1932	131	101	138	27	−1	396
1933	172	94	121	29	−7	409
1934	193	110	149	40	6	498
1935	184	121	154	48	11	518
1936	183	136	164	55	27	565
1937	171	166	166	60	21	584
1938	169	160	183	54	26	592
1939	110	180	180	50	10	530
1940	160		260	20	20	460
1941	120		200	20	30	370
1942	90		170	20	40	320
1943	60		100	30	30	220
1944	40		70	30	30	170
1945	70		70	30	20	190
1946	260		130	70	20	480
1947	140	130	180	80	30	560
1948	130	140	220	80	30	600

National Accounts 12. *continued*

C. 1948–65 at 1958 prices

(in £ million)

	Dwellings	Other New Buildings and Works (*a*)	Plant and Machinery	Vehicles (*b*) Ships	Total
1948	486	484	767	404	2,139
1949	476	594	845	424	2,339
1950	465	679	941	391	2,476
1951	456	690	1,023	347	2,516
1952	546	686	971	308	2,511
1953	711	735	981	363	2,790
1954	736	814	1,092	390	3,032
1955	688	906	1,183	431	3,208
1956	650	1,011	1,228	469	3,358
1957	620	1,072	1,331	518	3,541
1958	582	1,119	1,338	530	3,569
1959	659	1,194	1,416	580	3,849
1960	729	1,316	1,510	648	4,203
1961	776	1,506	1,725	601	4,608
1962	806	1,569	1,707	515	4,597
1963	868	1,541	1,777	543	4,729
1964	1,093	1,792	1,997	645	5,527
1965	1,110	1,860	2,119	640	5,729
D. 1962–80 at 1975 prices					
1962	2,758	5,348	4,164	1,169	13,096
1963	2,821	5,139	4,341	1,193	13,269
1964	3,522	5,981	4,885	1,425	15,494
1965	3,651	6,235	5,245	1,395	16,240
1966	3,754	6,297	5,608	1,250	16,643
1967	4,182	6,940	5,862	1,399	18,052
1968	4,379	7,279	5,864	1,722	18,878
1969	4,187	7,352	6,043	1,694	18,954
1970	3,850	7,655	6,365	1,819	19,460
1971	4,091	7,781	6,264	1,882	19,743
1972	4,309	7,607	6,055	2,148	19,823
1973	4,152	7,852	6,775	2,416	21,195
1974	3,826	7,469	6,963	2,304	20,562
1975	4,149	7,560	6,658	2,041	20,408
1976	4,264	7,546	6,812	2,018	20,640
1977	3,913	7,075	6,969	2,182	20,139
1978	4,061	6,996	7,502	2,286	20,845
1979	3,615	6,750	8,253	2,421	21,039
1980	3,106	6,378	8,658	2,301	20,443

(*a*) Including transfer costs of land and buildings.
(*b*) Railway rolling stock, trams, motor vehicles and aircraft.

National Accounts 13. Gross Domestic Fixed Capital Formation by Type of Asset – Republic of Ireland 1953–80

NOTES

[1] Source: Central Statistics Office, Dublin, *National Income and Expenditure*.

[2] The sum of the columns in this table is not always the same as the total for Gross Domestic Fixed Capital Formation in table 6 owing to the unavailability of all revised figures in the source.

A. At Current Prices

(in £ million)

	Dwellings	Roads	Other Construction	Transport Equipment	Agricultural Machinery	Other Machinery and Equipment
1953	16·3	5·1	28·5	7·7	4·9	18·2
1954	14·9	5·0	31·4	10·9	6·4	17·2
1955	15·8	5·0	35·8	10·6	5·4	18·9
1956	17·0	4·5	35·2	13·5	3·2	17·1
1957	11·7	4·1	31·8	11·7	5·0	15·0
	---(*a*)		---(*a*)			
1958	11·6	4·4	26·8	14·1	5·1	18·0
1959	12·8	4·5	29·0	13·1	5·0	18·9
1960	14·6	5·0	30·4	12·9	4·6	22·8
1961	16·1	6·6	34·6	16·8	6·3	28·5
1962	19·0	6·7	44·2	18·0	6·1	35·0
1963	23·4	6·9	50·9	18·5	7·1	40·9
1964	31·5	7·8	61·8	22·0	7·9	42·3
1965	40·5	7·9	66·5	26·8	7·9	50·5
1966	37·5	8·0	69·8	24·6	8·3	51·8
1967	46·2	7·9	75·0	26·5	8·6	56·7
1968	50·1	7·7	90·9	31·6	13·4	64·8
1969	57·2	8·4	109·6	55·8	16·8	84·7
1970	61·7	10·6	117·1	53·6	17·4	101·2
1971	81·9	11·4	139·6	65·8	15·7	115·3
1972	120·4	11·1	138·3	47·9	22·1	157·1
1973	150·1	13·7	170·8	87·1	25·4	209·2
1974	203·4	19·6	175·9	78·8	28·2	247·0
1975	209·7	19·3	230·5	89·9	37·4	298·5
1976	251·6	16·9	286·0	142·5	57·2	404·6
1977	304·0	27·2	317·7	208·2	94·5	462·7
1978	400·7	36·6	411·9	290·9	115·3	607·4
1979	558·2	46·9	611·1	356·2	130·7	743·1
1980	578·0	57·2	833·4	334·1	79·1	804·3

B. At Constant Prices

1953–58 at 1953 prices

	Dwellings	Roads	Other Construction	Transport Equipment	Agricultural Machinery	Other Machinery and Equipment
1953	16·3	5·1	28·5	7·7	4·9	18·2
1954	15·2	5·1	32·1	10·9	6·2	17·3
1955	15·8	5·0	35·8	10·6	5·0	18·1
1956	15·9	4·2	33·0	13·5	2·8	15·7
1957	10·5	3·6	28·5	11·7	4·1	13·3
	---(*a*)		---(*a*)			
1958	10·2	3·9	23·6	12·6	4·2	15·9

1958–65 at 1958 prices

	Dwellings	Roads	Other Construction	Transport Equipment	Agricultural Machinery	Other Machinery and Equipment
1958	11·6	4·4	26·8	14·1	5·1	18·0
1959	12·3	4·6	29·5	13·0	5·0	18·8
1960	13·6	5·0	30·2	12·8	4·4	22·5
1961	14·1	6·3	32·9	16·4	5·9	27·7
1962	16·2	6·0	40·0	17·3	5·6	33·4
1963	18·2	6·2	45·7	17·6	6·5	38·7
1964	22·7	6·5	51·5	20·5	7·0	38·7
1965	27·2	6·4	53·8	24·2	6·8	45·5

National Accounts 13. *continued*

(in £ million)

	Dwellings	Roads	Other Construction	Transport Equipment	Agricultural Machinery	Other Machinery and Equipment
B. At Constant Prices (*cont.*)						
1965–70 at 1968 prices						
1965	44·3	8·9	75·1	29·6	8·9	54·4
1966	40·4	8·7	75·4	26·4	9·0	54·5
1967	47·5	8·2	78·2	27·3	9·0	58·6
1968	50·1	7·7	90·9	31·6	13·4	64·8
1969	52·5	7·6	98·9	52·4	15·7	80·9
1970	52·6	8·6	95·0	47·1	14·8	91·4
1970–80 at 1975 prices						
1970	125·7	23·2	256·8	101·9	37·9	176·7
1971	150·5	22·6	277·1	110·0	31·6	192·3
1972	193·3	19·9	248·3	75·9	39·6	248·1
1973	219·2	21·6	270·3	123·3	39·6	300·2
1974	242·3	23·4	210·7	96·3	34·4	293·7
1975	209·7	19·3	230·5	89·9	37·4	298·5
1976	212·6	14·5	245·3	115·1	45·1	342·2
1977	228·8	19·9	232·4	140·3	60·2	339·5
1978	265·4	24·3	273·7	175·9	64·6	403·9
1979	304·9	26·9	351·0	195·1	67·3	433·3
1980	256·1	27·3	397·9	167·7	36·7	407·6

(*a*) There was some rearrangement of categories in 1958.

National Accounts 14. Capital Stock – Great Britain 1760–1850, United Kingdom 1850–1980

NOTES

[1] Parts A and B – Kindly supplied by C. H. Feinstein, which replace those in the source of Parts C, D to 1962 (1st line), E and F, which is C. H. Feinstein, *National Income, Expenditure and Output of the United Kingdom 1855–1965* (Cambridge, 1972), tables 43 and 46. Part D from 1962 (2nd line) and Part G – C.S.O., *National Income and Expenditure* (later *United Kingdom National Accounts*).

[2] The figures of gross stocks at current prices since 1948 have been obtained from the Blue Books by using the price indices given there, since they are only published in constant price form.

[3] Southern Ireland is included to 1920 (1st line) and excluded subsequently.

[4] The main reason for the differences between figures for 1938 and 1948 in Parts C and D is different treatment of "historic assets". See C. H. Feinstein, *op. cit.*, pp. 199–200.

A. Great Britain 1760–1860

(in £ million)

	at current prices				at 1851–60 prices			
	Total Gross Stock	*of which* Buildings and Works	Total Net Stock	*of which* Buildings and Works	Total Gross Stock	*of which* Buildings and Works	Total Net Stock	*of which* Buildings and Works
1760	239	204	133	113	449	400	248	221
1770	262	219	143	121	470	417	257	229
1780	303	254	166	140	507	447	281	248
1790	327	276	188	159	561	487	315	275
1800	587	482	334	277	637	549	364	316
1810	1,140	944	649	549	733	626	422	367
1820	1,017	861	593	511	851	726	497	432
1830	1,020	857	610	518	1,018	864	609	523
1840	1,388	1,144	856	712	1,277	1,067	789	665
1850	1,491	1,236	942	789	1,642(*a*)	1,346(*a*)	1,037(*a*)	860(*a*)

B. United Kingdom 1850–1920

					at 1900 prices			
1850	1,583	1,313	997	836	1,940	1,643	1,229	1,052
1851	1,591	1,317	1,001	838	1,985	1,677	1,258	1,074
1852	1,671	1,376	1,053	877	2,034	1,714	1,292	1,100
1853	1,925	1,583	1,213	1,009	2,084	1,750	1,324	1,123
1854	2,061	1,665	1,302	1,063	2,134	1,783	1,357	1,144
1855	2,103	1,677	1,328	1,069	2,179	1,812	1,385	1,161
1856	2,083	1,638	1,312	1,042	2,220	1,842	1,406	1,177
1857	2,113	1,665	1,326	1,056	2,261	1,872	1,427	1,192
1858	2,075	1,631	1,299	1,033	2,303	1,902	1,448	1,209
1859	2,089	1,644	1,301	1,039	2,347	1,936	1,472	1,230
1860	2,136	1,687	1,328	1,064	2,394	1,970	1,499	1,250
1861	2,162	1,705	1,345	1,078	2,448	2,010	1,532	1,276
1862	2,188	1,723	1,362	1,090	2,505	2,052	1,569	1,303
1863	2,291	1,801	1,430	1,142	2,571	2,098	1,613	1,336
1864	2,421	1,879	1,516	1,195	2,642	2,147	1,662	1,369
1865	2,478	1,906	1,558	1,216	2,716	2,199	1,714	1,405
1866	2,610	2,006	1,644	1,283	2,785	2,248	1,760	1,440
1867	2,620	2,018	1,648	1,291	2,848	2,295	1,798	1,470
1868	2,632	2,036	1,652	1,302	2,908	2,339	1,832	1,499
1869	2,687	2,082	1,678	1,327	2,967	2,384	1,865	1,527
1870	2,795	2,155	1,743	1,374	3,033	2,432	1,905	1,559
1871	2,929	2,256	1,829	1,440	3,106	2,485	1,953	1,595
1872	3,322	2,534	2,074	1,618	3,185	2,542	2,005	1,635
1873	3,740	2,830	2,335	1,811	3,261	2,599	2,054	1,674
1874	3,817	2,853	2,385	1,832	3,350	2,666	2,115	1,723
1875	3,666	2,731	2,301	1,768	3,445	2,738	2,183	1,778
1876	3,639	2,745	2,297	1,786	3,547	2,816	2,256	1,838
1877	3,638	2,776	2,305	1,812	3,648	2,892	2,327	1,895
1878	3,557	2,713	2,253	1,775	3,742	2,964	2,387	1,946
1879	3,485	2,652	2,202	1,735	3,825	3,026	2,436	1,987

See p. 868 for footnotes.

National Accounts 14. *continued*

B. United Kingdom 1850–1920 (*cont.*)

(in £ million)

	at current prices				at 1900 prices			
	Total Gross Stock	*of which* Buildings and Works	Total Net Stock	*of which* Buildings and Works	Total Gross Stock	*of which* Buildings and Works	Total Net Stock	*of which* Buildings and Works
1880	3,706	2,826	2,338	1,849	3,903	3,085	2,478	2,024
1881	3,665	2,797	2,311	1,830	3,983	3,145	2,526	2,063
1882	3,797	2,891	2,391	1,892	4,058	3,202	2,569	2,098
1883	3,791	2,883	2,385	1,885	4,134	3,259	2,614	2,132
1884	3,740	2,849	2,353	1,865	4,212	3,320	2,661	2,172
1885	3,721	2,857	2,336	1,865	4,279	3,375	2,697	2,203
1886	3,657	2,828	2,289	1,841	4,338	3,426	2,724	2,229
1887	3,659	2,846	2,283	1,847	4,401	3,477	2,753	2,257
1888	3,720	2,899	2,315	1,875	4,465	3,527	2,784	2,282
1889	3,911	3,047	2,426	1,964	4,535	3,577	2,819	2,308
1890	4,146	3,237	2,568	2,083	4,605	3,628	2,853	2,333
1891	4,117	3,206	2,540	2,057	4,684	3,682	2,894	2,362
1892	4,146	3,221	2,551	2,061	4,765	3,738	2,936	2,390
1893	4,122	3,212	2,532	2,051	4,847	3,799	2,980	2,423
1894	4,153	3,241	2,548	2,066	4,932	3,861	3,025	2,456
1895	4,178	3,265	2,564	2,080	5,019	3,925	3,075	2,494
1896	4,323	3,376	2,657	2,151	5,114	3,996	3,136	2,537
1897	4,512	3,527	2,782	2,248	5,220	4,075	3,211	2,589
1898	4,796	3,757	2,974	2,399	5,348	4,167	3,307	2,654
1899	5,160	4,020	3,216	2,571	5,483	4,262	3,412	2,721
1900	5,619	4,355	3,515	2,784	5,619	4,355	3,515	2,784
1901	5,621	4,339	3,537	2,783	5,771	4,452	3,628	2,852
1902	5,563	4,241	3,518	2,731	5,935	4,555	3,749	2,927
1903	5,606	4,264	3,561	2,751	6,096	4,656	3,865	2,997
1904	5,678	4,299	3,615	2,775	6,254	4,753	3,974	3,060
1905	5,767	4,330	3,676	2,796	6,401	4,843	4,072	3,118
1906	6,029	4,496	3,836	2,899	6,545	4,928	4,158	3,170
1907	6,309	4,692	3,995	3,016	6,669	5,001	4,220	3,209
1908	6,240	4,630	3,922	2,963	6,769	5,063	4,249	3,232
1909	6,275	4,633	3,917	2,951	6,875	5,125	4,287	3,257
1910	6,477	4,785	4,018	3,032	6,978	5,186	4,324	3,280
1911	6,733	4,971	4,150	3,133	7,077	5,241	4,357	3,296
1912	7,137	5,257	4,368	3,292	7,178	5,294	4,387	3,308
1913	7,502	5,510	4,565	3,431	7,290	5,352	4,429	3,327
1914	7,671	5,627	4,642	3,483	7,405	5,406	4,471	3,339
1915	8,866	6,584	5,298	4,026	7,488	5,439	4,471	3,329
1916	10,417	7,647	6,131	4,613	7,524	5,460	4,435	3,305
1917	12,261	8,891	7,112	5,300	7,526	5,475	4,375	3,275
1918	14,920	10,966	8,588	6,480	7,585	5,492	4,360	3,249
1919	18,419	13,634	10,558	7,996	7,703	5,517	4,404	3,237
1920	22,088	16,324	12,660	9,554	7,837	5,570	4,475	3,257

National Accounts 14. *continued*

C. United Kingdom (*a*) 1920–48 at Current Prices

(in £ thousand million)

	Total Gross Stock	*of which* Dwellings	*of which* Other Buildings and Works	*of which* Plant and Machinery	*of which* Vehicles, Ships and Aircraft	Total Net Stock	*of which* Dwellings	*of which* Other Buildings and Works	*of which* Plant, Vehicles etc.
1920	24·87	5·61	12·28	4·96	2·02	13·44	3·20	7·36	2·88
1921	20·43	4·69	10·43	3·38	1·93	11·06	2·67	6·17	2·22
1922	17·23	3·87	8·36	2·50	2·51	9·23	2·20	4·89	2·14
1923	15·91	3·69	7·91	2·53	1·78	8·51	2·10	4·58	1·83
1924	16·09	3·92	8·20	2·58	1·38	8·61	2·23	4·71	1·67
1925	16·26	4·05	8·29	2·55	1·38	8·70	2·31	4·72	1·67
1926	16·11	4·07	8·17	2·55	1·32	8·59	2·35	4·60	1·64
1927	16·02	4·14	8·14	2·58	1·16	8·56	2·42	4·54	1·60
1928	15·89	4·09	7·96	2·59	1·26	8·46	2·40	4·38	1·68
1929	16·28	4·23	8·03	2·72	1·29	8·66	2·50	4·39	1·77
1930	16·18	4·26	7·98	2·61	1·34	8·59	2·53	4·33	1·73
1931	15·87	4·21	7·83	2·50	1·34	8·41	2·51	4·22	1·68
1932	15·45	4·13	7·51	2·53	1·28	8·13	2·47	4·00	1·66
1933	15·42	4·20	7·42	2·59	1·21	8·08	2·53	3·92	1·63
1934	15·69	4·37	7·48	2·67	1·17	8·22	2·66	3·91	1·65
1935	16·37	4·61	7·69	2·81	1·26	8·56	2·84	3·97	1·75
1936	17·30	4·95	8·05	3·06	1·24	9·08	3·07	4·14	1·87
1937	18·82	5·35	8·59	3·58	1·31	9·86	3·34	4·39	2·13
1938	19·52	5·60	8·96	3·61	1·35	10·23	3·51	4·56	2·16
1948	49·25	15·46	21·23	9·63	2·93	24·97	9·20	10·35	5·42

D. United Kingdom 1938–80 at Current Prices

	Total Gross Stock	*of which* Dwellings	*of which* Other Buildings and Works	*of which* Plant and Machinery	*of which* Vehicles, Ships and Aircraft	Total Net Stock	*of which* Dwellings	*of which* Other Buildings and Works	*of which* Plant, Vehicles etc.
1938	18·01	5·30	7·64	3·80	1·27	...	...	...	...
1948	46·61	14·76	18·71	10·25	2·89	23·8	9·1	8·3	6·4
1949	47·82	15·14	18·83	10·76	3·09	24·6	9·3	8·5	6·8
1950	49·74	15·76	19·16	11·46	3·36	25·8	9·7	8·7	7·4
1951	56·77	18·55	21·80	12·79	3·63	30·0	11·5	10·0	8·5
1952	63·11	20·76	23·43	14·73	4·19	33·6	12·9	10·9	9·8
1953	65·07	20·87	23·91	15·79	4·50	34·7	12·9	11·3	10·5
1954	66·53	21·19	24·28	16·40	4·66	35·7	13·2	11·5	11·0
1955	71·94	22·99	26·32	17·79	4·84	39·1	14·4	12·7	12·0
1956	77·16	24·68	27·86	19·44	5·18	43·2	15·6	13·9	13·7
1957	81·90	25·62	29·73	20·89	5·66	46·6	16·3	15·2	15·1
1958	85·80	26·33	31·25	22·14	6·08	48·4	16·5	16·0	15·9
1959	87·29	26·38	31·62	23·07	6·22	49·1	16·4	16·2	16·5
1960	90·42	27·21	32·46	24·22	6·53	53·0	17·4	17·8	17·8
1961	95·72	28·61	33·94	26·24	6·93	57·1	18·6	19·3	19·2
1962	102·08 / 100·0 (*b*)	30·44 / 30·3 (*b*)	36·64 / 35·5 (*b*)	27·89 / 27·2 (*b*)	7·11 / 7·0 (*b*)	61·2	19·9	20·9	20·4
1963	106·2	31·9	37·7	29·3	7·3	65·3	21·1	22·5	21·7
1964	112·7	33·8	39·4	31·8	7·8	70·6 / 71·7 (*d*)	22·6 / 22·8 (*d*)	24·4 / 24·6 (*d*)	23·6 / 24·3 (*d*)
1965	120·4	35·8	42·0	34·4	8·2	77·8	24·4	26·7	26·7
1966	129·2	37·7	45·0	37·8	8·7	83·0	25·8	28·5	28·7

National Accounts 14. *continued*

D. United Kingdom (*a*) 1938–80 at Current Prices (*cont.*)

(in £ thousand million)

	Total Gross Stock	*of which* Dwellings	Other Buildings and Works	Plant and Machinery	Vehicles, Ships and Aircraft	Total Net Stock	*of which* Dwellings	Other Buildings and Works	Plant, Vehicles etc.
1967	137·9 ---- (*b*) 148·3	40·0 ---- (*b*) 46·7	47·9 ---- (*b*) 56·6	41·0 ---- (*b*) 36·3	9·0 ---- (*b*) 8·8	89·1	27·5	30·6	31·0
1968	158·2	50·5	60·2	38·2	9·2	97·6	30·0	33·9	33·8
1969	172·9	54·7	66·2	42·0	9·9	108·1	32·9	37·6	37·7
1970	195·5	61·3	75·0	48·1	11·2	122·6	36·7	42·8	43·1
1971	219·4	68·4	84·3	54·4	12·3	141·2	42·5	50·1	48·7
1972	253·0 ---- (*c*) 240·9	78·6 ---- (*c*) 75·5	97·2 ---- (*c*) 95·2	63·0 ---- (*c*) 57·2	14·2 ---- (*c*) 13·0	169·0 ---- (*c*) 162·3	53·3	61·7 ---- (*c*) 58·4	53·9 ---- (*c*) 50·6
1973	292·5 ---- (*c*) 297·6	91·1 ---- (*c*) 94·9	115·7 ---- (*c*) 115·6	70·0 ---- (*c*) 71·4	15·8 ---- (*c*) 15·7	207·5 ---- (*c*) 211·6	70·7 ---- (*c*) 74·0	77·7 ---- (*c*) 77·6	59·2 ---- (*c*) 60·0
1974	371·0 ---- (*c*) 381·9	117·6 ---- (*c*) 117·9	144·0 ---- (*c*) 149·6	89·7 ---- (*c*) 94·6	19·7 ---- (*c*) 19·8	270·8 ---- (*c*) 284·0	94·1 ---- (*c*) 94·3	101·9 ---- (*c*) 112·4	74·8 ---- (*c*) 77·2
1975	489·4	150·9	191·9	121·6	24·9	342·6	112·2	134·1	96·3
1976	572·9	176·6	224·9	142·9	28·6	393·8	127·2	150·6	115·9
1977	659·9	203·2	258·7	165·2	32·8	445·1	142·7	167·9	134·4
1978	761·2	234·3	297·8	191·6	37·6	517·7	166·6	198·0	153·1
1979	899·6	276·5	350·7	228·2	44·2	634·6	206·1	253·0	175·4
1980	1,097·3	336·8	426·3	280·6	53·7	751·6	247·5	306·2	197·8

E. United Kingdom (*a*) 1920–48 at 1938 replacement cost

	Total Gross Stock	Dwellings	Other Buildings and Works	Plant and Machinery	Vehicles, Ships and Aircraft	Total Net Stock	Dwellings	Other Buildings and Works	Plant, Vehicles etc.
1920	14·66	3·34	7·49	2·65	1·19	7·92	1·90	4·48	1·54
1921	14·83	3·42	7·56	2·66	1·20	7·98	1·94	4·47	1·57
1922	14·99	3·48	7·62	2·67	1·23	8·02	1·98	4·45	1·59
1923	15·15	3·54	7·69	2·69	1·24	8·06	2·00	4·45	1·61
1924	15·37	3·62	7·76	2·72	1·27	8·14	2·05	4·45	1·64
1925	15·64	3·73	7·85	2·76	1·31	8·27	2·13	4·46	1·69
1926	15·89	3·86	7·93	2·79	1·32	8·38	2·23	4·45	1·70
1927	16·16	4·00	8·00	2·84	1·32	8·53	2·34	4·45	1·75
1928	16·43	4·11	8·07	2·90	1·35	8·67	2·41	4·44	1·82
1929	16·72	4·24	8·16	2·95	1·38	8·83	2·50	4·45	1·88
1930	17·02	4·35	8·28	3·01	1·39	8·97	2·58	4·48	1·91
1931	17·29	4·48	8·36	3·10	1·36	9·10	2·67	4·49	1·94
1932	17·50	4·61	8·42	3·14	1·34	9·17	2·75	4·48	1·94
1933	17·72	4·77	8·47	3·18	1·30	9·24	2·88	4·46	1·91
1934	18·04	4·96	8·54	3·24	1·29	9·40	3·02	4·45	1·93
1935	18·37	5·13	8·63	3·31	1·29	9·58	3·15	4·46	1·97
1936	18·74	5·29	8·73	3·40	1·31	9·79	3·28	4·48	2·04
1937	19·13	5·45	8·85	3·50	1·32	10·01	3·40	4·52	2·09
1938	19·52	5·60	8·96	3·61	1·35	10·23	3·51	4·56	2·16
1948	20·70	5·88	9·23	4·34	1·24	10·40	3·50	4·50	2·40

F. United Kingdom 1938–62 at 1958 replacement cost

	Total Gross Stock	Dwellings	Other Buildings and Works	Plant and Machinery	Vehicles, Ships and Aircraft	Total Net Stock	Dwellings	Other Buildings and Works	Plant, Vehicles etc.
1938	65·28	20·22	26·36	13·45	5·25	...	...	...	...
1947	67·34	20·87	26·58	15·25	4·64	34·0	12·9	11·8	9·3
1948	68·51	21·30	26·73	15·67	4·81	34·9	13·2	11·9	9·8
1949	69·83	21·72	26·94	16·18	4·99	35·9	13·4	12·2	10·3
1950	71·42	22·13	27·30	16·78	5·21	37·0	13·6	12·4	11·0

National Accounts 14. *continued*

F. United Kingdom 1938–62 at 1958 replacement cost (*cont.*)

(in £ thousand million)

	Total Gross Stock	*of which* Dwellings	Other Buildings and Works	Plant and Machinery	Vehicles, Ships and Aircraft	Total Net Stock	*of which* Dwellings	Other Buildings and Works	Plant, Vehicles etc.
1951	72·86	22·49	27·63	17·45	5·29	38·1	13·9	12·7	11·5
1952	74·36	22·94	27·99	18·07	5·36	39·1	14·2	13·0	11·9
1953	76·10	23·55	28·40	18·71	5·44	40·4	14·6	13·4	12·4
1954	78·02	24·19	28·87	19·39	5·57	41·8	15·1	13·7	13·0
1955	79·87	24·75	29·38	20·06	5·68	43·3	15·5	14·2	13·6
1956	81·72	25·31	29·93	20·70	5·78	45·0	15·9	14·8	14·3
1957	83·78	25·83	30·59	21·45	5·91	46·7	16·2	15·4	15·1
1958	85·80	26·33	31·25	22·14	6·08	48·4	16·5	16·0	15·9
1959	88·16	26·89	32·00	23·00	6·27	50·3	16·9	16·7	16·7
1960	90·74	27·51	32·82	23·86	6·55	52·5	17·4	17·4	17·7
1961	93·81	28·05	33·91	25·04	6·81	55·0	17·9	18·4	18·7
1962	96·83	28·66	35·03	26·16	6·98	57·4	18·4	19·4	19·6

G. United Kingdom 1962–80 at 1975 replacement cost

	Total Gross Stock	*of which* Dwellings	Other Buildings and Works	Plant and Machinery	Vehicles, Ships and Aircraft	Total Net Stock	*of which* Dwellings	Other Buildings and Works	Plant, Vehicles etc.
1962	270·3	82·0	95·9	73·5	18·9	165·4	53·8	56·5	55·1
1963	279·6	84·0	99·1	77·2	19·3	171·8	55·5	59·2	57·1
1964	289·0	86·6	100·9	81·6	19·9	181·0 ---- (*d*) 183·8	57·9 ---- (*d*) 58·5	62·6 ---- (*d*) 63·1	60·5 ---- (*d*) 62·3
1965	300·9	89·4	105·0	86·1	20·5	194·5	61·0	66·8	66·8
1966	307·6	89·9	107·1	90·1	20·6	197·6	61·4	67·9	68·3
1967	328·3 ---- (*b*) 353·1	95·3 ---- (*b*) 111·1	114·1 ---- (*b*) 134·8	97·6 ---- (*b*) 86·4	21·3 ---- (*b*) 20·9	212·1	65·5	72·9	73·8
1968	368·0	117·5	140·1	88·9	21·5	227·0	69·8	78·8	78·6
1969	384·2	121·6	147·1	93·4	22·1	240·2	73·1	83·6	83·8
1970	399·0	125·1	153·0	98·1	22·8	250·2	74·9	87·3	88·0
1971	414·0	129·1	159·0	102·7	23·3	266·4	80·2	94·5	91·9
1972	428·8 ---- (*c*) 408·3	133·2 ---- (*c*) 128·0	164·7 ---- (*c*) 161·4	106·8 ---- (*c*) 97·0	24·1 ---- (*c*) 22·0	286·4 ---- (*c*) 275·1	90·3	104·6 ---- (*c*) 99·0	91·4 ---- (*c*) 85·8
1973	436·6 ---- (*c*) 444·2	136·0 ---- (*c*) 141·6	172·6 ---- (*c*) 172·5	104·5 ---- (*c*) 106·5	23·6 ---- (*c*) 23·5	309·7 ---- (*c*) 315·8	105·5 ---- (*c*) 110·4	116·0 ---- (*c*) 115·8	88·4 ---- (*c*) 89·6
1974	452·5 ---- (*c*) 465·7	143·5 ---- (*c*) 143·8	175·6 ---- (*c*) 182·4	109·5 ---- (*c*) 115·4	24·0 ---- (*c*) 24·2	330·2 ---- (*c*) 346·3	114·8 ---- (*c*) 115·0	124·3 ---- (*c*) 137·1	91·2 ---- (*c*) 94·1
1975	489·4	150·9	191·9	121·6	24·9	342·6	112·2	134·1	96·3
1976	502·5	154·9	197·3	125·4	25·1	345·4	111·6	132·1	101·7
1977	515·5	158·8	202·1	129·0	25·6	347·7	111·5	131·2	105·0
1978	532·3	163·8	208·2	134·0	26·3	362·0	116·5	138·5	107·1
1979	548·5	168·6	213·8	139·2	26·9	387·0	125·7	154·3	107·0
1980	568·5	174·5	220·9	145·4	27·8	389·4	128·2	158·7	102·5

(*a*) See note 3 above.
(*b*) These breaks are caused by changes in the weights used in the indices of replacement cost of fixed assets.
(*c*) Various changes in assumptions, mainly about the length of life of assets, were made in the 1983, 1984, and 1985 Blue Books which affect the comparability of series.
(*d*) A major revision in methodology was used in the 1975 Blue Book.

National Accounts 15. Balance of Payments – United Kingdom 1816–1980

NOTES TO PART A

[1] SOURCE: A. H. Imlah, *Economic Elements in the Pax Britannica* (Cambridge, Mass., 1958), pp. 70–5.

[2] The various minor breaks in the series have not been shown here. They are discussed at length in chapter III of his book.

Part A. 1816–1913

(Net balances in £ million)

	Merchandise Trade	Overseas Investment Earnings	All other Invisible Trade	Bullion and Specie	Overall Balance on Current Account
1816	+ 4·1	+ 0·6	+ 14·9	− 5·0	+ 14·6
1817	− 9·1	+ 1·5	+ 16·8	− 2·9	+ 6·3
1818	− 21·9	+ 1·9	+ 20·8	+ 3·9	+ 4·7
1819	− 10·6	+ 2·1	+ 14·4	+ 1·4	+ 7·3
1820	− 7·4	+ 2·6	+ 13·4	− 5·4	+ 3·2
1821	+ 0·6	+ 2·8	+ 12·6	− 2·2	+ 13·8
1822	+ 0·2	+ 3·6	+ 12·3	− 2·8	+ 13·3
1823	− 9·4	+ 4·4	+ 13·4	− 2·5	+ 5·9
1824	− 5·3	+ 4·7	+ 13·4	+ 3·5	+ 16·3
1825	− 26·5	+ 5·7	+ 17·8	+ 5·4	+ 2·4
1826	− 11·6	+ 5·4	+ 12·6	− 4·0	+ 2·4
1827	− 14·8	+ 5·0	+ 13·4	− 3·6	0·0
1828	− 14·0	+ 4·5	+ 13·0	+ 0·3	+ 3·8
1829	− 11·7	+ 4·2	+ 12·5	+ 1·1	+ 6·1
1830	− 12·0	+ 3·9	+ 12·2	− 3·5	+ 0·6
1831	− 18·1	+ 3·9	+ 13·1	+ 3·5	+ 2·4
1832	− 8·7	+ 4·3	+ 11·7	− 1·2	+ 6·1
1833	− 12·3	+ 4·8	+ 13·5	− 2·4	+ 3·6
1834	− 15·1	+ 6·1	+ 13·8	+ 2·3	+ 7·1
1835	− 11·4	+ 7·8	+ 15·5	+ 0·8	+ 12·7
1836	− 21·8	+ 8·6	+ 17·2	+ 1·5	+ 5·5
1837	− 19·0	+ 8·4	+ 14·9	− 2·0	+ 2·3
1838	− 20·8	+ 8·1	+ 17·5	0·0	+ 4·5
1839	− 28·4	+ 7·7	+ 19·4	+ 4·4	+ 3·1
1840	− 29·8	+ 7·1	+ 19·5	+ 0·9	− 2·3
1841	− 22·4	+ 6·2	+ 18·3	− 1·0	+ 1·1
1842	− 20·6	+ 6·3	+ 16·6	− 2·9	− 0·6
1843	− 10·9	+ 7·0	+ 16·8	− 3·6	+ 9·3
1844	− 12·3	+ 8·3	+ 17·4	− 3·0	+ 10·4
1845	− 19·0	+ 9·7	+ 19·6	− 1·0	+ 9·3
1846	− 20·3	+ 10·2	+ 19·5	− 1·4	+ 8·0
1847	− 41·6	+ 10·6	+ 24·6	+ 5·3	− 1·1
1848	− 26·9	+ 9·0	+ 19·0	+ 1·0	+ 2·1
1849	− 25·7	+ 8·2	+ 21·4	+ 1·0	+ 3·9
1850	− 19·6	+ 9·4	+ 21·8	− 1·0	+ 10·6
1851	− 22·6	+ 10·4	+ 22·6	− 1·2	+ 9·2
1852	− 18·9	+ 10·9	+ 23·5	− 7·8	+ 7·7
1853	− 32·8	+ 11·8	+ 30·8	− 6·5	+ 3·3
1854	− 36·6	+ 12·6	+ 33·4	− 3·6	+ 5·8
1855	− 25·9	+ 12·9	+ 34·7	− 7·8	+ 13·9
1856	− 32·1	+ 14·9	+ 40·9	− 1·9	+ 21·8
1857	− 40·4	+ 16·2	+ 44·8	+ 6·5	+ 27·1
1858	− 23·8	+ 15·9	+ 40·2	− 9·9	+ 22·4
1859	− 22·6	+ 16·9	+ 43·2	− 1·4	+ 36·1
1860	− 45·5	+ 18·7	+ 48·0	+ 2·5	+ 23·7

National Accounts 15. *continued*

Part A. 1816–1913 (*cont.*)

(Net balances in £ million)

	Merchandise Trade	Overseas Investment Earnings	All other Invisible Trade	Bullion and Specie	Overall Balance on Current Account
1861	− 57·6	+ 19·9	+ 50·0	+ 2·1	+ 14·4
1862	− 58·8	+ 20·7	+ 51·9	− 2·3	+ 11·5
1863	− 51·4	+ 21·3	+ 60·1	− 3·5	+ 26·5
1864	− 61·5	+ 22·9	+ 66·0	− 4·6	+ 22·8
1865	− 51·2	+ 24·1	+ 68·4	− 6·4	+ 34·9
1866	− 55·2	+ 26·4	+ 74·5	− 12·7	+ 33·0
1867	− 48·6	+ 28·2	+ 72·1	− 9·5	+ 42·2
1868	− 65·5	+ 31·1	+ 75·5	− 4·6	+ 36·5
1869	− 57·5	+ 33·1	+ 75·2	− 4·1	+ 46·7
1870	+ 57·5	+ 35·3	+ 76·8	− 10·5	+ 44·1
1871	− 46·0	+ 39·5	+ 82·4	− 4·4	+ 71·3
1872	− 36·8	+ 44·3	+ 89·8	+ 0·7	+ 98·0
1873	− 56·3	+ 51·7	+ 90·6	− 4·7	+ 81·3
1874	− 69·1	+ 56·6	+ 90·9	− 7·5	+ 70·9
1875	− 90·5	+ 57·8	+ 89·6	− 5·6	+ 51·3
1876	−117·8	+ 57·5	+ 91·1	− 7·6	+ 23·2
1877	−141·5	+ 55·5	+ 96·5	+ 2·6	+ 13·1
1878	−121·8	+ 55·1	+ 89·1	− 5·7	+ 16·9
1879	−111·8	+ 55·9	+ 88·0	+ 4·4	+ 35·5
1880	−121·1	+ 57·7	+ 96·4	+ 2·6	+ 35·6
1881	− 94·5	+ 59·5	+ 95·0	+ 5·6	+ 65·7
1882	−100·0	+ 62·8	+ 97·5	− 2·6	+ 58·7
1883	−116·9	+ 64·4	+102·1	− 0·8	+ 48·8
1884	− 91·1	+ 66·8	+ 95·0	+ 1·6	+ 72·3
1885	− 98·5	+ 70·3	+ 90·7	− 0·2	+ 62·3
1886	− 79·5	+ 74·0	+ 83·8	+ 0·6	+ 78·9
1887	− 78·5	+ 79·5	+ 87·3	− 0·6	+ 87·7
1888	− 85·9	+ 84·5	+ 92·7	+ 0·6	+ 91·9
1889	−105·0	+ 88·8	+ 99·1	− 2·0	+ 80·9
1890	− 86·3	+ 94·0	+ 99·6	− 8·8	+ 98·5
1891	−122·1	+ 94·3	+ 99·6	− 2·4	+ 69·4
1892	−128·9	+ 94·7	+ 96·7	− 3·4	+ 59·1
1893	−124·6	+ 94·7	+ 85·6	− 3·7	+ 53·0
1894	−131·5	+ 92·6	+ 88·4	− 10·8	+ 38·7
1895	−126·5	+ 93·6	+ 87·8	− 14·9	+ 40·0
1896	−137·9	+ 96·0	+ 92·3	+ 6·4	+ 56·8
1897	−153·9	+ 97·0	+ 94·7	+ 0·8	+ 41·6
1898	−168·9	+101·2	+ 96·8	− 6·2	+ 22·9
1899	−153·7	+103·2	+102·7	− 9·8	+ 42·4
1900	−167·0	+103·6	+109·1	− 7·5	+ 37·9
1901	−173·1	+106·5	+106·7	− 6·2	+ 33·9
1902	−178·4	+109·1	+107·9	− 5·3	+ 33·3
1903	−181·3	+112·2	+113·6	+ 0·3	+ 44·8
1904	−179·1	+113·4	+115·5	+ 0·7	+ 51·7
1905	−155·9	+123·5	+120·1	− 6·2	+ 81·5
1906	−146·0	+134·3	+131·0	− 1·8	+117·5
1907	−126·8	+143·8	+142·4	− 5·3	+154·1
1908	−135·6	+151·0	+132·5	+ 6·8	+154·7
1909	−154·2	+158·0	+138·3	− 6·5	+135·6
1910	−142·7	+170·0	+146·7	− 6·7	+167·3
1911	−121·2	+177·3	+146·8	− 6·0	+196·9
1912	−143·8	+186·9	+158·6	− 4·6	+197·1
1913	−131·6	+199·6	+168·2	− 11·9	+224·3

NOTES TO PART B

[1] SOURCES: C. H. Feinstein, *National Income, Expenditure and Output of the United Kingdom, 1855–1965* (Cambridge, 1972), table 15 to 1956, and C.S.O., *National Income and Expenditure*, subsequently.

[2] Southern Ireland is included to 1920 (1st line) and is excluded subsequently.

[3] The series presented here are on a national accounts basis, and differ slightly from those presented in the C.S.O. publication, *The U.K. Balance of Payments*, because of the different treatment of taxes on property income.

[4] The main differences in principle between this Part and Part A of this table are that imports are here valued f.o.b., and that bullion and specie movements are included in the overall current balance.

[5] Capital grants and transfers from abroad in the period 1946–55 are included with "current transfers", as follows:

1946	164	1951	78
1947	159	1952	35
1948	234	1953	17
1949	189	1954	1
1950	167	1955	1

[6] Except in the final column, rounding errors arising from the summation of individual items have not been eliminated.

B. 1870–1980

(in £ million)

	Merchandise Exports (*a*)	Merchandise Imports	Overall Visible Balance	Exports of Services	Imports of Services	Property Income from Abroad (*b*)	Property Income paid Abroad (*c*)	Balance of Current Transfers (*d*)	Overall Invisible Balance (*d*)	Overall Current Balance (*d*) (*e*)
1870	246	279	−33	80	25	37	2	−2	+88	+55
1871	285	304	−19	85	27	42	3	−2	+95	+76
1872	318	326	−8	93	30	47	3	−2	+105	+97
1873	315	342	−27	93	30	56	4	−2	+113	+86
1874	301	341	−40	92	29	61	4	−2	+118	+78
1875	283	344	−61	89	28	62	4	−1	+118	+57
1876	257	345	−88	89	27	61	4	—	+119	+31
1877	253	363	−110	94	29	59	4	—	+120	+10
1878	247	339	−92	88	27	59	4	−1	+115	+23
1879	251	334	−83	86	27	60	4	−1	+114	+31
1880	290	378	−88	96	31	62	4	−2	+121	+33
1881	303	365	−62	96	31	63	4	−2	+122	+60
1882	313	380	−67	99	32	68	5	−2	+128	+61
1883	310	393	−83	104	33	69	5	−3	+132	+49
1884	299	359	−60	96	31	72	5	−2	+130	+70
1885	272	341	−69	91	29	75	5	−1	+131	+62
1886	270	322	−52	85	28	80	6	−1	+130	+78
1887	283	333	−50	90	29	85	6	−2	+138	+88
1888	302	357	−55	94	30	90	6	−2	+146	+91
1889	323	393	−70	99	33	96	7	−2	+153	+83
1890	334	387	−53	100	33	101	7	−1	+160	+107
1891	313	400	−87	98	32	101	7	−1	+159	+72
1892	295	390	−95	95	31	102	7	−1	+158	+63
1893	280	372	−92	85	30	102	7	−1	+149	+57
1894	277	376	−99	86	30	100	7	—	+149	+50
1895	290	383	−93	85	30	101	7	−1	+148	+55
1896	304	407	−103	90	32	103	7	−1	+153	+50
1897	300	415	−115	92	32	105	8	−1	+156	+41
1898	302	433	−131	93	33	109	8	−1	+160	+29
1899	331	446	−115	100	40	111	8	−1	+162	+47
1900	356	485	−129	111	50	112	8	−2	+163	+34
1901	349	485	−136	109	55	115	9	−5	+155	+19
1902	350	491	−141	110	46	119	10	−8	+165	+24
1903	361	505	−144	118	38	122	10	−5	+187	+43
1904	372	512	−140	120	39	124	11	−2	+192	+52
1905	409	527	−118	126	40	135	12	−3	+206	+88
1906	462	568	−106	139	43	148	14	−3	+227	+121
1907	519	603	−84	152	46	160	16	−4	+246	+162
1908	457	550	−93	140	46	168	17	−2	+243	+150
1909	470	581	−111	145	47	175	17	−3	+253	+142

See p. 873 for footnotes.

National Accounts 15. *continued*

B. 1870–1980 (*cont.*)

(in £ million)

	Merchandise Exports (*a*)	Merchandise Imports	Overall Visible Balance	Exports of Services	Imports of Services	Property Income from Abroad (*b*)	Property Income paid Abroad (*c*)	Balance of Current Transfers (*d*)	Overall Invisible Balance (*d*)	Overall Current Balance (*d*) (*e*)
1910	536	632	−96	155	51	189	19	−4	+270	+174
1911	559	634	−75	156	51	197	20	−3	+279	+204
1912	600	694	−94	168	54	209	22	−4	+297	+203
1913	637	719	−82	179	58	224	24	−4	+317	+235
1914	540	660	−120	145	80	215	25	−1	+254	+134
1915	500	840	−340	250	130	190	25	—	+285	−55
1916	630	980	−350	370	160	230	30	+30	+440	+90
1917	620	1,040	−420	465	220	235	40	+30	+470	+50
1918	540	1,170	−630	400	230	240	65	+10	+415	−275
1919	990	1,460	−470	480	220	230	65	—	+425	−45
	1,585	1,761	−176	464	224	295	41	−1	+493	+317
1920	---(*f*)	---(*f*)	---(*f*)	---(*f*)	---(*f*)	---(*f*)	---(*f*)	---(*f*)	---(*f*)	---(*f*)
	1,664	1,812	−148	464	224	292	46	−1	+485	+337
1921	874	1,022	−148	292	172	222	44	+43	+341	+193
1922	888	951	−63	225	150	237	60	+12	+264	+201
1923	914	1,011	−97	247	146	240	64	+3	+280	+183
1924	958	1,172	−214	242	152	261	65	+6	+292	+78
1925	943	1,208	−265	215	149	295	63	+19	+317	+52
1926	794	1,140	−346	223	152	300	63	+20	+328	−18
1927	845	1,115	−270	245	142	302	63	+26	+368	+98
1928	858	1,095	−237	234	140	304	64	+27	+361	+124
1929	854	1,117	−263	242	152	307	64	+26	+359	+96
1930	670	953	−283	214	147	277	62	+37	+319	+36
1931	464	786	−322	168	140	211	48	+28	+219	−103
1932	425	641	−216	153	123	175	48	+8	+165	−51
1933	427	619	−192	146	120	183	29	+4	+184	−8
1934	463	683	−220	145	116	195	28	+2	+198	−22
1935	541	724	−183	149	124	212	31	—	+206	+23
1936	523	784	−261	174	135	229	34	—	+234	−27
1937	614	950	−336	229	144	242	37	−1	+289	−47
1938	564	849	−285	193	152	229	37	−3	+230	−55
1939	500	800	−300	200	300	[250](*h*)	[90] (*i*)	−10	+50	−250
1940	400	1,000	−600	200	550	[260](*h*)	[100](*i*)	−10	−200	−800
1941 (*g*)	400	1,100	−700	200	450	[270](*h*)	[130](*i*)	−10	−120	−820
1942 (*g*)	300	800	−500	300	550	[270](*h*)	[170](*i*)	−10	−160	−660
1943 (*g*)	240	800	−560	500	700	[280](*h*)	[190](*i*)	−10	−120	−680
1944 (*g*)	270	900	−630	700	800	[290](*h*)	[210](*i*)	−10	−30	−660
1945 (*g*)	450	700	−250	350	1,000	[310](*h*)	[230](*i*)	−50	−620	−870
1946	960	1,063	−103	470	762	198	113	+244	+37	−66
1947	1,180	1,541	−361	472	687	261	111	+204	+139	−222
1948	1,639	1,790	−151	557	644	360	125	+263	+411	+260
1949	1,863	2,000	−137	632	697	351	128	+171	+329	+192
1950	2,261	2,312	−51	734	764	558	162	+158	+524	+473
1951	2,735	3,424	−689	913	907	553	211	+50	+398	+182
1952	2,769	3,048	−279	991	885	500	248	+119	+477	+198
1953	2,683	2,927	−244	1,004	908	495	266	+81	+506	+262
1954	2,785	2,989	−204	1,052	972	540	290	−8	+322	+117
1955	3,073	3,386	−313	1,104	1,095	517	343	−24	+159	−155
1956	3,377	3,324	+53	1,221	1,230	571	342	−65	+155	+208
1957	3,509	3,538	−29	1,327	1,240	583	334	−74	+262	+233
1958	3,406	3,377	+29	1,304	1,206	682	389	−60	+331	+360
1959	3,527	3,642	−115	1,329	1,243	658	396	−51	+293	+172

National Accounts 15. *continued*

B. 1870–1980 (*cont.*)

(in £ million)

	Merchandise Exports (*a*)	Merchandise Imports	Overall Visible Balance	Exports of Services	Imports of Services	Property Income from Abroad (*b*)	Property Income paid Abroad (*c*)	Balance of Current Transfers (*d*)	Overall Invisible Balance (*d*)	Overall Current Balance (*d*) (*e*)
1960	3,737	4,138	−401	1,419	1,411	671	438	−68	+528	−228
1961	3,903	4,043	−140	1,488	1,467	676	422	−88	+185	+47
1962	4,003	4,103	−100	1,523	1,505	754	420	−97	+255	+155
1963	4,331	4,450	−119	1,546	1,577	842	444	−123	+244	+125
1964	4,568	5,111	−543	1,633	1,709	900	494	−158	+272	−371
1965	4,913	5,173	−260	1,701	1,799	1,005	557	−168	+182	−79
1966	5,276	5,384	−108	1,890	1,875	979	576	−181	+237	+129
1967	5,241	5,840	−599	2,146	2,015	1,001	601	−216	+315	−284
1968	6,433	7,145	−712	2,547	2,235	1,135	776	−223	+448	−264
1969	7,269	7,478	−209	2,820	2,452	1,376	844	−206	+694	+485
1970	8,150	8,184	−34	3,379	2,963	1,493	898	−182	+829	+795
1971	9,043	8,853	+190	3,884	3,340	1,535	984	−196	+899	+1,089
1972	9,437	10,185	−748	4,204	3,586	1,801	1,209	−272	+939	+191
1973	11,937	14,523	−2,586	5,185	4,501	4,924	3,597	−443	+1,568	−1,018
1974	16,394	21,745	−5,351	6,594	5,645	6,209	4,702	−422	+2,034	−3,317
1975	19,330	22,663	−3,333	7,677	6,341	6,565	5,675	−475	+1,751	−1,582
1976	25,191	29,120	−3,929	10,019	7,774	8,385	6,828	−786	+3,016	−913
1977	31,728	34,012	−2,284	11,625	8,587	8,796	8,550	−1,128	+2,156	−128
1978	35,063	36,605	−1,542	12,440	8,962	11,202	10,375	−1,791	+2,514	+972
1979	40,687	44,136	−3,449	14,336	10,532	17,526	16,338	−2,279	+2,713	−736
1980	47,422	46,061	+1,361	15,693	11,657	23,512	23,731	−2,078	+1,739	+3,100

(*a*) Including re-exports.
(*b*) Net of foreign taxes paid by U.K. residents.
(*c*) Net of U.K. taxes paid by non-residents.
(*d*) See note 5 above.
(*e*) Equals net investment abroad plus acquisition of gold and foreign exchange reserves.
(*f*) See note 2 above.
(*g*) Cash transactions only. Lend-lease and reciprocal aid.
(*h*) Including U.K. taxes paid by non-residents.
(*i*) Including foreign taxes paid by U.K. residents.

National Accounts 16. Balance of Payments – Republic of Ireland 1933–80

NOTE
SOURCES: *Statistical Abstract of Ireland* and *Revisions to the Balance of International Payments and the National Accounts* (Dublin, 1984).

(in £ million)

	Merchandise Exports (*a*)	Merchandise Imports (*b*)	Overall Visible Balance (*b*)	Exports of Services	Imports of Services	Capital Income Received	Capital Income Paid	Balance of Current Transfers (*c*)	Overall Invisible Balance (*b*) (*d*)	Overall Current Balance
1933	18·4	35·2	− 16·8	...	...	13·3	7·3	+ 3·5	+ 15·5	− 1·3
1934	17·6	38·8	− 21·2	...	...	14·1	7·8	+ 2·8	+ 16·9	− 4·3
1935	19·6	37·0	− 17·4	...	...	13·7	8·1	+ 2·9	+ 18·0	+ 0·6
1936	22·0	39·4	− 17·4	...	...	13·5	8·3	+ 3·1	+ 15·9	− 2·5
1937	22·2	43·5	− 21·3	...	...	13·4	8·1	+ 3·0	+ 18·8	− 2·5
1938	23·9	41·1	− 17·2	...	...	13·4	7·1	+ 3·0	+ 19·2	+ 2·0
1939	26·9	43·4	− 16·5	...	...	13·6	7·1	+ 2·8	+ 16·0	− 0·5
1940	33·0	46·8	− 13·8	...	...	14·0	7·0	+ 2·1	+ 16·1	+ 2·3
1941	31·8	29·5	+ 2·3	...	...	13·3	8·5	+ 3·6	+ 12·0	+ 14·3
1942	32·7	34·6	− 2·0	...	...	13·6	8·7	+ 6·5	+ 28·1	+ 26·1
1943	27·5	26·1	+ 1·4	...	...	14·0	7·4	+ 8·7	+ 33·8	+ 32·4
1944	29·6	28·2	+ 1·4	...	...	15·1	8·0	+ 9·3	+ 34·0	+ 32·6
1945	35·2	40·7	− 5·4	...	...	15·0	8·3	+ 9·6	+ 40·0	+ 34·6
1946	39·0	72·0	− 33·1	...	...	17·5	8·9	+ 9·8	+ 52·8	+ 19·7
1947	39·5	131·3	− 91·8	...	...	18·7	9·9	+ 9·7	+ 62·0	− 29·8
1948	48·8	135·8	− 87·0	...	...	19·5	9·3	+ 8·8	+ 67·4	− 19·6
1949	59·8	127·7	− 67·8	...	...	19·6	10·4	+ 10·0	+ 58·1	− 9·7
1950	71·4	157·3	− 85·9	...	...	20·5	11·5	+ 10·6	+ 55·7	− 30·2
1951	80·8	203·2	−122·5	...	...	21·8	11·2	+ 10·4	+ 60·9	− 61·6
1952	100·4	170·4	− 70·0	...	...	22·7	12·6	+ 10·2	+ 52·7	− 17·3
1953	109·7	178·2	− 67·6	...	...	23·8	13·1	+ 11·0	+ 51·0	− 16·6
1954	110·1	174·9	− 64·1	...	...	24·5	12·8	+ 11·1	+ 53·1	− 11·0
1955	104·7	202·3	− 97·5	...	...	25·9	15·9	+ 11·4	+ 52·7	− 44·8
1956	102·3	176·7	− 74·7	...	...	26·9	16·7	+ 11·6	+ 56·1	− 18·6
1957	123·7	176·9	− 53·6	...	...	27·0	14·5	+ 12·3	+ 49·5	− 4·1
1958	121·8	190·0	− 68·2	...	...	27·9	15·4	+ 12·3	+ 69·2	+ 1·0
1959	122·4	204·6	− 82·2	...	...	28·4	17·3	+ 12·5	+ 91·0	+ 8·8
1960	144·5	218·1	− 73·7	...	...	30·9	18·7	+ 13·3	+ 72·5	+ 0·8
1961	169·8	251·6	− 81·7	...	...	32·9	19·1	+ 13·9	+ 82·9	+ 1·2
1962	164·6	264·8	−100·3	...	...	33·9	20·2	+ 13·7	+ 86·8	− 13·5

1963	186·4	297·6	−111·2	...	...	34·9	21·7	+ 13·1	+ 89·1	− 22·1
1964	212·3	339·9	−127·6	...	...	38·8	25·9	+ 13·5	+ 96·2	− 31·4
1965	211·4	362·6	−151·3	...	...	44·2	24·5	+ 14·5	+109·5	−41·8
		--- (b)	--- (b)						--- (b)	
								+ 15·2		
1966	266·1	390·6	−124·5	99·6	45·1	44·9	27·5	--- (c)	+108·4	− 16·1
								+ 26·9		
1967	307·0	407·1	−100·1	107·0	45·6	46·1	27·7	+ 30·1	+115·3	+ 15·2
1968	355·8	509·0	−153·2	122·0	55·3	51·0	27·4	+ 37·1	+136·9	− 16·3
1969	395·9	607·2	−211·3	130·3	58·4	50·9	32·4	+ 39·4	+142·2	− 69·1
1970	455·0	667·0	−212·0	133·0	61·1	58·7	40·9	+ 43·6	+ 146·7	− 65·3
1971	522·3	738·6	−216·3	142·5	64·9	62·5	47·5	+ 45·6	+145·3	− 71·0
1972	632·5	823·3	−190·8	139·6	69·3	76·2	59·5	+ 50·1	+142·4	+ 48·4
1973	852·8	1,121·5	−268·7	170·2	89·1	99·4	93·3	+ 86·5	+186·4	− 82·3
1974	1,060·6	1,601·5	−540·9	210·2	106·6	130·9	121·1	+129·9	+260·7	−280·2
1975	1,370·8	1,672·1	−301·3	245·4	141·5	140·8	145·7	+175·0	+295·3	− 6·0
1976	1,851·1	2,302·0	−450·9	307·7	164·6	187·1	244·9	+167·4	+270·7	−180·2
1977	2,424·2	3,042·5	−618·3	395·1	213·7	186·3	300·7	+327·1	+427·1	−191·2
1978	2,921·6	3,656·3	−734·7	471·4	286·4	217·8	398·0	+446·8	+477·8	−256·9
1979	3,395·1	4,760·4	−1,365·3	577·7	373·0	272·9	510·9	+563·1	+327·4	−1,037·9
1980	4,004·4	5,346·1	−1,341·7	669·8	468·0	380·7	685·5	+590·9	+315·8	−1,025·9

(a) Including re-exports.
(b) Imports are valued c.i.f. to 1965, with consequences for both the visible and invisible balances.
(c) Balance of emigrants' remittances only to 1966 (1st line).
(d) Including the balance unaccounted for in the detailed classification, and the balance of current transfers.

INDEX